System
Concepts

Database System Concepts

FOURTH EDITION

Abraham Silberschatz
Bell Laboratories

Henry F. Korth
Bell Laboratories

S. Sudarshan
Indian Institute of Technology, Bombay

Boston   Burr Ridge, IL   Dubuque, IA   Madison, WI   New York   San Francisco   St. Louis
Bangkok   Bogotá   Caracas   Kuala Lumpur   Lisbon   London   Madrid   Mexico City
Milan   Montreal   New Delhi   Santiago   Seoul   Singapore   Sydney   Taipei   Toronto

McGraw-Hill Higher Education

*A Division of The **McGraw-Hill** Companies*

DATABASE SYSTEM CONCEPTS, FOURTH EDITION

Published by McGraw-Hill, a business unit of The McGraw-Hill Companies, Inc., 1221 Avenue of the Americas, New York, NY 10020. Copyright © 2002, 1999, 1991, 1986 by The McGraw-Hill Companies, Inc. All rights reserved. No part of this publication may be reproduced or distributed in any form or by any means, or stored in a database or retrieval system, without the prior written consent of The McGraw-Hill Companies, Inc., including, but not limited to, in any network or other electronic storage or transmission, or broadcast for distance learning.

Some ancillaries, including electronic and print components, may not be available to customers outside the United States.

This book is printed on acid-free paper.

1 2 3 4 5 6 7 8 9 0 DOC/DOC 0 9 8 7 6 5 4 3 2 1

ISBN 0–07–228363–7
ISBN 0–07–112268–0 (ISE)

General manager: *Thomas E. Casson*
Publisher: *Elizabeth A. Jones*
Senior developmental editor: *Kelley Butcher*
Executive marketing manager: *John Wannemacher*
Project manager: *Jill R. Peter*
Production supervisor: *Kara Kudronowicz*
Coordinator of freelance design: *Rick D. Noel*
Cover designer: *JoAnne Schopler*
Cover illustration: *Paul D. Turnbaugh*
Supplement producer: *Jodi K. Banowetz*
Media technology senior producer: *Phillip Meek*
Compositor: *Abraham Silberschatz/Techsetters*
Typeface: *10/12 Palatino*
Printer: *R. R. Donnelley & Sons Company/Crawfordsville, IN*

The credits section for this book begins on page 000 and is considered an extension of the copyright page.

Library of Congress Cataloging-in-Publication Data

Silberschatz, Abraham.
    Database system concepts / Abraham Silberschatz, Henry F. Korth, S. Sudarshan. — 4th ed.
        p.   cm.
    Includes bibliographical references and index.
    ISBN 0–07–228363–7
    1. Database management. I. Korth, Henry F. II. Sudarshan, S. III. Title.

    QA76.9.D3 S5637   2002
    005.74—dc21   2001030845
                                                       CIP

INTERNATIONAL EDITION ISBN 0–07–112268–0
Copyright © 2002. Exclusive rights by The McGraw-Hill Companies, Inc., for manufacture and export. This book cannot be re-exported from the country to which it is sold by McGraw-Hill. The International Edition is not available in North America.

www.mhhe.com

In memory of my father Joseph Silberschatz,
and my grandparents Stepha and Aaron Rosenblum

Avi Silberschatz

To my wife, Joan
my children, Abigail and Joseph
and my parents, Henry and Frances

Hank Korth

To my wife, Sita
my son, Madhur
and my mother, Indira

S. Sudarshan

Contents

PART 2 ■ RELATIONAL DATABASES

Chapter 7   Relational-Database Design

PART 3   ■   OBJECT-BASED DATABASES AND XML

Chapter 8   Object-Oriented Databases

Chapter 9   Object-Relational Databases

Chapter 10   XML

PART 4 ■ DATA STORAGE AND QUERYING

Chapter 11 Storage and File Structure

Chapter 12 Indexing and Hashing

Chapter 13 Query Processing

Chapter 14 Query Optimization

PART 5 ■ TRANSACTION MANAGEMENT

Chapter 15   Transactions

Chapter 16   Concurrency Control

Chapter 17   Recovery System

PART 6 ■ DATABASE SYSTEM ARCHITECTURE

Chapter 18   Database System Architectures

Chapter 19   Distributed Databases

Chapter 20   Parallel Databases

PART 7   ■   OTHER TOPICS

Chapter 21   Application Development and Administration

Chapter 22   Advanced Querying and Information Retrieval

Chapter 23   Advanced Data Types and New Applications

Chapter 24   Advanced Transaction Processing

PART 8   ■   CASE STUDIES

Chapter 25   Oracle

Chapter 26   IBM DB2 Universal Database

Chapter 27   Microsoft SQL Server

PART 9 ■ APPENDICES

Appendix A   Network Model (contents online)

Appendix B   Hierarchical Model (contents online)

Appendix C   Advanced Relational Design (contents online)

Preface

Database management has evolved from a specialized computer application to a central component of a modern computing environment, and, as a result, knowledge about database systems has become an essential part of an education in computer science. In this text, we present the fundamental concepts of database management. These concepts include aspects of database design, database languages, and database-system implementation.

This text is intended for a first course in databases at the junior or senior undergraduate, or first-year graduate, level. In addition to basic material for a first course, the text contains advanced material that can be used for course supplements, or as introductory material for an advanced course.

We assume only a familiarity with basic data structures, computer organization, and a high-level programming language such as Java, C, or Pascal. We present concepts as intuitive descriptions, many of which are based on our running example of a bank enterprise. Important theoretical results are covered, but formal proofs are omitted. The bibliographical notes contain pointers to research papers in which results were first presented and proved, as well as references to material for further reading. In place of proofs, figures and examples are used to suggest why a result is true.

The fundamental concepts and algorithms covered in the book are often based on those used in existing commercial or experimental database systems. Our aim is to present these concepts and algorithms in a general setting that is not tied to one particular database system. Details of particular commercial database systems are discussed in Part 8, "Case Studies."

In this fourth edition of *Database System Concepts*, we have retained the overall style of the first three editions, while addressing the evolution of database management. Several new chapters have been added to cover new technologies. Every chapter has been edited, and most have been modified extensively. We shall describe the changes in detail shortly.

Organization

The text is organized in eight major parts, plus three appendices:

- **Overview** (Chapter 1). Chapter 1 provides a general overview of the nature and purpose of database systems. We explain how the concept of a database system has developed, what the common features of database systems are, what a database system does for the user, and how a database system interfaces with operating systems. We also introduce an example database application: a banking enterprise consisting of multiple bank branches. This example is used as a running example throughout the book. This chapter is motivational, historical, and explanatory in nature.

- **Data models** (Chapters 2 and 3). Chapter 2 presents the entity-relationship model. This model provides a high-level view of the issues in database design, and of the problems that we encounter in capturing the semantics of realistic applications within the constraints of a data model. Chapter 3 focuses on the relational data model, covering the relevant relational algebra and relational calculus.

- **Relational databases** (Chapters 4 through 7). Chapter 4 focuses on the most influential of the user-oriented relational languages: SQL. Chapter 5 covers two other relational languages, QBE and Datalog. These two chapters describe data manipulation: queries, updates, insertions, and deletions. Algorithms and design issues are deferred to later chapters. Thus, these chapters are suitable for introductory courses or those individuals who want to learn the basics of database systems, without getting into the details of the internal algorithms and structure.

  Chapter 6 presents constraints from the standpoint of database integrity and security; Chapter 7 shows how constraints can be used in the design of a relational database. Referential integrity; mechanisms for integrity maintenance, such as triggers and assertions; and authorization mechanisms are presented in Chapter 6. The theme of this chapter is the protection of the database from accidental and intentional damage.

  Chapter 7 introduces the theory of relational database design. The theory of functional dependencies and normalization is covered, with emphasis on the motivation and intuitive understanding of each normal form. The overall process of database design is also described in detail.

- **Object-based databases and XML** (Chapters 8 through 10). Chapter 8 covers object-oriented databases. It introduces the concepts of object-oriented programming, and shows how these concepts form the basis for a data model. No prior knowledge of object-oriented languages is assumed. Chapter 9 covers object-relational databases, and shows how the SQL:1999 standard extends the relational data model to include object-oriented features, such as inheritance, complex types, and object identity.

Chapter 10 covers the XML standard for data representation, which is seeing increasing use in data communication and in the storage of complex data types. The chapter also describes query languages for XML.

- **Data storage and querying** (Chapters 11 through 14). Chapter 11 deals with disk, file, and file-system structure, and with the mapping of relational and object data to a file system. A variety of data-access techniques are presented in Chapter 12, including hashing, B^+-tree indices, and grid file indices. Chapters 13 and 14 address query-evaluation algorithms, and query optimization based on equivalence-preserving query transformations.

  These chapters provide an understanding of the internals of the storage and retrieval components of a database.

- **Transaction management** (Chapters 15 through 17). Chapter 15 focuses on the fundamentals of a transaction-processing system, including transaction atomicity, consistency, isolation, and durability, as well as the notion of serializability.

  Chapter 16 focuses on concurrency control and presents several techniques for ensuring serializability, including locking, timestamping, and optimistic (validation) techniques. The chapter also covers deadlock issues. Chapter 17 covers the primary techniques for ensuring correct transaction execution despite system crashes and disk failures. These techniques include logs, shadow pages, checkpoints, and database dumps.

- **Database system architecture** (Chapters 18 through 20). Chapter 18 covers computer-system architecture, and describes the influence of the underlying computer system on the database system. We discuss centralized systems, client–server systems, parallel and distributed architectures, and network types in this chapter. Chapter 19 covers distributed database systems, revisiting the issues of database design, transaction management, and query evaluation and optimization, in the context of distributed databases. The chapter also covers issues of system availability during failures and describes the LDAP directory system.

  Chapter 20, on parallel databases explores a variety of parallelization techniques, including I/O parallelism, interquery and intraquery parallelism, and interoperation and intraoperation parallelism. The chapter also describes parallel-system design.

- **Other topics** (Chapters 21 through 24). Chapter 21 covers database application development and administration. Topics include database interfaces, particularly Web interfaces, performance tuning, performance benchmarks, standardization, and database issues in e-commerce. Chapter 22 covers querying techniques, including decision support systems, and information retrieval. Topics covered in the area of decision support include online analytical processing (OLAP) techniques, SQL:1999 support for OLAP, data mining, and data warehousing. The chapter also describes information retrieval techniques for querying textual data, including hyperlink-based techniques used in Web search engines.

Chapter 23 covers advanced data types and new applications, including temporal data, spatial and geographic data, multimedia data, and issues in the management of mobile and personal databases. Finally, Chapter 24 deals with advanced transaction processing. We discuss transaction-processing monitors, high-performance transaction systems, real-time transaction systems, and transactional workflows.

- **Case studies** (Chapters 25 through 27). In this part we present case studies of three leading commercial database systems, including Oracle, IBM DB2, and Microsoft SQL Server. These chapters outline unique features of each of these products, and describe their internal structure. They provide a wealth of interesting information about the respective products, and help you see how the various implementation techniques described in earlier parts are used in real systems. They also cover several interesting practical aspects in the design of real systems.

- **Online appendices**. Although most new database applications use either the relational model or the object-oriented model, the network and hierarchical data models are still in use. For the benefit of readers who wish to learn about these data models, we provide appendices describing the network and hierarchical data models, in Appendices A and B respectively; the appendices are available only online (http://www.bell-labs.com/topic/books/db-book).

Appendix C describes advanced relational database design, including the theory of multivalued dependencies, join dependencies, and the project-join and domain-key normal forms. This appendix is for the benefit of individuals who wish to cover the theory of relational database design in more detail, and instructors who wish to do so in their courses. This appendix, too, is available only online, on the Web page of the book.

The Fourth Edition

The production of this fourth edition has been guided by the many comments and suggestions we received concerning the earlier editions, by our own observations while teaching at IIT Bombay, and by our analysis of the directions in which database technology is evolving.

Our basic procedure was to rewrite the material in each chapter, bringing the older material up to date, adding discussions on recent developments in database technology, and improving descriptions of topics that students found difficult to understand. Each chapter now has a list of review terms, which can help you review key topics covered in the chapter. We have also added a tools section at the end of most chapters, which provide information on software tools related to the topic of the chapter. We have also added new exercises, and updated references.

We have added a new chapter covering XML, and three case study chapters covering the leading commercial database systems, including Oracle, IBM DB2, and Microsoft SQL Server.

We have organized the chapters into several parts, and reorganized the contents of several chapters. For the benefit of those readers familiar with the third edition, we explain the main changes here:

- **Entity-relationship model**. We have improved our coverage of the entity-relationship (E-R) model. More examples have been added, and some changed, to give better intuition to the reader. A summary of alternative E-R notations has been added, along with a new section on UML.

- **Relational databases**. Our coverage of SQL in Chapter 4 now references the SQL:1999 standard, which was approved after publication of the third edition. SQL coverage has been significantly expanded to include the **with** clause, expanded coverage of embedded SQL, and coverage of ODBC and JDBC whose usage has increased greatly in the past few years. Coverage of Quel has been dropped from Chapter 5, since it is no longer in wide use. Coverage of QBE has been revised to remove some ambiguities and to add coverage of the QBE version used in the Microsoft Access database.

  Chapter 6 now covers integrity constraints and security. Coverage of security has been moved to Chapter 6 from its third-edition position of Chapter 19. Chapter 6 also covers triggers. Chapter 7 covers relational-database design and normal forms. Discussion of functional dependencies has been moved into Chapter 7 from its third-edition position of Chapter 6. Chapter 7 has been significantly rewritten, providing several short-cut algorithms for dealing with functional dependencies and extended coverage of the overall database design process. Axioms for multivalued dependency inference, PJNF and DKNF, have been moved into an appendix.

- **Object-based databases**. Coverage of object orientation in Chapter 8 has been improved, and the discussion of ODMG updated. Object-relational coverage in Chapter 9 has been updated, and in particular the SQL:1999 standard replaces the extended SQL used in the third edition.

- **XML**. Chapter 10, covering XML, is a new chapter in the fourth edition.

- **Storage, indexing, and query processing**. Coverage of storage and file structures, in Chapter 11, has been updated; this chapter was Chapter 10 in the third edition. Many characteristics of disk drives and other storage mechanisms have changed greatly in the past few years, and our coverage has been correspondingly updated. Coverage of RAID has been updated to reflect technology trends. Coverage of data dictionaries (catalogs) has been extended.

  Chapter 12, on indexing, now includes coverage of bitmap indices; this chapter was Chapter 11 in the third edition. The B^+-tree insertion algorithm has been simplified, and pseudocode has been provided for search. Partitioned hashing has been dropped, since it is not in significant use.

  Our treatment of query processing has been reorganized, with the earlier chapter (Chapter 12 in the third edition) split into two chapters, one on query processing (Chapter 13) and another on query optimization (Chapter 14). All details regarding cost estimation and query optimization have been moved to Chapter 14, allowing Chapter 13 to concentrate on query processing algorithms. We have dropped several detailed (and tedious) formulae for calculating the exact number of I/O operations for different operations. Chapter 14 now has pseudocode for optimization algorithms, and new sections on optimization of nested subqueries and on materialized views.

- **Transaction processing**. Chapter 15, which provides an introduction to transactions, has been updated; this chapter was numbered Chapter 13 in the third edition. Tests for view serializability have been dropped.

  Chapter 16, on concurrency control, includes a new section on implementation of lock managers, and a section on weak levels of consistency, which was in Chapter 20 of the third edition. Concurrency control of index structures has been expanded, providing details of the crabbing protocol, which is a simpler alternative to the B-link protocol, and next-key locking to avoid the phantom problem. Chapter 17, on recovery, now includes coverage of the ARIES recovery algorithm. This chapter also covers remote backup systems for providing high availability despite failures, an increasingly important feature in "24 × 7" applications.

  As in the third edition, instructors can choose between just introducing transaction-processing concepts (by covering only Chapter 15), or offering detailed coverage (based on Chapters 15 through 17).

- **Database system architectures**. Chapter 18, which provides an overview of database system architectures, has been updated to cover current technology; this was Chapter 16 in the third edition. The order of the parallel database chapter and the distributed database chapters has been flipped. While the coverage of parallel database query processing techniques in Chapter 20 (which was Chapter 16 in the third edition) is mainly of interest to those who wish to learn about database internals, distributed databases, now covered in Chapter 19, is a topic that is more fundamental; it is one that anyone dealing with databases should be familiar with.

  Chapter 19 on distributed databases has been significantly rewritten, to reduce the emphasis on naming and transparency and to increase coverage of operation during failures, including concurrency control techniques to provide high availability. Coverage of three-phase commit protocol has been abbreviated, as has distributed detection of global deadlocks, since neither is used much in practice. Coverage of query processing issues in heterogeneous databases has been moved up from Chapter 20 of the third edition. There is a new section on directory systems, in particular LDAP, since these are quite widely used as a mechanism for making information available in a distributed setting.

- **Other topics**. Although we have modified and updated the entire text, we concentrated our presentation of material pertaining to ongoing database research and new database applications in four new chapters, from Chapter 21 to Chapter 24.

Chapter 21 is new in the fourth edition and covers application development and administration. The description of how to build Web interfaces to databases, including servlets and other mechanisms for server-side scripting, is new. The section on performance tuning, which was earlier in Chapter 19, has new material on the famous 5-minute rule and the 1-minute rule, as well as some new examples. Coverage of materialized view selection is also new. Coverage of benchmarks and standards has been updated. There is a new section on e-commerce, focusing on database issues in e-commerce, and a new section on dealing with legacy systems.

Chapter 22, which covers advanced querying and information retrieval, includes new material on OLAP, particulary on SQL:1999 extensions for data analysis. Coverage of data warehousing and data mining has also been extended greatly. Coverage of information retrieval has been significantly extended, particulary in the area of Web searching. Earlier versions of this material were in Chapter 21 of the third edition.

Chapter 23, which covers advanced data types and new applications, has material on temporal data, spatial data, multimedia data, and mobile databases. This material is an updated version of material that was in Chapter 21 of the third edition. Chapter 24, which covers advanced transaction processing, contains updated versions of sections on TP monitors, workflow systems, main-memory and real-time databases, long-duration transactions, and transaction management in multidatabases, which appeared in Chapter 20 of the third edition.

- **Case studies**. The case studies covering Oracle, IBM DB2 and Microsoft SQL Server are new to the fourth edition. These chapters outline unique features of each of these products, and describe their internal structure.

Instructor's Note

The book contains both basic and advanced material, which might not be covered in a single semester. We have marked several sections as advanced, using the symbol "∗∗". These sections may be omitted if so desired, without a loss of continuity.

It is possible to design courses by using various subsets of the chapters. We outline some of the possibilities here:

- Chapter 5 can be omitted if students will not be using QBE or Datalog as part of the course.

- If object orientation is to be covered in a separate advanced course, Chapters 8 and 9, and Section 11.9, can be omitted. Alternatively, they could constitute the foundation of an advanced course in object databases.

- Chapter 10 (XML) and Chapter 14 (query optimization) can be omitted from an introductory course.

- Both our coverage of transaction processing (Chapters 15 through 17) and our coverage of database-system architecture (Chapters 18 through 20) consist of an overview chapter (Chapters 15 and 18, respectively), followed by chapters with details. You might choose to use Chapters 15 and 18, while omitting Chapters 16, 17, 19, and 20, if you defer these latter chapters to an advanced course.

- Chapters 21 through 24 are suitable for an advanced course or for self-study by students, although Section 21.1 may be covered in a first database course.

Model course syllabi, based on the text, can be found on the Web home page of the book (see the following section).

Web Page and Teaching Supplements

A Web home page for the book is available at the URL:

http://www.bell-labs.com/topic/books/db-book

The Web page contains:

- Slides covering all the chapters of the book

- Answers to selected exercises

- The three appendices

- An up-to-date errata list

- Supplementary material contributed by users of the book

A complete solution manual will be made available only to faculty. For more information about how to get a copy of the solution manual, please send electronic mail to customer.service@mcgraw-hill.com. In the United States, you may call 800-338-3987. The McGraw-Hill Web page for this book is

http://www.mhhe.com/silberschatz

Contacting Us and Other Users

We provide a mailing list through which users of our book can communicate among themselves and with us. If you wish to be on the list, please send a message to db-book@research.bell-labs.com, include your name, affiliation, title, and electronic mail address.

We have endeavored to eliminate typos, bugs, and the like from the text. But, as in new releases of software, bugs probably remain; an up-to-date errata list is accessible from the book's home page. We would appreciate it if you would notify us of any errors or omissions in the book that are not on the current list of errata.

We would be glad to receive suggestions on improvements to the books. We also welcome any contributions to the book Web page that could be of use to other readers, such as programming exercises, project suggestions, online labs and tutorials, and teaching tips.

E-mail should be addressed to db-book@research.bell-labs.com. Any other correspondence should be sent to Avi Silberschatz, Bell Laboratories, Room 2T-310, 600 Mountain Avenue, Murray Hill, NJ 07974, USA.

Acknowledgments

This edition has benefited from the many useful comments provided to us by the numerous students who have used the third edition. In addition, many people have written or spoken to us about the book, and have offered suggestions and comments. Although we cannot mention all these people here, we especially thank the following:

- Phil Bernhard, Florida Institute of Technology; Eitan M. Gurari, The Ohio State University; Irwin Levinstein, Old Dominion University; Ling Liu, Georgia Institute of Technology; Ami Motro, George Mason University; Bhagirath Narahari, Meral Ozsoyoglu, Case Western Reserve University; and Odinaldo Rodriguez, King's College London; who served as reviewers of the book and whose comments helped us greatly in formulating this fourth edition.

- Soumen Chakrabarti, Sharad Mehrotra, Krithi Ramamritham, Mike Reiter, Sunita Sarawagi, N. L. Sarda, and Dilys Thomas, for extensive and invaluable feedback on several chapters of the book.

- Phil Bohannon, for writing the first draft of Chapter 10 describing XML.

- Hakan Jakobsson (Oracle), Sriram Padmanabhan (IBM), and César Galindo-Legaria, Goetz Graefe, José A. Blakeley, Kalen Delaney, Michael Rys, Michael Zwilling, Sameet Agarwal, Thomas Casey (all of Microsoft) for writing the appendices describing the Oracle, IBM DB2, and Microsoft SQL Server database systems.

- Yuri Breitbart, for help with the distributed database chapter; Mike Reiter, for help with the security sections; and Jim Melton, for clarifications on SQL:1999.

- Marilyn Turnamian and Nandprasad Joshi, whose excellent secretarial assistance was essential for timely completion of this fourth edition.

The publisher was Betsy Jones. The senior developmental editor was Kelley Butcher. The project manager was Jill Peter. The executive marketing manager was John Wannemacher. The cover illustrator was Paul Tumbaugh while the cover designer was JoAnne Schopler. The freelance copyeditor was George Watson. The freelance proofreader was Marie Zartman. The supplement producer was Jodi Banowetz. The designer was Rick Noel. The freelance indexer was Tobiah Waldron.

This edition is based on the three previous editions, so we thank once again the many people who helped us with the first three editions, including R. B. Abhyankar, Don Batory, Haran Boral, Paul Bourgeois, Robert Brazile, Michael Carey, J. Edwards, Christos Faloutsos, Homma Farian, Alan Fekete, Shashi Gadia, Jim Gray, Le Gruenwald, Ron Hitchens, Yannis Ioannidis, Hyoung-Joo Kim, Won Kim, Henry Korth (father of Henry F.), Carol Kroll, Gary Lindstrom, Dave Maier, Keith Marzullo, Fletcher Mattox, Alberto Mendelzon, Hector Garcia-Molina, Ami Motro, Anil Nigam, Cyril Orji, Bruce Porter, Jim Peterson, K. V. Raghavan, Mark Roth, Marek Rusinkiewicz, S. Seshadri, Shashi Shekhar, Amit Sheth, Nandit Soparkar, Greg Speegle, and Marianne Winslett. Lyn Dupré copyedited the third edition and Sara Strandtman edited the text of the third edition. Greg Speegle, Dawn Bezviner, and K. V. Raghavan helped us to prepare the instructor's manual for earlier editions. The new cover is an evolution of the covers of the first three editions; Marilyn Turnamian created an early draft of the cover design for this edition. The idea of using ships as part of the cover concept was originally suggested to us by Bruce Stephan.

Finally, Sudarshan would like to acknowledge his wife, Sita, for her love and support, two-year old son Madhur for his love, and mother, Indira, for her support. Hank would like to acknowledge his wife, Joan, and his children, Abby and Joe, for their love and understanding. Avi would like to acknowledge his wife Haya, and his son, Aaron, for their patience and support during the revision of this book.

A. S.
H. F. K.
S. S.

CHAPTER 1

Introduction

A **database-management system** (DBMS) is a collection of interrelated data and a set of programs to access those data. The collection of data, usually referred to as the **database**, contains information relevant to an enterprise. The primary goal of a DBMS is to provide a way to store and retrieve database information that is both *convenient* and *efficient*.

Database systems are designed to manage large bodies of information. Management of data involves both defining structures for storage of information and providing mechanisms for the manipulation of information. In addition, the database system must ensure the safety of the information stored, despite system crashes or attempts at unauthorized access. If data are to be shared among several users, the system must avoid possible anomalous results.

Because information is so important in most organizations, computer scientists have developed a large body of concepts and techniques for managing data. These concepts and technique form the focus of this book. This chapter briefly introduces the principles of database systems.

1.1 Database System Applications

Databases are widely used. Here are some representative applications:

- *Banking*: For customer information, accounts, and loans, and banking transactions.

- *Airlines*: For reservations and schedule information. Airlines were among the first to use databases in a geographically distributed manner—terminals situated around the world accessed the central database system through phone lines and other data networks.

- *Universities*: For student information, course registrations, and grades.

- *Credit card transactions*: For purchases on credit cards and generation of monthly statements.

- *Telecommunication*: For keeping records of calls made, generating monthly bills, maintaining balances on prepaid calling cards, and storing information about the communication networks.

- *Finance*: For storing information about holdings, sales, and purchases of financial instruments such as stocks and bonds.

- *Sales*: For customer, product, and purchase information.

- *Manufacturing*: For management of supply chain and for tracking production of items in factories, inventories of items in warehouses/stores, and orders for items.

- *Human resources*: For information about employees, salaries, payroll taxes and benefits, and for generation of paychecks.

As the list illustrates, databases form an essential part of almost all enterprises today.

Over the course of the last four decades of the twentieth century, use of databases grew in all enterprises. In the early days, very few people interacted directly with database systems, although without realizing it they interacted with databases indirectly—through printed reports such as credit card statements, or through agents such as bank tellers and airline reservation agents. Then automated teller machines came along and let users interact directly with databases. Phone interfaces to computers (interactive voice response systems) also allowed users to deal directly with databases—a caller could dial a number, and press phone keys to enter information or to select alternative options, to find flight arrival/departure times, for example, or to register for courses in a university.

The internet revolution of the late 1990s sharply increased direct user access to databases. Organizations converted many of their phone interfaces to databases into Web interfaces, and made a variety of services and information available online. For instance, when you access an online bookstore and browse a book or music collection, you are accessing data stored in a database. When you enter an order online, your order is stored in a database. When you access a bank Web site and retrieve your bank balance and transaction information, the information is retrieved from the bank's database system. When you access a Web site, information about you may be retrieved from a database, to select which advertisements should be shown to you. Furthermore, data about your Web accesses may be stored in a database.

Thus, although user interfaces hide details of access to a database, and most people are not even aware they are dealing with a database, accessing databases forms an essential part of almost everyone's life today.

The importance of database systems can be judged in another way—today, database system vendors like Oracle are among the largest software companies in the world, and database systems form an important part of the product line of more diversified companies like Microsoft and IBM.

1.2   Database Systems versus File Systems

Consider part of a savings-bank enterprise that keeps information about all customers and savings accounts. One way to keep the information on a computer is to store it in operating system files. To allow users to manipulate the information, the system has a number of application programs that manipulate the files, including

- A program to debit or credit an account

- A program to add a new account

- A program to find the balance of an account

- A program to generate monthly statements

System programmers wrote these application programs to meet the needs of the bank.

New application programs are added to the system as the need arises. For example, suppose that the savings bank decides to offer checking accounts. As a result, the bank creates new permanent files that contain information about all the checking accounts maintained in the bank, and it may have to write new application programs to deal with situations that do not arise in savings accounts, such as overdrafts. Thus, as time goes by, the system acquires more files and more application programs.

This typical **file-processing system** is supported by a conventional operating system. The system stores permanent records in various files, and it needs different application programs to extract records from, and add records to, the appropriate files. Before database management systems (DBMSs) came along, organizations usually stored information in such systems.

Keeping organizational information in a file-processing system has a number of major disadvantages:

- **Data redundancy and inconsistency**. Since different programmers create the files and application programs over a long period, the various files are likely to have different formats and the programs may be written in several programming languages. Moreover, the same information may be duplicated in several places (files). For example, the address and telephone number of a particular customer may appear in a file that consists of savings-account records and in a file that consists of checking-account records. This redundancy leads to higher storage and access cost. In addition, it may lead to **data inconsistency**; that is, the various copies of the same data may no longer agree. For example, a changed customer address may be reflected in savings-account records but not elsewhere in the system.

- **Difficulty in accessing data**. Suppose that one of the bank officers needs to find out the names of all customers who live within a particular postal-code area. The officer asks the data-processing department to generate such a list. Because the designers of the original system did not anticipate this request, there is no application program on hand to meet it. There is, however, an application program to generate the list of *all* customers. The bank officer has now two choices: either obtain the list of all customers and extract the needed information manually or ask a system programmer to write the necessary application program. Both alternatives are obviously unsatisfactory. Suppose that such a program is written, and that, several days later, the same officer needs to trim that list to include only those customers who have an account balance of $10,000 or more. As expected, a program to generate such a list does not exist. Again, the officer has the preceding two options, neither of which is satisfactory.

The point here is that conventional file-processing environments do not allow needed data to be retrieved in a convenient and efficient manner. More responsive data-retrieval systems are required for general use.

- **Data isolation**. Because data are scattered in various files, and files may be in different formats, writing new application programs to retrieve the appropriate data is difficult.

- **Integrity problems**. The data values stored in the database must satisfy certain types of **consistency constraints**. For example, the balance of a bank account may never fall below a prescribed amount (say, $25). Developers enforce these constraints in the system by adding appropriate code in the various application programs. However, when new constraints are added, it is difficult to change the programs to enforce them. The problem is compounded when constraints involve several data items from different files.

- **Atomicity problems**. A computer system, like any other mechanical or electrical device, is subject to failure. In many applications, it is crucial that, if a failure occurs, the data be restored to the consistent state that existed prior to the failure. Consider a program to transfer $50 from account A to account B. If a system failure occurs during the execution of the program, it is possible that the $50 was removed from account A but was not credited to account B, resulting in an inconsistent database state. Clearly, it is essential to database consistency that either both the credit and debit occur, or that neither occur. That is, the funds transfer must be *atomic*—it must happen in its entirety or not at all. It is difficult to ensure atomicity in a conventional file-processing system.

- **Concurrent-access anomalies**. For the sake of overall performance of the system and faster response, many systems allow multiple users to update the data simultaneously. In such an environment, interaction of concurrent updates may result in inconsistent data. Consider bank account A, containing $500. If two customers withdraw funds (say $50 and $100 respectively) from account A at about the same time, the result of the concurrent executions may leave the account in an incorrect (or inconsistent) state. Suppose that the programs executing on behalf of each withdrawal read the old balance, reduce that value by the amount being withdrawn, and write the result back. If the two programs run concurrently, they may both read the value $500, and write back $450 and $400, respectively. Depending on which one writes the value last, the account may contain either $450 or $400, rather than the correct value of $350. To guard against this possibility, the system must maintain some form of supervision. But supervision is difficult to provide because data may be accessed by many different application programs that have not been coordinated previously.

- **Security problems**. Not every user of the database system should be able to access all the data. For example, in a banking system, payroll personnel need to see only that part of the database that has information about the various bank employees. They do not need access to information about customer accounts. But, since application programs are added to the system in an ad hoc manner, enforcing such security constraints is difficult.

These difficulties, among others, prompted the development of database systems. In what follows, we shall see the concepts and algorithms that enable database systems to solve the problems with file-processing systems. In most of this book, we use a bank enterprise as a running example of a typical data-processing application found in a corporation.

1.3   View of Data

A database system is a collection of interrelated files and a set of programs that allow users to access and modify these files. A major purpose of a database system is to provide users with an *abstract* view of the data. That is, the system hides certain details of how the data are stored and maintained.

1.3.1   Data Abstraction

For the system to be usable, it must retrieve data efficiently. The need for efficiency has led designers to use complex data structures to represent data in the database. Since many database-systems users are not computer trained, developers hide the complexity from users through several levels of abstraction, to simplify users' interactions with the system:

- **Physical level**. The lowest level of abstraction describes *how* the data are actually stored. The physical level describes complex low-level data structures in detail.

- **Logical level**. The next-higher level of abstraction describes *what* data are stored in the database, and what relationships exist among those data. The logical level thus describes the entire database in terms of a small number of relatively simple structures. Although implementation of the simple structures at the logical level may involve complex physical-level structures, the user of the logical level does not need to be aware of this complexity. Database administrators, who must decide what information to keep in the database, use the logical level of abstraction.

- **View level**. The highest level of abstraction describes only part of the entire database. Even though the logical level uses simpler structures, complexity remains because of the variety of information stored in a large database. Many users of the database system do not need all this information; instead, they need to access only a part of the database. The view level of abstraction exists to simplify their interaction with the system. The system may provide many views for the same database.

Figure 1.1 shows the relationship among the three levels of abstraction.

An analogy to the concept of data types in programming languages may clarify the distinction among levels of abstraction. Most high-level programming languages support the notion of a record type. For example, in a Pascal-like language, we may declare a record as follows:

```
type customer = record
            customer-id : string;
            customer-name : string;
            customer-street : string;
            customer-city : string;
        end;
```

This code defines a new record type called *customer* with four fields. Each field has a name and a type associated with it. A banking enterprise may have several such record types, including

- *account*, with fields *account-number* and *balance*

- *employee*, with fields *employee-name* and *salary*

At the physical level, a *customer*, *account*, or *employee* record can be described as a block of consecutive storage locations (for example, words or bytes). The language

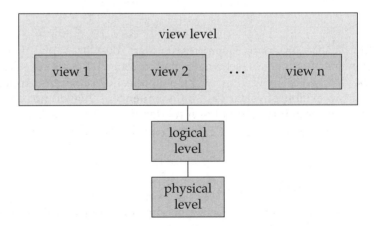

Figure 1.1   The three levels of data abstraction.

compiler hides this level of detail from programmers. Similarly, the database system hides many of the lowest-level storage details from database programmers. Database administrators, on the other hand, may be aware of certain details of the physical organization of the data.

At the logical level, each such record is described by a type definition, as in the previous code segment, and the interrelationship of these record types is defined as well. Programmers using a programming language work at this level of abstraction. Similarly, database administrators usually work at this level of abstraction.

Finally, at the view level, computer users see a set of application programs that hide details of the data types. Similarly, at the view level, several views of the database are defined, and database users see these views. In addition to hiding details of the logical level of the database, the views also provide a security mechanism to prevent users from accessing certain parts of the database. For example, tellers in a bank see only that part of the database that has information on customer accounts; they cannot access information about salaries of employees.

1.3.2   Instances and Schemas

Databases change over time as information is inserted and deleted. The collection of information stored in the database at a particular moment is called an **instance** of the database. The overall design of the database is called the database **schema**. Schemas are changed infrequently, if at all.

The concept of database schemas and instances can be understood by analogy to a program written in a programming language. A database schema corresponds to the variable declarations (along with associated type definitions) in a program. Each variable has a particular value at a given instant. The values of the variables in a program at a point in time correspond to an *instance* of a database schema.

Database systems have several schemas, partitioned according to the levels of abstraction. The **physical schema** describes the database design at the physical level, while the **logical schema** describes the database design at the logical level. A database may also have several schemas at the view level, sometimes called **subschemas**, that describe different views of the database.

Of these, the logical schema is by far the most important, in terms of its effect on application programs, since programmers construct applications by using the logical schema. The physical schema is hidden beneath the logical schema, and can usually be changed easily without affecting application programs. Application programs are said to exhibit **physical data independence** if they do not depend on the physical schema, and thus need not be rewritten if the physical schema changes.

We study languages for describing schemas, after introducing the notion of data models in the next section.

1.4   Data Models

Underlying the structure of a database is the **data model**: a collection of conceptual tools for describing data, data relationships, data semantics, and consistency constraints. To illustrate the concept of a data model, we outline two data models in this section: the entity-relationship model and the relational model. Both provide a way to describe the design of a database at the logical level.

1.4.1 The Entity-Relationship Model

The entity-relationship (E-R) data model is based on a perception of a real world that consists of a collection of basic objects, called *entities*, and of *relationships* among these objects. An entity is a "thing" or "object" in the real world that is distinguishable from other objects. For example, each person is an entity, and bank accounts can be considered as entities.

Entities are described in a database by a set of **attributes**. For example, the attributes *account-number* and *balance* may describe one particular account in a bank, and they form attributes of the *account* entity set. Similarly, attributes *customer-name*, *customer-street* address and *customer-city* may describe a *customer* entity.

An extra attribute *customer-id* is used to uniquely identify customers (since it may be possible to have two customers with the same name, street address, and city). A unique customer identifier must be assigned to each customer. In the United States, many enterprises use the social-security number of a person (a unique number the U.S. government assigns to every person in the United States) as a customer identifier.

A **relationship** is an association among several entities. For example, a *depositor* relationship associates a customer with each account that she has. The set of all entities of the same type and the set of all relationships of the same type are termed an **entity set** and **relationship set**, respectively.

The overall logical structure (schema) of a database can be expressed graphically by an *E-R diagram*, which is built up from the following components:

- **Rectangles**, which represent entity sets
- **Ellipses**, which represent attributes
- **Diamonds**, which represent relationships among entity sets
- **Lines**, which link attributes to entity sets and entity sets to relationships

Each component is labeled with the entity or relationship that it represents.

As an illustration, consider part of a database banking system consisting of customers and of the accounts that these customers have. Figure 1.2 shows the corresponding E-R diagram. The E-R diagram indicates that there are two entity sets, *customer* and *account*, with attributes as outlined earlier. The diagram also shows a relationship *depositor* between customer and account.

In addition to entities and relationships, the E-R model represents certain constraints to which the contents of a database must conform. One important constraint is **mapping cardinalities**, which express the number of entities to which another entity can be associated via a relationship set. For example, if each account must belong to only one customer, the E-R model can express that constraint.

The entity-relationship model is widely used in database design, and Chapter 2 explores it in detail.

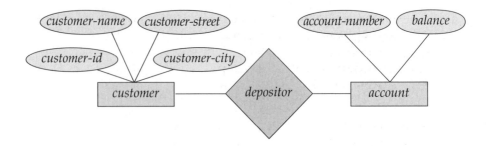

Figure 1.2   A sample E-R diagram.

1.4.2 Relational Model

The relational model uses a collection of tables to represent both data and the relationships among those data. Each table has multiple columns, and each column has a unique name. Figure 1.3 presents a sample relational database comprising three tables: One shows details of bank customers, the second shows accounts, and the third shows which accounts belong to which customers.

The first table, the *customer* table, shows, for example, that the customer identified by customer-id 192-83-7465 is named Johnson and lives at 12 Alma St. in Palo Alto. The second table, *account*, shows, for example, that account A-101 has a balance of $500, and A-201 has a balance of $900.

The third table shows which accounts belong to which customers. For example, account number A-101 belongs to the customer whose customer-id is 192-83-7465, namely Johnson, and customers 192-83-7465 (Johnson) and 019-28-3746 (Smith) share account number A-201 (they may share a business venture).

The relational model is an example of a record-based model. Record-based models are so named because the database is structured in fixed-format records of several types. Each table contains records of a particular type. Each record type defines a fixed number of fields, or attributes. The columns of the table correspond to the attributes of the record type.

It is not hard to see how tables may be stored in files. For instance, a special character (such as a comma) may be used to delimit the different attributes of a record, and another special character (such as a newline character) may be used to delimit records. The relational model hides such low-level implementation details from database developers and users.

The relational data model is the most widely used data model, and a vast majority of current database systems are based on the relational model. Chapters 3 through 7 cover the relational model in detail.

The relational model is at a lower level of abstraction than the E-R model. Database designs are often carried out in the E-R model, and then translated to the relational model; Chapter 2 describes the translation process. For example, it is easy to see that the tables *customer* and *account* correspond to the entity sets of the same name, while the table *depositor* corresponds to the relationship set *depositor*.

We also note that it is possible to create schemas in the relational model that have problems such as unnecessarily duplicated information. For example, suppose we

customer-id	customer-name	customer-street	customer-city
192-83-7465	Johnson	12 Alma St.	Palo Alto
019-28-3746	Smith	4 North St.	Rye
677-89-9011	Hayes	3 Main St.	Harrison
182-73-6091	Turner	123 Putnam Ave.	Stamford
321-12-3123	Jones	100 Main St.	Harrison
336-66-9999	Lindsay	175 Park Ave.	Pittsfield
019-28-3746	Smith	72 North St.	Rye

(a) The *customer* table

account-number	balance
A-101	500
A-215	700
A-102	400
A-305	350
A-201	900
A-217	750
A-222	700

(b) The *account* table

customer-id	account-number
192-83-7465	A-101
192-83-7465	A-201
019-28-3746	A-215
677-89-9011	A-102
182-73-6091	A-305
321-12-3123	A-217
336-66-9999	A-222
019-28-3746	A-201

(c) The *depositor* table

Figure 1.3 A sample relational database.

store *account-number* as an attribute of the *customer* record. Then, to represent the fact that accounts A-101 and A-201 both belong to customer Johnson (with customer-id 192-83-7465), we would need to store two rows in the *customer* table. The values for customer-name, customer-street, and customer-city for Johnson would get unnecessarily duplicated in the two rows. In Chapter 7, we shall study how to distinguish good schema designs from bad schema designs.

1.4.3 Other Data Models

The **object-oriented data model** is another data model that has seen increasing attention. The object-oriented model can be seen as extending the E-R model with notions

of encapsulation, methods (functions), and object identity. Chapter 8 examines the object-oriented data model.

The **object-relational data model** combines features of the object-oriented data model and relational data model. Chapter 9 examines it.

Semistructured data models permit the specification of data where individual data items of the same type may have different sets of attributes. This is in contrast with the data models mentioned earlier, where every data item of a particular type must have the same set of attributes. The **extensible markup language (XML)** is widely used to represent semistructured data. Chapter 10 covers it.

Historically, two other data models, the **network data model** and the **hierarchical data model**, preceded the relational data model. These models were tied closely to the underlying implementation, and complicated the task of modeling data. As a result they are little used now, except in old database code that is still in service in some places. They are outlined in Appendices A and B, for interested readers.

1.5   Database Languages

A database system provides a **data definition language** to specify the database schema and a **data manipulation language** to express database queries and updates. In practice, the data definition and data manipulation languages are not two separate languages; instead they simply form parts of a single database language, such as the widely used SQL language.

1.5.1   Data-Definition Language

We specify a database schema by a set of definitions expressed by a special language called a **data-definition language** (DDL).

For instance, the following statement in the SQL language defines the *account* table:

> **create table** *account*
> (*account-number* **char**(10),
> *balance* **integer**)

Execution of the above DDL statement creates the *account* table. In addition, it updates a special set of tables called the **data dictionary** or **data directory**.

A data dictionary contains **metadata**—that is, data about data. The schema of a table is an example of metadata. A database system consults the data dictionary before reading or modifying actual data.

We specify the storage structure and access methods used by the database system by a set of statements in a special type of DDL called a **data storage and definition** language. These statements define the implementation details of the database schemas, which are usually hidden from the users.

The data values stored in the database must satisfy certain **consistency constraints**. For example, suppose the balance on an account should not fall below $100. The DDL provides facilities to specify such constraints. The database systems check these constraints every time the database is updated.

1.5.2 Data-Manipulation Language

Data manipulation is

- The retrieval of information stored in the database

- The insertion of new information into the database

- The deletion of information from the database

- The modification of information stored in the database

A **data-manipulation language (DML)** is a language that enables users to access or manipulate data as organized by the appropriate data model. There are basically two types:

- **Procedural DMLs** require a user to specify *what* data are needed and *how* to get those data.

- **Declarative DMLs** (also referred to as **nonprocedural** DMLs) require a user to specify *what* data are needed *without* specifying how to get those data.

Declarative DMLs are usually easier to learn and use than are procedural DMLs. However, since a user does not have to specify how to get the data, the database system has to figure out an efficient means of accessing data. The DML component of the SQL language is nonprocedural.

A **query** is a statement requesting the retrieval of information. The portion of a DML that involves information retrieval is called a **query language**. Although technically incorrect, it is common practice to use the terms *query language* and *data-manipulation language* synonymously.

This query in the SQL language finds the name of the customer whose customer-id is 192-83-7465:

> **select** *customer.customer-name*
> **from** *customer*
> **where** *customer.customer-id* = 192-83-7465

The query specifies that those rows *from* the table *customer where* the *customer-id* is 192-83-7465 must be retrieved, and the *customer-name* attribute of these rows must be displayed. If the query were run on the table in Figure 1.3, the name Johnson would be displayed.

Queries may involve information from more than one table. For instance, the following query finds the balance of all accounts owned by the customer with customer-id 192-83-7465.

> **select** *account.balance*
> **from** *depositor, account*
> **where** *depositor.customer-id* = 192-83-7465 **and**
>   *depositor.account-number* = *account.account-number*

If the above query were run on the tables in Figure 1.3, the system would find that the two accounts numbered A-101 and A-201 are owned by customer 192-83-7465 and would print out the balances of the two accounts, namely 500 and 900.

There are a number of database query languages in use, either commercially or experimentally. We study the most widely used query language, SQL, in Chapter 4. We also study some other query languages in Chapter 5.

The levels of abstraction that we discussed in Section 1.3 apply not only to defining or structuring data, but also to manipulating data. At the physical level, we must define algorithms that allow efficient access to data. At higher levels of abstraction, we emphasize ease of use. The goal is to allow humans to interact efficiently with the system. The query processor component of the database system (which we study in Chapters 13 and 14) translates DML queries into sequences of actions at the physical level of the database system.

1.5.3   Database Access from Application Programs

Application programs are programs that are used to interact with the database. Application programs are usually written in a *host* language, such as Cobol, C, C++, or Java. Examples in a banking system are programs that generate payroll checks, debit accounts, credit accounts, or transfer funds between accounts.

To access the database, DML statements need to be executed from the host language. There are two ways to do this:

- By providing an application program interface (set of procedures) that can be used to send DML and DDL statements to the database, and retrieve the results.

    The Open Database Connectivity (ODBC) standard defined by Microsoft for use with the C language is a commonly used application program interface standard. The Java Database Connectivity (JDBC) standard provides corresponding features to the Java language.

- By extending the host language syntax to embed DML calls within the host language program. Usually, a special character prefaces DML calls, and a preprocessor, called the *DML* **precompiler**, converts the DML statements to normal procedure calls in the host language.

1.6   Database Users and Administrators

A primary goal of a database system is to retrieve information from and store new information in the database. People who work with a database can be categorized as database users or database administrators.

1.6.1   Database Users and User Interfaces

There are four different types of database-system users, differentiated by the way they expect to interact with the system. Different types of user interfaces have been designed for the different types of users.

- **Naive users** are unsophisticated users who interact with the system by invoking one of the application programs that have been written previously. For example, a bank teller who needs to transfer $50 from account *A* to account *B* invokes a program called *transfer*. This program asks the teller for the amount of money to be transferred, the account from which the money is to be transferred, and the account to which the money is to be transferred.

  As another example, consider a user who wishes to find her account balance over the World Wide Web. Such a user may access a form, where she enters her account number. An application program at the Web server then retrieves the account balance, using the given account number, and passes this information back to the user.

  The typical user interface for naive users is a forms interface, where the user can fill in appropriate fields of the form. Naive users may also simply read *reports* generated from the database.

- **Application programmers** are computer professionals who write application programs. Application programmers can choose from many tools to develop user interfaces. **Rapid application development (RAD)** tools are tools that enable an application programmer to construct forms and reports without writing a program. There are also special types of programming languages that combine imperative control structures (for example, for loops, while loops and if-then-else statements) with statements of the data manipulation language. These languages, sometimes called *fourth-generation languages*, often include special features to facilitate the generation of forms and the display of data on the screen. Most major commercial database systems include a fourth-generation language.

- **Sophisticated users** interact with the system without writing programs. Instead, they form their requests in a database query language. They submit each such query to a **query processor**, whose function is to break down DML statements into instructions that the storage manager understands. Analysts who submit queries to explore data in the database fall in this category.

  Online analytical processing (OLAP) tools simplify analysts' tasks by letting them view summaries of data in different ways. For instance, an analyst can see total sales by region (for example, North, South, East, and West), or by product, or by a combination of region and product (that is, total sales of each product in each region). The tools also permit the analyst to select specific regions, look at data in more detail (for example, sales by city within a region) or look at the data in less detail (for example, aggregate products together by category).

  Another class of tools for analysts is **data mining** tools, which help them find certain kinds of patterns in data.

  We study OLAP tools and data mining in Chapter 22.

- **Specialized users** are sophisticated users who write specialized database applications that do not fit into the traditional data-processing framework. Among these applications are computer-aided design systems, knowledge-base and expert systems, systems that store data with complex data types (for example, graphics data and audio data), and environment-modeling systems. Chapters 8 and 9 cover several of these applications.

1.6.2   Database Administrator

One of the main reasons for using DBMSs is to have central control of both the data and the programs that access those data. A person who has such central control over the system is called a **database administrator (DBA)**. The functions of a DBA include:

- **Schema definition**. The DBA creates the original database schema by executing a set of data definition statements in the DDL.

- **Storage structure and access-method definition**.

- **Schema and physical-organization modification**. The DBA carries out changes to the schema and physical organization to reflect the changing needs of the organization, or to alter the physical organization to improve performance.

- **Granting of authorization for data access**. By granting different types of authorization, the database administrator can regulate which parts of the database various users can access. The authorization information is kept in a special system structure that the database system consults whenever someone attempts to access the data in the system.

- **Routine maintenance**. Examples of the database administrator's routine maintenance activities are:
  - ☐ Periodically backing up the database, either onto tapes or onto remote servers, to prevent loss of data in case of disasters such as flooding.
  - ☐ Ensuring that enough free disk space is available for normal operations, and upgrading disk space as required.
  - ☐ Monitoring jobs running on the database and ensuring that performance is not degraded by very expensive tasks submitted by some users.

1.7   Transaction Management

Often, several operations on the database form a single logical unit of work. An example is a funds transfer, as in Section 1.2, in which one account (say A) is debited and another account (say B) is credited. Clearly, it is essential that either both the credit and debit occur, or that neither occur. That is, the funds transfer must happen in its entirety or not at all. This all-or-none requirement is called **atomicity**. In addition, it is essential that the execution of the funds transfer preserve the consistency of the database. That is, the value of the sum $A + B$ must be preserved. This correctness requirement is called **consistency**. Finally, after the successful execution of a funds transfer, the new values of accounts A and B must persist, despite the possibility of system failure. This persistence requirement is called **durability**.

A **transaction** is a collection of operations that performs a single logical function in a database application. Each transaction is a unit of both atomicity and consistency. Thus, we require that transactions do not violate any database-consistency constraints. That is, if the database was consistent when a transaction started, the database must be consistent when the transaction successfully terminates. However, during the execution of a transaction, it may be necessary temporarily to allow inconsistency, since either the debit of A or the credit of B must be done before the other. This temporary inconsistency, although necessary, may lead to difficulty if a failure occurs.

It is the programmer's responsibility to define properly the various transactions, so that each preserves the consistency of the database. For example, the transaction to transfer funds from account A to account B could be defined to be composed of two separate programs: one that debits account A, and another that credits account B. The execution of these two programs one after the other will indeed preserve consistency. However, each program by itself does not transform the database from a consistent state to a new consistent state. Thus, those programs are not transactions.

Ensuring the atomicity and durability properties is the responsibility of the database system itself—specifically, of the **transaction-management component**. In the absence of failures, all transactions complete successfully, and atomicity is achieved easily. However, because of various types of failure, a transaction may not always complete its execution successfully. If we are to ensure the atomicity property, a failed transaction must have no effect on the state of the database. Thus, the database must be restored to the state in which it was before the transaction in question started executing. The database system must therefore perform **failure recovery**, that is, detect system failures and restore the database to the state that existed prior to the occurrence of the failure.

Finally, when several transactions update the database concurrently, the consistency of data may no longer be preserved, even though each individual transaction is correct. It is the responsibility of the **concurrency-control manager** to control the interaction among the concurrent transactions, to ensure the consistency of the database.

Database systems designed for use on small personal computers may not have all these features. For example, many small systems allow only one user to access the database at a time. Others do not offer backup and recovery, leaving that to the user. These restrictions allow for a smaller data manager, with fewer requirements for physical resources—especially main memory. Although such a low-cost, low-feature approach is adequate for small personal databases, it is inadequate for a medium- to large-scale enterprise.

1.8 Database System Structure

A database system is partitioned into modules that deal with each of the responsibilites of the overall system. The functional components of a database system can be broadly divided into the storage manager and the query processor components.

The storage manager is important because databases typically require a large amount of storage space. Corporate databases range in size from hundreds of gigabytes to, for the largest databases, terabytes of data. A gigabyte is 1000 megabytes

(1 billion bytes), and a terabyte is 1 million megabytes (1 trillion bytes). Since the main memory of computers cannot store this much information, the information is stored on disks. Data are moved between disk storage and main memory as needed. Since the movement of data to and from disk is slow relative to the speed of the central processing unit, it is imperative that the database system structure the data so as to minimize the need to move data between disk and main memory.

The query processor is important because it helps the database system simplify and facilitate access to data. High-level views help to achieve this goal; with them, users of the system are not be burdened unnecessarily with the physical details of the implementation of the system. However, quick processing of updates and queries is important. It is the job of the database system to translate updates and queries written in a nonprocedural language, at the logical level, into an efficient sequence of operations at the physical level.

1.8.1 Storage Manager

A *storage manager* is a program module that provides the interface between the low-level data stored in the database and the application programs and queries submitted to the system. The storage manager is responsible for the interaction with the file manager. The raw data are stored on the disk using the file system, which is usually provided by a conventional operating system. The storage manager translates the various DML statements into low-level file-system commands. Thus, the storage manager is responsible for storing, retrieving, and updating data in the database.

The storage manager components include:

- **Authorization and integrity manager**, which tests for the satisfaction of integrity constraints and checks the authority of users to access data.

- **Transaction manager**, which ensures that the database remains in a consistent (correct) state despite system failures, and that concurrent transaction executions proceed without conflicting.

- **File manager**, which manages the allocation of space on disk storage and the data structures used to represent information stored on disk.

- **Buffer manager**, which is responsible for fetching data from disk storage into main memory, and deciding what data to cache in main memory. The buffer manager is a critical part of the database system, since it enables the database to handle data sizes that are much larger than the size of main memory.

The storage manager implements several data structures as part of the physical system implementation:

- **Data files**, which store the database itself.

- **Data dictionary**, which stores metadata about the structure of the database, in particular the schema of the database.

- **Indices**, which provide fast access to data items that hold particular values.

1.8.2 The Query Processor

The query processor components include

- **DDL interpreter**, which interprets DDL statements and records the definitions in the data dictionary.

- **DML** compiler, which translates DML statements in a query language into an evaluation plan consisting of low-level instructions that the query evaluation engine understands.

    A query can usually be translated into any of a number of alternative evaluation plans that all give the same result. The DML compiler also performs **query optimization**, that is, it picks the lowest cost evaluation plan from among the alternatives.

- **Query evaluation engine**, which executes low-level instructions generated by the DML compiler.

Figure 1.4 shows these components and the connections among them.

1.9 Application Architectures

Most users of a database system today are not present at the site of the database system, but connect to it through a network. We can therefore differentiate between **client** machines, on which remote database users work, and **server** machines, on which the database system runs.

Database applications are usually partitioned into two or three parts, as in Figure 1.5. In a **two-tier architecture**, the application is partitioned into a component that resides at the client machine, which invokes database system functionality at the server machine through query language statements. Application program interface standards like ODBC and JDBC are used for interaction between the client and the server.

In contrast, in a **three-tier architecture**, the client machine acts as merely a front end and does not contain any direct database calls. Instead, the client end communicates with an **application server**, usually through a forms interface. The application server in turn communicates with a database system to access data. The **business logic** of the application, which says what actions to carry out under what conditions, is embedded in the application server, instead of being distributed across multiple clients. Three-tier applications are more appropriate for large applications, and for applications that run on the World Wide Web.

1.10 History of Database Systems

Data processing drives the growth of computers, as it has from the earliest days of commercial computers. In fact, automation of data processing tasks predates computers. Punched cards, invented by Hollerith, were used at the very beginning of the twentieth century to record U.S. census data, and mechanical systems were used to

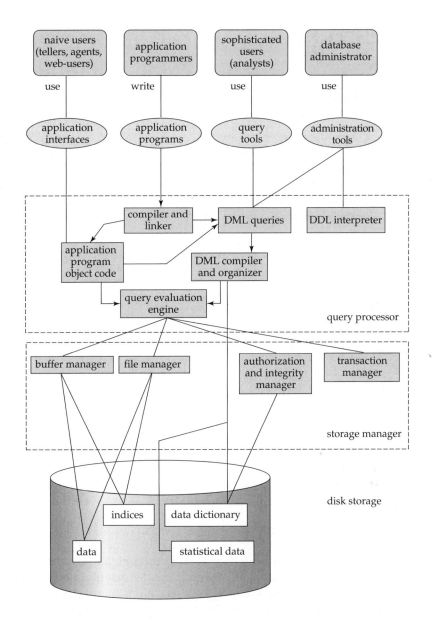

Figure 1.4   System structure.

process the cards and tabulate results. Punched cards were later widely used as a means of entering data into computers.

Techniques for data storage and processing have evolved over the years:

- **1950s and early 1960s**: Magnetic tapes were developed for data storage. Data processing tasks such as payroll were automated, with data stored on tapes. Processing of data consisted of reading data from one or more tapes and

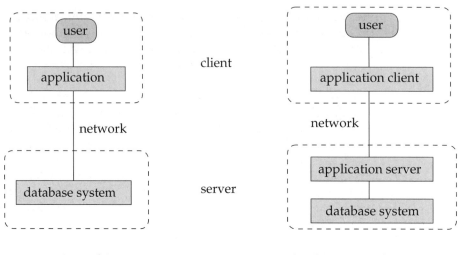

a. two-tier architecture   b. three-tier architecture

Figure 1.5   Two-tier and three-tier architectures.

writing data to a new tape. Data could also be input from punched card decks, and output to printers. For example, salary raises were processed by entering the raises on punched cards and reading the punched card deck in synchronization with a tape containing the master salary details. The records had to be in the same sorted order. The salary raises would be added to the salary read from the master tape, and written to a new tape; the new tape would become the new master tape.

Tapes (and card decks) could be read only sequentially, and data sizes were much larger than main memory; thus, data processing programs were forced to process data in a particular order, by reading and merging data from tapes and card decks.

- **Late 1960s and 1970s**: Widespread use of hard disks in the late 1960s changed the scenario for data processing greatly, since hard disks allowed direct access to data. The position of data on disk was immaterial, since any location on disk could be accessed in just tens of milliseconds. Data were thus freed from the tyranny of sequentiality. With disks, network and hierarchical databases could be created that allowed data structures such as lists and trees to be stored on disk. Programmers could construct and manipulate these data structures.

  A landmark paper by Codd [1970] defined the relational model, and non-procedural ways of querying data in the relational model, and relational databases were born. The simplicity of the relational model and the possibility of hiding implementation details completely from the programmer were enticing indeed. Codd later won the prestigious Association of Computing Machinery Turing Award for his work.

- **1980s:** Although academically interesting, the relational model was not used in practice initially, because of its perceived performance disadvantages; relational databases could not match the performance of existing network and hierarchical databases. That changed with System R, a groundbreaking project at IBM Research that developed techniques for the construction of an efficient relational database system. Excellent overviews of System R are provided by Astrahan et al. [1976] and Chamberlin et al. [1981]. The fully functional System R prototype led to IBM's first relational database product, SQL/DS. Initial commercial relational database systems, such as IBM DB2, Oracle, Ingres, and DEC Rdb, played a major role in advancing techniques for efficient processing of declarative queries. By the early 1980s, relational databases had become competitive with network and hierarchical database systems even in the area of performance. Relational databases were so easy to use that they eventually replaced network/hierarchical databases; programmers using such databases were forced to deal with many low-level implementation details, and had to code their queries in a procedural fashion. Most importantly, they had to keep efficiency in mind when designing their programs, which involved a lot of effort. In contrast, in a relational database, almost all these low-level tasks are carried out automatically by the database, leaving the programmer free to work at a logical level. Since attaining dominance in the 1980s, the relational model has reigned supreme among data models.

    The 1980s also saw much research on parallel and distributed databases, as well as initial work on object-oriented databases.

- **Early 1990s:** The SQL language was designed primarily for decision support applications, which are query intensive, yet the mainstay of databases in the 1980s was transaction processing applications, which are update intensive. Decision support and querying re-emerged as a major application area for databases. Tools for analyzing large amounts of data saw large growths in usage.

    Many database vendors introduced parallel database products in this period. Database vendors also began to add object-relational support to their databases.

- **Late 1990s:** The major event was the explosive growth of the World Wide Web. Databases were deployed much more extensively than ever before. Database systems now had to support very high transaction processing rates, as well as very high reliability and 24×7 availability (availability 24 hours a day, 7 days a week, meaning no downtime for scheduled maintenance activities). Database systems also had to support Web interfaces to data.

1.11 Summary

- A **database-management system** (DBMS) consists of a collection of interrelated data and a collection of programs to access that data. The data describe one particular enterprise.

- The primary goal of a DBMS is to provide an environment that is both convenient and efficient for people to use in retrieving and storing information.

- Database systems are ubiquitous today, and most people interact, either directly or indirectly, with databases many times every day.

- Database systems are designed to store large bodies of information. The management of data involves both the definition of structures for the storage of information and the provision of mechanisms for the manipulation of information. In addition, the database system must provide for the safety of the information stored, in the face of system crashes or attempts at unauthorized access. If data are to be shared among several users, the system must avoid possible anomalous results.

- A major purpose of a database system is to provide users with an abstract view of the data. That is, the system hides certain details of how the data are stored and maintained.

- Underlying the structure of a database is the **data model**: a collection of conceptual tools for describing data, data relationships, data semantics, and data constraints. The entity-relationship (E-R) data model is a widely used data model, and it provides a convenient graphical representation to view data, relationships and constraints. The relational data model is widely used to store data in databases. Other data models are the object-oriented model, the object-relational model, and semistructured data models.

- The overall design of the database is called the database **schema**. A database schema is specified by a set of definitions that are expressed using a **data-definition language (DDL)**.

- A **data-manipulation language (DML)** is a language that enables users to access or manipulate data. Nonprocedural DMLs, which require a user to specify only what data are needed, without specifying exactly how to get those data, are widely used today.

- Database users can be categorized into several classes, and each class of users usually uses a different type of interface to the database.

- A database system has several subsystems.
  - ☐ The **transaction manager** subsystem is responsible for ensuring that the database remains in a consistent (correct) state despite system failures. The transaction manager also ensures that concurrent transaction executions proceed without conflicting.
  - ☐ The **query processor** subsystem compiles and executes DDL and DML statements.
  - ☐ The **storage manager** subsystem provides the interface between the low-level data stored in the database and the application programs and queries submitted to the system.

- Database applications are typically broken up into a front-end part that runs at client machines and a part that runs at the back end. In two-tier architectures, the front-end directly communicates with a database running at the back end. In three-tier architectures, the back end part is itself broken up into an application server and a database server.

Review Terms

- Database management system (DBMS)
- Database systems applications
- File systems
- Data inconsistency
- Consistency constraints
- Data views
- Data abstraction
- Database instance
- Schema
    - ☐ Database schema
    - ☐ Physical schema
    - ☐ Logical schema
- Physical data independence
- Data models

- ☐ Entity-relationship model
- ☐ Relational data model
- ☐ Object-oriented data model
- ☐ Object-relational data model
- Database languages
    - ☐ Data definition language
    - ☐ Data manipulation language
    - ☐ Query language
- Data dictionary
- Metadata
- Application program
- Database administrator (DBA)
- Transactions
- Concurrency
- Client and server machines

Exercises

1.1 List four significant differences between a file-processing system and a DBMS.

1.2 This chapter has described several major advantages of a database system. What are two disadvantages?

1.3 Explain the difference between physical and logical data independence.

1.4 List five responsibilities of a database management system. For each responsibility, explain the problems that would arise if the responsibility were not discharged.

1.5 What are five main functions of a database administrator?

1.6 List seven programming languages that are procedural and two that are nonprocedural. Which group is easier to learn and use? Explain your answer.

1.7 List six major steps that you would take in setting up a database for a particular enterprise.

1.8 Consider a two-dimensional integer array of size $n \times m$ that is to be used in your favorite programming language. Using the array as an example, illustrate the difference (a) between the three levels of data abstraction, and (b) between a schema and instances.

Bibliographical Notes

We list below general purpose books, research paper collections, and Web sites on databases. Subsequent chapters provide references to material on each topic outlined in this chapter.

Textbooks covering database systems include Abiteboul et al. [1995], Date [1995], Elmasri and Navathe [2000], O'Neil and O'Neil [2000], Ramakrishnan and Gehrke [2000], and Ullman [1988]. Textbook coverage of transaction processing is provided by Bernstein and Newcomer [1997] and Gray and Reuter [1993].

Several books contain collections of research papers on database management. Among these are Bancilhon and Buneman [1990], Date [1986], Date [1990], Kim [1995], Zaniolo et al. [1997], and Stonebraker and Hellerstein [1998].

A review of accomplishments in database management and an assessment of future research challenges appears in Silberschatz et al. [1990], Silberschatz et al. [1996] and Bernstein et al. [1998]. The home page of the ACM Special Interest Group on Management of Data (see www.acm.org/sigmod) provides a wealth of information about database research. Database vendor Web sites (see the tools section below) provide details about their respective products.

Codd [1970] is the landmark paper that introduced the relational model. Discussions concerning the evolution of DBMSs and the development of database technology are offered by Fry and Sibley [1976] and Sibley [1976].

Tools

There are a large number of commercial database systems in use today. The major ones include: IBM DB2 (www.ibm.com/software/data), Oracle (www.oracle.com), Microsoft SQL Server (www.microsoft.com/sql), Informix (www.informix.com), and Sybase (www.sybase.com). Some of these systems are available free for personal or noncommercial use, or for development, but are not free for actual deployment.

There are also a number of free/public domain database systems; widely used ones include MySQL (www.mysql.com) and PostgresSQL (www.postgresql.org).

A more complete list of links to vendor Web sites and other information is available from the home page of this book, at www.research.bell-labs.com/topic/books/db-book.

PART 1

Data Models

A **data model** is a collection of conceptual tools for describing data, data relationships, data semantics, and consistency constraints. In this part, we study two data models—the entity–relationship model and the relational model.

The entity–relationship (E-R) model is a high-level data model. It is based on a perception of a real world that consists of a collection of basic objects, called *entities*, and of *relationships* among these objects.

The relational model is a lower-level model. It uses a collection of tables to represent both data and the relationships among those data. Its conceptual simplicity has led to its widespread adoption; today a vast majority of database products are based on the relational model. Designers often formulate database schema design by first modeling data at a high level, using the E-R model, and then translating it into the the relational model.

We shall study other data models later in the book. The object-oriented data model, for example, extends the representation of entities by adding notions of encapsulation, methods (functions), and object identity. The object-relational data model combines features of the object-oriented data model and the relational data model. Chapters 8 and 9, respectively, cover these two data models.

Entity-Relationship Model

The **entity-relationship** (**E-R**) data model perceives the real world as consisting of basic objects, called *entities*, and *relationships* among these objects. It was developed to facilitate database design by allowing specification of an *enterprise schema*, which represents the overall logical structure of a database. The E-R data model is one of several semantic data models; the semantic aspect of the model lies in its representation of the meaning of the data. The E-R model is very useful in mapping the meanings and interactions of real-world enterprises onto a conceptual schema. Because of this usefulness, many database-design tools draw on concepts from the E-R model.

2.1 Basic Concepts

The E-R data model employs three basic notions: entity sets, relationship sets, and attributes.

2.1.1 Entity Sets

An **entity** is a "thing" or "object" in the real world that is distinguishable from all other objects. For example, each person in an enterprise is an entity. An entity has a set of properties, and the values for some set of properties may uniquely identify an entity. For instance, a person may have a *person-id* property whose value uniquely identifies that person. Thus, the value 677-89-9011 for *person-id* would uniquely identify one particular person in the enterprise. Similarly, loans can be thought of as entities, and loan number L-15 at the Perryridge branch uniquely identifies a loan entity. An entity may be concrete, such as a person or a book, or it may be abstract, such as a loan, or a holiday, or a concept.

An **entity set** is a set of entities of the same type that share the same properties, or attributes. The set of all persons who are customers at a given bank, for example, can be defined as the entity set *customer*. Similarly, the entity set *loan* might represent the set of all loans awarded by a particular bank. The individual entities that constitute a set are said to be the *extension* of the entity set. Thus, all the individual bank customers are the extension of the entity set *customer*.

Entity sets do not need to be disjoint. For example, it is possible to define the entity set of all employees of a bank (*employee*) and the entity set of all customers of the bank (*customer*). A *person* entity may be an *employee* entity, a *customer* entity, both, or neither.

An entity is represented by a set of **attributes**. Attributes are descriptive properties possessed by each member of an entity set. The designation of an attribute for an entity set expresses that the database stores similar information concerning each entity in the entity set; however, each entity may have its own value for each attribute. Possible attributes of the *customer* entity set are *customer-id*, *customer-name*, *customer-street*, and *customer-city*. In real life, there would be further attributes, such as street number, apartment number, state, postal code, and country, but we omit them to keep our examples simple. Possible attributes of the *loan* entity set are *loan-number* and *amount*.

Each entity has a **value** for each of its attributes. For instance, a particular *customer* entity may have the value 321-12-3123 for *customer-id*, the value Jones for *customer-name*, the value Main for *customer-street*, and the value Harrison for *customer-city*.

The *customer-id* attribute is used to uniquely identify customers, since there may be more than one customer with the same name, street, and city. In the United States, many enterprises find it convenient to use the *social-security* number of a person[1] as an attribute whose value uniquely identifies the person. In general the enterprise would have to create and assign a unique identifier for each customer.

For each attribute, there is a set of permitted values, called the **domain**, or **value set**, of that attribute. The domain of attribute *customer-name* might be the set of all text strings of a certain length. Similarly, the domain of attribute *loan-number* might be the set of all strings of the form "L-n" where n is a positive integer.

A database thus includes a collection of entity sets, each of which contains any number of entities of the same type. Figure 2.1 shows part of a bank database that consists of two entity sets: *customer* and *loan*.

Formally, an attribute of an entity set is a function that maps from the entity set into a domain. Since an entity set may have several attributes, each entity can be described by a set of (attribute, data value) pairs, one pair for each attribute of the entity set. For example, a particular *customer* entity may be described by the set {(*customer-id*, 677-89-9011), (*customer-name*, Hayes), (*customer-street*, Main), (*customer-city*, Harrison)}, meaning that the entity describes a person named Hayes whose customer identifier is 677-89-9011 and who resides at Main Street in Harrison. We can see, at this point, an integration of the abstract schema with the actual enterprise being modeled. The attribute values describing an entity will constitute a significant portion of the data stored in the database.

An attribute, as used in the E-R model, can be characterized by the following attribute types.

---

1.   In the United States, the government assigns to each person in the country a unique number, called a social-security number, to identify that person uniquely. Each person is supposed to have only one social-security number, and no two people are supposed to have the same social-security number.

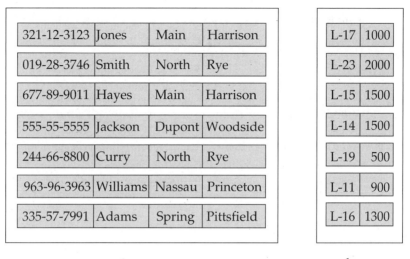

321-12-3123	Jones	Main	Harrison
019-28-3746	Smith	North	Rye
677-89-9011	Hayes	Main	Harrison
555-55-5555	Jackson	Dupont	Woodside
244-66-8800	Curry	North	Rye
963-96-3963	Williams	Nassau	Princeton
335-57-7991	Adams	Spring	Pittsfield

L-17	1000
L-23	2000
L-15	1500
L-14	1500
L-19	500
L-11	900
L-16	1300

customer   *loan*

Figure 2.1   Entity sets *customer* and *loan*.

- **Simple** and **composite** attributes. In our examples thus far, the attributes have been simple; that is, they are not divided into subparts. **Composite** attributes, on the other hand, can be divided into subparts (that is, other attributes). For example, an attribute *name* could be structured as a composite attribute consisting of *first-name*, *middle-initial*, and *last-name*. Using composite attributes in a design schema is a good choice if a user will wish to refer to an entire attribute on some occasions, and to only a component of the attribute on other occasions. Suppose we were to substitute for the *customer* entity-set attributes *customer-street* and *customer-city* the composite attribute *address* with the attributes *street*, *city*, *state*, and *zip-code*.[2] Composite attributes help us to group together related attributes, making the modeling cleaner.

  Note also that a composite attribute may appear as a hierarchy. In the composite attribute *address*, its component attribute *street* can be further divided into *street-number*, *street-name*, and *apartment-number*. Figure 2.2 depicts these examples of composite attributes for the *customer* entity set.

- **Single-valued** and **multivalued** attributes. The attributes in our examples all have a single value for a particular entity. For instance, the *loan-number* attribute for a specific loan entity refers to only one loan number. Such attributes are said to be **single valued**. There may be instances where an attribute has a set of values for a specific entity. Consider an *employee* entity set with the attribute *phone-number*. An employee may have zero, one, or several phone numbers, and different employees may have different numbers of phones. This type of attribute is said to be **multivalued**. As another example, an at-

---

2.   We assume the address format used in the United States, which includes a numeric postal code called a zip code.

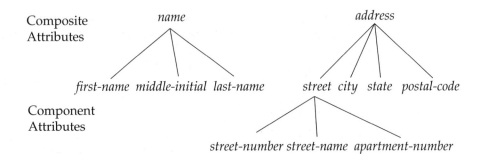

Figure 2.2 Composite attributes *customer-name* and *customer-address*.

tribute *dependent-name* of the *employee* entity set would be multivalued, since any particular employee may have zero, one, or more dependent(s).

Where appropriate, upper and lower bounds may be placed on the number of values in a multivalued attribute. For example, a bank may limit the number of phone numbers recorded for a single customer to two. Placing bounds in this case expresses that the *phone-number* attribute of the *customer* entity set may have between zero and two values.

- **Derived** attribute. The value for this type of attribute can be derived from the values of other related attributes or entities. For instance, let us say that the *customer* entity set has an attribute *loans-held*, which represents how many loans a customer has from the bank. We can derive the value for this attribute by counting the number of *loan* entities associated with that customer.

  As another example, suppose that the *customer* entity set has an attribute *age*, which indicates the customer's age. If the *customer* entity set also has an attribute *date-of-birth*, we can calculate *age* from *date-of-birth* and the current date. Thus, *age* is a derived attribute. In this case, *date-of-birth* may be referred to as a *base* attribute, or a *stored* attribute. The value of a derived attribute is not stored, but is computed when required.

An attribute takes a **null** value when an entity does not have a value for it. The *null* value may indicate "not applicable"—that is, that the value does not exist for the entity. For example, one may have no middle name. *Null* can also designate that an attribute value is unknown. An unknown value may be either *missing* (the value does exist, but we do not have that information) or *not known* (we do not know whether or not the value actually exists).

For instance, if the *name* value for a particular customer is *null*, we assume that the value is missing, since every customer must have a name. A null value for the *apartment-number* attribute could mean that the address does not include an apartment number (not applicable), that an apartment number exists but we do not know what it is (missing), or that we do not know whether or not an apartment number is part of the customer's address (unknown).

A database for a banking enterprise may include a number of different entity sets. For example, in addition to keeping track of customers and loans, the bank also provides accounts, which are represented by the entity set *account* with attributes *account-number* and *balance*. Also, if the bank has a number of different branches, then we may keep information about all the branches of the bank. Each *branch* entity set may be described by the attributes *branch-name*, *branch-city*, and *assets*.

2.1.2 Relationship Sets

A **relationship** is an association among several entities. For example, we can define a relationship that associates customer Hayes with loan L-15. This relationship specifies that Hayes is a customer with loan number L-15.

   A **relationship set** is a set of relationships of the same type. Formally, it is a mathematical relation on $n \geq 2$ (possibly nondistinct) entity sets. If E_1, $E_2, \ldots, E_n$ are entity sets, then a relationship set R is a subset of

$$\{(e_1, e_2, \ldots, e_n) \mid e_1 \in E_1, e_2 \in E_2, \ldots, e_n \in E_n\}$$

where $(e_1, e_2, \ldots, e_n)$ is a relationship.

   Consider the two entity sets *customer* and *loan* in Figure 2.1. We define the relationship set *borrower* to denote the association between customers and the bank loans that the customers have. Figure 2.3 depicts this association.

   As another example, consider the two entity sets *loan* and *branch*. We can define the relationship set *loan-branch* to denote the association between a bank loan and the branch in which that loan is maintained.

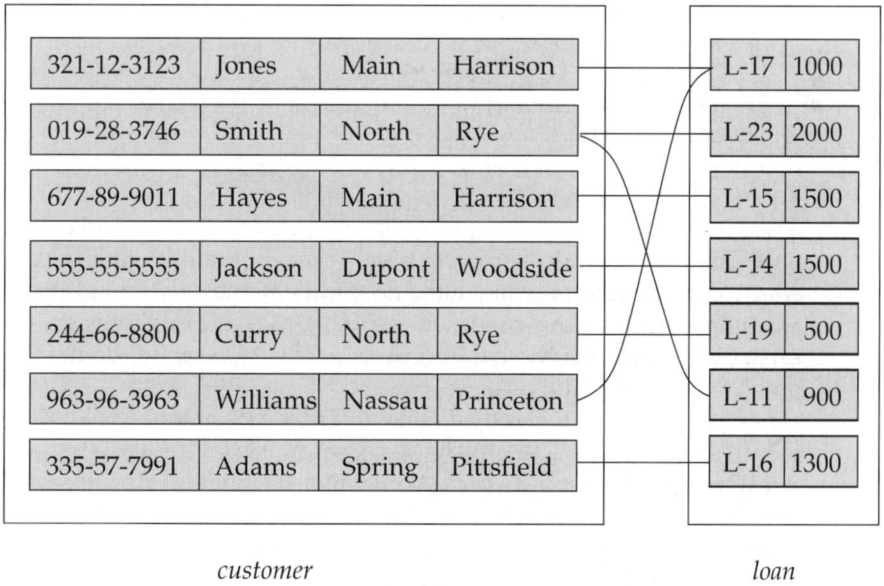

321-12-3123	Jones	Main	Harrison
019-28-3746	Smith	North	Rye
677-89-9011	Hayes	Main	Harrison
555-55-5555	Jackson	Dupont	Woodside
244-66-8800	Curry	North	Rye
963-96-3963	Williams	Nassau	Princeton
335-57-7991	Adams	Spring	Pittsfield

L-17	1000
L-23	2000
L-15	1500
L-14	1500
L-19	500
L-11	900
L-16	1300

customer   *loan*

Figure 2.3   Relationship set *borrower*.

The association between entity sets is referred to as participation; that is, the entity sets E_1, E_2, ..., E_n **participate** in relationship set R. A **relationship instance** in an E-R schema represents an association between the named entities in the real-world enterprise that is being modeled. As an illustration, the individual *customer* entity Hayes, who has customer identifier 677-89-9011, and the *loan* entity L-15 participate in a relationship instance of *borrower*. This relationship instance represents that, in the real-world enterprise, the person called Hayes who holds *customer-id* 677-89-9011 has taken the loan that is numbered L-15.

The function that an entity plays in a relationship is called that entity's **role**. Since entity sets participating in a relationship set are generally distinct, roles are implicit and are not usually specified. However, they are useful when the meaning of a relationship needs clarification. Such is the case when the entity sets of a relationship set are not distinct; that is, the same entity set participates in a relationship set more than once, in different roles. In this type of relationship set, sometimes called a **recursive** relationship set, explicit role names are necessary to specify how an entity participates in a relationship instance. For example, consider an entity set *employee* that records information about all the employees of the bank. We may have a relationship set *works-for* that is modeled by ordered pairs of *employee* entities. The first employee of a pair takes the role of *worker*, whereas the second takes the role of *manager*. In this way, all relationships of *works-for* are characterized by (worker, manager) pairs; (manager, worker) pairs are excluded.

A relationship may also have attributes called **descriptive attributes**. Consider a relationship set *depositor* with entity sets *customer* and *account*. We could associate the attribute *access-date* to that relationship to specify the most recent date on which a customer accessed an account. The *depositor* relationship among the entities corresponding to customer Jones and account A-217 has the value "23 May 2001" for attribute *access-date*, which means that the most recent date that Jones accessed account A-217 was 23 May 2001.

As another example of descriptive attributes for relationships, suppose we have entity sets *student* and *course* which participate in a relationship set *registered-for*. We may wish to store a descriptive attribute *for-credit* with the relationship, to record whether a student has taken the course for credit, or is auditing (or sitting in on) the course.

A relationship instance in a given relationship set must be uniquely identifiable from its participating entities, without using the descriptive attributes. To understand this point, suppose we want to model all the dates when a customer accessed an account. The single-valued attribute *access-date* can store a single access date only . We cannot represent multiple access dates by multiple relationship instances between the same customer and account, since the relationship instances would not be uniquely identifiable using only the participating entities. The right way to handle this case is to create a multivalued attribute *access-dates*, which can store all the access dates.

However, there can be more than one relationship set involving the same entity sets. In our example the *customer* and *loan* entity sets participate in the relationship set *borrower*. Additionally, suppose each loan must have another customer who serves as a guarantor for the loan. Then the *customer* and *loan* entity sets may participate in another relationship set, *guarantor*.

The relationship sets *borrower* and *loan-branch* provide an example of a **binary** relationship set—that is, one that involves two entity sets. Most of the relationship sets in a database system are binary. Occasionally, however, relationship sets involve more than two entity sets.

As an example, consider the entity sets *employee*, *branch*, and *job*. Examples of *job* entities could include manager, teller, auditor, and so on. Job entities may have the attributes *title* and *level*. The relationship set *works-on* among *employee*, *branch*, and *job* is an example of a ternary relationship. A ternary relationship among Jones, Perryridge, and manager indicates that Jones acts as a manager at the Perryridge branch. Jones could also act as auditor at the Downtown branch, which would be represented by another relationship. Yet another relationship could be between Smith, Downtown, and teller, indicating Smith acts as a teller at the Downtown branch.

The number of entity sets that participate in a relationship set is also the **degree** of the relationship set. A binary relationship set is of degree 2; a ternary relationship set is of degree 3.

2.2   Constraints

An E-R enterprise schema may define certain constraints to which the contents of a database must conform. In this section, we examine mapping cardinalities and participation constraints, which are two of the most important types of constraints.

2.2.1   Mapping Cardinalities

Mapping cardinalities, or cardinality ratios, express the number of entities to which another entity can be associated via a relationship set.

Mapping cardinalities are most useful in describing binary relationship sets, although they can contribute to the description of relationship sets that involve more than two entity sets. In this section, we shall concentrate on only binary relationship sets.

For a binary relationship set R between entity sets A and B, the mapping cardinality must be one of the following:

- **One to one**. An entity in A is associated with *at most* one entity in B, and an entity in B is associated with *at most* one entity in A. (See Figure 2.4a.)

- **One to many**. An entity in A is associated with any number (zero or more) of entities in B. An entity in B, however, can be associated with *at most* one entity in A. (See Figure 2.4b.)

- **Many to one**. An entity in A is associated with *at most* one entity in B. An entity in B, however, can be associated with any number (zero or more) of entities in A. (See Figure 2.5a.)

- **Many to many**. An entity in A is associated with any number (zero or more) of entities in B, and an entity in B is associated with any number (zero or more) of entities in A. (See Figure 2.5b.)

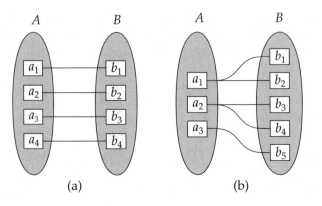

Figure 2.4   Mapping cardinalities. (a) One to one. (b) One to many.

The appropriate mapping cardinality for a particular relationship set obviously depends on the real-world situation that the relationship set is modeling.

As an illustration, consider the *borrower* relationship set. If, in a particular bank, a loan can belong to only one customer, and a customer can have several loans, then the relationship set from *customer* to *loan* is one to many. If a loan can belong to several customers (as can loans taken jointly by several business partners), the relationship set is many to many. Figure 2.3 depicts this type of relationship.

2.2.2 Participation Constraints

The participation of an entity set E in a relationship set R is said to be **total** if every entity in E participates in at least one relationship in R. If only some entities in E participate in relationships in R, the participation of entity set E in relationship R is said to be **partial**. For example, we expect every loan entity to be related to at least one customer through the *borrower* relationship. Therefore the participation of *loan* in

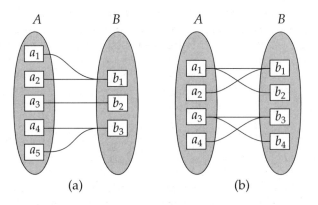

Figure 2.5   Mapping cardinalities. (a) Many to one. (b) Many to many.

the relationship set *borrower* is total. In contrast, an individual can be a bank customer whether or not she has a loan with the bank. Hence, it is possible that only some of the *customer* entities are related to the *loan* entity set through the *borrower* relationship, and the participation of *customer* in the *borrower* relationship set is therefore partial.

2.3 Keys

We must have a way to specify how entities within a given entity set are distinguished. Conceptually, individual entities are distinct; from a database perspective, however, the difference among them must be expressed in terms of their attributes.

Therefore, the values of the attribute values of an entity must be such that they can *uniquely identify* the entity. In other words, no two entities in an entity set are allowed to have exactly the same value for all attributes.

A *key* allows us to identify a set of attributes that suffice to distinguish entities from each other. Keys also help uniquely identify relationships, and thus distinguish relationships from each other.

2.3.1 Entity Sets

A **superkey** is a set of one or more attributes that, taken collectively, allow us to identify uniquely an entity in the entity set. For example, the *customer-id* attribute of the entity set *customer* is sufficient to distinguish one *customer* entity from another. Thus, *customer-id* is a superkey. Similarly, the combination of *customer-name* and *customer-id* is a superkey for the entity set *customer*. The *customer-name* attribute of *customer* is not a superkey, because several people might have the same name.

The concept of a superkey is not sufficient for our purposes, since, as we saw, a superkey may contain extraneous attributes. If K is a superkey, then so is any superset of K. We are often interested in superkeys for which no proper subset is a superkey. Such minimal superkeys are called **candidate keys**.

It is possible that several distinct sets of attributes could serve as a candidate key. Suppose that a combination of *customer-name* and *customer-street* is sufficient to distinguish among members of the *customer* entity set. Then, both {*customer-id*} and {*customer-name, customer-street*} are candidate keys. Although the attributes *customer-id* and *customer-name* together can distinguish *customer* entities, their combination does not form a candidate key, since the attribute *customer-id* alone is a candidate key.

We shall use the term **primary key** to denote a candidate key that is chosen by the database designer as the principal means of identifying entities within an entity set. A key (primary, candidate, and super) is a property of the entity set, rather than of the individual entities. Any two individual entities in the set are prohibited from having the same value on the key attributes at the same time. The designation of a key represents a constraint in the real-world enterprise being modeled.

Candidate keys must be chosen with care. As we noted, the name of a person is obviously not sufficient, because there may be many people with the same name. In the United States, the social-security number attribute of a person would be a candidate key. Since non-U.S. residents usually do not have social-security numbers, international enterprises must generate their own unique identifiers. An alternative is to use some unique combination of other attributes as a key.

The primary key should be chosen such that its attributes are never, or very rarely, changed. For instance, the address field of a person should not be part of the primary key, since it is likely to change. Social-security numbers, on the other hand, are guaranteed to never change. Unique identifiers generated by enterprises generally do not change, except if two enterprises merge; in such a case the same identifier may have been issued by both enterprises, and a reallocation of identifiers may be required to make sure they are unique.

2.3.2 Relationship Sets

The primary key of an entity set allows us to distinguish among the various entities of the set. We need a similar mechanism to distinguish among the various relationships of a relationship set.

Let R be a relationship set involving entity sets E_1, E_2, ..., E_n. Let *primary-key*(E_i) denote the set of attributes that forms the primary key for entity set E_i. Assume for now that the attribute names of all primary keys are unique, and each entity set participates only once in the relationship. The composition of the primary key for a relationship set depends on the set of attributes associated with the relationship set R.

If the relationship set R has no attributes associated with it, then the set of attributes

$$primary\text{-}key(E_1) \cup primary\text{-}key(E_2) \cup \cdots \cup primary\text{-}key(E_n)$$

describes an individual relationship in set R.

If the relationship set R has attributes $a_1, a_2, \cdots, a_m$ associated with it, then the set of attributes

$$primary\text{-}key(E_1) \cup primary\text{-}key(E_2) \cup \cdots \cup primary\text{-}key(E_n) \cup \{a_1, a_2, \ldots, a_m\}$$

describes an individual relationship in set R.

In both of the above cases, the set of attributes

$$primary\text{-}key(E_1) \cup primary\text{-}key(E_2) \cup \cdots \cup primary\text{-}key(E_n)$$

forms a superkey for the relationship set.

In case the attribute names of primary keys are not unique across entity sets, the attributes are renamed to distinguish them; the name of the entity set combined with the name of the attribute would form a unique name. In case an entity set participates more than once in a relationship set (as in the *works-for* relationship in Section 2.1.2), the role name is used instead of the name of the entity set, to form a unique attribute name.

The structure of the primary key for the relationship set depends on the mapping cardinality of the relationship set. As an illustration, consider the entity sets *customer* and *account*, and the relationship set *depositor*, with attribute *access-date*, in Section 2.1.2. Suppose that the relationship set is many to many. Then the primary key of *depositor* consists of the union of the primary keys of *customer* and *account*. However, if a customer can have only one account—that is, if the *depositor* relationship is many to one from *customer* to *account*—then the primary key of *depositor* is simply the primary key of *customer*. Similarly, if the relationship is many to one from *account* to *customer*—that is, each account is owned by at most one customer—then the primary key of *depositor* is simply the primary key of *account*. For one-to-one relationships either primary key can be used.

For nonbinary relationships, if no cardinality constraints are present then the superkey formed as described earlier in this section is the only candidate key, and it is chosen as the primary key. The choice of the primary key is more complicated if cardinality constraints are present. Since we have not discussed how to specify cardinality constraints on nonbinary relations, we do not discuss this issue further in this chapter. We consider the issue in more detail in Section 7.3.

2.4 Design Issues

The notions of an entity set and a relationship set are not precise, and it is possible to define a set of entities and the relationships among them in a number of different ways. In this section, we examine basic issues in the design of an E-R database schema. Section 2.7.4 covers the design process in further detail.

2.4.1 Use of Entity Sets versus Attributes

Consider the entity set *employee* with attributes *employee-name* and *telephone-number*. It can easily be argued that a telephone is an entity in its own right with attributes *telephone-number* and *location* (the office where the telephone is located). If we take this point of view, we must redefine the *employee* entity set as:

- The *employee* entity set with attribute *employee-name*

- The *telephone* entity set with attributes *telephone-number* and *location*

- The relationship set *emp-telephone*, which denotes the association between employees and the telephones that they have

What, then, is the main difference between these two definitions of an employee? Treating a telephone as an attribute *telephone-number* implies that employees have precisely one telephone number each. Treating a telephone as an entity *telephone* permits employees to have several telephone numbers (including zero) associated with them. However, we could instead easily define *telephone-number* as a multivalued attribute to allow multiple telephones per employee.

The main difference then is that treating a telephone as an entity better models a situation where one may want to keep extra information about a telephone, such as its location, or its type (mobile, video phone, or plain old telephone), or who all share the telephone. Thus, treating telephone as an entity is more general than treating it as an attribute and is appropriate when the generality may be useful.

In contrast, it would not be appropriate to treat the attribute *employee-name* as an entity; it is difficult to argue that *employee-name* is an entity in its own right (in contrast to the telephone). Thus, it is appropriate to have *employee-name* as an attribute of the *employee* entity set.

Two natural questions thus arise: What constitutes an attribute, and what constitutes an entity set? Unfortunately, there are no simple answers. The distinctions mainly depend on the structure of the real-world enterprise being modeled, and on the semantics associated with the attribute in question.

A common mistake is to use the primary key of an entity set as an attribute of another entity set, instead of using a relationship. For example, it is incorrect to model *customer-id* as an attribute of *loan* even if each loan had only one customer. The relationship *borrower* is the correct way to represent the connection between loans and customers, since it makes their connection explicit, rather than implicit via an attribute.

Another related mistake that people sometimes make is to designate the primary key attributes of the related entity sets as attributes of the relationship set. This should not be done, since the primary key attributes are already implicit in the relationship.

2.4.2   Use of Entity Sets versus Relationship Sets

It is not always clear whether an object is best expressed by an entity set or a relationship set. In Section 2.1.1, we assumed that a bank loan is modeled as an entity. An alternative is to model a loan not as an entity, but rather as a relationship between customers and branches, with *loan-number* and *amount* as descriptive attributes. Each loan is represented by a relationship between a customer and a branch.

If every loan is held by exactly one customer and is associated with exactly one branch, we may find satisfactory the design where a loan is represented as a relationship. However, with this design, we cannot represent conveniently a situation in which several customers hold a loan jointly. To handle such a situation, we must define a separate relationship for each holder of the joint loan. Then, we must replicate the values for the descriptive attributes *loan-number* and *amount* in each such relationship. Each such relationship must, of course, have the same value for the descriptive attributes *loan-number* and *amount*.

Two problems arise as a result of the replication: (1) the data are stored multiple times, wasting storage space, and (2) updates potentially leave the data in an inconsistent state, where the values differ in two relationships for attributes that are supposed to have the same value. The issue of how to avoid such replication is treated formally by *normalization theory*, discussed in Chapter 7.

The problem of replication of the attributes *loan-number* and *amount* is absent in the original design of Section 2.1.1, because there *loan* is an entity set.

One possible guideline in determining whether to use an entity set or a relationship set is to designate a relationship set to describe an action that occurs between entities. This approach can also be useful in deciding whether certain attributes may be more appropriately expressed as relationships.

2.4.3   Binary versus n-ary Relationship Sets

Relationships in databases are often binary. Some relationships that appear to be nonbinary could actually be better represented by several binary relationships. For instance, one could create a ternary relationship *parent*, relating a child to his/her mother and father. However, such a relationship could also be represented by two binary relationships, *mother* and *father*, relating a child to his/her mother and father separately. Using the two relationships *mother* and *father* allows us record a child's mother, even if we are not aware of the father's identity; a null value would be required if the ternary relationship *parent* is used. Using binary relationship sets is preferable in this case.

In fact, it is always possible to replace a nonbinary (n-ary, for $n > 2$) relationship set by a number of distinct binary relationship sets. For simplicity, consider the abstract ternary ($n = 3$) relationship set R, relating entity sets A, B, and C. We replace the relationship set R by an entity set E, and create three relationship sets:

- R_A, relating E and A

- R_B, relating E and B

- R_C, relating E and C

If the relationship set R had any attributes, these are assigned to entity set E; further, a special identifying attribute is created for E (since it must be possible to distinguish different entities in an entity set on the basis of their attribute values). For each relationship (a_i, b_i, c_i) in the relationship set R, we create a new entity e_i in the entity set E. Then, in each of the three new relationship sets, we insert a relationship as follows:

- (e_i, a_i) in R_A

- (e_i, b_i) in R_B

- (e_i, c_i) in R_C

We can generalize this process in a straightforward manner to n-ary relationship sets. Thus, conceptually, we can restrict the E-R model to include only binary relationship sets. However, this restriction is not always desirable.

- An identifying attribute may have to be created for the entity set created to represent the relationship set. This attribute, along with the extra relationship sets required, increases the complexity of the design and (as we shall see in Section 2.9) overall storage requirements.

- A n-ary relationship set shows more clearly that several entities participate in a single relationship.

- There may not be a way to translate constraints on the ternary relationship into constraints on the binary relationships. For example, consider a constraint that says that R is many-to-one from A, B to C; that is, each pair of entities from A and B is associated with at most one C entity. This constraint cannot be expressed by using cardinality constraints on the relationship sets R_A, R_B, and R_C.

Consider the relationship set *works-on* in Section 2.1.2, relating *employee*, *branch*, and *job*. We cannot directly split *works-on* into binary relationships between *employee* and *branch* and between *employee* and *job*. If we did so, we would be able to record that Jones is a manager and an auditor and that Jones works at Perryridge and Downtown; however, we would not be able to record that Jones is a manager at Perryridge and an auditor at Downtown, but is not an auditor at Perryridge or a manager at Downtown.

The relationship set *works-on* can be split into binary relationships by creating a new entity set as described above. However, doing so would not be very natural.

2.4.4   Placement of Relationship Attributes

The cardinality ratio of a relationship can affect the placement of relationship attributes. Thus, attributes of one-to-one or one-to-many relationship sets can be associated with one of the participating entity sets, rather than with the relationship set. For instance, let us specify that *depositor* is a one-to-many relationship set such that one customer may have several accounts, but each account is held by only one customer. In this case, the attribute *access-date*, which specifies when the customer last accessed that account, could be associated with the *account* entity set, as Figure 2.6 depicts; to keep the figure simple, only some of the attributes of the two entity sets are shown. Since each *account* entity participates in a relationship with at most one instance of *customer*, making this attribute designation would have the same meaning

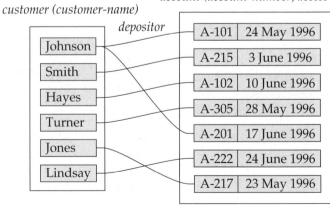

Figure 2.6   *Access-date* as attribute of the *account* entity set.

as would placing *access-date* with the *depositor* relationship set. Attributes of a one-to-many relationship set can be repositioned to only the entity set on the "many" side of the relationship. For one-to-one relationship sets, on the other hand, the relationship attribute can be associated with either one of the participating entities.

The design decision of where to place descriptive attributes in such cases—as a relationship or entity attribute—should reflect the characteristics of the enterprise being modeled. The designer may choose to retain *access-date* as an attribute of *depositor* to express explicitly that an access occurs at the point of interaction between the *customer* and *account* entity sets.

The choice of attribute placement is more clear-cut for many-to-many relationship sets. Returning to our example, let us specify the perhaps more realistic case that *depositor* is a many-to-many relationship set expressing that a customer may have one or more accounts, and that an account can be held by one or more customers. If we are to express the date on which a specific customer last accessed a specific account, *access-date* must be an attribute of the *depositor* relationship set, rather than either one of the participating entities. If *access-date* were an attribute of *account*, for instance, we could not determine which customer made the most recent access to a joint account. When an attribute is determined by the combination of participating entity sets, rather than by either entity separately, that attribute must be associated with the many-to-many relationship set. Figure 2.7 depicts the placement of *access-date* as a relationship attribute; again, to keep the figure simple, only some of the attributes of the two entity sets are shown.

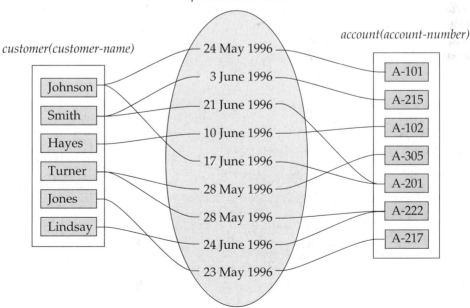

Figure 2.7   *Access-date* as attribute of the *depositor* relationship set.

2.5 Entity-Relationship Diagram

As we saw briefly in Section 1.4, an **E-R diagram** can express the overall logical structure of a database graphically. E-R diagrams are simple and clear—qualities that may well account in large part for the widespread use of the E-R model. Such a diagram consists of the following major components:

- **Rectangles**, which represent entity sets

- **Ellipses**, which represent attributes

- **Diamonds**, which represent relationship sets

- **Lines**, which link attributes to entity sets and entity sets to relationship sets

- **Double ellipses**, which represent multivalued attributes

- **Dashed ellipses**, which denote derived attributes

- **Double lines**, which indicate total participation of an entity in a relationship set

- **Double rectangles**, which represent weak entity sets (described later, in Section 2.6.)

Consider the entity-relationship diagram in Figure 2.8, which consists of two entity sets, *customer* and *loan*, related through a binary relationship set *borrower*. The attributes associated with *customer* are *customer-id*, *customer-name*, *customer-street*, and *customer-city*. The attributes associated with *loan* are *loan-number* and *amount*. In Figure 2.8, attributes of an entity set that are members of the primary key are underlined.

The relationship set *borrower* may be many-to-many, one-to-many, many-to-one, or one-to-one. To distinguish among these types, we draw either a directed line ($\rightarrow$) or an undirected line (—) between the relationship set and the entity set in question.

- A directed line from the relationship set *borrower* to the entity set *loan* specifies that *borrower* is either a one-to-one or many-to-one relationship set, from *customer* to *loan*; *borrower* cannot be a many-to-many or a one-to-many relationship set from *customer* to *loan*.

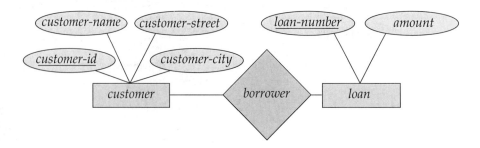

Figure 2.8   E-R diagram corresponding to customers and loans.

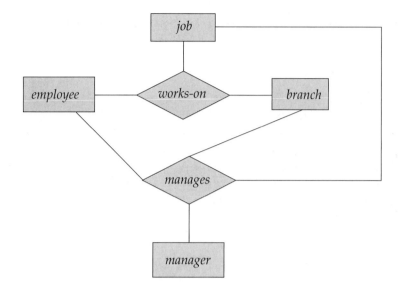

Figure 2.18   E-R diagram with redundant relationships.

There is redundant information in the resultant figure, however, since every *employee, branch, job* combination in *manages* is also in *works-on*. If the manager were a value rather than an *manager* entity, we could instead make *manager* a multivalued attribute of the relationship *works-on*. But doing so makes it more difficult (logically as well as in execution cost) to find, for example, employee-branch-job triples for which a manager is responsible. Since the manager is a *manager* entity, this alternative is ruled out in any case.

The best way to model a situation such as the one just described is to use aggregation. **Aggregation** is an abstraction through which relationships are treated as higher-level entities. Thus, for our example, we regard the relationship set *works-on* (relating the entity sets *employee*, *branch*, and *job*) as a higher-level entity set called *works-on*. Such an entity set is treated in the same manner as is any other entity set. We can then create a binary relationship *manages* between *works-on* and *manager* to represent who manages what tasks. Figure 2.19 shows a notation for aggregation commonly used to represent the above situation.

2.7.6   Alternative E-R Notations

Figure 2.20 summarizes the set of symbols we have used in E-R diagrams. There is no universal standard for E-R diagram notation, and different books and E-R diagram software use different notations; Figure 2.21 indicates some of the alternative notations that are widely used. An entity set may be represented as a box with the name outside, and the attributes listed one below the other within the box. The primary key attributes are indicated by listing them at the top, with a line separating them from the other attributes.

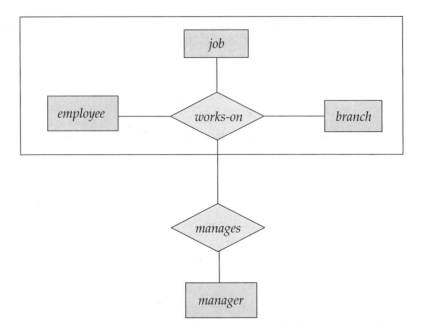

Figure 2.19 E-R diagram with aggregation.

Cardinality constraints can be indicated in several different ways, as Figure 2.21 shows. The labels ∗ and 1 on the edges out of the relationship are sometimes used for depicting many-to-many, one-to-one, and many-to-one relationships, as the figure shows. The case of one-to-many is symmetric to many-to-one, and is not shown. In another alternative notation in the figure, relationship sets are represented by lines between entity sets, without diamonds; only binary relationships can be modeled thus. Cardinality constraints in such a notation are shown by "crow's foot" notation, as in the figure.

2.8 Design of an E-R Database Schema

The E-R data model gives us much flexibility in designing a database schema to model a given enterprise. In this section, we consider how a database designer may select from the wide range of alternatives. Among the designer's decisions are:

- Whether to use an attribute or an entity set to represent an object (discussed earlier in Section 2.2.1)

- Whether a real-world concept is expressed more accurately by an entity set or by a relationship set (Section 2.2.2)

- Whether to use a ternary relationship or a pair of binary relationships (Section 2.2.3)

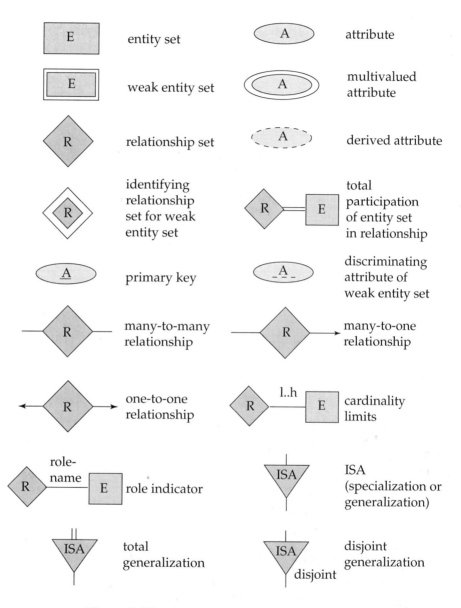

Figure 2.20   Symbols used in the E-R notation.

- Whether to use a strong or a weak entity set (Section 2.6); a strong entity set and its dependent weak entity sets may be regarded as a single "object" in the database, since weak entities are existence dependent on a strong entity

- Whether using generalization (Section 2.7.2) is appropriate; generalization, or a hierarchy of ISA relationships, contributes to modularity by allowing com-

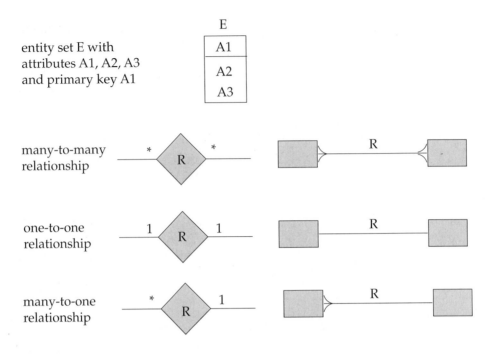

entity set E with
attributes A1, A2, A3
and primary key A1

many-to-many
relationship

one-to-one
relationship

many-to-one
relationship

Figure 2.21   Alternative E-R notations.

mon attributes of similar entity sets to be represented in one place in an E-R diagram

- Whether using aggregation (Section 2.7.5) is appropriate; aggregation groups a part of an E-R diagram into a single entity set, allowing us to treat the aggregate entity set as a single unit without concern for the details of its internal structure.

We shall see that the database designer needs a good understanding of the enterprise being modeled to make these decisions.

2.8.1 Design Phases

A high-level data model serves the database designer by providing a conceptual framework in which to specify, in a systematic fashion, what the data requirements of the database users are, and how the database will be structured to fulfill these requirements. The initial phase of database design, then, is to characterize fully the data needs of the prospective database users. The database designer needs to interact extensively with domain experts and users to carry out this task. The outcome of this phase is a specification of user requirements.

Next, the designer chooses a data model, and by applying the concepts of the chosen data model, translates these requirements into a conceptual schema of the database. The schema developed at this **conceptual-design** phase provides a detailed overview of the enterprise. Since we have studied only the E-R model so far, we shall use it to develop the conceptual schema. Stated in terms of the E-R model, the schema specifies all entity sets, relationship sets, attributes, and mapping constraints. The designer reviews the schema to confirm that all data requirements are indeed satisfied and are not in conflict with one another. She can also examine the design to remove any redundant features. Her focus at this point is describing the data and their relationships, rather than on specifying physical storage details.

A fully developed conceptual schema will also indicate the functional requirements of the enterprise. In a **specification of functional requirements**, users describe the kinds of operations (or transactions) that will be performed on the data. Example operations include modifying or updating data, searching for and retrieving specific data, and deleting data. At this stage of conceptual design, the designer can review the schema to ensure it meets functional requirements.

The process of moving from an abstract data model to the implementation of the database proceeds in two final design phases. In the **logical-design phase**, the designer maps the high-level conceptual schema onto the implementation data model of the database system that will be used. The designer uses the resulting system-specific database schema in the subsequent **physical-design phase**, in which the physical features of the database are specified. These features include the form of file organization and the internal storage structures; they are discussed in Chapter 11.

In this chapter, we cover only the concepts of the E-R model as used in the conceptual-schema-design phase. We have presented a brief overview of the database-design process to provide a context for the discussion of the E-R data model. Database design receives a full treatment in Chapter 7.

In Section 2.8.2, we apply the two initial database-design phases to our banking-enterprise example. We employ the E-R data model to translate user requirements into a conceptual design schema that is depicted as an E-R diagram.

2.8.2   Database Design for Banking Enterprise

We now look at the database-design requirements of a banking enterprise in more detail, and develop a more realistic, but also more complicated, design than what we have seen in our earlier examples. However, we do not attempt to model every aspect of the database-design for a bank; we consider only a few aspects, in order to illustrate the process of database design.

2.8.2.1   Data Requirements

The initial specification of user requirements may be based on interviews with the database users, and on the designer's own analysis of the enterprise. The description that arises from this design phase serves as the basis for specifying the conceptual structure of the database. Here are the major characteristics of the banking enterprise.

- The bank is organized into branches. Each branch is located in a particular city and is identified by a unique name. The bank monitors the assets of each branch.

- Bank customers are identified by their *customer-id* values. The bank stores each customer's name, and the street and city where the customer lives. Customers may have accounts and can take out loans. A customer may be associated with a particular banker, who may act as a loan officer or personal banker for that customer.

- Bank employees are identified by their *employee-id* values. The bank administration stores the name and telephone number of each employee, the names of the employee's dependents, and the *employee-id* number of the employee's manager. The bank also keeps track of the employee's start date and, thus, length of employment.

- The bank offers two types of accounts—savings and checking accounts. Accounts can be held by more than one customer, and a customer can have more than one account. Each account is assigned a unique account number. The bank maintains a record of each account's balance, and the most recent date on which the account was accessed by each customer holding the account. In addition, each savings account has an interest rate, and overdrafts are recorded for each checking account.

- A loan originates at a particular branch and can be held by one or more customers. A loan is identified by a unique loan number. For each loan, the bank keeps track of the loan amount and the loan payments. Although a loan-payment number does not uniquely identify a particular payment among those for all the bank's loans, a payment number does identify a particular payment for a specific loan. The date and amount are recorded for each payment.

In a real banking enterprise, the bank would keep track of deposits and withdrawals from savings and checking accounts, just as it keeps track of payments to loan accounts. Since the modeling requirements for that tracking are similar, and we would like to keep our example application small, we do not keep track of such deposits and withdrawals in our model.

2.8.2.2 Entity Sets Designation

Our specification of data requirements serves as the starting point for constructing a conceptual schema for the database. From the characteristics listed in Section 2.8.2.1, we begin to identify entity sets and their attributes:

- The *branch* entity set, with attributes *branch-name*, *branch-city*, and *assets*.

- The *customer* entity set, with attributes *customer-id*, *customer-name*, *customer-street*; and *customer-city*. A possible additional attribute is *banker-name*.

- The *employee* entity set, with attributes *employee-id*, *employee-name*, *telephone-number*, *salary*, and *manager*. Additional descriptive features are the multivalued attribute *dependent-name*, the base attribute *start-date*, and the derived attribute *employment-length*.

- Two account entity sets—*savings-account* and *checking-account*—with the common attributes of *account-number* and *balance*; in addition, *savings-account* has the attribute *interest-rate* and *checking-account* has the attribute *overdraft-amount*.

- The *loan* entity set, with the attributes *loan-number*, *amount*, and *originating-branch*.

- The weak entity set *loan-payment*, with attributes *payment-number*, *payment-date*, and *payment-amount*.

2.8.2.3   Relationship Sets Designation

We now return to the rudimentary design scheme of Section 2.8.2.2 and specify the following relationship sets and mapping cardinalities. In the process, we also refine some of the decisions we made earlier regarding attributes of entity sets.

- *borrower*, a many-to-many relationship set between *customer* and *loan*.

- *loan-branch*, a many-to-one relationship set that indicates in which branch a loan originated. Note that this relationship set replaces the attribute *originating-branch* of the entity set *loan*.

- *loan-payment*, a one-to-many relationship from *loan* to *payment*, which documents that a payment is made on a loan.

- *depositor*, with relationship attribute *access-date*, a many-to-many relationship set between *customer* and *account*, indicating that a customer owns an account.

- *cust-banker*, with relationship attribute *type*, a many-to-one relationship set expressing that a customer can be advised by a bank employee, and that a bank employee can advise one or more customers. Note that this relationship set has replaced the attribute *banker-name* of the entity set *customer*.

- *works-for*, a relationship set between *employee* entities with role indicators *manager* and *worker*; the mapping cardinalities express that an employee works for only one manager and that a manager supervises one or more employees. Note that this relationship set has replaced the *manager* attribute of *employee*.

2.8.2.4   E-R Diagram

Drawing on the discussions in Section 2.8.2.3, we now present the completed E-R diagram for our example banking enterprise. Figure 2.22 depicts the full representation of a conceptual model of a bank, expressed in terms of E-R concepts. The diagram includes the entity sets, attributes, relationship sets, and mapping cardinalities arrived at through the design processes of Sections 2.8.2.1 and 2.8.2.2, and refined in Section 2.8.2.3.

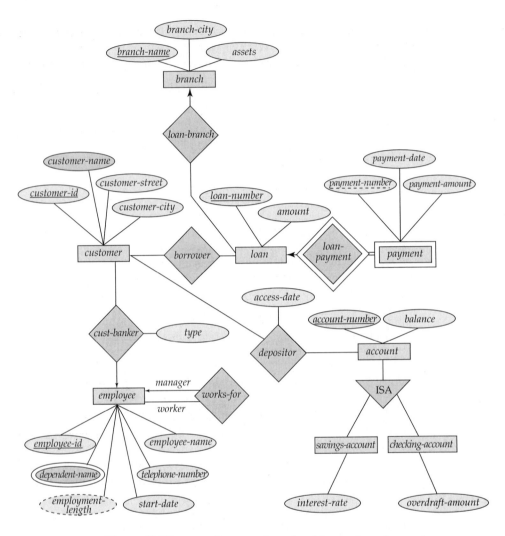

Figure 2.22 E-R diagram for a banking enterprise.

2.9 Reduction of an E-R Schema to Tables

We can represent a database that conforms to an E-R database schema by a collection of tables. For each entity set and for each relationship set in the database, there is a unique table to which we assign the name of the corresponding entity set or relationship set. Each table has multiple columns, each of which has a unique name.

Both the E-R model and the relational-database model are abstract, logical representations of real-world enterprises. Because the two models employ similar design principles, we can convert an E-R design into a relational design. Converting a database representation from an E-R diagram to a table format is the way we arrive at a relational-database design from an E-R diagram. Although important differences exist between a relation and a table, informally, a relation can be considered to be a table of values.

In this section, we describe how an E-R schema can be represented by tables; and in Chapter 3, we show how to generate a relational-database schema from an E-R schema.

The constraints specified in an E-R diagram, such as primary keys and cardinality constraints, are mapped to constraints on the tables generated from the E-R diagram. We provide more details about this mapping in Chapter 6 after describing how to specify constraints on tables.

2.9.1   Tabular Representation of Strong Entity Sets

Let E be a strong entity set with descriptive attributes $a_1, a_2, \ldots, a_n$. We represent this entity by a table called E with n distinct columns, each of which corresponds to one of the attributes of E. Each row in this table corresponds to one entity of the entity set E.

As an illustration, consider the entity set *loan* of the E-R diagram in Figure 2.8. This entity set has two attributes: *loan-number* and *amount*. We represent this entity set by a table called *loan*, with two columns, as in Figure 2.23. The row

$$(\text{L-17, 1000})$$

in the *loan* table means that loan number L-17 has a loan amount of $1000. We can add a new entity to the database by inserting a row into a table. We can also delete or modify rows.

Let D_1 denote the set of all loan numbers, and let D_2 denote the set of all balances. Any row of the *loan* table must consist of a 2-tuple (v_1, v_2), where v_1 is a loan (that is, v_1 is in set D_1) and v_2 is an amount (that is, v_2 is in set D_2). In general, the *loan* table will contain only a subset of the set of all possible rows. We refer to the set of all possible rows of *loan* as the *Cartesian product* of D_1 and D_2, denoted by

$$D_1 \times D_2$$

In general, if we have a table of n columns, we denote the Cartesian product of $D_1, D_2, \cdots, D_n$ by

$$D_1 \times D_2 \times \cdots \times D_{n-1} \times D_n$$

loan-number	amount
L-11	900
L-14	1500
L-15	1500
L-16	1300
L-17	1000
L-23	2000
L-93	500

Figure 2.23   The *loan* table.

customer-id	customer-name	customer-street	customer-city
019-28-3746	Smith	North	Rye
182-73-6091	Turner	Putnam	Stamford
192-83-7465	Johnson	Alma	Palo Alto
244-66-8800	Curry	North	Rye
321-12-3123	Jones	Main	Harrison
335-57-7991	Adams	Spring	Pittsfield
336-66-9999	Lindsay	Park	Pittsfield
677-89-9011	Hayes	Main	Harrison
963-96-3963	Williams	Nassau	Princeton

Figure 2.24   The *customer* table.

As another example, consider the entity set *customer* of the E-R diagram in Figure 2.8. This entity set has the attributes *customer-id*, *customer-name*, *customer-street*, and *customer-city*. The table corresponding to *customer* has four columns, as in Figure 2.24.

2.9.2 Tabular Representation of Weak Entity Sets

Let A be a weak entity set with attributes $a_1, a_2, \ldots, a_m$. Let B be the strong entity set on which A depends. Let the primary key of B consist of attributes $b_1, b_2, \ldots, b_n$. We represent the entity set A by a table called A with one column for each attribute of the set:

$$\{a_1, a_2, \ldots, a_m\} \cup \{b_1, b_2, \ldots, b_n\}$$

As an illustration, consider the entity set *payment* in the E-R diagram of Figure 2.16. This entity set has three attributes: *payment-number*, *payment-date*, and *payment-amount*. The primary key of the *loan* entity set, on which *payment* depends, is *loan-number*. Thus, we represent *payment* by a table with four columns labeled *loan-number*, *payment-number*, *payment-date*, and *payment-amount*, as in Figure 2.25.

2.9.3 Tabular Representation of Relationship Sets

Let R be a relationship set, let $a_1, a_2, \ldots, a_m$ be the set of attributes formed by the union of the primary keys of each of the entity sets participating in R, and let the descriptive attributes (if any) of R be $b_1, b_2, \ldots, b_n$. We represent this relationship set by a table called R with one column for each attribute of the set:

$$\{a_1, a_2, \ldots, a_m\} \cup \{b_1, b_2, \ldots, b_n\}$$

As an illustration, consider the relationship set *borrower* in the E-R diagram of Figure 2.8. This relationship set involves the following two entity sets:

- *customer*, with the primary key *customer-id*
- *loan*, with the primary key *loan-number*

loan-number	payment-number	payment-date	payment-amount
L-11	53	7 June 2001	125
L-14	69	28 May 2001	500
L-15	22	23 May 2001	300
L-16	58	18 June 2001	135
L-17	5	10 May 2001	50
L-17	6	7 June 2001	50
L-17	7	17 June 2001	100
L-23	11	17 May 2001	75
L-93	103	3 June 2001	900
L-93	104	13 June 2001	200

Figure 2.25   The *payment* table.

Since the relationship set has no attributes, the *borrower* table has two columns, labeled *customer-id* and *loan-number*, as shown in Figure 2.26.

2.9.3.1   Redundancy of Tables

A relationship set linking a weak entity set to the corresponding strong entity set is treated specially. As we noted in Section 2.6, these relationships are many-to-one and have no descriptive attributes. Furthermore, the primary key of a weak entity set includes the primary key of the strong entity set. In the E-R diagram of Figure 2.16, the weak entity set *payment* is dependent on the strong entity set *loan* via the relationship set *loan-payment*. The primary key of *payment* is {*loan-number, payment-number*}, and the primary key of *loan* is {*loan-number*}. Since *loan-payment* has no descriptive attributes, the *loan-payment* table would have two columns, *loan-number* and *payment-number*. The table for the entity set *payment* has four columns, *loan-number, payment-number, payment-date*, and *payment-amount*. Every (*loan-number, payment-number*) combination in *loan-payment* would also be present in the *payment* table, and vice versa. Thus, the *loan-payment* table is redundant. In general, the table for the relationship set

customer-id	loan-number
019-28-3746	L-11
019-28-3746	L-23
244-66-8800	L-93
321-12-3123	L-17
335-57-7991	L-16
555-55-5555	L-14
677-89-9011	L-15
963-96-3963	L-17

Figure 2.26   The *borrower* table.

linking a weak entity set to its corresponding strong entity set is redundant and does not need to be present in a tabular representation of an E-R diagram.

2.9.3.2 Combination of Tables

Consider a many-to-one relationship set AB from entity set A to entity set B. Using our table-construction scheme outlined previously, we get three tables: A, B, and AB. Suppose further that the participation of A in the relationship is total; that is, every entity a in the entity set A must participate in the relationship AB. Then we can combine the tables A and AB to form a single table consisting of the union of columns of both tables.

As an illustration, consider the E-R diagram of Figure 2.27. The double line in the E-R diagram indicates that the participation of *account* in the *account-branch* is total. Hence, an account cannot exist without being associated with a particular branch. Further, the relationship set *account-branch* is many to one from *account* to *branch*. Therefore, we can combine the table for *account-branch* with the table for *account* and require only the following two tables:

- *account*, with attributes *account-number*, *balance*, and *branch-name*
- *branch*, with attributes *branch-name*, *branch-city*, and *assets*

2.9.4 Composite Attributes

We handle composite attributes by creating a separate attribute for each of the component attributes; we do not create a separate column for the composite attribute itself. Suppose *address* is a composite attribute of entity set *customer*, and the components of *address* are *street* and *city*. The table generated from *customer* would then contain columns *address-street* and *address-city*; there is no separate column for *address*.

2.9.5 Multivalued Attributes

We have seen that attributes in an E-R diagram generally map directly into columns for the appropriate tables. Multivalued attributes, however, are an exception; new tables are created for these attributes.

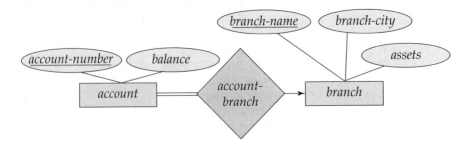

Figure 2.27 E-R diagram.

For a multivalued attribute M, we create a table T with a column C that corresponds to M and columns corresponding to the primary key of the entity set or relationship set of which M is an attribute. As an illustration, consider the E-R diagram in Figure 2.22. The diagram includes the multivalued attribute *dependent-name*. For this multivalued attribute, we create a table *dependent-name*, with columns *dname*, referring to the *dependent-name* attribute of *employee*, and *employee-id*, representing the primary key of the entity set *employee*. Each dependent of an employee is represented as a unique row in the table.

2.9.6   Tabular Representation of Generalization

There are two different methods for transforming to a tabular form an E-R diagram that includes generalization. Although we refer to the generalization in Figure 2.17 in this discussion, we simplify it by including only the first tier of lower-level entity sets—that is, *savings-account* and *checking-account*.

1. Create a table for the higher-level entity set. For each lower-level entity set, create a table that includes a column for each of the attributes of that entity set plus a column for each attribute of the primary key of the higher-level entity set. Thus, for the E-R diagram of Figure 2.17, we have three tables:
   - *account*, with attributes *account-number* and *balance*
   - *savings-account*, with attributes *account-number* and *interest-rate*
   - *checking-account*, with attributes *account-number* and *overdraft-amount*

2. An alternative representation is possible, if the generalization is disjoint and complete—that is, if no entity is a member of two lower-level entity sets directly below a higher-level entity set, and if every entity in the higher level entity set is also a member of one of the lower-level entity sets. Here, do not create a table for the higher-level entity set. Instead, for each lower-level entity set, create a table that includes a column for each of the attributes of that entity set plus a column for *each* attribute of the higher-level entity set. Then, for the E-R diagram of Figure 2.17, we have two tables.
   - *savings-account*, with attributes *account-number*, *balance*, and *interest-rate*
   - *checking-account*, with attributes *account-number*, *balance*, and *overdraft-amount*

   The *savings-account* and *checking-account* relations corresponding to these tables both have *account-number* as the primary key.

If the second method were used for an overlapping generalization, some values such as *balance* would be stored twice unnecessarily. Similarly, if the generalization were not complete—that is, if some accounts were neither savings nor checking accounts—then such accounts could not be represented with the second method.

2.9.7   Tabular Representation of Aggregation

Transforming an E-R diagram containing aggregation to a tabular form is straightforward. Consider the diagram of Figure 2.19. The table for the relationship set *manages* between the aggregation of *works-on* and the entity set *manager* includes a column for each attribute in the primary keys of the entity set *manager* and the relationship set *works-on*. It would also include a column for any descriptive attributes, if they exist, of the relationship set *manages*. We then transform the relationship sets and entity sets within the aggregated entity.

2.10   The Unified Modeling Language UML∗∗

Entity-relationship diagrams help model the data representation component of a software system. Data representation, however, forms only one part of an overall system design. Other components include models of user interactions with the system, specification of functional modules of the system and their interaction, etc. The **Unified Modeling Language** (UML), is a proposed standard for creating specifications of various components of a software system. Some of the parts of UML are:

- **Class diagram**. A class diagram is similar to an E-R diagram. Later in this section we illustrate a few features of class diagrams and how they relate to E-R diagrams.

- **Use case diagram**. Use case diagrams show the interaction between users and the system, in particular the steps of tasks that users perform (such as withdrawing money or registering for a course).

- **Activity diagram**. Activity diagrams depict the flow of tasks between various components of a system.

- **Implementation diagram**. Implementation diagrams show the system components and their interconnections, both at the software component level and the hardware component level.

We do not attempt to provide detailed coverage of the different parts of UML here. See the bibliographic notes for references on UML. Instead we illustrate some features of UML through examples.

Figure 2.28 shows several E-R diagram constructs and their equivalent UML class diagram constructs. We describe these constructs below. UML shows entity sets as boxes and, unlike E-R, shows attributes within the box rather than as separate ellipses. UML actually models objects, whereas E-R models entities. Objects are like entities, and have attributes, but additionally provide a set of functions (called methods) that can be invoked to compute values on the basis of attributes of the objects, or to update the object itself. Class diagrams can depict methods in addition to attributes. We cover objects in Chapter 8.

We represent binary relationship sets in UML by just drawing a line connecting the entity sets. We write the relationship set name adjacent to the line. We may also specify the role played by an entity set in a relationship set by writing the role name on the line, adjacent to the entity set. Alternatively, we may write the relationship set name in a box, along with attributes of the relationship set, and connect the box by a dotted line to the line depicting the relationship set. This box can then be treated as

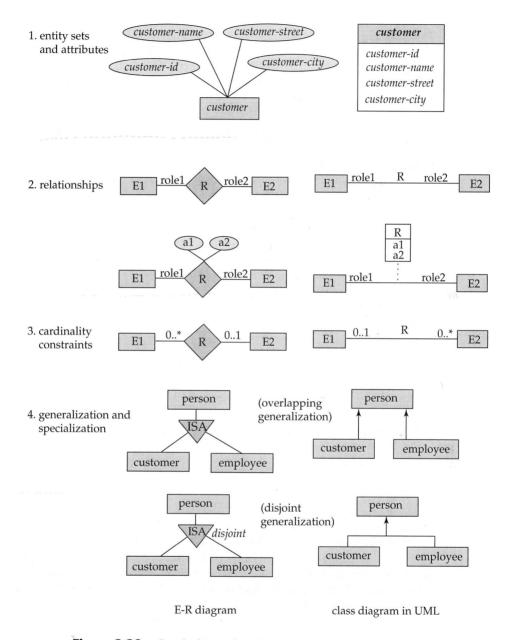

Figure 2.28   Symbols used in the UML class diagram notation.

an entity set, in the same way as an aggregation in E-R diagrams and can participate in relationships with other entity sets.

Nonbinary relationships cannot be directly represented in UML—they have to be converted to binary relationships by the technique we have seen earlier in Section 2.4.3.

Cardinality constraints are specified in UML in the same way as in E-R diagrams, in the form $l..h$, where l denotes the minimum and h the maximum number of relationships an entity can participate in. However, you should be aware that the positioning of the constraints is exactly the reverse of the positioning of constraints in E-R diagrams, as shown in Figure 2.28. The constraint $0..*$ on the $E2$ side and $0..1$ on the $E1$ side means that each $E2$ entity can participate in at most one relationship, whereas each $E1$ entity can participate in many relationships; in other words, the relationship is many to one from $E2$ to $E1$.

Single values such as 1 or $*$ may be written on edges; the single value 1 on an edge is treated as equivalent to $1..1$, while $*$ is equivalent to $0..*$.

We represent generalization and specialization in UML by connecting entity sets by a line with a triangle at the end corresponding to the more general entity set. For instance, the entity set *person* is a generalization of *customer* and *employee*. UML diagrams can also represent explicitly the constraints of disjoint/overlapping on generalizations. Figure 2.28 shows disjoint and overlapping generalizations of *customer* and *employee* to *person*. Recall that if the *customer/employee* to *person* generalization is disjoint, it means that no one can be both a *customer* and an *employee*. An overlapping generalization allows a person to be both a *customer* and an *employee*.

2.11 Summary

- The **entity-relationship (E-R)** data model is based on a perception of a real world that consists of a set of basic objects called **entities**, and of **relationships** among these objects.

- The model is intended primarily for the database-design process. It was developed to facilitate database design by allowing the specification of an **enterprise schema**. Such a schema represents the overall logical structure of the database. This overall structure can be expressed graphically by an **E-R diagram**.

- An **entity** is an object that exists in the real world and is distinguishable from other objects. We express the distinction by associating with each entity a set of attributes that describes the object.

- A **relationship** is an association among several entities. The collection of all entities of the same type is an **entity set**, and the collection of all relationships of the same type is a **relationship set**.

- **Mapping cardinalities** express the number of entities to which another entity can be associated via a relationship set.

- A **superkey** of an entity set is a set of one or more attributes that, taken collectively, allows us to identify uniquely an entity in the entity set. We choose a minimal superkey for each entity set from among its superkeys; the minimal superkey is termed the entity set's **primary key**. Similarly, a relationship set is a set of one or more attributes that, taken collectively, allows us to identify uniquely a relationship in the relationship set. Likewise, we choose a minimal superkey for each relationship set from among its superkeys; this is the relationship set's primary key.

- An entity set that does not have sufficient attributes to form a primary key is termed a **weak entity set**. An entity set that has a primary key is termed a **strong entity set**.

- **Specialization** and **generalization** define a containment relationship between a higher-level entity set and one or more lower-level entity sets. Specialization is the result of taking a subset of a higher-level entity set to form a lower-level entity set. Generalization is the result of taking the union of two or more disjoint (lower-level) entity sets to produce a higher-level entity set. The attributes of higher-level entity sets are inherited by lower-level entity sets.

- **Aggregation** is an abstraction in which relationship sets (along with their associated entity sets) are treated as higher-level entity sets, and can participate in relationships.

- The various features of the E-R model offer the database designer numerous choices in how to best represent the enterprise being modeled. Concepts and objects may, in certain cases, be represented by entities, relationships, or attributes. Aspects of the overall structure of the enterprise may be best described by using weak entity sets, generalization, specialization, or aggregation. Often, the designer must weigh the merits of a simple, compact model versus those of a more precise, but more complex, one.

- A database that conforms to an E-R diagram can be represented by a collection of tables. For each entity set and for each relationship set in the database, there is a unique table that is assigned the name of the corresponding entity set or relationship set. Each table has a number of columns, each of which has a unique name. Converting database representation from an E-R diagram to a table format is the basis for deriving a relational-database design from an E-R diagram.

- The **unified modeling language (UML)** provides a graphical means of modeling various components of a software system. The class diagram component of UML is based on E-R diagrams. However, there are some differences between the two that one must beware of.

Review Terms

- Entity-relationship data model
- Entity
- Entity set
- Attributes
- Domain
- Simple and composite attributes
- Single-valued and multivalued attributes
- Null value
- Derived attribute
- Relationship, and relationship set
- Role

- Recursive relationship set
- Descriptive attributes
- Binary relationship set
- Degree of relationship set
- Mapping cardinality:
  - ☐ One-to-one relationship
  - ☐ One-to-many relationship
  - ☐ Many-to-one relationship
  - ☐ Many-to-many relationship
- Participation
  - ☐ Total participation
  - ☐ Partial participation
- Superkey, candidate key, and primary key
- Weak entity sets and strong entity sets

- ☐ Discriminator attributes
- ☐ Identifying relationship
- Specialization and generalization
  - ☐ Superclass and subclass
  - ☐ Attribute inheritance
  - ☐ Single and multiple inheritance
  - ☐ Condition-defined and user-defined membership
  - ☐ Disjoint and overlapping generalization
- Completeness constraint
  - ☐ Total and partial generalization
- Aggregation
- E-R diagram
- Unified Modeling Language (UML)

Exercises

2.1 Explain the distinctions among the terms primary key, candidate key, and superkey.

2.2 Construct an E-R diagram for a car-insurance company whose customers own one or more cars each. Each car has associated with it zero to any number of recorded accidents.

2.3 Construct an E-R diagram for a hospital with a set of patients and a set of medical doctors. Associate with each patient a log of the various tests and examinations conducted.

2.4 A university registrar's office maintains data about the following entities: (a) courses, including number, title, credits, syllabus, and prerequisites; (b) course offerings, including course number, year, semester, section number, instructor(s), timings, and classroom; (c) students, including student-id, name, and program; and (d) instructors, including identification number, name, department, and title. Further, the enrollment of students in courses and grades awarded to students in each course they are enrolled for must be appropriately modeled.

Construct an E-R diagram for the registrar's office. Document all assumptions that you make about the mapping constraints.

2.5 Consider a database used to record the marks that students get in different exams of different course offerings.

   a. Construct an E-R diagram that models exams as entities, and uses a ternary relationship, for the above database.

b. Construct an alternative E-R diagram that uses only a binary relationship between *students* and *course-offerings*. Make sure that only one relationship exists between a particular student and course-offering pair, yet you can represent the marks that a student gets in different exams of a course offering.

2.6 Construct appropriate tables for each of the E-R diagrams in Exercises 2.2 to 2.4.

2.7 Design an E-R diagram for keeping track of the exploits of your favourite sports team. You should store the matches played, the scores in each match, the players in each match and individual player statistics for each match. Summary statistics should be modeled as derived attributes

2.8 Extend the E-R diagram of the previous question to track the same information for all teams in a league.

2.9 Explain the difference between a weak and a strong entity set.

2.10 We can convert any weak entity set to a strong entity set by simply adding appropriate attributes. Why, then, do we have weak entity sets?

2.11 Define the concept of aggregation. Give two examples of where this concept is useful.

2.12 Consider the E-R diagram in Figure 2.29, which models an online bookstore.
 a. List the entity sets and their primary keys.
 b. Suppose the bookstore adds music cassettes and compact disks to its collection. The same music item may be present in cassette or compact disk format, with differing prices. Extend the E-R diagram to model this addition, ignoring the effect on shopping baskets.
 c. Now extend the E-R diagram, using generalization, to model the case where a shopping basket may contain any combination of books, music cassettes, or compact disks.

2.13 Consider an E-R diagram in which the same entity set appears several times. Why is allowing this redundancy a bad practice that one should avoid whenever possible?

2.14 Consider a university database for the scheduling of classrooms for final exams. This database could be modeled as the single entity set *exam*, with attributes *course-name*, *section-number*, *room-number*, and *time*. Alternatively, one or more additional entity sets could be defined, along with relationship sets to replace some of the attributes of the *exam* entity set, as

 - *course* with attributes *name*, *department*, and *c-number*
 - *section* with attributes *s-number* and *enrollment*, and dependent as a weak entity set on *course*
 - *room* with attributes *r-number*, *capacity*, and *building*

 a. Show an E-R diagram illustrating the use of all three additional entity sets listed.

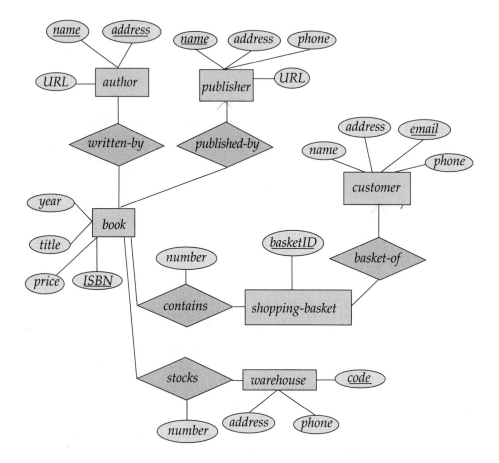

Figure 2.29 E-R diagram for Exercise 2.12.

b. Explain what application characteristics would influence a decision to include or not to include each of the additional entity sets.

2.15 When designing an E-R diagram for a particular enterprise, you have several alternatives from which to choose.

a. What criteria should you consider in making the appropriate choice?

b. Design three alternative E-R diagrams to represent the university registrar's office of Exercise 2.4. List the merits of each. Argue in favor of one of the alternatives.

2.16 An E-R diagram can be viewed as a graph. What do the following mean in terms of the structure of an enterprise schema?

a. The graph is disconnected.

b. The graph is acyclic.

2.17 In Section 2.4.3, we represented a ternary relationship (Figure 2.30a) using binary relationships, as shown in Figure 2.30b. Consider the alternative shown in

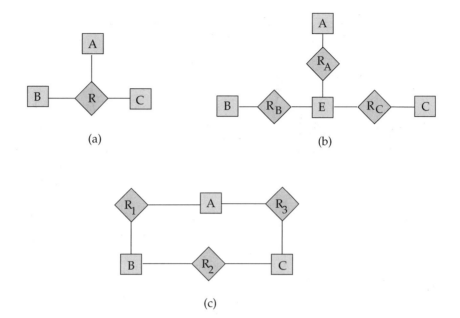

Figure 2.30   E-R diagram for Exercise 2.17 (attributes not shown).

Figure 2.30c. Discuss the relative merits of these two alternative representations of a ternary relationship by binary relationships.

2.18 Consider the representation of a ternary relationship using binary relationships as described in Section 2.4.3 (shown in Figure 2.30b.)

    a. Show a simple instance of E, A, B, C, R_A, R_B, and R_C that cannot correspond to any instance of A, B, C, and R.

    b. Modify the E-R diagram of Figure 2.30b to introduce constraints that will guarantee that any instance of E, A, B, C, R_A, R_B, and R_C that satisfies the constraints will correspond to an instance of A, B, C, and R.

    c. Modify the translation above to handle total participation constraints on the ternary relationship.

    d. The above representation requires that we create a primary key attribute for E. Show how to treat E as a weak entity set so that a primary key attribute is not required.

2.19 A weak entity set can always be made into a strong entity set by adding to its attributes the primary key attributes of its identifying entity set. Outline what sort of redundancy will result if we do so.

2.20 Design a generalization–specialization hierarchy for a motor-vehicle sales company. The company sells motorcycles, passenger cars, vans, and buses. Justify your placement of attributes at each level of the hierarchy. Explain why they should not be placed at a higher or lower level.

2.21 Explain the distinction between condition-defined and user-defined constraints. Which of these constraints can the system check automatically? Explain your answer.

2.22 Explain the distinction between disjoint and overlapping constraints.

2.23 Explain the distinction between total and partial constraints.

2.24 Figure 2.31 shows a lattice structure of generalization and specialization. For entity sets A, B, and C, explain how attributes are inherited from the higher-level entity sets X and Y. Discuss how to handle a case where an attribute of X has the same name as some attribute of Y.

2.25 Draw the UML equivalents of the E-R diagrams of Figures 2.9c, 2.10, 2.12, 2.13 and 2.17.

2.26 Consider two separate banks that decide to merge. Assume that both banks use exactly the same E-R database schema—the one in Figure 2.22. (This assumption is, of course, highly unrealistic; we consider the more realistic case in Section 19.8.) If the merged bank is to have a single database, there are several potential problems:

- The possibility that the two original banks have branches with the same name
- The possibility that some customers are customers of both original banks
- The possibility that some loan or account numbers were used at both original banks (for different loans or accounts, of course)

For each of these potential problems, describe why there is indeed a potential for difficulties. Propose a solution to the problem. For your solution, explain any changes that would have to be made and describe what their effect would be on the schema and the data.

2.27 Reconsider the situation described for Exercise 2.26 under the assumption that one bank is in the United States and the other is in Canada. As before, the banks use the schema of Figure 2.22, except that the Canadian bank uses the *social-insurance* number assigned by the Canadian government, whereas the U.S. bank uses the social-security number to identify customers. What problems (be-

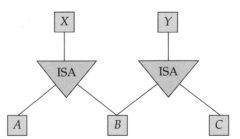

Figure 2.31   E-R diagram for Exercise 2.24 (attributes not shown).

yond those identified in Exercise 2.24) might occur in this multinational case? How would you resolve them? Be sure to consider both the scheme and the actual data values in constructing your answer.

Bibliographical Notes

The E-R data model was introduced by Chen [1976]. A logical design methodology for relational databases using the extended E-R model is presented by Teorey et al. [1986]. Mapping from extended E-R models to the relational model is discussed by Lyngbaek and Vianu [1987] and Markowitz and Shoshani [1992]. Various data-manipulation languages for the E-R model have been proposed: GERM (Benneworth et al. [1981]), GORDAS (Elmasri and Wiederhold [1981]), and ERROL (Markowitz and Raz [1983]). A graphical query language for the E-R database was proposed by Zhang and Mendelzon [1983] and Elmasri and Larson [1985].

Smith and Smith [1977] introduced the concepts of generalization, specialization, and aggregation and Hammer and McLeod [1980] expanded them. Lenzerini and Santucci [1983] used the concepts in defining cardinality constraints in the E-R model.

Thalheim [2000] provides a detailed textbook coverage of research in E-R modeling. Basic textbook discussions are offered by Batini et al. [1992] and Elmasri and Navathe [2000]. Davis et al. [1983] provide a collection of papers on the E-R model.

Tools

Many database systems provide tools for database design that support E-R diagrams. These tools help a designer create E-R diagrams, and they can automatically create corresponding tables in a database. See bibliographic notes of Chapter 1 for references to database system vendor's Web sites. There are also some database-independent data modeling tools that support E-R diagrams and UML class diagrams. These include Rational Rose (www.rational.com/products/rose), Visio Enterprise (see www.visio.com), and ERwin (search for ERwin at the site www.cai.com/products).

CHAPTER 3

Relational Model

The relational model is today the primary data model for commercial data-processing applications. It has attained its primary position because of its simplicity, which eases the job of the programmer, as compared to earlier data models such as the network model or the hierarchical model.

In this chapter, we first study the fundamentals of the relational model, which provides a very simple yet powerful way of representing data. We then describe three formal query languages; query languages are used to specify requests for information. The three we cover in this chapter are not user-friendly, but instead serve as the formal basis for user-friendly query languages that we study later. We cover the first query language, relational algebra, in great detail. The relational algebra forms the basis of the widely used SQL query language. We then provide overviews of the other two formal languages, the tuple relational calculus and the domain relational calculus, which are declarative query languages based on mathematical logic. The domain relational calculus is the basis of the QBE query language.

A substantial theory exists for relational databases. We study the part of this theory dealing with queries in this chapter. In Chapter 7 we shall examine aspects of relational database theory that help in the design of relational database schemas, while in Chapters 13 and 14 we discuss aspects of the theory dealing with efficient processing of queries.

3.1 Structure of Relational Databases

A relational database consists of a collection of **tables**, each of which is assigned a unique name. Each table has a structure similar to that presented in Chapter 2, where we represented E-R databases by tables. A row in a table represents a *relationship* among a set of values. Since a table is a collection of such relationships, there is a close correspondence between the concept of *table* and the mathematical concept of *relation,* from which the relational data model takes its name. In what follows, we introduce the concept of relation.

In this chapter, we shall be using a number of different relations to illustrate the various concepts underlying the relational data model. These relations represent part of a banking enterprise. They differ slightly from the tables that were used in Chapter 2, so that we can simplify our presentation. We shall discuss criteria for the appropriateness of relational structures in great detail in Chapter 7.

3.1.1 Basic Structure

Consider the *account* table of Figure 3.1. It has three column headers: *account-number, branch-name,* and *balance*. Following the terminology of the relational model, we refer to these headers as **attributes** (as we did for the E-R model in Chapter 2). For each attribute, there is a set of permitted values, called the **domain** of that attribute. For the attribute *branch-name,* for example, the domain is the set of all branch names. Let D_1 denote the set of all account numbers, D_2 the set of all branch names, and D_3 the set of all balances. As we saw in Chapter 2, any row of *account* must consist of a 3-tuple (v_1, v_2, v_3), where v_1 is an account number (that is, v_1 is in domain D_1), v_2 is a branch name (that is, v_2 is in domain D_2), and v_3 is a balance (that is, v_3 is in domain D_3). In general, *account* will contain only a subset of the set of all possible rows. Therefore, *account* is a subset of

$$D_1 \times D_2 \times D_3$$

In general, a **table** of n attributes must be a subset of

$$D_1 \times D_2 \times \cdots \times D_{n-1} \times D_n$$

Mathematicians define a **relation** to be a subset of a Cartesian product of a list of domains. This definition corresponds almost exactly with our definition of *table*. The only difference is that we have assigned names to attributes, whereas mathematicians rely on numeric "names," using the integer 1 to denote the attribute whose domain appears first in the list of domains, 2 for the attribute whose domain appears second, and so on. Because tables are essentially relations, we shall use the mathematical

account-number	branch-name	balance
A-101	Downtown	500
A-102	Perryridge	400
A-201	Brighton	900
A-215	Mianus	700
A-217	Brighton	750
A-222	Redwood	700
A-305	Round Hill	350

Figure 3.1   The *account* relation.

account-number	branch-name	balance
A-101	Downtown	500
A-215	Mianus	700
A-102	Perryridge	400
A-305	Round Hill	350
A-201	Brighton	900
A-222	Redwood	700
A-217	Brighton	750

Figure 3.2   The *account* relation with unordered tuples.

terms **relation** and **tuple** in place of the terms **table** and **row**. A **tuple variable** is a variable that stands for a tuple; in other words, a tuple variable is a variable whose domain is the set of all tuples.

In the *account* relation of Figure 3.1, there are seven tuples. Let the tuple variable t refer to the first tuple of the relation. We use the notation $t[account\text{-}number]$ to denote the value of t on the *account-number* attribute. Thus, $t[account\text{-}number] =$ "A-101," and $t[branch\text{-}name] =$ "Downtown". Alternatively, we may write $t[1]$ to denote the value of tuple t on the first attribute (*account-number*), $t[2]$ to denote *branch-name*, and so on. Since a relation is a set of tuples, we use the mathematical notation of $t \in r$ to denote that tuple t is in relation r.

The order in which tuples appear in a relation is irrelevant, since a relation is a *set* of tuples. Thus, whether the tuples of a relation are listed in sorted order, as in Figure 3.1, or are unsorted, as in Figure 3.2, does not matter; the relations in the two figures above are the same, since both contain the same set of tuples.

We require that, for all relations r, the domains of all attributes of r be atomic. A domain is **atomic** if elements of the domain are considered to be indivisible units. For example, the set of integers is an atomic domain, but the set of all sets of integers is a nonatomic domain. The distinction is that we do not normally consider integers to have subparts, but we consider sets of integers to have subparts—namely, the integers composing the set. The important issue is not what the domain itself is, but rather how we use domain elements in our database. The domain of all integers would be nonatomic if we considered each integer to be an ordered list of digits. In all our examples, we shall assume atomic domains. In Chapter 9, we shall discuss extensions to the relational data model to permit nonatomic domains.

It is possible for several attributes to have the same domain. For example, suppose that we have a relation *customer* that has the three attributes *customer-name*, *customer-street*, and *customer-city*, and a relation *employee* that includes the attribute *employee-name*. It is possible that the attributes *customer-name* and *employee-name* will have the same domain: the set of all person names, which at the physical level is the set of all character strings. The domains of *balance* and *branch-name*, on the other hand, certainly ought to be distinct. It is perhaps less clear whether *customer-name* and *branch-name* should have the same domain. At the physical level, both customer names and branch names are character strings. However, at the logical level, we may want *customer-name* and *branch-name* to have distinct domains.

One domain value that is a member of any possible domain is the **null** value, which signifies that the value is unknown or does not exist. For example, suppose that we include the attribute *telephone-number* in the *customer* relation. It may be that a customer does not have a telephone number, or that the telephone number is unlisted. We would then have to resort to null values to signify that the value is unknown or does not exist. We shall see later that null values cause a number of difficulties when we access or update the database, and thus should be eliminated if at all possible. We shall assume null values are absent initially, and in Section 3.3.4, we describe the effect of nulls on different operations.

3.1.2 Database Schema

When we talk about a database, we must differentiate between the **database schema**, which is the logical design of the database, and a **database instance**, which is a snapshot of the data in the database at a given instant in time.

The concept of a relation corresponds to the programming-language notion of a variable. The concept of a **relation schema** corresponds to the programming-language notion of type definition.

It is convenient to give a name to a relation schema, just as we give names to type definitions in programming languages. We adopt the convention of using lowercase names for relations, and names beginning with an uppercase letter for relation schemas. Following this notation, we use *Account-schema* to denote the relation schema for relation *account*. Thus,

$$Account\text{-}schema = (account\text{-}number, branch\text{-}name, balance)$$

We denote the fact that *account* is a relation on *Account-schema* by

$$account(Account\text{-}schema)$$

In general, a relation schema consists of a list of attributes and their corresponding domains. We shall not be concerned about the precise definition of the domain of each attribute until we discuss the SQL language in Chapter 4.

The concept of a **relation instance** corresponds to the programming language notion of a value of a variable. The value of a given variable may change with time; similarly the contents of a relation instance may change with time as the relation is updated. However, we often simply say "relation" when we actually mean "relation instance."

As an example of a relation instance, consider the *branch* relation of Figure 3.3. The schema for that relation is

$$Branch\text{-}schema = (branch\text{-}name, branch\text{-}city, assets)$$

Note that the attribute *branch-name* appears in both *Branch-schema* and *Account-schema*. This duplication is not a coincidence. Rather, using common attributes in relation schemas is one way of relating tuples of distinct relations. For example, suppose we wish to find the information about all of the accounts maintained in branches

branch-name	branch-city	assets
Brighton	Brooklyn	7100000
Downtown	Brooklyn	9000000
Mianus	Horseneck	400000
North Town	Rye	3700000
Perryridge	Horseneck	1700000
Pownal	Bennington	300000
Redwood	Palo Alto	2100000
Round Hill	Horseneck	8000000

Figure 3.3 The *branch* relation.

located in Brooklyn. We look first at the *branch* relation to find the names of all the branches located in Brooklyn. Then, for each such branch, we would look in the *account* relation to find the information about the accounts maintained at that branch. This is not surprising—recall that the primary key attributes of a strong entity set appear in the table created to represent the entity set, as well as in the tables created to represent relationships that the entity set participates in.

Let us continue our banking example. We need a relation to describe information about customers. The relation schema is

$$Customer\text{-}schema = (customer\text{-}name, customer\text{-}street, customer\text{-}city)$$

Figure 3.4 shows a sample relation *customer* (*Customer-schema*). Note that we have omitted the *customer-id* attribute, which we used Chapter 2, because now we want to have smaller relation schemas in our running example of a bank database. We assume that the customer name uniquely identifies a customer—obviously this may not be true in the real world, but the assumption makes our examples much easier to read.

customer-name	customer-street	customer-city
Adams	Spring	Pittsfield
Brooks	Senator	Brooklyn
Curry	North	Rye
Glenn	Sand Hill	Woodside
Green	Walnut	Stamford
Hayes	Main	Harrison
Johnson	Alma	Palo Alto
Jones	Main	Harrison
Lindsay	Park	Pittsfield
Smith	North	Rye
Turner	Putnam	Stamford
Williams	Nassau	Princeton

Figure 3.4 The *customer* relation.

In a real-world database, the *customer-id* (which could be a *social-security* number, or an identifier generated by the bank) would serve to uniquely identify customers.

We also need a relation to describe the association between customers and accounts. The relation schema to describe this association is

$$Depositor\text{-}schema = (customer\text{-}name, account\text{-}number)$$

Figure 3.5 shows a sample relation *depositor* (*Depositor-schema*).

It would appear that, for our banking example, we could have just one relation schema, rather than several. That is, it may be easier for a user to think in terms of one relation schema, rather than in terms of several. Suppose that we used only one relation for our example, with schema

> (*branch-name, branch-city, assets, customer-name, customer-street*
> *customer-city, account-number, balance*)

Observe that, if a customer has several accounts, we must list her address once for each account. That is, we must repeat certain information several times. This repetition is wasteful and is avoided by the use of several relations, as in our example.

In addition, if a branch has no accounts (a newly created branch, say, that has no customers yet), we cannot construct a complete tuple on the preceding single relation, because no data concerning *customer* and *account* are available yet. To represent incomplete tuples, we must use *null* values that signify that the value is unknown or does not exist. Thus, in our example, the values for *customer-name, customer-street*, and so on must be null. By using several relations, we can represent the branch information for a bank with no customers without using null values. We simply use a tuple on *Branch-schema* to represent the information about the branch, and create tuples on the other schemas only when the appropriate information becomes available.

In Chapter 7, we shall study criteria to help us decide when one set of relation schemas is more appropriate than another, in terms of information repetition and the existence of null values. For now, we shall assume that the relation schemas are given.

We include two additional relations to describe data about loans maintained in the various branches in the bank:

customer-name	account-number
Hayes	A-102
Johnson	A-101
Johnson	A-201
Jones	A-217
Lindsay	A-222
Smith	A-215
Turner	A-305

Figure 3.5   The *depositor* relation.

loan-number	branch-name	amount
L-11	Round Hill	900
L-14	Downtown	1500
L-15	Perryridge	1500
L-16	Perryridge	1300
L-17	Downtown	1000
L-23	Redwood	2000
L-93	Mianus	500

Figure 3.6   The *loan* relation.

$$Loan\text{-}schema = (loan\text{-}number, branch\text{-}name, amount)$$
$$Borrower\text{-}schema = (customer\text{-}name, loan\text{-}number)$$

Figures 3.6 and 3.7, respectively, show the sample relations *loan* (*Loan-schema*) and *borrower* (*Borrower-schema*).

The E-R diagram in Figure 3.8 depicts the banking enterprise that we have just described. The relation schemas correspond to the set of tables that we might generate by the method outlined in Section 2.9. Note that the tables for *account-branch* and *loan-branch* have been combined into the tables for *account* and *loan* respectively. Such combining is possible since the relationships are many to one from *account* and *loan*, respectively, to *branch*, and, further, the participation of *account* and *loan* in the corresponding relationships is total, as the double lines in the figure indicate. Finally, we note that the *customer* relation may contain information about customers who have neither an account nor a loan at the bank.

The banking enterprise described here will serve as our primary example in this chapter and in subsequent ones. On occasion, we shall need to introduce additional relation schemas to illustrate particular points.

3.1.3 Keys

The notions of *superkey*, *candidate key*, and *primary key*, as discussed in Chapter 2, are also applicable to the relational model. For example, in *Branch-schema*, {*branch-*

customer-name	loan-number
Adams	L-16
Curry	L-93
Hayes	L-15
Jackson	L-14
Jones	L-17
Smith	L-11
Smith	L-23
Williams	L-17

Figure 3.7   The *borrower* relation.

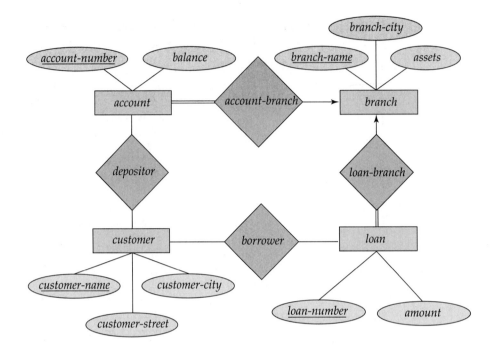

Figure 3.8 E-R diagram for the banking enterprise.

name} and {*branch-name, branch-city*} are both superkeys. {*branch-name, branch-city*} is not a candidate key, because {*branch-name*} is a subset of {*branch-name, branch-city*} and {*branch-name*} itself is a superkey. However, {*branch-name*} *is* a candidate key, and for our purpose also will serve as a primary key. The attribute *branch-city* is not a superkey, since two branches in the same city may have different names (and different asset figures).

Let R be a relation schema. If we say that a subset K of R is a *superkey* for R, we are restricting consideration to relations $r(R)$ in which no two distinct tuples have the same values on all attributes in K. That is, if t_1 *and* t_2 are in r and $t_1 \neq t_2$, then $t_1[K] \neq t_2[K]$.

If a relational database schema is based on tables derived from an E-R schema, it is possible to determine the primary key for a relation schema from the primary keys of the entity or relationship sets from which the schema is derived:

- **Strong entity set**. The primary key of the entity set becomes the primary key of the relation.

- **Weak entity set**. The table, and thus the relation, corresponding to a weak entity set includes
  - ☐ The attributes of the weak entity set
  - ☐ The primary key of the strong entity set on which the weak entity set depends

The primary key of the relation consists of the union of the primary key of the strong entity set and the discriminator of the weak entity set.

- **Relationship set**. The union of the primary keys of the related entity sets becomes a superkey of the relation. If the relationship is many-to-many, this superkey is also the primary key. Section 2.4.2 describes how to determine the primary keys in other cases. Recall from Section 2.9.3 that no table is generated for relationship sets linking a weak entity set to the corresponding strong entity set.

- **Combined tables**. Recall from Section 2.9.3 that a binary many-to-one relationship set from A to B can be represented by a table consisting of the attributes of A and attributes (if any exist) of the relationship set. The primary key of the "many" entity set becomes the primary key of the relation (that is, if the relationship set is many to one from A to B, the primary key of A is the primary key of the relation). For one-to-one relationship sets, the relation is constructed like that for a many-to-one relationship set. However, we can choose either entity set's primary key as the primary key of the relation, since both are candidate keys.

- **Multivalued attributes**. Recall from Section 2.9.5 that a multivalued attribute M is represented by a table consisting of the primary key of the entity set or relationship set of which M is an attribute plus a column C holding an individual value of M. The primary key of the entity or relationship set, together with the attribute C, becomes the primary key for the relation.

From the preceding list, we see that a relation schema, say r_1, derived from an E-R schema may include among its attributes the primary key of another relation schema, say r_2. This attribute is called a **foreign key** from r_1, referencing r_2. The relation r_1 is also called the **referencing relation** of the foreign key dependency, and r_2 is called the **referenced relation** of the foreign key. For example, the attribute *branch-name* in *Account-schema* is a foreign key from *Account-schema* referencing *Branch-schema*, since *branch-name* is the primary key of *Branch-schema*. In any database instance, given any tuple, say t_a, from the *account* relation, there must be some tuple, say t_b, in the *branch* relation such that the value of the *branch-name* attribute of t_a is the same as the value of the primary key, *branch-name*, of t_b.

It is customary to list the primary key attributes of a relation schema before the other attributes; for example, the *branch-name* attribute of *Branch-schema* is listed first, since it is the primary key.

3.1.4   Schema Diagram

A database schema, along with primary key and foreign key dependencies, can be depicted pictorially by **schema diagram**s. Figure 3.9 shows the schema diagram for our banking enterprise. Each relation appears as a box, with the attributes listed inside it and the relation name above it. If there are primary key attributes, a horizontal line crosses the box, with the primary key attributes listed above the line. Foreign

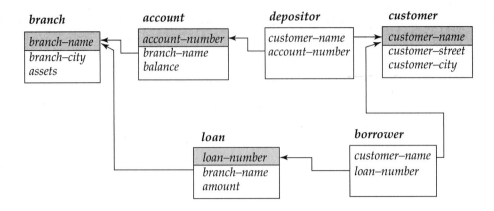

Figure 3.9   Schema diagram for the banking enterprise.

key dependencies appear as arrows from the foreign key attributes of the referencing relation to the primary key of the referenced relation.

Do not confuse a schema diagram with an E-R diagram. In particular, E-R diagrams do not show foreign key attributes explicitly, whereas schema diagrams show them explicity.

Many database systems provide design tools with a graphical user interface for creating schema diagrams.

3.1.5   Query Languages

A **query language** is a language in which a user requests information from the database. These languages are usually on a level higher than that of a standard programming language. Query languages can be categorized as either procedural or nonprocedural. In a **procedural language**, the user instructs the system to perform a sequence of operations on the database to compute the desired result. In a **nonprocedural language**, the user describes the desired information without giving a specific procedure for obtaining that information.

Most commercial relational-database systems offer a query language that includes elements of both the procedural and the nonprocedural approaches. We shall study the very widely used query language SQL in Chapter 4. Chapter 5 covers the query languages QBE and Datalog, the latter a query language that resembles the Prolog programming language.

In this chapter, we examine "pure" languages: The relational algebra is procedural, whereas the tuple relational calculus and domain relational calculus are nonprocedural. These query languages are terse and formal, lacking the "syntactic sugar" of commercial languages, but they illustrate the fundamental techniques for extracting data from the database.

Although we shall be concerned with only queries initially, a complete data-manipulation language includes not only a query language, but also a language for database modification. Such languages include commands to insert and delete tuples, as well as commands to modify parts of existing tuples. We shall examine database modification after we complete our discussion of queries.

3.2 The Relational Algebra

The relational algebra is a *procedural* query language. It consists of a set of operations that take one or two relations as input and produce a new relation as their result. The fundamental operations in the relational algebra are *select, project, union, set difference, Cartesian product,* and *rename*. In addition to the fundamental operations, there are several other operations—namely, set intersection, natural join, division, and assignment. We will define these operations in terms of the fundamental operations.

3.2.1 Fundamental Operations

The select, project, and rename operations are called *unary* operations, because they operate on one relation. The other three operations operate on pairs of relations and are, therefore, called *binary* operations.

3.2.1.1 The Select Operation

The **select** operation selects tuples that satisfy a given predicate. We use the lowercase Greek letter sigma (σ) to denote selection. The predicate appears as a subscript to σ. The argument relation is in parentheses after the σ. Thus, to select those tuples of the *loan* relation where the branch is "Perryridge," we write

$$\sigma_{branch\text{-}name\,=\,\text{"Perryridge"}}\,(loan)$$

If the *loan* relation is as shown in Figure 3.6, then the relation that results from the preceding query is as shown in Figure 3.10.

We can find all tuples in which the amount lent is more than \$1200 by writing

$$\sigma_{amount>1200}\,(loan)$$

In general, we allow comparisons using $=, \neq, <, \leq, >, \geq$ in the selection predicate. Furthermore, we can combine several predicates into a larger predicate by using the connectives *and* ($\wedge$), *or* ($\vee$), and *not* ($\neg$). Thus, to find those tuples pertaining to loans of more than \$1200 made by the Perryridge branch, we write

$$\sigma_{branch\text{-}name\,=\,\text{"Perryridge"}\,\wedge\,amount>1200}\,(loan)$$

loan-number	branch-name	amount
L-15	Perryridge	1500
L-16	Perryridge	1300

Figure 3.10   Result of $\sigma_{branch\text{-}name\,=\,\text{"Perryridge"}}\,(loan)$.

The selection predicate may include comparisons between two attributes. To illustrate, consider the relation *loan-officer* that consists of three attributes: *customer-name*, *banker-name*, and *loan-number*, which specifies that a particular banker is the loan officer for a loan that belongs to some customer. To find all customers who have the same name as their loan officer, we can write

$$\sigma_{customer\text{-}name\ =\ banker\text{-}name}(loan\text{-}officer)$$

3.2.1.2 The Project Operation

Suppose we want to list all loan numbers and the amount of the loans, but do not care about the branch name. The **project** operation allows us to produce this relation. The project operation is a unary operation that returns its argument relation, with certain attributes left out. Since a relation is a set, any duplicate rows are eliminated. Projection is denoted by the uppercase Greek letter pi (Π). We list those attributes that we wish to appear in the result as a subscript to Π. The argument relation follows in parentheses. Thus, we write the query to list all loan numbers and the amount of the loan as

$$\Pi_{loan\text{-}number,\ amount}(loan)$$

Figure 3.11 shows the relation that results from this query.

3.2.1.3 Composition of Relational Operations

The fact that the result of a relational operation is itself a relation is important. Consider the more complicated query "Find those customers who live in Harrison." We write:

$$\Pi_{customer\text{-}name}(\sigma_{customer\text{-}city\ =\ \text{``Harrison''}}(customer))$$

Notice that, instead of giving the name of a relation as the argument of the projection operation, we give an expression that evaluates to a relation.

In general, since the result of a relational-algebra operation is of the same type (relation) as its inputs, relational-algebra operations can be composed together into

loan-number	amount
L-11	900
L-14	1500
L-15	1500
L-16	1300
L-17	1000
L-23	2000
L-93	500

Figure 3.11   Loan number and the amount of the loan.

a **relational-algebra expression**. Composing relational-algebra operations into relational-algebra expressions is just like composing arithmetic operations (such as $+$, $-$, $*$, and $\div$) into arithmetic expressions. We study the formal definition of relational-algebra expressions in Section 3.2.2.

3.2.1.4   The Union Operation

Consider a query to find the names of all bank customers who have either an account or a loan or both. Note that the *customer* relation does not contain the information, since a customer does not need to have either an account or a loan at the bank. To answer this query, we need the information in the *depositor* relation (Figure 3.5) and in the *borrower* relation (Figure 3.7). We know how to find the names of all customers with a loan in the bank:

$$\Pi_{customer\text{-}name}\ (borrower)$$

We also know how to find the names of all customers with an account in the bank:

$$\Pi_{customer\text{-}name}\ (depositor)$$

To answer the query, we need the **union** of these two sets; that is, we need all customer names that appear in either or both of the two relations. We find these data by the binary operation union, denoted, as in set theory, by $\cup$. So the expression needed is

$$\Pi_{customer\text{-}name}\ (borrower)\ \cup\ \Pi_{customer\text{-}name}\ (depositor)$$

The result relation for this query appears in Figure 3.12. Notice that there are 10 tuples in the result, even though there are seven distinct borrowers and six depositors. This apparent discrepancy occurs because Smith, Jones, and Hayes are borrowers as well as depositors. Since relations are sets, duplicate values are eliminated.

customer-name
Adams
Curry
Hayes
Jackson
Jones
Smith
Williams
Lindsay
Johnson
Turner

Figure 3.12   Names of all customers who have either a loan or an account.

Observe that, in our example, we took the union of two sets, both of which consisted of *customer-name* values. In general, we must ensure that unions are taken between *compatible* relations. For example, it would not make sense to take the union of the *loan* relation and the *borrower* relation. The former is a relation of three attributes; the latter is a relation of two. Furthermore, consider a union of a set of customer names and a set of cities. Such a union would not make sense in most situations. Therefore, for a union operation $r \cup s$ to be valid, we require that two conditions hold:

1. The relations r and s must be of the same arity. That is, they must have the same number of attributes.

2. The domains of the ith attribute of r and the ith attribute of s must be the same, for all i.

Note that r and s can be, in general, temporary relations that are the result of relational-algebra expressions.

3.2.1.5 The Set Difference Operation

The **set-difference** operation, denoted by $-$, allows us to find tuples that are in one relation but are not in another. The expression $r - s$ produces a relation containing those tuples in r but not in s.

We can find all customers of the bank who have an account but not a loan by writing

$$\Pi_{customer\text{-}name}\,(depositor) - \Pi_{customer\text{-}name}\,(borrower)$$

The result relation for this query appears in Figure 3.13.

As with the union operation, we must ensure that set differences are taken between *compatible* relations. Therefore, for a set difference operation $r - s$ to be valid, we require that the relations r and s be of the same arity, and that the domains of the ith attribute of r and the ith attribute of s be the same.

3.2.1.6 The Cartesian-Product Operation

The **Cartesian-product** operation, denoted by a cross ($\times$), allows us to combine information from any two relations. We write the Cartesian product of relations r_1 and r_2 as $r_1 \times r_2$.

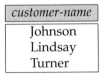

customer-name
Johnson
Lindsay
Turner

Figure 3.13   Customers with an account but no loan.

Recall that a relation is by definition a subset of a Cartesian product of a set of domains. From that definition, we should already have an intuition about the definition of the Cartesian-product operation. However, since the same attribute name may appear in both r_1 and r_2, we need to devise a naming schema to distinguish between these attributes. We do so here by attaching to an attribute the name of the relation from which the attribute originally came. For example, the relation schema for $r = borrower \times loan$ is

(*borrower.customer-name, borrower.loan-number, loan.loan-number,*
loan.branch-name, loan.amount)

With this schema, we can distinguish *borrower.loan-number* from *loan.loan-number*. For those attributes that appear in only one of the two schemas, we shall usually drop the relation-name prefix. This simplification does not lead to any ambiguity. We can then write the relation schema for r as

(*customer-name, borrower.loan-number, loan.loan-number,*
branch-name, amount)

This naming convention *requires* that the relations that are the arguments of the Cartesian-product operation have distinct names. This requirement causes problems in some cases, such as when the Cartesian product of a relation with itself is desired. A similar problem arises if we use the result of a relational-algebra expression in a Cartesian product, since we shall need a name for the relation so that we can refer to the relation's attributes. In Section 3.2.1.7, we see how to avoid these problems by using a rename operation.

Now that we know the relation schema for $r = borrower \times loan$, what tuples appear in r? As you may suspect, we construct a tuple of r out of each possible pair of tuples: one from the *borrower* relation and one from the *loan* relation. Thus, r is a large relation, as you can see from Figure 3.14, which includes only a portion of the tuples that make up r.

Assume that we have n_1 tuples in *borrower* and n_2 tuples in *loan*. Then, there are $n_1 * n_2$ ways of choosing a pair of tuples—one tuple from each relation; so there are $n_1 * n_2$ tuples in r. In particular, note that for some tuples t in r, it may be that $t[borrower.loan-number] \neq t[loan.loan-number]$.

In general, if we have relations $r_1(R_1)$ and $r_2(R_2)$, then $r_1 \times r_2$ is a relation whose schema is the concatenation of R_1 and R_2. Relation R contains all tuples t for which there is a tuple t_1 in r_1 and a tuple t_2 in r_2 for which $t[R_1] = t_1[R_1]$ and $t[R_2] = t_2[R_2]$.

Suppose that we want to find the names of all customers who have a loan at the Perryridge branch. We need the information in both the *loan* relation and the *borrower* relation to do so. If we write

$$\sigma_{branch-name = \text{“Perryridge”}}(borrower \times loan)$$

then the result is the relation in Figure 3.15. We have a relation that pertains to only the Perryridge branch. However, the *customer-name* column may contain customers

customer-name	borrower. loan-number	loan. loan-number	branch-name	amount
Adams	L-16	L-11	Round Hill	900
Adams	L-16	L-14	Downtown	1500
Adams	L-16	L-15	Perryridge	1500
Adams	L-16	L-16	Perryridge	1300
Adams	L-16	L-17	Downtown	1000
Adams	L-16	L-23	Redwood	2000
Adams	L-16	L-93	Mianus	500
Curry	L-93	L-11	Round Hill	900
Curry	L-93	L-14	Downtown	1500
Curry	L-93	L-15	Perryridge	1500
Curry	L-93	L-16	Perryridge	1300
Curry	L-93	L-17	Downtown	1000
Curry	L-93	L-23	Redwood	2000
Curry	L-93	L-93	Mianus	500
Hayes	L-15	L-11		900
Hayes	L-15	L-14		1500
Hayes	L-15	L-15		1500
Hayes	L-15	L-16		1300
Hayes	L-15	L-17		1000
Hayes	L-15	L-23		2000
Hayes	L-15	L-93		500
. . .	. . .	. . .	. . .	. . .
. . .	. . .	. . .	. . .	. . .
. . .	. . .	. . .	. . .	. . .
Smith	L-23	L-11	Round Hill	900
Smith	L-23	L-14	Downtown	1500
Smith	L-23	L-15	Perryridge	1500
Smith	L-23	L-16	Perryridge	1300
Smith	L-23	L-17	Downtown	1000
Smith	L-23	L-23	Redwood	2000
Smith	L-23	L-93	Mianus	500
Williams	L-17	L-11	Round Hill	900
Williams	L-17	L-14	Downtown	1500
Williams	L-17	L-15	Perryridge	1500
Williams	L-17	L-16	Perryridge	1300
Williams	L-17	L-17	Downtown	1000
Williams	L-17	L-23	Redwood	2000
Williams	L-17	L-93	Mianus	500

Figure 3.14 Result of *borrower* × *loan*.

customer-name	borrower. loan-number	loan. loan-number	branch-name	amount
Adams	L-16	L-15	Perryridge	1500
Adams	L-16	L-16	Perryridge	1300
Curry	L-93	L-15	Perryridge	1500
Curry	L-93	L-16	Perryridge	1300
Hayes	L-15	L-15	Perryridge	1500
Hayes	L-15	L-16	Perryridge	1300
Jackson	L-14	L-15	Perryridge	1500
Jackson	L-14	L-16	Perryridge	1300
Jones	L-17	L-15	Perryridge	1500
Jones	L-17	L-16	Perryridge	1300
Smith	L-11	L-15	Perryridge	1500
Smith	L-11	L-16	Perryridge	1300
Smith	L-23	L-15	Perryridge	1500
Smith	L-23	L-16	Perryridge	1300
Williams	L-17	L-15	Perryridge	1500
Williams	L-17	L-16	Perryridge	1300

Figure 3.15   Result of $\sigma_{branch\text{-}name = \text{"Perryridge"}}(borrower \times loan)$.

who do not have a loan at the Perryridge branch. (If you do not see why that is true, recall that the Cartesian product takes all possible pairings of one tuple from *borrower* with one tuple of *loan*.)

Since the Cartesian-product operation associates *every* tuple of *loan* with every tuple of *borrower*, we know that, if a customer has a loan in the Perryridge branch, then there is some tuple in *borrower* × *loan* that contains his name, and *borrower.loan-number* = *loan.loan-number*. So, if we write

$$\sigma_{borrower.loan\text{-}number = loan.loan\text{-}number}$$
$$(\sigma_{branch\text{-}name = \text{"Perryridge"}}(borrower \times loan))$$

we get only those tuples of *borrower* × *loan* that pertain to customers who have a loan at the Perryridge branch.

Finally, since we want only *customer-name*, we do a projection:

$$\Pi_{customer\text{-}name}(\sigma_{borrower.loan\text{-}number = loan.loan\text{-}number}$$
$$(\sigma_{branch\text{-}name = \text{"Perryridge"}}(borrower \times loan)))$$

The result of this expression, shown in Figure 3.16, is the correct answer to our query.

3.2.1.7   The Rename Operation

Unlike relations in the database, the results of relational-algebra expressions do not have a name that we can use to refer to them. It is useful to be able to give them names; the **rename** operator, denoted by the lowercase Greek letter rho (ρ), lets us do

customer-name
Adams
Hayes

Figure 3.16   Result of $\Pi_{customer\text{-}name}$
$(\sigma_{borrower.loan\text{-}number\,=\,loan.loan\text{-}number}$
$(\sigma_{branch\text{-}name\,=\,\text{"Perryridge"}}\,(borrower\,\times\,loan)))$.

this. Given a relational-algebra expression E, the expression

$$\rho_x\,(E)$$

returns the result of expression E under the name x.

A relation r by itself is considered a (trivial) relational-algebra expression. Thus, we can also apply the rename operation to a relation r to get the same relation under a new name.

A second form of the rename operation is as follows. Assume that a relational-algebra expression E has arity n. Then, the expression

$$\rho_{x(A_1,A_2,\ldots,A_n)}\,(E)$$

returns the result of expression E under the name x, and with the attributes renamed to $A_1, A_2, \ldots, A_n$.

To illustrate renaming a relation, we consider the query "Find the largest account balance in the bank." Our strategy is to (1) compute first a temporary relation consisting of those balances that are *not* the largest and (2) take the set difference between the relation $\Pi_{balance}\,(account)$ and the temporary relation just computed, to obtain the result.

Step 1: To compute the temporary relation, we need to compare the values of all account balances. We do this comparison by computing the Cartesian product $account\,\times\,account$ and forming a selection to compare the value of any two balances appearing in one tuple. First, we need to devise a mechanism to distinguish between the two *balance* attributes. We shall use the rename operation to rename one reference to the account relation; thus we can reference the relation twice without ambiguity.

balance
500
400
700
750
350

Figure 3.17   Result of the subexpression
$\Pi_{account.balance}\,(\sigma_{account.balance\,<\,d.balance}\,(account\,\times\,\rho_d\,(account)))$.

balance
900

Figure 3.18   Largest account balance in the bank.

We can now write the temporary relation that consists of the balances that are not the largest:

$$\Pi_{account.balance} \left(\sigma_{account.balance \, < \, d.balance} \left(account \, \times \, \rho_d \left(account \right) \right) \right)$$

This expression gives those balances in the *account* relation for which a larger balance appears somewhere in the *account* relation (renamed as *d*). The result contains all balances *except* the largest one. Figure 3.17 shows this relation.

Step 2: The query to find the largest account balance in the bank can be written as:

$$\Pi_{balance} \left(account \right) - $$
$$\Pi_{account.balance} \left(\sigma_{account.balance \, < \, d.balance} \left(account \, \times \, \rho_d \left(account \right) \right) \right)$$

Figure 3.18 shows the result of this query.

As one more example of the rename operation, consider the query "Find the names of all customers who live on the same street and in the same city as Smith." We can obtain Smith's street and city by writing

$$\Pi_{customer\text{-}street, \; customer\text{-}city} \left(\sigma_{customer\text{-}name \, = \, \text{``Smith''}} \left(customer \right) \right)$$

However, in order to find other customers with this street and city, we must reference the *customer* relation a second time. In the following query, we use the rename operation on the preceding expression to give its result the name *smith-addr*, and to rename its attributes to *street* and *city*, instead of *customer-street* and *customer-city*:

$$\Pi_{customer.customer\text{-}name}$$
$$\left(\sigma_{customer.customer\text{-}street = smith\text{-}addr.street \, \wedge \, customer.customer\text{-}city = smith\text{-}addr.city} \right.$$
$$\left(customer \, \times \, \rho_{smith\text{-}addr(street, city)} \right.$$
$$\left. \left. \left(\Pi_{customer\text{-}street, \; customer\text{-}city} \left(\sigma_{customer\text{-}name \, = \, \text{``Smith''}} \left(customer \right) \right) \right) \right) \right)$$

The result of this query, when we apply it to the *customer* relation of Figure 3.4, appears in Figure 3.19.

The rename operation is not strictly required, since it is possible to use a positional notation for attributes. We can name attributes of a relation implicitly by using a positional notation, where $1, $2, ... refer to the first attribute, the second attribute, and so on. The positional notation also applies to results of relational-algebra operations.

customer-name
Curry
Smith

Figure 3.19   Customers who live on the same street and in the same city as Smith.

The following relational-algebra expression illustrates the use of positional notation with the unary operator σ:

$$\sigma_{\$2=\$3}(R \times R)$$

If a binary operation needs to distinguish between its two operand relations, a similar positional notation can be used for relation names as well. For example, $\$R1$ could refer to the first operand, and $\$R2$ could refer to the second operand. However, the positional notation is inconvenient for humans, since the position of the attribute is a number, rather than an easy-to-remember attribute name. Hence, we do not use the positional notation in this textbook.

3.2.2   Formal Definition of the Relational Algebra

The operations in Section 3.2.1 allow us to give a complete definition of an expression in the relational algebra. A basic expression in the relational algebra consists of either one of the following:

- A relation in the database
- A constant relation

A constant relation is written by listing its tuples within { }, for example { (A-101, Downtown, 500) (A-215, Mianus, 700) }.

A general expression in relational algebra is constructed out of smaller subexpressions. Let E_1 and E_2 be relational-algebra expressions. Then, these are all relational-algebra expressions:

- $E_1 \cup E_2$
- $E_1 - E_2$
- $E_1 \times E_2$
- $\sigma_P(E_1)$, where P is a predicate on attributes in E_1
- $\Pi_S(E_1)$, where S is a list consisting of some of the attributes in E_1
- $\rho_x(E_1)$, where x is the new name for the result of E_1

3.2.3   Additional Operations

The fundamental operations of the relational algebra are sufficient to express any relational-algebra query.[1] However, if we restrict ourselves to just the fundamental operations, certain common queries are lengthy to express. Therefore, we define additional operations that do not add any power to the algebra, but simplify common queries. For each new operation, we give an equivalent expression that uses only the fundamental operations.

---

1.   In Section 3.3, we introduce operations that extend the power of the relational algebra, to handle null and aggregate values.

3.2.3.1 The Set-Intersection Operation

The first additional-relational algebra operation that we shall define is **set intersection** ($\cap$). Suppose that we wish to find all customers who have both a loan and an account. Using set intersection, we can write

$$\Pi_{customer\text{-}name} \, (borrower) \, \cap \, \Pi_{customer\text{-}name} \, (depositor)$$

The result relation for this query appears in Figure 3.20.

Note that we can rewrite any relational algebra expression that uses set intersection by replacing the intersection operation with a pair of set-difference operations as:

$$r \cap s = r - (r - s)$$

Thus, set intersection is not a fundamental operation and does not add any power to the relational algebra. It is simply more convenient to write $r \cap s$ than to write $r - (r - s)$.

3.2.3.2 The Natural-Join Operation

It is often desirable to simplify certain queries that require a Cartesian product. Usually, a query that involves a Cartesian product includes a selection operation on the result of the Cartesian product. Consider the query "Find the names of all customers who have a loan at the bank, along with the loan number and the loan amount." We first form the Cartesian product of the *borrower* and *loan* relations. Then, we select those tuples that pertain to only the same *loan-number*, followed by the projection of the resulting *customer-name*, *loan-number*, and *amount*:

$$\Pi_{customer\text{-}name, \; loan.loan\text{-}number, \; amount}$$
$$\left(\sigma_{borrower.loan\text{-}number \, = \, loan.loan\text{-}number} \, (borrower \, \times \, loan)\right)$$

The *natural join* is a binary operation that allows us to combine certain selections and a Cartesian product into one operation. It is denoted by the "join" symbol $\bowtie$. The natural-join operation forms a Cartesian product of its two arguments, performs a selection forcing equality on those attributes that appear in both relation schemas, and finally removes duplicate attributes.

Although the definition of natural join is complicated, the operation is easy to apply. As an illustration, consider again the example "Find the names of all customers who have a loan at the bank, and find the amount of the loan." We express this query

customer-name
Hayes
Jones
Smith

Figure 3.20   Customers with both an account and a loan at the bank.

customer-name	loan-number	amount
Adams	L-16	1300
Curry	L-93	500
Hayes	L-15	1500
Jackson	L-14	1500
Jones	L-17	1000
Smith	L-23	2000
Smith	L-11	900
Williams	L-17	1000

Figure 3.21 Result of $\Pi_{customer\text{-}name,\ loan\text{-}number,\ amount}\ (borrower \bowtie loan)$.

by using the natural join as follows:

$$\Pi_{customer\text{-}name,\ loan\text{-}number,\ amount}\ (borrower \bowtie loan)$$

Since the schemas for *borrower* and *loan* (that is, *Borrower-schema* and *Loan-schema*) have the attribute *loan-number* in common, the natural-join operation considers only pairs of tuples that have the same value on *loan-number*. It combines each such pair of tuples into a single tuple on the union of the two schemas (that is, *customer-name, branch-name, loan-number, amount*). After performing the projection, we obtain the relation in Figure 3.21.

Consider two relation schemas R and S—which are, of course, lists of attribute names. If we consider the schemas to be *sets*, rather than lists, we can denote those attribute names that appear in both R and S by $R \cap S$, and denote those attribute names that appear in R, in S, or in both by $R \cup S$. Similarly, those attribute names that appear in R but not S are denoted by $R - S$, whereas $S - R$ denotes those attribute names that appear in S but not in R. Note that the union, intersection, and difference operations here are on sets of attributes, rather than on relations.

We are now ready for a formal definition of the natural join. Consider two relations $r(R)$ and $s(S)$. The **natural join** of r and s, denoted by $r \bowtie s$, is a relation on schema $R \cup S$ formally defined as follows:

$$r \bowtie s = \Pi_{R \cup S} \left(\sigma_{r.A_1 = s.A_1 \wedge r.A_2 = s.A_2 \wedge \ldots \wedge r.A_n = s.A_n}\ r \times s \right)$$

where $R \cap S = \{A_1, A_2, \ldots, A_n\}$.

Because the natural join is central to much of relational-database theory and practice, we give several examples of its use.

branch-name
Brighton
Perryridge

Figure 3.22 Result of

$$\Pi_{branch\text{-}name} \left(\sigma_{customer\text{-}city\ =\ \text{“Harrison”}}\ (customer \bowtie account \bowtie depositor) \right).$$

- Find the names of all branches with customers who have an account in the bank and who live in Harrison.

$$\Pi_{branch\text{-}name}$$
$$(\sigma_{customer\text{-}city\,=\,\text{"Harrison"}}\,(customer \bowtie account \bowtie depositor))$$

The result relation for this query appears in Figure 3.22.

Notice that we wrote $customer \bowtie account \bowtie depositor$ without inserting parentheses to specify the order in which the natural-join operations on the three relations should be executed. In the preceding case, there are two possibilities:

- $(customer \bowtie account) \bowtie depositor$
- $customer \bowtie (account \bowtie depositor)$

We did not specify which expression we intended, because the two are equivalent. That is, the natural join is **associative**.

- Find all customers who have *both* a loan and an account at the bank.

$$\Pi_{customer\text{-}name}\,(borrower \bowtie depositor)$$

Note that in Section 3.2.3.1 we wrote an expression for this query by using set intersection. We repeat this expression here.

$$\Pi_{customer\text{-}name}\,(borrower) \cap \Pi_{customer\text{-}name}\,(depositor)$$

The result relation for this query appeared earlier in Figure 3.20. This example illustrates a general fact about the relational algebra: It is possible to write several equivalent relational-algebra expressions that are quite different from one another.

- Let $r(R)$ and $s(S)$ be relations without any attributes in common; that is, $R \cap S = \emptyset$. ($\emptyset$ denotes the empty set.) Then, $r \bowtie s = r \times s$.

The *theta join* operation is an extension to the natural-join operation that allows us to combine a selection and a Cartesian product into a single operation. Consider relations $r(R)$ and $s(S)$, and let θ be a predicate on attributes in the schema $R \cup S$. The **theta join** operation $r \bowtie_\theta s$ is defined as follows:

$$r \bowtie_\theta s = \sigma_\theta(r \times s)$$

3.2.3.3 The Division Operation

The **division** operation, denoted by $\div$, is suited to queries that include the phrase "for all." Suppose that we wish to find all customers who have an account at *all* the branches located in Brooklyn. We can obtain all branches in Brooklyn by the expression

$$r_1 = \Pi_{branch\text{-}name}\,(\sigma_{branch\text{-}city\,=\,\text{"Brooklyn"}}\,(branch))$$

The result relation for this expression appears in Figure 3.23.

branch-name
Brighton
Downtown

Figure 3.23   Result of $\Pi_{branch\text{-}name}(\sigma_{branch\text{-}city\,=\,\text{"Brooklyn"}}(branch))$.

We can find all (*customer-name, branch-name*) pairs for which the customer has an account at a branch by writing

$$r_2 = \Pi_{customer\text{-}name,\ branch\text{-}name}(depositor \bowtie account)$$

Figure 3.24 shows the result relation for this expression.

Now, we need to find customers who appear in r_2 with *every* branch name in r_1. The operation that provides exactly those customers is the divide operation. We formulate the query by writing

$$\Pi_{customer\text{-}name,\ branch\text{-}name}(depositor \bowtie account)$$
$$\div\ \Pi_{branch\text{-}name}(\sigma_{branch\text{-}city\,=\,\text{"Brooklyn"}}(branch))$$

The result of this expression is a relation that has the schema (*customer-name*) and that contains the tuple (Johnson).

Formally, let $r(R)$ and $s(S)$ be relations, and let $S \subseteq R$; that is, every attribute of schema S is also in schema R. The relation $r \div s$ is a relation on schema $R - S$ (that is, on the schema containing all attributes of schema R that are not in schema S). A tuple t is in $r \div s$ if and only if both of two conditions hold:

1. t is in $\Pi_{R-S}(r)$

2. For every tuple t_s in s, there is a tuple t_r in r satisfying both of the following:
   a. $t_r[S] = t_s[S]$
   b. $t_r[R - S] = t$

It may surprise you to discover that, given a division operation and the schemas of the relations, we can, in fact, define the division operation in terms of the fundamental operations. Let $r(R)$ and $s(S)$ be given, with $S \subseteq R$:

$$r \div s = \Pi_{R-S}(r) - \Pi_{R-S}((\Pi_{R-S}(r) \times s) - \Pi_{R-S,S}(r))$$

customer-name	branch-name
Hayes	Perryridge
Johnson	Downtown
Johnson	Brighton
Jones	Brighton
Lindsay	Redwood
Smith	Mianus
Turner	Round Hill

Figure 3.24   Result of $\Pi_{customer\text{-}name,\ branch\text{-}name}(depositor \bowtie account)$.

To see that this expression is true, we observe that $\Pi_{R-S}(r)$ gives us all tuples t that satisfy the first condition of the definition of division. The expression on the right side of the set difference operator

$$\Pi_{R-S}((\Pi_{R-S}(r) \times s) - \Pi_{R-S,S}(r))$$

serves to eliminate those tuples that fail to satisfy the second condition of the definition of division. Let us see how it does so. Consider $\Pi_{R-S}(r) \times s$. This relation is on schema R, and pairs every tuple in $\Pi_{R-S}(r)$ with every tuple in s. The expression $\Pi_{R-S,S}(r)$ merely reorders the attributes of r.

Thus, $(\Pi_{R-S}(r) \times s) - \Pi_{R-S,S}(r)$ gives us those pairs of tuples from $\Pi_{R-S}(r)$ and s that do not appear in r. If a tuple t_j is in

$$\Pi_{R-S}((\Pi_{R-S}(r) \times s) - \Pi_{R-S,S}(r))$$

then there is some tuple t_s in s that does not combine with tuple t_j to form a tuple in r. Thus, t_j holds a value for attributes $R - S$ that does not appear in $r \div s$. It is these values that we eliminate from $\Pi_{R-S}(r)$.

3.2.3.4   The Assignment Operation

It is convenient at times to write a relational-algebra expression by assigning parts of it to temporary relation variables. The **assignment** operation, denoted by $\leftarrow$, works like assignment in a programming language. To illustrate this operation, consider the definition of division in Section 3.2.3.3. We could write $r \div s$ as

$$temp1 \leftarrow \Pi_{R-S}(r)$$
$$temp2 \leftarrow \Pi_{R-S}((temp1 \times s) - \Pi_{R-S,S}(r))$$
$$result = temp1 - temp2$$

The evaluation of an assignment does not result in any relation being displayed to the user. Rather, the result of the expression to the right of the $\leftarrow$ is assigned to the relation variable on the left of the $\leftarrow$. This relation variable may be used in subsequent expressions.

With the assignment operation, a query can be written as a sequential program consisting of a series of assignments followed by an expression whose value is displayed as the result of the query. For relational-algebra queries, assignment must always be made to a temporary relation variable. Assignments to permanent relations constitute a database modification. We discuss this issue in Section 3.4. Note that the assignment operation does not provide any additional power to the algebra. It is, however, a convenient way to express complex queries.

3.3   Extended Relational-Algebra Operations

The basic relational-algebra operations have been extended in several ways. A simple extension is to allow arithmetic operations as part of projection. An important extension is to allow *aggregate operations* such as computing the sum of the elements of a

customer-name	limit	credit-balance
Curry	2000	1750
Hayes	1500	1500
Jones	6000	700
Smith	2000	400

Figure 3.25   The *credit-info* relation.

set, or their average. Another important extension is the *outer-join* operation, which allows relational-algebra expressions to deal with null values, which model missing information.

3.3.1 Generalized Projection

The **generalized-projection** operation extends the projection operation by allowing arithmetic functions to be used in the projection list. The generalized projection operation has the form

$$\Pi_{F_1, F_2, \ldots, F_n}(E)$$

where E is any relational-algebra expression, and each of $F_1, F_2, \ldots, F_n$ is an arithmetic expression involving constants and attributes in the schema of E. As a special case, the arithmetic expression may be simply an attribute or a constant.

For example, suppose we have a relation *credit-info*, as in Figure 3.25, which lists the credit limit and expenses so far (the *credit-balance* on the account). If we want to find how much more each person can spend, we can write the following expression:

$$\Pi_{customer\text{-}name, \; limit \, - \, credit\text{-}balance}(credit\text{-}info)$$

The attribute resulting from the expression $limit \; - \; credit\text{-}balance$ does not have a name. We can apply the rename operation to the result of generalized projection in order to give it a name. As a notational convenience, renaming of attributes can be combined with generalized projection as illustrated below:

$$\Pi_{customer\text{-}name, \; (limit \, - \, credit\text{-}balance) \; \textbf{as} \; credit\text{-}available}(credit\text{-}info)$$

The second attribute of this generalized projection has been given the name *credit-available*. Figure 3.26 shows the result of applying this expression to the relation in Figure 3.25.

3.3.2 Aggregate Functions

Aggregate functions take a collection of values and return a single value as a result. For example, the aggregate function **sum** takes a collection of values and returns the sum of the values. Thus, the function **sum** applied on the collection

$$\{1, 1, 3, 4, 4, 11\}$$

customer-name	credit-available
Curry	250
Jones	5300
Smith	1600
Hayes	0

Figure 3.26   The result of $\Pi_{customer\text{-}name,\ (limit\ -\ credit\text{-}balance)}$ **as** $credit\text{-}available$ ($credit\text{-}info$).

returns the value 24. The aggregate function **avg** returns the average of the values. When applied to the preceding collection, it returns the value 4. The aggregate function **count** returns the number of the elements in the collection, and returns 6 on the preceding collection. Other common aggregate functions include **min** and **max**, which return the minimum and maximum values in a collection; they return 1 and 11, respectively, on the preceding collection.

The collections on which aggregate functions operate can have multiple occurrences of a value; the order in which the values appear is not relevant. Such collections are called **multisets**. Sets are a special case of multisets where there is only one copy of each element.

To illustrate the concept of aggregation, we shall use the *pt-works* relation in Figure 3.27, for part-time employees. Suppose that we want to find out the total sum of salaries of all the part-time employees in the bank. The relational-algebra expression for this query is:

$$\mathcal{G}_{\textbf{sum}(salary)}(pt\text{-}works)$$

The symbol $\mathcal{G}$ is the letter G in calligraphic font; read it as "calligraphic G." The relational-algebra operation $\mathcal{G}$ signifies that aggregation is to be applied, and its subscript specifies the aggregate operation to be applied. The result of the expression above is a relation with a single attribute, containing a single row with a numerical value corresponding to the sum of all the salaries of all employees working part-time in the bank.

employee-name	branch-name	salary
Adams	Perryridge	1500
Brown	Perryridge	1300
Gopal	Perryridge	5300
Johnson	Downtown	1500
Loreena	Downtown	1300
Peterson	Downtown	2500
Rao	Austin	1500
Sato	Austin	1600

Figure 3.27   The *pt-works* relation.

There are cases where we must eliminate multiple occurrences of a value before computing an aggregate function. If we do want to eliminate duplicates, we use the same function names as before, with the addition of the hyphenated string "**distinct**" appended to the end of the function name (for example, **count-distinct**). An example arises in the query "Find the number of branches appearing in the *pt-works* relation." In this case, a branch name counts only once, regardless of the number of employees working that branch. We write this query as follows:

$$\mathcal{G}_{\textbf{count-distinct}(branch\text{-}name)}(pt\text{-}works)$$

For the relation in Figure 3.27, the result of this query is a single row containing the value 3.

Suppose we want to find the total salary sum of all part-time employees at each branch of the bank separately, rather than the sum for the entire bank. To do so, we need to partition the relation *pt-works* into **groups** based on the branch, and to apply the aggregate function on each group.

The following expression using the aggregation operator $\mathcal{G}$ achieves the desired result:

$$_{branch\text{-}name}\mathcal{G}_{\textbf{sum}(salary)}(pt\text{-}works)$$

In the expression, the attribute *branch-name* in the left-hand subscript of $\mathcal{G}$ indicates that the input relation *pt-works* must be divided into groups based on the value of *branch-name*. Figure 3.28 shows the resulting groups. The expression **sum**(*salary*) in the right-hand subscript of $\mathcal{G}$ indicates that for each group of tuples (that is, each branch), the aggregation function **sum** must be applied on the collection of values of the *salary* attribute. The output relation consists of tuples with the branch name, and the sum of the salaries for the branch, as shown in Figure 3.29.

The general form of the **aggregation operation** $\mathcal{G}$ is as follows:

$$_{G_1, G_2, \ldots, G_n}\mathcal{G}_{F_1(A_1),\ F_2(A_2), \ldots,\ F_m(A_m)}(E)$$

where E is any relational-algebra expression; $G_1, G_2, \ldots, G_n$ constitute a list of attributes on which to group; each F_i is an aggregate function; and each A_i is an at-

employee-name	branch-name	salary
Rao	Austin	1500
Sato	Austin	1600
Johnson	Downtown	1500
Loreena	Downtown	1300
Peterson	Downtown	2500
Adams	Perryridge	1500
Brown	Perryridge	1300
Gopal	Perryridge	5300

Figure 3.28   The *pt-works* relation after grouping.

branch-name	sum of salary
Austin	3100
Downtown	5300
Perryridge	8100

Figure 3.29   Result of ${}_{branch\text{-}name}\mathcal{G}_{\textbf{sum}(salary)}(pt\text{-}works)$.

tribute name. The meaning of the operation is as follows. The tuples in the result of expression E are partitioned into groups in such a way that

1. All tuples in a group have the same values for $G_1, G_2, \ldots, G_n$.

2. Tuples in different groups have different values for $G_1, G_2, \ldots, G_n$.

Thus, the groups can be identified by the values of attributes $G_1, G_2, \ldots, G_n$. For each group $(g_1, g_2, \ldots, g_n)$, the result has a tuple $(g_1, g_2, \ldots, g_n, a_1, a_2, \ldots, a_m)$ where, for each i, a_i is the result of applying the aggregate function F_i on the multiset of values for attribute A_i in the group.

As a special case of the aggregate operation, the list of attributes $G_1, G_2, \ldots, G_n$ can be empty, in which case there is a single group containing all tuples in the relation. This corresponds to aggregation without grouping.

Going back to our earlier example, if we want to find the maximum salary for part-time employees at each branch, in addition to the sum of the salaries, we write the expression

$${}_{branch\text{-}name}\mathcal{G}_{\textbf{sum}(salary),\textbf{max}(salary)}(pt\text{-}works)$$

As in generalized projection, the result of an aggregation operation does not have a name. We can apply a rename operation to the result in order to give it a name. As a notational convenience, attributes of an aggregation operation can be renamed as illustrated below:

$${}_{branch\text{-}name}\mathcal{G}_{\textbf{sum}(salary)\textbf{ as }sum\text{-}salary,\textbf{max}(salary)\textbf{ as }max\text{-}salary}(pt\text{-}works)$$

Figure 3.30 shows the result of the expression.

branch-name	sum-salary	max-salary
Austin	3100	1600
Downtown	5300	2500
Perryridge	8100	5300

Figure 3.30   Result of
${}_{branch\text{-}name}\mathcal{G}_{\textbf{sum}(salary)\textbf{ as }sum\text{-}salary,\textbf{max}(salary)\textbf{ as }max\text{-}salary}(pt\text{-}works)$.

employee-name	street	city
Coyote	Toon	Hollywood
Rabbit	Tunnel	Carrotville
Smith	Revolver	Death Valley
Williams	Seaview	Seattle

employee-name	branch-name	salary
Coyote	Mesa	1500
Rabbit	Mesa	1300
Gates	Redmond	5300
Williams	Redmond	1500

Figure 3.31   The *employee* and *ft-works* relations.

3.3.3   Outer Join

The **outer-join** operation is an extension of the join operation to deal with missing information. Suppose that we have the relations with the following schemas, which contain data on full-time employees:

$$employee \text{ (employee-name, street, city)}$$
$$ft\text{-}works \text{ (employee-name, branch-name, salary)}$$

Consider the *employee* and *ft-works* relations in Figure 3.31. Suppose that we want to generate a single relation with all the information (street, city, branch name, and salary) about full-time employees. A possible approach would be to use the natural-join operation as follows:

$$employee \bowtie ft\text{-}works$$

The result of this expression appears in Figure 3.32. Notice that we have lost the street and city information about Smith, since the tuple describing Smith is absent from the *ft-works* relation; similarly, we have lost the branch name and salary information about Gates, since the tuple describing Gates is absent from the *employee* relation.

We can use the *outer-join* operation to avoid this loss of information. There are actually three forms of the operation: *left outer join*, denoted ⟕; *right outer join*, denoted ⟖; and *full outer join*, denoted ⟗. All three forms of outer join compute the join, and add extra tuples to the result of the join. The results of the expressions

employee-name	street	city	branch-name	salary
Coyote	Toon	Hollywood	Mesa	1500
Rabbit	Tunnel	Carrotville	Mesa	1300
Williams	Seaview	Seattle	Redmond	1500

Figure 3.32   The result of *employee* ⋈ *ft-works*.

employee-name	street	city	branch-name	salary
Coyote	Toon	Hollywood	Mesa	1500
Rabbit	Tunnel	Carrotville	Mesa	1300
Williams	Seaview	Seattle	Redmond	1500
Smith	Revolver	Death Valley	null	null

Figure 3.33 Result of *employee* ⟕ *ft-works*.

employee ⟕ *ft-works*., *employee* ⟖ *ft-works*, and *employee* ⟗ *ft-works* appear in Figures 3.33, 3.34, and 3.35, respectively.

The **left outer join** (⟕) takes all tuples in the left relation that did not match with any tuple in the right relation, pads the tuples with null values for all other attributes from the right relation, and adds them to the result of the natural join. In Figure 3.33, tuple (Smith, Revolver, Death Valley, *null*, *null*) is such a tuple. All information from the left relation is present in the result of the left outer join.

The **right outer join** (⟖) is symmetric with the left outer join: It pads tuples from the right relation that did not match any from the left relation with nulls and adds them to the result of the natural join. In Figure 3.34, tuple (Gates, *null*, *null*, Redmond, 5300) is such a tuple. Thus, all information from the right relation is present in the result of the right outer join.

The **full outer join**(⟗) does both of those operations, padding tuples from the left relation that did not match any from the right relation, as well as tuples from the right relation that did not match any from the left relation, and adding them to the result of the join. Figure 3.35 shows the result of a full outer join.

Since outer join operations may generate results containing null values, we need to specify how the different relational-algebra operations deal with null values. Section 3.3.4 deals with this issue.

It is interesting to note that the outer join operations can be expressed by the basic relational-algebra operations. For instance, the left outer join operation, $r ⟕ s$, can be written as

$$(r \bowtie s) \cup (r - \Pi_R(r \bowtie s)) \times \{(null, \ldots, null)\}$$

where the constant relation $\{(null, \ldots, null)\}$ is on the schema $S - R$.

employee-name	street	city	branch-name	salary
Coyote	Toon	Hollywood	Mesa	1500
Rabbit	Tunnel	Carrotville	Mesa	1300
Williams	Seaview	Seattle	Redmond	1500
Gates	null	null	Redmond	5300

Figure 3.34 Result of *employee* ⟖ *ft-works*.

employee-name	street	city	branch-name	salary
Coyote	Toon	Hollywood	Mesa	1500
Rabbit	Tunnel	Carrotville	Mesa	1300
Williams	Seaview	Seattle	Redmond	1500
Smith	Revolver	Death Valley	null	null
Gates	null	null	Redmond	5300

Figure 3.35 Result of *employee* ⋈ *ft-works*.

3.3.4 Null Values∗∗

In this section, we define how the various relational algebra operations deal with null values and complications that arise when a null value participates in an arithmetic operation or in a comparison. As we shall see, there is often more than one possible way of dealing with null values, and as a result our definitions can sometimes be arbitrary. Operations and comparisons on null values should therefore be avoided, where possible.

Since the special value *null* indicates "value unknown or nonexistent," any arithmetic operations (such as $+, -, *, /$) involving null values must return a null result.

Similarly, any comparisons (such as $<, <=, >, >=, \neq$) involving a null value evaluate to special value **unknown**; we cannot say for sure whether the result of the comparison is true or false, so we say that the result is the new truth value *unknown*.

Comparisons involving nulls may occur inside Boolean expressions involving the and, or, and not operations. We must therefore define how the three Boolean operations deal with the truth value *unknown*.

- **and**: (*true* **and** *unknown*) = *unknown*; (*false* **and** *unknown*) = *false*; (*unknown* **and** *unknown*) = *unknown*.

- **or**: (*true* **or** *unknown*) = *true*; (*false* **or** *unknown*) = *unknown*; (*unknown* **or** *unknown*) = *unknown*.

- **not**: (**not** *unknown*) = *unknown*.

We are now in a position to outline how the different relational operations deal with null values. Our definitions follow those used in the SQL language.

- **select**: The selection operation evaluates predicate P in $\sigma_P(E)$ on each tuple t in E. If the predicate returns the value *true*, t is added to the result. Otherwise, if the predicate returns *unknown* or *false*, t is not added to the result.

- **join**: Joins can be expressed as a cross product followed by a selection. Thus, the definition of how selection handles nulls also defines how join operations handle nulls.

  In a natural join, say $r \bowtie s$, we can see from the above definition that if two tuples, $t_r \in r$ and $t_s \in s$, both have a null value in a common attribute, then the tuples do not match.

- **projection**: The projection operation treats nulls just like any other value when eliminating duplicates. Thus, if two tuples in the projection result are exactly the same, and both have nulls in the same fields, they are treated as duplicates.

  The decision is a little arbitrary since, without knowing the actual value, we do not know if the two instances of null are duplicates or not.

- **union**, **intersection**, **difference**: These operations treat nulls just as the projection operation does; they treat tuples that have the same values on all fields as duplicates even if some of the fields have null values in both tuples.

  The behavior is rather arbitrary, especially in the case of intersection and difference, since we do not know if the actual values (if any) represented by the nulls are the same.

- **generalized projection**: We outlined how nulls are handled in expressions at the beginning of Section 3.3.4. Duplicate tuples containing null values are handled as in the projection operation.

- **aggregate**: When nulls occur in grouping attributes, the aggregate operation treats them just as in projection: If two tuples are the same on all grouping attributes, the operation places them in the same group, even if some of their attribute values are null.

  When nulls occur in aggregated attributes, the operation deletes null values at the outset, before applying aggregation. If the resultant multiset is empty, the aggregate result is null.

  Note that the treatment of nulls here is different from that in ordinary arithmetic expressions; we could have defined the result of an aggregate operation as null if even one of the aggregated values is null. However, this would mean a single unknown value in a large group could make the aggregate result on the group to be null, and we would lose a lot of useful information.

- **outer join**: Outer join operations behave just like join operations, except on tuples that do not occur in the join result. Such tuples may be added to the result (depending on whether the operation is ⟖, ⟕, or ⟗), padded with nulls.

3.4   Modification of the Database

We have limited our attention until now to the extraction of information from the database. In this section, we address how to add, remove, or change information in the database.

We express database modifications by using the assignment operation. We make assignments to actual database relations by using the same notation as that described in Section 3.2.3 for assignment.

3.4.1   Deletion

We express a delete request in much the same way as a query. However, instead of displaying tuples to the user, we remove the selected tuples from the database. We can delete only whole tuples; we cannot delete values on only particular attributes. In relational algebra a deletion is expressed by

$$r \leftarrow r - E$$

where r is a relation and E is a relational-algebra query.

Here are several examples of relational-algebra delete requests:

- Delete all of Smith's account records.

$$depositor \leftarrow depositor - \sigma_{customer\text{-}name = \text{"Smith"}} (depositor)$$

- Delete all loans with amount in the range 0 to 50.

$$loan \leftarrow loan - \sigma_{amount \geq 0 \text{ and } amount \leq 50} (loan)$$

- Delete all accounts at branches located in Needham.

$$r_1 \leftarrow \sigma_{branch\text{-}city = \text{"Needham"}} (account \bowtie branch)$$
$$r_2 \leftarrow \Pi_{branch\text{-}name, \, account\text{-}number, \, balance} (r_1)$$
$$account \leftarrow account - r_2$$

Note that, in the final example, we simplified our expression by using assignment to temporary relations (r_1 and r_2).

3.4.2 Insertion

To insert data into a relation, we either specify a tuple to be inserted or write a query whose result is a set of tuples to be inserted. Obviously, the attribute values for inserted tuples must be members of the attribute's domain. Similarly, tuples inserted must be of the correct arity. The relational algebra expresses an insertion by

$$r \leftarrow r \cup E$$

where r is a relation and E is a relational-algebra expression. We express the insertion of a single tuple by letting E be a constant relation containing one tuple.

Suppose that we wish to insert the fact that Smith has $1200 in account A-973 at the Perryridge branch. We write

$$account \leftarrow account \cup \{(\text{A-973, "Perryridge", } 1200)\}$$
$$depositor \leftarrow depositor \cup \{(\text{"Smith", A-973})\}$$

More generally, we might want to insert tuples on the basis of the result of a query. Suppose that we want to provide as a gift for all loan customers of the Perryridge branch a new $200 savings account. Let the loan number serve as the account number for this savings account. We write

$$r_1 \leftarrow (\sigma_{branch\text{-}name = \text{"Perryridge"}} (borrower \bowtie loan))$$
$$r_2 \leftarrow \Pi_{loan\text{-}number, \, branch\text{-}name} (r_1)$$
$$account \leftarrow account \cup (r_2 \times \{(200)\})$$
$$depositor \leftarrow depositor \cup \Pi_{customer\text{-}name, \, loan\text{-}number} (r_1)$$

Instead of specifying a tuple as we did earlier, we specify a set of tuples that is inserted into both the *account* and *depositor* relation. Each tuple in the *account* relation has an *account-number* (which is the same as the loan number), a *branch-name* (Perryridge), and the initial balance of the new account ($200). Each tuple in the *depositor* relation has as *customer-name* the name of the loan customer who is being given the new account and the same account number as the corresponding *account* tuple.

3.4.3   Updating

In certain situations, we may wish to change a value in a tuple without changing *all* values in the tuple. We can use the generalized-projection operator to do this task:

$$r \leftarrow \Pi_{F_1, F_2, \ldots, F_n}(r)$$

where each F_i is either the ith attribute of r, if the ith attribute is not updated, or, if the attribute is to be updated, F_i is an expression, involving only constants and the attributes of r, that gives the new value for the attribute.

If we want to select some tuples from r and to update only them, we can use the following expression; here, P denotes the selection condition that chooses which tuples to update:

$$r \leftarrow \Pi_{F_1, F_2, \ldots, F_n}(\sigma_P(r)) \cup (r - \sigma_P(r))$$

To illustrate the use of the update operation, suppose that interest payments are being made, and that all balances are to be increased by 5 percent. We write

$$account \leftarrow \Pi_{account\text{-}number,\ branch\text{-}name,\ balance\ *1.05}(account)$$

Now suppose that accounts with balances over $10,000 receive 6 percent interest, whereas all others receive 5 percent. We write

$$account \leftarrow \Pi_{AN, BN,\ balance\ *1.06}(\sigma_{balance>10000}(account))$$
$$\cup\ \Pi_{AN,\ BN\ balance\ *1.05}(\sigma_{balance \leq 10000}(account))$$

where the abbreviations AN and BN stand for *account-number* and *branch-name*, respectively.

3.5   Views

In our examples up to this point, we have operated at the logical-model level. That is, we have assumed that the relations in thecollection we are given are the actual relations stored in the database.

It is not desirable for all users to see the entire logical model. Security considerations may require that certain data be hidden from users. Consider a person who needs to know a customer's loan number and branch name, but has no need to see the loan amount. This person should see a relation described, in the relational algebra, by

$$\Pi_{customer\text{-}name,\ loan\text{-}number,\ branch\text{-}name}(borrower \bowtie loan)$$

Aside from security concerns, we may wish to create a personalized collection of relations that is better matched to a certain user's intuition than is the logical model.

An employee in the advertising department, for example, might like to see a relation consisting of the customers who have either an account or a loan at the bank, and the branches with which they do business. The relation that we would create for that employee is

$$\Pi_{branch\text{-}name,\ customer\text{-}name}\ (depositor \bowtie\ account)$$
$$\cup\ \Pi_{branch\text{-}name,\ customer\text{-}name}\ (borrower \bowtie\ loan)$$

Any relation that is not part of the logical model, but is made visible to a user as a virtual relation, is called a **view**. It is possible to support a large number of views on top of any given set of actual relations.

3.5.1 View Definition

We define a view by using the **create view** statement. To define a view, we must give the view a name, and must state the query that computes the view. The form of the **create view** statement is

$$\textbf{create view } v \textbf{ as } <\text{query expression}>$$

where <query expression> is any legal relational-algebra query expression. The view name is represented by v.

As an example, consider the view consisting of branches and their customers. We wish this view to be called *all-customer*. We define this view as follows:

create view *all-customer* **as**
$$\Pi_{branch\text{-}name,\ customer\text{-}name}\ (depositor \bowtie\ account)$$
$$\cup\ \Pi_{branch\text{-}name,\ customer\text{-}name}\ (borrower \bowtie\ loan)$$

Once we have defined a view, we can use the view name to refer to the virtual relation that the view generates. Using the view *all-customer*, we can find all customers of the Perryridge branch by writing

$$\Pi_{customer\text{-}name}\ (\sigma_{branch\text{-}name\ =\ \text{“Perryridge”}}\ (all\text{-}customer))$$

Recall that we wrote the same query in Section 3.2.1 without using views.

View names may appear in any place where a relation name may appear, so long as no update operations are executed on the views. We study the issue of update operations on views in Section 3.5.2.

View definition differs from the relational-algebra assignment operation. Suppose that we define relation $r1$ as follows:

$$r1 \leftarrow \Pi_{branch\text{-}name,\ customer\text{-}name}\ (depositor \bowtie\ account)$$
$$\cup\ \Pi_{branch\text{-}name,\ customer\text{-}name}(borrower \bowtie\ loan)$$

We evaluate the assignment operation once, and $r1$ does not change when we update the relations *depositor, account, loan,* or *borrower*. In contrast, any modification we make to these relations changes the set of tuples in the view *all-customer* as well. Intuitively, at any given time, the set of tuples in the view relation is the result of evaluation of the query expression that defines the view at that time.

Thus, if a view relation is computed and stored, it may become out of date if the relations used to define it are modified. To avoid this, views are usually implemented as follows. When we define a view, the database system stores the definition of the view itself, rather than the result of evaluation of the relational-algebra expression that defines the view. Wherever a view relation appears in a query, it is replaced by the stored query expression. Thus, whenever we evaluate the query, the view relation gets recomputed.

Certain database systems allow view relations to be stored, but they make sure that, if the actual relations used in the view definition change, the view is kept up to date. Such views are called **materialized views**. The process of keeping the view up to date is called **view maintenance**, covered in Section 14.5. Applications that use a view frequently benefit from the use of materialized views, as do applications that demand fast response to certain view-based queries. Of course, the benefits to queries from the materialization of a view must be weighed against the storage costs and the added overhead for updates.

3.5.2   Updates through Views and Null Values

Although views are a useful tool for queries, they present serious problems if we express updates, insertions, or deletions with them. The difficulty is that a modification to the database expressed in terms of a view must be translated to a modification to the actual relations in the logical model of the database.

To illustrate the problem, consider a clerk who needs to see all loan data in the *loan* relation, except *loan-amount*. Let *loan-branch* be the view given to the clerk. We define this view as

$$\textbf{create view } \textit{loan-branch } \textbf{as}$$
$$\Pi_{loan\text{-}number,\ branch\text{-}name}\ (loan)$$

Since we allow a view name to appear wherever a relation name is allowed, the clerk can write:

$$loan\text{-}branch \ \leftarrow \ loan\text{-}branch \cup \{(\text{L-37, "Perryridge"})\}$$

This insertion must be represented by an insertion into the relation *loan*, since *loan* is the actual relation from which the database system constructs the view *loan-branch*. However, to insert a tuple into *loan*, we must have some value for *amount*. There are two reasonable approaches to dealing with this insertion:

- Reject the insertion, and return an error message to the user.

- Insert a tuple (L-37, "Perryridge", *null*) into the *loan* relation.

Another problem with modification of the database through views occurs with a view such as

$$\textbf{create view } \textit{loan-info } \textbf{as}$$
$$\Pi_{customer\text{-}name,\ amount}(borrower \bowtie loan)$$

loan-number	branch-name	amount
L-11	Round Hill	900
L-14	Downtown	1500
L-15	Perryridge	1500
L-16	Perryridge	1300
L-17	Downtown	1000
L-23	Redwood	2000
L-93	Mianus	500
null	*null*	1900

customer-name	loan-number
Adams	L-16
Curry	L-93
Hayes	L-15
Jackson	L-14
Jones	L-17
Smith	L-11
Smith	L-23
Williams	L-17
Johnson	*null*

Figure 3.36   Tuples inserted into *loan* and *borrower*.

This view lists the loan amount for each loan that any customer of the bank has. Consider the following insertion through this view:

$$loan\text{-}info \leftarrow loan\text{-}info \cup \{(\text{"Johnson"}, 1900)\}$$

The only possible method of inserting tuples into the *borrower* and *loan* relations is to insert ("Johnson", *null*) into *borrower* and (*null*, *null*, 1900) into *loan*. Then, we obtain the relations shown in Figure 3.36. However, this update does not have the desired effect, since the view relation *loan-info* still does *not* include the tuple ("Johnson", 1900). Thus, there is no way to update the relations *borrower* and *loan* by using nulls to get the desired update on *loan-info*.

Because of problems such as these, modifications are generally not permitted on view relations, except in limited cases. Different database systems specify different conditions under which they permit updates on view relations; see the database system manuals for details. The general problem of database modification through views has been the subject of substantial research, and the bibliographic notes provide pointers to some of this research.

3.5.3   Views Defined by Using Other Views

In Section 3.5.1 we mentioned that view relations may appear in any place that a relation name may appear, except for restrictions on the use of views in update expressions. Thus, one view may be used in the expression defining another view. For example, we can define the view *perryridge-customer* as follows:

create view *perryridge-customer* **as**
$$\Pi_{customer\text{-}name} \left(\sigma_{branch\text{-}name\,=\,\text{``Perryridge''}} \left(all\text{-}customer \right) \right)$$

where *all-customer* is itself a view relation.

View expansion is one way to define the meaning of views defined in terms of other views. The procedure assumes that view definitions are not **recursive**; that is, no view is used in its own definition, whether directly, or indirectly through other view definitions. For example, if $v1$ is used in the definition of $v2$, $v2$ is used in the definition of $v3$, and $v3$ is used in the definition of $v1$, then each of $v1$, $v2$, and $v3$ is recursive. Recursive view definitions are useful in some situations, and we revisit them in the context of the Datalog language, in Section 5.2.

Let view v_1 be defined by an expression e_1 that may itself contain uses of view relations. A view relation stands for the expression defining the view, and therefore a view relation can be replaced by the expression that defines it. If we modify an expression by replacing a view relation by the latter's definition, the resultant expression may still contain other view relations. Hence, view expansion of an expression repeats the replacement step as follows:

> **repeat**
>   Find any view relation v_i in e_1
>   Replace the view relation v_i by the expression defining v_i
> **until** no more view relations are present in e_1

As long as the view definitions are not recursive, this loop will terminate. Thus, an expression e containing view relations can be understood as the expression resulting from view expansion of e, which does not contain any view relations.

As an illustration of view expansion, consider the following expression:

$$\sigma_{customer\text{-}name=\text{``John''}} \left(perryridge\text{-}customer \right)$$

The view-expansion procedure initially generates

$$\sigma_{customer\text{-}name=\text{``John''}} \left( \Pi_{customer\text{-}name} \left( \sigma_{branch\text{-}name\,=\,\text{``Perryridge''}} \left(all\text{-}customer \right) \right) \right)$$

It then generates

$$\sigma_{customer\text{-}name=\text{``John''}} \left( \Pi_{customer\text{-}name} \left( \sigma_{branch\text{-}name\,=\,\text{``Perryridge''}} \right.\right.$$
$$\left(\Pi_{branch\text{-}name,\ customer\text{-}name} \left(depositor \bowtie account \right) \right.$$
$$\left.\left.\left. \cup\ \Pi_{branch\text{-}name,\ customer\text{-}name} \left(borrower \bowtie loan \right) \right) \right) \right)$$

There are no more uses of view relations, and view expansion terminates.

3.6 The Tuple Relational Calculus

When we write a relational-algebra expression, we provide a sequence of procedures that generates the answer to our query. The tuple relational calculus, by contrast, is a **nonprocedural** query language. It describes the desired information without giving a specific procedure for obtaining that information.

A query in the tuple relational calculus is expressed as

$$\{t \mid P(t)\}$$

that is, it is the set of all tuples t such that predicate P is true for t. Following our earlier notation, we use $t[A]$ to denote the value of tuple t on attribute A, and we use $t \in r$ to denote that tuple t is in relation r.

Before we give a formal definition of the tuple relational calculus, we return to some of the queries for which we wrote relational-algebra expressions in Section 3.2.

3.6.1 Example Queries

Say that we want to find the *branch-name*, *loan-number*, and *amount* for loans of over $1200:

$$\{t \mid t \in loan \wedge t[amount] > 1200\}$$

Suppose that we want only the *loan-number* attribute, rather than all attributes of the *loan* relation. To write this query in the tuple relational calculus, we need to write an expression for a relation on the schema (*loan-number*). We need those tuples on (*loan-number*) such that there is a tuple in *loan* with the *amount* attribute > 1200. To express this request, we need the construct "there exists" from mathematical logic. The notation

$$\exists \, t \in r \, (Q(t))$$

means "there exists a tuple t in relation r such that predicate $Q(t)$ is true."

Using this notation, we can write the query "Find the loan number for each loan of an amount greater than $1200" as

$$\{t \mid \exists \, s \in loan \, (t[loan\text{-}number] = s[loan\text{-}number] \\ \wedge \, s[amount] > 1200)\}$$

In English, we read the preceding expression as "The set of all tuples t such that there exists a tuple s in relation *loan* for which the values of t and s for the *loan-number* attribute are equal, and the value of s for the *amount* attribute is greater than $1200."

Tuple variable t is defined on only the *loan-number* attribute, since that is the only attribute having a condition specified for t. Thus, the result is a relation on (*loan-number*).

Consider the query "Find the names of all customers who have a loan from the Perryridge branch." This query is slightly more complex than the previous queries, since it involves two relations: *borrower* and *loan*. As we shall see, however, all it requires is that we have two "there exists" clauses in our tuple-relational-calculus expression, connected by *and* ($\wedge$). We write the query as follows:

$$\{t \mid \exists\, s \, \in \, borrower \, (t[customer\text{-}name] \, = \, s[customer\text{-}name]$$
$$\wedge\, \exists\, u \, \in \, loan \, (u[loan\text{-}number] \, = \, s[loan\text{-}number]$$
$$\wedge\, u[branch\text{-}name] \, = \, \text{``Perryridge''}))\}$$

In English, this expression is "The set of all (*customer-name*) tuples for which the customer has a loan that is at the Perryridge branch." Tuple variable *u* ensures that the customer is a borrower at the Perryridge branch. Tuple variable *s* is restricted to pertain to the same loan number as *s*. Figure 3.37 shows the result of this query.

To find all customers who have a loan, an account, or both at the bank, we used the union operation in the relational algebra. In the tuple relational calculus, we shall need two "there exists" clauses, connected by *or* ($\vee$):

$$\{t \mid \exists\, s \, \in \, borrower \, (t[customer\text{-}name] \, = \, s[customer\text{-}name])$$
$$\vee\, \exists\, u \, \in \, depositor \, (t[customer\text{-}name] \, = \, u[customer\text{-}name])\}$$

This expression gives us the set of all *customer-name* tuples for which at least one of the following holds:

- The *customer-name* appears in some tuple of the *borrower* relation as a borrower from the bank.

- The *customer-name* appears in some tuple of the *depositor* relation as a depositor of the bank.

If some customer has both a loan and an account at the bank, that customer appears only once in the result, because the mathematical definition of a set does not allow duplicate members. The result of this query appeared earlier in Figure 3.12.

If we now want *only* those customers who have *both* an account and a loan at the bank, all we need to do is to change the *or* ($\vee$) to *and* ($\wedge$) in the preceding expression.

$$\{t \mid \exists\, s \, \in \, borrower \, (t[customer\text{-}name] \, = \, s[customer\text{-}name])$$
$$\wedge\, \exists\, u \, \in \, depositor \, (t[customer\text{-}name] \, = \, u[customer\text{-}name])\}$$

The result of this query appeared in Figure 3.20.

Now consider the query "Find all customers who have an account at the bank but do not have a loan from the bank." The tuple-relational-calculus expression for this query is similar to the expressions that we have just seen, except for the use of the *not* ($\neg$) symbol:

$$\{t \mid \exists\, u \, \in \, depositor \, (t[customer\text{-}name] \, = \, u[customer\text{-}name])$$
$$\wedge\, \neg\, \exists\, s \, \in \, borrower \, (t[customer\text{-}name] \, = \, s[customer\text{-}name])\}$$

customer-name
Adams
Hayes

Figure 3.37   Names of all customers who have a loan at the Perryridge branch.

This tuple-relational-calculus expression uses the $\exists\, u\, \in\, depositor\, (\ldots)$ clause to require that the customer have an account at the bank, and it uses the $\neg\, \exists\, s\, \in$ *borrower* $(\ldots)$ clause to eliminate those customers who appear in some tuple of the *borrower* relation as having a loan from the bank. The result of this query appeared in Figure 3.13.

The query that we shall consider next uses implication, denoted by $\Rightarrow$. The formula $P \Rightarrow Q$ means "P implies Q"; that is, "if P is true, then Q must be true." Note that $P \Rightarrow Q$ is logically equivalent to $\neg P \vee Q$. The use of implication rather than *not* and *or* often suggests a more intuitive interpretation of a query in English.

Consider the query that we used in Section 3.2.3 to illustrate the division operation: "Find all customers who have an account at all branches located in Brooklyn." To write this query in the tuple relational calculus, we introduce the "for all" construct, denoted by $\forall$. The notation

$$\forall\, t\, \in\, r\, (Q(t))$$

means "Q is true for all tuples t in relation r."

We write the expression for our query as follows:

$$\{t \mid \exists\, r\, \in\, customer\, (r[customer\text{-}name] = t[customer\text{-}name]) \wedge$$
$$(\forall\, u\, \in\, branch\, (u[branch\text{-}city] = \text{``Brooklyn''} \Rightarrow$$
$$\exists\, s\, \in\, depositor\, (t[customer\text{-}name] = s[customer\text{-}name]$$
$$\wedge\, \exists\, w\, \in\, account\, (w[account\text{-}number] = s[account\text{-}number]$$
$$\wedge\, w[branch\text{-}name] = u[branch\text{-}name]))))\}$$

In English, we interpret this expression as "The set of all customers (that is, (*customer-name*) tuples t) such that, for *all* tuples u in the *branch* relation, if the value of u on attribute *branch-city* is Brooklyn, then the customer has an account at the branch whose name appears in the *branch-name* attribute of u."

Note that there is a subtlety in the above query: If there is no branch in Brooklyn, all customer names satisfy the condition. The first line of the query expression is critical in this case—without the condition

$$\exists\, r\, \in\, customer\, (r[customer\text{-}name] = t[customer\text{-}name])$$

if there is no branch in Brooklyn, any value of t (including values that are not customer names in the *depositor* relation) would qualify.

3.6.2 Formal Definition

We are now ready for a formal definition. A tuple-relational-calculus expression is of the form

$$\{t \mid P(t)\}$$

where P is a *formula*. Several tuple variables may appear in a formula. A tuple variable is said to be a *free variable* unless it is quantified by a $\exists$ or $\forall$. Thus, in

$$t \in loan\, \wedge\, \exists\, s\, \in\, customer(t[branch\text{-}name] = s[branch\text{-}name])$$

t is a free variable. Tuple variable s is said to be a *bound* variable.

A tuple-relational-calculus formula is built up out of *atoms*. An atom has one of the following forms:

- $s \in r$, where s is a tuple variable and r is a relation (we do not allow use of the $\notin$ operator)

- $s[x] \Theta u[y]$, where s and u are tuple variables, x is an attribute on which s is defined, y is an attribute on which u is defined, and Θ is a comparison operator ($<, \leq, =, \neq, >, \geq$); we require that attributes x and y have domains whose members can be compared by Θ

- $s[x] \Theta c$, where s is a tuple variable, x is an attribute on which s is defined, Θ is a comparison operator, and c is a constant in the domain of attribute x

We build up formulae from atoms by using the following rules:

- An atom is a formula.
- If P_1 is a formula, then so are $\neg P_1$ and (P_1).
- If P_1 and P_2 are formulae, then so are $P_1 \lor P_2$, $P_1 \land P_2$, and $P_1 \Rightarrow P_2$.
- If $P_1(s)$ is a formula containing a free tuple variable s, and r is a relation, then

$$\exists s \in r \, (P_1(s)) \quad \text{and} \quad \forall s \in r \, (P_1(s))$$

are also formulae.

As we could for the relational algebra, we can write equivalent expressions that are not identical in appearance. In the tuple relational calculus, these equivalences include the following three rules:

1. $P_1 \land P_2$ is equivalent to $\neg \, (\neg(P_1) \lor \neg(P_2))$.

2. $\forall t \in r \, (P_1(t))$ is equivalent to $\neg \exists t \in r \, (\neg P_1(t))$.

3. $P_1 \Rightarrow P_2$ is equivalent to $\neg(P_1) \lor P_2$.

3.6.3 Safety of Expressions

There is one final issue to be addressed. A tuple-relational-calculus expression may generate an infinite relation. Suppose that we write the expression

$$\{t \, | \, \neg \, (t \in \, loan)\}$$

There are infinitely many tuples that are not in *loan*. Most of these tuples contain values that do not even appear in the database! Clearly, we do not wish to allow such expressions.

To help us define a restriction of the tuple relational calculus, we introduce the concept of the **domain** of a tuple relational formula, P. Intuitively, the domain of P, denoted $dom(P)$, is the set of all values referenced by P. They include values mentioned in P itself, as well as values that appear in a tuple of a relation mentioned in P. Thus, the domain of P is the set of all values that appear explicitly in

P or that appear in one or more relations whose names appear in P. For example, $dom(t \in loan \wedge t[amount] > 1200)$ is the set containing 1200 as well as the set of all values appearing in *loan*. Also, $dom(\neg (t \in loan))$ is the set of all values appearing in *loan*, since the relation *loan* is mentioned in the expression.

We say that an expression $\{t \mid P(t)\}$ is *safe* if all values that appear in the result are values from $dom(P)$. The expression $\{t \mid \neg (t \in loan)\}$ is not safe. Note that $dom(\neg (t \in loan))$ is the set of all values appearing in *loan*. However, it is possible to have a tuple t not in *loan* that contains values that do not appear in *loan*. The other examples of tuple-relational-calculus expressions that we have written in this section are safe.

3.6.4 Expressive Power of Languages

The tuple relational calculus restricted to safe expressions is equivalent in expressive power to the basic relational algebra (with the operators $\cup$, $-$, $\times$, σ, and ρ, but without the extended relational operators such as generalized projection $\mathcal{G}$ and the outer-join operations) Thus, for every relational-algebra expression using only the basic operations, there is an equivalent expression in the tuple relational calculus, and for every tuple-relational-calculus expression, there is an equivalent relational-algebra expression. We will not prove this assertion here; the bibliographic notes contain references to the proof. Some parts of the proof are included in the exercises. We note that the tuple relational calculus does not have any equivalent of the aggregate operation, but it can be extended to support aggregation. Extending the tuple relational calculus to handle arithmetic expressions is straightforward.

3.7 The Domain Relational Calculus **

A second form of relational calculus, called **domain relational calculus**, uses *domain* variables that take on values from an attributes domain, rather than values for an entire tuple. The domain relational calculus, however, is closely related to the tuple relational calculus.

Domain relational calculus serves as the theoretical basis of the widely used QBE language, just as relational algebra serves as the basis for the SQL language.

3.7.1 Formal Definition

An expression in the domain relational calculus is of the form

$$\{< x_1, x_2, \ldots, x_n > \mid P(x_1, x_2, \ldots, x_n)\}$$

where $x_1, x_2, \ldots, x_n$ represent domain variables. P represents a formula composed of atoms, as was the case in the tuple relational calculus. An atom in the domain relational calculus has one of the following forms:

- $< x_1, x_2, \ldots, x_n > \in r$, where r is a relation on n attributes and $x_1, x_2, \ldots, x_n$ are domain variables or domain constants.

- $x \ominus y$, where x and y are domain variables and $\ominus$ is a comparison operator ($<, \leq, =, \neq, >, \geq$). We require that attributes x and y have domains that can be compared by $\ominus$.

- $x \ominus c$, where x is a domain variable, $\ominus$ is a comparison operator, and c is a constant in the domain of the attribute for which x is a domain variable.

We build up formulae from atoms by using the following rules:

- An atom is a formula.
- If P_1 is a formula, then so are $\neg P_1$ and (P_1).
- If P_1 and P_2 are formulae, then so are $P_1 \lor P_2$, $P_1 \land P_2$, and $P_1 \Rightarrow P_2$.
- If $P_1(x)$ is a formula in x, where x is a domain variable, then

$$\exists x \, (P_1(x)) \text{ and } \forall x \, (P_1(x))$$

are also formulae.

As a notational shorthand, we write

$$\exists a, b, c \, (P(a, b, c))$$

for

$$\exists a \, (\exists b \, (\exists c \, (P(a, b, c))))$$

3.7.2 Example Queries

We now give domain-relational-calculus queries for the examples that we considered earlier. Note the similarity of these expressions and the corresponding tuple-relational-calculus expressions.

- Find the loan number, branch name, and amount for loans of over $1200:

$$\{<l, b, a> \mid <l, b, a> \in \text{ loan } \land a > 1200\}$$

- Find all loan numbers for loans with an amount greater than $1200:

$$\{<l> \mid \exists b, a \, (<l, b, a> \in \text{ loan } \land a > 1200)\}$$

Although the second query appears similar to the one that we wrote for the tuple relational calculus, there is an important difference. In the tuple calculus, when we write $\exists s$ for some tuple variable s, we bind it immediately to a relation by writing $\exists s \in r$. However, when we write $\exists b$ in the domain calculus, b refers not to a tuple, but rather to a domain value. Thus, the domain of variable b is unconstrained until the subformula $<l, b, a> \in \text{ loan}$ constrains b to branch names that appear in the *loan* relation. For example,

- Find the names of all customers who have a loan from the Perryridge branch and find the loan amount:

$$\{< c, a > \; | \; \exists \; l \, (< c, l > \in \; borrower$$
$$\land \; \exists \, b \, (< l, b, a > \in \; loan \; \land \; b \; = \; \text{``Perryridge''}))\}$$

- Find the names of all customers who have a loan, an account, or both at the Perryridge branch:

$$\{< c > \; | \; \exists l \, (< c, l > \in \; borrower$$
$$\land \exists \, b, a \, (< l, b, a > \in \; loan \; \land \; b \; = \; \text{``Perryridge''}))$$
$$\lor \, \exists \, a \, (< c, a > \in \; depositor$$
$$\land \exists \, b, n \, (< a, b, n > \in \; account \; \land \; b \; = \; \text{``Perryridge''}))\}$$

- Find the names of all customers who have an account at all the branches located in Brooklyn:

$$\{< c > \; | \; \exists \, n \, (< c, n > \in \; customer) \; \land$$
$$\forall \, x, y, z \, (< x, y, z > \in \; branch \; \land \; y \; = \; \text{``Brooklyn''} \; \Rightarrow$$
$$\exists \, a, b \, (< a, x, b > \in \; account \; \land \; < c, a > \in \; depositor))\}$$

In English, we interpret this expression as "The set of all (*customer-name*) tuples c such that, for all (*branch-name, branch-city, assets*) tuples, x, y, z, if the branch city is Brooklyn, then the following is true":

- ☐ There exists a tuple in the relation *account* with account number a and branch name x.
- ☐ There exists a tuple in the relation *depositor* with customer c and account number a."

3.7.3 Safety of Expressions

We noted that, in the tuple relational calculus (Section 3.6), it is possible to write expressions that may generate an infinite relation. That led us to define *safety* for tuple-relational-calculus expressions. A similar situation arises for the domain relational calculus. An expression such as

$$\{< l, b, a > \; | \; \neg (< l, b, a > \in \; loan)\}$$

is unsafe, because it allows values in the result that are not in the domain of the expression.

For the domain relational calculus, we must be concerned also about the form of formulae within "there exists" and "for all" clauses. Consider the expression

$$\{< x > \; | \; \exists y \, (< x, y > \in \; r) \; \land \; \exists z \, (\neg (< x, z > \in \; r) \; \land \; P(x, z))\}$$

where P is some formula involving x and z. We can test the first part of the formula, $\exists \, y \, (< x, y > \in \; r)$, by considering only the values in r. However, to test the second part of the formula, $\exists \, z \, (\neg \, (< x, z > \in \; r) \; \land \; P(x, z))$, we must consider values for z that do not appear in r. Since all relations are finite, an infinite number of values do not appear in r. Thus, it is not possible, in general, to test the second part of the formula, without considering an infinite number of potential values for z. Instead, we add restrictions to prohibit expressions such as the preceding one.

In the tuple relational calculus, we restricted any existentially quantified variable to range over a specific relation. Since we did not do so in the domain calculus, we add rules to the definition of safety to deal with cases like our example. We say that an expression

$$\{< x_1,\, x_2, \ldots, x_n > \mid P(x_1,\, x_2, \ldots, x_n)\}$$

is safe if all of the following hold:

1. All values that appear in tuples of the expression are values from $dom(P)$.

2. For every "there exists" subformula of the form $\exists\, x\, (P_1(x))$, the subformula is true if and only if there is a value x in $dom(P_1)$ such that $P_1(x)$ is true.

3. For every "for all" subformula of the form $\forall x\, (P_1(x))$, the subformula is true if and only if $P_1(x)$ is true for all values x from $dom(P_1)$.

The purpose of the additional rules is to ensure that we can test "for all" and "there exists" subformulae without having to test infinitely many possibilities. Consider the second rule in the definition of safety. For $\exists\, x\, (P_1(x))$ to be true, we need to find only one x for which $P_1(x)$ is true. In general, there would be infinitely many values to test. However, if the expression is safe, we know that we can restrict our attention to values from $dom(P_1)$. This restriction reduces to a finite number the tuples we must consider.

The situation for subformulae of the form $\forall x\, (P_1(x))$ is similar. To assert that $\forall x\, (P_1(x))$ is true, we must, in general, test all possible values, so we must examine infinitely many values. As before, if we know that the expression is safe, it is sufficient for us to test $P_1(x)$ for those values taken from $dom(P_1)$.

All the domain-relational-calculus expressions that we have written in the example queries of this section are safe.

3.7.4   Expressive Power of Languages

When the domain relational calculus is restricted to safe expressions, it is equivalent in expressive power to the tuple relational calculus restricted to safe expressions. Since we noted earlier that the restricted tuple relational calculus is equivalent to the relational algebra, all three of the following are equivalent:

- The basic relational algebra (without the extended relational algebra operations)

- The tuple relational calculus restricted to safe expressions

- The domain relational calculus restricted to safe expressions

We note that the domain relational calculus also does not have any equivalent of the aggregate operation, but it can be extended to support aggregation, and extending it to handle arithmatic expressions is straightforward.

3.8 Summary

- The **relational data model** is based on a collection of tables. The user of the database system may query these tables, insert new tuples, delete tuples, and update (modify) tuples. There are several languages for expressing these operations.

- The **relational algebra** defines a set of algebraic operations that operate on tables, and output tables as their results. These operations can be combined to get expressions that express desired queries. The algebra defines the basic operations used within relational query languages.

- The operations in relational algebra can be divided into
    - ☐ Basic operations
    - ☐ Additional operations that can be expressed in terms of the basic operations
    - ☐ Extended operations, some of which add further expressive power to relational algebra

- Databases can be modified by **insertion, deletion,** or **update** of tuples. We used the relational algebra with the **assignment operator** to express these modifications.

- Different users of a shared database may benefit from individualized **views** of the database. Views are "virtual relations" defined by a query expression. We evaluate queries involving views by replacing the view with the expression that defines the view.

- Views are useful mechanisms for simplifying database queries, but modification of the database through views may cause problems. Therefore, database systems severely restrict updates through views.

- For reasons of query-processing efficiency, a view may be **materialized**—that is, the query is evaluated and the result stored physically. When database relations are updated, the materialized view must be correspondingly updated.

- The **tuple relational calculus** and the **domain relational calculus** are non-procedural languages that represent the basic power required in a relational query language. The basic relational algebra is a procedural language that is equivalent in power to both forms of the relational calculus when they are restricted to safe expressions.

- The relational algebra and the relational calculi are terse, formal languages that are inappropriate for casual users of a database system. Commercial database systems, therefore, use languages with more "syntactic sugar." In Chapters 4 and 5, we shall consider the three most influential languages: **SQL**, which is based on relational algebra, and **QBE** and **Datalog**, which are based on domain relational calculus.

Review Terms

- Table
- Relation
- Tuple variable
- Atomic domain
- Null value
- Database schema
- Database instance
- Relation schema
- Relation instance
- Keys
- Foreign key
  - ☐ Referencing relation
  - ☐ Referenced relation
- Schema diagram
- Query language
- Procedural language
- Nonprocedural language
- Relational algebra
- Relational algebra operations
  - ☐ Select σ
  - ☐ Project Π
  - ☐ Union $\cup$
  - ☐ Set difference $-$
  - ☐ Cartesian product $\times$
  - ☐ Rename ρ
- Additional operations
  - ☐ Set-intersection $\cap$
  - ☐ Natural-join $\bowtie$
  - ☐ Division $/$
- Assignment operation
- Extended relational-algebra operations
  - ☐ Generalized projection Π
  - ☐ Outer join
    - — Left outer join $\sqsupset\!\bowtie$
    - — Right outer join $\bowtie\!\sqsubset$
    - — Full outer join $\sqsupset\!\bowtie\!\sqsubset$
  - ☐ Aggregation $\mathcal{G}$
- Multisets
- Grouping
- Null values
- Modification of the database
  - ☐ Deletion
  - ☐ Insertion
  - ☐ Updating
- Views
- View definition
- Materialized views
- View update
- View expansion
- Recursive views
- Tuple relational calculus
- Domain relational calculus
- Safety of expressions
- Expressive power of languages

Exercises

3.1 Design a relational database for a university registrar's office. The office maintains data about each class, including the instructor, the number of students enrolled, and the time and place of the class meetings. For each student–class pair, a grade is recorded.

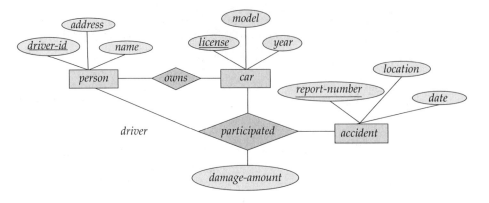

Figure 3.38   E-R diagram.

3.2 Describe the differences in meaning between the terms *relation* and *relation schema*. Illustrate your answer by referring to your solution to Exercise 3.1.

3.3 Design a relational database corresponding to the E-R diagram of Figure 3.38.

3.4 In Chapter 2, we saw how to represent many-to-many, many-to-one, one-to-many, and one-to-one relationship sets. Explain how primary keys help us to represent such relationship sets in the relational model.

3.5 Consider the relational database of Figure 3.39, where the primary keys are underlined. Give an expression in the relational algebra to express each of the following queries:

   a. Find the names of all employees who work for First Bank Corporation.

   b. Find the names and cities of residence of all employees who work for First Bank Corporation.

   c. Find the names, street address, and cities of residence of all employees who work for First Bank Corporation and earn more than $10,000 per annum.

   d. Find the names of all employees in this database who live in the same city as the company for which they work.

   e. Find the names of all employees who live in the same city and on the same street as do their managers.

   f. Find the names of all employees in this database who do not work for First Bank Corporation.

   g. Find the names of all employees who earn more than every employee of Small Bank Corporation.

   h. Assume the companies may be located in several cities. Find all companies located in every city in which Small Bank Corporation is located.

3.6 Consider the relation of Figure 3.21, which shows the result of the query "Find the names of all customers who have a loan at the bank." Rewrite the query to include not only the name, but also the city of residence for each customer. Observe that now customer Jackson no longer appears in the result, even though Jackson does in fact have a loan from the bank.

> *employee* (<u>*person-name*</u>, *street, city*)
> *works* (<u>*person-name, company-name*</u>, *salary*)
> *company* (<u>*company-name*</u>, *city*)
> *manages* (<u>*person-name*</u>, *manager-name*)

Figure 3.39   Relational database for Exercises 3.5, 3.8 and 3.10.

a. Explain why Jackson does not appear in the result.
b. Suppose that you want Jackson to appear in the result. How would you modify the database to achieve this effect?
c. Again, suppose that you want Jackson to appear in the result. Write a query using an outer join that accomplishes this desire without your having to modify the database.

3.7 The outer-join operations extend the natural-join operation so that tuples from the participating relations are not lost in the result of the join. Describe how the theta join operation can be extended so that tuples from the left, right, or both relations are not lost from the result of a theta join.

3.8 Consider the relational database of Figure 3.39. Give an expression in the relational algebra for each request:

a. Modify the database so that Jones now lives in Newtown.
b. Give all employees of First Bank Corporation a 10 percent salary raise.
c. Give all managers in this database a 10 percent salary raise.
d. Give all managers in this database a 10 percent salary raise, unless the salary would be greater than $100,000. In such cases, give only a 3 percent raise.
e. Delete all tuples in the *works* relation for employees of Small Bank Corporation.

3.9 Using the bank example, write relational-algebra queries to find the accounts held by more than two customers in the following ways:

a. Using an aggregate function.
b. Without using any aggregate functions.

3.10 Consider the relational database of Figure 3.39. Give a relational-algebra expression for each of the following queries:

a. Find the company with the most employees.
b. Find the company with the smallest payroll.
c. Find those companies whose employees earn a higher salary, on average, than the average salary at First Bank Corporation.

3.11 List two reasons why we may choose to define a view.

3.12 List two major problems with processing update operations expressed in terms of views.

3.13 Let the following relation schemas be given:

$$R = (A, B, C)$$

$$S = (D, E, F)$$

Let relations $r(R)$ and $s(S)$ be given. Give an expression in the tuple relational calculus that is equivalent to each of the following:

   a. $\Pi_A(r)$
   b. $\sigma_{B=17}(r)$
   c. $r \times s$
   d. $\Pi_{A,F}(\sigma_{C=D}(r \times s))$

3.14 Let $R = (A, B, C)$, and let r_1 and r_2 both be relations on schema R. Give an expression in the domain relational calculus that is equivalent to each of the following:

   a. $\Pi_A(r_1)$
   b. $\sigma_{B=17}(r_1)$
   c. $r_1 \cup r_2$
   d. $r_1 \cap r_2$
   e. $r_1 - r_2$
   f. $\Pi_{A,B}(r_1) \bowtie \Pi_{B,C}(r_2)$

3.15 Repeat Exercise 3.5 using the tuple relational calculus and the domain relational calculus.

3.16 Let $R = (A, B)$ and $S = (A, C)$, and let $r(R)$ and $s(S)$ be relations. Write relational-algebra expressions equivalent to the following domain-relational-calculus expressions:

   a. $\{< a > \mid \exists b (< a, b > \in r \wedge b = 17)\}$
   b. $\{< a, b, c > \mid < a, b > \in r \wedge < a, c > \in s\}$
   c. $\{< a > \mid \exists b (< a, b > \in r) \vee \forall c (\exists d (< d, c > \in s) \Rightarrow < a, c > \in s)\}$
   d. $\{< a > \mid \exists c (< a, c > \in s \wedge \exists b_1, b_2 (< a, b_1 > \in r \wedge < c, b_2 > \in r \wedge b_1 > b_2))\}$

3.17 Let $R = (A, B)$ and $S = (A, C)$, and let $r(R)$ and $s(S)$ be relations. Using the special constant *null*, write tuple-relational-calculus expressions equivalent to each of the following:

   a. $r \bowtie s$
   b. $r \bowtie s$
   c. $r \bowtie s$

3.18 List two reasons why null values might be introduced into the database.

3.19 Certain systems allow *marked* nulls. A marked null $\perp_i$ is equal to itself, but if $i \neq j$, then $\perp_i \neq \perp_j$. One application of marked nulls is to allow certain updates through views. Consider the view *loan-info* (Section 3.5). Show how you can use marked nulls to allow the insertion of the tuple ("Johnson", 1900) through *loan-info*.

Bibliographical Notes

E. F. Codd of the IBM San Jose Research Laboratory proposed the relational model in the late 1960s; Codd [1970]. This work led to the prestigious ACM Turing Award to Codd in 1981; Codd [1982].

After Codd published his original paper, several research projects were formed with the goal of constructing practical relational database systems, including System R at the IBM San Jose Research Laboratory, Ingres at the University of California at Berkeley, Query-by-Example at the IBM T. J. Watson Research Center, and the Peterlee Relational Test Vehicle (PRTV) at the IBM Scientific Center in Peterlee, United Kingdom. System R is discussed in Astrahan et al. [1976], Astrahan et al. [1979], and Chamberlin et al. [1981]. Ingres is discussed in Stonebraker [1980], Stonebraker [1986b], and Stonebraker et al. [1976]. Query-by-example is described in Zloof [1977]. PRTV is described in Todd [1976].

Many relational-database products are now commercially available. These include IBM's DB2, Ingres, Oracle, Sybase, Informix, and Microsoft SQL Server. Database products for personal computers include Microsoft Access, dBase, and FoxPro. Information about the products can be found in their respective manuals.

General discussion of the relational data model appears in most database texts. Atzeni and Antonellis [1993] and Maier [1983] are texts devoted exclusively to the relational data model. The original definition of relational algebra is in Codd [1970]; that of tuple relational calculus is in Codd [1972]. A formal proof of the equivalence of tuple relational calculus and relational algebra is in Codd [1972].

Several extensions to the relational calculus have been proposed. Klug [1982] and Escobar-Molano et al. [1993] describe extensions to scalar aggregate functions. Extensions to the relational model and discussions of incorporation of null values in the relational algebra (the RM/T model), as well as outer joins, are in Codd [1979]. Codd [1990] is a compendium of E. F. Codd's papers on the relational model. Outer joins are also discussed in Date [1993b]. The problem of updating relational databases through views is addressed by Bancilhon and Spyratos [1981], Cosmadakis and Papadimitriou [1984], Dayal and Bernstein [1978], and Langerak [1990]. Section 14.5 covers materialized view maintenance, and references to literature on view maintenance can be found at the end of that chapter.

PART 2

Relational Databases

A relational database is a shared repository of data. To make data from a relational database available to users, we have to address several issues. One is how users specify requests for data: Which of the various query languages do they use? Chapter 4 covers the SQL language, which is the most widely used query language today. Chapter 5 covers two other query languages, QBE and Datalog, which offer alternative approaches to querying relational data.

Another issue is data integrity and security; databases need to protect data from damage by user actions, whether unintentional or intentional. The integrity maintenance component of a database ensures that updates do not violate integrity constraints that have been specified on the data. The security component of a database includes authentication of users, and access control, to restrict the permissible actions for each user. Chapter 6 covers integrity and security issues. Security and integrity issues are present regardless of the data model, but for concreteness we study them in the context of the relational model. Integrity constraints form the basis of relational database design, which we study in Chapter 7.

Relational database design—the design of the relational schema—is the first step in building a database application. Schema design was covered informally in earlier chapters. There are, however, principles that can be used to distinguish good database designs from bad ones. These are formalized by means of several "normal forms," which offer different tradeoffs between the possibility of inconsistencies and the efficiency of certain queries. Chapter 7 describes the formal design of relational schemas.

C H A P T E R 4

SQL

The formal languages described in Chapter 3 provide a concise notation for representing queries. However, commercial database systems require a query language that is more user friendly. In this chapter, we study SQL, the most influential commercially marketed query language, SQL. SQL uses a combination of relational-algebra and relational-calculus constructs.

Although we refer to the SQL language as a "query language," it can do much more than just query a database. It can define the structure of the data, modify data in the database, and specify security constraints.

It is not our intention to provide a complete users' guide for SQL. Rather, we present SQL's fundamental constructs and concepts. Individual implementations of SQL may differ in details, or may support only a subset of the full language.

4.1 Background

IBM developed the original version of SQL at its San Jose Research Laboratory (now the Almaden Research Center). IBM implemented the language, originally called Sequel, as part of the System R project in the early 1970s. The Sequel language has evolved since then, and its name has changed to SQL (Structured Query Language). Many products now support the SQL language. SQL has clearly established itself as *the* standard relational-database language.

In 1986, the American National Standards Institute (ANSI) and the International Organization for Standardization (ISO) published an SQL standard, called SQL-86. IBM published its own corporate SQL standard, the Systems Application Architecture Database Interface (SAA-SQL) in 1987. ANSI published an extended standard for SQL, SQL-89, in 1989. The next version of the standard was SQL-92 standard, and the most recent version is SQL:1999. The bibliographic notes provide references to these standards.

In this chapter, we present a survey of SQL, based mainly on the widely implemented SQL-92 standard. The SQL:1999 standard is a superset of the SQL-92 standard; we cover some features of SQL:1999 in this chapter, and provide more detailed coverage in Chapter 9. Many database systems support some of the new constructs in SQL:1999, although currently no database system supports all the new constructs. You should also be aware that some database systems do not even support all the features of SQL-92, and that many databases provide nonstandard features that we do not cover here.

The SQL language has several parts:

- **Data-definition language** (DDL). The SQL DDL provides commands for defining relation schemas, deleting relations, and modifying relation schemas.

- **Interactive data-manipulation language** (DML). The SQL DML includes a query language based on both the relational algebra and the tuple relational calculus. It includes also commands to insert tuples into, delete tuples from, and modify tuples in the database.

- **View definition**. The SQL DDL includes commands for defining views.

- **Transaction control**. SQL includes commands for specifying the beginning and ending of transactions.

- **Embedded SQL** and **dynamic SQL**. Embedded and dynamic SQL define how SQL statements can be embedded within general-purpose programming languages, such as C, C++, Java, PL/I, Cobol, Pascal, and Fortran.

- **Integrity**. The SQL DDL includes commands for specifying integrity constraints that the data stored in the database must satisfy. Updates that violate integrity constraints are disallowed.

- **Authorization**. The SQL DDL includes commands for specifying access rights to relations and views.

In this chapter, we cover the DML and the basic DDL features of SQL. We also briefly outline embedded and dynamic SQL, including the ODBC and JDBC standards for interacting with a database from programs written in the C and Java languages. SQL features supporting integrity and authorization are described in Chapter 6, while Chapter 9 outlines object-oriented extensions to SQL.

The enterprise that we use in the examples in this chapter, and later chapters, is a banking enterprise with the following relation schemas:

Branch-schema = (*branch-name, branch-city, assets*)
Customer-schema = (*customer-name, customer-street, customer-city*)
Loan-schema = (*loan-number, branch-name, amount*)
Borrower-schema = (*customer-name, loan-number*)
Account-schema = (*account-number, branch-name, balance*)
Depositor-schema = (*customer-name, account-number*)

Note that in this chapter, as elsewhere in the text, we use hyphenated names for schema, relations, and attributes for ease of reading. In actual SQL systems, however, hyphens are not valid parts of a name (they are treated as the minus operator). A simple way of translating the names we use to valid SQL names is to replace all hyphens by the underscore symbol ("_"). For example, we use *branch_name* in place of *branch-name*.

4.2 Basic Structure

A relational database consists of a collection of relations, each of which is assigned a unique name. Each relation has a structure similar to that presented in Chapter 3. SQL allows the use of null values to indicate that the value either is unknown or does not exist. It allows a user to specify which attributes cannot be assigned null values, as we shall discuss in Section 4.11.

The basic structure of an SQL expression consists of three clauses: **select**, **from**, and **where**.

- The **select** clause corresponds to the projection operation of the relational algebra. It is used to list the attributes desired in the result of a query.

- The **from** clause corresponds to the Cartesian-product operation of the relational algebra. It lists the relations to be scanned in the evaluation of the expression.

- The **where** clause corresponds to the selection predicate of the relational algebra. It consists of a predicate involving attributes of the relations that appear in the **from** clause.

That the term *select* has different meaning in SQL than in the relational algebra is an unfortunate historical fact. We emphasize the different interpretations here to minimize potential confusion.

A typical SQL query has the form

select $A_1, A_2, \ldots, A_n$
from $r_1, r_2, \ldots, r_m$
where P

Each A_i represents an attribute, and each r_i a relation. P is a predicate. The query is equivalent to the relational-algebra expression

$$\Pi_{A_1, A_2, \ldots, A_n}(\sigma_P(r_1 \times r_2 \times \cdots \times r_m))$$

If the **where** clause is omitted, the predicate P is **true**. However, unlike the result of a relational-algebra expression, the result of the SQL query may contain multiple copies of some tuples; we shall return to this issue in Section 4.2.8.

SQL forms the Cartesian product of the relations named in the **from** clause, performs a relational-algebra selection using the **where** clause predicate, and then projects the result onto the attributes of the **select** clause. In practice, SQL may convert the expression into an equivalent form that can be processed more efficiently. However, we shall defer concerns about efficiency to Chapters 13 and 14.

4.2.1 The select Clause

The result of an SQL query is, of course, a relation. Let us consider a simple query using our banking example, "Find the names of all branches in the *loan* relation":

select *branch-name*
from *loan*

The result is a relation consisting of a single attribute with the heading *branch-name*.

Formal query languages are based on the mathematical notion of a relation being a set. Thus, duplicate tuples never appear in relations. In practice, duplicate elimination is time-consuming. Therefore, SQL (like most other commercial query languages) allows duplicates in relations as well as in the results of SQL expressions. Thus, the preceding query will list each *branch-name* once for every tuple in which it appears in the *loan* relation.

In those cases where we want to force the elimination of duplicates, we insert the keyword **distinct** after **select**. We can rewrite the preceding query as

select distinct *branch-name*
from *loan*

if we want duplicates removed.

SQL allows us to use the keyword **all** to specify explicitly that duplicates are not removed:

select all *branch-name*
from *loan*

Since duplicate retention is the default, we will not use **all** in our examples. To ensure the elimination of duplicates in the results of our example queries, we will use **distinct** whenever it is necessary. In most queries where **distinct** is not used, the exact number of duplicate copies of each tuple present in the query result is not important. However, the number is important in certain applications; we return to this issue in Section 4.2.8.

The asterisk symbol " * " can be used to denote "all attributes." Thus, the use of *loan*.* in the preceding **select** clause would indicate that all attributes of *loan* are to be selected. A select clause of the form **select *** indicates that all attributes of all relations appearing in the **from** clause are selected.

The **select** clause may also contain arithmetic expressions involving the operators $+$, $-$, $*$, and $/$ operating on constants or attributes of tuples. For example, the query

select *loan-number, branch-name, amount* * 100
from *loan*

even if an attribute name can be derived from the base relations as in the preceding example, we may want to change the attribute name in the result. Hence, SQL provides a way of renaming the attributes of a result relation.

For example, if we want the attribute name *loan-number* to be replaced with the name *loan-id*, we can rewrite the preceding query as

> **select** *customer-name, borrower.loan-number* **as** *loan-id, amount*
> **from** *borrower, loan*
> **where** *borrower.loan-number = loan.loan-number*

4.2.5   Tuple Variables

The **as** clause is particularly useful in defining the notion of tuple variables, as is done in the tuple relational calculus. A tuple variable in SQL must be associated with a particular relation. Tuple variables are defined in the **from** clause by way of the **as** clause. To illustrate, we rewrite the query "For all customers who have a loan from the bank, find their names, loan numbers, and loan amount" as

> **select** *customer-name, T.loan-number, S.amount*
> **from** *borrower* **as** *T, loan* **as** *S*
> **where** *T.loan-number = S.loan-number*

Note that we define a tuple variable in the **from** clause by placing it after the name of the relation with which it is associated, with the keyword **as** in between (the keyword **as** is optional). When we write expressions of the form *relation-name.attribute-name*, the relation name is, in effect, an implicitly defined tuple variable.

Tuple variables are most useful for comparing two tuples in the same relation. Recall that, in such cases, we could use the rename operation in the relational algebra. Suppose that we want the query "Find the names of all branches that have assets greater than at least one branch located in Brooklyn." We can write the SQL expression

> **select distinct** *T.branch-name*
> **from** *branch* **as** *T, branch* **as** *S*
> **where** *T.assets > S.assets* **and** *S.branch-city = 'Brooklyn'*

Observe that we could not use the notation *branch.asset*, since it would not be clear which reference to *branch* is intended.

SQL permits us to use the notation $(v_1, v_2, \ldots, v_n)$ to denote a tuple of arity n containing values $v_1, v_2, \ldots, v_n$. The comparison operators can be used on tuples, and the ordering is defined lexicographically. For example, $(a_1, a_2) <= (b_1, b_2)$ is true if $a_1 < b_1$, or $(a_1 = b_1) \wedge (a_2 <= b_2)$; similarly, the two tuples are equal if all their attributes are equal.

4.2.6   String Operations

SQL specifies strings by enclosing them in single quotes, for example, 'Perryridge', as we saw earlier. A single quote character that is part of a string can be specified by using two single quote characters; for example the string "It's right" can be specified by 'It''s right'.

The most commonly used operation on strings is pattern matching using the operator **like**. We describe patterns by using two special characters:

- Percent (%): The % character matches any substring.

- Underscore (_): The _ character matches any character.

Patterns are case sensitive; that is, uppercase characters do not match lowercase characters, or vice versa. To illustrate pattern matching, we consider the following examples:

- 'Perry%' matches any string beginning with "Perry".

- '%idge%' matches any string containing "idge" as a substring, for example, 'Perryridge', 'Rock Ridge', 'Mianus Bridge', and 'Ridgeway'.

- '_ _ _' matches any string of exactly three characters.

- '_ _ _%' matches any string of at least three characters.

SQL expresses patterns by using the **like** comparison operator. Consider the query "Find the names of all customers whose street address includes the substring 'Main'." This query can be written as

> **select** *customer-name*
> **from** *customer*
> **where** *customer-street* **like** '%Main%'

For patterns to include the special pattern characters (that is, % and _), SQL allows the specification of an escape character. The escape character is used immediately before a special pattern character to indicate that the special pattern character is to be treated like a normal character. We define the escape character for a **like** comparison using the **escape** keyword. To illustrate, consider the following patterns, which use a backslash (\) as the escape character:

- **like** 'ab\%cd%' **escape** '\' matches all strings beginning with "ab%cd".

- **like** 'ab\\cd%' **escape** '\' matches all strings beginning with "ab\cd".

SQL allows us to search for mismatches instead of matches by using the **not like** comparison operator.

SQL also permits a variety of functions on character strings, such as concatenating (using "‖"), extracting substrings, finding the length of strings, converting between uppercase and lowercase, and so on. SQL:1999 also offers a **similar to** operation, which provides more powerful pattern matching than the **like** operation; the syntax for specifying patterns is similar to that used in Unix regular expressions.

4.2.7   Ordering the Display of Tuples

SQL offers the user some control over the order in which tuples in a relation are displayed. The **order by** clause causes the tuples in the result of a query to appear in sorted order. To list in alphabetic order all customers who have a loan at the Perryridge branch, we write

> **select distinct** *customer-name*
> **from** *borrower, loan*
> **where** *borrower.loan-number* = *loan.loan-number* **and**
>   *branch-name* = 'Perryridge'
> **order by** *customer-name*

By default, the **order by** clause lists items in ascending order. To specify the sort order, we may specify **desc** for descending order or **asc** for ascending order. Furthermore, ordering can be performed on multiple attributes. Suppose that we wish to list the entire *loan* relation in descending order of *amount*. If several loans have the same amount, we order them in ascending order by loan number. We express this query in SQL as follows:

> **select** *
> **from** *loan*
> **order by** *amount* **desc**, *loan-number* **asc**

To fulfill an **order by** request, SQL must perform a sort. Since sorting a large number of tuples may be costly, it should be done only when necessary.

4.2.8   Duplicates

Using relations with duplicates offers advantages in several situations. Accordingly, SQL formally defines not only what tuples are in the result of a query, but also how many copies of each of those tuples appear in the result. We can define the duplicate semantics of an SQL query using *multiset* versions of the relational operators. Here, we define the multiset versions of several of the relational-algebra operators. Given multiset relations r_1 and r_2,

1. If there are c_1 copies of tuple t_1 in r_1, and t_1 satisfies selection σ_θ, then there are c_1 copies of t_1 in $\sigma_\theta(r_1)$.

2. For each copy of tuple t_1 in r_1, there is a copy of tuple $\Pi_A(t_1)$ in $\Pi_A(r_1)$, where $\Pi_A(t_1)$ denotes the projection of the single tuple t_1.

3. If there are c_1 copies of tuple t_1 in r_1 and c_2 copies of tuple t_2 in r_2, there are $c_1 * c_2$ copies of the tuple $t_1.t_2$ in $r_1 \times r_2$.

For example, suppose that relations r_1 with schema (A, B) and r_2 with schema (C) are the following multisets:

$$r_1 = \{(1, a), (2, a)\} \quad r_2 = \{(2), (3), (3)\}$$

Then $\Pi_B(r_1)$ would be $\{(a),(a)\}$, whereas $\Pi_B(r_1) \times r_2$ would be

$$\{(a,2),(a,2),(a,3),(a,3),(a,3),(a,3)\}$$

We can now define how many copies of each tuple occur in the result of an SQL query. An SQL query of the form

> **select** $A_1,\ A_2,\ldots,A_n$
> **from** $r_1,\ r_2,\ldots,r_m$
> **where** P

is equivalent to the relational-algebra expression

$$\Pi_{A_1,\ A_2,\ldots,A_n}(\sigma_P(r_1\ \times\ r_2\ \times\ \cdots\ \times\ r_m))$$

using the multiset versions of the relational operators σ, Π, and $\times$.

4.3   Set Operations

The SQL operations **union**, **intersect**, and **except** operate on relations and correspond to the relational-algebra operations $\cup$, $\cap$, and $-$. Like union, intersection, and set difference in relational algebra, the relations participating in the operations must be *compatible*; that is, they must have the same set of attributes.

Let us demonstrate how several of the example queries that we considered in Chapter 3 can be written in SQL. We shall now construct queries involving the **union**, **intersect**, and **except** operations of two sets: the set of all customers who have an account at the bank, which can be derived by

> **select** *customer-name*
> **from** *depositor*

and the set of customers who have a loan at the bank, which can be derived by

> **select** *customer-name*
> **from** *borrower*

We shall refer to the relations obtained as the result of the preceding queries as *d* and *b*, respectively.

4.3.1   The Union Operation

To find all customers having a loan, an account, or both at the bank, we write

> (**select** *customer-name*
> **from** *depositor*)
> **union**
> (**select** *customer-name*
> **from** *borrower*)

The **union** operation automatically eliminates duplicates, unlike the **select** clause. Thus, in the preceding query, if a customer—say, Jones—has several accounts or loans (or both) at the bank, then Jones will appear only once in the result.

If we want to retain all duplicates, we must write **union all** in place of **union**:

> (**select** *customer-name*
>   **from** *depositor*)
> **union all**
> (**select** *customer-name*
>   **from** *borrower*)

The number of duplicate tuples in the result is equal to the total number of duplicates that appear in both *d* and *b*. Thus, if Jones has three accounts and two loans at the bank, then there will be five tuples with the name Jones in the result.

4.3.2 The Intersect Operation

To find all customers who have both a loan and an account at the bank, we write

> (**select distinct** *customer-name*
>   **from** *depositor*)
> **intersect**
> (**select distinct** *customer-name*
>   **from** *borrower*)

The **intersect** operation automatically eliminates duplicates. Thus, in the preceding query, if a customer—say, Jones—has several accounts and loans at the bank, then Jones will appear only once in the result.

If we want to retain all duplicates, we must write **intersect all** in place of **intersect**:

> (**select** *customer-name*
>   **from** *depositor*)
> **intersect all**
> (**select** *customer-name*
>   **from** *borrower*)

The number of duplicate tuples that appear in the result is equal to the minimum number of duplicates in both *d* and *b*. Thus, if Jones has three accounts and two loans at the bank, then there will be two tuples with the name Jones in the result.

4.3.3 The Except Operation

To find all customers who have an account but no loan at the bank, we write

> (**select distinct** *customer-name*
> **from** *depositor*)
> **except**
> (**select** *customer-name*
> **from** *borrower*)

The **except** operation automatically eliminates duplicates. Thus, in the preceding query, a tuple with customer name Jones will appear (exactly once) in the result only if Jones has an account at the bank, but has no loan at the bank.

If we want to retain all duplicates, we must write **except all** in place of **except**:

> (**select** *customer-name*
> **from** *depositor*)
> **except all**
> (**select** *customer-name*
> **from** *borrower*)

The number of duplicate copies of a tuple in the result is equal to the number of duplicate copies of the tuple in *d* minus the number of duplicate copies of the tuple in *b*, provided that the difference is positive. Thus, if Jones has three accounts and one loan at the bank, then there will be two tuples with the name Jones in the result. If, instead, this customer has two accounts and three loans at the bank, there will be no tuple with the name Jones in the result.

4.4 Aggregate Functions

Aggregate functions are functions that take a collection (a set or multiset) of values as input and return a single value. SQL offers five built-in aggregate functions:

- Average: **avg**

- Minimum: **min**

- Maximum: **max**

- Total: **sum**

- Count: **count**

The input to **sum** and **avg** must be a collection of numbers, but the other operators can operate on collections of nonnumeric data types, such as strings, as well.

As an illustration, consider the query "Find the average account balance at the Perryridge branch." We write this query as follows:

> **select avg** (*balance*)
> **from** *account*
> **where** *branch-name* = 'Perryridge'

The result of this query is a relation with a single attribute, containing a single tuple with a numerical value corresponding to the average balance at the Perryridge branch. Optionally, we can give a name to the attribute of the result relation by using the **as** clause.

There are circumstances where we would like to apply the aggregate function not only to a single set of tuples, but also to a group of sets of tuples; we specify this wish in SQL using the **group by** clause. The attribute or attributes given in the **group by** clause are used to form groups. Tuples with the same value on all attributes in the **group by** clause are placed in one group.

As an illustration, consider the query "Find the average account balance at each branch." We write this query as follows:

> **select** *branch-name*, **avg** (*balance*)
> **from** *account*
> **group by** *branch-name*

Retaining duplicates is important in computing an average. Suppose that the account balances at the (small) Brighton branch are $1000, $3000, $2000, and $1000. The average balance is $7000/4 = $1750.00. If duplicates were eliminated, we would obtain the wrong answer ($6000/3 = $2000).

There are cases where we must eliminate duplicates before computing an aggregate function. If we do want to eliminate duplicates, we use the keyword **distinct** in the aggregate expression. An example arises in the query "Find the number of depositors for each branch." In this case, a depositor counts only once, regardless of the number of accounts that depositor may have. We write this query as follows:

> **select** *branch-name*, **count** (**distinct** *customer-name*)
> **from** *depositor, account*
> **where** *depositor.account-number = account.account-number*
> **group by** *branch-name*

At times, it is useful to state a condition that applies to groups rather than to tuples. For example, we might be interested in only those branches where the average account balance is more than $1200. This condition does not apply to a single tuple; rather, it applies to each group constructed by the **group by** clause. To express such a query, we use the **having** clause of SQL. SQL applies predicates in the **having** clause after groups have been formed, so aggregate functions may be used. We express this query in SQL as follows:

> **select** *branch-name*, **avg** (*balance*)
> **from** *account*
> **group by** *branch-name*
> **having avg** (*balance*) > 1200

At times, we wish to treat the entire relation as a single group. In such cases, we do not use a **group by** clause. Consider the query "Find the average balance for all accounts." We write this query as follows:

$$\textbf{select avg } (balance)$$
$$\textbf{from } account$$

We use the aggregate function **count** frequently to count the number of tuples in a relation. The notation for this function in SQL is **count** (*). Thus, to find the number of tuples in the *customer* relation, we write

$$\textbf{select count } (*)$$
$$\textbf{from } customer$$

SQL does not allow the use of **distinct** with **count**(*). It is legal to use **distinct** with **max** and **min**, even though the result does not change. We can use the keyword **all** in place of **distinct** to specify duplicate retention, but, since **all** is the default, there is no need to do so.

If a **where** clause and a **having** clause appear in the same query, SQL applies the predicate in the **where** clause first. Tuples satisfying the **where** predicate are then placed into groups by the **group by** clause. SQL then applies the **having** clause, if it is present, to each group; it removes the groups that do not satisfy the **having** clause predicate. The **select** clause uses the remaining groups to generate tuples of the result of the query.

To illustrate the use of both a **having** clause and a **where** clause in the same query, we consider the query "Find the average balance for each customer who lives in Harrison and has at least three accounts."

select *depositor.customer-name*, **avg** (*balance*)
from *depositor, account, customer*
where *depositor.account-number* = *account.account-number* **and**
    depositor.customer-name = *customer.customer-name* **and**
    customer-city = 'Harrison'
group by *depositor.customer-name*
having count (**distinct** *depositor.account-number*) >= 3

4.5 Null Values

SQL allows the use of *null* values to indicate absence of information about the value of an attribute.

We can use the special keyword **null** in a predicate to test for a null value. Thus, to find all loan numbers that appear in the *loan* relation with null values for *amount*, we write

select *loan-number*
from *loan*
where *amount* **is null**

The predicate **is not null** tests for the absence of a null value.

The use of a *null* value in arithmetic and comparison operations causes several complications. In Section 3.3.4 we saw how null values are handled in the relational algebra. We now outline how SQL handles null values.

The result of an arithmetic expression (involving, for example $+$, $-$, $*$ or $/$) is null if any of the input values is null. SQL treats as **unknown** the result of any comparison involving a *null* value (other than **is null** and **is not null**).

Since the predicate in a **where** clause can involve Boolean operations such as **and**, **or**, and **not** on the results of comparisons, the definitions of the Boolean operations are extended to deal with the value **unknown**, as outlined in Section 3.3.4.

- **and**: The result of *true* **and** *unknown* is *unknown*, *false* **and** *unknown* is *false*, while *unknown* **and** *unknown* is *unknown*.

- **or**: The result of *true* **or** *unknown* is *true*, *false* **or** *unknown* is *unknown*, while *unknown* **or** *unknown* is *unknown*.

- **not**: The result of **not** *unknown* is *unknown*.

SQL defines the result of an SQL statement of the form

$$\textbf{select} \ldots \textbf{from } R_1, \cdots, R_n \textbf{ where } P$$

to contain (projections of) tuples in $R_1 \times \cdots \times R_n$ for which predicate P evaluates to **true**. If the predicate evaluates to either **false** or **unknown** for a tuple in $R_1 \times \cdots \times R_n$ (the projection of) the tuple is not added to the result.

SQL also allows us to test whether the result of a comparison is unknown, rather than true or false, by using the clauses **is unknown** and **is not unknown**.

Null values, when they exist, also complicate the processing of aggregate operators. For example, assume that some tuples in the *loan* relation have a null value for *amount*. Consider the following query to total all loan amounts:

$$\textbf{select sum } (amount)$$
$$\textbf{from } loan$$

The values to be summed in the preceding query include null values, since some tuples have a null value for *amount*. Rather than say that the overall sum is itself *null*, the SQL standard says that the **sum** operator should ignore *null* values in its input.

In general, aggregate functions treat nulls according to the following rule: All aggregate functions except **count(*)** ignore null values in their input collection. As a result of null values being ignored, the collection of values may be empty. The **count** of an empty collection is defined to be 0, and all other aggregate operations return a value of null when applied on an empty collection. The effect of null values on some of the more complicated SQL constructs can be subtle.

A **boolean** type data, which can take values **true**, **false**, and **unknown**, was introduced in SQL:1999. The aggregate functions **some** and **every**, which mean exactly what you would intuitively expect, can be applied on a collection of Boolean values.

4.6 Nested Subqueries

SQL provides a mechanism for nesting subqueries. A subquery is a **select-from-where** expression that is nested within another query. A common use of subqueries is to perform tests for set membership, make set comparisons, and determine set cardinality. We shall study these uses in subsequent sections.

4.6.1 Set Membership

SQL draws on the relational calculus for operations that allow testing tuples for membership in a relation. The **in** connective tests for set membership, where the set is a collection of values produced by a **select** clause. The **not in** connective tests for the absence of set membership. As an illustration, reconsider the query "Find all customers who have both a loan and an account at the bank." Earlier, we wrote such a query by intersecting two sets: the set of depositors at the bank, and the set of borrowers from the bank. We can take the alternative approach of finding all account holders at the bank who are members of the set of borrowers from the bank. Clearly, this formulation generates the same results as the previous one did, but it leads us to write our query using the **in** connective of SQL. We begin by finding all account holders, and we write the subquery

> (**select** *customer-name*
> **from** *depositor*)

We then need to find those customers who are borrowers from the bank and who appear in the list of account holders obtained in the subquery. We do so by nesting the subquery in an outer **select**. The resulting query is

> **select distinct** *customer-name*
> **from** *borrower*
> **where** *customer-name* **in** (**select** *customer-name*
>   **from** *depositor*)

This example shows that it is possible to write the same query several ways in SQL. This flexibility is beneficial, since it allows a user to think about the query in the way that seems most natural. We shall see that there is a substantial amount of redundancy in SQL.

In the preceding example, we tested membership in a one-attribute relation. It is also possible to test for membership in an arbitrary relation in SQL. We can thus write the query "Find all customers who have both an account and a loan at the Perryridge branch" in yet another way:

> **select distinct** *customer-name*
> **from** *borrower, loan*
> **where** *borrower.loan-number = loan.loan-number* **and**
>   *branch-name =* 'Perryridge' **and**
>   (*branch-name, customer-name*) **in**
>   (**select** *branch-name, customer-name*
>   **from** *depositor, account*
>   **where** *depositor.account-number = account.account-number*)

We use the **not in** construct in a similar way. For example, to find all customers who do have a loan at the bank, but do not have an account at the bank, we can write

> **select distinct** *customer-name*
> **from** *borrower*
> **where** *customer-name* **not in** (**select** *customer-name*
>   **from** *depositor*)

The **in** and **not in** operators can also be used on enumerated sets. The following query selects the names of customers who have a loan at the bank, and whose names are neither Smith nor Jones.

> **select distinct** *customer-name*
> **from** *borrower*
> **where** *customer-name* **not in** ('Smith', 'Jones')

4.6.2   Set Comparison

As an example of the ability of a nested subquery to compare sets, consider the query "Find the names of all branches that have assets greater than those of at least one branch located in Brooklyn." In Section 4.2.5, we wrote this query as follows:

> **select distinct** *T.branch-name*
> **from** *branch* **as** *T*, *branch* **as** *S*
> **where** *T.assets* > *S.assets* **and** *S.branch-city* = 'Brooklyn'

SQL does, however, offer an alternative style for writing the preceding query. The phrase "greater than at least one" is represented in SQL by > **some**. This construct allows us to rewrite the query in a form that resembles closely our formulation of the query in English.

> **select** *branch-name*
> **from** *branch*
> **where** *assets* > **some** (**select** *assets*
>   **from** *branch*
>   **where** *branch-city* = 'Brooklyn')

The subquery

> (**select** *assets*
> **from** *branch*
> **where** *branch-city* = 'Brooklyn')

generates the set of all asset values for all branches in Brooklyn. The > **some** comparison in the **where** clause of the outer **select** is true if the *assets* value of the tuple is greater than at least one member of the set of all asset values for branches in Brooklyn.

SQL also allows $<$ **some**, $<=$ **some**, $>=$ **some**, $=$ **some**, and $<>$ **some** comparisons. As an exercise, verify that $=$ **some** is identical to **in**, whereas $<>$ **some** is *not* the same as **not in**. The keyword **any** is synonymous to **some** in SQL. Early versions of SQL allowed only **any**. Later versions added the alternative **some** to avoid the linguistic ambiguity of the word *any* in English.

Now we modify our query slightly. Let us find the names of all branches that have an asset value greater than that of each branch in Brooklyn. The construct $>$ **all** corresponds to the phrase "greater than all." Using this construct, we write the query as follows:

> **select** *branch-name*
> **from** *branch*
> **where** *assets* $>$ **all** (**select** *assets*
> > **from** *branch*
> > **where** *branch-city* $=$ 'Brooklyn')

As it does for **some**, SQL also allows $<$ **all**, $<=$ **all**, $>=$ **all**, $=$ **all**, and $<>$ **all** comparisons. As an exercise, verify that $<>$ **all** is identical to **not in**.

As another example of set comparisons, consider the query "Find the branch that has the highest average balance." Aggregate functions cannot be composed in SQL. Thus, we cannot use **max** (**avg** $(\ldots)$). Instead, we can follow this strategy: We begin by writing a query to find all average balances, and then nest it as a subquery of a larger query that finds those branches for which the average balance is greater than or equal to all average balances:

> **select** *branch-name*
> **from** *account*
> **group by** *branch-name*
> **having avg** (*balance*) $>=$ **all** (**select avg** (*balance*)
> > **from** *account*
> > **group by** *branch-name*)

4.6.3   Test for Empty Relations

SQL includes a feature for testing whether a subquery has any tuples in its result. The **exists** construct returns the value **true** if the argument subquery is nonempty. Using the **exists** construct, we can write the query "Find all customers who have both an account and a loan at the bank" in still another way:

> **select** *customer-name*
> **from** *borrower*
> **where exists** (**select** *
> > **from** *depositor*
> > **where** *depositor.customer-name* $=$ *borrower.customer-name*)

We can test for the nonexistence of tuples in a subquery by using the **not exists** construct. We can use the **not exists** construct to simulate the set containment (that is, superset) operation: We can write "relation A contains relation B" as "**not exists** (B **except** A)." (Although it is not part of the SQL-92 and SQL:1999 standards, the **contains** operator was present in some early relational systems.) To illustrate the **not exists** operator, consider again the query "Find all customers who have an account at all the branches located in Brooklyn." For each customer, we need to see whether the set of all branches at which that customer has an account contains the set of all branches in Brooklyn. Using the **except** construct, we can write the query as follows:

> **select distinct** *S.customer-name*
> **from** *depositor* **as** *S*
> **where not exists** ((**select** *branch-name*
>   **from** *branch*
>   **where** *branch-city* = 'Brooklyn')
>   **except**
>   (**select** *R.branch-name*
>   **from** *depositor* **as** *T, account* **as** *R*
>   **where** *T.account-number* = *R.account-number* **and**
>   *S.customer-name* = *T.customer-name*))

Here, the subquery

> (**select** *branch-name*
> **from** *branch*
> **where** *branch-city* = 'Brooklyn')

finds all the branches in Brooklyn. The subquery

> (**select** *R.branch-name*
> **from** *depositor* **as** *T, account* **as** *R*
> **where** *T.account-number* = *R.account-number* **and**
>   *S.customer-name* = *T.customer-name*)

finds all the branches at which customer *S.customer-name* has an account. Thus, the outer **select** takes each customer and tests whether the set of all branches at which that customer has an account contains the set of all branches located in Brooklyn.

In queries that contain subqueries, a scoping rule applies for tuple variables. In a subquery, according to the rule, it is legal to use only tuple variables defined in the subquery itself or in any query that contains the subquery. If a tuple variable is defined both locally in a subquery and globally in a containing query, the local definition applies. This rule is analogous to the usual scoping rules used for variables in programming languages.

4.6.4   Test for the Absence of Duplicate Tuples

SQL includes a feature for testing whether a subquery has any duplicate tuples in its result. The **unique** construct returns the value **true** if the argument subquery contains no duplicate tuples. Using the **unique** construct, we can write the query "Find all customers who have at most one account at the Perryridge branch" as follows:

> **select** *T.customer-name*
> **from** *depositor* **as** *T*
> **where unique** (**select** *R.customer-name*
>   **from** *account, depositor* **as** *R*
>   **where** *T.customer-name* = *R.customer-name* **and**
>   *R.account-number* = *account.account-number* **and**
>   *account.branch-name* = 'Perryridge')

We can test for the existence of duplicate tuples in a subquery by using the **not unique** construct. To illustrate this construct, consider the query "Find all customers who have at least two accounts at the Perryridge branch," which we write as

> **select distinct** *T.customer-name*
> **from** *depositor T*
> **where not unique** (**select** *R.customer-name*
>   **from** *account, depositor* **as** *R*
>   **where** *T.customer-name* = *R.customer-name* **and**
>   *R.account-number* = *account.account-number* **and**
>   *account.branch-name* = 'Perryridge')

Formally, the **unique** test on a relation is defined to fail if and only if the relation contains two tuples t_1 and t_2 such that $t_1 = t_2$. Since the test $t_1 = t_2$ fails if any of the fields of t_1 or t_2 are null, it is possible for **unique** to be true even if there are multiple copies of a tuple, as long as at least one of the attributes of the tuple is null.

4.7 Views

We define a view in SQL by using the **create view** command. To define a view, we must give the view a name and must state the query that computes the view. The form of the **create view** command is

> **create view** *v* **as** <query expression>

where <query expression> is any legal query expression. The view name is represented by *v*. Observe that the notation that we used for view definition in the relational algebra (see Chapter 3) is based on that of SQL.

As an example, consider the view consisting of branch names and the names of customers who have either an account or a loan at that branch. Assume that we want this view to be called *all-customer*. We define this view as follows:

```
create view all-customer as
    (select branch-name, customer-name
     from depositor, account
     where depositor.account-number = account.account-number)
  union
    (select branch-name, customer-name
     from borrower, loan
     where borrower.loan-number = loan.loan-number)
```

The attribute names of a view can be specified explicitly as follows:

```
create view branch-total-loan(branch-name, total-loan) as
select branch-name, sum(amount)
from loan
groupby branch-name
```

The preceding view gives for each branch the sum of the amounts of all the loans at the branch. Since the expression **sum**(*amount*) does not have a name, the attribute name is specified explicitly in the view definition.

View names may appear in any place that a relation name may appear. Using the view *all-customer*, we can find all customers of the Perryridge branch by writing

```
select customer-name
from all-customer
where branch-name = 'Perryridge'
```

4.8 Complex Queries

Complex queries are often hard or impossible to write as a single SQL block or a union/intersection/difference of SQL blocks. (An SQL block consists of a single **select from where** statement, possibly with **groupby** and **having** clauses.) We study here two ways of composing multiple SQL blocks to express a complex query: derived relations and the **with** clause.

4.8.1 Derived Relations

SQL allows a subquery expression to be used in the **from** clause. If we use such an expression, then we must give the result relation a name, and we can rename the attributes. We do this renaming by using the **as** clause. For example, consider the subquery

```
(select branch-name, avg (balance)
 from account
 group by branch-name)
as result (branch-name, avg-balance)
```

This subquery generates a relation consisting of the names of all branches and their corresponding average account balances. The subquery result is named *result*, with the attributes *branch-name* and *avg-balance*.

To illustrate the use of a subquery expression in the **from** clause, consider the query "Find the average account balance of those branches where the average account balance is greater than \$1200." We wrote this query in Section 4.4 by using the **having** clause. We can now rewrite this query, without using the **having** clause, as follows:

> **select** *branch-name, avg-balance*
> **from** (**select** *branch-name*, **avg** (*balance*)
>   **from** *account*
>   **group by** *branch-name*)
>   **as** *branch-avg (branch-name, avg-balance)*
> **where** *avg-balance* > 1200

Note that we do not need to use the **having** clause, since the subquery in the **from** clause computes the average balance, and its result is named as *branch-avg*; we can use the attributes of *branch-avg* directly in the **where** clause.

As another example, suppose we wish to find the maximum across all branches of the total balance at each branch. The **having** clause does not help us in this task, but we can write this query easily by using a subquery in the **from** clause, as follows:

> **select max**(*tot-balance*)
> **from** (**select** *branch-name*, **sum**(*balance*)
>   **from** *account*
>   **group by** *branch-name*) as *branch-total (branch-name, tot-balance)*

4.8.2 The with Clause

Complex queries are much easier to write and to understand if we structure them by breaking them into smaller views that we then combine, just as we structure programs by breaking their task into procedures. However, unlike a procedure definition, a **create view** clause creates a view definition in the database, and the view definition stays in the database until a command **drop view** *view-name* is executed.

The **with** clause provides a way of defining a temporary view whose definition is available only to the query in which the **with** clause occurs. Consider the following query, which selects accounts with the maximum balance; if there are many accounts with the same maximum balance, all of them are selected.

> **with** *max-balance* (*value*) **as**
>   **select max**(*balance*)
>   **from** *account*
> **select** *account-number*
> **from** *account, max-balance*
> **where** *account.balance* = *max-balance.value*

The **with** clause introduced in SQL:1999, is currently supported only by some databases.

We could have written the above query by using a nested subquery in either the **from** clause or the **where** clause. However, using nested subqueries would have made the query harder to read and understand. The **with** clause makes the query logic clearer; it also permits a view definition to be used in multiple places within a query.

For example, suppose we want to find all branches where the total account deposit is less than the average of the total account deposits at all branches. We can write the query using the **with** clause as follows.

> **with** *branch-total (branch-name, value)* **as**
>   **select** *branch-name,* **sum**(*balance*)
>   **from** *account*
>   **group by** *branch-name*
> **with** *branch-total-avg*(*value*) **as**
>   **select avg**(*value*)
>   **from** *branch-total*
> **select** *branch-name*
> **from** *branch-total, branch-total-avg*
> **where** *branch-total.value* $>=$ *branch-total-avg.value*

We can, of course, create an equivalent query without the **with** clause, but it would be more complicated and harder to understand. You can write the equivalent query as an exercise.

4.9   Modification of the Database

We have restricted our attention until now to the extraction of information from the database. Now, we show how to add, remove, or change information with SQL.

4.9.1   Deletion

A delete request is expressed in much the same way as a query. We can delete only whole tuples; we cannot delete values on only particular attributes. SQL expresses a deletion by

> **delete from** *r*
> **where** *P*

where *P* represents a predicate and *r* represents a relation. The **delete** statement first finds all tuples *t* in *r* for which *P(t)* is true, and then deletes them from *r*. The **where** clause can be omitted, in which case all tuples in *r* are deleted.

Note that a **delete** command operates on only one relation. If we want to delete tuples from several relations, we must use one **delete** command for each relation.

The predicate in the **where** clause may be as complex as a **select** command's **where** clause. At the other extreme, the **where** clause may be empty. The request

delete from *loan*

deletes all tuples from the *loan* relation. (Well-designed systems will seek confirmation from the user before executing such a devastating request.)

Here are examples of SQL delete requests:

- Delete all account tuples in the Perryridge branch.

delete from *account*
where *branch-name* = 'Perryridge'

- Delete all loans with loan amounts between $1300 and $1500.

delete from *loan*
where *amount* **between** 1300 **and** 1500

- Delete all account tuples at every branch located in Needham.

delete from *account*
where *branch-name* **in** (**select** *branch-name*
     from *branch*
     where *branch-city* = 'Needham')

This **delete** request first finds all branches in Needham, and then deletes all *account* tuples pertaining to those branches.

Note that, although we may delete tuples from only one relation at a time, we may reference any number of relations in a **select-from-where** nested in the **where** clause of a **delete**. The **delete** request can contain a nested **select** that references the relation from which tuples are to be deleted. For example, suppose that we want to delete the records of all accounts with balances below the average at the bank. We could write

delete from *account*
where *balance* < (**select avg** (*balance*)
     from *account*)

The **delete** statement first tests each tuple in the relation *account* to check whether the account has a balance less than the average at the bank. Then, all tuples that fail the test—that is, represent an account with a lower-than-average balance—are deleted. Performing all the tests before performing any deletion is important—if some tuples are deleted before other tuples have been tested, the average balance may change, and the final result of the **delete** would depend on the order in which the tuples were processed!

4.9.2 Insertion

To insert data into a relation, we either specify a tuple to be inserted or write a query whose result is a set of tuples to be inserted. Obviously, the attribute values for inserted tuples must be members of the attribute's domain. Similarly, tuples inserted must be of the correct arity.

The simplest **insert** statement is a request to insert one tuple. Suppose that we wish to insert the fact that there is an account A-9732 at the Perryridge branch and that is has a balance of $1200. We write

> **insert into** *account*
>   **values** ('A-9732', 'Perryridge', 1200)

In this example, the values are specified in the order in which the corresponding attributes are listed in the relation schema. For the benefit of users who may not remember the order of the attributes, SQL allows the attributes to be specified as part of the **insert** statement. For example, the following SQL **insert** statements are identical in function to the preceding one:

> **insert into** *account* (*account-number, branch-name, balance*)
>   **values** ('A-9732', 'Perryridge', 1200)

> **insert into** *account* (*branch-name, account-number, balance*)
>   **values** ('Perryridge', 'A-9732', 1200)

More generally, we might want to insert tuples on the basis of the result of a query. Suppose that we want to present a new $200 savings acocunt as a gift to all loan customers of the Perryridge branch, for each loan they have. Let the loan number serve as the account number for the savings account. We write

> **insert into** *account*
>   **select** *loan-number, branch-name*, 200
>   **from** *loan*
>   **where** *branch-name* = 'Perryridge'

Instead of specifying a tuple as we did earlier in this section, we use a **select** to specify a set of tuples. SQL evaluates the **select** statement first, giving a set of tuples that is then inserted into the *account* relation. Each tuple has a *loan-number* (which serves as the account number for the new account), a *branch-name* (Perryridge), and an initial balance of the new account ($200).

We also need to add tuples to the *depositor* relation; we do so by writing

> **insert into** *depositor*
>   **select** *customer-name, loan-number*
>   **from** *borrower, loan*
>   **where** *borrower.loan-number* = *loan.loan-number* **and**
>   *branch-name* = 'Perryridge'

This query inserts a tuple (*customer-name, loan-number*) into the *depositor* relation for each *customer-name* who has a loan in the Perryridge branch with loan number *loan-number*.

It is important that we evaluate the **select** statement fully before we carry out any insertions. If we carry out some insertions even as the **select** statement is being evaluated, a request such as

> **insert into** *account*
> **select** *
> **from** *account*

might insert an infinite number of tuples! The request would insert the first tuple in *account* again, creating a second copy of the tuple. Since this second copy is part of *account* now, the **select** statement may find it, and a third copy would be inserted into *account*. The **select** statement may then find this third copy and insert a fourth copy, and so on, forever. Evaluating the **select** statement completely before performing insertions avoids such problems.

Our discussion of the **insert** statement considered only examples in which a value is given for every attribute in inserted tuples. It is possible, as we saw in Chapter 3, for inserted tuples to be given values on only some attributes of the schema. The remaining attributes are assigned a null value denoted by *null*. Consider the request

> **insert into** *account*
> **values** ('A-401', *null*, 1200)

We know that account A-401 has $1200, but the branch name is not known. Consider the query

> **select** *account-number*
> **from** *account*
> **where** *branch-name* = 'Perryridge'

Since the branch at which account A-401 is maintained is not known, we cannot determine whether it is equal to "Perryridge".

We can prohibit the insertion of null values on specified attributes by using the SQL DDL, which we discuss in Section 4.11.

4.9.3 Updates

In certain situations, we may wish to change a value in a tuple without changing *all* values in the tuple. For this purpose, the **update** statement can be used. As we could for **insert** and **delete**, we can choose the tuples to be updated by using a query.

Suppose that annual interest payments are being made, and all balances are to be increased by 5 percent. We write

> **update** *account*
> **set** *balance* = *balance* * 1.05

The preceding update statement is applied once to each of the tuples in *account* relation.

If interest is to be paid only to accounts with a balance of $1000 or more, we can write

> **update** *account*
> **set** *balance* = *balance* * 1.05
> **where** *balance* >= 1000

In general, the **where** clause of the **update** statement may contain any construct legal in the **where** clause of the **select** statement (including nested **select**s). As with **insert** and **delete**, a nested **select** within an **update** statement may reference the relation that is being updated. As before, SQL first tests all tuples in the relation to see whether they should be updated, and carries out the updates afterward. For example, we can write the request "Pay 5 percent interest on accounts whose balance is greater than average" as follows:

> **update** *account*
> **set** *balance* = *balance* * 1.05
> **where** *balance* > **select avg** (*balance*)
>   **from** *account*

Let us now suppose that all accounts with balances over $10,000 receive 6 percent interest, whereas all others receive 5 percent. We could write two **update** statements:

> **update** *account*
> **set** *balance* = *balance* * 1.06
> **where** *balance* > 10000

> **update** *account*
> **set** *balance* = *balance* * 1.05
> **where** *balance* <= 10000

Note that, as we saw in Chapter 3, the order of the two **update** statements is important. If we changed the order of the two statements, an account with a balance just under $10,000 would receive 11.3 percent interest.

SQL provides a **case** construct, which we can use to perform both the updates with a single **update** statement, avoiding the problem with order of updates.

> **update** *account*
> **set** *balance* = **case**
>   **when** *balance* <= 10000 **then** *balance* * 1.05
>   **else** *balance* * 1.06
>   **end**

The general form of the case statement is as follows.

case
    when $pred_1$ **then** $result_1$
    when $pred_2$ **then** $result_2$

    . . .

    when $pred_n$ **then** $result_n$
    else $result_0$
end

The operation returns $result_i$, where i is the first of $pred_1, pred_2, \ldots, pred_n$ that is satisfied; if none of the predicates is satisfied, the operation returns $result_0$. Case statements can be used in any place where a value is expected.

4.9.4 Update of a View

The view-update anomaly that we discussed in Chapter 3 exists also in SQL. As an illustration, consider the following view definition:

    create view *loan-branch* **as**
        select *branch-name, loan-number*
      from *loan*

Since SQL allows a view name to appear wherever a relation name is allowed, we can write

    insert into *loan-branch*
        values ('Perryridge', 'L-307')

SQL represents this insertion by an insertion into the relation *loan*, since *loan* is the actual relation from which the view *loan-branch* is constructed. We must, therefore, have some value for *amount*. This value is a null value. Thus, the preceding **insert** results in the insertion of the tuple

    ('L-307', 'Perryridge', *null*)

into the *loan* relation.

    As we saw in Chapter 3, the view-update anomaly becomes more difficult to handle when a view is defined in terms of several relations. As a result, many SQL-based database systems impose the following constraint on modifications allowed through views:

- A modification is permitted through a view only if the view in question is defined in terms of one relation of the actual relational database—that is, of the logical-level database.

Under this constraint, the **update**, **insert**, and **delete** operations would be forbidden on the example view *all-customer* that we defined previously.

4.9.5   Transactions

A **transaction** consists of a sequence of query and/or update statements. The SQL standard specifies that a transaction begins implicitly when an SQL statement is executed. One of the following SQL statements must end the transaction:

- **Commit work** commits the current transaction; that is, it makes the updates performed by the transaction become permanent in the database. After the transaction is committed, a new transaction is automatically started.

- **Rollback work** causes the current transaction to be rolled back; that is, it undoes all the updates performed by the SQL statements in the transaction. Thus, the database state is restored to what it was before the first statement of the transaction was executed.

The keyword **work** is optional in both the statements.

Transaction rollback is useful if some error condition is detected during execution of a transaction. Commit is similar, in a sense, to saving changes to a document that is being edited, while rollback is similar to quitting the edit session without saving changes. Once a transaction has executed **commit work**, its effects can no longer be undone by **rollback work**. The database system guarantees that in the event of some failure, such as an error in one of the SQL statements, a power outage, or a system crash, a transaction's effects will be rolled back if it has not yet executed **commit work**. In the case of power outage or other system crash, the rollback occurs when the system restarts.

For instance, to transfer money from one account to another we need to update two account balances. The two update statements would form a transaction. An error while a transaction executes one of its statements would result in undoing of the effects of the earlier statements of the transaction, so that the database is not left in a partially updated state. We study further properties of transactions in Chapter 15.

If a program terminates without executing either of these commands, the updates are either committed or rolled back. The standard does not specify which of the two happens, and the choice is implementation dependent. In many SQL implementations, by default each SQL statement is taken to be a transaction on its own, and gets committed as soon as it is executed. Automatic commit of individual SQL statements must be turned off if a transaction consisting of multiple SQL statements needs to be executed. How to turn off automatic commit depends on the specific SQL implementation.

A better alternative, which is part of the SQL:1999 standard (but supported by only some SQL implementations currently), is to allow multiple SQL statements to be enclosed between the keywords **begin atomic** ... **end**. All the statements between the keywords then form a single transaction.

4.10   Joined Relations**

SQL provides not only the basic Cartesian-product mechanism for joining tuples of relations found in its earlier versions, but, SQL also provides various other mecha-

loan-number	branch-name	amount
L-170	Downtown	3000
L-230	Redwood	4000
L-260	Perryridge	1700

loan

customer-name	loan-number
Jones	L-170
Smith	L-230
Hayes	L-155

borrower

Figure 4.1   The *loan* and *borrower* relations.

nisms for joining relations, including condition joins and natural joins, as well as various forms of outer joins. These additional operations are typically used as subquery expressions in the **from** clause.

4.10.1 Examples

We illustrate the various join operations by using the relations *loan* and *borrower* in Figure 4.1. We start with a simple example of inner joins. Figure 4.2 shows the result of the expression

$$loan \text{ inner join } borrower \text{ on } loan.loan\text{-}number = borrower.loan\text{-}number$$

The expression computes the theta join of the *loan* and the *borrower* relations, with the join condition being *loan.loan-number = borrower.loan-number*. The attributes of the result consist of the attributes of the left-hand-side relation followed by the attributes of the right-hand-side relation.

Note that the attribute *loan-number* appears twice in the figure—the first occurrence is from *loan*, and the second is from *borrower*. The SQL standard does not require attribute names in such results to be unique. An **as** clause should be used to assign unique names to attributes in query and subquery results.

We rename the result relation of a join and the attributes of the result relation by using an **as** clause, as illustrated here:

$$loan \text{ inner join } borrower \text{ on } loan.loan\text{-}number = borrower.loan\text{-}number$$
$$\textbf{as } lb(loan\text{-}number, branch, amount, cust, cust\text{-}loan\text{-}num)$$

We rename the second occurrence of *loan-number* to *cust-loan-num*. The ordering of the attributes in the result of the join is important for the renaming.

Next, we consider an example of the **left outer join** operation:

$$loan \text{ left outer join } borrower \text{ on } loan.loan\text{-}number = borrower.loan\text{-}number$$

loan-number	branch-name	amount	customer-name	loan-number
L-170	Downtown	3000	Jones	L-170
L-230	Redwood	4000	Smith	L-230

Figure 4.2   The result of *loan* **inner join** *borrower* **on**
loan.loan-number = borrower.loan-number.

loan-number	branch-name	amount	customer-name	loan-number
L-170	Downtown	3000	Jones	L-170
L-230	Redwood	4000	Smith	L-230
L-260	Perryridge	1700	*null*	*null*

Figure 4.3   The result of *loan* **left outer join** *borrower* **on**
$loan.loan\text{-}number = borrower.loan\text{-}number$.

We can compute the left outer join operation logically as follows. First, compute the result of the inner join as before. Then, for every tuple t in the left-hand-side relation *loan* that does not match any tuple in the right-hand-side relation *borrower* in the inner join, add a tuple r to the result of the join: The attributes of tuple r that are derived from the left-hand-side relation are filled in with the values from tuple t, and the remaining attributes of r are filled with null values. Figure 4.3 shows the resultant relation. The tuples (L-170, Downtown, 3000) and (L-230, Redwood, 4000) join with tuples from *borrower* and appear in the result of the inner join, and hence in the result of the left outer join. On the other hand, the tuple (L-260, Perryridge, 1700) did not match any tuple from *borrower* in the inner join, and hence a tuple (L-260, Perryridge, 1700, null, null) is present in the result of the left outer join.

Finally, we consider an example of the **natural join** operation:

loan **natural inner join** *borrower*

This expression computes the natural join of the two relations. The only attribute name common to *loan* and *borrower* is *loan-number*. Figure 4.4 shows the result of the expression. The result is similar to the result of the inner join with the **on** condition in Figure 4.2, since they have, in effect, the same join condition. However, the attribute *loan-number* appears only once in the result of the natural join, whereas it appears twice in the result of the join with the **on** condition.

4.10.2   Join Types and Conditions

In Section 4.10.1, we saw examples of the join operations permitted in SQL. Join operations take two relations and return another relation as the result. Although outer-join expressions are typically used in the **from** clause, they can be used anywhere that a relation can be used.

Each of the variants of the join operations in SQL consists of a *join type* and a *join condition*. The join condition defines which tuples in the two relations match and what attributes are present in the result of the join. The join type defines how tuples in each

loan-number	branch-name	amount	customer-name
L-170	Downtown	3000	Jones
L-230	Redwood	4000	Smith

Figure 4.4   The result of *loan* **natural inner join** *borrower*.

Join types
inner join
left outer join
right outer join
full outer join

Join Conditions
natural
on < predicate>
using $(A_1, A_1, \ldots, A_n)$

Figure 4.5   Join types and join conditions.

relation that do not match any tuple in the other relation (based on the join condition) are treated. Figure 4.5 shows some of the allowed join types and join conditions. The first join type is the inner join, and the other three are the outer joins. Of the three join conditions, we have seen the **natural** join and the **on** condition before, and we shall discuss the **using** condition, later in this section.

The use of a join condition is mandatory for outer joins, but is optional for inner joins (if it is omitted, a Cartesian product results). Syntactically, the keyword **natural** appears before the join type, as illustrated earlier, whereas the **on** and **using** conditions appear at the end of the join expression. The keywords **inner** and **outer** are optional, since the rest of the join type enables us to deduce whether the join is an inner join or an outer join.

The meaning of the join condition **natural**, in terms of which tuples from the two relations match, is straightforward. The ordering of the attributes in the result of a natural join is as follows. The join attributes (that is, the attributes common to both relations) appear first, in the order in which they appear in the left-hand-side relation. Next come all nonjoin attributes of the left-hand-side relation, and finally all nonjoin attributes of the right-hand-side relation.

The **right outer join** is symmetric to the **left outer join**. Tuples from the right-hand-side relation that do not match any tuple in the left-hand-side relation are padded with nulls and are added to the result of the right outer join.

Here is an example of combining the natural join condition with the right outer join type:

loan **natural right outer join** *borrower*

Figure 4.6 shows the result of this expression. The attributes of the result are defined by the join type, which is a natural join; hence, *loan-number* appears only once. The first two tuples in the result are from the inner natural join of *loan* and *borrower*. The tuple (Hayes, L-155) from the right-hand-side relation does not match any tuple from the left-hand-side relation *loan* in the natural inner join. Hence, the tuple (L-155, null, null, Hayes) appears in the join result.

The join condition **using**$(A_1, A_2, \ldots, A_n)$ is similar to the natural join condition, except that the join attributes are the attributes $A_1, A_2, \ldots, A_n$, rather than all attributes that are common to both relations. The attributes $A_1, A_2, \ldots, A_n$ must consist of only attributes that are common to both relations, and they appear only once in the result of the join.

The **full outer join** is a combination of the left and right outer-join types. After the operation computes the result of the inner join, it extends with nulls tuples from

loan-number	branch-name	amount	customer-name
L-170	Downtown	3000	Jones
L-230	Redwood	4000	Smith
L-155	*null*	*null*	Hayes

Figure 4.6   The result of *loan* **natural right outer join** *borrower*.

the left-hand-side relation that did not match with any from the right-hand-side, and adds them to the result. Similarly, it extends with nulls tuples from the right-hand-side relation that did not match with any tuples from the left-hand-side relation and adds them to the result.

For example, Figure 4.7 shows the result of the expression

$$loan \text{ \textbf{full outer join} } borrower \text{ \textbf{using} (loan-number)}$$

As another example of the use of the outer-join operation, we can write the query "Find all customers who have an account but no loan at the bank" as

> **select** *d-CN*
> **from** (*depositor* **left outer join** *borrower*
>   **on** *depositor.customer-name = borrower.customer-name*)
>   **as** *db*1 (*d-CN, account-number, b-CN, loan-number*)
> **where** *b-CN* **is** *null*

Similarly, we can write the query "Find all customers who have either an account or a loan (but not both) at the bank," with natural full outer joins as:

> **select** *customer-name*
> **from** (*depositor* **natural full outer join** *borrower*)
> **where** *account-number* **is** *null* **or** *loan-number* **is** *null*

SQL-92 also provides two other join types, called **cross join** and **union join**. The first is equivalent to an inner join without a join condition; the second is equivalent to a full outer join on the "false" condition—that is, where the inner join is empty.

loan-number	branch-name	amount	customer-name
L-170	Downtown	3000	Jones
L-230	Redwood	4000	Smith
L-260	Perryridge	1700	*null*
L-155	*null*	*null*	Hayes

Figure 4.7   The result of *loan* **full outer join** *borrower* **using**(*loan-number*).

4.11 Data-Definition Language

In most of our discussions of SQL and relational databases, we have accepted a set of relations as given. Of course, the set of relations in a database must be specified to the system by means of a data definition language (DDL).

The SQL DDL allows specification of not only a set of relations, but also information about each relation, including

- The schema for each relation

- The domain of values associated with each attribute

- The integrity constraints

- The set of indices to be maintained for each relation

- The security and authorization information for each relation

- The physical storage structure of each relation on disk

We discuss here schema definition and domain values; we defer discussion of the other SQL DDL features to Chapter 6.

4.11.1 Domain Types in SQL

The SQL standard supports a variety of built-in domain types, including:

- **char**(n): A fixed-length character string with user-specified length n. The full form, **character**, can be used instead.

- **varchar**(n): A variable-length character string with user-specified maximum length n. The full form, **character varying**, is equivalent.

- **int**: An integer (a finite subset of the integers that is machine dependent). The full form, **integer**, is equivalent.

- **smallint**: A small integer (a machine-dependent subset of the integer domain type).

- **numeric**(p, d): A fixed-point number with user-specified precision. The number consists of p digits (plus a sign), and d of the p digits are to the right of the decimal point. Thus, **numeric**(3,1) allows 44.5 to be stored exactly, but neither 444.5 or 0.32 can be stored exactly in a field of this type.

- **real, double precision**: Floating-point and double-precision floating-point numbers with machine-dependent precision.

- **float**(n): A floating-point number, with precision of at least n digits.

- **date**: A calendar date containing a (four-digit) year, month, and day of the month.

- **time**: The time of day, in hours, minutes, and seconds. A variant, **time**(p), can be used to specify the number of fractional digits for seconds (the default being 0). It is also possible to store time zone information along with the time.

- **timestamp**: A combination of **date** and **time**. A variant, **timestamp**(p), can be used to specify the number of fractional digits for seconds (the default here being 6).

Date and time values can be specified like this:

date '2001-04-25'
time '09:30:00'
timestamp '2001-04-25 10:29:01.45'

Dates must be specified in the format year followed by month followed by day, as shown. The seconds field of **time** or **timestamp** can have a fractional part, as in the timestamp above. We can use an expression of the form **cast** e **as** t to convert a character string (or string valued expression) e to the type t, where t is one of **date, time,** or **timestamp**. The string must be in the appropriate format as illustrated at the beginning of this paragraph.

To extract individual fields of a **date** or **time** value d, we can use **extract** (*field* **from** d), where *field* can be one of **year, month, day, hour, minute**, or **second**.

SQL allows comparison operations on all the domains listed here, and it allows both arithmetic and comparison operations on the various numeric domains. SQL also provides a data type called **interval**, and it allows computations based on dates and times and on intervals. For example, if x and y are of type **date**, then $x - y$ is an interval whose value is the number of days from date x to date y. Similarly, adding or subtracting an interval to a date or time gives back a date or time, respectively.

It is often useful to compare values from **compatible** domains. For example, since every small integer is an integer, a comparison $x < y$, where x is a small integer and y is an integer (or vice versa), makes sense. We make such a comparison by casting small integer x as an integer. A transformation of this sort is called a **type coercion**. Type coercion is used routinely in common programming languages, as well as in database systems.

As an illustration, suppose that the domain of *customer-name* is a character string of length 20, and the domain of *branch-name* is a character string of length 15. Although the string lengths might differ, standard SQL will consider the two domains compatible.

As we discussed in Chapter 3, the *null* value is a member of all domains. For certain attributes, however, null values may be inappropriate. Consider a tuple in the *customer* relation where *customer-name* is null. Such a tuple gives a street and city for an anonymous customer; thus, it does not contain useful information. In cases such as this, we wish to forbid null values, and we do so by restricting the domain of *customer-name* to exclude null values.

SQL allows the domain declaration of an attribute to include the specification **not null** and thus prohibits the insertion of a null value for this attribute. Any database modification that would cause a null to be inserted in a **not null** domain generates an error diagnostic. There are many situations where we want to avoid null values. In particular, it is essential to prohibit null values in the primary key of a relation schema. Thus, in our bank example, in the *customer* relation, we must prohibit a null value for the attribute *customer-name*, which is the primary key for *customer*.

4.11.2 Schema Definition in SQL

We define an SQL relation by using the **create table** command:

$$\textbf{create table } r(A_1D_1, A_2D_2, \ldots, A_nD_n,$$
$$\langle \text{integrity-constraint}_1 \rangle,$$
$$\ldots,$$
$$\langle \text{integrity-constraint}_k \rangle)$$

where r is the name of the relation, each A_i is the name of an attribute in the schema of relation r, and D_i is the domain type of values in the domain of attribute A_i. The allowed integrity constraints include

- **primary key** $(A_{j_1}, A_{j_2}, \ldots, A_{j_m})$: The **primary key** specification says that attributes $A_{j_1}, A_{j_2}, \ldots, A_{j_m}$ form the primary key for the relation. The primary key attributes are required to be *non-null* and *unique*; that is, no tuple can have a null value for a primary key attribute, and no two tuples in the relation can be equal on all the primary-key attributes.[1] Although the primary key specification is optional, it is generally a good idea to specify a primary key for each relation.

- **check**(P): The **check** clause specifies a predicate P that must be satisfied by every tuple in the relation.

The **create table** command also includes other integrity constraints, which we shall discuss in Chapter 6.

Figure 4.8 presents a partial SQL DDL definition of our bank database. Note that, as in earlier chapters, we do not attempt to model precisely the real world in the bank-database example. In the real world, multiple people may have the same name, so *customer-name* would not be a primary key *customer*; a *customer-id* would more likely be used as a primary key. We use *customer-name* as a primary key to keep our database schema simple and short.

If a newly inserted or modified tuple in a relation has null values for any primary-key attribute, or if the tuple has the same value on the primary-key attributes as does another tuple in the relation, SQL flags an error and prevents the update. Similarly, it flags an error and prevents the update if the **check** condition on the tuple fails.

By default **null** is a legal value for every attribute in SQL, unless the attribute is specifically stated to be **not null**. An attribute can be declared to be not null in the following way:

account-number **char**(10) **not null**

---

1. In SQL-89, primary-key attributes were not implicitly declared to be **not null**; an explicit **not null** declaration was required.

```
create table customer
    (customer-name    char(20),
     customer-street  char(30),
     customer-city    char(30),
     primary key (customer-name))

create table branch
    (branch-name      char(15),
     branch-city      char(30),
     assets           integer,
     primary key (branch-name),
     check (assets >= 0))

create table account
    (account-number   char(10),
     branch-name      char(15),
     balance          integer,
     primary key (account-number),
     check (balance >= 0))

create table depositor
    (customer-name    char(20),
     account-number   char(10),
     primary key (customer-name, account-number))
```

Figure 4.8   SQL data definition for part of the bank database.

SQL also supports an integrity constraint

$$\textbf{unique } (A_{j_1}, A_{j_2}, \ldots, A_{j_m})$$

The **unique** specification says that attributes $A_{j_1}, A_{j_2}, \ldots, A_{j_m}$ form a candidate key; that is, no two tuples in the relation can be equal on all the primary-key attributes. However, candidate key attributes are permitted to be null unless they have explicitly been declared to be **not null**. Recall that a null value does not equal any other value. The treatment of nulls here is the same as that of the **unique** construct defined in Section 4.6.4.

A common use of the **check** clause is to ensure that attribute values satisfy specified conditions, in effect creating a powerful type system. For instance, the **check** clause in the **create table** command for relation *branch* checks that the value of **assets** is nonnegative. As another example, consider the following:

```
create table student
    (name             char(15)  not null,
     student-id       char(10),
     degree-level     char(15),
     primary key (student-id),
     check (degree-level in ('Bachelors', 'Masters', 'Doctorate')))
```

Here, we use the **check** clause to simulate an enumerated type, by specifying that *degree-level* must be one of 'Bachelors', 'Masters', or 'Doctorate'. We consider more general forms of **check** conditions, as well as a class of constraints called referential integrity constraints, in Chapter 6.

A newly created relation is empty initially. We can use the **insert** command to load data into the relation. Many relational-database products have special bulk loader utilities to load an initial set of tuples into a relation.

To remove a relation from an SQL database, we use the **drop table** command. The **drop table** command deletes all information about the dropped relation from the database. The command

$$\textbf{drop table } r$$

is a more drastic action than

$$\textbf{delete from } r$$

The latter retains relation r, but deletes all tuples in r. The former deletes not only all tuples of r, but also the schema for r. After r is dropped, no tuples can be inserted into r unless it is re-created with the **create table** command.

We use the **alter table** command to add attributes to an existing relation. All tuples in the relation are assigned *null* as the value for the new attribute. The form of the **alter table** command is

$$\textbf{alter table } r \textbf{ add } A \ D$$

where r is the name of an existing relation, A is the name of the attribute to be added, and D is the domain of the added attribute. We can drop attributes from a relation by the command

$$\textbf{alter table } r \textbf{ drop } A$$

where r is the name of an existing relation, and A is the name of an attribute of the relation. Many database systems do not support dropping of attributes, although they will allow an entire table to be dropped.

4.12 Embedded SQL

SQL provides a powerful declarative query language. Writing queries in SQL is usually much easier than coding the same queries in a general-purpose programming language. However, a programmer must have access to a database from a general-purpose programming language for at least two reasons:

1. Not all queries can be expressed in SQL, since SQL does not provide the full expressive power of a general-purpose language. That is, there exist queries that can be expressed in a language such as C, Java, or Cobol that cannot be expressed in SQL. To write such queries, we can embed SQL within a more powerful language.

SQL is designed so that queries written in it can be optimized automatically and executed efficiently—and providing the full power of a programming language makes automatic optimization exceedingly difficult.

2. Nondeclarative actions—such as printing a report, interacting with a user, or sending the results of a query to a graphical user interface—cannot be done from within SQL. Applications usually have several components, and querying or updating data is only one component; other components are written in general-purpose programming languages. For an integrated application, the programs written in the programming language must be able to access the database.

The SQL standard defines embeddings of SQL in a variety of programming languages, such as C, Cobol, Pascal, Java, PL/I, and Fortran. A language in which SQL queries are embedded is referred to as a *host* language, and the SQL structures permitted in the host language constitute *embedded* SQL.

Programs written in the host language can use the embedded SQL syntax to access and update data stored in a database. This embedded form of SQL extends the programmer's ability to manipulate the database even further. In embedded SQL, all query processing is performed by the database system, which then makes the result of the query available to the program one tuple (record) at a time.

An embedded SQL program must be processed by a special preprocessor prior to compilation. The preprocessor replaces embedded SQL requests with host-language declarations and procedure calls that allow run-time execution of the database accesses. Then, the resulting program is compiled by the host-language compiler. To identify embedded SQL requests to the preprocessor, we use the EXEC SQL statement; it has the form

EXEC SQL <embedded SQL statement > END-EXEC

The exact syntax for embedded SQL requests depends on the language in which SQL is embedded. For instance, a semicolon is used instead of END-EXEC when SQL is embedded in C. The Java embedding of SQL (called SQLJ) uses the syntax

SQL { <embedded SQL statement > };

We place the statement SQL INCLUDE in the program to identify the place where the preprocessor should insert the special variables used for communication between the program and the database system. Variables of the host language can be used within embedded SQL statements, but they must be preceded by a colon (:) to distinguish them from SQL variables.

Embedded SQL statements are similar in form to the SQL statements that we described in this chapter. There are, however, several important differences, as we note here.

To write a relational query, we use the **declare cursor** statement. The result of the query is not yet computed. Rather, the program must use the **open** and **fetch** commands (discussed later in this section) to obtain the result tuples.

Consider the banking schema that we have used in this chapter. Assume that we have a host-language variable *amount*, and that we wish to find the names and cities of residence of customers who have more than *amount* dollars in any account. We can write this query as follows:

> EXEC SQL
>> **declare** *c* **cursor for**
>> **select** *customer-name, customer-city*
>> **from** *depositor, customer, account*
>> **where** *depositor.customer-name* = *customer.customer-name* **and**
>>> *account.account-number* = *depositor.account-number* **and**
>>> *account.balance* > *:amount*
>
> END-EXEC

The variable *c* in the preceding expression is called a *cursor* for the query. We use this variable to identify the query in the **open** statement, which causes the query to be evaluated, and in the **fetch** statement, which causes the values of one tuple to be placed in host-language variables.

The **open** statement for our sample query is as follows:

EXEC SQL **open** *c* END-EXEC

This statement causes the database system to execute the query and to save the results within a temporary relation. The query has a host-language variable (*:amount*); the query uses the value of the variable at the time the **open** statement was executed.

If the SQL query results in an error, the database system stores an error diagnostic in the SQL communication-area (SQLCA) variables, whose declarations are inserted by the SQL INCLUDE statement.

An embedded SQL program executes a series of **fetch** statements to retrieve tuples of the result. The **fetch** statement requires one host-language variable for each attribute of the result relation. For our example query, we need one variable to hold the *customer-name* value and another to hold the *customer-city* value. Suppose that those variables are *cn* and *cc*, respectively. Then the statement:

EXEC SQL **fetch** *c* **into** :*cn*, :*cc* END-EXEC

produces a tuple of the result relation. The program can then manipulate the variables *cn* and *cc* by using the features of the host programming language.

A single **fetch** request returns only one tuple. To obtain all tuples of the result, the program must contain a loop to iterate over all tuples. Embedded SQL assists the programmer in managing this iteration. Although a relation is conceptually a set, the tuples of the result of a query are in some fixed physical order. When the program executes an **open** statement on a cursor, the cursor is set to point to the first tuple of the result. Each time it executes a **fetch** statement, the cursor is updated to point to the next tuple of the result. When no further tuples remain to be processed, the variable SQLSTATE in the SQLCA is set to '02000' (meaning "no data"). Thus, we can use a **while** loop (or equivalent loop) to process each tuple of the result.

We must use the **close** statement to tell the database system to delete the temporary relation that held the result of the query. For our example, this statement takes the form

EXEC SQL close c END-EXEC

SQLJ, the Java embedding of SQL, provides a variation of the above scheme, where Java iterators are used in place of cursors. SQLJ associates the results of a query with an iterator, and the next() method of the Java iterator interface can be used to step through the result tuples, just as the preceding examples use **fetch** on the cursor.

Embedded SQL expressions for database modification (**update**, **insert**, and **delete**) do not return a result. Thus, they are somewhat simpler to express. A database-modification request takes the form

EXEC SQL < any valid update, insert, or delete> END-EXEC

Host-language variables, preceded by a colon, may appear in the SQL database-modification expression. If an error condition arises in the execution of the statement, a diagnostic is set in the SQLCA.

Database relations can also be updated through cursors. For example, if we want to add 100 to the *balance* attribute of every *account* where the branch name is "Perryridge", we could declare a cursor as follows.

declare *c* **cursor for**
select *
from *account*
where *branch-name* = 'Perryridge'
for update

We then iterate through the tuples by performing **fetch** operations on the cursor (as illustrated earlier), and after fetching each tuple we execute the following code

update *account*
set *balance* = *balance* + 100
where current of *c*

Embedded SQL allows a host-language program to access the database, but it provides no assistance in presenting results to the user or in generating reports. Most commercial database products include tools to assist application programmers in creating user interfaces and formatted reports. We discuss such tools in Chapter 5 (Section 5.3).

4.13 Dynamic SQL

The *dynamic SQL* component of SQL allows programs to construct and submit SQL queries at run time. In contrast, embedded SQL statements must be completely present at compile time; they are compiled by the embedded SQL preprocessor. Using dynamic SQL, programs can create SQL queries as strings at run time (perhaps based on input from the user) and can either have them executed immediately or have them *prepared* for subsequent use. Preparing a dynamic SQL statement compiles it, and subsequent uses of the prepared statement use the compiled version.

SQL defines standards for embedding dynamic SQL calls in a host language, such as C, as in the following example.

> **char** * *sqlprog* = "**update** *account* **set** *balance* = *balance* *1.05*
>   **where** *account-number* = ?"
> EXEC SQL **prepare** *dynprog* **from** :*sqlprog*;
> **char** *account*[10] = "A-101";
> EXEC SQL **execute** *dynprog* **using** :*account*;

The dynamic SQL program contains a ?, which is a place holder for a value that is provided when the SQL program is executed.

However, the syntax above requires extensions to the language or a preprocessor for the extended language. An alternative that is very widely used is to use an application program interface to send SQL queries or updates to a database system, and not make any changes in the programming language itself.

In the rest of this section, we look at two standards for connecting to an SQL database and performing queries and updates. One, ODBC, is an application program interface for the C language, while the other, JDBC, is an application program interface for the Java language.

To understand these standards, we need to understand the concept of SQL sessions. The user or application *connects* to an SQL server, establishing a session; executes a series of statements; and finally *disconnects* the session. Thus, all activities of the user or application are in the context of an SQL session. In addition to the normal SQL commands, a session can also contain commands to *commit* the work carried out in the session, or to *rollback* the work carried out in the session.

4.13.1   ODBC**

The **Open DataBase Connectivity** (ODBC) standard defines a way for an application program to communicate with a database server. ODBC defines an **application program interface (API)** that applications can use to open a connection with a database, send queries and updates, and get back results. Applications such as graphical user interfaces, statistics packages, and spreadsheets can make use of the same ODBC API to connect to any database server that supports ODBC.

Each database system supporting ODBC provides a library that must be linked with the client program. When the client program makes an ODBC API call, the code in the library communicates with the server to carry out the requested action, and fetch results.

Figure 4.9 shows an example of C code using the ODBC API. The first step in using ODBC to communicate with a server is to set up a connection with the server. To do so, the program first allocates an SQL environment, then a database connection handle. ODBC defines the types HENV, HDBC, and RETCODE. The program then opens the database connection by using SQLConnect. This call takes several parameters, in-

```
int ODBCexample()
{
    RETCODE error;
    HENV env; /* environment */
    HDBC conn; /* database connection */

    SQLAllocEnv(&env);
    SQLAllocConnect(env, &conn);
    SQLConnect(conn, "aura.bell-labs.com", SQL_NTS, "avi", SQL_NTS,
                "avipasswd", SQL_NTS);
    {
        char branchname[80];
        float balance;
        int lenOut1, lenOut2;
        HSTMT stmt;

        SQLAllocStmt(conn, &stmt);
        char * sqlquery = "select branch_name, sum (balance)
                        from account
                        group by branch_name";
        error = SQLExecDirect(stmt, sqlquery, SQL_NTS);
        if (error == SQL_SUCCESS) {
            SQLBindCol(stmt, 1, SQL_C_CHAR, branchname , 80, &lenOut1);
            SQLBindCol(stmt, 2, SQL_C_FLOAT, &balance, 0 , &lenOut2);
            while (SQLFetch(stmt) >= SQL_SUCCESS) {
                printf (" %s %g\n", branchname, balance);
            }
        }
    }
    SQLFreeStmt(stmt, SQL_DROP);
    SQLDisconnect(conn);
    SQLFreeConnect(conn);
    SQLFreeEnv(env);
}
```

Figure 4.9   ODBC code example.

cluding the connection handle, the server to which to connect, the user identifier, and the password for the database. The constant SQL_NTS denotes that the previous argument is a null-terminated string.

Once the connection is set up, the program can send SQL commands to the database by using SQLExecDirect C language variables can be bound to attributes of the query result, so that when a result tuple is fetched using SQLFetch, its attribute values are stored in corresponding C variables. The SQLBindCol function does this task; the second argument identifies the position of the attribute in the query result, and the third argument indicates the type conversion required from SQL to C. The next argument gives the address of the variable. For variable-length types like character arrays, the last two arguments give the maximum length of the variable and a location where the actual length is to be stored when a tuple is fetched. A negative value returned for the length field indicates that the value is **null**.

The SQLFetch statement is in a **while** loop that gets executed until SQLFetch returns a value other than SQL_SUCCESS. On each fetch, the program stores the values in C variables as specified by the calls on SQLBindCol and prints out these values.

At the end of the session, the program frees the statement handle, disconnects from the database, and frees up the connection and SQL environment handles. Good programming style requires that the result of every function call must be checked to make sure there are no errors; we have omitted most of these checks for brevity.

It is possible to create an SQL statement with parameters; for example, consider the statement insert into account values(?,?,?). The question marks are placeholders for values which will be supplied later. The above statement can be "prepared," that is, compiled at the database, and repeatedly executed by providing actual values for the placeholders—in this case, by providing an account number, branch name, and balance for the relation *account*.

ODBC defines functions for a variety of tasks, such as finding all the relations in the database and finding the names and types of columns of a query result or a relation in the database.

By default, each SQL statement is treated as a separate transaction that is committed automatically. The call SQLSetConnectOption(conn, SQL_AUTOCOMMIT, 0) turns off automatic commit on connection conn, and transactions must then be committed explicitly by SQLTransact(conn, SQL_COMMIT) or rolled back by SQLTransact(conn, SQL_ROLLBACK).

The more recent versions of the ODBC standard add new functionality. Each version defines *conformance levels*, which specify subsets of the functionality defined by the standard. An ODBC implementation may provide only core level features, or it may provide more advanced (level 1 or level 2) features. Level 1 requires support for fetching information about the catalog, such as information about what relations are present and the types of their attributes. Level 2 requires further features, such as ability to send and retrieve arrays of parameter values and to retrieve more detailed catalog information.

The more recent SQL standards (SQL-92 and SQL:1999) define a **call level interface (CLI)** that is similar to the ODBC interface, but with some minor differences.

4.13.2   JDBC**

The **JDBC** standard defines an API that Java programs can use to connect to database servers. (The word JDBC was originally an abbreviation for "Java Database Connectivity", but the full form is no longer used.) Figure 4.10 shows an example Java program that uses the JDBC interface. The program must first open a connection to a database, and can then execute SQL statements, but before opening a connection, it loads the appropriate drivers for the database by using Class.forName. The first parameter to the getConnection call specifies the machine name where the server

```
public static void JDBCexample(String dbid, String userid, String passwd)
{
    try
    {
        Class.forName ("oracle.jdbc.driver.OracleDriver");
        Connection conn = DriverManager.getConnection(
                "jdbc:oracle:thin: @ aura.bell-labs.com:2000:bankdb",
                userid, passwd);
        Statement stmt = conn.createStatement();
        try {
            stmt.executeUpdate(
                    "insert into account values('A-9732', 'Perryridge', 1200)");
        } catch (SQLException sqle)
        {
            System.out.println("Could not insert tuple. " + sqle);
        }
        ResultSet rset = stmt.executeQuery(
                "select branch_name, avg (balance)
                from account
                group by branch_name");
        while (rset.next()) {
            System.out.println(rset.getString("branch_name") + " " +
                    rset.getFloat(2));
        }
        stmt.close();
        conn.close();
    }
    catch (SQLException sqle)
    {
        System.out.println("SQLException : " + sqle);
    }
}
```

Figure 4.10   An example of JDBC code.

runs (in our example, aura.bell-labs.com), the port number it uses for communication (in our example, 2000). The parameter also specifies which schema on the server is to be used (in our example, bankdb), since a database server may support multiple schemas. The first parameter also specifies the protocol to be used to communicate with the database (in our example, jdbc:oracle:thin:). Note that JDBC specifies only the API, not the communication protocol. A JDBC driver may support multiple protocols, and we must specify one supported by both the database and the driver. The other two arguments to **getConnection** are a user identifier and a password.

The program then creates a statement handle on the connection and uses it to execute an SQL statement and get back results. In our example, stmt.executeUpdate executes an update statement. The try { ... } catch { ... } construct permits us to

```
PreparedStatement pStmt = conn.prepareStatement(
                    "insert into account values(?,?,?)");
pStmt.setString(1, "A-9732");
pStmt.setString(2, "Perryridge");
pStmt.setInt(3, 1200);
pStmt.executeUpdate();
pStmt.setString(1, "A-9733");
pStmt.executeUpdate();
```

Figure 4.11   Prepared statements in JDBC code.

catch any exceptions (error conditions) that arise when JDBC calls are made, and print an appropriate message to the user.

The program can execute a query by using stmt.executeQuery. It can retrieve the set of rows in the result into a ResultSet and fetch them one tuple at a time using the next() function on the result set. Figure 4.10 shows two ways of retrieving the values of attributes in a tuple: using the name of the attribute (*branch-name*) and using the position of the attribute (2, to denote the second attribute).

We can also create a prepared statement in which some values are replaced by "?", thereby specifying that actual values will be provided later. We can then provide the values by using setString(). The database can compile the query when it is prepared, and each time it is executed (with new values), the database can reuse the previously compiled form of the query. The code fragment in Figure 4.11 shows how prepared statements can be used.

JDBC provides a number of other features, such as **updatable result sets**. It can create an updatable result set from a query that performs a selection and/or a projection on a database relation. An update to a tuple in the result set then results in an update to the corresponding tuple of the database relation. JDBC also provides an API to examine database schemas and to find the types of attributes of a result set.

For more information about JDBC, refer to the bibliographic information at the end of the chapter.

4.14   Other SQL Features ✶✶

The SQL language has grown over the past two decades from a simple language with a few features to a rather complex language with features to satisfy many different types of users. We covered the basics of SQL earlier in this chapter. In this section we introduce the reader to some of the more complex features of SQL.

4.14.1   Schemas, Catalogs, and Environments

To understand the motivation for schemas and catalogs, consider how files are named in a file system. Early file systems were flat; that is, all files were stored in a single directory. Current generation file systems of course have a directory structure, with files stored within subdirectories. To name a file uniquely, we must specify the full path name of the file, for example, /users/avi/db-book/chapter4.tex.

Like early file systems, early database systems also had a single name space for all relations. Users had to coordinate to make sure they did not try to use the same name for different relations. Contemporary database systems provide a three-level hierarchy for naming relations. The top level of the hierarchy consists of **catalogs**, each of which can contain **schemas**. SQL objects such as relations and views are contained within a **schema**.

In order to perform any actions on a database, a user (or a program) must first *connect* to the database. The user must provide the user name and usually, a secret password for verifying the identity of the user, as we saw in the ODBC and JDBC examples in Sections 4.13.1 and 4.13.2. Each user has a default catalog and schema, and the combination is unique to the user. When a user connects to a database system, the default catalog and schema are set up for for the connection; this corresponds to the current directory being set to the user's home directory when the user logs into an operating system.

To identify a relation uniquely, a three-part name must be used, for example,

catalog5.bank-schema.account

We may omit the catalog component, in which case the catalog part of the name is considered to be the default catalog for the connection. Thus if catalog5 is the default catalog, we can use bank-schema.account to identify the same relation uniquely. Further, we may also omit the schema name, and the schema part of the name is again considered to be the default schema for the connection. Thus we can use just account if the default catalog is catalog5 and the default schema is bank-schema.

With multiple catalogs and schemas available, different applications and different users can work independently without worrying about name clashes. Moreover, multiple versions of an application—one a production version, other test versions—can run on the same database system.

The default catalog and schema are part of an **SQL environment** that is set up for each connection. The environment additionally contains the user identifier (also referred to as the *authorization identifier*). All the usual SQL statements, including the DDL and DML statements, operate in the context of a schema. We can create and drop schemas by means of **create schema** and **drop schema** statements. Creation and dropping of catalogs is implementation dependent and not part of the SQL standard.

4.14.2   Procedural Extensions and Stored Procedures

SQL provides a **module** language, which allows procedures to be defined in SQL. A module typically contains multiple SQL procedures. Each procedure has a name, optional arguments, and an SQL statement. An extension of the SQL-92 standard language also permits procedural constructs, such as **for**, **while**, and **if-then-else**, and compound SQL statements (multiple SQL statements between a **begin** and an **end**).

We can store procedures in the database and then execute them by using the **call** statement. Such procedures are also called **stored procedures**. Stored procedures are particularly useful because they permit operations on the database to be made available to external applications, without exposing any of the internal details of the database.

Chapter 9 covers procedural extensions of SQL as well as many other new features of SQL:1999.

4.15 Summary

- Commercial database systems do not use the terse, formal query languages covered in Chapter 3. The widely used SQL language, which we studied in this chapter, is based on the formal relational algebra, but includes much "syntactic sugar."

- SQL includes a variety of language constructs for queries on the database. All the relational-algebra operations, including the extended relational-algebra operations, can be expressed by SQL. SQL also allows ordering of query results by sorting on specified attributes.

- View relations can be defined as relations containing the result of queries. Views are useful for hiding unneeded information, and for collecting together information from more than one relation into a single view.

- Temporary views defined by using the **with** clause are also useful for breaking up complex queries into smaller and easier-to-understand parts.

- SQL provides constructs for updating, inserting, and deleting information. A transaction consists of a sequence of operations, which must appear to be atomic. That is, all the operations are carried out successfully, or none is carried out. In practice, if a transaction cannot complete successfully, any partial actions it carried out are undone.

- Modifications to the database may lead to the generation of null values in tuples. We discussed how nulls can be introduced, and how the SQL query language handles queries on relations containing null values.

- The SQL data definition language is used to create relations with specified schemas. The SQL DDL supports a number of types including **date** and **time** types. Further details on the SQL DDL, in particular its support for integrity constraints, appear in Chapter 6.

- SQL queries can be invoked from host languages, via embedded and dynamic SQL. The ODBC and JDBC standards define application program interfaces to access SQL databases from C and Java language programs. Increasingly, programmers use these APIs to access databases.

- We also saw a brief overview of some advanced features of SQL, such as procedural extensions, catalogs, schemas and stored procedures.

Review Terms

- DDL: data definition language
- DML: data manipulation language
- **select** clause
- **from** clause
- **where** clause
- **as** clause
- Tuple variable
- **order** by clause
- Duplicates
- Set operations
  - □ **union, intersect, except**
- Aggregate functions
  - □ **avg, min, max, sum, count**
  - □ **group by**
- Null values
  - □ Truth value "unknown"
- Nested subqueries
- Set operations
  - □ $\{<, <=, >, >=\}$ { **some, all** }
  - □ **exists**
  - □ **unique**

- Views
- Derived relations (in **from** clause)
- **with** clause
- Database modification
  - □ **delete, insert, update**
  - □ View update
- Join types
  - □ Inner and outer join
  - □ left, right and full outer join
  - □ natural, using, and on
- Transaction
- Atomicity
- Index
- Schema
- Domains
- Embedded SQL
- Dynamic SQL
- ODBC
- JDBC
- Catalog
- Stored procedures

Exercises

4.1 Consider the insurance database of Figure 4.12, where the primary keys are underlined. Construct the following SQL queries for this relational database.

    a. Find the total number of people who owned cars that were involved in accidents in 1989.

    b. Find the number of accidents in which the cars belonging to "John Smith" were involved.

    c. Add a new accident to the database; assume any values for required attributes.

    d. Delete the Mazda belonging to "John Smith".

    e. Update the damage amount for the car with license number "AABB2000" in the accident with report number "AR2197" to $3000.

4.2 Consider the employee database of Figure 4.13, where the primary keys are underlined. Give an expression in SQL for each of the following queries.

    a. Find the names of all employees who work for First Bank Corporation.

person (*driver-id#*, *name*, *address*)
car (*license*, *model*, *year*)
accident (*report-number*, *date*, *location*)
owns (*driver-id#*, *license*)
participated (*driver-id*, *car*, *report-number*, *damage-amount*)

Figure 4.12   Insurance database.

employee (*employee-name*, *street*, *city*)
works (*employee-name*, *company-name*, *salary*)
company (*company-name*, *city*)
manages (*employee-name*, *manager-name*)

Figure 4.13   Employee database.

  b. Find the names and cities of residence of all employees who work for First Bank Corporation.
  c. Find the names, street addresses, and cities of residence of all employees who work for First Bank Corporation and earn more than $10,000.
  d. Find all employees in the database who live in the same cities as the companies for which they work.
  e. Find all employees in the database who live in the same cities and on the same streets as do their managers.
  f. Find all employees in the database who do not work for First Bank Corporation.
  g. Find all employees in the database who earn more than each employee of Small Bank Corporation.
  h. Assume that the companies may be located in several cities. Find all companies located in every city in which Small Bank Corporation is located.
  i. Find all employees who earn more than the average salary of all employees of their company.
  j. Find the company that has the most employees.
  k. Find the company that has the smallest payroll.
  l. Find those companies whose employees earn a higher salary, on average, than the average salary at First Bank Corporation.

4.3 Consider the relational database of Figure 4.13. Give an expression in SQL for each of the following queries.

  a. Modify the database so that Jones now lives in Newtown.
  b. Give all employees of First Bank Corporation a 10 percent raise.
  c. Give all managers of First Bank Corporation a 10 percent raise.
  d. Give all managers of First Bank Corporation a 10 percent raise unless the salary becomes greater than $100,000; in such cases, give only a 3 percent raise.
  e. Delete all tuples in the *works* relation for employees of Small Bank Corporation.

4.4 Let the following relation schemas be given:

$$R = (A, B, C)$$
$$S = (D, E, F)$$

Let relations $r(R)$ and $s(S)$ be given. Give an expression in SQL that is equivalent to each of the following queries.

  a. $\Pi_A(r)$
  b. $\sigma_{B=17}(r)$
  c. $r \times s$
  d. $\Pi_{A,F}(\sigma_{C=D}(r \times s))$

4.5 Let $R = (A, B, C)$, and let r_1 and r_2 both be relations on schema R. Give an expression in SQL that is equivalent to each of the following queries.

  a. $r_1 \cup r_2$
  b. $r_1 \cap r_2$
  c. $r_1 - r_2$
  d. $\Pi_{AB}(r_1) \bowtie \Pi_{BC}(r_2)$

4.6 Let $R = (A, B)$ and $S = (A, C)$, and let $r(R)$ and $s(S)$ be relations. Write an expression in SQL for each of the queries below:

  a. $\{<a> \mid \exists b \, (<a, b> \in r \wedge b = 17)\}$
  b. $\{<a, b, c> \mid <a, b> \in r \wedge <a, c> \in s\}$
  c. $\{<a> \mid \exists c \, (<a, c> \in s \wedge \exists b_1, b_2 \, (<a, b_1> \in r \wedge <c, b_2> \in r \wedge b_1 > b_2))\}$

4.7 Show that, in SQL, $<>$ **all** is identical to **not in**.

4.8 Consider the relational database of Figure 4.13. Using SQL, define a view consisting of *manager-name* and the average salary of all employees who work for that manager. Explain why the database system should not allow updates to be expressed in terms of this view.

4.9 Consider the SQL query

> **select** $p.a1$
> **from** $p, r1, r2$
> **where** $p.a1 = r1.a1$ **or** $p.a1 = r2.a1$

Under what conditions does the preceding query select values of $p.a1$ that are either in $r1$ or in $r2$? Examine carefully the cases where one of $r1$ or $r2$ may be empty.

4.10 Write an SQL query, without using a **with** clause, to find all branches where the total account deposit is less than the average total account deposit at all branches,

  a. Using a nested query in the **from** clauser.

b. Using a nested query in a **having** clause.

4.11 Suppose that we have a relation *marks(student-id, score)* and we wish to assign grades to students based on the score as follows: grade F if $score < 40$, grade C if $40 \leq score < 60$, grade B if $60 \leq score < 80$, and grade A if $80 \leq score$. Write SQL queries to do the following:

   a. Display the grade for each student, based on the *marks* relation.
   b. Find the number of students with each grade.

4.12 SQL-92 provides an n-ary operation called **coalesce**, which is defined as follows: **coalesce**$(A_1, A_2, \ldots, A_n)$ returns the first nonnull A_i in the list $A_1, A_2, \ldots, A_n$, and returns null if all of $A_1, A_2, \ldots, A_n$ are null. Show how to express the **coalesce** operation using the **case** operation.

4.13 Let a and b be relations with the schemas $A(name, address, title)$ and $B(name, address, salary)$, respectively. Show how to express a **natural full outer join** b using the **full outer join** operation with an **on** condition and the **coalesce** operation. Make sure that the result relation does not contain two copies of the attributes *name* and *address*, and that the solution is correct even if some tuples in a and b have null values for attributes *name* or *address*.

4.14 Give an SQL schema definition for the employee database of Figure 4.13. Choose an appropriate domain for each attribute and an appropriate primary key for each relation schema.

4.15 Write **check** conditions for the schema you defined in Exercise 4.14 to ensure that:

   a. Every employee works for a company located in the same city as the city in which the employee lives.
   b. No employee earns a salary higher than that of his manager.

4.16 Describe the circumstances in which you would choose to use embedded SQL rather than SQL alone or only a general-purpose programming language.

Bibliographical Notes

The original version of SQL, called Sequel 2, is described by Chamberlin et al. [1976]. Sequel 2 was derived from the languages Square Boyce et al. [1975] and Chamberlin and Boyce [1974]. The American National Standard SQL-86 is described in ANSI [1986]. The IBM Systems Application Architecture definition of SQL is defined by IBM [1987]. The official standards for SQL-89 and SQL-92 are available as ANSI [1989] and ANSI [1992], respectively.

Textbook descriptions of the SQL-92 language include Date and Darwen [1997], Melton and Simon [1993], and Cannan and Otten [1993]. Melton and Eisenberg [2000] provides a guide to SQLJ, JDBC, and related technologies. More information on SQLJ and SQLJ software can be obtained from http://www.sqlj.org. Date and Darwen [1997] and Date [1993a] include a critique of SQL-92.

Eisenberg and Melton [1999] provide an overview of SQL:1999. The standard is published as a sequence of five ISO/IEC standards documents, with several more parts describing various extensions under development. Part 1 (SQL/Framework), gives an overview of the other parts. Part 2 (SQL/Foundation) outlines the basics of the language. Part 3 (SQL/CLI) describes the Call-Level Interface. Part 4 (SQL/PSM) describes Persistent Stored Modules, and Part 5 (SQL/Bindings) describes host language bindings. The standard is useful to database implementers but is very hard to read. If you need them, you can purchase them electronically from the Web site http://webstore.ansi.org.

Many database products support SQL features beyond those specified in the standards, and may not support some features of the standard. More information on these features may be found in the SQL user manuals of the respective products. http://java.sun.com/docs/books/tutorial is an excellent source for more (and up-to-date) information on JDBC, and on Java in general. References to books on Java (including JDBC) are also available at this URL. The ODBC API is described in Microsoft [1997] and Sanders [1998].

The processing of SQL queries, including algorithms and performance issues, is discussed in Chapters 13 and 14. Bibliographic references on these matters appear in that chapter.

CHAPTER 5

Other Relational Languages

In Chapter 4, we described SQL—the most influential commercial relational-database language. In this chapter, we study two more languages: QBE and Datalog. Unlike SQL, QBE is a graphical language, where queries *look* like tables. QBE and its variants are widely used in database systems on personal computers. Datalog has a syntax modeled after the Prolog language. Although not used commercially at present, Datalog has been used in several research database systems.

Here, we present fundamental constructs and concepts rather than a complete users' guide for these languages. Keep in mind that individual implementations of a language may differ in details, or may support only a subset of the full language.

In this chapter, we also study forms interfaces and tools for generating reports and analyzing data. While these are not strictly speaking languages, they form the main interface to a database for many users. In fact, most users do not perform explicit querying with a query language at all, and access data only via forms, reports, and other data analysis tools.

5.1 Query-by-Example

Query-by-Example (QBE) is the name of both a data-manipulation language and an early database system that included this language. The QBE database system was developed at IBM's T. J. Watson Research Center in the early 1970s. The QBE data-manipulation language was later used in IBM's Query Management Facility (QMF). Today, many database systems for personal computers support variants of QBE language. In this section, we consider only the data-manipulation language. It has two distinctive features:

1. Unlike most query languages and programming languages, QBE has a **two-dimensional syntax**: Queries *look* like tables. A query in a one-dimensional

language (for example, SQL) *can* be written in one (possibly long) line. A two-dimensional language *requires* two dimensions for its expression. (There is a one-dimensional version of QBE, but we shall not consider it in our discussion).

2. QBE queries are expressed "by example." Instead of giving a procedure for obtaining the desired answer, the user gives an example of what is desired. The system generalizes this example to compute the answer to the query.

Despite these unusual features, there is a close correspondence between QBE and the domain relational calculus.

We express queries in QBE by **skeleton tables**. These tables show the relation schema, as in Figure 5.1. Rather than clutter the display with all skeletons, the user selects those skeletons needed for a given query and fills in the skeletons with **example rows**. An example row consists of constants and *example elements*, which are domain variables. To avoid confusion between the two, QBE uses an underscore character (_) before domain variables, as in _x, and lets constants appear without any qualification.

branch	branch-name	branch-city	assets

customer	customer-name	customer-street	customer-city

loan	loan-number	branch-name	amount

borrower	customer-name	loan-number

account	account-number	branch-name	balance

depositor	customer-name	account-number

Figure 5.1 QBE skeleton tables for the bank example.

This convention is in contrast to those in most other languages, in which constants are quoted and variables appear without any qualification.

5.1.1 Queries on One Relation

Returning to our ongoing bank example, to find all loan numbers at the Perryridge branch, we bring up the skeleton for the *loan* relation, and fill it in as follows:

loan	loan-number	branch-name	amount
	P._x	Perryridge	

This query tells the system to look for tuples in *loan* that have "Perryridge" as the value for the *branch-name* attribute. For each such tuple, the system assigns the value of the *loan-number* attribute to the variable x. It "prints" (actually, displays) the value of the variable x, because the command P. appears in the *loan-number* column next to the variable x. Observe that this result is similar to what would be done to answer the domain-relational-calculus query

$$\{\langle x \rangle \mid \exists \, b, a (\langle x, b, a \rangle \in \, loan \, \land \, b \, = \, \text{"Perryridge"})\}$$

QBE assumes that a blank position in a row contains a unique variable. As a result, if a variable does not appear more than once in a query, it may be omitted. Our previous query could thus be rewritten as

loan	loan-number	branch-name	amount
	P.	Perryridge	

QBE (unlike SQL) performs duplicate elimination automatically. To suppress duplicate elimination, we insert the command ALL. after the P. command:

loan	loan-number	branch-name	amount
	P.ALL.	Perryridge	

To display the entire *loan* relation, we can create a single row consisting of P. in every field. Alternatively, we can use a shorthand notation by placing a single P. in the column headed by the relation name:

loan	loan-number	branch-name	amount
P.			

QBE allows queries that involve arithmetic comparisons (for example, $>$), rather than equality comparisons, as in "Find the loan numbers of all loans with a loan amount of more than \$700":

loan	loan-number	branch-name	amount
	P.		>700

Comparisons can involve only one arithmetic expression on the right-hand side of the comparison operation (for example, $> (\_x +\_y - 20)$). The expression can include both variables and constants. The space on the left-hand side of the comparison operation must be blank. The arithmetic operations that QBE supports are $=, <, \le, >, \ge$, and $\neg$.

Note that requiring the left-hand side to be blank implies that we cannot compare two distinct named variables. We shall deal with this difficulty shortly.

As yet another example, consider the query "Find the names of all branches that are not located in Brooklyn." This query can be written as follows:

branch	branch-name	branch-city	assets
	P.	¬ Brooklyn	

The primary purpose of variables in QBE is to force values of certain tuples to have the same value on certain attributes. Consider the query "Find the loan numbers of all loans made jointly to Smith and Jones":

borrower	customer-name	loan-number
	"Smith"	P._x
	"Jones"	_x

To execute this query, the system finds all pairs of tuples in *borrower* that agree on the *loan-number* attribute, where the value for the *customer-name* attribute is "Smith" for one tuple and "Jones" for the other. The system then displays the value of the *loan-number* attribute.

In the domain relational calculus, the query would be written as

$$\{\langle l \rangle \mid \exists\, x\, (\langle x, l \rangle \in \ borrower\ \wedge\ x = \text{``Smith''})$$

$$\wedge\, \exists\, x\, (\langle x, l \rangle \in \ borrower\ \wedge\ x = \text{``Jones''})\}$$

As another example, consider the query "Find all customers who live in the same city as Jones":

customer	customer-name	customer-street	customer-city
	P._x		_y
	Jones		_y

5.1.2 Queries on Several Relations

QBE allows queries that span several different relations (analogous to Cartesian product or natural join in the relational algebra). The connections among the various relations are achieved through variables that force certain tuples to have the same value on certain attributes. As an illustration, suppose that we want to find the names of all customers who have a loan from the Perryridge branch. This query can be written as

loan	loan-number	branch-name	amount
	_x	Perryridge	

borrower	customer-name	loan-number
	P._y	_x

To evaluate the preceding query, the system finds tuples in *loan* with "Perryridge" as the value for the *branch-name* attribute. For each such tuple, the system finds tuples in *borrower* with the same value for the *loan-number* attribute as the *loan* tuple. It displays the values for the *customer-name* attribute.

We can use a technique similar to the preceding one to write the query "Find the names of all customers who have both an account and a loan at the bank":

depositor	customer-name	account-number
	P._x	

borrower	customer-name	loan-number
	_x	

Now consider the query "Find the names of all customers who have an account at the bank, but who do not have a loan from the bank." We express queries that involve negation in QBE by placing a **not** sign ($\neg$) under the relation name and next to an example row:

depositor	customer-name	account-number
	P._x	

borrower	customer-name	loan-number
$\neg$	_x	

Compare the preceding query with our earlier query "Find the names of all customers who have both an account and a loan at the bank." The only difference is the $\neg$ appearing next to the example row in the *borrower* skeleton. This difference, however, has a major effect on the processing of the query. QBE finds all x values for which

1. There is a tuple in the *depositor* relation whose *customer-name* is the domain variable x.

2. There is no tuple in the *borrower* relation whose *customer-name* is the same as in the domain variable x.

The $\neg$ can be read as "there does not exist."

The fact that we placed the $\neg$ under the relation name, rather than under an attribute name, is important. A $\neg$ under an attribute name is shorthand for $\neq$. Thus, to find all customers who have at least two accounts, we write

depositor	customer-name	account-number
	P._x	_y
	_x	¬ _y

In English, the preceding query reads "Display all *customer-name* values that appear in at least two tuples, with the second tuple having an *account-number* different from the first."

5.1.3 The Condition Box

At times, it is either inconvenient or impossible to express all the constraints on the domain variables within the skeleton tables. To overcome this difficulty, QBE includes a **condition box** feature that allows the expression of general constraints over any of the domain variables. QBE allows logical expressions to appear in a condition box. The logical operators are the words **and** and **or**, or the symbols "&" and "|".

For example, the query "Find the loan numbers of all loans made to Smith, to Jones (or to both jointly)" can be written as

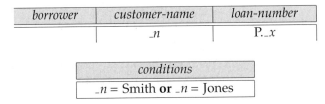

borrower	customer-name	loan-number
	_n	P._x

conditions
_n = Smith **or** _n = Jones

It is possible to express the above query without using a condition box, by using P. in multiple rows. However, queries with P. in multiple rows are sometimes hard to understand, and are best avoided.

As yet another example, suppose that we modify the final query in Section 5.1.2 to be "Find all customers who are not named 'Jones' and who have at least two accounts." We want to include an "$x \neq$ Jones" constraint in this query. We do that by bringing up the condition box and entering the constraint "$x \neg =$ Jones":

conditions
$x \neg =$ Jones

Turning to another example, to find all account numbers with a balance between $1300 and $1500, we write

account	account-number	branch-name	balance
	P.		_x

conditions
_x ≥ 1300
_x ≤ 1500

As another example, consider the query "Find all branches that have assets greater than those of at least one branch located in Brooklyn." This query can be written as

branch	branch-name	branch-city	assets
	P._x		_y
		Brooklyn	_z

conditions
_y > _z

QBE allows complex arithmetic expressions to appear in a condition box. We can write the query "Find all branches that have assets that are at least twice as large as the assets of one of the branches located in Brooklyn" much as we did in the preceding query, by modifying the condition box to

conditions
_y ≥ 2 * _z

To find all account numbers of account with a balance between $1300 and $2000, but not exactly $1500, we write

account	account-number	branch-name	balance
	P.		_x

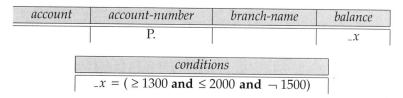

conditions
_x = (≥ 1300 **and** ≤ 2000 **and** ¬ 1500)

QBE uses the **or** construct in an unconventional way to allow comparison with a set of constant values. To find all branches that are located in either Brooklyn or Queens, we write

branch	branch-name	branch-city	assets
	P.	_x	

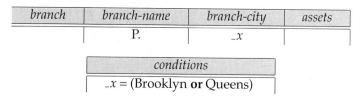

conditions
_x = (Brooklyn **or** Queens)

5.1.4   The Result Relation

The queries that we have written thus far have one characteristic in common: The results to be displayed appear in a single relation schema. If the result of a query includes attributes from several relation schemas, we need a mechanism to display the desired result in a single table. For this purpose, we can declare a temporary *result* relation that includes all the attributes of the result of the query. We print the desired result by including the command P. in only the *result* skeleton table.

As an illustration, consider the query "Find the *customer-name, account-number,* and *balance* for all accounts at the Perryridge branch." In relational algebra, we would construct this query as follows:

1. Join *depositor* and *account.*

2. Project *customer-name, account-number,* and *balance.*

To construct the same query in QBE, we proceed as follows:

1. Create a skeleton table, called *result,* with attributes *customer-name, account-number,* and *balance.* The name of the newly created skeleton table (that is, *result*) must be different from any of the previously existing database relation names.

2. Write the query.

The resulting query is

account	account-number	branch-name	balance
	_y	Perryridge	_z

depositor	customer-name	account-number
	_x	_y

result	customer-name	account-number	balance
P.	_x	_y	_z

5.1.5 Ordering of the Display of Tuples

QBE offers the user control over the order in which tuples in a relation are displayed. We gain this control by inserting either the command AO. (ascending order) or the command DO. (descending order) in the appropriate column. Thus, to list in ascending alphabetic order all customers who have an account at the bank, we write

depositor	customer-name	account-number
	P.AO.	

QBE provides a mechanism for sorting and displaying data in multiple columns. We specify the order in which the sorting should be carried out by including, with each sort operator (AO or DO), an integer surrounded by parentheses. Thus, to list all account numbers at the Perryridge branch in ascending alphabetic order with their respective account balances in descending order, we write

account	account-number	branch-name	balance
	P.AO(1).	Perryridge	P.DO(2).

The command P.AO(1). specifies that the account number should be sorted first; the command P.DO(2). specifies that the balances for each account should then be sorted.

5.1.6 Aggregate Operations

QBE includes the aggregate operators AVG, MAX, MIN, SUM, and CNT. We must post-fix these operators with ALL. to create a multiset on which the aggregate operation is evaluated. The ALL. operator ensures that duplicates are not eliminated. Thus, to find the total balance of all the accounts maintained at the Perryridge branch, we write

account	account-number	branch-name	balance
		Perryridge	P.SUM.ALL.

We use the operator UNQ to specify that we want duplicates eliminated. Thus, to find the total number of customers who have an account at the bank, we write

depositor	customer-name	account-number
	P.CNT.UNQ.	

QBE also offers the ability to compute functions on groups of tuples using the G. operator, which is analogous to SQL's **group by** construct. Thus, to find the average balance at each branch, we can write

account	account-number	branch-name	balance
		P.G.	P.AVG.ALL._x

The average balance is computed on a branch-by-branch basis. The keyword ALL. in the P.AVG.ALL. entry in the *balance* column ensures that all the balances are considered. If we wish to display the branch names in ascending order, we replace P.G. by P.AO.G.

To find the average account balance at only those branches where the average account balance is more than $1200, we add the following condition box:

conditions
AVG.ALL._x > 1200

As another example, consider the query "Find all customers who have accounts at each of the branches located in Brooklyn":

depositor	customer-name	account-number
	P.G._x	_y

account	account-number	branch-name	balance
	_y	_z	

branch	branch-name	branch-city	assets
	_z	Brooklyn	
	_w	Brooklyn	

conditions
CNT.UNQ._z =
CNT.UNQ._w

The domain variable w can hold the value of names of branches located in Brooklyn. Thus, CNT.UNQ._w is the number of distinct branches in Brooklyn. The domain variable z can hold the value of branches in such a way that both of the following hold:

- The branch is located in Brooklyn.

- The customer whose name is x has an account at the branch.

Thus, CNT.UNQ._z is the number of distinct branches in Brooklyn at which customer x has an account. If CNT.UNQ._z = CNT.UNQ._w, then customer x must have an account at all of the branches located in Brooklyn. In such a case, the displayed result includes x (because of the P.).

5.1.7   Modification of the Database

In this section, we show how to add, remove, or change information in QBE.

5.1.7.1   Deletion

Deletion of tuples from a relation is expressed in much the same way as a query. The major difference is the use of D. in place of P. QBE (unlike SQL), lets us delete whole tuples, as well as values in selected columns. When we delete information in only some of the columns, null values, specified by −, are inserted.

We note that a D. command operates on only one relation. If we want to delete tuples from several relations, we must use one D. operator for each relation.

Here are some examples of QBE delete requests:

- Delete customer Smith.

customer	customer-name	customer-street	customer-city
D.	Smith		

- Delete the *branch-city* value of the branch whose name is "Perryridge."

branch	branch-name	branch-city	assets
	Perryridge	D.	

Thus, if before the delete operation the *branch* relation contains the tuple (Perryridge, Brooklyn, 50000), the delete results in the replacement of the preceding tuple with the tuple (Perryridge, $-$, 50000).

- Delete all loans with a loan amount between $1300 and $1500.

loan	loan-number	branch-name	amount
D.	_y		_x

borrower	customer-name	loan-number
D.		_y

conditions
_x = ($\geq$ 1300 **and** $\leq$ 1500)

Note that to delete loans we must delete tuples from both the *loan* and *borrower* relations.

- Delete all accounts at all branches located in Brooklyn.

account	account-number	branch-name	balance
D.	_y	_x	

depositor	customer-name	account-number
D.		_y

branch	branch-name	branch-city	assets
	_x	Brooklyn	

Note that, in expressing a deletion, we can reference relations other than those from which we are deleting information.

5.1.7.2   Insertion

To insert data into a relation, we either specify a tuple to be inserted or write a query whose result is a set of tuples to be inserted. We do the insertion by placing the I. operator in the query expression. Obviously, the attribute values for inserted tuples must be members of the attribute's domain.

The simplest insert is a request to insert one tuple. Suppose that we wish to insert the fact that account A-9732 at the Perryridge branch has a balance of $700. We write

account	account-number	branch-name	balance
I.	A-9732	Perryridge	700

We can also insert a tuple that contains only partial information. To insert information into the *branch* relation about a new branch with name "Capital" and city "Queens," but with a null asset value, we write

branch	branch-name	branch-city	assets
I.	Capital	Queens	

More generally, we might want to insert tuples on the basis of the result of a query. Consider again the situation where we want to provide as a gift, for all loan customers of the Perryridge branch, a new $200 savings account for every loan account that they have, with the loan number serving as the account number for the savings account. We write

account	account-number	branch-name	balance
I.	_x	Perryridge	200

depositor	customer-name	account-number
I.	_y	_x

loan	loan-number	branch-name	amount
	_x	Perryridge	

borrower	customer-name	loan-number
	_y	_x

To execute the preceding insertion request, the system must get the appropriate information from the *borrower* relation, then must use that information to insert the appropriate new tuple in the *depositor* and *account* relations.

5.1.7.3 Updates

There are situations in which we wish to change one value in a tuple without changing *all* values in the tuple. For this purpose, we use the U. operator. As we could for insert and delete, we can choose the tuples to be updated by using a query. QBE, however, does not allow users to update the primary key fields.

Suppose that we want to update the asset value of the of the Perryridge branch to $10,000,000. This update is expressed as

branch	branch-name	branch-city	assets
	Perryridge		U.10000000

The blank field of attribute *branch-city* implies that no updating of that value is required.

The preceding query updates the assets of the Perryridge branch to $10,000,000, regardless of the old value. There are circumstances, however, where we need to update a value by using the previous value. Suppose that interest payments are being made, and all balances are to be increased by 5 percent. We write

account	*account-number*	*branch-name*	*balance*
			U._x * 1.05

This query specifies that we retrieve one tuple at a time from the *account* relation, determine the balance x, and update that balance to $x * 1.05$.

5.1.8   QBE in Microsoft Access

In this section, we survey the QBE version supported by Microsoft Access. While the original QBE was designed for a text-based display environment, Access QBE is designed for a graphical display environment, and accordingly is called **graphical query-by-example (GQBE)**.

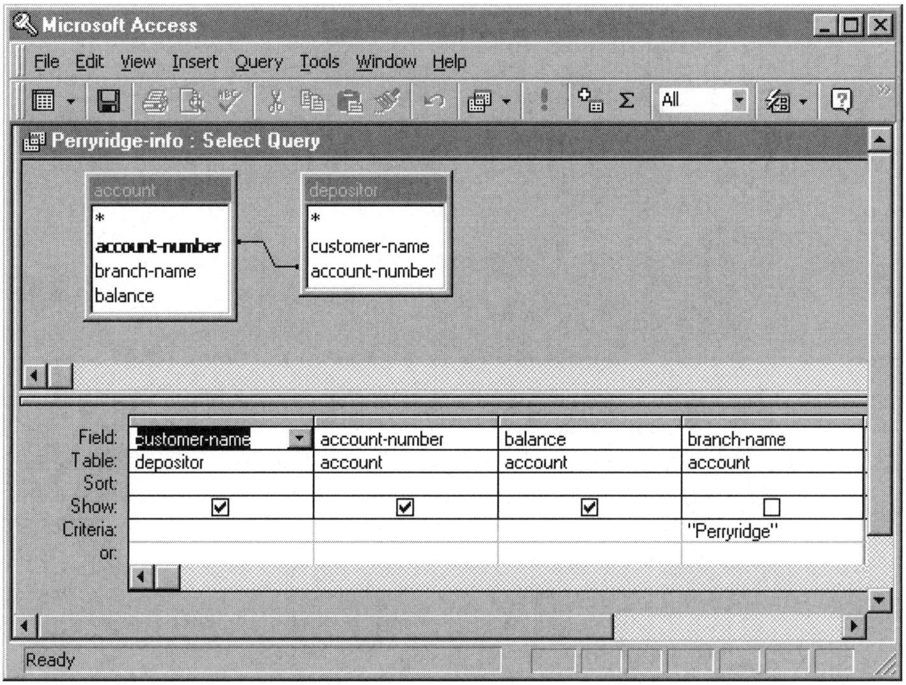

Figure 5.2   An example query in Microsoft Access QBE.

Figure 5.2 shows a sample GQBE query. The query can be described in English as "Find the *customer-name*, *account-number*, and *balance* for all accounts at the Perryridge branch." Section 5.1.4 showed how it is expressed in QBE.

A minor difference in the GQBE version is that the attributes of a table are written one below the other, instead of horizontally. A more significant difference is that the graphical version of QBE uses a line linking attributes of two tables, instead of a shared variable, to specify a join condition.

An interesting feature of QBE in Access is that links between tables are created automatically, on the basis of the attribute name. In the example in Figure 5.2, the two tables *account* and *depositor* were added to the query. The attribute *account-number* is shared between the two selected tables, and the system automatically inserts a link between the two tables. In other words, a natural join condition is imposed by default between the tables; the link can be deleted if it is not desired. The link can also be specified to denote a natural outer-join, instead of a natural join.

Another minor difference in Access QBE is that it specifies attributes to be printed in a separate box, called the **design grid**, instead of using a P. in the table. It also specifies selections on attribute values in the design grid.

Queries involving group by and aggregation can be created in Access as shown in Figure 5.3. The query in the figure finds the name, street, and city of all customers who have more than one account at the bank; we saw the QBE version of the query earlier in Section 5.1.6. The group by attributes as well as the aggregate functions

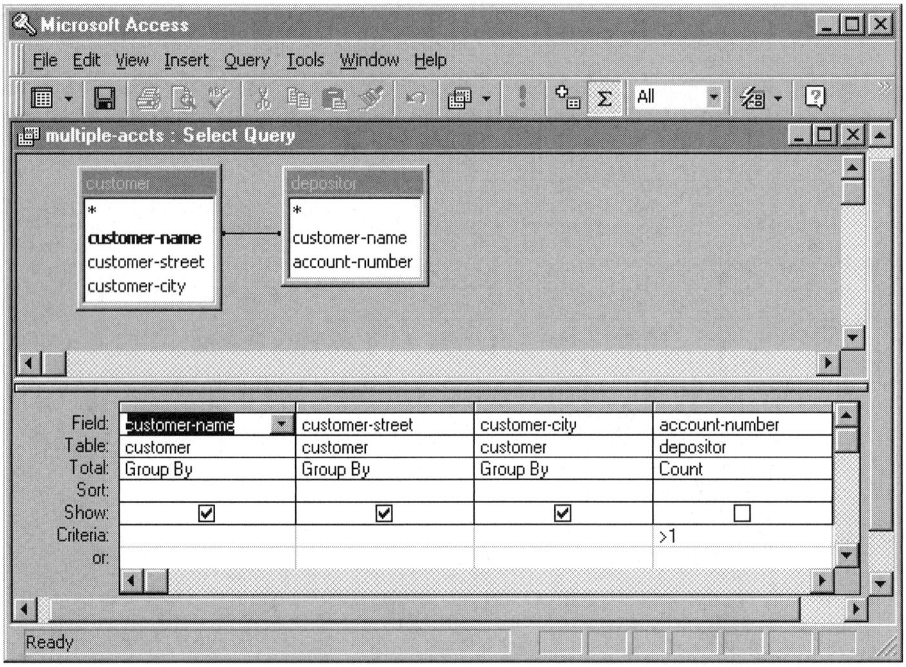

Figure 5.3 An aggregation query in Microsoft Access QBE.

are noted in the design grid. If an attribute is to be printed, it must appear in the design grid, and must be specified in the "Total" row to be either a group by, or have an aggregate function applied to it. SQL has a similar requirement. Attributes that participate in selection conditions but are not to be printed can alternatively be marked as "Where" in the row "Total", indicating that the attribute is neither a group by attribute, nor one to be aggregated on.

Queries are created through a graphical user interface, by first selecting tables. Attributes can then be added to the design grid by dragging and dropping them from the tables. Selection conditions, grouping and aggregation can then be specified on the attributes in the design grid. Access QBE supports a number of other features too, including queries to modify the database through insertion, deletion, or update.

5.2   Datalog

Datalog is a nonprocedural query language based on the logic-programming language Prolog. As in the relational calculus, a user describes the information desired without giving a specific procedure for obtaining that information. The syntax of Datalog resembles that of Prolog. However, the meaning of Datalog programs is defined in a purely declarative manner, unlike the more procedural semantics of Prolog, so Datalog simplifies writing simple queries and makes query optimization easier.

5.2.1   Basic Structure

A Datalog program consists of a set of **rules**. Before presenting a formal definition of Datalog rules and their formal meaning, we consider examples. Consider a Datalog rule to define a view relation $v1$ containing account numbers and balances for accounts at the Perryridge branch with a balance of over \$700:

$$v1(A, B) \ :- account(A, \text{"Perryridge"}, B), B > 700$$

Datalog rules define views; the preceding rule **uses** the relation *account*, and **defines** the view relation $v1$. The symbol :– is read as "if," and the comma separating the "*account*(A, "Perryridge", B)" from "$B > 700$" is read as "and." Intuitively, the rule is understood as follows:

> **for all** A, B
> **if** $(A, \text{"Perryridge"}, B) \in account$ **and** $B > 700$
> **then** $(A, B) \in v1$

Suppose that the relation *account* is as shown in Figure 5.4. Then, the view relation $v1$ contains the tuples in Figure 5.5.

To retrieve the balance of account number A-217 in the view relation $v1$, we can write the following query:

$$? \ v1(\text{"A-217"}, B)$$

The answer to the query is

$$(A\text{-}217, 750)$$

account-number	branch-name	balance
A-101	Downtown	500
A-215	Mianus	700
A-102	Perryridge	400
A-305	Round Hill	350
A-201	Perryridge	900
A-222	Redwood	700
A-217	Perryridge	750

Figure 5.4   The *account* relation.

To get the account number and balance of all accounts in relation *v1*, where the balance is greater than 800, we can write

$$? v1(A, B), B > 800$$

The answer to this query is

$$(A\text{-}201, 900)$$

In general, we need more than one rule to define a view relation. Each rule defines a set of tuples that the view relation must contain. The set of tuples in the view relation is then defined as the union of all these sets of tuples. The following Datalog program specifies the interest rates for accounts:

$$interest\text{-}rate(A, 5) :- account(A, N, B), B < 10000$$
$$interest\text{-}rate(A, 6) :- account(A, N, B), B >= 10000$$

The program has two rules defining a view relation *interest-rate*, whose attributes are the account number and the interest rate. The rules say that, if the balance is less than $10000, then the interest rate is 5 percent, and if the balance is greater than or equal to $10000, the interest rate is 6 percent.

Datalog rules can also use negation. The following rules define a view relation *c* that contains the names of all customers who have a deposit, but have no loan, at the bank:

$$c(N) :- depositor(N,A), \textbf{not } is\text{-}borrower(N)$$
$$is\text{-}borrower(N) :- borrower(N, L),$$

Prolog and most Datalog implementations recognize attributes of a relation by position and omit attribute names. Thus, Datalog rules are compact, compared to SQL

account-number	balance
A-201	900
A-217	750

Figure 5.5   The *v1* relation.

queries. However, when relations have a large number of attributes, or the order or number of attributes of relations may change, the positional notation can be cumbersome and error prone. It is not hard to create a variant of Datalog syntax using named attributes, rather than positional attributes. In such a system, the Datalog rule defining *v1* can be written as

> *v1(account-number A, balance B)* :–
> > *account(account-number A, branch-name* "Perryridge", *balance B),*
> > $B > 700$

Translation between the two forms can be done without significant effort, given the relation schema.

5.2.2   Syntax of Datalog Rules

Now that we have informally explained rules and queries, we can formally define their syntax; we discuss their meaning in Section 5.2.3. We use the same conventions as in the relational algebra for denoting relation names, attribute names, and constants (such as numbers or quoted strings). We use uppercase (capital) letters and words starting with uppercase letters to denote variable names, and lowercase letters and words starting with lowercase letters to denote relation names and attribute names. Examples of constants are 4, which is a number, and "John," which is a string; X and *Name* are variables. A **positive literal** has the form

$$p(t_1, t_2, \ldots, t_n)$$

where p is the name of a relation with n attributes, and $t_1, t_2, \ldots, t_n$ are either constants or variables. A **negative literal** has the form

$$\textbf{not } p(t_1, t_2, \ldots, t_n)$$

where relation p has n attributes. Here is an example of a literal:

$$account(A, \text{``Perryridge''}, B)$$

Literals involving arithmetic operations are treated specially. For example, the literal $B > 700$, although not in the syntax just described, can be conceptually understood to stand for $> (B, 700)$, which *is* in the required syntax, and where $>$ is a relation.

But what does this notation mean for arithmetic operations such as ">"? The relation $>$ (conceptually) contains tuples of the form (x, y) for every possible pair of values x, y such that $x > y$. Thus, $(2, 1)$ and $(5, -33)$ are both tuples in $>$. Clearly, the (conceptual) relation $>$ is infinite. Other arithmetic operations (such as $>, =, +$ or $-$) are also treated conceptually as relations. For example, A = B + C stands conceptually for +(B, C, A), where the relation + contains every tuple (x, y, z) such that $z = x + y$.

A **fact** is written in the form

$$p(v_1, v_2, \ldots, v_n)$$

and denotes that the tuple $(v_1, v_2, \ldots, v_n)$ is in relation p. A set of facts for a relation can also be written in the usual tabular notation. A set of facts for the relations in a database schema is equivalent to an instance of the database schema. **Rules** are built out of literals and have the form

$$p(t_1, t_2, \ldots, t_n) :\!- L_1, L_2, \ldots, L_n$$

where each L_i is a (positive or negative) literal. The literal $p(t_1, t_2, \ldots, t_n)$ is referred to as the **head** of the rule, and the rest of the literals in the rule constitute the **body** of the rule.

A **Datalog program** consists of a set of rules; the order in which the rules are written has no significance. As mentioned earlier, there may be several rules defining a relation.

Figure 5.6 shows a Datalog program that defines the interest on each account in the Perryridge branch. The first rule of the program defines a view relation *interest*, whose attributes are the account number and the interest earned on the account. It uses the relation *account* and the view relation *interest-rate*. The last two rules of the program are rules that we saw earlier.

A view relation v_1 is said to **depend directly on** a view relation v_2 if v_2 is used in the expression defining v_1. In the above program, view relation *interest* depends directly on relations *interest-rate* and *account*. Relation *interest-rate* in turn depends directly on *account*.

A view relation v_1 is said to **depend indirectly on** view relation v_2 if there is a sequence of intermediate relations $i_1, i_2, \ldots, i_n$, for some n, such that v_1 depends directly on i_1, i_1 depends directly on i_2, and so on till i_{n-1} depends on i_n.

In the example in Figure 5.6, since we have a chain of dependencies from *interest* to *interest-rate* to *account*, relation *interest* also depends indirectly on *account*.

Finally, a view relation v_1 is said to **depend on** view relation v_2 if v_1 either depends directly or indirectly on v_2.

A view relation v is said to be **recursive** if it depends on itself. A view relation that is not recursive is said to be **nonrecursive**.

Consider the program in Figure 5.7. Here, the view relation *empl* depends on itself (becasue of the second rule), and is therefore recursive. In contrast, the program in Figure 5.6 is nonrecursive.

$$
\begin{aligned}
&interest(A, I) :\!- account(A, \text{``Perryridge''}, B),\\
&\qquad\qquad\qquad interest\text{-}rate(A, R),\, I = B * R/100.\\
&interest\text{-}rate(A, 5) :\!- account(A, N, B),\, B < 10000.\\
&interest\text{-}rate(A, 6) :\!- account(A, N, B),\, B >= 10000.
\end{aligned}
$$

Figure 5.6   Datalog program that defines interest on Perryridge accounts.

$$empl(X, Y) :- manager(X, Y).$$
$$empl(X, Y) :- manager(X, Z), empl(Z, Y).$$

Figure 5.7   Recursive Datalog program.

5.2.3   Semantics of Nonrecursive Datalog

We consider the formal semantics of Datalog programs. For now, we consider only programs that are nonrecursive. The semantics of recursive programs is somewhat more complicated; it is discussed in Section 5.2.6. We define the semantics of a program by starting with the semantics of a single rule.

5.2.3.1   Semantics of a Rule

A **ground instantiation of a rule** is the result of replacing each variable in the rule by some constant. If a variable occurs multiple times in a rule, all occurrences of the variable must be replaced by the same constant. Ground instantiations are often simply called **instantiations**.

Our example rule defining $v1$, and an instantiation of the rule, are:

$$v1(A, B) :- account(A, \text{“Perryridge”}, B), B > 700$$
$$v1(\text{“A-217”}, 750) :- account(\text{“A-217”}, \text{“Perryridge”}, 750), 750 > 700$$

Here, variable A was replaced by "A-217," and variable B by 750.

A rule usually has many possible instantiations. These instantiations correspond to the various ways of assigning values to each variable in the rule.

Suppose that we are given a rule R,

$$p(t_1, t_2, \ldots, t_n) :- L_1, L_2, \ldots, L_n$$

and a set of facts I for the relations used in the rule (I can also be thought of as a database instance). Consider any instantiation R' of rule R:

$$p(v_1, v_2, \ldots, v_n) :- l_1, l_2, \ldots, l_n$$

where each literal l_i is either of the form $q_i(v_{i,1}, v_{1,2}, \ldots, v_{i,n_i})$ or of the form **not** $q_i(v_{i,1}, v_{1,2}, \ldots, v_{i,n_i})$, and where each v_i and each $v_{i,j}$ is a constant.

We say that the body of rule instantiation R' is **satisfied** in I if

1. For each positive literal $q_i(v_{i,1}, \ldots, v_{i,n_i})$ in the body of R', the set of facts I contains the fact $q(v_{i,1}, \ldots, v_{i,n_i})$.

2. For each negative literal **not** $q_j(v_{j,1}, \ldots, v_{j,n_j})$ in the body of R', the set of facts I does not contain the fact $q_j(v_{j,1}, \ldots, v_{j,n_j})$.

account-number	balance
A-201	900
A-217	750

Figure 5.8   Result of $infer(R, I)$.

We define the set of facts that can be **inferred** from a given set of facts I using rule R as

$$infer(R, I) = \{p(t_1, \ldots, t_{n_i}) \mid \text{there is an instantiation } R' \text{ of } R,$$
$$\text{where } p(t_1, \ldots, t_{n_i}) \text{ is the head of } R', \text{ and}$$
$$\text{the body of } R' \text{ is satisfied in } I\}.$$

Given a set of rules $\mathcal{R} = \{R_1, R_2, \ldots, R_n\}$, we define

$$infer(\mathcal{R}, I) = infer(R_1, I) \cup infer(R_2, I) \cup \ldots \cup infer(R_n, I)$$

Suppose that we are given a set of facts I containing the tuples for relation *account* in Figure 5.4. One possible instantiation of our running-example rule R is

$$v1(\text{``A-217''}, 750) :- account(\text{``A-217''}, \text{``Perryridge''}, 750), 750 > 700.$$

The fact *account*("A-217", "Perryridge", 750) is in the set of facts I. Further, 750 is greater than 700, and hence conceptually $(750, 700)$ is in the relation ">". Hence, the body of the rule instantiation is satisfied in I. There are other possible instantiations of R, and using them we find that $infer(R, I)$ has exactly the set of facts for *v1* that appears in Figure 5.8.

5.2.3.2 Semantics of a Program

When a view relation is defined in terms of another view relation, the set of facts in the first view depends on the set of facts in the second one. We have assumed, in this section, that the definition is nonrecursive; that is, no view relation depends (directly or indirectly) on itself. Hence, we can layer the view relations in the following way, and can use the layering to define the semantics of the program:

- A relation is in layer 1 if all relations used in the bodies of rules defining it are stored in the database.

- A relation is in layer 2 if all relations used in the bodies of rules defining it either are stored in the database or are in layer 1.

- In general, a relation p is in layer $i + 1$ if (1) it is not in layers $1, 2, \ldots, i$, and (2) all relations used in the bodies of rules defining p either are stored in the database or are in layers $1, 2, \ldots, i$.

Consider the program in Figure 5.6. The layering of view relations in the program appears in Figure 5.9. The relation *account* is in the database. Relation *interest-rate* is

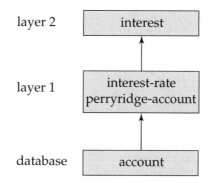

Figure 5.9   Layering of view relations.

in level 1, since all the relations used in the two rules defining it are in the database. Relation *perryridge-account* is similarly in layer 1. Finally, relation *interest* is in layer 2, since it is not in layer 1 and all the relations used in the rule defining it are in the database or in layers lower than 2.

We can now define the semantics of a Datalog program in terms of the layering of view relations. Let the layers in a given program be $1, 2, \ldots, n$. Let $\mathcal{R}_i$ denote the set of all rules defining view relations in layer i.

- We define I_0 to be the set of facts stored in the database, and define I_1 as

$$I_1 = I_0 \cup \mathit{infer}(\mathcal{R}_1, I_0)$$

- We proceed in a similar fashion, defining I_2 in terms of I_1 and $\mathcal{R}_2$, and so on, using the following definition:

$$I_{i+1} = I_i \cup \mathit{infer}(\mathcal{R}_{i+1}, I_i)$$

- Finally, the set of facts in the view relations defined by the program (also called the **semantics of the program**) is given by the set of facts I_n corresponding to the highest layer n.

For the program in Figure 5.6, I_0 is the set of facts in the database, and I_1 is the set of facts in the database along with all facts that we can infer from I_0 using the rules for relations *interest-rate* and *perryridge-account*. Finally, I_2 contains the facts in I_1 along with the facts for relation *interest* that we can infer from the facts in I_1 by the rule defining *interest*. The semantics of the program—that is, the set of those facts that are in each of the view relations—is defined as the set of facts I_2.

Recall that, in Section 3.5.3, we saw how to define the meaning of nonrecursive relational-algebra views by a technique known as view expansion. View expansion can be used with nonrecursive Datalog views as well; conversely, the layering technique described here can also be used with relational-algebra views.

5.2.4 Safety

It is possible to write rules that generate an infinite number of answers. Consider the rule

$$gt(X, Y) :- X > Y$$

Since the relation defining $>$ is infinite, this rule would generate an infinite number of facts for the relation gt, which calculation would, correspondingly, take an infinite amount of time and space.

The use of negation can also cause similar problems. Consider the rule:

$$not\text{-}in\text{-}loan(L, B, A) :- \textbf{not } loan(L, B, A)$$

The idea is that a tuple *(loan-number, branch-name, amount)* is in view relation *not-in-loan* if the tuple is not present in the *loan* relation. However, if the set of possible account numbers, branch-names, and balances is infinite, the relation *not-in-loan* would be infinite as well.

Finally, if we have a variable in the head that does not appear in the body, we may get an infinite number of facts where the variable is instantiated to different values.

So that these possibilities are avoided, Datalog rules are required to satisfy the following **safety** conditions:

1. Every variable that appears in the head of the rule also appears in a nonarithmetic positive literal in the body of the rule.

2. Every variable appearing in a negative literal in the body of the rule also appears in some positive literal in the body of the rule.

If all the rules in a nonrecursive Datalog program satisfy the preceding safety conditions, then all the view relations defined in the program can be shown to be finite, as long as all the database relations are finite. The conditions can be weakened somewhat to allow variables in the head to appear only in an arithmetic literal in the body in some cases. For example, in the rule

$$p(A) :- q(B), A = B + 1$$

we can see that if relation q is finite, then so is p, according to the properties of addition, even though variable A appears in only an arithmetic literal.

5.2.5 Relational Operations in Datalog

Nonrecursive Datalog expressions without arithmetic operations are equivalent in expressive power to expressions using the basic operations in relational algebra ($\cup$, $-$, $\times$, σ, Π and ρ). We shall not formally prove this assertion here. Rather, we shall show through examples how the various relational-algebra operations can be expressed in Datalog. In all cases, we define a view relation called *query* to illustrate the operations.

We have already seen how to do selection by using Datalog rules. We perform projections simply by using only the required attributes in the head of the rule. To project attribute *account-name* from account, we use

$$query(A) :- account(A, N, B)$$

We can obtain the Cartesian product of two relations r_1 and r_2 in Datalog as follows:

$$query(X_1, X_2, \ldots, X_n, Y_1, Y_2, \ldots, Y_m) :- r_1(X_1, X_2, \ldots, X_n), r_2(Y_1, Y_2, \ldots, Y_m)$$

where r_1 is of arity n, and r_2 is of arity m, and the $X_1, X_2, \ldots, X_n, Y_1, Y_2, \ldots, Y_m$ are all distinct variable names.

We form the union of two relations r_1 and r_2 (both of arity n) in this way:

$$query(X_1, X_2, \ldots, X_n) :- r_1(X_1, X_2, \ldots, X_n)$$
$$query(X_1, X_2, \ldots, X_n) :- r_2(X_1, X_2, \ldots, X_n)$$

We form the set difference of two relations r_1 and r_2 in this way:

$$query(X_1, X_2, \ldots, X_n) :- r_1(X_1, X_2, \ldots, X_n), \textbf{not } r_2(X_1, X_2, \ldots, X_n)$$

Finally, we note that with the positional notation used in Datalog, the renaming operator ρ is not needed. A relation can occur more than once in the rule body, but instead of renaming to give distinct names to the relation occurrences, we can use different variable names in the different occurrences.

It is possible to show that we can express any nonrecursive Datalog query without arithmetic by using the relational-algebra operations. We leave this demonstration as an exercise for you to carry out. You can thus establish the equivalence of the basic operations of relational algebra and nonrecursive Datalog without arithmetic operations.

Certain extensions to Datalog support the extended relational update operations of insertion, deletion, and update. The syntax for such operations varies from implementation to implementation. Some systems allow the use of + or − in rule heads to denote relational insertion and deletion. For example, we can move all accounts at the Perryridge branch to the Johnstown branch by executing

$$+ \, account(A, \text{``Johnstown''}, B) :- account(A, \text{``Perryridge''}, B)$$
$$- \, account(A, \text{``Perryridge''}, B) :- account(A, \text{``Perryridge''}, B)$$

Some implementations of Datalog also support the aggregation operation of extended relational algebra. Again, there is no standard syntax for this operation.

5.2.6   Recursion in Datalog

Several database applications deal with structures that are similar to tree data structures. For example, consider employees in an organization. Some of the employees are managers. Each manager manages a set of people who report to him or her. But

> **procedure** Datalog-Fixpoint
> I = set of facts in the database
> **repeat**
> $Old\_I = I$
> $I = I \cup infer(\mathcal{R}, I)$
> **until** $I = Old\_I$

Figure 5.10 Datalog-Fixpoint procedure.

each of these people may in turn be managers, and they in turn may have other people who report to them. Thus employees may be organized in a structure similar to a tree.

Suppose that we have a relation schema

$$Manager\text{-}schema = (employee\text{-}name, manager\text{-}name)$$

Let *manager* be a relation on the preceding schema.

Suppose now that we want to find out which employees are supervised, directly or indirectly by a given manager—say, Jones. Thus, if the manager of Alon is Barinsky, and the manager of Barinsky is Estovar, and the manager of Estovar is Jones, then Alon, Barinsky, and Estovar are the employees controlled by Jones. People often write programs to manipulate tree data structures by recursion. Using the idea of recursion, we can define the set of employees controlled by Jones as follows. The people supervised by Jones are (1) people whose manager is Jones and (2) people whose manager is supervised by Jones. Note that case (2) is recursive.

We can encode the preceding recursive definition as a recursive Datalog view, called *empl-jones*:

$$empl\text{-}jones(X) \ :\!\!-\ manager(X, \text{``Jones''})$$
$$empl\text{-}jones(X) \ :\!\!-\ manager(X, Y), empl\text{-}jones(Y)$$

The first rule corresponds to case (1); the second rule corresponds to case (2). The view *empl-jones* depends on itself because of the second rule; hence, the preceding Datalog program is recursive. We *assume* that recursive Datalog programs contain no rules with negative literals. The reason will become clear later. The bibliographical

employee-name	manager-name
Alon	Barinsky
Barinsky	Estovar
Corbin	Duarte
Duarte	Jones
Estovar	Jones
Jones	Klinger
Rensal	Klinger

Figure 5.11 The *manager* relation.

Iteration number	Tuples in *empl-jones*
0	
1	(Duarte), (Estovar)
2	(Duarte), (Estovar), (Barinsky), (Corbin)
3	(Duarte), (Estovar), (Barinsky), (Corbin), (Alon)
4	(Duarte), (Estovar), (Barinsky), (Corbin), (Alon)

Figure 5.12 Employees of Jones in iterations of procedure Datalog-Fixpoint.

notes refer to papers that describe where negation can be used in recursive Datalog programs.

The view relations of a recursive program that contains a set of rules $\mathcal{R}$ are defined to contain exactly the set of facts I computed by the iterative procedure Datalog-Fixpoint in Figure 5.10. The recursion in the Datalog program has been turned into an iteration in the procedure. At the end of the procedure, $infer(\mathcal{R}, I) = I$, and I is called a **fixed point** of the program.

Consider the program defining *empl-jones*, with the relation *manager*, as in Figure 5.11. The set of facts computed for the view relation *empl-jones* in each iteration appears in Figure 5.12. In each iteration, the program computes one more level of employees under Jones and adds it to the set *empl-jones*. The procedure terminates when there is no change to the set *empl-jones*, which the system detects by finding $I = Old\_I$. Such a termination point must be reached, since the set of managers and employees is finite. On the given *manager* relation, the procedure Datalog-Fixpoint terminates after iteration 4, when it detects that no new facts have been inferred.

You should verify that, at the end of the iteration, the view relation *empl-jones* contains exactly those employees who work under Jones. To print out the names of the employees supervised by Jones defined by the view, you can use the query

$$? \; empl\text{-}jones(N)$$

To understand procedure Datalog-Fixpoint, we recall that a rule infers new facts from a given set of facts. Iteration starts with a set of facts I set to the facts in the database. These facts are all known to be true, but there may be other facts that are true as well.[1] Next, the set of rules $\mathcal{R}$ in the given Datalog program is used to infer what facts are true, given that facts in I are true. The inferred facts are added to I, and the rules are used again to make further inferences. This process is repeated until no new facts can be inferred.

For safe Datalog programs, we can show that there will be some point where no more new facts can be derived; that is, for some k, $I_{k+1} = I_k$. At this point, then, we have the final set of true facts. Further, given a Datalog program and a database, the fixed-point procedure infers all the facts that can be inferred to be true.

---

1. The word "fact" is used in a technical sense to note membership of a tuple in a relation. Thus, in the Datalog sense of "fact," a fact may be true (the tuple is indeed in the relation) or false (the tuple is not in the relation).

If a recursive program contains a rule with a negative literal, the following problem can arise. Recall that when we make an inference by using a ground instantiation of a rule, for each negative literal **not**q in the rule body we check that q is not present in the set of facts I. This test assumes that q cannot be inferred later. However, in the fixed-point iteration, the set of facts I grows in each iteration, and even if q is not present in I at one iteration, it may appear in I later. Thus, we may have made an inference in one iteration that can no longer be made at an earlier iteration, and the inference was incorrect. We require that a recursive program should not contain negative literals, in order to avoid such problems.

Instead of creating a view for the employees supervised by a specific manager Jones, we can create a more general view relation *empl* that contains every tuple (X, Y) such that X is directly or indirectly managed by Y, using the following program (also shown in Figure 5.7):

$$empl(X, Y) \;:\!- \; manager(X, Y)$$
$$empl(X, Y) \;:\!- \; manager(X, Z), empl(Z, Y)$$

To find the direct and indirect subordinates of Jones, we simply use the query

$$? \; empl(X, \text{``Jones''})$$

which gives the same set of values for X as the view *empl-jones*. Most Datalog implementations have sophisticated query optimizers and evaluation engines that can run the preceding query at about the same speed they could evaluate the view *empl-jones*.

The view *empl* defined previously is called the **transitive closure** of the relation *manager*. If the relation *manager* were replaced by any other binary relation R, the preceding program would define the transitive closure of R.

5.2.7 The Power of Recursion

Datalog with recursion has more expressive power than Datalog without recursion. In other words, there are queries on the database that we can answer by using recursion, but cannot answer without using it. For example, we cannot express transitive closure in Datalog without using recursion (or for that matter, in SQL or QBE without recursion). Consider the transitive closure of the relation *manager*. Intuitively, a fixed number of joins can find only those employees that are some (other) fixed number of levels down from any manager (we will not attempt to prove this result here). Since any given nonrecursive query has a fixed number of joins, there is a limit on how many levels of employees the query can find. If the number of levels of employees in the *manager* relation is more than the limit of the query, the query will miss some levels of employees. Thus, a nonrecursive Datalog program cannot express transitive closure.

An alternative to recursion is to use an external mechanism, such as embedded SQL, to iterate on a nonrecursive query. The iteration in effect implements the fixed-point loop of Figure 5.10. In fact, that is how such queries are implemented on database systems that do not support recursion. However, writing such queries by iteration is more complicated than using recursion, and evaluation by recursion can be optimized to run faster than evaluation by iteration.

The expressive power provided by recursion must be used with care. It is relatively easy to write recursive programs that will generate an infinite number of facts, as this program illustrates:

$$number(0)$$
$$number(A) :- number(B), A = B + 1$$

The program generates $number(n)$ for all positive integers n, which is clearly infinite, and will not terminate. The second rule of the program does not satisfy the safety condition in Section 5.2.4. Programs that satisfy the safety condition will terminate, even if they are recursive, provided that all database relations are finite. For such programs, tuples in view relations can contain only constants from the database, and hence the view relations must be finite. The converse is not true; that is, there are programs that do not satisfy the safety conditions, but that do terminate.

5.2.8   Recursion in Other Languages

The SQL:1999 standard supports a limited form of recursion, using the **with recursive** clause. Suppose the relation *manager* has attributes *emp* and *mgr*. We can find every pair (X, Y) such that X is directly or indirectly managed by Y, using this SQL:1999 query:

```
with recursive empl(emp, mgr) as (
        select emp, mgr
        from manager
    union
        select emp, empl.mgr
        from manager, empl
        where manager.mgr = empl.emp
)
select *
from empl
```

Recall that the **with** clause is used to define a temporary view whose definition is available only to the query where it is defined. The additional keyword **recursive** specifies that the view is recursive. The SQL definition of the view *empl* above is equivalent to the Datalog version we saw in Section 5.2.6.

The procedure Datalog-Fixpoint iteratively uses the function $infer(\mathcal{R}, I)$ to compute what facts are true, given a recursive Datalog program. Although we considered only the case of Datalog programs without negative literals, the procedure can also be used on views defined in other languages, such as SQL or relational algebra, provided that the views satisfy the conditions described next. Regardless of the language used to define a view V, the view can be thought of as being defined by an expression E_V that, given a set of facts I, returns a set of facts $E_V(I)$ for the view relation V. Given a set of view definitions $\mathcal{R}$ (in any language), we can define a function

$infer(\mathcal{R}, I)$ that returns $I \cup \bigcup_{V \in \mathcal{R}} E_V(I)$. The preceding function has the same form as the *infer* function for Datalog.

A view V is said to be **monotonic** if, given any two sets of facts I_1 and I_2 such that $I_1 \subseteq I_2$, then $E_V(I_1) \subseteq E_V(I_2)$, where E_V is the expression used to define V. Similarly, the function *infer* is said to be monotonic if

$$I_1 \subseteq I_2 \Rightarrow infer(\mathcal{R}, I_1) \subseteq infer(\mathcal{R}, I_2)$$

Thus, if *infer* is monotonic, given a set of facts I_0 that is a subset of the true facts, we can be sure that all facts in $infer(\mathcal{R}, I_0)$ are also true. Using the same reasoning as in Section 5.2.6, we can then show that procedure Datalog-Fixpoint is sound (that is, it computes only true facts), provided that the function *infer* is monotonic.

Relational-algebra expressions that use only the operators $\Pi, \sigma, \times, \bowtie, \cup, \cap$, or ρ are monotonic. Recursive views can be defined by using such expressions.

However, relational expressions that use the operator $-$ are not monotonic. For example, let $manager_1$ and $manager_2$ be relations with the same schema as the *manager* relation. Let

$$I_1 = \{ \ manager_1(\text{"Alon", "Barinsky"}), \ manager_1(\text{"Barinsky", "Estovar"}),$$
$$manager_2(\text{"Alon", "Barinsky"}) \ \}$$

and let

$$I_2 = \{ \ manager_1(\text{"Alon", "Barinsky"}), \ manager_1(\text{"Barinsky", "Estovar"}),$$
$$manager_2(\text{"Alon", "Barinsky"}), \ manager_2(\text{"Barinsky", "Estovar"})\}$$

Consider the expression $manager_1 - manager_2$. Now the result of the preceding expression on I_1 is ("Barinsky", "Estovar"), whereas the result of the expression on I_2 is the empty relation. But $I_1 \subseteq I_2$; hence, the expression is not monotonic. Expressions using the grouping operation of extended relational algebra are also nonmonotonic.

The fixed-point technique does not work on recursive views defined with nonmonotonic expressions. However, there are instances where such views are useful, particularly for defining aggregates on "part–subpart" relationships. Such relationships define what subparts make up each part. Subparts themselves may have further subparts, and so on; hence, the relationships, like the manager relationship, have a natural recursive structure. An example of an aggregate query on such a structure would be to compute the total number of subparts of each part. Writing this query in Datalog or in SQL (without procedural extensions) would require the use of a recursive view on a nonmonotonic expression. The bibliographic notes provide references to research on defining such views.

It is possible to define some kinds of recursive queries without using views. For example, extended relational operations have been proposed to define transitive closure, and extensions to the SQL syntax to specify (generalized) transitive closure have been proposed. However, recursive view definitions provide more expressive power than do the other forms of recursive queries.

5.3 User Interfaces and Tools

Although many people interact with databases, few people use a query language to directly interact with a database system. Most people interact with a database system through one of the following means:

1. **Forms and graphical user interfaces** allow users to enter values that complete predefined queries. The system executes the queries and appropriately formats and displays the results to the user. Graphical user interfaces provide an easy-to-use way to interact with the database system.

2. **Report generators** permit predefined reports to be generated on the current database contents. Analysts or managers view such reports in order to make business decisions.

3. **Data analysis tools** permit users to interactively browse and analyze data.

It is worth noting that such interfaces use query languages to communicate with database systems.

In this section, we provide an overview of forms, graphical user interfaces, and report generators. Chapter 22 covers data analysis tools in more detail. Unfortunately, there are no standards for user interfaces, and each database system usually provides its own user interface. In this section, we describe the basic concepts, without going into the details of any particular user interface product.

5.3.1 Forms and Graphical User Interfaces

Forms interfaces are widely used to enter data into databases, and extract information from databases, via predefined queries. For example, World Wide Web search engines provide forms that are used to enter key words. Hitting a "submit" button causes the search engine to execute a query using the entered key words and display the result to the user.

As a more database-oriented example, you may connect to a university registration system, where you are asked to fill in your roll number and password into a form. The system uses this information to verify your identity, as well as to extract information, such as your name and the courses you have registered for, from the database and display it. There may be further links on the Web page that let you search for courses and find further information about courses such as the syllabus and the instructor.

Web browsers supporting HTML constitute the most widely used forms and graphical user interface today. Most database system vendors also provide proprietary forms interfaces that offer facilities beyond those present in HTML forms.

Programmers can create forms and graphical user interfaces by using HTML or programming languages such as C or Java. Most database system vendors also provide tools that simplify the creation of graphical user interfaces and forms. These tools allow application developers to create forms in an easy declarative fashion, using form-editor programs. Users can define the type, size, and format of each field in a form by using the form editor. System actions can be associated with user actions, such as filling in a field, hitting a function key on the keyboard, or submitting a form. For instance, the execution of a query to fill in name and address fields may be associated with filling in a roll number field, and execution of an update statement may be associated with submitting a form.

Simple error checks can be performed by defining constraints on the fields in the form.[2] For example, a constraint on the course number field may check that the course number typed in by the user corresponds to an actual course. Although such constraints can be checked when the transaction is executed, detecting errors early helps the user to correct errors quickly. Menus that indicate the valid values that can be entered in a field can help eliminate the possibility of many types of errors. System developers find that the ability to control such features declaratively with the help of a user interface development tool, instead of creating a form directly by using a scripting or programming language, makes their job much easier.

5.3.2 Report Generators

Report generators are tools to generate human-readable summary reports from a database. They integrate querying the database with the creation of formatted text and summary charts (such as bar or pie charts). For example, a report may show the total sales in each of the past two months for each sales region.

The application developer can specify report formats by using the formatting facilities of the report generator. Variables can be used to store parameters such as the month and the year and to define fields in the report. Tables, graphs, bar charts, or other graphics can be defined via queries on the database. The query definitions can make use of the parameter values stored in the variables.

Once we have defined a report structure on a report-generator facility, we can store it, and can execute it at any time to generate a report. Report-generator systems provide a variety of facilities for structuring tabular output, such as defining table and column headers, displaying subtotals for each group in a table, automatically splitting long tables into multiple pages, and displaying subtotals at the end of each page.

Figure 5.13 is an example of a formatted report. The data in the report are generated by aggregation on information about orders.

The Microsoft Office suite provides a convenient way of embedding formatted query results from a database, such as MS Access, into a document created with a text editor, such as MS Word. The query results can be formatted in a tabular fashion or graphically (as charts) by the report generator facility of MS Access. A feature called OLE (Object Linking and Embedding) links the resulting structure into a text document.

The collections of application-development tools provided by database systems, such as forms packages and report generator, used to be referred to as *fourth-generation languages* (4GLs). The name emphasizes that these tools offer a programming paradigm that is different from the imperative programming paradigm offered by third-

---

2. These are called "form triggers" in Oracle, but in this book we use the term "trigger" in a different sense, which we cover in Chapter 6.

Acme Supply Company Inc.
Quarterly Sales Report

Period: Jan. 1 to March 31, 2001

Region	Category	Sales	Subtotal
North	Computer Hardware	1,000,000	
	Computer Software	500,000	
	All categories		1,500,000
South	Computer Hardware	200,000	
	Computer Software	400,000	
	All categories		600,000

Total Sales   2,100,000

Figure 5.13   A formatted report.

generation programming languages, such as Pascal and C. However, this term is less relevant today, since forms and report generators are typically created with graphical tools, rather than with programming languages.

5.4 Summary

- We have considered two query languages: QBE, and Datalog.

- QBE is based on a visual paradigm: The queries look much like tables.

- QBE and its variants have become popular with nonexpert database users because of the intuitive simplicity of the visual paradigm. The widely used Microsoft Access database system supports a graphical version of QBE, called GQBE.

- Datalog is derived from Prolog, but unlike Prolog, it has a declarative semantics, making simple queries easier to write and query evaluation easier to optimize.

- Defining views is particularly easy in Datalog, and the recursive views that Datalog supports makes it possible to write queries, such as transitive-closure queries, that cannot be written without recursion or iteration. However, no accepted standards exist for important features, such as grouping and aggregation, in Datalog. Datalog remains mainly a research language.

- Most users interact with databases via forms and graphical user interfaces, and there are numerous tools to simplify the construction of such interfaces. Report generators are tools that help create human-readable reports from the contents of the database.

Review Terms

- Query-by-Example (QBE)
- Two-dimensional syntax
- Skeleton tables
- Example rows
- Condition box
- Result relation
- Microsoft Access
- Graphical Query-By-Example (GQBE)
- Design grid
- Datalog
- Rules
- Uses
- Defines
- Positive literal
- Negative literal
- Fact
- Rule
  - ☐ Head
  - ☐ Body

- Datalog program
- Depend on
  - ☐ Directly
  - ☐ Indirectly
- Recursive view
- Nonrecursive view
- Instantiation
  - ☐ Ground instantiation
  - ☐ Satisfied
- Infer
- Semantics
  - ☐ Of a rule
  - ☐ Of a program
- Safety
- Fixed point
- Transitive closure
- Monotonic view definition
- Forms
- Graphical user interfaces
- Report generators

Exercises

5.1 Consider the insurance database of Figure 5.14, where the primary keys are underlined. Construct the following QBE queries for this relational-database.

   a. Find the total number of people who owned cars that were involved in accidents in 1989.

   b. Find the number of accidents in which the cars belonging to "John Smith" were involved.

   c. Add a new accident to the database; assume any values for required attributes.

   d. Delete the Mazda belonging to "John Smith."

   e. Update the damage amount for the car with license number "AABB2000" in the accident with report number "AR2197" to $3000.

5.2 Consider the employee database of Figure 5.15. Give expressions in QBE, and Datalog for each of the following queries:

   a. Find the names of all employees who work for First Bank Corporation.

   b. Find the names and cities of residence of all employees who work for First Bank Corporation.

person (<u>driver-id#</u>, name, address)
car (<u>license</u>, model, year)
accident (<u>report-number</u>, <u>date</u>, location)
owns (<u>driver-id#</u>, <u>license</u>)
participated (<u>driver-id</u>, <u>car</u>, <u>report-number</u>, damage-amount)

Figure 5.14   Insurance database.

   c. Find the names, street addresses, and cities of residence of all employees who work for First Bank Corporation and earn more than $10,000 per annum.

   d. Find all employees who live in the same city as the company for which they work is located.

   e. Find all employees who live in the same city and on the same street as their managers.

   f. Find all employees in the database who do not work for First Bank Corporation.

   g. Find all employees who earn more than every employee of Small Bank Corporation.

   h. Assume that the companies may be located in several cities. Find all companies located in every city in which Small Bank Corporation is located.

5.3 Consider the relational database of Figure 5.15. where the primary keys are underlined. Give expressions in QBE for each of the following queries:

   a. Find all employees who earn more than the average salary of all employees of their company.

   b. Find the company that has the most employees.

   c. Find the company that has the smallest payroll.

   d. Find those companies whose employees earn a higher salary, on average, than the average salary at First Bank Corporation.

5.4 Consider the relational database of Figure 5.15. Give expressions in QBE for each of the following queries:

   a. Modify the database so that Jones now lives in Newtown.

   b. Give all employees of First Bank Corporation a 10 percent raise.

   c. Give all managers in the database a 10 percent raise.

   d. Give all managers in the database a 10 percent raise, unless the salary would be greater than $100,000. In such cases, give only a 3 percent raise.

employee (<u>person-name</u>, street, city)
works (<u>person-name</u>, company-name, salary)
company (<u>company-name</u>, city)
manages (<u>person-name</u>, manager-name)

Figure 5.15   Employee database.

e. Delete all tuples in the *works* relation for employees of Small Bank Corporation.

5.5 Let the following relation schemas be given:

$$R = (A, B, C)$$
$$S = (D, E, F)$$

Let relations $r(R)$ and $s(S)$ be given. Give expressions in QBE, and Datalog equivalent to each of the following queries:

a. $\Pi_A(r)$
b. $\sigma_{B=17}(r)$
c. $r \times s$
d. $\Pi_{A,F}(\sigma_{C=D}(r \times s))$

5.6 Let $R = (A, B, C)$, and let r_1 and r_2 both be relations on schema R. Give expressions in QBE, and Datalog equivalent to each of the following queries:

a. $r_1 \cup r_2$
b. $r_1 \cap r_2$
c. $r_1 - r_2$
d. $\Pi_{AB}(r_1) \bowtie \Pi_{BC}(r_2)$

5.7 Let $R = (A, B)$ and $S = (A, C)$, and let $r(R)$ and $s(S)$ be relations. Write expressions in QBE and Datalog for each of the following queries:

a. $\{<a> \mid \exists b\,(<a,b> \in r \wedge b = 17)\}$
b. $\{<a,b,c> \mid <a,b> \in r \wedge <a,c> \in s\}$
c. $\{<a> \mid \exists c\,(<a,c> \in s \wedge \exists b_1, b_2\,(<a,b_1> \in r \wedge <c, b_2> \in r \wedge b_1 > b_2))\}$

5.8 Consider the relational database of Figure 5.15. Write a Datalog program for
each of the following queries:

a. Find all employees who work (directly or indirectly) under the manager
"Jones".
b. Find all cities of residence of all employees who work (directly or indirectly)
under the manager "Jones".
c. Find all pairs of employees who have a (direct or indirect) manager in common.
d. Find all pairs of employees who have a (direct or indirect) manager in common, and are at the same number of levels of supervision below the common manager.

5.9 Write an extended relational-algebra view equivalent to the Datalog rule

$$p(A, C, D) :- q1(A, B),\ q2(B, C),\ q3(4, B),\ D = B + 1\,.$$

5.10 Describe how an arbitrary Datalog rule can be expressed as an extended relational algebra view.

Bibliographical Notes

The experimental version of Query-by-Example is described in Zloof [1977]; the commercial version is described in IBM [1978]. Numerous database systems—in particular, database systems that run on personal computers—implement QBE or variants. Examples are Microsoft Access and Borland Paradox.

Implementations of Datalog include LDL system (described in Tsur and Zaniolo [1986] and Naqvi and Tsur [1988]), Nail! (described in Derr et al. [1993]), and Coral (described in Ramakrishnan et al. [1992b] and Ramakrishnan et al. [1993]). Early discussions concerning logic databases were presented in Gallaire and Minker [1978] and Gallaire et al. [1984]. Ullman [1988] and Ullman [1989] provide extensive textbook discussions of logic query languages and implementation techniques. Ramakrishnan and Ullman [1995] provides a more recent survey on deductive databases.

Datalog programs that have both recursion and negation can be assigned a simple semantics if the negation is "stratified"—that is, if there is no recursion through negation. Chandra and Harel [1982] and Apt and Pugin [1987] discuss stratified negation. An important extension, called the *modular-stratification semantics*, which handles a class of recursive programs with negative literals, is discussed in Ross [1990]; an evaluation technique for such programs is described by Ramakrishnan et al. [1992a].

Tools

The Microsoft Access QBE is probably the most widely used implementation of QBE. IBM DB2 QMF and Borland Paradox also support QBE.

The Coral system from the University of Wisconsin–Madison is a widely used implementation of Datalog (see (http://www.cs.wisc.edu/coral). The XSB system from the State University of New York (SUNY) Stony Brook (http://xsb.sourceforge.net) is a widely used Prolog implementation that supports database querying; recall that Datalog is a nonprocedural subset of Prolog.

Integrity and Security

Integrity constraints ensure that changes made to the database by authorized users do not result in a loss of data consistency. Thus, integrity constraints guard against accidental damage to the database.

We have already seen two forms of integrity constraints for the E-R model in Chapter 2:

- **Key declarations**—the stipulation that certain attributes form a candidate key for a given entity set.

- **Form of a relationship**—many to many, one to many, one to one.

In general, an integrity constraint can be an arbitrary predicate pertaining to the database. However, arbitrary predicates may be costly to test. Thus, we concentrate on integrity constraints that can be tested with minimal overhead. We study some such forms of integrity constraints in Sections 6.1 and 6.2, and cover a more complex form in Section 6.3. In Chapter 7 we study another form of integrity constraint, called "functional dependency," which is primarily used in the process of schema design.

In Section 6.4 we study *triggers*, which are statements that are executed automatically by the system as a side effect of a modification to the database. Triggers are used to ensure some types of integrity.

In addition to protecting against accidental introduction of inconsistency, the data stored in the database need to be protected from unauthorized access and malicious destruction or alteration. In Sections 6.5 through 6.7, we examine ways in which data may be misused or intentionally made inconsistent, and present security mechanisms to guard against such occurrences.

6.1 Domain Constraints

We have seen that a domain of possible values must be associated with every attribute. In Chapter 4, we saw a number of standard domain types, such as integer types, character types, and date/time types defined in SQL. Declaring an attribute to be of a particular domain acts as a constraint on the values that it can take. Domain constraints are the most elementary form of integrity constraint. They are tested easily by the system whenever a new data item is entered into the database.

It is possible for several attributes to have the same domain. For example, the attributes *customer-name* and *employee-name* might have the same domain: the set of all person names. However, the domains of *balance* and *branch-name* certainly ought to be distinct. It is perhaps less clear whether *customer-name* and *branch-name* should have the same domain. At the implementation level, both customer names and branch names are character strings. However, we would normally not consider the query "Find all customers who have the same name as a branch" to be a meaningful query. Thus, if we view the database at the conceptual, rather than the physical, level, *customer-name* and *branch-name* should have distinct domains.

From the above discussion, we can see that a proper definition of domain constraints not only allows us to test values inserted in the database, but also permits us to test queries to ensure that the comparisons made make sense. The principle behind attribute domains is similar to that behind typing of variables in programming languages. Strongly typed programming languages allow the compiler to check the program in greater detail.

The **create domain** clause can be used to define new domains. For example, the statements:

create domain *Dollars* **numeric(12,2)**
create domain *Pounds* **numeric(12,2)**

define the domains *Dollars* and *Pounds* to be decimal numbers with a total of 12 digits, two of which are placed after the decimal point. An attempt to assign a value of type *Dollars* to a variable of type *Pounds* would result in a syntax error, although both are of the same numeric type. Such an assignment is likely to be due to a programmer error, where the programmer forgot about the differences in currency. Declaring different domains for different currencies helps catch such errors.

Values of one domain can be *cast* (that is, converted) to another domain. If the attribute *A* or relation *r* is of type *Dollars*, we can convert it to *Pounds* by writing

cast *r.A* **as** *Pounds*

In a real application we would of course multiply *r.A* by a currency conversion factor before casting it to pounds. SQL also provides **drop domain** and **alter domain** clauses to drop or modify domains that have been created earlier.

The **check** clause in SQL permits domains to be restricted in powerful ways that most programming language type systems do not permit. Specifically, the **check** clause permits the schema designer to specify a predicate that must be satisfied by any value assigned to a variable whose type is the domain. For instance, a **check** clause can ensure that an hourly wage domain allows only values greater than a specified value (such as the minimum wage):

> **create domain** *HourlyWage* **numeric**(5,2)
>   **constraint** *wage-value-test* **check**(**value** $>=$ 4.00)

The domain *HourlyWage* has a constraint that ensures that the hourly wage is greater than 4.00. The clause **constraint** *wage-value-test* is optional, and is used to give the name *wage-value-test* to the constraint. The name is used to indicate which constraint an update violated.

The **check** clause can also be used to restrict a domain to not contain any null values:

> **create domain** *AccountNumber* **char**(10)
>   **constraint** *account-number-null-test* **check**(**value not null**)

As another example, the domain can be restricted to contain only a specified set of values by using the **in** clause:

> **create domain** *AccountType* **char**(10)
>   **constraint** *account-type-test*
>   **check**(**value in** ('Checking', 'Saving'))

The preceding **check** conditions can be tested quite easily, when a tuple is inserted or modified. However, in general, the **check** conditions can be more complex (and harder to check), since subqueries that refer to other relations are permitted in the **check** condition. For example, this constraint could be specified on the relation *deposit*:

> **check** (*branch-name* **in** (**select** *branch-name* **from** *branch*))

The **check** condition verifies that the *branch-name* in each tuple in the *deposit* relation is actually the name of a branch in the *branch* relation. Thus, the condition has to be checked not only when a tuple is inserted or modified in *deposit*, but also when the relation *branch* changes (in this case, when a tuple is deleted or modified in relation *branch*).

The preceding constraint is actually an example of a class of constraints called *referential-integrity* constraints. We discuss such constraints, along with a simpler way of specifying them in SQL, in Section 6.2.

Complex **check** conditions can be useful when we want to ensure integrity of data, but we should use them with care, since they may be costly to test.

6.2 Referential Integrity

Often, we wish to ensure that a value that appears in one relation for a given set of attributes also appears for a certain set of attributes in another relation. This condition is called **referential integrity**.

6.2.1 Basic Concepts

Consider a pair of relations $r(R)$ and $s(S)$, and the natural join $r \bowtie s$. There may be a tuple t_r in r that does not join with any tuple in s. That is, there is no t_s in s such that $t_r[R \cap S] = t_s[R \cap S]$. Such tuples are called *dangling* tuples. Depending on the entity set or relationship set being modeled, dangling tuples may or may not be acceptable. In Section 3.3.3, we considered a modified form of join—the outer join—to operate on relations containing dangling tuples. Here, our concern is not with queries, but rather with when we should permit dangling tuples to exist in the database.

Suppose there is a tuple t_1 in the *account* relation with $t_1[branch\text{-}name]$ = "Lunartown," but there is no tuple in the *branch* relation for the Lunartown branch. This situation would be undesirable. We expect the *branch* relation to list all bank branches. Therefore, tuple t_1 would refer to an account at a branch that does not exist. Clearly, we would like to have an integrity constraint that prohibits dangling tuples of this sort.

Not all instances of dangling tuples are undesirable, however. Assume that there is a tuple t_2 in the *branch* relation with $t_2[branch\text{-}name]$ = "Mokan," but there is no tuple in the *account* relation for the Mokan branch. In this case, a branch exists that has no accounts. Although this situation is not common, it may arise when a branch is opened or is about to close. Thus, we do not want to prohibit this situation.

The distinction between these two examples arises from two facts:

- The attribute *branch-name* in *Account-schema* is a foreign key referencing the primary key of *Branch-schema*.

- The attribute *branch-name* in *Branch-schema* is not a foreign key.

(Recall from Section 3.1.3 that a foreign key is a set of attributes in a relation schema that forms a primary key for another schema.)

In the Lunartown example, tuple t_1 in *account* has a value on the foreign key *branch-name* that does not appear in *branch*. In the Mokan-branch example, tuple t_2 in *branch* has a value on *branch-name* that does not appear in *account*, but *branch-name* is not a foreign key. Thus, the distinction between our two examples of dangling tuples is the presence of a foreign key.

Let $r_1(R_1)$ and $r_2(R_2)$ be relations with primary keys K_1 and K_2, respectively. We say that a subset α of R_2 is a **foreign key** referencing K_1 in relation r_1 if it is required that, for every t_2 in r_2, there must be a tuple t_1 in r_1 such that $t_1[K_1] = t_2[\alpha]$. Requirements of this form are called **referential integrity constraints**, or **subset dependencies**. The latter term arises because the preceding referential-integrity constraint can be written as $\Pi_\alpha(r_2) \subseteq \Pi_{K_1}(r_1)$. Note that, for a referential-integrity constraint to make sense, either α must be equal to K_1, or α and K_1 must be compatible sets of attributes.

6.2.2 Referential Integrity and the E-R Model

Referential-integrity constraints arise frequently. If we derive our relational-database schema by constructing tables from E-R diagrams, as we did in Chapter 2, then every

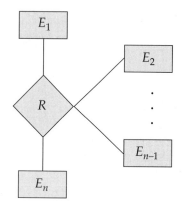

Figure 6.1   An n-ary relationship set.

relation arising from a relationship set has referential-integrity constraints. Figure 6.1 shows an n-ary relationship set R, relating entity sets $E_1, E_2, \ldots, E_n$. Let K_i denote the primary key of E_i. The attributes of the relation schema for relationship set R include $K_1 \cup K_2 \cup \cdots \cup K_n$. The following referential integrity constraints are then present: For each i, K_i in the schema for R is a foreign key referencing K_i in the relation schema generated from entity set E_i

Another source of referential-integrity constraints is weak entity sets. Recall from Chapter 2 that the relation schema for a weak entity set must include the primary key of the entity set on which the weak entity set depends. Thus, the relation schema for each weak entity set includes a foreign key that leads to a referential-integrity constraint.

6.2.3   Database Modification

Database modifications can cause violations of referential integrity. We list here the test that we must make for each type of database modification to preserve the following referential-integrity constraint:

$$\Pi_\alpha (r_2) \subseteq \Pi_K (r_1)$$

- **Insert**. If a tuple t_2 is inserted into r_2, the system must ensure that there is a tuple t_1 in r_1 such that $t_1[K] = t_2[\alpha]$. That is,

$$t_2[\alpha] \in \Pi_K (r_1)$$

- **Delete**. If a tuple t_1 is deleted from r_1, the system must compute the set of tuples in r_2 that reference t_1:

$$\sigma_{\alpha = t_1[K]} (r_2)$$

If this set is not empty, either the delete command is rejected as an error, or the tuples that reference t_1 must themselves be deleted. The latter solution may lead to cascading deletions, since tuples may reference tuples that reference t_1, and so on.

- **Update**. We must consider two cases for update: updates to the referencing relation (r_2), and updates to the referenced relation (r_1).

  □ If a tuple t_2 is updated in relation r_2, and the update modifies values for the foreign key α, then a test similar to the insert case is made. Let t_2' denote the new value of tuple t_2. The system must ensure that

  $$t_2'[\alpha] \in \Pi_K (r_1)$$

  □ If a tuple t_1 is updated in r_1, and the update modifies values for the primary key (K), then a test similar to the delete case is made. The system must compute

  $$\sigma_{\alpha = t_1[K]} (r_2)$$

  using the old value of t_1 (the value before the update is applied). If this set is not empty, the update is rejected as an error, or the update is cascaded in a manner similar to delete.

6.2.4   Referential Integrity in SQL

Foreign keys can be specified as part of the SQL **create table** statement by using the **foreign key** clause. We illustrate foreign-key declarations by using the SQL DDL definition of part of our bank database, shown in Figure 6.2.

By default, a foreign key references the primary key attributes of the referenced table. SQL also supports a version of the **references** clause where a list of attributes of the referenced relation can be specified explicitly. The specified list of attributes must be declared as a candidate key of the referenced relation.

We can use the following short form as part of an attribute definition to declare that the attribute forms a foreign key:

branch-name **char**(15) **references** *branch*

When a referential-integrity constraint is violated, the normal procedure is to reject the action that caused the violation. However, a **foreign key** clause can specify that if a delete or update action on the referenced relation violates the constraint, then, instead of rejecting the action, the system must take steps to change the tuple in the referencing relation to restore the constraint. Consider this definition of an integrity constraint on the relation *account*:

```
create table account
  ( . . .
  foreign key (branch-name) references branch
                        on delete cascade
                        on update cascade,
  . . . )
```

Because of the clause **on delete cascade** associated with the foreign-key declaration, if a delete of a tuple in *branch* results in this referential-integrity constraint being violated, the system does not reject the delete. Instead, the delete "cascades" to the

```
create table customer
   (customer-name    char(20),
    customer-street  char(30),
    customer-city    char(30),
    primary key (customer-name))

create table branch
   (branch-name   char(15),
    branch-city   char(30),
    assets        integer,
    primary key (branch-name),
    check (assets >= 0))

create table account
   (account-number  char(10),
    branch-name     char(15),
    balance         integer,
    primary key (account-number),
    foreign key (branch-name) references branch,
    check (balance >= 0))

create table depositor
   (customer-name    char(20),
    account-number   char(10),
    primary key (customer-name, account-number),
    foreign key (customer-name) references customer,
    foreign key (account-number) references account)
```

Figure 6.2   SQL data definition for part of the bank database.

account relation, deleting the tuple that refers to the branch that was deleted. Similarly, the system does not reject an update to a field referenced by the constraint if it violates the constraint; instead, the system updates the field *branch-name* in the referencing tuples in *account* to the new value as well. SQL also allows the **foreign key** clause to specify actions other than **cascade**, if the constraint is violated: The referencing field (here, *branch-name*) can be set to null (by using **set null** in place of **cascade**), or to the default value for the domain (by using **set default**).

If there is a chain of foreign-key dependencies across multiple relations, a deletion or update at one end of the chain can propagate across the entire chain. An interesting case where the **foreign key** constraint on a relation references the same relation appears in Exercise 6.4. If a cascading update or delete causes a constraint violation that cannot be handled by a further cascading operation, the system aborts the transaction. As a result, all the changes caused by the transaction and its cascading actions are undone.

Null values complicate the semantics of referential integrity constraints in SQL. Attributes of foreign keys are allowed to be null, provided that they have not otherwise been declared to be non-null. If all the columns of a foreign key are non-null in a given tuple, the usual definition of foreign-key constraints is used for that tuple. If any of the foreign-key columns is null, the tuple is defined automatically to satisfy the constraint.

This definition may not always be the right choice, so SQL also provides constructs that allow you to change the behavior with null values; we do not discuss the constructs here. To avoid such complexity, it is best to ensure that all columns of a **foreign key** specification are declared to be non-null.

Transactions may consist of several steps, and integrity constraints may be violated temporarily after one step, but a later step may remove the violation. For instance, suppose we have a relation *marriedperson* with primary key *name*, and an attribute *spouse*, and suppose that *spouse* is a foreign key on *marriedperson*. That is, the constraint says that the *spouse* attribute must contain a name that is present in the *person* table. Suppose we wish to note the fact that John and Mary are married to each other by inserting two tuples, one for John and one for Mary, in the above relation. The insertion of the first tuple would violate the foreign key constraint, regardless of which of the two tuples is inserted first. After the second tuple is inserted the foreign key constraint would hold again.

To handle such situations, integrity constraints are checked at the end of a transaction, and not at intermediate steps.[1]

6.3 Assertions

An **assertion** is a predicate expressing a condition that we wish the database always to satisfy. Domain constraints and referential-integrity constraints are special forms of assertions. We have paid substantial attention to these forms of assertion because they are easily tested and apply to a wide range of database applications. However, there are many constraints that we cannot express by using only these special forms. Two examples of such constraints are:

- The sum of all loan amounts for each branch must be less than the sum of all account balances at the branch.

- Every loan has at least one customer who maintains an account with a minimum balance of $1000.00.

An assertion in SQL takes the form

create assertion <assertion-name> **check** <predicate>

Here is how the two examples of constraints can be written. Since SQL does not provide a "for all X, $P(X)$" construct (where P is a predicate), we are forced to im-

---

1. We can work around the problem in the above example in another way, if the *spouse* attribute can be set to null: We set the spouse attributes to null when inserting the tuples for John and Mary, and we update them later. However, this technique is rather messy, and does not work if the attributes cannot be set to null.

plement the construct by the equivalent "not exists X such that not $P(X)$" construct, which can be written in SQL. We write

> **create assertion** *sum-constraint* **check**
>   **(not exists (select** * **from** *branch*
>   **where (select sum**(*amount*) **from** *loan*
>   **where** *loan.branch-name* $=$ *branch.branch-name*)
> $>=$ **(select sum**(*balance*) **from** *account*
>   **where** *account.branch-name* $=$ *branch.branch-name*)))

> **create assertion** *balance-constraint* **check**
>   **(not exists (select** * **from** *loan*
>   **where not exists (select** *
>   **from** *borrower, depositor, account*
>   **where** *loan.loan-number* $=$ *borrower.loan-number*
>   **and** *borrower.customer-name* $=$ *depositor.customer-name*
>   **and** *depositor.account-number* $=$ *account.account-number*
>   **and** *account.balance* $>=$ 1000)))

When an assertion is created, the system tests it for validity. If the assertion is valid, then any future modification to the database is allowed only if it does not cause that assertion to be violated. This testing may introduce a significant amount of overhead if complex assertions have been made. Hence, assertions should be used with great care. The high overhead of testing and maintaining assertions has led some system developers to omit support for general assertions, or to provide specialized forms of assertions that are easier to test.

6.4 Triggers

A **trigger** is a statement that the system executes automatically as a side effect of a modification to the database. To design a trigger mechanism, we must meet two requirements:

1. Specify when a trigger is to be executed. This is broken up into an *event* that causes the trigger to be checked and a *condition* that must be satisfied for trigger execution to proceed.

2. Specify the *actions* to be taken when the trigger executes.

The above model of triggers is referred to as the **event-condition-action model** for triggers.

The database stores triggers just as if they were regular data, so that they are persistent and are accessible to all database operations. Once we enter a trigger into the database, the database system takes on the responsibility of executing it whenever the specified event occurs and the corresponding condition is satisfied.

6.4.1 Need for Triggers

Triggers are useful mechanisms for alerting humans or for starting certain tasks automatically when certain conditions are met. As an illustration, suppose that, instead of allowing negative account balances, the bank deals with overdrafts by setting the account balance to zero, and creating a loan in the amount of the overdraft. The bank gives this loan a loan number identical to the account number of the overdrawn account. For this example, the condition for executing the trigger is an update to the *account* relation that results in a negative *balance* value. Suppose that Jones' withdrawal of some money from an account made the account balance negative. Let t denote the account tuple with a negative *balance* value. The actions to be taken are:

- Insert a new tuple s in the *loan* relation with

$$s[loan\text{-}number] = t[account\text{-}number]$$
$$s[branch\text{-}name] = t[branch\text{-}name]$$
$$s[amount] = -t[balance]$$

  (Note that, since $t[balance]$ is negative, we negate $t[balance]$ to get the loan amount—a positive number.)

- Insert a new tuple u in the *borrower* relation with

$$u[customer\text{-}name] = \text{``Jones''}$$
$$u[loan\text{-}number] = t[account\text{-}number]$$

- Set $t[balance]$ to 0.

As another example of the use of triggers, suppose a warehouse wishes to maintain a minimum inventory of each item; when the inventory level of an item falls below the minimum level, an order should be placed automatically. This is how the business rule can be implemented by triggers: On an update of the inventory level of an item, the trigger should compare the level with the minimum inventory level for the item, and if the level is at or below the minimum, a new order is added to an *orders* relation.

Note that trigger systems cannot usually perform updates outside the database, and hence in the inventory replenishment example, we cannot use a trigger to directly place an order in the external world. Instead, we add an order to the *orders* relation as in the inventory example. We must create a separate permanently running system process that periodically scans the *orders* relation and places orders. This system process would also note which tuples in the *orders* relation have been processed and when each order was placed. The process would also track deliveries of orders, and alert managers in case of exceptional conditions such as delays in deliveries.

6.4.2 Triggers in SQL

SQL-based database systems use triggers widely, although before SQL:1999 they were not part of the SQL standard. Unfortunately, each database system implemented its

```
create trigger overdraft-trigger after update on account
referencing new row as nrow
for each row
when nrow.balance < 0
begin atomic
    insert into borrower
            (select customer-name, account-number
             from depositor
             where nrow.account-number = depositor.account-number);
        insert into loan values
            (nrow.account-number, nrow.branch-name, − nrow.balance);
        update account set balance = 0
            where account.account-number = nrow.account-number
end
```

Figure 6.3   Example of SQL:1999 syntax for triggers.

own syntax for triggers, leading to incompatibilities. We outline in Figure 6.3 the SQL:1999 syntax for triggers (which is similar to the syntax in the IBM DB2 and Oracle database systems).

This trigger definition specifies that the trigger is initiated *after* any update of the relation *account* is executed. An SQL update statement could update multiple tuples of the relation, and the **for each row** clause in the trigger code would then explicitly iterate over each updated row. The **referencing new row as** clause creates a variable *nrow* (called a **transition variable**), which stores the value of an updated row after the update.

The **when** statement specifies a condition, namely *nrow.balance* < 0. The system executes the rest of the trigger body only for tuples that satisfy the condition. The **begin atomic** ... **end** clause serves to collect multiple SQL statements into a single compound statement. The two **insert** statements with the **begin** ... **end** structure carry out the specific tasks of creating new tuples in the *borrower* and *loan* relations to represent the new loan. The **update** statement serves to set the account balance back to 0 from its earlier negative value.

The triggering event and actions can take many forms:

- The triggering *event* can be **insert** or **delete**, instead of **update**.

    For example, the action on **delete** of an account could be to check if the holders of the account have any remaining accounts, and if they do not, to delete them from the *depositor* relation. You can define this trigger as an exercise (Exercise 6.7).

    As another example, if a new *depositor* is inserted, the triggered action could be to send a welcome letter to the depositor. Obviously a trigger cannot directly cause such an action outside the database, but could instead add a tuple to a relation storing addresses to which welcome letters need to be sent. A separate process would go over this table, and print out letters to be sent.

- For updates, the trigger can specify columns whose update causes the trigger to execute. For instance if the first line of the overdraft trigger were replaced by

  create trigger *overdraft-trigger* **after update of** *balance* **on** *account*

  then the trigger would be executed only on updates to *balance*; updates to other attributes would not cause it to be executed.

- The **referencing old row as** clause can be used to create a variable storing the old value of an updated or deleted row. The **referencing new row as** clause can be used with inserts in addition to updates.

- Triggers can be activated **before** the event (insert/delete/update) instead of **after** the event.

  Such triggers can serve as extra constraints that can prevent invalid updates. For instance, if we wish not to permit overdrafts, we can create a **before** trigger that rolls back the transaction if the new balance is negative.

  As another example, suppose the value in a phone number field of an inserted tuple is blank, which indicates absence of a phone number. We can define a trigger that replaces the value by the **null** value. The **set** statement can be used to carry out such modifications.

  > **create trigger** *setnull-trigger* **before update on** *r*
  > **referencing new row as** *nrow*
  > **for each row**
  > **when** *nrow.phone-number* = ' '
  > **set** *nrow.phone-number* = **null**

- Instead of carrying out an action for each affected row, we can carry out a single action for the entire SQL statement that caused the insert/delete/update. To do so, we use the **for each statement** clause instead of the **for each row** clause.

  The clauses **referencing old table as** or **referencing new table as** can then be used to refer to temporary tables (called *transition tables*) containing all the affected rows. Transition tables cannot be used with **before** triggers, but can be used with **after** triggers, regardless of whether they are statement triggers or row triggers.

  A single SQL statement can then be used to carry out multiple actions on the basis of the transition tables.

Returning to our warehouse inventory example, suppose we have the following relations:

- *inventory(item, level)*, which notes the current amount (number/weight/volume) of the item in the warehouse

```
create trigger reorder-trigger after update of amount on inventory
referencing old row as orow, new row as nrow
for each row
when nrow.level <= (select level
                    from minlevel
                    where minlevel.item = orow.item)
and orow.level > (select level
                  from minlevel
                  where minlevel.item = orow.item)
begin
      insert into orders
          (select item, amount
          from reorder
          where reorder.item = orow.item)
end
```

Figure 6.4   Example of trigger for reordering an item.

- *minlevel(item, level)*, which notes the minimum amount of the item to be maintained

- *reorder(item, amount)*, which notes the amount of the item to be ordered when its level falls below the minimum

- *orders(item, amount)*, which notes the amount of the item to be ordered.

We can then use the trigger shown in Figure 6.4 for reordering the item.

Note that we have been careful to place an order only when the amount falls from above the minimum level to below the minimum level. If we only check that the new value after an update is below the minimum level, we may place an order erroneously when the item has already been reordered.

Many database systems provide nonstandard trigger implementations, or implement only some of the trigger features. For instance, many database systems do not implement the **before** clause, and the keyword **on** is used instead of **after**. They may not implement the **referencing** clause. Instead, they may specify transition tables by using the keywords **inserted** or **deleted**. Figure 6.5 illustrates how the overdraft trigger would be written in MS-SQLServer. Read the user manual for the database system you use for more information about the trigger features it supports.

6.4.3 When Not to Use Triggers

There are many good uses for triggers, such as those we have just seen in Section 6.4.2, but some uses are best handled by alternative techniques. For example, in the past, system designers used triggers to maintain summary data. For instance, they used triggers on insert/delete/update of a *employee* relation containing *salary* and *dept* attributes to maintain the total salary of each department. However, many database systems today support materialized views (see Section 3.5.1), which provide a much

```
create trigger overdraft-trigger on account
for update
as
if nrow.balance < 0
begin
    insert into borrower
            (select customer-name, account-number
             from depositor, inserted
             where inserted.account-number = depositor.account-number)
      insert into loan values
            (inserted.account-number, inserted.branch-name, − inserted.balance)
    update account set balance = 0
            from account, inserted
            where account.account-number = inserted.account-number
end
```

Figure 6.5   Example of trigger in MS-SQL server syntax

easier way to maintain summary data. Designers also used triggers extensively for replicating databases; they used triggers on insert/delete/update of each relation to record the changes in relations called **change** or **delta** relations. A separate process copied over the changes to the replica (copy) of the database, and the system executed the changes on the replica. Modern database systems, however, provide built-in facilities for database replication, making triggers unnecessary for replication in most cases.

In fact, many trigger applications, including our example overdraft trigger, can be substituted by "encapsulation" features being introduced in SQL:1999. Encapsulation can be used to ensure that updates to the *balance* attribute of *account* are done only through a special procedure. That procedure would in turn check for negative balance, and carry out the actions of the overdraft trigger. Encapsulations can replace the reorder trigger in a similar manner.

Triggers should be written with great care, since a trigger error detected at run time causes the failure of the insert/delete/update statement that set off the trigger. Furthermore, the action of one trigger can set off another trigger. In the worst case, this could even lead to an infinite chain of triggering. For example, suppose an insert trigger on a relation has an action that causes another (new) insert on the same relation. The insert action then triggers yet another insert action, and so on ad infinitum. Database systems typically limit the length of such chains of triggers (for example to 16 or 32), and consider longer chains of triggering an error.

Triggers are occasionally called *rules*, or *active rules*, but should not be confused with Datalog rules (see Section 5.2), which are really view definitions.

6.5 Security and Authorization

The data stored in the database need protection from unauthorized access and malicious destruction or alteration, in addition to the protection against accidental introduction of inconsistency that integrity constraints provide. In this section, we examine the ways in which data may be misused or intentionally made inconsistent. We then present mechanisms to guard against such occurrences.

6.5.1 Security Violations

Among the forms of malicious access are:

- Unauthorized reading of data (theft of information)

- Unauthorized modification of data

- Unauthorized destruction of data

Database security refers to protection from malicious access. Absolute protection of the database from malicious abuse is not possible, but the cost to the perpetrator can be made high enough to deter most if not all attempts to access the database without proper authority.

To protect the database, we must take security measures at several levels:

- **Database system**. Some database-system users may be authorized to access only a limited portion of the database. Other users may be allowed to issue queries, but may be forbidden to modify the data. It is the responsibility of the database system to ensure that these authorization restrictions are not violated.

- **Operating system**. No matter how secure the database system is, weakness in operating-system security may serve as a means of unauthorized access to the database.

- **Network**. Since almost all database systems allow remote access through terminals or networks, software-level security within the network software is as important as physical security, both on the Internet and in private networks.

- **Physical**. Sites with computer systems must be physically secured against armed or surreptitious entry by intruders.

- **Human**. Users must be authorized carefully to reduce the chance of any user giving access to an intruder in exchange for a bribe or other favors.

Security at all these levels must be maintained if database security is to be ensured. A weakness at a low level of security (physical or human) allows circumvention of strict high-level (database) security measures.

In the remainder of this section, we shall address security at the database-system level. Security at the physical and human levels, although important, is beyond the scope of this text.

Security within the operating system is implemented at several levels, ranging from passwords for access to the system to the isolation of concurrent processes running within the system. The file system also provides some degree of protection. The bibliographical notes reference coverage of these topics in operating-system texts. Finally, network-level security has gained widespread recognition as the Internet has evolved from an academic research platform to the basis of international electronic commerce. The bibliographic notes list textbook coverage of the basic principles of network security. We shall present our discussion of security in terms of the relational-data model, although the concepts of this chapter are equally applicable to all data models.

6.5.2 Authorization

We may assign a user several forms of authorization on parts of the database. For example,

- **Read authorization** allows reading, but not modification, of data.

- **Insert authorization** allows insertion of new data, but not modification of existing data.

- **Update authorization** allows modification, but not deletion, of data.

- **Delete authorization** allows deletion of data.

We may assign the user all, none, or a combination of these types of authorization.

In addition to these forms of authorization for access to data, we may grant a user authorization to modify the database schema:

- **Index authorization** allows the creation and deletion of indices.

- **Resource authorization** allows the creation of new relations.

- **Alteration authorization** allows the addition or deletion of attributes in a relation.

- **Drop authorization** allows the deletion of relations.

The **drop** and **delete** authorization differ in that **delete** authorization allows deletion of tuples only. If a user deletes all tuples of a relation, the relation still exists, but it is empty. If a relation is dropped, it no longer exists.

We regulate the ability to create new relations through **resource** authorization. A user with **resource** authorization who creates a new relation is given all privileges on that relation automatically.

Index authorization may appear unnecessary, since the creation or deletion of an index does not alter data in relations. Rather, indices are a structure for performance enhancements. However, indices also consume space, and all database modifications are required to update indices. If **index** authorization were granted to all users, those who performed updates would be tempted to delete indices, whereas those who issued queries would be tempted to create numerous indices. To allow the *database administrator* to regulate the use of system resources, it is necessary to treat index creation as a privilege.

The ultimate form of authority is that given to the database administrator. The database administrator may authorize new users, restructure the database, and so on. This form of authorization is analogous to that of a **superuser** or operator for an operating system.

6.5.3   Authorization and Views

In Chapter 3, we introduced the concept of *views* as a means of providing a user with a personalized model of the database. A view can hide data that a user does not need to see. The ability of views to hide data serves both to simplify usage of the system and to enhance security. Views simplify system usage because they restrict the user's attention to the data of interest. Although a user may be denied direct access to a relation, that user may be allowed to access part of that relation through a view. Thus, a combination of relational-level security and view-level security limits a user's access to precisely the data that the user needs.

In our banking example, consider a clerk who needs to know the names of all customers who have a loan at each branch. This clerk is not authorized to see information regarding specific loans that the customer may have. Thus, the clerk must be denied direct access to the *loan* relation. But, if she is to have access to the information needed, the clerk must be granted access to the view *cust-loan*, which consists of only the names of customers and the branches at which they have a loan. This view can be defined in SQL as follows:

> **create view** *cust-loan* **as**
> (**select** *branch-name, customer-name*
> **from** *borrower, loan*
> **where** *borrower.loan-number = loan.loan-number*)

Suppose that the clerk issues the following SQL query:

> **select** *
> **from** *cust-loan*

Clearly, the clerk is authorized to see the result of this query. However, when the query processor translates it into a query on the actual relations in the database, it produces a query on *borrower* and *loan*. Thus, the system must check authorization on the clerk's query before it begins query processing.

Creation of a view does not require **resource** authorization. A user who creates a view does not necessarily receive all privileges on that view. She receives only those privileges that provide no additional authorization beyond those that she already had. For example, a user cannot be given **update** authorization on a view without having **update** authorization on the relations used to define the view. If a user creates a view on which no authorization can be granted, the system will deny the view creation request. In our *cust-loan* view example, the creator of the view must have **read** authorization on both the *borrower* and *loan* relations.

6.5.4 Granting of Privileges

A user who has been granted some form of authorization may be allowed to pass on this authorization to other users. However, we must be careful how authorization may be passed among users, to ensure that such authorization can be revoked at some future time.

Consider, as an example, the granting of update authorization on the *loan* relation of the bank database. Assume that, initially, the database administrator grants update authorization on *loan* to users U_1, U_2, and U_3, who may in turn pass on this authorization to other users. The passing of authorization from one user to another can be represented by an **authorization graph**. The nodes of this graph are the users. The graph includes an edge $U_i \rightarrow U_j$ if user U_i grants update authorization on *loan* to U_j. The root of the graph is the database administrator. In the sample graph in Figure 6.6, observe that user U_5 is granted authorization by both U_1 and U_2; U_4 is granted authorization by only U_1.

A user has an authorization *if and only if* there is a path from the root of the authorization graph (namely, the node representing the database administrator) down to the node representing the user.

Suppose that the database administrator decides to revoke the authorization of user U_1. Since U_4 has authorization from U_1, that authorization should be revoked as well. However, U_5 was granted authorization by both U_1 and U_2. Since the database administrator did not revoke update authorization on *loan* from U_2, U_5 retains update authorization on *loan*. If U_2 eventually revokes authorization from U_5, then U_5 loses the authorization.

A pair of devious users might attempt to defeat the rules for revocation of authorization by granting authorization to each other, as shown in Figure 6.7a. If the database administrator revokes authorization from U_2, U_2 retains authorization through U_3, as in Figure 6.7b. If authorization is revoked subsequently from U_3, U_3 appears to retain authorization through U_2, as in Figure 6.7c. However, when the database administrator revokes authorization from U_3, the edges from U_3 to U_2 and from U_2 to U_3 are no longer part of a path starting with the database administrator.

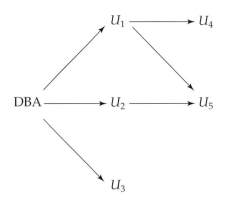

Figure 6.6 Authorization-grant graph.

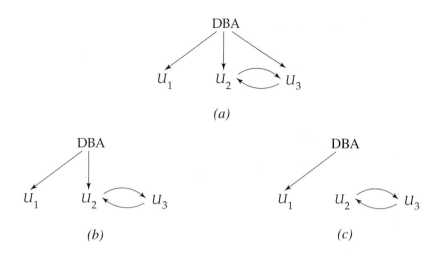

(a)

(b)   (c)

Figure 6.7   Attempt to defeat authorization revocation.

We require that all edges in an authorization graph be part of some path originating with the database administrator. The edges between U_2 and U_3 are deleted, and the resulting authorization graph is as in Figure 6.8.

6.5.5 Notion of Roles

Consider a bank where there are many tellers. Each teller must have the same types of authorizations to the same set of relations. Whenever a new teller is appointed, she will have to be given all these authorizations individually.

A better scheme would be to specify the authorizations that every teller is to be given, and to separately identify which database users are tellers. The system can use these two pieces of information to determine the authorizations of each person who is a teller. When a new person is hired as a teller, a user identifier must be allocated to him, and he must be identified as a teller. Individual permissions given to tellers need not be specified again.

The notion of **roles** captures this scheme. A set of roles is created in the database. Authorizations can be granted to roles, in exactly the same fashion as they are granted to individual users. Each database user is granted a set of roles (which may be empty) that he or she is authorized to perform.

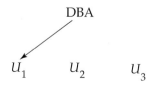

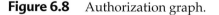

Figure 6.8   Authorization graph.

In our bank database, examples of roles could include *teller*, *branch-manager*, *auditor*, and *system-administrator*.

A less preferable alternative would be to create a *teller* userid, and permit each teller to connect to the database using the *teller* userid. The problem with this scheme is that it would not be possible to identify exactly which teller carried out a transaction, leading to security risks. The use of roles has the benefit of requiring users to connect to the database with their own userid.

Any authorization that can be granted to a user can be granted to a role. Roles are granted to users just as authorizations are. And like other authorizations, a user may also be granted authorization to grant a particular role to others. Thus, branch managers may be granted authorization to grant the *teller* role.

6.5.6 Audit Trails

Many secure database applications require an **audit trail** be maintained. An audit trail is a log of all changes (inserts/deletes/updates) to the database, along with information such as which user performed the change and when the change was performed.

The audit trail aids security in several ways. For instance, if the balance on an account is found to be incorrect, the bank may wish to trace all the updates performed on the account, to find out incorrect (or fraudulent) updates, as well as the persons who carried out the updates. The bank could then also use the audit trail to trace all the updates performed by these persons, in order to find other incorrect or fraudulent updates.

It is possible to create an audit trail by defining appropriate triggers on relation updates (using system-defined variables that identify the user name and time). However, many database systems provide built-in mechanisms to create audit trails, which are much more convenient to use. Details of how to create audit trails vary across database systems, and you should refer the database system manuals for details.

6.6 Authorization in SQL

The SQL language offers a fairly powerful mechanism for defining authorizations. We describe these mechanisms, as well as their limitations, in this section.

6.6.1 Privileges in SQL

The SQL standard includes the privileges **delete**, **insert**, **select**, and **update**. The **select** privilege corresponds to the **read** privilege. SQL also includes a **references** privilege that permits a user/role to declare foreign keys when creating relations. If the relation to be created includes a foreign key that references attributes of another relation, the user/role must have been granted **references** privilege on those attributes. The reason that the **references** privilege is a useful feature is somewhat subtle; we explain the reason later in this section.

The SQL data-definition language includes commands to grant and revoke privileges. The **grant** statement is used to confer authorization. The basic form of this statement is:

grant <privilege list> **on** <relation name or view name> **to** <user/role list>

The *privilege list* allows the granting of several privileges in one command.

The following **grant** statement grants users U_1, U_2, and U_3 **select** authorization on the *account* relation:

grant select on *account* **to** U_1, U_2, U_3

The **update** authorization may be given either on all attributes of the relation or on only some. If **update** authorization is included in a **grant** statement, the list of attributes on which update authorization is to be granted optionally appears in parentheses immediately after the **update** keyword. If the list of attributes is omitted, the update privilege will be granted on all attributes of the relation.

This **grant** statement gives users U_1, U_2, and U_3 update authorization on the *amount* attribute of the *loan* relation:

grant update (*amount*) **on** *loan* **to** U_1, U_2, U_3

The **insert** privilege may also specify a list of attributes; any inserts to the relation must specify only these attributes, and the system either gives each of the remaining attributes default values (if a default is defined for the attribute) or sets them to null.

The SQL **references** privilege is granted on specific attributes in a manner like that for the **update** privilege. The following **grant** statement allows user U_1 to create relations that reference the key *branch-name* of the *branch* relation as a foreign key:

grant references (*branch-name*) **on** *branch* **to** U_1

Initially, it may appear that there is no reason ever to prevent users from creating foreign keys referencing another relation. However, recall from Section 6.2 that foreign-key constraints restrict deletion and update operations on the referenced relation. In the preceding example, if U_1 creates a foreign key in a relation r referencing the *branch-name* attribute of the *branch* relation, and then inserts a tuple into r pertaining to the Perryridge branch, it is no longer possible to delete the Perryridge branch from the *branch* relation without also modifying relation r. Thus, the definition of a foreign key by U_1 restricts future activity by other users; therefore, there is a need for the **references** privilege.

The privilege **all privileges** can be used as a short form for all the allowable privileges. Similarly, the user name **public** refers to all current and future users of the system. SQL also includes a **usage** privilege that authorizes a user to use a specified domain (recall that a domain corresponds to the programming-language notion of a type, and may be user defined).

6.6.2 Roles

Roles can be created in SQL:1999 as follows

create role *teller*

Roles can then be granted privileges just as the users can, as illustrated in this statement:

grant select on *account*
to *teller*

Roles can be asigned to the users, as well as to some other roles, as these statements show.

grant *teller* **to** john
create role *manager*
grant *teller* **to** *manager*
grant *manager* **to** mary

Thus the privileges of a user or a role consist of

- All privileges directly granted to the user/role

- All privileges granted to roles that have been granted to the user/role

Note that there can be a chain of roles; for example, the role *employee* may be granted to all *teller*s. In turn the role *teller* is granted to all *manager*s. Thus, the *manager* role inherits all privileges granted to the roles *employee* and to *teller* in addition to privileges granted directly to *manager*.

6.6.3 The Privilege to Grant Privileges

By default, a user/role that is granted a privilege is not authorized to grant that privilege to another user/role. If we wish to grant a privilege and to allow the recipient to pass the privilege on to other users, we append the **with grant option** clause to the appropriate **grant** command. For example, if we wish to allow U_1 the **select** privilege on *branch* and allow U_1 to grant this privilege to others, we write

grant select on *branch* **to** U_1 **with grant option**

To revoke an authorization, we use the **revoke** statement. It takes a form almost identical to that of **grant**:

revoke <privilege list> **on** <relation name or view name>
from <user/role list> [**restrict** | **cascade**]

Thus, to revoke the privileges that we granted previously, we write

> **revoke select on** *branch* **from** U_1, U_2, U_3
> **revoke update** (*amount*) **on** *loan* **from** U_1, U_2, U_3
> **revoke references** (*branch-name*) **on** *branch* **from** U_1

As we saw in Section 6.5.4, the revocation of a privilege from a user/role may cause other users/roles also to lose that privilege. This behavior is called *cascading of the revoke*. In most database systems, cascading is the default behavior; the keyword **cascade** can thus be omitted, as we have done in the preceding examples. The **revoke** statement may alternatively specify **restrict**:

> **revoke select on** *branch* **from** U_1, U_2, U_3 **restrict**

In this case, the system returns an error if there are any cascading revokes, and does not carry out the revoke action. The following **revoke** statement revokes only the grant option, rather than the actual **select** privilege:

> **revoke grant option for select on** *branch* **from** U_1

6.6.4   Other Features

The creator of an object (relation/view/role) gets all privileges on the object, including the privilege to grant privileges to others.

The SQL standard specifies a primitive authorization mechanism for the database schema: Only the owner of the schema can carry out any modification to the schema. Thus, schema modifications—such as creating or deleting relations, adding or dropping attributes of relations, and adding or dropping indices—may be executed by only the owner of the schema. Several database implementations have more powerful authorization mechanisms for database schemas, similar to those discussed earlier, but these mechanisms are nonstandard.

6.6.5   Limitations of SQL Authorization

The current SQL standards for authorization have some shortcomings. For instance, suppose you want all students to be able to see their own grades, but not the grades of anyone else. Authorization must then be at the level of individual tuples, which is not possible in the SQL standards for authorization.

Furthermore, with the growth in the Web, database accesses come primarily from Web application servers. The end users may not have individual user identifiers on the database, and indeed there may only be a single user identifier in the database corresponding to all users of an application server.

The task of authorization then falls on the application server; the entire authorization scheme of SQL is bypassed. The benefit is that fine-grained authorizations, such as those to individual tuples, can be implemented by the application. The problems are these:

- The code for checking authorization becomes intermixed with the rest of the application code.

- Implementing authorization through application code, rather than specifying it declaratively in SQL, makes it hard to ensure the absence of loopholes. Because of an oversight, one of the application programs may not check for authorization, allowing unauthorized users access to confidential data. Verifying that all application programs make all required authorization checks involves reading through all the application server code, a formidable task in a large system.

6.7 Encryption and Authentication

The various provisions that a database system may make for authorization may still not provide sufficient protection for highly sensitive data. In such cases, data may be stored in **encrypt**ed form. It is not possible for encrypted data to be read unless the reader knows how to decipher (**decrypt**) them. Encryption also forms the basis of good schemes for authenticating users to a database.

6.7.1 Encryption Techniques

There are a vast number of techniques for the encryption of data. Simple encryption techniques may not provide adequate security, since it may be easy for an unauthorized user to break the code. As an example of a weak encryption technique, consider the substitution of each character with the next character in the alphabet. Thus,

Perryridge

becomes

Qfsszsjehf

If an unauthorized user sees only "Qfsszsjehf," she probably has insufficient information to break the code. However, if the intruder sees a large number of encrypted branch names, she could use statistical data regarding the relative frequency of characters to guess what substitution is being made (for example, *E* is the most common letter in English text, followed by *T, A, O, N, I* and so on).

A good encryption technique has the following properties:

- It is relatively simple for authorized users to encrypt and decrypt data.

- It depends not on the secrecy of the algorithm, but rather on a parameter of the algorithm called the *encryption key*.

- Its encryption key is extremely difficult for an intruder to determine.

One approach, the *Data Encryption Standard* (DES), issued in 1977, does both a substitution of characters and a rearrangement of their order on the basis of an encryption key. For this scheme to work, the authorized users must be provided with the encryption key via a secure mechanism. This requirement is a major weakness, since the scheme is no more secure than the security of the mechanism by which the encryption key is transmitted. The DES standard was reaffirmed in 1983, 1987, and again in 1993. However, weakness in DES was recongized in 1993 as reaching a point where a new standard to be called the **Advanced Encryption Standard** (AES), needed to be selected. In 2000, the **Rijndael algorithm** (named for the inventors V. Rijmen and J. Daemen), was selected to be the AES. The Rijndael algorithm was chosen for its significantly stronger level of security and its relative ease of implementation on current computer systems as well as such devices as smart cards. Like the DES standard, the Rijndael algorithm is a shared-key (or, symmetric key) algorithm in which the authorized users share a key.

Public-key encryption is an alternative scheme that avoids some of the problems that we face with the DES. It is based on two keys; a *public key* and a *private key*. Each user U_i has a public key E_i and a private key D_i. All public keys are published: They can be seen by anyone. Each private key is known to only the one user to whom the key belongs. If user U_1 wants to store encrypted data, U_1 encrypts them using public key E_1. Decryption requires the private key D_1.

Because the encryption key for each user is public, it is possible to exchange information securely by this scheme. If user U_1 wants to share data with U_2, U_1 encrypts the data using E_2, the public key of U_2. Since only user U_2 knows how to decrypt the data, information is transferred securely.

For public-key encryption to work, there must be a scheme for encryption that can be made public without making it easy for people to figure out the scheme for decryption. In other words, it must be hard to deduce the private key, given the public key. Such a scheme does exist and is based on these conditions:

- There is an efficient algorithm for testing whether or not a number is prime.

- No efficient algorithm is known for finding the prime factors of a number.

For purposes of this scheme, data are treated as a collection of integers. We create a public key by computing the product of two large prime numbers: P_1 and P_2. The private key consists of the pair (P_1, P_2). The decryption algorithm cannot be used successfully if only the product $P_1 P_2$ is known; it needs the individual values P_1 and P_2. Since all that is published is the product $P_1 P_2$, an unauthorized user would need to be able to factor $P_1 P_2$ to steal data. By choosing P_1 and P_2 to be sufficiently large (over 100 digits), we can make the cost of factoring $P_1 P_2$ prohibitively high (on the order of years of computation time, on even the fastest computers).

The details of public-key encryption and the mathematical justification of this technique's properties are referenced in the bibliographic notes.

Although public-key encryption by this scheme is secure, it is also computationally expensive. A hybrid scheme used for secure communication is as follows: DES keys are exchanged via a public-key–encryption scheme, and DES encryption is used on the data transmitted subsequently.

6.7.2 Authentication

Authentication refers to the task of verifying the identity of a person/software connecting to a database. The simplest form of authentication consists of a secret password which must be presented when a connection is opened to a database.

Password-based authentication is used widely by operating systems as well as databases. However, the use of passwords has some drawbacks, especially over a network. If an eavesdropper is able to "sniff" the data being sent over the network, she may be able to find the password as it is being sent across the network. Once the eavesdropper has a user name and password, she can connect to the database, pretending to be the legitimate user.

A more secure scheme involves a **challenge-response** system. The database system sends a challenge string to the user. The user encrypts the challenge string using a secret password as encryption key, and then returns the result. The database system can verify the authenticity of the user by decrypting the string with the same secret password, and checking the result with the original challenge string. This scheme ensures that no passwords travel across the network.

Public-key systems can be used for encryption in challenge–response systems. The database system encrypts a challenge string using the user's public key and sends it to the user. The user decrypts the string using her private key, and returns the result to the database system. The database system then checks the response. This scheme has the added benefit of not storing the secret password in the database, where it could potentially be seen by system administrators.

Another interesting application of public-key encryption is in **digital signatures** to verify authenticity of data; digital signatures play the electronic role of physical signatures on documents. The private key is used to sign data, and the signed data can be made public. Anyone can verify them by the public key, but no one could have generated the signed data without having the private key. Thus, we can **authenticate** the data; that is, we can verify that the data were indeed created by the person who claims to have created them.

Furthermore, digital signatures also serve to ensure **nonrepudiation**. That is, in case the person who created the data later claims she did not create it (the electronic equivalent of claiming not to have signed the check), we can prove that that person must have created the data (unless her private key was leaked to others).

6.8 Summary

- Integrity constraints ensure that changes made to the database by authorized users do not result in a loss of data consistency.

- In earlier chapters, we considered several forms of constraints, including key declarations and the declaration of the form of a relationship (many to many, many to one, one to one). In this chapter, we considered several additional forms of constraints, and discussed mechanisms for ensuring the maintenance of these constraints.

- Domain constraints specify the set of possible values that may be associated with an attribute. Such constraints may also prohibit the use of null values for particular attributes.

- Referential-integrity constraints ensure that a value that appears in one relation for a given set of attributes also appears for a certain set of attributes in another relation.

- Domain constraints, and referential-integrity constraints are relatively easy to test. Use of more complex constraints may lead to substantial overhead. We saw two ways to express more general constraints. Assertions are declarative expressions that state predicates that we require always to be true.

- Triggers define actions to be executed automatically when certain events occur and corresponding conditions are satisfied. Triggers have many uses, such as implementing business rules, audit logging, and even carrying out actions outside the database system. Although triggers were added only lately to the SQL standard as part of SQL:1999, most database systems have long implemented triggers.

- The data stored in the database need to be protected from unauthorized access, malicious destruction or alteration, and accidental introduction of inconsistency.

- It is easier to protect against accidental loss of data consistency than to protect against malicious access to the database. Absolute protection of the database from malicious abuse is not possible, but the cost to the perpetrator can be made sufficiently high to deter most, if not all, attempts to access the database without proper authority.

- A user may have several forms of authorization on parts of the database. Authorization is a means by which the database system can be protected against malicious or unauthorized access.

- A user who has been granted some form of authority may be allowed to pass on this authority to other users. However, we must be careful about how authorization can be passed among users if we are to ensure that such authorization can be revoked at some future time.

- Roles help to assign a set of privileges to a user according to on the role that the user plays in the organization.

- The various authorization provisions in a database system may not provide sufficient protection for highly sensitive data. In such cases, data can be *encrypted*. Only a user who knows how to decipher (*decrypt*) the encrypted data can read them. Encryption also forms the basis for secure authentication of users.

Review Terms

- Domain constraints
- Check clause
- Referential integrity

- Primary key constraint
- Unique constraint
- Foreign key constraint

- Cascade
- Assertion
- Trigger
- Event-condition-action model
- Before and after triggers
- Transition variables and tables
- Database security
- Levels of security
- Authorization
- Privileges
  - ☐ Read
  - ☐ Insert
  - ☐ Update
  - ☐ Delete
  - ☐ Index
  - ☐ Resource
  - ☐ Alteration
  - ☐ Drop
  - ☐ Grant
  - ☐ All privileges
- Authorization graph
- Granting of privileges
- Roles
- Encryption
- Secret-key encryption
- Public-key encryption
- Authentication
- Challenge–response system
- Digital signature
- Nonrepudiation

Exercises

6.1 Complete the SQL DDL definition of the bank database of Figure 6.2 to include the relations *loan* and *borrower*.

6.2 Consider the following relational database:

$$employee\ (\underline{employee\text{-}name},\ street,\ city)$$
$$works\ (\underline{employee\text{-}name},\ company\text{-}name,\ salary)$$
$$company\ (\underline{company\text{-}name},\ city)$$
$$manages\ (\underline{employee\text{-}name},\ manager\text{-}name)$$

Give an SQL DDL definition of this database. Identify referential-integrity constraints that should hold, and include them in the DDL definition.

6.3 Referential-integrity constraints as defined in this chapter involve exactly two relations. Consider a database that includes the following relations:

$$salaried\text{-}worker\ (name,\ office,\ phone,\ salary)$$
$$hourly\text{-}worker\ (name,\ hourly\text{-}wage)$$
$$address\ (name,\ street,\ city)$$

Suppose that we wish to require that every name that appears in *address* appear in either *salaried-worker* or *hourly-worker*, but not necessarily in both.

  a. Propose a syntax for expressing such constraints.

  b. Discuss the actions that the system must take to enforce a constraint of this form.

6.4 SQL allows a foreign-key dependency to refer to the same relation, as in the following example:

> **create table** *manager*
>   (*employee-name*   **char**(20) **not null**
>   *manager-name*   **char**(20) **not null**,
>   **primary key** *employee-name,*
>   **foreign key** (*manager-name*) **references** *manager*
>   **on delete cascade**)

Here, *employee-name* is a key to the table *manager*, meaning that each employee has at most one manager. The foreign-key clause requires that every manager also be an employee. Explain exactly what happens when a tuple in the relation *manager* is deleted.

6.5 Suppose there are two relations r and s, such that the foreign key B of r references the primary key A of s. Describe how the trigger mechanism can be used to implement the **on delete cascade** option, when a tuple is deleted from s.

6.6 Write an assertion for the bank database to ensure that the assets value for the Perryridge branch is equal to the sum of all the amounts lent by the Perryridge branch.

6.7 Write an SQL trigger to carry out the following action: On **delete** of an account, for each owner of the account, check if the owner has any remaining accounts, and if she does not, delete her from the *depositor* relation.

6.8 Consider a view *branch-cust* defined as follows:

> **create view** *branch-cust* **as**
>   **select** *branch-name, customer-name*
>   **from** *depositor, account*
>   **where** *depositor.account-number = account.account-number*

Suppose that the view is *materialized*, that is, the view is computed and stored. Write active rules to *maintain* the view, that is, to keep it up to date on insertions to and deletions from *depositor* or *account*. Do not bother about updates.

6.9 Make a list of security concerns for a bank. For each item on your list, state whether this concern relates to physical security, human security, operating-system security, or database security.

6.10 Using the relations of our sample bank database, write an SQL expression to define the following views:

    a. A view containing the account numbers and customer names (but not the balances) for all accounts at the Deer Park branch.

    b. A view containing the names and addresses of all customers who have an account with the bank, but do not have a loan.

    c. A view containing the name and average account balance of every customer of the Rock Ridge branch.

6.11 For each of the views that you defined in Exercise 6.10, explain how updates would be performed (if they should be allowed at all). *Hint*: See the discussion of views in Chapter 3.

6.12 In Chapter 3, we described the use of views to simplify access to the database by users who need to see only part of the database. In this chapter, we described the use of views as a security mechanism. Do these two purposes for views ever conflict? Explain your answer.

6.13 What is the purpose of having separate categories for index authorization and resource authorization?

6.14 Database systems that store each relation in a separate operating-system file may use the operating system's security and authorization scheme, instead of defining a special scheme themselves. Discuss an advantage and a disadvantage of such an approach.

6.15 What are two advantages of encrypting data stored in the database?

6.16 Perhaps the most important data items in any database system are the passwords that control access to the database. Suggest a scheme for the secure storage of passwords. Be sure that your scheme allows the system to test passwords supplied by users who are attempting to log into the system.

Bibliographical Notes

Discussions of integrity constraints in the relational model are offered by Hammer and McLeod [1975], Stonebraker [1975], Eswaran and Chamberlin [1975], Schmid and Swenson [1975] and Codd [1979]. The original SQL proposals for assertions and triggers are discussed in Astrahan et al. [1976], Chamberlin et al. [1976], and Chamberlin et al. [1981]. See the bibliographic notes of Chapter 4 for references to SQL standards and books on SQL.

    Discussions of efficient maintenance and checking of semantic-integrity assertions are offered by Hammer and Sarin [1978], Badal and Popek [1979], Bernstein et al. [1980a], Hsu and Imielinski [1985], McCune and Henschen [1989], and Chomicki [1992]. An alternative to using run-time integrity checking is certifying the correctness of programs that access the database. Sheard and Stemple [1989] discusses this approach.

    Active databases are databases that support triggers and other mechanisms that permit the database to take actions on occurrence of events. McCarthy and Dayal [1989] discuss the architecture of an active database system based on the event–condition–action formalism. Widom and Finkelstein [1990] describe the architecture of a rule system based on set-oriented rules; the implementation of the rule system on the Starburst extensible database system is presented in Widom et al. [1991]. Consider an execution mechanism that allows a nondeterministic choice of which rule to execute next. A rule system is said to be **confluent** if, regardless of the rule chosen, the final state is the same. Issues of termination, nondeterminism, and confluence of rule systems are discussed in Aiken et al. [1995].

Security aspects of computer systems in general are discussed in Bell and La-Padula [1976] and by US Dept. of Defense [1985]. Security aspects of SQL can be found in the SQL standards and textbooks on SQL referenced in the bibliographic notes of Chapter 4.

Stonebraker and Wong [1974] discusses the Ingres approach to security, which involves modification of users' queries to ensure that users do not access data for which authorization has not been granted. Denning and Denning [1979] survey database security.

Database systems that can produce incorrect answers when necessary for security maintenance are discussed in Winslett et al. [1994] and Tendick and Matloff [1994]. Work on security in relational databases includes that of Stachour and Thuraisingham [1990], Jajodia and Sandhu [1990], and Qian and Lunt [1996]. Operating-system security issues are discussed in most operating-system texts, including Silberschatz and Galvin [1998].

Stallings [1998] provides a textbook description of cryptography. Daemen and Rijmen [2000] present the Rijndael algorithm. The Data Encryption Standard is presented by US Dept. of Commerce [1977]. Public-key encryption is discussed by Rivest et al. [1978]. Other discussions on cryptography include Diffie and Hellman [1979], Simmons [1979], Fernandez et al. [1981], and Akl [1983].

CHAPTER 7

Relational-Database Design

This chapter continues our discussion of design issues in relational databases. In general, the goal of a relational-database design is to generate a set of relation schemas that allows us to store information without unnecessary redundancy, yet also allows us to retrieve information easily. One approach is to design schemas that are in an appropriate *normal form*. To determine whether a relation schema is in one of the desirable normal forms, we need additional information about the real-world enterprise that we are modeling with the database. In this chapter, we introduce the notion of functional dependencies. We then define normal forms in terms of functional dependencies and other types of data dependencies.

7.1 First Normal Form

The first of the normal forms that we study, **first normal form**, imposes a very basic requirement on relations; unlike the other normal forms, it does not require additional information such as functional dependencies.

A domain is **atomic** if elements of the domain are considered to be indivisible units. We say that a relation schema R is in **first normal form** (1NF) if the domains of all attributes of R are atomic.

A set of names is an example of a nonatomic value. For example, if the schema of a relation *employee* included an attribute *children* whose domain elements are sets of names, the schema would not be in first normal form.

Composite attributes, such as an attribute *address* with component attributes *street* and *city*, also have nonatomic domains.

Integers are assumed to be atomic, so the set of integers is an atomic domain; the set of all sets of integers is a nonatomic domain. The distinction is that we do not normally consider integers to have subparts, but we consider sets of integers to have subparts—namely, the integers making up the set. But the important issue is not what the domain itself is, but rather how we use domain elements in our database.

The domain of all integers would be nonatomic if we considered each integer to be an ordered list of digits.

As a practical illustration of the above point, consider an organization that assigns employees identification numbers of the following form: The first two letters specify the department and the remaining four digits are a unique number within the department for the employee. Examples of such numbers would be $CS0012$ and $EE1127$. Such identification numbers can be divided into smaller units, and are therefore nonatomic. If a relation schema had an attribute whose domain consists of identification numbers encoded as above, the schema would not be in first normal form.

When such identification numbers are used, the department of an employee can be found by writing code that breaks up the structure of an identification number. Doing so requires extra programming, and information gets encoded in the application program rather than in the database. Further problems arise if such identification numbers are used as primary keys: When an employee changes department, the employee's identification number must be changed everywhere it occurs, which can be a difficult task, or the code that interprets the number would give a wrong result.

The use of set valued attributes can lead to designs with redundant storage of data, which in turn can result in inconsistencies. For instance, instead of the relationship between accounts and customers being represented as a separate relation *depositor*, a database designer may be tempted to store a set of *owners* with each account, and a set of *accounts* with each customer. Whenever an account is created, or the set of owners of an account is updated, the update has to be performed at two places; failure to perform both updates can leave the database in an inconsistent state. Keeping only one of these sets would avoid repeated information, but would complicate some queries. Set valued attributes are also more complicated to write queries with, and more complicated to reason about.

In this chapter we consider only atomic domains, and assume that relations are in first normal form. Although we have not mentioned first normal form earlier, when we introduced the relational model in Chapter 3 we stated that attribute values must be atomic.

Some types of nonatomic values can be useful, although they should be used with care. For example, composite valued attributes are often useful, and set valued attributes are also useful in many cases, which is why both are supported in the E-R model. In many domains where entities have a complex structure, forcing a first normal form representation represents an unnecessary burden on the application programmer, who has to write code to convert data into atomic form. There is also a run-time overhead of converting data back and forth from the atomic form. Support for nonatomic values can thus be very useful in such domains. In fact, modern database systems do support many types of nonatomic values, as we will see in Chapters 8 and 9. However, in this chapter we restrict ourselves to relations in first normal form.

7.2   Pitfalls in Relational-Database Design

Before we continue our discussion of normal forms, let us look at what can go wrong in a bad database design. Among the undesirable properties that a bad design may have are:

- Repetition of information

- Inability to represent certain information

We shall discuss these problems with the help of a modified database design for our banking example: In contrast to the relation schema used in Chapters 3 to 6, suppose the information concerning loans is kept in one single relation, *lending*, which is defined over the relation schema

$$Lending\text{-}schema = (branch\text{-}name, branch\text{-}city, assets, customer\text{-}name,$$
$$loan\text{-}number, amount)$$

Figure 7.1 shows an instance of the relation *lending* (*Lending-schema*). A tuple *t* in the *lending* relation has the following intuitive meaning:

- *t*[*assets*] is the asset figure for the branch named *t*[*branch-name*].

- *t*[*branch-city*] is the city in which the branch named *t*[*branch-name*] is located.

- *t*[*loan-number*] is the number assigned to a loan made by the branch named *t*[*branch-name*] to the customer named *t*[*customer-name*].

- *t*[*amount*] is the amount of the loan whose number is *t*[*loan-number*].

Suppose that we wish to add a new loan to our database. Say that the loan is made by the Perryridge branch to Adams in the amount of $1500. Let the *loan-number* be L-31. In our design, we need a tuple with values on all the attributes of *Lending-schema*. Thus, we must repeat the asset and city data for the Perryridge branch, and must add the tuple

(Perryridge, Horseneck, 1700000, Adams, L-31, 1500)

branch-name	branch-city	assets	customer-name	loan-number	amount
Downtown	Brooklyn	9000000	Jones	L-17	1000
Redwood	Palo Alto	2100000	Smith	L-23	2000
Perryridge	Horseneck	1700000	Hayes	L-15	1500
Downtown	Brooklyn	9000000	Jackson	L-14	1500
Mianus	Horseneck	400000	Jones	L-93	500
Round Hill	Horseneck	8000000	Turner	L-11	900
Pownal	Bennington	300000	Williams	L-29	1200
North Town	Rye	3700000	Hayes	L-16	1300
Downtown	Brooklyn	9000000	Johnson	L-18	2000
Perryridge	Horseneck	1700000	Glenn	L-25	2500
Brighton	Brooklyn	7100000	Brooks	L-10	2200

Figure 7.1 Sample *lending* relation.

to the *lending* relation. In general, the asset and city data for a branch must appear once for each loan made by that branch.

The repetition of information in our alternative design is undesirable. Repeating information wastes space. Furthermore, it complicates updating the database. Suppose, for example, that the assets of the Perryridge branch change from 1700000 to 1900000. Under our original design, one tuple of the *branch* relation needs to be changed. Under our alternative design, many tuples of the *lending* relation need to be changed. Thus, updates are more costly under the alternative design than under the original design. When we perform the update in the alternative database, we must ensure that *every* tuple pertaining to the Perryridge branch is updated, or else our database will show two different asset values for the Perryridge branch.

That observation is central to understanding why the alternative design is bad. We know that a bank branch has a unique value of assets, so given a branch name we can uniquely identify the assets value. On the other hand, we know that a branch may make many loans, so given a branch name, we cannot uniquely determine a loan number. In other words, we say that the *functional dependency*

$$branch\text{-}name \rightarrow assets$$

holds on *Lending-schema*, but we do not expect the functional dependency *branch-name → loan-number* to hold. The fact that a branch has a particular value of assets, and the fact that a branch makes a loan are independent, and, as we have seen, these facts are best represented in separate relations. We shall see that we can use functional dependencies to specify formally when a database design is good.

Another problem with the *Lending-schema* design is that we cannot represent directly the information concerning a branch (*branch-name*, *branch-city*, *assets*) unless there exists at least one loan at the branch. This is because tuples in the *lending* relation require values for *loan-number*, *amount*, and *customer-name*.

One solution to this problem is to introduce *null values*, as we did to handle updates through views. Recall, however, that null values are difficult to handle, as we saw in Section 3.3.4. If we are not willing to deal with null values, then we can create the branch information only when the first loan application at that branch is made. Worse, we would have to delete this information when all the loans have been paid. Clearly, this situation is undesirable, since, under our original database design, the branch information would be available regardless of whether or not loans are currently maintained in the branch, and without resorting to null values.

7.3 Functional Dependencies

Functional dependencies play a key role in differentiating good database designs from bad database designs. A **functional dependency** is a type of constraint that is a generalization of the notion of *key*, as discussed in Chapters 2 and 3.

7.3.1 Basic Concepts

Functional dependencies are constraints on the set of legal relations. They allow us to express facts about the enterprise that we are modeling with our database.

In Chapter 2, we defined the notion of a *superkey* as follows. Let R be a relation schema. A subset K of R is a **superkey** of R if, in any legal relation $r(R)$, for all pairs t_1 and t_2 of tuples in r such that $t_1 \neq t_2$, then $t_1[K] \neq t_2[K]$. That is, no two tuples in any legal relation $r(R)$ may have the same value on attribute set K.

The notion of functional dependency generalizes the notion of superkey. Consider a relation schema R, and let $\alpha \subseteq R$ and $\beta \subseteq R$. The **functional dependency**

$$\alpha \rightarrow \beta$$

holds on schema R if, in any legal relation $r(R)$, for all pairs of tuples t_1 and t_2 in r such that $t_1[\alpha] = t_2[\alpha]$, it is also the case that $t_1[\beta] = t_2[\beta]$.

Using the functional-dependency notation, we say that K is a superkey of R if $K \rightarrow R$. That is, K is a superkey if, whenever $t_1[K] = t_2[K]$, it is also the case that $t_1[R] = t_2[R]$ (that is, $t_1 = t_2$).

Functional dependencies allow us to express constraints that we cannot express with superkeys. Consider the schema

$$\textit{Loan-info-schema} = (\textit{loan-number, branch-name, customer-name, amount})$$

which is simplification of the *Lending-schema* that we saw earlier. The set of functional dependencies that we expect to hold on this relation schema is

$$\textit{loan-number} \rightarrow \textit{amount}$$
$$\textit{loan-number} \rightarrow \textit{branch-name}$$

We would not, however, expect the functional dependency

$$\textit{loan-number} \rightarrow \textit{customer-name}$$

to hold, since, in general, a given loan can be made to more than one customer (for example, to both members of a husband–wife pair).

We shall use functional dependencies in two ways:

1. To test relations to see whether they are legal under a given set of functional dependencies. If a relation r is legal under a set F of functional dependencies, we say that r **satisfies** F.

2. To specify constraints on the set of legal relations. We shall thus concern ourselves with *only* those relations that satisfy a given set of functional dependencies. If we wish to constrain ourselves to relations on schema R that satisfy a set F of functional dependencies, we say that F **holds** on R.

Let us consider the relation r of Figure 7.2, to see which functional dependencies are satisfied. Observe that $A \rightarrow C$ is satisfied. There are two tuples that have an A value of a_1. These tuples have the same C value—namely, c_1. Similarly, the two tuples with an A value of a_2 have the same C value, c_2. There are no other pairs of distinct tuples that have the same A value. The functional dependency $C \rightarrow A$ is not satisfied, however. To see that it is not, consider the tuples $t_1 = (a_2, b_3, c_2, d_3)$ and

A	B	C	D
a_1	b_1	c_1	d_1
a_1	b_2	c_1	d_2
a_2	b_2	c_2	d_2
a_2	b_2	c_2	d_3
a_3	b_3	c_2	d_4

Figure 7.2   Sample relation r.

$t_2 = (a_3, b_3, c_2, d_4)$. These two tuples have the same C values, c_2, but they have different A values, a_2 and a_3, respectively. Thus, we have found a pair of tuples t_1 and t_2 such that $t_1[C] = t_2[C]$, but $t_1[A] \neq t_2[A]$.

Many other functional dependencies are satisfied by r, including, for example, the functional dependency $AB \rightarrow D$. Note that we use AB as a shorthand for $\{A,B\}$, to conform with standard practice. Observe that there is no pair of distinct tuples t_1 and t_2 such that $t_1[AB] = t_2[AB]$. Therefore, if $t_1[AB] = t_2[AB]$, it must be that $t_1 = t_2$ and, thus, $t_1[D] = t_2[D]$. So, r satisfies $AB \rightarrow D$.

Some functional dependencies are said to be **trivial** because they are satisfied by all relations. For example, $A \rightarrow A$ is satisfied by all relations involving attribute A. Reading the definition of functional dependency literally, we see that, for all tuples t_1 and t_2 such that $t_1[A] = t_2[A]$, it is the case that $t_1[A] = t_2[A]$. Similarly, $AB \rightarrow A$ is satisfied by all relations involving attribute A. In general, a functional dependency of the form $\alpha \rightarrow \beta$ is **trivial** if $\beta \subseteq \alpha$.

To distinguish between the concepts of a relation satisfying a dependency and a dependency holding on a schema, we return to the banking example. If we consider the *customer* relation (on *Customer-schema*) in Figure 7.3, we see that *customer-street* $\rightarrow$ *customer-city* is satisfied. However, we believe that, in the real world, two cities

customer-name	customer-street	customer-city
Jones	Main	Harrison
Smith	North	Rye
Hayes	Main	Harrison
Curry	North	Rye
Lindsay	Park	Pittsfield
Turner	Putnam	Stamford
Williams	Nassau	Princeton
Adams	Spring	Pittsfield
Johnson	Alma	Palo Alto
Glenn	Sand Hill	Woodside
Brooks	Senator	Brooklyn
Green	Walnut	Stamford

Figure 7.3   The *customer* relation.

loan-number	branch-name	amount
L-17	Downtown	1000
L-23	Redwood	2000
L-15	Perryridge	1500
L-14	Downtown	1500
L-93	Mianus	500
L-11	Round Hill	900
L-29	Pownal	1200
L-16	North Town	1300
L-18	Downtown	2000
L-25	Perryridge	2500
L-10	Brighton	2200

Figure 7.4   The *loan* relation.

can have streets with the same name. Thus, it is possible, at some time, to have an instance of the *customer* relation in which *customer-street* → *customer-city* is not satisfied. So, we would not include *customer-street* → *customer-city* in the set of functional dependencies that hold on *Customer-schema*.

In the *loan* relation (on *Loan-schema*) of Figure 7.4, we see that the dependency *loan-number* → *amount* is satisfied. In contrast to the case of *customer-city* and *customer-street* in *Customer-schema*, we do believe that the real-world enterprise that we are modeling requires each loan to have only one amount. Therefore, we want to require that *loan-number* → *amount* be satisfied by the *loan* relation at all times. In other words, we require that the constraint *loan-number* → *amount* hold on *Loan-schema*.

In the *branch* relation of Figure 7.5, we see that *branch-name* → *assets* is satisfied, as is *assets* → *branch-name*. We want to require that *branch-name* → *assets* hold on *Branch-schema*. However, we do not wish to require that *assets* → *branch-name* hold, since it is possible to have several branches that have the same asset value.

In what follows, we assume that, when we design a relational database, we first list those functional dependencies that must always hold. In the banking example, our list of dependencies includes the following:

branch-name	branch-city	assets
Downtown	Brooklyn	9000000
Redwood	Palo Alto	2100000
Perryridge	Horseneck	1700000
Mianus	Horseneck	400000
Round Hill	Horseneck	8000000
Pownal	Bennington	300000
North Town	Rye	3700000
Brighton	Brooklyn	7100000

Figure 7.5   The *branch* relation.

- On *Branch-schema*:

$$branch\text{-}name \rightarrow branch\text{-}city$$
$$branch\text{-}name \rightarrow assets$$

- On *Customer-schema*:

$$customer\text{-}name \rightarrow customer\text{-}city$$
$$customer\text{-}name \rightarrow customer\text{-}street$$

- On *Loan-schema*:

$$loan\text{-}number \rightarrow amount$$
$$loan\text{-}number \rightarrow branch\text{-}name$$

- On *Borrower-schema*:

No functional dependencies

- On *Account-schema*:

$$account\text{-}number \rightarrow branch\text{-}name$$
$$account\text{-}number \rightarrow balance$$

- On *Depositor-schema*:

No functional dependencies

7.3.2 Closure of a Set of Functional Dependencies

It is not sufficient to consider the given set of functional dependencies. Rather, we need to consider *all* functional dependencies that hold. We shall see that, given a set F of functional dependencies, we can prove that certain other functional dependencies hold. We say that such functional dependencies are "logically implied" by F.

More formally, given a relational schema R, a functional dependency f on R is **logically implied** by a set of functional dependencies F on R if every relation instance $r(R)$ that satisfies F also satisfies f.

Suppose we are given a relation schema $R = (A, B, C, G, H, I)$ and the set of functional dependencies

$$A \rightarrow B$$
$$A \rightarrow C$$
$$CG \rightarrow H$$
$$CG \rightarrow I$$
$$B \rightarrow H$$

The functional dependency

$$A \rightarrow H$$

is logically implied. That is, we can show that, whenever our given set of functional dependencies holds on a relation, $A \rightarrow H$ must also hold on the relation. Suppose that t_1 and t_2 are tuples such that

$$t_1[A] = t_2[A]$$

Since we are given that $A \rightarrow B$, it follows from the definition of functional dependency that

$$t_1[B] = t_2[B]$$

Then, since we are given that $B \rightarrow H$, it follows from the definition of functional dependency that

$$t_1[H] = t_2[H]$$

Therefore, we have shown that, whenever t_1 and t_2 are tuples such that $t_1[A] = t_2[A]$, it must be that $t_1[H] = t_2[H]$. But that is exactly the definition of $A \rightarrow H$.

Let F be a set of functional dependencies. The **closure** of F, denoted by F^+, is the set of all functional dependencies logically implied by F. Given F, we can compute F^+ directly from the formal definition of functional dependency. If F were large, this process would be lengthy and difficult. Such a computation of F^+ requires arguments of the type just used to show that $A \rightarrow H$ is in the closure of our example set of dependencies.

Axioms, or rules of inference, provide a simpler technique for reasoning about functional dependencies. In the rules that follow, we use Greek letters (α, β, γ, ...) for sets of attributes, and uppercase Roman letters from the beginning of the alphabet for individual attributes. We use $\alpha\beta$ to denote $\alpha \cup \beta$.

We can use the following three rules to find logically implied functional dependencies. By applying these rules *repeatedly*, we can find all of F^+, given F. This collection of rules is called **Armstrong's axioms** in honor of the person who first proposed it.

- **Reflexivity rule**. If α is a set of attributes and $\beta \subseteq \alpha$, then $\alpha \rightarrow \beta$ holds.

- **Augmentation rule**. If $\alpha \rightarrow \beta$ holds and γ is a set of attributes, then $\gamma\alpha \rightarrow \gamma\beta$ holds.

- **Transitivity rule**. If $\alpha \rightarrow \beta$ holds and $\beta \rightarrow \gamma$ holds, then $\alpha \rightarrow \gamma$ holds.

Armstrong's axioms are **sound**, because they do not generate any incorrect functional dependencies. They are **complete**, because, for a given set F of functional dependencies, they allow us to generate all F^+. The bibliographical notes provide references for proofs of soundness and completeness.

Although Armstrong's axioms are complete, it is tiresome to use them directly for the computation of F^+. To simplify matters further, we list additional rules. It is possible to use Armstrong's axioms to prove that these rules are correct (see Exercises 7.8, 7.9, and 7.10).

- **Union rule**. If $\alpha \rightarrow \beta$ holds and $\alpha \rightarrow \gamma$ holds, then $\alpha \rightarrow \beta\gamma$ holds.

- **Decomposition rule**. If $\alpha \rightarrow \beta\gamma$ holds, then $\alpha \rightarrow \beta$ holds and $\alpha \rightarrow \gamma$ holds.

- **Pseudotransitivity rule**. If $\alpha \rightarrow \beta$ holds and $\gamma\beta \rightarrow \delta$ holds, then $\alpha\gamma \rightarrow \delta$ holds.

Let us apply our rules to the example of schema $R = (A, B, C, G, H, I)$ and the set F of functional dependencies $\{A \rightarrow B, A \rightarrow C, CG \rightarrow H, CG \rightarrow I, B \rightarrow H\}$. We list several members of F^+ here:

- $A \rightarrow H$. Since $A \rightarrow B$ and $B \rightarrow H$ hold, we apply the transitivity rule. Observe that it was much easier to use Armstrong's axioms to show that $A \rightarrow H$ holds than it was to argue directly from the definitions, as we did earlier in this section.

- $CG \rightarrow HI$. Since $CG \rightarrow H$ and $CG \rightarrow I$, the union rule implies that $CG \rightarrow HI$.

- $AG \rightarrow I$. Since $A \rightarrow C$ and $CG \rightarrow I$, the pseudotransitivity rule implies that $AG \rightarrow I$ holds.

    Another way of finding that $AG \rightarrow I$ holds is as follows. We use the augmentation rule on $A \rightarrow C$ to infer $AG \rightarrow CG$. Applying the transitivity rule to this dependency and $CG \rightarrow I$, we infer $AG \rightarrow I$.

Figure 7.6 shows a procedure that demonstrates formally how to use Armstrong's axioms to compute F^+. In this procedure, when a functional dependency is added to F^+, it may be already present, and in that case there is no change to F^+. We will also see an alternative way of computing F^+ in Section 7.3.3.

The left-hand and right-hand sides of a functional dependency are both subsets of R. Since a set of size n has 2^n subsets, there are a total of $2 \times 2^n = 2^{n+1}$ possible functional dependencies, where n is the number of attributes in R. Each iteration of the repeat loop of the procedure, except the last iteration, adds at least one functional dependency to F^+. Thus, the procedure is guaranteed to terminate.

7.3.3 Closure of Attribute Sets

To test whether a set α is a superkey, we must devise an algorithm for computing the set of attributes functionally determined by α. One way of doing this is to compute F^+, take all functional dependencies with α as the left-hand side, and take the union of the right-hand sides of all such dependencies. However, doing so can be expensive, since F^+ can be large.

```
F+ = F
repeat
      for each functional dependency f in F+
            apply reflexivity and augmentation rules on f
            add the resulting functional dependencies to F+
      for each pair of functional dependencies f1 and f2 in F+
            if f1 and f2 can be combined using transitivity
                  add the resulting functional dependency to F+
until F+ does not change any further
```

Figure 7.6   A procedure to compute F^+.

An efficient algorithm for computing the set of attributes functionally determined by α is useful not only for testing whether α is a superkey, but also for several other tasks, as we will see later in this section.

Let α be a set of attributes. We call the set of all attributes functionally determined by α under a set F of functional dependencies the **closure** of α under F; we denote it by α^+. Figure 7.7 shows an algorithm, written in pseudocode, to compute α^+. The input is a set F of functional dependencies and the set α of attributes. The output is stored in the variable *result*.

To illustrate how the algorithm works, we shall use it to compute $(AG)^+$ with the functional dependencies defined in Section 7.3.2. We start with *result* $= AG$. The first time that we execute the **while** loop to test each functional dependency, we find that

- $A \rightarrow B$ causes us to include B in *result*. To see this fact, we observe that $A \rightarrow B$ is in F, $A \subseteq$ *result* (which is AG), so *result* := *result* $\cup B$.

- $A \rightarrow C$ causes *result* to become $ABCG$.

- $CG \rightarrow H$ causes *result* to become $ABCGH$.

- $CG \rightarrow I$ causes *result* to become $ABCGHI$.

The second time that we execute the **while** loop, no new attributes are added to *result*, and the algorithm terminates.

Let us see why the algorithm of Figure 7.7 is correct. The first step is correct, since $\alpha \rightarrow \alpha$ always holds (by the reflexivity rule). We claim that, for any subset β of *result*, $\alpha \rightarrow \beta$. Since we start the **while** loop with $\alpha \rightarrow$ *result* being true, we can add γ to *result* only if $\beta \subseteq$ *result* and $\beta \rightarrow \gamma$. But then *result* $\rightarrow \beta$ by the reflexivity rule, so $\alpha \rightarrow \beta$ by transitivity. Another application of transitivity shows that $\alpha \rightarrow \gamma$ (using $\alpha \rightarrow \beta$ and $\beta \rightarrow \gamma$). The union rule implies that $\alpha \rightarrow$ *result* $\cup \gamma$, so α functionally determines any new result generated in the **while** loop. Thus, any attribute returned by the algorithm is in α^+.

It is easy to see that the algorithm finds all α^+. If there is an attribute in α^+ that is not yet in *result*, then there must be a functional dependency $\beta \rightarrow \gamma$ for which $\beta \subseteq$ *result*, and at least one attribute in γ is not in *result*.

It turns out that, in the worst case, this algorithm may take an amount of time quadratic in the size of F. There is a faster (although slightly more complex) algorithm that runs in time linear in the size of F; that algorithm is presented as part of Exercise 7.14.

$result := \alpha;$
while (changes to *result*) **do**
    for each functional dependency $\beta \rightarrow \gamma$ **in** F **do**
        begin
            if $\beta \subseteq$ *result* **then** *result* := *result* $\cup \gamma;$
        end

Figure 7.7   An algorithm to compute α^+, the closure of α under F.

There are several uses of the attribute closure algorithm:

- To test if α is a superkey, we compute α^+, and check if α^+ contains all attributes of R.

- We can check if a functional dependency $\alpha \rightarrow \beta$ holds (or, in other words, is in F^+), by checking if $\beta \subseteq \alpha^+$. That is, we compute α^+ by using attribute closure, and then check if it contains β. This test is particularly useful, as we will see later in this chapter.

- It gives us an alternative way to compute F^+: For each $\gamma \subseteq R$, we find the closure γ^+, and for each $S \subseteq \gamma^+$, we output a functional dependency $\gamma \rightarrow S$.

7.3.4 Canonical Cover

Suppose that we have a set of functional dependencies F on a relation schema. Whenever a user performs an update on the relation, the database system must ensure that the update does not violate any functional dependencies, that is, all the functional dependencies in F are satisfied in the new database state.

The system must roll back the update if it violates any functional dependencies in the set F.

We can reduce the effort spent in checking for violations by testing a simplified set of functional dependencies that has the same closure as the given set. Any database that satisfies the simplified set of functional dependencies will also satisfy the original set, and vice versa, since the two sets have the same closure. However, the simplified set is easier to test. We shall see how the simplified set can be constructed in a moment. First, we need some definitions.

An attribute of a functional dependency is said to be **extraneous** if we can remove it without changing the closure of the set of functional dependencies. The formal definition of **extraneous attributes** is as follows. Consider a set F of functional dependencies and the functional dependency $\alpha \rightarrow \beta$ in F.

- Attribute A is extraneous in α if $A \in \alpha$, and F logically implies $(F - \{\alpha \rightarrow \beta\}) \cup \{(\alpha - A) \rightarrow \beta\}$.

- Attribute A is extraneous in β if $A \in \beta$, and the set of functional dependencies $(F - \{\alpha \rightarrow \beta\}) \cup \{\alpha \rightarrow (\beta - A)\}$ logically implies F.

For example, suppose we have the functional dependencies $AB \rightarrow C$ and $A \rightarrow C$ in F. Then, B is extraneous in $AB \rightarrow C$. As another example, suppose we have the functional dependencies $AB \rightarrow CD$ and $A \rightarrow C$ in F. Then C would be extraneous in the right-hand side of $AB \rightarrow CD$.

Beware of the direction of the implications when using the definition of extraneous attributes: If you exchange the left-hand side with right-hand side, the implication will *always* hold. That is, $(F - \{\alpha \rightarrow \beta\}) \cup \{(\alpha - A) \rightarrow \beta\}$ always logically implies F, and also F always logically implies $(F - \{\alpha \rightarrow \beta\}) \cup \{\alpha \rightarrow (\beta - A)\}$

Here is how we can test efficiently if an attribute is extraneous. Let R be the relation schema, and let F be the given set of functional dependencies that hold on R. Consider an attribute A in a dependency $\alpha \rightarrow \beta$.

- If $A \in \beta$, to check if A is extraneous consider the set
$$F' = (F - \{\alpha \rightarrow \beta\}) \cup \{\alpha \rightarrow (\beta - A)\}$$
  and check if $\alpha \rightarrow A$ can be inferred from F'. To do so, compute α^+ (the closure of α) under F'; if α^+ includes A, then A is extraneous in β.

- If $A \in \alpha$, to check if A is extraneous, let $\gamma = \alpha - \{A\}$, and check if $\gamma \rightarrow \beta$ can be inferred from F. To do so, compute γ^+ (the closure of γ) under F; if γ^+ includes all attributes in β, then A is extraneous in α.

For example, suppose F contains $AB \rightarrow CD$, $A \rightarrow E$, and $E \rightarrow C$. To check if C is extraneous in $AB \rightarrow CD$, we compute the attribute closure of AB under $F' = \{AB \rightarrow D, A \rightarrow E, \text{ and } E \rightarrow C\}$. The closure is $ABCDE$, which includes CD, so we infer that C is extraneous.

A **canonical cover** F_c for F is a set of dependencies such that F logically implies all dependencies in F_c, and F_c logically implies all dependencies in F. Furthermore, F_c must have the following properties:

- No functional dependency in F_c contains an extraneous attribute.

- Each left side of a functional dependency in F_c is unique. That is, there are no two dependencies $\alpha_1 \rightarrow \beta_1$ and $\alpha_2 \rightarrow \beta_2$ in F_c such that $\alpha_1 = \alpha_2$.

A canonical cover for a set of functional dependencies F can be computed as depicted in Figure 7.8. It is important to note that when checking if an attribute is extraneous, the check uses the dependencies in the current value of F_c, and **not** the dependencies in F. If a functional dependency contains only one attribute in its right-hand side, for example $A \rightarrow C$, and that attribute is found to be extraneous, we would get a functional dependency with an empty right-hand side. Such functional dependencies should be deleted.

The canonical cover of F, F_c, can be shown to have the same closure as F; hence, testing whether F_c is satisfied is equivalent to testing whether F is satisfied. However, F_c is minimal in a certain sense—it does not contain extraneous attributes, and it

$F_c = F$
repeat
      Use the union rule to replace any dependencies in F_c of the form
          $\alpha_1 \rightarrow \beta_1$ and $\alpha_1 \rightarrow \beta_2$ with $\alpha_1 \rightarrow \beta_1 \beta_2$.
      Find a functional dependency $\alpha \rightarrow \beta$ in F_c with an extraneous
          attribute either in α or in β.
          /* Note: the test for extraneous attributes is done using F_c, not F */
      If an extraneous attribute is found, delete it from $\alpha \rightarrow \beta$.
until F_c does not change.

Figure 7.8   Computing canonical cover

combines functional dependencies with the same left side. It is cheaper to test F_c than it is to test F itself.

Consider the following set F of functional dependencies on schema (A, B, C):

$$A \rightarrow BC$$
$$B \rightarrow C$$
$$A \rightarrow B$$
$$AB \rightarrow C$$

Let us compute the canonical cover for F.

- There are two functional dependencies with the same set of attributes on the left side of the arrow:

$$A \rightarrow BC$$
$$A \rightarrow B$$

We combine these functional dependencies into $A \rightarrow BC$.

- A is extraneous in $AB \rightarrow C$ because F logically implies $(F - \{AB \rightarrow C\}) \cup \{B \rightarrow C\}$. This assertion is true because $B \rightarrow C$ is already in our set of functional dependencies.

- C is extraneous in $A \rightarrow BC$, since $A \rightarrow BC$ is logically implied by $A \rightarrow B$ and $B \rightarrow C$.

Thus, our canonical cover is

$$A \rightarrow B$$
$$B \rightarrow C$$

Given a set F of functional dependencies, it may be that an entire functional dependency in the set is extraneous, in the sense that dropping it does not change the closure of F. We can show that a canonical cover F_c of F contains no such extraneous functional dependency. Suppose that, to the contrary, there were such an extraneous functional dependency in F_c. The right-side attributes of the dependency would then be extraneous, which is not possible by the definition of canonical covers.

A canonical cover might not be unique. For instance, consider the set of functional dependencies $F = \{A \rightarrow BC, B \rightarrow AC, \text{and } C \rightarrow AB\}$. If we apply the extraneity test to $A \rightarrow BC$, we find that both B and C are extraneous under F. However, it is incorrect to delete both! The algorithm for finding the canonical cover picks one of the two, and deletes it. Then,

1. If C is deleted, we get the set $F' = \{A \rightarrow B, B \rightarrow AC, \text{and } C \rightarrow AB\}$. Now, B is not extraneous in the righthand side of $A \rightarrow B$ under F'. Continuing the algorithm, we find A and B are extraneous in the right-hand side of $C \rightarrow AB$, leading to two canonical covers

$$F_c = \{A \rightarrow B, B \rightarrow C, \text{and } C \rightarrow A\}, \text{and}$$
$$F_c = \{A \rightarrow B, B \rightarrow AC, \text{and } C \rightarrow B\}.$$

2. If B is deleted, we get the set $\{A \rightarrow C, B \rightarrow AC,$ and $C \rightarrow AB\}$. This case is symmetrical to the previous case, leading to the canonical covers

$$F_c = \{A \rightarrow C, C \rightarrow B, \text{ and } B \rightarrow A\}, \text{ and}$$
$$F_c = \{A \rightarrow C, B \rightarrow C, \text{ and } C \rightarrow AB\}.$$

As an exercise, can you find one more canonical cover for F?

7.4 Decomposition

The bad design of Section 7.2 suggests that we should *decompose* a relation schema that has many attributes into several schemas with fewer attributes. Careless decomposition, however, may lead to another form of bad design.

Consider an alternative design in which we decompose *Lending-schema* into the following two schemas:

Branch-customer-schema = (*branch-name, branch-city, assets, customer-name*)
Customer-loan-schema = (*customer-name, loan-number, amount*)

Using the *lending* relation of Figure 7.1, we construct our new relations *branch-customer* (*Branch-customer*) and *customer-loan* (*Customer-loan-schema*):

$$\text{branch-customer} = \Pi_{\text{branch-name, branch-city, assets, customer-name}} (\text{lending})$$
$$\text{customer-loan} = \Pi_{\text{customer-name, loan-number, amount}} (\text{lending})$$

Figures 7.9 and 7.10, respectively, show the resulting *branch-customer* and *customer-name* relations.

Of course, there are cases in which we need to reconstruct the *loan* relation. For example, suppose that we wish to find all branches that have loans with amounts less than $1000. No relation in our alternative database contains these data. We need to reconstruct the *lending* relation. It appears that we can do so by writing

$$\text{branch-customer} \bowtie \text{customer-loan}$$

branch-name	branch-city	assets	customer-name
Downtown	Brooklyn	9000000	Jones
Redwood	Palo Alto	2100000	Smith
Perryridge	Horseneck	1700000	Hayes
Downtown	Brooklyn	9000000	Jackson
Mianus	Horseneck	400000	Jones
Round Hill	Horseneck	8000000	Turner
Pownal	Bennington	300000	Williams
North Town	Rye	3700000	Hayes
Downtown	Brooklyn	9000000	Johnson
Perryridge	Horseneck	1700000	Glenn
Brighton	Brooklyn	7100000	Brooks

Figure 7.9   The relation *branch-customer*.

customer-name	loan-number	amount
Jones	L-17	1000
Smith	L-23	2000
Hayes	L-15	1500
Jackson	L-14	1500
Jones	L-93	500
Turner	L-11	900
Williams	L-29	1200
Hayes	L-16	1300
Johnson	L-18	2000
Glenn	L-25	2500
Brooks	L-10	2200

Figure 7.10   The relation *customer-loan*.

Figure 7.11 shows the result of computing *branch-customer* ⋈ *customer-loan*. When we compare this relation and the *lending* relation with which we started (Figure 7.1), we notice a difference: Although every tuple that appears in the *lending* relation appears in *branch-customer* ⋈ *customer-loan*, there are tuples in *branch-customer* ⋈ *customer-loan* that are not in *lending*. In our example, *branch-customer* ⋈ *customer-loan* has the following additional tuples:

(Downtown, Brooklyn, 9000000, Jones, L-93, 500)
(Perryridge, Horseneck, 1700000, Hayes, L-16, 1300)
(Mianus, Horseneck, 400000, Jones, L-17, 1000)
(North Town, Rye, 3700000, Hayes, L-15, 1500)

Consider the query, "Find all bank branches that have made a loan in an amount less than \$1000." If we look back at Figure 7.1, we see that the only branches with loan amounts less than \$1000 are Mianus and Round Hill. However, when we apply the expression

$$\Pi_{branch\text{-}name} \left(\sigma_{amount\,<\,1000} \left(branch\text{-}customer \ \bowtie \ customer\text{-}loan \right) \right)$$

we obtain *three* branch names: Mianus, Round Hill, and Downtown.

A closer examination of this example shows why. If a customer happens to have several loans from different branches, we cannot tell which loan belongs to which branch. Thus, when we join *branch-customer* and *customer-loan*, we obtain not only the tuples we had originally in *lending*, but also several additional tuples. Although we have *more* tuples in *branch-customer* ⋈ *customer-loan*, we actually have *less* information. We are no longer able, in general, to represent in the database information about which customers are borrowers from which branch. Because of this loss of information, we call the decomposition of *Lending-schema* into *Branch-customer-schema* and *customer-loan-schema* a **lossy decomposition**, or a **lossy-join decomposition**. A decomposition that is not a lossy-join decomposition is a **lossless-join decomposi-**

branch-name	branch-city	assets	customer-name	loan-number	amount
Downtown	Brooklyn	9000000	Jones	L-17	1000
Downtown	Brooklyn	9000000	Jones	L-93	500
Redwood	Palo Alto	2100000	Smith	L-23	2000
Perryridge	Horseneck	1700000	Hayes	L-15	1500
Perryridge	Horseneck	1700000	Hayes	L-16	1300
Downtown	Brooklyn	9000000	Jackson	L-14	1500
Mianus	Horseneck	400000	Jones	L-17	1000
Mianus	Horseneck	400000	Jones	L-93	500
Round Hill	Horseneck	8000000	Turner	L-11	900
Pownal	Bennington	300000	Williams	L-29	1200
North Town	Rye	3700000	Hayes	L-15	1500
North Town	Rye	3700000	Hayes	L-16	1300
Downtown	Brooklyn	9000000	Johnson	L-18	2000
Perryridge	Horseneck	1700000	Glenn	L-25	2500
Brighton	Brooklyn	7100000	Brooks	L-10	2200

Figure 7.11   The relation *branch-customer* ⋈ *customer-loan*.

tion. It should be clear from our example that a lossy-join decomposition is, in general, a bad database design.

Why is the decomposition lossy? There is one attribute in common between *Branch-customer-schema* and *Customer-loan-schema*:

$$Branch\text{-}customer\text{-}schema \cap Customer\text{-}loan\text{-}schema = \{customer\text{-}name\}$$

The only way that we can represent a relationship between, for example, *loan-number* and *branch-name* is through *customer-name*. This representation is not adequate because a customer may have several loans, yet these loans are not necessarily obtained from the same branch.

Let us consider another alternative design, in which we decompose *Lending-schema* into the following two schemas:

$$Branch\text{-}schema = (branch\text{-}name, branch\text{-}city, assets)$$
$$Loan\text{-}info\text{-}schema = (branch\text{-}name, customer\text{-}name, loan\text{-}number, amount)$$

There is one attribute in common between these two schemas:

$$Branch\text{-}loan\text{-}schema \cap Customer\text{-}loan\text{-}schema = \{branch\text{-}name\}$$

Thus, the only way that we can represent a relationship between, for example, *customer-name* and *assets* is through *branch-name*. The difference between this example and the preceding one is that the assets of a branch are the same, regardless of the customer to which we are referring, whereas the lending branch associated with a certain loan amount *does* depend on the customer to which we are referring. For a given *branch-name*, there is exactly one *assets* value and exactly one *branch-city*;

whereas a similar statement cannot be made for *customer-name*. That is, the functional dependency

$$branch\text{-}name \rightarrow assets\ branch\text{-}city$$

holds, but *customer-name* does not functionally determine *loan-number*.

The notion of lossless joins is central to much of relational-database design. Therefore, we restate the preceding examples more concisely and more formally. Let R be a relation schema. A set of relation schemas $\{R_1, R_2, \ldots, R_n\}$ is a **decomposition** of R if

$$R = R_1 \cup R_2 \cup \cdots \cup R_n$$

That is, $\{R_1, R_2, \ldots, R_n\}$ is a decomposition of R if, for $i = 1, 2, \ldots, n$, each R_i is a subset of R, and every attribute in R appears in at least one R_i.

Let r be a relation on schema R, and let $r_i = \Pi_{R_i}(r)$ for $i = 1, 2, \ldots, n$. That is, $\{r_1, r_2, \ldots, r_n\}$ is the database that results from decomposing R into $\{R_1, R_2, \ldots, R_n\}$. It is always the case that

$$r \subseteq r_1 \bowtie r_2 \bowtie \cdots \bowtie r_n$$

To see that this assertion is true, consider a tuple t in relation r. When we compute the relations $r_1, r_2, \ldots, r_n$, the tuple t gives rise to one tuple t_i in each r_i, $i = 1, 2, \ldots, n$. These n tuples combine to regenerate t when we compute $r_1 \bowtie r_2 \bowtie \cdots \bowtie r_n$. The details are left for you to complete as an exercise. Therefore, every tuple in r appears in $r_1 \bowtie r_2 \bowtie \cdots \bowtie r_n$.

In general, $r \neq r_1 \bowtie r_2 \bowtie \cdots \bowtie r_n$. As an illustration, consider our earlier example, in which

- $n = 2$.
- $R = Lending\text{-}schema$.
- $R_1 = Branch\text{-}customer\text{-}schema$.
- $R_2 = Customer\text{-}loan\text{-}schema$.
- $r = $ the relation shown in Figure 7.1.
- $r_1 = $ the relation shown in Figure 7.9.
- $r_2 = $ the relation shown in Figure 7.10.
- $r_1 \bowtie r_2 = $ the relation shown in Figure 7.11.

Note that the relations in Figures 7.1 and 7.11 are not the same.

To have a lossless-join decomposition, we need to impose constraints on the set of possible relations. We found that the decomposition of *Lending-schema* into *Branch-schema* and *Loan-info-schema* is lossless because the functional dependency

$$branch\text{-}name \rightarrow branch\text{-}city\ assets$$

holds on *Branch-schema*.

Later in this chapter, we shall introduce constraints other than functional dependencies. We say that a relation is **legal** if it satisfies all rules, or constraints, that we impose on our database.

Let C represent a set of constraints on the database, and let R be a relation schema. A decomposition $\{R_1, R_2, \ldots, R_n\}$ of R is a **lossless-join decomposition** if, for all relations r on schema R that are legal under C,

$$r = \Pi_{R_1}(r) \bowtie \Pi_{R_2}(r) \bowtie \cdots \bowtie \Pi_{R_n}(r)$$

We shall show how to test whether a decomposition is a lossless-join decomposition in the next few sections. A major part of this chapter deals with the questions of how to specify constraints on the database, and how to obtain lossless-join decompositions that avoid the pitfalls represented by the examples of bad database designs that we have seen in this section.

7.5   Desirable Properties of Decomposition

We can use a given set of functional dependencies in designing a relational database in which most of the undesirable properties discussed in Section 7.2 do not occur. When we design such systems, it may become necessary to decompose a relation into several smaller relations.

In this section, we outline the desirable properties of a decomposition of a relational schema. In later sections, we outline specific ways of decomposing a relational schema to get the properties we desire. We illustrate our concepts with the *Lending-schema* schema of Section 7.2:

$$\textit{Lending-schema} = (\textit{branch-name, branch-city, assets, customer-name,}$$
$$\textit{loan-number, amount})$$

The set F of functional dependencies that we require to hold on *Lending-schema* are

$$\textit{branch-name} \rightarrow \textit{branch-city assets}$$
$$\textit{loan-number} \rightarrow \textit{amount branch-name}$$

As we discussed in Section 7.2, *Lending-schema* is an example of a bad database design. Assume that we decompose it to the following three relations:

$$\textit{Branch-schema} = (\textit{branch-name, branch-city, assets})$$
$$\textit{Loan-schema} = (\textit{loan-number, branch-name, amount})$$
$$\textit{Borrower-schema} = (\textit{customer-name, loan-number})$$

We claim that this decomposition has several desirable properties, which we discuss next. Note that these three relation schemas are precisely the ones that we used previously, in Chapters 3 through 5.

7.5.1   Lossless-Join Decomposition

In Section 7.2, we argued that, when we decompose a relation into a number of smaller relations, it is crucial that the decomposition be lossless. We claim that the decomposition in Section 7.5 is indeed lossless. To demonstrate our claim, we must first present a criterion for determining whether a decomposition is lossy.

Let R be a relation schema, and let F be a set of functional dependencies on R. Let R_1 and R_2 form a decomposition of R. This decomposition is a lossless-join decomposition of R if at least one of the following functional dependencies is in F^+:

- $R_1 \cap R_2 \rightarrow R_1$
- $R_1 \cap R_2 \rightarrow R_2$

In other words, if $R_1 \cap R_2$ forms a superkey of either R_1 or R_2, the decomposition of R is a lossless-join decomposition. We can use attribute closure to efficiently test for superkeys, as we have seen earlier.

We now demonstrate that our decomposition of *Lending-schema* is a lossless-join decomposition by showing a sequence of steps that generate the decomposition. We begin by decomposing *Lending-schema* into two schemas:

> *Branch-schema = (branch-name, branch-city, assets)*
> *Loan-info-schema = (branch-name, customer-name, loan-number, amount)*

Since *branch-name → branch-city assets*, the augmentation rule for functional dependencies (Section 7.3.2) implies that

> *branch-name → branch-name branch-city assets*

Since *Branch-schema ∩ Loan-info-schema = {branch-name}*, it follows that our initial decomposition is a lossless-join decomposition.

Next, we decompose *Loan-info-schema* into

> *Loan-schema = (loan-number, branch-name, amount)*
> *Borrower-schema = (customer-name, loan-number)*

This step results in a lossless-join decomposition, since *loan-number* is a common attribute and *loan-number → amount branch-name*.

For the general case of decomposition of a relation into multiple parts at once, the test for lossless join decomposition is more complicated. See the bibliographical notes for references on the topic.

While the test for binary decomposition is clearly a sufficient condition for lossless join, it is a necessary condition only if all constraints are functional dependencies. We shall see other types of constraints later (in particular, a type of constraint called multivalued dependencies), that can ensure that a decomposition is lossless join even if no functional dependencies are present.

7.5.2 Dependency Preservation

There is another goal in relational-database design: *dependency preservation*. When an update is made to the database, the system should be able to check that the update will not create an illegal relation—that is, one that does not satisfy all the given functional dependencies. If we are to check updates efficiently, we should design relational-database schemas that allow update validation without the computation of joins.

To decide whether joins must be computed to check an update, we need to determine what functional dependencies can be tested by checking each relation individually. Let F be a set of functional dependencies on a schema R, and let $R_1, R_2, \ldots, R_n$ be a decomposition of R. The **restriction** of F to R_i is the set F_i of all functional dependencies in F^+ that include *only* attributes of R_i. Since all functional dependencies in a restriction involve attributes of only one relation schema, it is possible to test such a dependency for satisfaction by checking only one relation.

Note that the definition of restriction uses all dependencies in F^+, not just those in F. For instance, suppose $F = \{A \rightarrow B, B \rightarrow C\}$, and we have a decomposition into AC and AB. The restriction of F to AC is then $A \rightarrow C$, since $A \rightarrow C$ is in F^+, even though it is not in F.

The set of restrictions $F_1, F_2, \ldots, F_n$ is the set of dependencies that can be checked efficiently. We now must ask whether testing only the restrictions is sufficient. Let $F' = F_1 \cup F_2 \cup \cdots \cup F_n$. F' is a set of functional dependencies on schema R, but, in general, $F' \neq F$. However, even if $F' \neq F$, it may be that $F'^+ = F^+$. If the latter is true, then every dependency in F is logically implied by F', and, if we verify that F' is satisfied, we have verified that F is satisfied. We say that a decomposition having the property $F'^+ = F^+$ is a **dependency-preserving decomposition**.

Figure 7.12 shows an algorithm for testing dependency preservation. The input is a set $D = \{R_1, R_2, \ldots, R_n\}$ of decomposed relation schemas, and a set F of functional dependencies. This algorithm is expensive since it requires computation of F^+; we will describe another algorithm that is more efficient after giving an example of testing for dependency preservation.

We can now show that our decomposition of *Lending-schema* is dependency preserving. Instead of applying the algorithm of Figure 7.12, we consider an easier alternative: We consider each member of the set F of functional dependencies that we

```
compute F⁺;
for each schema Rᵢ in D do
    begin
        Fᵢ := the restriction of F⁺ to Rᵢ;
    end
F' := ∅
for each restriction Fᵢ do
    begin
        F' = F' ∪ Fᵢ
    end
compute F'⁺;
if (F'⁺ = F⁺) then return (true)
            else return (false);
```

Figure 7.12   Testing for dependency preservation.

require to hold on *Lending-schema*, and show that each one can be tested in at least one relation in the decomposition.

- We can test the functional dependency: *branch-name* → *branch-city assets* using *Branch-schema* = (*branch-name, branch-city, assets*).

- We can test the functional dependency: *loan-number* → *amount branch-name* using *Loan-schema* = (*branch-name, loan-number, amount*).

If each member of F can be tested on one of the relations of the decomposition, then the decomposition is dependency preserving. However, there are cases where, even though the decomposition is dependency preserving, there is a dependency in F that cannot be tested in any one relation in the decomposition. The alternative test can therefore be used as a sufficient condition that is easy to check; if it fails we cannot conclude that the decomposition is not dependency preserving, instead we will have to apply the general test.

We now give a more efficient test for dependency preservation, which avoids computing F^+. The idea is to test each functional dependency $\alpha \rightarrow \beta$ in F by using a modified form of attribute closure to see if it is preserved by the decomposition. We apply the following procedure to each $\alpha \rightarrow \beta$ in F.

$$result = \alpha$$
while (changes to *result*) **do**
  for each R_i in the decomposition
    $t = (result \cap R_i)^+ \cap R_i$
    $result = result \cup t$

The attribute closure is with respect to the functional dependencies in F. If *result* contains all attributes in β, then the functional dependency $\alpha \rightarrow \beta$ is preserved. The decomposition is dependency preserving if and only if all the dependencies in F are preserved.

Note that instead of precomputing the restriction of F on R_i and using it for computing the attribute closure of *result*, we use attribute closure on (*result* $\cap R_i$) with respect to F, and then intersect it with R_i, to get an equivalent result. This procedure takes polynomial time, instead of the exponential time required to compute F^+.

7.5.3 Repetition of Information

The decomposition of *Lending-schema* does not suffer from the problem of repetition of information that we discussed in Section 7.2. In *Lending-schema*, it was necessary to repeat the city and assets of a branch for each loan. The decomposition separates branch and loan data into distinct relations, thereby eliminating this redundancy. Similarly, observe that, if a single loan is made to several customers, we must repeat the amount of the loan once for each customer (as well as the city and assets of the branch) in *lending-schema*. In the decomposition, the relation on schema *Borrower-schema* contains the *loan-number, customer-name* relationship, and no other schema does. Therefore, we have one tuple for each customer for a loan in only the relation on *Borrower-schema*. In the other relations involving *loan-number* (those on schemas *Loan-schema* and *Borrower-schema*), only one tuple per loan needs to appear.

Clearly, the lack of redundancy in our decomposition is desirable. The degree to which we can achieve this lack of redundancy is represented by several *normal forms*, which we shall discuss in the remainder of this chapter.

7.6   Boyce–Codd Normal Form

Using functional dependencies, we can define several *normal forms* that represent "good" database designs. In this section we cover BCNF (defined below), and later, in Section 7.7, we cover 3NF.

7.6.1   Definition

One of the more desirable normal forms that we can obtain is **Boyce–Codd normal form** (**BCNF**). A relation schema R is in BCNF with respect to a set F of functional dependencies if, for all functional dependencies in F^+ of the form $\alpha \rightarrow \beta$, where $\alpha \subseteq R$ and $\beta \subseteq R$, at least one of the following holds:

- $\alpha \rightarrow \beta$ is a trivial functional dependency (that is, $\beta \subseteq \alpha$).

- α is a superkey for schema R.

A database design is in BCNF if each member of the set of relation schemas that constitutes the design is in BCNF.

As an illustration, consider the following relation schemas and their respective functional dependencies:

- *Customer-schema* = (*customer-name, customer-street, customer-city*)
  customer-name → *customer-street customer-city*

- *Branch-schema* = (*branch-name, assets, branch-city*)
  branch-name → *assets branch-city*

- *Loan-info-schema* = (*branch-name, customer-name, loan-number, amount*)
  loan-number → *amount branch-name*

We claim that *Customer-schema* is in BCNF. We note that a candidate key for the schema is *customer-name*. The only nontrivial functional dependencies that hold on *Customer-schema* have *customer-name* on the left side of the arrow. Since *customer-name* is a candidate key, functional dependencies with *customer-name* on the left side do not violate the definition of BCNF. Similarly, it can be shown easily that the relation schema *Branch-schema* is in BCNF.

The schema *Loan-info-schema*, however, is *not* in BCNF. First, note that *loan-number* is not a superkey for *Loan-info-schema*, since we *could* have a pair of tuples representing a single loan made to two people—for example,

(Downtown, John Bell, L-44, 1000)
(Downtown, Jane Bell, L-44, 1000)

Because we did not list functional dependencies that rule out the preceding case, *loan-number* is not a candidate key. However, the functional dependency *loan-number* → *amount* is nontrivial. Therefore, *Loan-info-schema* does not satisfy the definition of BCNF.

We claim that *Loan-info-schema* is not in a desirable form, since it suffers from the problem of *repetition of information* that we described in Section 7.2. We observe that, if there are several customer names associated with a loan, in a relation on *Loan-info-schema*, then we are forced to repeat the branch name and the amount once for each customer. We can eliminate this redundancy by redesigning our database such that all schemas are in BCNF. One approach to this problem is to take the existing non-BCNF design as a starting point, and to decompose those schemas that are not in BCNF. Consider the decomposition of *Loan-info-schema* into two schemas:

$$Loan\text{-}schema = (loan\text{-}number,\ branch\text{-}name,\ amount)$$
$$Borrower\text{-}schema = (customer\text{-}name,\ loan\text{-}number)$$

This decomposition is a lossless-join decomposition.

To determine whether these schemas are in BCNF, we need to determine what functional dependencies apply to them. In this example, it is easy to see that

$$loan\text{-}number \rightarrow amount\ branch\text{-}name$$

applies to the *Loan-schema*, and that only trivial functional dependencies apply to *Borrower-schema*. Although *loan-number* is not a superkey for *Loan-info-schema*, it is a candidate key for *Loan-schema*. Thus, both schemas of our decomposition are in BCNF.

It is now possible to avoid redundancy in the case where there are several customers associated with a loan. There is exactly one tuple for each loan in the relation on *Loan-schema*, and one tuple for each customer of each loan in the relation on *Borrower-schema*. Thus, we do not have to repeat the branch name and the amount once for each customer associated with a loan.

Often testing of a relation to see if it satisfies BCNF can be simplified:

- To check if a nontrivial dependency $\alpha \rightarrow \beta$ causes a violation of BCNF, compute α^+ (the attribute closure of α), and verify that it includes all attributes of R; that is, it is a superkey of R.

- To check if a relation schema R is in BCNF, it suffices to check only the dependencies in the given set F for violation of BCNF, rather than check all dependencies in F^+.

  We can show that if none of the dependencies in F causes a violation of BCNF, then none of the dependencies in F^+ will cause a violation of BCNF either.

Unfortunately, the latter procedure does not work when a relation is decomposed. That is, it *does not* suffice to use F when we test a relation R_i, in a decomposition of R, for violation of BCNF. For example, consider relation schema $R\ (A, B, C, D, E)$, with functional dependencies F containing $A \rightarrow B$ and $BC \rightarrow D$. Suppose this were decomposed into $R1(A, B)$ and $R2(A, C, D, E)$. Now, neither of the dependencies in F contains only attributes from (A, C, D, E) so we might be misled into thinking $R2$ satisfies BCNF. In fact, there is a dependency $AC \rightarrow D$ in F^+ (which can be inferred using the pseudotransitivity rule from the two dependencies in F), which shows that $R2$ is not in BCNF. Thus, we may need a dependency that is in F^+, but is not in F, to show that a decomposed relation is not in BCNF.

An alternative BCNF test is sometimes easier than computing every dependency in F^+. To check if a relation R_i in a decomposition of R is in BCNF, we apply this test:

- For every subset α of attributes in R_i, check that α^+ (the attribute closure of α under F) either includes no attribute of $R_i - \alpha$, or includes all attributes of R_i.

If the condition is violated by some set of attributes α in R_i, consider the following functional dependency, which can be shown to be present in F^+:

$$\alpha \rightarrow (\alpha^+ - \alpha) \cap R_i.$$

The above dependency shows that R_i violates BCNF, and is a "witness" for the violation. The BCNF decomposition algorithm, which we shall see in Section 7.6.2, makes use of the witness.

7.6.2 Decomposition Algorithm

We are now able to state a general method to decompose a relation schema so as to satisfy BCNF. Figure 7.13 shows an algorithm for this task. If R is not in BCNF, we can decompose R into a collection of BCNF schemas $R_1, R_2, \ldots, R_n$ by the algorithm. The algorithm uses dependencies ("witnesses") that demonstrate violation of BCNF to perform the decomposition.

The decomposition that the algorithm generates is not only in BCNF, but is also a lossless-join decomposition. To see why our algorithm generates only lossless-join decompositions, we note that, when we replace a schema R_i with $(R_i - \beta)$ and (α, β), the dependency $\alpha \rightarrow \beta$ holds, and $(R_i - \beta) \cap (\alpha, \beta) = \alpha$.

> $result := \{R\};$
> $done :=$ false;
> compute F^+;
> **while** (**not** $done$) **do**
>   **if** (there is a schema R_i in $result$ that is not in BCNF)
>   **then begin**
>   let $\alpha \rightarrow \beta$ be a nontrivial functional dependency that holds
>   on R_i such that $\alpha \rightarrow R_i$ is not in F^+, and $\alpha \cap \beta = \emptyset$;
> $result := (result - R_i) \cup (R_i - \beta) \cup (\alpha, \beta);$
>   **end**
>   **else** $done :=$ true;

Figure 7.13   BCNF decomposition algorithm.

We apply the BCNF decomposition algorithm to the *Lending-schema* schema that we used in Section 7.2 as an example of a poor database design:

$$Lending\text{-}schema = (branch\text{-}name, branch\text{-}city, assets, customer\text{-}name,$$
$$loan\text{-}number, amount)$$

The set of functional dependencies that we require to hold on *Lending-schema* are

$$branch\text{-}name \rightarrow assets\ branch\text{-}city$$
$$loan\text{-}number \rightarrow amount\ branch\text{-}name$$

A candidate key for this schema is {*loan-number, customer-name*}.

We can apply the algorithm of Figure 7.13 to the *Lending-schema* example as follows:

- The functional dependency

$$branch\text{-}name \rightarrow assets\ branch\text{-}city$$

  holds on *Lending-schema*, but *branch-name* is not a superkey. Thus, *Lending-schema* is not in BCNF. We replace *Lending-schema* by

  $$Branch\text{-}schema = (branch\text{-}name, branch\text{-}city, assets)$$
  $$Loan\text{-}info\text{-}schema = (branch\text{-}name, customer\text{-}name, loan\text{-}number, amount)$$

- The only nontrivial functional dependencies that hold on *Branch-schema* include *branch-name* on the left side of the arrow. Since *branch-name* is a key for *Branch-schema*, the relation *Branch-schema* is in BCNF.

- The functional dependency

$$loan\text{-}number \rightarrow amount\ branch\text{-}name$$

  holds on *Loan-info-schema*, but *loan-number* is not a key for *Loan-info-schema*. We replace *Loan-info-schema* by

  $$Loan\text{-}schema = (loan\text{-}number, branch\text{-}name, amount)$$
  $$Borrower\text{-}schema = (customer\text{-}name, loan\text{-}number)$$

- *Loan-schema* and *Borrower-schema* are in BCNF.

Thus, the decomposition of *Lending-schema* results in the three relation schemas *Branch-schema*, *Loan-schema*, and *Borrower-schema*, each of which is in BCNF. These relation schemas are the same as those in Section 7.5, where we demonstrated that the resulting decomposition is both a lossless-join decomposition and a dependency-preserving decomposition.

The BCNF decomposition algorithm takes time exponential in the size of the initial schema, since the algorithm for checking if a relation in the decomposition satisfies BCNF can take exponential time. The bibliographical notes provide references to an algorithm that can compute a BCNF decomposition in polynomial time. However, the algorithm may "overnormalize," that is, decompose a relation unnecessarily.

7.6.3 Dependency Preservation

Not every BCNF decomposition is dependency preserving. As an illustration, consider the relation schema

$$Banker\text{-}schema = (branch\text{-}name, customer\text{-}name, banker\text{-}name)$$

which indicates that a customer has a "personal banker" in a particular branch. The set Γ of functional dependencies that we require to hold on the *Banker-schema* is

$$banker\text{-}name \rightarrow branch\text{-}name$$
$$branch\text{-}name\ customer\text{-}name\ \rightarrow banker\text{-}name$$

Clearly, *Banker-schema* is not in BCNF since *banker-name* is not a superkey.

If we apply the algorithm of Figure 7.13, we obtain the following BCNF decomposition:

$$Banker\text{-}branch\text{-}schema = (banker\text{-}name, branch\text{-}name)$$
$$Customer\text{-}banker\text{-}schema = (customer\text{-}name, banker\text{-}name)$$

The decomposed schemas preserve only *banker-name* $\rightarrow$ *branch-name* (and trivial dependencies), but the closure of {*banker-name* $\rightarrow$ *branch-name*} does not include *customer-name branch-name* $\rightarrow$ *banker-name*. The violation of this dependency cannot be detected unless a join is computed.

To see why the decomposition of *Banker-schema* into the schemas *Banker-branch-schema* and *Customer-banker-schema* is not dependency preserving, we apply the algorithm of Figure 7.12. We find that the restrictions F_1 and F_2 of F to each schema are:

$$F_1 = \{banker\text{-}name \rightarrow branch\text{-}name\}$$
$$F_2 = \emptyset\ (only\ trivial\ dependencies\ hold\ on\ Customer\text{-}banker\text{-}schema)$$

(For brevity, we do not show trivial functional dependencies.) It is easy to see that the dependency *customer-name branch-name* $\rightarrow$ *banker-name* is not in $(F_1 \cup F_2)^+$ even though it *is* in F^+. Therefore, $(F_1 \cup F_2)^+ \neq F^+$, and the decomposition is not dependency preserving.

This example demonstrates that not every BCNF decomposition is dependency preserving. Moreover, it is easy to see that *any* BCNF decomposition of *Banker-schema* must fail to preserve *customer-name branch-name* $\rightarrow$ *banker-name*. Thus, the example shows that we cannot always satisfy all three design goals:

1. Lossless join

2. BCNF

3. Dependency preservation

Recall that lossless join is an essential condition for a decomposition, to avoid loss of information. We are therefore forced to give up either BCNF or dependency preservation. In Section 7.7 we present an alternative normal form, called **third normal form**, which is a small relaxation of BCNF; the motivation for using third normal form is that there is always a dependency preserving decomposition into third normal form.

There are situations where there is more than one way to decompose a schema into BCNF. Some of these decompositions may be dependency preserving, while others may not. For instance, suppose we have a relation schema $R(A, B, C)$ with the functional dependencies $A \rightarrow B$ and $B \rightarrow C$. From this set we can derive the further dependency $A \rightarrow C$. If we used the dependency $A \rightarrow B$ (or equivalently, $A \rightarrow C$) to decompose R, we would end up with two relations $R1(A, B)$ and $R2(A, C)$; the dependency $B \rightarrow C$ would not be preserved.

If instead we used the dependency $B \rightarrow C$ to decompose R, we would end up with two relations $R1(A, B)$ and $R2(B, C)$, which are in BCNF, and the decomposition is also dependency preserving. Clearly the decomposition into $R1(A, B)$ and $R2(B, C)$ is preferable. In general, the database designer should therefore look at alternative decompositions, and pick a dependency preserving decomposition where possible.

7.7 Third Normal Form

As we saw earlier, there are relational schemas where a BCNF decomposition cannot be dependency preserving. For such schemas, we have two alternatives if we wish to check if an update violates any functional dependencies:

- Pay the extra cost of computing joins to test for violations.

- Use an alternative decomposition, third normal form (3NF), which we present below, which makes testing of updates cheaper. Unlike BCNF, 3NF decompositions may contain some redundancy in the decomposed schema.

We shall see that it is always possible to find a lossless-join, dependency-preserving decomposition that is in 3NF. Which of the two alternatives to choose is a design decision to be made by the database designer on the basis of the application requirements.

7.7.1 Definition

BCNF requires that all nontrivial dependencies be of the form $\alpha \rightarrow \beta$, where α is a superkey. 3NF relaxes this constraint slightly by allowing nontrivial functional dependencies whose left side is not a superkey.

A relation schema R is in **third normal form (3NF)** with respect to a set F of functional dependencies if, for all functional dependencies in F^+ of the form $\alpha \rightarrow \beta$, where $\alpha \subseteq R$ and $\beta \subseteq R$, at least one of the following holds:

- $\alpha \rightarrow \beta$ is a trivial functional dependency.

- α is a superkey for R.

- Each attribute A in $\beta - \alpha$ is contained in a candidate key for R.

Note that the third condition above does not say that a single candidate key should contain all the attributes in $\beta - \alpha$; each attribute A in $\beta - \alpha$ may be contained in a *different* candidate key.

The first two alternatives are the same as the two alternatives in the definition of BCNF. The third alternative of the 3NF definition seems rather unintuitive, and it is not obvious why it is useful. It represents, in some sense, a minimal relaxation of the BCNF conditions that helps ensure that every schema has a dependency-preserving decomposition into 3NF. Its purpose will become more clear later, when we study decomposition into 3NF.

Observe that any schema that satisfies BCNF also satisfies 3NF, since each of its functional dependencies would satisfy one of the first two alternatives. BCNF is therefore a more restrictive constraint than is 3NF.

The definition of 3NF allows certain functional dependencies that are not allowed in BCNF. A dependency $\alpha \rightarrow \beta$ that satisfies only the third alternative of the 3NF definition is not allowed in BCNF, but is allowed in 3NF.[1]

Let us return to our *Banker-schema* example (Section 7.6). We have shown that this relation schema does not have a dependency-preserving, lossless-join decomposition into BCNF. This schema, however, turns out to be in 3NF. To see that it is, we note that {*customer-name, branch-name*} is a candidate key for *Banker-schema*, so the only attribute not contained in a candidate key for *Banker-schema* is *banker-name*. The only nontrivial functional dependencies of the form

$$\alpha \rightarrow \textit{banker-name}$$

include {*customer-name, branch-name*} as part of α. Since {*customer-name, branch-name*} is a candidate key, these dependencies do not violate the definition of 3NF.

As an optimization when testing for 3NF, we can consider only functional dependencies in the given set F, rather than in F^+. Also, we can decompose the dependencies in F so that their right-hand side consists of only single attributes, and use the resultant set in place of F.

Given a dependency $\alpha \rightarrow \beta$, we can use the same attribute-closure–based technique that we used for BCNF to check if α is a superkey. If α is not a superkey, we have to verify whether each attribute in β is contained in a candidate key of R; this test is rather more expensive, since it involves finding candidate keys. In fact, testing for 3NF has been shown to be NP-hard; thus, it is very unlikely that there is a polynomial time complexity algorithm for the task.

7.7.2   Decomposition Algorithm

Figure 7.14 shows an algorithm for finding a dependency-preserving, lossless-join decomposition into 3NF. The set of dependencies F_c used in the algorithm is a canoni-

---

1. These dependencies are examples of **transitive dependencies** (see Exercise 7.25). The original definition of 3NF was in terms of transitive dependencies. The definition we use is equivalent but easier to understand.

let F_c be a canonical cover for F;
$i := 0$;
for each functional dependency $\alpha \rightarrow \beta$ in F_c **do**
    if none of the schemas $R_j, j = 1, 2, \ldots, i$ contains $\alpha \beta$
      then begin
          $i := i + 1$;
          $R_i := \alpha \beta$;
      end
    if none of the schemas $R_j, j = 1, 2, \ldots, i$ contains a candidate key for R
      then begin
          $i := i + 1$;
          $R_i :=$ any candidate key for R;
    end
return $(R_1, R_2, \ldots, R_i)$

Figure 7.14   Dependency-preserving, lossless-join decomposition into 3NF.

cal cover for F. Note that the algorithm considers the set of schemas $R_j, j = 1, 2, \ldots, i$; initially $i = 0$, and in this case the set is empty.

To illustrate the algorithm of Figure 7.14, consider the following extension to the *Banker-schema* in Section 7.6:

$$Banker\text{-}info\text{-}schema = (branch\text{-}name, customer\text{-}name, banker\text{-}name, \\ office\text{-}number)$$

The main difference here is that we include the banker's office number as part of the information. The functional dependencies for this relation schema are

$$banker\text{-}name \rightarrow branch\text{-}name\ office\text{-}number$$
$$customer\text{-}name\ branch\text{-}name \rightarrow banker\text{-}name$$

The **for** loop in the algorithm causes us to include the following schemas in our decomposition:

$$Banker\text{-}office\text{-}schema = (banker\text{-}name, branch\text{-}name, office\text{-}number)$$
$$Banker\text{-}schema = (customer\text{-}name, branch\text{-}name, banker\text{-}name)$$

Since *Banker-schema* contains a candidate key for *Banker-info-schema*, we are finished with the decomposition process.

The algorithm ensures the preservation of dependencies by explicitly building a schema for each dependency in a canonical cover. It ensures that the decomposition is a lossless-join decomposition by guaranteeing that at least one schema contains a candidate key for the schema being decomposed. Exercise 7.19 provides some insight into the proof that this suffices to guarantee a lossless join.

This algorithm is also called the **3NF synthesis algorithm**, since it takes a set of dependencies and adds one schema at a time, instead of decomposing the initial schema repeatedly. The result is not uniquely defined, since a set of functional dependencies can have more than one canonical cover, and, further, in some cases the result of the algorithm depends on the order in which it considers the dependencies in F_c.

If a relation R_i is in the decomposition generated by the synthesis algorithm, then R_i is in 3NF. Recall that when we test for 3NF, it suffices to consider functional dependencies whose right-hand side is a single attribute. Therefore, to see that R_i is in 3NF, you must convince yourself that any functional dependency $\gamma \rightarrow B$ that holds on R_i satisfies the definition of 3NF. Assume that the dependency that generated R_i in the synthesis algorithm is $\alpha \rightarrow \beta$. Now, B must be in α or β, since B is in R_i and $\alpha \rightarrow \beta$ generated R_i. Let us consider the three possible cases:

- B is in both α and β. In this case, the dependency $\alpha \rightarrow \beta$ would not have been in F_c since B would be extraneous in β. Thus, this case cannot hold.

- B is in β but not α. Consider two cases:

  ☐ γ is a superkey. The second condition of 3NF is satisfied.

  ☐ γ is not a superkey. Then α must contain some attribute not in γ. Now, since $\gamma \rightarrow B$ is in F^+, it must be derivable from F_c by using the attribute closure algorithm on γ. The derivation could not have used $\alpha \rightarrow \beta$— if it had been used, α must be contained in the attribute closure of γ, which is not possible, since we assumed γ is not a superkey. Now, using $\alpha \rightarrow (\beta - \{B\})$ and $\gamma \rightarrow B$, we can derive $\alpha \rightarrow B$ (since $\gamma \subseteq \alpha\beta$, and γ cannot contain B because $\gamma \rightarrow B$ is nontrivial). This would imply that B is extraneous in the right-hand side of $\alpha \rightarrow \beta$, which is not possible since $\alpha \rightarrow \beta$ is in the canonical cover F_c. Thus, if B is in β, then γ must be a superkey, and the second condition of 3NF must be satisfied.

- B is in α but not β.

  Since α is a candidate key, the third alternative in the definition of 3NF is satisfied.

Interestingly, the algorithm we described for decomposition into 3NF can be implemented in polynomial time, even though testing a given relation to see if it satisfies 3NF is NP-hard.

7.7.3 Comparison of BCNF and 3NF

Of the two normal forms for relational-database schemas, 3NF and BCNF, there are advantages to 3NF in that we know that it is always possible to obtain a 3NF design without sacrificing a lossless join or dependency preservation. Nevertheless, there are disadvantages to 3NF: If we do not eliminate all transitive relations schema dependencies, we may have to use null values to represent some of the possible meaningful relationships among data items, and there is the problem of repetition of information.

As an illustration of the null value problem, consider again the *Banker-schema* and its associated functional dependencies. Since *banker-name* $\rightarrow$ *branch-name*, we may want to represent relationships between values for *banker-name* and values for *branch-name* in our database. If we are to do so, however, either there must be a corresponding value for *customer-name*, or we must use a null value for the attribute *customer-name*.

customer-name	banker-name	branch-name
Jones	Johnson	Perryridge
Smith	Johnson	Perryridge
Hayes	Johnson	Perryridge
Jackson	Johnson	Perryridge
Curry	Johnson	Perryridge
Turner	Johnson	Perryridge

Figure 7.15   An instance of *Banker-schema*.

As an illustration of the repetition of information problem, consider the instance of *Banker-schema* in Figure 7.15. Notice that the information indicating that Johnson is working at the Perryridge branch is repeated.

Recall that our goals of database design with functional dependencies are:

1. BCNF

2. Lossless join

3. Dependency preservation

Since it is not always possible to satisfy all three, we may be forced to choose between BCNF and dependency preservation with 3NF.

It is worth noting that SQL does not provide a way of specifying functional dependencies, except for the special case of declaring superkeys by using the **primary key** or **unique** constraints. It is possible, although a little complicated, to write assertions that enforce a functional dependency (see Exercise 7.15); unfortunately, testing the assertions would be very expensive in most database systems. Thus even if we had a dependency-preserving decomposition, if we use standard SQL we would not be able to efficiently test a functional dependency whose left-hand side is not a key.

Although testing functional dependencies may involve a join if the decomposition is not dependency preserving, we can reduce the cost by using materialized views, which many database systems support. Given a BCNF decomposition that is not dependency preserving, we consider each dependency in a minimum cover F_c that is not preserved in the decomposition. For each such dependency $\alpha \rightarrow \beta$, we define a materialized view that computes a join of all relations in the decomposition, and projects the result on $\alpha\beta$. The functional dependency can be easily tested on the materialized view, by means of a constraint **unique** (α). On the negative side, there is a space and time overhead due to the materialized view, but on the positive side, the application programmer need not worry about writing code to keep redundant data consistent on updates; it is the job of the database system to maintain the materialized view, that is, keep up up to date when the database is updated. (Later in the book, in Section 14.5, we outline how a database system can perform materialized view maintenance efficiently.)

Thus, in case we are not able to get a dependency-preserving BCNF decomposition, it is generally preferable to opt for BCNF, and use techniques such as materialized views to reduce the cost of checking functional dependencies.

7.8 Fourth Normal Form

Some relation schemas, even though they are in BCNF, do not seem to be sufficiently normalized, in the sense that they still suffer from the problem of repetition of information. Consider again our banking example. Assume that, in an alternative design for the bank database schema, we have the schema

$$BC\text{-}schema = (loan\text{-}number, customer\text{-}name, customer\text{-}street, customer\text{-}city)$$

The astute reader will recognize this schema as a non-BCNF schema because of the functional dependency

$$customer\text{-}name \rightarrow customer\text{-}street\ customer\text{-}city$$

that we asserted earlier, and because *customer-name* is not a key for *BC-schema*. However, assume that our bank is attracting wealthy customers who have several addresses (say, a winter home and a summer home). Then, we no longer wish to enforce the functional dependency *customer-name* → *customer-street customer-city*. If we remove this functional dependency, we find *BC-schema* to be in BCNF with respect to our modified set of functional dependencies. Yet, even though *BC-schema* is now in BCNF, we still have the problem of repetition of information that we had earlier.

   To deal with this problem, we must define a new form of constraint, called a *multivalued dependency*. As we did for functional dependencies, we shall use multivalued dependencies to define a normal form for relation schemas. This normal form, called **fourth normal form** (4NF), is more restrictive than BCNF. We shall see that every 4NF schema is also in BCNF, but there are BCNF schemas that are not in 4NF.

7.8.1 Multivalued Dependencies

Functional dependencies rule out certain tuples from being in a relation. If $A \rightarrow B$, then we cannot have two tuples with the same A value but different B values. Multivalued dependencies, on the other hand, do not rule out the existence of certain tuples. Instead, they *require* that other tuples of a certain form be present in the relation. For this reason, functional dependencies sometimes are referred to as **equality-generating dependencies**, and multivalued dependencies are referred to as **tuple-generating dependencies**.

   Let R be a relation schema and let $\alpha \subseteq R$ and $\beta \subseteq R$. The **multivalued dependency**

$$\alpha \rightarrow\!\!\!\rightarrow \beta$$

holds on R if, in any legal relation $r(R)$, for all pairs of tuples t_1 and t_2 in r such that $t_1[\alpha] = t_2[\alpha]$, there exist tuples t_3 and t_4 in r such that

$$t_1[\alpha] = t_2[\alpha] = t_3[\alpha] = t_4[\alpha]$$
$$t_3[\beta] = t_1[\beta]$$
$$t_3[R - \beta] = t_2[R - \beta]$$
$$t_4[\beta] = t_2[\beta]$$
$$t_4[R - \beta] = t_1[R - \beta]$$

	α	β	$R - \alpha - \beta$
t_1	$a_1 \ldots a_i$	$a_{i+1} \ldots a_j$	$a_{j+1} \ldots a_n$
t_2	$a_1 \ldots a_i$	$b_{i+1} \ldots b_j$	$b_{j+1} \ldots b_n$
t_3	$a_1 \ldots a_i$	$a_{i+1} \ldots a_j$	$b_{j+1} \ldots b_n$
t_4	$a_1 \ldots a_i$	$b_{i+1} \ldots b_j$	$a_{j+1} \ldots a_n$

Figure 7.16   Tabular representation of $\alpha \twoheadrightarrow \beta$.

This definition is less complicated than it appears to be. Figure 7.16 gives a tabular picture of t_1, t_2, t_3, and t_4. Intuitively, the multivalued dependency $\alpha \twoheadrightarrow \beta$ says that the relationship between α and β is independent of the relationship between α and $R - \beta$. If the multivalued dependency $\alpha \twoheadrightarrow \beta$ is satisfied by all relations on schema R, then $\alpha \twoheadrightarrow \beta$ is a *trivial* multivalued dependency on schema R. Thus, $\alpha \twoheadrightarrow \beta$ is trivial if $\beta \subseteq \alpha$ or $\beta \cup \alpha = R$.

To illustrate the difference between functional and multivalued dependencies, we consider the *BC-schema* again, and the relation *bc* (*BC-schema*) of Figure 7.17. We must repeat the loan number once for each address a customer has, and we must repeat the address for each loan a customer has. This repetition is unnecessary, since the relationship between a customer and his address is independent of the relationship between that customer and a loan. If a customer (say, Smith) has a loan (say, loan number L-23), we want that loan to be associated with all Smith's addresses. Thus, the relation of Figure 7.18 is illegal. To make this relation legal, we need to add the tuples (L-23, Smith, Main, Manchester) and (L-27, Smith, North, Rye) to the *bc* relation of Figure 7.18.

Comparing the preceding example with our definition of multivalued dependency, we see that we want the multivalued dependency

$$customer\text{-}name \twoheadrightarrow customer\text{-}street \; customer\text{-}city$$

to hold. (The multivalued dependency *customer-name* $\twoheadrightarrow$ *loan-number* will do as well. We shall soon see that they are equivalent.)

As with functional dependencies, we shall use multivalued dependencies in two ways:

1. To test relations to determine whether they are legal under a given set of functional and multivalued dependencies

2. To specify constraints on the set of legal relations; we shall thus concern ourselves with *only* those relations that satisfy a given set of functional and multivalued dependencies

loan-number	customer-name	customer-street	customer-city
L-23	Smith	North	Rye
L-23	Smith	Main	Manchester
L-93	Curry	Lake	Horseneck

Figure 7.17   Relation *bc*: An example of redundancy in a BCNF relation.

loan-number	customer-name	customer-street	customer-city
L-23	Smith	North	Rye
L-27	Smith	Main	Manchester

Figure 7.18   An illegal *bc* relation.

Note that, if a relation *r* fails to satisfy a given multivalued dependency, we can construct a relation *r'* that *does* satisfy the multivalued dependency by adding tuples to *r*.

Let *D* denote a set of functional and multivalued dependencies. The **closure** D^+ of *D* is the set of all functional and multivalued dependencies logically implied by *D*. As we did for functional dependencies, we can compute D^+ from *D*, using the formal definitions of functional dependencies and multivalued dependencies. We can manage with such reasoning for very simple multivalued dependencies. Luckily, multivalued dependencies that occur in practice appear to be quite simple. For complex dependencies, it is better to reason about sets of dependencies by using a system of inference rules. (Section C.1.1 of the appendix outlines a system of inference rules for multivalued dependencies.)

From the definition of multivalued dependency, we can derive the following rule:

- If $\alpha \rightarrow \beta$, then $\alpha \twoheadrightarrow \beta$.

In other words, every functional dependency is also a multivalued dependency.

7.8.2   Definition of Fourth Normal Form

Consider again our *BC-schema* example in which the multivalued dependency *customer-name* $\twoheadrightarrow$ *customer-street customer-city* holds, but no nontrivial functional dependencies hold. We saw in the opening paragraphs of Section 7.8 that, although *BC-schema* is in BCNF, the design is not ideal, since we must repeat a customer's address information for each loan. We shall see that we can use the given multivalued dependency to improve the database design, by decomposing *BC-schema* into a **fourth normal form** decomposition.

A relation schema *R* is in **fourth normal form** (4NF) with respect to a set *D* of functional and multivalued dependencies if, for all multivalued dependencies in D^+ of the form $\alpha \twoheadrightarrow \beta$, where $\alpha \subseteq R$ and $\beta \subseteq R$, at least one of the following holds

- $\alpha \twoheadrightarrow \beta$ is a trivial multivalued dependency.
- α is a superkey for schema *R*.

A database design is in 4NF if each member of the set of relation schemas that constitutes the design is in 4NF.

Note that the definition of 4NF differs from the definition of BCNF in only the use of multivalued dependencies instead of functional dependencies. Every 4NF schema is in BCNF. To see this fact, we note that, if a schema *R* is not in BCNF, then there is

result := {*R*};
done := false;
compute D^+; Given schema R_i, let D_i denote the restriction of D^+ to R_i
while (**not** *done*) **do**
    if (there is a schema R_i in *result* that is not in 4NF w.r.t. D_i)
      then begin
            let $\alpha \twoheadrightarrow \beta$ be a nontrivial multivalued dependency that holds
            on R_i such that $\alpha \rightarrow R_i$ is not in D_i, and $\alpha \cap \beta = \emptyset$;
            result := (*result* − R_i) ∪ (R_i − β) ∪ (α, β);
      end
    else *done* := true;

Figure 7.19   4NF decomposition algorithm.

a nontrivial functional dependency $\alpha \rightarrow \beta$ holding on R, where α is not a superkey. Since $\alpha \rightarrow \beta$ implies $\alpha \twoheadrightarrow \beta$, R cannot be in 4NF.

Let R be a relation schema, and let $R_1, R_2, \ldots, R_n$ be a decomposition of R. To check if each relation schema R_i in the decomposition is in 4NF, we need to find what multivalued dependencies hold on each R_i. Recall that, for a set F of functional dependencies, the restriction F_i of F to R_i is all functional dependencies in F^+ that include *only* attributes of R_i. Now consider a set D of both functional and multivalued dependencies. The **restriction** of D to R_i is the set D_i consisting of

1. All functional dependencies in D^+ that include only attributes of R_i

2. All multivalued dependencies of the form

$$\alpha \twoheadrightarrow \beta \cap R_i$$

where $\alpha \subseteq R_i$ and $\alpha \twoheadrightarrow \beta$ is in D^+.

7.8.3 Decomposition Algorithm

The analogy between 4NF and BCNF applies to the algorithm for decomposing a schema into 4NF. Figure 7.19 shows the 4NF decomposition algorithm. It is identical to the BCNF decomposition algorithm of Figure 7.13, except that it uses multivalued, instead of functional, dependencies and uses the restriction of D^+ to R_i.

If we apply the algorithm of Figure 7.19 to *BC-schema*, we find that *customer-name* $\twoheadrightarrow$ *loan-number* is a nontrivial multivalued dependency, and *customer-name* is not a superkey for *BC-schema*. Following the algorithm, we replace *BC-schema* by two schemas:

        Borrower-schema = (*customer-name, loan-number*)
        Customer-schema = (*customer-name, customer-street, customer-city*).

This pair of schemas, which is in 4NF, eliminates the problem we encountered earlier with the redundancy of *BC-schema*.

As was the case when we were dealing solely with functional dependencies, we are interested in decompositions that are lossless-join decompositions and that preserve dependencies. The following fact about multivalued dependencies and lossless joins shows that the algorithm of Figure 7.19 generates only lossless-join decompositions:

- Let R be a relation schema, and let D be a set of functional and multivalued dependencies on R. Let R_1 and R_2 form a decomposition of R. This decomposition is a lossless-join decomposition of R if and only if at least one of the following multivalued dependencies is in D^+:

$$R_1 \cap R_2 \twoheadrightarrow R_1$$
$$R_1 \cap R_2 \twoheadrightarrow R_2$$

Recall that we stated in Section 7.5.1 that, if $R_1 \cap R_2 \to R_1$ or $R_1 \cap R_2 \to R_2$, then R_1 and R_2 are a lossless-join decomposition of R. The preceding fact about multivalued dependencies is a more general statement about lossless joins. It says that, for *every* lossless-join decomposition of R into two schemas R_1 and R_2, one of the two dependencies $R_1 \cap R_2 \twoheadrightarrow R_1$ or $R_1 \cap R_2 \twoheadrightarrow R_2$ must hold.

The issue of dependency preservation when we decompose a relation becomes more complicated in the presence of multivalued dependencies. Section C.1.2 of the appendix pursues this topic.

7.9   More Normal Forms

The fourth normal form is by no means the "ultimate" normal form. As we saw earlier, multivalued dependencies help us understand and tackle some forms of repetition of information that cannot be understood in terms of functional dependencies. There are types of constraints called **join dependencies** that generalize multivalued dependencies, and lead to another normal form called **project-join normal form (PJNF)** (PJNF is called **fifth normal form** in some books). There is a class of even more general constraints, which leads to a normal form called **domain-key normal form**.

A practical problem with the use of these generalized constraints is that they are not only hard to reason with, but there is also no set of sound and complete inference rules for reasoning about the constraints. Hence PJNF and domain-key normal form are used quite rarely. Appendix C provides more details about these normal forms.

Conspicuous by its absence from our discussion of normal forms is **second normal form** (2NF). We have not discussed it, because it is of historical interest only. We simply define it, and let you experiment with it in Exercise 7.26.

7.10   Overall Database Design Process

So far we have looked at detailed issues about normal forms and normalization. In this section we study how normalization fits into the overall database design process.

Earlier in the chapter, starting in Section 7.4, we assumed that a relation schema R is given, and proceeded to normalize it. There are several ways in which we could have come up with the schema R:

1. R could have been generated when converting a E-R diagram to a set of tables.

2. R could have been a single relation containing *all* attributes that are of interest. The normalization process then breaks up R into smaller relations.

3. R could have been the result of some ad hoc design of relations, which we then test to verify that it satisfies a desired normal form.

In the rest of this section we examine the implications of these approaches. We also examine some practical issues in database design, including denormalization for performance and examples of bad design that are not detected by normalization.

7.10.1   E-R Model and Normalization

When we carefully define an E-R diagram, identifying all entities correctly, the tables generated from the E-R diagram should not need further normalization. However, there can be functional dependencies between attributes of an entity. For instance, suppose an *employee* entity had attributes *department-number* and *department-address*, and there is a functional dependency *department-number* → *department-address*. We would then need to normalize the relation generated from *employee*.

Most examples of such dependencies arise out of poor E-R diagram design. In the above example, if we did the E-R diagram correctly, we would have created a *department* entity with attribute *department-address* and a relationship between *employee* and *department*. Similarly, a relationship involving more than two entities may not be in a desirable normal form. Since most relationships are binary, such cases are relatively rare. (In fact, some E-R diagram variants actually make it difficult or impossible to specify nonbinary relations.)

Functional dependencies can help us detect poor E-R design. If the generated relations are not in desired normal form, the problem can be fixed in the E-R diagram. That is, normalization can be done formally as part of data modeling. Alternatively, normalization can be left to the designer's intuition during E-R modeling, and can be done formally on the relations generated from the E-R model.

7.10.2   The Universal Relation Approach

The second approach to database design is to start with a single relation schema containing all attributes of interest, and decompose it. One of our goals in choosing a decomposition was that it be a lossless-join decomposition. To consider losslessness, we assumed that it is valid to talk about the join of all the relations of the decomposed database.

Consider the database of Figure 7.20, showing a decomposition of the *loan-info* relation. The figure depicts a situation in which we have not yet determined the amount of loan L-58, but wish to record the remainder of the data on the loan. If we compute the natural join of these relations, we discover that all tuples referring to loan L-58 disappear. In other words, there is no *loan-info* relation corresponding to the relations of Figure 7.20. Tuples that disappear when we compute the join are *dangling tuples* (see Section 6.2.1). Formally, let $r_1(R_1)$, $r_2(R_2), \ldots, r_n(R_n)$ be a set of relations. A

branch-name	loan-number
Round Hill	L-58

loan-number	amount

loan-number	customer-name
L-58	Johnson

Figure 7.20   Decomposition of *loan-info*.

tuple t of relation r_i is a dangling tuple if t is not in the relation

$$\Pi_{R_i} \ (r_1 \Join r_2 \Join \cdots \Join r_n)$$

Dangling tuples may occur in practical database applications. They represent incomplete information, as they do in our example, where we wish to store data about a loan that is still in the process of being negotiated. The relation $r_1 \Join r_2 \Join \cdots \Join r_n$ is called a **universal relation**, since it involves all the attributes in the universe defined by $R_1 \cup R_2 \cup \cdots \cup R_n$.

The only way that we can write a universal relation for the example of Figure 7.20 is to include *null values* in the universal relation. We saw in Chapter 3 that null values present several difficulties. Because of them, it may be better to view the relations of the decomposed design as representing the database, rather than as the universal relation whose schema we decomposed during the normalization process. (The bibliographical notes discuss research on null values and universal relations.)

Note that we cannot enter all incomplete information into the database of Figure 7.20 without resorting to null values. For example, we cannot enter a loan number unless we know at least one of the following:

- The customer name
- The branch name
- The amount of the loan

Thus, a particular decomposition defines a restricted form of incomplete information that is acceptable in our database.

The normal forms that we have defined generate good database designs from the point of view of representation of incomplete information. Returning again to the example of Figure 7.20, we would not want to allow storage of the following fact: "There is a loan (whose number is unknown) to Jones in the amount of $100." This is because

$$loan\text{-}number \rightarrow customer\text{-}name \ amount$$

and therefore the only way that we can relate *customer-name* and *amount* is through *loan-number*. If we do not know the loan number, we cannot distinguish this loan from other loans with unknown numbers.

In other words, we do not want to store data for which the key attributes are un-known. Observe that the normal forms that we have defined do not allow us to store that type of information unless we use null values. Thus, our normal forms allow representation of acceptable incomplete information via dangling tuples, while pro-hibiting the storage of undesirable incomplete information.

Another consequence of the universal relation approach to database design is that attribute names must be unique in the universal relation. We cannot use *name* to refer to both *customer-name* and to *branch-name*. It is generally preferable to use unique names, as we have done. Nevertheless, if we defined our relation schemas directly, rather than in terms of a universal relation, we could obtain relations on schemas such as the following for our banking example:

> *branch-loan (name, number)*
> *loan-customer (number, name)*
> *amt (number, amount)*

Observe that, with the preceding relations, expressions such as *branch-loan ⋈ loan-customer* are meaningless. Indeed, the expression *branch-loan ⋈ loan-customer* finds loans made by branches to customers who have the same name as the name of the branch.

In a language such as SQL, however, a query involving *branch-loan* and *loan-custom-er* must remove ambiguity in references to *name* by prefixing the relation name. In such environments, the multiple roles for *name* (as branch name and as customer name) are less troublesome and may be simpler to use.

We believe that using the **unique-role assumption**—that each attribute name has a unique meaning in the database—is generally preferable to reusing of the same name in multiple roles. When the unique-role assumption is not made, the database designer must be especially careful when constructing a normalized relational-data-base design.

7.10.3   Denormalization for Performance

Occasionally database designers choose a schema that has redundant information; that is, it is not normalized. They use the redundancy to improve performance for specific applications. The penalty paid for not using a normalized schema is the extra work (in terms of coding time and execution time) to keep redundant data consistent.

For instance, suppose that the name of an account holder has to be displayed along with the account number and balance, every time the account is accessed. In our normalized schema, this requires a join of *account* with *depositor*.

One alternative to computing the join on the fly is to store a relation containing all the attributes of *account* and *depositor*. This makes displaying the account information faster. However, the balance information for an account is repeated for every person who owns the account, and all copies must be updated by the application, when-ever the account balance is updated. The process of taking a normalized schema and making it non-normalized is called **denormalization**, and designers use it to tune performance of systems to support time-critical operations.

A better alternative, supported by many database systems today, is to use the normalized schema, and additionally store the join or *account* and *depositor* as a materialized view. (Recall that a materialized view is a view whose result is stored in the database, and brought up to date when the relations used in the view are updated.) Like denormalization, using materialized view does have space and time overheads; however, it has the advantage that keeping the view up to date is the job of the database system, not the application programmer.

7.10.4   Other Design Issues

There are some aspects of database design that are not addressed by normalization, and can thus lead to bad database design. We give examples here; obviously, such designs should be avoided.

Consider a company database, where we want to store earnings of companies in different years. A relation *earnings(company-id, year, amount)* could be used to store the earnings information. The only functional dependency on this relation is *company-id, year → amount*, and the relation is in BCNF.

An alternative design is to use multiple relations, each storing the earnings for a different year. Let us say the years of interest are 2000, 2001, and 2002; we would then have relations of the form *earnings-2000, earnings-2001, earnings-2002*, all of which are on the schema *(company-id, earnings)*. The only functional dependency here on each relation would be *company-id → earnings*, so these relations are also in BCNF.

However, this alternative design is clearly a bad idea—we would have to create a new relation every year, and would also have to write new queries every year, to take each new relation into account. Queries would also be more complicated since they may have to refer to many relations.

Yet another way of representing the same data is to have a single relation *company-year(company-id, earnings-2000, earnings-2001, earnings-2002)*. Here the only functional dependencies are from *company-id* to the other attributes, and again the relation is in BCNF. This design is also a bad idea since it has problems similar to the previous design—namely we would have to modify the relation schema and write new queries, every year. Queries would also be more complicated, since they may have to refer to many attributes.

Representations such as those in the *company-year* relation, with one column for each value of an attribute, are called **crosstabs**; they are widely used in spreadsheets and reports and in data analysis tools. While such representations are useful for display to users, for the reasons just given, they are not desirable in a database design. SQL extensions have been proposed to convert data from a normal relational representation to a crosstab, for display.

7.11   Summary

- We showed pitfalls in database design, and how to systematically design a database schema that avoids the pitfalls. The pitfalls included repeated information and inability to represent some information.

- We introduced the concept of functional dependencies, and showed how to reason with functional dependencies. We laid special emphasis on what dependencies are logically implied by a set of dependencies. We also defined the notion of a canonical cover, which is a minimal set of functional dependencies equivalent to a given set of functional dependencies.

- We introduced the concept of decomposition, and showed that decompositions must be lossless-join decompositions, and should preferably be dependency preserving.

- If the decomposition is dependency preserving, given a database update, all functional dependencies can be verifiable from individual relations, without computing a join of relations in the decomposition.

- We then presented Boyce–Codd Normal Form (BCNF); relations in BCNF are free from the pitfalls outlined earlier. We outlined an algorithm for decomposing relations into BCNF. There are relations for which there is no dependency-preserving BCNF decomposition.

- We used the canonical covers to decompose a relation into 3NF, which is a small relaxation of the BCNF condition. Relations in 3NF may have some redundancy, but there is always a dependency-preserving decomposition into 3NF.

- We presented the notion of multivalued dependencies, which specify constraints that cannot be specified with functional dependencies alone. We defined fourth normal form (4NF) with multivalued dependencies. Section C.1.1 of the appendix gives details on reasoning about multivalued dependencies.

- Other normal forms, such as PJNF and DKNF, eliminate more subtle forms of redundancy. However, these are hard to work with and are rarely used. Appendix C gives details on these normal forms.

- In reviewing the issues in this chapter, note that the reason we could define rigorous approaches to relational-database design is that the relational data model rests on a firm mathematical foundation. That is one of the primary advantages of the relational model compared with the other data models that we have studied.

Review Terms

- Atomic domains
- First normal form
- Pitfalls in relational-database design
- Functional dependencies
- Superkey

- F holds on R
- R satisfies F
- Trivial functional dependencies
- Closure of a set of functional dependencies
- Armstrong's axioms

- Closure of attribute sets
- Decomposition
- Lossless-join decomposition
- Legal relations
- Dependency preservation
- Restriction of F to R_i
- Boyce–Codd normal form (BCNF)
- BCNF decomposition algorithm
- Canonical cover
- Extraneous attributes
- Third normal form

- 3NF decomposition algorithm
- Multivalued dependencies
- Fourth normal form
- restriction of a multivalued dependency
- Project-join normal form (PJNF)
- Domain-key normal form
- E-R model and normalization
- Universal relation
- Unique-role assumption
- Denormalization

Exercises

7.1 Explain what is meant by *repetition of information* and *inability to represent information*. Explain why each of these properties may indicate a bad relational-database design.

7.2 Suppose that we decompose the schema $R = (A, B, C, D, E)$ into

$$(A, B, C)$$
$$(A, D, E)$$

Show that this decomposition is a lossless-join decomposition if the following set F of functional dependencies holds:

$$A \rightarrow BC$$
$$CD \rightarrow E$$
$$B \rightarrow D$$
$$E \rightarrow A$$

7.3 Why are certain functional dependencies called *trivial* functional dependencies?

7.4 List all functional dependencies satisfied by the relation of Figure 7.21.

A	B	C
a_1	b_1	c_1
a_1	b_1	c_2
a_2	b_1	c_1
a_2	b_1	c_3

Figure 7.21   Relation of Exercise 7.4.

7.5 Use the definition of functional dependency to argue that each of Armstrong's axioms (reflexivity, augmentation, and transitivity) is sound.

7.6 Explain how functional dependencies can be used to indicate the following:

- A one-to-one relationship set exists between entity sets *account* and *customer*.
- A many-to-one relationship set exists between entity sets *account* and *customer*.

7.7 Consider the following proposed rule for functional dependencies: If $\alpha \rightarrow \beta$ and $\gamma \rightarrow \beta$, then $\alpha \rightarrow \gamma$. Prove that this rule is *not* sound by showing a relation r that satisfies $\alpha \rightarrow \beta$ and $\gamma \rightarrow \beta$, but does not satisfy $\alpha \rightarrow \gamma$.

7.8 Use Armstrong's axioms to prove the soundness of the union rule. (*Hint*: Use the augmentation rule to show that, if $\alpha \rightarrow \beta$, then $\alpha \rightarrow \alpha\beta$. Apply the augmentation rule again, using $\alpha \rightarrow \gamma$, and then apply the transitivity rule.)

7.9 Use Armstrong's axioms to prove the soundness of the decomposition rule.

7.10 Use Armstrong's axioms to prove the soundness of the pseudotransitivity rule.

7.11 Compute the closure of the following set F of functional dependencies for relation schema $R = (A, B, C, D, E)$.

$$A \rightarrow BC$$
$$CD \rightarrow E$$
$$B \rightarrow D$$
$$E \rightarrow A$$

List the candidate keys for R.

7.12 Using the functional dependencies of Exercise 7.11, compute B^+.

7.13 Using the functional dependencies of Exercise 7.11, compute the canonical cover F_c.

7.14 Consider the algorithm in Figure 7.22 to compute α^+. Show that this algorithm is more efficient than the one presented in Figure 7.7 (Section 7.3.3) and that it computes α^+ correctly.

7.15 Given the database schema $R(a, b, c)$, and a relation r on the schema R, write an SQL query to test whether the functional dependency $b \rightarrow c$ holds on relation r. Also write an SQL assertion that enforces the functional dependency. Assume that no null values are present.

7.16 Show that the following decomposition of the schema R of Exercise 7.2 is not a lossless-join decomposition:

$$(A, B, C)$$
$$(C, D, E)$$

Hint: Give an example of a relation r on schema R such that

$$\Pi_{A, B, C} (r) \bowtie \Pi_{C, D, E} (r) \neq r$$

```
result  :=  ∅;
/* fdcount is an array whose ith element contains the number
     of attributes on the left side of the ith FD that are
     not yet known to be in α⁺ */
for i  :=  1 to |F| do
    begin
        let β  →  γ denote the ith FD;
        fdcount [i]  :=  |β|;
    end
/* appears is an array with one entry for each attribute. The
     entry for attribute A is a list of integers. Each integer
     i on the list indicates that A appears on the left side
     of the ith FD */
for each attribute A do
    begin
        appears [A]  :=  NIL;
        for i  :=  1 to |F| do
            begin
                let β  →  γ denote the ith FD;
                if A  ∈  β then add i to appears [A];
            end
    end
addin (α);
return (result);


procedure addin (α);
for each attribute A in α do
    begin
        if A  ∉  result then
            begin
                result := result ∪ {A};
                for each element i of appears[A] do
                    begin
                        fdcount [i]  := fdcount [i]  − 1;
                        if fdcount [i]  :=  0 then
                            begin
                                let β  →  γ denote the ith FD;
                                addin (γ);
                            end
                    end
            end
    end
```

Figure 7.22   An algorithm to compute α^+.

7.17 Let $R_1, R_2, \ldots, R_n$ be a decomposition of schema U. Let $u(U)$ be a relation, and let $r_i = \Pi_{R_i}(u)$. Show that

$$u \subseteq r_1 \bowtie r_2 \bowtie \cdots \bowtie r_n$$

7.18 Show that the decomposition in Exercise 7.2 is not a dependency-preserving decomposition.

7.19 Show that it is possible to ensure that a dependency-preserving decomposition into 3NF is a lossless-join decomposition by guaranteeing that at least one schema contains a candidate key for the schema being decomposed. (*Hint*: Show that the join of all the projections onto the schemas of the decomposition cannot have more tuples than the original relation.)

7.20 List the three design goals for relational databases, and explain why each is desirable.

7.21 Give a lossless-join decomposition into BCNF of schema R of Exercise 7.2.

7.22 Give an example of a relation schema R' and set F' of functional dependencies such that there are at least three distinct lossless-join decompositions of R' into BCNF.

7.23 In designing a relational database, why might we choose a non-BCNF design?

7.24 Give a lossless-join, dependency-preserving decomposition into 3NF of schema R of Exercise 7.2.

7.25 Let a *prime* attribute be one that appears in at least one candidate key. Let α and β be sets of attributes such that $\alpha \to \beta$ holds, but $\beta \to \alpha$ does not hold. Let A be an attribute that is not in α, is not in β, and for which $\beta \to A$ holds. We say that A is *transitively dependent* on α. We can restate our definition of 3NF as follows: A relation schema R is in 3NF with respect to a set F of functional dependencies if there are no nonprime attributes A in R for which A is transitively dependent on a key for R.

Show that this new definition is equivalent to the original one.

7.26 A functional dependency $\alpha \to \beta$ is called a **partial dependency** if there is a proper subset γ of α such that $\gamma \to \beta$. We say that β is *partially dependent* on α. A relation schema R is in **second normal form** (2NF) if each attribute A in R meets one of the following criteria:

- It appears in a candidate key.
- It is not partially dependent on a candidate key.

Show that every 3NF schema is in 2NF. (*Hint*: Show that every partial dependency is a transitive dependency.)

7.27 Given the three goals of relational-database design, is there any reason to design a database schema that is in 2NF, but is in no higher-order normal form? (See Exercise 7.26 for the definition of 2NF.)

7.28 Give an example of a relation schema R and a set of dependencies such that R is in BCNF, but is not in 4NF.

7.29 Explain why 4NF is a normal form more desirable than BCNF.

7.30 Explain how dangling tuples may arise. Explain problems that they may cause.

Bibliographical Notes

The first discussion of relational-database design theory appeared in an early paper by Codd [1970]. In that paper, Codd also introduced functional dependencies, and first, second, and third normal forms.

Armstrong's axioms were introduced in Armstrong [1974]. Ullman [1988] is an easily accessible source of proofs of soundness and completeness of Armstrong's axioms. Ullman [1988] also provides an algorithm for testing for lossless-join decomposition for general (nonbinary) decompositions, and many other algorithms, theorems, and proofs concerning dependency theory. Maier [1983] discusses the theory of functional dependencies.Graham et al. [1986] discusses formal aspects of the concept of a legal relation.

BCNF was introduced in Codd [1972]. The desirability of BCNF is discussed in Bernstein et al. [1980a]. A polynomial-time algorithm for BCNF decomposition appears in Tsou and Fischer [1982], and can also be found in Ullman [1988]. Biskup et al. [1979] gives the algorithm we used to find a lossless-join dependency-preserving decomposition into 3NF. Fundamental results on the lossless-join property appear in Aho et al. [1979a].

Multivalued dependencies are discussed in Zaniolo [1976]. Beeri et al. [1977] gives a set of axioms for multivalued dependencies, and proves that the authors axioms are sound and complete. Our axiomatization is based on theirs. The notions of 4NF, PJNF, and DKNF are from Fagin [1977], Fagin [1979], and Fagin [1981], respectively.

Maier [1983] presents the design theory of relational databases in detail. Ullman [1988] and Abiteboul et al. [1995] present a more theoretic coverage of many of the dependencies and normal forms presented here. See the bibliographical notes of Appendix C for further references to literature on normalization.

PART 3

Object-based Databases and XML

Several application areas for database systems are limited by the restrictions of the relational data model. As a result, researchers have developed several data models to deal with these application domains. In this part, we study the object-oriented data model and the object-relational data model. In addition, we study XML, a language that can represent data that is less structured than that of the other data models.

The object-oriented data model, described in Chapter 8, is based on the object-oriented-programming language paradigm, which is now in wide use. Inheritance, object-identity, and encapsulation (information hiding), with methods to provide an interface to objects, are among the key concepts of object-oriented programming that have found applications in data modeling. The object-oriented data model also supports a rich type system, including structured and collection types. While inheritance and, to some extent, complex types are also present in the E-R model, encapsulation and object-identity distinguish the object-oriented data model from the E-R model.

The object-relational model, described in Chapter 9, combines features of the relational and object-oriented models. This model provides the rich type system of object-oriented databases, combined with relations as the basis for storage of data. It applies inheritance to relations, not just to types. The object-relational data model provides a smooth migration path from relational databases, which is attractive to relational database vendors. As a result, the SQL:1999 standard includes a number of object-oriented features in its type system, while continuing to use the relational model as the underlying model.

The XML language was initially designed as a way of adding markup information to text documents, but has become important because of its applications in data exchange. XML provides a way to represent data that have nested structure, and furthermore allows a great deal of flexibility in structuring of data, which is important for certain kinds of nontraditional data. Chapter 10 describes the XML language, and then presents different ways of expressing queries on data represented in XML, and transforming XML data from one form to another.

Object-Oriented Databases

As database systems were applied to a wider range of applications including, for example, computer-aided design, limitations imposed by the relational model emerged as obstacles. As a result, database researchers invented new data models that overcame the relational model's restrictions. This chapter concentrates on one of them, the *object-oriented model*, which is based on the object-oriented–programming paradigm. Chapter 9 deals with another data model, the object-relational data model, which combines features of the object-oriented and relational data models.

The object-oriented approach to programming was first introduced by the language Simula 67, which was designed for programming simulations. Smalltalk was one of the early object-oriented programming languages for general applications. Today, the languages C++ and Java are the most widely used object-oriented programming languages.

Here, we introduce the concepts of object-oriented programming and then consider the use of these concepts in database systems.

8.1 Need for Complex Data Types

Traditional database applications consist of data processing tasks, such as banking and payroll management. Such applications have conceptually simple data types. The basic data items are records that are fairly small and whose fields are atomic—that is, they are not further structured, and first normal form holds (see Chapter 7). Further, there are only a few record types.

In recent years, demand has grown for ways to deal with more complex data types. Consider, for example, addresses. While an entire address could be viewed as an atomic data item of type string, this view would hide details such as the street address, city, state, and postal code, which could be of interest to queries. On the other hand, if an address were represented by breaking it into the components (street address, city, state, and postal code), writing queries would be more complicated since they would have to mention each field. A better alternative is to allow structured data types, which allow a type *address* with subparts *street-address, city, state,* and *postal-code.*

As another example, consider multivalued attributes from the E-R model. Such attributes are natural, for example, for representing phone numbers, since people may have more than one phone. The alternative of normalization by creating a new relation is expensive and artificial for this example.

As yet another example, consider a computer-aided design database for an electronic circuit. A circuit uses many parts, of different types, and parts have to refer to other parts to which they are connected. All parts of a type have the same properties. Modeling of the circuit in the database is simpler if we can view each part in the design as an *instance* of a part type, and give each instance a unique *identifier.* Parts of the circuit can then *refer* to other parts by means of their unique identifier.

Now suppose an engineer wants to find the power consumption of the whole circuit. A good way of doing this is to view each part as an *object* providing a function *powerusage()* that tells how much power the part uses. The function that computes overall power usage need not know anything about the internals of the part; it just needs to invoke the *powerusage()* function on each part and add up the results.

We examine the above issues in more detail in the rest of this chapter.

8.2 The Object-Oriented Data Model

In this section we present the main concepts of the object-oriented data model: the structure of objects and the notions of classes, inheritance, and object identity.

8.2.1 Object Structure

Loosely speaking, an **object** corresponds to an entity in the E-R model. The object-oriented paradigm is based on **encapsulation** of data and code related to an object into a single unit, whose contents are not visible to the outside world. Conceptually, all interactions between an object and the rest of the system are via messages. Thus, the interface between an object and the rest of the system is defined by a set of allowed *messages.*

In general, an object has associated with it

- A set of **variables** that contain the data for the object; variables correspond to attributes in the E-R model.

- A set of **messages** to which the object responds; each message may have zero, one, or more *parameters.*

- A set of **methods**, each of which is a body of code to implement a message; a method returns a value as the *response* to the message.

The term *message* in an object-oriented context does not imply the use of a physical message in a computer network. Rather, it refers to the passing of requests among objects without regard to specific implementation details. The term **invoke a method** is sometimes used to denote the act of sending a message to an object and the execution of the corresponding method.

We can illustrate the motivation for using this approach by considering *employee* entities in a bank database. Suppose the annual salary of an employee is calculated in different ways for different employees. For instance, managers may get a bonus depending on the bank's performance, while tellers may get a bonus depending on how many hours they have worked. We can (conceptually) encapsulate the code for computing the salary with each employee as a method that is executed in response to an *annual-salary* message.

All *employee* objects respond to the *annual-salary* message, but they do so in different ways. By encapsulating within the *employee* object itself the information about how to compute the annual salary, all employee objects present the same interface. Since the only external interface presented by an object is the set of messages to which that object responds, it is possible to modify the definitions of methods and variables without affecting the rest of the system. The ability to modify the definition of an object without affecting the rest of the system is one of the major advantages of the object-oriented–programming paradigm.

Methods of an object may be classified as either *read-only* or *update*. A read-only method does not affect the values of the variables in an object, whereas an update method may change the values of the variables. The messages to which an object responds can be similarly classified as read-only or update, depending on the method that implements the message.

In the object-oriented model, we express derived attributes of an E-R model entity as read-only messages. For example, we can express the derived attribute *employment-length* of an *employee* entity as an *employment-length* message of an *employee* object. The method implementing the message may determine the employment length by subtracting the *start-date* of the employee from the current date.

Strictly speaking, every attribute of an entity must be expressed as a variable and a pair of messages of the corresponding object in the object-oriented model. We use the variable to store the value of the attribute, one message to read the value of the attribute, and the other message to update the value. For instance, the attribute *address* of the *employee* entity can be represented by:

- A variable *address*

- A message *get-address*, the response to which is the address

- A message *set-address*, which takes a parameter *new-address*, to update the address

However, for simplicity, many object-oriented data models allow variables to be read or updated directly, without defining messages to read and update them.

8.2.2   Object Classes

Usually, there are many similar objects in a database. By *similar*, we mean that they respond to the same messages, use the same methods, and have variables of the same

```
class employee {
    /* Variables */
        string name;
        string address;
        date   start-date;
        int    salary;
    /* Messages */
        int    annual-salary();
        string get-name();
        string get-address();
        int    set-address(string new-address);
        int    employment-length();
};
```

Figure 8.1   Definition of the class *employee*.

name and type. It would be wasteful to define each such object separately. Therefore, we group similar objects to form a **class**. Each such object is called an **instance** of its class. All objects in a class share a common definition, although they differ in the values assigned to the variables.

The notion of a class in the object-oriented data model corresponds to the notion of an entity set in the E-R model. Examples of classes in our bank database are employees, customers, accounts, and loans.

Figure 8.1 defines the class *employee* in pseudocode. The definition shows the variables and the messages to which the objects of the class respond. In this definition, each object of the class *employee* contains the variables *name* and *address*, both of which are strings; *start-date*, which is a date; and *salary*, which is an integer. Each object responds to the five messages, namely *annual-salary*, *get-name*, *get-address*, *set-address*, and *employment-length*. The type name before each message name indicates the type of the response to the message. Observe that the message *set-address* takes a parameter *new-address*, which specifies the new value of the address. Although we have not shown them here, the class *employee* would also support messages that set the name, salary, and start date.

The methods for handling the messages are usually defined separately from the class definition. The methods *get-address*() and *set-address*() would be defined, for example, by the pseudocode:

```
string get-address() {
    return address;
}
int set-address(string new-address) {
    address = new-address;
}
```

while the method *employment-length*() would be defined as:

```
int employment-length() {
    return today() − start-date;
}
```

Here we assume that *today*() is a function that returns the current date, and the "−" operation on dates returns the interval between the two dates.

The concept of classes is similar to the concept of abstract data types. However, there are several additional aspects to the class concept, beyond those of abstract data types. To represent these additional properties, we treat each class as itself being an object. A class object includes

- A set-valued variable whose value is the set of all objects that are instances of the class

- Implementation of a method for the message *new*, which creates a new instance of the class

We return to these features in Section 8.5.2.

8.2.3 Inheritance

An object-oriented database schema usually requires a large number of classes. Often, however, several classes are similar. For example, assume that we have an object-oriented database for our bank application. We would expect the class of bank customers to be similar to the class of bank employees, in that both define variables for *name, address*, and so on. However, there are variables specific to employees (*salary*, for example) and variables specific to customers (*credit-rating*, for example). It would be desirable to define a representation for the common variables in one place. We can define one only if we combine employees and customers into one class.

To allow the direct representation of similarities among classes, we need to place classes in a specialization hierarchy (the "ISA" relationship) like that defined in Chapter 2 for the entity-relationship model. For instance, we say that *employee* is a specialization of *person*, because the set of all employees is a subset of the set of all persons. That is, every employee is a person. Similarly, *customer* is a specialization of *person*.

The concept of a **class hierarchy** is similar to the concept of specialization hierarchy in the entity-relationship model. Employees and customers can be represented by classes that are specializations of a *person* class. Variables and methods specific to employees are associated with the *employee* class. Variables and methods specific to customers are associated with the *customer* class. Variables and methods that apply both to employees and to customers are associated with the *person* class.

Figure 8.2 shows an E-R diagram with a specialization hierarchy to represent people involved in the operation of our bank example. Figure 8.3 shows the corresponding class hierarchy. The classes shown in the hierarchy can be defined in pseudocode as shown in Figure 8.4. For brevity, we do not present all the messages and methods associated with these classes, although they would be included in a full definition of the bank database.

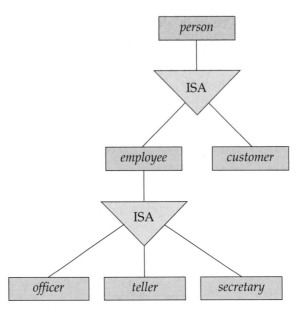

Figure 8.2   Specialization hierarchy for the bank example.

We use the keyword **isa** to indicate that a class is a specialization of another class. The specializations of a class are called **subclasses**. Thus, for example, *employee* is a subclass of *person*, and *teller* is a subclass of *employee*. Conversely, *employee* is a **superclass** of *teller*, and *person* is a superclass of *employee*.

An object representing an officer contains all the variables of class *officer*; in addition the object representing an officer also contains all the variables of classes *employee* and *person*. This is because every officer is defined to be an employee, and since in turn every employee is defined to be a person, we can infer that every officer is also a person. We refer to this property—that objects of a class contain variables defined in its superclasses—as the **inheritance** of variables.

Messages and methods are inherited in the same way that variables are inherited. An important benefit of inheritance in object-oriented systems is **substitutability**: Any method of a class—say, *A* (or a function that takes an object of a class *A* as an argument)—can equally well be invoked with any object belonging to any subclass *B* of *A*. This characteristic leads to code reuse, since the messages, methods, and

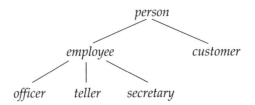

Figure 8.3   Class hierarchy corresponding to Figure 8.2.

```
class person {
    string  name;
    string  address;
    string  get-name();
    string  get-address();
    int     set-address(string new-address);
};
class customer isa person {
    int     credit-rating;
};
class employee isa person {
    date    start-date;
    int     salary;
    int     annual-salary();
    int     employment-length();
};
class officer isa employee {
    int     office-number;
    int     expense-account-number;
};
class teller isa employee {
    int     hours-per-week;
    int     station-number;
};
class secretary isa employee {
    int     hours-per-week;
    string  manager;
};
```

Figure 8.4   Definition of class hierarchy in pseudocode.

functions do not have to be written again for objects of class B. For instance, the message *get-name*() is defined for the class *person*, and it can be invoked with a *person* object, or with any object belonging to any subclass of *person*, such as *customer* or *officer*.

In Section 8.2.2, we noted that each class is itself an object, and that object includes a variable containing the set of all instances of the class. It is easy to determine which objects are associated with classes at the leaves of the hierarchy. For example, we associate with the *customer* class the set of all customers of the bank. For nonleaf classes, however, the issue is more complex. In the hierarchy of Figure 8.3, there are two plausible ways of associating objects with classes:

1. We could associate with the *employee* class all employee objects including those that are instances of *officer*, *teller*, and *secretary*.

2. We could associate with the *employee* class only those employee objects that are instances of neither *officer* nor *teller* nor *secretary*.

Usually, we make the latter choice in object-oriented systems. It is possible to determine the set of all employee objects in this case by taking the union of those objects associated with all subclasses of *employee*. Most object-oriented systems allow the specialization to be partial; that is, they allow objects that belong to a class such as *employee* but that do not belong to any of that class's subclasses.

8.2.4   Multiple Inheritance

In most cases, a **tree-structured organization** of classes is adequate to describe applications—in tree-structured organizations, each class can have at most one superclass. However, there are situations that cannot be represented well in a tree-structured class hierarchy.

Multiple inheritance permits a class to inherit variables and methods from multiple superclasses. The class–subclass relationship is represented by a **directed acyclic graph** (DAG) in which a class may have more than one superclass.

For example, suppose employees can be either temporary (for a limited period) or permanent. We may then create subclasses *temporary* and *permanent*, of the class *employee*. The subclass *temporary* would have an attribute *termination-date* specifying when the employment term ends. The subclass *permanent* may have a method for computing contributions to a company pension plan, which is not applicable to temporary employees.

The above categorization of employees as temporary or permanent is independent of their categorization based on the job they perform, namely, officer, teller, or secretary. We could have officers who are permanent, officers who are temporary, tellers who are permanent, and tellers who are temporary. Using multiple inheritance, we simply create new classes, such as *temporary-teller*, which is a subclass of *temporary* and *teller*, and *permanent-teller*, which is a subclass of *permanent* and *teller*. Combinations that cannot occur in real life need not be created; for example, if all officers are permanent, there is no need to create a class of temporary officers. The resulting class hierarchy appears in Figure 8.5.

Thanks to multiple inheritance, attributes and methods specific to temporary and permanent employees are specified only once and are inherited by all the subclasses. In contrast, without multiple inheritance, we would, for example, define *temporary-officer* as a subclass of *officer*, and *temporary-teller* as a subclass of *teller*. The attributes and methods specific to temporary employees would have to be repeated in each of the above subclasses.

As another example of multiple inheritance, consider a university database, where a person can be a student or a teacher. The university database may have classes *student* and *teacher*, which are subclasses of *person*, to model this situation. Now, there is also a category of students who also work as teaching assistants; to model this situation, a class *teaching-assistant* may be created as a subclass of *student* as well as of *teacher*.

When multiple inheritance is used, there is potential ambiguity if the same variable or method can be inherited from more than one superclass. For instance, the *student* class may have a variable *dept* identifying a student's department, and the *teacher* class may correspondingly have a variable *dept* identifying a teacher's department.

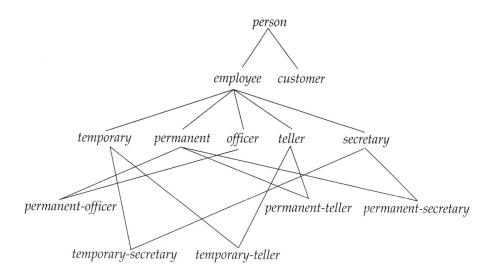

Figure 8.5   Class DAG for the bank example.

The class *teaching-assistant* inherits both these definitions of the variable *dept*; thus the use of the variable *dept* in the context of teaching assistants becomes ambiguous.

The result of using *dept* varies, depending on the particular implementation of the object-oriented model. For example, the implementation may handle *dept* in one of these ways:

- Include both variables, renaming them to *student.dept* and *teacher.dept*.

- Choose one or the other, according to the order in which the classes *student* and *teacher* were created.

- Force the user to make a choice explicitly in the definition of the class *teaching-assistant*.

- Treat the situation as an error.

No single solution has been accepted as best, and different systems make different choices.

Not all cases of multiple inheritance lead to ambiguity. For example, the variable *salary* is defined in class *employee*; classes *officer*, *teller*, and *secretary* as well as *temporary* and *permanent* all inherit *salary* from *employee*. Since all three classes share the same definition of *salary*, no ambiguity results from the inheritance of *salary* by *permanent-teller*, *temporary-officer*, and so on.

Consider the university database again. The database may have several subclasses of *person*, including *student* and *teacher* as we saw earlier in this section, and additional subclasses such as *council-member* (that is, a member of a council of students and teachers that is in charge of student affairs). An object can belong to several of these categories at once, and each of these categories is called a *role*. The notion of role here is similar in spirit to that of roles used for authorization in SQL (see Chapter 6).

Many object-oriented programming languages insist that an object must have a **most-specific class**, that is, if the object belongs to many classes, it must belong to one class that is a (direct or indirect) subclass of all the other classes to which the object belongs. For example, if an object belongs to the *person* and *teacher* classes, it must belong to some class that is a subclass of both these classes. We must then use multiple inheritance to create all required subclasses such as *teaching-assistant* (which is a subclass of *student* and *teacher*), *student-council-member*, *teaching-assistant-council-member*, and so on, to model the possibility of an object simultaneously having multiple roles.

Clearly creating many such subclasses is rather inconvenient, and systems that do not have a requirement of objects having a most-specific class are preferable for modeling roles. In Chapter 9, we discuss extensions to SQL that provide alternative ways of modeling roles.

8.2.5   Object Identity

Objects in an object-oriented database usually correspond to an entity in the enterprise being modeled by the database. An entity retains its identity even if some of its properties change over time. Likewise, an object retains its identity even if some or all of the values of variables or definitions of methods change over time. This concept of identity does not apply to tuples of a relational database. In relational systems, the tuples of a relation are distinguished only by the values that they contain.

Object identity is a stronger notion of identity than that usually found in programming languages or in data models not based on object orientation. We illustrate several forms of identity next.

- **Value**. A data value is used for identity. This form of identity is used in relational systems. For instance, the primary key value of a tuple identifies the tuple.

- **Name**. A user-supplied name is used for identity. This form of identity is used for files in file systems. The user gives each file a name that uniquely identifies it, regardless of its contents.

- **Built-in**. A notion of identity is built into the data model or programming language, and no user-supplied identifier is required. This form of identity is used in object-oriented systems. The system automatically gives each object an identifier when that object is created.

The identity of objects is a conceptual notion; actual systems require a physical mechanism to *identify* objects uniquely. For identifying humans, names along with other information, such as date and place of birth, are often used as identifiers. Object-oriented systems use an **object identifier** to identify objects. Object identifiers are **unique**; that is, each object has a single identifier, and no two objects have the same identifier. Object identifiers are not necessarily in a form with which humans are comfortable—they could be long numbers, for example. The ability to store the identifier of an object as a field of another object is more important than having a name that is easy to remember.

As an example of the use of object identifiers, one of the attributes of a *person* object may be a *spouse* attribute, which is actually the identifier of the *person* object corresponding to the first person's spouse. Thus, the *person* object can store a *reference* to the object representing the person's spouse.

Usually, the identifier is generated automatically by the system. In contrast, in a relational database, the *spouse* field of a *person* relation would typically be a unique identifier (perhaps a social-security number) of the person's spouse, generated outside the database system. There are many situations where having the system generate identifiers automatically is a benefit, since it frees humans from that task. However, this ability should be used with care. System-generated identifiers are usually specific to the system, and they have to be translated if data are moved to a different database system. Moreover, system-generated identifiers may be redundant if the entities being modeled already have unique identifiers external to the system. For example, social-security numbers are often used as unique identifiers for people in the United States.

8.2.6   Object Containment

References between objects can be used to model different real-world concepts. One such concept is that of *object containment*. For an illustration of containment, consider the simplified bicycle-design database of Figure 8.6. Each bicycle design contains wheels, a frame, brakes, and gears. Wheels, in turn, contain a rim, a set of spokes, and a tire. Each of the components of the design can be modeled as an object, and the containment of components can be modeled as containment of objects.

Objects that contain other objects are called **complex objects** or **composite objects**. There can be multiple levels of containment, as Figure 8.6 shows. This situation creates a **containment hierarchy** among objects.

The hierarchy of Figure 8.6 shows the containment relationship among objects in a schematic way by listing class names, rather than individual objects. The links between classes must be interpreted as **is-part-of**, rather than the **is-a** interpretation of links in an inheritance hierarchy.

The figure does not show the variables of the various classes. Consider the class *bicycle*. It may include variables, such as *brand-name*, containing descriptive data about an instance of the class *bicycle*. In addition, class *bicycle* includes variables that con-

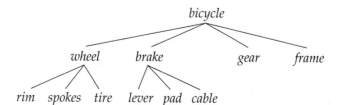

Figure 8.6   Containment hierarchy for bicycle-design database.

tain a reference, or a set of references, to objects from the classes *wheel*, *brake*, *gear*, and *frame*.

Containment is an important concept in object-oriented systems because it allows different users to view data at different granularities. A wheel designer can focus on instances of class *wheel* without much, if any, concern about the objects of class *gear* or *brake*. A marketing-staff person, attempting to price an entire bicycle, can reference all data pertaining to the bicycle by referencing the appropriate instance of class *bicycle*. She can use the containment hierarchy to find all objects contained in a *bicycle* object.

In certain applications, an object may be contained in several objects. In such cases, the containment relationship is represented by a DAG, rather than by a hierarchy.

8.3 Object-Oriented Languages

Until now, we have covered the basic concepts of object orientation at an abstract level. To use the concepts in practice in a database system, however, we have to express them in some language. We can do this in either of two ways:

1. We use the concepts of object orientation purely as a design tool, and encode them into, for example, a relational database. We follow this approach when we use entity-relationship diagrams to model data, and we then manually convert the diagrams into a set of relations.

2. We incorporate the concepts of object orientation into a language that we use to manipulate the database. With this approach, there are several possible languages into which the concepts can be integrated:

   - One choice is to extend a data-manipulation language such as SQL by adding complex types and object orientation. Systems that provide object-oriented extensions to relational systems are called *object-relational* systems. We describe object-relational systems, and in particular object-oriented extensions to SQL, in Chapter 9.
   - Another choice is to take an existing object-oriented programming language and to extend it to deal with databases. Such languages are called **persistent programming** languages.

There are different situations in which one approach is better than the other. We study the latter approach in succeeding sections of this chapter. We discuss the relationship between the two approaches in Chapter 9, after describing object-relational systems.

8.4 Persistent Programming Languages

Database languages differ from traditional programming languages in that they directly manipulate data that are persistent—that is, data that continue to exist even after the program that created it has terminated. A relation in a database and tuples in a relation are examples of persistent data. In contrast, the only persistent data that traditional programming languages directly manipulate are files.

Access to a database is only one component of any real-world application. While a data manipulation language like SQL is quite effective for accessing data, a programming language is required for implementing other components of the application such as user interfaces or communication with other computers. The traditional way of interfacing database languages to programming languages is by embedding SQL within the programming language.

A **persistent programming language** is a programming language extended with constructs to handle persistent data. Persistent programming languages can be distinguished from languages with embedded SQL in at least two ways:

1. With an embedded language, the type system of the host language usually differs from the type system of the data manipulation language. The programmer is responsible for any type conversions between the host language and SQL. Having the programmer carry out this task has several drawbacks:

   - The code to convert between objects and tuples operates outside the object-oriented type system, and hence has a higher chance of having undetected errors.

   - Conversion between the object-oriented format and the relational format of tuples in the database takes a substantial amount of code. The format translation code, along with the code for loading and unloading data from a database, can form a significant percentage of the total code required for an application.

   In contrast, in a persistent programming language, the query language is fully integrated with the host language, and both share the same type system. Objects can be created and stored in the database without any explicit type or format changes; any format changes required are carried out transparently.

2. The programmer using an embedded query language is responsible for writing explicit code to fetch data from the database into memory. If any updates are performed, the programmer must write code explicitly to store the updated data back in the database.

   In contrast, in a persistent programming language, the programmer can manipulate persistent data without writing code explicitly to fetch it into memory or store it back to disk.

In the past, database system developers have proposed persistent versions of programming languages such as Pascal. In recent years, developers have focused their attention on persistent versions of object-oriented languages such as C++, Java, and Smalltalk. These language versions allow programmers to manipulate data directly from the programming language, without having to go through a data-manipulation language such as SQL. Thereby, they provide tighter integration of the programming languages with the database than, for example, embedded SQL.

There are certain drawbacks to persistent programming languages, however, that we must keep in mind when deciding whether to use them. Since the programming language is usually a powerful one, it is relatively easy to make programming errors that damage the database. The complexity of the language makes automatic high-level optimization, such as to reduce disk I/O, harder. Support for declarative querying is important for many applications, but persistent programming languages currently do not support declarative querying well.

We outline below several issues that any persistent programming language must deal with, and in later sections we describe extensions to C++ that make it a persistent programming language.

8.4.1 Persistence of Objects

Object-oriented programming languages already have a concept of objects, a type system to define object types, and constructs to create objects. However, these objects are *transient*—they vanish when the program terminates, just as variables in a Pascal or C program vanish when the program terminates. If we wish to turn such a language into a database programming language, the first step is to provide a way to make objects persistent. Several approaches have been proposed.

- **Persistence by class**. The simplest, but least convenient, way is to declare that a class is persistent. All objects of the class are then persistent objects by default. Objects of nonpersistent classes are all transient.

  This approach is not flexible, since it is often useful to have both transient and persistent objects in a single class. Many object-oriented database systems interpret declaring a class to be persistent as saying that objects in the class potentially can be made persistent, rather than that all objects in the class are persistent. Such classes might more appropriately be called "persistable" classes.

- **Persistence by creation**. In this approach, new syntax is introduced to create persistent objects, by extending the syntax for creating transient objects. Thus, an object is either persistent or transient, depending on how it was created. Several object-oriented database systems follow this approach.

- **Persistence by marking**. A variant of the preceding approach is to mark objects as persistent after they are created. All objects are created as transient objects, but, if an object is to persist beyond the execution of the program, it must be marked explicitly as persistent before the program terminates. This approach, unlike the previous one, postpones the decision on persistence or transience until after the object is created.

- **Persistence by reachability**. One or more objects are explicitly declared as (root) persistent objects. All other objects are persistent if (and only if) they are referred to directly, or indirectly, from a root persistent object.

  Thus, all objects referenced from the root persistent objects are persistent. But also, all objects referenced from these objects are persistent, and objects to which they refer are in turn persistent, and so on. Thus, the persistent objects are exactly those reachable from a persistent root.

  A benefit of this scheme is that it is easy to make entire data structures persistent by merely declaring the root of such structures as persistent. However, the database system has the burden of following chains of references to detect which objects are persistent, and that can be expensive.

8.4.2 Object Identity and Pointers

In an object-oriented programming language that has not been extended to handle persistence, when an object is created, the system returns a transient object identifier. Transient object identifiers are valid only when the program that created them is executing; after that program terminates, the objects are deleted, and the identifier is meaningless. When a persistent object is created, it is assigned a persistent object identifier.

The notion of object identity has an interesting relationship to pointers in programming languages. A simple way to achieve built-in identity is through pointers to physical locations in storage. In particular, in many object-oriented languages such as C++, a transient object identifier is actually an in-memory pointer.

However, the association of an object with a physical location in storage may change over time. There are several degrees of permanence of identity:

- **Intraprocedure**. Identity persists only during the execution of a single procedure. Examples of intraprogram identity are local variables within procedures.

- **Intraprogram**. Identity persists only during the execution of a single program or query. Examples of intraprogram identity are global variables in programming languages. Main-memory or virtual-memory pointers offer only intraprogram identity.

- **Interprogram**. Identity persists from one program execution to another. Pointers to file-system data on disk offer interprogram identity, but they may change if the way data is stored in the file system is changed.

- **Persistent**. Identity persists not only among program executions, but also among structural reorganizations of the data. It is the persistent form of identity that is required for object-oriented systems.

In persistent extensions of languages such as C++, object identifiers for persistent objects are implemented as "persistent pointers." A *persistent pointer* is a type of pointer that, unlike in-memory pointers, remains valid even after the end of a program execution, and across some forms of data reorganization. A programmer may use a persistent pointer in the same ways that she may use an in-memory pointer in a programming language. Conceptually, we may think of a persistent pointer as a pointer to an object in the database.

8.4.3 Storage and Access of Persistent Objects

What does it mean to store an object in a database? Clearly, the data part of an object has to be stored individually for each object. Logically, the code that implements methods of a class should be stored in the database as part of the database schema, along with the type definitions of the classes. However, many implementations simply store the code in files outside the database, to avoid having to integrate system software such as compilers with the database system.

There are several ways to find objects in the database. One way is to give names to objects, just as we give names to files. This approach works for a relatively small number of objects, but does not scale to millions of objects. A second way is to expose object identifiers or persistent pointers to the objects, which can be stored externally. Unlike names, these pointers do not have to be mnemonic, and can even be physical pointers into a database.

A third way is to store collections of objects, and to allow programs to iterate over the collections to find required objects. Collections of objects can themselves be modeled as objects of a *collection type*. Collection types include sets, multisets (that is, sets with possibly many occurrences of a value), lists, and so on. A special case of a collection is a *class extent*, which is the collection of all objects belonging to the class. If a class extent is present for a class, then, whenever an object of the class is created, that object is inserted in the class extent automatically, and, whenever an object is deleted, that object is removed from the class extent. Class extents allow classes to be treated like relations in that we can examine all objects in the class, just as we can examine all tuples in a relation.

Most object-oriented database systems support all three ways of accessing persistent objects. They give identifiers to all objects. They usually give names only to class extents and other collection objects, and perhaps to other selected objects, but not to most objects. They usually maintain class extents for all classes that can have persistent objects, but, in many of the implementations, the class extents contain only persistent objects of the class.

8.5 Persistent C++ Systems

Several object-oriented databases based on persistent extensions to C++ have appeared in the past few years (see the bibliographical notes). There are differences between them in terms of the system architecture, yet they have many common features in terms of the programming language.

Several of the object-oriented features of the C++ language help in providing a good deal of support for persistence without changing the language itself. For example, we can declare a class called Persistent_Object with attributes and methods to support persistence; any other class that should be persistent can be made a subclass of this class, and thereby inherit the support for persistence. The C++ language (like some other modern programming languages) also lets us redefine standard function names and operators—such as $+$, $-$, the pointer dereference operator $-$>, and so on —according to the type of the operands on which they are applied. This ability is called *overloading*; it is used to redefine operators to behave in the required manner when they are operating on persistent objects. Examples of the use of such features appear in the next section.

Providing persistence support via class libraries has the benefit of making only minimal changes to C++ necessary; moreover, it is relatively easy to implement. However, it has the drawback that the programmer has to spend much more time to write a program that handles persistent objects, and it is not easy for the programmer to specify integrity constraints on the schema or to provide support for declarative querying. Some persistent C++ implementations support extensions to the C++ syntax to make these tasks easier.

8.5.1   The ODMG C++ Object-Definition Language

The Object Database Management Group (ODMG) has been working on standardizing language extensions to C++ and Smalltalk to support persistence, and on defining class libraries to support persistence. ODMG published the first version of its standard in 1993. The group published the second version, ODMG-2.0, which we cover in this chapter, in 1997.

The ODMG standard provides all functionality via class libraries, without any extensions to the language. We describe the ODMG standard by using examples. You must have prior knowledge of the C++ programming language to understand the examples fully. (See the bibliographical notes for references to C++ texts.)

There are two parts to the ODMG C++ extension: (1) the C++ *Object Definition Language* (C++ *ODL*) and (2) the C++ *Object Manipulation Language* (C++ *OML*). The C++ ODL extends the C++ type definition syntax.

Figure 8.7 shows a sample of code written in the ODMG C++ ODL. The sample defines the schemas of four classes. It defines each class as a subclass of d_Object so as to permit creation of persistent objects belonging to the class. The classes Branch, Account, and Person are direct subclasses of d_Object. The class Customer is a subclass of Person and is therefore indirectly also a subclass of d_Object. The types d_String, d_Date, and d_Long are among the standard types defined by ODMG-2.0. The type d_Long denotes 32-bit integers.

C++ does not support the concept of messages directly. Instead, methods may be directly invoked, and behave like procedure calls. The declaration of class Account illustrates methods find_balance() and update_balance(d_Long delta), which are used to read and update the balance attribute (we have not presented the code for the methods).

The declaration of class Account also illustrates the "encapsulation" features of C++ (these are not specific to ODMG). The keyword private indicates that the following attributes or methods are visible to only methods of the class; public indicates that the attributes or methods are visible to other code as well. The attribute balance of Account is declared to be private, meaning that no function other than methods of the class can read or write it. The Account class has two other variables that occur after the public keyword, meaning they can be accessed by code other than the methods of class Account.

The use of the keyword public just before the name of a superclass indicates that public attributes or methods inherited from the superclass remain public in the subclass. These features are part of standard C++, and not specific to ODMG.

The type d_Ref<Branch> used in the Customer class is a *reference*, or persistent pointer, to an object of type Branch. The type d_Set<d_Ref<Customer>> used in Account is a set of persistent pointers to objects of type Account.

The classes d_Ref<> and d_Set<> are *template* classes defined in the ODMG-2.0 standard; the standard defines them in a type-independent way, and the programmer can instantiate them to the required types (such as d_Ref<Branch>) as desired.

```
class Branch : public d_Object {
public:
    d_String branch_name;
    d_String address;
    d_Long assets;
};

class Account : public d_Object {
private:
    d_Long balance;
public:
    d_Long account_number;
    d_Set<d_Ref<Customer>> owners;
    d_Long find_balance();
    int update_balance(d_Long delta);
};

class Person : public d_Object {
public:
    d_String name;
    d_String address;
};

class Customer : public Person {
public:
    d_Date member_from;
    d_Long customer_id;
    d_Ref<Branch> home_branch;
    d_Set<d_Ref<Account>> accounts;
};
```

Figure 8.7   Example of ODMG C++ Object-Definition Language.

The references between Customer and Account represent a relationship between Customer and Account objects. The relationship results in the following referential integrity constraint: "If a Customer object has a reference to an Account object from its accounts attribute, there must also be an **inverse reference** from the Account object back to the Customer object through the owners attribute."

The programmer can specify referential integrity constraints in ODMG-2.0, and the system will automatically maintain them, in a way we describe in the following paragraphs. The programmer specifies the referential integrity constraint between the Account and Owner classes by declaring the owners and accounts attributes of the two classes, as in Figure 8.8. the standard defines these attributes as instances of a template class d_Rel_Set<T,A>. An instance of this class contains a set of references to objects of type T. There must be an attribute in class T that stores the inverse reference; the name of this attribute is stored in A. Because of restrictions of the C++

```
extern const char _owners[], _accounts[];
class Customer : public Person {
public:

    . . .
    d_Rel_Set<Account,_owners> accounts;
};

class Account : public d_Object {
public:

    . . .
    d_Rel_Set<Customer, _accounts> owners;
    . . .
};
const char _owners[] = "owners";
const char _accounts[] = "accounts";
```

Figure 8.8 Referential integrity constraints in ODMG C++ ODL.

language, we cannot directly use the string "owners" or "accounts" as a parameter to a template class, so we use the variables _owners and _accounts, which store the strings "owners" and "accounts" respectively.

ODMG-2.0 maintains referential integrity automatically: The template class d_Rel_Ref<T,A> provides a method for inserting a reference; this method also inserts an inverse reference (if it is not already present) in the attribute, whose name is stored in A, of class T. For example, to add a new account to a customer we insert a reference to the account in the accounts attribute of Customer; using the insert method of the class d_Rel_Set<Account,_owners>. This method maintains the referential integrity constraint by automatically inserting a reference to the owner in the owners variable of the account. Similarly, when the system carries out a deletion, the method correspondingly deletes the inverse reference. Thus, the method guarantees that the referential integrity constraint is not violated.

ODMG-2.0 also provides a template class d_Rel_Ref<T,A> which provides referential integrity to attributes that store a single reference. In this case, assignment to a variable of type d_Rel_Ref<T,A> is redefined to automatically maintain inverse references. Suppose Branch objects has an attribute customers that stores inverse references to Customer objects. We can then declare the attribute home_branch of Customer to be of type d_Rel_Ref<Branch,_customers>, where _customers is a variable initialized to the string "customers." The attribute customers of Branch would be of type d_Rel_Set<Customer,_home_branch>, where _home_branch is a variable initialized to the string "home_branch." The referential integrity constraints are then maintained automatically.

8.5.2 The ODMG C++ Object Manipulation Language

Figure 8.9 shows code written in the ODMG C++ OML. First, the program opens a database, then starts a transaction. Recall the notion of transactions from Section 4.9.5;

```
int create_account_owner(String name, String address) {
    d_Database bank_db_obj;
    d_Database * bank_db = & bank_db_obj;
    bank_db->open("Bank-DB");
    d_Transaction Trans;
    Trans.begin();

    d_Ref<Account> account = new(bank_db, "Account") Account;
    d_Ref<Customer> cust = new(bank_db, "Customer") Customer;
    cust->name = name;
    cust->address = address;
    cust->accounts.insert_element(account);
    account->owners.insert_element(cust);
    .. Code to initialize customer_id, account number etc.
    Trans.commit();
    bank_db->close();
}
```

Figure 8.9   Example of ODMG C++ Object Manipulation Language.

transactions form a unit of work that is atomic; that is, if the transaction is not successfully completed, the system undoes the the actions of the transaction.

As the next step, the program creates an account and an owner object by using the new operator. The class d_Object implements several methods, including the persistent version of the C++ memory-allocation operator new that is used in the example code. This version of the new operator allocates the object in the specified database, rather than in memory. The operator also takes a parameter that specifies the class name of the object being allocated; the class name is used to keep track of which objects in a database belong to a particular class.

The program then initializes the account and owner objects. We use the method insert_element of the template class d_Set<> to insert customer and account references in the appropriate sets after creating the customer and account objects. If we had declared accounts and owners to be of type d_Rel_Set, as soon as an account is added to the set of accounts of a customer, the reverse references from the account object (through the owners attribute) would get created automatically. Thus, inserting the customer into the set of owners of the account becomes unnecessary (although not incorrect). Similarly, if we deleted an account from a customer, the set of owners of the account would also get updated automatically, by removing the customer.

At the end, the program commits the transaction and closes the database. A **transaction** consists of all steps between a call from begin a call to commit or abort the transaction. The steps of the transaction form an atomic unit. That is, the database system guarantees that (1) if the commit() operation is executed for a transaction, all the updates it made will be persistent in the database and (2) if an abort() operation is executed, or if the program executing the transaction terminates without executing commit(), all the updates performed as part of the transaction will be undone. If there is any form of system failure before a transaction commits, the system undoes all the updates of the transaction when it comes back up.

8.5.2.1 Class Extents

In the code in Figure 8.9, the identifiers of the customer and account objects are not explicitly stored anywhere, although the objects are still in the database. The natural question is, once the program that created these objects terminates, how do we get to the objects? There are two ways to do so.

In the first method, ODMG provides a mechanism to specify, as part of the schema of a class in a database, that a class extent should be maintained for the class. This specification can be done by administrative tools provided by an ODMG implementation, or by a function call. Once this specification has been done, whenever a programmer creates an object of the class, say C, in that database, the system adds the object identifier to the class extent of class C. Whenever the programmer deletes an object, the system deletes its identifier from the class extent of C. The template class d_Extent is used to access the elements in a class extent. In Section 8.5.2.2 we outline how.

The second method is to give names to objects, just as we give names to files in a file system. Since a database may contain a very large number of objects of each class, giving names to every object becomes problematic. Instead, we can create a persistent set that contains the identifiers of all objects in a class, and give a name to the set. In other words, we manually create a class extent for the class. We describe details in Section 8.5.2.4.

8.5.2.2 Iterators

We can iterate over a collection of references by using an *iterator*. We create an iterator with the method create_iterator() that is provided by collection classes, such as d_Set, as well as by the special class d_Extent, which is used to access class extents.

In the code in Figure 8.10, the line

d_Extent<Customer> all_customers(bank_db);

declares all_customers to be a class extent of class Customer, and initializes it to be the class extent of Customer in the database bank_db. The variable iter is then set to be an iterator on the objects in the class extent of Customer.

We use the method next(), provided by the iterator, to step through consecutive elements of the collection of customers. For each customer, the program calls the function print_cust (which, we assume, the programmer has already defined) to print out information about the customer.

Collection classes and the d_Extent class also provide a method select(), which is like create_iterator(), but takes a selection condition as argument, and iterates over only those objects that satisfy the selection condition.

```
int print_customers() {
    d_Database bank_db_obj;
    d_Database * bank_db = & bank_db_obj;
    bank_db->open("Bank-DB");
    d_Transaction Trans;
    Trans.begin();
    d_Extent<Customer> all_customers(bank_db);

    d_Iterator<d_Ref<Customer>> iter = all_customers.create_iterator();
    d_Ref<Customer> p;
    while(iter.next(p)) {
        print_cust(p);
    }
    Trans.commit();
}
```

Figure 8.10   Example of use of ODMG C++ iterators.

8.5.2.3 Updating Objects

If an object is to be updated, ODMG requires that the database system be notified of the update. To do so, the program must invoke the method mark_modified() on the object *before* it is updated.

For example, the method update_balance(d_Long delta) of the class Account must invoke mark_modified() before it updates the balance. Failure to do so can result in the update not being reflected in the database.

So far, our example program has modified only objects that have just been created, and there is no need to invoke mark_modified() for such objects. Also, system-defined methods like insert_element() automatically invoke mark_modified().

The need to mark objects as modified before updating them can lead to bugs, since programmers may easily forget to do so. Some object-oriented databases implement techniques for automatically determining when an object is modified, freeing the programmer from this task.

8.5.2.4 Creating Class Extents Manually

As an exercise in writing an ODMG program, consider how to create a class extent manually for Customer objects. It is convenient to store the identifier of the set in a global variable associated with the classes Customer. We declare the global variable by adding the following line as part of the Customer class declaration.

```
static d_Ref<d_Set<d_Ref<Customer>>> all_customers;
```

We initially allocate the persistent set for Customer in the database and store its identifier in the global variable as follows:

```
Customer::all_customers =
          new(bank_db) d_Set<d_Ref<Customer>>;
```

When we create a customer object, we insert its identifier in the set of customers by using a statement of the form

```
Customer::all_customers->insert_element(cust);
```

We can create a a persistent set for storing identifiers of the Account objects, and store the identifiers of the account objects in it, similarly. However, the value of the variable Customer::all_customers, and thus the identifier of the persistent set, would be lost when the transaction ends. In order to find the set in the database later on, when we initially allocate the set we give its object identifier a name in the database, as follows:

```
bank_db->set_object_name(Customer::all_customers, "All_Customers");
```

When a later transaction starts up, it first opens the database, and then finds the set created earlier and initializes Customer::all_customers:

```
Customer::all_customers =
          bank_db->lookup_object("All_Customers");
```

   A **constructor** for a class is a special method that is used to initialize objects when they are created; it is called automatically when the new operator is executed. Similarly, a **destructor** for a class is a special method that is called when objects in the class are deleted. By adding the insert_element statement to the constructors of a class, and adding a corresponding delete_element statement to the destructor of the class, a programmer can ensure that the collection Customer::all_customers is maintained correctly. As we noted in Section 8.5.2.1, ODMG implementations may maintain class extents automatically, and there is then no need for manual maintenance.

8.5.2.5 Object Query Language

ODMG provides a declarative query language, OQL. OQL has the look and feel of SQL. The following code creates and executes an OQL query to find all accounts owned by "Jones" that have a balance greater than 100. The results are stored in the set-valued variable result.

```
d_Set<d_Ref<Account>> result;
d_OQL_Query q1("select a
          from Customer c, c.accounts a
          where c.name = 'Jones'
               and a.find_balance() > 100");
d_oql_execute(q1, result);
```

8.5.2.6 Making Pointer Persistence Transparent

One drawback of the ODMG approach is that the programmer has to deal with two types of pointers—in-memory pointers and d_Ref references—and code written for one type will not work with the other. Further, the programmer must make sure to call mark_modified() when an object is updated.

In contrast, the **ObjectStore** database system permits database objects to be referenced by using the normal C++ style pointers, instead of using d_Refs. To the programmer, pointers to persistent objects appear to be the same as pointers to regular in-memory objects. Persistence of pointers is transparent, and having only one pointer type makes programming much easier. ObjectStore programmers write programs exactly as with normal C++ with the only difference being that, as in ODMG, objects can be created in a database by using a special form of new.

This functionality is implemented by means of a translation mechanism called *swizzling*, which converts between persistent pointers and in-memory pointers; swizzling is described in Chapter 11.

ObjectStore also provides extensions of the C++ language that permit referential integrity constraints to be specified more easily. It also automatically detects updates, and does not require calls to mark_modified().

8.6 Persistent Java Systems

The Java language has seen an enormous growth in usage in recent years. Demand for support for persistence of data in Java programs has grown correspondingly, and the ODMG consortium has defined standards for persistence support in Java.

The ODMG model for object persistence in Java programs differs from the model for persistence support in C++ programs. The biggest difference is the use of **persistence by reachability** in Java. Objects are not explicitly created in a database. Instead, names are given to objects in the database that serve as **roots** for persistence. These objects, and any objects reachable from these objects, are persistent.

Persistence by reachability implies that persistent pointers must be of the same type as transient pointers, so there is no equivalent to the C++ d_Ref template class. Another result of persistence by reachability is that objects in the database may become garbage if the object becomes unreachable from all persistent roots in the database, and no active transaction has stored a pointer to the object. Such objects must be removed by periodically running a **garbage collection** procedure on the database. Garbage collection generally runs concurrently with other database activities.

If an object of a class is reachable from a persistent root, the class must be made *persistence capable*. A class is typically made persistence capable (that is, objects of that class may become persistent) by running a postprocessor on the class code generated by compiling the Java program. It is also possible to manually make a class persistence capable by inserting appropriate declarations in the Java code, but this approach is relatively complicated and not favored.

The postprocessor also inserts code to automatically mark objects as modified whenever they are updated, unlike in the ODMG C++ binding where updated objects must be explicitly marked by using mark_modified().

When a transaction wishes to access objects in a database, it must start at one of the database root objects, which the transaction looks up by its name. The system fetches the root object from the database into memory. Implementations may choose to fetch all objects referenced from the root object immediately, or fetch referenced objects in a lazy fashion. In lazy fetching of objects, the root object is initially "hollow", that is, it is assigned a memory location but its fields are not initialized. When a hollow object h is accessed for the first time, its fields are filled in from the database. The hollow object h may contain references to other objects; if any such object is already in memory, its in-memory address is used to replace the reference in h. If the referenced object is not in memory, a hollow object is created for it, and the in-memory address of the hollow object is used to replace the reference in h.

The ODMG standard for Java defines collection types such as DSet, DBag, and DList that extend the standard Java collection types. Java already defines an iterator type to iterate over collections.

8.7 Summary

- Current-generation database applications often do not fit the set of assumptions made for older, data-processing–style applications. The object-oriented data model has been developed to deal with several of these new type of applications.

- The object-oriented data model is an adaptation to database systems of the object-oriented–programming paradigm. It is based on the concept of encapsulating in an object the data and the code that operates on those data.

- Similarly structured objects are grouped into classes. The set of classes is structured into sub- and superclasses according to an extension of the ISA concept of the entity-relationship model.

- The value of a data item in an object can be an object, making it possible to represent object containment, resulting in a composite object.

- There are two approaches to creating an object-oriented database: We can add the concepts of object orientation to existing database languages, or we can extend existing object-oriented languages to deal with databases by adding concepts such as persistence and collections. Extended relational databases take the former approach. Persistent programming languages follow the latter approach.

- Persistent extensions to C++ and Java have appeared in recent years. They integrate persistence seamlessly and orthogonally with existing language constructs and so are easy to use.

- The ODMG standard defines classes and other constructs for creating and accessing persistent objects from C++ and from Java.

Review Terms

- Object
- Encapsulation
- Variables
- Messages
- Methods
- Class
- Instance
- Inheritance
- Class hierarchy
- Subclasses
- Superclass
- Substitutability
- Multiple inheritance
- Directed acyclic graph (DAG)
- Ambiguity in inheritance
- Most-specific class
- Roles
- Object identity
  - ☐ Value
  - ☐ Name
  - ☐ Built-in

- Object identifier
- Object containment
- Persistent programming languages
- Persistence by
  - ☐ Class
  - ☐ Creation
  - ☐ Marking
  - ☐ Reachability
- ODMG C++ ODL
  - ☐ d_Ref, d_Set
  - ☐ Referential integrity
    — d_Rel_Set, d_Ref_Ref
- ODMG C++ OML
  - ☐ Class extents (d_Extent)
  - ☐ Iterators (d_Iterator)
  - ☐ Object query language
- Object store
- ODMG Java
  - ☐ Persistence by reachability
  - ☐ Roots
  - ☐ Garbage collection

Exercises

8.1 For each of the following application areas, explain why a relational database system would be inadequate. List all specific system components that would need to be modified.

   a. Computer-aided design

   b. Multimedia databases

8.2 How does the concept of an object in the object-oriented model differ from the concept of an entity in the entity-relationship model?

8.3 A car-rental company maintains a vehicle database for all vehicles in its current fleet. For all vehicles, it includes the vehicle identification number, license number, manufacturer, model, date of purchase, and color. Special data are included for certain types of vehicles:

- Trucks: cargo capacity
- Sports cars: horsepower, renter age requirement

- Vans: number of passengers
- Off-road vehicles: ground clearance, drivetrain (four- or two-wheel drive)

Construct an object-oriented database schema definition for this database. Use inheritance where appropriate.

8.4 Explain why ambiguity potentially exists with multiple inheritance. Illustrate your explanation with an example.

8.5 Explain how the concept of object identity in the object-oriented model differs from the concept of tuple equality in the relational model.

8.6 Explain the distinction in meaning between edges in a DAG representing inheritance and a DAG representing object containment.

8.7 Why do persistent programming languages allow transient objects? Might it be simpler to use only persistent objects, with unneeded objects deleted at the end of an execution? Explain your answer.

8.8 Using ODMG C++

   a. Give schema definitions corresponding to the relational schema shown in Figure 3.39, using references to express foreign-key relationships.
   b. Write programs to compute each of the queries in Exercise 3.10.

8.9 Using ODMG C++, give schema definitions corresponding to the E-R diagram in Figure 2.29, using references to implement relationships.

8.10 Explain, using an example, how to represent a ternary relationship in an object-oriented data model such as ODMG C++.

8.11 Explain how a persistent pointer is implemented. Contrast this implementation with that of pointers as they exist in general-purpose languages, such as C or Pascal.

8.12 If an object is created without any references to it, how can that object be deleted?

8.13 Consider a system that provides persistent objects. Is such a system necessarily a database system? Explain your answer.

Bibliographical Notes

Applications of database concepts to CAD are discussed in Haskin and Lorie [1982] and Lorie et al. [1985].

Object-oriented programming is discussed in Goldberg and Robson [1983], Stefik and Bobrow [1986], and Stroustrup [1988]. Stroustrup [1997] describes the C++ programming language.

There are numerous implemented object-oriented database systems, including (in alphabetical order) Cactis (Hudson and King [1989]); E/Exodus, developed at the University of Wisconsin (Carey et al. [1990]); Gemstone (Maier et al. [1986]); Iris, developed at Hewlett-Packard (Fishman et al. [1990]); Jasmine, developed at Fujitsu Labs (Ishikawa et al. [1993]); O_2 (Lecluse et al. [1988]); ObjectStore (Lamb et al.

[1991]); Ode, developed at Bell Laboratories (Agrawal and Gehani [1989]); Ontos; Open-OODB; Orion (Kim et al. [1988]); Versant, and others.

The object database standard ODMG is described in detail in Cattell [2000].

Overviews of object-oriented database research include Kim [1990], Zdonik and Maier [1990], and Dogac et al. [1994]. Object identity is characterized in detail by Khoshafian and Copeland [1990].

Schema modification in object-oriented databases is more complicated than schema modification in relational databases, since object-oriented databases have complex type systems with inheritance. Schema modification is discussed in Skarra and Zdonik [1986], Banerjee et al. [1987], and Penney and Stein [1987].

Goodman [1995] describes the benefits and drawbacks of using an object-oriented databases in a genome database application. Lunt [1995] provides an overview of issues in authorization in object-oriented databases.

Object-Relational Databases

Persistent programming languages add persistence and other database features to existing programming languages by using an existing object-oriented type system. In contrast, *object-relational data models* extend the relational data model by providing a richer type system including complex data types and object orientation. Relational query languages, in particular SQL, need to be correspondingly extended to deal with the richer type system. Such extensions attempt to preserve the relational foundations—in particular, the declarative access to data—while extending the modeling power. Object-relational database systems (that is, database systems based on the object-relation model) provide a convenient migration path for users of relational databases who wish to use object-oriented features.

We first present the motivation for the nested relational model, which allows relations that are not in first normal form, and allows direct representation of hierarchical structures. We then show how to extend SQL by adding a variety of object-relational features. Our discussion is based on the SQL:1999 standard.

Finally, we discuss differences between persistent programming languages and object-relational systems, and mention criteria for choosing between them.

9.1 Nested Relations

In Chapter 7, we defined *first normal form* (1NF), which requires that all attributes have *atomic domains*. Recall that a domain is *atomic* if elements of the domain are considered to be indivisible units.

The assumption of 1NF is a natural one in the bank examples we have considered. However, not all applications are best modeled by 1NF relations. For example, rather than view a database as a set of records, users of certain applications view it as a set of objects (or entities). These objects may require several records for their representation. We shall see that a simple, easy-to-use interface requires a one-to-one correspondence

title	author-set	publisher (name, branch)	keyword-set
Compilers	{Smith, Jones}	(McGraw-Hill, New York)	{parsing, analysis}
Networks	{Jones, Frick}	(Oxford, London)	{Internet, Web}

Figure 9.1   Non-1NF books relation, *books*.

between the user's intuitive notion of an object and the database system's notion of a data item.

The **nested relational model** is an extension of the relational model in which domains may be either atomic or relation valued. Thus, the value of a tuple on an attribute may be a relation, and relations may be contained within relations. A complex object thus can be represented by a single tuple of a nested relation. If we view a tuple of a nested relation as a data item, we have a one-to-one correspondence between data items and objects in the user's view of the database.

We illustrate nested relations by an example from a library. Suppose we store for each book the following information:

- Book title

- Set of authors

- Publisher

- Set of keywords

We can see that, if we define a relation for the preceding information, several domains will be nonatomic.

- **Authors**. A book may have a set of authors. Nevertheless, we may want to find all books of which Jones was one of the authors. Thus, we are interested in a subpart of the domain element "set of authors."

- **Keywords**. If we store a set of keywords for a book, we expect to be able to retrieve all books whose keywords include one or more keywords. Thus, we view the domain of the set of keywords as nonatomic.

- **Publisher**. Unlike *keywords* and *authors*, *publisher* does not have a set-valued domain. However, we may view *publisher* as consisting of the subfields *name* and *branch*. This view makes the domain of *publisher* nonatomic.

Figure 9.1 shows an example relation, *books*. The *books* relation can be represented in 1NF, as in Figure 9.2. Since we must have atomic domains in 1NF, yet want access to individual authors and to individual keywords, we need one tuple for each (keyword, author) pair. The *publisher* attribute is replaced in the 1NF version by two attributes: one for each subfield of *publisher*.

title	author	pub-name	pub-branch	keyword
Compilers	Smith	McGraw-Hill	New York	parsing
Compilers	Jones	McGraw-Hill	New York	parsing
Compilers	Smith	McGraw-Hill	New York	analysis
Compilers	Jones	McGraw-Hill	New York	analysis
Networks	Jones	Oxford	London	Internet
Networks	Frick	Oxford	London	Internet
Networks	Jones	Oxford	London	Web
Networks	Frick	Oxford	London	Web

Figure 9.2   *flat-books*, a 1NF version of non-1NF relation *books*.

Much of the awkwardness of the *flat-books* relation in Figure 9.2 disappears if we assume that the following multivalued dependencies hold:

- *title* $\rightarrow\rightarrow$ *author*
- *title* $\rightarrow\rightarrow$ *keyword*
- *title* $\rightarrow$ *pub-name, pub-branch*

Then, we can decompose the relation into 4NF using the schemas:

- *authors*(*title, author*)
- *keywords*(*title, keyword*)
- *books4*(*title, pub-name, pub-branch*)

Figure 9.3 shows the projection of the relation *flat-books* of Figure 9.2 onto the preceding decomposition.

Although our example book database can be adequately expressed without using nested relations, the use of nested relations leads to an easier-to-understand model: The typical user of an information-retrieval system thinks of the database in terms of books having sets of authors, as the non-1NF design models. The 4NF design would require users to include joins in their queries, thereby complicating interaction with the system.

We could define a non-nested relational view (whose contents are identical to *flat-books*) that eliminates the need for users to write joins in their query. In such a view, however, we lose the one-to-one correspondence between tuples and books.

9.2   Complex Types

Nested relations are just one example of extensions to the basic relational model; other nonatomic data types, such as nested records, have also proved useful. The object-oriented data model has caused a need for features such as inheritance and references to objects. With complex type systems and object orientation, we can represent E-R model concepts, such as identity of entities, multivalued attributes, and generalization and specialization directly, without a complex translation to the relational model.

title	author
Compilers	Smith
Compilers	Jones
Networks	Jones
Networks	Frick

authors

title	keyword
Compilers	parsing
Compilers	analysis
Networks	Internet
Networks	Web

keywords

title	pub-name	pub-branch
Compilers	McGraw-Hill	New York
Networks	Oxford	London

books4

Figure 9.3   4NF version of the relation *flat-books* of Figure 9.2.

In this section, we describe extensions to SQL to allow complex types, including nested relations, and object-oriented features. Our presentation is based on the SQL:1999 standard, but we also outline features that are not currently in the standard but may be introduced in future versions of SQL standards.

9.2.1   Collection and Large Object Types

Consider this fragment of code.

create table *books* (
   . . .
   keyword-set **setof(varchar**(20))
   . . .
)

This table definition differs from table definitions in ordinary relational databases, since it allows attributes that are **sets**, thereby permitting multivalued attributes of E-R diagrams to be represented directly.

Sets are an instance of **collection type**s. Other instances of collection types include **array**s and **multiset**s (that is, unordered collections, where an element may occur multiple times). The following attribute definitions illustrate the declaration of an array:

author-array **varchar**(20) **array** [10]

Here, *author-array* is an array of up to 10 author names. We can access elements of an array by specifying the array index, for example *author-array*[1].

Arrays are the only collection type supported by SQL:1999; the syntax used is as in the preceding declaration. SQL:1999 does *not* support unordered sets or multisets, although they may appear in future versions of SQL.[1]

Many current-generation database applications need to store attributes that can be large (of the order of many kilobytes), such as a photograph of a person, or very large (of the order of many megabytes or even gigabytes), such as a high-resolution medical image or video clip. SQL:1999 therefore provides new large-object data types for character data (**clob**) and binary data (**blob**). The letters "lob" in these data types stand for "Large OBject". For example, we may declare attributes

> *book-review* **clob**(10KB)
> *image* **blob**(10MB)
> *movie* **blob**(2GB))

Large objects are typically used in external applications, and it makes little sense to retrieve them in their entirety by SQL. Instead, an application would usually retrieve a "locator" for a large object and then use the locator to manipulate the object from the host language. For instance, JDBC permits the programmer to fetch a large object in small pieces, rather than all at once, much like fetching data from an operating system file.

9.2.2 Structured Types

Structured types can be declared and used in SQL:1999 as in the following example:

> **create type** *Publisher* **as**
>   (*name* **varchar**(20),
>   *branch* **varchar**(20))
> **create type** *Book* **as**
>   (*title* **varchar**(20),
>   *author-array* **varchar**(20) **array** [10],
>   *pub-date* **date**,
>   *publisher Publisher*,
>   *keyword-set* **setof**(**varchar**(20)))
> **create table** *books* **of** *Book*

The first statement defines a type called *Publisher*, which has two components: a name and a branch. The second statement defines a structured type *Book*, which contains a *title*, an *author-array*, which is an array of authors, a publication date, a publisher (of type *Publisher*), and a set of keywords. (The declaration of *keyword-set* as a set uses our extended syntax, and is not supported by the SQL:1999 standard.) The types illustrated above are called **structured type**s in SQL:1999.

---

1. The Oracle 8 database system supports nested relations, but uses a syntax different from that in this chapter.

Finally, a table *books* containing tuples of type *Book* is created. The table is similar to the nested relation *books* in Figure 9.1, except we have decided to create an array of author names instead of a set of author names. The array permits us to record the order of author names.

Structured types allow composite attributes of E-R diagrams to be represented directly. Unnamed **row type**s can also be used in SQL:1999 to define composite attributes. For instance, we could have defined an attribute *publisher1* as

$$publisher1 \textbf{ row } (name \textbf{ varchar}(20),$$
$$branch \textbf{ varchar}(20))$$

instead of creating a named type *Publisher*.

We can of course create tables without creating an intermediate type for the table. For example, the table *books* could also be defined as follows:

> **create table** *books*
> (*title* **varchar**(20),
> *author-array* **varchar**(20) **array**[10],
> *pub-date* **date**,
> *publisher Publisher*,
> *keyword-set* **setof**(**varchar**(20)))

With the above declaration, there is no explicit type for rows of the table. [2]

A structured type can have **method**s defined on it. We declare methods as part of the type definition of a structured type:

> **create type** *Employee* **as** (
> *name* **varchar**(20),
> *salary* **integer**)
> **method** *giveraise* (*percent* **integer**)

We create the method body separately:

> **create method** *giveraise* (*percent* **integer**) **for** *Employee*
> **begin**
>   **set self**.*salary* = **self**.*salary* + (**self**.*salary* * *percent*) / 100;
> **end**

The variable **self** refers to the structured type instance on which the method is invoked. The body of the method can contain procedural statements, which we shall study in Section 9.6.

---

2. In Oracle PL/SQL, given a table *t*, *t***%rowtype** denotes the type of the rows of the table. Similarly, *t.a***%type** denotes the type of attribute *a* of table *t*.

9.2.3 Creation of Values of Complex Types

In SQL:1999 **constructor functions** are used to create values of structured types. A function with the same name as a structured type is a constructor function for the structured type. For instance, we could declare a constructor for the type *Publisher* like this:

> **create function** *Publisher* (*n* **varchar**(20), *b* **varchar**(20))
> **returns** *Publisher*
> **begin**
>   **set** *name = n;*
>   **set** *branch = b;*
> **end**

We can then use *Publisher*('McGraw-Hill', 'New York') to create a value of the type *Publisher*.

SQL:1999 also supports functions other than constructors, as we shall see in Section 9.6; the names of such functions must be different from the name of any structured type.

Note that in SQL:1999, unlike in object-oriented databases, a constructor creates a value of the type, not an object of the type. That is, the value the constructor creates has no object identity. In SQL:1999 objects correspond to tuples of a relation, and are created by inserting a tuple in a relation.

By default every structured type has a constructor with no arguments, which sets the attributes to their default values. Any other constructors have to be created explicitly. There can be more than one constructor for the same structured type; although they have the same name, they must be distinguishable by the number of arguments and types of their arguments.

An array of values can be created in SQL:1999 in this way:

> **array**['Silberschatz', 'Korth', 'Sudarshan']

We can construct a row value by listing its attributes within parentheses. For instance, if we declare an attribute *publisher1* as a row type (as in Section 9.2.2), we can construct this value for it:

> ('McGraw-Hill', 'New York')

without using a constructor.

We create set-valued attributes, such as *keyword-set*, by enumerating their elements within parentheses following the keyword **set**. We can create multiset values just like set values, by replacing **set** by **multiset**.[3]

Thus, we can create a tuple of the type defined by the *books* relation as:

> ('Compilers', **array**['Smith', 'Jones'], *Publisher*('McGraw-Hill', 'New York'),
>   **set**('parsing', 'analysis'))

---

3. Although sets and multisets are not part of the SQL:1999 standard, the other constructs shown in this section are part of the standard. Future versions of SQL are likely to support sets and multisets.

Here we have created a value for the attribute *Publisher* by invoking a *constructor* function for *Publisher* with appropriate arguments.

If we want to insert the preceding tuple into the relation *books*, we could execute the statement

insert into *books*
values
('Compilers', **array**['Smith', 'Jones'], *Publisher*('McGraw-Hill', 'New York'),
                                    set('parsing', 'analysis'))

9.3 Inheritance

Inheritance can be at the level of types, or at the level of tables. We first consider inheritance of types, then inheritance at the level of tables.

9.3.1 Type Inheritance

Suppose that we have the following type definition for people:

create type *Person*
    (*name* **varchar**(20),
        address **varchar**(20))

We may want to store extra information in the database about people who are students, and about people who are teachers. Since students and teachers are also people, we can use inheritance to define the student and teacher types in SQL:1999:

create type *Student*
        under *Person*
        (*degree* **varchar**(20),
            department **varchar**(20))
create type *Teacher*
        under *Person*
        (*salary* **integer**,
            department **varchar**(20))

Both *Student* and *Teacher* inherit the attributes of *Person*—namely, *name* and *address*. *Student* and *Teacher* are said to be subtypes of *Person*, and *Person* is a supertype of *Student*, as well as of *Teacher*.

Methods of a structured type are inherited by its subtypes, just as attributes are. However, a subtype can redefine the effect of a method by declaring the method again, using **overriding method** in place of **method** in the method declaration.

Now suppose that we want to store information about teaching assistants, who are simultaneously students and teachers, perhaps even in different departments. We can do this by using **multiple inheritance**, which we studied in Chapter 8. The SQL:1999 standard does not support multiple inheritance. However, draft versions of the SQL:1999 standard provided for multiple inheritance, and although the final

SQL:1999 omitted it, future versions of the SQL standard may introduce it. We base our discussion on the draft versions of the SQL:1999 standard.

For instance, if our type system supports multiple inheritance, we can define a type for teaching assistant as follows:

create type *TeachingAssistant*
under *Student, Teacher*

TeachingAssistant would inherit all the attributes of *Student* and *Teacher*. There is a problem, however, since the attributes *name*, *address*, and *department* are present in *Student*, as well as in *Teacher*.

The attributes *name* and *address* are actually inherited from a common source, *Person*. So there is no conflict caused by inheriting them from *Student* as well as *Teacher*. However, the attribute *department* is defined separately in *Student* and *Teacher*. In fact, a teaching assistant may be a student of one department and a teacher in another department. To avoid a conflict between the two occurrences of *department*, we can rename them by using an **as** clause, as in this definition of the type *TeachingAssistant*:

create type *TeachingAssistant*
under *Student* **with** (*department* **as** *student-dept*),
Teacher **with** (*department* **as** *teacher-dept*)

We note that SQL:1999 supports only single inheritance— that is, a type can inherit from only a single type; the syntax used is as in our earlier examples. Multiple inheritance as in the *TeachingAssistant* example is *not* supported in SQL:1999. The SQL:1999 standard also requires an extra field at the end of the type definition, whose value is either **final** or **not final**. The keyword **final** says that subtypes may not be created from the given type, while **not final** says that subtypes may be created.

In SQL as in most other languages, a value of a structured type must have exactly one "most-specific type." That is, each value must be associated with one specific type, called its **most-specific type**, when it is created. By means of inheritance, it is also associated with each of the supertypes of its most specific type. For example, suppose that an entity has the type *Person*, as well as the type *Student*. Then, the most-specific type of the entity is *Student*, since *Student* is a subtype of *Person*. However, an entity cannot have the type *Student*, as well as the type *Teacher*, unless it has a type, such as *TeachingAssistant*, that is a subtype of *Teacher*, as well as of *Student*.

9.3.2   Table Inheritance

Subtables in SQL:1999 correspond to the E-R notion of specialization/generalization. For instance, suppose we define the *people* table as follows:

create table *people* **of** *Person*

We can then define tables *students* and *teachers* as **subtable**s of *people*, as follows:

> **create table** *students* **of** *Student*
> **under** *people*
> **create table** *teachers* **of** *Teacher*
> **under** *people*

The types of the subtables must be subtypes of the type of the parent table. Thereby, every attribute present in *people* is also present in the subtables.

Further, when we declare *students* and *teachers* as subtables of *people*, every tuple present in *students* or *teachers* becomes also implicitly present in *people*. Thus, if a query uses the table *people*, it will find not only tuples directly inserted into that table, but also tuples inserted into its subtables, namely *students* and *teachers*. However, only those attributes that are present in *people* can be accessed.

Multiple inheritance is possible with tables, just as it is possible with types. (We note, however, that multiple inheritance of tables is not supported by SQL:1999.) For example, we can create a table of type *TeachingAssistant*:

> **create table** *teaching-assistants*
> **of** *TeachingAssistant*
> **under** *students*, *teachers*

As a result of the declaration, every tuple present in the *teaching-assistants* table is also implicitly present in the *teachers* and in the *students* table, and in turn in the *people* table.

SQL:1999 permits us to find tuples that are in *people* but not in its subtables by using "**only** *people*" in place of *people* in a query.

There are some consistency requirements for subtables. Before we state the constraints, we need a definition: We say that tuples in a subtable **corresponds** to tuples in a parent table if they have the same values for all inherited attributes. Thus, corresponding tuples represent the same entity.

The consistency requirements for subtables are:

1. Each tuple of the supertable can correspond to at most one tuple in each of its immediate subtables.

2. SQL:1999 has an additional constraint that all the tuples corresponding to each other must be derived from one tuple (inserted into one table).

For example, without the first condition, we could have two tuples in *students* (or *teachers*) that correspond to the same person.

The second condition rules out a tuple in *people* corresponding to both a tuple in *students* and a tuple in *teachers*, unless all these tuples are implicitly present because a tuple was inserted in a table *teaching-assistants*, which is a subtable of both *teachers* and *students*.

Since SQL:1999 does not support multiple inheritance, the second condition actually prevents a person from being both a teacher and a student. The same problem would arise if the subtable *teaching-assistants* is absent, even if multiple inheritance were supported. Obviously it would be useful to model a situation where a person can be a teacher and a student, even if a common subtable *teaching-assistants* is not present. Thus, it can be useful to remove the second consistency constraint. We return to this issue in Section 9.3.3.

Subtables can be stored in an efficient manner without replication of all inherited fields, in one of two ways:

- Each table stores the primary key (which may be inherited from a parent table) and the attributes defined locally. Inherited attributes (other than the primary key) do not need to be stored, and can be derived by means of a join with the supertable, based on the primary key.

- Each table stores all inherited and locally defined attributes. When a tuple is inserted, it is stored only in the table in which it is inserted, and its presence is inferred in each of the supertables. Access to all attributes of a tuple is faster, since a join is not required. However, in case the second consistency constraint is absent—that is, an entity can be represented in two subtables without being present in a common subtable of both—this representation can result in replication of information.

9.3.3   Overlapping Subtables

Inheritance of types should be used with care. A university database may have many subtypes of *Person*, such as *Student*, *Teacher*, *FootballPlayer*, *ForeignCitizen*, and so on. *Student* may itself have subtypes such as *UndergraduateStudent*, *GraduateStudent*, and *PartTimeStudent*. Clearly, a person can belong to several of these categories at once. As Chapter 8 mentions, each of these categories is sometimes called a *role*.

For each entity to have exactly one most-specific type, we would have to create a subtype for every possible combination of the supertypes. In the preceding example, we would have subtypes such as *ForeignUndergraduateStudent*, *ForeignGraduateStudentFootballPlayer*, and so on. Unfortunately, we would end up with an enormous number of subtypes of *Person*.

A better approach in the context of database systems is to allow an object to have multiple types, without having a most-specific type. Object-relational systems can model such a feature by using inheritance at the level of tables, rather than of types, and allowing an entity to exist in more than one table at once.

For example, suppose we again have the type *Person*, with subtypes *Student* and *Teacher*, and the corresponding table *people*, with subtables *teachers* and *students*. We can then have a tuple in *teachers* and a tuple in *students* corresponding to the same tuple in *people*.

There is no need to have a type *TeachingAssistant* that is a subtype of both *Student* and *Teacher*. We need not create a type *TeachingAssistant* unless we wish to store extra attributes or redefine methods in a manner specific to people who are both students and teachers.

We note, however, that SQL:1999 prohibits such a situation, because of consistency requirement 2 from Section 9.3.2. Since SQL:1999 also does not support multiple inheritance, we cannot use inheritance to model a situation where a person can be both a student and a teacher. We can of course create separate tables to represent the information without using inheritance. We would have to add appropriate referential integrity constraints to ensure that students and teachers are also represented in the *people* table.

9.4 Reference Types

Object-oriented languages provide the ability to refer to objects. An attribute of a type can be a reference to an object of a specified type. For example, in SQL:1999 we can define a type *Department* with a field *name* and a field *head* which is a reference to the type *Person*, and a table *departments* of type *Department*, as follows:

> **create type** *Department* (
>   *name* **varchar(20)**,
>   *head* **ref**(*Person*) **scope** *people*
>)
> **create table** *departments* **of** *Department*

Here, the reference is restricted to tuples of the table *people*. The restriction of the **scope** of a reference to tuples of a table is mandatory in SQL:1999, and it makes references behave like foreign keys.

We can omit the declaration **scope** *people* from the type declaration and instead make an addition to the **create table** statement:

> **create table** *departments* **of** *Department*
>   (*head* **with options scope** *people*)

In order to initialize a reference attribute, we need to get the identifier of the tuple that is to be referenced. We can get the identifier value of a tuple by means of a query. Thus, to create a tuple with the reference value, we may first create the tuple with a null reference and then set the reference separately:

> **insert into** *departments*
>   **values** ('CS', null)
> **update** *departments*
>   **set** *head* = (**select ref**(*p*)
>   **from** *people* **as** *p*
>   **where** *name* = 'John')
> **where** *name* = 'CS'

This syntax for accessing the identifier of a tuple is based on the Oracle syntax. SQL:1999 adopts a different approach, one where the referenced table must have an attribute that stores the identifier of the tuple. We declare this attribute, called the **self-referential attribute**, by adding a **ref is** clause to the **create table** statement:

> **create table** *people* **of** *Person*
>   **ref is** *oid* **system generated**

Here, *oid* is an attribute name, not a keyword. The subquery above would then use

select *p.oid*

instead of **select ref**(*p*).

An alternative to system-generated identifiers is to allow users to generate identifiers. The type of the self-referential attribute must be specified as part of the type definition of the referenced table, and the table definition must specify that the reference is **user generated**:

> **create type** *Person*
> (*name* **varchar**(20),
> *address* **varchar**(20))
> **ref using varchar**(20)
> **create table** *people* **of** *Person*
> **ref is** *oid* **user generated**

When inserting a tuple in *people*, we must provide a value for the identifier:

> **insert into** *people* **values**
> ('01284567', 'John', '23 Coyote Run')

No other tuple for *people* or its supertables or subtables can have the same identifier. We can then use the identifier value when inserting a tuple into *departments*, without the need for a separate query to retrieve the identifier:

> **insert into** *departments*
> **values** ('CS', '01284567')

It is even possible to use an existing primary key value as the identifier, by including the **ref from** clause in the type definition:

> **create type** *Person*
> (*name* **varchar**(20) **primary key**,
> *address* **varchar**(20))
> **ref from**(*name*)
> **create table** *people* **of** *Person*
> **ref is** *oid* **derived**

Note that the table definition must specify that the reference is derived, and must still specify a self-referential attribute name. When inserting a tuple for *departments*, we can then use

> **insert into** *departments*
> **values** ('CS', 'John')

9.5   Querying with Complex Types

In this section, we present extensions of the SQL query language to deal with complex types. Let us start with a simple example: Find the title and the name of the publisher of each book. This query carries out the task:

$$\textbf{select } \textit{title, publisher.name}$$
$$\textbf{from } \textit{books}$$

Notice that the field *name* of the composite attribute *publisher* is referred to by a dot notation.

9.5.1   Path Expressions

References are dereferenced in SQL:1999 by the $->$ symbol. Consider the *departments* table defined earlier. We can use this query to find the names and addresses of the heads of all departments:

$$\textbf{select } \textit{head}->\textit{name}, \textit{head}->\textit{address}$$
$$\textbf{from } \textit{departments}$$

An expression such as "*head*->*name*" is called a **path expression**.

Since *head* is a reference to a tuple in the *people* table, the attribute *name* in the preceding query is the *name* attribute of the tuple from the *people* table. References can be used to hide join operations; in the preceding example, without the references, the *head* field of *department* would be declared a foreign key of the table *people*. To find the name and address of the head of a department, we would require an explicit join of the relations *departments* and *people*. The use of references simplifies the query considerably.

9.5.2   Collection-Valued Attributes

We now consider how to handle collection-valued attributes. Arrays are the only collection type supported by SQL:1999, but we use the same syntax for relation-valued attributes also. An expression evaluating to a collection can appear anywhere that a relation name may appear, such as in a **from** clause, as the following paragraphs illustrate. We use the table *books* which we defined earlier.

If we want to find all books that have the word "database" as one of their keywords, we can use this query:

$$\textbf{select } \textit{title}$$
$$\textbf{from } \textit{books}$$
$$\textbf{where } \text{'database'} \textbf{ in } (\textbf{unnest}(\textit{keyword-set}))$$

Note that we have used **unnest**(*keyword-set*) in a position where SQL without nested relations would have required a **select-from-where** subexpression.

If we know that a particular book has three authors, we could write:

> **select** *author-array*[1], *author-array*[2], *author-array*[3]
> **from** *books*
> **where** *title* = 'Database System Concepts'

Now, suppose that we want a relation containing pairs of the form "title, author-name" for each book and each author of the book. We can use this query:

> **select** *B.title, A.name*
> **from** *books* **as** *B,* **unnest**(*B.author-array*) **as** *A*

Since the *author-array* attribute of *books* is a collection-valued field, it can be used in a **from** clause, where a relation is expected.

9.5.3 Nesting and Unnesting

The transformation of a nested relation into a form with fewer (or no) relation-valued attributes is called **unnesting**. The *books* relation has two attributes, *author-array* and *keyword-set*, that are collections, and two attributes, *title* and *publisher*, that are not. Suppose that we want to convert the relation into a single flat relation, with no nested relations or structured types as attributes. We can use the following query to carry out the task:

> **select** *title, A* **as** *author, publisher.name* **as** *pub-name, publisher.branch*
> **as** *pub-branch, K* **as** *keyword*
> **from** *books* **as** *B,* **unnest**(*B.author-array*) **as** *A,* **unnest** (*B.keyword-set*) **as** *K*

The variable *B* in the from clause is declared to range over *books*. The variable *A* is declared to range over the authors in *author-array* for the book *B*, and *K* is declared to range over the keywords in the *keyword-set* of the book *B*. Figure 9.1 (in Section 9.1) shows an instance *books* relation, and Figure 9.2 shows the 1NF relation that is the result of the preceding query.

The reverse process of transforming a 1NF relation into a nested relation is called **nesting**. Nesting can be carried out by an extension of grouping in SQL. In the normal use of grouping in SQL, a temporary multiset relation is (logically) created for each group, and an aggregate function is applied on the temporary relation. By returning the multiset instead of applying the aggregate function, we can create a nested relation. Suppose that we are given a 1NF relation *flat-books*, as in Figure 9.2. The following query nests the relation on the attribute *keyword*:

> **select** *title, author,* Publisher(*pub-name, pub-branch*) **as** *publisher,*
> **set**(*keyword*) **as** *keyword-set*
> **from** *flat-books*
> **groupby** *title, author, publisher*

The result of the query on the *books* relation from Figure 9.2 appears in Figure 9.4. If we want to nest the author attribute as well, and thereby to convert the 1NF table

title	author	publisher	keyword-set
		(pub-name, pub-branch)	
Compilers	Smith	(McGraw-Hill, New York)	{parsing, analysis}
Compilers	Jones	(McGraw-Hill, New York)	{parsing, analysis}
Networks	Jones	(Oxford, London)	{Internet, Web}
Networks	Frick	(Oxford, London)	{Internet, Web}

Figure 9.4   A partially nested version of the *flat-books* relation.

flat-books in Figure 9.2 back to the nested table *books* in Figure 9.1, we can use the query:

> **select** *title*, **set**(*author*) **as** *author-set*, *Publisher*(*pub-name, pub-branch*) **as** *publisher*,
>   **set**(*keyword*) **as** *keyword-set*
> **from** *flat-books*
> **groupby** *title, publisher*

Another approach to creating nested relations is to use subqueries in the **select** clause. The following query, which performs the same task as the previous query, illustrates this approach.

> **select** *title*,
>   (**select** *author*
>   **from** *flat-books* **as** *M*
>   **where** *M.title = O.title*) **as** *author-set*,
>   *Publisher*(*pub-name, pub-branch*) **as** *publisher*,
>   (**select** *keyword*
>   **from** *flat-books* **as** *N*
>   **where** *N.title = O.title*) **as** *keyword-set*,
> **from** *flat-books* **as** *O*

The system executes the nested subqueries in the **select** clause for each tuple generated by the **from** and *where* clauses of the outer query. Observe that the attribute *O.title* from the outer query is used in the nested queries, to ensure that only the correct sets of authors and keywords are generated for each title. An advantage of this approach is that an **orderby** clause can be used in the nested query, to generate results in a desired order. An array or a list could be constructed from the result of the nested query. Without such an ordering, arrays and lists would not be uniquely determined.

We note that while unnesting of array-valued attributes can be carried out in SQL:1999 as shown above, the reverse process of nesting is not supported in SQL:1999. The extensions we have shown for nesting illustrate features from some proposals for extending SQL, but are not part of any standard currently.

9.6 Functions and Procedures

SQL:1999 allows the definition of functions, procedures, and methods. These can be defined either by the procedural component of SQL:1999, or by an external programming language such as Java, C, or C++. We look at definitions in SQL:1999 first, and then see how to use definitions in external languages. Several database systems support their own procedural languages, such as PL/SQL in Oracle and TransactSQL in Microsoft SQLServer. These resemble the procedural part of SQL:1999, but there are differences in syntax and semantics; see the respective system manuals for further details.

9.6.1 SQL Functions and Procedures

Suppose that we want a function that, given the title of a book, returns the count of the number of authors, using the 4NF schema. We can define the function this way:

```
create function author-count(title varchar(20))
      returns integer
      begin
      declare a-count integer;
            select count(author) into a-count
            from authors
            where authors.title = title
      return a-count;
      end
```

This function can be used in a query that returns the titles of all books that have more than one author:

```
select title
from books4
where author-count(title) > 1
```

Functions are particularly useful with specialized data types such as images and geometric objects. For instance, a polygon data type used in a map database may have an associated function that checks if two polygons overlap, and an image data type may have associated functions to compare two images for similarity. Functions may be written in an external language such as C, as we see in Section 9.6.2. Some database systems also support functions that return relations, that is, multisets of tuples, although such functions are not supported by SQL:1999.

Methods, which we saw in Section 9.2.2, can be viewed as functions associated with structured types. They have an implicit first parameter called **self**, which is set to the structured type value on which the method is invoked. Thus, the body of the method can refer to an attribute a of the value by using **self**.a. These attributes can also be updated by the method.

SQL:1999 also supports procedures. The *author-count* function could instead be written as a procedure:

```
create procedure author-count-proc(in title varchar(20), out a-count integer)
    begin
        select count(author) into a-count
        from authors
        where authors.title = title
    end
```

Procedures can be invoked either from an SQL procedure or from embedded SQL by the **call** statement:

```
declare a-count integer;
call author-count-proc('Database Systems Concepts', a-count);
```

SQL:1999 permits more than one procedure of the same name, so long as the number of arguments of the procedures with the same name is different. The name, along with the number of arguments, is used to identify the procedure. SQL:1999 also permits more than one function with the same name, so long as the different functions with the same name either have different numbers of arguments, or for functions with the same number of arguments, differ in the type of at least one argument.

9.6.2 External Language Routines

SQL:1999 allows us to define functions in a programming language such as C or C++. Functions defined in this fashion can be more efficient than functions defined in SQL, and computations that cannot be carried out in SQL can be executed by these functions. An example of the use of such functions would be to perform a complex arithmetic computation on the data in a tuple.

External procedures and functions can be specified in this way:

```
create procedure author-count-proc( in title varchar(20), out count integer)
language C
external name '/usr/avi/bin/author-count-proc'
```

```
create function author-count (title varchar(20))
returns integer
language C
external name '/usr/avi/bin/author-count'
```

The external language procedures need to deal with null values and exceptions. They must therefore have several extra parameters: an **sqlstate** value to indicate failure/success status, a parameter to store the return value of the function, and indicator variables for each parameter/function result to indicate if the value is null. An extra line **parameter style general** added to the declaration above indicates that the external procedures/functions take only the arguments shown and do not deal with null values or exceptions.

Functions defined in a programming language and compiled outside the database system may be loaded and executed with the database system code. However, doing so carries the risk that a bug in the program can corrupt the database internal structures, and can bypass the access-control functionality of the database system. Database systems that are concerned more about efficient performance than about security may execute procedures in such a fashion.

Database systems that are concerned about security would typically execute such code as part of a separate process, communicate the parameter values to it, and fetch results back, via interprocess communication.

If the code is written in a language such as Java, there is a third possibility: executing the code in a "*sandbox*" within the database process itself. The sandbox prevents the Java code from carrying out any reads or updates directly on the database.

9.6.3 Procedural Constructs

SQL:1999 supports a variety of procedural constructs, which gives it almost all the power of a general purpose programming language. The part of the SQL:1999 standard that deals with these constructs is called the **Persistent Storage Module (PSM)**.

A compound statement is of the form **begin** ... **end**, and it may contain multiple SQL statements between the **begin** and the **end**. Local variables can be declared within a compound statement, as we have seen in Section 9.6.1.

SQL:1999 supports while statements and repeat statements by this syntax:

> **declare** n **integer default** 0;
> **while** $n < 10$ **do**
>   **set** $n = n + 1$;
> **end while**
> **repeat**
>   **set** $n = n - 1$;
> **until** $n = 0$
> **end repeat**

This code does not do anything useful; it is simply meant to show the syntax of while and repeat loops. We will see more meaningful uses later.

There is also a **for** loop, which permits iteration over all results of a query:

> **declare** n **integer default** 0;
> **for** r **as**
>   **select** *balance* **from** *account*
>   **where** *branch-name* = 'Perryridge'
> **do**
>   **set** $n = n + r.balance$
> **end for**

The program implicitly opens a cursor when the **for** loop begins execution and uses it to fetch the values one row at a time into the **for** loop variable (r, in the above example). It is possible to give a name to the cursor, by inserting the text *cn* **cursor for** just after the keyword **as**, where *cn* is the name we wish to give to the cursor. The cursor name can be used to perform update/delete operations on the tuple being pointed to by the cursor. The statement **leave** can be used to exit the loop, while **iterate** starts on the next tuple, from the beginning of the loop, skipping the remaining statements.

The conditional statements supported by SQL:1999 include if-then-else statements statements by using this syntax:

> **if** *r.balance* < 1000
>   **then set** $l = l+$ *r.balance*
> **elseif** *r.balance* < 5000
>   **then set** $m = m+$ *r.balance*
> **else set** $h = h+$ *r.balance*
> **end if**

This code assumes that l, m, and h are integer variables, and r is a row variable. If we replace the line "**set** $n = n+$ *r.balance*" in the **for** loop of the preceding paragraph by the **if-then-else** code, the loop would compute the total balances of accounts that fall under the low, medium, and high balance categories respectively.

SQL:1999 also supports a case statement similar to the C/C++ language case statement (in addition to case expressions, which we saw in Chapter 4).

Finally, SQL:1999 includes the concept of signaling **exception conditions**, and declaring **handlers** that can handle the exception, as in this code:

> **declare** *out-of-stock* **condition**
> **declare exit handler for** *out-of-stock*
> **begin**
>   . . .
> **end**

The statements between the **begin** and the **end** can raise an exception by executing **signal** *out-of-stock*. The handler says that if the condition arises, the action to be taken is to exit the enclosing **begin end** statement. Alternative actions would be **continue**, which continues execution from the next statement following the one that raised the exception. In addition to explicitly defined conditions, there are also predefined conditions such as **sqlexception**, **sqlwarning**, and **not found**.

Figure 9.5 provides a larger example of the use of SQL:1999 procedural constructs. The procedure *findEmpl* computes the set of all direct and indirect employees of a given manager (specified by the parameter *mgr*), and stores the resulting employee names in a relation called *empl*, which is assumed to exist already. The relation *manager(empname, mgrname)*, specifying who works directly for which manager, is assumed to be available. The set of all direct/indirect employees is basically the transitive closure of the relation *manager*. We saw how to express such a query by recursion in Chapter 5 (Section 5.2.6).

The procedure uses two temporary tables, *newemp* and *temp*. The procedure inserts all employees who directly work for *mgr* into *newemp* before the **repeat** loop. The **repeat** loop first adds all employees in *newemp* to *empl*. Next, it computes employees who work for those in *newemp*, except those who have already been found to be

create procedure *findEmpl*(**in** *mgr* **char(10)**)
– – Finds all employees who work directly or indirectly for *mgr*
– – and adds them to the relation *empl*(*name*).
– – The relation *manager*(*empname*, *mgrname*) specifies who directly
– – works for whom.
begin
    create temporary table *newemp* (*name* **char(10)**);
    create temporary table *temp* (*name* **char(10)**);
    insert into *newemp*
        select *empname*
        from *manager*
        where *mgrname* = *mgr*
    repeat
        insert into *empl*
           select *name*
           from *newemp*;

        insert into *temp*
           (**select** *manager.empname*
               from *newemp, manager*
               where *newemp.empname* = *manager.mgrname*;
)
           except (
               select *empname*
               from *empl*
           );
        delete from *newemp*;
        insert into *newemp*
           select *
           from *temp*;
        delete from *temp*;

    until not exists (**select** * **from** *newemp*)
    end repeat;
end

Figure 9.5   Finding all employees of a manager.

employees of *mgr*, and stores them in the temporary table *temp*. Finally, it replaces the contents of *newemp* by the contents of *temp*. The **repeat** loop terminates when it finds no new (indirect) employees.

    We note that the use of the **except** clause in the procedure ensures that the procedure works even in the (abnormal) case where there is a cycle of management. For example, if *a* works for *b*, *b* works for *c*, and *c* works for *a*, there is a cycle.

    While cycles may be unrealistic in management control, cycles are possible in other applications. For instance, suppose we have a relation *flights*(*to, from*) that says which cities can be reached from which other cities by a direct flight. We can modify the *findEmpl* procedure to find all cities that are reachable by a sequence of one or more flights from a given city. All we have to do is to replace *manager* by *flight* and replace attribute names correspondingly. In this situation there can be cycles of reachability, but the procedure would work correctly since it would eliminate cities that have already been seen.

9.7   Object-Oriented versus Object-Relational

We have now studied object-oriented databases built around persistent programming languages, as well as object-relational databases, which are object-oriented databases built on top of the relation model. Database systems of both types are on the market, and a database designer needs to choose the kind of system that is appropriate to the needs of the application.

Persistent extensions to programming languages and object-relational systems target different markets. The declarative nature and limited power (compared to a programming language) of the SQL language provides good protection of data from programming errors, and makes high-level optimizations, such as reducing I/O, relatively easy. (We cover optimization of relational expressions in Chapter 13.) Object-relational systems aim at making data modeling and querying easier by using complex data types. Typical applications include storage and querying of complex data, including multimedia data.

A declarative language such as SQL, however, imposes a significant performance penalty for certain kinds of applications that run primarily in main memory, and that perform a large number of accesses to the database. Persistent programming languages target such applications that have high performance requirements. They provide low-overhead access to persistent data, and eliminate the need for data translation if the data are to be manipulated by a programming language. However, they are more susceptible to data corruption by programming errors, and usually do not have a powerful querying capability. Typical applications include CAD databases.

We can summarize the strengths of the various kinds of database systems in this way:

- **Relational systems**: simple data types, powerful query languages, high protection

- **Persistent-programming-language–based OODBs**: complex data types, integration with programming language, high performance

- **Object-relational systems**: complex data types, powerful query languages, high protection

These descriptions hold in general, but keep in mind that some database systems blur the boundaries. For example, some object-oriented database systems built around a persistent programming language are implemented on top of a relational database system. Such systems may provide lower performance than object-oriented database systems built directly on a storage system, but provide some of the stronger protection guarantees of relational systems.

Many object-relational database systems are built on top of existing relational database systems. To do so, the complex data types supported by object-relational systems need to be translated to the simpler type system of relational databases.

To understand how the translation is done, we need only look at how some features of the E-R model are translated into relations. For instance, multivalued attributes in the E-R model correspond to set-valued attributes in the object-relational model. Composite attributes roughly correspond to structured types. ISA hierarchies in the E-R model correspond to table inheritance in the object-relational model. The techniques for converting E-R model features to tables, which we saw in Section 2.9, can be used, with some extensions, to translate object-relational data to relational data.

9.8 Summary

- The object-relational data model extends the relational data model by providing a richer type system including collection types, and object orientation.

- Object orientation provides inheritance with subtypes and subtables, as well as object (tuple) references.

- Collection types include nested relations, sets, multisets, and arrays, and the object-relational model permits attributes of a table to be collections.

- The SQL:1999 standard extends the SQL data definition and query language to deal with the new data types and with object orientation.

- We saw a variety of features of the extended data-definition language, as well as the query language, and in particular support for collection-valued attributes, inheritance, and tuple references. Such extensions attempt to preserve the relational foundations—in particular, the declarative access to data —while extending the modeling power.

- Object-relational database systems (that is, database systems based on the object-relation model) provide a convenient migration path for users of relational databases who wish to use object-oriented features.

- We have also outlined the procedural extensions provided by SQL:1999.

- We discussed differences between persistent programming languages and object-relational systems, and mention criteria for choosing between them.

Review Terms

- Nested relations
- Nested relational model
- Complex types
- Collection types
- Large object types
- Sets
- Arrays
- Multisets
- Character large object (clob)
- Binary large object (blob)

- Structured types
- Methods
- Row types
- Constructors
- Inheritance
  - ☐ Single inheritance
  - ☐ Multiple inheritance
- Type inheritance
- Most-specific type
- Table inheritance
- Subtable

- Overlapping subtables
- Reference types
- Scope of a reference
- Self-referential attribute
- Path expressions
- Nesting and unnesting
- SQL functions and procedures
- Procedural constructs
- Exceptions
- Handlers
- External language routines

Exercises

9.1 Consider the database schema

$$Emp = (ename, \textbf{setof}(Children), \textbf{setof}(Skills))$$
$$Children = (name, Birthday)$$
$$Birthday = (day, month, year)$$
$$Skills = (type, \textbf{setof}(Exams))$$
$$Exams = (year, city)$$

Assume that attributes of type **setof**(*Children*), **setof**(*Skills*), and **setof**(*Exams*), have attribute names *ChildrenSet*, *SkillsSet*, and *ExamsSet*, respectively. Suppose that the database contains a relation *emp (Emp)*. Write the following queries in SQL:1999 (with the extensions described in this chapter).

  a. Find the names of all employees who have a child who has a birthday in March.
  b. Find those employees who took an examination for the skill type "typing" in the city "Dayton".
  c. List all skill types in the relation *emp*.

9.2 Redesign the database of Exercise 9.1 into first normal form and fourth normal form. List any functional or multivalued dependencies that you assume. Also list all referential-integrity constraints that should be present in the first- and fourth-normal-form schemas.

9.3 Consider the schemas for the table *people*, and the tables *students* and *teachers*, which were created under *people*, in Section 9.3. Give a relational schema in third normal form that represents the same information. Recall the constraints on subtables, and give all constraints that must be imposed on the relational schema so that every database instance of the relational schema can also be represented by an instance of the schema with inheritance.

9.4 A car-rental company maintains a vehicle database for all vehicles in its current fleet. For all vehicles, it includes the vehicle identification number, license number, manufacturer, model, date of purchase, and color. Special data are included for certain types of vehicles:

- Trucks: cargo capacity
- Sports cars: horsepower, renter age requirement
- Vans: number of passengers
- Off-road vehicles: ground clearance, drivetrain (four- or two-wheel drive)

Construct an SQL:1999 schema definition for this database. Use inheritance where appropriate.

9.5 Explain the distinction between a type x and a reference type **ref**(x). Under what circumstances would you choose to use a reference type?

9.6 Consider the E-R diagram in Figure 2.11, which contains composite, multivalued and derived attributes.

    a. Give an SQL:1999 schema definition corresponding to the E-R diagram. Use an array to represent the multivalued attribute, and appropriate SQL:1999 constructs to represent the other attribute types.

    b. Give constructors for each of the structured types defined above.

9.7 Give an SQL:1999 schema definition of the E-R diagram in Figure 2.17, which contains specializations.

9.8 Consider the relational schema shown in Figure 3.39.

    a. Give a schema definition in SQL:1999 corresponding to the relational schema, but using references to express foreign-key relationships.

    b. Write each of the queries given in Exercise 3.10 on the above schema, using SQL:1999.

9.9 Consider an employee database with two relations

$$employee\ (\underline{employee\text{-}name},\ street,\ city)$$
$$works\ (\underline{employee\text{-}name},\ company\text{-}name,\ salary)$$

where the primary keys are underlined. Write a query to find companies whose employees earn a higher salary, on average, than the average salary at First Bank Corporation.

    a. Using SQL:1999 functions as appropriate.

    b. Without using SQL:1999 functions.

9.10 Rewrite the query in Section 9.6.1 that returns the titles of all books that have more than one author, using the **with** clause in place of the function.

9.11 Compare the use of embedded SQL with the use in SQL of functions defined in a general-purpose programming language. Under what circumstances would you use each of these features?

9.12 Suppose that you have been hired as a consultant to choose a database system for your client's application. For each of the following applications, state what type of database system (relational, persistent-programming-language–based OODB, object relational; do not specify a commercial product) you would recommend. Justify your recommendation.

    a. A computer-aided design system for a manufacturer of airplanes

    b. A system to track contributions made to candidates for public office

    c. An information system to support the making of movies

Bibliographical Notes

The nested relational model was introduced in Makinouchi [1977] and Jaeschke and Schek [1982]. Various algebraic query languages are presented in Fischer and Thomas [1983], Zaniolo [1983], Ozsoyoglu et al. [1987], Gucht [1987], and Roth et al. [1988]. The management of null values in nested relations is discussed in Roth et al. [1989]. Design and normalization issues are discussed in Ozsoyoglu and Yuan [1987], Roth and Korth [1987], and Mok et al. [1996]. A collection of papers on nested relations appears in

    Several object-oriented extensions to SQL have been proposed. POSTGRES (Stonebraker and Rowe [1986] and Stonebraker [1986a]) was an early implementation of an object-relational system. Illustra was the commercial object-relational system that is the successor of POSTGRES (Illustra was later acquired by Informix, which itself was recently acquired by IBM). The Iris database system from Hewlett-Packard (Fishman et al. [1990] and Wilkinson et al. [1990]) provides object-oriented extensions on top of a relational database system. The O_2 query language described in Bancilhon et al. [1989] is an object-oriented extension of SQL implemented in the O_2 object-oriented database system (Deux [1991]). UniSQL is described in UniSQL [1991]. XSQL is an object-oriented extension of SQL proposed by Kifer et al. [1992].

    SQL:1999 was the product of an extensive (and long-delayed) standardization effort, which originally started off as adding object-oriented features to SQL and ended up adding many more features, such as control flow, as we have seen. The official standard documents are available (for a fee) from http://webstore.ansi.org. However, standards documents are very hard to read, and are best left to SQL:1999 implementers. Books on SQL:1999 were still in press at the time of writing this book, see the Web site of the book for current information.

Tools

The Informix database system provides support for many object-relational features. Oracle introduced several object-relational features in Oracle 8.0. Both these systems provided object-relational features before the SQL:1999 standard was finalized, and have some features that are not part of SQL:1999. IBM DB2 supports many of the SQL:1999 features.

CHAPTER 10

XML

Unlike most of the technologies presented in the preceding chapters, the **Extensible Markup Language** (**XML**) was not originally conceived as a database technology. In fact, like the *Hyper-Text Markup Language* (HTML) on which the World Wide Web is based, XML has its roots in document management, and is derived from a language for structuring large documents known as the *Standard Generalized Markup Language* (SGML). However, unlike SGML and HTML, XML can represent database data, as well as many other kinds of structured data used in business applications. It is particularly useful as a data format when an application must communicate with another application, or integrate information from several other applications. When XML is used in these contexts, many database issues arise, including how to organize, manipulate, and query the XML data. In this chapter, we introduce XML and discuss both the management of XML data with database techniques and the exchange of data formatted as XML documents.

10.1 Background

To understand XML, it is important to understand its roots as a document markup language. The term **markup** refers to anything in a document that is not intended to be part of the printed output. For example, a writer creating text that will eventually be typeset in a magazine may want to make notes about how the typesetting should be done. It would be important to type these notes in a way so that they could be distinguished from the actual content, so that a note like "do not break this paragraph" does not end up printed in the magazine. In electronic document processing, a **markup language** is a formal description of what part of the document is content, what part is markup, and what the markup means.

Just as database systems evolved from physical file processing to provide a separate logical view, markup languages evolved from specifying instructions for how to print parts of the document to specify the *function* of the content. For instance, with functional markup, text representing section headings (for this section, the words "Background") would be marked up as being a section heading, instead of being marked up as text to be printed in large size, bold font. Such functional markup allowed the document to be formatted differently in different situations. It also helps different parts of a large document, or different pages in a large Web site to be formatted in a uniform manner. Functional markup also helps automate extraction of key parts of documents.

For the family of markup languages that includes HTML, SGML, and XML the markup takes the form of **tags** enclosed in angle-brackets, <>. Tags are used in pairs, with <tag> and </tag> delimiting the beginning and the end of the portion of the document to which the tag refers. For example, the title of a document might be marked up as follows.

<title>Database System Concepts</title>

Unlike HTML, XML does not prescribe the set of tags allowed, and the set may be specialized as needed. This feature is the key to XML's major role in data representation and exchange, whereas HTML is used primarily for document formatting.

For example, in our running banking application, account and customer information can be represented as part of an XML document as in Figure 10.1. Observe the use of tags such as account and account-number. These tags provide context for each value and allow the semantics of the value to be identified.

Compared to storage of data in a database, the XML representation may be inefficient, since tag names are repeated throughout the document. However, in spite of this disadvantage, an XML representation has significant advantages when it is used to exchange data, for example, as part of a message:

- First, the presence of the tags makes the message **self-documenting**; that is, a schema need not be consulted to understand the meaning of the text. We can readily read the fragment above, for example.

- Second, the format of the document is not rigid. For example, if some sender adds additional information, such as a tag last-accessed noting the last date on which an account was accessed, the recipient of the XML data may simply ignore the tag. The ability to recognize and ignore unexpected tags allows the format of the data to evolve over time, without invalidating existing applications.

- Finally, since the XML format is widely accepted, a wide variety of tools are available to assist in its processing, including browser software and database tools.

Just as SQL is the dominant *language* for querying relational data, XML is becoming the dominant *format* for data exchange.

```
<bank>
    <account>
        <account-number> A-101 </account-number>
        <branch-name> Downtown </branch-name>
        <balance> 500 </balance>
    </account>
    <account>
        <account-number> A-102 </account-number>
        <branch-name> Perryridge </branch-name>
        <balance> 400 </balance>
    </account>
    <account>
        <account-number> A-201 </account-number>
        <branch-name> Brighton </branch-name>
        <balance> 900 </balance>
    </account>
    <customer>
        <customer-name> Johnson </customer-name>
        <customer-street> Alma </customer-street>
        <customer-city> Palo Alto </customer-city>
    </customer>
    <customer>
        <customer-name> Hayes </customer-name>
        <customer-street> Main </customer-street>
        <customer-city> Harrison </customer-city>
    </customer>
    <depositor>
        <account-number> A-101 </account-number>
        <customer-name> Johnson </customer-name>
    </depositor>
    <depositor>
        <account-number> A-201 </account-number>
        <customer-name> Johnson </customer-name>
    </depositor>
    <depositor>
        <account-number> A-102 </account-number>
        <customer-name> Hayes </customer-name>
    </depositor>
</bank>
```

Figure 10.1   XML representation of bank information.

10.2 Structure of XML Data

The fundamental construct in an XML document is the **element**. An element is simply a pair of matching start- and end-tags, and all the text that appears between them.

XML documents must have a single **root** element that encompasses all other elements in the document. In the example in Figure 10.1, the <bank> element forms the root element. Further, elements in an XML document must **nest** properly. For instance,

<account> ... <balance> ... </balance> ... </account>

is properly nested, whereas

<account> ... <balance> ... </account> ... </balance>

is not properly nested.

While proper nesting is an intuitive property, we may define it more formally. Text is said to appear **in the context of** an element if it appears between the start-tag and end-tag of that element. Tags are properly nested if every start-tag has a unique matching end-tag that is in the context of the same parent element.

Note that text may be mixed with the subelements of an element, as in Figure 10.2. As with several other features of XML, this freedom makes more sense in a document-processing context than in a data-processing context, and is not particularly useful for representing more structured data such as database content in XML.

The ability to nest elements within other elements provides an alternative way to represent information. Figure 10.3 shows a representation of the bank information from Figure 10.1, but with account elements nested within customer elements. The nested representation makes it easy to find all accounts of a customer, although it would store account elements redundantly if they are owned by multiple customers.

Nested representations are widely used in XML data interchange applications to avoid joins. For instance, a shipping application would store the full address of sender and receiver redundantly on a shipping document associated with each shipment, whereas a normalized representation may require a join of shipping records with a *company-address* relation to get address information.

In addition to elements, XML specifies the notion of an **attribute**. For instance, the type of an account can represented as an attribute, as in Figure 10.4. The attributes of

```
      . . .
          <account>
              This account is seldom used any more.
              <account-number> A-102 </account-number>
              <branch-name> Perryridge </branch-name>
              <balance> 400 </balance>
          </account>
      . . .
```

Figure 10.2 Mixture of text with subelements.

```
<bank-1>
    <customer>
        <customer-name> Johnson </customer-name>
        <customer-street> Alma </customer-street>
        <customer-city> Palo Alto </customer-city>
        <account>
            <account-number> A-101 </account-number>
            <branch-name> Downtown </branch-name>
            <balance> 500 </balance>
        </account>
        <account>
            <account-number> A-201 </account-number>
            <branch-name> Brighton </branch-name>
            <balance> 900 </balance>
        </account>
    </customer>
    <customer>
        <customer-name> Hayes </customer-name>
        <customer-street> Main </customer-street>
        <customer-city> Harrison </customer-city>
        <account>
            <account-number> A-102 </account-number>
            <branch-name> Perryridge </branch-name>
            <balance> 400 </balance>
        </account>
    </customer>
</bank-1>
```

Figure 10.3   Nested XML representation of bank information.

an element appear as *name=value* pairs before the closing ">" of a tag. Attributes are strings, and do not contain markup. Furthermore, attributes can appear only once in a given tag, unlike subelements, which may be repeated.

Note that in a document construction context, the distinction between subelement and attribute is important—an attribute is implicitly text that does not appear in the printed or displayed document. However, in database and data exchange applications of XML, this distinction is less relevant, and the choice of representing data as an attribute or a subelement is frequently arbitrary.

One final syntactic note is that an element of the form <element></element>, which contains no subelements or text, can be abbreviated as <element/>; abbreviated elements may, however, contain attributes.

Since XML documents are designed to be exchanged between applications, a **namespace** mechanism has been introduced to allow organizations to specify globally unique names to be used as element tags in documents. The idea of a namespace is to prepend each tag or attribute with a universal resource identifier (for example, a Web address) Thus, for example, if First Bank wanted to ensure that XML documents

. . .

```
<account acct-type= "checking">
    <account-number> A-102 </account-number>
    <branch-name> Perryridge </branch-name>
    <balance> 400 </balance>
</account>
```

. . .

Figure 10.4 Use of attributes.

it created would not duplicate tags used by any business partner's XML documents, it can prepend a unique identifier with a colon to each tag name. The bank may use a Web URL such as

http://www.FirstBank.com

as a unique identifier. Using long unique identifiers in every tag would be rather inconvenient, so the namespace standard provides a way to define an abbreviation for identifiers.

In Figure 10.5, the root element (bank) has an attribute xmlns:FB, which declares that FB is defined as an abbreviation for the URL given above. The abbreviation can then be used in various element tags, as illustrated in the figure.

A document can have more than one namespace, declared as part of the root element. Different elements can then be associated with different namespaces. A *default namespace* can be defined, by using the attribute xmlns instead of xmlns:FB in the root element. Elements without an explicit namespace prefix would then belong to the default namespace.

Sometimes we need to store values containing tags without having the tags interpreted as XML tags. So that we can do so, XML allows this construct:

<![CDATA[<account> ···</account>]]>

Because it is enclosed within CDATA, the text <account> is treated as normal text data, not as a tag. The term CDATA stands for character data.

```
<bank xmlns:FB="http://www.FirstBank.com">
    . . .
    <FB:branch>
        <FB:branchname> Downtown </FB:branchname>
        <FB:branchcity> Brooklyn </FB:branchcity>
    </FB:branch>
    . . .
</bank>
```

Figure 10.5 Unique tag names through the use of namespaces.

10.3 XML Document Schema

Databases have schemas, which are used to constrain what information can be stored in the database and to constrain the data types of the stored information. In contrast, by default, XML documents can be created without any associated schema: An element may then have any subelement or attribute. While such freedom may occasionally be acceptable given the self-describing nature of the data format, it is not generally useful when XML documents must be processesed automatically as part of an application, or even when large amounts of related data are to be formatted in XML.

Here, we describe the document-oriented schema mechanism included as part of the XML standard, the *Document Type Definition*, as well as the more recently defined *XMLSchema*.

10.3.1 Document Type Definition

The **document type definition** (DTD) is an optional part of an XML document. The main purpose of a DTD is much like that of a schema: to constrain and type the information present in the document. However, the DTD does not in fact constrain types in the sense of basic types like integer or string. Instead, it only constrains the appearance of subelements and attributes within an element. The DTD is primarily a list of rules for what pattern of subelements appear within an element. Figure 10.6 shows a part of an example DTD for a bank information document; the XML document in Figure 10.1 conforms to this DTD.

Each declaration is in the form of a regular expression for the subelements of an element. Thus, in the DTD in Figure 10.6, a bank element consists of one or more account, customer, or depositor elements; the | operator specifies "or" while the + operator specifies "one or more." Although not shown here, the * operator is used to specify "zero or more," while the ? operator is used to specify an optional element (that is, "zero or one").

```
<!DOCTYPE bank [
    <!ELEMENT bank ( (account—customer—depositor)+)>
    <!ELEMENT account ( account-number branch-name balance )>
    <!ELEMENT customer ( customer-name customer-street customer-city )>
    <!ELEMENT depositor ( customer-name account-number )>
    <!ELEMENT account-number ( #PCDATA )>
    <!ELEMENT branch-name ( #PCDATA )>
    <!ELEMENT balance( #PCDATA )>
    <!ELEMENT customer-name( #PCDATA )>
    <!ELEMENT customer-street( #PCDATA )>
    <!ELEMENT customer-city( #PCDATA )>
] >
```

Figure 10.6   Example of a DTD.

The account element is defined to contain subelements account-number, branch-name and balance (in that order). Similarly, customer and depositor have the attributes in their schema defined as subelements.

Finally, the elements account-number, branch-name, balance, customer-name, customer-street, and customer-city are all declared to be of type #PCDATA. The keyword #PCDATA indicates text data; it derives its name, historically, from "parsed character data." Two other special type declarations are empty, which says that the element has no contents, and any, which says that there is no constraint on the subelements of the element; that is, any elements, even those not mentioned in the DTD, can occur as subelements of the element. The absence of a declaration for an element is equivalent to explicitly declaring the type as any.

The allowable attributes for each element are also declared in the DTD. Unlike subelements, no order is imposed on attributes. Attributes may specified to be of type CDATA, ID, IDREF, or IDREFS; the type CDATA simply says that the attribute contains character data, while the other three are not so simple; they are explained in more detail shortly. For instance, the following line from a DTD specifies that element account has an attribute of type acct-type, with default value checking.

<!ATTLIST account acct-type CDATA "checking" >

Attributes must have a type declaration and a default declaration. The default declaration can consist of a default value for the attribute or #REQUIRED, meaning that a value must be specified for the attribute in each element, or #IMPLIED, meaning that no default value has been provided. If an attribute has a default value, for every element that does not specify a value for the attribute, the default value is filled in automatically when the XML document is read

An attribute of type ID provides a unique identifier for the element; a value that occurs in an ID attribute of an element must not occur in any other element in the same document. At most one attribute of an element is permitted to be of type ID.

```
<!DOCTYPE bank-2 [
    <!ELEMENT account ( branch, balance )>
    <!ATTLIST account
        account-number ID #REQUIRED
        owners IDREFS #REQUIRED >
    <!ELEMENT customer ( customer-name, customer-street, customer-city )>
    <!ATTLIST customer
        customer-id ID #REQUIRED
        accounts IDREFS #REQUIRED >
    ··· declarations for branch, balance, customer-name,
        customer-street and customer-city ···
] >
```

Figure 10.7   DTD with ID and IDREF attribute types.

An attribute of type IDREF is a reference to an element; the attribute must contain a value that appears in the ID attribute of some element in the document. The type IDREFS allows a list of references, separated by spaces.

Figure 10.7 shows an example DTD in which customer account relationships are represented by ID and IDREFS attributes, instead of depositor records. The account elements use account-number as their identifier attribute; to do so, account-number has been made an attribute of account instead of a subelement. The customer elements have a new identifier attribute called customer-id. Additionally, each customer element contains an attribute accounts, of type IDREFS, which is a list of identifiers of accounts that are owned by the customer. Each account element has an attribute owners, of type IDREFS, which is a list of owners of the account.

Figure 10.8 shows an example XML document based on the DTD in Figure 10.7. Note that we use a different set of accounts and customers from our earlier example, in order to illustrate the IDREFS feature better.

The ID and IDREF attributes serve the same role as reference mechanisms in object-oriented and object-relational databases, permitting the construction of complex data relationships.

```
<bank-2>
    <account account-number="A-401" owners="C100 C102">
        <branch-name> Downtown </branch-name>
        <balance> 500 </balance>
    </account>
    <account account-number="A-402" owners="C102 C101">
        <branch-name> Perryridge </branch-name>
        <balance> 900 </balance>
    </account>
    <customer customer-id="C100" accounts="A-401">
        <customer-name>Joe</customer-name>
        <customer-street> Monroe </customer-street>
        <customer-city> Madison </customer-city>
    </customer>
    <customer customer-id="C101" accounts="A-402">
        <customer-name>Lisa</customer-name>
        <customer-street> Mountain </customer-street>
        <customer-city> Murray Hill </customer-city>
    </customer>
    <customer customer-id="C102" accounts="A-401 A-402">
        <customer-name>Mary</customer-name>
        <customer-street> Erin </customer-street>
        <customer-city> Newark </customer-city>
    </customer>
</bank-2>
```

Figure 10.8   XML data with ID and IDREF attributes.

Document type definitions are strongly connected to the document formatting heritage of XML. Because of this, they are unsuitable in many ways for serving as the type structure of XML for data processing applications. Nevertheless, a tremendous number of data exchange formats are being defined in terms of DTDs, since they were part of the original standard. Here are some of the limitations of DTDs as a schema mechanism.

- Individual text elements and attributes cannot be further typed. For instance, the element balance cannot be constrained to be a positive number. The lack of such constraints is problematic for data processing and exchange applications, which must then contain code to verify the types of elements and attributes.

- It is difficult to use the DTD mechanism to specify unordered sets of subelements. Order is seldom important for data exchange (unlike document layout, where it is crucial). While the combination of alternation (the | operation) and the ∗ operation as in Figure 10.6 permits the specification of unordered collections of tags, it is much more difficult to specify that each tag may only appear once.

- There is a lack of typing in IDs and IDREFs. Thus, there is no way to specify the type of element to which an IDREF or IDREFS attribute should refer. As a result, the DTD in Figure 10.7 does not prevent the "owners" attribute of an account element from referring to other accounts, even though this makes no sense.

10.3.2 XML Schema

An effort to redress many of these DTD deficiencies resulted in a more sophisticated schema language, **XMLSchema**. We present here an example of XMLSchema, and list some areas in which it improves DTDs, without giving full details of XMLSchema's syntax.

Figure 10.9 shows how the DTD in Figure 10.6 can be represented by XMLSchema. The first element is the root element bank, whose type is declared later. The example then defines the types of elements account, customer, and depositor. Observe the use of types xsd:string and xsd:decimal to constrain the types of data elements. Finally the example defines the type BankType as containing zero or more occurrences of each of account, customer and depositor. XMLSchema can define the minimum and maximum number of occurrences of subelements by using minOccurs and maxOccurs. The default for both minimum and maximum occurrences is 1, so these have to be explicit specified to allow zero or more accounts, deposits, and customers.

Among the benefits that XMLSchema offers over DTDs are these:

- It allows user-defined types to be created.

- It allows the text that appears in elements to be constrained to specific types, such as numeric types in specific formats or even more complicated types such as lists or union.

```
<xsd:schema xmlns:xsd="http://www.w3.org/2001/XMLSchema">
<xsd:element name="bank" type="BankType" />
<xsd:element name="account">
    <xsd:complexType>
        <xsd:sequence>
            <xsd:element name="account-number" type="xsd:string"/>
            <xsd:element name="branch-name" type="xsd:string"/>
            <xsd:element name="balance" type="xsd:decimal"/>
        </xsd:sequence>
    </xsd:complexType>
</xsd:element>
<xsd:element name="customer">
            <xsd:element name="customer-number" type="xsd:string"/>
            <xsd:element name="customer-street" type="xsd:string"/>
            <xsd:element name="customer-city" type="xsd:string"/>
</xsd:element>
<xsd:element name="depositor">
    <xsd:complexType>
        <xsd:sequence>
            <xsd:element name="customer-name" type="xsd:string"/>
            <xsd:element name="account-number" type="xsd:string"/>
        </xsd:sequence>
    </xsd:complexType>
</xsd:element>
<xsd:complexType name="BankType">
    <xsd:sequence>
        <xsd:element ref="account" minOccurs="0" maxOccurs="unbounded"/>
        <xsd:element ref="customer" minOccurs="0" maxOccurs="unbounded"/>
        <xsd:element ref="depositor" minOccurs="0" maxOccurs="unbounded"/>
    </xsd:sequence>
</xsd:complexType>
</xsd:schema>
```

Figure 10.9   XMLSchema version of DTD from Figure 10.6.

- It allows types to be restricted to create specialized types, for instance by specifying minimum and maximum values.

- It allows complex types to be extended by using a form of inheritance.

- It is a superset of DTDs.

- It allows uniqueness and foreign key constraints.

- It is integrated with namespaces to allow different parts of a document to conform to different schema.

- It is itself specified by XML syntax, as Figure 10.9 shows.

However, the price paid for these features is that XMLSchema is significantly more complicated than DTDs.

10.4 Querying and Transformation

Given the increasing number of applications that use XML to exchange, mediate, and store data, tools for effective management of XML data are becoming increasingly important. In particular, tools for querying and transformation of XML data are essential to extract information from large bodies of XML data, and to convert data between different representations (schemas) in XML. Just as the output of a relational query is a relation, the output of an XML query can be an XML document. As a result, querying and transformation can be combined into a single tool.

Several languages provide increasing degrees of querying and transformation capabilities:

- XPath is a language for path expressions, and is actually a building block for the remaining two query languages.

- XSLT was designed to be a transformation language, as part of the XSL style sheet system, which is used to control the formatting of XML data into HTML or other print or display languages. Although designed for formatting, XSLT can generate XML as output, and can express many interesting queries. Furthermore, it is currently the most widely available language for manipulating XML data.

- XQuery has been proposed as a standard for querying of XML data. XQuery combines features from many of the earlier proposals for querying XML, in particular the language Quilt.

A **tree model** of XML data is used in all these languages. An XML document is modeled as a **tree**, with **nodes** corresponding to elements and attributes. Element nodes can have children nodes, which can be subelements or attributes of the element. Correspondingly, each node (whether attribute or element), other than the root element, has a parent node, which is an element. The order of elements and attributes in the XML document is modeled by the ordering of children of nodes of the tree. The terms parent, child, ancestor, descendant, and siblings are interpreted in the tree model of XML data.

The text content of an element can be modeled as a text node child of the element. Elements containing text broken up by intervening subelements can have multiple text node children. For instance, an element containing "this is a <bold> wonderful </bold> book" would have a subelement child corresponding to the element bold and two text node children corresponding to "this is a" and "book". Since such structures are not commonly used in database data, we shall assume that elements do not contain both text and subelements.

10.4.1 XPath

XPath addresses parts of an XML document by means of path expressions. The language can be viewed as an extension of the simple path expressions in object-oriented and object-relational databases (See Section 9.5.1).

A **path expression** in XPath is a sequence of location steps separated by "/" (instead of the "." operator that separates steps in SQL:1999). The result of a path expression is a set of values. For instance, on the document in Figure 10.8, the XPath expression

/bank-2/customer/name

would return these elements:

<name>Joe</name>
<name>Lisa</name>
<name>Mary</name>

The expression

/bank-2/customer/name/text()

would return the same names, but without the enclosing tags.

Like a directory hierarchy, the initial '/' indicates the root of the document. (Note that this is an abstract root "above" <bank-2> that is the document tag.) Path expressions are evaluated from left to right. As a path expression is evaluated, the result of the path at any point consists of a set of nodes from the document.

When an element name, such as customer, appears before the next '/', it refers to all elements of the specified name that are children of elements in the current element set. Since multiple children can have the same name, the number of nodes in the node set can increase or decrease with each step. Attribute values may also be accessed, using the "@" symbol. For instance, /bank-2/account/@account-number returns a set of all values of account-number attributes of account elements. By default, IDREF links are not followed; we shall see how to deal with IDREFs later.

XPath supports a number of other features:

- Selection predicates may follow any step in a path, and are contained in square brackets. For example,

/bank-2/account[balance > 400]

returns account elements with a balance value greater than 400, while

/bank-2/account[balance > 400]/@account-number

returns the account numbers of those accounts.

We can test the existence of a subelement by listing it without any comparison operation; for instance, if we removed just "> 400" from the above, the expression would return account numbers of all accounts that have a balance subelement, regardless of its value.

- XPath provides several functions that can be used as part of predicates, including testing the position of the current node in the sibling order and counting the number of nodes matched. For example, the path expression

/bank-2/account/[customer/count()> 2]

returns accounts with more than 2 customers. Boolean connectives and and or can be used in predicates, while the function not(. . .) can be used for negation.

- The function id("foo") returns the node (if any) with an attribute of type ID and value "foo". The function id can even be applied on sets of references, or even strings containing multiple references separated by blanks, such as IDREFS. For instance, the path

/bank-2/account/id(@owner)

returns all customers referred to from the owners attribute of account elements.

- The | operator allows expression results to be unioned. For example, if the DTD of bank-2 also contained elements for loans, with attribute borrower of type IDREFS identifying loan borrower, the expression

/bank-2/account/id(@owner) | /bank-2/loan/id(@borrower)

gives customers with either accounts or loans. However, the | operator cannot be nested inside other operators.

- An XPath expression can skip multiple levels of nodes by using "//". For instance, the expression /bank-2//name finds any name element *anywhere* under the /bank-2 element, regardless of the element in which it is contained. This example illustrates the ability to find required data without full knowledge of the schema.

- Each step in the path need not select from the children of the nodes in the current node set. In fact, this is just one of several directions along which a step in the path may proceed, such as parents, siblings, ancestors and descendants. We omit details, but note that "//", described above, is a short form for specifying "all descendants," while ".." specifies the parent.

10.4.2 XSLT

A **style sheet** is a representation of formatting options for a document, usually stored outside the document itself, so that formatting is separate from content. For example, a style sheet for HTML might specify the font to be used on all headers, and thus

```
<xsl:template match="/bank-2/customer">
    <customer>
    <xsl:value-of select="customer-name"/>
    </customer>
</xsl:template>
<xsl:template match="."/>
```

Figure 10.10   Using XSLT to wrap results in new XML elements.

replace a large number of font declarations in the HTML page. The **XML Stylesheet Language (XSL)** was originally designed for generating HTML from XML, and is thus a logical extension of HTML style sheets. The language includes a general-purpose transformation mechanism, called **XSL Transformations (XSLT)**, which can be used to transform one XML document into another XML document, or to other formats such as HTML.[1] XSLT transformations are quite powerful, and in fact XSLT can even act as a query language.

XSLT transformations are expressed as a series of recursive rules, called **templates**. In their basic form, templates allow selection of nodes in an XML tree by an XPath expression. However, templates can also generate new XML content, so that selection and content generation can be mixed in natural and powerful ways. While XSLT can be used as a query language, its syntax and semantics are quite dissimilar from those of SQL.

A simple template for XSLT consists of a **match** part and a **select** part. Consider this XSLT code:

```
<xsl:template match="/bank-2/customer">
    <xsl:value-of select="customer-name"/>
</xsl:template>
<xsl:template match="."/>
```

The xsl:template match statement contains an XPath expression that selects one or more nodes. The first template matches customer elements that occur as children of the bank-2 root element. The xsl:value-of statement enclosed in the match statement outputs values from the nodes in the result of the XPath expression. The first template outputs the value of the customer-name subelement; note that the value does not contain the element tag.

Note that the second template matches all nodes. This is required because the default behavior of XSLT on subtrees of the input document that do not match any template is to copy the subtrees to the output document.

XSLT copies any tag that is not in the xsl namespace unchanged to the output. Figure 10.10 shows how to use this feature to make each customer name from our example appear as a subelement of a "<customer>" element, by placing the xsl:value-of statement between <customer> and </customer>.

---

1. The XSL standard now consists of XSLT and a standard for specifying formatting features such as fonts, page margins, and tables. Formatting is not relevant from a database perspective, so we do not cover it here.

```
<xsl:template match="/bank">
    <customers>
    <xsl:apply-templates/>
    </customers>
</xsl:template>
<xsl:template match="/customer">
    <customer>
    <xsl:value-of select="customer-name"/>
    </customer>
</xsl:template>
<xsl:template match="."/>
```

Figure 10.11   Applying rules recursively.

Structural recursion is a key part of XSLT. Recall that elements and subelements naturally form a tree structure. The idea of structural recursion is this: When a template matches an element in the tree structure, XSLT can use structural recursion to apply template rules recursively on subtrees, instead of just outputting a value. It applies rules recursively by the xsl:apply-templates directive, which appears inside other templates.

For example, the results of our previous query can be placed in a surrounding <customers> element by the addition of a rule using xsl:apply-templates, as in Figure 10.11 The new rule matches the outer "bank" tag, and constructs a result document by applying all other templates to the subtrees appearing within the bank element, but wrapping the results in the given <customers> </customers> element. Without recursion forced by the <xsl:apply-templates/> clause, the template would output <customers> </customers>, and then apply the other templates on the subelements.

In fact, the structural recursion is critical to constructing well-formed XML documents, since XML documents must have a single top-level element containing all other elements in the document.

XSLT provides a feature called **keys**, which permit lookup of elements by using values of subelements or attributes; the goals are similar to that of the id() function in XPath, but permits attributes other than the ID attributes to be used. Keys are defined by an xsl:key directive, which has three parts, for example:

<xsl:key name="acctno" match="account" use="account-number"/>

The name attribute is used to distinguish different keys. The match attribute specifies which nodes the key applies to. Finally, the use attribute specifies the expression to be used as the value of the key. Note that the expression need not be unique to an element; that is, more than one element may have the same expression value. In the example, the key named acctno specifies that the account-number subelement of account should be used as a key for that account.

Keys can be subsequently used in templates as part of any pattern through the key function. This function takes the name of the key and a value, and returns the

```
<xsl:key name="acctno" match="account"use="account-number"/>
<xsl:key name="custno" match="customer" use="customer-name"/>
<xsl:template match="depositor">
       <cust-acct>
       <xsl:value-of select=key("custno", "customer-name")/>
       <xsl:value-of select=key("acctno", "account-number")/>
       </cust-acct>
</xsl:template>
<xsl:template match=".."/>
```

Figure 10.12   Joins in XSLT.

set of nodes that match that value. Thus, the XML node for account "A-401" can be referenced as key("acctno", "A-401").

Keys can be used to implement some types of joins, as in Figure 10.12. The code in the figure can be applied to XML data in the format in Figure 10.1. Here, the key function joins the depositor elements with matching customer and account elements. The result of the query consists of pairs of customer and account elements enclosed within cust-acct elements.

XSLT allows nodes to be sorted. A simple example shows how xsl:sort would be used in our style sheet to return customer elements sorted by name:

```
<xsl:template match="/bank">
       <xsl:apply-templates select="customer">
       <xsl:sort select="customer-name"/>
       </xsl:apply-templates>
</xsl:template>
<xsl:template match="customer">
       <customer>
              <xsl:value-of select="customer-name"/>
              <xsl:value-of select="customer-street"/>
              <xsl:value-of select="customer-city"/>
       </customer>
</xsl:template>
<xsl:template match=".."/>
```

Here, the xsl:apply-template has a select attribute, which constrains it to be applied only on customer subelements. The xsl:sort directive within the xsl:apply-template element causes nodes to be sorted *before* they are processed by the next set of templates. Options exist to allow sorting on multiple subelements/attributes, by numeric value, and in descending order.

10.4.3   XQuery

The World Wide Web Consortium (W3C) is developing XQuery, a query language for XML. Our discusssion here is based on a draft of the language standard, so the final standard may differ; however we expect the main features we cover here will not change substantially. The XQuery language derives from an XML query language called Quilt; most of the XQuery features we outline here are part of Quilt. Quilt itself includes features from earlier languages such as XPath, discussed in Section 10.4.1, and two other XML query languages, XQL and XML-QL.

Unlike XSLT, XQuery does not represent queries in XML. Instead, they appear more like SQL queries, and are organized into "FLWR" (pronounced "flower") expressions comprising four sections: **for**, **let**, **where**, and **return**. The **for** section gives a series of variables that range over the results of XPath expressions. When more than one variable is specified, the results include the Cartesian product of the possible values the variables can take, making the **for** clause similar in spirit to the **from** clause of an SQL query. The **let** clause simply allows complicated expressions to be assigned to variable names for simplicity of representation. The **where** section, like the SQL **where** clause, performs additional tests on the joined tuples from the **for** section. Finally, the **return** section allows the construction of results in XML.

A simple FLWR expression that returns the account numbers for checking accounts is based on the XML document of Figure 10.8, which uses ID and IDREFS:

> **for** $x **in** /bank-2/account
> **let** $acctno := $x/@account-number
> **where** $x/balance > 400
> **return** <account-number> $acctno </account-number>

Since this query is simple, the **let** clause is not essential, and the variable $acctno in the **return** clause could be replaced with $x/@account-number. Note further that, since the **for** clause uses XPath expressions, selections may occur within the XPath expression. Thus, an equivalent query may have only **for** and **return** clauses:

> **for** $x **in** /bank-2/account[balance > 400]
> **return** <account-number> $x/@account-number </account-number>

However, the **let** clause simplifies complex queries.

Path expressions in XQuery may return a multiset, with repeated nodes. The function distinct applied on a multiset, returns a set without duplication. The distinct function can be used even within a **for** clause. XQuery also provides aggregate functions such as sum and count that can be applied on collections such as sets and multisets. While XQuery does not provide a **group by** construct, aggregate queries can be written by using nested FLWR constructs in place of grouping; we leave details as an exercise for you. Note also that variables assigned by **let** clauses may be set- or multiset-valued, if the path expression on the right-hand side returns a set or multiset value.

Joins are specified in XQuery much as they are in SQL. The join of depositor, account and customer elements in Figure 10.1, which we wrote in XSLT in Section 10.4.2, can be written in XQuery this way:

```
for $b in /bank/account,
       $c in /bank/customer,
       $d in /bank/depositor
where $a/account-number = $d/account-number
       and $c/customer-name = $d/customer-name
return <cust-acct> $c $a </cust-acct>
```

The same query can be expressed with the selections specified as XPath selections:

```
for $a in /bank/account,
    $c in /bank/customer,
    $d in /bank/depositor[account-number = $a/account-number
          and customer-name = $c/customer-name]
return <cust-acct> $c $a</cust-acct>
```

XQuery FLWR expressions can be nested in the **return** clause, in order to generate element nestings that do not appear in the source document. This feature is similar to nested subqueries in the **from** clause of SQL queries in Section 9.5.3.

For instance, the XML structure shown in Figure 10.3, with account elements nested within customer elements, can be generated from the structure in Figure 10.1 by this query:

```
<bank-1>
    for $c in /bank/customer
    return
        <customer>
            $c/*
            for $d in /bank/depositor[customer-name = $c/customer-name],
                $a in /bank/account[account-number=$d/account-number]
            return $a
        </customer>
</bank-1>
```

The query also introduces the syntax $c/*, which refers to all the children of the node, which is bound to the variable $c. Similarly, $c/text() gives the text content of an element, without the tags.

Path expressions in XQuery are based on path expressions in XPath, but XQuery provides some extensions (which may eventually be added to XPath itself). One of the useful syntax extensions is the operator - >, which can be used to dereference IDREFs, just like the function id(). The operator can be applied on a value of type IDREFS to get a set of elements. It can be used, for example, to find all the accounts associated with a customer, with the ID/IDREFS representation of bank information. We leave details to the reader.

Results can be sorted in XQuery if a **sortby** clause is included at the end of any expression; the clause specifies how the instances of that expression should be sorted. For instance, this query outputs all customer elements sorted by the name subelement:

```
for $c in /bank/customer,
return <customer> $c/* </customer> sortby(name)
```

To sort in descending order, we can use **sortby**(name **descending**).

Sorting can be done at multiple levels of nesting. For instance, we can get a nested representation of bank information sorted in customer name order, with accounts of each customer sorted by account number, as follows.

```
<bank-1>
     for $c in /bank/customer
     return
          <customer>
               $c/*
               for $d in /bank/depositor[customer-name = $c/customer-name],
                    $a in /bank/account[account-number=$d/account-number]
               return <account> $a/* </account> sortby(account-number)
          </customer> sortby(customer-name)
</bank-1>
```

XQuery provides a variety of built-in functions, and supports user-defined functions. For instance, the built-in function document(name) returns the root of a named document; the root can then be used in a path expression to access the contents of the document. Users can define functions as illustrated by this function, which returns a list of all balances of a customer with a specified name:

```
function balances(xsd:string $c) returns list(xsd:numeric) {
     for $d in /bank/depositor[customer-name = $c],
          $a in /bank/account[account-number=$d/account-number]
     return $a/balance
}
```

XQuery uses the type system of XMLSchema. XQuery also provides functions to convert between types. For instance, number(x) converts a string to a number.

XQuery offers a variety of other features, such as if-then-else clauses, which can be used within **return** clauses, and existential and universal quantification, which can be used in predicates in **where** clauses. For example, existential quantification can be expressed using **some** $e **in** path **satisfies** P where path is a path expression, and P is a predicate which can use $e. Universal quantification can be expressed by using **every** in place of **some**.

10.5   The Application Program Interface

With the wide acceptance of XML as a data representation and exchange format, software tools are widely available for manipulation of XML data. In fact, there are two standard models for programmatic manipulation of XML, each available for use with a wide variety of popular programming languages.

One of the standard APIs for manipulating XML is the *document object model* (DOM), which treats XML content as a tree, with each element represented by a node, called a DOMNode. Programs may access parts of the document in a navigational fashion, beginning with the root.

DOM libraries are available for most common programming langauges and are even present in Web browsers, where it may be used to manipulate the document displayed to the user. We outline here some of the interfaces and methods in the Java API for DOM, to give a flavor of DOM. The Java DOM API provides an interface called Node, and interfaces Element and Attribute, which inherit from the Node interface. The Node interface provides methods such as getParentNode(), getFirstChild(), and getNextSibling(), to navigate the DOM tree, starting with the root node. Subelements of an element can be accessed by name getElementsByTagName(name), which returns a list of all child elements with a specified tag name; individual members of the list can be accessed by the method item(i), which returns the ith element in the list. Attribute values of an element can be accessed by name, using the method getAttribute(name). The text value of an element is modeled as a Text node, which is a child of the element node; an element node with no subelements has only one such child node. The method getData() on the Text node returns the text contents. DOM also provides a variety of functions for updating the document by adding and deleting attribute and element children of a node, setting node values, and so on.

Many more details are required for writing an actual DOM program; see the bibliographical notes for references to further information.

DOM can be used to access XML data stored in databases, and an XML database can be built using DOM as its primary interface for accessing and modifying data. However, the DOM interface does not support any form of declarative querying.

The second programming interface we discuss, the *Simple API for XML* (SAX) is an *event* model, designed to provide a common interface between parsers and applications. This API is built on the notion of *event handlers*, which consists of user-specified functions associated with parsing events. Parsing events correspond to the recognition of parts of a document; for example, an event is generated when the start-tag is found for an element, and another event is generated when the end-tag is found. The pieces of a document are always encountered in order from start to finish. SAX is not appropriate for database applications.

10.6   Storage of XML Data

Many applications require storage of XML data. One way to store XML data is to convert it to relational representation, and store it in a relational database. There are several alternatives for storing XML data, briefly outlined here.

10.6.1   Relational Databases

Since relational databases are widely used in existing applications, there is a great benefit to be had in storing XML data in relational databases, so that the data can be accessed from existing applications.

Converting XML data to relational form is usually straightforward if the data were generated from a relational schema in the first place, and XML was used merely as a data exchange format for relational data. However, there are many applications where the XML data is not generated from a relational schema, and translating the data to relational form for storage may not be straightforward. In particular, nested elements and elements that recur (corresponding to set valued attributes) complicate storage of XML data in relational format. Several alternative approaches are available:

- **Store as string.** A simple way to store XML data in a relational database is to store each child element of the top-level element as a string in a separate tuple in the database. For instance, the XML data in Figure 10.1 could be stored as a set of tuples in a relation *elements*(*data*), with the attribute *data* of each tuple storing one XML element (account, customer, or depositor) in string form.

  While the above representation is easy to use, the database system does not know the schema of the stored elements. As a result, it is not possible to query the data directly. In fact, it is not even possible to implement simple selections such as finding all account elements, or finding the account element with account number A-401, without scanning all tuples of the relation and examining the contents of the string stored in the tuple.

  A partial solution to this problem is to store different types of elements in different relations, and also store the values of some critical elements as attributes of the relation to enable indexing. For instance, in our example, the relations would be *account-elements*, *customer-elements*, and *depositor-elements*, each with an attribute *data*. Each relation may have extra attributes to store the values of some subelements, such as *account-number* or *customer-name*. Thus, a query that requires account elements with a specified account number can be answered efficiently with this representation. Such an approach depends on type information about XML data, such as the DTD of the data.

  Some database systems, such as Oracle 9, support **function indices**, which can help avoid replication of attributes between the XML string and relation attributes. Unlike normal indices, which are on attribute values, function indices can be built on the result of applying user-defined functions on tuples. For instance, a function index can be built on a user-defined function that returns the value of the account-number subelement of the XML string in a tuple. The index can then be used in the same way as an index on a *account-number* attribute.

  The above approaches have the drawback that a large part of the XML information is stored within strings. It is possible to store all the information in relations in one of several ways which we examine next.

- **Tree representation.** Arbitrary XML data can be modeled as a tree and stored using a pair of relations:

  nodes(*id, type, label, value*)
  child(*child-id, parent-id*)

Each element and attribute in the XML data is given a unique identifier. A tuple inserted in the *nodes* relation for each element and attribute with its identifier (*id*), its type (attribute or element), the name of the element or attribute (*label*), and the text value of the element or attribute (*value*). The relation *child* is used to record the parent element of each element and attribute. If order information of elements and attributes must be preserved, an extra attribute *position* can be added to the *child* relation to indicate the relative position of the child among the children of the parent. As an exercise, you can represent the XML data of Figure 10.1 by using this technique.

This representation has the advantage that all XML information can be represented directly in relational form, and many XML queries can be translated into relational queries and executed inside the database system. However, it has the drawback that each element gets broken up into many pieces, and a large number of joins are required to reassemble elements.

- **Map to relations.** In this approach, XML elements whose schema is known are mapped to relations and attributes. Elements whose schema is unknown are stored as strings, or as a tree representation.

  A relation is created for each element type whose schema is known. All attributes of these elements are stored as attributes of the relation. All subelements that occur at most once inside these element (as specified in the DTD) can also be represented as attributes of the relation; if the subelement can contain only text, the attribute stores the text value. Otherwise, the relation corresponding to the subelement stores the contents of the subelement, along with an identifier for the parent type and the attribute stores the identifier of the subelement. If the subelement has further nested subelements, the same procedure is applied to the subelement.

  If a subelement can occur multiple times in an element, the map-to-relations approach stores the contents of the subelements in the relation corresponding to the subelement. It gives both parent and subelement unique identifiers, and creates a separate relation, similar to the child relation we saw earlier in the tree representation, to identify which subelement occurs under which parent.

  Note that when we apply this appoach to the DTD of the data in Figure 10.1, we get back the original relational schema that we have used in earlier chapters. The bibliographical notes provide references to such hybrid approaches.

10.6.2   Nonrelational Data Stores

There are several alternatives for storing XML data in nonrelational data storage systems:

- **Store in flat files.** Since XML is primarily a file format, a natural storage mechanism is simply a flat file. This approach has many of the drawbacks, outlined in Chapter 1, of using file systems as the basis for database applications. In particular, it lacks data isolation, integrity checks, atomicity, concurrent access, and security. However, the wide availability of XML tools that work on file data makes it relatively easy to access and query XML data stored in files. Thus, this storage format may be sufficient for some applications.

- **Store in an XML Database.** XML databases are databases that use XML as their basic data model. Early XML databases implemented the Document Object Model on a C++-based object-oriented database. This allows much of the object-oriented database infrastucture to be reused, while using a standard XML interface. The addition of an XML query language provides declarative querying. It is also possible to build XML databases as a layer on top of relational databases.

10.7 XML Applications

A central design goal for XML is to make it easier to communicate information, on the Web and between applications, by allowing the semantics of the data to be described with the data itself. Thus, while the large amount of XML data and its use in business applications will undoubtably require and benefit from database technologies, XML is foremost a means of communication. Two applications of XML for communication —exchange of data, and mediation of Web information resources—illustrate how XML achieves its goal of supporting data exchange and demonstrate how database technology and interaction are key in supporting exchange-based applications.

10.7.1 Exchange of Data

Standards are being developed for XML representation of data for a variety of specialized applications ranging from business applications such as banking and shipping to scientific applications such as chemistry and molecular biology. Some examples:

- The chemical industry needs information about chemicals, such as their molecular structure, and a variety of important properties such as boiling and melting points, calorific values, solubility in various solvents, and so on. *ChemML* is a standard for representing such information.

- In shipping, carriers of goods and customs and tax officials need shipment records containing detailed information about the goods being shipped, from whom and to where they were sent, to whom and to where they are being shipped, the monetary value of the goods, and so on.

- An online marketplace in which business can buy and sell goods (a so-called business-to-business B2B market) requires information such as product catalogs, including detailed product descriptions and price information, product inventories, offers to buy, and quotes for a proposed sale.

Using normalized relational schemas to model such complex data requirements results in a large number of relations, which is often hard for users to manage. The relations often have large numbers of attributes; explicit representation of attribute/-element names along with values in XML helps avoid confusion between attributes. Nested element representations help reduce the number of relations that must be represented, as well as the number of joins required to get required information, at the possible cost of redundancy. For instance, in our bank example, listing customers with account elements nested within account elements, as in Figure 10.3, results in a format that is more natural for some applications, in particular for humans to read, than is the normalized representation in Figure 10.1.

When XML is used to exchange data between business applications, the data most often originate in relational databases. Data in relational databases must be *published*, that is, converted to XML form, for export to other applications. Incoming data must be *shredded*, that is, converted back from XML to normalized relation form and stored in a relational database. While application code can perform the publishing and shredding operations, the operations are so common that the conversions should be done automatically, without writing application code, where possible. Database vendors are therefore working to *XML-enable* their database products.

An XML-enabled database supports an automatic mapping from its internal model (relational, object-relational or object-oriented) to XML. These mappings may be simple or complex. A simple mapping might assign an element to every row of a table, and make each column in that row either an attribute or a subelement of the row's element. Such a mapping is straightforward to generate automatically. A more complicated mapping would allow nested structures to be created. Extensions of SQL with nested queries in the **select** clause have been developed to allow easy creation of nested XML output. Some database products also allow XML queries to access relational data by treating the XML form of relational data as a *virtual* XML document.

10.7.1.1   Data Mediation

Comparison shopping is an example of a mediation application, in which data about items, inventory, pricing, and shipping costs are extracted from a variety of Web sites offering a particular item for sale. The resulting aggregated information is significantly more valuable than the individual information offered by a single site.

A personal financial manager is a similar application in the context of banking. Consider a consumer with a variety of accounts to manage, such as bank accounts, savings accounts, and retirement accounts. Suppose that these accounts may be held at different institutions. Providing centralized management for all accounts of a customer is a major challenge. XML-based mediation addresses the problem by extracting an XML representation of account information from the respective Web sites of the financial institutions where the individual holds accounts. This information may be extracted easily if the institution exports it in a standard XML format, and undoubtedly some will. For those that do not, *wrapper* software is used to generate XML data from HTML Web pages returned by the Web site. Wrapper applications need constant maintenance, since they depend on formatting details of Web pages, which change often. Nevertheless, the value provided by mediation often justifies the effort required to develop and maintain wrappers.

Once the basic tools are available to extract information from each source, a *mediator* application is used to combine the extracted information under a single schema. This may require further transformation of the XML data from each site, since different sites may structure the same information differently. For instance, one of the banks may export information in the format in Figure 10.1, while another may use the nested format in Figure 10.3. They may also use different names for the same information (for instance, acct-number and account-id), or may even use the same name for different information. The mediator must decide on a single schema that represents all required information, and must provide code to transform data between different representations. Such issues are discussed in more detail in Section 19.8, in the context of distributed databases. XML query languages such as XSLT and XQuery play an important role in the task of transformation between different XML representations.

10.8 Summary

- Like the Hyper-Text Markup Language, HTML, on which the Web is based, the Extensible Markup Language, XML, is a descendant of the Standard Generalized Markup Language (SGML). XML was originally intended for providing functional markup for Web documents, but has now become the defacto standard data format for data exchange between applications.

- XML documents contain elements, with matching starting and ending tags indicating the beginning and end of an element. Elements may have subelements nested within them, to any level of nesting. Elements may also have attributes. The choice between representing information as attributes and subelements is often arbitrary in the context of data representation.

- Elements may have an attribute of type ID that stores a unique identifier for the element. Elements may also store references to other elements using attributes of type IDREF. Attributes of type IDREFS can store a list of references.

- Documents may optionally have their schema specified by a Document Type Declaration, DTD. The DTD of a document specifies what elements may occur, how they may be nested, and what attributes each element may have.

- Although DTDs are widely used, they have several limitations. For instance, they do not provide a type system. XMLSchema is a new standard for specifying the schema of a document. While it provides more expressive power, including a powerful type system, it is also more complicated.

- XML data can be represented as tree structures, with nodes corresponding to elements and attributes. Nesting of elements is reflected by the parent-child structure of the tree representation.

- Path expressions can be used to traverse the XML tree structure, to locate required data. XPath is a standard language for path expressions, and allows required elements to be specified by a file-system-like path, and additionally allows selections and other features. XPath also forms part of other XML query languages.

- The XSLT language was originally designed as the transformation language for a style sheet facility, in other words, to apply formatting information to

XML documents. However, XSLT offers quite powerful querying and transformation features and is widely available, so it is used for quering XML data.

- XSLT programs contain a series of templates, each with a **match** part and a **select** part. Each element in the input XML data is matched against available templates, and the select part of the first matching template is applied to the element.

    Templates can be applied recursively, from within the body of another template, a procedure known as structural recursion. XSLT supports keys, which can be used to implement some types of joins. It also supports sorting and other querying facilities.

- The XQuery language, which is currently being standardized, is based on the Quilt query language. The XQuery language is similar to SQL, with **for**, **let**, **where**, and **return** clauses.

    However, it supports many extensions to deal with the tree nature of XML and to allow for the transformation of XML documents into other documents with a significantly different structure.

- XML data can be stored in any of several different ways. For example, XML data can be stored as strings in a relational database. Alternatively, relations can represent XML data as trees. As another alternative, XML data can be mapped to relations in the same way that E-R schemas are mapped to relational schemas.

    XML data may also be stored in file systems, or in XML-databases, which use XML as their internal representation.

- The ability to transform documents in languages such as XSLT and XQuery is a key to the use of XML in mediation applications, such as electronic business exchanges and the extraction and combination of Web data for use by a personal finance manager or comparison shopper.

Review Terms

- Extensible Markup Language (XML)
- Hyper-Text Markup Language (HTML)
- Standard Generalized Markup Language
- Markup language
- Tags
- Self-documenting
- Element
- Root element

- Nested elements
- Attribute
- Namespace
- Default namespace
- Schema definition
    - ☐ Document Type Definition (DTD)
    - ☐ XMLSchema
- ID
- IDREF and IDREFS
- Tree model of XML data

- Nodes
- Querying and transformation
- Path expressions
- XPath
- Style sheet
- XML Style sheet Language (XSL)
- XSL Transformations (XSLT)
    - ☐ Templates
        - — Match
        - — Select
    - ☐ Structural recursion
    - ☐ Keys
    - ☐ Sorting
- XQuery
    - ☐ FLWR expressions
        - — **for**
        - — **let**
        - — **where**
        - — **return**

- ☐ Joins
- ☐ Nested FLWR expression
- ☐ Sorting
- XML API
- Document Object Model (DOM)
- Simple API for XML (SAX)
- Storage of XML data
    - ☐ In relational databases
        - — Store as string
        - — Tree representation
        - — Map to relations
    - ☐ In nonrelational data stores
        - — Files
        - — XML-databases
- XML Applications
    - ☐ Exchange of data
        - — Publish and shred
    - ☐ Data mediation
        - — Wrapper software
- XML-Enabled database

Exercises

10.1 Give an alternative representation of bank information containing the same data as in Figure 10.1, but using attributes instead of subelements. Also give the DTD for this representation.

10.2 Show, by giving a DTD, how to represent the *books* nested-relation from Section 9.1, using XML.

10.3 Give the DTD for an XML representation of the following nested-relational schema

> *Emp = (ename, ChildrenSet* **setof**(*Children*), *SkillsSet* **setof**(*Skills*))
> *Children = (name, Birthday)*
> *Birthday = (day, month, year)*
> *Skills = (type, ExamsSet* **setof**(*Exams*))
> *Exams = (year, city)*

10.4 Write the following queries in XQuery, assuming the DTD from Exercise 10.3.

    a. Find the names of all employees who have a child who has a birthday in March.

    b. Find those employees who took an examination for the skill type "typing" in the city "Dayton".

    c. List all skill types in *Emp*.

```
<!DOCTYPE bibliography [
    <!ELEMENT book (title, author+, year, publisher, place?)>
    <!ELEMENT article (title, author+, journal, year, number, volume, pages?)>
    <!ELEMENT author ( last-name, first-name) >
    <!ELEMENT title ( #PCDATA )>
    · · · similar PCDATA declarations for year, publisher, place, journal, year,
        number, volume, pages, last-name and first-name
] >
```

Figure 10.13   DTD for bibliographical data.

10.5 Write queries in XSLT and in XPath on the DTD of Exercise 10.3 to list all skill types in *Emp*.

10.6 Write a query in XQuery on the XML representation in Figure 10.1 to find the total balance, across all accounts, at each branch. (Hint: Use a nested query to get the effect of an SQL **group by**.)

10.7 Write a query in XQuery on the XML representation in Figure 10.1 to compute the left outer join of **customer** elements with **account** elements. (Hint: Use universal quantification.)

10.8 Give a query in XQuery to flip the nesting of data from Exercise 10.2. That is, at the outermost level of nesting the output must have elements corresponding to authors, and each such element must have nested within it items corresponding to all the books written by the author.

10.9 Give the DTD for an XML representation of the information in Figure 2.29. Create a separate element type to represent each relationship, but use ID and IDREF to implement primary and foreign keys.

10.10 Write queries in XSLT and XQuery to output customer elements with associated account elements nested within the customer elements, given the bank information representation using ID and IDREFS in Figure 10.8.

10.11 Give a relational schema to represent bibliographical information specified as per the DTD fragment in Figure 10.13. The relational schema must keep track of the order of author elements. You can assume that only books and articles appear as top level elements in XML documents.

10.12 Consider Exercise 10.11, and suppose that authors could also appear as top level elements. What change would have to be done to the relational schema.

10.13 Write queries in XQuery on the bibliography DTD fragment in Figure 10.13, to do the following.
   a. Find all authors who have authored a book and an article in the same year.
   b. Display books and articles sorted by year.
   c. Display books with more than one author.

10.14 Show the tree representation of the XML data in Figure 10.1, and the representation of the tree using *nodes* and *child* relations described in Section 10.6.1.

10.15 Consider the following recursive DTD.

```
<!DOCTYPE parts [
    <!ELEMENT part (name, subpartinfo*)>
    <!ELEMENT subpartinfo (part, quantity)>
    <!ELEMENT name ( #PCDATA )>
    <!ELEMENT quantity ( #PCDATA )>
] >
```

  a. Give a small example of data corresponding to the above DTD.
  b. Show how to map this DTD to a relational schema. You can assume that part names are unique, that is, whereever a part appears, its subpart structure will be the same.

Bibliographical Notes

The XML Cover Pages site (www.oasis-open.org/cover/) contains a wealth of XML information, including tutorial introductions to XML, standards, publications, and software. The World Wide Web Consortium (W3C) acts as the standards body for Web-related standards, including basic XML and all the XML-related languages such as XPath, XSLT and XQuery. A large number of technical reports defining the XML related standards are available at www.w3c.org.

Fernandez et al. [2000] gives an algebra for XML. Quilt is described in Chamberlin et al. [2000]. Sahuguet [2001] describes a system, based on the Quilt language, for querying XML. Deutsch et al. [1999b] describes the XML-QL language. Integration of keyword querying into XML is outlined by Florescu et al. [2000]. Query optimization for XML is described in McHugh and Widom [1999]. Fernandez and Morishima [2001] describe efficient evaluation of XML queries in middleware systems. Other work on querying and manipulating XML data includes Chawathe [1999], Deutsch et al. [1999a], and Shanmugasundaram et al. [2000].

Florescu and Kossmann [1999], Kanne and Moerkotte [2000], and Shanmugasundaram et al. [1999] describe storage of XML data. Schning [2001] describes a database designed for XML. XML support in commercial databases is described in Banerjee et al. [2000], Cheng and Xu [2000] and Rys [2001]. See Chapters 25 through 27 for more information on XML support in commercial databases. The use of XML for data integration is described by Liu et al. [2000], Draper et al. [2001], Baru et al. [1999], and Carey et al. [2000].

Tools

A number of tools to deal with XML are available in the public domain. The site www.oasis-open.org/cover/ contains links to a variety of software tools for XML and XSL (including XSLT). Kweelt (available at http://db.cis.upenn.edu/Kweelt/) is a publicly available XML querying system based on the Quilt language.

PART 4

Data Storage and Querying

Although a database system provides a high-level view of data, ultimately data have to be stored as bits on one or more storage devices. A vast majority of databases today store data on magnetic disk and fetch data into main space memory for processing, or copy data onto tapes and other backup devices for archival storage. The physical characteristics of storage devices play a major role in the way data are stored, in particular because access to a random piece of data on disk is much slower than memory access: Disk access takes tens of milliseconds, whereas memory access takes a tenth of a microsecond.

Chapter 11 begins with an overview of physical storage media, including mechanisms to minimize the chance of data loss due to failures. The chapter then describes how records are mapped to files, which in turn are mapped to bits on the disk. Storage and retrieval of objects is also covered in Chapter 11.

Many queries reference only a small proportion of the records in a file. An index is a structure that helps locate desired records of a relation quickly, without examining all records. The index in this textbook is an example, although, unlike database indices, it is meant for human use. Chapter 12 describes several types of indices used in database systems.

User queries have to be executed on the database contents, which reside on storage devices. It is usually convenient to break up queries into smaller operations, roughly corresponding to the relational algebra operations. Chapter 13 describes how queries are processed, presenting algorithms for implementing individual operations, and then outlining how the operations are executed in synchrony, to process a query.

There are many alternative ways of processing a query, which can have widely varying costs. Query optimization refers to the process of finding the lowest-cost method of evaluating a given query. Chapter 14 describes the process of query optimization.

CHAPTER 11

Storage and File Structure

In preceding chapters, we have emphasized the higher-level models of a database. For example, at the *conceptual* or *logical* level, we viewed the database, in the relational model, as a collection of tables. Indeed, the logical model of the database is the correct level for database *users* to focus on. This is because the goal of a database system is to simplify and facilitate access to data; users of the system should not be burdened unnecessarily with the physical details of the implementation of the system.

In this chapter, however, as well as in Chapters 12, 13, and 14, we probe below the higher levels as we describe various methods for implementing the data models and languages presented in preceding chapters. We start with characteristics of the underlying storage media, such as disk and tape systems. We then define various data structures that will allow fast access to data. We consider several alternative structures, each best suited to a different kind of access to data. The final choice of data structure needs to be made on the basis of the expected use of the system and of the physical characteristics of the specific machine.

11.1 Overview of Physical Storage Media

Several types of data storage exist in most computer systems. These storage media are classified by the speed with which data can be accessed, by the cost per unit of data to buy the medium, and by the medium's reliability. Among the media typically available are these:

- **Cache**. The cache is the fastest and most costly form of storage. Cache memory is small; its use is managed by the computer system hardware. We shall not be concerned about managing cache storage in the database system.

- **Main memory**. The storage medium used for data that are available to be operated on is main memory. The general-purpose machine instructions operate on main memory. Although main memory may contain many megabytes of data, or even gigabytes of data in large server systems, it is generally too small (or too expensive) for storing the entire database. The contents of main memory are usually lost if a power failure or system crash occurs.

- **Flash memory**. Also known as *electrically erasable programmable read-only memory (EEPROM)*, flash memory differs from main memory in that data survive power failure. Reading data from flash memory takes less than 100 nanoseconds (a nanosecond is $1/1000$ of a microsecond), which is roughly as fast as reading data from main memory. However, writing data to flash memory is more complicated—data can be written once, which takes about 4 to 10 microseconds, but cannot be overwritten directly. To overwrite memory that has been written already, we have to erase an entire bank of memory at once; it is then ready to be written again. A drawback of flash memory is that it can support only a limited number of erase cycles, ranging from 10,000 to 1 million. Flash memory has found popularity as a replacement for magnetic disks for storing small volumes of data (5 to 10 megabytes) in low-cost computer systems, such as computer systems that are embedded in other devices, in hand-held computers, and in other digital electronic devices such as digital cameras.

- **Magnetic-disk storage**. The primary medium for the long-term on-line storage of data is the magnetic disk. Usually, the entire database is stored on magnetic disk. The system must move the data from disk to main memory so that they can be accessed. After the system has performed the designated operations, the data that have been modified must be written to disk.

   The size of magnetic disks currently ranges from a few gigabytes to 80 gigabytes. Both the lower and upper end of this range have been growing at about 50 percent per year, and we can expect much larger capacity disks every year. Disk storage survives power failures and system crashes. Disk-storage devices themselves may sometimes fail and thus destroy data, but such failures usually occur much less frequently than do system crashes.

- **Optical storage**. The most popular forms of optical storage are the *compact disk* (CD), which can hold about 640 megabytes of data, and the *digital video disk* (DVD) which can hold 4.7 or 8.5 gigabytes of data per side of the disk (or up to 17 gigabytes on a two-sided disk). Data are stored optically on a disk, and are read by a laser. The optical disks used in read-only compact disks (CD-ROM) or read-only digital video disk (DVD-ROM) cannot be written, but are supplied with data prerecorded.

   There are "record-once" versions of compact disk (called CD-R) and digital video disk (called DVD-R), which can be written only once; such disks are also called **write-once, read-many** (WORM) disks. There are also "multiple-write" versions of compact disk (called CD-RW) and digital video disk (DVD-RW and DVD-RAM), which can be written multiple times. Recordable compact disks are magnetic–optical storage devices that use optical means to read magnetically encoded data. Such disks are useful for archival storage of data as well as distribution of data.

Jukebox systems contain a few drives and numerous disks that can be loaded into one of the drives automatically (by a robot arm) on demand.

- **Tape storage**. Tape storage is used primarily for backup and archival data. Although magnetic tape is much cheaper than disks, access to data is much slower, because the tape must be accessed sequentially from the beginning. For this reason, tape storage is referred to as **sequential-access** storage. In contrast, disk storage is referred to as **direct-access** storage because it is possible to read data from any location on disk.

  Tapes have a high capacity (40 gigabyte to 300 gigabytes tapes are currently available), and can be removed from the tape drive, so they are well suited to cheap archival storage. Tape jukeboxes are used to hold exceptionally large collections of data, such as remote-sensing data from satellites, which could include as much as hundreds of terabytes (1 terabyte = 10^{12} bytes), or even a petabyte (1 petabyte = 10^{15} bytes) of data.

The various storage media can be organized in a hierarchy (Figure 11.1) according to their speed and their cost. The higher levels are expensive, but are fast. As we move down the hierarchy, the cost per bit decreases, whereas the access time increases. This trade-off is reasonable; if a given storage system were both faster and less expensive than another—other properties being the same—then there would be no reason to use the slower, more expensive memory. In fact, many early storage devices, including paper tape and core memories, are relegated to museums now that magnetic tape and semiconductor memory have become faster and cheaper. Magnetic tapes themselves were used to store active data back when disks were expensive and had low

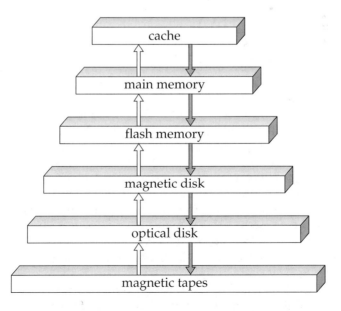

Figure 11.1   Storage-device hierarchy.

storage capacity. Today, almost all active data are stored on disks, except in rare cases where they are stored on tape or in optical jukeboxes.

The fastest storage media—for example, cache and main memory—are referred to as **primary storage**. The media in the next level in the hierarchy—for example, magnetic disks—are referred to as **secondary storage**, or **online storage**. The media in the lowest level in the hierarchy—for example, magnetic tape and optical-disk jukeboxes—are referred to as **tertiary storage**, or **offline storage**.

In addition to the speed and cost of the various storage systems, there is also the issue of storage volatility. **Volatile storage** loses its contents when the power to the device is removed. In the hierarchy shown in Figure 11.1, the storage systems from main memory up are volatile, whereas the storage systems below main memory are nonvolatile. In the absence of expensive battery and generator backup systems, data must be written to **nonvolatile storage** for safekeeping. We shall return to this subject in Chapter 17.

11.2 Magnetic Disks

Magnetic disks provide the bulk of secondary storage for modern computer systems. Disk capacities have been growing at over 50 percent per year, but the storage requirements of large applications have also been growing very fast, in some cases even faster than the growth rate of disk capacities. A large database may require hundreds of disks.

11.2.1 Physical Characteristics of Disks

Physically, disks are relatively simple (Figure 11.2). Each disk **platter** has a flat circular shape. Its two surfaces are covered with a magnetic material, and information is recorded on the surfaces. Platters are made from rigid metal or glass and are covered (usually on both sides) with magnetic recording material. We call such magnetic disks **hard disks**, to distinguish them from **floppy disks**, which are made from flexible material.

When the disk is in use, a drive motor spins it at a constant high speed (usually 60, 90, or 120 revolutions per second, but disks running at 250 revolutions per second are available). There is a read–write head positioned just above the surface of the platter. The disk surface is logically divided into **tracks**, which are subdivided into **sectors**. A **sector** is the smallest unit of information that can be read from or written to the disk. In currently available disks, sector sizes are typically 512 bytes; there are over 16,000 tracks on each platter, and 2 to 4 platters per disk. The inner tracks (closer to the spindle) are of smaller length, and in current-generation disks, the outer tracks contain more sectors than the inner tracks; typical numbers are around 200 sectors per track in the inner tracks, and around 400 sectors per track in the outer tracks. The numbers above vary among different models; higher-capacity models usually have more sectors per track and more tracks on each platter.

The **read–write head** stores information on a sector magnetically as reversals of the direction of magnetization of the magnetic material. There may be hundreds of concentric tracks on a disk surface, containing thousands of sectors.

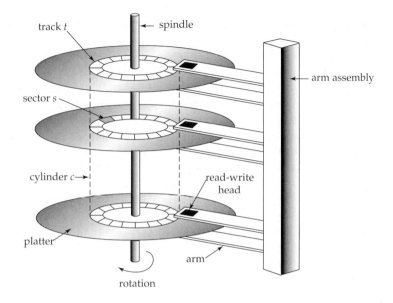

Figure 11.2   Moving-head disk mechanism.

Each side of a platter of a disk has a read–write head, which moves across the platter to access different tracks. A disk typically contains many platters, and the read–write heads of all the tracks are mounted on a single assembly called a **disk arm**, and move together. The disk platters mounted on a spindle and the heads mounted on a disk arm are together known as **head–disk assemblies**. Since the heads on all the platters move together, when the head on one platter is on the ith track, the heads on all other platters are also on the ith track of their respective platters. Hence, the ith tracks of all the platters together are called the ith **cylinder**.

Today, disks with a platter diameter of $3\frac{1}{2}$ inches dominate the market. They have a lower cost and faster seek times (due to smaller seek distances) than do the larger-diameter disks (up to 14 inches) that were common earlier, yet they provide high storage capacity. Smaller-diameter disks are used in portable devices such as laptop computers.

The read–write heads are kept as close as possible to the disk surface to increase the recording density. The head typically floats or flies only microns from the disk surface; the spinning of the disk creates a small breeze, and the head assembly is shaped so that the breeze keeps the head floating just above the disk surface. Because the head floats so close to the surface, platters must be machined carefully to be flat. Head crashes can be a problem. If the head contacts the disk surface, the head can scrape the recording medium off the disk, destroying the data that had been there. Usually, the head touching the surface causes the removed medium to become air-borne and to come between the other heads and their platters, causing more crashes. Under normal circumstances, a head crash results in failure of the entire disk, which must then be replaced. Current-generation disk drives use a thin film of magnetic metal as recording medium. They are much less susceptible to failure by head crashes than the older oxide-coated disks.

A *fixed-head disk* has a separate head for each track. This arrangement allows the computer to switch from track to track quickly, without having to move the head assembly, but because of the large number of heads, the device is extremely expensive. Some disk systems have multiple disk arms, allowing more than one track on the same platter to be accessed at a time. Fixed-head disks and multiple-arm disks were used in high-performance mainframe systems, but are no longer in production.

A **disk controller** interfaces between the computer system and the actual hardware of the disk drive. It accepts high-level commands to read or write a sector, and initiates actions, such as moving the disk arm to the right track and actually reading or writing the data. Disk controllers also attach **checksums** to each sector that is written; the checksum is computed from the data written to the sector. When the sector is read back, the controller computes the checksum again from the retrieved data and compares it with the stored checksum; if the data are corrupted, with a high probability the newly computed checksum will not match the stored checksum. If such an error occurs, the controller will retry the read several times; if the error continues to occur, the controller will signal a read failure.

Another interesting task that disk controllers perform is **remapping of bad sectors**. If the controller detects that a sector is damaged when the disk is initially formatted, or when an attempt is made to write the sector, it can logically map the sector to a different physical location (allocated from a pool of extra sectors set aside for this purpose). The remapping is noted on disk or in nonvolatile memory, and the write is carried out on the new location.

Figure 11.3 shows how disks are connected to a computer system. Like other storage units, disks are connected to a computer system or to a controller through a high-speed interconnection. In modern disk systems, lower-level functions of the disk controller, such as control of the disk arm, computing and verification of checksums, and remapping of bad sectors, are implemented within the disk drive unit.

The **AT attachment** (**ATA**) interface (which is a faster version of the **integrated drive electronics** (IDE) interface used earlier in IBM PCs) and a **small-computer-system interconnect** (SCSI; pronounced "scuzzy") are commonly used to connect

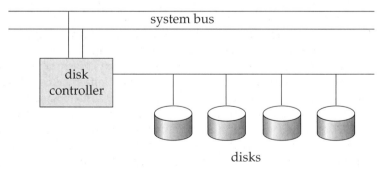

Figure 11.3 Disk subsystem.

disks to personal computers and workstations. Mainframe and server systems usually have a faster and more expensive interface, such as high-capacity versions of the SCSI interface, and the Fibre Channel interface.

While disks are usually connected directly by cables to the disk controller, they can be situated remotely and connected by a high-speed network to the disk controller. In the **storage area network** (**SAN**) architecture, large numbers of disks are connected by a high-speed network to a number of server computers. The disks are usually organized locally using **redundant arrays of independent disks** (**RAID**) storage organizations, but the RAID organization may be hidden from the server computers: the disk subsystems pretend each RAID system is a very large and very reliable disk. The controller and the disk continue to use SCSI or Fibre Channel interfaces to talk with each other, although they may be separated by a network. Remote access to disks across a storage area network means that disks can be shared by multiple computers, which could run different parts of an application in parallel. Remote access also means that disks containing important data can be kept in a central server room where they can be monitored and maintained by system administrators, instead of being scattered in different parts of an organization.

11.2.2   Performance Measures of Disks

The main measures of the qualities of a disk are capacity, access time, data-transfer rate, and reliability.

Access time is the time from when a read or write request is issued to when data transfer begins. To access (that is, to read or write) data on a given sector of a disk, the arm first must move so that it is positioned over the correct track, and then must wait for the sector to appear under it as the disk rotates. The time for repositioning the arm is called the **seek time**, and it increases with the distance that the arm must move. Typical seek times range from 2 to 30 milliseconds, depending on how far the track is from the initial arm position. Smaller disks tend to have lower seek times since the head has to travel a smaller distance.

The **average seek time** is the average of the seek times, measured over a sequence of (uniformly distributed) random requests. If all tracks have the same number of sectors, and we disregard the time required for the head to start moving and to stop moving, we can show that the average seek time is one-third the worst case seek time. Taking these factors into account, the average seek time is around one-half of the maximum seek time. Average seek times currently range between 4 milliseconds and 10 milliseconds, depending on the disk model.

Once the seek has started, the time spent waiting for the sector to be accessed to appear under the head is called the **rotational latency time**. Rotational speeds of disks today range from 5400 rotations per minute (90 rotations per second) up to 15,000 rotations per minute (250 rotations per second), or, equivalently, 4 milliseconds to 11.1 milliseconds per rotation. On an average, one-half of a rotation of the disk is required for the beginning of the desired sector to appear under the head. Thus, the **average latency time** of the disk is one-half the time for a full rotation of the disk.

The access time is then the sum of the seek time and the latency, and ranges from 8 to 20 milliseconds. Once the first sector of the data to be accessed has come under the head, data transfer begins. The **data-transfer rate** is the rate at which data can be retrieved from or stored to the disk. Current disk systems claim to support maximum transfer rates of about 25 to 40 megabytes per second, although actual transfer rates may be significantly less, at about 4 to 8 megabytes per second.

The final commonly used measure of a disk is the **mean time to failure (MTTF)**, which is a measure of the reliability of the disk. The mean time to failure of a disk (or of any other system) is the amount of time that, on average, we can expect the system to run continuously without any failure. According to vendors' claims, the mean time to failure of disks today ranges from 30,000 to 1,200,000 hours—about 3.4 to 136 years. In practice the claimed mean time to failure is computed on the probability of failure when the disk is new—the figure means that given 1000 relatively new disks, if the MTTF is 1,200,000 hours, on an average one of them will fail in 1200 hours. A mean time to failure of 1,200,000 hours does not imply that the disk can be expected to function for 136 years! Most disks have an expected life span of about 5 years, and have significantly higher rates of failure once they become more than a few years old.

There may be multiple disks sharing a disk interface. The widely used ATA-4 interface standard (also called Ultra-DMA) supports 33 megabytes per second transfer rates, while ATA-5 supports 66 megabytes per second. SCSI-3 (Ultra2 wide SCSI) supports 40 megabytes per second, while the more expensive Fibre Channel interface supports up to 256 megabytes per second. The transfer rate of the interface is shared between all disks attached to the interface.

11.2.3 Optimization of Disk-Block Access

Requests for disk I/O are generated both by the file system and by the virtual memory manager found in most operating systems. Each request specifies the address on the disk to be referenced; that address is in the form of a *block number*. A **block** is a contiguous sequence of sectors from a single track of one platter. Block sizes range from 512 bytes to several kilobytes. Data are transferred between disk and main memory in units of blocks. The lower levels of the file-system manager convert block addresses into the hardware-level cylinder, surface, and sector number.

Since access to data on disk is several orders of magnitude slower than access to data in main memory, equipment designers have focused on techniques for improving the speed of access to blocks on disk. One such technique, buffering of blocks in memory to satisfy future requests, is discussed in Section 11.5. Here, we discuss several other techniques.

- **Scheduling**. If several blocks from a cylinder need to be transferred from disk to main memory, we may be able to save access time by requesting the blocks in the order in which they will pass under the heads. If the desired blocks are on different cylinders, it is advantageous to request the blocks in an order that minimizes disk-arm movement. **Disk-arm–scheduling** algorithms attempt to order accesses to tracks in a fashion that increases the number of accesses that can be processed. A commonly used algorithm is the **elevator algorithm**, which works in the same way many elevators do. Suppose that, initially, the arm is moving from the innermost track toward the outside of the disk. Under the elevator algorithms control, for each track for which there is an access request, the arm stops at that track, services requests for the track, and then continues moving outward until there are no waiting requests for tracks farther out. At this point, the arm changes direction, and moves toward the inside, again stopping at each track for which there is a request, until it reaches a track where there is no request for tracks farther toward the center. Now, it reverses direction and starts a new cycle. Disk controllers usually perform the task of reordering read requests to improve performance, since they are intimately aware of the organization of blocks on disk, of the rotational position of the disk platters, and of the position of the disk arm.

- **File organization**. To reduce block-access time, we can organize blocks on disk in a way that corresponds closely to the way we expect data to be accessed. For example, if we expect a file to be accessed sequentially, then we should ideally keep all the blocks of the file sequentially on adjacent cylinders. Older operating systems, such as the IBM mainframe operating systems, provided programmers fine control on placement of files, allowing a programmer to reserve a set of cylinders for storing a file. However, this control places a burden on the programmer or system administrator to decide, for example, how many cylinders to allocate for a file, and may require costly reorganization if data are inserted to or deleted from the file.

  Subsequent operating systems, such as Unix and personal-computer operating systems, hide the disk organization from users, and manage the allocation internally. However, over time, a sequential file may become **fragmented**; that is, its blocks become scattered all over the disk. To reduce fragmentation, the system can make a backup copy of the data on disk and restore the entire disk. The restore operation writes back the blocks of each file contiguously (or nearly so). Some systems (such as different versions of the Windows operating system) have utilities that scan the disk and then move blocks to decrease the fragmentation. The performance increases realized from these techniques can be large, but the system is generally unusable while these utilities operate.

- **Nonvolatile write buffers**. Since the contents of main memory are lost in a power failure, information about database updates has to be recorded on disk to survive possible system crashes. For this reason, the performance of update-intensive database applications, such as transaction-processing systems, is heavily dependent on the speed of disk writes.

  We can use **nonvolatile random-access memory** (NV-RAM) to speed up disk writes drastically. The contents of nonvolatile RAM are not lost in power failure. A common way to implement nonvolatile RAM is to use battery–backed-up RAM. The idea is that, when the database system (or the operating system) requests that a block be written to disk, the disk controller writes the block to a nonvolatile RAM buffer, and immediately notifies the operating system that the write completed successfully. The controller writes the data to their destination on disk whenever the disk does not have any other requests, or when the nonvolatile RAM buffer becomes full. When the database system requests a block write, it notices a delay only if the nonvolatile RAM buffer is full. On recovery from a system crash, any pending buffered writes in the nonvolatile RAM are written back to the disk.

An example illustrates how much nonvolatile RAM improves performance. Assume that write requests are received in a random fashion, with the disk being busy on average 90 percent of the time.[1] If we have a nonvolatile RAM buffer of 50 blocks, then, on average, only once per minute will a write find the buffer to be full (and therefore have to wait for a disk write to finish). Doubling the buffer to 100 blocks results in approximately only one write per hour finding the buffer to be full. Thus, in most cases, disk writes can be executed without the database system waiting for a seek or rotational latency.

- **Log disk**. Another approach to reducing write latencies is to use a log disk—that is, a disk devoted to writing a sequential log—in much the same way as a nonvolatile RAM buffer. All access to the log disk is sequential, essentially eliminating seek time, and several consecutive blocks can be written at once, making writes to the log disk several times faster than random writes. As before, the data have to be written to their actual location on disk as well, but the log disk can do the write later, without the database system having to wait for the write to complete. Furthermore, the log disk can reorder the writes to minimize disk arm movement. If the system crashes before some writes to the actual disk location have completed, when the system comes back up it reads the log disk to find those writes that had not been completed, and carries them out then.

  File systems that support log disks as above are called **journaling file systems**. Journaling file systems can be implemented even without a separate log disk, keeping data and the log on the same disk. Doing so reduces the monetary cost, at the expense of lower performance.

  The **log-based file system** is an extreme version of the log-disk approach. Data are not written back to their original destination on disk; instead, the file system keeps track of where in the log disk the blocks were written most recently, and retrieves them from that location. The log disk itself is compacted periodically, so that old writes that have subsequently been overwritten can be removed. This approach improves write performance, but generates a high degree of fragmentation for files that are updated often. As we noted earlier, such fragmentation increases seek time for sequential reading of files.

11.3   RAID

The data storage requirements of some applications (in particular Web, database, and multimedia data applications) have been growing so fast that a large number of disks are needed to store data for such applications, even though disk drive capacities have been growing very fast.

---

1.   For the statistically inclined reader, we assume Poisson distribution of arrivals. The exact arrival rate and rate of service are not needed since the disk utilization provides enough information for our calculations.

Having a large number of disks in a system presents opportunities for improving the rate at which data can be read or written, if the disks are operated in parallel. Parallelism can also be used to perform several independent reads or writes in parallel. Furthermore, this setup offers the potential for improving the reliability of data storage, because redundant information can be stored on multiple disks. Thus, failure of one disk does not lead to loss of data.

A variety of disk-organization techniques, collectively called **redundant arrays of independent disks (RAID)**, have been proposed to achieve improved performance and reliability.

In the past, system designers viewed storage systems composed of several small cheap disks as a cost-effective alternative to using large, expensive disks; the cost per megabyte of the smaller disks was less than that of larger disks. In fact, the I in RAID, which now stands for *independent*, originally stood for *inexpensive*. Today, however, all disks are physically small, and larger-capacity disks actually have a lower cost per megabyte. RAID systems are used for their higher reliability and higher performance rate, rather than for economic reasons.

11.3.1 Improvement of Reliability via Redundancy

Let us first consider reliability. The chance that some disk out of a set of N disks will fail is much higher than the chance that a specific single disk will fail. Suppose that the mean time to failure of a disk is 100,000 hours, or slightly over 11 years. Then, the mean time to failure of some disk in an array of 100 disks will be 100,000 / 100 = 1000 hours, or around 42 days, which is not long at all! If we store only one copy of the data, then each disk failure will result in loss of a significant amount of data (as discussed in Section 11.2.1). Such a high rate of data loss is unacceptable.

The solution to the problem of reliability is to introduce **redundancy**; that is, we store extra information that is not needed normally, but that can be used in the event of failure of a disk to rebuild the lost information. Thus, even if a disk fails, data are not lost, so the effective mean time to failure is increased, provided that we count only failures that lead to loss of data or to nonavailability of data.

The simplest (but most expensive) approach to introducing redundancy is to duplicate every disk. This technique is called **mirroring** (or, sometimes, *shadowing*). A logical disk then consists of two physical disks, and every write is carried out on both disks. If one of the disks fails, the data can be read from the other. Data will be lost only if the second disk fails before the first failed disk is repaired.

The mean time to failure (where failure is the loss of data) of a mirrored disk depends on the mean time to failure of the individual disks, as well as on the **mean time to repair**, which is the time it takes (on an average) to replace a failed disk and to restore the data on it. Suppose that the failures of the two disks are *independent*; that is, there is no connection between the failure of one disk and the failure of the other. Then, if the mean time to failure of a single disk is 100,000 hours, and the mean time to repair is 10 hours, then the **mean time to data loss** of a mirrored disk system is $100000^2/(2 * 10) = 500 * 10^6$ hours, or 57,000 years! (We do not go into the derivations here; references in the bibliographical notes provide the details.)

You should be aware that the assumption of independence of disk failures is not valid. Power failures, and natural disasters such as earthquakes, fires, and floods, may result in damage to both disks at the same time. As disks age, the probability of failure increases, increasing the chance that a second disk will fail while the first is being repaired. In spite of all these considerations, however, mirrored-disk systems offer much higher reliability than do single-disk systems. Mirrored-disk systems with mean time to data loss of about 500,000 to 1,000,000 hours, or 55 to 110 years, are available today.

Power failures are a particular source of concern, since they occur far more frequently than do natural disasters. Power failures are not a concern if there is no data transfer to disk in progress when they occur. However, even with mirroring of disks, if writes are in progress to the same block in both disks, and power fails before both blocks are fully written, the two blocks can be in an inconsistent state. The solution to this problem is to write one copy first, then the next, so that one of the two copies is always consistent. Some extra actions are required when we restart after a power failure, to recover from incomplete writes. This matter is examined in Exercise 11.4.

11.3.2 Improvement in Performance via Parallelism

Now let us consider the benefit of parallel access to multiple disks. With disk mirroring, the rate at which read requests can be handled is doubled, since read requests can be sent to either disk (as long as both disks in a pair are functional, as is almost always the case). The transfer rate of each read is the same as in a single-disk system, but the number of reads per unit time has doubled.

With multiple disks, we can improve the transfer rate as well (or instead) by **striping data** across multiple disks. In its simplest form, data striping consists of splitting the bits of each byte across multiple disks; such striping is called **bit-level striping**. For example, if we have an array of eight disks, we write bit i of each byte to disk i. The array of eight disks can be treated as a single disk with sectors that are eight times the normal size, and, more important, that has eight times the transfer rate. In such an organization, every disk participates in every access (read or write), so the number of accesses that can be processed per second is about the same as on a single disk, but each access can read eight times as many data in the same time as on a single disk. Bit-level striping can be generalized to a number of disks that either is a multiple of 8 or a factor of 8. For example, if we use an array of four disks, bits i and $4 + i$ of each byte go to disk i.

Block-level striping stripes blocks across multiple disks. It treats the array of disks as a single large disk, and it gives blocks logical numbers; we assume the block numbers start from 0. With an array of n disks, block-level striping assigns logical block i of the disk array to disk $(i \bmod n) + 1$; it uses the $\lfloor i/n \rfloor$th physical block of the disk to store logical block i. For example, with 8 disks, logical block 0 is stored in physical block 0 of disk 1, while logical block 11 is stored in physical block 1 of disk 4. When reading a large file, block-level striping fetches n blocks at a time in parallel from the n disks, giving a high data transfer rate for large reads. When a single block is read, the data transfer rate is the same as on one disk, but the remaining $n - 1$ disks are free to perform other actions.

Block level striping is the most commonly used form of data striping. Other levels of striping, such as bytes of a sector or sectors of a block also are possible.

In summary, there are two main goals of parallelism in a disk system:

1. Load-balance multiple small accesses (block accesses), so that the throughput of such accesses increases.

2. Parallelize large accesses so that the response time of large accesses is reduced.

11.3.3   RAID Levels

Mirroring provides high reliability, but it is expensive. Striping provides high data-transfer rates, but does not improve reliability. Various alternative schemes aim to provide redundancy at lower cost by combining disk striping with "parity" bits (which we describe next). These schemes have different cost–performance trade-offs. The schemes are classified into **RAID levels**, as in Figure 11.4. (In the figure, P indicates error-correcting bits, and C indicates a second copy of the data.) For all levels, the figure depicts four disk's worth of data, and the extra disks depicted are used to store redundant information for failure recovery.

- **RAID level 0** refers to disk arrays with striping at the level of blocks, but without any redundancy (such as mirroring or parity bits). Figure 11.4a shows an array of size 4.

- **RAID level 1** refers to disk mirroring with block striping. Figure 11.4b shows a mirrored organization that holds four disks worth of data.

- **RAID level 2**, known as memory-style error-correcting-code (ECC) organization, employs parity bits. Memory systems have long used parity bits for error detection and correction. Each byte in a memory system may have a parity bit associated with it that records whether the numbers of bits in the byte that are set to 1 is even (parity = 0) or odd (parity = 1). If one of the bits in the byte gets damaged (either a 1 becomes a 0, or a 0 becomes a 1), the parity of the byte changes and thus will not match the stored parity. Similarly, if the stored parity bit gets damaged, it will not match the computed parity. Thus, all 1-bit errors will be detected by the memory system. Error-correcting schemes store 2 or more extra bits, and can reconstruct the data if a single bit gets damaged.

  The idea of error-correcting codes can be used directly in disk arrays by striping bytes across disks. For example, the first bit of each byte could be stored in disk 1, the second bit in disk 2, and so on until the eighth bit is stored in disk 8, and the error-correction bits are stored in further disks.

  Figure 11.4c shows the level 2 scheme. The disks labeled P store the error-correction bits. If one of the disks fails, the remaining bits of the byte and the associated error-correction bits can be read from other disks, and can be used to reconstruct the damaged data. Figure 11.4c shows an array of size 4; note RAID level 2 requires only three disks' overhead for four disks of data, unlike RAID level 1, which required four disks' overhead.

(a) RAID 0: nonredundant striping

(b) RAID 1: mirrored disks

(c) RAID 2: memory-style error-correcting codes

(d) RAID 3: bit-interleaved parity

(e) RAID 4: block-interleaved parity

(f) RAID 5: block-interleaved distributed parity

(g) RAID 6: P + Q redundancy

Figure 11.4   RAID levels.

- **RAID level 3**, bit-interleaved parity organization, improves on level 2 by exploiting the fact that disk controllers, unlike memory systems, can detect whether a sector has been read correctly, so a single parity bit can be used for error correction, as well as for detection. The idea is as follows. If one of the sectors gets damaged, the system knows exactly which sector it is, and, for each bit in the sector, the system can figure out whether it is a 1 or a 0 by computing the parity of the corresponding bits from sectors in the other disks. If the parity of the remaining bits is equal to the stored parity, the missing bit is 0; otherwise, it is 1.

RAID level 3 is as good as level 2, but is less expensive in the number of extra disks (it has only a one-disk overhead), so level 2 is not used in practice. Figure 11.4d shows the level 3 scheme.

RAID level 3 has two benefits over level 1. It needs only one parity disk for several regular disks, whereas Level 1 needs one mirror disk for every disk, and thus reduces the storage overhead. Since reads and writes of a byte are spread out over multiple disks, with N-way striping of data, the transfer rate for reading or writing a single block is N times faster than a RAID level 1 organization using N-way striping. On the other hand, RAID level 3 supports a lower number of I/O operations per second, since every disk has to participate in every I/O request.

- **RAID level 4**, block-interleaved parity organization, uses block level striping, like RAID 0, and in addition keeps a parity block on a separate disk for corresponding blocks from N other disks. This scheme is shown pictorially in Figure 11.4e. If one of the disks fails, the parity block can be used with the corresponding blocks from the other disks to restore the blocks of the failed disk.

  A block read accesses only one disk, allowing other requests to be processed by the other disks. Thus, the data-transfer rate for each access is slower, but multiple read accesses can proceed in parallel, leading to a higher overall I/O rate. The transfer rates for large reads is high, since all the disks can be read in parallel; large writes also have high transfer rates, since the data and parity can be written in parallel.

  Small independent writes, on the other hand, cannot be performed in parallel. A write of a block has to access the disk on which the block is stored, as well as the parity disk, since the parity block has to be updated. Moreover, both the old value of the parity block and the old value of the block being written have to be read for the new parity to be computed. Thus, a single write requires four disk accesses: two to read the two old blocks, and two to write the two blocks.

- **RAID level 5**, block-interleaved distributed parity, improves on level 4 by partitioning data and parity among all $N + 1$ disks, instead of storing data in N disks and parity in one disk. In level 5, all disks can participate in satisfying read requests, unlike RAID level 4, where the parity disk cannot participate, so level 5 increases the total number of requests that can be met in a given amount of time. For each set of N logical blocks, one of the disks stores the parity, and the other N disks store the blocks.

  Figure 11.4f shows the setup. The P's are distributed across all the disks. For example, with an array of 5 disks, the parity block, labelled Pk, for logical blocks $4k, 4k + 1, 4k + 2, 4k + 3$ is stored in disk $(k \bmod 5) + 1$; the corresponding blocks of the other four disks store the 4 data blocks $4k$ to $4k + 3$. The following table indicates how the first 20 blocks, numbered 0 to 19, and their parity blocks are laid out. The pattern shown gets repeated on further blocks.

P0	0	1	2	3
4	P1	5	6	7
8	9	P2	10	11
12	13	14	P3	15
16	17	18	19	P4

Note that a parity block cannot store parity for blocks in the same disk, since then a disk failure would result in loss of data as well as of parity, and hence would not be recoverable. Level 5 subsumes level 4, since it offers better read–write performance at the same cost, so level 4 is not used in practice.

- **RAID level 6**, the P + Q redundancy scheme, is much like RAID level 5, but stores extra redundant information to guard against multiple disk failures. Instead of using parity, level 6 uses error-correcting codes such as the Reed–Solomon codes (see the bibliographical notes). In the scheme in Figure 11.4g, 2 bits of redundant data are stored for every 4 bits of data—unlike 1 parity bit in level 5—and the system can tolerate two disk failures.

Finally, we note that several variations have been proposed to the basic RAID schemes described here.

Some vendors use their own terminology to describe their RAID implementations.[2] However, the terminology we have presented is the most widely used.

11.3.4 Choice of RAID Level

The factors to be taken into account when choosing a RAID level are

- Monetary cost of extra disk storage requirements

- Performance requirements in terms of number of I/O operations

- Performance when a disk has failed

- Performance during rebuild (that is, while the data in a failed disk is being rebuilt on a new disk)

The time to rebuild the data of a failed disk can be significant, and varies with the RAID level that is used. Rebuilding is easiest for RAID level 1, since data can be copied from another disk; for the other levels, we need to access all the other disks in the array to rebuild data of a failed disk. The **rebuild performance** of a RAID system may be an important factor if continuous availability of data is required, as it is in high-performance database systems. Furthermore, since rebuild time can form a significant part of the repair time, rebuild performance also influences the mean time to data loss.

---

2. For example, some products use RAID level 1 to refer to mirroring without striping, and level 1+0 or level 10 to refer to mirroring with striping. Such a distinction is not really necessary since not striping can simply be viewed as a special case of striping, namely striping across 1 disk.

RAID level 0 is used in high-performance applications where data safety is not critical. Since RAID levels 2 and 4 are subsumed by RAID levels 3 and 5, the choice of RAID levels is restricted to the remaining levels. Bit striping (level 3) is rarely used since block striping (level 5) gives as good data transfer rates for large transfers, while using fewer disks for small transfers. For small transfers, the disk access time dominates anyway, so the benefit of parallel reads diminishes. In fact, level 3 may perform worse than level 5 for a small transfer, since the transfer completes only when corresponding sectors on all disks have been fetched; the average latency for the disk array thus becomes very close to the worst-case latency for a single disk, negating the benefits of higher transfer rates. Level 6 is not supported currently by many RAID implementations, but it offers better reliability than level 5 and can be used in applications where data safety is very important.

The choice between RAID level 1 and level 5 is harder to make. RAID level 1 is popular for applications such as storage of log files in a database system, since it offers the best write performance. RAID level 5 has a lower storage overhead than level 1, but has a higher time overhead for writes. For applications where data are read frequently, and written rarely, level 5 is the preferred choice.

Disk storage capacities have been growing at a rate of over 50 percent per year for many years, and the cost per byte has been falling at the same rate. As a result, for many existing database applications with moderate storage requirements, the monetary cost of the extra disk storage needed for mirroring has become relatively small (the extra monetary cost, however, remains a significant issue for storage-intensive applications such as video data storage). Access speeds have improved at a much slower rate (around a factor of 3 over 10 years), while the number of I/O operations required per second has increased tremendously, particularly for Web application servers.

RAID level 5, which increases the number of I/O operations needed to write a single logical block, pays a significant time penalty in terms of write performance. RAID level 1 is therefore the RAID level of choice for many applications with moderate storage requirements, and high I/O requirements.

RAID system designers have to make several other decisions as well. For example, how many disks should there be in an array? How many bits should be protected by each parity bit? If there are more disks in an array, data-transfer rates are higher, but the system would be more expensive. If there are more bits protected by a parity bit, the space overhead due to parity bits is lower, but there is an increased chance that a second disk will fail before the first failed disk is repaired, and that will result in data loss.

11.3.5 Hardware Issues

Another issue in the choice of RAID implementations is at the level of hardware. RAID can be implemented with no change at the hardware level, using only software modification. Such RAID implementations are called **software RAID**. However, there are significant benefits to be had by building special-purpose hardware to support RAID, which we outline below; systems with special hardware support are called **hardware RAID** systems.

Hardware RAID implementations can use nonvolatile RAM to record writes that need to be executed; in case of power failure before a write is completed, when the system comes back up, it retrieves information about incomplete writes from non-volatile RAM and then completes the writes. Without such hardware support, extra work needs to be done to detect blocks that may have been partially written before power failure (see Exercise 11.4).

Some hardware RAID implementations permit **hot swapping**; that is, faulty disks can be removed and replaced by new ones without turning power off. Hot swapping reduces the mean time to repair, since replacement of a disk does not have to wait until a time when the system can be shut down. In fact many critical systems today run on a 24 × 7 schedule; that is, they run 24 hours a day, 7 days a week, providing no time for shutting down and replacing a failed disk. Further, many RAID imple-mentations assign a spare disk for each array (or for a set of disk arrays). If a disk fails, the spare disk is immediately used as a replacement. As a result, the mean time to repair is reduced greatly, minimizing the chance of any data loss. The failed disk can be replaced at leisure.

The power supply, or the disk controller, or even the system interconnection in a RAID system could become a single point of failure, that could stop functioning of the RAID system. To avoid this possibility, good RAID implementations have multiple redundant power supplies (with battery backups so they continue to function even if power fails). Such RAID systems have multiple disk controllers, and multiple in-terconnections to connect them to the computer system (or to a network of computer systems). Thus, failure of any single component will not stop the functioning of the RAID system.

11.3.6   Other RAID Applications

The concepts of RAID have been generalized to other storage devices, including ar-rays of tapes, and even to the broadcast of data over wireless systems. When applied to arrays of tapes, the RAID structures are able to recover data even if one of the tapes in an array of tapes is damaged. When applied to broadcast of data, a block of data is split into short units and is broadcast along with a parity unit; if one of the units is not received for any reason, it can be reconstructed from the other units.

11.4   Tertiary Storage

In a large database system, some of the data may have to reside on tertiary storage. The two most common tertiary storage media are optical disks and magnetic tapes.

11.4.1   Optical Disks

Compact disks are a popular medium for distributing software, multimedia data such as audio and images, and other electronically published information. They have a fairly large capacity (640 megabytes), and they are cheap to mass-produce.

Digital video disks (DVDs) are replacing compact disks in applications that require very large amounts of data. Disks in the DVD-5 format can store 4.7 gigabytes of data (in one recording layer), while disks in the DVD-9 format can store 8.5 gigabytes of data (in two recording layers). Recording on both sides of a disk yields even larger capacities; DVD-10 and DVD-18 formats, which are the two-sided versions of DVD-5 and DVD-9, can store 9.4 gigabytes and 17 gigabytes respectively.

CD and DVD drives have much longer seek times (100 milliseconds is common) than do magnetic-disk drives, since the head assembly is heavier. Rotational speeds are typically lower than those of magnetic disks, although the faster CD and DVD drives have rotation speeds of about 3000 rotations per minute, which is comparable to speeds of lower-end magnetic-disk drives. Rotational speeds of CD drives originally corresponded to the audio CD standards, and the speeds of DVD drives originally corresponded to the DVD video standards, but current-generation drives rotate at many times the standard rate.

Data transfer rates are somewhat less than for magnetic disks. Current CD drives read at around 3 to 6 megabytes per second, and current DVD drives read at 8 to 15 megabytes per second. Like magnetic disk drives, optical disks store more data in outside tracks and less data in inner tracks. The transfer rate of optical drives is characterized as $n\times$, which means the drive supports transfers at n times the standard rate; rates of around $50\times$ for CD and $12\times$ for DVD are now common.

The record-once versions of optical disks (CD-R, and increasingly, DVD-R) are popular for distribution of data and particularly for archival storage of data because they have a high capacity, have a longer lifetime than magnetic disks, and can be removed and stored at a remote location. Since they cannot be overwritten, they can be used to store information that should not be modified, such as audit trails. The multiple-write versions (CD-RW, DVD-RW, and DVD-RAM) are also used for archival purposes.

Jukeboxes are devices that store a large number of optical disks (up to several hundred) and load them automatically on demand to one of a small number (usually, 1 to 10) of drives. The aggregate storage capacity of such a system can be many terabytes. When a disk is accessed, it is loaded by a mechanical arm from a rack onto a drive (any disk that was already in the drive must first be placed back on the rack). The disk load/unload time is usually of the order of a few seconds—very much slower than disk access times.

11.4.2 Magnetic Tapes

Although magnetic tapes are relatively permanent, and can hold large volumes of data, they are slow in comparison to magnetic and optical disks. Even more important, magnetic tapes are limited to sequential access. Thus, they cannot provide random access for secondary-storage requirements, although historically, prior to the use of magnetic disks, tapes were used as a secondary-storage medium.

Tapes are used mainly for backup, for storage of infrequently used information, and as an offline medium for transferring information from one system to another. Tapes are also used for storing large volumes of data, such as video or image data, that either do not need to be accessible quickly or are so voluminous that magnetic-disk storage would be too expensive.

A tape is kept in a spool, and is wound or rewound past a read–write head. Moving to the correct spot on a tape can take seconds or even minutes, rather than milliseconds; once positioned, however, tape drives can write data at densities and speeds approaching those of disk drives. Capacities vary, depending on the length and width of the tape and on the density at which the head can read and write. The market is currently fragmented among a wide variety of tape formats. Currently available tape capacities range from a few gigabytes [with the **Digital Audio Tape** (DAT) format], 10 to 40 gigabytes [with the **Digital Linear Tape** (DLT) format], 100 gigabytes and higher (with the **Ultrium** format), to 330 gigabytes (with **Ampex helical scan** tape formats). Data transfer rates are of the order of a few to tens of megabytes per second.

Tape devices are quite reliable, and good tape drive systems perform a read of the just-written data to ensure that it has been recorded correctly. Tapes, however, have limits on the number of times that they can be read or written reliably.

Some tape formats (such as the **Accelis** format) support faster seek times (of the order of tens of seconds), which is important for applications that need quick access to very large amounts of data, larger than what would fit economically on a disk drive. Most other tape formats provide larger capacities, at the cost of slower access; such formats are ideal for data backup, where fast seeks are not important.

Tape jukeboxes, like optical disk jukeboxes, hold large numbers of tapes, with a few drives onto which the tapes can be mounted; they are used for storing large volumes of data, ranging up to many terabytes (10^{12} bytes), with access times on the order of seconds to a few minutes. Applications that need such enormous data storage include imaging systems that gather data by remote-sensing satellites, and large video libraries for television broadcasters.

11.5 Storage Access

A database is mapped into a number of different files, which are maintained by the underlying operating system. These files reside permanently on disks, with backups on tapes. Each file is partitioned into fixed-length storage units called **blocks**, which are the units of both storage allocation and data transfer. We shall discuss in Section 11.6 various ways to organize the data logically in files.

A block may contain several data items. The exact set of data items that a block contains is determined by the form of physical data organization being used (see Section 11.6). We shall assume that no data item spans two or more blocks. This assumption is realistic for most data-processing applications, such as our banking example.

A major goal of the database system is to minimize the number of block transfers between the disk and memory. One way to reduce the number of disk accesses is to keep as many blocks as possible in main memory. The goal is to maximize the chance that, when a block is accessed, it is already in main memory, and, thus, no disk access is required.

Since it is not possible to keep all blocks in main memory, we need to manage the allocation of the space available in main memory for the storage of blocks. The **buffer** is that part of main memory available for storage of copies of disk blocks. There is always a copy kept on disk of every block, but the copy on disk may be a version of the block older than the version in the buffer. The subsystem responsible for the allocation of buffer space is called the **buffer manager**.

11.5.1 Buffer Manager

Programs in a database system make requests (that is, calls) on the buffer manager when they need a block from disk. If the block is already in the buffer, the buffer manager passes the address of the block in main memory to the requester. If the block is not in the buffer, the buffer manager first allocates space in the buffer for the block, throwing out some other block, if necessary, to make space for the new block. The thrown-out block is written back to disk only if it has been modified since the most recent time that it was written to the disk. Then, the buffer manager reads in the requested block from the disk to the buffer, and passes the address of the block in main memory to the requester. The internal actions of the buffer manager are transparent to the programs that issue disk-block requests.

If you are familiar with operating-system concepts, you will note that the buffer manager appears to be nothing more than a virtual-memory manager, like those found in most operating systems. One difference is that the size of the database may be much more than the hardware address space of a machine, so memory addresses are not sufficient to address all disk blocks. Further, to serve the database system well, the buffer manager must use techniques more sophisticated than typical virtual-memory management schemes:

- **Buffer replacement strategy**. When there is no room left in the buffer, a block must be removed from the buffer before a new one can be read in. Most operating systems use a **least recently used (LRU)** scheme, in which the block that was referenced least recently is written back to disk and is removed from the buffer. This simple approach can be improved on for database applications.

- **Pinned blocks**. For the database system to be able to recover from crashes (Chapter 17), it is necessary to restrict those times when a block may be written back to disk. For instance, most recovery systems require that a block should not be written to disk while an update on the block is in progress. A block that is not allowed to be written back to disk is said to be **pinned**. Although many operating systems do not support pinned blocks, such a feature is essential for a database system that is resilient to crashes.

- **Forced output of blocks**. There are situations in which it is necessary to write back the block to disk, even though the buffer space that it occupies is not needed. This write is called the **forced output** of a block. We shall see the reason for forced output in Chapter 17; briefly, main-memory contents and thus buffer contents are lost in a crash, whereas data on disk usually survive a crash.

11.5.2 Buffer-Replacement Policies

The goal of a replacement strategy for blocks in the buffer is to minimize accesses to the disk. For general-purpose programs, it is not possible to predict accurately

```
for each tuple b of borrower do
    for each tuple c of customer do
        if b[customer-name] = c[customer-name]
        then begin
                let x be a tuple defined as follows:
                x[customer-name] := b[customer-name]
                x[loan-number] := b[loan-number]
                x[customer-street] := c[customer-street]
                x[customer-city] := c[customer-city]
                include tuple x as part of result of borrower ⋈ customer
            end
    end
end
```

Figure 11.5   Procedure for computing join.

which blocks will be referenced. Therefore, operating systems use the past pattern of block references as a predictor of future references. The assumption generally made is that blocks that have been referenced recently are likely to be referenced again. Therefore, if a block must be replaced, the least recently referenced block is replaced. This approach is called the **least recently used** (**LRU**) block-replacement scheme.

LRU is an acceptable replacement scheme in operating systems. However, a database system is able to predict the pattern of future references more accurately than an operating system. A user request to the database system involves several steps. The database system is often able to determine in advance which blocks will be needed by looking at each of the steps required to perform the user-requested operation. Thus, unlike operating systems, which must rely on the past to predict the future, database systems may have information regarding at least the short-term future.

To illustrate how information about future block access allows us to improve the LRU strategy, consider the processing of the relational-algebra expression

$$borrower \bowtie customer$$

Assume that the strategy chosen to process this request is given by the pseudocode program shown in Figure 11.5. (We shall study other strategies in Chapter 13.)

Assume that the two relations of this example are stored in separate files. In this example, we can see that, once a tuple of *borrower* has been processed, that tuple is not needed again. Therefore, once processing of an entire block of *borrower* tuples is completed, that block is no longer needed in main memory, even though it has been used recently. The buffer manager should be instructed to free the space occupied by a *borrower* block as soon as the final tuple has been processed. This buffer-management strategy is called the **toss-immediate** strategy.

Now consider blocks containing *customer* tuples. We need to examine every block of *customer* tuples once for each tuple of the *borrower* relation. When processing of a *customer* block is completed, we know that that block will not be accessed again until all other *customer* blocks have been processed. Thus, the most recently used *customer* block will be the final block to be re-referenced, and the least recently used *customer* block is the block that will be referenced next. This assumption set is the exact opposite of the one that forms the basis for the LRU strategy. Indeed, the optimal strategy for block replacement is the **most recently used (MRU)** strategy. If a *customer* block must be removed from the buffer, the MRU strategy chooses the most recently used block.

For the MRU strategy to work correctly for our example, the system must pin the *customer* block currently being processed. After the final *customer* tuple has been processed, the block is unpinned, and it becomes the most recently used block.

In addition to using knowledge that the system may have about the request being processed, the buffer manager can use statistical information about the probability that a request will reference a particular relation. For example, the data dictionary that (as we will see in detail in Section 11.8) keeps track of the logical schema of the relations as well as their physical storage information is one of the most frequently accessed parts of the database. Thus, the buffer manager should try not to remove data-dictionary blocks from main memory, unless other factors dictate that it do so. In Chapter 12, we discuss indices for files. Since an index for a file may be accessed more frequently than the file itself, the buffer manager should, in general, not remove index blocks from main memory if alternatives are available.

The ideal database block-replacement strategy needs knowledge of the database operations—both those being performed and those that will be performed in the future. No single strategy is known that handles all the possible scenarios well. Indeed, a surprisingly large number of database systems use LRU, despite that strategy's faults. The exercises explore alternative strategies.

The strategy that the buffer manager uses for block replacement is influenced by factors other than the time at which the block will be referenced again. If the system is processing requests by several users concurrently, the concurrency-control subsystem (Chapter 16) may need to delay certain requests, to ensure preservation of database consistency. If the buffer manager is given information from the concurrency-control subsystem indicating which requests are being delayed, it can use this information to alter its block-replacement strategy. Specifically, blocks needed by active (nondelayed) requests can be retained in the buffer at the expense of blocks needed by the delayed requests.

The crash-recovery subsystem (Chapter 17) imposes stringent constraints on block replacement. If a block has been modified, the buffer manager is not allowed to write back the new version of the block in the buffer to disk, since that would destroy the old version. Instead, the block manager must seek permission from the crash-recovery subsystem before writing out a block. The crash-recovery subsystem may demand that certain other blocks be force-output before it grants permission to the buffer manager to output the block requested. In Chapter 17, we define precisely the interaction between the buffer manager and the crash-recovery subsystem.

11.6 File Organization

A **file** is organized logically as a sequence of records. These records are mapped onto disk blocks. Files are provided as a basic construct in operating systems, so we shall

record 0	A-102	Perryridge	400
record 1	A-305	Round Hill	350
record 2	A-215	Mianus	700
record 3	A-101	Downtown	500
record 4	A-222	Redwood	700
record 5	A-201	Perryridge	900
record 6	A-217	Brighton	750
record 7	A-110	Downtown	600
record 8	A-218	Perryridge	700

Figure 11.6   File containing *account* records.

assume the existence of an underlying *file system*. We need to consider ways of representing logical data models in terms of files.

Although blocks are of a fixed size determined by the physical properties of the disk and by the operating system, record sizes vary. In a relational database, tuples of distinct relations are generally of different sizes.

One approach to mapping the database to files is to use several files, and to store records of only one fixed length in any given file. An alternative is to structure our files so that we can accommodate multiple lengths for records; however, files of fixed-length records are easier to implement than are files of variable-length records. Many of the techniques used for the former can be applied to the variable-length case. Thus, we begin by considering a file of fixed-length records.

11.6.1 Fixed-Length Records

As an example, let us consider a file of *account* records for our bank database. Each record of this file is defined as:

$$\textbf{type } \textit{deposit} = \textbf{record}$$
$$\textit{account-number} : \text{char}(10);$$
$$\textit{branch-name} : \text{char }(22);$$
$$\textit{balance} : \text{real};$$
$$\textbf{end}$$

If we assume that each character occupies 1 byte and that a real occupies 8 bytes, our *account* record is 40 bytes long. A simple approach is to use the first 40 bytes for the first record, the next 40 bytes for the second record, and so on (Figure 11.6). However, there are two problems with this simple approach:

1. It is difficult to delete a record from this structure. The space occupied by the record to be deleted must be filled with some other record of the file, or we must have a way of marking deleted records so that they can be ignored.

record 0	A-102	Perryridge	400
record 1	A-305	Round Hill	350
record 3	A-101	Downtown	500
record 4	A-222	Redwood	700
record 5	A-201	Perryridge	900
record 6	A-217	Brighton	750
record 7	A-110	Downtown	600
record 8	A-218	Perryridge	700

Figure 11.7   File of Figure 11.6, with record 2 deleted and all records moved.

2. Unless the block size happens to be a multiple of 40 (which is unlikely), some records will cross block boundaries. That is, part of the record will be stored in one block and part in another. It would thus require two block accesses to read or write such a record.

When a record is deleted, we could move the record that came after it into the space formerly occupied by the deleted record, and so on, until every record following the deleted record has been moved ahead (Figure 11.7). Such an approach requires moving a large number of records. It might be easier simply to move the final record of the file into the space occupied by the deleted record (Figure 11.8).

It is undesirable to move records to occupy the space freed by a deleted record, since doing so requires additional block accesses. Since insertions tend to be more frequent than deletions, it is acceptable to leave open the space occupied by the deleted record, and to wait for a subsequent insertion before reusing the space. A simple marker on a deleted record is not sufficient, since it is hard to find this available space when an insertion is being done. Thus, we need to introduce an additional structure.

At the beginning of the file, we allocate a certain number of bytes as a **file header**. The header will contain a variety of information about the file. For now, all we need to store there is the address of the first record whose contents are deleted. We use this

record 0	A-102	Perryridge	400
record 1	A-305	Round Hill	350
record 8	A-218	Perryridge	700
record 3	A-101	Downtown	500
record 4	A-222	Redwood	700
record 5	A-201	Perryridge	900
record 6	A-217	Brighton	750
record 7	A-110	Downtown	600

Figure 11.8   File of Figure 11.6, with record 2 deleted and final record moved.

header				
record 0	A-102	Perryridge	400	
record 1				
record 2	A-215	Mianus	700	
record 3	A-101	Downtown	500	
record 4				
record 5	A-201	Perryridge	900	
record 6				
record 7	A-110	Downtown	600	
record 8	A-218	Perryridge	700	

Figure 11.9 File of Figure 11.6, with free list after deletion of records 1, 4, and 6.

first record to store the address of the second available record, and so on. Intuitively, we can think of these stored addresses as *pointers*, since they point to the location of a record. The deleted records thus form a linked list, which is often referred to as a **free list**. Figure 11.9 shows the file of Figure 11.6, with the free list, after records 1, 4, and 6 have been deleted.

On insertion of a new record, we use the record pointed to by the header. We change the header pointer to point to the next available record. If no space is available, we add the new record to the end of the file.

Insertion and deletion for files of fixed-length records are simple to implement, because the space made available by a deleted record is exactly the space needed to insert a record. If we allow records of variable length in a file, this match no longer holds. An inserted record may not fit in the space left free by a deleted record, or it may fill only part of that space.

11.6.2 Variable-Length Records

Variable-length records arise in database systems in several ways:

- Storage of multiple record types in a file

- Record types that allow variable lengths for one or more fields

- Record types that allow repeating fields

Different techniques for implementing variable-length records exist. For purposes of illustration, we shall use one example to demonstrate the various implementation techniques. We shall consider a different representation of the *account* information stored in the file of Figure 11.6, in which we use one variable-length record for each branch name and for all the account information for that branch. The format of the record is

```
type account-list = record
                      branch-name : char (22);
                      account-info : array [1 .. ∞] of
                              record;
                                account-number : char(10);
                                balance : real;
                              end
         end
```

We define *account-info* as an array with an arbitrary number of elements. That is, the type definition does not limit the number of elements in the array, although any actual record will have a specific number of elements in its array. There is no limit on how large a record can be (up to, of course, the size of the disk storage!).

11.6.2.1 Byte-String Representation

A simple method for implementing variable-length records is to attach a special *end-of-record* (⊥) symbol to the end of each record. We can then store each record as a string of consecutive bytes. Figure 11.10 shows such an organization to represent the file of fixed-length records of Figure 11.6 as variable-length records. An alternative version of the byte-string representation stores the record length at the beginning of each record, instead of using end-of-record symbols.

The byte-string representation as described in Figure 11.10 has some disadvantages:

- It is not easy to reuse space occupied formerly by a deleted record. Although techniques exist to manage insertion and deletion, they lead to a large number of small fragments of disk storage that are wasted.

- There is no space, in general, for records to grow longer. If a variable-length record becomes longer, it must be moved—movement is costly if pointers to the record are stored elsewhere in the database (e.g., in indices, or in other records), since the pointers must be located and updated.

Thus, the basic byte-string representation described here not usually used for implementing variable-length records. However, a modified form of the byte-string repre-

0	Perryridge	A-102	400	A-201	900	A-218	700	⊥
1	Round Hill	A-305	350	⊥				
2	Mianus	A-215	700	⊥				
3	Downtown	A-101	500	A-110	600	⊥		
4	Redwood	A-222	700	⊥				
5	Brighton	A-217	750	⊥				

Figure 11.10   Byte-string representation of variable-length records.

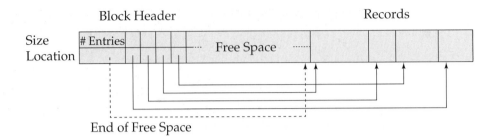

Figure 11.11 Slotted-page structure.

sentation, called the slotted-page structure, is commonly used for organizing records *within* a single block.

The **slotted-page structure** appears in Figure 11.11. There is a header at the beginning of each block, containing the following information:

1. The number of record entries in the header

2. The end of free space in the block

3. An array whose entries contain the location and size of each record

The actual records are allocated *contiguously* in the block, starting from the end of the block. The free space in the block is contiguous, between the final entry in the header array, and the first record. If a record is inserted, space is allocated for it at the end of free space, and an entry containing its size and location is added to the header.

If a record is deleted, the space that it occupies is freed, and its entry is set to deleted (its size is set to −1, for example). Further, the records in the block before the deleted record are moved, so that the free space created by the deletion gets occupied, and all free space is again between the final entry in the header array and the first record. The end-of-free-space pointer in the header is appropriately updated as well. Records can be grown or shrunk by similar techniques, as long as there is space in the block. The cost of moving the records is not too high, since the size of a block is limited: A typical value is 4 kilobytes.

The slotted-page structure requires that there be no pointers that point directly to records. Instead, pointers must point to the entry in the header that contains the actual location of the record. This level of indirection allows records to be moved to prevent fragmentation of space inside a block, while supporting indirect pointers to the record.

11.6.2.2 Fixed-Length Representation

Another way to implement variable-length records efficiently in a file system is to use one or more fixed-length records to represent one variable-length record.

There are two ways of doing this:

1. **Reserved space**. If there is a maximum record length that is never exceeded, we can use fixed-length records of that length. Unused space (for records

0	Perryridge	A-102	400	A-201	900	A-218	700
1	Round Hill	A-305	350	⊥	⊥	⊥	⊥
2	Mianus	A-215	700	⊥	⊥	⊥	⊥
3	Downtown	A-101	500	A-110	600	⊥	⊥
4	Redwood	A-222	700	⊥	⊥	⊥	⊥
5	Brighton	A-217	750	⊥	⊥	⊥	⊥

Figure 11.12   File of Figure 11.10, using the reserved-space method.

shorter than the maximum space) is filled with a special null, or end-of-record, symbol.

2. **List representation**. We can represent variable-length records by lists of fixed-length records, chained together by pointers.

If we choose to apply the reserved-space method to our account example, we need to select a maximum record length. Figure 11.12 shows how the file of Figure 11.10 would be represented if we allowed a maximum of three accounts per branch. A record in this file is of the *account-list* type, but with the array containing exactly three elements. Those branches with fewer than three accounts (for example, Round Hill) have records with null fields. We use the symbol ⊥ to represent this situation in Figure 11.12. In practice, a particular value that can never represent real data is used (for example, an account number that is blank, or a name beginning with "*").

The reserved-space method is useful when most records have a length close to the maximum. Otherwise, a significant amount of space may be wasted. In our bank example, some branches may have many more accounts than others. This situation leads us to consider the linked list method. To represent the file by the linked list method, we add a pointer field as we did in Figure 11.9. The resulting structure appears in Figure 11.13.

0	Perryridge	A-102	400	
1	Round Hill	A-305	350	
2	Mianus	A-215	700	
3	Downtown	A-101	500	
4	Redwood	A-222	700	
5		A-201	900	
6	Brighton	A-217	750	
7		A-110	600	
8		A-218	700	

Figure 11.13   File of Figure 11.10 using linked lists.

anchor block

Perryridge	A-102	400	
Round Hill	A-305	350	
Mianus	A-215	700	
Downtown	A-101	500	
Redwood	A-222	700	
Brighton	A-217	750	

overflow block

A-201	900	
A-218	700	
A-110	600	

Figure 11.14   Anchor-block and overflow-block structures.

The file structures of Figures 11.9 and 11.13 both use pointers; the difference is that, in Figure 11.9, we use pointers to chain together only deleted records, whereas in Figure 11.13, we chain together all records pertaining to the same branch.

A disadvantage to the structure of Figure 11.13 is that we waste space in all records except the first in a chain. The first record needs to have the *branch-name* value, but subsequent records do not. Nevertheless, we need to include a field for *branch-name* in all records, lest the records not be of fixed length. This wasted space is significant, since we expect, in practice, that each branch has a large number of accounts. To deal with this problem, we allow two kinds of blocks in our file:

1. **Anchor block**, which contains the first record of a chain

2. **Overflow block**, which contains records other than those that are the first record of a chain

Thus, all records *within a block* have the same length, even though not all records in the file have the same length. Figure 11.14 shows this file structure.

11.7 Organization of Records in Files

So far, we have studied how records are represented in a file structure. An instance of a relation is a set of records. Given a set of records, the next question is how to organize them in a file. Several of the possible ways of organizing records in files are:

- **Heap file organization**. Any record can be placed anywhere in the file where there is space for the record. There is no ordering of records. Typically, there is a single file for each relation

- **Sequential file organization**. Records are stored in sequential order, according to the value of a "search key" of each record. Section 11.7.1 describes this organization.

- **Hashing file organization**. A hash function is computed on some attribute of each record. The result of the hash function specifies in which block of the file the record should be placed. Chapter 12 describes this organization; it is closely related to the indexing structures described in that chapter.

Generally, a separate file is used to store the records of each relation. However, in a **clustering file organization**, records of several different relations are stored in the same file; further, related records of the different relations are stored on the same block, so that one I/O operation fetches related records from all the relations. For example, records of the two relations can be considered to be related if they would match in a join of the two relations. Section 11.7.2 describes this organization.

11.7.1   Sequential File Organization

A **sequential file** is designed for efficient processing of records in sorted order based on some search-key. A **search key** is any attribute or set of attributes; it need not be the primary key, or even a superkey. To permit fast retrieval of records in search-key order, we chain together records by pointers. The pointer in each record points to the next record in search-key order. Furthermore, to minimize the number of block accesses in sequential file processing, we store records physically in search-key order, or as close to search-key order as possible.

Figure 11.15 shows a sequential file of *account* records taken from our banking example. In that example, the records are stored in search-key order, using *branch-name* as the search key.

The sequential file organization allows records to be read in sorted order; that can be useful for display purposes, as well as for certain query-processing algorithms that we shall study in Chapter 13.

It is difficult, however, to maintain physical sequential order as records are inserted and deleted, since it is costly to move many records as a result of a single

A-217	Brighton	750	
A-101	Downtown	500	
A-110	Downtown	600	
A-215	Mianus	700	
A-102	Perryridge	400	
A-201	Perryridge	900	
A-218	Perryridge	700	
A-222	Redwood	700	
A-305	Round Hill	350	

Figure 11.15   Sequential file for *account* records.

A-217	Brighton	750	
A-101	Downtown	500	
A-110	Downtown	600	
A-215	Mianus	700	
A-102	Perryridge	400	
A-201	Perryridge	900	
A-218	Perryridge	700	
A-222	Redwood	700	
A-305	Round Hill	350	

A-888	North Town	800	

Figure 11.16 Sequential file after an insertion.

insertion or deletion. We can manage deletion by using pointer chains, as we saw previously. For insertion, we apply the following rules:

1. Locate the record in the file that comes before the record to be inserted in search-key order.

2. If there is a free record (that is, space left after a deletion) within the same block as this record, insert the new record there. Otherwise, insert the new record in an *overflow block*. In either case, adjust the pointers so as to chain together the records in search-key order.

Figure 11.16 shows the file of Figure 11.15 after the insertion of the record (North Town, A-888, 800). The structure in Figure 11.16 allows fast insertion of new records, but forces sequential file-processing applications to process records in an order that does not match the physical order of the records.

If relatively few records need to be stored in overflow blocks, this approach works well. Eventually, however, the correspondence between search-key order and physical order may be totally lost, in which case sequential processing will become much less efficient. At this point, the file should be **reorganized** so that it is once again physically in sequential order. Such reorganizations are costly, and must be done during times when the system load is low. The frequency with which reorganizations are needed depends on the frequency of insertion of new records. In the extreme case in which insertions rarely occur, it is possible always to keep the file in physically sorted order. In such a case, the pointer field in Figure 11.15 is not needed.

11.7.2 Clustering File Organization

Many relational-database systems store each relation in a separate file, so that they can take full advantage of the file system that the operating system provides. Usually, tuples of a relation can be represented as fixed-length records. Thus, relations can be mapped to a simple file structure. This simple implementation of a relational database system is well suited to low-cost database implementations as in, for example, embedded systems or portable devices. In such systems, the size of the database is small, so little is gained from a sophisticated file structure. Furthermore, in such environments, it is essential that the overall size of the object code for the database system be small. A simple file structure reduces the amount of code needed to implement the system.

This simple approach to relational-database implementation becomes less satisfactory as the size of the database increases. We have seen that there are performance advantages to be gained from careful assignment of records to blocks, and from careful organization of the blocks themselves. Clearly, a more complicated file structure may be beneficial, even if we retain the strategy of storing each relation in a separate file.

However, many large-scale database systems do not rely directly on the underlying operating system for file management. Instead, one large operating-system file is allocated to the database system. The database system stores all relations in this one file, and manages the file itself. To see the advantage of storing many relations in one file, consider the following SQL query for the bank database:

> **select** *account-number, customer-name, customer-street, customer-city*
> **from** *depositor, customer*
> **where** *depositor.customer-name = customer.customer-name*

This query computes a join of the *depositor* and *customer* relations. Thus, for each tuple of *depositor*, the system must locate the *customer* tuples with the same value for *customer-name*. Ideally, these records will be located with the help of *indices*, which we shall discuss in Chapter 12. Regardless of how these records are located, however, they need to be transferred from disk into main memory. In the worst case, each record will reside on a different block, forcing us to do one block read for each record required by the query.

As a concrete example, consider the *depositor* and *customer* relations of Figures 11.17 and 11.18, respectively. In Figure 11.19, we show a file structure designed for efficient execution of queries involving *depositor* ⋈ *customer*. The *depositor* tuples for each *customer-name* are stored near the *customer* tuple for the corresponding *customer-name*. This structure mixes together tuples of two relations, but allows for efficient processing of the join. When a tuple of the *customer* relation is read, the entire block containing that tuple is copied from disk into main memory. Since the corresponding

customer-name	account-number
Hayes	A-102
Hayes	A-220
Hayes	A-503
Turner	A-305

Figure 11.17   The *depositor* relation.

customer-name	customer-street	customer-city
Hayes	Main	Brooklyn
Turner	Putnam	Stamford

Figure 11.18 The *customer* relation.

depositor tuples are stored on the disk near the *customer* tuple, the block containing the *customer* tuple contains tuples of the *depositor* relation needed to process the query. If a customer has so many accounts that the *depositor* records do not fit in one block, the remaining records appear on nearby blocks.

A **clustering file organization** is a file organization, such as that illustrated in Figure 11.19 that stores related records of two or more relations in each block. Such a file organization allows us to read records that would satisfy the join condition by using one block read. Thus, we are able to process this particular query more efficiently.

Our use of clustering has enhanced processing of a particular join (*depositor ⋈ customer*), but it results in slowing processing of other types of query. For example,

> **select** *
> **from** *customer*

requires more block accesses than it did in the scheme under which we stored each relation in a separate file. Instead of several *customer* records appearing in one block, each record is located in a distinct block. Indeed, simply finding all the *customer* records is not possible without some additional structure. To locate all tuples of the *customer* relation in the structure of Figure 11.19, we need to chain together all the records of that relation using pointers, as in Figure 11.20.

When clustering is to be used depends on the types of query that the database designer believes to be most frequent. Careful use of clustering can produce significant performance gains in query processing.

11.8 Data-Dictionary Storage

So far, we have considered only the representation of the relations themselves. A relational-database system needs to maintain data *about* the relations, such as the

Hayes	Main	Brooklyn
Hayes	A-102	
Hayes	A-220	
Hayes	A-503	
Turner	Putnam	Stamford
Turner	A-305	

Figure 11.19 Clustering file structure.

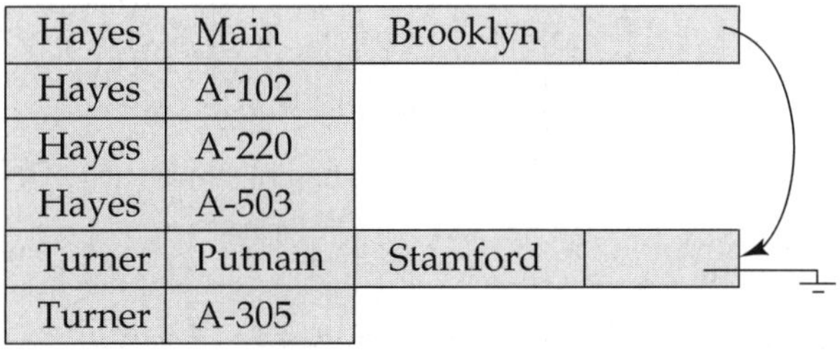

Hayes	Main	Brooklyn	
Hayes	A-102		
Hayes	A-220		
Hayes	A-503		
Turner	Putnam	Stamford	
Turner	A-305		

Figure 11.20   Clustering file structure with pointer chains.

schema of the relations. This information is called the **data dictionary**, or **system catalog**. Among the types of information that the system must store are these:

- Names of the relations

- Names of the attributes of each relation

- Domains and lengths of attributes

- Names of views defined on the database, and definitions of those views

- Integrity constraints (for example, key constraints)

In addition, many systems keep the following data on users of the system:

- Names of authorized users

- Accounting information about users

- Passwords or other information used to authenticate users

Further, the database may store statistical and descriptive data about the relations, such as:

- Number of tuples in each relation

- Method of storage for each relation (for example, clustered or nonclustered)

The data dictionary may also note the storage organization (sequential, hash or heap) of relations, and the location where each relation is stored:

- If relations are stored in operating system files, the dictionary would note the names of the file (or files) containing each relation.

- If the database stores all relations in a single file, the dictionary may note blocks containing records of each relation in a data structure such as a list.

In Chapter 12, in which we study indices, we shall see a need to st about each index on each of the relations:

- Name of the index

- Name of the relation being indexed

- Attributes on which the index is defined

- Type of index formed

All this information constitutes, in effect, a miniature database. Some database systems store this information by using special-purpose data structures and code. It is generally preferable to store the data about the database in the database itself. By using the database to store system data, we simplify the overall structure of the system and harness the full power of the database for fast access to system data.

The exact choice of how to represent system data by relations must be made by the system designers. One possible representation, with primary keys underlined, is

Relation-metadata (<u>*relation-name*</u>, *number-of-attributes*, *storage-organization*, *location*)
Attribute-metadata (<u>*attribute-name*</u>, <u>*relation-name*</u>, *domain-type*, *position*, *length*)
User-metadata (<u>*user-name*</u>, *encrypted-password*, *group*)
Index-metadata (<u>*index-name*</u>, *relation-name*, *index-type*, *index-attributes*)
View-metadata (<u>*view-name*</u>, *definition*)

In this representation, the attribute *index-attributes* of the relation *Index-metadata* is assumed to contain a list of one or more attributes, which can be represented by a character string such as "*branch-name, branch-city*". The *Index-metadata* relation is thus not in first normal form; it can be normalized, but the above representation is likely to be more efficient to access. The data dictionary is often stored in a non-normalized form to achieve fast access.

The storage organization and location of the *Relation-metadata* itself must be recorded elsewhere (for example, in the database code itself), since we need this information to find the contents of *Relation-metadata*.

11.9 Storage for Object-Oriented Databases∗∗

The file-organization techniques described in Section 11.7—the heap, sequential, hashing and clustering organizations—can also be used for storing objects in an object-oriented database. However, some extra features are needed to support object-　　　　base features, such as set-valued fields and persistent pointers.

pping of Objects to Files

f objects to files is in many ways like the mapping of tuples to files in a
n. At the lowest level of data representation, both tuples and the data
are simply sequences of bytes. We can therefore store object data in
s described in this chapter, with some modifications which we note

ct-oriented databases may lack the uniformity of tuples in relational
ample, fields of records may be sets; in relational databases, in con-

trast, data are typically required to be (at least) in first normal form. Furthermore, objects may be extremely large. Such objects have to be managed differently from records in a relational system.

We can implement set-valued fields that have a small number of elements using data structures such as linked lists. Set-valued fields that have a larger number of elements can be implemented as relations in the database. Set-valued fields of objects can also be eliminated at the *storage level* by normalization: A relation is created containing one tuple for each value of a set-valued field of an object. Each tuple also contains the object identifier of the object. However, this relation is not made visible to the upper levels of the database system. The storage system gives the upper levels of the database system the view of a set-valued field, even though the set-valued field has actually been normalized by creating a new relation.

Some applications include extremely large objects that are not easily decomposed into smaller components. Such large objects may each be stored in a separate file. We discuss this idea further in Section 11.9.6.

11.9.2   Implementation of Object Identifiers

Since objects are identified by object identifiers (OIDs), an object-storage system needs a mechanism to locate an object, given an OID. If the OIDs are **logical OIDs**—that is, they do not specify the location of the object—then the storage system must maintain an index that maps OIDs to the actual location of the object. If the OIDs are **physical OIDs**—that is, they encode the location of the object—then the object can be found directly. Physical OIDs typically have the following three parts:

1. A volume or file identifier

2. A block identifier within the volume or file

3. An offset within the block

A volume is a logical unit of storage that usually corresponds to a disk.

In addition, physical OIDs may contain a **unique identifier**, which is an integer that distinguishes the OID from the identifiers of other objects that happened to be stored at the same location earlier, and were deleted or moved elsewhere. The unique identifier is also stored with the object, and the identifiers in an OID and the corresponding object should match. If the unique identifier in a physical OID does not match the unique identifier in the object to which that OID points, the system detects that the pointer is a dangling pointer, and signals an error. (A **dangling pointer** is a pointer that does not point to a valid object.) Figure 11.21 illustrates this scheme.

Such pointer errors occur when physical OIDs corresponding to old objects that have been deleted are used accidentally. If the space occupied by the object had been reallocated, there may be a new object in the location, and it may get incorrectly addressed by the identifier of the old object. If a dangling pointer is not detected, it could cause corruption of a new object stored at the same location. The unique identifier helps to detect such errors, since the unique identifiers of the old physical OID and the new object will not match.

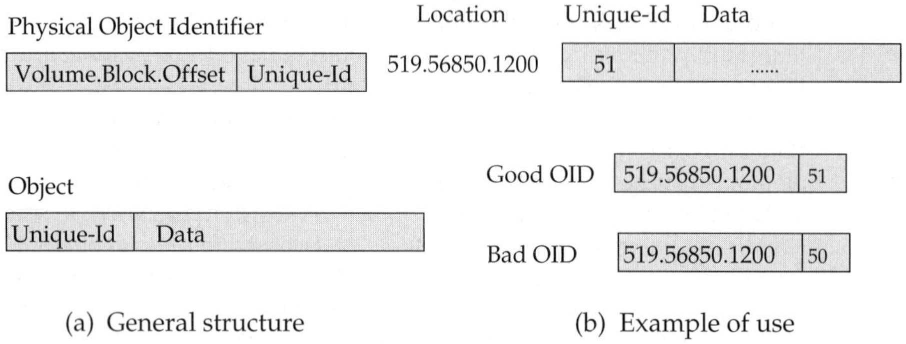

Physical Object Identifier

Volume.Block.Offset	Unique-Id

Location	Unique-Id	Data
519.56850.1200	51	......

Object

Unique-Id	Data

Good OID	519.56850.1200	51

Bad OID	519.56850.1200	50

(a) General structure   (b) Example of use

Figure 11.21   Unique identifiers in an OID.

Suppose that an object has to be moved to a new block, perhaps because the size of the object has increased, and the old block has no extra space. Then, the physical OID will point to the old block, which no longer contains the object. Rather than change the OID of the object (which involves changing every object that points to this one), we leave behind a **forwarding address** at the old location. When the database tries to locate the object, it finds the forwarding address instead of the object; it then uses the forwarding address to locate the object.

11.9.3 Management of Persistent Pointers

We implement persistent pointers in a persistent programming language by using OIDs. In some implementations, persistent pointers are physical OIDs; in others, they are logical OIDs. An important difference between persistent pointers and in-memory pointers is the size of the pointer. In-memory pointers need to be only big enough to address all virtual memory. On most current computers, in-memory pointers are usually 4 bytes long, which is sufficient to address 4 gigabytes of memory. The most recent computer architectures have pointers that are 8 bytes long,

Persistent pointers need to address all the data in a database. Since database systems are often bigger than 4 gigabytes, persistent pointers are usually at least 8 bytes long. Many object-oriented databases also provide unique identifiers in persistent pointers, to catch dangling references. This feature further increases the size of persistent pointers. Thus, persistent pointers may be substantially longer than in-memory pointers.

The action of looking up an object, given its identifier, is called **dereferencing**. Given an in-memory pointer (as in C++), looking up the object is merely a memory reference. Given a persistent pointer, dereferencing an object has an extra step—finding the actual location of the object in memory by looking up the persistent pointer in a table. If the object is not already in memory, it has to be loaded from disk. We can implement the table lookup fairly efficiently by using a hash table data structure, but the lookup is still slow compared to a pointer dereference, even if the object is already in memory.

Pointer swizzling is a way to cut down the cost of locating persistent objects that are already present in memory. The idea is that, when a persistent pointer is first dereferenced, the system locates the object and brings it into memory if it is not already there. Now the system carries out an extra step—it stores an in-memory pointer to the object in place of the persistent pointer. The next time that the *same* persistent pointer is dereferenced, the in-memory location can be read out directly, so the costs of locating the object are avoided. (When persistent objects have to be moved from memory back to disk to make space for other persistent objects, the system must carry out an extra step to ensure that the object is still in memory. Correspondingly, when an object is written out, any persistent pointers that it contained and that were swizzled have to be **deswizzled**, that is, converted back to their persistent representation. Pointer swizzling on pointer dereference, as described here, is called **software swizzling**.

Buffer management is more complicated if pointer swizzling is used, since the physical location of an object must not change once that object is brought into the buffer. One way to ensure that it will not change is to pin pages containing swizzled objects in the buffer pool, so that they are never replaced until the program that performed the swizzling has finished execution. See the bibliographical notes for more complex buffer-management schemes, based on virtual-memory mapping techniques, that make it unnecessary to pin the buffer pages.

11.9.4   Hardware Swizzling

Having two types of pointers, persistent and transient (in-memory), is inconvenient. Programmers have to remember the type of the pointers, and may have to write code twice—once for the persistent pointers and once for the in-memory pointers. It would be simpler if both persistent and in-memory pointers were of the same type.

A simple way to merge persistent and in-memory pointer types is just to extend the length of in-memory pointers to the same size as persistent pointers, and to use 1 bit of the identifier to distinguish between persistent and in-memory pointers. However, the storage cost of longer persistent pointers will have to be borne by in-memory pointers as well; understandably, this scheme is unpopular.

We shall describe a technique called **hardware swizzling**, which uses the virtual-memory-management hardware present in most current computer systems to address this problem. When data in a virtual memory page are accessed, and the operating system detects that the page does not have real storage allocated for it, or has been access protected, then a **segmentation violation** is said to occur.[3] Many operating systems provide a mechanism to specify a function to be called when a segmentation violation occurs, and a mechanism to allocate storage for a page in virtual address space, and to set that page's access permissions. In most Unix systems, the mmap system call provides this latter functionality. Hardware swizzling makes clever use of the above mechanisms.

---

3.   The term **page fault** is sometimes used instead of *segmentation violation*, although access protection violations are generally not considered to be page faults.

Hardware swizzling has two major advantages over software swizzling:

1. It is able to store persistent pointers in objects in the same amount of space as in-memory pointers require (along with extra storage external to the object).

2. It transparently converts between persistent pointers and in-memory pointers in a clever and efficient way. Software written to deal with in-memory pointers can thereby deal with persistent pointers as well, without any changes.

11.9.4.1 Pointer Representation

Hardware swizzling uses the following representation of persistent pointers contained in objects that are on disk. A persistent pointer is conceptually split into two parts: a page identifier in the database, and an offset within the page.[4] The page identifier in a persistent pointer is actually a small indirect pointer, which we call the short page identifier. Each page (or other unit of storage) has a translation table that provides a mapping from the short page identifiers to full database page identifiers. The system has to look up the short page identifier in a persistent pointer in the translation table to find the full page identifier.

The translation table, in the worst case, will be only as big as the maximum number of pointers that can be contained in objects in a page; with a page size of 4096, and a pointer size of 4 bytes, the maximum number of pointers is 1024. In practice, the translation table is likely to contain much less than the maximum number of elements (1024 in our example) and will not consume excessive space. The short page identifier needs to have only enough bits to identify a row in the table; with a maximum table size of 1024, only 10 bits are required. Hence, a small number of bits is enough to store the short page identifier. Thus, the translation table permits an entire persistent pointer to fit into the same space as an in-memory pointer. Even though only a few bits are needed for the short page identifier, all the bits of an in-memory pointer, other than the page-offset bits, are used as the short page identifier. This architecture facilitates swizzling, as we shall see.

The persistent-pointer representation scheme appears in Figure 11.22, where there are three objects in the page, each containing a persistent pointer. The translation table gives the mapping between short page identifiers and the full database page identifiers for each of the short page identifiers in these persistent pointers. The database page identifiers are shown in the format *volume.page.offset*.

Each page maintains extra information so that all persistent pointers in the page can be found. The system updates the information when an object is created or deleted in the page. The need to locate all the persistent pointers in a page will become clear later.

---

4. The term **page** is generally used to refer to a real-memory or virtual-memory page, and the term **block** is used to refer to disk blocks in the database. In hardware swizzling, these have to be of the same size, and database blocks are fetched into virtual memory pages. We shall use the terms *page* and *block* interchangeably in this section.

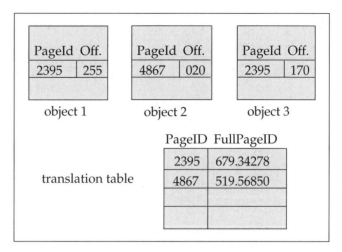

Figure 11.22   Page image before swizzling.

11.9.4.2 Swizzling Pointers on a Page

Initially no page of the database has been allocated a page in virtual memory. Virtual-memory pages may be allocated to database pages even before they are actually loaded, as we will see shortly. Database pages get loaded into virtual-memory when the database system needs to access data on the page. Before a database page is loaded, the system allocates a virtual-memory page to the database page if one has not already been allocated. The system then loads the database page into the virtual-memory page it has allocated to it.

When the system loads a database page P into virtual memory, it does pointer swizzling on the page: It locates all persistent pointers contained in objects in page P, using the extra information stored in the page. It takes the following actions for each persistent pointer in the page. (Let the value of the persistent pointer be $\langle p_i, o_i \rangle$, where p_i is the short page identifier and o_i is the offset within the page. Let P_i be the full page identifier of p_i, found in the translation table in page P.)

1. If page P_i does not already have a virtual-memory page allocated to it, the system now allocates a free page in virtual memory to it. The page P_i will reside at this virtual-memory location if and when it is brought in. At this point, the page in virtual address space does not have any storage allocated for it, either in memory or on disk; it is merely a range of addresses reserved for the database page. The system allocates actual space when it actually loads the database page P_i into virtual memory.

2. Let the virtual-memory page allocated (either earlier or in the preceding step) for P_i be v_i. The system updates the persistent pointer being considered, whose value is $\langle p_i, o_i \rangle$, by replacing p_i with v_i.

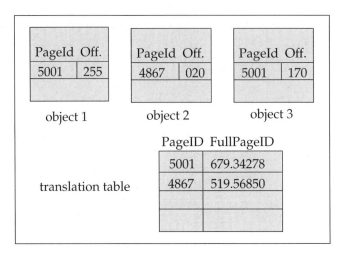

Figure 11.23 Page image after swizzling.

Figure 11.23 shows the state of the page from Figure 11.22 after the system has brought that page into memory and swizzled the pointers in it. Here, we assume that the page whose database page identifier is 679.34278 has been mapped to page 5001 in memory, whereas the page whose identifier is 519.56850 has been mapped to page 4867 (which is the same as the short page identifier). All the pointers in objects have been updated to reflect the new mapping, and can now be used as in-memory pointers.

At the end of the translation phase for a page, the objects in the page satisfy an important property: All persistent pointers contained in objects in the page have been converted to in-memory pointers. Thus, objects in in-memory pages contain only in-memory pointers. Routines that use these objects do not even need to know about the existence of persistent pointers! For example, existing libraries written for in-memory objects can be used unchanged for persistent objects. That is indeed an important advantage!

11.9.4.3 Pointer Dereference

Consider the first time that an in-memory pointer to a virtual-memory page v_i is dereferenced, when storage has not yet been allocated for the page. As we described, a segmentation violation will occur, and will result in a function call on the database system. The database system takes the following actions:

1. It first determines what database page was allocated to virtual-memory page v_i; let the full page identifier of the database page be P_i. (If no database page has been allocated to v_i, the pointer is incorrect, and the system flags an error.)

2. It allocates storage space for page v_i, and loads the database page P_i into virtual-memory page v_i.

3. It carries out pointer swizzling out on page P_i, as described earlier in "Swizzling Pointer on a Page".

4. After swizzling all persistent pointers in P, the system allows the pointer dereference that resulted in the segmentation violation to continue. The pointer dereference will find the object for which it was looking loaded in memory.

If any swizzled pointer that points to an object in page v_i is dereferenced later, the dereference proceeds just like any other virtual-memory access, with no extra overheads. In contrast, if swizzling is not used, there is considerable overhead in locating the buffer page containing the object and then accessing it. This overhead has to be incurred on *every* access to objects in the page, whereas when swizzling is performed, the overhead is incurred only on the *first* access to an object in the page. Later accesses operate at regular virtual-memory access speeds. Hardware swizzling thus gives excellent performance benefits to applications that repeatedly dereference pointers.

11.9.4.4   Optimizations

Software swizzling performs a deswizzling operation when a page in memory has to be written back to the database, to convert in-memory pointers back to persistent pointers. Hardware swizzling can avoid this step—when the system does pointer swizzling for the page, it simply updates the translation table for the page, so that the page-identifier part of the swizzled in-memory pointers can be used to look up the table. For example, as shown in Figure 11.23, database page 679.34278 (with short identifier 2395 in the page shown) is mapped to virtual-memory page 5001. At this point, not only is the pointer in object 1 updated from 2395255 to 5001255, but also the short identifier in the table is updated to 5001. Thus, the short identifier 5001 in object 1 and in the table match each other again. Therefore, the page can be written back to disk without any deswizzling.

Several optimizations can be carried out on the basic scheme described here. When the system swizzles page P, for each page P' referred to by any persistent pointer in P, it attempts to allocate P' to the virtual address location indicated by the short page identifier of P' on page P. If the system can allocate the page in this attempt, pointers to it do not need to be updated. In our swizzling example, page 519.56850 with short page identifier 4867 was mapped to virtual-memory page 4867, which is the same as its short page identifier. We can see that the pointer in object 2 to this page did not need to be changed during swizzling. If every page can be allocated to its appropriate location in virtual address space, none of the pointers need to be translated, and the cost of swizzling is reduced significantly.

Hardware swizzling works even if the database is bigger than virtual memory, but only as long as all the pages that a particular process accesses fit into the virtual memory of the process. If they do not, a page that has been brought into virtual memory will have to be replaced, and that replacement is hard to do, since there may be in-memory pointers to objects in that page.

Hardware swizzling can also be used at the level of sets of pages (often called segments), instead of for a single page. For set-level swizzling, the system uses a single translation table for all pages in the segment. It loads pages in the segment and swizzles them as and when they are required; they need not be loaded all together.

11.9.5   Disk Versus Memory Structure of Objects

The format in which objects are stored in memory may be different from the format in which they are stored on disk in the database. One reason may be the use of software swizzling, where the structures of persistent and in-memory pointers are different. Another reason may be that we want to have the database accessible from different machines, possibly based on different architectures, and from different languages, and from programs compiled under different compilers, all of which result in differences in the in-memory representation.

Consider, for example, a data-structure definition in a programming language such as C++. The physical structure (such as sizes and representation of integers) in the object depends on the machine on which the program is run.[5] Further, the physical structure may also depend on which compiler is used—in a language as complex as C++, different choices for translation from the high-level description to the physical structure are possible, and each compiler can make its own choice.

The solution to this problem is to make the physical representation of objects in the database independent of the machine and of the compiler. The system can convert the object from the disk representation to the form that is required on the specific machine, language, and compiler, when that object is brought into memory. It can do this conversion transparently at the same time that it swizzles pointers in the object, so the programmer does not need to worry about the conversion.

The first step in implementing such a scheme is to define a common language for describing the structure of objects—that is, a data-definition language. One such language is the Object Definition Language (ODL) developed by the Object Database Management Group (ODMG). ODL has mappings defined to the Java, C++, and Smalltalk languages, so potentially we may manipulate objects in an ODMG-compliant database using any of these languages.

The definition of the structure of each class in the database is stored (logically) in the databases. The code to translate an object in the database to the representation that is manipulated with the programming language (and vice versa) depends on the machine as well as on the compiler for the language. We can generate this code automatically, using the stored definition of the class of the object.

An unexpected source of differences between the disk and in-memory representations of data is the hidden-pointers in objects. **Hidden pointers** are transient pointers

---

5. For instance, the Motorola 680x0 architectures, the IBM 360 architecture, and the Intel 80386/80486/Pentium/Pentium-II/Pentium-III architectures all have 4-byte integers. However, they differ in how the bits of an integer are laid out within a word. In earlier-generation personal computers, integers were 2 bytes long; in newer workstation architectures, such as the Compaq Alpha, Intel Itanium, and Sun UltraSparc architectures, integers can be 8 bytes long.

that compilers generate and store in objects. These pointers point (indirectly) to tables used to implement certain methods of the object. The tables are typically compiled into executable object code, and their exact location depends on the executable object code; hence, they may be different for different processes. Therefore, when a process accesses an object, the hidden pointers must be fixed to point to the correct location. The hidden pointers can be initialized at the same time that data-representation conversions are carried out.

11.9.6   Large Objects

Objects may also be extremely large; for instance, multimedia objects may occupy several megabytes of space. Exceptionally large data items, such as video sequences, may run into gigabytes, although they are usually split into multiple objects, each on the order of a few megabytes or less. Large objects containing binary data are called binary large objects (blobs), while large objects containing character data, are called character large objects (clobs), as we saw in Section 9.2.1.

Most relational databases restrict the size of a record to be no larger than the size of a page, to simplify buffer management and free-space management. Large objects and long fields are often stored in a special file (or collection of files) reserved for long-field storage.

Allocation of buffer pages presents a problem with managing large objects. Large objects may need to be stored in a contiguous sequence of bytes when they are brought into memory; in that case, if an object is bigger than a page, contiguous pages of the buffer pool must be allocated to store it, which makes buffer management more difficult.

We often modify large objects by updating part of the object, or by inserting or deleting parts of the object, rather than by writing the entire object. If inserts and deletes need to be supported, we can handle large objects by using B-tree structures (which we study in Chapter 12). B-tree structures permit us to read the entire object, as well as to insert and delete parts of the object.

For practical reasons, we may manipulate large objects by using application programs, instead of doing so within the database:

- **Text data**. Text is usually treated as a byte string manipulated by editors and formatters.

- **Image/Graphical data**. Graphical data may be represented as a bitmap or as a set of lines, boxes, and other geometric objects. Although some graphical data often are managed within the database system itself, special application software is used for many cases, such as integrated circuit design.

- **Audio and video data**. Audio and video data are typically a digitized, compressed representation created and displayed by separate application software. Data are usually modified with special-purpose editing software, outside the database system.

The most widely used method for updating such data is the **checkout/checkin** method. A user or an application would **check out** a copy of a long-field object, operate on this copy with special-purpose application programs, and then **check in** the modified copy. *Checkout* and a *checkin* correspond roughly to read and write. In some systems, a checkin may create a new version of the object without deleting the old version.

11.10 Summary

- Several types of data storage exist in most computer systems. They are classified by the speed with which they can access data, by their cost per unit of data to buy the memory, and by their reliability. Among the media available are cache, main memory, flash memory, magnetic disks, optical disks, and magnetic tapes.

- Two factors determine the reliability of storage media: whether a power failure or system crash causes data to be lost, and what the likelihood is of physical failure of the storage devise.

- We can reduce the likelihood of physical failure by retaining multiple copies of data. For disks, we can use mirroring. Or we can use more sophisticated methods based on redundant arrays of independent disks (RAIDs). By striping data across disks, these methods offer high throughput rates on large accesses; by introducing redundancy across disks, they improve reliability greatly. Several different RAID organizations are possible, each with different cost, performance and reliability characteristics. RAID level 1 (mirroring) and RAID level 5 are the most commonly used.

- We can organize a file logically as a sequence of records mapped onto disk blocks. One approach to mapping the database to files is to use several files, and to store records of only one fixed length in any given file. An alternative is to structure files so that they can accommodate multiple lengths for records. There are different techniques for implementing variable-length records, including the slotted-page method, the pointer method, and the reserved-space method.

- Since data are transferred between disk storage and main memory in units of a block, it is worthwhile to assign file records to blocks in such a way that a single block contains related records. If we can access several of the records we want with only one block access, we save disk accesses. Since disk accesses are usually the bottleneck in the performance of a database system, careful assignment of records to blocks can pay significant performance dividends.

- One way to reduce the number of disk accesses is to keep as many blocks as possible in main memory. Since it is not possible to keep all blocks in main memory, we need to manage the allocation of the space available in main memory for the storage of blocks. The *buffer* is that part of main memory available for storage of copies of disk blocks. The subsystem responsible for the allocation of buffer space is called the *buffer manager*.

- Storage systems for object-oriented databases are somewhat different from storage systems for relational databases: They must deal with large objects, for example, and must support persistent pointers. There are schemes to detect dangling persistent pointers.

- Software- and hardware-based swizzling schemes permit efficient dereferencing of persistent pointers. The hardware-based schemes use the virtual-memory-management support implemented in hardware, and made accessible to user programs by many current-generation operating systems.

Review Terms

- Physical storage media
  - ☐ Cache
  - ☐ Main memory
  - ☐ Flash memory
  - ☐ Magnetic disk
  - ☐ Optical storage
- Magnetic disk
  - ☐ Platter
  - ☐ Hard disks
  - ☐ Floppy disks
  - ☐ Tracks
  - ☐ Sectors
  - ☐ Read–write head
  - ☐ Disk arm
  - ☐ Cylinder
  - ☐ Disk controller
  - ☐ Checksums
  - ☐ Remapping of bad sectors
- Performance measures of disks
  - ☐ Access time
  - ☐ Seek time
  - ☐ Rotational latency
  - ☐ Data-transfer rate
  - ☐ Mean time to failure (MTTF)
- Disk block
- Optimization of disk-block access
  - ☐ Disk-arm scheduling
  - ☐ Elevator algorithm

- ☐ File organization
- ☐ Defragmenting
- ☐ Nonvolatile write buffers
- ☐ Nonvolatile random-access memory (NV-RAM)
- ☐ Log disk
- ☐ Log-based file system
- Redundant arrays of independent disks (RAID)
  - ☐ Mirroring
  - ☐ Data striping
  - ☐ Bit-level striping
  - ☐ Block-level striping
- RAID levels
  - ☐ Level 0 (block striping, no redundancy)
  - ☐ Level 1 (block striping, mirroring)
  - ☐ Level 3 (bit striping, parity)
  - ☐ Level 5 (block striping, distributed parity)
  - ☐ Level 6 (block striping, $P + Q$ redundancy)
- Rebuild performance
- Software RAID
- Hardware RAID
- Hot swapping

- Tertiary storage
  - ☐ Optical disks
  - ☐ Magnetic tapes
  - ☐ Jukeboxes
- Buffer
  - ☐ Buffer manager
  - ☐ Pinned blocks
  - ☐ Forced output of blocks
- Buffer-replacement policies
  - ☐ Least recently used (LRU)
  - ☐ Toss-immediate
  - ☐ Most recently used (MRU)
- File
- File organization
  - ☐ File header
  - ☐ Free list
- Variable-length records
  - ☐ Byte-string representation
  - ☐ Slotted-page structure
  - ☐ Reserved space
  - ☐ List representation
- Heap file organization

- Sequential file organization
- Hashing file organization
- Clustering file organization
- Search key
- Data dictionary
- System catalog
- Storage structures for OODBs
- Object identifier (OID)
  - ☐ Logical OID
  - ☐ Physical OID
  - ☐ Unique identifier
  - ☐ Dangling pointer
  - ☐ Forwarding address
- Pointer swizzling
  - ☐ Dereferencing
  - ☐ Deswizzling
  - ☐ Software swizzling
  - ☐ Hardware swizzling
  - ☐ Segmentation violation
  - ☐ Page fault
- Hidden pointers
- Large objects

Exercises

11.1 List the physical storage media available on the computers you use routinely. Give the speed with which data can be accessed on each medium.

11.2 How does the remapping of bad sectors by disk controllers affect data-retrieval rates?

11.3 Consider the following data and parity-block arrangement on four disks:

Disk 1	Disk 2	Disk 3	Disk 4
B_1	B_2	B_3	B_4
P_1	B_5	B_6	B_7
B_8	P_2	B_9	B_{10}
$\vdots$	$\vdots$	$\vdots$	$\vdots$

The B_i's represent data blocks; the P_i's represent parity blocks. Parity block P_i is the parity block for data blocks B_{4i-3} to B_{4i}. What, if any, problem might this arrangement present?

11.4 A power failure that occurs while a disk block is being written could result in the block being only partially written. Assume that partially written blocks can be detected. An atomic block write is one where either the disk block is fully written or nothing is written (i.e., there are no partial writes). Suggest schemes for getting the effect of atomic block writes with the following RAID schemes. Your schemes should involve work on recovery from failure.

  a. RAID level 1 (mirroring)
  b. RAID level 5 (block interleaved, distributed parity)

11.5 RAID systems typically allow you to replace failed disks without stopping access to the system. Thus, the data in the failed disk must be rebuilt and written to the replacement disk while the system is in operation. With which of the RAID levels is the amount of interference between the rebuild and ongoing disk accesses least? Explain your answer.

11.6 Give an example of a relational-algebra expression and a query-processing strategy in each of the following situations:

  a. MRU is preferable to LRU.
  b. LRU is preferable to MRU.

11.7 Consider the deletion of record 5 from the file of Figure 11.8. Compare the relative merits of the following techniques for implementing the deletion:

  a. Move record 6 to the space occupied by record 5, and move record 7 to the space occupied by record 6.
  b. Move record 7 to the space occupied by record 5.
  c. Mark record 5 as deleted, and move no records.

11.8 Show the structure of the file of Figure 11.9 after each of the following steps:

  a. Insert (Brighton, A-323, 1600).
  b. Delete record 2.
  c. Insert (Brighton, A-626, 2000).

11.9 Give an example of a database application in which the reserved-space method of representing variable-length records is preferable to the pointer method. Explain your answer.

11.10 Give an example of a database application in which the pointer method of representing variable-length records is preferable to the reserved-space method. Explain your answer.

11.11 Show the structure of the file of Figure 11.12 after each of the following steps:

  a. Insert (Mianus, A-101, 2800).
  b. Insert (Brighton, A-323, 1600).
  c. Delete (Perryridge, A-102, 400).

11.12 What happens if you attempt to insert the record

(Perryridge, A-929, 3000)

into the file of Figure 11.12?

11.13 Show the structure of the file of Figure 11.13 after each of the following steps:
   a. Insert (Mianus, A-101, 2800).
   b. Insert (Brighton, A-323, 1600).
   c. Delete (Perryridge, A-102, 400).

11.14 Explain why the allocation of records to blocks affects database-system performance significantly.

11.15 If possible, determine the buffer-management strategy used by the operating system running on your local computer system, and what mechanisms it provides to control replacement of pages. Discuss how the control on replacement that it provides would be useful for the implementation of database systems.

11.16 In the sequential file organization, why is an overflow *block* used even if there is, at the moment, only one overflow record?

11.17 List two advantages and two disadvantages of each of the following strategies for storing a relational database:
   a. Store each relation in one file.
   b. Store multiple relations (perhaps even the entire database) in one file.

11.18 Consider a relational database with two relations:

course (*course-name, room, instructor*)
enrollment (*course-name, student-name, grade*)

Define instances of these relations for three courses, each of which enrolls five students. Give a file structure of these relations that uses clustering.

11.19 Consider the following bitmap technique for tracking free space in a file. For each block in the file, two bits are maintained in the bitmap. If the block is between 0 and 30 percent full the bits are 00, between 30 and 60 percent the bits are 01, between 60 and 90 percent the bits are 10, and above 90 percent the bits are 11. Such bitmaps can be kept in memory even for quite large files.
   a. Describe how to keep the bitmap up-to-date on record insertions and deletions.
   b. Outline the benefit of the bitmap technique over free lists when searching for free space and when updating free space information.

11.20 Give a normalized version of the *Index-metadata* relation, and explain why using the normalized version would result in worse performance.

11.21 Explain why a physical OID must contain more information than a pointer to a physical storage location.

11.22 If physical OIDs are used, an object can be relocated by keeping a forwarding pointer to its new location. In case an object gets forwarded multiple times, what would be the effect on retrieval speed? Suggest a technique to avoid multiple accesses in such a case.

11.23 Define the term *dangling pointer*. Describe how the unique-id scheme helps in detecting dangling pointers in an object-oriented database.

11.24 Consider the example on page 435, which shows that there is no need for deswizzling if hardware swizzling is used. Explain why, in that example, it is safe to change the short identifier of page 679.34278 from 2395 to 5001. Can some other page already have short identifier 5001? If it could, how can you handle that situation?

Bibliographical Notes

Patterson and Hennessy [1995] discusses the hardware aspects of translation look-aside buffers, caches and memory-management units. Rosch and Wethington [1999] presents an excellent overview of computer hardware, including extensive coverage of all types of storage technology such as floppy disks, magnetic disks, optical disks, tapes, and storage interfaces. Ruemmler and Wilkes [1994] presents a survey of magnetic-disk technology. Flash memory is discussed by Dippert and Levy [1993].

The specifications of current-generation disk drives can be obtained from the Web sites of their manufacturers, such as IBM, Seagate, and Maxtor.

Alternative disk organizations that provide a high degree of fault tolerance include those described by Gray et al. [1990] and Bitton and Gray [1988]. Disk striping is described by Salem and Garcia-Molina [1986]. Discussions of redundant arrays of inexpensive disks (RAID) are presented by Patterson et al. [1988] and Chen and Patterson [1990]. Chen et al. [1994] presents an excellent survey of RAID principles and implementation. Reed–Solomon codes are covered in Pless [1989]. The log-based file system, which makes disk access sequential, is described in Rosenblum and Ousterhout [1991].

In systems that support mobile computing, data may be broadcast repeatedly. The broadcast medium can be viewed as a level of the storage hierarchy—as a broadcast disk with high latency. These issues are discussed in Acharya et al. [1995]. Caching and buffer management for mobile computing is discussed in Barbará and Imielinski [1994]. Further discussion of storage issues in mobile computing appears in Douglis et al. [1994].

Basic data structures are discussed in Cormen et al. [1990]. There are several papers describing the storage structure of specific database systems. Astrahan et al. [1976] discusses System R. Chamberlin et al. [1981] reviews System R in retrospect. The *Oracle 8 Concepts Manual* (Oracle [1997]) describes the storage organization of the Oracle 8 database system. The structure of the Wisconsin Storage System (WiSS) is described in Chou et al. [1985]. A software tool for the physical design of relational databases is described by Finkelstein et al. [1988].

Buffer management is discussed in most operating system texts, including in Silberschatz and Galvin [1998]. Stonebraker [1981] discusses the relationship between database-system buffer managers and operating-system buffer managers. Chou and Dewitt [1985] presents algorithms for buffer management in database systems, and describes a performance evaluation. Bridge et al. [1997] describes techniques used in the buffer manager of the Oracle database system.

Descriptions and performance comparisons of different swizzling techniques are given in Wilson [1990], Moss [1990], and White and DeWitt [1992]. White and DeWitt [1994] describes the virtual-memory-mapped buffer-management scheme used in the ObjectStore OODB system and in the QuickStore storage manager. Using this scheme, we can map disk pages to a fixed virtual-memory address, even if they are not pinned in the buffer. The Exodus object storage manager is described in Carey et al. [1986]. Biliris and Orenstein [1994] provides a survey of storage systems for object-oriented databases. Jagadish et al. [1994] describes a storage manager for main-memory databases.

C H A P T E R   1 2

Indexing and Hashing

Many queries reference only a small proportion of the records in a file. For example, a query like "Find all accounts at the Perryridge branch" or "Find the balance of account number A-101" references only a fraction of the account records. It is inefficient for the system to read every record and to check the *branch-name* field for the name "Perryridge," or the *account-number* field for the value A-101. Ideally, the system should be able to locate these records directly. To allow these forms of access, we design additional structures that we associate with files.

12.1 Basic Concepts

An index for a file in a database system works in much the same way as the index in this textbook. If we want to learn about a particular topic (specified by a word or a phrase) in this textbook, we can search for the topic in the index at the back of the book, find the pages where it occurs, and then read the pages to find the information we are looking for. The words in the index are in sorted order, making it easy to find the word we are looking for. Moreover, the index is much smaller than the book, further reducing the effort needed to find the words we are looking for.

Card catalogs in libraries worked in a similar manner (although they are rarely used any longer). To find a book by a particular author, we would search in the author catalog, and a card in the catalog tells us where to find the book. To assist us in searching the catalog, the library would keep the cards in alphabetic order by authors, with one card for each author of each book.

Database system indices play the same role as book indices or card catalogs in libraries. For example, to retrieve an *account* record given the account number, the database system would look up an index to find on which disk block the corresponding record resides, and then fetch the disk block, to get the *account* record.

Keeping a sorted list of account numbers would not work well on very large databases with millions of accounts, since the index would itself be very big; further, even though keeping the index sorted reduces the search time, finding an account can still be rather time-consuming. Instead, more sophisticated indexing techniques may be used. We shall discuss several of these techniques in this chapter.

There are two basic kinds of indices:

- **Ordered indices**. Based on a sorted ordering of the values.

- **Hash indices**. Based on a uniform distribution of values across a range of buckets. The bucket to which a value is assigned is determined by a function, called a *hash function*.

We shall consider several techniques for both ordered indexing and hashing. No one technique is the best. Rather, each technique is best suited to particular database applications. Each technique must be evaluated on the basis of these factors:

- **Access types**: The types of access that are supported efficiently. Access types can include finding records with a specified attribute value and finding records whose attribute values fall in a specified range.

- **Access time**: The time it takes to find a particular data item, or set of items, using the technique in question.

- **Insertion time**: The time it takes to insert a new data item. This value includes the time it takes to find the correct place to insert the new data item, as well as the time it takes to update the index structure.

- **Deletion time**: The time it takes to delete a data item. This value includes the time it takes to find the item to be deleted, as well as the time it takes to update the index structure.

- **Space overhead**: The additional space occupied by an index structure. Provided that the amount of additional space is moderate, it is usually worthwhile to sacrifice the space to achieve improved performance.

We often want to have more than one index for a file. For example, libraries maintained several card catalogs: for author, for subject, and for title.

An attribute or set of attributes used to look up records in a file is called a **search key**. Note that this definition of *key* differs from that used in *primary key*, *candidate key*, and *superkey*. This duplicate meaning for *key* is (unfortunately) well established in practice. Using our notion of a search key, we see that if there are several indices on a file, there are several search keys.

12.2 Ordered Indices

To gain fast random access to records in a file, we can use an index structure. Each index structure is associated with a particular search key. Just like the index of a book or a library catalog, an ordered index stores the values of the search keys in sorted order, and associates with each search key the records that contain it.

The records in the indexed file may themselves be stored in some sorted order, just as books in a library are stored according to some attribute such as the Dewey deci-

A-217	Brighton	750	
A-101	Downtown	500	
A-110	Downtown	600	
A-215	Mianus	700	
A-102	Perryridge	400	
A-201	Perryridge	900	
A-218	Perryridge	700	
A-222	Redwood	700	
A-305	Round Hill	350	

Brighton	
Mianus	
Redwood	

Figure 12.1   Sequential file for *account* records.

mal number. A file may have several indices, on different search keys. If the file containing the records is sequentially ordered, a **primary index** is an index whose search key also defines the sequential order of the file. (The term *primary index* is sometimes used to mean an index on a primary key. However, such usage is nonstandard and should be avoided.) Primary indices are also called **clustering indices**. The search key of a primary index is usually the primary key, although that is not necessarily so. Indices whose search key specifies an order different from the sequential order of the file are called **secondary indices**, or **nonclustering** indices.

12.2.1 Primary Index

In this section, we assume that all files are ordered sequentially on some search key. Such files, with a primary index on the search key, are called **index-sequential files**. They represent one of the oldest index schemes used in database systems. They are designed for applications that require both sequential processing of the entire file and random access to individual records.

Figure 12.1 shows a sequential file of *account* records taken from our banking example. In the example of Figure 12.1, the records are stored in search-key order, with *branch-name* used as the search key.

12.2.1.1 Dense and Sparse Indices

An **index record**, or **index entry**, consists of a search-key value, and pointers to one or more records with that value as their search-key value. The pointer to a record consists of the identifier of a disk block and an offset within the disk block to identify the record within the block.

There are two types of ordered indices that we can use:

- **Dense index**: An index record appears for every search-key value in the file. In a dense primary index, the index record contains the search-key value and a pointer to the first data record with that search-key value. The rest of the records with the same search key-value would be stored sequentially after the first record, since, because the index is a primary one, records are sorted on the same search key.

Dense index implementations may store a list of pointers to all records with the same search-key value; doing so is not essential for primary indices.

- **Sparse index**: An index record appears for only some of the search-key values. As is true in dense indices, each index record contains a search-key value and a pointer to the first data record with that search-key value. To locate a record, we find the index entry with the largest search-key value that is less than or equal to the search-key value for which we are looking. We start at the record pointed to by that index entry, and follow the pointers in the file until we find the desired record.

Figures 12.2 and 12.3 show dense and sparse indices, respectively, for the *account* file. Suppose that we are looking up records for the Perryridge branch. Using the dense index of Figure 12.2, we follow the pointer directly to the first Perryridge record. We process this record, and follow the pointer in that record to locate the next record in search-key (*branch-name*) order. We continue processing records until we encounter a record for a branch other than Perryridge. If we are using the sparse index (Figure 12.3), we do not find an index entry for "Perryridge." Since the last entry (in alphabetic order) before "Perryridge" is "Mianus," we follow that pointer. We then read the *account* file in sequential order until we find the first Perryridge record, and begin processing at that point.

As we have seen, it is generally faster to locate a record if we have a dense index rather than a sparse index. However, sparse indices have advantages over dense indices in that they require less space and they impose less maintenance overhead for insertions and deletions.

There is a trade-off that the system designer must make between access time and space overhead. Although the decision regarding this trade-off depends on the specific application, a good compromise is to have a sparse index with one index entry per block. The reason this design is a good trade-off is that the dominant cost in pro-

Brighton	—	A-217	Brighton	750	
Downtown	—	A-101	Downtown	500	
Mianus	—	A-110	Downtown	600	
Perryridge	—	A-215	Mianus	700	
Redwood	—	A-102	Perryridge	400	
Round Hill	—	A-201	Perryridge	900	
		A-218	Perryridge	700	
		A-222	Redwood	700	
		A-305	Round Hill	350	

Figure 12.2 Dense index.

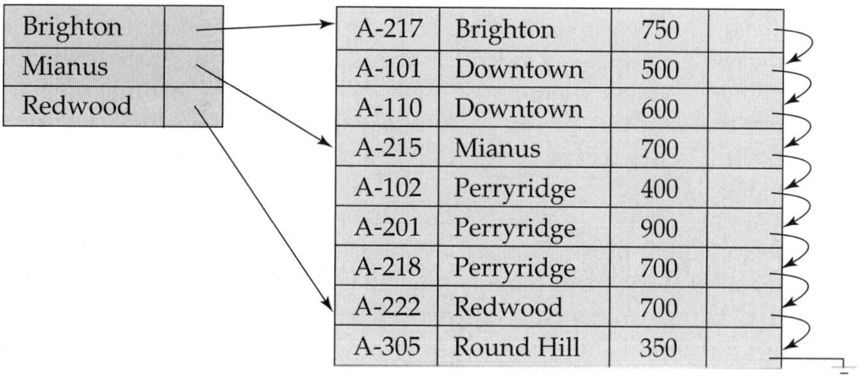

Figure 12.3   Sparse index.

cessing a database request is the time that it takes to bring a block from disk into main memory. Once we have brought in the block, the time to scan the entire block is negligible. Using this sparse index, we locate the block containing the record that we are seeking. Thus, unless the record is on an overflow block (see Section 11.7.1), we minimize block accesses while keeping the size of the index (and thus, our space overhead) as small as possible.

For the preceding technique to be fully general, we must consider the case where records for one search-key value occupy several blocks. It is easy to modify our scheme to handle this situation.

12.2.1.2   Multilevel Indices

Even if we use a sparse index, the index itself may become too large for efficient processing. It is not unreasonable, in practice, to have a file with 100,000 records, with 10 records stored in each block. If we have one index record per block, the index has 10,000 records. Index records are smaller than data records, so let us assume that 100 index records fit on a block. Thus, our index occupies 100 blocks. Such large indices are stored as sequential files on disk.

If an index is sufficiently small to be kept in main memory, the search time to find an entry is low. However, if the index is so large that it must be kept on disk, a search for an entry requires several disk block reads. Binary search can be used on the index file to locate an entry, but the search still has a large cost. If the index occupies b blocks, binary search requires as many as $\lceil \log_2(b) \rceil$ blocks to be read. ($\lceil x \rceil$ denotes the least integer that is greater than or equal to x; that is, we round upward.) For our 100-block index, binary search requires seven block reads. On a disk system where a block read takes 30 milliseconds, the search will take 210 milliseconds, which is long. Note that, if overflow blocks have been used, binary search will not be possible. In that case, a sequential search is typically used, and that requires b block reads, which will take even longer. Thus, the process of searching a large index may be costly.

To deal with this problem, we treat the index just as we would treat any other sequential file, and construct a sparse index on the primary index, as in Figure 12.4.

To locate a record, we first use binary search on the outer index to find the record for the largest search-key value less than or equal to the one that we desire. The pointer points to a block of the inner index. We scan this block until we find the record that has the largest search-key value less than or equal to the one that we desire. The pointer in this record points to the block of the file that contains the record for which we are looking.

Using the two levels of indexing, we have read only one index block, rather than the seven we read with binary search, if we assume that the outer index is already in main memory. If our file is extremely large, even the outer index may grow too large to fit in main memory. In such a case, we can create yet another level of index. Indeed, we can repeat this process as many times as necessary. Indices with two or more levels are called **multilevel** indices. Searching for records with a multilevel index requires significantly fewer I/O operations than does searching for records by binary search. Each level of index could correspond to a unit of physical storage. Thus, we may have indices at the track, cylinder, and disk levels.

A typical dictionary is an example of a multilevel index in the nondatabase world. The header of each page lists the first word alphabetically on that page. Such a book

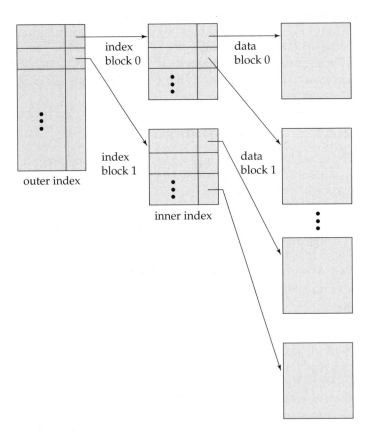

Figure 12.4 Two-level sparse index.

index is a multilevel index: The words at the top of each page of the book index form a sparse index on the contents of the dictionary pages.

Multilevel indices are closely related to tree structures, such as the binary trees used for in-memory indexing. We shall examine the relationship later, in Section 12.3.

12.2.1.3   Index Update

Regardless of what form of index is used, every index must be updated whenever a record is either inserted into or deleted from the file. We first describe algorithms for updating single-level indices.

- **Insertion**. First, the system performs a lookup using the search-key value that appears in the record to be inserted. Again, the actions the system takes next depend on whether the index is dense or sparse:

  □ Dense indices:

  1. If the search-key value does not appear in the index, the system inserts an index record with the search-key value in the index at the appropriate position.

  2. Otherwise the following actions are taken:

     a. If the index record stores pointers to all records with the same search-key value, the system adds a pointer to the new record to the index record.

     b. Otherwise, the index record stores a pointer to only the first record with the search-key value. The system then places the record being inserted after the other records with the same search-key values.

  □ Sparse indices: We assume that the index stores an entry for each block. If the system creates a new block, it inserts the first search-key value (in search-key order) appearing in the new block into the index. On the other hand, if the new record has the least search-key value in its block, the system updates the index entry pointing to the block; if not, the system makes no change to the index.

- **Deletion**. To delete a record, the system first looks up the record to be deleted. The actions the system takes next depend on whether the index is dense or sparse:

  □ Dense indices:

  1. If the deleted record was the only record with its particular search-key value, then the system deletes the corresponding index record from the index.

  2. Otherwise the following actions are taken:

     a. If the index record stores pointers to all records with the same search-key value, the system deletes the pointer to the deleted record from the index record.

b. Otherwise, the index record stores a pointer to only the first record with the search-key value. In this case, if the deleted record was the first record with the search-key value, the system updates the index record to point to the next record.

☐ Sparse indices:

1. If the index does not contain an index record with the search-key value of the deleted record, nothing needs to be done to the index.

2. Otherwise the system takes the following actions:

a. If the deleted record was the only record with its search key, the system replaces the corresponding index record with an index record for the next search-key value (in search-key order). If the next search-key value already has an index entry, the entry is deleted instead of being replaced.

b. Otherwise, if the index record for the search-key value points to the record being deleted, the system updates the index record to point to the next record with the same search-key value.

Insertion and deletion algorithms for multilevel indices are a simple extension of the scheme just described. On deletion or insertion, the system updates the lowest-level index as described. As far as the second level is concerned, the lowest-level index is merely a file containing records—thus, if there is any change in the lowest-level index, the system updates the second-level index as described. The same technique applies to further levels of the index, if there are any.

12.2.2 Secondary Indices

Secondary indices must be dense, with an index entry for every search-key value, and a pointer to every record in the file. A primary index may be sparse, storing only some of the search-key values, since it is always possible to find records with intermediate search-key values by a sequential access to a part of the file, as described earlier. If a secondary index stores only some of the search-key values, records with intermediate search-key values may be anywhere in the file and, in general, we cannot find them without searching the entire file.

A secondary index on a candidate key looks just like a dense primary index, except that the records pointed to by successive values in the index are not stored sequentially. In general, however, secondary indices may have a different structure from primary indices. If the search key of a primary index is not a candidate key, it suffices if the index points to the first record with a particular value for the search key, since the other records can be fetched by a sequential scan of the file.

In contrast, if the search key of a secondary index is not a candidate key, it is not enough to point to just the first record with each search-key value. The remaining records with the same search-key value could be anywhere in the file, since the records are ordered by the search key of the primary index, rather than by the search key of the secondary index. Therefore, a secondary index must contain pointers to all the records.

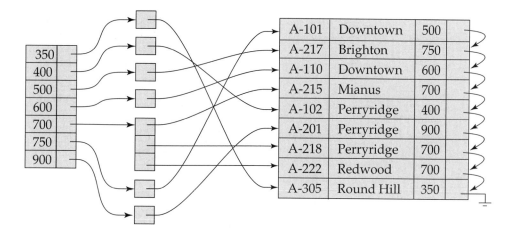

Figure 12.5   Secondary index on *account* file, on noncandidate key *balance*.

We can use an extra level of indirection to implement secondary indices on search keys that are not candidate keys. The pointers in such a secondary index do not point directly to the file. Instead, each points to a bucket that contains pointers to the file. Figure 12.5 shows the structure of a secondary index that uses an extra level of indirection on the *account* file, on the search key *balance*.

A sequential scan in primary index order is efficient because records in the file are stored physically in the same order as the index order. However, we cannot (except in rare special cases) store a file physically ordered both by the search key of the primary index, and the search key of a secondary index. Because secondary-key order and physical-key order differ, if we attempt to scan the file sequentially in secondary-key order, the reading of each record is likely to require the reading of a new block from disk, which is very slow.

The procedure described earlier for deletion and insertion can also be applied to secondary indices; the actions taken are those described for dense indices storing a pointer to every record in the file. If a file has multiple indices, whenever the file is modified, *every* index must be updated.

Secondary indices improve the performance of queries that use keys other than the search key of the primary index. However, they impose a significant overhead on modification of the database. The designer of a database decides which secondary indices are desirable on the basis of an estimate of the relative frequency of queries and modifications.

12.3   B$^+$-Tree Index Files

The main disadvantage of the index-sequential file organization is that performance degrades as the file grows, both for index lookups and for sequential scans through the data. Although this degradation can be remedied by reorganization of the file, frequent reorganizations are undesirable.

P_1	K_1	P_2	$\cdots$	P_{n-1}	K_{n-1}	P_n

Figure 12.6 Typical node of a B^+-tree.

The **B^+-tree** index structure is the most widely used of several index structures that maintain their efficiency despite insertion and deletion of data. A B^+-tree index takes the form of a **balanced tree** in which every path from the root of the tree to a leaf of the tree is of the same length. Each nonleaf node in the tree has between $\lceil n/2 \rceil$ and n children, where n is fixed for a particular tree.

We shall see that the B^+-tree structure imposes performance overhead on insertion and deletion, and adds space overhead. The overhead is acceptable even for frequently modified files, since the cost of file reorganization is avoided. Furthermore, since nodes may be as much as half empty (if they have the minimum number of children), there is some wasted space. This space overhead, too, is acceptable given the performance benefits of the B^+-tree structure.

12.3.1 Structure of a B^+-Tree

A B^+-tree index is a multilevel index, but it has a structure that differs from that of the multilevel index-sequential file. Figure 12.6 shows a typical node of a B^+-tree. It contains up to $n - 1$ search-key values $K_1, K_2, \ldots, K_{n-1}$, and n pointers $P_1, P_2, \ldots, P_n$. The search-key values within a node are kept in sorted order; thus, if $i < j$, then $K_i < K_j$.

We consider first the structure of the leaf nodes. For $i = 1, 2, \ldots, n - 1$, pointer P_i points to either a file record with search-key value K_i or to a bucket of pointers, each of which points to a file record with search-key value K_i. The bucket structure is used only if the search key does not form a primary key, and if the file is not sorted in the search-key value order. Pointer P_n has a special purpose that we shall discuss shortly.

Figure 12.7 shows one leaf node of a B^+-tree for the *account* file, in which we have chosen n to be 3, and the search key is *branch-name*. Note that, since the account file is ordered by *branch-name*, the pointers in the leaf node point directly to the file.

Now that we have seen the structure of a leaf node, let us consider how search-key values are assigned to particular nodes. Each leaf can hold up to $n - 1$ values. We allow leaf nodes to contain as few as $\lceil (n-1)/2 \rceil$ values. The ranges of values in each leaf do not overlap. Thus, if L_i and L_j are leaf nodes and $i < j$, then every search-key value in L_i is less than every search-key value in L_j. If the B^+-tree index is to be a dense index, every search-key value must appear in some leaf node.

Now we can explain the use of the pointer P_n. Since there is a linear order on the leaves based on the search-key values that they contain, we use P_n to chain together the leaf nodes in search-key order. This ordering allows for efficient sequential processing of the file.

The nonleaf nodes of the B^+-tree form a multilevel (sparse) index on the leaf nodes. The structure of nonleaf nodes is the same as that for leaf nodes, except that all pointers are pointers to tree nodes. A nonleaf node may hold up to n pointers, and *must*

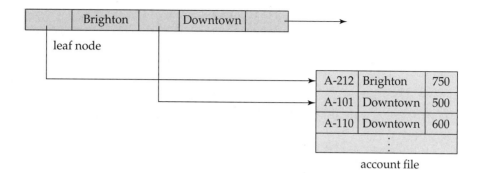

Figure 12.7   A leaf node for *account* B$^+$-tree index ($n = 3$).

hold at least $\lceil n/2 \rceil$ pointers. The number of pointers in a node is called the *fanout* of the node.

Let us consider a node containing m pointers. For $i = 2, 3, \ldots, m - 1$, pointer P_i points to the subtree that contains search-key values less than K_i and greater than or equal to K_{i-1}. Pointer P_m points to the part of the subtree that contains those key values greater than or equal to K_{m-1}, and pointer P_1 points to the part of the subtree that contains those search-key values less than K_1.

Unlike other nonleaf nodes, the root node can hold fewer than $\lceil n/2 \rceil$ pointers; however, it must hold at least two pointers, unless the tree consists of only one node. It is always possible to construct a B$^+$-tree, for any n, that satisfies the preceding requirements. Figure 12.8 shows a complete B$^+$-tree for the *account* file ($n = 3$). For simplicity, we have omitted both the pointers to the file itself and the null pointers. As an example of a B$^+$-tree for which the root must have less than $\lceil n/2 \rceil$ values, Figure 12.9 shows a B$^+$-tree for the *account* file with $n = 5$.

These examples of B$^+$-trees are all balanced. That is, the length of every path from the root to a leaf node is the same. This property is a requirement for a B$^+$-tree. Indeed, the "B" in B$^+$-tree stands for "balanced." It is the balance property of B$^+$-trees that ensures good performance for lookup, insertion, and deletion.

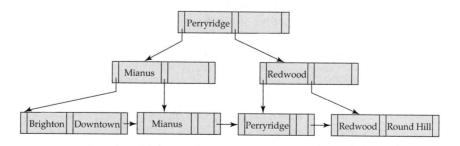

Figure 12.8   B$^+$-tree for *account* file ($n = 3$).

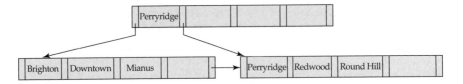

Figure 12.9 B$^+$-tree for *account* file with $n = 5$.

12.3.2 Queries on B$^+$-Trees

Let us consider how we process queries on a B$^+$-tree. Suppose that we wish to find all records with a search-key value of V. Figure 12.10 presents pseudocode for doing so. Intuitively, the procedure works as follows. First, we examine the root node, looking for the smallest search-key value greater than V. Suppose that we find that this search-key value is K_i. We then follow pointer P_i to another node. If we find no such value, then $k \geq K_{m-1}$, where m is the number of pointers in the node. In this case we follow P_m to another node. In the node we reached above, again we look for the smallest search-key value greater than V, and once again follow the corresponding pointer as above. Eventually, we reach a leaf node. At the leaf node, if we find search-key value K_i equals V, then pointer P_i directs us to the desired record or bucket. If the value V is not found in the leaf node, no record with key value V exists.

Thus, in processing a query, we traverse a path in the tree from the root to some leaf node. If there are K search-key values in the file, the path is no longer than $\lceil \log_{\lceil n/2 \rceil}(K) \rceil$.

In practice, only a few nodes need to be accessed, Typically, a node is made to be the same size as a disk block, which is typically 4 kilobytes. With a search-key size of 12 bytes, and a disk-pointer size of 8 bytes, n is around 200. Even with a more conservative estimate of 32 bytes for the search-key size, n is around 100. With $n = 100$, if we have 1 million search-key values in the file, a lookup requires only

```
procedure find(value V)
    set C = root node
    while C is not a leaf node begin
        Let K_i = smallest search-key value, if any, greater than V
        if there is no such value then begin
            Let m = the number of pointers in the node
            set C = node pointed to by P_m
        end
            else set C = the node pointed to by P_i
    end
    if there is a key value K_i in C such that K_i = V
        then pointer P_i directs us to the desired record or bucket
        else no record with key value k exists
end procedure
```

Figure 12.10 Querying a B$^+$-tree.

$\lceil \log_{50}(1,000,000) \rceil = 4$ nodes to be accessed. Thus, at most four blocks need to be read from disk for the lookup. The root node of the tree is usually heavily accessed and is likely to be in the buffer, so typically only three or fewer blocks need to be read from disk.

An important difference between B⁺-tree structures and in-memory tree structures, such as binary trees, is the size of a node, and as a result, the height of the tree. In a binary tree, each node is small, and has at most two pointers. In a B⁺-tree, each node is large—typically a disk block—and a node can have a large number of pointers. Thus, B⁺-trees tend to be fat and short, unlike thin and tall binary trees. In a balanced binary tree, the path for a lookup can be of length $\lceil \log_2(K) \rceil$, where K is the number of search-key values. With $K = 1,000,000$ as in the previous example, a balanced binary tree requires around 20 node accesses. If each node were on a different disk block, 20 block reads would be required to process a lookup, in contrast to the four block reads for the B⁺-tree.

12.3.3 Updates on B⁺-Trees

Insertion and deletion are more complicated than lookup, since it may be necessary to **split** a node that becomes too large as the result of an insertion, or to **coalesce** nodes (that is, combine nodes) if a node becomes too small (fewer than $\lceil n/2 \rceil$ pointers). Furthermore, when a node is split or a pair of nodes is combined, we must ensure that balance is preserved. To introduce the idea behind insertion and deletion in a B⁺-tree, we shall assume temporarily that nodes never become too large or too small. Under this assumption, insertion and deletion are performed as defined next.

- **Insertion**. Using the same technique as for lookup, we find the leaf node in which the search-key value would appear. If the search-key value already appears in the leaf node, we add the new record to the file and, if necessary, add to the bucket a pointer to the record. If the search-key value does not appear, we insert the value in the leaf node, and position it such that the search keys are still in order. We then insert the new record in the file and, if necessary, create a new bucket with the appropriate pointer.

- **Deletion**. Using the same technique as for lookup, we find the record to be deleted, and remove it from the file. We remove the search-key value from the leaf node if there is no bucket associated with that search-key value or if the bucket becomes empty as a result of the deletion.

We now consider an example in which a node must be split. Assume that we wish to insert a record with a *branch-name* value of "Clearview" into the B⁺-tree of Figure 12.8. Using the algorithm for lookup, we find that "Clearview" should appear in the node containing "Brighton" and "Downtown." There is no room to insert the search-key value "Clearview." Therefore, the node is *split* into two nodes. Figure 12.11 shows the two leaf nodes that result from inserting "Clearview" and splitting the node containing "Brighton" and "Downtown." In general, we take the n search-key

Figure 12.11   Split of leaf node on insertion of "Clearview."

values (the $n - 1$ values in the leaf node plus the value being inserted), and put the first $\lceil n/2 \rceil$ in the existing node and the remaining values in a new node.

Having split a leaf node, we must insert the new leaf node into the B$^+$-tree structure. In our example, the new node has "Downtown" as its smallest search-key value. We need to insert this search-key value into the parent of the leaf node that was split. The B$^+$-tree of Figure 12.12 shows the result of the insertion. The search-key value "Downtown" was inserted into the parent. It was possible to perform this insertion because there was room for an added search-key value. If there were no room, the parent would have had to be split. In the worst case, all nodes along the path to the root must be split. If the root itself is split, the entire tree becomes deeper.

The general technique for insertion into a B$^+$-tree is to determine the leaf node l into which insertion must occur. If a split results, insert the new node into the parent of node l. If this insertion causes a split, proceed recursively up the tree until either an insertion does not cause a split or a new root is created.

Figure 12.13 outlines the insertion algorithm in pseudocode. In the pseudocode, $L.K_i$ and $L.P_i$ denote the ith value and the ith pointer in node L, respectively. The pseudocode also makes use of the function $parent(L)$ to find the parent of a node L. We can compute a list of nodes in the path from the root to the leaf while initially finding the leaf node, and can use it later to find the parent of any node in the path efficiently. The pseudocode refers to inserting an entry (V, P) into a node. In the case of leaf nodes, the pointer to an entry actually precedes the key value, so the leaf node actually stores P before V. For internal nodes, P is stored just after V.

We now consider deletions that cause tree nodes to contain too few pointers. First, let us delete "Downtown" from the B$^+$-tree of Figure 12.12. We locate the entry for "Downtown" by using our lookup algorithm. When we delete the entry for "Downtown" from its leaf node, the leaf becomes empty. Since, in our example, $n = 3$ and $0 < \lceil (n-1)/2 \rceil$, this node must be eliminated from the B$^+$-tree. To delete a leaf node,

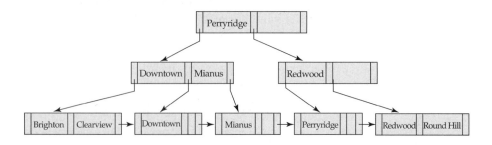

Figure 12.12   Insertion of "Clearview" into the B$^+$-tree of Figure 12.8.

procedure insert(*value V*, *pointer P*)
    find the leaf node L that should contain value V
    insert_entry(L, V, P)
end procedure

procedure insert_entry(*node L*, *value V*, *pointer P*)
    if (L has space for (V, P))
        then insert (V, P) in L
        else begin /* Split L */
            Create node L'
            Let V' be the value in $L.K_1, \ldots, L.K_{n-1}, V$ such that exactly
                $\lceil n/2 \rceil$ of the values $L.K_1, \ldots, L.K_{n-1}, V$ are less than V'
            Let m be the lowest value such that $L.K_m \geq V'$
            /* Note: V' must be either $L.K_m$ or V */
            if (L is a leaf) **then begin**
                move $L.P_m, L.K_m, \ldots, L.P_{n-1}, L.K_{n-1}$ to L'
                if $(V < V')$ **then** insert (P, V) in L
                else insert (P, V) in L'
            end
            else begin
                if $(V = V')$ /* V is smallest value to go to L' */
                    then add $P, L.K_m, \ldots, L.P_{n-1}, L.K_{n-1}, L.P_n$ to L'
                    else add $L.P_m, \ldots, L.P_{n-1}, L.K_{n-1}, L.P_n$ to L'
                delete $L.K_m, \ldots, L.P_{n-1}, L.K_{n-1}, L.P_n$ from L
                if $(V < V')$ **then** insert (V, P) in L
                else if $(V > V')$ **then** insert (V, P) in L'
                /* Case of $V = V'$ handled already */
            end
            if (L is not the root of the tree)
                then insert_entry(*parent*(L), V', L');
                else begin
                    create a new node R with child nodes L and L' and
                        the single value V'
                    make R the root of the tree
                end
            if (L) is a leaf node **then begin** /* Fix next child pointers */
                set $L'.P_n = L.P_n$;
                set $L.P_n = L'$
         end
      end
end procedure

Figure 12.13   Insertion of entry in a B$^+$-tree.

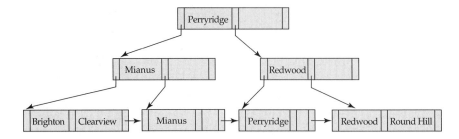

Figure 12.14 Deletion of "Downtown" from the B$^+$-tree of Figure 12.12.

we must delete the pointer to it from its parent. In our example, this deletion leaves the parent node, which formerly contained three pointers, with only two pointers. Since $2 \geq \lceil n/2 \rceil$, the node is still sufficiently large, and the deletion operation is complete. The resulting B$^+$-tree appears in Figure 12.14.

When we make a deletion from a parent of a leaf node, the parent node itself may become too small. That is exactly what happens if we delete "Perryridge" from the B$^+$-tree of Figure 12.14. Deletion of the Perryridge entry causes a leaf node to become empty. When we delete the pointer to this node in the latter's parent, the parent is left with only one pointer. Since $n = 3$, $\lceil n/2 \rceil = 2$, and thus only one pointer is too few. However, since the parent node contains useful information, we cannot simply delete it. Instead, we look at the sibling node (the nonleaf node containing the one search key, Mianus). This sibling node has room to accommodate the information contained in our now-too-small node, so we coalesce these nodes, such that the sibling node now contains the keys "Mianus" and "Redwood." The other node (the node containing only the search key "Redwood") now contains redundant information and can be deleted from its parent (which happens to be the root in our example). Figure 12.15 shows the result. Notice that the root has only one child pointer after the deletion, so it is deleted and its sole child becomes the root. So the depth of the B$^+$-tree has been decreased by 1.

It is not always possible to coalesce nodes. As an illustration, delete "Perryridge" from the B$^+$-tree of Figure 12.12. In this example, the "Downtown" entry is still part of the tree. Once again, the leaf node containing "Perryridge" becomes empty. The parent of the leaf node becomes too small (only one pointer). However, in this example, the sibling node already contains the maximum number of pointers: three. Thus, it cannot accommodate an additional pointer. The solution in this case is to **redistribute** the pointers such that each sibling has two pointers. The result appears in

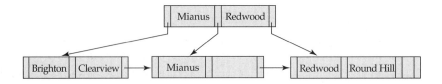

Figure 12.15 Deletion of "Perryridge" from the B$^+$-tree of Figure 12.14.

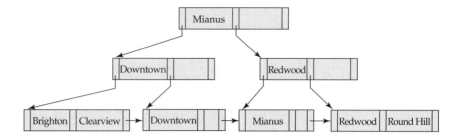

Figure 12.16   Deletion of "Perryridge" from the B$^+$-tree of Figure 12.12.

Figure 12.16. Note that the redistribution of values necessitates a change of a search-key value in the parent of the two siblings.

In general, to delete a value in a B$^+$-tree, we perform a lookup on the value and delete it. If the node is too small, we delete it from its parent. This deletion results in recursive application of the deletion algorithm until the root is reached, a parent remains adequately full after deletion, or redistribution is applied.

Figure 12.17 outlines the pseudocode for deletion from a B$^+$-tree. The procedure swap_variables(L, L') merely swaps the values of the (pointer) variables L and L'; this swap has no effect on the tree itself. The pseudocode uses the condition "too few pointers/values." For nonleaf nodes, this criterion means less than $\lceil n/2 \rceil$ pointers; for leaf nodes, it means less than $\lceil (n - 1)/2 \rceil$ values. The pseudocode redistributes entries by borrowing a single entry from an adjacent node. We can also redistribute entries by repartitioning entries equally between the two nodes. The pseudocode refers to deleting an entry (V, P) from a node. In the case of leaf nodes, the pointer to an entry actually precedes the key value, so the pointer P precedes the key value V. For internal nodes, P follows the key value V.

It is worth noting that, as a result of deletion, a key value that is present in an internal node of the B$^+$-tree may not be present at any leaf of the tree.

Although insertion and deletion operations on B$^+$-trees are complicated, they require relatively few I/O operations, which is an important benefit since I/O operations are expensive. It can be shown that the number of I/O operations needed for a worst-case insertion or deletion is proportional to $\log_{\lceil n/2 \rceil}(K)$, where n is the maximum number of pointers in a node, and K is the number of search-key values. In other words, the cost of insertion and deletion operations is proportional to the height of the B$^+$-tree, and is therefore low. It is the speed of operation on B$^+$-trees that makes them a frequently used index structure in database implementations.

12.3.4   B$^+$-Tree File Organization

As mentioned in Section 12.3, the main drawback of index-sequential file organization is the degradation of performance as the file grows: With growth, an increasing percentage of index records and actual records become out of order, and are stored in overflow blocks. We solve the degradation of index lookups by using B$^+$-tree indices on the file. We solve the degradation problem for storing the actual records by using the leaf level of the B$^+$-tree to organize the blocks containing the actual records. We

procedure delete(*value V*, *pointer P*)
    find the leaf node L that contains (V, P)
    delete_entry(L, V, P)
end procedure
procedure delete_entry(*node L*, *value V*, *pointer P*)
    delete (V, P) from L
    if (L is the root **and** L has only one remaining child)
    then make the child of L the new root of the tree and delete L
    else if (L has too few values/pointers) **then begin**
        Let L' be the previous or next child of $parent(L)$
        Let V' be the value between pointers L and L' in $parent(L)$
        if (entries in L and L' can fit in a single node)
            then begin /* Coalesce nodes */
                if (L is a predecessor of L') **then** swap_variables(L, L')
                if (L is not a leaf)
                    then append V' and all pointers and values in L to L'
                    else append all (K_i, P_i) pairs in L to L'; set $L'.P_n = L.P_n$
                delete_entry($parent(L), V', L$); delete node L
            end
        else begin /* Redistribution: borrow an entry from L' */
            if (L' is a predecessor of L) **then begin**
                if (L is a non-leaf node) **then begin**
                    let m be such that $L'.P_m$ is the last pointer in L'
                    remove $(L'.K_{m-1}, L'.P_m)$ from L'
                    insert $(L'.P_m, V')$ as the first pointer and value in L,
                        by shifting other pointers and values right
                    replace V' in $parent(L)$ by $L'.K_{m-1}$
                end
                else begin
                    let m be such that $(L'.P_m, L'.K_m)$ is the last pointer/value
                        pair in L'
                    remove $(L'.P_m, L'.K_m)$ from L'
                    insert $(L'.P_m, L'.K_m)$ as the first pointer and value in L,
                        by shifting other pointers and values right
                    replace V' in $parent(L)$ by $L'.K_m$
                end
            end
            else ... symmetric to the **then** case ...
        end
    end
end procedure

Figure 12.17 Deletion of entry from a B$^+$-tree.

use the B$^+$-tree structure not only as an index, but also as an organizer for records in a file. In a **B$^+$-tree file organization**, the leaf nodes of the tree store records, instead of storing pointers to records. Figure 12.18 shows an example of a B$^+$-tree file organization. Since records are usually larger than pointers, the maximum number of records that can be stored in a leaf node is less than the number of pointers in a nonleaf node. However, the leaf nodes are still required to be at least half full.

Insertion and deletion of records from a B$^+$-tree file organization are handled in the same way as insertion and deletion of entries in a B$^+$-tree index. When a record with a given key value v is inserted, the system locates the block that should contain the record by searching the B$^+$-tree for the largest key in the tree that is $\leq v$. If the block located has enough free space for the record, the system stores the record in the block. Otherwise, as in B$^+$-tree insertion, the system splits the block in two, and redistributes the records in it (in the B$^+$-tree–key order) to create space for the new record. The split propagates up the B$^+$-tree in the normal fashion. When we delete a record, the system first removes it from the block containing it. If a block B becomes less than half full as a result, the records in B are redistributed with the records in an adjacent block B'. Assuming fixed-sized records, each block will hold at least one-half as many records as the maximum that it can hold. The system updates the nonleaf nodes of the B$^+$-tree in the usual fashion.

When we use a B$^+$-tree for file organization, space utilization is particularly important, since the space occupied by the records is likely to be much more than the space occupied by keys and pointers. We can improve the utilization of space in a B$^+$-tree by involving more sibling nodes in redistribution during splits and merges. The technique is applicable to both leaf nodes and internal nodes, and works as follows.

During insertion, if a node is full the system attempts to redistribute some of its entries to one of the adjacent nodes, to make space for a new entry. If this attempt fails because the adjacent nodes are themselves full, the system splits the node, and splits the entries evenly among one of the adjacent nodes and the two nodes that it obtained by splitting the original node. Since the three nodes together contain one more record than can fit in two nodes, each node will be about two-thirds full. More precisely, each node will have at least $\lfloor 2n/3 \rfloor$ entries, where n is the maximum number of entries that the node can hold. ($\lfloor x \rfloor$ denotes the greatest integer that is less than or equal to x; that is, we drop the fractional part, if any.)

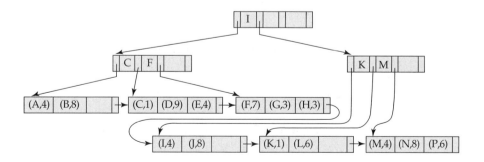

Figure 12.18   B$^+$-tree file organization.

During deletion of a record, if the occupancy of a node falls below $\lfloor 2n/3 \rfloor$, the system attempts to borrow an entry from one of the sibling nodes. If both sibling nodes have $\lfloor 2n/3 \rfloor$ records, instead of borrowing an entry, the system redistributes the entries in the node and in the two siblings evenly between two of the nodes, and deletes the third node. We can use this approach because the total number of entries is $3\lfloor 2n/3 \rfloor - 1$, which is less than $2n$. With three adjacent nodes used for redistribution, each node can be guaranteed to have $\lfloor 3n/4 \rfloor$ entries. In general, if m nodes ($m - 1$ siblings) are involved in redistribution, each node can be guaranteed to contain at least $\lfloor (m - 1)n/m \rfloor$ entries. However, the cost of update becomes higher as more sibling nodes are involved in the redistribution.

12.4 B-Tree Index Files

B-tree indices are similar to B$^+$-tree indices. The primary distinction between the two approaches is that a B-tree eliminates the redundant storage of search-key values. In the B$^+$-tree of Figure 12.12, the search keys "Downtown," "Mianus," "Redwood," and "Perryridge" appear twice. Every search-key value appears in some leaf node; several are repeated in nonleaf nodes.

A B-tree allows search-key values to appear only once. Figure 12.19 shows a B-tree that represents the same search keys as the B$^+$-tree of Figure 12.12. Since search keys are not repeated in the B-tree, we may be able to store the index in fewer tree nodes than in the corresponding B$^+$-tree index. However, since search keys that appear in nonleaf nodes appear nowhere else in the B-tree, we are forced to include an additional pointer field for each search key in a nonleaf node. These additional pointers point to either file records or buckets for the associated search key.

A generalized B-tree leaf node appears in Figure 12.20a; a nonleaf node appears in Figure 12.20b. Leaf nodes are the same as in B$^+$-trees. In nonleaf nodes, the pointers P_i are the tree pointers that we used also for B$^+$-trees, while the pointers B_i are bucket or file-record pointers. In the generalized B-tree in the figure, there are $n - 1$ keys in the leaf node, but there are $m - 1$ keys in the nonleaf node. This discrepancy occurs because nonleaf nodes must include pointers B_i, thus reducing the number of

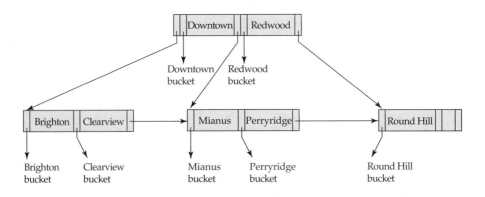

Figure 12.19 B-tree equivalent of B$^+$-tree in Figure 12.12.

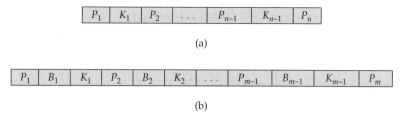

(a)

(b)

Figure 12.20   Typical nodes of a B-tree. (a) Leaf node. (b) Nonleaf node.

search keys that can be held in these nodes. Clearly, $m < n$, but the exact relationship between m and n depends on the relative size of search keys and pointers.

The number of nodes accessed in a lookup in a B-tree depends on where the search key is located. A lookup on a B^+-tree requires traversal of a path from the root of the tree to some leaf node. In contrast, it is sometimes possible to find the desired value in a B-tree before reaching a leaf node. However, roughly n times as many keys are stored in the leaf level of a B-tree as in the nonleaf levels, and, since n is typically large, the benefit of finding certain values early is relatively small. Moreover, the fact that fewer search keys appear in a nonleaf B-tree node, compared to B^+-trees, implies that a B-tree has a smaller fanout and therefore may have depth greater than that of the corresponding B^+-tree. Thus, lookup in a B-tree is faster for some search keys but slower for others, although, in general, lookup time is still proportional to the logarithm of the number of search keys.

Deletion in a B-tree is more complicated. In a B^+-tree, the deleted entry always appears in a leaf. In a B-tree, the deleted entry may appear in a nonleaf node. The proper value must be selected as a replacement from the subtree of the node containing the deleted entry. Specifically, if search key K_i is deleted, the smallest search key appearing in the subtree of pointer P_{i+1} must be moved to the field formerly occupied by K_i. Further actions need to be taken if the leaf node now has too few entries. In contrast, insertion in a B-tree is only slightly more complicated than is insertion in a B^+-tree.

The space advantages of B-trees are marginal for large indices, and usually do not outweigh the disadvantages that we have noted. Thus, many database system implementers prefer the structural simplicity of a B^+-tree. The exercises explore details of the insertion and deletion algorithms for B-trees.

12.5 Static Hashing

One disadvantage of sequential file organization is that we must access an index structure to locate data, or must use binary search, and that results in more I/O operations. File organizations based on the technique of **hashing** allow us to avoid accessing an index structure. Hashing also provides a way of constructing indices. We study file organizations and indices based on hashing in the following sections.

12.5.1 Hash File Organization

In a **hash file organization**, we obtain the address of the disk block containing a desired record directly by computing a function on the search-key value of the record. In our description of hashing, we shall use the term **bucket** to denote a unit of storage that can store one or more records. A bucket is typically a disk block, but could be chosen to be smaller or larger than a disk block.

Formally, let K denote the set of all search-key values, and let B denote the set of all bucket addresses. A **hash function** h is a function from K to B. Let h denote a hash function.

To insert a record with search key K_i, we compute $h(K_i)$, which gives the address of the bucket for that record. Assume for now that there is space in the bucket to store the record. Then, the record is stored in that bucket.

To perform a lookup on a search-key value K_i, we simply compute $h(K_i)$, then search the bucket with that address. Suppose that two search keys, K_5 and K_7, have the same hash value; that is, $h(K_5) = h(K_7)$. If we perform a lookup on K_5, the bucket $h(K_5)$ contains records with search-key values K_5 and records with search-key values K_7. Thus, we have to check the search-key value of every record in the bucket to verify that the record is one that we want.

Deletion is equally straightforward. If the search-key value of the record to be deleted is K_i, we compute $h(K_i)$, then search the corresponding bucket for that record, and delete the record from the bucket.

12.5.1.1 Hash Functions

The worst possible hash function maps all search-key values to the same bucket. Such a function is undesirable because all the records have to be kept in the same bucket. A lookup has to examine every such record to find the one desired. An ideal hash function distributes the stored keys uniformly across all the buckets, so that every bucket has the same number of records.

Since we do not know at design time precisely which search-key values will be stored in the file, we want to choose a hash function that assigns search-key values to buckets in such a way that the distribution has these qualities:

- The distribution is *uniform*. That is, the hash function assigns each bucket the same number of search-key values from the set of *all* possible search-key values.

- The distribution is *random*. That is, in the average case, each bucket will have nearly the same number of values assigned to it, regardless of the actual distribution of search-key values. More precisely, the hash value will not be correlated to any externally visible ordering on the search-key values, such as alphabetic ordering or ordering by the length of the search keys; the hash function will appear to be random.

As an illustration of these principles, let us choose a hash function for the *account* file using the search key *branch-name*. The hash function that we choose must have the desirable properties not only on the example *account* file that we have been using, but also on an *account* file of realistic size for a large bank with many branches.

Assume that we decide to have 26 buckets, and we define a hash function that maps names beginning with the *i*th letter of the alphabet to the *i*th bucket. This hash function has the virtue of simplicity, but it fails to provide a uniform distribution, since we expect more branch names to begin with such letters as B and R than Q and X, for example.

Now suppose that we want a hash function on the search key *balance*. Suppose that the minimum balance is 1 and the maximum balance is 100,000, and we use a hash function that divides the values into 10 ranges, 1–10,000, 10,001–20,000 and so on. The distribution of search-key values is uniform (since each bucket has the same number of different *balance* values), but is not random. But records with balances between 1 and 10,000 are far more common than are records with balances between 90,001 and 100,000. As a result, the distribution of records is not uniform—some buckets receive more records than others do. If the function has a random distribution, even if there are such correlations in the search keys, the randomness of the distribution will make it very likely that all buckets will have roughly the same number of records, as long as each search key occurs in only a small fraction of the records. (If a single search key occurs in a large fraction of the records, the bucket containing it is likely to have more records than other buckets, regardless of the hash function used.)

Typical hash functions perform computation on the internal binary machine representation of characters in the search key. A simple hash function of this type first computes the sum of the binary representations of the characters of a key, then returns the sum modulo the number of buckets. Figure 12.21 shows the application of such a scheme, with 10 buckets, to the *account* file, under the assumption that the *i*th letter in the alphabet is represented by the integer *i*.

Hash functions require careful design. A bad hash function may result in lookup taking time proportional to the number of search keys in the file. A well-designed function gives an average-case lookup time that is a (small) constant, independent of the number of search keys in the file.

12.5.1.2 Handling of Bucket Overflows

So far, we have assumed that, when a record is inserted, the bucket to which it is mapped has space to store the record. If the bucket does not have enough space, a **bucket overflow** is said to occur. Bucket overflow can occur for several reasons:

- **Insufficient buckets**. The number of buckets, which we denote n_B, must be chosen such that $n_B > n_r/f_r$, where n_r denotes the total number of records that will be stored, and f_r denotes the number of records that will fit in a bucket. This designation, of course, assumes that the total number of records is known when the hash function is chosen.

- **Skew**. Some buckets are assigned more records than are others, so a bucket may overflow even when other buckets still have space. This situation is called bucket **skew**. Skew can occur for two reasons:

bucket 0

bucket 5

A-102	Perryridge	400
A-201	Perryridge	900
A-218	Perryridge	700

bucket 1

bucket 6

bucket 2

bucket 7

A-215	Mianus	700

bucket 3

A-217	Brighton	750
A-305	Round Hill	350

bucket 8

A-101	Downtown	500
A-110	Downtown	600

bucket 4

A-222	Redwood	700

bucket 9

Figure 12.21   Hash organization of *account* file, with *branch-name* as the key.

1. Multiple records may have the same search key.
2. The chosen hash function may result in nonuniform distribution of search keys.

So that the probability of bucket overflow is reduced, the number of buckets is chosen to be $(n_r/f_r) * (1 + d)$, where d is a fudge factor, typically around 0.2. Some space is wasted: About 20 percent of the space in the buckets will be empty. But the benefit is that the probability of overflow is reduced.

Despite allocation of a few more buckets than required, bucket overflow can still occur. We handle bucket overflow by using **overflow buckets**. If a record must be inserted into a bucket b, and b is already full, the system provides an overflow bucket for b, and inserts the record into the overflow bucket. If the overflow bucket is also full, the system provides another overflow bucket, and so on. All the overflow buck-

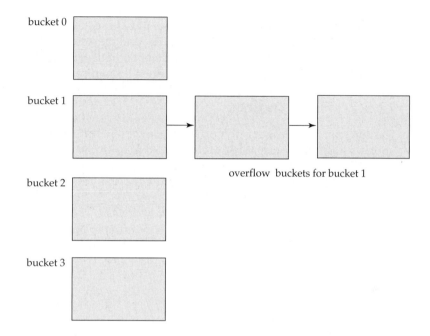

Figure 12.22   Overflow chaining in a hash structure.

ets of a given bucket are chained together in a linked list, as in Figure 12.22. Overflow handling using such a linked list is called **overflow chaining**.

We must change the lookup algorithm slightly to handle overflow chaining. As before, the system uses the hash function on the search key to identify a bucket b. The system must examine all the records in bucket b to see whether they match the search key, as before. In addition, if bucket b has overflow buckets, the system must examine the records in all the overflow buckets also.

The form of hash structure that we have just described is sometimes referred to as **closed hashing**. Under an alternative approach, called **open hashing**, the set of buckets is fixed, and there are no overflow chains. Instead, if a bucket is full, the system inserts records in some other bucket in the initial set of buckets B. One policy is to use the next bucket (in cyclic order) that has space; this policy is called *linear probing*. Other policies, such as computing further hash functions, are also used. Open hashing has been used to construct symbol tables for compilers and assemblers, but closed hashing is preferable for database systems. The reason is that deletion under open hashing is troublesome. Usually, compilers and assemblers perform only lookup and insertion operations on their symbol tables. However, in a database system, it is important to be able to handle deletion as well as insertion. Thus, open hashing is of only minor importance in database implementation.

An important drawback to the form of hashing that we have described is that we must choose the hash function when we implement the system, and it cannot be changed easily thereafter if the file being indexed grows or shrinks. Since the function h maps search-key values to a fixed set B of bucket addresses, we waste space if B is made large to handle future growth of the file. If B is too small, the buckets contain records of many different search-key values, and bucket overflows can occur. As the file grows, performance suffers. We study later, in Section 12.6, how the number of buckets and the hash function can be changed dynamically.

12.5.2 Hash Indices

Hashing can be used not only for file organization, but also for index-structure creation. A **hash index** organizes the search keys, with their associated pointers, into a hash file structure. We construct a hash index as follows. We apply a hash function on a search key to identify a bucket, and store the key and its associated pointers in the bucket (or in overflow buckets). Figure 12.23 shows a secondary hash index on the *account* file, for the search key *account-number*. The hash function in the figure computes the sum of the digits of the account number modulo 7. The hash index has seven buckets, each of size 2 (realistic indices would, of course, have much larger

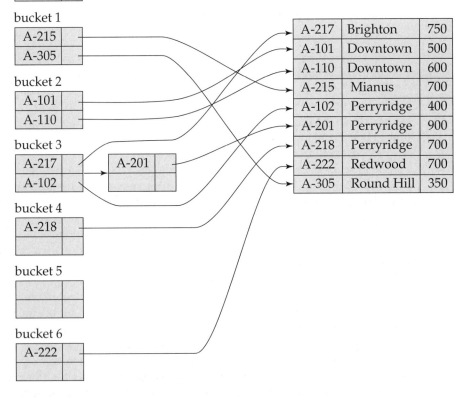

Figure 12.23   Hash index on search key *account-number* of *account* file.

bucket sizes). One of the buckets has three keys mapped to it, so it has an overflow bucket. In this example, *account-number* is a primary key for *account*, so each search-key has only one associated pointer. In general, multiple pointers can be associated with each key.

We use the term *hash index* to denote hash file structures as well as secondary hash indices. Strictly speaking, hash indices are only secondary index structures. A hash index is never needed as a primary index structure, since, if a file itself is organized by hashing, there is no need for a separate hash index structure on it. However, since hash file organization provides the same direct access to records that indexing provides, we pretend that a file organized by hashing also has a primary hash index on it.

12.6   Dynamic Hashing

As we have seen, the need to fix the set B of bucket addresses presents a serious problem with the static hashing technique of the previous section. Most databases grow larger over time. If we are to use static hashing for such a database, we have three classes of options:

1. Choose a hash function based on the current file size. This option will result in performance degradation as the database grows.

2. Choose a hash function based on the anticipated size of the file at some point in the future. Although performance degradation is avoided, a significant amount of space may be wasted initially.

3. Periodically reorganize the hash structure in response to file growth. Such a reorganization involves choosing a new hash function, recomputing the hash function on every record in the file, and generating new bucket assignments. This reorganization is a massive, time-consuming operation. Furthermore, it is necessary to forbid access to the file during reorganization.

Several **dynamic hashing** techniques allow the hash function to be modified dynamically to accommodate the growth or shrinkage of the database. In this section we describe one form of dynamic hashing, called **extendable hashing**. The bibliographical notes provide references to other forms of dynamic hashing.

12.6.1   Data Structure

Extendable hashing copes with changes in database size by splitting and coalescing buckets as the database grows and shrinks. As a result, space efficiency is retained. Moreover, since the reorganization is performed on only one bucket at a time, the resulting performance overhead is acceptably low.

With extendable hashing, we choose a hash function h with the desirable properties of uniformity and randomness. However, this hash function generates values over a relatively large range—namely, b-bit binary integers. A typical value for b is 32.

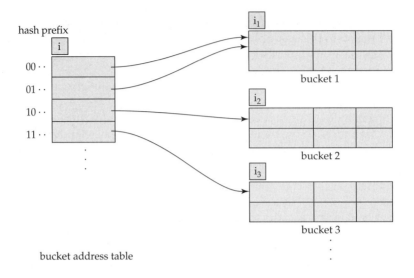

Figure 12.24   General extendable hash structure.

We do not create a bucket for each hash value. Indeed, 2^{32} is over 4 billion, and that many buckets is unreasonable for all but the largest databases. Instead, we create buckets on demand, as records are inserted into the file. We do not use the entire b bits of the hash value initially. At any point, we use i bits, where $0 \leq i \leq b$. These i bits are used as an offset into an additional table of bucket addresses. The value of i grows and shrinks with the size of the database.

Figure 12.24 shows a general extendable hash structure. The i appearing above the bucket address table in the figure indicates that i bits of the hash value $h(K)$ are required to determine the correct bucket for K. This number will, of course, change as the file grows. Although i bits are required to find the correct entry in the bucket address table, several consecutive table entries may point to the same bucket. All such entries will have a common hash prefix, but the length of this prefix may be less than i. Therefore, we associate with each bucket an integer giving the length of the common hash prefix. In Figure 12.24 the integer associated with bucket j is shown as i_j. The number of bucket-address-table entries that point to bucket j is

$$2^{(i - i_j)}$$

12.6.2 Queries and Updates

We now see how to perform lookup, insertion, and deletion on an extendable hash structure.

To locate the bucket containing search-key value K_l, the system takes the first i high-order bits of $h(K_l)$, looks at the corresponding table entry for this bit string, and follows the bucket pointer in the table entry.

To insert a record with search-key value K_l, the system follows the same procedure for lookup as before, ending up in some bucket—say, j. If there is room in the bucket, the system inserts the record in the bucket. If, on the other hand, the bucket is full, it must split the bucket and redistribute the current records, plus the new one. To split the bucket, the system must first determine from the hash value whether it needs to increase the number of bits that it uses.

- If $i = i_j$, only one entry in the bucket address table points to bucket j. Therefore, the system needs to increase the size of the bucket address table so that it can include pointers to the two buckets that result from splitting bucket j. It does so by considering an additional bit of the hash value. It increments the value of i by 1, thus doubling the size of the bucket address table. It replaces each entry by two entries, both of which contain the same pointer as the original entry. Now two entries in the bucket address table point to bucket j. The system allocates a new bucket (bucket z), and sets the second entry to point to the new bucket. It sets i_j and i_z to i. Next, it rehashes each record in bucket j and, depending on the first i bits (remember the system has added 1 to i), either keeps it in bucket j or allocates it to the newly created bucket.

    The system now reattempts the insertion of the new record. Usually, the attempt will succeed. However, if all the records in bucket j, as well as the new record, have the same hash-value prefix, it will be necessary to split a bucket again, since all the records in bucket j and the new record are assigned to the same bucket. If the hash function has been chosen carefully, it is unlikely that a single insertion will require that a bucket be split more than once, unless there are a large number of records with the same search key. If all the records in bucket j have the same search-key value, no amount of splitting will help. In such cases, overflow buckets are used to store the records, as in static hashing.

- If $i > i_j$, then more than one entry in the bucket address table points to bucket j. Thus, the system can split bucket j without increasing the size of the bucket address table. Observe that all the entries that point to bucket j correspond to hash prefixes that have the same value on the leftmost i_j bits. The system allocates a new bucket (bucket z), and set i_j and i_z to the value that results from adding 1 to the original i_j value. Next, the system needs to adjust the entries in the bucket address table that previously pointed to bucket j. (Note that with the new value for i_j, not all the entries correspond to hash prefixes that have the same value on the leftmost i_j bits.) The system leaves the first half of the entries as they were (pointing to bucket j), and sets all the remaining entries to point to the newly created bucket (bucket z). Next, as in the previous case, the system rehashes each record in bucket j, and allocates it either to bucket j or to the newly created bucket z.

    The system then reattempts the insert. In the unlikely case that it again fails, it applies one of the two cases, $i = i_j$ or $i > i_j$, as appropriate.

Note that, in both cases, the system needs to recompute the hash function on only the records in bucket j.

To delete a record with search-key value K_l, the system follows the same procedure for lookup as before, ending up in some bucket—say, j. It removes both the

A-217	Brighton	750
A-101	Downtown	500
A-110	Downtown	600
A-215	Mianus	700
A-102	Perryridge	400
A-201	Perryridge	900
A-218	Perryridge	700
A-222	Redwood	700
A-305	Round Hill	350

Figure 12.25 Sample *account* file.

search key from the bucket and the record from the file. The bucket too is removed if it becomes empty. Note that, at this point, several buckets can be coalesced, and the size of the bucket address table can be cut in half. The procedure for deciding on which buckets can be coalesced and how to coalesce buckets is left to you to do as an exercise. The conditions under which the bucket address table can be reduced in size are also left to you as an exercise. Unlike coalescing of buckets, changing the size of the bucket address table is a rather expensive operation if the table is large. Therefore it may be worthwhile to reduce the bucket address table size only if the number of buckets reduces greatly.

Our example *account* file in Figure 12.25 illustrates the operation of insertion. The 32-bit hash values on *branch-name* appear in Figure 12.26. Assume that, initially, the file is empty, as in Figure 12.27. We insert the records one by one. To illustrate all the features of extendable hashing in a small structure, we shall make the unrealistic assumption that a bucket can hold only two records.

We insert the record (A-217, Brighton, 750). The bucket address table contains a pointer to the one bucket, and the system inserts the record. Next, we insert the record (A-101, Downtown, 500). The system also places this record in the one bucket of our structure.

When we attempt to insert the next record (Downtown, A-110, 600), we find that the bucket is full. Since $i = i_0$, we need to increase the number of bits that we use from the hash value. We now use 1 bit, allowing us $2^1 = 2$ buckets. This increase in

branch-name	h(*branch-name*)
Brighton	0010 1101 1111 1011 0010 1100 0011 0000
Downtown	1010 0011 1010 0000 1100 0110 1001 1111
Mianus	1100 0111 1110 1101 1011 1111 0011 1010
Perryridge	1111 0001 0010 0100 1001 0011 0110 1101
Redwood	0011 0101 1010 0110 1100 1001 1110 1011
Round Hill	1101 1000 0011 1111 1001 1100 0000 0001

Figure 12.26 Hash function for *branch-name*.

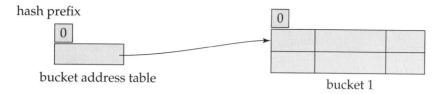

hash prefix

bucket address table

bucket 1

Figure 12.27   Initial extendable hash structure.

the number of bits necessitates doubling the size of the bucket address table to two entries. The system splits the bucket, placing in the new bucket those records whose search key has a hash value beginning with 1, and leaving in the original bucket the other records. Figure 12.28 shows the state of our structure after the split.

Next, we insert (A-215, Mianus, 700). Since the first bit of h(Mianus) is 1, we must insert this record into the bucket pointed to by the "1" entry in the bucket address table. Once again, we find the bucket full and $i = i_1$. We increase the number of bits that we use from the hash to 2. This increase in the number of bits necessitates doubling the size of the bucket address table to four entries, as in Figure 12.29. Since the bucket of Figure 12.28 for hash prefix 0 was not split, the two entries of the bucket address table of 00 and 01 both point to this bucket.

For each record in the bucket of Figure 12.28 for hash prefix 1 (the bucket being split), the system examines the first 2 bits of the hash value to determine which bucket of the new structure should hold it.

Next, we insert (A-102, Perryridge, 400), which goes in the same bucket as Mianus. The following insertion, of (A-201, Perryridge, 900), results in a bucket overflow, leading to an increase in the number of bits, and a doubling of the size of the bucket address table. The insertion of the third Perryridge record, (A-218, Perryridge, 700), leads to another overflow. However, this overflow cannot be handled by increasing the number of bits, since there are three records with exactly the same hash value. Hence the system uses an overflow bucket, as in Figure 12.30.

We continue in this manner until we have inserted all the *account* records of Figure 12.25. The resulting structure appears in Figure 12.31.

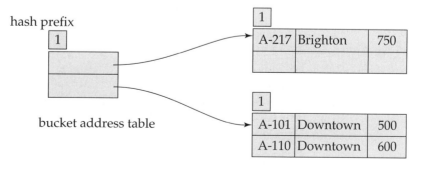

hash prefix

bucket address table

1		
A-217	Brighton	750

1		
A-101	Downtown	500
A-110	Downtown	600

Figure 12.28   Hash structure after three insertions.

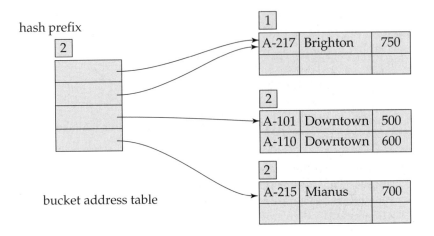

Figure 12.29 Hash structure after four insertions.

12.6.3 Comparison with Other Schemes

We now examine the advantages and disadvantages of extendable hashing, compared with the other schemes that we have discussed. The main advantage of extendable hashing is that performance does not degrade as the file grows. Furthermore, there is minimal space overhead. Although the bucket address table incurs additional overhead, it contains one pointer for each hash value for the current pre-

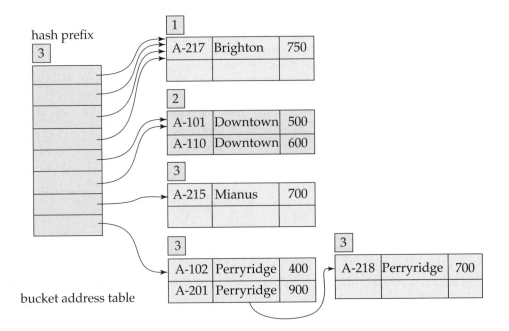

Figure 12.30 Hash structure after seven insertions.

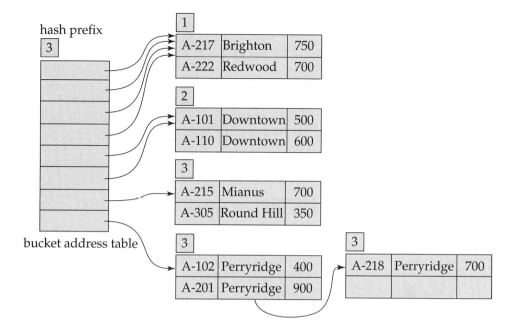

Figure 12.31   Extendable hash structure for the *account* file.

fix length. This table is thus small. The main space saving of extendable hashing over other forms of hashing is that no buckets need to be reserved for future growth; rather, buckets can be allocated dynamically.

A disadvantage of extendable hashing is that lookup involves an additional level of indirection, since the system must access the bucket address table before accessing the bucket itself. This extra reference has only a minor effect on performance. Although the hash structures that we discussed in Section 12.5 do not have this extra level of indirection, they lose their minor performance advantage as they become full.

Thus, extendable hashing appears to be a highly attractive technique, provided that we are willing to accept the added complexity involved in its implementation. The bibliographical notes reference more detailed descriptions of extendable hashing implementation. The bibliographical notes also provide references to another form of dynamic hashing called **linear hashing**, which avoids the extra level of indirection associated with extendable hashing, at the possible cost of more overflow buckets.

12.7   Comparison of Ordered Indexing and Hashing

We have seen several ordered-indexing schemes and several hashing schemes. We can organize files of records as ordered files, by using index-sequential organization or B+-tree organizations. Alternatively, we can organize the files by using hashing. Finally, we can organize them as heap files, where the records are not ordered in any particular way.

Each scheme has advantages in certain situations. A database-system implementor could provide many schemes, leaving the final decision of which schemes to use to the database designer. However, such an approach requires the implementor to write more code, adding both to the cost of the system and to the space that the system occupies. Most database systems support B^+-trees and may additionally support some form of hash file organization or hash indices.

To make a wise choice of file organization and indexing techniques for a relation, the implementor or the database designer must consider the following issues:

- Is the cost of periodic reorganization of the index or hash organization acceptable?

- What is the relative frequency of insertion and deletion?

- Is it desirable to optimize average access time at the expense of increasing the worst-case access time?

- What types of queries are users likely to pose?

We have already examined the first three of these issues, first in our review of the relative merits of specific indexing techniques, and again in our discussion of hashing techniques. The fourth issue, the expected type of query, is critical to the choice of ordered indexing or hashing.

If most queries are of the form

> **select** $A_1, A_2, \ldots, A_n$
> **from** r
> **where** $A_i = c$

then, to process this query, the system will perform a lookup on an ordered index or a hash structure for attribute A_i, for value c. For queries of this form, a hashing scheme is preferable. An ordered-index lookup requires time proportional to the log of the number of values in r for A_i. In a hash structure, however, the average lookup time is a constant independent of the size of the database. The only advantage to an index over a hash structure for this form of query is that the worst-case lookup time is proportional to the log of the number of values in r for A_i. By contrast, for hashing, the worst-case lookup time is proportional to the number of values in r for A_i. However, the worst-case lookup time is unlikely to occur with hashing, and hashing is preferable in this case.

Ordered-index techniques are preferable to hashing in cases where the query specifies a range of values. Such a query takes the following form:

> **select** $A_1, A_2, \ldots, A_n$
> **from** r
> **where** $A_i \leq c_2$ **and** $A_i \geq c_1$

In other words, the preceding query finds all the records with A_i values between c_1 and c_2.

Let us consider how we process this query using an ordered index. First, we perform a lookup on value c_1. Once we have found the bucket for value c_1, we follow the pointer chain in the index to read the next bucket in order, and we continue in this manner until we reach c_2.

If, instead of an ordered index, we have a hash structure, we can perform a lookup on c_1 and can locate the corresponding bucket—but it is not easy, in general, to determine the next bucket that must be examined. The difficulty arises because a good hash function assigns values randomly to buckets. Thus, there is no simple notion of "next bucket in sorted order." The reason we cannot chain buckets together in sorted order on A_i is that each bucket is assigned many search-key values. Since values are scattered randomly by the hash function, the values in the specified range are likely to be scattered across many or all of the buckets. Therefore, we have to read all the buckets to find the required search keys.

Usually the designer will choose ordered indexing unless it is known in advance that range queries will be infrequent, in which case hashing would be chosen. Hash organizations are particularly useful for temporary files created during query processing, if lookups based on a key value are required, but no range queries will be performed.

12.8 Index Definition in SQL

The SQL standard does not provide any way for the database user or administrator to control what indices are created and maintained in the database system. Indices are not required for correctness, since they are redundant data structures. However, indices are important for efficient processing of transactions, including both update transactions and queries. Indices are also important for efficient enforcement of integrity constraints. For example, typical implementations enforce a key declaration (Chapter 6) by creating an index with the declared key as the search key of the index.

In principle, a database system can decide automatically what indices to create. However, because of the space cost of indices, as well as the effect of indices on update processing, it is not easy to automatically make the right choices about what indices to maintain. Therefore, most SQL implementations provide the programmer control over creation and removal of indices via data-definition-language commands.

We illustrate the syntax of these commands next. Although the syntax that we show is widely used and supported by many database systems, it is not part of the SQL:1999 standard. The SQL standards (up to SQL:1999, at least) do not support control of the physical database schema, and have restricted themselves to the logical database schema.

We create an index by the **create index** command, which takes the form

create index <index-name> **on** <relation-name> (<attribute-list>)

The *attribute-list* is the list of attributes of the relations that form the search key for the index.

To define an index name *b-index* on the *branch* relation with *branch-name* as the search key, we write

> **create index** *b-index* **on** *branch* (*branch-name*)

If we wish to declare that the search key is a candidate key, we add the attribute **unique** to the index definition. Thus, the command

> **create unique index** *b-index* **on** *branch* (*branch-name*)

declares *branch-name* to be a candidate key for *branch*. If, at the time we enter the **create unique index** command, *branch-name* is not a candidate key, the system will display an error message, and the attempt to create the index will fail. If the index-creation attempt succeeds, any subsequent attempt to insert a tuple that violates the key declaration will fail. Note that the **unique** feature is redundant if the database system supports the **unique** declaration of the SQL standard.

Many database systems also provide a way to specify the type of index to be used (such as B$^+$-tree or hashing). Some database systems also permit one of the indices on a relation to be declared to be clustered; the system then stores the relation sorted by the search-key of the clustered index.

The index name we specified for an index is required to drop an index. The **drop index** command takes the form:

> **drop index** <index-name>

12.9 Multiple-Key Access

Until now, we have assumed implicitly that only one index (or hash table) is used to process a query on a relation. However, for certain types of queries, it is advantageous to use multiple indices if they exist.

12.9.1 Using Multiple Single-Key Indices

Assume that the *account* file has two indices: one for *branch-name* and one for *balance*. Consider the following query: "Find all account numbers at the Perryridge branch with balances equal to $1000." We write

> **select** *loan-number*
> **from** *account*
> **where** *branch-name* = "Perryridge" **and** *balance* = 1000

There are three strategies possible for processing this query:

1. Use the index on *branch-name* to find all records pertaining to the Perryridge branch. Examine each such record to see whether *balance* = 1000.

2. Use the index on *balance* to find all records pertaining to accounts with balances of $1000. Examine each such record to see whether *branch-name* = "Perryridge."

3. Use the index on *branch-name* to find *pointers* to all records pertaining to the Perryridge branch. Also, use the index on *balance* to find pointers to all records

pertaining to accounts with a balance of $1000. Take the intersection of these two sets of pointers. Those pointers that are in the intersection point to records pertaining to both Perryridge and accounts with a balance of $1000.

The third strategy is the only one of the three that takes advantage of the existence of multiple indices. However, even this strategy may be a poor choice if all of the following hold:

- There are many records pertaining to the Perryridge branch.

- There are many records pertaining to accounts with a balance of $1000.

- There are only a few records pertaining to *both* the Perryridge branch and accounts with a balance of $1000.

If these conditions hold, we must scan a large number of pointers to produce a small result. An index structure called a "bitmap index" greatly speeds up the intersection operation used in the third strategy. Bitmap indices are outlined in Section 12.9.4.

12.9.2 Indices on Multiple Keys

An alternative strategy for this case is to create and use an index on a search key (*branch-name, balance*)—that is, the search key consisting of the branch name concatenated with the account balance. The structure of the index is the same as that of any other index, the only difference being that the search key is not a single attribute, but rather is a list of attributes. The search key can be represented as a tuple of values, of the form $(a_1, \ldots, a_n)$, where the indexed attributes are $A_1, \ldots, A_n$. The ordering of search-key values is the *lexicographic ordering*. For example, for the case of two attribute search keys, $(a_1, a_2) < (b_1, b_2)$ if either $a_1 < b_1$ or $a_1 = b_1$ and $a_2 < b_2$. Lexicographic ordering is basically the same as alphabetic ordering of words.

The use of an ordered-index structure on multiple attributes has a few shortcomings. As an illustration, consider the query

> **select** *loan-number*
> **from** *account*
> **where** *branch-name* < "Perryridge" **and** *balance* = 1000

We can answer this query by using an ordered index on the search key (*branch-name, balance*): For each value of *branch-name* that is less than "Perryridge" in alphabetic order, the system locates records with a *balance* value of 1000. However, each record is likely to be in a different disk block, because of the ordering of records in the file, leading to many I/O operations.

The difference between this query and the previous one is that the condition on *branch-name* is a comparison condition, rather than an equality condition.

To speed the processing of general multiple search-key queries (which can involve one or more comparison operations), we can use several special structures. We shall consider the *grid file* in Section 12.9.3. There is another structure, called the *R-tree*, that can be used for this purpose. The R-tree is an extension of the B^+-tree to handle indexing on multiple dimensions. Since the R-tree is used primarily with geographical data types, we describe the structure in Chapter 23.

12.9.3   Grid Files

Figure 12.32 shows part of a **grid file** for the search keys *branch-name* and *balance* on the *account* file. The two-dimensional array in the figure is called the *grid array,* and the one-dimensional arrays are called *linear scales*. The grid file has a single grid array, and one linear scale for each search-key attribute.

Search keys are mapped to cells in this way. Each cell in the grid array has a pointer to a bucket that contains the search-key values and pointers to records. Only some of the buckets and pointers from the cells are shown in the figure. To conserve space, multiple elements of the array can point to the same bucket. The dotted boxes in the figure indicate which cells point to the same bucket.

Suppose that we want to insert in the grid-file index a record whose search-key value is ("Brighton", 500000). To find the cell to which the key is mapped, we independently locate the row and column to which the cell belongs.

We first use the linear scales on *branch-name* to locate the row of the cell to which the search key maps. To do so, we search the array to find the least element that is greater than "Brighton". In this case, it is the first element, so the search key maps to the row marked 0. If it were the ith element, the search key would map to row $i - 1$. If the search key is greater than or equal to all elements in the linear scale, it maps to

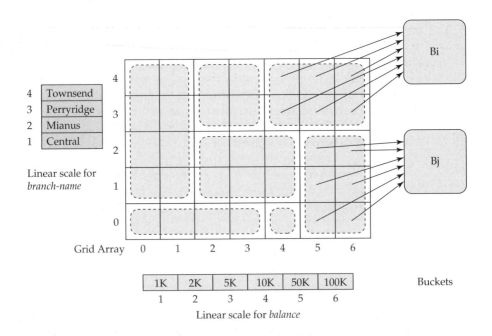

Figure 12.32   Grid file on keys *branch-name* and *balance* of the *account* file.

the final row. Next, we use the linear scale on *balance* to find out similarly to which column the search key maps. In this case, the balance 500000 maps to column 6.

Thus, the search-key value ("Brighton", 500000) maps to the cell in row 0, column 6. Similarly, ("Downtown", 60000) would map to the cell in row 1 column 5. Both cells point to the same bucket (as indicated by the dotted box), so, in both cases, the system stores the search-key values and the pointer to the record in the bucket labeled B_j in the figure.

To perform a lookup to answer our example query, with the search condition of

$$branch\text{-}name < \text{``Perryridge''} \textbf{ and } balance = 1000$$

we find all rows that can contain branch names less than "Perryridge", using the linear scale on *branch-name*. In this case, these rows are 0, 1, and 2. Rows 3 and beyond contain branch names greater than or equal to "Perryridge". Similarly, we find that only column 1 can contain a *balance* value of 1000. In this case, only column 1 satisfies this condition. Thus, only the cells in column 1, rows 0, 1, and 2, can contain entries that satisfy the search condition.

We therefore look up all entries in the buckets pointed to from these three cells. In this case, there are only two buckets, since two of the cells point to the same bucket, as indicated by the dotted boxes in the figure. The buckets may contain some search keys that do not satisfy the required condition, so each search key in the buckets must be tested again to see whether it satisfies the search condition. We have to examine only a small number of buckets, however, to answer this query.

We must choose the linear scales in such a way that the records are uniformly distributed across the cells. When a bucket—call it A—becomes full and an entry has to be inserted in it, the system allocates an extra bucket, B. If more than one cell points to A, the system changes the cell pointers so that some point to A and others to B. The entries in bucket A and the new entry are then redistributed between A and B according to the cells to which they map. If only one cell points to bucket A, B becomes an overflow bucket for A. To improve performance in such a situation, we must reorganize the grid file, with an expanded grid array and expanded linear scales. The process is much like the expansion of the bucket address table in extensible hashing, and is left for you to do as an exercise.

It is conceptually simple to extend the grid-file approach to any number of search keys. If we want our structure to be used for queries on n keys, we construct an n-dimensional grid array with n linear scales.

The grid structure is suitable also for queries involving one search key. Consider this query:

> **select** *
> **from** *account*
> **where** *branch-name* = "Perryridge"

The linear scale on *branch-name* tells us that only cells in row 3 can satisfy this condition. Since there is no condition on *balance*, we examine all buckets pointed to by cells in row 3 to find entries pertaining to Perryridge. Thus, we can use a grid-file index on two search keys to answer queries on either search key by itself, as well as to answer queries on both search keys. Thus, a single grid-file index can serve the role of three separate indices. If each index were maintained separately, the three together would occupy more space, and the cost of updating them would be high.

Grid files provide a significant decrease in processing time for multiple-key queries. However, they impose a space overhead (the grid directory can become large), as well as a performance overhead on record insertion and deletion. Further, it is hard to choose partitioning ranges for the keys such that the distribution of records is uniform. If insertions to the file are frequent, reorganization will have to be carried out periodically, and that can have a high cost.

12.9.4 Bitmap Indices

Bitmap indices are a specialized type of index designed for easy querying on multiple keys, although each bitmap index is built on a single key.

For bitmap indices to be used, records in a relation must be numbered sequentially, starting from, say, 0. Given a number n, it must be easy to retrieve the record numbered n. This is particularly easy to achieve if records are fixed in size, and allocated on consecutive blocks of a file. The record number can then be translated easily into a block number and a number that identifies the record within the block.

Consider a relation r, with an attribute A that can take on only one of a small number (for example, 2 to 20) values. For instance, a relation *customer-info* may have an attribute *gender*, which can take only values m (male) or f (female). Another example would be an attribute *income-level*, where income has been broken up into 5 levels: $L1: \$0 - 9999$, $L2: \$10,000 - 19,999$, $L3: 20,000 - 39,999$, $L4: 40,000 - 74,999$, and $L5: 75,000 - \infty$. Here, the raw data can take on many values, but a data analyst has split the values into a small number of ranges to simplify analysis of the data.

12.9.4.1 Bitmap Index Structure

A **bitmap** is simply an array of bits. In its simplest form, a **bitmap index** on the attribute A of relation r consists of one bitmap for each value that A can take. Each bitmap has as many bits as the number of records in the relation. The ith bit of the bitmap for value v_j is set to 1 if the record numbered i has the value v_j for attribute A. All other bits of the bitmap are set to 0.

In our example, there is one bitmap for the value m and one for f. The ith bit of the bitmap for m is set to 1 if the *gender* value of the record numbered i is m. All other bits of the bitmap for m are set to 0. Similarly, the bitmap for f has the value 1 for bits corresponding to records with the value f for the *gender* attribute; all other bits have the value 0. Figure 12.33 shows an example of bitmap indices on a relation *customer-info*.

We now consider when bitmaps are useful. The simplest way of retrieving all records with value m (or value f) would be to simply read all records of the relation and select those records with value m (or f, respectively). The bitmap index doesn't really help to speed up such a selection.

record number	name	gender	address	income-level
0	John	m	Perryridge	L1
1	Diana	f	Brooklyn	L2
2	Mary	f	Jonestown	L1
3	Peter	m	Brooklyn	L4
4	Kathy	f	Perryridge	L3

Bitmaps for *gender*

m 10010
f 01101

Bitmaps for *income-level*

L1 10100
L2 01000
L3 00001
L4 00010
L5 00000

Figure 12.33   Bitmap indices on relation *customer-info*.

In fact, bitmap indices are useful for selections mainly when there are selections on multiple keys. Suppose we create a bitmap index on attribute *income-level*, which we described earlier, in addition to the bitmap index on *gender*.

Consider now a query that selects women with income in the range $10,000 - 19,999$. This query can be expressed as $\sigma_{gender=f \wedge income\text{-}level=L2}(r)$. To evaluate this selection, we fetch the bitmaps for *gender* value f and the bitmap for *income-level* value $L2$, and perform an **intersection** (logical-and) of the two bitmaps. In other words, we compute a new bitmap where bit i has value 1 if the ith bit of the two bitmaps are both 1, and has a value 0 otherwise. In the example in Figure 12.33, the intersection of the bitmap for $gender = $ f (01101) and the bitmap for $income\text{-}level = L1$ (10100) gives the bitmap 00100.

Since the first attribute can take 2 values, and the second can take 5 values, we would expect only about 1 in 10 records, on an average, to satisfy a combined condition on the two attributes. If there are further conditions, the fraction of records satisfying all the conditions is likely to be quite small. The system can then compute the query result by finding all bits with value 1 in the intersection bitmap, and retrieving the corresponding records. If the fraction is large, scanning the entire relation would remain the cheaper alternative.

Another important use of bitmaps is to count the number of tuples satisfying a given selection. Such queries are important for data analysis. For instance, if we wish to find out how many women have an income level $L2$, we compute the intersection of the two bitmaps, and then count the number of bits that are 1 in the intersection bitmap. We can thus get the desired result from the bitmap index, without even accessing the relation.

Bitmap indices are generally quite small compared to the actual relation size. Records are typically at least tens of bytes to hundreds of bytes long, whereas a single bit represents the record in a bitmap. Thus the space occupied by a single bitmap is usually less than 1 percent of the space occupied by the relation. For instance, if the record size for a given relation is 100 bytes, then the space occupied by a single bitmap would be $\frac{1}{8}$ of 1 percent of the space occupied by the relation. If an attribute A of the relation can take on only one of 8 values, a bitmap index on attribute A would consist of 8 bitmaps, which together occupy only 1 percent of the size of the relation.

Deletion of records creates gaps in the sequence of records, since shifting records (or record numbers) to fill gaps would be extremely expensive. To recognize deleted records, we can store an **existence bitmap**, in which bit i is 0 if record i does not exist and 1 otherwise. We will see the need for existence bitmaps in Section 12.9.4.2. Insertion of records should not affect the sequence numbering of other records. Therefore, we can do insertion either by appending records to the end of the file or by replacing deleted records.

12.9.4.2 Efficient Implementation of Bitmap Operations

We can compute the intersection of two bitmaps easily by using a **for** loop: the ith iteration of the loop computes the **and** of the ith bits of the two bitmaps. We can speed up computation of the intersection greatly by using bit-wise **and** instructions supported by most computer instruction sets. A *word* usually consists of 32 or 64 bits, depending on the architecture of the computer. A bit-wise **and** instruction takes two words as input and outputs a word where each bit is the logical **and** of the bits in corresponding positions of the input words. What is important to note is that a single bit-wise **and** instruction can compute the intersection of 32 or 64 bits *at once*.

If a relation had 1 million records, each bitmap would contain 1 million bits, or equivalently 128 Kbytes. Only 31,250 instructions are needed to compute the intersection of two bitmaps for our relation, assuming a 32-bit word length. Thus, computing bitmap intersections is an extremely fast operation.

Just like bitmap intersection is useful for computing the **and** of two conditions, bitmap union is useful for computing the **or** of two conditions. The procedure for bitmap union is exactly the same as for intersection, except we use bit-wise **or** instructions instead of bit-wise **and** instructions.

The complement operation can be used to compute a predicate involving the negation of a condition, such as **not** (*income-level* = $L1$). The complement of a bitmap is generated by complementing every bit of the bitmap (the complement of 1 is 0 and the complement of 0 is 1). It may appear that **not** (*income-level* = $L1$) can be implemented by just computing the complement of the bitmap for income level $L1$. If some records have been deleted, however, just computing the complement of a bitmap is not sufficient. Bits corresponding to such records would be 0 in the original bitmap, but would become 1 in the complement, although the records don't exist. A similar problem also arises when the value of an attribute is *null*. For instance, if the value of *income-level* is null, the bit would be 0 in the original bitmap for value $L1$, and 1 in the complement bitmap.

To make sure that the bits corresponding to deleted records are set to 0 in the result, the complement bitmap must be intersected with the existence bitmap to turn off the bits for deleted records. Similarly, to handle null values, the complement bitmap must also be intersected with the complement of the bitmap for the value *null*.[1]

Counting the number of bits that are 1 in a bitmap can be done fast by a clever technique. We can maintain an array with 256 entries, where the ith entry stores the

---

1. Handling predicates such as **is unknown** would cause further complications, which would in general require use of an extra bitmap to to track which operation results are unknown.

number of bits that are 1 in the binary representation of i. Set the total count initially to 0. We take each byte of the bitmap, use it to index into this array, and add the stored count to the total count. The number of addition operations would be $\frac{1}{8}$ of the number of tuples, and thus the counting process is very efficient. A large array (using $2^{16} = 65536$ entries), indexed by pairs of bytes, would give even higher speedup, but at a higher storage cost.

12.9.4.3 Bitmaps and B$^+$-Trees

Bitmaps can be combined with regular B$^+$-tree indices for relations where a few attribute values are extremely common, and other values also occur, but much less frequently. In a B$^+$-tree index leaf, for each value we would normally maintain a list of all records with that value for the indexed attribute. Each element of the list would be a record identifier, consisting of at least 32 bits, and usually more. For a value that occurs in many records, we store a bitmap instead of a list of records.

Suppose a particular value v_i occurs in $\frac{1}{16}$ of the records of a relation. Let N be the number of records in the relation, and assume that a record has a 64-bit number identifying it. The bitmap needs only 1 bit per record, or N bits in total. In contrast, the list representation requires 64 bits per record where the value occurs, or $64 * N/16 = 4N$ bits. Thus, a bitmap is preferable for representing the list of records for value v_i. In our example (with a 64-bit record identifier), if fewer than 1 in 64 records have a particular value, the list representation is preferable for identifying records with that value, since it uses fewer bits than the bitmap representation. If more than 1 in 64 records have that value, the bitmap representation is preferable.

Thus, bitmaps can be used as a compressed storage mechanism at the leaf nodes of B$^+$-trees, for those values that occur very frequently.

12.10 Summary

- Many queries reference only a small proportion of the records in a file. To reduce the overhead in searching for these records, we can construct *indices* for the files that store the database.

- Index-sequential files are one of the oldest index schemes used in database systems. To permit fast retrieval of records in stored sequentially, and out-of-order records a fast random access, we use an index structure.

- There are two types of indices that we can u indices. Dense indices contain entries for eve sparse indices contain entries only for some sea

- If the sort order of a search key matches the so on the search key is called a *primary index.* Th *ondary indices.* Secondary indices improve the p search keys other than the primary one. Howe on modification of the database.

- The primary disadvantage of the index-sequential file organization is that performance degrades as the file grows. To overcome this deficiency, we can use a B^+-*tree index*.

- A B^+-tree index takes the form of a *balanced* tree, in which every path from the root of the tree to a leaf of the tree is of the same length. The height of a B^+-tree is proportional to the logarithm to the base N of the number of records in the relation, where each nonleaf node stores N pointers; the value of N is often around 50 or 100. B^+-trees are much shorter than other balanced binary-tree structures such as AVL trees, and therefore require fewer disk accesses to locate records.

- Lookup on B^+-trees is straightforward and efficient. Insertion and deletion, however, are somewhat more complicated, but still efficient. The number of operations required for lookup, insertion, and deletion on B^+-trees is proportional to the logarithm to the base N of the number of records in the relation, where each nonleaf node stores N pointers.

- We can use B^+-trees for indexing a file containing records, as well as to organize records into a file.

- B-tree indices are similar to B^+-tree indices. The primary advantage of a B-tree is that the B-tree eliminates the redundant storage of search-key values. The major disadvantages are overall complexity and reduced fanout for a given node size. System designers almost universally prefer B^+-tree indices over B-tree indices in practice.

- Sequential file organizations require an index structure to locate data. File organizations based on hashing, by contrast, allow us to find the address of a data item directly by computing a function on the search-key value of the desired record. Since we do not know at design time precisely which search-key values will be stored in the file, a good hash function to choose is one that assigns search-key values to buckets such that the distribution is both uniform and random.

- *Static hashing* uses hash functions in which the set of bucket addresses is fixed. Such hash functions cannot easily accommodate databases that grow significantly larger over time. There are several *dynamic hashing techniques* that allow the hash function to be modified. One example is *extendable hashing*, which copes with changes in database size by splitting and coalescing buckets as the database grows and shrinks.

- We can also use hashing to create secondary indices; such indices are called *hash indices*. For notational convenience, we assume hash file organizations have an implicit hash index on the search key used for hashing.

- Ordered indices such as B^+-trees and hash indices can be used for selections based on equality conditions involving single attributes. When multiple attributes are involved in a selection condition, we can intersect record identifiers retrieved from multiple indices.

- Grid files provide a general means of indexing on multiple attributes.

- Bitmap indices provide a very compact representation for indexing attributes with very few distinct values. Intersection operations are extremely fast on bitmaps, making them ideal for supporting queries on multiple attributes.

Review Terms

- Access types
- Access time
- Insertion time
- Deletion time
- Space overhead
- Ordered index
- Primary index
- Clustering index
- Secondary index
- Nonclustering index
- Index-sequential file
- Index record/entry
- Dense index
- Sparse index
- Multilevel index
- Sequential scan
- B^+-Tree index
- Balanced tree
- B^+-Tree file organization

- B-Tree index
- Static hashing
- Hash file organization
- Hash index
- Bucket
- Hash function
- Bucket overflow
- Skew
- Closed hashing
- Dynamic hashing
- Extendable hashing
- Multiple-key access
- Indices on multiple keys
- Grid files
- Bitmap index
- Bitmap operations
  - ☐ Intersection
  - ☐ Union
  - ☐ Complement
  - ☐ Existence bitmap

Exercises

12.1 When is it preferable to use a dense index rather than a sparse index? Explain your answer.

12.2 Since indices speed query processing, why might they not be kept on several search keys? List as many reasons as possible.

12.3 What is the difference between a primary index and a secondary index?

12.4 Is it possible in general to have two primary indices on the same relation for different search keys? Explain your answer.

12.5 Construct a B$^+$-tree for the following set of key values:

$$(2, 3, 5, 7, 11, 17, 19, 23, 29, 31)$$

Assume that the tree is initially empty and values are added in ascending order. Construct B$^+$-trees for the cases where the number of pointers that will fit in one node is as follows:

a. Four
b. Six
c. Eight

12.6 For each B$^+$-tree of Exercise 12.5, show the steps involved in the following queries:

a. Find records with a search-key value of 11.
b. Find records with a search-key value between 7 and 17, inclusive.

12.7 For each B$^+$-tree of Exercise 12.5, show the form of the tree after each of the following series of operations:

a. Insert 9.
b. Insert 10.
c. Insert 8.
d. Delete 23.
e. Delete 19.

12.8 Consider the modified redistribution scheme for B$^+$-trees described in page 463. What is the expected height of the tree as a function of n?

12.9 Repeat Exercise 12.5 for a B-tree.

12.10 Explain the distinction between closed and open hashing. Discuss the relative merits of each technique in database applications.

12.11 What are the causes of bucket overflow in a hash file organization? What can be done to reduce the occurrence of bucket overflows?

12.12 Suppose that we are using extendable hashing on a file that contains records with the following search-key values:

$$2, 3, 5, 7, 11, 17, 19, 23, 29, 31$$

Show the extendable hash structure for this file if the hash function is $h(x) = x$ mod 8 and buckets can hold three records.

12.13 Show how the extendable hash structure of Exercise 12.12 changes as the result of each of the following steps:

a. Delete 11.
b. Delete 31.
c. Insert 1.
d. Insert 15.

12.14 Give pseudocode for deletion of entries from an extendable hash structure, including details of when and how to coalesce buckets. Do not bother about reducing the size of the bucket address table.

12.15 Suggest an efficient way to test if the bucket address table in extendable hashing can be reduced in size, by storing an extra count with the bucket address table. Give details of how the count should be maintained when buckets are split, coalesced or deleted.

(Note: Reducing the size of the bucket address table is an expensive operation, and subsequent inserts may cause the table to grow again. Therefore, it is best not to reduce the size as soon as it is possible to do so, but instead do it only if the number of index entries becomes small compared to the bucket address table size.)

12.16 Why is a hash structure not the best choice for a search key on which range queries are likely?

12.17 Consider a grid file in which we wish to avoid overflow buckets for performance reasons. In cases where an overflow bucket would be needed, we instead reorganize the grid file. Present an algorithm for such a reorganization.

12.18 Consider the *account* relation shown in Figure 12.25.

    a. Construct a bitmap index on the attributes *branch-name* and *balance*, dividing *balance* values into 4 ranges: below 250, 250 to below 500, 500 to below 750, and 750 and above.

    b. Consider a query that requests all accounts in Downtown with a balance of 500 or more. Outline the steps in answering the query, and show the final and intermediate bitmaps constructed to answer the query.

12.19 Show how to compute existence bitmaps from other bitmaps. Make sure that your technique works even in the presence of null values, by using a bitmap for the value *null*.

12.20 How does data encryption affect index schemes? In particular, how might it affect schemes that attempt to store data in sorted order?

Bibliographical Notes

Discussions of the basic data structures in indexing and hashing can be found in Cormen et al. [1990]. B-tree indices were first introduced in Bayer [1972] and Bayer and McCreight [1972]. B$^+$-trees are discussed in Comer [1979], Bayer and Unterauer [1977] and Knuth [1973]. The bibliographic notes in Chapter 16 provides references to research on allowing concurrent accesses and updates on B$^+$-trees. Gray and Reuter [1993] provide a good description of issues in the implementation of B$^+$-trees.

Several alternative tree and treelike search structures have been proposed. **Tries** are trees whose structure is based on the "digits" of keys (for example, a dictionary thumb index, which has one entry for each letter). Such trees may not be balanced in the sense that B$^+$-trees are. Tries are discussed by Ramesh et al. [1989], Orenstein

[1982], Litwin [1981] and Fredkin [1960]. Related work includes the digital B-trees of Lomet [1981].

Knuth [1973] analyzes a large number of different hashing techniques. Several dynamic hashing schemes exist. Extendable hashing was introduced by Fagin et al. [1979]. Linear hashing was introduced by Litwin [1978] and Litwin [1980]; Larson [1982] presents a performance analysis of linear hashing. Ellis [1987] examined concurrency with linear hashing. Larson [1988] presents a variant of linear hashing. Another scheme, called dynamic hashing, was proposed by Larson [1978]. An alternative given by Ramakrishna and Larson [1989] allows retrieval in a single disk access at the price of a high overhead for a small fraction of database modifications. Partitioned hashing is an extension of hashing to multiple attributes, and is covered in Rivest [1976], Burkhard [1976] and Burkhard [1979].

The grid file structure appears in Nievergelt et al. [1984] and Hinrichs [1985]. Bitmap indices, and variants called **bit-sliced indices** and **projection indices** are described in O'Neil and Quass [1997]. They were first introduced in the IBM Model 204 file manager on the AS 400 platform. They provide very large speedups on certain types of queries, and are today implemented on most database systems. Recent research on bitmap indices includes Wu and Buchmann [1998], Chan and Ioannidis [1998], Chan and Ioannidis [1999], and Johnson [1999a].

CHAPTER 13

Query Processing

Query processing refers to the range of activities involved in extracting data from a database. The activities include translation of queries in high-level database languages into expressions that can be used at the physical level of the file system, a variety of query-optimizing transformations, and actual evaluation of queries.

13.1 Overview

The steps involved in processing a query appear in Figure 13.1. The basic steps are

1. Parsing and translation

2. Optimization

3. Evaluation

Before query processing can begin, the system must translate the query into a usable form. A language such as SQL is suitable for human use, but is ill-suited to be the system's internal representation of a query. A more useful internal representation is one based on the extended relational algebra.

Thus, the first action the system must take in query processing is to translate a given query into its internal form. This translation process is similar to the work performed by the parser of a compiler. In generating the internal form of the query, the parser checks the syntax of the user's query, verifies that the relation names appearing in the query are names of the relations in the database, and so on. The system constructs a parse-tree representation of the query, which it then translates into a relational-algebra expression. If the query was expressed in terms of a view, the translation phase also replaces all uses of the view by the relational-algebra expres-

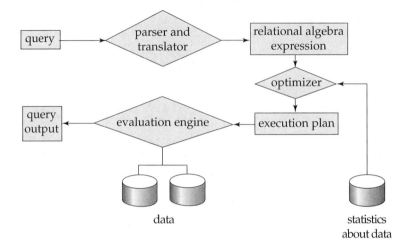

Figure 13.1   Steps in query processing.

sion that defines the view.[1] Most compiler texts cover parsing (see the bibliographical notes).

Given a query, there are generally a variety of methods for computing the answer. For example, we have seen that, in SQL, a query could be expressed in several different ways. Each SQL query can itself be translated into a relational-algebra expression in one of several ways. Furthermore, the relational-algebra representation of a query specifies only partially how to evaluate a query; there are usually several ways to evaluate relational-algebra expressions. As an illustration, consider the query

> **select** *balance*
> **from** *account*
> **where** *balance* < 2500

This query can be translated into either of the following relational-algebra expressions:

- $\sigma_{balance<2500} \left(\Pi_{balance} \left(account \right) \right)$

- $\Pi_{balance} \left(\sigma_{balance<2500} \left(account \right) \right)$

Further, we can execute each relational-algebra operation by one of several different algorithms. For example, to implement the preceding selection, we can search every tuple in *account* to find tuples with balance less than 2500. If a B^+-tree index is available on the attribute *balance*, we can use the index instead to locate the tuples.

To specify fully how to evaluate a query, we need not only to provide the relational-algebra expression, but also to annotate it with instructions specifying how to eval-

---

1. For materialized views, the expression defining the view has already been evaluated and stored. Therefore, the stored relation can be used, instead of uses of the view being replaced by the expression defining the view. Recursive views are handled differently, via a fixed-point procedure, as discussed in Section 5.2.6.

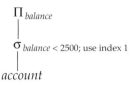

Figure 13.2   A query-evaluation plan.

uate each operation. Annotations may state the algorithm to be used for a specific operation, or the particular index or indices to use. A relational-algebra operation annotated with instructions on how to evaluate it is called an **evaluation primitive**. A sequence of primitive operations that can be used to evaluate a query is a **query-execution plan** or **query-evaluation plan**. Figure 13.2 illustrates an evaluation plan for our example query, in which a particular index (denoted in the figure as "index 1") is specified for the selection operation. The **query-execution engine** takes a query-evaluation plan, executes that plan, and returns the answers to the query.

The different evaluation plans for a given query can have different costs. We do not expect users to write their queries in a way that suggests the most efficient evaluation plan. Rather, it is the responsibility of the system to construct a query-evaluation plan that minimizes the cost of query evaluation. Chapter 14 describes query optimization in detail.

Once the query plan is chosen, the query is evaluated with that plan, and the result of the query is output.

The sequence of steps already described for processing a query is representative; not all databases exactly follow those steps. For instance, instead of using the relational-algebra representation, several databases use an annotated parse-tree representation based on the structure of the given SQL query. However, the concepts that we describe here form the basis of query processing in databases.

In order to optimize a query, a query optimizer must know the cost of each operation. Although the exact cost is hard to compute, since it depends on many parameters such as actual memory available to the operation, it is possible to get a rough estimate of execution cost for each operation.

Section 13.2 outlines how we measure the cost of a query. Sections 13.3 through 13.6 cover the evaluation of individual relational-algebra operations. Several operations may be grouped together into a **pipeline**, in which each of the operations starts working on its input tuples even as they are being generated by another operation. In Section 13.7, we examine how to coordinate the execution of multiple operations in a query evaluation plan, in particular, how to use pipelined operations to avoid writing intermediate results to disk.

13.2   Measures of Query Cost

The cost of query evaluation can be measured in terms of a number of different resources, including disk accesses, CPU time to execute a query, and, in a distributed or parallel database system, the cost of communication (which we discuss later, in

Chapters 19 and 20). The response time for a query-evaluation plan (that is, the clock time required to execute the plan), assuming no other activity is going on on the computer, would account for all these costs, and could be used as a good measure of the cost of the plan.

In large database systems, however, disk accesses (which we measure as the number of transfers of blocks from disk) are usually the most important cost, since disk accesses are slow compared to in-memory operations. Moreover, CPU speeds have been improving much faster than have disk speeds. Thus, it is likely that the time spent in disk activity will continue to dominate the total time to execute a query. Finally, estimating the CPU time is relatively hard, compared to estimating the disk-access cost. Therefore, most people consider the disk-access cost a reasonable measure of the cost of a query-evaluation plan.

We use the *number of block transfers* from disk as a measure of the actual cost. To simplify our computation of disk-access cost, we assume that all transfers of blocks have the same cost. This assumption ignores the variance arising from rotational latency (waiting for the desired data to spin under the read–write head) and seek time (the time that it takes to move the head over the desired track or cylinder). To get more precise numbers, we need to distinguish between **sequential I/O**, where the blocks read are contiguous on disk, and **random I/O**, where the blocks are non-contiguous, and an extra seek cost must be paid for each disk I/O operation. We also need to distinguish between reads and writes of blocks, since it takes more time to write a block to disk than to read a block from disk. A more accurate measure would therefore estimate

1. The number of seek operations performed

2. The number of blocks read

3. The number of blocks written

and then add up these numbers after multiplying them by the average seek time, average transfer time for reading a block, and average transfer time for writing a block, respectively. Real-life query optimizers also take CPU costs into account when computing the cost of an operation. For simplicity we ignore these details, and leave it to you to work out more precise cost estimates for various operations.

The cost estimates we give ignore the cost of writing the final result of an operation back to disk. These are taken into account separately where required. The costs of all the algorithms that we consider depend on the size of the buffer in main memory. In the best case, all data can be read into the buffers, and the disk does not need to be accessed again. In the worst case, we assume that the buffer can hold only a few blocks of data—approximately one block per relation. When presenting cost estimates, we generally assume the worst case.

13.3 Selection Operation

In query processing, the **file scan** is the lowest-level operator to access data. File scans are search algorithms that locate and retrieve records that fulfill a selection condition.

In relational systems, a file scan allows an entire relation to be read in those cases where the relation is stored in a single, dedicated file.

13.3.1 Basic Algorithms

Consider a selection operation on a relation whose tuples are stored together in one file. Two scan algorithms to implement the selection operation are:

- **A1 (linear search)**. In a linear search, the system scans each file block and tests all records to see whether they satisfy the selection condition. For a selection on a key attribute, the system can terminate the scan if the required record is found, without looking at the other records of the relation.

  The cost of linear search, in terms of number of I/O operations, is b_r, where b_r denotes the number of blocks in the file. Selections on key attributes have an average cost of $b_r/2$, but still have a worst-case cost of b_r.

  Although it may be slower than other algorithms for implementing selection, the linear search algorithm can be applied to any file, regardless of the ordering of the file, or the availability of indices, or the nature of the selection operation. The other algorithms that we shall study are not applicable in all cases, but when applicable they are generally faster than linear search.

- **A2 (binary search)**. If the file is ordered on an attribute, and the selection condition is an equality comparison on the attribute, we can use a binary search to locate records that satisfy the selection. The system performs the binary search on the blocks of the file.

  The number of blocks that need to be examined to find a block containing the required records is $\lceil \log_2(b_r) \rceil$, where b_r denotes the number of blocks in the file. If the selection is on a nonkey attribute, more than one block may contain required records, and the cost of reading the extra blocks has to be added to the cost estimate. We can estimate this number by estimating the size of the selection result (which we cover in Section 14.2), and dividing it by the average number of records that are stored per block of the relation.

13.3.2 Selections Using Indices

Index structures are referred to as **access paths**, since they provide a path through which data can be located and accessed. In Chapter 12, we pointed out that it is efficient to read the records of a file in an order corresponding closely to physical order. Recall that a *primary index* is an index that allows the records of a file to be read in an order that corresponds to the physical order in the file. An index that is not a primary index is called a *secondary index*.

Search algorithms that use an index are referred to as **index scans**. Ordered indices, such as B$^+$-trees, also permit access to tuples in a sorted order, which is useful for implementing range queries. Although indices can provide fast, direct, and ordered access, they impose the overhead of access to those blocks containing the index. We use the selection predicate to guide us in the choice of the index to use in processing the query. Search algorithms that use an index are:

- **A3 (primary index, equality on key).** For an equality comparison on a key attribute with a primary index, we can use the index to retrieve a single record that satisfies the corresponding equality condition.

  If a B$^+$-tree is used, the cost of the operation, in terms of I/O operations, is equal to the height of the tree plus one I/O to fetch the record.

- **A4 (primary index, equality on nonkey).** We can retrieve multiple records by using a primary index when the selection condition specifies an equality comparison on a nonkey attribute, A. The only difference from the previous case is that multiple records may need to be fetched. However, the records would be stored consecutively in the file since the file is sorted on the search key.

  The cost of the operation is proportional to the height of the tree, plus the number of blocks containing records with the specified search key.

- **A5 (secondary index, equality).** Selections specifying an equality condition can use a secondary index. This strategy can retrieve a single record if the equality condition is on a key; multiple records may get retrieved if the indexing field is not a key.

  In the first case, only one record is retrieved, and the cost is equal to the height of the tree plus one I/O operation to fetch the record. In the second case each record may be resident on a different block, which may result in one I/O operation per retrieved record. The cost could become even worse than that of linear search if a large number of records are retrieved.

If B$^+$-tree file organizations are used to store relations, records may be moved between blocks when leaf nodes are split or merged, and when records are redistributed. If secondary indices store pointers to records' physical location, the pointers will have to be updated when records are moved. In some systems, such as Compaq's Non-Stop SQL System, the secondary indices instead store the key value in the B$^+$-tree file organization. Accessing a record through a secondary index is then even more expensive since a search has to be performed on the B$^+$-tree used in the file organization. The cost formulae described for secondary indices will have to be modified appropriately if such indices are used.

13.3.3   Selections Involving Comparisons

Consider a selection of the form $\sigma_{A \le v}(r)$. We can implement the selection either by using a linear or binary search or by using indices in one of the following ways:

- **A6 (primary index, comparison).** A primary ordered index (for example, a primary B$^+$-tree index) can be used when the selection condition is a comparison. For comparison conditions of the form $A > v$ or $A \ge v$, a primary index on A can be used to direct the retrieval of tuples, as follows. For $A \ge v$, we look up the value v in the index to find the first tuple in the file that has a value of $A = v$. A file scan starting from that tuple up to the end of the file returns all tuples that satisfy the condition. For $A > v$, the file scan starts with the first tuple such that $A > v$.

For comparisons of the form $A < v$ or $A \leq v$, an index lookup is not required. For $A < v$, we use a simple file scan starting from the beginning of the file, and continuing up to (but not including) the first tuple with attribute $A = v$. The case of $A \leq v$ is similar, except that the scan continues up to (but not including) the first tuple with attribute $A > v$. In either case, the index is not useful.

- **A7 (secondary index, comparison).** We can use a secondary ordered index to guide retrieval for comparison conditions involving $<, \leq, \geq$, or $>$. The lowest-level index blocks are scanned, either from the smallest value up to v (for $<$ and $\leq$), or from v up to the maximum value (for $>$ and $\geq$).

  The secondary index provides pointers to the records, but to get the actual records we have to fetch the records by using the pointers. This step may require an I/O operation for each record fetched, since consecutive records may be on different disk blocks. If the number of retrieved records is large, using the secondary index may be even more expensive than using linear search. Therefore the secondary index should be used only if very few records are selected.

13.3.4   Implementation of Complex Selections

So far, we have considered only simple selection conditions of the form A *op* B, where *op* is an equality or comparison operation. We now consider more complex selection predicates.

- **Conjunction:** A *conjunctive selection* is a selection of the form

  $$\sigma_{\theta_1 \wedge \theta_2 \wedge \cdots \wedge \theta_n} (r)$$

- **Disjunction:** A *disjunctive selection* is a selection of the form

  $$\sigma_{\theta_1 \vee \theta_2 \vee \cdots \vee \theta_n} (r)$$

  A disjunctive condition is satisfied by the union of all records satisfying the individual, simple conditions θ_i.

- **Negation:** The result of a selection $\sigma_{\neg\theta}(r)$ is the set of tuples of r for which the condition θ evaluates to false. In the absence of nulls, this set is simply the set of tuples that are not in $\sigma_{\theta}(r)$.

We can implement a selection operation involving either a conjunction or a disjunction of simple conditions by using one of the following algorithms:

- **A8 (conjunctive selection using one index).** We first determine whether an access path is available for an attribute in one of the simple conditions. If one is, one of the selection algorithms A2 through A7 can retrieve records satisfying that condition. We complete the operation by testing, in the memory buffer, whether or not each retrieved record satisfies the remaining simple conditions.

To reduce the cost, we choose a θ_i and one of algorithms A1 through A7 for which the combination results in the least cost for $\sigma_{\theta_i}(r)$. The cost of algorithm A8 is given by the cost of the chosen algorithm.

- **A9 (conjunctive selection using composite index)**. An appropriate *composite index* (that is, an index on multiple attributes) may be available for some conjunctive selections. If the selection specifies an equality condition on two or more attributes, and a composite index exists on these combined attribute fields, then the index can be searched directly. The type of index determines which of algorithms A3, A4, or A5 will be used.

- **A10 (conjunctive selection by intersection of identifiers)**. Another alternative for implementing conjunctive selection operations involves the use of record pointers or record identifiers. This algorithm requires indices with record pointers, on the fields involved in the individual conditions. The algorithm scans each index for pointers to tuples that satisfy an individual condition. The intersection of all the retrieved pointers is the set of pointers to tuples that satisfy the conjunctive condition. The algorithm then uses the pointers to retrieve the actual records. If indices are not available on all the individual conditions, then the algorithm tests the retrieved records against the remaining conditions.

  The cost of algorithm **A10** is the sum of the costs of the individual index scans, plus the cost of retrieving the records in the intersection of the retrieved lists of pointers. This cost can be reduced by sorting the list of pointers and retrieving records in the sorted order. Thereby, (1) all pointers to records in a block come together, hence all selected records in the block can be retrieved using a single I/O operation, and (2) blocks are read in sorted order, minimizing disk arm movement. Section 13.4 describes sorting algorithms.

- **A11 (disjunctive selection by union of identifiers)**. If access paths are available on all the conditions of a disjunctive selection, each index is scanned for pointers to tuples that satisfy the individual condition. The union of all the retrieved pointers yields the set of pointers to all tuples that satisfy the disjunctive condition. We then use the pointers to retrieve the actual records.

  However, if even one of the conditions does not have an access path, we will have to perform a linear scan of the relation to find tuples that satisfy the condition. Therefore, if there is even one such condition in the disjunct, the most efficient access method is a linear scan, with the disjunctive condition tested on each tuple during the scan.

The implementation of selections with negation conditions is left to you as an exercise (Exercise 13.10).

13.4 Sorting

Sorting of data plays an important role in database systems for two reasons. First, SQL queries can specify that the output be sorted. Second, and equally important for query processing, several of the relational operations, such as joins, can be implemented efficiently if the input relations are first sorted. Thus, we discuss sorting here before discussing the join operation in Section 13.5.

We can sort a relation by building an index on the sort key, and then using that index to read the relation in sorted order. However, such a process orders the relation only *logically*, through an index, rather than *physically*. Hence, the reading of tuples in the sorted order may lead to a disk access for each record, which can be very expensive, since the number of records can be much larger than the number of blocks. For this reason, it may be desirable to order the records physically.

The problem of sorting has been studied extensively, both for relations that fit entirely in main memory, and for relations that are bigger than memory. In the first case, standard sorting techniques such as quick-sort can be used. Here, we discuss how to handle the second case.

Sorting of relations that do not fit in memory is called **external sorting**. The most commonly used technique for external sorting is the **external sort–merge** algorithm. We describe the external sort–merge algorithm next. Let M denote the number of page frames in the main-memory buffer (the number of disk blocks whose contents can be buffered in main memory).

1. In the first stage, a number of sorted **runs** are created; each run is sorted, but contains only some of the records of the relation.

   $i = 0;$
   repeat
     read M blocks of the relation, or the rest of the relation,
       whichever is smaller;
     sort the in-memory part of the relation;
     write the sorted data to run file R_i;
     $i = i + 1;$
   until the end of the relation

2. In the second stage, the runs are *merged*. Suppose, for now, that the total number of runs, N, is less than M, so that we can allocate one page frame to each run and have space left to hold one page of output. The merge stage operates as follows:

   read one block of each of the N files R_i into a buffer page in memory;
   repeat
     choose the first tuple (in sort order) among all buffer pages;
     write the tuple to the output, and delete it from the buffer page;
     if the buffer page of any run R_i is empty **and not** end-of-file(R_i)
       then read the next block of R_i into the buffer page;
   until all buffer pages are empty

The output of the merge stage is the sorted relation. The output file is buffered to reduce the number of disk write operations. The preceding merge operation is a generalization of the two-way merge used by the standard in-memory sort–merge algorithm; it merges N runs, so it is called an **N-way merge**.

In general, if the relation is much larger than memory, there may be M or more runs generated in the first stage, and it is not possible to allocate a page frame for each run during the merge stage. In this case, the merge operation proceeds in multiple passes. Since there is enough memory for $M - 1$ input buffer pages, each merge can take $M - 1$ runs as input.

The initial *pass* functions in this way: It merges the first $M - 1$ runs (as described in item 2 above) to get a single run for the next pass. Then, it merges the next $M - 1$ runs similarly, and so on, until it has processed all the initial runs. At this point, the number of runs has been reduced by a factor of $M - 1$. If this reduced number of runs is still greater than or equal to M, another pass is made, with the runs created by the first pass as input. Each pass reduces the number of runs by a factor of $M - 1$. The passes repeat as many times as required, until the number of runs is less than M; a final pass then generates the sorted output.

Figure 13.3 illustrates the steps of the external sort–merge for an example relation. For illustration purposes, we assume that only one tuple fits in a block ($f_r = 1$), and we assume that memory holds at most three page frames. During the merge stage, two page frames are used for input and one for output.

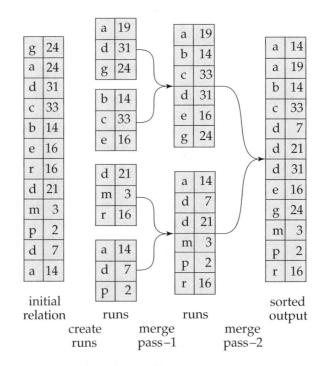

Figure 13.3   External sorting using sort–merge.

We compute how many block transfers are required for the external sort merge in this way: Let b_r denote the number of blocks containing records of relation r. The first stage reads every block of the relation and writes them out again, giving a total of $2b_r$ disk accesses. The initial number of runs is $\lceil b_r/M \rceil$. Since the number of runs decreases by a factor of $M - 1$ in each merge pass, the total number of merge passes required is $\lceil \log_{M-1}(b_r/M) \rceil$. Each of these passes reads every block of the relation once and writes it out once, with two exceptions. First, the final pass can produce the sorted output without writing its result to disk. Second, there may be runs that are not read in or written out during a pass—for example, if there are M runs to be merged in a pass, $M - 1$ are read in and merged, and one run is not accessed during the pass. Ignoring the (relatively small) savings due to the latter effect, the total number of disk accesses for external sorting of the relation is

$$b_r(2\lceil \log_{M-1}(b_r/M) \rceil + 1)$$

Applying this equation to the example in Figure 13.3, we get a total of $12 * (4+1) =$ 60 block transfers, as you can verify from the figure. Note that this value does not include the cost of writing out the final result.

13.5 Join Operation

In this section, we study several algorithms for computing the join of relations, and we analyze their respective costs.

We use the term **equi-join** to refer to a join of the form $r \bowtie_{r.A=s.B} s$, where A and B are attributes or sets of attributes of relations r and s respectively.

We use as a running example the expression

$$depositor \bowtie customer$$

We assume the following information about the two relations:

- Number of records of *customer*: $n_{customer} = 10,000$.

- Number of blocks of *customer*: $b_{customer} = 400$.

- Number of records of *depositor*: $n_{depositor} = 5000$.

- Number of blocks of *depositor*: $b_{depositor} = 100$.

13.5.1 Nested-Loop Join

Figure 13.4 shows a simple algorithm to compute the theta join, $r \bowtie_\theta s$, of two relations r and s. This algorithm is called the **nested-loop join** algorithm, since it basically consists of a pair of nested **for** loops. Relation r is called the **outer relation** and relation s the **inner relation** of the join, since the loop for r encloses the loop for s. The algorithm uses the notation $t_r \cdot t_s$, where t_r and t_s are tuples; $t_r \cdot t_s$ denotes the tuple constructed by concatenating the attribute values of tuples t_r and t_s.

Like the linear file-scan algorithm for selection, the nested-loop join algorithm requires no indices, and it can be used regardless of what the join condition is. Extending the algorithm to compute the natural join is straightforward, since the natural

```
for each tuple t_r in r do begin
    for each tuple t_s in s do begin
        test pair (t_r, t_s) to see if they satisfy the join condition θ
        if they do, add t_r · t_s to the result.
    end
end
```

Figure 13.4 Nested-loop join.

join can be expressed as a theta join followed by elimination of repeated attributes by a projection. The only change required is an extra step of deleting repeated attributes from the tuple $t_r \cdot t_s$, before adding it to the result.

The nested-loop join algorithm is expensive, since it examines every pair of tuples in the two relations. Consider the cost of the nested-loop join algorithm. The number of pairs of tuples to be considered is $n_r * n_s$, where n_r denotes the number of tuples in r, and n_s denotes the number of tuples in s. For each record in r, we have to perform a complete scan on s. In the worst case, the buffer can hold only one block of each relation, and a total of $n_r * b_s + b_r$ block accesses would be required, where b_r and b_s denote the number of blocks containing tuples of r and s respectively. In the best case, there is enough space for both relations to fit simultaneously in memory, so each block would have to be read only once; hence, only $b_r + b_s$ block accesses would be required.

If one of the relations fits entirely in main memory, it is beneficial to use that relation as the inner relation, since the inner relation would then be read only once. Therefore, if s is small enough to fit in main memory, our strategy requires only a total $b_r + b_s$ accesses—the same cost as that for the case where both relations fit in memory.

Now consider the natural join of *depositor* and *customer*. Assume for now that we have no indices whatsoever on either relation, and that we are not willing to create any index. We can use the nested loops to compute the join; assume that *depositor* is the outer relation and *customer* is the inner relation in the join. We will have to examine $5000 * 10000 = 50 * 10^6$ pairs of tuples. In the worst case, the number of block accesses is $5000 * 400 + 100 = 2{,}000{,}100$. In the best-case scenario, however, we can read both relations only once, and perform the computation. This computation requires at most $100 + 400 = 500$ block accesses—a significant improvement over the worst-case scenario. If we had used *customer* as the relation for the outer loop and *depositor* for the inner loop, the worst-case cost of our final strategy would have been lower: $10000 * 100 + 400 = 1{,}000{,}400$.

13.5.2 Block Nested-Loop Join

If the buffer is too small to hold either relation entirely in memory, we can still obtain a major saving in block accesses if we process the relations on a per-block basis, rather than on a per-tuple basis. Figure 13.5 shows **block nested-loop join**, which is a variant of the nested-loop join where every block of the inner relation is paired with every block of the outer relation. Within each pair of blocks, every tuple in one block

```
for each block B_r of r do begin
    for each block B_s of s do begin
        for each tuple t_r in B_r do begin
            for each tuple t_s in B_s do begin
                test pair (t_r, t_s) to see if they satisfy the join condition
                if they do, add t_r · t_s to the result.
            end
        end
    end
end
```

Figure 13.5   Block nested-loop join.

is paired with every tuple in the other block, to generate all pairs of tuples. As before, all pairs of tuples that satisfy the join condition are added to the result.

The primary difference in cost between the block nested-loop join and the basic nested-loop join is that, in the worst case, each block in the inner relation s is read only once for each *block* in the outer relation, instead of once for each *tuple* in the outer relation. Thus, in the worst case, there will be a total of $b_r * b_s + b_r$ block accesses, where b_r and b_s denote the number of blocks containing records of r and s respectively. Clearly, it is more efficient to use the smaller relation as the outer relation, in case neither of the relations fits in memory. In the best case, there will be $b_r + b_s$ block accesses.

Now return to our example of computing *depositor* ⋈ *customer*, using the block nested-loop join algorithm. In the worst case we have to read each block of *customer* once for each block of *depositor*. Thus, in the worst case, a total of $100 * 400 + 100 = 40,100$ block accesses are required. This cost is a significant improvement over the $5000 * 400 + 100 = 2,000,100$ block accesses needed in the worst case for the basic nested-loop join. The number of block accesses in the best case remains the same— namely, $100 + 400 = 500$.

The performance of the nested-loop and block nested-loop procedures can be further improved:

- If the join attributes in a natural join or an equi-join form a key on the inner relation, then for each outer relation tuple the inner loop can terminate as soon as the first match is found.

- In the block nested-loop algorithm, instead of using disk blocks as the blocking unit for the outer relation, we can use the biggest size that can fit in memory, while leaving enough space for the buffers of the inner relation and the output. In other words, if memory has M blocks, we read in $M - 2$ blocks of the outer relation at a time, and when we read each block of the inner relation we join it with all the $M - 2$ blocks of the outer relation. This change reduces the number of scans of the inner relation from b_r to $\lceil b_r/(M - 2) \rceil$, where b_r is the number of blocks of the outer relation. The total cost is then $\lceil b_r/(M - 2) \rceil * b_s + b_r$.

- We can scan the inner loop alternately forward and backward. This scanning method orders the requests for disk blocks so that the data remaining in the buffer from the previous scan can be reused, thus reducing the number of disk accesses needed.

- If an index is available on the inner loop's join attribute, we can replace file scans with more efficient index lookups. Section 13.5.3 describes this optimization.

13.5.3 Indexed Nested-Loop Join

In a nested-loop join (Figure 13.4), if an index is available on the inner loop's join attribute, index lookups can replace file scans. For each tuple t_r in the outer relation r, the index is used to look up tuples in s that will satisfy the join condition with tuple t_r.

This join method is called an **indexed nested-loop join**; it can be used with existing indices, as well as with temporary indices created for the sole purpose of evaluating the join.

Looking up tuples in s that will satisfy the join conditions with a given tuple t_r is essentially a selection on s. For example, consider *depositor* ⋈ *customer*. Suppose that we have a *depositor* tuple with *customer-name* "John". Then, the relevant tuples in s are those that satisfy the selection "*customer-name* = John".

The cost of an indexed nested-loop join can be computed as follows. For each tuple in the outer relation r, a lookup is performed on the index for s, and the relevant tuples are retrieved. In the worst case, there is space in the buffer for only one page of r and one page of the index. Then, b_r disk accesses are needed to read relation r, where b_r denotes the number of blocks containing records of r. For each tuple in r, we perform an index lookup on s. Then, the cost of the join can be computed as $b_r + n_r * c$, where n_r is the number of records in relation r, and c is the cost of a single selection on s using the join condition. We have seen in Section 13.3 how to estimate the cost of a single selection algorithm (possibly using indices); that estimate gives us the value of c.

The cost formula indicates that, if indices are available on both relations r and s, it is generally most efficient to use the one with fewer tuples as the outer relation.

For example, consider an indexed nested-loop join of *depositor* ⋈ *customer*, with *depositor* as the outer relation. Suppose also that *customer* has a primary B$^+$-tree index on the join attribute *customer-name*, which contains 20 entries on an average in each index node. Since *customer* has 10,000 tuples, the height of the tree is 4, and one more access is needed to find the actual data. Since $n_{depositor}$ is 5000, the total cost is $100 + 5000 * 5 = 25,100$ disk accesses. This cost is lower than the $40,100$ accesses needed for a block nested-loop join.

13.5.4 Merge Join

The **merge join** algorithm (also called the **sort–merge join** algorithm) can be used to compute natural joins and equi-joins. Let $r(R)$ and $s(S)$ be the relations whose natural join is to be computed, and let $R \cap S$ denote their common attributes. Suppose

```
pr := address of first tuple of r;
ps := address of first tuple of s;
while (ps ≠ null and pr ≠ null) do
    begin
        t_s := tuple to which ps points;
        S_s := {t_s};
        set ps to point to next tuple of s;
        done := false;
        while (not done and ps ≠ null) do
            begin
                t_s' := tuple to which ps points;
                if (t_s'[JoinAttrs] = t_s[JoinAttrs])
                    then begin
                            S_s := S_s ∪ {t_s'};
                            set ps to point to next tuple of s;
                        end
                    else done := true;
            end
        t_r := tuple to which pr points;
        while (pr ≠ null and t_r[JoinAttrs] < t_s[JoinAttrs]) do
            begin
                set pr to point to next tuple of r;
                t_r := tuple to which pr points;
            end
        while (pr ≠ null and t_r[JoinAttrs] = t_s[JoinAttrs]) do
            begin
                for each t_s in S_s do
                    begin
                        add t_s ⋈ t_r to result ;
                    end
                set pr to point to next tuple of r;
                t_r := tuple to which pr points;
            end
    end.
```

Figure 13.6   Merge join.

that both relations are sorted on the attributes $R \cap S$. Then, their join can be computed by a process much like the merge stage in the merge–sort algorithm.

Figure 13.6 shows the merge join algorithm. In the algorithm, *JoinAttrs* refers to the attributes in $R \cap S$, and $t_r \bowtie t_s$, where t_r and t_s are tuples that have the same values for *JoinAttrs*, denotes the concatenation of the attributes of the tuples, followed by projecting out repeated attributes. The merge join algorithm associates one pointer with each relation. These pointers point initially to the first tuple of the respective relations. As the algorithm proceeds, the pointers move through the relation. A group of tuples of one relation with the same value on the join attributes is read into S_s.

The algorithm in Figure 13.6 *requires* that every set of tuples S_s fit in main memory; we shall look at extensions of the algorithm to avoid this requirement later in this section. Then, the corresponding tuples (if any) of the other relation are read in, and are processed as they are read.

Figure 13.7 shows two relations that are sorted on their join attribute $a1$. It is instructive to go through the steps of the merge join algorithm on the relations shown in the figure.

Since the relations are in sorted order, tuples with the same value on the join attributes are in consecutive order. Thereby, each tuple in the sorted order needs to be read only once, and, as a result, each block is also read only once. Since it makes only a single pass through both files, the merge join method is efficient; the number of block accesses is equal to the sum of the number of blocks in both files, $b_r + b_s$.

If either of the input relations r and s is not sorted on the join attributes, they can be sorted first, and then the merge join algorithm can be used. The merge join algorithm can also be easily extended from natural joins to the more general case of equi-joins.

Suppose the merge join scheme is applied to our example of *depositor* ⋈ *customer*. The join attribute here is *customer-name*. Suppose that the relations are already sorted on the join attribute *customer-name*. In this case, the merge join takes a total of $400 + 100 = 500$ block accesses. Suppose the relations are not sorted, and the memory size is the worst case of three blocks. Sorting *customer* takes $400 * (2\lceil\log_2(400/3)\rceil + 1)$, or 6800, block transfers, with 400 more transfers to write out the result. Similarly, sorting *depositor* takes $100 * (2\lceil\log_2(100/3)\rceil + 1)$, or 1300, transfers, with 100 more transfers to write it out. Thus, the total cost is 9100 block transfers if the relations are not sorted, and the memory size is just 3 blocks.

With a memory size of 25 blocks, sorting the relation *customer* takes a total of just $400 * (2\lceil\log_{24}(400/25) + 1) = 1200$ block transfers, while sorting *depositor* takes 300 block transfers. Adding the cost of writing out the sorted results and reading them back gives a total cost of 2500 block transfers if the relations are not sorted and the memory size is 25 blocks.

As mentioned earlier, the merge join algorithm of Figure 13.6 requires that the set S_s of all tuples with the same value for the join attributes must fit in main memory.

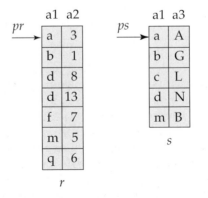

Figure 13.7   Sorted relations for merge join.

This requirement can usually be met, even if the relation s is large. If it cannot be met, a block nested-loop join must be performed between S_s and the tuples in r with the same values for the join attributes. The overall cost of the merge join increases as a result.

It is also possible to perform a variation of the merge join operation on unsorted tuples, if secondary indices exist on both join attributes. The algorithm scans the records through the indices, resulting in their being retrieved in sorted order. This variation presents a significant drawback, however, since records may be scattered throughout the file blocks. Hence, each tuple access could involve accessing a disk block, and that is costly.

To avoid this cost, we can use a hybrid merge–join technique, which combines indices with merge join. Suppose that one of the relations is sorted; the other is unsorted, but has a secondary B^+-tree index on the join attributes. The **hybrid merge–join algorithm** merges the sorted relation with the leaf entries of the secondary B^+-tree index. The result file contains tuples from the sorted relation and addresses for tuples of the unsorted relation. The result file is then sorted on the addresses of tuples of the unsorted relation, allowing efficient retrieval of the corresponding tuples, in physical storage order, to complete the join. Extensions of the technique to handle two unsorted relations are left as an exercise for you.

13.5.5   Hash Join

Like the merge join algorithm, the hash join algorithm can be used to implement natural joins and equi-joins. In the hash join algorithm, a hash function h is used to partition tuples of both relations. The basic idea is to partition the tuples of each of the relations into sets that have the same hash value on the join attributes.

We assume that

- h is a hash function mapping *JoinAttrs* values to $\{0, 1, \ldots, n_h\}$, where *JoinAttrs* denotes the common attributes of r and s used in the natural join.

- $H_{r_0}, H_{r_1}, \ldots, H_{r_{n_h}}$ denote partitions of r tuples, each initially empty. Each tuple $t_r \in r$ is put in partition H_{r_i}, where $i = h(t_r[\textit{JoinAttrs}])$.

- $H_{s_0}, H_{s_1}, \ldots, H_{s_{n_h}}$ denote partitions of s tuples, each initially empty. Each tuple $t_s \in s$ is put in partition H_{s_i}, where $i = h(t_s[\textit{JoinAttrs}])$.

The hash function h should have the "goodness" properties of randomness and uniformity that we discussed in Chapter 12. Figure 13.8 depicts the partitioning of the relations.

The idea behind the hash join algorithm is this: Suppose that an r tuple and an s tuple satisfy the join condition; then, they will have the same value for the join attributes. If that value is hashed to some value i, the r tuple has to be in H_{r_i} and the s tuple in H_{s_i}. Therefore, r tuples in H_{r_i} need only to be compared with s tuples in H_{s_i}; they do not need to be compared with s tuples in any other partition.

For example, if d is a tuple in *depositor*, c a tuple in *customer*, and h a hash function on the *customer-name* attributes of the tuples, then d and c must be tested only if

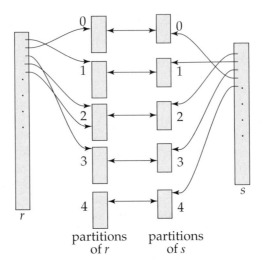

partitions
of r

partitions
of s

Figure 13.8 Hash partitioning of relations.

$h(c) = h(d)$. If $h(c) \neq h(d)$, then c and d must have different values for *customer-name*. However, if $h(c) = h(d)$, we must test c and d to see whether the values in their join attributes are the same, since it is possible that c and d have different *customer-names* that have the same hash value.

Figure 13.9 shows the details of the **hash join** algorithm to compute the natural join of relations r and s. As in the merge join algorithm, $t_r \bowtie t_s$ denotes the concatenation of the attributes of tuples t_r and t_s, followed by projecting out repeated attributes. After the partitioning of the relations, the rest of the hash join code performs a separate indexed nested-loop join on each of the partition pairs i, for $i = 0, \ldots, n_h$. To do so, it first **builds** a hash index on each H_{s_i}, and then **probes** (that is, looks up H_{s_i}) with tuples from H_{r_i}. The relation s is the **build input**, and r is the **probe input**.

The hash index on H_{s_i} is built in memory, so there is no need to access the disk to retrieve the tuples. The hash function used to build this hash index is different from the hash function h used earlier, but is still applied to only the join attributes. In the course of the indexed nested-loop join, the system uses this hash index to retrieve records that will match records in the probe input.

The build and probe phases require only a single pass through both the build and probe inputs. It is straightforward to extend the hash join algorithm to compute general equi-joins.

The value n_h must be chosen to be large enough such that, for each i, the tuples in the partition H_{s_i} of the build relation, along with the hash index on the partition, will fit in memory. It is not necessary for the partitions of the probe relation to fit in memory. Clearly, it is best to use the smaller input relation as the build relation. If the size of the build relation is b_s blocks, then, for each of the n_h partitions to be of size less than or equal to M, n_h must be at least $\lceil b_s/M \rceil$. More precisely stated, we have

```
/* Partition s */
for each tuple t_s in s do begin
    i := h(t_s[JoinAttrs]);
    H_{s_i} := H_{s_i} ∪ {t_s};
end
/* Partition r */
for each tuple t_r in r do begin
    i := h(t_r[JoinAttrs]);
    H_{r_i} := H_{r_i} ∪ {t_r};
end
/* Perform join on each partition */
for i := 0 to n_h do begin
    read H_{s_i} and build an in-memory hash index on it
    for each tuple t_r in H_{r_i} do begin
        probe the hash index on H_{s_i} to locate all tuples t_s
            such that t_s[JoinAttrs] = t_r[JoinAttrs]
        for each matching tuple t_s in H_{s_i} do begin
            add t_r ⋈ t_s to the result
        end
    end
end
```

Figure 13.9   Hash join.

to account for the extra space occupied by the hash index on the partition as well, so n_h should be correspondingly larger. For simplicity, we sometimes ignore the space requirement of the hash index in our analysis.

13.5.5.1 Recursive Partitioning

If the value of n_h is greater than or equal to the number of page frames of memory, the relations cannot be partitioned in one pass, since there will not be enough buffer pages. Instead, partitioning has to be done in repeated passes. In one pass, the input can be split into at most as many partitions as there are page frames available for use as output buffers. Each bucket generated by one pass is separately read in and partitioned again in the next pass, to create smaller partitions. The hash function used in a pass is, of course, different from the one used in the previous pass. The system repeats this splitting of the input until each partition of the build input fits in memory. Such partitioning is called **recursive partitioning**.

A relation does not need recursive partitioning if $M > n_h + 1$, or equivalently $M > (b_s/M) + 1$, which simplifies (approximately) to $M > \sqrt{b_s}$. For example, consider a memory size of 12 megabytes, divided into 4-kilobyte blocks; it would contain a total of 3000 blocks. We can use a memory of this size to partition relations of size 9 million blocks, which is 36 gigabytes. Similarly, a relation of size 1 gigabyte requires $\sqrt{250000}$ blocks, or about 2 megabytes, to avoid recursive partitioning.

13.5.5.2 Handling of Overflows

Hash-table overflow occurs in partition i of the build relation s if the hash index on H_{s_i} is larger than main memory. Hash-table overflow can occur if there are many tuples in the build relation with the same values for the join attributes, or if the hash function does not have the properties of randomness and uniformity. In either case, some of the partitions will have more tuples than the average, whereas others will have fewer; partitioning is then said to be **skewed**.

We can handle a small amount of skew by increasing the number of partitions so that the expected size of each partition (including the hash index on the partition) is somewhat less than the size of memory. The number of partitions is therefore increased by a small value called the **fudge factor**, which is usually about 20 percent of the number of hash partitions computed as described in Section 13.5.5.

Even if we are conservative on the sizes of the partitions, by using a fudge factor, overflows can still occur. Hash-table overflows can be handled by either *overflow resolution* or *overflow avoidance*. **Overflow resolution** is performed during the build phase, if a hash-index overflow is detected. Overflow resolution proceeds in this way: If H_{s_i}, for any i, is found to be too large, it is further partitioned into smaller partitions by using a different hash function. Similarly, H_{r_i} is also partitioned using the new hash function, and only tuples in the matching partitions need to be joined.

In contrast, **overflow avoidance** performs the partitioning carefully, so that overflows never occur during the build phase. In overflow avoidance, the build relation s is initially partitioned into many small partitions, and then some partitions are combined in such a way that each combined partition fits in memory. The probe relation r is partitioned in the same way as the combined partitions on s, but the sizes of H_{r_i} do not matter.

If a large number of tuples in s have the same value for the join attributes, the resolution and avoidance techniques may fail on some partitions. In that case, instead of creating an in-memory hash index and using a nested-loop join to join the partitions, we can use other join techniques, such as block nested-loop join, on those partitions.

13.5.5.3 Cost of Hash Join

We now consider the cost of a hash join. Our analysis assumes that there is no hash-table overflow. First, consider the case where recursive partitioning is not required. The partitioning of the two relations r and s calls for a complete reading of both relations, and a subsequent writing back of them. This operation requires $2(b_r + b_s)$ block accesses, where b_r and b_s denote the number of blocks containing records of relations r and s respectively. The build and probe phases read each of the partitions once, calling for a further $b_r + b_s$ accesses. The number of blocks occupied by partitions could be slightly more than $b_r + b_s$, as a result of partially filled blocks. Accessing such partially filled blocks can add an overhead of at most $2n_h$ for each of the relations, since each of the n_h partitions could have a partially filled block that has to be written and read back. Thus, the cost estimate for a hash join is

$$3(b_r + b_s) + 4n_h$$

The overhead $4n_h$ is quite small compared to $b_r + b_s$, and can be ignored.

Now consider the case where recursive partitioning is required. Each pass reduces the size of each of the partitions by an expected factor of $M - 1$; and passes are repeated until each partition is of size at most M blocks. The expected number of passes required for partitioning s is therefore $\lceil \log_{M-1}(b_s) - 1 \rceil$. Since, in each pass, every block of s is read in and written out, the total block transfers for partitioning of s is $2b_s \lceil \log_{M-1}(b_s) - 1 \rceil$. The number of passes for partitioning of r is the same as the number of passes for partitioning of s, therefore the cost estimate for the join is

$$2(b_r + b_s)\lceil \log_{M-1}(b_s) - 1 \rceil + b_r + b_s$$

Consider, for example, the join *customer* ⋈ *depositor*. With a memory size of 20 blocks, *depositor* can be partitioned into five partitions, each of size 20 blocks, which size will fit into memory. Only one pass is required for the partitioning. The relation *customer* is similarly partitioned into five partitions, each of size 80. Ignoring the cost of writing partially filled blocks, the cost is $3(100 + 400) = 1500$ block transfers.

The hash join can be improved if the main memory size is large. When the entire build input can be kept in main memory, n_h can be set to 0; then, the hash join algorithm executes quickly, without partitioning the relations into temporary files, regardless of the probe input's size. The cost estimate goes down to $b_r + b_s$.

13.5.5.4 Hybrid Hash–Join

The **hybrid hash–join** algorithm performs another optimization; it is useful when memory sizes are relatively large, but not all of the build relation fits in memory. The partitioning phase of the hash join algorithm needs one block of memory as a buffer for each partition that is created, and one block of memory as an input buffer. Hence, a total of $n_h + 1$ blocks of memory are needed for the partitioning the two relations. If memory is larger than $n_h + 1$, we can use the rest of memory ($M - n_h - 1$ blocks) to buffer the first partition of the build input (that is, H_{s_0}), so that it will not need to be written out and read back in. Further, the hash function is designed in such a way that the hash index on H_{s_0} fits in $M - n_h - 1$ blocks, in order that, at the end of partitioning of s, H_{s_0} is completely in memory and a hash index can be built on H_{s_0}.

When the system partitions r it again does not write tuples in H_{r_0} to disk; instead, as it generates them, the system uses them to probe the memory-resident hash index on H_{s_0}, and to generate output tuples of the join. After they are used for probing, the tuples can be discarded, so the partition H_{r_0} does not occupy any memory space. Thus, a write and a read access have been saved for each block of both H_{r_0} and H_{s_0}. The system writes out tuples in the other partitions as usual, and joins them later. The savings of hybrid hash–join can be significant if the build input is only slightly bigger than memory.

If the size of the build relation is b_s, n_h is approximately equal to b_s/M. Thus, hybrid hash–join is most useful if $M \gg b_s/M$, or $M \gg \sqrt{b_s}$, where the notation $\gg$ denotes *much larger than*. For example, suppose the block size is 4 kilobytes, and the build relation size is 1 gigabyte. Then, the hybrid hash–join algorithm is useful if the size of memory is significantly more than 2 megabytes; memory sizes of 100 megabytes or more are common on computers today.

Consider the join *customer* ⋈ *depositor* again. With a memory size of 25 blocks, *depositor* can be partitioned into five partitions, each of size 20 blocks, and the first of the partitions of the build relation can be kept in memory. It occupies 20 blocks of memory; one block is for input and one block each is for buffering the other four partitions. The relation *customer* can be similarly partitioned into five partitions each of size 80, the first of which the system uses right away for probing, instead of writing it out and reading it back in. Ignoring the cost of writing partially filled blocks, the cost is $3(80 + 320) + 20 + 80 = 1300$ block transfers, instead of 1500 block transfers without the hybrid hashing optimization.

13.5.6 Complex Joins

Nested-loop and block nested-loop joins can be used regardless of the join conditions. The other join techniques are more efficient than the nested-loop join and its variants, but can handle only simple join conditions, such as natural joins or equijoins. We can implement joins with complex join conditions, such as conjunctions and disjunctions, by using the efficient join techniques, if we apply the techniques developed in Section 13.3.4 for handling complex selections.

Consider the following join with a conjunctive condition:

$$r \bowtie_{\theta_1 \wedge \theta_2 \wedge \cdots \wedge \theta_n} s$$

One or more of the join techniques described earlier may be applicable for joins on the individual conditions $r \bowtie_{\theta_1} s$, $r \bowtie_{\theta_2} s$, $r \bowtie_{\theta_3} s$, and so on. We can compute the overall join by first computing the result of one of these simpler joins $r \bowtie_{\theta_i} s$; each pair of tuples in the intermediate result consists of one tuple from r and one from s. The result of the complete join consists of those tuples in the intermediate result that satisfy the remaining conditions

$$\theta_1 \wedge \cdots \wedge \theta_{i-1} \wedge \theta_{i+1} \wedge \cdots \wedge \theta_n$$

These conditions can be tested as tuples in $r \bowtie_{\theta_i} s$ are being generated.

A join whose condition is disjunctive can be computed in this way: Consider

$$r \bowtie_{\theta_1 \vee \theta_2 \vee \cdots \vee \theta_n} s$$

The join can be computed as the union of the records in individual joins $r \bowtie_{\theta_i} s$:

$$(r \bowtie_{\theta_1} s) \cup (r \bowtie_{\theta_2} s) \cup \cdots \cup (r \bowtie_{\theta_n} s)$$

Section 13.6 describes algorithms for computing the union of relations.

13.6 Other Operations

Other relational operations and extended relational operations—such as duplicate elimination, projection, set operations, outer join, and aggregation—can be implemented as outlined in Sections 13.6.1 through 13.6.5.

13.6.1 Duplicate Elimination

We can implement duplicate elimination easily by sorting. Identical tuples will appear adjacent to each other during sorting, and all but one copy can be removed. With external sort–merge, duplicates found while a run is being created can be removed before the run is written to disk, thereby reducing the number of block transfers. The remaining duplicates can be eliminated during merging, and the final sorted run will have no duplicates. The worst-case cost estimate for duplicate elimination is the same as the worst-case cost estimate for sorting of the relation.

We can also implement duplicate elimination by hashing, as in the hash join algorithm. First, the relation is partitioned on the basis of a hash function on the whole tuple. Then, each partition is read in, and an in-memory hash index is constructed. While constructing the hash index, a tuple is inserted only if it is not already present. Otherwise, the tuple is discarded. After all tuples in the partition have been processed, the tuples in the hash index are written to the result. The cost estimate is the same as that for the cost of processing (partitioning and reading each partition) of the build relation in a hash join.

Because of the relatively high cost of duplicate elimination, SQL requires an explicit request by the user to remove duplicates; otherwise, the duplicates are retained.

13.6.2 Projection

We can implement projection easily by performing projection on each tuple, which gives a relation that could have duplicate records, and then removing duplicate records. Duplicates can be eliminated by the methods described in Section 13.6.1. If the attributes in the projection list include a key of the relation, no duplicates will exist; hence, duplicate elimination is not required. Generalized projection (which was discussed in Section 3.3.1) can be implemented in the same way as projection.

13.6.3 Set Operations

We can implement the *union, intersection,* and *set-difference* operations by first sorting both relations, and then scanning once through each of the sorted relations to produce the result. In $r \cup s$, when a concurrent scan of both relations reveals the same tuple in both files, only one of the tuples is retained. The result of $r \cap s$ will contain only those tuples that appear in both relations. We implement *set difference,* $r - s$, similarly, by retaining tuples in r only if they are absent in s.

For all these operations, only one scan of the two input relations is required, so the cost is $b_r + b_s$. If the relations are not sorted initially, the cost of sorting has to be included. Any sort order can be used in evaluation of set operations, provided that both inputs have that same sort order.

Hashing provides another way to implement these set operations. The first step in each case is to partition the two relations by the same hash function, and thereby create the partitions $H_{r_0}, H_{r_1}, \ldots, H_{r_{n_h}}$ and $H_{s_0}, H_{s_1}, \ldots, H_{s_{n_h}}$. Depending on the operation, the system then takes these steps on each partition $i = 0, 1 \ldots, n_h$:

- $r \cup s$

    1. Build an in-memory hash index on H_{r_i}.
    2. Add the tuples in H_{s_i} to the hash index only if they are not already present.
    3. Add the tuples in the hash index to the result.

- $r \cap s$

    1. Build an in-memory hash index on H_{r_i}.
    2. For each tuple in H_{s_i}, probe the hash index, and output the tuple to the result only if it is already present in the hash index.

- $r - s$

    1. Build an in-memory hash index on H_{r_i}.
    2. For each tuple in H_{s_i}, probe the hash index, and, if the tuple is present in the hash index, delete it from the hash index.
    3. Add the tuples remaining in the hash index to the result.

13.6.4 Outer Join

Recall the *outer-join operations* described in Section 3.3.3. For example, the natural left outer join *customer* $\bowtie$ *depositor* contains the join of *customer* and *depositor*, and, in addition, for each *customer* tuple t that has no matching tuple in *depositor* (that is, where *customer-name* is not in *depositor*), the following tuple t_1 is added to the result. For all attributes in the schema of *customer*, tuple t_1 has the same values as tuple t. The remaining attributes (from the schema of *depositor*) of tuple t_1 contain the value null.

We can implement the outer-join operations by using one of two strategies:

1. Compute the corresponding join, and then add further tuples to the join result to get the outer-join result. Consider the left outer-join operation and two relations: $r(R)$ and $s(S)$. To evaluate $r \bowtie_\theta s$, we first compute $r \bowtie_\theta s$, and save that result as temporary relation q_1. Next, we compute $r - \Pi_R(q_1)$, which gives tuples in r that did not participate in the join. We can use any of the algorithms for computing the joins, projection, and set difference described earlier to compute the outer joins. We pad each of these tuples with null values for attributes from s, and add it to q_1 to get the result of the outer join.

    The right outer-join operation $r \bowtie_\theta s$ is equivalent to $s \bowtie_\theta r$, and can therefore be implemented in a symmetric fashion to the left outer join. We can implement the full outer-join operation $r \bowtie_\theta s$ by computing the join $r \bowtie s$, and then adding the extra tuples of both the left and right outer-join operations, as before.

2. Modify the join algorithms. It is easy to extend the nested-loop join algorithms to compute the left outer join: Tuples in the outer relation that do not match any tuple in the inner relation are written to the output after being padded with null values. However, it is hard to extend the nested-loop join to compute the full outer join.

Natural outer joins and outer joins with an equi-join condition can be computed by extensions of the merge join and hash join algorithms. Merge join can be extended to compute the full outer join as follows: When the merge of the two relations is being done, tuples in either relation that did not match any tuple in the other relation can be padded with nulls and written to the output. Similarly, we can extend merge join to compute the left and right outer joins by writing out nonmatching tuples (padded with nulls) from only one of the relations. Since the relations are sorted, it is easy to detect whether or not a tuple matches any tuples from the other relation. For example, when a merge join of *customer* and *depositor* is done, the tuples are read in sorted order of *customer-name*, and it is easy to check, for each tuple, whether there is a matching tuple in the other.

The cost estimates for implementing outer joins using the merge join algorithm are the same as are those for the corresponding join. The only difference lies in size of the result, and therefore in the block transfers for writing it out, which we did not count in our earlier cost estimates.

The extension of the hash join algorithm to compute outer joins is left for you to do as an exercise (Exercise 13.11).

13.6.5   Aggregation

Recall the aggregation operator $\mathcal{G}$, discussed in Section 3.3.2. For example, the operation

$$_{branch\text{-}name}\mathcal{G}_{\mathbf{sum}(balance)}(account)$$

groups *account* tuples by branch, and computes the total balance of all the accounts at each branch.

The aggregation operation can be implemented in the same way as duplicate elimination. We use either sorting or hashing, just as we did for duplicate elimination, but based on the grouping attributes (*branch-name* in the preceding example). However, instead of eliminating tuples with the same value for the grouping attribute, we gather them into groups, and apply the aggregation operations on each group to get the result.

The cost estimate for implementing the aggregation operation is the same as the cost of duplicate elimination, for aggregate functions such as **min, max, sum, count,** and **avg**.

Instead of gathering all the tuples in a group and then applying the aggregation operations, we can implement the aggregation operations **sum, min, max, count,** and **avg** on the fly as the groups are being constructed. For the case of **sum, min,** and **max,** when two tuples in the same group are found, the system replaces them by a single tuple containing the **sum, min,** or **max,** respectively, of the columns being aggregated. For the **count** operation, it maintains a running count for each group for which a tuple has been found. Finally, we implement the **avg** operation by computing the sum and the count values on the fly, and finally dividing the sum by the count to get the average.

If all tuples of the result will fit in memory, both the sort-based and the hash-based implementations do not need to write any tuples to disk. As the tuples are read in, they can be inserted in a sorted tree structure or in a hash index. When we use on the fly aggregation techniques, only one tuple needs to be stored for each of the groups. Hence, the sorted tree structure or hash index will fit in memory, and the aggregation can be processed with just b_r block transfers, instead of with the $3b_r$ transfers that would be required otherwise.

13.7 Evaluation of Expressions

So far, we have studied how individual relational operations are carried out. Now we consider how to evaluate an expression containing multiple operations. The obvious way to evaluate an expression is simply to evaluate one operation at a time, in an appropriate order. The result of each evaluation is **materialized** in a temporary relation for subsequent use. A disadvantage to this approach is the need to construct the temporary relations, which (unless they are small) must be written to disk. An alternative approach is to evaluate several operations simultaneously in a **pipeline**, with the results of one operation passed on to the next, without the need to store a temporary relation.

In Sections 13.7.1 and 13.7.2, we consider both the *materialization* approach and the *pipelining* approach. We shall see that the costs of these approaches can differ substantially, but also that there are cases where only the materialization approach is feasible.

13.7.1 Materialization

It is easiest to understand intuitively how to evaluate an expression by looking at a pictorial representation of the expression in an **operator tree**. Consider the expression

$$\Pi_{customer\text{-}name} (\sigma_{balance<2500} (account) \bowtie customer)$$

in Figure 13.10.

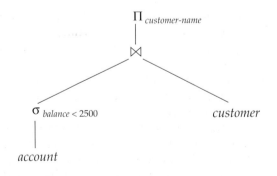

Figure 13.10   Pictorial representation of an expression.

If we apply the materialization approach, we start from the lowest-level operations in the expression (at the bottom of the tree). In our example, there is only one such operation; the selection operation on *account*. The inputs to the lowest-level operations are relations in the database. We execute these operations by the algorithms that we studied earlier, and we store the results in temporary relations. We can use these temporary relations to execute the operations at the next level up in the tree, where the inputs now are either temporary relations or relations stored in the database. In our example, the inputs to the join are the *customer* relation and the temporary relation created by the selection on *account*. The join can now be evaluated, creating another temporary relation.

By repeating the process, we will eventually evaluate the operation at the root of the tree, giving the final result of the expression. In our example, we get the final result by executing the projection operation at the root of the tree, using as input the temporary relation created by the join.

Evaluation as just described is called **materialized evaluation**, since the results of each intermediate operation are created (materialized) and then are used for evaluation of the next-level operations.

The cost of a materialized evaluation is not simply the sum of the costs of the operations involved. When we computed the cost estimates of algorithms, we ignored the cost of writing the result of the operation to disk. To compute the cost of evaluating an expression as done here, we have to add the costs of all the operations, as well as the cost of writing the intermediate results to disk. We assume that the records of the result accumulate in a buffer, and, when the buffer is full, they are written to disk. The cost of writing out the result can be estimated as n_r/f_r, where n_r is the estimated number of tuples in the result relation r, and f_r is the *blocking factor* of the result relation, that is, the number of records of r that will fit in a block.

Double buffering (using two buffers, with one continuing execution of the algorithm while the other is being written out) allows the algorithm to execute more quickly by performing CPU activity in parallel with I/O activity.

13.7.2 Pipelining

We can improve query-evaluation efficiency by reducing the number of temporary files that are produced. We achieve this reduction by combining several relational operations into a *pipeline* of operations, in which the results of one operation are passed along to the next operation in the pipeline. Evaluation as just described is called **pipelined evaluation**. Combining operations into a pipeline eliminates the cost of reading and writing temporary relations.

For example, consider the expression $(\Pi_{a1,a2}(r \bowtie s))$. If materialization were applied, evaluation would involve creating a temporary relation to hold the result of the join, and then reading back in the result to perform the projection. These operations can be combined: When the join operation generates a tuple of its result, it passes that tuple immediately to the project operation for processing. By combining the join and the projection, we avoid creating the intermediate result, and instead create the final result directly.

13.7.2.1 Implementation of Pipelining

We can implement a pipeline by constructing a single, complex operation that combines the operations that constitute the pipeline. Although this approach may be feasible for various frequently occurring situations, it is desirable in general to reuse the code for individual operations in the construction of a pipeline. Therefore, each operation in the pipeline is modeled as a separate process or thread within the system, which takes a stream of tuples from its pipelined inputs, and generates a stream of tuples for its output. For each pair of adjacent operations in the pipeline, the system creates a buffer to hold tuples being passed from one operation to the next.

In the example of Figure 13.10, all three operations can be placed in a pipeline, which passes the results of the selection to the join as they are generated. In turn, it passes the results of the join to the projection as they are generated. The memory requirements are low, since results of an operation are not stored for long. However, as a result of pipelining, the inputs to the operations are not available all at once for processing.

Pipelines can be executed in either of two ways:

1. Demand driven

2. Producer driven

In a **demand-driven pipeline**, the system makes repeated requests for tuples from the operation at the top of the pipeline. Each time that an operation receives a request for tuples, it computes the next tuple (or tuples) to be returned, and then returns that tuple. If the inputs of the operation are not pipelined, the next tuple(s) to be returned can be computed from the input relations, while the system keeps track of what has been returned so far. If it has some pipelined inputs, the operation also makes requests for tuples from its pipelined inputs. Using the tuples received from its pipelined inputs, the operation computes tuples for its output, and passes them up to its parent.

In a **producer-driven pipeline**, operations do not wait for requests to produce tuples, but instead generate the tuples **eagerly**. Each operation at the bottom of a pipeline continually generates output tuples, and puts them in its output buffer, until the buffer is full. An operation at any other level of a pipeline generates output tuples when it gets input tuples from lower down in the pipeline, until its output buffer is full. Once the operation uses a tuple from a pipelined input, it removes the tuple from its input buffer. In either case, once the output buffer is full, the operation waits until its parent operation removes tuples from the buffer, so that the buffer has space for more tuples. At this point, the operation generates more tuples, until the buffer is full again. The operation repeats this process until all the output tuples have been generated.

It is necessary for the system to switch between operations only when an output buffer is full, or an input buffer is empty and more input tuples are needed to generate any more output tuples. In a parallel-processing system, operations in a pipeline may be run concurrently on distinct processors (see Chapter 20).

Using producer-driven pipelining can be thought of as **pushing** data up an operation tree from below, whereas using demand-driven pipelining can be thought of as

pulling data up an operation tree from the top. Whereas tuples are generated *eagerly* in producer-driven pipelining, they are generated **lazily**, on demand, in demand-driven pipelining.

Each operation in a demand-driven pipeline can be implemented as an **iterator**, which provides the following functions: open(), next(), and close(). After a call to open(), each call to next() returns the next output tuple of the operation. The implementation of the operation in turn calls open() and next() on its inputs, to get its input tuples when required. The function close() tells an iterator that no more tuples are required. The iterator maintains the **state** of its execution in between calls, so that successive next() requests receive successive result tuples.

For example, for an iterator implementing the select operation using linear search, the open() operation starts a file scan, and the iterator's state records the point to which the file has been scanned. When the next() function is called, the file scan continues from after the previous point; when the next tuple satisfying the selection is found by scanning the file, the tuple is returned after storing the point where it was found in the iterator state. A merge–join iterator's open() operation would open its inputs, and if they are not already sorted, it would also sort the inputs. On calls to next(), it would return the next pair of matching tuples. The state information would consist of up to where each input had been scanned.

Details of the implementation of iterators are left for you to complete in Exercise 13.12. Demand-driven pipelining is used more commonly than producer-driven pipelining, because it is easier to implement.

13.7.2.2   Evaluation Algorithms for Pipelining

Consider a join operation whose left-hand–side input is pipelined. Since it is pipelined, the input is not available all at once for processing by the join operation. This unavailability limits the choice of join algorithm to be used. Merge join, for example, cannot be used if the inputs are not sorted, since it is not possible to sort a relation until all the tuples are available—thus, in effect, turning pipelining into materialization. However, indexed nested-loop join can be used: As tuples are received for the left-hand side of the join, they can be used to index the right-hand–side relation, and to generate tuples in the join result. This example illustrates that choices regarding the algorithm used for an operation and choices regarding pipelining are not independent.

The restrictions on the evaluation algorithms that are eligible for use are a limiting factor for pipelining. As a result, despite the apparent advantages of pipelining, there are cases where materialization achieves lower overall cost. Suppose that the join of r and s is required, and input r is pipelined. If indexed nested-loop join is used to support pipelining, one access to disk may be needed for every tuple in the pipelined input relation. The cost of this technique is $n_r * \text{HT}_i$, where HT_i is the height of the index on s. With materialization, the cost of writing out r would be b_r. With a join technique such as hash join, it may be possible to perform the join with a cost of about $3(b_r + b_s)$. If n_r is substantially more than $4b_r + 3b_s$, materialization would be cheaper.

$done_r := false;$
$done_s := false;$
$r := \emptyset;$
$s := \emptyset;$
$result := \emptyset;$
while not $done_r$ **or not** $done_s$ **do**
    begin
        if queue is empty, **then** wait until queue is not empty;
        $t :=$ top entry in queue;
        if $t = End_r$ **then** $done_r := true$
          else if $t = End_s$ **then** $done_s := true$
            else if t is from input r
            then
                begin
                  $r := r \cup \{t\};$
                  $result := result \cup (\{t\} \bowtie s);$
                end
              else /* t is from input s */
                begin
                  $s := s \cup \{t\};$
                  $result := result \cup (r \bowtie \{t\});$
                end
end

Figure 13.11 Pipelined join algorithm.

The effective use of pipelining requires the use of evaluation algorithms that can generate output tuples even as tuples are received for the inputs to the operation. We can distinguish between two cases:

1. Only one of the inputs to a join is pipelined.

2. Both inputs to the join are pipelined.

If only one of the inputs to a join is pipelined, indexed nested-loop join is a natural choice. If the pipelined input tuples are sorted on the join attributes, and the join condition is an equi-join, merge join can also be used. Hybrid hash–join can be used too, with the pipelined input as the probe relation. However, tuples that are not in the first partition will be output only after the entire pipelined input relation is received. Hybrid hash–join is useful if the nonpipelined input fits entirely in memory, or if at least most of that input fits in memory.

If both inputs are pipelined, the choice of join algorithms is more restricted. If both inputs are sorted on the join attribute, and the join condition is an equi-join, merge join can be used. Another alternative is the **pipelined join** technique, shown in Figure 13.11. The algorithm assumes that the input tuples for both input relations, r and s, are pipelined. Tuples made available for both relations are queued for processing in a single queue. Special queue entries, called End_r and End_s, which serve as end-of-file markers, are inserted in the queue after all tuples from r and s (respectively) have been generated. For efficient evaluation, appropriate indices should be built on the relations r and s. As tuples are added to r and s, the indices must be kept up to date.

13.8 Summary

- The first action that the system must perform on a query is to translate the query into its internal form, which (for relational database systems) is usually based on the relational algebra. In the process of generating the internal form of the query, the parser checks the syntax of the user's query, verifies that the relation names appearing in the query are names of relations in the database, and so on. If the query was expressed in terms of a view, the parser replaces all references to the view name with the relational-algebra expression to compute the view.

- Given a query, there are generally a variety of methods for computing the answer. It is the responsibility of the query optimizer to transform the query as entered by the user into an equivalent query that can be computed more efficiently. Chapter 14 covers query optimization.

- We can process simple selection operations by performing a linear scan, by doing a binary search, or by making use of indices. We can handle complex selections by computing unions and intersections of the results of simple selections.

- We can sort relations larger than memory by the external merge–sort algorithm.

- Queries involving a natural join may be processed in several ways, depending on the availability of indices and the form of physical storage for the relations.
  - ☐ If the join result is almost as large as the Cartesian product of the two relations, a *block nested-loop* join strategy may be advantageous.
  - ☐ If indices are available, the *indexed nested-loop* join can be used.
  - ☐ If the relations are sorted, a *merge join* may be desirable. It may be advantageous to sort a relation prior to join computation (so as to allow use of the merge join strategy).
  - ☐ The *hash join* algorithm partitions the relations into several pieces, such that each piece of one of the relations fits in memory. The partitioning is carried out with a hash function on the join attributes, so that corresponding pairs of partitions can be joined independently.

- Duplicate elimination, projection, set operations (union, intersection and difference), and aggregation can be done by sorting or by hashing.

- Outer join operations can be implemented by simple extensions of join algorithms.

- Hashing and sorting are dual, in the sense that any operation such as duplicate elimination, projection, aggregation, join, and outer join that can be implemented by hashing can also be implemented by sorting, and vice versa; that is, any operation that can be implemented by sorting can also be implemented by hashing.

- An expression can be evaluated by means of materialization, where the system computes the result of each subexpression and stores it on disk, and then uses it to compute the result of the parent expression.

- Pipelining helps to avoid writing the results of many subexpressions to disk, by using the results in the parent expression even as they are being generated.

Review Terms

- Query processing
- Evaluation primitive
- Query-execution plan
- Query-evaluation plan
- Query-execution engine
- Measures of query cost
- Sequential I/O
- Random I/O
- File scan
- Linear search
- Binary search
- Selections using indices
- Access paths
- Index scans
- Conjunctive selection
- Disjunctive selection
- Composite index
- Intersection of identifiers
- External sorting
- External sort–merge
- Runs
- N-way merge
- Equi-join
- Nested-loop join

- Block nested-loop join
- Indexed nested-loop join
- Merge join
- Sort–merge join
- Hybrid merge–join
- Hash join
  - ☐ Build
  - ☐ Probe
  - ☐ Build input
  - ☐ Probe input
  - ☐ Recursive partitioning
  - ☐ Hash-table overflow
  - ☐ Skew
  - ☐ Fudge factor
  - ☐ Overflow resolution
  - ☐ Overflow avoidance
- Hybrid hash–join
- Operator tree
- Materialized evaluation
- Double buffering
- Pipelined evaluation
  - ☐ Demand-driven pipeline (lazy, pulling)
  - ☐ Producer-driven pipeline (eager, pushing)
  - ☐ Iterator
- Pipelined join

Exercises

13.1 Why is it not desirable to force users to make an explicit choice of a query-processing strategy? Are there cases in which it *is* desirable for users to be aware of the costs of competing query-processing strategies? Explain your answer.

13.2 Consider the following SQL query for our bank database:

> **select** *T.branch-name*
> **from** *branch T, branch S*
> **where** *T.assets* > *S.assets* **and** *S.branch-city* = "Brooklyn"

Write an efficient relational-algebra expression that is equivalent to this query. Justify your choice.

13.3 What are the advantages and disadvantages of hash indices relative to B^+-tree indices? How might the type of index available influence the choice of a query-processing strategy?

13.4 Assume (for simplicity in this exercise) that only one tuple fits in a block and memory holds at most 3 page frames. Show the runs created on each pass of the sort-merge algorithm, when applied to sort the following tuples on the first attribute: (kangaroo, 17), (wallaby, 21), (emu, 1), (wombat, 13), (platypus, 3), (lion, 8), (warthog, 4), (zebra, 11), (meerkat, 6), (hyena, 9), (hornbill, 2), (baboon, 12).

13.5 Let relations $r_1(A, B, C)$ and $r_2(C, D, E)$ have the following properties: r_1 has 20,000 tuples, r_2 has 45,000 tuples, 25 tuples of r_1 fit on one block, and 30 tuples of r_2 fit on one block. Estimate the number of block accesses required, using each of the following join strategies for $r_1 \bowtie r_2$:

   a. Nested-loop join
   b. Block nested-loop join
   c. Merge join
   d. Hash join

13.6 Design a variant of the hybrid merge–join algorithm for the case where both relations are not physically sorted, but both have a sorted secondary index on the join attributes.

13.7 The indexed nested-loop join algorithm described in Section 13.5.3 can be inefficient if the index is a secondary index, and there are multiple tuples with the same value for the join attributes. Why is it inefficient? Describe a way, using sorting, to reduce the cost of retrieving tuples of the inner relation. Under what conditions would this algorithm be more efficient than hybrid merge–join?

13.8 Estimate the number of block accesses required by your solution to Exercise 13.6 for $r_1 \bowtie r_2$, where r_1 and r_2 are as defined in Exercise 13.5.

13.9 Let r and s be relations with no indices, and assume that the relations are not sorted. Assuming infinite memory, what is the lowest cost way (in terms of I/O operations) to compute $r \bowtie s$? What is the amount of memory required for this algorithm?

13.10 Suppose that a B^+-tree index on *branch-city* is available on relation *branch*, and that no other index is available. List different ways to handle the following selections that involve negation?

   a. $\sigma_{\neg(branch\text{-}city<\text{"Brooklyn"})}(branch)$
   b. $\sigma_{\neg(branch\text{-}city=\text{"Brooklyn"})}(branch)$
   c. $\sigma_{\neg(branch\text{-}city<\text{"Brooklyn"} \vee assets<5000)}(branch)$

13.11 The hash join algorithm as described in Section 13.5.5 computes the natural join of two relations. Describe how to extend the hash join algorithm to compute the natural left outer join, the natural right outer join and the natural full outer join. (Hint: Keep extra information with each tuple in the hash index, to detect whether any tuple in the probe relation matches the tuple in the hash index.) Try out your algorithm on the *customer* and *depositor* relations.

13.12 Write pseudocode for an iterator that implements indexed nested-loop join, where the outer relation is pipelined. Use the standard iterator functions in your pseudocode. Show what state information the iterator must maintain between calls.

13.13 Design sorting based and hashing algorithms for computing the division operation.

Bibliographical Notes

A query processor must parse statements in the query language, and must translate them into an internal form. Parsing of query languages differs little from parsing of traditional programming languages. Most compiler texts, such as Aho et al. [1986], cover the main parsing techniques, and present optimization from a programming-language point of view.

Knuth [1973] presents an excellent description of external sorting algorithms, including an optimization that can create initial runs that are (on the average) twice the size of memory. Based on performance studies conducted in the mid-1970s, database systems of that period used only nested-loop join and merge join. These studies, which were related to the development of System R, determined that either the nested-loop join or merge join nearly always provided the optimal join method (Blasgen and Eswaran [1976]); hence, these two were the only join algorithms implemented in System R. The System R study, however, did not include an analysis of hash join algorithms. Today, hash joins are considered to be highly efficient.

Hash join algorithms were initially developed for parallel database systems. Hash join techniques are described in Kitsuregawa et al. [1983], and extensions including hybrid hash join are described in Shapiro [1986]. Zeller and Gray [1990] and Davison and Graefe [1994] describe hash join techniques that can adapt to the available memory, which is important in systems where multiple queries may be running at the same time. Graefe et al. [1998] describes the use of hash joins and *hash teams*, which allow pipelining of hash-joins by using the same partitioning for all hash-joins in a pipeline sequence, in the Microsoft SQL Server.

Graefe [1993] presents an excellent survey of query-evaluation techniques. An earlier survey of query-processing techniques appears in Jarke and Koch [1984].

Query processing in main memory database is covered by DeWitt et al. [1984] and Whang and Krishnamurthy [1990]. Kim [1982] and Kim [1984] describe join strategies and the optimal use of available main memory.

CHAPTER 14

Query Optimization

Query optimization is the process of selecting the most efficient query-evaluation plan from among the many strategies usually possible for processing a given query, especially if the query is complex. We do not expect users to write their queries so that they can be processed efficiently. Rather, we expect the system to construct a query-evaluation plan that minimizes the cost of query evaluation. This is where query optimization comes into play.

One aspect of optimization occurs at the relational-algebra level, where the system attempts to find an expression that is equivalent to the given expression, but more efficient to execute. Another aspect is selecting a detailed strategy for processing the query, such as choosing the algorithm to use for executing an operation, choosing the specific indices to use, and so on.

The difference in cost (in terms of evaluation time) between a good strategy and a bad strategy is often substantial, and may be several orders of magnitude. Hence, it is worthwhile for the system to spend a substantial amount of time on the selection of a good strategy for processing a query, even if the query is executed only once.

14.1 Overview

Consider the relational-algebra expression for the query "Find the names of all customers who have an account at any branch located in Brooklyn."

$$\Pi_{customer\text{-}name} \left(\sigma_{branch\text{-}city\,=\,\text{"Brooklyn"}} \left(branch \bowtie \left(account \bowtie depositor \right) \right) \right)$$

This expression constructs a large intermediate relation, $branch \bowtie account \bowtie depositor$. However, we are interested in only a few tuples of this relation (those pertaining to branches located in Brooklyn), and in only one of the six attributes of this relation. Since we are concerned with only those tuples in the $branch$ relation that pertain to branches located in Brooklyn, we do not need to consider those tuples that do not

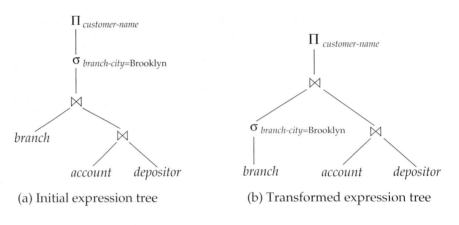

(a) Initial expression tree   (b) Transformed expression tree

Figure 14.1   Equivalent expressions.

have *branch-city* = "Brooklyn". By reducing the number of tuples of the *branch* relation that we need to access, we reduce the size of the intermediate result. Our query
is now represented by the relational-algebra expression

$$\Pi_{customer-name} \left(\left(\sigma_{branch-city\,=\,\text{"Brooklyn"}} (branch) \right) \bowtie (account \bowtie depositor) \right)$$

which is equivalent to our original algebra expression, but which generates smaller
intermediate relations. Figure 14.1 depicts the initial and transformed expressions.

Given a relational-algebra expression, it is the job of the query optimizer to come
up with a query-evaluation plan that computes the same result as the given expression, and is the least costly way of generating the result (or, at least, is not much
costlier than the least costly way).

To choose among different query-evaluation plans, the optimizer has to **estimate**
the cost of each evaluation plan. Computing the precise cost of evaluation of a plan is
usually not possible without actually evaluating the plan. Instead, optimizers make
use of statistical information about the relations, such as relation sizes and index
depths, to make a good estimate of the cost of a plan. Disk access, which is slow
compared to memory access, usually dominates the cost of processing a query.

In Section 14.2 we describe how to estimate statistics of the results of each operation in a query plan. Using these statistics with the cost formulae in Chapter 13 allows
us to estimate the costs of individual operation. The individual costs are combined to
determine the estimated cost of evaluating a given relational-algebra expression, as
outlined earlier in Section 13.7.

To find the least-costly query-evaluation plan, the optimizer needs to generate alternative plans that produce the same result as the given expression, and to choose
the least costly one. Generation of query-evaluation plans involves two steps: (1) generating expressions that are logically equivalent to the given expression and (2) annotating the resultant expressions in alternative ways to generate alternative query
evaluation plans. The two steps are interleaved in the query optimizer—some expressions are generated and annotated, then further expressions are generated and
annotated, and so on.

To implement the first step, the query optimizer must generate expressions equivalent to a given expression. It does so by means of *equivalence rules* that specify how to transform an expression into a logically equivalent one. We describe these rules in Section 14.3.1. In Section 14.4, we describe how to choose a query-evaluation plan. We can choose one based on the estimated cost of the plans. Since the cost is an estimate, the selected plan is not necessarily the least costly plan; however, as long as the estimates are good, the plan is likely to be the least costly one, or not much more costly than it. Such optimization, called **cost-based optimization**, is described in Section 14.4.2.

Materialized views help to speed up processing of certain queries. In Section 14.5, we study how to "maintain" materialized views—that is, to keep them up-to-date—and how to perform query optimization with materialized views.

14.2   Estimating Statistics of Expression Results

The cost of an operation depends on the size and other statistics of its inputs. Given an expression such as $a \bowtie (b \bowtie c)$ to estimate the cost of joining a with $(b \bowtie c)$, we need to have estimates of statistics such as the size of $b \bowtie c$.

In this section we first list some statistics about database relations that are stored in database system catalogs, and then show how to use the statistics to estimate statistics on the results of various relational operations.

One thing that will become clear later in this section is that the estimates are not very accurate, since they are based on assumptions that may not hold exactly. A query evaluation plan that has the lowest estimated execution cost may therefore not actually have the lowest actual execution cost. However, real-world experience has shown that even if estimates are not precise, the plans with the lowest estimated costs usually have actual execution costs that are either the lowest actual execution costs, or are close to the lowest actual execution costs.

14.2.1   Catalog Information

The DBMS catalog stores the following statistical information about database relations:

- n_r, the number of tuples in the relation r.

- b_r, the number of blocks containing tuples of relation r.

- l_r, the size of a tuple of relation r in bytes.

- f_r, the blocking factor of relation r—that is, the number of tuples of relation r that fit into one block.

- $V(A, r)$, the number of distinct values that appear in the relation r for attribute A. This value is the same as the size of $\Pi_A(r)$. If A is a key for relation r, $V(A, r)$ is n_r.

The last statistic, $V(A, r)$, can also be maintained for sets of attributes, if desired, instead of just for individual attributes. Thus, given a set of attributes, A, $V(A, r)$ is the size of $\Pi_A(r)$.

If we assume that the tuples of relation r are stored together physically in a file, the following equation holds:

$$b_r = \left\lceil \frac{n_r}{f_r} \right\rceil$$

Statistics about indices, such as the heights of B^+-tree indices and number of leaf pages in the indices, are also maintained in the catalog.

If we wish to maintain accurate statistics, then, every time a relation is modified, we must also update the statistics. This update incurs a substantial amount of overhead. Therefore, most systems do not update the statistics on every modification. Instead, they update the statistics during periods of light system load. As a result, the statistics used for choosing a query-processing strategy may not be completely accurate. However, if not too many updates occur in the intervals between the updates of the statistics, the statistics will be sufficiently accurate to provide a good estimation of the relative costs of the different plans.

The statistical information noted here is simplified. Real-world optimizers often maintain further statistical information to improve the accuracy of their cost estimates of evaluation plans. For instance, some databases store the distribution of values for each attribute as a **histogram**: in a histogram the values for the attribute are divided into a number of ranges, and with each range the histogram associates the number of tuples whose attribute value lies in that range. As an example of a histogram, the range of values for an attribute *age* of a relation *person* could be divided into 0–9, 10–19, ..., 90–99 (assuming a maximum age of 99). With each range we store a count of the number of *person* tuples whose *age* values lie in that range. Without such histogram information, an optimizer would have to assume that the distribution of values is uniform; that is, each range has the same count.

14.2.2 Selection Size Estimation

The size estimate of the result of a selection operation depends on the selection predicate. We first consider a single equality predicate, then a single comparison predicate, and finally combinations of predicates.

- $\sigma_{A=a}(r)$: If we assume uniform distribution of values (that is, each value appears with equal probability), the selection result can be estimated to have $n_r/V(A, r)$ tuples, assuming that the value a appears in attribute A of some record of r. The assumption that the value a in the selection appears in some record is generally true, and cost estimates often make it implicitly. However, it is often not realistic to assume that each value appears with equal probability. The *branch-name* attribute in the *account* relation is an example where the assumption is not valid. There is one tuple in the *account* relation for each account. It is reasonable to expect that the large branches have more accounts than smaller branches. Therefore, certain *branch-name* values appear with greater probability than do others. Despite the fact that the uniform-distribution assumption is often not correct, it is a reasonable approximation of reality in many cases, and it helps us to keep our presentation relatively simple.

- $\sigma_{A \leq v}(r)$: Consider a selection of the form $\sigma_{A \leq v}(r)$. If the actual value used in the comparison (v) is available at the time of cost estimation, a more accurate estimate can be made. The lowest and highest values ($\min(A, r)$ and $\max(A, r)$) for the attribute can be stored in the catalog. Assuming that values are uniformly distributed, we can estimate the number of records that will satisfy the condition $A \leq v$ as 0 if $v < \min(A, r)$, as n_r if $v \geq \max(A, r)$, and

$$n_r \cdot \frac{v - \min(A, r)}{\max(A, r) - \min(A, r)}$$

otherwise.

In some cases, such as when the query is part of a stored procedure, the value v may not be available when the query is optimized. In such cases, we will assume that approximately one-half the records will satisfy the comparison condition. That is, we assume the result has $n_r/2$ tuples; the estimate may be very inaccurate, but is the best we can do without any further information.

- Complex selections:

  - ☐ **Conjunction:** A *conjunctive selection* is a selection of the form

  $$\sigma_{\theta_1 \wedge \theta_2 \wedge \cdots \wedge \theta_n}(r)$$

  We can estimate the result size of such a selection: For each θ_i, we estimate the size of the selection $\sigma_{\theta_i}(r)$, denoted by s_i, as described previously. Thus, the probability that a tuple in the relation satisfies selection condition θ_i is s_i/n_r.

  The preceding probability is called the **selectivity** of the selection $\sigma_{\theta_i}(r)$. Assuming that the conditions are *independent* of each other, the probability that a tuple satisfies all the conditions is simply the product of all these probabilities. Thus, we estimate the number of tuples in the full selection as

  $$n_r * \frac{s_1 * s_2 * \cdots * s_n}{n_r^n}$$

  - ☐ **Disjunction:** A *disjunctive selection* is a selection of the form

  $$\sigma_{\theta_1 \vee \theta_2 \vee \cdots \vee \theta_n}(r)$$

  A disjunctive condition is satisfied by the union of all records satisfying the individual, simple conditions θ_i.

  As before, let s_i/n_r denote the probability that a tuple satisfies condition θ_i. The probability that the tuple will satisfy the disjunction is then 1 minus the probability that it will satisfy *none* of the conditions:

  $$1 - \left(1 - \frac{s_1}{n_r}\right) * \left(1 - \frac{s_2}{n_r}\right) * \cdots * \left(1 - \frac{s_n}{n_r}\right)$$

  Multiplying this value by n_r gives us the estimated number of tuples that satisfy the selection.

☐ **Negation:** In the absence of nulls, the result of a selection $\sigma_{\neg\theta}(r)$ is simply the tuples of r that are not in $\sigma_\theta(r)$. We already know how to estimate the number of tuples in $\sigma_\theta(r)$. The number of tuples in $\sigma_{\neg\theta}(r)$ is therefore estimated to be $n(r)$ minus the estimated number of tuples in $\sigma_\theta(r)$.

We can account for nulls by estimating the number of tuples for which the condition θ would evaluate to *unknown*, and subtracting that number from the above estimate ignoring nulls. Estimating that number would require extra statistics to be maintained in the catalog.

14.2.3 Join Size Estimation

In this section, we see how to estimate the size of the result of a join.

The Cartesian product $r \times s$ contains $n_r * n_s$ tuples. Each tuple of $r \times s$ occupies $l_r + l_s$ bytes, from which we can calculate the size of the Cartesian product.

Estimating the size of a natural join is somewhat more complicated than estimating the size of a selection or of a Cartesian product. Let $r(R)$ and $s(S)$ be relations.

- If $R \cap S = \emptyset$—that is, the relations have no attribute in common—then $r \bowtie s$ is the same as $r \times s$, and we can use our estimation technique for Cartesian products.

- If $R \cap S$ is a key for R, then we know that a tuple of s will join with at most one tuple from r. Therefore, the number of tuples in $r \bowtie s$ is no greater than the number of tuples in s. The case where $R \cap S$ is a key for S is symmetric to the case just described. If $R \cap S$ forms a foreign key of S, referencing R, the number of tuples in $r \bowtie s$ is exactly the same as the number of tuples in s.

- The most difficult case is when $R \cap S$ is a key for neither R nor S. In this case, we assume, as we did for selections, that each value appears with equal probability. Consider a tuple t of r, and assume $R \cap S = \{A\}$. We estimate that tuple t produces

$$\frac{n_s}{V(A, s)}$$

tuples in $r \bowtie s$, since this number is the average number of tuples in s with a given value for the attributes A. Considering all the tuples in r, we estimate that there are

$$\frac{n_r * n_s}{V(A, s)}$$

tuples in $r \bowtie s$. Observe that, if we reverse the roles of r and s in the preceding estimate, we obtain an estimate of

$$\frac{n_r * n_s}{V(A, r)}$$

tuples in $r \bowtie s$. These two estimates differ if $V(A, r) \neq V(A, s)$. If this situation occurs, there are likely to be dangling tuples that do not participate in the join. Thus, the lower of the two estimates is probably the more accurate one.

The preceding estimate of join size may be too high if the $V(A, r)$ values for attribute A in r have few values in common with the $V(A, s)$ values for attribute A in s. However, this situation is unlikely to happen in the real world, since dangling tuples either do not exist, or constitute only a small fraction of the tuples, in most real-world relations. More important, the preceding estimate depends on the assumption that each value appears with equal probability. More sophisticated techniques for size estimation have to be used if this assumption does not hold.

We can estimate the size of a theta join $r \bowtie_\theta s$ by rewriting the join as $\sigma_\theta(r \times s)$, and using the size estimates for Cartesian products along with the size estimates for selections, which we saw in Section 14.2.2.

To illustrate all these ways of estimating join sizes, consider the expression

$$depositor \bowtie customer$$

Assume the following catalog information about the two relations:

- $n_{customer} = 10000$.

- $f_{customer} = 25$, which implies that $b_{customer} = 10000/25 = 400$.

- $n_{depositor} = 5000$.

- $f_{depositor} = 50$, which implies that $b_{depositor} = 5000/50 = 100$.

- $V(customer\text{-}name, depositor) = 2500$, which implies that, on average, each customer has two accounts.

Also assume that *customer-name* in *depositor* is a foreign key on *customer*.

In our example of *depositor* $\bowtie$ *customer*, *customer-name* in *depositor* is a foreign key referencing *customer*; hence, the size of the result is exactly $n_{depositor}$, which is 5000.

Let us now compute the size estimates for *depositor* $\bowtie$ *customer* without using information about foreign keys. Since $V(customer\text{-}name, depositor) = 2500$ and $V(customer\text{-}name, customer) = 10000$, the two estimates we get are $5000 * 10000/2500 = 20,000$ and $5000 * 10000/10000 = 5000$, and we choose the lower one. In this case, the lower of these estimates is the same as that which we computed earlier from information about foreign keys.

14.2.4 Size Estimation for Other Operations

We outline below how to estimate the sizes of the results of other relational algebra operations.

Projection: The estimated size (number of records or number of tuples) of a projection of the form $\Pi_A(r)$ is $V(A, r)$, since projection eliminates duplicates.

Aggregation: The size of $_A\mathcal{G}_F(r)$ is simply $V(A, r)$, since there is one tuple in $_A\mathcal{G}_F(r)$ for each distinct value of A.

Set operations: If the two inputs to a set operation are selections on the same relation, we can rewrite the set operation as disjunctions, conjunctions, or negations. For example, $\sigma_{\theta_1}(r) \cup \sigma_{\theta_2}(r)$ can be rewritten as $\sigma_{\theta_1 \vee \theta_2}(r)$. Similarly, we can rewrite intersections as conjunctions, and we can rewrite set difference by using negation, so long as the two relations participating in the set operations are selections on the same relation. We can then use the estimates for selections involving conjunctions, disjunctions, and negation in Section 14.2.2.

If the inputs are not selections on the same relation, we estimate the sizes this way: The estimated size of $r \cup s$ is the sum of the sizes of r and s. The estimated size of $r \cap s$ is the minimum of the sizes of r and s. The estimated size of $r - s$ is the same size as r. All three estimates may be inaccurate, but provide upper bounds on the sizes.

Outer join: The estimated size of $r \rightJoin s$ is the size of $r \Join s$ plus the size of r; that of $r \leftJoin s$ is symmetric, while that of $r \fullJoin s$ is the size of $r \Join s$ plus the sizes of r and s. All three estimates may be inaccurate, but provide upper bounds on the sizes.

14.2.5 Estimation of Number of Distinct Values

For selections, the number of distinct values of an attribute (or set of attributes) A in the result of a selection, $V(A, \sigma_\theta(r))$, can be estimated in these ways:

- If the selection condition θ forces A to take on a specified value (e.g., $A = 3$), $V(A, \sigma_\theta(r)) = 1$.

- If θ forces A to take on one of a specified set of values (e.g., $(A = 1 \lor A = 3 \lor A = 4)$), then $V(A, \sigma_\theta(r))$ is set to the number of specified values.

- If the selection condition θ is of the form A op v, where op is a comparison operator, $V(A, \sigma_\theta(r))$ is estimated to be $V(A, r) * s$, where s is the selectivity of the selection.

- In all other cases of selections, we assume that the distribution of A values is independent of the distribution of the values on which selection conditions are specified, and use an approximate estimate of $\min(V(A, r), n_{\sigma_\theta(r)})$. A more accurate estimate can be derived for this case using probability theory, but the above approximation works fairly well.

For joins, the number of distinct values of an attribute (or set of attributes) A in the result of a join, $V(A, r \Join s)$, can be estimated in these ways:

- If all attributes in A are from r, $V(A, r \Join s)$ is estimated as $\min(V(A, r), n_{r \Join s})$, and similarly if all attributes in A are from s, $V(A, r \Join s)$ is estimated to be $\min(V(A, s), n_{r \Join s})$.

- If A contains attributes $A1$ from r and $A2$ from s, then $V(A, r \Join s)$ is estimated as

$$\min(V(A1, r) * V(A2 - A1, s), V(A1 - A2, r) * V(A2, s), n_{r \Join s})$$

Note that some attributes may be in $A1$ as well as in $A2$, and $A1 - A2$ and $A2 - A1$ denote, respectively, attributes in A that are only from r and attributes in A that are only from s. Again, more accurate estimates can be derived by using probability theory, but the above approximations work fairly well.

The estimates of distinct values are straightforward for projections: They are the same in $\Pi_A(r)$ as in r. The same holds for grouping attributes of aggregation. For results of **sum**, **count**, and **average**, we can assume, for simplicity, that all aggregate values are distinct. For $\mathbf{min}(A)$ and $\mathbf{max}(A)$, the number of distinct values can be estimated as $\min(V(A, r), V(G, r))$, where G denotes the grouping attributes. We omit details of estimating distinct values for other operations.

14.3   Transformation of Relational Expressions

So far, we have studied algorithms to evaluate extended relational-algebra operations, and have estimated their costs. As mentioned at the start of this chapter, a query can be expressed in several different ways, with different costs of evaluation. In this section, rather than take the relational expression as given, we consider alternative, equivalent expressions.

Two relational-algebra expressions are said to be **equivalent** if, on every legal database instance, the two expressions generate the same set of tuples. (Recall that a legal database instance is one that satisfies all the integrity constraints specified in the database schema.) Note that the order of the tuples is irrelevant; the two expressions may generate the tuples in different orders, but would be considered equivalent as long as the set of tuples is the same.

In SQL, the inputs and outputs are multisets of tuples, and a multiset version of the relational algebra is used for evaluating SQL queries. Two expressions in the *multiset* version of the relational algebra are said to be equivalent if on every legal database the two expressions generate the same multiset of tuples. The discussion in this chapter is based on the relational algebra. We leave extensions to the multiset version of the relational algebra to you as exercises.

14.3.1   Equivalence Rules

An **equivalence rule** says that expressions of two forms are equivalent. We can replace an expression of the first form by an expression of the second form, or vice versa—that is we can replace an expression of the second form by an expression of the first form—since the two expressions would generate the same result on any valid database. The optimizer uses equivalence rules to transform expressions into other logically equivalent expressions.

We now list a number of general equivalence rules on relational-algebra expressions. Some of the equivalences listed appear in Figure 14.2. We use $\theta, \theta_1, \theta_2$, and so on to denote predicates, L_1, L_2, L_3, and so on to denote lists of attributes, and E, E_1, E_2, and so on to denote relational-algebra expressions. A relation name r is simply a special case of a relational-algebra expression, and can be used wherever E appears.

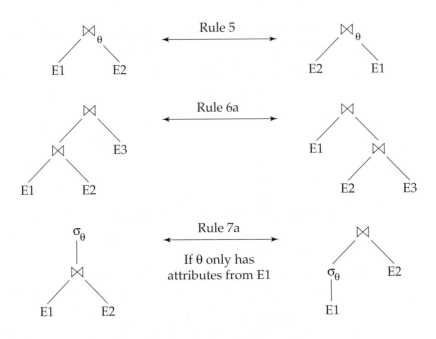

Figure 14.2   Pictorial representation of equivalences.

1. Conjunctive selection operations can be deconstructed into a sequence of individual selections. This transformation is referred to as a cascade of σ.

$$\sigma_{\theta_1 \wedge \theta_2}(E) = \sigma_{\theta_1}(\sigma_{\theta_2}(E))$$

2. Selection operations are **commutative**.

$$\sigma_{\theta_1}(\sigma_{\theta_2}(E)) = \sigma_{\theta_2}(\sigma_{\theta_1}(E))$$

3. Only the final operations in a sequence of projection operations are needed, the others can be omitted. This transformation can also be referred to as a cascade of Π.

$$\Pi_{L_1}(\Pi_{L_2}(\dots (\Pi_{L_n}(E))\dots)) = \Pi_{L_1}(E)$$

4. Selections can be combined with Cartesian products and theta joins.
   a. $\sigma_\theta(E_1 \times E_2) = E_1 \bowtie_\theta E_2$
      This expression is just the definition of the theta join.
   b. $\sigma_{\theta_1}(E_1 \bowtie_{\theta_2} E_2) = E_1 \bowtie_{\theta_1 \wedge \theta_2} E_2$

5. Theta-join operations are commutative.

$$E_1 \bowtie_\theta E_2 = E_2 \bowtie_\theta E_1$$

Actually, the order of attributes differs between the left-hand side and right-hand side, so the equivalence does not hold if the order of attributes is taken into account. A projection operation can be added to one of the sides of the equivalence to appropriately reorder attributes, but for simplicity we omit the projection and ignore the attribute order in most of our examples.

Recall that the natural-join operator is simply a special case of the theta-join operator; hence, natural joins are also commutative.

6. **a.** Natural-join operations are **associative**.

$$(E_1 \bowtie E_2) \bowtie E_3 \; = \; E_1 \bowtie (E_2 \bowtie E_3)$$

b. Theta joins are associative in the following manner:

$$(E_1 \bowtie_{\theta_1} E_2) \bowtie_{\theta_2 \wedge \theta_3} E_3 \; = \; E_1 \bowtie_{\theta_1 \wedge \theta_3} (E_2 \bowtie_{\theta_2} E_3)$$

where θ_2 involves attributes from only E_2 and E_3. Any of these conditions may be empty; hence, it follows that the Cartesian product ($\times$) operation is also associative. The commutativity and associativity of join operations are important for join reordering in query optimization.

7. The selection operation distributes over the theta-join operation under the following two conditions:

a. It distributes when all the attributes in selection condition θ_0 involve only the attributes of one of the expressions (say, E_1) being joined.

$$\sigma_{\theta_0}(E_1 \bowtie_\theta E_2) = (\sigma_{\theta_0}(E_1)) \bowtie_\theta E_2$$

b. It distributes when selection condition θ_1 involves only the attributes of E_1 and θ_2 involves only the attributes of E_2.

$$\sigma_{\theta_1 \wedge \theta_2}(E_1 \bowtie_\theta E_2) = (\sigma_{\theta_1}(E_1)) \bowtie_\theta (\sigma_{\theta_2}(E_2))$$

8. The projection operation distributes over the theta-join operation under the following conditions.

a. Let L_1 and L_2 be attributes of E_1 and E_2, respectively. Suppose that the join condition θ involves only attributes in $L_1 \cup L_2$. Then,

$$\Pi_{L_1 \cup L_2}(E_1 \bowtie_\theta E_2) = (\Pi_{L_1}(E_1)) \bowtie_\theta (\Pi_{L_2}(E_2))$$

b. Consider a join $E_1 \bowtie_\theta E_2$. Let L_1 and L_2 be sets of attributes from E_1 and E_2, respectively. Let L_3 be attributes of E_1 that are involved in join condition θ, but are not in $L_1 \cup L_2$, and let L_4 be attributes of E_2 that are involved in join condition θ, but are not in $L_1 \cup L_2$. Then,

$$\Pi_{L_1 \cup L_2}(E_1 \bowtie_\theta E_2) = \Pi_{L_1 \cup L_2}((\Pi_{L_1 \cup L_3}(E_1)) \bowtie_\theta (\Pi_{L_2 \cup L_4}(E_2)))$$

9. The set operations union and intersection are commutative.

$$E_1 \cup E_2 \; = \; E_2 \cup E_1$$

$$E_1 \cap E_2 \; = \; E_2 \cap E_1$$

Set difference is not commutative.

10. Set union and intersection are associative.

$$(E_1 \cup E_2) \cup E_3 \; = \; E_1 \cup (E_2 \cup E_3)$$

$$(E_1 \cap E_2) \cap E_3 \; = \; E_1 \cap (E_2 \cap E_3)$$

11. The selection operation distributes over the union, intersection, and set–difference operations.

$$\sigma_P(E_1 - E_2) = \sigma_P(E_1) - \sigma_P(E_2)$$

Similarly, the preceding equivalence, with − replaced with either ∪ or ∩, also holds. Further,

$$\sigma_P(E_1 - E_2) = \sigma_P(E_1) - E_2$$

The preceding equivalence, with − replaced by ∩, also holds, but does not hold if − is replaced by ∪.

12. The projection operation distributes over the union operation.

$$\Pi_L(E_1 \cup E_2) = (\Pi_L(E_1)) \cup (\Pi_L(E_2))$$

This is only a partial list of equivalences. More equivalences involving extended relational operators, such as the outer join and aggregation, are discussed in the exercises.

14.3.2 Examples of Transformations

We now illustrate the use of the equivalence rules. We use our bank example with the relation schemas:

$$Branch\text{-}schema = (branch\text{-}name, branch\text{-}city, assets)$$
$$Account\text{-}schema = (account\text{-}number, branch\text{-}name, balance)$$
$$Depositor\text{-}schema = (customer\text{-}name, account\text{-}number)$$

The relations *branch*, *account*, and *depositor* are instances of these schemas.

In our example in Section 14.1, the expression

$$\Pi_{customer\text{-}name}(\sigma_{branch\text{-}city\,=\,\text{“Brooklyn”}}(branch \bowtie (account \bowtie depositor)))$$

was transformed into the following expression,

$$\Pi_{customer\text{-}name}((\sigma_{branch\text{-}city\,=\,\text{“Brooklyn”}}(branch)) \bowtie (account \bowtie depositor))$$

which is equivalent to our original algebra expression, but generates smaller intermediate relations. We can carry out this transformation by using rule 7.a. Remember that the rule merely says that the two expressions are equivalent; it does not say that one is better than the other.

Multiple equivalence rules can be used, one after the other, on a query or on parts of the query. As an illustration, suppose that we modify our original query to restrict attention to customers who have a balance over $1000. The new relational-algebra query is

$$\Pi_{customer\text{-}name}(\sigma_{branch\text{-}city\,=\,\text{“Brooklyn”}\,\wedge\,balance\,>\,1000}$$
$$(branch \bowtie (account \bowtie depositor)))$$

We cannot apply the selection predicate directly to the *branch* relation, since the predicate involves attributes of both the *branch* and *account* relation. However, we can first apply rule 6.a (associativity of natural join) to transform the join *branch* ⋈ (*account* ⋈ *depositor*) into (*branch* ⋈ *account*) ⋈ *depositor*:

$$\Pi_{customer\text{-}name} \left(\sigma_{branch\text{-}city\,=\,\text{``Brooklyn''}\,\wedge\,balance\,>1000} \right. \\ \left. ((branch \bowtie account) \bowtie depositor)\right)$$

Then, using rule 7.a, we can rewrite our query as

$$\Pi_{customer\text{-}name} \left((\sigma_{branch\text{-}city\,=\,\text{``Brooklyn''}\wedge\,balance>1000} \right. \\ \left. (branch \bowtie account)) \bowtie depositor\right)$$

Let us examine the selection subexpression within this expression. Using rule 1, we can break the selection into two selections, to get the following subexpression:

$$\sigma_{branch\text{-}city\,=\,\text{``Brooklyn''}} \left(\sigma_{balance\,>\,1000} (branch \bowtie account)\right)$$

Both of the preceding expressions select tuples with *branch-city* = "Brooklyn" and *balance* > 1000. However, the latter form of the expression provides a new opportunity to apply the "perform selections early" rule, resulting in the subexpression

$$\sigma_{branch\text{-}city\,=\,\text{``Brooklyn''}} (branch) \bowtie \sigma_{balance>1000} (account)$$

Figure 14.3 depicts the initial expression and the final expression after all these transformations. We could equally well have used rule 7.b to get the final expression directly, without using rule 1 to break the selection into two selections. In fact, rule 7.b can itself be derived from rules 1 and 7.a

A set of equivalence rules is said to be **minimal** if no rule can be derived from any combination of the others. The preceding example illustrates that the set of equivalence rules in Section 14.3.1 is not minimal. An expression equivalent to the original expression may be generated in different ways; the number of different ways of generating an expression increases when we use a nonminimal set of equivalence rules. Query optimizers therefore use minimal sets of equivalence rules.

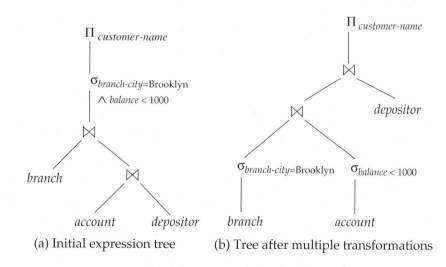

(a) Initial expression tree   (b) Tree after multiple transformations

Figure 14.3   Multiple transformations.

Now consider the following form of our example query:

$$\Pi_{customer\text{-}name} \left((\sigma_{branch\text{-}city = \text{``Brooklyn''}} \, (branch) \bowtie account) \bowtie depositor \right)$$

When we compute the subexpression

$$(\sigma_{branch\text{-}city = \text{``Brooklyn''}} \, (branch) \bowtie account)$$

we obtain a relation whose schema is

(branch-name, branch-city, assets, account-number, balance)

We can eliminate several attributes from the schema, by pushing projections based on equivalence rules 8.a and 8.b. The only attributes that we must retain are those that either appear in the result of the query or are needed to process subsequent operations. By eliminating unneeded attributes, we reduce the number of columns of the intermediate result. Thus, we reduce the size of the intermediate result. In our example, the only attribute we need from the join of *branch* and *account* is *account-number*. Therefore, we can modify the expression to

$$\Pi_{customer\text{-}name} \, (\\ (\, \Pi_{account\text{-}number} \, ((\sigma_{branch\text{-}city = \text{``Brooklyn''}} \, (branch)) \bowtie account)) \bowtie depositor)$$

The projection $\Pi_{account\text{-}number}$ reduces the size of the intermediate join results.

14.3.3 Join Ordering

A good ordering of join operations is important for reducing the size of temporary results; hence, most query optimizers pay a lot of attention to the join order. As mentioned in Chapter 3 and in equivalence rule 6.a, the natural-join operation is associative. Thus, for all relations r_1, r_2, and r_3,

$$(r_1 \bowtie r_2) \bowtie r_3 \; = \; r_1 \bowtie (r_2 \bowtie r_3)$$

Although these expressions are equivalent, the costs of computing them may differ. Consider again the expression

$$\Pi_{customer\text{-}name} \left((\sigma_{branch\text{-}city = \text{``Brooklyn''}} \, (branch)) \bowtie account \bowtie depositor \right)$$

We could choose to compute *account* $\bowtie$ *depositor* first, and then to join the result with

$$\sigma_{branch\text{-}city = \text{``Brooklyn''}} \, (branch)$$

However, *account* $\bowtie$ *depositor* is likely to be a large relation, since it contains one tuple for every account. In contrast,

$$\sigma_{branch\text{-}city = \text{``Brooklyn''}} \, (branch) \bowtie account$$

is probably a small relation. To see that it is, we note that, since the bank has a large number of widely distributed branches, it is likely that only a small fraction of the bank's customers have accounts in branches located in Brooklyn. Thus, the preceding expression results in one tuple for each account held by a resident of Brooklyn. Therefore, the temporary relation that we must store is smaller than it would have been had we computed *account* $\bowtie$ *depositor* first.

There are other options to consider for evaluating our query. We do not care about the order in which attributes appear in a join, since it is easy to change the order before displaying the result. Thus, for all relations r_1 and r_2,

$$r_1 \bowtie r_2 = r_2 \bowtie r_1$$

That is, natural join is commutative (equivalence rule 5).

Using the associativity and commutativity of the natural join (rules 5 and 6), we can consider rewriting our relational-algebra expression as

$$\Pi_{customer\text{-}name} \left(\left(\left(\sigma_{branch\text{-}city = \text{"Brooklyn"}} (branch) \right) \bowtie depositor \right) \bowtie account \right)$$

That is, we could compute

$$\left(\sigma_{branch\text{-}city = \text{"Brooklyn"}} (branch) \right) \bowtie depositor$$

first, and, after that, join the result with *account*. Note, however, that there are no attributes in common between *Branch-schema* and *Depositor-schema*, so the join is just a Cartesian product. If there are *b* branches in Brooklyn and *d* tuples in the *depositor* relation, this Cartesian product generates $b * d$ tuples, one for every possible pair of depositor tuple and branches (without regard for whether the account in *depositor* is maintained at the branch). Thus, it appears that this Cartesian product will produce a large temporary relation. As a result, we would reject this strategy. However, if the user had entered the preceding expression, we could use the associativity and commutativity of the natural join to transform this expression to the more efficient expression that we used earlier.

14.3.4   Enumeration of Equivalent Expressions

Query optimizers use equivalence rules to systematically generate expressions equivalent to the given query expression. Conceptually, the process proceeds as follows. Given an expression, if any subexpression matches one side of an equivalence rule, the optimizer generates a new expression where the subexpression is transformed to match the other side of the rule. This process continues until no more new expressions can be generated.

The preceding process is costly both in space and in time. Here is how the space requirement can be reduced: If we generate an expression E_1 from an expression E_2 by using an equivalence rule, then E_1 and E_2 are similar in structure, and have subexpressions that are identical. Expression-representation techniques that allow both expressions to point to shared subexpressions can reduce the space requirement significantly, and many query optimizers use them.

Moreover, it is not always necessary to generate every expression that can be generated with the equivalence rules. If an optimizer takes cost estimates of evaluation into account, it may be able to avoid examining some of the expressions, as we shall see in Section 14.4. We can reduce the time required for optimization by using techniques such as these.

14.4 Choice of Evaluation Plans

Generation of expressions is only part of the query-optimization process, since each operation in the expression can be implemented with different algorithms. An evaluation plan is therefore needed to define exactly what algorithm should be used for each operation, and how the execution of the operations should be coordinated. Figure 14.4 illustrates one possible evaluation plan for the expression from Figure 14.3. As we have seen, several different algorithms can be used for each relational operation, giving rise to alternative evaluation plans. Further, decisions about pipelining have to be made. In the figure, the edges from the selection operations to the merge join operation are marked as pipelined; pipelining is feasible if the selection operations generate their output sorted on the join attributes. They would do so if the indices on *branch* and *account* store records with equal values for the index attributes sorted by *branch-name*.

14.4.1 Interaction of Evaluation Techniques

One way to choose an evaluation plan for a query expression is simply to choose for each operation the cheapest algorithm for evaluating it. We can choose any ordering of the operations that ensures that operations lower in the tree are executed before operations higher in the tree.

However, choosing the cheapest algorithm for each operation independently is not necessarily a good idea. Although a merge join at a given level may be costlier than a hash join, it may provide a sorted output that makes evaluating a later operation (such as duplicate elimination, intersection, or another merge join) cheaper. Similarly, a nested-loop join with indexing may provide opportunities for pipelining the results to the next operation, and thus may be useful even if it is not the cheapest way of

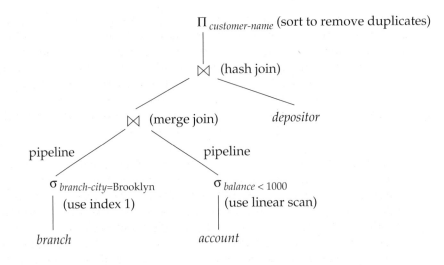

Figure 14.4   An evaluation plan.

performing the join. To choose the best overall algorithm, we must consider even nonoptimal algorithms for individual operations.

Thus, in addition to considering alternative expressions for a query, we must also consider alternative algorithms for each operation in an expression. We can use rules much like the equivalence rules to define what algorithms can be used for each operation, and whether its result can be pipelined or must be materialized. We can use these rules to generate all the query-evaluation plans for a given expression.

Given an evaluation plan, we can estimate its cost using statistics estimated by the techniques in Section 14.2 coupled with cost estimates for various algorithms and evaluation methods described in Chapter 13. That still leaves the problem of choosing the best evaluation plan for a query. There are two broad approaches: The first searches all the plans, and chooses the best plan in a cost-based fashion. The second uses heuristics to choose a plan. We discuss these approaches next. Practical query optimizers incorporate elements of both approaches.

14.4.2   Cost-Based Optimization

A **cost-based optimizer** generates a range of query-evaluation plans from the given query by using the equivalence rules, and chooses the one with the least cost. For a complex query, the number of different query plans that are equivalent to a given plan can be large. As an illustration, consider the expression

$$r_1 \bowtie r_2 \bowtie \cdots \bowtie r_n$$

where the joins are expressed without any ordering. With $n = 3$, there are 12 different join orderings:

$r_1 \bowtie (r_2 \bowtie r_3)$	$r_1 \bowtie (r_3 \bowtie r_2)$	$(r_2 \bowtie r_3) \bowtie r_1$	$(r_3 \bowtie r_2) \bowtie r_1$
$r_2 \bowtie (r_1 \bowtie r_3)$	$r_2 \bowtie (r_3 \bowtie r_1)$	$(r_1 \bowtie r_3) \bowtie r_2$	$(r_3 \bowtie r_1) \bowtie r_2$
$r_3 \bowtie (r_1 \bowtie r_2)$	$r_3 \bowtie (r_2 \bowtie r_1)$	$(r_1 \bowtie r_2) \bowtie r_3$	$(r_2 \bowtie r_1) \bowtie r_3$

In general, with n relations, there are $(2(n-1))!/(n-1)!$ different join orders. (We leave the computation of this expression for you to do in Exercise 14.10.) For joins involving small numbers of relations, this number is acceptable; for example, with $n = 5$, the number is 1680. However, as n increases, this number rises quickly. With $n = 7$, the number is 665280; with $n = 10$, the number is greater than 17.6 billion!

Luckily, it is not necessary to generate all the expressions equivalent to a given expression. For example, suppose we want to find the best join order of the form

$$(r_1 \bowtie r_2 \bowtie r_3) \bowtie r_4 \bowtie r_5$$

which represents all join orders where r_1, r_2, and r_3 are joined first (in some order), and the result is joined (in some order) with r_4 and r_5. There are 12 different join orders for computing $r_1 \bowtie r_2 \bowtie r_3$, and 12 orders for computing the join of this result with r_4 and r_5. Thus, there appear to be 144 join orders to examine. However, once we have found the best join order for the subset of relations $\{r_1, r_2, r_3\}$, we can use that order for further joins with r_4 and r_5, and can ignore all costlier join orders of $r_1 \bowtie r_2 \bowtie r_3$. Thus, instead of 144 choices to examine, we need to examine only 12 + 12 choices.

procedure findbestplan(S)
    if ($bestplan[S].cost \neq \infty$)
        return $bestplan[S]$
    // else $bestplan[S]$ has not been computed earlier, compute it now
    for each non-empty subset $S1$ of S such that $S1 \neq S$
        P1 = findbestplan($S1$)
        P2 = findbestplan($S - S1$)
        A = best algorithm for joining results of $P1$ and $P2$
        cost = $P1.cost + P2.cost$ + cost of A
        if cost $< bestplan[S].cost$
            $bestplan[S].cost$ = cost
            $bestplan[S].plan$ = "execute $P1.plan$; execute $P2.plan$;
                          join results of $P1$ and $P2$ using A"
    return $bestplan[S]$

Figure 14.5   Dynamic programming algorithm for join order optimization.

Using this idea, we can develop a *dynamic-programming* algorithm for finding optimal join orders. Dynamic programming algorithms store results of computations
and reuse them, a procedure that can reduce execution time greatly. A recursive procedure implementing the dynamic programming algorithm appears in Figure 14.5.

The procedure stores the evaluation plans it computes in an associative array
bestplan, which is indexed by sets of relations. Each element of the associative array contains two components: the cost of the best plan of S, and the plan itself. The
value of $bestplan[S].cost$ is assumed to be initialized to ∞ if $bestplan[S]$ has not yet
been computed.

The procedure first checks if the best plan for computing the join of the given
set of relations S has been computed already (and stored in the associative array
bestplan); if so it returns the already computed plan. Otherwise, the procedure tries
every way of dividing S into two disjoint subsets. For each division, the procedure
recursively finds the best plans for each of the two subsets, and then computes the
cost of the overall plan by using that division. The procedure picks the cheapest plan
from among all the alternatives for dividing S into two sets. The cheapest plan and
its cost are stored in the array *bestplan*, and returned by the procedure. The time
complexity of the procedure can be shown to be $O(3^n)$ (see Exercise 14.11).

Actually, the order in which tuples are generated by the join of a set of relations
is also important for finding the best overall join order, since it can affect the cost of
further joins (for instance, if merge join is used). A particular sort order of the tuples
is said to be an **interesting sort order** if it could be useful for a later operation. For
instance, generating the result of $r_1 \bowtie r_2 \bowtie r_3$ sorted on the attributes common with
r_4 or r_5 may be useful, but generating it sorted on the attributes common to only r_1
and r_2 is not useful. Using merge join for computing $r_1 \bowtie r_2 \bowtie r_3$ may be costlier than
using some other join technique, but may provide an output sorted in an interesting
sort order.

Hence, it is not sufficient to find the best join order for each subset of the set of
n given relations. Instead, we have to find the best join order for each subset, for

each interesting sort order of the join result for that subset. The number of subsets of n relations is 2^n. The number of interesting sort orders is generally not large. Thus, about 2^n join expressions need to be stored. The dynamic-programming algorithm for finding the best join order can be easily extended to handle sort orders. The cost of the extended algorithm depends on the number of interesting orders for each subset of relations; since this number has been found to be small in practice, the cost remains at $O(3^n)$.

With $n = 10$, this number is around 59000, which is much better than the 17.6 billion different join orders. More important, the storage required is much less than before, since we need to store only one join order for each interesting sort order of each of 1024 subsets of $r_1, \ldots, r_{10}$. Although both numbers still increase rapidly with n, commonly occurring joins usually have less than 10 relations, and can be handled easily.

We can use several techniques to reduce further the cost of searching through a large number of plans. For instance, when examining the plans for an expression, we can terminate after we examine only a part of the expression, if we determine that the cheapest plan for that part is already costlier than the cheapest evaluation plan for a full expression examined earlier. Similarly, suppose that we determine that the cheapest way of evaluating a subexpression is costlier than the cheapest evaluation plan for a full expression examined earlier. Then, no full expression involving that subexpression needs to be examined. We can further reduce the number of evaluation plans that need to be considered fully by first making a heuristic guess of a good plan, and estimating that plan's cost. Then, only a few competing plans will require a full analysis of cost. These optimizations can reduce the overhead of query optimization significantly.

14.4.3   Heuristic Optimization

A drawback of cost-based optimization is the cost of optimization itself. Although the cost of query processing can be reduced by clever optimizations, cost-based optimization is still expensive. Hence, many systems use **heuristics** to reduce the number of choices that must be made in a cost-based fashion. Some systems even choose to use only heuristics, and do not use cost-based optimization at all.

An example of a heuristic rule is the following rule for transforming relational-algebra queries:

- Perform selection operations as early as possible.

A heuristic optimizer would use this rule without finding out whether the cost is reduced by this transformation. In the first transformation example in Section 14.3, the selection operation was pushed into a join.

We say that the preceding rule is a heuristic because it usually, but not always, helps to reduce the cost. For an example of where it can result in an increase in cost, consider an expression $\sigma_\theta(r \bowtie s)$, where the condition θ refers to only attributes in s. The selection can certainly be performed before the join. However, if r is extremely small compared to s, and if there is an index on the join attributes of s, but no index on the attributes used by θ, then it is probably a bad idea to perform the selection early. Performing the selection early—that is, directly on s—would require doing a scan of all tuples in s. It is probably cheaper, in this case, to compute the join by using the index, and then to reject tuples that fail the selection.

The projection operation, like the selection operation, reduces the size of relations. Thus, whenever we need to generate a temporary relation, it is advantageous to apply immediately any projections that are possible. This advantage suggests a companion to the "perform selections early" heuristic:

- Perform projections early.

It is usually better to perform selections earlier than projections, since selections have the potential to reduce the sizes of relations greatly, and selections enable the use of indices to access tuples. An example similar to the one used for the selection heuristic should convince you that this heuristic does not always reduce the cost.

Drawing on the equivalences discussed in Section 14.3.1, a heuristic optimization algorithm will reorder the components of an initial query tree to achieve improved query execution. We now present an overview of the steps in a typical heuristic optimization algorithm. You can understand the heuristics by visualizing a query expression as a tree, as illustrated in Figure 14.3

1. Deconstruct conjunctive selections into a sequence of single selection operations. This step, based on equivalence rule 1, facilitates moving selection operations down the query tree.

2. Move selection operations down the query tree for the earliest possible execution. This step uses the commutativity and distributivity properties of the selection operation noted in equivalence rules 2, 7.a, 7.b, and 11.

   For instance, this step transforms $\sigma_\theta(r \bowtie s)$ into either $\sigma_\theta(r) \bowtie s$ or $r \bowtie \sigma_\theta(s)$ whenever possible. Performing value-based selections as early as possible reduces the cost of sorting and merging intermediate results. The degree of reordering permitted for a particular selection is determined by the attributes involved in that selection condition.

3. Determine which selection operations and join operations will produce the smallest relations—that is, will produce the relations with the least number of tuples. Using associativity of the $\bowtie$ operation, rearrange the tree so that the leaf-node relations with these restrictive selections are executed first.

   This step considers the selectivity of a selection or join condition. Recall that the most restrictive selection—that is, the condition with the smallest selectivity—retrieves the fewest records. This step relies on the associativity of binary operations given in equivalence rule 6.

4. Replace with join operations those Cartesian product operations that are followed by a selection condition (rule 4.a). The Cartesian product operation is often expensive to implement since $r_1 \times r_2$ includes a record for each combination of records from r_1 and r_2. The selection may significantly reduce the number of records, making the join much less expensive than the Cartesian product.

5. Deconstruct and move as far down the tree as possible lists of projection attributes, creating new projections where needed. This step draws on the properties of the projection operation given in equivalence rules 3, 8.a, 8.b, and 12.

6. Identify those subtrees whose operations can be pipelined, and execute them using pipelining.

In summary, the heuristics listed here reorder an initial query-tree representation in such a way that the operations that reduce the size of intermediate results are applied first; early selection reduces the number of tuples, and early projection reduces the number of attributes. The heuristic transformations also restructure the tree so that the system performs the most restrictive selection and join operations before other similar operations.

Heuristic optimization further maps the heuristically transformed query expression into alternative sequences of operations to produce a set of candidate evaluation plans. An evaluation plan includes not only the relational operations to be performed, but also the indices to be used, the order in which tuples are to be accessed, and the order in which the operations are to be performed. The **access-plan –selection** phase of a heuristic optimizer chooses the most efficient strategy for each operation.

14.4.4   Structure of Query Optimizers**

So far, we have described the two basic approaches to choosing an evaluation plan; as noted, most practical query optimizers combine elements of both approaches. For example, certain query optimizers, such as the System R optimizer, do not consider all join orders, but rather restrict the search to particular kinds of join orders. The System R optimizer considers only those join orders where the right operand of each join is one of the initial relations $r_1, \ldots, r_n$. Such join orders are called **left-deep join orders**. Left-deep join orders are particularly convenient for pipelined evaluation, since the right operand is a stored relation, and thus only one input to each join is pipelined.

Figure 14.6 illustrates the difference between left-deep join trees and non-left-deep join trees. The time it takes to consider all left-deep join orders is $O(n!)$, which is much less than the time to consider all join orders. With the use of dynamic programming optimizations, the System R optimizer can find the best join order in time $O(n2^n)$. Contrast this cost with the $O(3^n)$ time required to find the best overall join order. The System R optimizer uses heuristics to push selections and projections down the query tree.

The cost estimate that we presented for scanning by secondary indices assumed that every tuple access results in an I/O operation. The estimate is likely to be accurate with small buffers; with large buffers, however, the page containing the tuple may already be in the buffer. Some optimizers incorporate a better cost-estimation technique for such scans: They take into account the probability that the page containing the tuple is in the buffer.

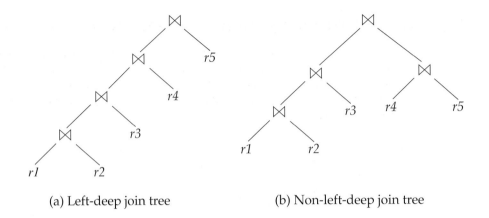

(a) Left-deep join tree   (b) Non-left-deep join tree

Figure 14.6   Left-deep join trees.

Query optimization approaches that integrate heuristic selection and the genera-tion of alternative access plans have been adopted in several systems. The approach used in System R and in its successor, the Starburst project, is a hierarchical procedure based on the nested-block concept of SQL. The cost-based optimization techniques described here are used for each block of the query separately.

The heuristic approach in some versions of Oracle works roughly this way: For an n-way join, it considers n evaluation plans. Each plan uses a left-deep join order, starting with a different one of the n relations. The heuristic constructs the join or-der for each of the n evaluation plans by repeatedly selecting the "best" relation to join next, on the basis of a ranking of the available access paths. Either nested-loop or sort–merge join is chosen for each of the joins, depending on the available access paths. Finally, the heuristic chooses one of the n evaluation plans in a heuristic man-ner, based on minimizing the number of nested-loop joins that do not have an index available on the inner relation, and on the number of sort–merge joins.

The intricacies of SQL introduce a good deal of complexity into query optimizers. In particular, it is hard to translate nested subqueries in SQL into relational algebra. We briefly outline how to handle nested subqueries in Section 14.4.5. For compound SQL queries (using the $\cup, \cap,$ or $-$ operation), the optimizer processes each component separately, and combines the evaluation plans to form the overall evaluation plan.

Even with the use of heuristics, cost-based query optimization imposes a substan-tial overhead on query processing. However, the added cost of cost-based query op-timization is usually more than offset by the saving at query-execution time, which is dominated by slow disk accesses. The difference in execution time between a good plan and a bad one may be huge, making query optimization essential. The achieved saving is magnified in those applications that run on a regular basis, where the query can be optimized once, and the selected query plan can be used on each run. There-fore, most commercial systems include relatively sophisticated optimizers. The bib-liographical notes give references to descriptions of the query optimizers of actual database systems.

14.4.5 Optimizing Nested Subqueries**

SQL conceptually treats nested subqueries in the **where** clause as functions that take parameters and return either a single value or a set of values (possibly an empty set). The parameters are the variables from outer level query that are used in the nested subquery (these variables are called **correlation variables**). For instance, suppose we have the following query.

> **select** *customer-name*
> **from** *borrower*
> **where exists** (**select** *
>   **from** *depositor*
>   **where** *depositor.customer-name = borrower.customer-name*)

Conceptually, the subquery can be viewed as a function that takes a parameter (here, *borrower.customer-name*) and returns the set of all depositors with the same name.

SQL evaluates the overall query (conceptually) by computing the Cartesian product of the relations in the outer **from** clause and then testing the predicates in the **where** clause for each tuple in the product. In the preceding example, the predicate tests if the result of the subquery evaluation is empty.

This technique for evaluating a query with a nested subquery is called **correlated evaluation**. Correlated evaluation is not very efficient, since the subquery is separately evaluated for each tuple in the outer level query. A large number of random disk I/O operations may result.

SQL optimizers therefore attempt to transform nested subqueries into joins, where possible. Efficient join algorithms help avoid expensive random I/O. Where the transformation is not possible, the optimizer keeps the subqueries as separate expressions, optimizes them separately, and then evaluates them by correlated evaluation.

As an example of transforming a nested subquery into a join, the query in the preceding example can be rewritten as

> **select** *customer-name*
> **from** *borrower, depositor*
> **where** *depositor.customer-name = borrower.customer-name*

(To properly reflect SQL semantics, the number of duplicate derivations should not change because of the rewriting; the rewritten query can be modified to ensure this property, as we will see shortly.)

In the example, the nested subquery was very simple. In general, it may not be possible to directly move the nested subquery relations into the **from** clause of the outer query. Instead, we create a temporary relation that contains the results of the nested query *without* the selections using correlation variables from the outer query, and join the temporary table with the outer level query. For instance, a query of the form

$$\textbf{select} \ldots$$
$$\textbf{from } L_1$$
$$\textbf{where } P_1 \textbf{ and exists (select *}$$
$$\textbf{from } L_2$$
$$\textbf{where } P_2)$$

where P_2 is a conjunction of simpler predicates, can be rewritten as

$$\textbf{create table } t_1 \textbf{ as}$$
$$\textbf{select distinct } V$$
$$\textbf{from } L_2$$
$$\textbf{where } P_2^1$$
$$\textbf{select} \ldots$$
$$\textbf{from } L_1, t_1$$
$$\textbf{where } P_1 \textbf{ and } P_2^2$$

where P_2^1 contains predicates in P_2 without selections involving correlation variables, and P_2^2 reintroduces the selections involving correlation variables (with relations referenced in the predicate appropriately renamed). Here, V contains all attributes that are used in selections with correlation variables in the nested subquery.

In our example, the original query would have been transformed to

$$\textbf{create table } t_1 \textbf{ as}$$
$$\textbf{select distinct } customer\text{-}name$$
$$\textbf{from } depositor$$
$$\textbf{select } customer\text{-}name$$
$$\textbf{from } borrower, t_1$$
$$\textbf{where } t_1.customer\text{-}name = borrower.customer\text{-}name$$

The query we rewrote to illustrate creation of a temporary relation can be obtained by simplifying the above transformed query, assuming the number of duplicates of each tuple does not matter.

The process of replacing a nested query by a query with a join (possibly with a temporary relation) is called **decorrelation**.

Decorrelation is more complicated when the nested subquery uses aggregation, or when the result of the nested subquery is used to test for equality, or when the condition linking the nested subquery to the outer query is **not exists**, and so on. We do not attempt to give algorithms for the general case, and instead refer you to relevant items in the bibliographical notes.

Optimization of complex nested subqueries is a difficult task, as you can infer from the above discussion, and many optimizers do only a limited amount of decorrelation. It is best to avoid using complex nested subqueries, where possible, since we cannot be sure that the query optimizer will succeed in converting them to a form that can be evaluated efficiently.

14.5   Materialized Views∗∗

When a view is defined, normally the database stores only the query defining the view. In contrast, a **materialized view** is a view whose contents are computed and stored. Materialized views constitute redundant data, in that their contents can be inferred from the view definition and the rest of the database contents. However, it is much cheaper in many cases to read the contents of a materialized view than to compute the contents of the view by executing the query defining the view.

Materialized views are important for improving performance in some applications. Consider this view, which gives the total loan amount at each branch:

> **create view** *branch-total-loan(branch-name, total-loan)* **as**
> **select** *branch-name*, **sum**(*amount*)
> **from** *loan*
> **groupby** *branch-name*

Suppose the total loan amount at the branch is required frequently (before making a new loan, for example). Computing the view requires reading every *loan* tuple pertaining to the branch, and summing up the loan amounts, which can be time-consuming.

In contrast, if the view definition of the total loan amount were materialized, the total loan amount could be found by looking up a single tuple in the materialized view.

14.5.1   View Maintenance

A problem with materialized views is that they must be kept up-to-date when the data used in the view definition changes. For instance, if the *amount* value of a loan is updated, the materialized view would become inconsistent with the underlying data, and must be updated. The task of keeping a materialized view up-to-date with the underlying data is known as **view maintenance**.

Views can be maintained by manually written code: That is, every piece of code that updates the *amount* value of a loan can be modified to also update the total loan amount for the corresponding branch.

Another option for maintaining materialized views is to define triggers on insert, delete, and update of each relation in the view definition. The triggers must modify the contents of the materialized view, to take into account the change that caused the trigger to fire. A simplistic way of doing so is to completely recompute the materialized view on every update.

A better option is to modify only the affected parts of the materialized view, which is known as **incremental view maintenance**. We describe how to perform incremental view maintenance in Section 14.5.2.

Modern database systems provide more direct support for incremental view maintenance. Database system programmers no longer need to define triggers for view maintenance. Instead, once a view is declared to be materialized, the database system computes the contents of the view, and incrementally updates the contents when the underlying data changes.

14.5.2 Incremental View Maintenance

To understand how to incrementally maintain materialized views, we start off by considering individual operations, and then see how to handle a complete expression.

The changes to a relation that can cause a materialized view to become out-of-date are inserts, deletes, and updates. To simplify our description, we replace updates to a tuple by deletion of the tuple followed by insertion of the updated tuple. Thus, we need to consider only inserts and deletes. The changes (inserts and deletes) to a relation or expression are referred to as its **differential**.

14.5.2.1 Join Operation

Consider the materialized view $v = r \bowtie s$. Suppose we modify r by inserting a set of tuples denoted by i_r. If the old value of r is denoted by r^{old}, and the new value of r by r^{new}, $r^{new} = r^{old} \cup i_r$. Now, the old value of the view, v^{old} is given by $r^{old} \bowtie s$, and the new value v^{new} is given by $r^{new} \bowtie s$. We can rewrite $r^{new} \bowtie s$ as $(r^{old} \cup i_r) \bowtie s$, which we can again rewrite as $(r^{old} \bowtie s) \cup (i_r \bowtie s)$. In other words,

$$v^{new} = v^{old} \cup (i_r \bowtie s)$$

Thus, to update the materialized view v, we simply need to add the tuples $i_r \bowtie s$ to the old contents of the materialized view. Inserts to s are handled in an exactly symmetric fashion.

Now suppose r is modified by deleting a set of tuples denoted by d_r. Using the same reasoning as above, we get

$$v^{new} = v^{old} - (d_r \bowtie s)$$

Deletes on s are handled in an exactly symmetric fashion.

14.5.2.2 Selection and Projection Operations

Consider a view $v = \sigma_\theta(r)$. If we modify r by inserting a set of tuples i_r, the new value of v can be computed as

$$v^{new} = v^{old} \cup \sigma_\theta(i_r)$$

Similarly, if r is modified by deleting a set of tuples d_r, the new value of v can be computed as

$$v^{new} = v^{old} - \sigma_\theta(d_r)$$

Projection is a more difficult operation with which to deal. Consider a materialized view $v = \Pi_A(r)$. Suppose the relation r is on the schema $R = (A, B)$, and r contains two tuples $(a, 2)$ and $(a, 3)$. Then, $\Pi_A(r)$ has a single tuple (a). If we delete the tuple $(a, 2)$ from r, we cannot delete the tuple (a) from $\Pi_A(r)$: If we did so, the result would be an empty relation, whereas in reality $\Pi_A(r)$ still has a single tuple (a). The reason is that the same tuple (a) is derived in two ways, and deleting one tuple from r removes only one of the ways of deriving (a); the other is still present.

This reason also gives us the intuition for solution: For each tuple in a projection such as $\Pi_A(r)$, we will keep a count of how many times it was derived.

When a set of tuples d_r is deleted from r, for each tuple t in d_r we do the following. Let $t.A$ denote the projection of t on the attribute A. We find $(t.A)$ in the materialized view, and decrease the count stored with it by 1. If the count becomes 0, $(t.A)$ is deleted from the materialized view.

Handling insertions is relatively straightforward. When a set of tuples i_r is inserted into r, for each tuple t in i_r we do the following. If $(t.A)$ is already present in the materialized view, we increase the count stored with it by 1. If not, we add $(t.A)$ to the materialized view, with the count set to 1.

14.5.2.3 Aggregation Operations

Aggregation operations proceed somewhat like projections. The aggregate operations in SQL are **count, sum, avg, min,** and **max**:

- **count**: Consider a materialized view $v = {}_A\mathcal{G}_{count(B)}(r)$, which computes the count of the attribute B, after grouping r by attribute A.

    When a set of tuples i_r is inserted into r, for each tuple t in i_r we do the following. We look for the group $t.A$ in the materialized view. If it is not present, we add $(t.A, 1)$ to the materialized view. If the group $t.A$ is present, we add 1 to the count of the group.

    When a set of tuples d_r is deleted from r, for each tuple t in d_r we do the following. We look for the group $t.A$ in the materialized view, and subtract 1 from the count for the group. If the count becomes 0, we delete the tuple for the group $t.A$ from the materialized view.

- **sum**: Consider a materialized view $v = {}_A\mathcal{G}_{sum(B)}(r)$.

    When a set of tuples i_r is inserted into r, for each tuple t in i_r we do the following. We look for the group $t.A$ in the materialized view. If it is not present, we add $(t.A, t.B)$ to the materialized view; in addition, we store a count of 1 associated with $(t.A, t.B)$, just as we did for projection. If the group $t.A$ is present, we add the value of $t.B$ to the aggregate value for the group, and add 1 to the count of the group.

    When a set of tuples d_r is deleted from r, for each tuple t in d_r we do the following. We look for the group $t.A$ in the materialized view, and subtract $t.B$ from the aggregate value for the group. We also subtract 1 from the count for the group, and if the count becomes 0, we delete the tuple for the group $t.A$ from the materialized view.

    Without keeping the extra count value, we would not be able to distinguish a case where the sum for a group is 0 from the case where the last tuple in a group is deleted.

- **avg**: Consider a materialized view $v = {}_A\mathcal{G}_{avg(B)}(r)$.

    Directly updating the average on an insert or delete is not possible, since it depends not only on the old average and the tuple being inserted/deleted, but also on the number of tuples in the group.

Instead, to handle the case of **avg**, we maintain the **sum** and **count** aggregate values as described earlier, and compute the average as the sum divided by the count.

- **min, max**: Consider a materialized view $v = {}_A\mathcal{G}_{min(B)}(r)$. (The case of **max** is exactly equivalent.)

  Handling insertions on r is straightforward. Maintaining the aggregate values **min** and **max** on deletions may be more expensive. For example, if the tuple corresponding to the minimum value for a group is deleted from r, we have to look at the other tuples of r that are in the same group to find the new minimum value.

14.5.2.4   Other Operations

The set operation *intersection* is maintained as follows. Given materialized view $v = r \cap s$, when a tuple is inserted in r we check if it is present in s, and if so we add it to v. If a tuple is deleted from r, we delete it from the intersection if it is present. The other set operations, *union* and *set difference*, are handled in a similar fashion; we leave details to you.

Outer joins are handled in much the same way as joins, but with some extra work. In the case of deletion from r we have to handle tuples in s that no longer match any tuple in r. In the case of insertion to r, we have to handle tuples in s that did not match any tuple in r. Again we leave details to you.

14.5.2.5   Handling Expressions

So far we have seen how to update incrementally the result of a single operation. To handle an entire expression, we can derive expressions for computing the incremental change to the result of each subexpression, starting from the smallest subexpressions.

For example, suppose we wish to incrementally update a materialized view $E_1 \bowtie E_2$ when a set of tuples i_r is inserted into relation r. Let us assume r is used in E_1 alone. Suppose the set of tuples to be inserted into E_1 is given by expression D_1. Then the expression $D_1 \bowtie E_2$ gives the set of tuples to be inserted into $E_1 \bowtie E_2$.

See the bibliographical notes for further details on incremental view maintenance with expressions.

14.5.3   Query Optimization and Materialized Views

Query optimization can be performed by treating materialized views just like regular relations. However, materialized views offer further opportunities for optimization:

- Rewriting queries to use materialized views:

  Suppose a materialized view $v = r \bowtie s$ is available, and a user submits a query $r \bowtie s \bowtie t$. Rewriting the query as $v \bowtie t$ may provide a more efficient query plan than optimizing the query as submitted. Thus, it is the job of the query optimizer to recognize when a materialized view can be used to speed up a query.

- Replacing a use of a materialized view by the view definition:
    Suppose a materialized view $v = r \bowtie s$ is available, but without any index on it, and a user submits a query $\sigma_{A=10}(v)$. Suppose also that s has an index on the common attribute B, and r has an index on attribute A. The best plan for this query may be to replace v by $r \bowtie s$, which can lead to the query plan $\sigma_{A=10}(r) \bowtie s$; the selection and join can be performed efficiently by using the indices on $r.A$ and $s.B$, respectively. In contrast, evaluating the selection directly on v may require a full scan of v, which may be more expensive.

The bibliographical notes give pointers to research showing how to efficiently perform query optimization with materialized views.

Another related optimization problem is that of **materialized view selection**, namely, "What is the best set of views to materialize?" This decision must be made on the basis of the system **workload**, which is a sequence of queries and updates that reflects the typical load on the system. One simple criterion would be to select a set of materialized views that minimizes the overall execution time of the workload of queries and updates, including the time taken to maintain the materialized views. Database administrators usually modify this criterion to take into account the importance of different queries and updates: Fast response may be required for some queries and updates, but a slow response may be acceptable for others.

Indices are just like materialized views, in that they too are derived data, can speed up queries, and may slow down updates. Thus, the problem of **index selection** is closely related, to that of materialized view selection, although it is simpler.

We examine these issues in more detail in Sections 21.2.5 and 21.2.6.

Some database systems, such as Microsoft SQL Server 7.5, and the RedBrick Data Warehouse from Informix, provide tools to help the database administrator with index and materialized view selection. These tools examine the history of queries and updates, and suggest indices and views to be materialized.

14.6   Summary

- Given a query, there are generally a variety of methods for computing the answer. It is the responsibility of the system to transform the query as entered by the user into an equivalent query that can be computed more efficiently. The process of finding a good strategy for processing a query, is called *query optimization*.

- The evaluation of complex queries involves many accesses to disk. Since the transfer of data from disk is slow relative to the speed of main memory and the CPU of the computer system, it is worthwhile to allocate a considerable amount of processing to choose a method that minimizes disk accesses.

- The strategy that the database system chooses for evaluating an operation depends on the size of each relation and on the distribution of values within columns. So that they can base the strategy choice on reliable information, database systems may store statistics for each relation r. These statistics include

- ☐ The number of tuples in the relation r
- ☐ The size of a record (tuple) of relation r in bytes
- ☐ The number of distinct values that appear in the relation r for a particular attribute

- These statistics allow us to estimate the sizes of the results of various operations, as well as the cost of executing the operations. Statistical information about relations is particularly useful when several indices are available to assist in the processing of a query. The presence of these structures has a significant influence on the choice of a query-processing strategy.

- Each relational-algebra expression represents a particular sequence of operations. The first step in selecting a query-processing strategy is to find a relational-algebra expression that is equivalent to the given expression and is estimated to cost less to execute.

- There are a number of equivalence rules that we can use to transform an expression into an equivalent one. We use these rules to generate systematically all expressions equivalent to the given query.

- Alternative evaluation plans for each expression can be generated by similar rules, and the cheapest plan across all expressions can be chosen. Several optimization techniques are available to reduce the number of alternative expressions and plans that need to be generated.

- We use heuristics to reduce the number of plans considered, and thereby to reduce the cost of optimization. Heuristic rules for transforming relational-algebra queries include "Perform selection operations as early as possible," "Perform projections early," and "Avoid Cartesian products."

- Materialized views can be used to speed up query processing. Incremental view maintenance is needed to efficiently update materialized views when the underlying relations are modified. The differential of an operation can be computed by means of algebraic expressions involving differentials of the inputs of the operation. Other issues related to materialized views include how to optimize queries by making use of available materialized views, and how to select views to be materialized.

Review Terms

- Query optimization
- Statistics estimation
- Catalog information

- Size estimation
  - ☐ Selection
  - ☐ Selectivity
  - ☐ Join

- Distinct value estimation
- Transformation of expressions
- Cost-based optimization
- Equivalence of expressions
- Equivalence rules
    - ☐ Join commutativity
    - ☐ Join associativity
- Minimal set of equivalence rules
- Enumeration of equivalent expressions
- Choice of evaluation plans
- Interaction of evaluation techniques
- Join order optimization
    - ☐ Dynamic-programming algorithm

- ☐ Left-deep join order
- Heuristic optimization
- Access-plan selection
- Correlated evaluation
- Decorrelation
- Materialized views
- Materialized view maintenance
    - ☐ Recomputation
    - ☐ Incremental maintenance
    - ☐ Insertion,
    - ☐ Deletion
    - ☐ Updates
- Query optimization with materialized views
- Index selection
- Materialized view selection

Exercises

14.1 Clustering indices may allow faster access to data than a nonclustering index affords. When must we create a nonclustering index, despite the advantages of a clustering index? Explain your answer.

14.2 Consider the relations $r_1(A, B, C)$, $r_2(C, D, E)$, and $r_3(E, F)$, with primary keys A, C, and E, respectively. Assume that r_1 has 1000 tuples, r_2 has 1500 tuples, and r_3 has 750 tuples. Estimate the size of $r_1 \bowtie r_2 \bowtie r_3$, and give an efficient strategy for computing the join.

14.3 Consider the relations $r_1(A, B, C)$, $r_2(C, D, E)$, and $r_3(E, F)$ of Exercise 14.2. Assume that there are no primary keys, except the entire schema. Let $V(C, r_1)$ be 900, $V(C, r_2)$ be 1100, $V(E, r_2)$ be 50, and $V(E, r_3)$ be 100. Assume that r_1 has 1000 tuples, r_2 has 1500 tuples, and r_3 has 750 tuples. Estimate the size of $r_1 \bowtie r_2 \bowtie r_3$, and give an efficient strategy for computing the join.

14.4 Suppose that a B$^+$-tree index on *branch-city* is available on relation *branch*, and that no other index is available. What would be the best way to handle the following selections that involve negation?

   a. $\sigma_{\neg(branch\text{-}city<\text{"Brooklyn"})}(branch)$
   b. $\sigma_{\neg(branch\text{-}city=\text{"Brooklyn"})}(branch)$
   c. $\sigma_{\neg(branch\text{-}city<\text{"Brooklyn"}\ \vee\ assets<5000)}(branch)$

14.5 Suppose that a B$^+$-tree index on (*branch-name, branch-city*) is available on relation *branch*. What would be the best way to handle the following selection?

   $\sigma_{(branch\text{-}city<\text{"Brooklyn"})\ \wedge\ (assets<5000)\wedge(branch\text{-}name=\text{"Downtown"})}(branch)$

14.6 Show that the following equivalences hold. Explain how you can apply then to improve the efficiency of certain queries:

    a. $E_1 \bowtie_\theta (E_2 - E_3) = (E_1 \bowtie_\theta E_2 - E_1 \bowtie_\theta E_3)$.

    b. $\sigma_\theta(\,_A\mathcal{G}_F(E)) = \,_A\mathcal{G}_F(\sigma_\theta(E))$, where θ uses only attributes from A.

    c. $\sigma_\theta(E_1 \bowtie E_2) = \sigma_\theta(E_1) \bowtie E_2$ where θ uses only attributes from E_1.

14.7 Show how to derive the following equivalences by a sequence of transformations using the equivalence rules in Section 14.3.1.

    a. $\sigma_{\theta_1 \wedge \theta_2 \wedge \theta_3}(E) = \sigma_{\theta_1}(\sigma_{\theta_2}(\sigma_{\theta_3}(E)))$

    b. $\sigma_{\theta_1 \wedge \theta_2}(E_1 \bowtie_{\theta_3} E_2) = \sigma_{\theta_1}(E_1 \bowtie_{\theta_3} (\sigma_{\theta_2}(E_2)))$, where θ_2 involves only attributes from E_2

14.8 For each of the following pairs of expressions, give instances of relations that show the expressions are not equivalent.

    a. $\Pi_A(R - S)$ and $\Pi_A(R) - \Pi_A(S)$

    b. $\sigma_{B<4}(\,_A\mathcal{G}_{max(B)}(R))$ and $\,_A\mathcal{G}_{max(B)}(\sigma_{B<4}(R))$

    c. In the preceding expressions, if both occurrences of max were replaced by min would the expressions be equivalent?

    d. $(R \bowtie S) \bowtie T$ and $R \bowtie (S \bowtie T)$

    In other words, the natural left outer join is not associative.

    (Hint: Assume that the schemas of the three relations are $R(a, b1)$, $S(a, b2)$, and $T(a, b3)$, respectively.)

    e. $\sigma_\theta(E_1 \bowtie E_2)$ and $E_1 \bowtie \sigma_\theta(E_2)$, where θ uses only attributes from E_2

14.9 SQL allows relations with duplicates (Chapter 4).

    a. Define versions of the basic relational-algebra operations σ, Π, $\times$, $\bowtie$, $-$, $\cup$, and $\cap$ that work on relations with duplicates, in a way consistent with SQL.

    b. Check which of the equivalence rules 1 through 7.b hold for the multiset version of the relational-algebra defined in part a.

14.10 ∗∗ Show that, with n relations, there are $(2(n-1))!/(n-1)!$ different join orders.

    Hint: A **complete binary tree** is one where every internal node has exactly two children. Use the fact that the number of different complete binary trees with n leaf nodes is $\frac{1}{n}\binom{2(n-1)}{(n-1)}$.

    If you wish, you can derive the formula for the number of complete binary trees with n nodes from the formula for the number of binary trees with n nodes. The number of binary trees with n nodes is $\frac{1}{n+1}\binom{2n}{n}$; this number is known as the Catalan number, and its derivation can be found in any standard textbook on data structures or algorithms.

14.11 ∗∗ Show that the lowest-cost join order can be computed in time $O(3^n)$. Assume that you can store and look up information about a set of relations (such as the optimal join order for the set, and the cost of that join order) in constant time. (If you find this exercise difficult, at least show the looser time bound of $O(2^{2n})$.)

14.12 Show that, if only left-deep join trees are considered, as in the System R optimizer, the time taken to find the most efficient join order is around $n2^n$. Assume that there is only one interesting sort order.

14.13 A set of equivalence rules is said to be *complete* if, whenever two expressions are equivalent, one can be derived from the other by a sequence of uses of the equivalence rules. Is the set of equivalence rules that we considered in Section 14.3.1 complete? Hint: Consider the equivalence $\sigma_{3=5}(r) = \{\ \}$.

14.14 Decorrelation:

    a. Write a nested query on the relation *account* to find for each branch with name starting with "B", all accounts with the maximum balance at the branch.

    b. Rewrite the preceding query, without using a nested subquery; in other words, decorrelate the query.

    c. Give a procedure (similar that that described in Section 14.4.5) for decorrelating such queries.

14.15 Describe how to incrementally maintain the results of the following operations, on both insertions and deletions.

    a. Union and set difference

    b. Left outer join

14.16 Give an example of an expression defining a materialized view and two situations (sets of statistics for the input relations and the differentials) such that incremental view maintenance is better than recomputation in one situation, and recomputation is better in the other situation.

Bibliographical Notes

The seminal work of Selinger et al. [1979] describes access-path selection in the System R optimizer, which was one of the earliest relational-query optimizers. Graefe and McKenna [1993] describe Volcano, an equivalence-rule based query optimizer. Query processing in Starburst is described in Haas et al. [1989]. Query optimization in Oracle is briefly outlined in Oracle [1997].

Estimation of statistics of query results, such as result size, is addressed by Ioannidis and Poosala [1995], Poosala et al. [1996], and Ganguly et al. [1996], among others. Nonuniform distributions of values causes problems for estimation of query size and cost. Cost-estimation techniques that use histograms of value distributions have been proposed to tackle the problem. Ioannidis and Christodoulakis [1993], Ioannidis and Poosala [1995], and Poosala et al. [1996] present results in this area.

Exhaustive searching of all query plans is impractical for optimization of joins involving many relations, and techniques based on randomized searching, which do not examine all alternatives, have been proposed. Ioannidis and Wong [1987], Swami and Gupta [1988], and Ioannidis and Kang [1990] present results in this area.

Parametric query-optimization techniques have been proposed by Ioannidis et al. [1992] and Ganguly [1998], to handle query processing when the selectivity of query parameters is not known at optimization time. A set of plans—one for each of several different query selectivities—is computed, and is stored by the optimizer, at compile time. One of these plans is chosen at run time, on the basis of the actual selectivities, avoiding the cost of full optimization at run time.

Klug [1982] was an early work on optimization of relational-algebra expressions with aggregate functions. More recent work in this area includes Yan and Larson [1995] and Chaudhuri and Shim [1994]. Optimization of queries containing outer joins is described in Rosenthal and Reiner [1984], Galindo-Legaria and Rosenthal [1992], and Galindo-Legaria [1994].

The SQL language poses several challenges for query optimization, including the presence of duplicates and nulls, and the semantics of nested subqueries. Extension of relational algebra to duplicates is described in Dayal et al. [1982]. Optimization of nested subqueries is discussed in Kim [1982], Ganski and Wong [1987], Dayal [1987], and more recently, in Seshadri et al. [1996].

When queries are generated through views, more relations often are joined than is necessary for computation of the query. A collection of techniques for join minimization has been grouped under the name *tableau optimization*. The notion of a tableau was introduced by Aho et al. [1979b] and Aho et al. [1979a], and was further extended by Sagiv and Yannakakis [1981]. Ullman [1988] andMaier [1983] provide a textbook coverage of tableaux.

Sellis [1988] and Roy et al. [2000] describe *multiquery optimization*, which is the problem of optimizing the execution of several queries as a group. If an entire group of queries is considered, it is possible to discover *common subexpressions* that can be evaluated once for the entire group. Finkelstein [1982] and Hall [1976] consider optimization of a group of queries and the use of common subexpressions. Dalvi et al. [2001] discuss optimization issues in pipelining with limited buffer space combined with sharing of common subexpressions.

Query optimization can make use of semantic information, such as functional dependencies and other integrity constraints. *Semantic query-optimization* in relational databases is covered by King [1981], Chakravarthy et al. [1990], and in the context of aggregation, by Sudarshan and Ramakrishnan [1991].

Query-processing and optimization techniques for Datalog, in particular techniques to handle queries on recursive views, are described in Bancilhon and Ramakrishnan [1986], Beeri and Ramakrishnan [1991], Ramakrishnan et al. [1992c], Srivastava et al. [1995] and Mumick et al. [1996]. Query processing and optimization techniques for object-oriented databases are discussed in Maier and Stein [1986], Beech [1988], Bertino and Kim [1989], and Blakeley et al. [1993].

Blakeley et al. [1986], Blakeley et al. [1989], and Griffin and Libkin [1995] describe techniques for maintenance of materialized views. Gupta and Mumick [1995] provides a survey of materialized view maintenance. Optimization of materialized view maintenance plans is described by Vista [1998] and Mistry et al. [2001]. Query optimization in the presence of materialized views is addressed by Larson and Yang [1985], Chaudhuri et al. [1995], Dar et al. [1996], and Roy et al. [2000]. Index selection and materialized view selection are addressed by Ross et al. [1996], Labio et al. [1997], Gupta [1997], Chaudhuri and Narasayya [1997], and Roy et al. [2000].

PART 5

Transaction Management

The term transaction refers to a collection of operations that form a single logical unit of work. For instance, transfer of money from one account to another is a transaction consisting of two updates, one to each account.

It is important that either all actions of a transaction be executed completely, or, in case of some failure, partial effects of a transaction be undone. This property is called *atomicity*. Further, once a transaction is successfully executed, its effects must persist in the database—a system failure should not result in the database forgetting about a transaction that successfully completed. This property is called *durability*.

In a database system where multiple transactions are executing concurrently, if updates to shared data are not controlled there is potential for transactions to see inconsistent intermediate states created by updates of other transactions. Such a situation can result in erroneous updates to data stored in the database. Thus, database systems must provide mechanisms to isolate transactions from the effects of other concurrently executing transactions. This property is called *isolation*.

Chapter 15 describes the concept of a transaction in detail, including the properties of atomicity, durability, isolation, and other properties provided by the transaction abstraction. In particular, the chapter makes precise the notion of isolation by means of a concept called serializability.

Chapter 16 describes several concurrency control techniques that help implement the isolation property.

Chapter 17 describes the recovery management component of a database, which implements the atomicity and durability properties.

CHAPTER 15

Transactions

Often, a collection of several operations on the database appears to be a single unit from the point of view of the database user. For example, a transfer of funds from a checking account to a savings account is a single operation from the customer's standpoint; within the database system, however, it consists of several operations. Clearly, it is essential that all these operations occur, or that, in case of a failure, none occur. It would be unacceptable if the checking account were debited, but the savings account were not credited.

Collections of operations that form a single logical unit of work are called **transactions**. A database system must ensure proper execution of transactions despite failures—either the entire transaction executes, or none of it does. Furthermore, it must manage concurrent execution of transactions in a way that avoids the introduction of inconsistency. In our funds-transfer example, a transaction computing the customer's total money might see the checking-account balance before it is debited by the funds-transfer transaction, but see the savings balance after it is credited. As a result, it would obtain an incorrect result.

This chapter introduces the basic concepts of transaction processing. Details on concurrent transaction processing and recovery from failures are in Chapters 16 and 17, respectively. Further topics in transaction processing are discussed in Chapter 24.

15.1 Transaction Concept

A **transaction** is a **unit** of program execution that accesses and possibly updates various data items. Usually, a transaction is initiated by a user program written in a high-level data-manipulation language or programming language (for example, SQL, COBOL, C, C++, or Java), where it is delimited by statements (or function calls) of the form **begin transaction** and **end transaction**. The transaction consists of all operations executed between the **begin transaction** and **end transaction**.

To ensure integrity of the data, we require that the database system maintain the following properties of the transactions:

- **Atomicity**. Either all operations of the transaction are reflected properly in the database, or none are.

- **Consistency**. Execution of a transaction in isolation (that is, with no other transaction executing concurrently) preserves the consistency of the database.

- **Isolation**. Even though multiple transactions may execute concurrently, the system guarantees that, for every pair of transactions T_i and T_j, it appears to T_i that either T_j finished execution before T_i started, or T_j started execution after T_i finished. Thus, each transaction is unaware of other transactions executing concurrently in the system.

- **Durability**. After a transaction completes successfully, the changes it has made to the database persist, even if there are system failures.

These properties are often called the **ACID properties**; the acronym is derived from the first letter of each of the four properties.

To gain a better understanding of ACID properties and the need for them, consider a simplified banking system consisting of several accounts and a set of transactions that access and update those accounts. For the time being, we assume that the database permanently resides on disk, but that some portion of it is temporarily residing in main memory.

Transactions access data using two operations:

- read(X), which transfers the data item X from the database to a local buffer belonging to the transaction that executed the read operation.

- write(X), which transfers the data item X from the the local buffer of the transaction that executed the write back to the database.

In a real database system, the write operation does not necessarily result in the immediate update of the data on the disk; the write operation may be temporarily stored in memory and executed on the disk later. For now, however, we shall assume that the write operation updates the database immediately. We shall return to this subject in Chapter 17.

Let T_i be a transaction that transfers \$50 from account A to account B. This transaction can be defined as

$$
\begin{aligned}
T_i:\ &\text{read}(A); \\
&A := A - 50; \\
&\text{write}(A); \\
&\text{read}(B); \\
&B := B + 50; \\
&\text{write}(B).
\end{aligned}
$$

Let us now consider each of the ACID requirements. (For ease of presentation, we consider them in an order different from the order A-C-I-D).

- **Consistency**: The consistency requirement here is that the sum of A and B be unchanged by the execution of the transaction. Without the consistency requirement, money could be created or destroyed by the transaction! It can be verified easily that, if the database is consistent before an execution of the transaction, the database remains consistent after the execution of the transaction.

Ensuring consistency for an individual transaction is the responsibility of the application programmer who codes the transaction. This task may be facilitated by automatic testing of integrity constraints, as we discussed in Chapter 6.

- **Atomicity**: Suppose that, just before the execution of transaction T_i the values of accounts A and B are $1000 and $2000, respectively. Now suppose that, during the execution of transaction T_i, a failure occurs that prevents T_i from completing its execution successfully. Examples of such failures include power failures, hardware failures, and software errors. Further, suppose that the failure happened after the write(A) operation but before the write(B) operation. In this case, the values of accounts A and B reflected in the database are $950 and $2000. The system destroyed $50 as a result of this failure. In particular, we note that the sum $A + B$ is no longer preserved.

  Thus, because of the failure, the state of the system no longer reflects a real state of the world that the database is supposed to capture. We term such a state an **inconsistent state**. We must ensure that such inconsistencies are not visible in a database system. Note, however, that the system must at some point be in an inconsistent state. Even if transaction T_i is executed to completion, there exists a point at which the value of account A is $950 and the value of account B is $2000, which is clearly an inconsistent state. This state, however, is eventually replaced by the consistent state where the value of account A is $950, and the value of account B is $2050. Thus, if the transaction never started or was guaranteed to complete, such an inconsistent state would not be visible except during the execution of the transaction. That is the reason for the atomicity requirement: If the atomicity property is present, all actions of the transaction are reflected in the database, or none are.

  The basic idea behind ensuring atomicity is this: The database system keeps track (on disk) of the old values of any data on which a transaction performs a write, and, if the transaction does not complete its execution, the database system restores the old values to make it appear as though the transaction never executed. We discuss these ideas further in Section 15.2. Ensuring atomicity is the responsibility of the database system itself; specifically, it is handled by a component called the **transaction-management component**, which we describe in detail in Chapter 17.

- **Durability:** Once the execution of the transaction completes successfully, and the user who initiated the transaction has been notified that the transfer of funds has taken place, it must be the case that no system failure will result in a loss of data corresponding to this transfer of funds.

  The durability property guarantees that, once a transaction completes successfully, all the updates that it carried out on the database persist, even if there is a system failure after the transaction completes execution.

We assume for now that a failure of the computer system may result in loss of data in main memory, but data written to disk are never lost. We can guarantee durability by ensuring that either

1. The updates carried out by the transaction have been written to disk before the transaction completes.
2. Information about the updates carried out by the transaction and written to disk is sufficient to enable the database to reconstruct the updates when the database system is restarted after the failure.

Ensuring durability is the responsibility of a component of the database system called the **recovery-management component**. The transaction-management component and the recovery-management component are closely related, and we describe them in Chapter 17.

- **Isolation:** Even if the consistency and atomicity properties are ensured for each transaction, if several transactions are executed concurrently, their operations may interleave in some undesirable way, resulting in an inconsistent state.

  For example, as we saw earlier, the database is temporarily inconsistent while the transaction to transfer funds from A to B is executing, with the deducted total written to A and the increased total yet to be written to B. If a second concurrently running transaction reads A and B at this intermediate point and computes $A + B$, it will observe an inconsistent value. Furthermore, if this second transaction then performs updates on A and B based on the inconsistent values that it read, the database may be left in an inconsistent state even after both transactions have completed.

  A way to avoid the problem of concurrently executing transactions is to execute transactions serially—that is, one after the other. However, concurrent execution of transactions provides significant performance benefits, as we shall see in Section 15.4. Other solutions have therefore been developed; they allow multiple transactions to execute concurrently.

  We discuss the problems caused by concurrently executing transactions in Section 15.4. The isolation property of a transaction ensures that the concurrent execution of transactions results in a system state that is equivalent to a state that could have been obtained had these transactions executed one at a time in some order. We shall discuss the principles of isolation further in Section 15.5. Ensuring the isolation property is the responsibility of a component of the database system called the **concurrency-control component**, which we discuss later, in Chapter 16.

15.2 Transaction State

In the absence of failures, all transactions complete successfully. However, as we noted earlier, a transaction may not always complete its execution successfully. Such a transaction is termed **aborted**. If we are to ensure the atomicity property, an aborted transaction must have no effect on the state of the database. Thus, any changes that the aborted transaction made to the database must be undone. Once the changes caused by an aborted transaction have been undone, we say that the transaction has been **rolled back**. It is part of the responsibility of the recovery scheme to manage transaction aborts.

A transaction that completes its execution successfully is said to be **committed**. A committed transaction that has performed updates transforms the database into a new consistent state, which must persist even if there is a system failure.

Once a transaction has committed, we cannot undo its effects by aborting it. The only way to undo the effects of a committed transaction is to execute a **compensating transaction**. For instance, if a transaction added $20 to an account, the compensating transaction would subtract $20 from the account. However, it is not always possible to create such a compensating transaction. Therefore, the responsibility of writing and executing a compensating transaction is left to the user, and is not handled by the database system. Chapter 24 includes a discussion of compensating transactions.

We need to be more precise about what we mean by *successful completion* of a transaction. We therefore establish a simple abstract transaction model. A transaction must be in one of the following states:

- **Active**, the initial state; the transaction stays in this state while it is executing

- **Partially committed**, after the final statement has been executed

- **Failed**, after the discovery that normal execution can no longer proceed

- **Aborted**, after the transaction has been rolled back and the database has been restored to its state prior to the start of the transaction

- **Committed**, after successful completion

The state diagram corresponding to a transaction appears in Figure 15.1. We say that a transaction has committed only if it has entered the committed state. Similarly, we say that a transaction has aborted only if it has entered the aborted state. A transaction is said to have **terminated** if has either committed or aborted.

A transaction starts in the active state. When it finishes its final statement, it enters the partially committed state. At this point, the transaction has completed its execution, but it is still possible that it may have to be aborted, since the actual output may still be temporarily residing in main memory, and thus a hardware failure may preclude its successful completion.

The database system then writes out enough information to disk that, even in the event of a failure, the updates performed by the transaction can be re-created when the system restarts after the failure. When the last of this information is written out, the transaction enters the committed state.

As mentioned earlier, we assume for now that failures do not result in loss of data on disk. Chapter 17 discusses techniques to deal with loss of data on disk.

A transaction enters the failed state after the system determines that the transaction can no longer proceed with its normal execution (for example, because of hardware or logical errors). Such a transaction must be rolled back. Then, it enters the aborted state. At this point, the system has two options:

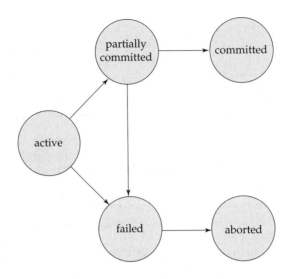

Figure 15.1 State diagram of a transaction.

- It can **restart** the transaction, but only if the transaction was aborted as a result of some hardware or software error that was not created through the internal logic of the transaction. A restarted transaction is considered to be a new transaction.

- It can **kill** the transaction. It usually does so because of some internal logical error that can be corrected only by rewriting the application program, or because the input was bad, or because the desired data were not found in the database.

We must be cautious when dealing with **observable external writes**, such as writes to a terminal or printer. Once such a write has occurred, it cannot be erased, since it may have been seen external to the database system. Most systems allow such writes to take place only after the transaction has entered the committed state. One way to implement such a scheme is for the database system to store any value associated with such external writes temporarily in nonvolatile storage, and to perform the actual writes only after the transaction enters the committed state. If the system should fail after the transaction has entered the committed state, but before it could complete the external writes, the database system will carry out the external writes (using the data in nonvolatile storage) when the system is restarted.

Handling external writes can be more complicated in some situations. For example suppose the external action is that of dispensing cash at an automated teller machine, and the system fails just before the cash is actually dispensed (we assume that cash can be dispensed atomically). It makes no sense to dispense cash when the system is restarted, since the user may have left the machine. In such a case a compensating transaction, such as depositing the cash back in the users account, needs to be executed when the system is restarted.

For certain applications, it may be desirable to allow active transactions to display data to users, particularly for long-duration transactions that run for minutes or hours. Unfortunately, we cannot allow such output of observable data unless we are willing to compromise transaction atomicity. Most current transaction systems ensure atomicity and, therefore, forbid this form of interaction with users. In Chapter 24, we discuss alternative transaction models that support long-duration, interactive transactions.

15.3   Implementation of Atomicity and Durability

The recovery-management component of a database system can support atomicity and durability by a variety of schemes. We first consider a simple, but extremely inefficient, scheme called the **shadow copy** scheme. This scheme, which is based on making copies of the database, called *shadow* copies, assumes that only one transaction is active at a time. The scheme also assumes that the database is simply a file on disk. A pointer called db-pointer is maintained on disk; it points to the current copy of the database.

In the shadow-copy scheme, a transaction that wants to update the database first creates a complete copy of the database. All updates are done on the new database copy, leaving the original copy, the **shadow copy**, untouched. If at any point the transaction has to be aborted, the system merely deletes the new copy. The old copy of the database has not been affected.

If the transaction completes, it is committed as follows. First, the operating system is asked to make sure that all pages of the new copy of the database have been written out to disk. (Unix systems use the flush command for this purpose.) After the operating system has written all the pages to disk, the database system updates the pointer db-pointer to point to the new copy of the database; the new copy then becomes the current copy of the database. The old copy of the database is then deleted. Figure 15.2 depicts the scheme, showing the database state before and after the update.

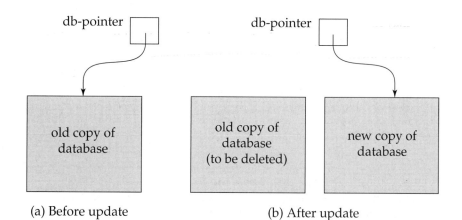

(a) Before update   (b) After update

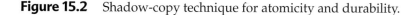

Figure 15.2   Shadow-copy technique for atomicity and durability.

The transaction is said to have been *committed* at the point where the updated db-pointer is written to disk.

We now consider how the technique handles transaction and system failures. First, consider transaction failure. If the transaction fails at any time before db-pointer is updated, the old contents of the database are not affected. We can abort the transaction by just deleting the new copy of the database. Once the transaction has been committed, all the updates that it performed are in the database pointed to by db-pointer. Thus, either all updates of the transaction are reflected, or none of the effects are reflected, regardless of transaction failure.

Now consider the issue of system failure. Suppose that the system fails at any time before the updated db-pointer is written to disk. Then, when the system restarts, it will read db-pointer and will thus see the original contents of the database, and none of the effects of the transaction will be visible on the database. Next, suppose that the system fails after db-pointer has been updated on disk. Before the pointer is updated, all updated pages of the new copy of the database were written to disk. Again, we assume that, once a file is written to disk, its contents will not be damaged even if there is a system failure. Therefore, when the system restarts, it will read db-pointer and will thus see the contents of the database *after* all the updates performed by the transaction.

The implementation actually depends on the write to db-pointer being atomic; that is, either all its bytes are written or none of its bytes are written. If some of the bytes of the pointer were updated by the write, but others were not, the pointer is meaningless, and neither old nor new versions of the database may be found when the system restarts. Luckily, disk systems provide atomic updates to entire blocks, or at least to a disk sector. In other words, the disk system guarantees that it will update db-pointer atomically, as long as we make sure that db-pointer lies entirely in a single sector, which we can ensure by storing db-pointer at the beginning of a block.

Thus, the atomicity and durability properties of transactions are ensured by the shadow-copy implementation of the recovery-management component.

As a simple example of a transaction outside the database domain, consider a text-editing session. An entire editing session can be modeled as a transaction. The actions executed by the transaction are reading and updating the file. Saving the file at the end of editing corresponds to a commit of the editing transaction; quitting the editing session without saving the file corresponds to an abort of the editing transaction.

Many text editors use essentially the implementation just described, to ensure that an editing session is transactional. A new file is used to store the updated file. At the end of the editing session, if the updated file is to be saved, the text editor uses a file *rename* command to rename the new file to have the actual file name. The rename, assumed to be implemented as an atomic operation by the underlying file system, deletes the old file as well.

Unfortunately, this implementation is extremely inefficient in the context of large databases, since executing a single transaction requires copying the *entire* database. Furthermore, the implementation does not allow transactions to execute concurrently with one another. There are practical ways of implementing atomicity and durability that are much less expensive and more powerful. We study these recovery techniques in Chapter 17.

15.4 Concurrent Executions

Transaction-processing systems usually allow multiple transactions to run concurrently. Allowing multiple transactions to update data concurrently causes several complications with consistency of the data, as we saw earlier. Ensuring consistency in spite of concurrent execution of transactions requires extra work; it is far easier to insist that transactions run **serially**—that is, one at a time, each starting only after the previous one has completed. However, there are two good reasons for allowing concurrency:

- **Improved throughput and resource utilization**. A transaction consists of many steps. Some involve I/O activity; others involve CPU activity. The CPU and the disks in a computer system can operate in parallel. Therefore, I/O activity can be done in parallel with processing at the CPU. The parallelism of the CPU and the I/O system can therefore be exploited to run multiple transactions in parallel. While a read or write on behalf of one transaction is in progress on one disk, another transaction can be running in the CPU, while another disk may be executing a read or write on behalf of a third transaction. All of this increases the **throughput** of the system—that is, the number of transactions executed in a given amount of time. Correspondingly, the processor and disk **utilization** also increase; in other words, the processor and disk spend less time idle, or not performing any useful work.

- **Reduced waiting time**. There may be a mix of transactions running on a system, some short and some long. If transactions run serially, a short transaction may have to wait for a preceding long transaction to complete, which can lead to unpredictable delays in running a transaction. If the transactions are operating on different parts of the database, it is better to let them run concurrently, sharing the CPU cycles and disk accesses among them. Concurrent execution reduces the unpredictable delays in running transactions. Moreover, it also reduces the **average response time**: the average time for a transaction to be completed after it has been submitted.

The motivation for using concurrent execution in a database is essentially the same as the motivation for using **multiprogramming** in an operating system.

When several transactions run concurrently, database consistency can be destroyed despite the correctness of each individual transaction. In this section, we present the concept of schedules to help identify those executions that are guaranteed to ensure consistency.

The database system must control the interaction among the concurrent transactions to prevent them from destroying the consistency of the database. It does so through a variety of mechanisms called **concurrency-control schemes**. We study concurrency-control schemes in Chapter 16; for now, we focus on the concept of correct concurrent execution.

Consider again the simplified banking system of Section 15.1, which has several accounts, and a set of transactions that access and update those accounts. Let T_1 and

T_2 be two transactions that transfer funds from one account to another. Transaction T_1 transfers \$50 from account A to account B. It is defined as

$$T_1: \text{read}(A);$$
$$A := A - 50;$$
$$\text{write}(A);$$
$$\text{read}(B);$$
$$B := B + 50;$$
$$\text{write}(B).$$

Transaction T_2 transfers 10 percent of the balance from account A to account B. It is defined as

$$T_2: \text{read}(A);$$
$$temp := A * 0.1;$$
$$A := A - temp;$$
$$\text{write}(A);$$
$$\text{read}(B);$$
$$B := B + temp;$$
$$\text{write}(B).$$

Suppose the current values of accounts A and B are \$1000 and \$2000, respectively. Suppose also that the two transactions are executed one at a time in the order T_1 followed by T_2. This execution sequence appears in Figure 15.3. In the figure, the sequence of instruction steps is in chronological order from top to bottom, with instructions of T_1 appearing in the left column and instructions of T_2 appearing in the right column. The final values of accounts A and B, after the execution in Figure 15.3 takes place, are \$855 and \$2145, respectively. Thus, the total amount of money in

T_1	T_2
read(A)	
$A := A - 50$	
write (A)	
read(B)	
$B := B + 50$	
write(B)	
	read(A)
	$temp := A * 0.1$
	$A := A - temp$
	write(A)
	read(B)
	$B := B + temp$
	write(B)

Figure 15.3   Schedule 1—a serial schedule in which T_1 is followed by T_2.

accounts A and B—that is, the sum $A + B$—is preserved after the execution of both transactions.

Similarly, if the transactions are executed one at a time in the order T_2 followed by T_1, then the corresponding execution sequence is that of Figure 15.4. Again, as expected, the sum $A + B$ is preserved, and the final values of accounts A and B are $850 and $2150, respectively.

The execution sequences just described are called **schedules.** They represent the chronological order in which instructions are executed in the system. Clearly, a schedule for a set of transactions must consist of all instructions of those transactions, and must preserve the order in which the instructions appear in each individual transaction. For example, in transaction T_1, the instruction write(A) must appear before the instruction read(B), in any valid schedule. In the following discussion, we shall refer to the first execution sequence (T_1 followed by T_2) as schedule 1, and to the second execution sequence (T_2 followed by T_1) as schedule 2.

These schedules are **serial**: Each serial schedule consists of a sequence of instructions from various transactions, where the instructions belonging to one single transaction appear together in that schedule. Thus, for a set of n transactions, there exist $n!$ different valid serial schedules.

When the database system executes several transactions concurrently, the corresponding schedule no longer needs to be serial. If two transactions are running concurrently, the operating system may execute one transaction for a little while, then perform a context switch, execute the second transaction for some time, and then switch back to the first transaction for some time, and so on. With multiple transactions, the CPU time is shared among all the transactions.

Several execution sequences are possible, since the various instructions from both transactions may now be interleaved. In general, it is not possible to predict exactly how many instructions of a transaction will be executed before the CPU switches to

T_1	T_2
	read(A)
	$temp := A * 0.1$
	$A := A - temp$
	write(A)
	read(B)
	$B := B + temp$
	write(B)
read(A)	
$A := A - 50$	
write(A)	
read(B)	
$B := B + 50$	
write(B)	

Figure 15.4   Schedule 2—a serial schedule in which T_2 is followed by T_1.

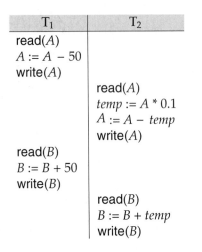

T_1	T_2
read(A) $A := A - 50$ write(A)	
	read(A) $temp := A * 0.1$ $A := A - temp$ write(A)
read(B) $B := B + 50$ write(B)	
	read(B) $B := B + temp$ write(B)

Figure 15.5 Schedule 3—a concurrent schedule equivalent to schedule 1.

another transaction. Thus, the number of possible schedules for a set of n transactions is much larger than $n!$.

Returning to our previous example, suppose that the two transactions are executed concurrently. One possible schedule appears in Figure 15.5. After this execution takes place, we arrive at the same state as the one in which the transactions are executed serially in the order T_1 followed by T_2. The sum $A + B$ is indeed preserved.

Not all concurrent executions result in a correct state. To illustrate, consider the schedule of Figure 15.6. After the execution of this schedule, we arrive at a state where the final values of accounts A and B are $950 and $2100, respectively. This final state is an *inconsistent state*, since we have gained $50 in the process of the concurrent execution. Indeed, the sum $A + B$ is not preserved by the execution of the two transactions.

If control of concurrent execution is left entirely to the operating system, many possible schedules, including ones that leave the database in an inconsistent state, such as the one just described, are possible. It is the job of the database system to ensure that any schedule that gets executed will leave the database in a consistent state. The **concurrency-control component** of the database system carries out this task.

We can ensure consistency of the database under concurrent execution by making sure that any schedule that executed has the same effect as a schedule that could have occurred without any concurrent execution. That is, the schedule should, in some sense, be equivalent to a serial schedule. We examine this idea in Section 15.5.

15.5 Serializability

The database system must control concurrent execution of transactions, to ensure that the database state remains consistent. Before we examine how the database

T_1	T_2
read(A)	
$A := A - 50$	
	read(A)
	$temp := A * 0.1$
	$A := A - temp$
	write(A)
	read(B)
write(A)	
read(B)	
$B := B + 50$	
write(B)	
	$B := B + temp$
	write(B)

Figure 15.6   Schedule 4—a concurrent schedule.

system can carry out this task, we must first understand which schedules will ensure consistency, and which schedules will not.

Since transactions are programs, it is computationally difficult to determine exactly what operations a transaction performs and how operations of various transactions interact. For this reason, we shall not interpret the type of operations that a transaction can perform on a data item. Instead, we consider only two operations: read and write. We thus assume that, between a read(Q) instruction and a write(Q) instruction on a data item Q, a transaction may perform an arbitrary sequence of operations on the copy of Q that is residing in the local buffer of the transaction. Thus, the only significant operations of a transaction, from a scheduling point of view, are its read and write instructions. We shall therefore usually show only read and write instructions in schedules, as we do in schedule 3 in Figure 15.7.

In this section, we discuss different forms of schedule equivalence; they lead to the notions of **conflict serializability** and **view serializability**.

T_1	T_2
read(A)	
write(A)	
	read(A)
	write(A)
read(B)	
write(B)	
	read(B)
	write(B)

Figure 15.7   Schedule 3—showing only the read and write instructions.

15.5.1 Conflict Serializability

Let us consider a schedule S in which there are two consecutive instructions I_i and I_j, of transactions T_i and T_j, respectively ($i \neq j$). If I_i and I_j refer to different data items, then we can swap I_i and I_j without affecting the results of any instruction in the schedule. However, if I_i and I_j refer to the same data item Q, then the order of the two steps may matter. Since we are dealing with only read and write instructions, there are four cases that we need to consider:

1. $I_i =$ read(Q), $I_j =$ read(Q). The order of I_i and I_j does not matter, since the same value of Q is read by T_i and T_j, regardless of the order.

2. $I_i =$ read(Q), $I_j =$ write(Q). If I_i comes before I_j, then T_i does not read the value of Q that is written by T_j in instruction I_j. If I_j comes before I_i, then T_i reads the value of Q that is written by T_j. Thus, the order of I_i and I_j matters.

3. $I_i =$ write(Q), $I_j =$ read(Q). The order of I_i and I_j matters for reasons similar to those of the previous case.

4. $I_i =$ write(Q), $I_j =$ write(Q). Since both instructions are write operations, the order of these instructions does not affect either T_i or T_j. However, the value obtained by the next read(Q) instruction of S is affected, since the result of only the latter of the two write instructions is preserved in the database. If there is no other write(Q) instruction after I_i and I_j in S, then the order of I_i and I_j directly affects the final value of Q in the database state that results from schedule S.

Thus, only in the case where both I_i and I_j are read instructions does the relative order of their execution not matter.

We say that I_i and I_j **conflict** if they are operations by different transactions on the same data item, and at least one of these instructions is a write operation.

To illustrate the concept of conflicting instructions, we consider schedule 3, in Figure 15.7. The write(A) instruction of T_1 conflicts with the read(A) instruction of T_2. However, the write(A) instruction of T_2 does not conflict with the read(B) instruction of T_1, because the two instructions access different data items.

Let I_i and I_j be consecutive instructions of a schedule S. If I_i and I_j are instructions of different transactions and I_i and I_j do not conflict, then we can swap the order of I_i and I_j to produce a new schedule S'. We expect S to be equivalent to S', since all instructions appear in the same order in both schedules except for I_i and I_j, whose order does not matter.

Since the write(A) instruction of T_2 in schedule 3 of Figure 15.7 does not conflict with the read(B) instruction of T_1, we can swap these instructions to generate an equivalent schedule, schedule 5, in Figure 15.8. Regardless of the initial system state, schedules 3 and 5 both produce the same final system state.

We continue to swap nonconflicting instructions:

- Swap the read(B) instruction of T_1 with the read(A) instruction of T_2.
- Swap the write(B) instruction of T_1 with the write(A) instruction of T_2.
- Swap the write(B) instruction of T_1 with the read(A) instruction of T_2.

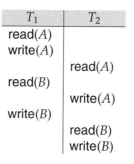

T_1	T_2
read(A)	
write(A)	
	read(A)
read(B)	
	write(A)
write(B)	
	read(B)
	write(B)

Figure 15.8   Schedule 5—schedule 3 after swapping of a pair of instructions.

The final result of these swaps, schedule 6 of Figure 15.9, is a serial schedule. Thus, we have shown that schedule 3 is equivalent to a serial schedule. This equivalence implies that, regardless of the initial system state, schedule 3 will produce the same final state as will some serial schedule.

If a schedule S can be transformed into a schedule S' by a series of swaps of non-conflicting instructions, we say that S and S' are **conflict equivalent**.

In our previous examples, schedule 1 is not conflict equivalent to schedule 2. However, schedule 1 is conflict equivalent to schedule 3, because the read(B) and write(B) instruction of T_1 can be swapped with the read(A) and write(A) instruction of T_2.

The concept of conflict equivalence leads to the concept of conflict serializability. We say that a schedule S is **conflict serializable** if it is conflict equivalent to a serial schedule. Thus, schedule 3 is conflict serializable, since it is conflict equivalent to the serial schedule 1.

Finally, consider schedule 7 of Figure 15.10; it consists of only the significant operations (that is, the read and write) of transactions T_3 and T_4. This schedule is not conflict serializable, since it is not equivalent to either the serial schedule $<T_3,T_4>$ or the serial schedule $<T_4,T_3>$.

It is possible to have two schedules that produce the same outcome, but that are not conflict equivalent. For example, consider transaction T_5, which transfers $10

T_1	T_2
read(A)	
write(A)	
read(B)	
write(B)	
	read(A)
	write(A)
	read(B)
	write(B)

Figure 15.9   Schedule 6—a serial schedule that is equivalent to schedule 3.

T_3	T_4
read(Q)	
	write(Q)
write(Q)	

Figure 15.10   Schedule 7.

from account B to account A. Let schedule 8 be as defined in Figure 15.11. We claim that schedule 8 is not conflict equivalent to the serial schedule $<T_1,T_5>$, since, in schedule 8, the write(B) instruction of T_5 conflicts with the read(B) instruction of T_1. Thus, we cannot move all the instructions of T_1 before those of T_5 by swapping consecutive nonconflicting instructions. However, the final values of accounts A and B after the execution of either schedule 8 or the serial schedule $<T_1,T_5>$ are the same —$960 and $2040, respectively.

We can see from this example that there are less stringent definitions of schedule equivalence than conflict equivalence. For the system to determine that schedule 8 produces the same outcome as the serial schedule $<T_1,T_5>$, it must analyze the computation performed by T_1 and T_5, rather than just the read and write operations. In general, such analysis is hard to implement and is computationally expensive. However, there are other definitions of schedule equivalence based purely on the read and write operations. We will consider one such definition in the next section.

15.5.2   View Serializability

In this section, we consider a form of equivalence that is less stringent than conflict equivalence, but that, like conflict equivalence, is based on only the read and write operations of transactions.

T_1	T_5
read(A)	
$A := A - 50$	
write(A)	
	read(B)
	$B := B - 10$
	write(B)
read(B)	
$B := B + 50$	
write(B)	
	read(A)
	$A := A + 10$
	write(A)

Figure 15.11   Schedule 8.

Consider two schedules S and S', where the same set of transactions participates in both schedules. The schedules S and S' are said to be **view equivalent** if three conditions are met:

1. For each data item Q, if transaction T_i reads the initial value of Q in schedule S, then transaction T_i must, in schedule S', also read the initial value of Q.

2. For each data item Q, if transaction T_i executes read(Q) in schedule S, and if that value was produced by a write(Q) operation executed by transaction T_j, then the read(Q) operation of transaction T_i must, in schedule S', also read the value of Q that was produced by the same write(Q) operation of transaction T_j.

3. For each data item Q, the transaction (if any) that performs the final write(Q) operation in schedule S must perform the final write(Q) operation in schedule S'.

Conditions 1 and 2 ensure that each transaction reads the same values in both schedules and, therefore, performs the same computation. Condition 3, coupled with conditions 1 and 2, ensures that both schedules result in the same final system state.

In our previous examples, schedule 1 is not view equivalent to schedule 2, since, in schedule 1, the value of account A read by transaction T_2 was produced by T_1, whereas this case does not hold in schedule 2. However, schedule 1 is view equivalent to schedule 3, because the values of account A and B read by transaction T_2 were produced by T_1 in both schedules.

The concept of view equivalence leads to the concept of view serializability. We say that a schedule S is **view serializable** if it is view equivalent to a serial schedule.

As an illustration, suppose that we augment schedule 7 with transaction T_6, and obtain schedule 9 in Figure 15.12. Schedule 9 is view serializable. Indeed, it is view equivalent to the serial schedule $<T_3, T_4, T_6>$, since the one read(Q) instruction reads the initial value of Q in both schedules, and T_6 performs the final write of Q in both schedules.

Every conflict-serializable schedule is also view serializable, but there are view-serializable schedules that are not conflict serializable. Indeed, schedule 9 is not conflict serializable, since every pair of consecutive instructions conflicts, and, thus, no swapping of instructions is possible.

Observe that, in schedule 9, transactions T_4 and T_6 perform write(Q) operations without having performed a read(Q) operation. Writes of this sort are called **blind writes**. Blind writes appear in any view-serializable schedule that is not conflict serializable.

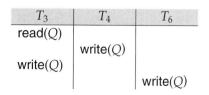

T_3	T_4	T_6
read(Q)		
	write(Q)	
write(Q)		
		write(Q)

Figure 15.12 Schedule 9—a view-serializable schedule.

15.6 Recoverability

So far, we have studied what schedules are acceptable from the viewpoint of consistency of the database, assuming implicitly that there are no transaction failures. We now address the effect of transaction failures during concurrent execution.

If a transaction T_i fails, for whatever reason, we need to undo the effect of this transaction to ensure the atomicity property of the transaction. In a system that allows concurrent execution, it is necessary also to ensure that any transaction T_j that is dependent on T_i (that is, T_j has read data written by T_i) is also aborted. To achieve this surety, we need to place restrictions on the type of schedules permitted in the system.

In the following two subsections, we address the issue of what schedules are acceptable from the viewpoint of recovery from transaction failure. We describe in Chapter 16 how to ensure that only such acceptable schedules are generated.

15.6.1 Recoverable Schedules

Consider schedule 11 in Figure 15.13, in which T_9 is a transaction that performs only one instruction: read(A). Suppose that the system allows T_9 to commit immediately after executing the read(A) instruction. Thus, T_9 commits before T_8 does. Now suppose that T_8 fails before it commits. Since T_9 has read the value of data item A written by T_8, we must abort T_9 to ensure transaction atomicity. However, T_9 has already committed and cannot be aborted. Thus, we have a situation where it is impossible to recover correctly from the failure of T_8.

Schedule 11, with the commit happening immediately after the read(A) instruction, is an example of a *nonrecoverable* schedule, which should not be allowed. Most database system require that all schedules be *recoverable*. A **recoverable schedule** is one where, for each pair of transactions T_i and T_j such that T_j reads a data item previously written by T_i, the commit operation of T_i appears before the commit operation of T_j.

15.6.2 Cascadeless Schedules

Even if a schedule is recoverable, to recover correctly from the failure of a transaction T_i, we may have to roll back several transactions. Such situations occur if transactions have read data written by T_i. As an illustration, consider the partial schedule

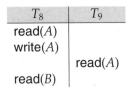

T_8	T_9
read(A)	
write(A)	
	read(A)
read(B)	

Figure 15.13 Schedule 11.

T_{10}	T_{11}	T_{12}
read(A)		
read(B)		
write(A)		
	read(A)	
	write(A)	
		read(A)

Figure 15.14   Schedule 12.

of Figure 15.14. Transaction T_{10} writes a value of A that is read by transaction T_{11}. Transaction T_{11} writes a value of A that is read by transaction T_{12}. Suppose that, at this point, T_{10} fails. T_{10} must be rolled back. Since T_{11} is dependent on T_{10}, T_{11} must be rolled back. Since T_{12} is dependent on T_{11}, T_{12} must be rolled back. This phenomenon, in which a single transaction failure leads to a series of transaction rollbacks, is called **cascading rollback**.

Cascading rollback is undesirable, since it leads to the undoing of a significant amount of work. It is desirable to restrict the schedules to those where cascading rollbacks cannot occur. Such schedules are called *cascadeless* schedules. Formally, a **cascadeless schedule** is one where, for each pair of transactions T_i and T_j such that T_j reads a data item previously written by T_i, the commit operation of T_i appears before the read operation of T_j. It is easy to verify that every cascadeless schedule is also recoverable.

15.7   Implementation of Isolation

So far, we have seen what properties a schedule must have if it is to leave the database in a consistent state and allow transaction failures to be handled in a safe manner. Specifically, schedules that are conflict or view serializable and cascadeless satisfy these requirements.

There are various **concurrency-control scheme**s that we can use to ensure that, even when multiple transactions are executed concurrently, only acceptable schedules are generated, regardless of how the operating-system time-shares resources (such as CPU time) among the transactions.

As a trivial example of a concurrency-control scheme, consider this scheme: A transaction acquires a **lock** on the entire database before it starts and releases the lock after it has committed. While a transaction holds a lock, no other transaction is allowed to acquire the lock, and all must therefore wait for the lock to be released. As a result of the locking policy, only one transaction can execute at a time. Therefore, only serial schedules are generated. These are trivially serializable, and it is easy to verify that they are cascadeless as well.

A concurrency-control scheme such as this one leads to poor performance, since it forces transactions to wait for preceding transactions to finish before they can start. In other words, it provides a poor degree of concurrency. As explained in Section 15.4, concurrent execution has several performance benefits.

The goal of concurrency-control schemes is to provide a high degree of concurrency, while ensuring that all schedules that can be generated are conflict or view serializable, and are cascadeless.

We study a number of concurrency-control schemes in Chapter 16. The schemes have different trade-offs in terms of the amount of concurrency they allow and the amount of overhead that they incur. Some of them allow only conflict serializable schedules to be generated; others allow certain view-serializable schedules that are not conflict-serializable to be generated.

15.8 Transaction Definition in SQL

A data-manipulation language must include a construct for specifying the set of actions that constitute a transaction.

The SQL standard specifies that a transaction begins implicitly. Transactions are ended by one of these SQL statements:

- **Commit work** commits the current transaction and begins a new one.

- **Rollback work** causes the current transaction to abort.

The keyword **work** is optional in both the statements. If a program terminates without either of these commands, the updates are either committed or rolled back—which of the two happens is not specified by the standard and depends on the implementation.

The standard also specifies that the system must ensure both serializability and freedom from cascading rollback. The definition of serializability used by the standard is that a schedule must have the *same effect* as would some serial schedule. Thus, conflict and view serializability are both acceptable.

The SQL-92 standard also allows a transaction to specify that it may be executed in a manner that causes it to become nonserializable with respect to other transactions. We study such weaker levels of consistency in Section 16.8.

15.9 Testing for Serializability

When designing concurrency control schemes, we must show that schedules generated by the scheme are serializable. To do that, we must first understand how to determine, given a particular schedule S, whether the schedule is serializable.

We now present a simple and efficient method for determining conflict serializability of a schedule. Consider a schedule S. We construct a directed graph, called a **precedence graph**, from S. This graph consists of a pair $G = (V, E)$, where V is a set of vertices and E is a set of edges. The set of vertices consists of all the transactions participating in the schedule. The set of edges consists of all edges $T_i \rightarrow T_j$ for which one of three conditions holds:

1. T_i executes write(Q) before T_j executes read(Q).
2. T_i executes read(Q) before T_j executes write(Q).
3. T_i executes write(Q) before T_j executes write(Q).

Figure 15.15   Precedence graph for (a) schedule 1 and (b) schedule 2.

If an edge $T_i \rightarrow T_j$ exists in the precedence graph, then, in any serial schedule S' equivalent to S, T_i must appear before T_j.

For example, the precedence graph for schedule 1 in Figure 15.15a contains the single edge $T_1 \rightarrow T_2$, since all the instructions of T_1 are executed before the first instruction of T_2 is executed. Similarly, Figure 15.15b shows the precedence graph for schedule 2 with the single edge $T_2 \rightarrow T_1$, since all the instructions of T_2 are executed before the first instruction of T_1 is executed.

The precedence graph for schedule 4 appears in Figure 15.16. It contains the edge $T_1 \rightarrow T_2$, because T_1 executes read(A) before T_2 executes write(A). It also contains the edge $T_2 \rightarrow T_1$, because T_2 executes read(B) before T_1 executes write(B).

If the precedence graph for S has a cycle, then schedule S is not conflict serializable. If the graph contains no cycles, then the schedule S is conflict serializable.

A **serializability order** of the transactions can be obtained through **topological sorting**, which determines a linear order consistent with the partial order of the precedence graph. There are, in general, several possible linear orders that can be obtained through a topological sorting. For example, the graph of Figure 15.17a has the two acceptable linear orderings shown in Figures 15.17b and 15.17c.

Thus, to test for conflict serializability, we need to construct the precedence graph and to invoke a cycle-detection algorithm. Cycle-detection algorithms can be found in standard textbooks on algorithms. Cycle-detection algorithms, such as those based on depth-first search, require on the order of n^2 operations, where n is the number of vertices in the graph (that is, the number of transactions). Thus, we have a practical scheme for determining conflict serializability.

Returning to our previous examples, note that the precedence graphs for schedules 1 and 2 (Figure 15.15) indeed do not contain cycles. The precedence graph for schedule 4 (Figure 15.16), on the other hand, contains a cycle, indicating that this schedule is not conflict serializable.

Testing for view serializability is rather complicated. In fact, it has been shown that the problem of testing for view serializability is itself *NP*-complete. Thus, almost certainly there exists no efficient algorithm to test for view serializability. See

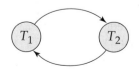

Figure 15.16   Precedence graph for schedule 4.

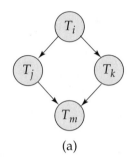

(a)

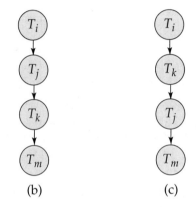

(b)   (c)

Figure 15.17   Illustration of topological sorting.

the bibliographical notes for references on testing for view serializability. However, concurrency-control schemes can still use *sufficient conditions* for view serializability. That is, if the sufficient conditions are satisfied, the schedule is view serializable, but there may be view-serializable schedules that do not satisfy the sufficient conditions.

15.10 Summary

- A *transaction* is a *unit* of program execution that accesses and possibly updates various data items. Understanding the concept of a transaction is critical for understanding and implementing updates of data in a database, in such a way that concurrent executions and failures of various forms do not result in the database becoming inconsistent.

- Transactions are required to have the ACID properties: atomicity, consistency, isolation, and durability.

  □ Atomicity ensures that either all the effects of a transaction are reflected in the database, or none are; a failure cannot leave the database in a state where a transaction is partially executed.

  □ Consistency ensures that, if the database is initially consistent, the execution of the transaction (by itself) leaves the database in a consistent state.

☐ Isolation ensures that concurrently executing transactions are isolated from one another, so that each has the impression that no other transaction is executing concurrently with it.

☐ Durability ensures that, once a transaction has been committed, that transaction's updates do not get lost, even if there is a system failure.

• Concurrent execution of transactions improves throughput of transactions and system utilization, and also reduces waiting time of transactions.

• When several transactions execute concurrently in the database, the consistency of data may no longer be preserved. It is therefore necessary for the system to control the interaction among the concurrent transactions.

☐ Since a transaction is a unit that preserves consistency, a serial execution of transactions guarantees that consistency is preserved.

☐ A *schedule* captures the key actions of transactions that affect concurrent execution, such as read and write operations, while abstracting away internal details of the execution of the transaction.

☐ We require that any schedule produced by concurrent processing of a set of transactions will have an effect equivalent to a schedule produced when these transactions are run serially in some order.

☐ A system that guarantees this property is said to ensure *serializability*.

☐ There are several different notions of equivalence leading to the concepts of *conflict serializability* and *view serializability*.

• Serializability of schedules generated by concurrently executing transactions can be ensured through one of a variety of mechanisms called *concurrency-control* schemes.

• Schedules must be recoverable, to make sure that if transaction a sees the effects of transaction b, and b then aborts, then a also gets aborted.

• Schedules should preferably be cascadeless, so that the abort of a transaction does not result in cascading aborts of other transactions. Cascadelessness is ensured by allowing transactions to only read committed data.

• The concurrency-control–management component of the database is responsible for handling the concurrency-control schemes. Chapter 16 describes concurrency-control schemes.

• The recovery-management component of a database is responsible for ensuring the atomicity and durability properties of transactions.

   The shadow copy scheme is used for ensuring atomicity and durability in text editors; however, it has extremely high overheads when used for database systems, and, moreover, it does not support concurrent execution. Chapter 17 covers better schemes.

• We can test a given schedule for conflict serializability by constructing a *precedence graph* for the schedule, and by searching for absence of cycles in the graph. However, there are more efficient concurrency control schemes for ensuring serializability.

Review Terms

- Transaction
- ACID properties
  - ☐ Atomicity
  - ☐ Consistency
  - ☐ Isolation
  - ☐ Durability
- Inconsistent state
- Transaction state
  - ☐ Active
  - ☐ Partially committed
  - ☐ Failed
  - ☐ Aborted
  - ☐ Committed
  - ☐ Terminated
- Transaction
  - ☐ Restart
  - ☐ Kill
- Observable external writes
- Shadow copy scheme

- Concurrent executions
- Serial execution
- Schedules
- Conflict of operations
- Conflict equivalence
- Conflict serializability
- View equivalence
- View serializability
- Blind writes
- Recoverability
- Recoverable schedules
- Cascading rollback
- Cascadeless schedules
- Concurrency-control scheme
- Lock
- Serializability testing
- Precedence graph
- Serializability order

Exercises

15.1 List the ACID properties. Explain the usefulness of each.

15.2 Suppose that there is a database system that never fails. Is a recovery manager required for this system?

15.3 Consider a file system such as the one on your favorite operating system.

    a. What are the steps involved in creation and deletion of files, and in writing data to a file?

    b. Explain how the issues of atomicity and durability are relevant to the creation and deletion of files, and to writing data to files.

15.4 Database-system implementers have paid much more attention to the ACID properties than have file-system implementers. Why might this be the case?

15.5 During its execution, a transaction passes through several states, until it finally commits or aborts. List all possible sequences of states through which a transaction may pass. Explain why each state transition may occur.

15.6 Justify the following statement: Concurrent execution of transactions is more important when data must be fetched from (slow) disk or when transactions are long, and is less important when data is in memory and transactions are very short.

15.7 Explain the distinction between the terms *serial schedule* and *serializable schedule*.

15.8 Consider the following two transactions:

$$T_1: \mathsf{read}(A);$$
$$\mathsf{read}(B);$$
$$\textbf{if } A = 0 \textbf{ then } B := B + 1;$$
$$\mathsf{write}(B).$$
$$T_2: \mathsf{read}(B);$$
$$\mathsf{read}(A);$$
$$\textbf{if } B = 0 \textbf{ then } A := A + 1;$$
$$\mathsf{write}(A).$$

Let the consistency requirement be $A = 0 \lor B = 0$, with $A = B = 0$ the initial values.

   a. Show that every serial execution involving these two transactions preserves the consistency of the database.

   b. Show a concurrent execution of T_1 and T_2 that produces a nonserializable schedule.

   c. Is there a concurrent execution of T_1 and T_2 that produces a serializable schedule?

15.9 Since every conflict-serializable schedule is view serializable, why do we emphasize conflict serializability rather than view serializability?

15.10 Consider the precedence graph of Figure 15.18. Is the corresponding schedule conflict serializable? Explain your answer.

15.11 What is a recoverable schedule? Why is recoverability of schedules desirable? Are there any circumstances under which it would be desirable to allow nonrecoverable schedules? Explain your answer.

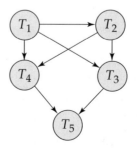

Figure 15.18   Precedence graph.

15.12 What is a cascadeless schedule? Why is cascadelessness of schedules desirable? Are there any circumstances under which it would be desirable to allow noncascadeless schedules? Explain your answer.

Bibliographical Notes

Gray and Reuter [1993] provides detailed textbook coverage of transaction-processing concepts, techniques and implementation details, including concurrency control and recovery issues. Bernstein and Newcomer [1997] provides textbook coverage of various aspects of transaction processing.

Early textbook discussions of concurrency control and recovery included Papadimitriou [1986] and Bernstein et al. [1987]. An early survey paper on implementation issues in concurrency control and recovery is presented by Gray [1978].

The concept of serializability was formalized by Eswaran et al. [1976] in connection to work on concurrency control for System R. The results concerning serializability testing and NP-completeness of testing for view serializability are from Papadimitriou et al. [1977] and Papadimitriou [1979]. Cycle-detection algorithms as well as an introduction to NP-completeness can be found in standard algorithm textbooks such as Cormen et al. [1990].

References covering specific aspects of transaction processing, such as concurrency control and recovery, are cited in Chapters 16, 17, and 24.

C H A P T E R 1 6

Concurrency Control

We saw in Chapter 15 that one of the fundamental properties of a transaction is isolation. When several transactions execute concurrently in the database, however, the isolation property may no longer be preserved. To ensure that it is, the system must control the interaction among the concurrent transactions; this control is achieved through one of a variety of mechanisms called *concurrency-control* schemes.

The concurrency-control schemes that we discuss in this chapter are all based on the serializability property. That is, all the schemes presented here ensure that the schedules are serializable. In Chapter 24, we discuss concurrency control schemes that admit nonserializable schedules. In this chapter, we consider the management of concurrently executing transactions, and we ignore failures. In Chapter 17, we shall see how the system can recover from failures.

16.1 Lock-Based Protocols

One way to ensure serializability is to require that data items be accessed in a mutually exclusive manner; that is, while one transaction is accessing a data item, no other transaction can modify that data item. The most common method used to implement this requirement is to allow a transaction to access a data item only if it is currently holding a lock on that item.

16.1.1 Locks

There are various modes in which a data item may be locked. In this section, we restrict our attention to two modes:

1. **Shared**. If a transaction T_i has obtained a **shared-mode lock** (denoted by S) on item Q, then T_i can read, but cannot write, Q.

2. **Exclusive**. If a transaction T_i has obtained an **exclusive-mode lock** (denoted by X) on item Q, then T_i can both read and write Q.

	S	X
S	true	false
X	false	false

Figure 16.1   Lock-compatibility matrix comp.

We require that every transaction **request** a lock in an appropriate mode on data item Q, depending on the types of operations that it will perform on Q. The transaction makes the request to the concurrency-control manager. The transaction can proceed with the operation only after the concurrency-control manager **grants** the lock to the transaction.

Given a set of lock modes, we can define a **compatibility function** on them as follows. Let A and B represent arbitrary lock modes. Suppose that a transaction T_i requests a lock of mode A on item Q on which transaction T_j ($T_i \neq T_j$) currently holds a lock of mode B. If transaction T_i can be granted a lock on Q immediately, in spite of the presence of the mode B lock, then we say mode A is **compatible** with mode B. Such a function can be represented conveniently by a matrix. The compatibility relation between the two modes of locking discussed in this section appears in the matrix comp of Figure 16.1. An element comp(A, B) of the matrix has the value *true* if and only if mode A is compatible with mode B.

Note that shared mode is compatible with shared mode, but not with exclusive mode. At any time, several shared-mode locks can be held simultaneously (by different transactions) on a particular data item. A subsequent exclusive-mode lock request has to wait until the currently held shared-mode locks are released.

A transaction requests a shared lock on data item Q by executing the lock-S(Q) instruction. Similarly, a transaction requests an exclusive lock through the lock-X(Q) instruction. A transaction can unlock a data item Q by the unlock(Q) instruction.

To access a data item, transaction T_i must first lock that item. If the data item is already locked by another transaction in an incompatible mode, the concurrency-control manager will not grant the lock until all incompatible locks held by other transactions have been released. Thus, T_i is made to **wait** until all incompatible locks held by other transactions have been released.

T_1: lock-X(B);
   read(B);
   $B := B - 50$;
   write(B);
   unlock(B);
   lock-X(A);
   read(A);
   $A := A + 50$;
   write(A);
   unlock(A).

Figure 16.2   Transaction T_1.

$$T_2: \text{lock-S}(A);$$
$$\text{read}(A);$$
$$\text{unlock}(A);$$
$$\text{lock-S}(B);$$
$$\text{read}(B);$$
$$\text{unlock}(B);$$
$$\text{display}(A + B).$$

Figure 16.3   Transaction T_2.

Transaction T_i may unlock a data item that it had locked at some earlier point. Note that a transaction must hold a lock on a data item as long as it accesses that item. Moreover, for a transaction to unlock a data item immediately after its final access of that data item is not always desirable, since serializability may not be ensured.

As an illustration, consider again the simplified banking system that we introduced in Chapter 15. Let A and B be two accounts that are accessed by transactions T_1 and T_2. Transaction T_1 transfers \$50 from account B to account A (Figure 16.2). Transaction T_2 displays the total amount of money in accounts A and B—that is, the sum $A + B$ (Figure 16.3).

T_1	T_2	concurrency-control manager
lock-x(B)		
		grant-x(B, T_1)
read(B)		
$B := B - 50$		
write(B)		
unlock(B)		
	lock-S(A)	
		grant-S(A, T_2)
	read(A)	
	unlock(A)	
	lock-S(B)	
		grant-S(B, T_2)
	read(B)	
	unlock(B)	
	display($A + B$)	
lock-x(A)		
		grant-x(A, T_2)
read(A)		
$A := A + 50$		
write(A)		
unlock(A)		

Figure 16.4   Schedule 1.

$$T_3: \text{lock-X}(B);$$
$$\text{read}(B);$$
$$B := B - 50;$$
$$\text{write}(B);$$
$$\text{lock-X}(A);$$
$$\text{read}(A);$$
$$A := A + 50;$$
$$\text{write}(A);$$
$$\text{unlock}(B);$$
$$\text{unlock}(A).$$

Figure 16.5 Transaction T_3.

Suppose that the values of accounts A and B are \$100 and \$200, respectively. If these two transactions are executed serially, either in the order T_1, T_2 or the order T_2, T_1, then transaction T_2 will display the value \$300. If, however, these transactions are executed concurrently, then schedule 1, in Figure 16.4 is possible. In this case, transaction T_2 displays \$250, which is incorrect. The reason for this mistake is that the transaction T_1 unlocked data item B too early, as a result of which T_2 saw an inconsistent state.

The schedule shows the actions executed by the transactions, as well as the points at which the concurrency-control manager grants the locks. The transaction making a lock request cannot execute its next action until the concurrency-control manager grants the lock. Hence, the lock must be granted in the interval of time between the lock-request operation and the following action of the transaction. Exactly when within this interval the lock is granted is not important; we can safely assume that the lock is granted just before the following action of the transaction. We shall therefore drop the column depicting the actions of the concurrency-control manager from all schedules depicted in the rest of the chapter. We let you infer when locks are granted.

Suppose now that unlocking is delayed to the end of the transaction. Transaction T_3 corresponds to T_1 with unlocking delayed (Figure 16.5). Transaction T_4 corresponds to T_2 with unlocking delayed (Figure 16.6).

You should verify that the sequence of reads and writes in schedule 1, which lead to an incorrect total of \$250 being displayed, is no longer possible with T_3 and T_4.

$$T_4: \text{lock-S}(A);$$
$$\text{read}(A);$$
$$\text{lock-S}(B);$$
$$\text{read}(B);$$
$$\text{display}(A + B);$$
$$\text{unlock}(A);$$
$$\text{unlock}(B).$$

Figure 16.6 Transaction T_4.

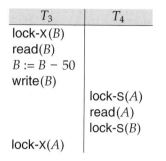

T_3	T_4
lock-X(B)	
read(B)	
$B := B - 50$	
write(B)	
	lock-S(A)
	read(A)
	lock-S(B)
lock-X(A)	

Figure 16.7   Schedule 2.

Other schedules are possible. T_4 will not print out an inconsistent result in any of them; we shall see why later.

Unfortunately, locking can lead to an undesirable situation. Consider the partial schedule of Figure 16.7 for T_3 and T_4. Since T_3 is holding an exclusive-mode lock on B and T_4 is requesting a shared-mode lock on B, T_4 is waiting for T_3 to unlock B. Similarly, since T_4 is holding a shared-mode lock on A and T_3 is requesting an exclusive-mode lock on A, T_3 is waiting for T_4 to unlock A. Thus, we have arrived at a state where neither of these transactions can ever proceed with its normal execution. This situation is called **deadlock**. When deadlock occurs, the system must roll back one of the two transactions. Once a transaction has been rolled back, the data items that were locked by that transaction are unlocked. These data items are then available to the other transaction, which can continue with its execution. We shall return to the issue of deadlock handling in Section 16.6.

If we do not use locking, or if we unlock data items as soon as possible after reading or writing them, we may get inconsistent states. On the other hand, if we do not unlock a data item before requesting a lock on another data item, deadlocks may occur. There are ways to avoid deadlock in some situations, as we shall see in Section 16.1.5. However, in general, deadlocks are a necessary evil associated with locking, if we want to avoid inconsistent states. Deadlocks are definitely preferable to inconsistent states, since they can be handled by rolling back of transactions, whereas inconsistent states may lead to real-world problems that cannot be handled by the database system.

We shall require that each transaction in the system follow a set of rules, called a **locking protocol**, indicating when a transaction may lock and unlock each of the data items. Locking protocols restrict the number of possible schedules. The set of all such schedules is a proper subset of all possible serializable schedules. We shall present several locking protocols that allow only conflict-serializable schedules. Before doing so, we need a few definitions.

Let $\{T_0, T_1, \ldots, T_n\}$ be a set of transactions participating in a schedule S. We say that T_i **precedes** T_j in S, written $T_i \rightarrow T_j$, if there exists a data item Q such that T_i has held lock mode A on Q, and T_j has held lock mode B on Q later, and comp(A,B) = false. If $T_i \rightarrow T_j$, then that precedence implies that in any equivalent serial schedule, T_i must appear before T_j. Observe that this graph is similar to the precedence graph that we used in Section 15.9 to test for conflict serializability. Conflicts between instructions correspond to noncompatibility of lock modes.

We say that a schedule S is **legal** under a given locking protocol if S is a possible schedule for a set of transactions that follow the rules of the locking protocol. We say that a locking protocol **ensures** conflict serializability if and only if all legal schedules are conflict serializable; in other words, for all legal schedules the associated $\rightarrow$ relation is acyclic.

16.1.2 Granting of Locks

When a transaction requests a lock on a data item in a particular mode, and no other transaction has a lock on the same data item in a conflicting mode, the lock can be granted. However, care must be taken to avoid the following scenario. Suppose a transaction T_2 has a shared-mode lock on a data item, and another transaction T_1 requests an exclusive-mode lock on the data item. Clearly, T_1 has to wait for T_2 to release the shared-mode lock. Meanwhile, a transaction T_3 may request a shared-mode lock on the same data item. The lock request is compatible with the lock granted to T_2, so T_3 may be granted the shared-mode lock. At this point T_2 may release the lock, but still T_1 has to wait for T_3 to finish. But again, there may be a new transaction T_4 that requests a shared-mode lock on the same data item, and is granted the lock before T_3 releases it. In fact, it is possible that there is a sequence of transactions that each requests a shared-mode lock on the data item, and each transaction releases the lock a short while after it is granted, but T_1 never gets the exclusive-mode lock on the data item. The transaction T_1 may never make progress, and is said to be **starved**.

We can avoid starvation of transactions by granting locks in the following manner: When a transaction T_i requests a lock on a data item Q in a particular mode M, the concurrency-control manager grants the lock provided that

1. There is no other other transaction holding a lock on Q in a mode that conflicts with M.

2. There is no other transaction that is waiting for a lock on Q, and that made its lock request before T_i.

Thus, a lock request will never get blocked by a lock request that is made later.

16.1.3 The Two-Phase Locking Protocol

One protocol that ensures serializability is the **two-phase locking protocol**. This protocol requires that each transaction issue lock and unlock requests in two phases:

1. **Growing phase**. A transaction may obtain locks, but may not release any lock.

2. **Shrinking phase**. A transaction may release locks, but may not obtain any new locks.

Initially, a transaction is in the growing phase. The transaction acquires locks as needed. Once the transaction releases a lock, it enters the shrinking phase, and it can issue no more lock requests.

For example, transactions T_3 and T_4 are two phase. On the other hand, transactions T_1 and T_2 are not two phase. Note that the unlock instructions do not need to appear at the end of the transaction. For example, in the case of transaction T_3, we could move the unlock(B) instruction to just after the lock-X(A) instruction, and still retain the two-phase locking property.

We can show that the two-phase locking protocol ensures conflict serializability. Consider any transaction. The point in the schedule where the transaction has obtained its final lock (the end of its growing phase) is called the **lock point** of the transaction. Now, transactions can be ordered according to their lock points—this ordering is, in fact, a serializability ordering for the transactions. We leave the proof as an exercise for you to do (see Exercise 16.1).

Two-phase locking does *not* ensure freedom from deadlock. Observe that transactions T_3 and T_4 are two phase, but, in schedule 2 (Figure 16.7), they are deadlocked.

Recall from Section 15.6.2 that, in addition to being serializable, schedules should be cascadeless. Cascading rollback may occur under two-phase locking. As an illustration, consider the partial schedule of Figure 16.8. Each transaction observes the two-phase locking protocol, but the failure of T_5 after the read(A) step of T_7 leads to cascading rollback of T_6 and T_7.

Cascading rollbacks can be avoided by a modification of two-phase locking called the **strict two-phase locking protocol**. This protocol requires not only that locking be two phase, but also that all exclusive-mode locks taken by a transaction be held until that transaction commits. This requirement ensures that any data written by an uncommitted transaction are locked in exclusive mode until the transaction commits, preventing any other transaction from reading the data.

Another variant of two-phase locking is the **rigorous two-phase locking protocol**, which requires that all locks be held until the transaction commits. We can easily

T_5	T_6	T_7
lock-X(A)		
read(A)		
lock-S(B)		
read(B)		
write(A)		
unlock(A)		
	lock-X(A)	
	read(A)	
	write(A)	
	unlock(A)	
		lock-S(A)
		read(A)

Figure 16.8   Partial schedule under two-phase locking.

verify that, with rigorous two-phase locking, transactions can be serialized in the order in which they commit. Most database systems implement either strict or rigorous two-phase locking.

Consider the following two transactions, for which we have shown only some of the significant **read** and **write** operations:

$$T_8: \text{read}(a_1);$$
$$\text{read}(a_2);$$
$$\cdots$$
$$\text{read}(a_n);$$
$$\text{write}(a_1).$$

$$T_9: \text{read}(a_1);$$
$$\text{read}(a_2);$$
$$\text{display}(a_1 + a_2).$$

If we employ the two-phase locking protocol, then T_8 must lock a_1 in exclusive mode. Therefore, any concurrent execution of both transactions amounts to a serial execution. Notice, however, that T_8 needs an exclusive lock on a_1 only at the end of its execution, when it writes a_1. Thus, if T_8 could initially lock a_1 in shared mode, and then could later change the lock to exclusive mode, we could get more concurrency, since T_8 and T_9 could access a_1 and a_2 simultaneously.

This observation leads us to a refinement of the basic two-phase locking protocol, in which **lock conversions** are allowed. We shall provide a mechanism for upgrading a shared lock to an exclusive lock, and downgrading an exclusive lock to a shared lock. We denote conversion from shared to exclusive modes by **upgrade**, and from exclusive to shared by **downgrade**. Lock conversion cannot be allowed arbitrarily. Rather, upgrading can take place in only the growing phase, whereas downgrading can take place in only the shrinking phase.

Returning to our example, transactions T_8 and T_9 can run concurrently under the refined two-phase locking protocol, as shown in the incomplete schedule of Figure 16.9, where only some of the locking instructions are shown.

T_8	T_9
lock-S (a_1)	
	lock-S (a_1)
lock-S (a_2)	
	lock-S (a_2)
lock-S (a_3)	
lock-S (a_4)	
	unlock(a_1)
	unlock(a_2)
lock-S (a_n)	
upgrade (a_1)	

Figure 16.9   Incomplete schedule with a lock conversion.

Note that a transaction attempting to upgrade a lock on an item Q may be forced to wait. This enforced wait occurs if Q is currently locked by *another* transaction in shared mode.

Just like the basic two-phase locking protocol, two-phase locking with lock conversion generates only conflict-serializable schedules, and transactions can be serialized by their lock points. Further, if exclusive locks are held until the end of the transaction, the schedules are cascadeless.

For a set of transactions, there may be conflict-serializable schedules that cannot be obtained through the two-phase locking protocol. However, to obtain conflict-serializable schedules through non-two-phase locking protocols, we need either to have additional information about the transactions or to impose some structure or ordering on the set of data items in the database. In the absence of such information, two-phase locking is necessary for conflict serializability—if T_i is a non-two-phase transaction, it is always possible to find another transaction T_j that is two-phase so that there is a schedule possible for T_i and T_j that is not conflict serializable.

Strict two-phase locking and rigorous two-phase locking (with lock conversions) are used extensively in commercial database systems.

A simple but widely used scheme automatically generates the appropriate lock and unlock instructions for a transaction, on the basis of read and write requests from the transaction:

- When a transaction T_i issues a read(Q) operation, the system issues a lock-S(Q) instruction followed by the read(Q) instruction.

- When T_i issues a write(Q) operation, the system checks to see whether T_i already holds a shared lock on Q. If it does, then the system issues an upgrade(Q) instruction, followed by the write(Q) instruction. Otherwise, the system issues a lock-X(Q) instruction, followed by the write(Q) instruction.

- All locks obtained by a transaction are unlocked after that transaction commits or aborts.

16.1.4 Implementation of Locking**

A **lock manager** can be implemented as a process that receives messages from transactions and sends messages in reply. The lock-manager process replies to lock-request messages with lock-grant messages, or with messages requesting rollback of the transaction (in case of deadlocks). Unlock messages require only an acknowledgment in response, but may result in a grant message to another waiting transaction.

The lock manager uses this data structure: For each data item that is currently locked, it maintains a linked list of records, one for each request, in the order in which the requests arrived. It uses a hash table, indexed on the name of a data item, to find the linked list (if any) for a data item; this table is called the **lock table**. Each record of the linked list for a data item notes which transaction made the request, and what lock mode it requested. The record also notes if the request has currently been granted.

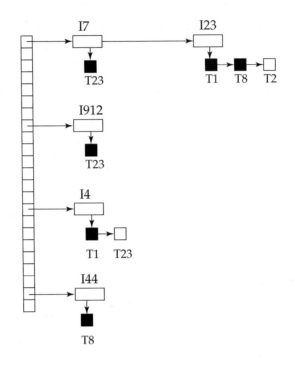

Figure 16.10   Lock table.

Figure 16.10 shows an example of a lock table. The table contains locks for five different data items, I4, I7, I23, I44, and I912. The lock table uses overflow chaining, so there is a linked list of data items for each entry in the lock table. There is also a list of transactions that have been granted locks, or are waiting for locks, for each of the data items. Granted locks are the filled-in (black) rectangles, while waiting requests are the empty rectangles. We have omitted the lock mode to keep the figure simple. It can be seen, for example, that T23 has been granted locks on I912 and I7, and is waiting for a lock on I4.

Although the figure does not show it, the lock table should also maintain an index on transaction identifiers, so that it is possible to determine efficiently the set of locks held by a given transaction.

The lock manager processes requests this way:

- When a lock request message arrives, it adds a record to the end of the linked list for the data item, if the linked list is present. Otherwise it creates a new linked list, containing only the record for the request.

   It always grants the first lock request on a data item. But if the transaction requests a lock on an item on which a lock has already been granted, the lock manager grants the request only if it is compatible with all earlier requests, and all earlier requests have been granted already. Otherwise the request has to wait.

- When the lock manager receives an unlock message from a transaction, it deletes the record for that data item in the linked list corresponding to that transaction. It tests the record that follows, if any, as described in the previous paragraph, to see if that request can now be granted. If it can, the lock manager grants that request, and processes the record following it, if any, similarly, and so on.

- If a transaction aborts, the lock manager deletes any waiting request made by the transaction. Once the database system has taken appropriate actions to undo the transaction (see Section 17.3), it releases all locks held by the aborted transaction.

This algorithm guarantees freedom from starvation for lock requests, since a request can never be granted while a request received earlier is waiting to be granted. We study how to detect and handle deadlocks later, in Section 16.6.3. Section 18.2.1 describes an alternative implementation—one that uses shared memory instead of message passing for lock request/grant.

16.1.5 Graph-Based Protocols

As noted in Section 16.1.3, the two-phase locking protocol is both necessary and sufficient for ensuring serializability in the absence of information concerning the manner in which data items are accessed. But, if we wish to develop protocols that are not two phase, we need additional information on how each transaction will access the database. There are various models that can give us the additional information, each differing in the amount of information provided. The simplest model requires that we have prior knowledge about the order in which the database items will be accessed. Given such information, it is possible to construct locking protocols that are not two phase, but that, nevertheless, ensure conflict serializability.

To acquire such prior knowledge, we impose a partial ordering $\rightarrow$ on the set $\mathbf{D} = \{d_1, d_2, \ldots, d_h\}$ of all data items. If $d_i \rightarrow d_j$, then any transaction accessing both d_i and d_j must access d_i before accessing d_j. This partial ordering may be the result of either the logical or the physical organization of the data, or it may be imposed solely for the purpose of concurrency control.

The partial ordering implies that the set $\mathbf{D}$ may now be viewed as a directed acyclic graph, called a **database graph**. In this section, for the sake of simplicity, we will restrict our attention to only those graphs that are rooted trees. We will present a simple protocol, called the *tree protocol*, which is restricted to employ only *exclusive* locks. References to other, more complex, graph-based locking protocols are in the bibliographical notes.

In the **tree protocol**, the only lock instruction allowed is lock-X. Each transaction T_i can lock a data item at most once, and must observe the following rules:

1. The first lock by T_i may be on any data item.

2. Subsequently, a data item Q can be locked by T_i only if the parent of Q is currently locked by T_i.

3. Data items may be unlocked at any time.

4. A data item that has been locked and unlocked by T_i cannot subsequently be relocked by T_i.

All schedules that are legal under the tree protocol are conflict serializable.

To illustrate this protocol, consider the database graph of Figure 16.11. The following four transactions follow the tree protocol on this graph. We show only the lock and unlock instructions:

T_{10}: lock-X(B); lock-X(E); lock-X(D); unlock(B); unlock(E); lock-X(G);
       unlock(D); unlock(G).
T_{11}: lock-X(D); lock-X(H); unlock(D); unlock(H).
T_{12}: lock-X(B); lock-X(E); unlock(E); unlock(B).
T_{13}: lock-X(D); lock-X(H); unlock(D); unlock(H).

One possible schedule in which these four transactions participated appears in Figure 16.12. Note that, during its execution, transaction T_{10} holds locks on two *disjoint* subtrees.

Observe that the schedule of Figure 16.12 is conflict serializable. It can be shown not only that the tree protocol ensures conflict serializability, but also that this protocol ensures freedom from deadlock.

The tree protocol in Figure 16.12 does not ensure recoverability and cascadelessness. To ensure recoverability and cascadelessness, the protocol can be modified to not permit release of exclusive locks until the end of the transaction. Holding exclusive locks until the end of the transaction reduces concurrency. Here is an alternative that improves concurrency, but ensures only recoverability: For each data item with an uncommitted write we record which transaction performed the last write to the data item. Whenever a transaction T_i performs a read of an uncommitted data item, we record a **commit dependency** of T_i on the transaction that performed the

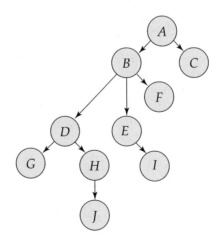

Figure 16.11   Tree-structured database graph.

T_{10}	T_{11}	T_{12}	T_{13}
lock-x(B)			
	lock-x(D)		
	lock-x(H)		
	unlock(D)		
lock-x(E)			
lock-x(D)			
unlock(B)			
unlock(E)			
		lock-x(B)	
		lock-x(E)	
	unlock(H)		
lock-x(G)			
unlock(D)			
			lock-x(D)
			lock-x(H)
			unlock(D)
			unlock(H)
		unlock(E)	
		unlock(B)	
unlock (G)			

Figure 16.12   Serializable schedule under the tree protocol.

last write to the data item. Transaction T_i is then not permitted to commit until the commit of all transactions on which it has a commit dependency. If any of these trans-actions aborts, T_i must also be aborted.

The tree-locking protocol has an advantage over the two-phase locking protocol in that, unlike two-phase locking, it is deadlock-free, so no rollbacks are required. The tree-locking protocol has another advantage over the two-phase locking protocol in that unlocking may occur earlier. Earlier unlocking may lead to shorter waiting times, and to an increase in concurrency.

However, the protocol has the disadvantage that, in some cases, a transaction may have to lock data items that it does not access. For example, a transaction that needs to access data items A and J in the database graph of Figure 16.11 must lock not only A and J, but also data items B, D, and H. This additional locking results in increased locking overhead, the possibility of additional waiting time, and a potential decrease in concurrency. Further, without prior knowledge of what data items will need to be locked, transactions will have to lock the root of the tree, and that can reduce concurrency greatly.

For a set of transactions, there may be conflict-serializable schedules that cannot be obtained through the tree protocol. Indeed, there are schedules possible under the two-phase locking protocol that are not possible under the tree protocol, and vice versa. Examples of such schedules are explored in the exercises.

16.2 Timestamp-Based Protocols

The locking protocols that we have described thus far determine the order between every pair of conflicting transactions at execution time by the first lock that both members of the pair request that involves incompatible modes. Another method for determining the serializability order is to select an ordering among transactions in advance. The most common method for doing so is to use a *timestamp-ordering* scheme.

16.2.1 Timestamps

With each transaction T_i in the system, we associate a unique fixed timestamp, denoted by TS(T_i). This timestamp is assigned by the database system before the transaction T_i starts execution. If a transaction T_i has been assigned timestamp TS(T_i), and a new transaction T_j enters the system, then TS(T_i) < TS(T_j). There are two simple methods for implementing this scheme:

1. Use the value of the *system clock* as the timestamp; that is, a transaction's timestamp is equal to the value of the clock when the transaction enters the system.

2. Use a **logical counter** that is incremented after a new timestamp has been assigned; that is, a transaction's timestamp is equal to the value of the counter when the transaction enters the system.

The timestamps of the transactions determine the serializability order. Thus, if TS(T_i) < TS(T_j), then the system must ensure that the produced schedule is equivalent to a serial schedule in which transaction T_i appears before transaction T_j.

To implement this scheme, we associate with each data item Q two timestamp values:

- **W-timestamp**(Q) denotes the largest timestamp of any transaction that executed write(Q) successfully.

- **R-timestamp**(Q) denotes the largest timestamp of any transaction that executed read(Q) successfully.

These timestamps are updated whenever a new read(Q) or write(Q) instruction is executed.

16.2.2 The Timestamp-Ordering Protocol

The **timestamp-ordering protocol** ensures that any conflicting read and write operations are executed in timestamp order. This protocol operates as follows:

1. Suppose that transaction T_i issues read(Q).

    a. If TS(T_i) < W-timestamp(Q), then T_i needs to read a value of Q that was already overwritten. Hence, the read operation is rejected, and T_i is rolled back.

    b. If $TS(T_i) \geq$ W-timestamp(Q), then the read operation is executed, and R-timestamp(Q) is set to the maximum of R-timestamp(Q) and $TS(T_i)$.

2. Suppose that transaction T_i issues write(Q).

    a. If $TS(T_i) <$ R-timestamp(Q), then the value of Q that T_i is producing was needed previously, and the system assumed that that value would never be produced. Hence, the system rejects the write operation and rolls T_i back.

    b. If $TS(T_i) <$ W-timestamp(Q), then T_i is attempting to write an obsolete value of Q. Hence, the system rejects this write operation and rolls T_i back.

    c. Otherwise, the system executes the write operation and sets W-timestamp(Q) to $TS(T_i)$.

If a transaction T_i is rolled back by the concurrency-control scheme as result of issuance of either a read or write operation, the system assigns it a new timestamp and restarts it.

To illustrate this protocol, we consider transactions T_{14} and T_{15}. Transaction T_{14} displays the contents of accounts A and B:

$$T_{14}: \text{ read}(B);$$
$$\text{read}(A);$$
$$\text{display}(A + B).$$

Transaction T_{15} transfers \$50 from account A to account B, and then displays the contents of both:

$$T_{15}: \text{ read}(B);$$
$$B := B - 50;$$
$$\text{write}(B);$$
$$\text{read}(A);$$
$$A := A + 50;$$
$$\text{write}(A);$$
$$\text{display}(A + B).$$

In presenting schedules under the timestamp protocol, we shall assume that a transaction is assigned a timestamp immediately before its first instruction. Thus, in schedule 3 of Figure 16.13, $TS(T_{14}) < TS(T_{15})$, and the schedule is possible under the timestamp protocol.

We note that the preceding execution can also be produced by the two-phase locking protocol. There are, however, schedules that are possible under the two-phase locking protocol, but are not possible under the timestamp protocol, and vice versa (see Exercise 16.20).

The timestamp-ordering protocol ensures conflict serializability. This is because conflicting operations are processed in timestamp order.

The protocol ensures freedom from deadlock, since no transaction ever waits. However, there is a possibility of starvation of long transactions if a sequence of conflicting short transactions causes repeated restarting of the long transaction. If

T_{14}	T_{15}
read (B)	
	read (B)
	$B := B - 50$
	write (B)
read (A)	
	read (A)
display ($A + B$)	
	$A := A + 50$
	write (A)
	display ($A + B$)

Figure 16.13   Schedule 3.

a transaction is found to be getting restarted repeatedly, conflicting transactions need to be temporarily blocked to enable the transaction to finish.

The protocol can generate schedules that are not recoverable. However, it can be extended to make the schedules recoverable, in one of several ways:

- Recoverability and cascadelessness can be ensured by performing all writes together at the end of the transaction. The writes must be atomic in the following sense: While the writes are in progress, no transaction is permitted to access any of the data items that have been written.

- Recoverability and cascadelessness can also be guaranteed by using a limited form of locking, whereby reads of uncommitted items are postponed until the transaction that updated the item commits (see Exercise 16.22).

- Recoverability alone can be ensured by tracking uncommitted writes, and allowing a transaction T_i to commit only after the commit of any transaction that wrote a value that T_i read. Commit dependencies, outlined in Section 16.1.5, can be used for this purpose.

16.2.3 Thomas' Write Rule

We now present a modification to the timestamp-ordering protocol that allows greater potential concurrency than does the protocol of Section 16.2.2. Let us consider schedule 4 of Figure 16.14, and apply the timestamp-ordering protocol. Since T_{16} starts before T_{17}, we shall assume that TS(T_{16}) < TS(T_{17}). The read(Q) operation of T_{16} succeeds, as does the write(Q) operation of T_{17}. When T_{16} attempts its write(Q) operation, we find that TS(T_{16}) < W-timestamp(Q), since W-timestamp(Q) = TS(T_{17}). Thus, the write(Q) by T_{16} is rejected and transaction T_{16} must be rolled back.

Although the rollback of T_{16} is required by the timestamp-ordering protocol, it is unnecessary. Since T_{17} has already written Q, the value that T_{16} is attempting to write is one that will never need to be read. Any transaction T_i with TS(T_i) < TS(T_{17}) that attempts a read(Q) will be rolled back, since TS(T_i) < W-timestamp(Q). Any

T_{16}	T_{17}
read(Q)	
	write(Q)
write(Q)	

Figure 16.14   Schedule 4.

transaction T_j with TS(T_j) > TS(T_{17}) must read the value of Q written by T_{17}, rather than the value written by T_{16}.

This observation leads to a modified version of the timestamp-ordering protocol in which obsolete write operations can be ignored under certain circumstances. The protocol rules for read operations remain unchanged. The protocol rules for write operations, however, are slightly different from the timestamp-ordering protocol of Section 16.2.2.

The modification to the timestamp-ordering protocol, called **Thomas' write rule**, is this: Suppose that transaction T_i issues write(Q).

1. If TS(T_i) < R-timestamp(Q), then the value of Q that T_i is producing was previously needed, and it had been assumed that the value would never be produced. Hence, the system rejects the write operation and rolls T_i back.

2. If TS(T_i) < W-timestamp(Q), then T_i is attempting to write an obsolete value of Q. Hence, this write operation can be ignored.

3. Otherwise, the system executes the write operation and sets W-timestamp(Q) to TS(T_i).

The difference between these rules and those of Section 16.2.2 lies in the second rule. The timestamp-ordering protocol requires that T_i be rolled back if T_i issues write(Q) and TS(T_i) < W-timestamp(Q). However, here, in those cases where TS(T_i) ≥ R-timestamp(Q), we ignore the obsolete write.

Thomas' write rule makes use of view serializability by, in effect, deleting obsolete write operations from the transactions that issue them. This modification of transactions makes it possible to generate serializable schedules that would not be possible under the other protocols presented in this chapter. For example, schedule 4 of Figure 16.14 is not conflict serializable and, thus, is not possible under any of two-phase locking, the tree protocol, or the timestamp-ordering protocol. Under Thomas' write rule, the write(Q) operation of T_{16} would be ignored. The result is a schedule that is view equivalent to the serial schedule <T_{16}, T_{17}>.

16.3 Validation-Based Protocols

In cases where a majority of transactions are read-only transactions, the rate of conflicts among transactions may be low. Thus, many of these transactions, if executed without the supervision of a concurrency-control scheme, would nevertheless leave the system in a consistent state. A concurrency-control scheme imposes overhead of code execution and possible delay of transactions. It may be better to use an alternative scheme that imposes less overhead. A difficulty in reducing the overhead is that we do not know in advance which transactions will be involved in a conflict. To gain that knowledge, we need a scheme for **monitoring** the system.

We assume that each transaction T_i executes in two or three different phases in its lifetime, depending on whether it is a read-only or an update transaction. The phases are, in order,

1. **Read phase**. During this phase, the system executes transaction T_i. It reads the values of the various data items and stores them in variables local to T_i. It performs all write operations on temporary local variables, without updates of the actual database.

2. **Validation phase**. Transaction T_i performs a validation test to determine whether it can copy to the database the temporary local variables that hold the results of write operations without causing a violation of serializability.

3. **Write phase**. If transaction T_i succeeds in validation (step 2), then the system applies the actual updates to the database. Otherwise, the system rolls back T_i.

Each transaction must go through the three phases in the order shown. However, all three phases of concurrently executing transactions can be interleaved.

To perform the validation test, we need to know when the various phases of transactions T_i took place. We shall, therefore, associate three different timestamps with transaction T_i:

1. **Start**(T_i), the time when T_i started its execution.

2. **Validation**(T_i), the time when T_i finished its read phase and started its validation phase.

3. **Finish**(T_i), the time when T_i finished its write phase.

We determine the serializability order by the timestamp-ordering technique, using the value of the timestamp Validation(T_i). Thus, the value TS(T_i) = Validation(T_i) and, if TS(T_j) < TS(T_k), then any produced schedule must be equivalent to a serial schedule in which transaction T_j appears before transaction T_k. The reason we have chosen Validation(T_i), rather than Start(T_i), as the timestamp of transaction T_i is that we can expect faster response time provided that conflict rates among transactions are indeed low.

The **validation test** for transaction T_j requires that, for all transactions T_i with TS(T_i) < TS(T_j), one of the following two conditions must hold:

1. Finish(T_i) < Start(T_j). Since T_i completes its execution before T_j started, the serializability order is indeed maintained.

2. The set of data items written by T_i does not intersect with the set of data items read by T_j, and T_i completes its write phase before T_j starts its validation phase (Start(T_j) < Finish(T_i) < Validation(T_j)). This condition ensures that

T_{14}	T_{15}
read(B)	
	read(B)
	$B := B - 50$
	read(A)
	$A := A + 50$
read(A)	
$\langle validate \rangle$	
display$(A + B)$	
	$\langle validate \rangle$
	write(B)
	write(A)

Figure 16.15   Schedule 5, a schedule produced by using validation.

the writes of T_i and T_j do not overlap. Since the writes of T_i do not affect the read of T_j, and since T_j cannot affect the read of T_i, the serializability order is indeed maintained.

As an illustration, consider again transactions T_{14} and T_{15}. Suppose that TS(T_{14}) < TS(T_{15}). Then, the validation phase succeeds in the schedule 5 in Figure 16.15. Note that the writes to the actual variables are performed only after the validation phase of T_{15}. Thus, T_{14} reads the old values of B and A, and this schedule is serializable.

The validation scheme automatically guards against cascading rollbacks, since the actual writes take place only after the transaction issuing the write has committed. However, there is a possibility of starvation of long transactions, due to a sequence of conflicting short transactions that cause repeated restarts of the long transaction. To avoid starvation, conflicting transactions must be temporarily blocked, to enable the long transaction to finish.

This validation scheme is called the **optimistic concurrency control** scheme since transactions execute optimistically, assuming they will be able to finish execution and validate at the end. In contrast, locking and timestamp ordering are pessimistic in that they force a wait or a rollback whenever a conflict is detected, even though there is a chance that the schedule may be conflict serializable.

16.4 Multiple Granularity

In the concurrency-control schemes described thus far, we have used each individual data item as the unit on which synchronization is performed.

There are circumstances, however, where it would be advantageous to group several data items, and to treat them as one individual synchronization unit. For example, if a transaction T_i needs to access the entire database, and a locking protocol is used, then T_i must lock each item in the database. Clearly, executing these locks is time consuming. It would be better if T_i could issue a *single* lock request to lock the

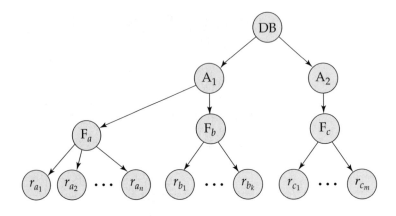

Figure 16.16 Granularity hierarchy.

entire database. On the other hand, if transaction T_j needs to access only a few data items, it should not be required to lock the entire database, since otherwise concurrency is lost.

What is needed is a mechanism to allow the system to define multiple levels of **granularity**. We can make one by allowing data items to be of various sizes and defining a hierarchy of data granularities, where the small granularities are nested within larger ones. Such a hierarchy can be represented graphically as a tree. Note that the tree that we describe here is significantly different from that used by the tree protocol (Section 16.1.5). A nonleaf node of the multiple-granularity tree represents the data associated with its descendants. In the tree protocol, each node is an independent data item.

As an illustration, consider the tree of Figure 16.16, which consists of four levels of nodes. The highest level represents the entire database. Below it are nodes of type *area*; the database consists of exactly these areas. Each area in turn has nodes of type *file* as its children. Each area contains exactly those files that are its child nodes. No file is in more than one area. Finally, each file has nodes of type *record*. As before, the file consists of exactly those records that are its child nodes, and no record can be present in more than one file.

Each node in the tree can be locked individually. As we did in the two-phase locking protocol, we shall use **shared** and **exclusive** lock modes. When a transaction locks a node, in either shared or exclusive mode, the transaction also has implicitly locked all the descendants of that node in the same lock mode. For example, if transaction T_i gets an **explicit lock** on file F_c of Figure 16.16, in exclusive mode, then it has an **implicit lock** in exclusive mode all the records belonging to that file. It does not need to lock the individual records of F_c explicitly.

Suppose that transaction T_j wishes to lock record r_{b_6} of file F_b. Since T_i has locked F_b explicitly, it follows that r_{b_6} is also locked (implicitly). But, when T_j issues a lock request for r_{b_6}, r_{b_6} is not explicitly locked! How does the system determine whether T_j can lock r_{b_6}? T_j must traverse the tree from the root to record r_{b_6}. If any node in that path is locked in an incompatible mode, then T_j must be delayed.

	IS	IX	S	SIX	X
IS	true	true	true	true	false
IX	true	true	false	false	false
S	true	false	true	false	false
SIX	true	false	false	false	false
X	false	false	false	false	false

Figure 16.17   Compatibility matrix.

Suppose now that transaction T_k wishes to lock the entire database. To do so, it simply must lock the root of the hierarchy. Note, however, that T_k should not succeed in locking the root node, since T_i is currently holding a lock on part of the tree (specifically, on file F_b). But how does the system determine if the root node can be locked? One possibility is for it to search the entire tree. This solution, however, defeats the whole purpose of the multiple-granularity locking scheme. A more efficient way to gain this knowledge is to introduce a new class of lock modes, called **intention lock modes**. If a node is locked in an intention mode, explicit locking is being done at a lower level of the tree (that is, at a finer granularity). Intention locks are put on all the ancestors of a node before that node is locked explicitly. Thus, a transaction does not need to search the entire tree to determine whether it can lock a node successfully. A transaction wishing to lock a node—say, Q—must traverse a path in the tree from the root to Q. While traversing the tree, the transaction locks the various nodes in an intention mode.

There is an intention mode associated with shared mode, and there is one with exclusive mode. If a node is locked in **intention-shared (IS) mode**, explicit locking is being done at a lower level of the tree, but with only shared-mode locks. Similarly, if a node is locked in **intention-exclusive (IX) mode**, then explicit locking is being done at a lower level, with exclusive-mode or shared-mode locks. Finally, if a node is locked in **shared and intention-exclusive (SIX) mode**, the subtree rooted by that node is locked explicitly in shared mode, and that explicit locking is being done at a lower level with exclusive-mode locks. The compatibility function for these lock modes is in Figure 16.17.

The **multiple-granularity locking protocol**, which ensures serializability, is this: Each transaction T_i can lock a node Q by following these rules:

1. It must observe the lock-compatibility function of Figure 16.17.

2. It must lock the root of the tree first, and can lock it in any mode.

3. It can lock a node Q in S or IS mode only if it currently has the parent of Q locked in either IX or IS mode.

4. It can lock a node Q in X, SIX, or IX mode only if it currently has the parent of Q locked in either IX or SIX mode.

5. It can lock a node only if it has not previously unlocked any node (that is, T_i is two phase).

6. It can unlock a node Q only if it currently has none of the children of Q locked.

Observe that the multiple-granularity protocol requires that locks be acquired in *top-down* (root-to-leaf) order, whereas locks must be released in *bottom-up* (leaf-to-root) order.

As an illustration of the protocol, consider the tree of Figure 16.16 and these transactions:

- Suppose that transaction T_{18} reads record r_{a_2} in file F_a. Then, T_{18} needs to lock the database, area A_1, and F_a in IS mode (and in that order), and finally to lock r_{a_2} in S mode.

- Suppose that transaction T_{19} modifies record r_{a_9} in file F_a. Then, T_{19} needs to lock the database, area A_1, and file F_a in IX mode, and finally to lock r_{a_9} in X mode.

- Suppose that transaction T_{20} reads all the records in file F_a. Then, T_{20} needs to lock the database and area A_1 (in that order) in IS mode, and finally to lock F_a in S mode.

- Suppose that transaction T_{21} reads the entire database. It can do so after locking the database in S mode.

We note that transactions T_{18}, T_{20}, and T_{21} can access the database concurrently. Transaction T_{19} can execute concurrently with T_{18}, but not with either T_{20} or T_{21}.

This protocol enhances concurrency and reduces lock overhead. It is particularly useful in applications that include a mix of

- Short transactions that access only a few data items

- Long transactions that produce reports from an entire file or set of files

There is a similar locking protocol that is applicable to database systems in which data granularities are organized in the form of a directed acyclic graph. See the bibliographical notes for additional references. Deadlock is possible in the protocol that we have, as it is in the two-phase locking protocol. There are techniques to reduce deadlock frequency in the multiple-granularity protocol, and also to eliminate deadlock entirely. These techniques are referenced in the bibliographical notes.

16.5 Multiversion Schemes

The concurrency-control schemes discussed thus far ensure serializability by either delaying an operation or aborting the transaction that issued the operation. For example, a read operation may be delayed because the appropriate value has not been written yet; or it may be rejected (that is, the issuing transaction must be aborted) because the value that it was supposed to read has already been overwritten. These difficulties could be avoided if old copies of each data item were kept in a system.

In **multiversion concurrency control** schemes, each write(Q) operation creates a new **version** of Q. When a transaction issues a read(Q) operation, the concurrency-control manager selects one of the versions of Q to be read. The concurrency-control scheme must ensure that the version to be read is selected in a manner that ensures serializability. It is also crucial, for performance reasons, that a transaction be able to determine easily and quickly which version of the data item should be read.

16.5.1 Multiversion Timestamp Ordering

The most common transaction ordering technique used by multiversion schemes is timestamping. With each transaction T_i in the system, we associate a unique static timestamp, denoted by $TS(T_i)$. The database system assigns this timestamp before the transaction starts execution, as described in Section 16.2.

With each data item Q, a sequence of versions $<Q_1, Q_2, \ldots, Q_m>$ is associated. Each version Q_k contains three data fields:

- **Content** is the value of version Q_k.

- **W-timestamp**(Q_k) is the timestamp of the transaction that created version Q_k.

- **R-timestamp**(Q_k) is the largest timestamp of any transaction that successfully read version Q_k.

A transaction—say, T_i—creates a new version Q_k of data item Q by issuing a write(Q) operation. The content field of the version holds the value written by T_i. The system initializes the W-timestamp and R-timestamp to $TS(T_i)$. It updates the R-timestamp value of Q_k whenever a transaction T_j reads the content of Q_k, and R-timestamp(Q_k) $< TS(T_j)$.

The **multiversion timestamp-ordering scheme** presented next ensures serializability. The scheme operates as follows. Suppose that transaction T_i issues a read(Q) or write(Q) operation. Let Q_k denote the version of Q whose write timestamp is the largest write timestamp less than or equal to $TS(T_i)$.

1. If transaction T_i issues a read(Q), then the value returned is the content of version Q_k.

2. If transaction T_i issues write(Q), and if $TS(T_i) < $ R-timestamp(Q_k), then the system rolls back transaction T_i. On the other hand, if $TS(T_i) = $ W-timestamp(Q_k), the system overwrites the contents of Q_k; otherwise it creates a new version of Q.

The justification for rule 1 is clear. A transaction reads the most recent version that comes before it in time. The second rule forces a transaction to abort if it is "too late" in doing a write. More precisely, if T_i attempts to write a version that some other transaction would have read, then we cannot allow that write to succeed.

Versions that are no longer needed are removed according to the following rule. Suppose that there are two versions, Q_k and Q_j, of a data item, and that both versions have a W-timestamp less than the timestamp of the oldest transaction in the system. Then, the older of the two versions Q_k and Q_j will not be used again, and can be deleted.

The multiversion timestamp-ordering scheme has the desirable property that a read request never fails and is never made to wait. In typical database systems, where reading is a more frequent operation than is writing, this advantage may be of major practical significance.

The scheme, however, suffers from two undesirable properties. First, the reading of a data item also requires the updating of the R-timestamp field, resulting in two potential disk accesses, rather than one. Second, the conflicts between transactions are resolved through rollbacks, rather than through waits. This alternative may be expensive. Section 16.5.2 describes an algorithm to alleviate this problem.

This multiversion timestamp-ordering scheme does not ensure recoverability and cascadelessness. It can be extended in the same manner as the basic timestamp-ordering scheme, to make it recoverable and cascadeless.

16.5.2 Multiversion Two-Phase Locking

The **multiversion two-phase locking protocol** attempts to combine the advantages of multiversion concurrency control with the advantages of two-phase locking. This protocol differentiates between **read-only transactions** and **update transactions**.

Update transactions perform rigorous two-phase locking; that is, they hold all locks up to the end of the transaction. Thus, they can be serialized according to their commit order. Each version of a data item has a single timestamp. The timestamp in this case is not a real clock-based timestamp, but rather is a counter, which we will call the ts-counter, that is incremented during commit processing.

Read-only transactions are assigned a timestamp by reading the current value of ts-counter before they start execution; they follow the multiversion timestamp-ordering protocol for performing reads. Thus, when a read-only transaction T_i issues a read(Q), the value returned is the contents of the version whose timestamp is the largest timestamp less than $\text{TS}(T_i)$.

When an update transaction reads an item, it gets a shared lock on the item, and reads the latest version of that item. When an update transaction wants to write an item, it first gets an exclusive lock on the item, and then creates a new version of the data item. The write is performed on the new version, and the timestamp of the new version is initially set to a value ∞, a value greater than that of any possible timestamp.

When the update transaction T_i completes its actions, it carries out commit processing: First, T_i sets the timestamp on every version it has created to 1 more than the value of ts-counter; then, T_i increments ts-counter by 1. Only one update transaction is allowed to perform commit processing at a time.

As a result, read-only transactions that start after T_i increments ts-counter will see the values updated by T_i, whereas those that start before T_i increments ts-counter will see the value before the updates by T_i. In either case, read-only transactions never need to wait for locks. Multiversion two-phase locking also ensures that schedules are recoverable and cascadeless.

Versions are deleted in a manner like that of multiversion timestamp ordering. Suppose there are two versions, Q_k and Q_j, of a data item, and that both versions have a timestamp less than the timestamp of the oldest read-only transaction in the system. Then, the older of the two versions Q_k and Q_j will not be used again and can be deleted.

Multiversion two-phase locking or variations of it are used in some commercial database systems.

16.6 Deadlock Handling

A system is in a deadlock state if there exists a set of transactions such that every transaction in the set is waiting for another transaction in the set. More precisely, there exists a set of waiting transactions $\{T_0, T_1, \ldots, T_n\}$ such that T_0 is waiting for a data item that T_1 holds, and T_1 is waiting for a data item that T_2 holds, and ..., and T_{n-1} is waiting for a data item that T_n holds, and T_n is waiting for a data item that T_0 holds. None of the transactions can make progress in such a situation.

The only remedy to this undesirable situation is for the system to invoke some drastic action, such as rolling back some of the transactions involved in the deadlock. Rollback of a transaction may be partial: That is, a transaction may be rolled back to the point where it obtained a lock whose release resolves the deadlock.

There are two principal methods for dealing with the deadlock problem. We can use a **deadlock prevention** protocol to ensure that the system will *never* enter a deadlock state. Alternatively, we can allow the system to enter a deadlock state, and then try to recover by using a **deadlock detection** and **deadlock recovery** scheme. As we shall see, both methods may result in transaction rollback. Prevention is commonly used if the probability that the system would enter a deadlock state is relatively high; otherwise, detection and recovery are more efficient.

Note that a detection and recovery scheme requires overhead that includes not only the run-time cost of maintaining the necessary information and of executing the detection algorithm, but also the potential losses inherent in recovery from a deadlock.

16.6.1 Deadlock Prevention

There are two approaches to deadlock prevention. One approach ensures that no cyclic waits can occur by ordering the requests for locks, or requiring all locks to be acquired together. The other approach is closer to deadlock recovery, and performs transaction rollback instead of waiting for a lock, whenever the wait could potentially result in a deadlock.

The simplest scheme under the first approach requires that each transaction locks all its data items before it begins execution. Moreover, either all are locked in one step or none are locked. There are two main disadvantages to this protocol: (1) it is often hard to predict, before the transaction begins, what data items need to be locked; (2) data-item utilization may be very low, since many of the data items may be locked but unused for a long time.

Another approach for preventing deadlocks is to impose an ordering of all data items, and to require that a transaction lock data items only in a sequence consistent with the ordering. We have seen one such scheme in the tree protocol, which uses a partial ordering of data items.

A variation of this approach is to use a total order of data items, in conjunction with two-phase locking. Once a transaction has locked a particular item, it cannot request locks on items that precede that item in the ordering. This scheme is easy to implement, as long as the set of data items accessed by a transaction is known when the transaction starts execution. There is no need to change the underlying concurrency-control system if two-phase locking is used: All that is needed it to ensure that locks are requested in the right order.

The second approach for preventing deadlocks is to use preemption and transaction rollbacks. In preemption, when a transaction T_2 requests a lock that transaction T_1 holds, the lock granted to T_1 may be **preempted** by rolling back of T_1, and granting of the lock to T_2. To control the preemption, we assign a unique timestamp to each transaction. The system uses these timestamps only to decide whether a transaction should wait or roll back. Locking is still used for concurrency control. If a transaction is rolled back, it retains its *old* timestamp when restarted. Two different deadlock-prevention schemes using timestamps have been proposed:

1. The **wait–die** scheme is a nonpreemptive technique. When transaction T_i requests a data item currently held by T_j, T_i is allowed to wait only if it has a timestamp smaller than that of T_j (that is, T_i is older than T_j). Otherwise, T_i is rolled back (dies).

   For example, suppose that transactions T_{22}, T_{23}, and T_{24} have timestamps 5, 10, and 15, respectively. If T_{22} requests a data item held by T_{23}, then T_{22} will wait. If T_{24} requests a data item held by T_{23}, then T_{24} will be rolled back.

2. The **wound–wait** scheme is a preemptive technique. It is a counterpart to the wait–die scheme. When transaction T_i requests a data item currently held by T_j, T_i is allowed to wait only if it has a timestamp larger than that of T_j (that is, T_i is younger than T_j). Otherwise, T_j is rolled back (T_j is *wounded* by T_i).

   Returning to our example, with transactions T_{22}, T_{23}, and T_{24}, if T_{22} requests a data item held by T_{23}, then the data item will be preempted from T_{23}, and T_{23} will be rolled back. If T_{24} requests a data item held by T_{23}, then T_{24} will wait.

Whenever the system rolls back transactions, it is important to ensure that there is no **starvation**—that is, no transaction gets rolled back repeatedly and is never allowed to make progress.

Both the wound–wait and the wait–die schemes avoid starvation: At any time, there is a transaction with the smallest timestamp. This transaction *cannot* be required to roll back in either scheme. Since timestamps always increase, and since transactions are *not* assigned new timestamps when they are rolled back, a transaction that is rolled back repeatedly will eventually have the smallest timestamp, at which point it will not be rolled back again.

There are, however, significant differences in the way that the two schemes operate.

- In the wait–die scheme, an older transaction must wait for a younger one to release its data item. Thus, the older the transaction gets, the more it tends to wait. By contrast, in the wound–wait scheme, an older transaction never waits for a younger transaction.

- In the wait–die scheme, if a transaction T_i dies and is rolled back because it requested a data item held by transaction T_j, then T_i may reissue the same sequence of requests when it is restarted. If the data item is still held by T_j, then T_i will die again. Thus, T_i may die several times before acquiring the needed data item. Contrast this series of events with what happens in the wound–wait scheme. Transaction T_i is wounded and rolled back because T_j requested a data item that it holds. When T_i is restarted and requests the data item now being held by T_j, T_i waits. Thus, there may be fewer rollbacks in the wound–wait scheme.

The major problem with both of these schemes is that unnecessary rollbacks may occur.

16.6.2   Timeout-Based Schemes

Another simple approach to deadlock handling is based on **lock timeouts**. In this approach, a transaction that has requested a lock waits for at most a specified amount of time. If the lock has not been granted within that time, the transaction is said to time out, and it rolls itself back and restarts. If there was in fact a deadlock, one or more transactions involved in the deadlock will time out and roll back, allowing the others to proceed. This scheme falls somewhere between deadlock prevention, where a deadlock will never occur, and deadlock detection and recovery, which Section 16.6.3 discusses.

The timeout scheme is particularly easy to implement, and works well if transactions are short and if long waits are likely to be due to deadlocks. However, in general it is hard to decide how long a transaction must wait before timing out. Too long a wait results in unnecessary delays once a deadlock has occurred. Too short a wait results in transaction rollback even when there is no deadlock, leading to wasted resources. Starvation is also a possibility with this scheme. Hence, the timeout-based scheme has limited applicability.

16.6.3   Deadlock Detection and Recovery

If a system does not employ some protocol that ensures deadlock freedom, then a detection and recovery scheme must be used. An algorithm that examines the state of the system is invoked periodically to determine whether a deadlock has occurred. If one has, then the system must attempt to recover from the deadlock. To do so, the system must:

- Maintain information about the current allocation of data items to transactions, as well as any outstanding data item requests.

- Provide an algorithm that uses this information to determine whether the system has entered a deadlock state.

- Recover from the deadlock when the detection algorithm determines that a deadlock exists.

In this section, we elaborate on these issues.

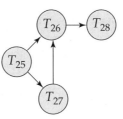

Figure 16.18 Wait-for graph with no cycle.

16.6.3.1 Deadlock Detection

Deadlocks can be described precisely in terms of a directed graph called a **wait-for graph**. This graph consists of a pair $G = (V, E)$, where V is a set of vertices and E is a set of edges. The set of vertices consists of all the transactions in the system. Each element in the set E of edges is an ordered pair $T_i \rightarrow T_j$. If $T_i \rightarrow T_j$ is in E, then there is a directed edge from transaction T_i to T_j, implying that transaction T_i is waiting for transaction T_j to release a data item that it needs.

When transaction T_i requests a data item currently being held by transaction T_j, then the edge $T_i \rightarrow T_j$ is inserted in the wait-for graph. This edge is removed only when transaction T_j is no longer holding a data item needed by transaction T_i.

A deadlock exists in the system if and only if the wait-for graph contains a cycle. Each transaction involved in the cycle is said to be deadlocked. To detect deadlocks, the system needs to maintain the wait-for graph, and periodically to invoke an algorithm that searches for a cycle in the graph.

To illustrate these concepts, consider the wait-for graph in Figure 16.18, which depicts the following situation:

- Transaction T_{25} is waiting for transactions T_{26} and T_{27}.

- Transaction T_{27} is waiting for transaction T_{26}.

- Transaction T_{26} is waiting for transaction T_{28}.

Since the graph has no cycle, the system is not in a deadlock state.

Suppose now that transaction T_{28} is requesting an item held by T_{27}. The edge $T_{28} \rightarrow T_{27}$ is added to the wait-for graph, resulting in the new system state in Figure 16.19. This time, the graph contains the cycle

$$T_{26} \rightarrow T_{28} \rightarrow T_{27} \rightarrow T_{26}$$

implying that transactions T_{26}, T_{27}, and T_{28} are all deadlocked.

Consequently, the question arises: When should we invoke the detection algorithm? The answer depends on two factors:

1. How often does a deadlock occur?

2. How many transactions will be affected by the deadlock?

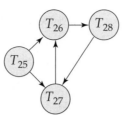

Figure 16.19   Wait-for graph with a cycle.

If deadlocks occur frequently, then the detection algorithm should be invoked more frequently than usual. Data items allocated to deadlocked transactions will be unavailable to other transactions until the deadlock can be broken. In addition, the number of cycles in the graph may also grow. In the worst case, we would invoke the detection algorithm every time a request for allocation could not be granted immediately.

16.6.3.2   Recovery from Deadlock

When a detection algorithm determines that a deadlock exists, the system must **recover** from the deadlock. The most common solution is to roll back one or more transactions to break the deadlock. Three actions need to be taken:

1. **Selection of a victim**. Given a set of deadlocked transactions, we must determine which transaction (or transactions) to roll back to break the deadlock. We should roll back those transactions that will incur the minimum cost. Unfortunately, the term *minimum cost* is not a precise one. Many factors may determine the cost of a rollback, including

    a. How long the transaction has computed, and how much longer the transaction will compute before it completes its designated task.

    b. How many data items the transaction has used.

    c. How many more data items the transaction needs for it to complete.

    d. How many transactions will be involved in the rollback.

2. **Rollback**. Once we have decided that a particular transaction must be rolled back, we must determine how far this transaction should be rolled back.

    The simplest solution is a **total rollback**: Abort the transaction and then restart it. However, it is more effective to roll back the transaction only as far as necessary to break the deadlock. Such **partial rollback** requires the system to maintain additional information about the state of all the running transactions. Specifically, the sequence of lock requests/grants and updates performed by the transaction needs to be recorded. The deadlock detection mechanism should decide which locks the selected transaction needs to release in order to break the deadlock. The selected transaction must be rolled back to the point where it obtained the first of these locks, undoing all actions it took after that point. The recovery mechanism must be capable of performing such partial rollbacks. Furthermore, the transactions must be capable of resuming execution after a partial rollback. See the bibliographical notes for relevant references.

3. **Starvation**. In a system where the selection of victims is based primarily on cost factors, it may happen that the same transaction is always picked as a victim. As a result, this transaction never completes its designated task, thus there is **starvation**. We must ensure that transaction can be picked as a victim only a (small) finite number of times. The most common solution is to include the number of rollbacks in the cost factor.

16.7 Insert and Delete Operations

Until now, we have restricted our attention to read and write operations. This restriction limits transactions to data items already in the database. Some transactions require not only access to existing data items, but also the ability to create new data items. Others require the ability to delete data items. To examine how such transactions affect concurrency control, we introduce these additional operations:

- **delete**(Q) deletes data item Q from the database.

- **insert**(Q) inserts a new data item Q into the database and assigns Q an initial value.

An attempt by a transaction T_i to perform a read(Q) operation after Q has been deleted results in a logical error in T_i. Likewise, an attempt by a transaction T_i to perform a read(Q) operation before Q has been inserted results in a logical error in T_i. It is also a logical error to attempt to delete a nonexistent data item.

16.7.1 Deletion

To understand how the presence of **delete** instructions affects concurrency control, we must decide when a **delete** instruction conflicts with another instruction. Let I_i and I_j be instructions of T_i and T_j, respectively, that appear in schedule S in consecutive order. Let $I_i = $ **delete**(Q). We consider several instructions I_j.

- $I_j = $ read(Q). I_i and I_j conflict. If I_i comes before I_j, T_j will have a logical error. If I_j comes before I_i, T_j can execute the read operation successfully.

- $I_j = $ write(Q). I_i and I_j conflict. If I_i comes before I_j, T_j will have a logical error. If I_j comes before I_i, T_j can execute the write operation successfully.

- $I_j = $ **delete**(Q). I_i and I_j conflict. If I_i comes before I_j, T_i will have a logical error. If I_j comes before I_i, T_i will have a logical error.

- $I_j = $ **insert**(Q). I_i and I_j conflict. Suppose that data item Q did not exist prior to the execution of I_i and I_j. Then, if I_i comes before I_j, a logical error results for T_i. If I_j comes before I_i, then no logical error results. Likewise, if Q existed prior to the execution of I_i and I_j, then a logical error results if I_j comes before I_i, but not otherwise.

We can conclude the following:

- Under the two-phase locking protocol, an exclusive lock is required on a data item before that item can be deleted.

- Under the timestamp-ordering protocol, a test similar to that for a write must be performed. Suppose that transaction T_i issues **delete**(Q).
  - □ If TS(T_i) < R-timestamp(Q), then the value of Q that T_i was to delete has already been read by a transaction T_j with TS(T_j) > TS(T_i). Hence, the **delete** operation is rejected, and T_i is rolled back.
  - □ If TS(T_i) < W-timestamp(Q), then a transaction T_j with TS(T_j) > TS(T_i) has written Q. Hence, this **delete** operation is rejected, and T_i is rolled back.
  - □ Otherwise, the **delete** is executed.

16.7.2   Insertion

We have already seen that an **insert**(Q) operation conflicts with a **delete**(Q) operation. Similarly, **insert**(Q) conflicts with a read(Q) operation or a write(Q) operation; no read or write can be performed on a data item before it exists.

Since an **insert**(Q) assigns a value to data item Q, an **insert** is treated similarly to a write for concurrency-control purposes:

- Under the two-phase locking protocol, if T_i performs an **insert**(Q) operation, T_i is given an exclusive lock on the newly created data item Q.

- Under the timestamp-ordering protocol, if T_i performs an **insert**(Q) operation, the values R-timestamp(Q) and W-timestamp(Q) are set to TS(T_i).

16.7.3   The Phantom Phenomenon

Consider transaction T_{29} that executes the following SQL query on the bank database:

> **select sum**(*balance*)
> **from** *account*
> **where** *branch-name* = 'Perryridge'

Transaction T_{29} requires access to all tuples of the *account* relation pertaining to the Perryridge branch.

Let T_{30} be a transaction that executes the following SQL insertion:

> **insert into** *account*
> **values** (A-201, 'Perryridge', 900)

Let S be a schedule involving T_{29} and T_{30}. We expect there to be potential for a conflict for the following reasons:

- If T_{29} uses the tuple newly inserted by T_{30} in computing **sum**(*balance*), then T_{29} read a value written by T_{30}. Thus, in a serial schedule equivalent to S, T_{30} must come before T_{29}.

- If T_{29} does not use the tuple newly inserted by T_{30} in computing **sum**(*balance*), then in a serial schedule equivalent to S, T_{29} must come before T_{30}.

The second of these two cases is curious. T_{29} and T_{30} do not access any tuple in common, yet they conflict with each other! In effect, T_{29} and T_{30} conflict on a phantom tuple. If concurrency control is performed at the tuple granularity, this conflict would go undetected. This problem is called the **phantom phenomenon**.

To prevent the phantom phenomenon, we allow T_{29} to prevent other transactions from creating new tuples in the *account* relation with *branch-name* = "Perryridge."

To find all *account* tuples with *branch-name* = "Perryridge", T_{29} must search either the whole *account* relation, or at least an index on the relation. Up to now, we have assumed implicitly that the only data items accessed by a transaction are tuples. However, T_{29} is an example of a transaction that reads information about what tuples are in a relation, and T_{30} is an example of a transaction that updates that information.

Clearly, it is not sufficient merely to lock the tuples that are accessed; the information used to find the tuples that are accessed by the transaction must also be locked.

The simplest solution to this problem is to associate a data item with the relation; the data item represents the information used to find the tuples in the relation. Transactions, such as T_{29}, that read the information about what tuples are in a relation would then have to lock the data item corresponding to the relation in shared mode. Transactions, such as T_{30}, that update the information about what tuples are in a relation would have to lock the data item in exclusive mode. Thus, T_{29} and T_{30} would conflict on a real data item, rather than on a phantom.

Do not confuse the locking of an entire relation, as in multiple granularity locking, with the locking of the data item corresponding to the relation. By locking the data item, a transaction only prevents other transactions from updating information about what tuples are in the relation. Locking is still required on tuples. A transaction that directly accesses a tuple can be granted a lock on the tuples even when another transaction has an exclusive lock on the data item corresponding to the relation itself.

The major disadvantage of locking a data item corresponding to the relation is the low degree of concurrency— two transactions that insert different tuples into a relation are prevented from executing concurrently.

A better solution is the **index-locking** technique. Any transaction that inserts a tuple into a relation must insert information into every index maintained on the relation. We eliminate the phantom phenomenon by imposing a locking protocol for indices. For simplicity we shall only consider B^+-tree indices.

As we saw in Chapter 12, every search-key value is associated with an index leaf node. A query will usually use one or more indices to access a relation. An insert must insert the new tuple in all indices on the relation. In our example, we assume that there is an index on *account* for *branch-name*. Then, T_{30} must modify the leaf containing the key Perryridge. If T_{29} reads the same leaf node to locate all tuples pertaining to the Perryridge branch, then T_{29} and T_{30} conflict on that leaf node.

The **index-locking protocol** takes advantage of the availability of indices on a relation, by turning instances of the phantom phenomenon into conflicts on locks on index leaf nodes. The protocol operates as follows:

- Every relation must have at least one index.

- A transaction T_i can access tuples of a relation only after first finding them through one or more of the indices on the relation.

- A transaction T_i that performs a lookup (whether a range lookup or a point lookup) must acquire a shared lock on all the index leaf nodes that it accesses.

- A transaction T_i may not insert, delete, or update a tuple t_i in a relation r without updating all indices on r. The transaction must obtain exclusive locks on all index leaf nodes that are affected by the insertion, deletion, or update. For insertion and deletion, the leaf nodes affected are those that contain (after insertion) or contained (before deletion) the search-key value of the tuple. For updates, the leaf nodes affected are those that (before the modification) contained the old value of the search-key, and nodes that (after the modification) contain the new value of the search-key.

- The rules of the two-phase locking protocol must be observed.

Variants of the index-locking technique exist for eliminating the phantom phenomenon under the other concurrency-control protocols presented in this chapter.

16.8 Weak Levels of Consistency

Serializability is a useful concept because it allows programmers to ignore issues related to concurrency when they code transactions. If every transaction has the property that it maintains database consistency if executed alone, then serializability ensures that concurrent executions maintain consistency. However, the protocols required to ensure serializability may allow too little concurrency for certain applications. In these cases, weaker levels of consistency are used. The use of weaker levels of consistency places additional burdens on programmers for ensuring database correctness.

16.8.1 Degree-Two Consistency

The purpose of **degree-two consistency** is to avoid cascading aborts without necessarily ensuring serializability. The locking protocol for degree-two consistency uses the same two lock modes that we used for the two-phase locking protocol: shared (S) and exclusive (X). A transaction must hold the appropriate lock mode when it accesses a data item.

In contrast to the situation in two-phase locking, S-locks may be released at any time, and locks may be acquired at any time. Exclusive locks cannot be released until the transaction either commits or aborts. Serializability is not ensured by this protocol. Indeed, a transaction may read the same data item twice and obtain different

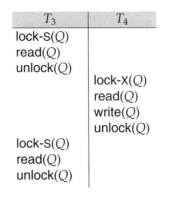

Figure 16.20   Nonserializable schedule with degree-two consistency.

results. In Figure 16.20, T_3 reads the value of Q before and after that value is written by T_4.

The potential for inconsistency due to nonserializable schedules under degree-two consistency makes this approach undesirable for many applications.

16.8.2 Cursor Stability

Cursor stability is a form of degree-two consistency designed for programs written in host languages, which iterate over tuples of a relation by using cursors. Instead of locking the entire relation, cursor stability ensures that

- The tuple that is currently being processed by the iteration is locked in shared mode.

- Any modified tuples are locked in exclusive mode until the transaction commits.

These rules ensure that degree-two consistency is obtained. Two-phase locking is not required. Serializability is not guaranteed. Cursor stability is used in practice on heavily accessed relations as a means of increasing concurrency and improving system performance. Applications that use cursor stability must be coded in a way that ensures database consistency despite the possibility of nonserializable schedules. Thus, the use of cursor stability is limited to specialized situations with simple consistency constraints.

16.8.3 Weak Levels of Consistency in SQL

The SQL standard also allows a transaction to specify that it may be executed in such a way that it becomes nonserializable with respect to other transactions. For instance, a transaction may operate at the level of **read uncommitted**, which permits the transaction to read records even if they have not been committed. SQL provides such features for long transactions whose results do not need to be precise. For instance, approximate information is usually sufficient for statistics used for query optimization. If these transactions were to execute in a serializable fashion, they could interfere with other transactions, causing the others' execution to be delayed.

The levels of consistency specified by SQL-92 are as follows:

- **Serializable** is the default.

- **Repeatable read** allows only committed records to be read, and further requires that, between two reads of a record by a transaction, no other transaction is allowed to update the record. However, the transaction may not be serializable with respect to other transactions. For instance, when it is searching for records satisfying some conditions, a transaction may find some of the records inserted by a committed transaction, but may not find others.

- **Read committed** allows only committed records to be read, but does not require even repeatable reads. For instance, between two reads of a record by the transaction, the records may have been updated by other committed transactions. This is basically the same as degree-two consistency; most systems supporting this level of consistency would actually implement cursor stability, which is a special case of degree-two consistency.

- **Read uncommitted** allows even uncommitted records to be read. It is the lowest level of consistency allowed by SQL-92.

16.9 Concurrency in Index Structures**

It is possible to treat access to index structures like any other database structure, and to apply the concurrency-control techniques discussed earlier. However, since indices are accessed frequently, they would become a point of great lock contention, leading to a low degree of concurrency. Luckily, indices do not have to be treated like other database structures. It is perfectly acceptable for a transaction to perform a lookup on an index twice, and to find that the structure of the index has changed in between, as long as the index lookup returns the correct set of tuples. Thus, it is acceptable to have nonserializable concurrent access to an index, as long as the accuracy of the index is maintained.

We outline two techniques for managing concurrent access to B^+-trees. The bibliographical notes reference other techniques for B^+-trees, as well as techniques for other index structures.

The techniques that we present for concurrency control on B^+-trees are based on locking, but neither two-phase locking nor the tree protocol is employed. The algorithms for lookup, insertion, and deletion are those used in Chapter 12, with only minor modifications.

The first technique is called the **crabbing protocol**:

- When searching for a key value, the crabbing protocol first locks the root node in shared mode. When traversing down the tree, it acquires a shared lock on the child node to be traversed further. After acquiring the lock on the child node, it releases the lock on the parent node. It repeats this process until it reaches a leaf node.

- When inserting or deleting a key value, the crabbing protocol takes these actions:
  - ☐ It follows the same protocol as for searching until it reaches the desired leaf node. Up to this point, it obtains only shared locks.
  - ☐ It locks the leaf node in exclusive mode and inserts or deletes the key value.
  - ☐ If it needs to split a node or coalesce it with its siblings, or redistribute key values between siblings, the crabbing protocol locks the parent of the node in exclusive mode. After performing these actions, it releases the locks on the node and siblings.

    If the parent requires splitting, coalescing, or redistribution of key values, the protcol retains the lock on the parent, and splitting, coalescing, or redistribution propagates further in the same manner. Otherwise, it releases the lock on the parent.

The protocol gets its name from the way in which crabs advance by moving sideways, moving the legs on one side, then the legs on the other, and so on alternately. The progress of locking while the protocol both goes down the tree and goes back up (in case of splits, coalescing, or redistribution) proceeds in a similar crab-like manner.

Once a particular operation releases a lock on a node, other operations can access that node. There is a possibility of deadlocks between search operations coming down the tree, and splits, coalescing or redistribution propagating up the tree. The system can easily handle such deadlocks by restarting the search operation from the root, after releasing the locks held by the operation.

The second technique achieves even more concurrency, avoiding even holding the lock on one node while acquiring the lock on another node, by using a modified version of B^+-trees called **B-link trees**; B-link trees require that every node (including internal nodes, not just the leaves) maintain a pointer to its right sibling. This pointer is required because a lookup that occurs while a node is being split may have to search not only that node but also that node's right sibling (if one exists). We shall illustrate this technique with an example later, but we first present the modified procedures of the **B-link-tree locking protocol**.

- **Lookup**. Each node of the B^+-tree must be locked in shared mode before it is accessed. A lock on a nonleaf node is released before any lock on any other node in the B^+-tree is requested. If a split occurs concurrently with a lookup, the desired search-key value may no longer appear within the range of values represented by a node accessed during lookup. In such a case, the search-key value is in the range represented by a sibling node, which the system locates by following the pointer to the right sibling. However, the system locks leaf nodes following the two-phase locking protocol, as Section 16.7.3 describes, to avoid the phantom phenomenon.

- **Insertion and deletion**. The system follows the rules for lookup to locate the leaf node into which it will make the insertion or deletion. It upgrades the shared-mode lock on this node to exclusive mode, and performs the insertion or deletion. It locks leaf nodes affected by insertion or deletion following the two-phase locking protocol, as Section 16.7.3 describes, to avoid the phantom phenomenon.

- **Split**. If the transaction splits a node, it creates a new node according to the algorithm of Section 12.3 and makes it the right sibling of the original node. The right-sibling pointers of both the original node and the new node are set. Following this, the transaction releases the exclusive lock on the original node and requests an exclusive lock on the parent, so that it can insert a pointer to the new node.

- **Coalescence**. If a node has too few search-key values after a deletion, the node with which it will be coalesced must be locked in exclusive mode. Once the transaction has coalesced these two nodes, it requests an exclusive lock on the parent so that the deleted node can be removed. At this point, the transaction releases the locks on the coalesced nodes. Unless the parent node must be coalesced also, its lock is released.

Observe this important fact: An insertion or deletion may lock a node, unlock it, and subsequently relock it. Furthermore, a lookup that runs concurrently with a split or coalescence operation may find that the desired search key has been moved to the right-sibling node by the split or coalescence operation.

As an illustration, consider the B$^+$-tree in Figure 16.21. Assume that there are two concurrent operations on this B$^+$-tree:

1. Insert "Clearview"

2. Look up "Downtown"

Let us assume that the insertion operation begins first. It does a lookup on "Clearview," and finds that the node into which "Clearview" should be inserted is full. It therefore converts its shared lock on the node to exclusive mode, and creates a new node. The original node now contains the search-key values "Brighton" and "Clearview." The new node contains the search-key value "Downtown."

Now assume that a context switch occurs that results in control passing to the lookup operation. This lookup operation accesses the root, and follows the pointer

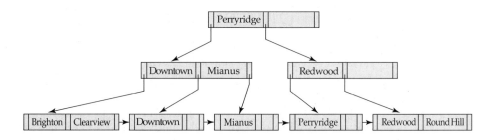

Figure 16.21   B$^+$-tree for *account* file with $n = 3$.

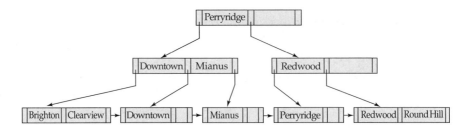

Figure 16.22 Insertion of "Clearview" into the B^+-tree of Figure 16.21.

to the left child of the root. It then accesses that node, and obtains a pointer to the left child. This left-child node originally contained the search-key values "Brighton" and "Downtown." Since this node is currently locked by the insertion operation in exclusive mode, the lookup operation must wait. Note that, at this point, the lookup operation holds no locks at all!

The insertion operation now unlocks the leaf node and relocks its parent, this time in exclusive mode. It completes the insertion, leaving the B^+-tree as in Figure 16.22. The lookup operation proceeds. However, it is holding a pointer to an incorrect leaf node. It therefore follows the right-sibling pointer to locate the next node. If this node, too, turns out to be incorrect, the lookup follows that node's right-sibling pointer. It can be shown that, if a lookup holds a pointer to an incorrect node, then, by following right-sibling pointers, the lookup must eventually reach the correct node.

Lookup and insertion operations cannot lead to deadlock. Coalescing of nodes during deletion can cause inconsistencies, since a lookup may have read a pointer to a deleted node from its parent, before the parent node was updated, and may then try to access the deleted node. The lookup would then have to restart from the root. Leaving nodes uncoalesced avoids such inconsistencies. This solution results in nodes that contain too few search-key values and that violate some properties of B^+-trees. In most databases, however, insertions are more frequent than deletions, so it is likely that nodes that have too few search-key values will gain additional values relatively quickly.

Instead of locking index leaf nodes in a two-phase manner, some index concurrency control schemes use **key-value locking** on individual key values, allowing other key values to be inserted or deleted from the same leaf. Key-value locking thus provides increased concurrency. Using key-value locking naively, however, would allow the phantom phenomenon to occur; to prevent the phantom phenomenon, the **next-key locking** technique is used. In this technique, every index lookup must lock not only the keys found within the range (or the single key, in case of a point lookup) but also the next key value—that is, the key value just greater than the last key value that was within the range. Also, every insert must lock not only the value that is inserted, but also the next key value. Thus, if a transaction attempts to insert a value that was within the range of the index lookup of another transaction, the two transactions would conflict on the key value next to the inserted key value. Similarly, deletes must also lock the next key value to the value being deleted, to ensure that conflicts with subsequent range lookups of other queries are detected.

16.10 Summary

- When several transactions execute concurrently in the database, the consistency of data may no longer be preserved. It is necessary for the system to control the interaction among the concurrent transactions, and this control is achieved through one of a variety of mechanisms called *concurrency-control* schemes.

- To ensure serializability, we can use various concurrency-control schemes. All these schemes either delay an operation or abort the transaction that issued the operation. The most common ones are locking protocols, timestamp-ordering schemes, validation techniques, and multiversion schemes.

- A locking protocol is a set of rules that state when a transaction may lock and unlock each of the data items in the database.

- The two-phase locking protocol allows a transaction to lock a new data item only if that transaction has not yet unlocked any data item. The protocol ensures serializability, but not deadlock freedom. In the absence of information concerning the manner in which data items are accessed, the two-phase locking protocol is both necessary and sufficient for ensuring serializability.

- The strict two-phase locking protocol permits release of exclusive locks only at the end of transaction, in order to ensure recoverability and cascadelessness of the resulting schedules. The rigorous two-phase locking protocol releases all locks only at the end of the transaction.

- A timestamp-ordering scheme ensures serializability by selecting an ordering in advance between every pair of transactions. A unique fixed timestamp is associated with each transaction in the system. The timestamps of the transactions determine the serializability order. Thus, if the timestamp of transaction T_i is smaller than the timestamp of transaction T_j, then the scheme ensures that the produced schedule is equivalent to a serial schedule in which transaction T_i appears before transaction T_j. It does so by rolling back a transaction whenever such an order is violated.

- A validation scheme is an appropriate concurrency-control method in cases where a majority of transactions are read-only transactions, and thus the rate of conflicts among these transactions is low. A unique fixed timestamp is associated with each transaction in the system. The serializability order is determined by the timestamp of the transaction. A transaction in this scheme is never delayed. It must, however, pass a validation test to complete. If it does not pass the validation test, the system rolls it back to its initial state.

- There are circumstances where it would be advantageous to group several data items, and to treat them as one aggregate data item for purposes of working, resulting in multiple levels of granularity. We allow data items of various sizes, and define a hierarchy of data items, where the small items are nested within larger ones. Such a hierarchy can be represented graphically as a tree.

Locks are acquired in root-to-leaf order; they are released in leaf-to-root order. The protocol ensures serializability, but not freedom from deadlock.

- A multiversion concurrency-control scheme is based on the creation of a new version of a data item for each transaction that writes that item. When a read operation is issued, the system selects one of the versions to be read. The concurrency-control scheme ensures that the version to be read is selected in a manner that ensures serializability, by using timestamps. A read operation always succeeds.
  - ☐ In multiversion timestamp ordering, a write operation may result in the rollback of the transaction.
  - ☐ In multiversion two-phase locking, write operations may result in a lock wait or, possibly, in deadlock.

- Various locking protocols do not guard against deadlocks. One way to prevent deadlock is to use an ordering of data items, and to request locks in a sequence consistent with the ordering.

- Another way to prevent deadlock is to use preemption and transaction rollbacks. To control the preemption, we assign a unique timestamp to each transaction. The system uses these timestamps to decide whether a transaction should wait or roll back. If a transaction is rolled back, it retains its old timestamp when restarted. The wound–wait scheme is a preemptive scheme.

- If deadlocks are not prevented, the system must deal with them by using a deadlock detection and recovery scheme. To do so, the system constructs a wait-for graph. A system is in a deadlock state if and only if the wait-for graph contains a cycle. When the deadlock detection algorithm determines that a deadlock exists, the system must recover from the deadlock. It does so by rolling back one or more transactions to break the deadlock.

- A **delete** operation may be performed only if the transaction deleting the tuple has an exclusive lock on the tuple to be deleted. A transaction that inserts a new tuple into the database is given an exclusive lock on the tuple.

- Insertions can lead to the phantom phenomenon, in which an insertion logically conflicts with a query even though the two transactions may access no tuple in common. Such conflict cannot be detected if locking is done only on tuples accessed by the transactions. Locking is required on the data used to find the tuples in the relation. The index-locking technique solves this problem by requiring locks on certain index buckets. These locks ensure that all conflicting transactions conflict on a real data item, rather than on a phantom.

- Weak levels of consistency are used in some applications where consistency of query results is not critical, and using serializability would result in queries adversely affecting transaction processing. Degree-two consistency is one such weaker level of consistency; cursor stability is a special case of degree-two consistency, and is widely used. SQL:1999 allows queries to specify the level of consistency that they require.

- Special concurrency-control techniques can be developed for special data structures. Often, special techniques are applied in B^+-trees to allow greater concurrency. These techniques allow nonserializable access to the B^+-tree, but they ensure that the B^+-tree structure is correct, and ensure that accesses to the database itself are serializable.

Review Terms

- Concurrency control
- Lock types
  - □ Shared-mode (S) lock
  - □ Exclusive-mode (X) lock
- Lock
  - □ Compatibility
  - □ Request
  - □ Wait
  - □ Grant
- Deadlock
- Starvation
- Locking protocol
- Legal schedule
- Two-phase locking protocol
  - □ Growing phase
  - □ Shrinking phase
  - □ Lock point
  - □ Strict two-phase locking
  - □ Rigorous two-phase locking
- Lock conversion
  - □ Upgrade
  - □ Downgrade
- Graph-based protocols
  - □ Tree protocol
  - □ Commit dependency
- Timestamp-based protocols
- Timestamp
  - □ System clock
  - □ Logical counter
  - □ W-timestamp(Q)
  - □ R-timestamp(Q)
- Timestamp-ordering protocol

- □ Thomas' write rule
- Validation-based protocols
  - □ Read phase
  - □ Validation phase
  - □ Write phase
  - □ Validation test
- Multiple granularity
  - □ Explicit locks
  - □ Implicit locks
  - □ Intention locks
- Intention lock modes
  - □ Intention-shared (IS)
  - □ Intention-exclusive (IX)
  - □ Shared and intention-exclusive (SIX)
- Multiple-granularity locking protocol
- Multiversion concurrency control
- Versions
- Multiversion timestamp ordering
- Multiversion two-phase locking
  - □ Read-only transactions
  - □ Update transactions
- Deadlock handling
  - □ Prevention
  - □ Detection
  - □ Recovery
- Deadlock prevention
  - □ Ordered locking
  - □ Preemption of locks
  - □ Wait–die scheme
  - □ Wound–wait scheme
  - □ Timeout-based schemes

- Deadlock detection
    - ☐ Wait-for graph
- Deadlock recovery
    - ☐ Total rollback
    - ☐ Partial rollback
- Insert and delete operations
- Phantom phenomenon
    - ☐ Index-locking protocol
- Weak levels of consistency

- ☐ Degree-two consistency
- ☐ Cursor stability
- ☐ Repeatable read
- ☐ Read committed
- ☐ Read uncommitted
- Concurrency in indices
    - ☐ Crabbing
    - ☐ B-link trees
    - ☐ B-link-tree locking protocol
    - ☐ Next-key locking

Exercises

16.1 Show that the two-phase locking protocol ensures conflict serializability, and that transactions can be serialized according to their lock points.

16.2 Consider the following two transactions:

$$T_{31}: \text{read}(A);$$
$$\text{read}(B);$$
$$\textbf{if } A = 0 \textbf{ then } B := B + 1;$$
$$\text{write}(B).$$

$$T_{32}: \text{read}(B);$$
$$\text{read}(A);$$
$$\textbf{if } B = 0 \textbf{ then } A := A + 1;$$
$$\text{write}(A).$$

Add lock and unlock instructions to transactions T_{31} and T_{32}, so that they observe the two-phase locking protocol. Can the execution of these transactions result in a deadlock?

16.3 What benefit does strict two-phase locking provide? What disadvantages result?

16.4 What benefit does rigorous two-phase locking provide? How does it compare with other forms of two-phase locking?

16.5 Most implementations of database systems use strict two-phase locking. Suggest three reasons for the popularity of this protocol.

16.6 Consider a database organized in the form of a rooted tree. Suppose that we insert a dummy vertex between each pair of vertices. Show that, if we follow the tree protocol on the new tree, we get better concurrency than if we follow the tree protocol on the original tree.

16.7 Show by example that there are schedules possible under the tree protocol that are not possible under the two-phase locking protocol, and vice versa.

16.8 Consider the following extension to the tree-locking protocol, which allows both shared and exclusive locks:

- A transaction can be either a read-only transaction, in which case it can request only shared locks, or an update transaction, in which case it can request only exclusive locks.
- Each transaction must follow the rules of the tree protocol. Read-only transactions may lock any data item first, whereas update transactions must lock the root first.

Show that the protocol ensures serializability and deadlock freedom.

16.9 Consider the following graph-based locking protocol, which allows only exclusive lock modes, and which operates on data graphs that are in the form of a rooted directed acyclic graph.

- A transaction can lock any vertex first.
- To lock any other vertex, the transaction must be holding a lock on the majority of the parents of that vertex.

Show that the protocol ensures serializability and deadlock freedom.

16.10 Consider the following graph-based locking protocol that allows only exclusive lock modes, and that operates on data graphs that are in the form of a rooted directed acyclic graph.

- A transaction can lock any vertex first.
- To lock any other vertex, the transaction must have visited all the parents of that vertex, and must be holding a lock on one of the parents of the vertex.

Show that the protocol ensures serializability and deadlock freedom.

16.11 Consider a variant of the tree protocol called the *forest* protocol. The database is organized as a forest of rooted trees. Each transaction T_i must follow the following rules:

- The first lock in each tree may be on any data item.
- The second, and all subsequent, locks in a tree may be requested only if the parent of the requested node is currently locked.
- Data items may be unlocked at any time.
- A data item may not be relocked by T_i after it has been unlocked by T_i.

Show that the forest protocol does *not* ensure serializability.

16.12 Locking is not done explicitly in persistent programming languages. Rather, objects (or the corresponding pages) must be locked when the objects are accessed. Most modern operating systems allow the user to set access protections (no access, read, write) on pages, and memory access that violate the access protections result in a protection violation (see the Unix `mprotect` command, for example). Describe how the access-protection mechanism can be

	S	X	I
S	true	false	false
X	false	false	false
I	false	false	true

Figure 16.23   Lock-compatibility matrix.

used for page-level locking in a persistent programming language. (Hint: The technique is similar to that used for hardware swizzling in Section 11.9.4).

16.13 Consider a database system that includes an atomic **increment** operation, in addition to the read and write operations. Let V be the value of data item X. The operation

$$\text{increment}(X) \text{ by } C$$

sets the value of X to $V + C$ in an atomic step. The value of X is not available to the transaction unless the latter executes a read(X). Figure 16.23 shows a lock-compatibility matrix for three lock modes: share mode, exclusive mode, and incrementation mode.

   a. Show that, if all transactions lock the data that they access in the corresponding mode, then two-phase locking ensures serializability.

   b. Show that the inclusion of **increment** mode locks allows for increased concurrency. (Hint: Consider check-clearing transactions in our bank example.)

16.14 In timestamp ordering, **W-timestamp**(Q) denotes the largest timestamp of any transaction that executed write(Q) successfully. Suppose that, instead, we defined it to be the timestamp of the most recent transaction to execute write(Q) successfully. Would this change in wording make any difference? Explain your answer.

16.15 When a transaction is rolled back under timestamp ordering, it is assigned a new timestamp. Why can it not simply keep its old timestamp?

16.16 In multiple-granularity locking, what is the difference between implicit and explicit locking?

16.17 Although SIX mode is useful in multiple-granularity locking, an exclusive and intend-shared (XIS) mode is of no use. Why is it useless?

16.18 Use of multiple-granularity locking may require more or fewer locks than an equivalent system with a single lock granularity. Provide examples of both situations, and compare the relative amount of concurrency allowed.

16.19 Consider the validation-based concurrency-control scheme of Section 16.3. Show that by choosing Validation(T_i), rather than Start(T_i), as the timestamp of transaction T_i, we can expect better response time provided that conflict rates among transactions are indeed low.

16.20 Show that there are schedules that are possible under the two-phase locking protocol, but are not possible under the timestamp protocol, and vice versa.

16.21 For each of the following protocols, describe aspects of practical applications that would lead you to suggest using the protocol, and aspects that would suggest not using the protocol:
- Two-phase locking
- Two-phase locking with multiple-granularity locking
- The tree protocol
- Timestamp ordering
- Validation
- Multiversion timestamp ordering
- Multiversion two-phase locking

16.22 Under a modified version of the timestamp protocol, we require that a commit bit be tested to see whether a **read** request must wait. Explain how the commit bit can prevent cascading abort. Why is this test not necessary for **write** requests?

16.23 Explain why the following technique for transaction execution may provide better performance than just using strict two-phase locking: First execute the transaction without acquiring any locks and without performing any writes to the database as in the validation based techniques, but unlike in the validation techniques do not perform either validation or perform writes on the database. Instead, rerun the transaction using strict two-phase locking. (Hint: Consider waits for disk I/O.)

16.24 Under what conditions is it less expensive to avoid deadlock than to allow deadlocks to occur and then to detect them?

16.25 If deadlock is avoided by deadlock avoidance schemes, is starvation still possible? Explain your answer.

16.26 Consider the timestamp ordering protocol, and two transactions, one that writes two data items p and q, and another that reads the same two data items. Give a schedule whereby the timestamp test for a **write** operation fails and causes the first transaction to be restarted, in turn causing a cascading abort of the other transaction. Show how this could result in starvation of both transactions. (Such a situation, where two or more processes carry out actions, but are unable to complete their task because of interaction with the other processes, is called a **livelock**.)

16.27 Explain the phantom phenomenon. Why may this phenomenon lead to an incorrect concurrent execution despite the use of the two-phase locking protocol?

16.28 Devise a timestamp-based protocol that avoids the phantom phenomenon.

16.29 Explain the reason for the use of degree-two consistency. What disadvantages does this approach have?

16.30 Suppose that we use the tree protocol of Section 16.1.5 to manage concurrent access to a B^+-tree. Since a split may occur on an insert that affects the root, it appears that an insert operation cannot release any locks until it has completed the entire operation. Under what circumstances is it possible to release a lock earlier?

16.31 Give example schedules to show that if any of lookup, insert or delete do not lock the next key value, the phantom phenomemon could go undetected.

Bibliographical Notes

Gray and Reuter [1993] provides detailed textbook coverage of transaction-processing concepts, including concurrency control concepts and implementation details. Bernstein and Newcomer [1997] provides textbook coverage of various aspects of transaction processing including concurrency control.

Early textbook discussions of concurrency control and recovery included Papadimitriou [1986] and Bernstein et al. [1987]. An early survey paper on implementation issues in concurrency control and recovery is presented by Gray [1978].

The two-phase locking protocol was introduced by Eswaran et al. [1976]. The tree-locking protocol is from Silberschatz and Kedem [1980]. Other non-two-phase locking protocols that operate on more general graphs are described in Yannakakis et al. [1979], Kedem and Silberschatz [1983], and Buckley and Silberschatz [1985]. General discussions concerning locking protocols are offered by Lien and Weinberger [1978], Yannakakis et al. [1979], Yannakakis [1981], and Papadimitriou [1982]. Korth [1983] explores various lock modes that can be obtained from the basic shared and exclusive lock modes.

Exercise 16.6 is from Buckley and Silberschatz [1984]. Exercise 16.8 is from Kedem and Silberschatz [1983]. Exercise 16.9 is from Kedem and Silberschatz [1979]. Exercise 16.10 is from Yannakakis et al. [1979]. Exercise 16.13 is from Korth [1983].

The timestamp-based concurrency-control scheme is from Reed [1983]. An exposition of various timestamp-based concurrency-control algorithms is presented by Bernstein and Goodman [1980]. A timestamp algorithm that does not require any rollback to ensure serializability is presented by Buckley and Silberschatz [1983]. The validation concurrency-control scheme is from Kung and Robinson [1981].

The locking protocol for multiple-granularity data items is from Gray et al. [1975]. A detailed description is presented by Gray et al. [1976]. The effects of locking granularity are discussed by Ries and Stonebraker [1977]. Korth [1983] formalizes multiple-granularity locking for an arbitrary collection of lock modes (allowing for more semantics than simply read and write). This approach includes a class of lock modes called *update* modes to deal with lock conversion. Carey [1983] extends the multiple-granularity idea to timestamp-based concurrency control. An extension of the protocol to ensure deadlock freedom is presented by Korth [1982]. Multiple-granularity locking for object-oriented database systems is discussed in Lee and Liou [1996].

Discussions concerning multiversion concurrency control are offered by Bernstein et al. [1983]. A multiversion tree-locking algorithm appears in Silberschatz [1982].

Multiversion timestamp order was introduced in Reed [1978] and Reed [1983]. Lai and Wilkinson [1984] describes a multiversion two-phase locking certifier.

Dijkstra [1965] was one of the first and most influential contributors in the deadlock area. Holt [1971] and Holt [1972] were the first to formalize the notion of deadlocks in terms of a graph model similar to the one presented in this chapter. An analysis of the probability of waiting and deadlock is presented by Gray et al. [1981a]. Theoretical results concerning deadlocks and serializability are presented by Fussell et al. [1981] and Yannakakis [1981]. Cycle-detection algorithms can be found in standard algorithm textbooks, such as Cormen et al. [1990].

Degree-two consistency was introduced in Gray et al. [1975]. The levels of consistency—or isolation—offered in SQL are explained and critiqued in Berenson et al. [1995].

Concurrency in B^+-trees was studied by Bayer and Schkolnick [1977] and Johnson and Shasha [1993]. The techniques presented in Section 16.9 are based on Kung and Lehman [1980] and Lehman and Yao [1981]. The technique of key-value locking used in ARIES provides for very high concurrency on B^+-tree access, and is described in Mohan [1990a] and Mohan and Levine [1992].

Shasha and Goodman [1988] presents a good characterization of concurrency protocols for index structures. Ellis [1987] presents a concurrency-control technique for linear hashing. Lomet and Salzberg [1992] present some extensions of B-link trees. Concurrency-control algorithms for other index structures appear in Ellis [1980a] and Ellis [1980b].

Recovery System

A computer system, like any other device, is subject to failure from a variety of causes: disk crash, power outage, software error, a fire in the machine room, even sabotage. In any failure, information may be lost. Therefore, the database system must take actions in advance to ensure that the atomicity and durability properties of transactions, introduced in Chapter 15, are preserved. An integral part of a database system is a **recovery scheme** that can restore the database to the consistent state that existed before the failure. The recovery scheme must also provide **high availability**; that is, it must minimize the time for which the database is not usable after a crash.

17.1 Failure Classification

There are various types of failure that may occur in a system, each of which needs to be dealt with in a different manner. The simplest type of failure is one that does not result in the loss of information in the system. The failures that are more difficult to deal with are those that result in loss of information. In this chapter, we shall consider only the following types of failure:

- **Transaction failure.** There are two types of errors that may cause a transaction to fail:
  - ☐ **Logical error.** The transaction can no longer continue with its normal execution because of some internal condition, such as bad input, data not found, overflow, or resource limit exceeded.
  - ☐ **System error.** The system has entered an undesirable state (for example, deadlock), as a result of which a transaction cannot continue with its normal execution. The transaction, however, can be reexecuted at a later time.

- **System crash.** There is a hardware malfunction, or a bug in the database software or the operating system, that causes the loss of the content of volatile storage, and brings transaction processing to a halt. The content of nonvolatile storage remains intact, and is not corrupted.

The assumption that hardware errors and bugs in the software bring the system to a halt, but do not corrupt the nonvolatile storage contents, is known as the **fail-stop assumption**. Well-designed systems have numerous internal checks, at the hardware and the software level, that bring the system to a halt when there is an error. Hence, the fail-stop assumption is a reasonable one.

- **Disk failure**. A disk block loses its content as a result of either a head crash or failure during a data transfer operation. Copies of the data on other disks, or archival backups on tertiary media, such as tapes, are used to recover from the failure.

To determine how the system should recover from failures, we need to identify the failure modes of those devices used for storing data. Next, we must consider how these failure modes affect the contents of the database. We can then propose algorithms to ensure database consistency and transaction atomicity despite failures. These algorithms, known as recovery algorithms, have two parts:

1. Actions taken during normal transaction processing to ensure that enough information exists to allow recovery from failures.

2. Actions taken after a failure to recover the database contents to a state that ensures database consistency, transaction atomicity, and durability.

17.2 Storage Structure

As we saw in Chapter 11, the various data items in the database may be stored and accessed in a number of different storage media. To understand how to ensure the atomicity and durability properties of a transaction, we must gain a better understanding of these storage media and their access methods.

17.2.1 Storage Types

In Chapter 11 we saw that storage media can be distinguished by their relative speed, capacity, and resilience to failure, and classified as volatile storage or nonvolatile storage. We review these terms, and introduce another class of storage, called stable storage.

- **Volatile storage**. Information residing in volatile storage does not usually survive system crashes. Examples of such storage are main memory and cache memory. Access to volatile storage is extremely fast, both because of the speed of the memory access itself, and because it is possible to access any data item in volatile storage directly.

- **Nonvolatile storage**. Information residing in nonvolatile storage survives system crashes. Examples of such storage are disk and magnetic tapes. Disks are used for online storage, whereas tapes are used for archival storage. Both, however, are subject to failure (for example, head crash), which may result in loss of information. At the current state of technology, nonvolatile storage is slower than volatile storage by several orders of magnitude. This is because disk and tape devices are electromechanical, rather than based entirely on chips, as is volatile storage. In database systems, disks are used for most nonvolatile storage. Other nonvolatile media are normally used only for backup data. Flash storage (see Section 11.1), though nonvolatile, has insufficient capacity for most database systems.

- **Stable storage**. Information residing in stable storage is *never* lost (*never* should be taken with a grain of salt, since theoretically *never* cannot be guaranteed—for example, it is possible, although extremely unlikely, that a black hole may envelop the earth and permanently destroy all data!). Although stable storage is theoretically impossible to obtain, it can be closely approximated by techniques that make data loss extremely unlikely. Section 17.2.2 discusses stable-storage implementation.

The distinctions among the various storage types are often less clear in practice than in our presentation. Certain systems provide battery backup, so that some main memory can survive system crashes and power failures. Alternative forms of nonvolatile storage, such as optical media, provide an even higher degree of reliability than do disks.

17.2.2   Stable-Storage Implementation

To implement stable storage, we need to replicate the needed information in several nonvolatile storage media (usually disk) with independent failure modes, and to update the information in a controlled manner to ensure that failure during data transfer does not damage the needed information.

Recall (from Chapter 11) that RAID systems guarantee that the failure of a single disk (even during data transfer) will not result in loss of data. The simplest and fastest form of RAID is the mirrored disk, which keeps two copies of each block, on separate disks. Other forms of RAID offer lower costs, but at the expense of lower performance.

RAID systems, however, cannot guard against data loss due to disasters such as fires or flooding. Many systems store archival backups of tapes off-site to guard against such disasters. However, since tapes cannot be carried off-site continually, updates since the most recent time that tapes were carried off-site could be lost in such a disaster. More secure systems keep a copy of each block of stable storage at a remote site, writing it out over a computer network, in addition to storing the block on a local disk system. Since the blocks are output to a remote system as and when they are output to local storage, once an output operation is complete, the output is not lost, even in the event of a disaster such as a fire or flood. We study such *remote backup* systems in Section 17.10.

In the remainder of this section, we discuss how storage media can be protected from failure during data transfer. Block transfer between memory and disk storage can result in

- **Successful completion**. The transferred information arrived safely at its destination.

- **Partial failure**. A failure occurred in the midst of transfer, and the destination block has incorrect information.

- **Total failure**. The failure occurred sufficiently early during the transfer that the destination block remains intact.

We require that, if a **data-transfer failure** occurs, the system detects it and invokes a recovery procedure to restore the block to a consistent state. To do so, the system must maintain two physical blocks for each logical database block; in the case of mirrored disks, both blocks are at the same location; in the case of remote backup, one of the blocks is local, whereas the other is at a remote site. An output operation is executed as follows:

1. Write the information onto the first physical block.

2. When the first write completes successfully, write the same information onto the second physical block.

3. The output is completed only after the second write completes successfully.

During recovery, the system examines each pair of physical blocks. If both are the same and no detectable error exists, then no further actions are necessary. (Recall that errors in a disk block, such as a partial write to the block, are detected by storing a checksum with each block.) If the system detects an error in one block, then it replaces its content with the content of the other block. If both blocks contain no detectable error, but they differ in content, then the system replaces the content of the first block with the value of the second. This recovery procedure ensures that a write to stable storage either succeeds completely (that is, updates all copies) or results in no change.

The requirement of comparing every corresponding pair of blocks during recovery is expensive to meet. We can reduce the cost greatly by keeping track of block writes that are in progress, using a small amount of nonvolatile RAM. On recovery, only blocks for which writes were in progress need to be compared.

The protocols for writing out a block to a remote site are similar to the protocols for writing blocks to a mirrored disk system, which we examined in Chapter 11, and particularly in Exercise 11.4.

We can extend this procedure easily to allow the use of an arbitrarily large number of copies of each block of stable storage. Although a large number of copies reduces the probability of a failure to even lower than two copies do, it is usually reasonable to simulate stable storage with only two copies.

17.2.3 Data Access

As we saw in Chapter 11, the database system resides permanently on nonvolatile storage (usually disks), and is partitioned into fixed-length storage units called **blocks**. Blocks are the units of data transfer to and from disk, and may contain several data

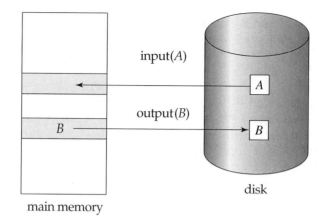

Figure 17.1   Block storage operations.

items. We shall assume that no data item spans two or more blocks. This assumption is realistic for most data-processing applications, such as our banking example.

Transactions input information from the disk to main memory, and then output the information back onto the disk. The input and output operations are done in block units. The blocks residing on the disk are referred to as **physical blocks**; the blocks residing temporarily in main memory are referred to as **buffer blocks**. The area of memory where blocks reside temporarily is called the **disk buffer**.

Block movements between disk and main memory are initiated through the following two operations:

1. input(B) transfers the physical block B to main memory.

2. output(B) transfers the buffer block B to the disk, and replaces the appropriate physical block there.

Figure 17.1 illustrates this scheme.

Each transaction T_i has a private work area in which copies of all the data items accessed and updated by T_i are kept. The system creates this work area when the transaction is initiated; the system removes it when the transaction either commits or aborts. Each data item X kept in the work area of transaction T_i is denoted by x_i. Transaction T_i interacts with the database system by transferring data to and from its work area to the system buffer. We transfer data by these two operations:

1. read(X) assigns the value of data item X to the local variable x_i. It executes this operation as follows:

   a. If block B_X on which X resides is not in main memory, it issues input(B_X).
   b. It assigns to x_i the value of X from the buffer block.

2. write(X) assigns the value of local variable x_i to data item X in the buffer block. It executes this operation as follows:

   a. If block B_X on which X resides is not in main memory, it issues input(B_X).
   b. It assigns the value of x_i to X in buffer B_X.

Note that both operations may require the transfer of a block from disk to main memory. They do not, however, specifically require the transfer of a block from main memory to disk.

A buffer block is eventually written out to the disk either because the buffer manager needs the memory space for other purposes or because the database system wishes to reflect the change to B on the disk. We shall say that the database system performs a **force-output** of buffer B if it issues an output(B).

When a transaction needs to access a data item X for the first time, it must execute read(X). The system then performs all updates to X on x_i. After the transaction accesses X for the final time, it must execute write(X) to reflect the change to X in the database itself.

The output(B_X) operation for the buffer block B_X on which X resides does not need to take effect immediately after write(X) is executed, since the block B_X may contain other data items that are still being accessed. Thus, the actual output may take place later. Notice that, if the system crashes after the write(X) operation was executed but before output(B_X) was executed, the new value of X is never written to disk and, thus, is lost.

17.3 Recovery and Atomicity

Consider again our simplified banking system and transaction T_i that transfers $50 from account A to account B, with initial values of A and B being $1000 and $2000, respectively. Suppose that a system crash has occurred during the execution of T_i, after output(B_A) has taken place, but before output(B_B) was executed, where B_A and B_B denote the buffer blocks on which A and B reside. Since the memory contents were lost, we do not know the fate of the transaction; thus, we could invoke one of two possible recovery procedures:

- **Reexecute** T_i. This procedure will result in the value of A becoming $900, rather than $950. Thus, the system enters an inconsistent state.

- **Do not reexecute** T_i. The current system state has values of $950 and $2000 for A and B, respectively. Thus, the system enters an inconsistent state.

In either case, the database is left in an inconsistent state, and thus this simple recovery scheme does not work. The reason for this difficulty is that we have modified the database without having assurance that the transaction will indeed commit. Our goal is to perform either all or no database modifications made by T_i. However, if T_i performed multiple database modifications, several output operations may be required, and a failure may occur after some of these modifications have been made, but before all of them are made.

To achieve our goal of atomicity, we must first output information describing the modifications to stable storage, without modifying the database itself. As we shall see, this procedure will allow us to output all the modifications made by a committed transaction, despite failures. There are two ways to perform such outputs; we study them in Sections 17.4 and 17.5. In these two sections, we shall assume that *transactions are executed serially*; in other words, only a single transaction is active at a time. We shall describe how to handle concurrently executing transactions later, in Section 17.6.

17.4 Log-Based Recovery

The most widely used structure for recording database modifications is the **log**. The log is a sequence of **log records**, recording all the update activities in the database. There are several types of log records. An **update log record** describes a single database write. It has these fields:

- **Transaction identifier** is the unique identifier of the transaction that performed the write operation.

- **Data-item identifier** is the unique identifier of the data item written. Typically, it is the location on disk of the data item.

- **Old value** is the value of the data item prior to the write.

- **New value** is the value that data item will have after the write.

Other special log records exist to record significant events during transaction processing, such as the start of a transaction and the commit or abort of a transaction. We denote the various types of log records as:

- $<T_i \text{ start}>$. Transaction T_i has started.

- $<T_i, X_j, V_1, V_2>$. Transaction T_i has performed a write on data item X_j. X_j had value V_1 before the write, and will have value V_2 after the write.

- $<T_i \text{ commit}>$. Transaction T_i has committed.

- $<T_i \text{ abort}>$. Transaction T_i has aborted.

Whenever a transaction performs a write, it is essential that the log record for that write be created before the database is modified. Once a log record exists, we can output the modification to the database if that is desirable. Also, we have the ability to *undo* a modification that has already been output to the database. We undo it by using the old-value field in log records.

For log records to be useful for recovery from system and disk failures, the log must reside in stable storage. For now, we assume that every log record is written to the end of the log on stable storage as soon as it is created. In Section 17.7, we shall see when it is safe to relax this requirement so as to reduce the overhead imposed by logging. In Sections 17.4.1 and 17.4.2, we shall introduce two techniques for using the log to ensure transaction atomicity despite failures. Observe that the log contains a complete record of all database activity. As a result, the volume of data stored in the log may become unreasonably large. In Section 17.4.3, we shall show when it is safe to erase log information.

17.4.1   Deferred Database Modification

The **deferred-modification technique** ensures transaction atomicity by recording all database modifications in the log, but deferring the execution of all write operations of a transaction until the transaction partially commits. Recall that a transaction is said to be partially committed once the final action of the transaction has been executed. The version of the deferred-modification technique that we describe in this section assumes that transactions are executed serially.

When a transaction partially commits, the information on the log associated with the transaction is used in executing the deferred writes. If the system crashes before the transaction completes its execution, or if the transaction aborts, then the information on the log is simply ignored.

The execution of transaction T_i proceeds as follows. Before T_i starts its execution, a record $<T_i$ start$>$ is written to the log. A write(X) operation by T_i results in the writing of a new record to the log. Finally, when T_i partially commits, a record $<T_i$ commit$>$ is written to the log.

When transaction T_i partially commits, the records associated with it in the log are used in executing the deferred writes. Since a failure may occur while this updating is taking place, we must ensure that, before the start of these updates, all the log records are written out to stable storage. Once they have been written, the actual updating takes place, and the transaction enters the committed state.

Observe that only the new value of the data item is required by the deferred-modification technique. Thus, we can simplify the general update-log record structure that we saw in the previous section, by omitting the old-value field.

To illustrate, reconsider our simplified banking system. Let T_0 be a transaction that transfers \$50 from account A to account B:

$$T_0: \text{read}(A);$$
$$A := A - 50;$$
$$\text{write}(A);$$
$$\text{read}(B);$$
$$B := B + 50;$$
$$\text{write}(B).$$

Let T_1 be a transaction that withdraws \$100 from account C:

$$T_1: \text{read}(C);$$
$$C := C - 100;$$
$$\text{write}(C).$$

Suppose that these transactions are executed serially, in the order T_0 followed by T_1, and that the values of accounts A, B, and C before the execution took place were \$1000, \$2000, and \$700, respectively. The portion of the log containing the relevant information on these two transactions appears in Figure 17.2.

There are various orders in which the actual outputs can take place to both the database system and the log as a result of the execution of T_0 and T_1. One such order

$$<T_0 \text{ start}>$$
$$<T_0, A, 950>$$
$$<T_0, B, 2050>$$
$$<T_0 \text{ commit}>$$
$$<T_1 \text{ start}>$$
$$<T_1, C, 600>$$
$$<T_1 \text{ commit}>$$

Figure 17.2   Portion of the database log corresponding to T_0 and T_1.

appears in Figure 17.3. Note that the value of A is changed in the database only after the record $<T_0, A, 950>$ has been placed in the log.

Using the log, the system can handle any failure that results in the loss of information on volatile storage. The recovery scheme uses the following recovery procedure:

- redo(T_i) sets the value of all data items updated by transaction T_i to the new values.

The set of data items updated by T_i and their respective new values can be found in the log.

The redo operation must be **idempotent**; that is, executing it several times must be equivalent to executing it once. This characteristic is required if we are to guarantee correct behavior even if a failure occurs during the recovery process.

After a failure, the recovery subsystem consults the log to determine which transactions need to be redone. Transaction T_i needs to be redone if and only if the log contains both the record $<T_i \text{ start}>$ and the record $<T_i \text{ commit}>$. Thus, if the system crashes after the transaction completes its execution, the recovery scheme uses the information in the log to restore the system to a previous consistent state after the transaction had completed.

As an illustration, let us return to our banking example with transactions T_0 and T_1 executed one after the other in the order T_0 followed by T_1. Figure 17.2 shows the log that results from the complete execution of T_0 and T_1. Let us suppose that the

Log	Database
$<T_0 \text{ start}>$	
$<T_0, A, 950>$	
$<T_0, B, 2050>$	
$<T_0 \text{ commit}>$	
	$A = 950$
	$B = 2050$
$<T_1 \text{ start}>$	
$<T_1, C, 600>$	
$<T_1 \text{ commit}>$	
	$C = 600$

Figure 17.3   State of the log and database corresponding to T_0 and T_1.

$<T_0$ start>	$<T_0$ start>	$<T_0$ start>
$<T_0, A, 950>$	$<T_0, A, 950>$	$<T_0, A, 950>$
$<T_0, B, 2050>$	$<T_0, B, 2050>$	$<T_0, B, 2050>$
	$<T_0$ commit>	$<T_0$ commit>
	$<T_1$ start>	$<T_1$ start>
	$<T_1, C, 600>$	$<T_1, C, 600>$
		$<T_1$ commit>
(a)	(b)	(c)

Figure 17.4   The same log as that in Figure 17.3, shown at three different times.

system crashes before the completion of the transactions, so that we can see how the recovery technique restores the database to a consistent state. Assume that the crash occurs just after the log record for the step

$$\text{write}(B)$$

of transaction T_0 has been written to stable storage. The log at the time of the crash appears in Figure 17.4a. When the system comes back up, no redo actions need to be taken, since no commit record appears in the log. The values of accounts A and B remain \$1000 and \$2000, respectively. The log records of the incomplete transaction T_0 can be deleted from the log.

Now, let us assume the crash comes just after the log record for the step

$$\text{write}(C)$$

of transaction T_1 has been written to stable storage. In this case, the log at the time of the crash is as in Figure 17.4b. When the system comes back up, the operation redo(T_0) is performed, since the record

$$<T_0 \text{ commit}>$$

appears in the log on the disk. After this operation is executed, the values of accounts A and B are \$950 and \$2050, respectively. The value of account C remains \$700. As before, the log records of the incomplete transaction T_1 can be deleted from the log.

Finally, assume that a crash occurs just after the log record

$$<T_1 \text{ commit}>$$

is written to stable storage. The log at the time of this crash is as in Figure 17.4c. When the system comes back up, two commit records are in the log: one for T_0 and one for T_1. Therefore, the system must perform operations redo(T_0) and redo(T_1), in the order in which their commit records appear in the log. After the system executes these operations, the values of accounts A, B, and C are \$950, \$2050, and \$600, respectively.

Finally, let us consider a case in which a second system crash occurs during re-covery from the first crash. Some changes may have been made to the database as a result of the redo operations, but all changes may not have been made. When the system comes up after the second crash, recovery proceeds exactly as in the preceding examples. For each commit record

$$<T_i \text{ commit}>$$

found in the log, the the system performs the operation redo(T_i). In other words, it restarts the recovery actions from the beginning. Since redo writes values to the database independent of the values currently in the database, the result of a successful second attempt at redo is the same as though redo had succeeded the first time.

17.4.2   Immediate Database Modification

The **immediate-modification technique** allows database modifications to be output to the database while the transaction is still in the active state. Data modifications written by active transactions are called **uncommitted modifications**. In the event of a crash or a transaction failure, the system must use the old-value field of the log records described in Section 17.4 to restore the modified data items to the value they had prior to the start of the transaction. The undo operation, described next, accomplishes this restoration.

Before a transaction T_i starts its execution, the system writes the record $<T_i$ start$>$ to the log. During its execution, any write(X) operation by T_i is *preceded* by the writing of the appropriate new update record to the log. When T_i partially commits, the system writes the record $<T_i$ commit$>$ to the log.

Since the information in the log is used in reconstructing the state of the database, we cannot allow the actual update to the database to take place before the corresponding log record is written out to stable storage. We therefore require that, before execution of an output(B) operation, the log records corresponding to B be written onto stable storage. We shall return to this issue in Section 17.7.

As an illustration, let us reconsider our simplified banking system, with transactions T_0 and T_1 executed one after the other in the order T_0 followed by T_1. The portion of the log containing the relevant information concerning these two transactions appears in Figure 17.5.

Figure 17.6 shows one possible order in which the actual outputs took place in both the database system and the log as a result of the execution of T_0 and T_1. Notice that

$<T_0$ start$>$
$<T_0,\ A,\ 1000,\ 950>$
$<T_0,\ B,\ 2000,\ 2050>$
$<T_0$ commit$>$
$<T_1$ start$>$
$<T_1,\ C,\ 700,\ 600>$
$<T_1$ commit$>$

Figure 17.5   Portion of the system log corresponding to T_0 and T_1.

Log	**Database**
$<T_0$ start>	
$<T_0,\ A,\ 1000,\ 950>$	
$<T_0,\ B,\ 2000,\ 2050>$	
	$A = 950$
	$B = 2050$
$<T_0$ commit>	
$<T_1$ start>	
$<T_1,\ C,\ 700,\ 600>$	
	$C = 600$
$<T_1$ commit>	

Figure 17.6 State of system log and database corresponding to T_0 and T_1.

this order could not be obtained in the deferred-modification technique of Section 17.4.1.

Using the log, the system can handle any failure that does not result in the loss of information in nonvolatile storage. The recovery scheme uses two recovery procedures:

- undo(T_i) restores the value of all data items updated by transaction T_i to the old values.

- redo(T_i) sets the value of all data items updated by transaction T_i to the new values.

The set of data items updated by T_i and their respective old and new values can be found in the log.

The undo and redo operations must be idempotent to guarantee correct behavior even if a failure occurs during the recovery process.

After a failure has occurred, the recovery scheme consults the log to determine which transactions need to be redone, and which need to be undone:

- Transaction T_i needs to be undone if the log contains the record $<T_i$ start>, but does not contain the record $<T_i$ commit>.

- Transaction T_i needs to be redone if the log contains both the record $<T_i$ start> and the record $<T_i$ commit>.

As an illustration, return to our banking example, with transaction T_0 and T_1 executed one after the other in the order T_0 followed by T_1. Suppose that the system crashes before the completion of the transactions. We shall consider three cases. The state of the logs for each of these cases appears in Figure 17.7.

First, let us assume that the crash occurs just after the log record for the step

write(B)

<T_0 start>	<T_0 start>	<T_0 start>
<T_0, A, 1000, 950>	<T_0, A, 1000, 950>	<T_0, A, 1000, 950>
<T_0, B, 2000, 2050>	<T_0, B, 2000, 2050>	<T_0, B, 2000, 2050>
	<T_0 commit>	<T_0 commit>
	<T_1 start>	<T_1 start>
	<T_1, C, 700, 600>	<T_1, C, 700, 600>
		<T_1 commit>
(a)	(b)	(c)

Figure 17.7   The same log, shown at three different times.

of transaction T_0 has been written to stable storage (Figure 17.7a). When the system comes back up, it finds the record <T_0 start> in the log, but no corresponding <T_0 commit> record. Thus, transaction T_0 must be undone, so an undo(T_0) is performed. As a result, the values in accounts A and B (on the disk) are restored to $1000 and $2000, respectively.

Next, let us assume that the crash comes just after the log record for the step

$$write(C)$$

of transaction T_1 has been written to stable storage (Figure 17.7b). When the system comes back up, two recovery actions need to be taken. The operation undo(T_1) must be performed, since the record <T_1 start> appears in the log, but there is no record <T_1 commit>. The operation redo(T_0) must be performed, since the log contains both the record <T_0 start> and the record <T_0 commit>. At the end of the entire recovery procedure, the values of accounts A, B, and C are $950, $2050, and $700, respectively. Note that the undo(T_1) operation is performed before the redo(T_0). In this example, the same outcome would result if the order were reversed. However, the order of doing undo operations first, and then redo operations, is important for the recovery algorithm that we shall see in Section 17.6.

Finally, let us assume that the crash occurs just after the log record

$$<T_1 \text{ commit}>$$

has been written to stable storage (Figure 17.7c). When the system comes back up, both T_0 and T_1 need to be redone, since the records <T_0 start> and <T_0 commit> appear in the log, as do the records <T_1 start> and <T_1 commit>. After the system performs the recovery procedures redo(T_0) and redo(T_1), the values in accounts A, B, and C are $950, $2050, and $600, respectively.

17.4.3 Checkpoints

When a system failure occurs, we must consult the log to determine those transactions that need to be redone and those that need to be undone. In principle, we need to search the entire log to determine this information. There are two major difficulties with this approach:

1. The search process is time consuming.

2. Most of the transactions that, according to our algorithm, need to be redone have already written their updates into the database. Although redoing them will cause no harm, it will nevertheless cause recovery to take longer.

To reduce these types of overhead, we introduce checkpoints. During execution, the system maintains the log, using one of the two techniques described in Sections 17.4.1 and 17.4.2. In addition, the system periodically performs **checkpoints**, which require the following sequence of actions to take place:

1. Output onto stable storage all log records currently residing in main memory.

2. Output to the disk all modified buffer blocks.

3. Output onto stable storage a log record <checkpoint>.

Transactions are not allowed to perform any update actions, such as writing to a buffer block or writing a log record, while a checkpoint is in progress.

The presence of a <checkpoint> record in the log allows the system to streamline its recovery procedure. Consider a transaction T_i that committed prior to the checkpoint. For such a transaction, the $<T_i$ commit> record appears in the log before the <checkpoint> record. Any database modifications made by T_i must have been written to the database either prior to the checkpoint or as part of the checkpoint itself. Thus, at recovery time, there is no need to perform a redo operation on T_i.

This observation allows us to refine our previous recovery schemes. (We continue to assume that transactions are run serially.) After a failure has occurred, the recovery scheme examines the log to determine the most recent transaction T_i that started executing before the most recent checkpoint took place. It can find such a transaction by searching the log backward, from the end of the log, until it finds the first <checkpoint> record (since we are searching backward, the record found is the final <checkpoint> record in the log); then it continues the search backward until it finds the next $<T_i$ start> record. This record identifies a transaction T_i.

Once the system has identified transaction T_i, the redo and undo operations need to be applied to only transaction T_i and all transactions T_j that started executing after transaction T_i. Let us denote these transactions by the set T. The remainder (earlier part) of the log can be ignored, and can be erased whenever desired. The exact recovery operations to be performed depend on the modification technique being used. For the immediate-modification technique, the recovery operations are:

- For all transactions T_k in T that have no $<T_k$ commit> record in the log, execute undo(T_k).

- For all transactions T_k in T such that the record $<T_k$ commit> appears in the log, execute redo(T_k).

Obviously, the undo operation does not need to be applied when the deferred-modification technique is being employed.

As an illustration, consider the set of transactions $\{T_0, T_1, \ldots, T_{100}\}$ executed in the order of the subscripts. Suppose that the most recent checkpoint took place during the execution of transaction T_{67}. Thus, only transactions $T_{67}, T_{68}, \ldots, T_{100}$ need to be considered during the recovery scheme. Each of them needs to be redone if it has committed; otherwise, it needs to be undone.

In Section 17.6.3, we consider an extension of the checkpoint technique for concurrent transaction processing.

17.5   Shadow Paging

An alternative to log-based crash-recovery techniques is **shadow paging**. The shadow-paging technique is essentially an improvement on the shadow-copy technique that we saw in Section 15.3. Under certain circumstances, shadow paging may require fewer disk accesses than do the log-based methods discussed previously. There are, however, disadvantages to the shadow-paging approach, as we shall see, that limit its use. For example, it is hard to extend shadow paging to allow multiple transactions to execute concurrently.

As before, the database is partitioned into some number of fixed-length blocks, which are referred to as **pages**. The term *page* is borrowed from operating systems, since we are using a paging scheme for memory management. Assume that there are n pages, numbered 1 through n. (In practice, n may be in the hundreds of thousands.) These pages do not need to be stored in any particular order on disk (there are many reasons why they do not, as we saw in Chapter 11). However, there must be a way to find the ith page of the database for any given i. We use a **page table**, as in Figure 17.8, for this purpose. The page table has n entries—one for each database page. Each entry contains a pointer to a page on disk. The first entry contains a pointer to the first page of the database, the second entry points to the second page, and so on. The example in Figure 17.8 shows that the logical order of database pages does not need to correspond to the physical order in which the pages are placed on disk.

The key idea behind the shadow-paging technique is to maintain *two* page tables during the life of a transaction: the **current page table** and the **shadow page table**. When the transaction starts, both page tables are identical. The shadow page table is never changed over the duration of the transaction. The current page table may be changed when a transaction performs a write operation. All input and output operations use the current page table to locate database pages on disk.

Suppose that the transaction T_j performs a write(X) operation, and that X resides on the ith page. The system executes the write operation as follows:

1. If the ith page (that is, the page on which X resides) is not already in main memory, then the system issues input(X).

2. If this is the write first performed on the ith page by this transaction, then the system modifies the current page table as follows:

   a. It finds an unused page on disk. Usually, the database system has access to a list of unused (free) pages, as we saw in Chapter 11.

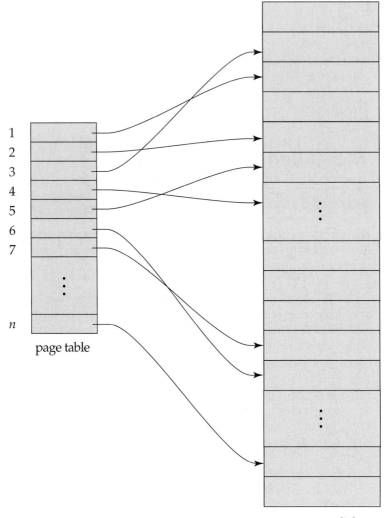

1
2
3
4
5
6
7

n

page table

pages on disk

Figure 17.8   Sample page table.

     b. It deletes the page found in step 2a from the list of free page frames; it copies the contents of the ith page to the page found in step 2a.

     c. It modifies the current page table so that the ith entry points to the page found in step 2a.

   3. It assigns the value of x_j to X in the buffer page.

Compare this action for a **write** operation with that described in Section 17.2.3 The only difference is that we have added a new step. Steps 1 and 3 here correspond to steps 1 and 2 in Section 17.2.3. The added step, step 2, manipulates the current

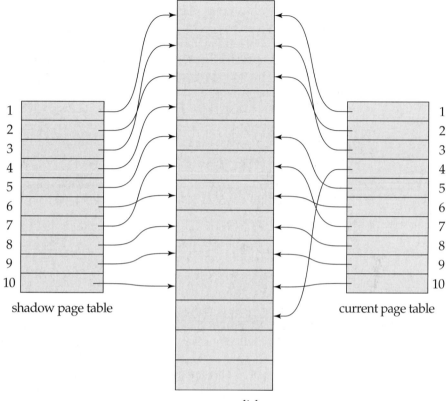

1
2
3
4
5
6
7
8
9
10

shadow page table

1
2
3
4
5
6
7
8
9
10

current page table

pages on disk

Figure 17.9   Shadow and current page tables.

page table. Figure 17.9 shows the shadow and current page tables for a transaction performing a write to the fourth page of a database consisting of 10 pages.

Intuitively, the shadow-page approach to recovery is to store the shadow page table in nonvolatile storage, so that the state of the database prior to the execution of the transaction can be recovered in the event of a crash, or transaction abort. When the transaction commits, the system writes the current page table to nonvolatile storage. The current page table then becomes the new shadow page table, and the next transaction is allowed to begin execution. It is important that the shadow page table be stored in nonvolatile storage, since it provides the only means of locating database pages. The current page table may be kept in main memory (volatile storage). We do not care whether the current page table is lost in a crash, since the system recovers by using the shadow page table.

Successful recovery requires that we find the shadow page table on disk after a crash. A simple way of finding it is to choose one fixed location in stable storage that contains the disk address of the shadow page table. When the system comes back up after a crash, it copies the shadow page table into main memory and uses it for subsequent transaction processing. Because of our definition of the write operation, we are guaranteed that the shadow page table will point to the database pages corresponding to the state of the database prior to any transaction that was active at the time of the crash. Thus, aborts are automatic. Unlike our log-based schemes, shadow paging needs to invoke no undo operations.

To commit a transaction, we must do the following:

1. Ensure that all buffer pages in main memory that have been changed by the transaction are output to disk. (Note that these output operations will not change database pages pointed to by some entry in the shadow page table.)

2. Output the current page table to disk. Note that we must not overwrite the shadow page table, since we may need it for recovery from a crash.

3. Output the disk address of the current page table to the fixed location in stable storage containing the address of the shadow page table. This action overwrites the address of the old shadow page table. Therefore, the current page table has become the shadow page table, and the transaction is committed.

If a crash occurs prior to the completion of step 3, we revert to the state just prior to the execution of the transaction. If the crash occurs after the completion of step 3, the effects of the transaction will be preserved; no redo operations need to be invoked.

Shadow paging offers several advantages over log-based techniques. The overhead of log-record output is eliminated, and recovery from crashes is significantly faster (since no undo or redo operations are needed). However, there are drawbacks to the shadow-page technique:

- **Commit overhead**. The commit of a single transaction using shadow paging requires multiple blocks to be output—the actual data blocks, the current page table, and the disk address of the current page table. Log-based schemes need to output only the log records, which, for typical small transactions, fit within one block.

  The overhead of writing an entire page table can be reduced by implementing the page table as a tree structure, with page table entries at the leaves. We outline the idea below, and leave it to the reader to fill in missing details. The nodes of the tree are pages and have a high fanout, like B$^+$-trees. The current page table's tree is initially the same as the shadow page table's tree. When a page is to be updated for the first time, the system changes the entry in the current page table to point to the copy of the page. If the leaf page containing the entry has been copied already, the system directly updates it. Otherwise, the system first copies it, and updates the copy. In turn, the parent of the copied page needs to be updated to point to the new copy, which the system does by applying the same procedure to its parent, copying it if it was not already copied. The process of copying proceeds up to the root of the tree. Changes are made only to the copied nodes, so the shadow page table's tree does not get modified.

The benefit of the tree representation is that the only pages that need to be copied are the leaf pages that are updated, and all their ancestors in the tree. All the other parts of the tree are shared between the shadow and the current page table, and do not need to be copied. The reduction in copying costs can be very significant for large databases. However, several pages of the page table still need to copied for each transaction, and the log-based schemes continue to be superior as long as most transactions update only small parts of the database.

- **Data fragmentation**. In Chapter 11, we considered strategies to ensure locality —that is, to keep related database pages close physically on the disk. Locality allows for faster data transfer. Shadow paging causes database pages to change location when they are updated. As a result, either we lose the locality property of the pages or we must resort to more complex, higher-overhead schemes for physical storage management. (See the bibliographical notes for references.)

- **Garbage collection**. Each time that a transaction commits, the database pages containing the old version of data changed by the transaction become inaccessible. In Figure 17.9, the page pointed to by the fourth entry of the shadow page table will become inaccessible once the transaction of that example commits. Such pages are considered **garbage**, since they are not part of free space and do not contain usable information. Garbage may be created also as a side effect of crashes. Periodically, it is necessary to find all the garbage pages, and to add them to the list of free pages. This process, called **garbage collection**, imposes additional overhead and complexity on the system. There are several standard algorithms for garbage collection. (See the bibliographical notes for references.)

In addition to the drawbacks of shadow paging just mentioned, shadow paging is more difficult than logging to adapt to systems that allow several transactions to execute concurrently. In such systems, some logging is usually required, even if shadow paging is used. The System R prototype, for example, used a combination of shadow paging and a logging scheme similar to that presented in Section 17.4.2. It is relatively easy to extend the log-based recovery schemes to allow concurrent transactions, as we shall see in Section 17.6. For these reasons, shadow paging is not widely used.

17.6   Recovery with Concurrent Transactions

Until now, we considered recovery in an environment where only a single transaction at a time is executing. We now discuss how we can modify and extend the log-based recovery scheme to deal with multiple concurrent transactions. Regardless of the number of concurrent transactions, the system has a single disk buffer and a single log. All transactions share the buffer blocks. We allow immediate modification, and permit a buffer block to have data items updated by one or more transactions.

17.6.1 Interaction with Concurrency Control

The recovery scheme depends greatly on the concurrency-control scheme that is used. To roll back a failed transaction, we must undo the updates performed by the transaction. Suppose that a transaction T_0 has to be rolled back, and a data item Q that was updated by T_0 has to be restored to its old value. Using the log-based schemes for recovery, we restore the value by using the undo information in a log record. Suppose now that a second transaction T_1 has performed yet another update on Q *before* T_0 is rolled back. Then, the update performed by T_1 will be lost if T_0 is rolled back.

Therefore, we require that, if a transaction T has updated a data item Q, no other transaction may update the same data item until T has committed or been rolled back. We can ensure this requirement easily by using strict two-phase locking—that is, two-phase locking with exclusive locks held until the end of the transaction.

17.6.2 Transaction Rollback

We roll back a failed transaction, T_i, by using the log. The system scans the log backward; for every log record of the form $<T_i, X_j, V_1, V_2>$ found in the log, the system restores the data item X_j to its old value V_1. Scanning of the log terminates when the log record $<T_i, \text{start}>$ is found.

Scanning the log backward is important, since a transaction may have updated a data item more than once. As an illustration, consider the pair of log records

$$<T_i, \ A, \ 10, \ 20>$$
$$<T_i, \ A, \ 20, \ 30>$$

The log records represent a modification of data item A by T_i, followed by another modification of A by T_i. Scanning the log backward sets A correctly to 10. If the log were scanned in the forward direction, A would be set to 20, which is incorrect.

If strict two-phase locking is used for concurrency control, locks held by a transaction T may be released only after the transaction has been rolled back as described. Once transaction T (that is being rolled back) has updated a data item, no other transaction could have updated the same data item, because of the concurrency-control requirements mentioned in Section 17.6.1. Therefore, restoring the old value of the data item will not erase the effects of any other transaction.

17.6.3 Checkpoints

In Section 17.4.3, we used checkpoints to reduce the number of log records that the system must scan when it recovers from a crash. Since we assumed no concurrency, it was necessary to consider only the following transactions during recovery:

- Those transactions that started after the most recent checkpoint

- The one transaction, if any, that was active at the time of the most recent checkpoint

The situation is more complex when transactions can execute concurrently, since several transactions may have been active at the time of the most recent checkpoint.

In a concurrent transaction-processing system, we require that the checkpoint log record be of the form <checkpoint L>, where L is a list of transactions active at the time of the checkpoint. Again, we assume that transactions do not perform updates either on the buffer blocks or on the log while the checkpoint is in progress.

The requirement that transactions must not perform any updates to buffer blocks or to the log during checkpointing can be bothersome, since transaction processing will have to halt while a checkpoint is in progress. A **fuzzy checkpoint** is a checkpoint where transactions are allowed to perform updates even while buffer blocks are being written out. Section 17.9.5 describes fuzzy checkpointing schemes.

17.6.4 Restart Recovery

When the system recovers from a crash, it constructs two lists: The undo-list consists of transactions to be undone, and the redo-list consists of transactions to be redone.

The system constructs the two lists as follows: Initially, they are both empty. The system scans the log backward, examining each record, until it finds the first <checkpoint> record:

- For each record found of the form <T_i commit>, it adds T_i to redo-list.

- For each record found of the form <T_i start>, if T_i is not in redo-list, then it adds T_i to undo-list.

When the system has examined all the appropriate log records, it checks the list L in the checkpoint record. For each transaction T_i in L, if T_i is not in redo-list then it adds T_i to the undo-list.

Once the redo-list and undo-list have have been constructed, the recovery proceeds as follows:

1. The system rescans the log from the most recent record backward, and performs an undo for each log record that belongs transaction T_i on the undo-list. Log records of transactions on the redo-list are ignored in this phase. The scan stops when the <T_i start> records have been found for every transaction T_i in the undo-list.

2. The system locates the most recent <checkpoint L> record on the log. Notice that this step may involve scanning the log forward, if the checkpoint record was passed in step 1.

3. The system scans the log forward from the most recent <checkpoint L> record, and performs redo for each log record that belongs to a transaction T_i that is on the redo-list. It ignores log records of transactions on the undo-list in this phase.

It is important in step 1 to process the log backward, to ensure that the resulting state of the database is correct.

After the system has undone all transactions on the undo-list, it redoes those transactions on the redo-list. It is important, in this case, to process the log forward. When the recovery process has completed, transaction processing resumes.

It is important to undo the transaction in the undo-list before redoing transactions in the redo-list, using the algorithm in steps 1 to 3; otherwise, a problem may occur. Suppose that data item A initially has the value 10. Suppose that a transaction T_i updated data item A to 20 and aborted; transaction rollback would restore A to the value 10. Suppose that another transaction T_j then updated data item A to 30 and committed, following which the system crashed. The state of the log at the time of the crash is

$$<T_i, \; A, \; 10, \; 20>$$
$$<T_j, \; A, \; 10, \; 30>$$
$$<T_j \; \text{commit}>$$

If the redo pass is performed first, A will be set to 30; then, in the undo pass, A will be set to 10, which is wrong. The final value of Q should be 30, which we can ensure by performing undo before performing redo.

17.7 Buffer Management

In this section, we consider several subtle details that are essential to the implementation of a crash-recovery scheme that ensures data consistency and imposes a minimal amount of overhead on interactions with the database.

17.7.1 Log-Record Buffering

So far, we have assumed that every log record is output to stable storage at the time it is created. This assumption imposes a high overhead on system execution for several reasons: Typically, output to stable storage is in units of blocks. In most cases, a log record is much smaller than a block. Thus, the output of each log record translates to a much larger output at the physical level. Furthermore, as we saw in Section 17.2.2, the output of a block to stable storage may involve several output operations at the physical level.

The cost of performing the output of a block to stable storage is sufficiently high that it is desirable to output multiple log records at once. To do so, we write log records to a log buffer in main memory, where they stay temporarily until they are output to stable storage. Multiple log records can be gathered in the log buffer, and output to stable storage in a single output operation. The order of log records in the stable storage must be exactly the same as the order in which they were written to the log buffer.

As a result of log buffering, a log record may reside in only main memory (volatile storage) for a considerable time before it is output to stable storage. Since such log records are lost if the system crashes, we must impose additional requirements on the recovery techniques to ensure transaction atomicity:

- Transaction T_i enters the commit state after the $<T_i$ commit$>$ log record has been output to stable storage.

- Before the $<T_i$ commit$>$ log record can be output to stable storage, all log records pertaining to transaction T_i must have been output to stable storage.

- Before a block of data in main memory can be output to the database (in non-volatile storage), all log records pertaining to data in that block must have been output to stable storage.

    This rule is called the **write-ahead logging (WAL)** rule. (Strictly speaking, the WAL rule requires only that the undo information in the log have been output to stable storage, and permits the redo information to be written later. The difference is relevant in systems where undo information and redo information are stored in separate log records.)

The three rules state situations in which certain log records *must* have been output to stable storage. There is no problem resulting from the output of log records *earlier* than necessary. Thus, when the system finds it necessary to output a log record to stable storage, it outputs an entire block of log records, if there are enough log records in main memory to fill a block. If there are insufficient log records to fill the block, all log records in main memory are combined into a partially full block, and are output to stable storage.

Writing the buffered log to disk is sometimes referred to as a **log force**.

17.7.2 Database Buffering

In Section 17.2, we described the use of a two-level storage hierarchy. The system stores the database in nonvolatile storage (disk), and brings blocks of data into main memory as needed. Since main memory is typically much smaller than the entire database, it may be necessary to overwrite a block B_1 in main memory when another block B_2 needs to be brought into memory. If B_1 has been modified, B_1 must be output prior to the input of B_2. As discussed in Section 11.5.1 in Chapter 11, this storage hierarchy is the standard operating system concept of *virtual memory*.

The rules for the output of log records limit the freedom of the system to output blocks of data. If the input of block B_2 causes block B_1 to be chosen for output, all log records pertaining to data in B_1 must be output to stable storage before B_1 is output. Thus, the sequence of actions by the system would be:

- Output log records to stable storage until all log records pertaining to block B_1 have been output.

- Output block B_1 to disk.

- Input block B_2 from disk to main memory.

It is important that no writes to the block B_1 be in progress while the system carries out this sequence of actions. We can ensure that there are no writes in progress by using a special means of locking: Before a transaction performs a write on a data item, it must acquire an exclusive lock on the block in which the data item resides. The lock can be released immediately after the update has been performed. Before a block is output, the system obtains an exclusive lock on the block, to ensure that no transaction is updating the block. It releases the lock once the block output has completed. Locks that are held for a short duration are often called **latches**. Latches are treated as distinct from locks used by the concurrency-control system. As a result, they may be released without regard to any locking protocol, such as two-phase locking, required by the concurrency-control system.

To illustrate the need for the write-ahead logging requirement, consider our banking example with transactions T_0 and T_1. Suppose that the state of the log is

$$<T_0 \text{ start}>$$
$$<T_0, A, 1000, 950>$$

and that transaction T_0 issues a read(B). Assume that the block on which B resides is not in main memory, and that main memory is full. Suppose that the block on which A resides is chosen to be output to disk. If the system outputs this block to disk and then a crash occurs, the values in the database for accounts A, B, and C are $950, $2000, and $700, respectively. This database state is inconsistent. However, because of the WAL requirements, the log record

$$<T_0, A, 1000, 950>$$

must be output to stable storage prior to output of the block on which A resides. The system can use the log record during recovery to bring the database back to a consistent state.

17.7.3 Operating System Role in Buffer Management

We can manage the database buffer by using one of two approaches:

1. The database system reserves part of main memory to serve as a buffer that it, rather than the operating system, manages. The database system manages data-block transfer in accordance with the requirements in Section 17.7.2.

   This approach has the drawback of limiting flexibility in the use of main memory. The buffer must be kept small enough that other applications have sufficient main memory available for their needs. However, even when the other applications are not running, the database will not be able to make use of all the available memory. Likewise, nondatabase applications may not use that part of main memory reserved for the database buffer, even if some of the pages in the database buffer are not being used.

2. The database system implements its buffer within the virtual memory provided by the operating system. Since the operating system knows about the memory requirements of all processes in the system, ideally it should be in charge of deciding what buffer blocks must be force-output to disk, and when. But, to ensure the write-ahead logging requirements in Section 17.7.1, the operating system should not write out the database buffer pages itself, but in-

stead should request the database system to force-output the buffer blocks. The database system in turn would force-output the buffer blocks to the database, after writing relevant log records to stable storage.

Unfortunately, almost all current-generation operating systems retain complete control of virtual memory. The operating system reserves space on disk for storing virtual-memory pages that are not currently in main memory; this space is called **swap space**. If the operating system decides to output a block B_x, that block is output to the swap space on disk, and there is no way for the database system to get control of the output of buffer blocks.

Therefore, if the database buffer is in virtual memory, transfers between database files and the buffer in virtual memory must be managed by the database system, which enforces the write-ahead logging requirements that we discussed.

This approach may result in extra output of data to disk. If a block B_x is output by the operating system, that block is not output to the database. Instead, it is output to the swap space for the operating system's virtual memory. When the database system needs to output B_x, the operating system may need first to input B_x from its swap space. Thus, instead of a single output of B_x, there may be two outputs of B_x (one by the operating system, and one by the database system) and one extra input of B_x.

Although both approaches suffer from some drawbacks, one or the other must be chosen unless the operating system is designed to support the requirements of database logging. Only a few current operating systems, such as the Mach operating system, support these requirements.

17.8   Failure with Loss of Nonvolatile Storage

Until now, we have considered only the case where a failure results in the loss of information residing in volatile storage while the content of the nonvolatile storage remains intact. Although failures in which the content of nonvolatile storage is lost are rare, we nevertheless need to be prepared to deal with this type of failure. In this section, we discuss only disk storage. Our discussions apply as well to other nonvolatile storage types.

The basic scheme is to **dump** the entire content of the database to stable storage periodically—say, once per day. For example, we may dump the database to one or more magnetic tapes. If a failure occurs that results in the loss of physical database blocks, the system uses the most recent dump in restoring the database to a previous consistent state. Once this restoration has been accomplished, the system uses the log to bring the database system to the most recent consistent state.

More precisely, no transaction may be active during the dump procedure, and a procedure similar to checkpointing must take place:

1. Output all log records currently residing in main memory onto stable storage.

2. Output all buffer blocks onto the disk.

3. Copy the contents of the database to stable storage.

4. Output a log record <dump> onto the stable storage.

Steps 1, 2, and 4 correspond to the three steps used for checkpoints in Section 17.4.3.

To recover from the loss of nonvolatile storage, the system restores the database to disk by using the most recent dump. Then, it consults the log and redoes all the transactions that have committed since the most recent dump occurred. Notice that no undo operations need to be executed.

A dump of the database contents is also referred to as an **archival dump**, since we can archive the dumps and use them later to examine old states of the database. Dumps of a database and checkpointing of buffers are similar.

The simple dump procedure described here is costly for the following two reasons. First, the entire database must be be copied to stable storage, resulting in considerable data transfer. Second, since transaction processing is halted during the dump procedure, CPU cycles are wasted. **Fuzzy dump** schemes have been developed, which allow transactions to be active while the dump is in progress. They are similar to fuzzy checkpointing schemes; see the bibliographical notes for more details.

17.9 Advanced Recovery Techniques**

The recovery techniques described in Section 17.6 require that, once a transaction updates a data item, no other transaction may update the same data item until the first commits or is rolled back. We ensure the condition by using strict two-phase locking. Although strict two-phase locking is acceptable for records in relations, as discussed in Section 16.9, it causes a significant decrease in concurrency when applied to certain specialized structures, such as B^+-tree index pages.

To increase concurrency, we can use the B^+-tree concurrency-control algorithm described in Section 16.9 to allow locks to be released early, in a non-two-phase manner. As a result, however, the recovery techniques from Section 17.6 will become inapplicable. Several alternative recovery techniques, applicable even with early lock release, have been proposed. These schemes can be used in a variety of applications, not just for recovery of B^+-trees. We first describe an advanced recovery scheme supporting early lock release. We then outline the ARIES recovery scheme, which is widely used in the industry. ARIES is more complex than our advanced recovery scheme, but incorporates a number of optimizations to minimize recovery time, and provides a number of other useful features.

17.9.1 Logical Undo Logging

For operations where locks are released early, we cannot perform the undo actions by simply writing back the old value of the data items. Consider a transaction T that inserts an entry into a B^+-tree, and, following the B^+-tree concurrency-control protocol, releases some locks after the insertion operation completes, but before the transaction commits. After the locks are released, other transactions may perform further insertions or deletions, thereby causing further changes to the B^+-tree nodes.

Even though the operation releases some locks early, it must retain enough locks to ensure that no other transaction is allowed to execute any conflicting operation (such as reading the inserted value or deleting the inserted value). For this reason, the B^+-tree concurrency-control protocol in Section 16.9 holds locks on the leaf level of the B^+-tree until the end of the transaction.

Now let us consider how to perform transaction rollback. If **physical undo** is used, that is, the old values of the internal B^+-tree nodes (before the insertion operation was executed) are written back during transaction rollback, some of the updates performed by later insertion or deletion operations executed by other transactions could be lost. Instead, the insertion operation has to be undone by a **logical undo**—that is, in this case, by the execution of a delete operation.

Therefore, when the insertion operation completes, before it releases any locks, it writes a log record $<T_i, O_j,$ operation-end, $U>$, where the U denotes undo information and O_j denotes a unique identifier for (the instance of) the operation. For example, if the operation inserted an entry in a B^+-tree, the undo information U would indicate that a deletion operation is to be performed, and would identify the B^+-tree and what to delete from the tree. Such logging of information about operations is called **logical logging**. In contrast, logging of old-value and new-value information is called **physical logging**, and the corresponding log records are called **physical log records**.

The insertion and deletion operations are examples of a class of operations that require logical undo operations since they release locks early; we call such operations **logical operations**. Before a logical operation begins, it writes a log record $<T_i, O_j,$ operation-begin$>$, where O_j is the unique identifier for the operation. While the system is executing the operation, it does physical logging in the normal fashion for all updates performed by the operation. Thus, the usual old-value and new-value information is written out for each update. When the operation finishes, it writes an operation-end log record as described earlier.

17.9.2   Transaction Rollback

First consider transaction rollback during normal operation (that is, not during recovery from system failure). The system scans the log backward and uses log records belonging to the transaction to restore the old values of data items. Unlike rollback in normal operation, however, rollback in our advanced recovery scheme writes out special redo-only log records of the form $<T_i, X_j, V>$ containing the value V being restored to data item X_j during the rollback. These log records are sometimes called **compensation log records**. Such records do not need undo information, since we will never need to undo such an undo operation.

Whenever the system finds a log record $<T_i, O_j,$ operation-end, $U>$, it takes special actions:

1. It rolls back the operation by using the undo information U in the log record. It logs the updates performed during the rollback of the operation just like updates performed when the operation was first executed. In other words, the system logs physical undo information for the updates performed during

rollback, instead of using compensation log records. This is because a crash may occur while a logical undo is in progress, and on recovery the system has to complete the logical undo; to do so, restart recovery will undo the partial effects of the earlier undo, using the physical undo information, and then perform the logical undo again, as we will see in Section 17.9.4.

At the end of the operation rollback, instead of generating a log record $< T_i, O_j,$ operation-end, $U >$, the system generates a log record $< T_i, O_j,$ operation-abort>.

2. When the backward scan of the log continues, the system skips all log records of the transaction until it finds the log record $<T_i, O_j,$ operation-begin>. After it finds the operation-begin log record, it processes log records of the transaction in the normal manner again.

Observe that skipping over physical log records when the operation-end log record is found during rollback ensures that the old values in the physical log record are not used for rollback, once the operation completes.

If the system finds a record $< T_i, O_j,$ operation-abort>, it skips all preceding records until it finds the record $< T_i, O_j,$ operation-begin>. These preceding log records must be skipped to prevent multiple rollback of the same operation, in case there had been a crash during an earlier rollback, and the transaction had already been partly rolled back. When the transaction T_i has been rolled back, the system adds a record $<T_i$ abort> to the log.

If failures occur while a logical operation is in progress, the operation-end log record for the operation will not be found when the transaction is rolled back. However, for every update performed by the operation, undo information—in the form of the old value in the physical log records—is available in the log. The physical log records will be used to roll back the incomplete operation.

17.9.3 Checkpoints

Checkpointing is performed as described in Section 17.6. The system suspends updates to the database temporarily and carries out these actions:

1. It outputs to stable storage all log records currently residing in main memory.

2. It outputs to the disk all modified buffer blocks.

3. It outputs onto stable storage a log record <checkpoint L>, where L is a list of all active transactions.

17.9.4 Restart Recovery

Recovery actions, when the database system is restarted after a failure, take place in two phases:

1. In the **redo phase**, the system replays updates of *all* transactions by scanning the log forward from the last checkpoint. The log records that are replayed include log records for transactions that were rolled back before sys-

tem crash, and those that had not committed when the system crash occurred. The records are the usual log records of the form $<T_i,\ X_j,\ V_1,\ V_2>$ as well as the special log records of the form $<T_i,\ X_j,\ V_2>$; the value V_2 is written to data item X_j in either case. This phase also determines all transactions that are either in the transaction list in the checkpoint record, or started later, but did not have either a $<T_i$ abort$>$ or a $<T_i$ commit$>$ record in the log. All these transactions have to be rolled back, and the system puts their transaction identifiers in an undo-list.

2. In the **undo phase**, the system rolls back all transactions in the undo-list. It performs rollback by scanning the log backward from the end. Whenever it finds a log record belonging to a transaction in the undo-list, it performs undo actions just as if the log record had been found during the rollback of a failed transaction. Thus, log records of a transaction preceding an operation-end record, but after the corresponding operation-begin record, are ignored.

    When the system finds a $<T_i$ start$>$ log record for a transaction T_i in undo-list, it writes a $<T_i$ abort$>$ log record to the log. Scanning of the log stops when the system has found $<T_i$ start$>$ log records for all transactions in the undo-list.

The redo phase of restart recovery replays every physical log record since the most recent checkpoint record. In other words, this phase of restart recovery repeats all the update actions that were executed after the checkpoint, and whose log records reached the stable log. The actions include actions of incomplete transactions and the actions carried out to roll failed transactions back. The actions are repeated in the same order in which they were carried out; hence, this process is called **repeating history**. Repeating history simplifies recovery schemes greatly.

Note that if an operation undo was in progress when the system crash occurred, the physical log records written during operation undo would be found, and the partial operation undo would itself be undone on the basis of these physical log records. After that the original operation's operation-end record would be found during recovery, and the operation undo would be executed again.

17.9.5 Fuzzy Checkpointing

The checkpointing technique described in Section 17.6.3 requires that all updates to the database be temporarily suspended while the checkpoint is in progress. If the number of pages in the buffer is large, a checkpoint may take a long time to finish, which can result in an unacceptable interruption in processing of transactions.

To avoid such interruptions, the checkpointing technique can be modified to permit updates to start once the checkpoint record has been written, but before the modified buffer blocks are written to disk. The checkpoint thus generated is a **fuzzy checkpoint**.

Since pages are output to disk only after the checkpoint record has been written, it is possible that the system could crash before all pages are written. Thus, a checkpoint on disk may be incomplete. One way to deal with incomplete checkpoints is this: The location in the log of the checkpoint record of the last completed checkpoint is stored in a fixed position, last-checkpoint, on disk. The system does not update this information when it writes the checkpoint record. Instead, before it writes the checkpoint record, it creates a list of all modified buffer blocks. The last-checkpoint information is updated only after all buffer blocks in the list of modified buffer blocks have been output to disk.

Even with fuzzy checkpointing, a buffer block must not be updated while it is being output to disk, although other buffer blocks may be updated concurrently. The write-ahead log protocol must be followed so that (undo) log records pertaining to a block are on stable storage before the block is output.

Note that, in our scheme, logical logging is used only for undo purposes, whereas physical logging is used for redo and undo purposes. There are recovery schemes that use logical logging for redo purposes. To perform logical redo, the database state on disk must be **operation consistent**, that is, it should not have partial effects of any operation. It is difficult to guarantee operation consistency of the database on disk if an operation can affect more than one page, since it is not possible to write two or more pages atomically. Therefore, logical redo logging is usually restricted only to operations that affect a single page; we will see how to handle such logical redos in Section 17.9.6. In contrast, logical undos are performed on an operation-consistent database state achieved by repeating history, and then performing physical undo of partially completed operations.

17.9.6 ARIES

The state of the art in recovery methods is best illustrated by the ARIES recovery method. The advanced recovery technique which we have described is modeled after ARIES, but has been simplified significantly to bring out key concepts and make it easier to understand. In contrast, ARIES uses a number of techniques to reduce the time taken for recovery, and to reduce the overheads of checkpointing. In particular, ARIES is able to avoid redoing many logged operations that have already been applied and to reduce the amount of information logged. The price paid is greater complexity; the benefits are worth the price.

The major differences between ARIES and our advanced recovery algorithm are that ARIES:

1. Uses a **log sequence number** (LSN) to identify log records, and the use of LSNs in database pages to identify which operations have been applied to a database page.

2. Supports **physiological redo** operations, which are physical in that the affected page is physically identified, but can be logical within the page.

   For instance, the deletion of a record from a page may result in many other records in the page being shifted, if a slotted page structure is used. With physical redo logging, all bytes of the page affected by the shifting of records must be logged. With physiological logging, the deletion operation can be logged, resulting in a much smaller log record. Redo of the deletion operation would delete the record and shift other records as required.

3. Uses a **dirty page table** to minimize unnecessary redos during recovery. Dirty pages are those that have been updated in memory, and the disk version is not up-to-date.

4. Uses fuzzy checkpointing scheme that only records information about dirty pages and associated information, and does not even require writing of dirty pages to disk. It flushes dirty pages in the background, continuously, instead of writing them during checkpoints.

In the rest of this section we provide an overview of ARIES. The bibliographical notes list references that provide a complete description of ARIES.

17.9.6.1 Data Structures

Each log record in ARIES has a **log sequence number** (**LSN**) that uniquely identifies the record. The number is conceptually just a logical identifier whose value is greater for log records that occur later in the log. In practice, the LSN is generated in such a way that it can also be used to locate the log record on disk. Typically, ARIES splits a log into multiple log files, each of which has a file number. When a log file grows to some limit, ARIES appends further log records to a new log file; the new log file has a file number that is higher by 1 than the previous log file. The LSN then consists of a file number and an offset within the file.

Each page also maintains an identifier called the **PageLSN**. Whenever an operation (whether physical or logical) occurs on a page, the operation stores the LSN of its log record in the PageLSN field of the page. During the redo phase of recovery, any log records with LSN less than or equal to the PageLSN of a page should not be executed on the page, since their actions are already reflected on the page. In combination with a scheme for recording PageLSNs as part of checkpointing, which we present later, ARIES can avoid even reading many pages for which logged operations are already reflected on disk. Thereby recovery time is reduced significantly.

The PageLSN is essential for ensuring idempotence in the presence of physiological redo operations, since reapplying a physiological redo that has already been applied to a page could cause incorrect changes to a page.

Pages should not be flushed to disk while an update is in progress, since physiological operations cannot be redone on the partially updated state of the page on disk. Therefore, ARIES uses latches on buffer pages to prevent them from being written to disk while they are being updated. It releases the buffer page latch only after the update is completed, and the log record for the update has been written to the log.

Each log record also contains the LSN of the previous log record of the same transaction. This value, stored in the PrevLSN field, permits log records of a transaction to be fetched backward, without reading the whole log. There are special redo-only log records generated during transaction rollback, called **compensation log records** (**CLRs**) in ARIES. These serve the same purpose as the redo-only log records in our advanced recovery scheme. In addition CLRs serve the role of the operation-abort log records in our scheme. The CLRs have an extra field, called the UndoNextLSN, that records the LSN of the log that needs to be undone next, when the transaction is being rolled back. This field serves the same purpose as the operation identifier in the operation-abort log record in our scheme, which helps to skip over log records that have already been rolled back. The **DirtyPageTable** contains a list of pages that have been updated in the database buffer. For each page, it stores the PageLSN and a field called the RecLSN which helps identify log records that have been applied already to the version of the page on disk. When a page is inserted into the DirtyPageTable (when it is first modified in the buffer pool) the value of RecLSN is set to the current end of log. Whenever the page is flushed to disk, the page is removed from the DirtyPageTable.

A **checkpoint log record** contains the DirtyPageTable and a list of active transactions. For each transaction, the checkpoint log record also notes LastLSN, the LSN of the last log record written by the transaction. A fixed position on disk also notes the LSN of the last (complete) checkpoint log record.

17.9.6.2 Recovery Algorithm

ARIES recovers from a system crash in three passes.

- **Analysis pass**: This pass determines which transactions to undo, which pages were dirty at the time of the crash, and the LSN from which the redo pass should start.

- **Redo pass**: This pass starts from a position determined during analysis, and performs a redo, repeating history, to bring the database to a state it was in before the crash.

- **Undo pass**: This pass rolls back all transactions that were incomplete at the time of crash.

Analysis Pass: The analysis pass finds the last complete checkpoint log record, and reads in the DirtyPageTable from this record. It then sets RedoLSN to the minimum of the RecLSNs of the pages in the DirtyPageTable. If there are no dirty pages, it sets RedoLSN to the LSN of the checkpoint log record. The redo pass starts its scan of the log from RedoLSN. All the log records earlier than this point have already been applied to the database pages on disk. The analysis pass initially sets the list of transactions to be undone, undo-list, to the list of transactions in the checkpoint log record. The analysis pass also reads from the checkpoint log record the LSNs of the last log record for each transaction in undo-list.

The analysis pass continues scanning forward from the checkpoint. Whenever it finds a log record for a transaction not in the undo-list, it adds the transaction to undo-list. Whenever it finds a transaction end log record, it deletes the transaction from undo-list. All transactions left in undo-list at the end of analysis have to be rolled back later, in the undo pass. The analysis pass also keeps track of the last record of each transaction in undo-list, which is used in the undo pass.

The analysis pass also updates DirtyPageTable whenever it finds a log record for an update on a page. If the page is not in DirtyPageTable, the analysis pass adds it to DirtyPageTable, and sets the RecLSN of the page to the LSN of the log record.

Redo Pass: The redo pass repeats history by replaying every action that is not already reflected in the page on disk. The redo pass scans the log forward from RedoLSN. Whenever it finds an update log record, it takes this action:

1. If the page is not in DirtyPageTable or the LSN of the update log record is less than the RecLSN of the page in DirtyPageTable, then the redo pass skips the log record.

2. Otherwise the redo pass fetches the page from disk, and if the PageLSN is less than the LSN of the log record, it redoes the log record.

Note that if either of the tests is negative, then the effects of the log record have already appeared on the page. If the first test is negative, it is not even necessary to fetch the page from disk.

Undo Pass and Transaction Rollback: The undo pass is relatively straightforward. It performs a backward scan of the log, undoing all transactions in undo-list. If a CLR is found, it uses the UndoNextLSN field to skip log records that have already been rolled back. Otherwise, it uses the PrevLSN field of the log record to find the next log record to be undone.

Whenever an update log record is used to perform an undo (whether for transaction rollback during normal processing, or during the restart undo pass), the undo pass generates a CLR containing the undo action performed (which must be physiological). It sets the UndoNextLSN of the CLR to the PrevLSN value of the update log record.

17.9.6.3 Other Features

Among other key features that ARIES provides are:

- **Recovery independence**: Some pages can be recovered independently from others, so that they can be used even while other pages are being recovered. If some pages of a disk fail, they can be recovered without stopping transaction processing on other pages.

- **Savepoints**: Transactions can record savepoints, and can be rolled back partially, up to a savepoint. This can be quite useful for deadlock handling, since transactions can be rolled back up to a point that permits release of required locks, and then restarted from that point.

- **Fine-grained locking**: The ARIES recovery algorithm can be used with index concurrency control algorithms that permit tuple level locking on indices, instead of page level locking, which improves concurrency significantly.

- **Recovery optimizations**: The DirtyPageTable can be used to prefetch pages during redo, instead of fetching a page only when the system finds a log record to be applied to the page. Out-of-order redo is also possible: Redo can be postponed on a page being fetched from disk, and performed when the page is fetched. Meanwhile, other log records can continue to be processed.

In summary, the ARIES algorithm is a state-of-the-art recovery algorithm, incorporating a variety of optimizations designed to improve concurrency, reduce logging overhead, and reduce recovery time.

17.10 Remote Backup Systems

Traditional transaction-processing systems are centralized or client–server systems. Such systems are vulnerable to environmental disasters such as fire, flooding, or earthquakes. Increasingly, there is a need for transaction-processing systems that can function in spite of system failures or environmental disasters. Such systems must provide **high availability**, that is, the time for which the system is unusable must be extremely small.

We can achieve high availability by performing transaction processing at one site, called the **primary site**, and having a **remote backup** site where all the data from the primary site are replicated. The remote backup site is sometimes also called the **secondary site**. The remote site must be kept synchronized with the primary site, as updates are performed at the primary. We achieve synchronization by sending all log records from primary site to the remote backup site. The remote backup site must be physically separated from the primary—for example, we can locate it in a different state—so that a disaster at the primary does not damage the remote backup site. Figure 17.10 shows the architecture of a remote backup system.

When the primary site fails, the remote backup site takes over processing. First, however, it performs recovery, using its (perhaps outdated) copy of the data from the primary, and the log records received from the primary. In effect, the remote backup site is performing recovery actions that would have been performed at the primary site when the latter recovered. Standard recovery algorithms, with minor modifications, can be used for recovery at the remote backup site. Once recovery has been performed, the remote backup site starts processing transactions.

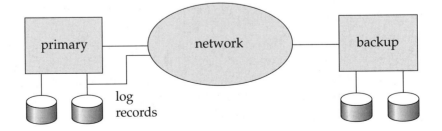

Figure 17.10   Architecture of remote backup system.

Availability is greatly increased over a single-site system, since the system can recover even if all data at the primary site are lost. The performance of a remote backup system is better than the performance of a distributed system with two-phase commit.

Several issues must be addressed in designing a remote backup system:

- **Detection of failure**. As in failure-handling protocols for distributed system, it is important for the remote backup system to detect when the primary has failed. Failure of communication lines can fool the remote backup into believing that the primary has failed. To avoid this problem, we maintain several communication links with independent modes of failure between the primary and the remote backup. For example, in addition to the network connection, there may be a separate modem connection over a telephone line, with services provided by different telecommunication companies. These connections may be backed up via manual intervention by operators, who can communicate over the telephone system.

- **Transfer of control**. When the primary fails, the backup site takes over processing and becomes the new primary. When the original primary site recovers, it can either play the role of remote backup, or take over the role of primary site again. In either case, the old primary must receive a log of updates carried out by the backup site while the old primary was down.

  The simplest way of transferring control is for the old primary to receive redo logs from the old backup site, and to catch up with the updates by applying them locally. The old primary can then act as a remote backup site. If control must be transferred back, the old backup site can pretend to have failed, resulting in the old primary taking over.

- **Time to recover**. If the log at the remote backup grows large, recovery will take a long time. The remote backup site can periodically process the redo log records that it has received, and can perform a checkpoint, so that earlier parts of the log can be deleted. The delay before the remote backup takes over can be significantly reduced as a result.

  A **hot-spare** configuration can make takeover by the backup site almost instantaneous. In this configuration, the remote backup site continually processes redo log records as they arrive, applying the updates locally. As soon as the failure of the primary is detected, the backup site completes recovery by rolling back incomplete transactions; it is then ready to process new transactions.

- **Time to commit**. To ensure that the updates of a committed transaction are durable, a transaction must not be declared committed until its log records have reached the backup site. This delay can result in a longer wait to commit a transaction, and some systems therefore permit lower degrees of durability. The degrees of durability can be classified as follows.

  □ **One-safe**. A transaction commits as soon as its commit log record is written to stable storage at the primary site.

The problem with this scheme is that the updates of a committed transaction may not have made it to the backup site, when the backup site takes over processing. Thus, the updates may appear to be lost. When the primary site recovers, the lost updates cannot be merged in directly, since the updates may conflict with later updates performed at the backup site. Thus, human intervention may be required to bring the database to a consistent state.

□ **Two-very-safe**. A transaction commits as soon as its commit log record is written to stable storage at the primary and the backup site.

The problem with this scheme is that transaction processing cannot proceed if either the primary or the backup site is down. Thus, availability is actually less than in the single-site case, although the probability of data loss is much less.

□ **Two-safe**. This scheme is the same as two-very-safe if both primary and backup sites are active. If only the primary is active, the transaction is allowed to commit as soon as its commit log record is written to stable storage at the primary site.

This scheme provides better availability than does two-very-safe, while avoiding the problem of lost transactions faced by the one-safe scheme. It results in a slower commit than the one-safe scheme, but the benefits generally outweigh the cost.

Several commercial shared-disk systems provide a level of fault tolerance that is intermediate between centralized and remote backup systems. In these systems, the failure of a CPU does not result in system failure. Instead, other CPUs take over, and they carry out recovery. Recovery actions include rollback of transactions running on the failed CPU, and recovery of locks held by those transactions. Since data are on a shared disk, there is no need for transfer of log records. However, we should safeguard the data from disk failure by using, for example, a RAID disk organization.

An alternative way of achieving high availability is to use a distributed database, with data replicated at more than one site. Transactions are then required to update all replicas of any data item that they update. We study distributed databases, including replication, in Chapter 19.

17.11 Summary

- A computer system, like any other mechanical or electrical device, is subject to failure. There are a variety of causes of such failure, including disk crash, power failure, and software errors. In each of these cases, information concerning the database system is lost.

- In addition to system failures, transactions may also fail for various reasons, such as violation of integrity constraints or deadlocks.

- An integral part of a database system is a recovery scheme that is responsible for the detection of failures and for the restoration of the database to a state that existed before the occurrence of the failure.

- The various types of storage in a computer are volatile storage, nonvolatile storage, and stable storage. Data in volatile storage, such as in RAM, are lost when the computer crashes. Data in nonvolatile storage, such as disk, are not lost when the computer crashes, but may occasionally be lost because of failures such as disk crashes. Data in stable storage are never lost.

- Stable storage that must be accessible online is approximated with mirrored disks, or other forms of RAID, which provide redundant data storage. Offline, or archival, stable storage may consist of multiple tape copies of data stored in a physically secure location.

- In case of failure, the state of the database system may no longer be consistent; that is, it may not reflect a state of the world that the database is supposed to capture. To preserve consistency, we require that each transaction be atomic. It is the responsibility of the recovery scheme to ensure the atomicity and durability property. There are basically two different approaches for ensuring atomicity: log-based schemes and shadow paging.

- In log-based schemes, all updates are recorded on a log, which must be kept in stable storage.
  - □ In the deferred-modifications scheme, during the execution of a transaction, all the write operations are deferred until the transaction partially commits, at which time the system uses the information on the log associated with the transaction in executing the deferred writes.
  - □ In the immediate-modifications scheme, the system applies all updates directly to the database. If a crash occurs, the system uses the information in the log in restoring the state of the system to a previous consistent state.

  To reduce the overhead of searching the log and redoing transactions, we can use the checkpointing technique.

- In shadow paging, two page tables are maintained during the life of a transaction: the current page table and the shadow page table. When the transaction starts, both page tables are identical. The shadow page table and pages it points to are never changed during the duration of the transaction. When the transaction partially commits, the shadow page table is discarded, and the current table becomes the new page table. If the transaction aborts, the current page table is simply discarded.

- If multiple transactions are allowed to execute concurrently, then the shadow-paging technique is not applicable, but the log-based technique can be used.

  No transaction can be allowed to update a data item that has already been updated by an incomplete transaction. We can use strict two-phase locking to ensure this condition.

- Transaction processing is based on a storage model in which main memory holds a log buffer, a database buffer, and a system buffer. The system buffer holds pages of system object code and local work areas of transactions.

- Efficient implementation of a recovery scheme requires that the number of writes to the database and to stable storage be minimized. Log records may be kept in volatile log buffer initially, but must be written to stable storage when one of the following conditions occurs:

  ☐ Before the $<T_i$ commit$>$ log record may be output to stable storage, all log records pertaining to transaction T_i must have been output to stable storage.

  ☐ Before a block of data in main memory is output to the database (in non-volatile storage), all log records pertaining to data in that block must have been output to stable storage.

- To recover from failures that result in the loss of nonvolatile storage, we must dump the entire contents of the database onto stable storage periodically—say, once per day. If a failure occurs that results in the loss of physical database blocks, we use the most recent dump in restoring the database to a previous consistent state. Once this restoration has been accomplished, we use the log to bring the database system to the most recent consistent state.

- Advanced recovery techniques support high-concurrency locking techniques, such as those used for B^+-tree concurrency control. These techniques are based on logical (operation) undo, and follow the principle of repeating history. When recovering from system failure, the system performs a redo pass using the log, followed by an undo pass on the log to roll back incomplete transactions.

- The ARIES recovery scheme is a state-of-the-art scheme that supports a number of features to provide greater concurrency, reduce logging overheads, and minimize recovery time. It is also based on repeating of history, and allows logical undo operations. The scheme flushes pages on a continuous basis and does not need to flush all pages at the time of a checkpoint. It uses log sequence numbers (LSNs) to implement a variety of optimizations that reduce the time taken for recovery.

- Remote backup systems provide a high degree of availability, allowing transaction processing to continue even if the primary site is destroyed by a fire, flood, or earthquake.

Review Terms

- Recovery scheme

- Failure classification
  - ☐ Transaction failure
  - ☐ Logical error
  - ☐ System error
  - ☐ System crash
  - ☐ Data-transfer failure

- Fail-stop assumption

- Disk failure

- Storage types
  - ☐ Volatile storage
  - ☐ Nonvolatile storage
  - ☐ Stable storage

- Blocks
  - ☐ Physical blocks
  - ☐ Buffer blocks
- Disk buffer
- Force-output
- Log-based recovery
- Log
- Log records
- Update log record
- Deferred modification
- Idempotent
- Immediate modification
- Uncommitted modifications
- Checkpoints
- Shadow paging
  - ☐ Page table
  - ☐ Current page table
  - ☐ Shadow page table
- Garbage collection
- Recovery with concurrent transactions
  - ☐ Transaction rollback
  - ☐ Fuzzy checkpoint
  - ☐ Restart recovery
- Buffer management
- Log-record buffering
- Write-ahead logging (WAL)
- Log force
- Database buffering
- Latches
- Operating system and buffer management
- Loss of nonvolatile storage

- Archival dump
- Fuzzy dump
- Advanced recovery technique
  - ☐ Physical undo
  - ☐ Logical undo
  - ☐ Physical logging
  - ☐ Logical logging
  - ☐ Logical operations
  - ☐ Transaction rollback
  - ☐ Checkpoints
  - ☐ Restart recovery
  - ☐ Redo phase
  - ☐ Undo phase
- Repeating history
- Fuzzy checkpointing
- ARIES
  - ☐ Log sequence number (LSN)
  - ☐ PageLSN
  - ☐ Physiological redo
  - ☐ Compensation log record (CLR)
  - ☐ DirtyPageTable
  - ☐ Checkpoint log record
- High availability
- Remote backup systems
  - ☐ Primary site
  - ☐ Remote backup site
  - ☐ Secondary site
- Detection of failure
- Transfer of control
- Time to recover
- Hot-spare configuration
- Time to commit
  - ☐ One-safe
  - ☐ Two-very-safe
  - ☐ Two-safe

Exercises

17.1 Explain the difference between the three storage types—volatile, nonvolatile, and stable—in terms of I/O cost.

17.2 Stable storage cannot be implemented.

   a. Explain why it cannot be.
   b. Explain how database systems deal with this problem.

17.3 Compare the deferred- and immediate-modification versions of the log-based recovery scheme in terms of ease of implementation and overhead cost.

17.4 Assume that immediate modification is used in a system. Show, by an example, how an inconsistent database state could result if log records for a transaction are not output to stable storage prior to data updated by the transaction being written to disk.

17.5 Explain the purpose of the checkpoint mechanism. How often should checkpoints be performed? How does the frequency of checkpoints affect

   • System performance when no failure occurs
   • The time it takes to recover from a system crash
   • The time it takes to recover from a disk crash

17.6 When the system recovers from a crash (see Section 17.6.4), it constructs an undo-list and a redo-list. Explain why log records for transactions on the undo-list must be processed in reverse order, while those log records for transactions on the redo-list are processed in a forward direction.

17.7 Compare the shadow-paging recovery scheme with the log-based recovery schemes in terms of ease of implementation and overhead cost.

17.8 Consider a database consisting of 10 consecutive disk blocks (block 1, block 2, ..., block 10). Show the buffer state and a possible physical ordering of the blocks after the following updates, assuming that shadow paging is used, that the buffer in main memory can hold only three blocks, and that a least recently used (LRU) strategy is used for buffer management.

> read block 3
> read block 7
> read block 5
> read block 3
> read block 1
> modify block 1
> read block 10
> modify block 5

17.9 Explain how the buffer manager may cause the database to become inconsistent if some log records pertaining to a block are not output to stable storage before the block is output to disk.

17.10 Explain the benefits of logical logging. Give examples of one situation where logical logging is preferable to physical logging and one situation where physical logging is preferable to logical logging.

17.11 Explain the reasons why recovery of interactive transactions is more difficult to deal with than is recovery of batch transactions. Is there a simple way to deal with this difficulty? (Hint: Consider an automatic teller machine transaction in which cash is withdrawn.)

17.12 Sometimes a transaction has to be undone after it has commited, because it was erroneously executed, for example because of erroneous input by a bank teller.

a. Give an example to show that using the normal transaction undo mechanism to undo such a transaction could lead to an inconsistent state.

b. One way to handle this situation is to bring the whole database to a state prior to the commit of the erroneous transaction (called *point-in-time* recovery). Transactions that committed later have their effects rolled back with this scheme.

Suggest a modification to the advanced recovery mechanism to implement point-in-time recovery.

c. Later non-erroneous transactions can be reexecuted logically, but cannot be reexecuted using their log records. Why?

17.13 Logging of updates is not done explicitly in persistent programming languages. Describe how page access protections provided by modern operating systems can be used to create before and after images of pages that are updated. (Hint: See Exercise 16.12.)

17.14 ARIES assumes there is space in each page for an LSN. When dealing with large objects that span multiple pages, such as operating system files, an entire page may be used by an object, leaving no space for the LSN. Suggest a technique to handle such a situation; your technique must support physical redos but need not support physiological redos.

17.15 Explain the difference between a system crash and a "disaster."

17.16 For each of the following requirements, identify the best choice of degree of durability in a remote backup system:

a. Data loss must be avoided but some loss of availability may be tolerated.

b. Transaction commit must be accomplished quickly, even at the cost of loss of some committed transactions in a disaster.

c. A high degree of availability and durability is required, but a longer running time for the transaction commit protocol is acceptable.

Bibliographical Notes

Gray and Reuter [1993] is an excellent textbook source of information about recovery, including interesting implementation and historical details. Bernstein et al. [1987] is an early textbook source of information on concurrency control and recovery.

Two early papers that present initial theoretical work in the area of recovery are Davies [1973] and Bjork [1973]. Chandy et al. [1975], which describes analytic models for rollback and recovery strategies in database systems, is another early work in this area.

An overview of the recovery scheme of System R is presented by Gray et al. [1981b]. The shadow-paging mechanism of System R is described by Lorie [1977]. Tutorial and survey papers on various recovery techniques for database systems include Gray [1978], Lindsay et al. [1980], and Verhofstad [1978]. The concepts of fuzzy checkpointing and fuzzy dumps are described in Lindsay et al. [1980]. A comprehensive presentation of the principles of recovery is offered by Haerder and Reuter [1983].

The state of the art in recovery methods is best illustrated by the ARIES recovery method, described in Mohan et al. [1992] and Mohan [1990b]. Aries and its variants are used in several database products, including IBM DB2 and Microsoft SQL Server. Recovery in Oracle is described in Lahiri et al. [2001].

Specialized recovery techniques for index structures are described in Mohan and Levine [1992] and Mohan [1993]; Mohan and Narang [1994] describes recovery techniques for client–server architectures, while Mohan and Narang [1991] and Mohan and Narang [1992] describe recovery techniques for parallel database architectures.

Remote backup for disaster recovery (loss of an entire computing facility by, for example, fire, flood, or earthquake) is considered in King et al. [1991] and Polyzois and Garcia-Molina [1994].

Chapter 24 lists references pertaining to long-duration transactions and related recovery issues.

PART 6

Database System Architecture

The architecture of a database system is greatly influenced by the underlying computer system on which the database system runs. Database systems can be centralized, or client–server, where one server machine executes work on behalf of multiple client machines. Database systems can also be designed to exploit parallel computer architectures. Distributed databases span multiple geographically separated machines.

Chapter 18 first outlines the architectures of database systems running on server systems, which are used in centralized and client–server architectures. The various processes that together implement the functionality of a database are outlined here. The chapter then outlines parallel computer architectures, and parallel database architectures designed for different types of parallel computers. Finally, the chapter outlines architectural issues in building a distributed database system.

Chapter 19 presents a number of issues that arise in a distributed database, and describes how to deal with each issue. The issues include how to store data, how to ensure atomicity of transactions that execute at multiple sites, how to perform concurrency control, and how to provide high availability in the presence of failures. Distributed query processing and directory systems are also described in this chapter.

Chapter 20 describes how various actions of a database, in particular query processing, can be implemented to exploit parallel processing.

Database System Architectures

The architecture of a database system is greatly influenced by the underlying computer system on which it runs, in particular by such aspects of computer architecture as networking, parallelism, and distribution:

- Networking of computers allows some tasks to be executed on a server system, and some tasks to be executed on client systems. This division of work has led to *client–server database systems*.

- Parallel processing within a computer system allows database-system activities to be speeded up, allowing faster response to transactions, as well as more transactions per second. Queries can be processed in a way that exploits the parallelism offered by the underlying computer system. The need for parallel query processing has led to *parallel database systems*.

- Distributing data across sites or departments in an organization allows those data to reside where they are generated or most needed, but still to be accessible from other sites and from other departments. Keeping multiple copies of the database across different sites also allows large organizations to continue their database operations even when one site is affected by a natural disaster, such as flood, fire, or earthquake. *Distributed database systems* handle geographically or administratively distributed data spread across multiple database systems.

We study the architecture of database systems in this chapter, starting with the traditional centralized systems, and covering client–server, parallel, and distributed database systems.

18.1   Centralized and Client—Server Architectures

Centralized database systems are those that run on a single computer system and do not interact with other computer systems. Such database systems span a range from single-user database systems running on personal computers to high-performance database systems running on high-end server systems. Client–server systems, on the other hand, have functionality split between a server system, and multiple client systems.

18.1.1 Centralized Systems

A modern, general-purpose computer system consists of one to a few CPUs and a number of device controllers that are connected through a common bus that provides access to shared memory (Figure 18.1). The CPUs have local cache memories that store local copies of parts of the memory, to speed up access to data. Each device controller is in charge of a specific type of device (for example, a disk drive, an audio device, or a video display). The CPUs and the device controllers can execute concurrently, competing for memory access. Cache memory reduces the contention for memory access, since it reduces the number of times that the CPU needs to access the shared memory.

We distinguish two ways in which computers are used: as single-user systems and as multiuser systems. Personal computers and workstations fall into the first category. A typical **single-user system** is a desktop unit used by a single person, usually with only one CPU and one or two hard disks, and usually only one person using the

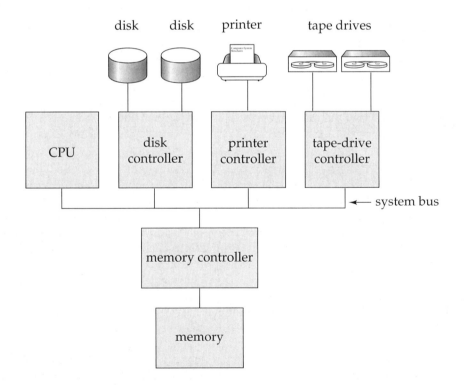

Figure 18.1   A centralized computer system.

machine at a time. A typical **multiuser system**, on the other hand, has more disks and more memory, may have multiple CPUs and has a multiuser operating system. It serves a large number of users who are connected to the system via terminals.

Database systems designed for use by single users usually do not provide many of the facilities that a multiuser database provides. In particular, they may not support concurrency control, which is not required when only a single user can generate updates. Provisions for crash-recovery in such systems are either absent or primitive– for example, they may consist of simply making a backup of the database before any update. Many such systems do not support SQL, and provide a simpler query language, such as a variant of QBE. In contrast, database systems designed for multiuser systems support the full transactional features that we have studied earlier.

Although general-purpose computer systems today have multiple processors, they have **coarse-granularity parallelism**, with only a few processors (about two to four, typically), all sharing the main memory. Databases running on such machines usually do not attempt to partition a single query among the processors; instead, they run each query on a single processor, allowing multiple queries to run concurrently. Thus, such systems support a higher throughput; that is, they allow a greater number of transactions to run per second, although individual transactions do not run any faster.

Databases designed for single-processor machines already provide multitasking, allowing multiple processes to run on the same processor in a time-shared manner, giving a view to the user of multiple processes running in parallel. Thus, coarse-granularity parallel machines logically appear to be identical to single-processor machines, and database systems designed for time-shared machines can be easily adapted to run on them.

In contrast, machines with **fine-granularity parallelism** have a large number of processors, and database systems running on such machines attempt to parallelize single tasks (queries, for example) submitted by users. We study the architecture of parallel database systems in Section 18.3.

18.1.2   Client–Server Systems

As personal computers became faster, more powerful, and cheaper, there was a shift away from the centralized system architecture. Personal computers supplanted terminals connected to centralized systems. Correspondingly, personal computers assumed the user-interface functionality that used to be handled directly by the centralized systems. As a result, centralized systems today act as **server systems** that satisfy requests generated by *client systems*. Figure 18.2 shows the general structure of a client–server system.

Database functionality can be broadly divided into two parts—the front end and the back end—as in Figure 18.3. The back end manages access structures, query evaluation and optimization, concurrency control, and recovery. The front end of a database system consists of tools such as forms, report writers, and graphical user-interface facilities. The interface between the front end and the back end is through SQL, or through an application program.

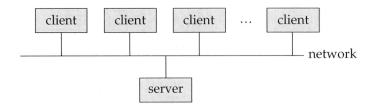

Figure 18.2   General structure of a client–server system.

Standards such as *ODBC* and *JDBC*, which we saw in Chapter 4, were developed to interface clients with servers. Any client that uses the ODBC or JDBC interfaces can connect to any server that provides the interface.

In earlier-generation database systems, the lack of such standards necessitated that the front end and the back end be provided by the same software vendor. With the growth of interface standards, the front-end user interface and the back-end server are often provided by different vendors. *Application development tools* are used to construct user interfaces; they provide graphical tools that can be used to construct interfaces without any programming. Some of the popular application development tools are PowerBuilder, Magic, and Borland Delphi; Visual Basic is also widely used for application development.

Further, certain application programs, such as spreadsheets and statistical-analysis packages, use the client–server interface directly to access data from a back-end server. In effect, they provide front ends specialized for particular tasks.

Some transaction-processing systems provide a **transactional remote procedure call** interface to connect clients with a server. These calls appear like ordinary procedure calls to the programmer, but all the remote procedure calls from a client are enclosed in a single transaction at the server end. Thus, if the transaction aborts, the server can undo the effects of the individual remote procedure calls.

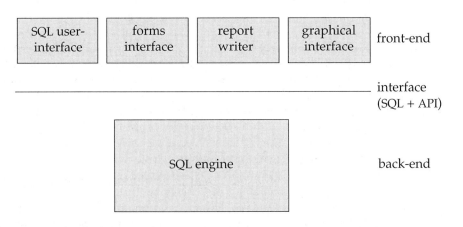

Figure 18.3   Front-end and back-end functionality.

18.2   Server System Architectures

Server systems can be broadly categorized as transaction servers and data servers.

- **Transaction-server** systems, also called **query-server** systems, provide an interface to which clients can send requests to perform an action, in response to which they execute the action and send back results to the client. Usually, client machines ship transactions to the server systems, where those transactions are executed, and results are shipped back to clients that are in charge of displaying the data. Requests may be specified by using SQL, or through a specialized application program interface.

- **Data-server systems** allow clients to interact with the servers by making requests to read or update data, in units such as files or pages. For example, file servers provide a file-system interface where clients can create, update, read, and delete files. Data servers for database systems offer much more functionality; they support units of data—such as pages, tuples, or objects—that are smaller than a file. They provide indexing facilities for data, and provide transaction facilities so that the data are never left in an inconsistent state if a client machine or process fails.

Of these, the transaction-server architecture is by far the more widely used architecture. We shall elaborate on the transaction-server and data-server architectures in Sections 18.2.1 and 18.2.2.

18.2.1   Transaction Server Process Structure

A typical transaction server system today consists of multiple processes accessing data in shared memory, as in Figure 18.4. The processes that form part of the database system include

- **Server processes**: These are processes that receive user queries (transactions), execute them, and send the results back. The queries may be submitted to the server processes from a a user interface, or from a user process running embedded SQL, or via JDBC, ODBC, or similar protocols. Some database systems use a separate process for each user session, and a few use a single database process for all user sessions, but with multiple threads so that multiple queries can execute concurrently. (A **thread** is like a process, but multiple threads execute as part of the same process, and all threads within a process run in the same virtual memory space. Multiple threads within a process can execute concurrently.) Many database systems use a hybrid architecture, with multiple processes, each one running multiple threads.

- **Lock manager process**: This process implements lock manager functionality, which includes lock grant, lock release, and deadlock detection.

- **Database writer process**: There are one or more processes that output modified buffer blocks back to disk on a continuous basis.

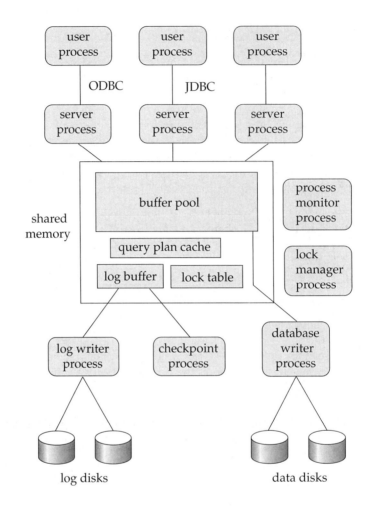

Figure 18.4 Shared memory and process structure.

- **Log writer process**: This process outputs log records from the log record buffer to stable storage. Server processes simply add log records to the log record buffer in shared memory, and if a log force is required, they request the log writer process to output log records.

- **Checkpoint process**: This process performs periodic checkpoints.

- **Process monitor process**: This process monitors other processes, and if any of them fails, it takes recovery actions for the process, such as aborting any transaction being executed by the failed process, and then restarting the process.

The shared memory contains all shared data, such as:

- Buffer pool

- Lock table

- Log buffer, containing log records waiting to be output to the log on stable storage

- Cached query plans, which can be reused if the same query is submitted again

All database processes can access the data in shared memory. Since multiple processes may read or perform updates on data structures in shared memory, there must be a mechanism to ensure that only one of them is modifying any data structure at a time, and no process is reading a data structure while it is being written by others. Such **mutual exclusion** can be implemented by means of operating system functions called semaphores. Alternative implementations, with less overheads, use special **atomic instructions** supported by the computer hardware; one type of atomic instruction tests a memory location and sets it to 1 atomically. Further implementation details of mutual exclusion can be found in any standard operating system textbook. The mutual exclusion mechanisms are also used to implement latches.

To avoid the overhead of message passing, in many database systems, server processes implement locking by directly updating the lock table (which is in shared memory), instead of sending lock request messages to a lock manager process. The lock request procedure executes the actions that the lock manager process would take on getting a lock request. The actions on lock request and release are like those in Section 16.1.4, but with two significant differences:

- Since multiple server processes may access shared memory, mutual exclusion must be ensured on the lock table.

- If a lock cannot be obtained immediately because of a lock conflict, the lock request code keeps monitoring the lock table to check when the lock has been granted. The lock release code updates the lock table to note which process has been granted the lock.

    To avoid repeated checks on the lock table, operating system semaphores can be used by the lock request code to wait for a lock grant notification. The lock release code must then use the semaphore mechanism to notify waiting transactions that their locks have been granted.

Even if the system handles lock requests through shared memory, it still uses the lock manager process for deadlock detection.

18.2.2 Data Servers

Data-server systems are used in local-area networks, where there is a high-speed connection between the clients and the server, the client machines are comparable in processing power to the server machine, and the tasks to be executed are computation intensive. In such an environment, it makes sense to ship data to client machines, to perform all processing at the client machine (which may take a while), and then to ship the data back to the server machine. Note that this architecture requires full back-end functionality at the clients. Data-server architectures have been particularly popular in object-oriented database systems.

Interesting issues arise in such an architecture, since the time cost of communication between the client and the server is high compared to that of a local memory reference (milliseconds, versus less than 100 nanoseconds):

- **Page shipping versus item shipping**. The unit of communication for data can be of coarse granularity, such as a page, or fine granularity, such as a tuple (or an object, in the context of object-oriented database systems). We use the term **item** to refer to both tuples and objects.

    If the unit of communication is a single item, the overhead of message passing is high compared to the amount of data transmitted. Instead, when an item is requested, it makes sense also to send back other items that are likely to be used in the near future. Fetching items even before they are requested is called **prefetching**. Page shipping can be considered a form of prefetching if multiple items reside on a page, since all the items in the page are shipped when a process desires to access a single item in the page.

- **Locking**. Locks are usually granted by the server for the data items that it ships to the client machines. A disadvantage of page shipping is that client machines may be granted locks of too coarse a granularity—a lock on a page implicitly locks all items contained in the page. Even if the client is not accessing some items in the page, it has implicitly acquired locks on all prefetched items. Other client machines that require locks on those items may be blocked unnecessarily. Techniques for lock **de-escalation**, have been proposed where the server can request its clients to transfer back locks on prefetched items. If the client machine does not need a prefetched item, it can transfer locks on the item back to the server, and the locks can then be allocated to other clients.

- **Data caching**. Data that are shipped to a client on behalf of a transaction can be **cached** at the client, even after the transaction completes, if sufficient storage space is available. Successive transactions at the same client may be able to make use of the cached data. However, **cache coherency** is an issue: Even if a transaction finds cached data, it must make sure that those data are up to date, since they may have been updated by a different client after they were cached. Thus, a message must still be exchanged with the server to check validity of the data, and to acquire a lock on the data.

- **Lock caching**. If the use of data is mostly partitioned among the clients, with clients rarely requesting data that are also requested by other clients, locks can also be cached at the client machine. Suppose that a client finds a data item in the cache, and that it also finds the lock required for an access to the data item in the cache. Then, the access can proceed without any communication with the server. However, the server must keep track of cached locks; if a client requests a lock from the server, the server must **call back** all conflicting locks on the data item from any other client machines that have cached the locks. The task becomes more complicated when machine failures are taken into account. This technique differs from lock de-escalation in that lock caching takes place across transactions; otherwise, the two techniques are similar.

The bibliographical references provide more information about client–server database systems.

18.3 Parallel Systems

Parallel systems improve processing and I/O speeds by using multiple CPUs and disks in parallel. Parallel machines are becoming increasingly common, making the study of parallel database systems correspondingly more important. The driving force behind parallel database systems is the demands of applications that have to query extremely large databases (of the order of terabytes—that is, 10^{12} bytes) or that have to process an extremely large number of transactions per second (of the order of thousands of transactions per second). Centralized and client–server database systems are not powerful enough to handle such applications.

In parallel processing, many operations are performed simultaneously, as opposed to serial processing, in which the computational steps are performed sequentially. A **coarse-grain** parallel machine consists of a small number of powerful processors; a **massively parallel** or **fine-grain parallel** machine uses thousands of smaller processors. Most high-end machines today offer some degree of coarse-grain parallelism: Two or four processor machines are common. Massively parallel computers can be distinguished from the coarse-grain parallel machines by the much larger degree of parallelism that they support. Parallel computers with hundreds of CPUs and disks are available commercially.

There are two main measures of performance of a database system: (1) **throughput**, the number of tasks that can be completed in a given time interval, and (2) **response time**, the amount of time it takes to complete a single task from the time it is submitted. A system that processes a large number of small transactions can improve throughput by processing many transactions in parallel. A system that processes large transactions can improve response time as well as throughput by performing subtasks of each transaction in parallel.

18.3.1 Speedup and Scaleup

Two important issues in studying parallelism are speedup and scaleup. Running a given task in less time by increasing the degree of parallelism is called **speedup**. Handling larger tasks by increasing the degree of parallelism is called **scaleup**.

Consider a database application running on a parallel system with a certain number of processors and disks. Now suppose that we increase the size of the system by increasing the number or processors, disks, and other components of the system. The goal is to process the task in time inversely proportional to the number of processors and disks allocated. Suppose that the execution time of a task on the larger machine is T_L, and that the execution time of the same task on the smaller machine is T_S. The speedup due to parallelism is defined as T_S/T_L. The parallel system is said to demonstrate **linear speedup** if the speedup is N when the larger system has N times the resources (CPU, disk, and so on) of the smaller system. If the speedup is less than N, the system is said to demonstrate **sublinear speedup**. Figure 18.5 illustrates linear and sublinear speedup.

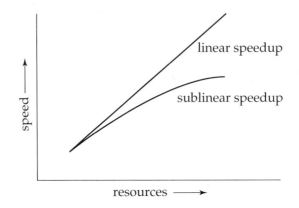

Figure 18.5   Speedup with increasing resources.

Scaleup relates to the ability to process larger tasks in the same amount of time by providing more resources. Let Q be a task, and let Q_N be a task that is N times bigger than Q. Suppose that the execution time of task Q on a given machine M_S is T_S, and the execution time of task Q_N on a parallel machine M_L, which is N times larger than M_S, is T_L. The scaleup is then defined as T_S/T_L. The parallel system M_L is said to demonstrate **linear scaleup** on task Q if $T_L = T_S$. If $T_L > T_S$, the system is said to demonstrate **sublinear scaleup**. Figure 18.6 illustrates linear and sublinear scaleups (where the resources increase proportional to problem size). There are two kinds of scaleup that are relevant in parallel database systems, depending on how the size of the task is measured:

- In **batch scaleup**, the size of the database increases, and the tasks are large jobs whose runtime depends on the size of the database. An example of such a task is a scan of a relation whose size is proportional to the size of the database. Thus, the size of the database is the measure of the size of the problem. Batch scaleup also applies in scientific applications, such as executing a query at an N-times finer resolution or performing an N-times longer simulation.

- In **transaction scaleup**, the rate at which transactions are submitted to the database increases and the size of the database increases proportionally to the transaction rate. This kind of scaleup is what is relevant in transaction-processing systems where the transactions are small updates—for example, a deposit or withdrawal from an account—and transaction rates grow as more accounts are created. Such transaction processing is especially well adapted for parallel execution, since transactions can run concurrently and independently on separate processors, and each transaction takes roughly the same amount of time, even if the database grows.

Scaleup is usually the more important metric for measuring efficiency of parallel database systems. The goal of parallelism in database systems is usually to make sure that the database system can continue to perform at an acceptable speed, even as the

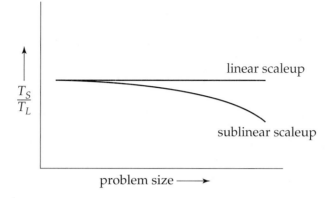

Figure 18.6   Scaleup with increasing problem size and resources.

size of the database and the number of transactions increases. Increasing the capacity of the system by increasing the parallelism provides a smoother path for growth for an enterprise than does replacing a centralized system by a faster machine (even assuming that such a machine exists). However, we must also look at absolute performance numbers when using scaleup measures; a machine that scales up linearly may perform worse than a machine that scales less than linearly, simply because the latter machine is much faster to start off with.

A number of factors work against efficient parallel operation and can diminish both speedup and scaleup.

- **Startup costs**. There is a startup cost associated with initiating a single process. In a parallel operation consisting of thousands of processes, the *startup time* may overshadow the actual processing time, affecting speedup adversely.

- **Interference**. Since processes executing in a parallel system often access shared resources, a slowdown may result from the *interference* of each new process as it competes with existing processes for commonly held resources, such as a system bus, or shared disks, or even locks. Both speedup and scaleup are affected by this phenomenon.

- **Skew**. By breaking down a single task into a number of parallel steps, we reduce the size of the average step. Nonetheless, the service time for the single slowest step will determine the service time for the task as a whole. It is often difficult to divide a task into exactly equal-sized parts, and the way that the sizes are distributed is therefore *skewed*. For example, if a task of size 100 is divided into 10 parts, and the division is skewed, there may be some tasks of size less than 10 and some tasks of size more than 10; if even one task happens to be of size 20, the speedup obtained by running the tasks in parallel is only five, instead of ten as we would have hoped.

18.3.2 Interconnection Networks

Parallel systems consist of a set of components (processors, memory, and disks) that can communicate with each other via an **interconnection network**. Figure 18.7 shows three commonly used types of interconnection networks:

- **Bus**. All the system components can send data on and receive data from a single communication bus. This type of interconnection is shown in Figure 18.7a. The bus could be an Ethernet or a parallel interconnect. Bus architectures work well for small numbers of processors. However, they do not scale well with increasing parallelism, since the bus can handle communication from only one component at a time.

- **Mesh**. The components are nodes in a grid, and each component connects to all its adjacent components in the grid. In a two-dimensional mesh each node connects to four adjacent nodes, while in a three-dimensional mesh each node connects to six adjacent nodes. Figure 18.7b shows a two-dimensional mesh. Nodes that are not directly connected can communicate with one another by routing messages via a sequence of intermediate nodes that are directly connected to one another. The number of communication links grows as the number of components grows, and the communication capacity of a mesh therefore scales better with increasing parallelism.

- **Hypercube**. The components are numbered in binary, and a component is connected to another if the binary representations of their numbers differ in exactly one bit. Thus, each of the n components is connected to $\log(n)$ other components. Figure 18.7c shows a hypercube with 8 nodes. In a hypercube interconnection, a message from a component can reach any other component by going through at most $\log(n)$ links. In contrast, in a mesh architecture a component may be $2(\sqrt{n} - 1)$ links away from some of the other components (or $\sqrt{n}$ links away, if the mesh interconnection wraps around at the edges of the grid). Thus communication delays in a hypercube are significantly lower than in a mesh.

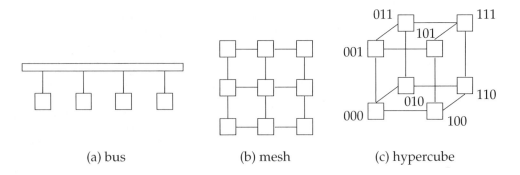

(a) bus   (b) mesh   (c) hypercube

Figure 18.7 Interconnection networks.

18.3.3 Parallel Database Architectures

There are several architectural models for parallel machines. Among the most prominent ones are those in Figure 18.8 (in the figure, M denotes memory, P denotes a processor, and disks are shown as cylinders):

- **Shared memory**. All the processors share a common memory (Figure 18.8a).

- **Shared disk**. All the processors share a common set of disks (Figure 18.8b). Shared-disk systems are sometimes called **clusters**.

- **Shared nothing**. The processors share neither a common memory nor common disk (Figure 18.8c).

- **Hierarchical**. This model is a hybrid of the preceding three architectures (Figure 18.8d).

In Sections 18.3.3.1 through 18.3.3.4, we elaborate on each of these models.

Techniques used to speed up transaction processing on data-server systems, such as data and lock caching and lock de-escalation, outlined in Section 18.2.2, can also be used in shared-disk parallel databases as well as in shared-nothing parallel databases. In fact, they are very important for efficient transaction processing in such systems.

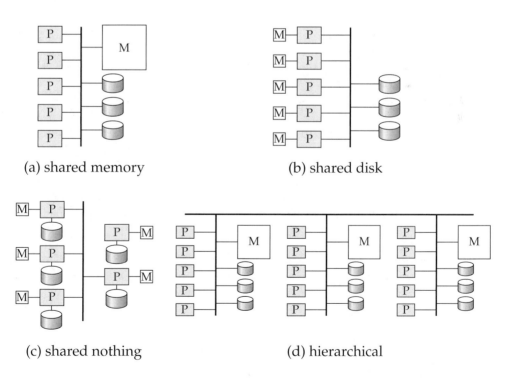

(a) shared memory   (b) shared disk

(c) shared nothing   (d) hierarchical

Figure 18.8   Parallel database architectures.

18.3.3.1 Shared Memory

In a **shared-memory** architecture, the processors and disks have access to a common memory, typically via a bus or through an interconnection network. The benefit of shared memory is extremely efficient communication between processors—data in shared memory can be accessed by any processor without being moved with software. A processor can send messages to other processors much faster by using memory writes (which usually take less than a microsecond) than by sending a message through a communication mechanism. The downside of shared-memory machines is that the architecture is not scalable beyond 32 or 64 processors because the bus or the interconnection network becomes a bottleneck (since it is shared by all processors). Adding more processors does not help after a point, since the processors will spend most of their time waiting for their turn on the bus to access memory.

Shared-memory architectures usually have large memory caches at each processor, so that referencing of the shared memory is avoided whenever possible. However, at least some of the data will not be in the cache, and accesses will have to go to the shared memory. Moreover, the caches need to be kept coherent; that is, if a processor performs a write to a memory location, the data in that memory location should be either updated at or removed from any processor where the data is cached. Maintaining cache-coherency becomes an increasing overhead with increasing number of processors. Consequently, shared-memory machines are not capable of scaling up beyond a point; current shared-memory machines cannot support more than 64 processors.

18.3.3.2 Shared Disk

In the **shared-disk** model, all processors can access all disks directly via an interconnection network, but the processors have private memories. There are two advantages of this architecture over a shared-memory architecture. First, since each processor has its own memory, the memory bus is not a bottleneck. Second, it offers a cheap way to provide a degree of **fault tolerance**: If a processor (or its memory) fails, the other processors can take over its tasks, since the database is resident on disks that are accessible from all processors. We can make the disk subsystem itself fault tolerant by using a RAID architecture, as described in Chapter 11. The shared-disk architecture has found acceptance in many applications.

The main problem with a shared-disk system is again scalability. Although the memory bus is no longer a bottleneck, the interconnection to the disk subsystem is now a bottleneck; it is particularly so in a situation where the database makes a large number of accesses to disks. Compared to shared-memory systems, shared-disk systems can scale to a somewhat larger number of processors, but communication across processors is slower (up to a few milliseconds in the absence of special-purpose hardware for communication), since it has to go through a communication network.

DEC clusters running Rdb were one of the early commercial users of the shared-disk database architecture. (Rdb is now owned by Oracle, and is called Oracle Rdb. Digital Equipment Corporation (DEC) is now owned by Compaq.)

18.3.3.3   Shared Nothing

In a **shared-nothing** system, each node of the machine consists of a processor, memory, and one or more disks. The processors at one node may communicate with another processor at another node by a high-speed interconnection network. A node functions as the server for the data on the disk or disks that the node owns. Since local disk references are serviced by local disks at each processor, the shared-nothing model overcomes the disadvantage of requiring all I/O to go through a single interconnection network; only queries, accesses to nonlocal disks, and result relations pass through the network. Moreover, the interconnection networks for shared-nothing systems are usually designed to be scalable, so that their transmission capacity increases as more nodes are added. Consequently, shared-nothing architectures are more scalable and can easily support a large number of processors. The main drawbacks of shared-nothing systems are the costs of communication and of nonlocal disk access, which are higher than in a shared-memory or shared-disk architecture since sending data involves software interaction at both ends.

The Teradata database machine was among the earliest commercial systems to use the shared-nothing database architecture. The Grace and the Gamma research prototypes also used shared-nothing architectures.

18.3.3.4   Hierarchical

The **hierarchical architecture** combines the characteristics of shared-memory, shared-disk, and shared-nothing architectures. At the top level, the system consists of nodes connected by an interconnection network, and do not share disks or memory with one another. Thus, the top level is a shared-nothing architecture. Each node of the system could actually be a shared-memory system with a few processors. Alternatively, each node could be a shared-disk system, and each of the systems sharing a set of disks could be a shared-memory system. Thus, a system could be built as a hierarchy, with shared-memory architecture with a few processors at the base, and a shared-nothing architecture at the top, with possibly a shared-disk architecture in the middle. Figure 18.8d illustrates a hierarchical architecture with shared-memory nodes connected together in a shared-nothing architecture. Commercial parallel database systems today run on several of these architectures.

Attempts to reduce the complexity of programming such systems have yielded **distributed virtual-memory** architectures, where logically there is a single shared memory, but physically there are multiple disjoint memory systems; the virtual-memory-mapping hardware, coupled with system software, allows each processor to view the disjoint memories as a single virtual memory. Since access speeds differ, depending on whether the page is available locally or not, such an architecture is also referred to as a **nonuniform memory architecture** (NUMA).

18.4   Distributed Systems

In a **distributed database system**, the database is stored on several computers. The computers in a distributed system communicate with one another through various communication media, such as high-speed networks or telephone lines. They do not share main memory or disks. The computers in a distributed system may vary in size and function, ranging from workstations up to mainframe systems.

The computers in a distributed system are referred to by a number of different names, such as **sites** or **nodes**, depending on the context in which they are mentioned. We mainly use the term **site**, to emphasize the physical distribution of these systems. The general structure of a distributed system appears in Figure 18.9.

The main differences between shared-nothing parallel databases and distributed databases are that distributed databases are typically geographically separated, are separately administered, and have a slower interconnection. Another major difference is that, in a distributed database system, we differentiate between local and global transactions. A **local transaction** is one that accesses data only from sites where the transaction was initiated. A **global transaction**, on the other hand, is one that either accesses data in a site different from the one at which the transaction was initiated, or accesses data in several different sites.

There are several reasons for building distributed database systems, including sharing of data, autonomy, and availability.

- **Sharing data.** The major advantage in building a distributed database system is the provision of an environment where users at one site may be able to access the data residing at other sites. For instance, in a distributed banking system, where each branch stores data related to that branch, it is possible for a user in one branch to access data in another branch. Without this capability, a user wishing to transfer funds from one branch to another would have to resort to some external mechanism that would couple existing systems.

- **Autonomy.** The primary advantage of sharing data by means of data distribution is that each site is able to retain a degree of control over data that

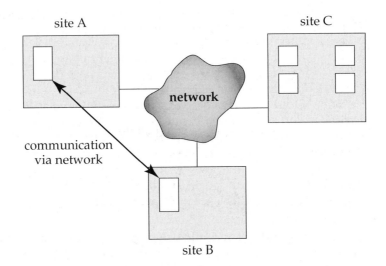

Figure 18.9   A distributed system.

are stored locally. In a centralized system, the database administrator of the central site controls the database. In a distributed system, there is a global database administrator responsible for the entire system. A part of these responsibilities is delegated to the local database administrator for each site. Depending on the design of the distributed database system, each administrator may have a different degree of **local autonomy**. The possibility of local autonomy is often a major advantage of distributed databases.

- **Availability.** If one site fails in a distributed system, the remaining sites may be able to continue operating. In particular, if data items are **replicated** in several sites, a transaction needing a particular data item may find that item in any of several sites. Thus, the failure of a site does not necessarily imply the shutdown of the system.

  The failure of one site must be detected by the system, and appropriate action may be needed to recover from the failure. The system must no longer use the services of the failed site. Finally, when the failed site recovers or is repaired, mechanisms must be available to integrate it smoothly back into the system.

  Although recovery from failure is more complex in distributed systems than in centralized systems, the ability of most of the system to continue to operate despite the failure of one site results in increased availability. Availability is crucial for database systems used for real-time applications. Loss of access to data by, for example, an airline may result in the loss of potential ticket buyers to competitors.

18.4.1   An Example of a Distributed Database

Consider a banking system consisting of four branches in four different cities. Each branch has its own computer, with a database of all the accounts maintained at that branch. Each such installation is thus a site. There also exists one single site that maintains information about all the branches of the bank. Each branch maintains (among others) a relation *account*(*Account-schema*), where

$$\text{\textit{Account-schema} = (\textit{account-number, branch-name, balance})}$$

The site containing information about all the branches of the bank maintains the relation *branch*(*Branch-schema*), where

$$\text{\textit{Branch-schema} = (\textit{branch-name, branch-city, assets})}$$

There are other relations maintained at the various sites; we ignore them for the purpose of our example.

To illustrate the difference between the two types of transactions—local and global—at the sites, consider a transaction to add $50 to account number A-177 located at the Valleyview branch. If the transaction was initiated at the Valleyview branch, then it is considered local; otherwise, it is considered global. A transaction to transfer $50 from account A-177 to account A-305, which is located at the Hillside branch, is a global transaction, since accounts in two different sites are accessed as a result of its execution.

In an ideal distributed database system, the sites would share a common global schema (although some relations may be stored only at some sites), all sites would run the same distributed database-management software, and the sites would be aware of each other's existence. If a distributed database is built from scratch, it would indeed be possible to achieve the above goals. However, in reality a distributed database has to be constructed by linking together multiple already-existing database systems, each with its own schema and possibly running different database-management software. Such systems are sometimes called **multidatabase systems** or **heterogeneous distributed database systems**. We discuss these systems in Section 19.8, where we show how to achieve a degree of global control despite the heterogeneity of the component systems.

18.4.2 Implementation Issues

Atomicity of transactions is an important issue in building a distributed database system. If a transaction runs across two sites, unless the system designers are careful, it may commit at one site and abort at another, leading to an inconsistent state. Transaction commit protocols ensure such a situation cannot arise. The *two-phase commit protocol* (2PC) is the most widely used of these protocols.

The basic idea behind 2PC is for each site to execute the transaction till just before commit, and then leave the commit decision to a single coordinator site; the transaction is said to be in the *ready* state at a site at this point. The coordinator decides to commit the transaction only if the transaction reaches the ready state at every site where it executed; otherwise (for example, if the transaction aborts at any site), the coordinator decides to abort the transaction. Every site where the transaction executed must follow the decision of the coordinator. If a site fails when a transaction is in ready state, when the site recovers from failure it should be in a position to either commit or abort the transaction, depending on the decision of the coordinator. The 2PC protocol is described in detail in Section 19.4.1.

Concurrency control is another issue in a distributed database. Since a transaction may access data items at several sites, transaction managers at several sites may need to coordinate to implement concurrency control. If locking is used (as is almost always the case in practice), locking can be performed locally at the sites containing accessed data items, but there is also a possibility of deadlock involving transactions originating at multiple sites. Therefore deadlock detection needs to be carried out across multiple sites. Failures are more common in distributed systems since not only may computers fail, but communication links may also fail. Replication of data items, which is the key to the continued functioning of distributed databases when failures occur, further complicates concurrency control. Section 19.5 provides detailed coverage of concurrency control in distributed databases.

The standard transaction models, based on multiple actions carried out by a single program unit, are often inappropriate for carrying out tasks that cross the boundaries of databases that cannot or will not cooperate to implement protocols such as 2PC.

Alternative approaches, based on *persistent messaging* for communication, are generally used for such tasks.

When the tasks to be carried out are complex, involving multiple databases and/or multiple interactions with humans, coordination of the tasks and ensuring transaction properties for the tasks become more complicated. *Workflow management systems* are systems designed to help with carrying out such tasks. Section 19.4.3 describes persistent messaging, while Section 24.2 describes workflow management systems.

In case an organization has to choose between a distributed architecture and a centralized architecture for implementing an application, the system architect must balance the advantages against the disadvantages of distribution of data. We have already seen the advantages of using distributed databases. The primary disadvantage of distributed database systems is the added complexity required to ensure proper coordination among the sites. This increased complexity takes various forms:

- **Software-development cost**. It is more difficult to implement a distributed database system; thus, it is more costly.

- **Greater potential for bugs**. Since the sites that constitute the distributed system operate in parallel, it is harder to ensure the correctness of algorithms, especially operation during failures of part of the system, and recovery from failures. The potential exists for extremely subtle bugs.

- **Increased processing overhead**. The exchange of messages and the additional computation required to achieve intersite coordination are a form of overhead that does not arise in centralized systems.

There are several approaches to distributed database design, ranging from fully distributed designs to ones that include a large degree of centralization. We study them in Chapter 19.

18.5 Network Types

Distributed databases and client–server systems are built around communication networks. There are basically two types of networks: **local-area networks** and **wide-area networks**. The main difference between the two is the way in which they are distributed geographically. In local-area networks, processors are distributed over small geographical areas, such as a single building or a number of adjacent buildings. In wide-area networks, on the other hand, a number of autonomous processors are distributed over a large geographical area (such as the United States or the entire world). These differences imply major variations in the speed and reliability of the communication network, and are reflected in the distributed operating-system design.

18.5.1 Local-Area Networks

Local-area networks (**LAN**s) (Figure 18.10) emerged in the early 1970s as a way for computers to communicate and to share data with one another. People recognized that, for many enterprises, numerous small computers, each with its own self-

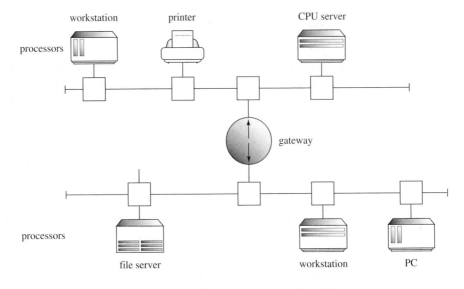

Figure 18.10 Local-area network.

contained applications, are more economical than a single large system. Because each small computer is likely to need access to a full complement of peripheral devices (such as disks and printers), and because some form of data sharing is likely to occur in a single enterprise, it was a natural step to connect these small systems into a network.

LANs are generally used in an office environment. All the sites in such systems are close to one another, so the communication links tend to have a higher speed and lower error rate than do their counterparts in wide-area networks. The most common links in a local-area network are twisted pair, coaxial cable, fiber optics, and, increasingly, wireless connections. Communication speeds range from a few megabits per second (for wireless local-area networks), to 1 gigabit per second for Gigabit Ethernet. Standard Ethernet runs at 10 megabits per second, while Fast Ethernet run at 100 megabits per second.

A **storage-area network** (**SAN**) is a special type of high-speed local-area network designed to connect large banks of storage devices (disks) to computers that use the data. Thus storage-area networks help build large-scale *shared-disk systems*. The motivation for using storage-area networks to connect multiple computers to large banks of storage devices is essentially the same as that for shared-disk databases, namely

- Scalability by adding more computers

- High availability, since data is still accessible even if a computer fails

RAID organizations are used in the storage devices to ensure high availability of the data, permitting processing to continue even if individual disks fail. Storage area networks are usually built with redundancy, such as multiple paths between nodes, so if a component such as a link or a connection to the network fails, the network continues to function.

18.5.2   Wide-Area Networks

Wide-area networks (WANs) emerged in the late 1960s, mainly as an academic research project to provide efficient communication among sites, allowing hardware and software to be shared conveniently and economically by a wide community of users. Systems that allowed remote terminals to be connected to a central computer via telephone lines were developed in the early 1960s, but they were not true WANs. The first WAN to be designed and developed was the *Arpanet*. Work on the Arpanet began in 1968. The Arpanet has grown from a four-site experimental network to a worldwide network of networks, the **Internet**, comprising hundreds of millions of computer systems. Typical links on the Internet are fiber-optic lines and, sometimes, satellite channels. Data rates for wide-area links typically range from a few megabits per second to hundreds of gigabits per second. The last link, to end user sites, is often based on *digital subscriber loop* (DSL) technology supporting a few megabits per second), or cable modem (supporting 10 megabits per second), or dial-up modem connections over phone lines (supporting up to 56 kilobits per second).

WANs can be classified into two types:

- In **discontinuous connection** WANs, such as those based on wireless connections, hosts are connected to the network only part of the time.

- In **continuous connection** WANs, such as the wired Internet, hosts are connected to the network at all times.

Networks that are not continuously connected typically do not allow transactions across sites, but may keep local copies of remote data, and refresh the copies periodically (every night, for instance). For applications where consistency is not critical, such as sharing of documents, groupware systems such as Lotus Notes allow updates of remote data to be made locally, and the updates are then propagated back to the remote site periodically. There is a potential for conflicting updates at different sites, conflicts that have to be detected and resolved. A mechanism for detecting conflicting updates is described later, in Section 23.5.4; the resolution mechanism for conflicting updates is, however, application dependent.

18.6   Summary

- Centralized database systems run entirely on a single computer. With the growth of personal computers and local-area networking, the database front-end functionality has moved increasingly to clients, with server systems providing the back-end functionality. Client–server interface protocols have helped the growth of client–server database systems.

- Servers can be either transaction servers or data servers, although the use of transaction servers greatly exceeds the use of data servers for providing database services.

  □ Transaction servers have multiple processes, possibly running on multiple processors. So that these processes have access to common data, such as the database buffer, systems store such data in shared memory. In addition to processes that handle queries, there are system processes that carry out tasks such as lock and log management and checkpointing.

☐ Data server systems supply raw data to clients. Such systems strive to minimize communication between clients and servers by caching data and locks at the clients. Parallel database systems use similar optimizations.

- Parallel database systems consist of multiple processors and multiple disks connected by a fast interconnection network. Speedup measures how much we can increase processing speed by increasing parallelism, for a single transaction. Scaleup measures how well we can handle an increased number of transactions by increasing parallelism. Interference, skew, and start–up costs act as barriers to getting ideal speedup and scaleup.

- Parallel database architectures include the shared-memory, shared-disk, shared-nothing, and hierarchical architectures. These architectures have different tradeoffs of scalability versus communication speed.

- A distributed database is a collection of partially independent databases that (ideally) share a common schema, and coordinate processing of transactions that access nonlocal data. The processors communicate with one another through a communication network that handles routing and connection strategies.

- Principally, there are two types of communication networks: local-area networks and wide-area networks. Local-area networks connect nodes that are distributed over small geographical areas, such as a single building or a few adjacent buildings. Wide-area networks connect nodes spread over a large geographical area. The Internet is the most extensively used wide-area network today.

    Storage-area networks are a special type of local-area network designed to provide fast interconnection between large banks of storage devices and multiple computers.

Review Terms

- Centralized systems
- Server systems
- Coarse-granularity parallelism
- Fine-granularity parallelism
- Database process structure
- Mutual exclusion
- Thread

- Server processes
    - ☐ Lock manager process
    - ☐ Database writer process
    - ☐ Log writer process
    - ☐ Checkpoint process
    - ☐ Process monitor process
- Client–server systems

- Transaction-server

- Query-server
- Data server
    - Prefetching
    - De-escalation
    - Data caching
    - Cache coherency
    - Lock caching
    - Call back
- Parallel systems
- Throughput
- Response time
- Speedup
    - Linear speedup
    - Sublinear speedup
- Scaleup
    - Linear scaleup
    - Sublinear scaleup
    - Batch scaleup
    - Transaction scaleup
- Startup costs
- Interference
- Skew
- Interconnection networks

- Bus
- Mesh
- Hypercube
- Parallel database architectures
    - Shared memory
    - Shared disk (clusters)
    - Shared nothing
    - Hierarchical
- Fault tolerance
- Distributed virtual-memory
- Nonuniform memory architecture (NUMA)
- Distributed systems
- Distributed database
    - Sites (nodes)
    - Local transaction
    - Global transaction
    - Local autonomy
- Multidatabase systems
- Network types
    - Local-area networks (LAN)
    - Wide-area networks (WAN)
    - Storage-area network (SAN)

Exercises

18.1 Why is it relatively easy to port a database from a single processor machine to a multiprocessor machine if individual queries need not be parallelized?

18.2 Transaction server architectures are popular for client-server relational databases, where transactions are short. On the other hand, data server architectures are popular for client-server object-oriented database systems, where transactions are expected to be relatively long. Give two reasons why data servers may be popular for object-oriented databases but not for relational databases.

18.3 Instead of storing shared structures in shared memory, an alternative architecture would be to store them in the local memory of a special process, and access the shared data by interprocess communication with the process. What would be the drawback of such an architecture?

18.4 In typical client–server systems the server machine is much more powerful than the clients; that is, its processor is faster, it may have multiple processors, and it has more memory and disk capacity. Consider instead a scenario where client and server machines have exactly the same power. Would it make sense to build a client–server system in such a scenario? Why? Which scenario would be better suited to a data-server architecture?

18.5 Consider an object-oriented database system based on a client-server architecture, with the server acting as a data server.

a. What is the effect of the speed of the interconnection between the client and the server on the choice between object and page shipping?

b. If page shipping is used, the cache of data at the client can be organized either as an object cache or a page cache. The page cache stores data in units of a page, while the object cache stores data in units of objects. Assume objects are smaller than a page. Describe one benefit of an object cache over a page cache.

18.6 What is lock de-escalation, and under what conditions is it required? Why is it not required if the unit of data shipping is an item?

18.7 Suppose you were in charge of the database operations of a company whose main job is to process transactions. Suppose the company is growing rapidly each year, and has outgrown its current computer system. When you are choosing a new parallel computer, what measure is most relevant—speedup, batch scaleup, or transaction scaleup? Why?

18.8 Suppose a transaction is written in C with embedded SQL, and about 80 percent of the time is spent in the SQL code, with the remaining 20 percent spent in C code. How much speedup can one hope to attain if parallelism is used only for the SQL code? Explain.

18.9 What are the factors that can work against linear scaleup in a transaction processing system? Which of the factors are likely to be the most important in each of the following architectures: shared memory, shared disk, and shared nothing?

18.10 Consider a bank that has a collection of sites, each running a database system. Suppose the only way the databases interact is by electronic transfer of money between one another. Would such a system qualify as a distributed database? Why?

18.11 Consider a network based on dial-up phone lines, where sites communicate periodically, such as every night. Such networks are often configured with a server site and multiple client sites. The client sites connect only to the server, and exchange data with other clients by storing data at the server and retrieving data stored at the server by other clients. What is the advantage of such an architecture over one where a site can exchange data with another site only by first dialing it up?

Bibliographical Notes

Patterson and Hennessy [1995] and Stone [1993] are textbooks that provide a good introduction to the area of computer architecture.

Gray and Reuter [1993] provides a textbook description of transaction processing, including the architecture of client–server and distributed systems. Geiger [1995] and Signore et al. [1995] describe the ODBC standard for client–server connectivity. North [1995] describes the use of a variety of tools for client–server database access.

Carey et al. [1991] and Franklin et al. [1993] describe data-caching techniques for client–server database systems. Biliris and Orenstein [1994] survey object storage management systems, including client–server related issues. Franklin et al. [1992] and Mohan and Narang [1994] describe recovery techniques for client-server systems.

DeWitt and Gray [1992] survey parallel database systems, including their architecture and performance measures. A survey of parallel computer architectures is presented by Duncan [1990]. Dubois and Thakkar [1992] is a collection of papers on scalable shared-memory architectures.

Ozsu and Valduriez [1999], Bell and Grimson [1992] and Ceri and Pelagatti [1984] provide textbook coverage of distributed database systems. Further references pertaining to parallel and distributed database systems appear in the bibliographical notes of Chapters 20 and 19, respectively.

Comer and Droms [1999] and Thomas [1996] describe the computer networking and the Internet. Tanenbaum [1996] and Halsall [1992] provide general overviews of computer networks. Discussions concerning ATM networks and switches are offered by de Prycker [1993].

CHAPTER 19

Distributed Databases

Unlike parallel systems, in which the processors are tightly coupled and constitute a single database system, a distributed database system consists of loosely coupled sites that share no physical components. Furthermore, the database systems that run on each site may have a substantial degree of mutual independence. We discussed the basic structure of distributed systems in Chapter 18.

Each site may participate in the execution of transactions that access data at one site, or several sites. The main difference between centralized and distributed database systems is that, in the former, the data reside in one single location, whereas in the latter, the data reside in several locations. This distribution of data is the cause of many difficulties in transaction processing and query processing. In this chapter, we address these difficulties.

We start by classifying distributed databases as homogeneous or heterogeneous, in Section 19.1. We then address the question of how to store data in a distributed database in Section 19.2. In Section 19.3, we outline a model for transaction processing in a distributed database. In Section 19.4, we describe how to implement atomic transactions in a distributed database by using special commit protocols. In Section 19.5, we describe concurrency control in distributed databases. In Section 19.6, we outline how to provide high availability in a distributed database by exploiting replication, so the system can continue processing transactions even when there is a failure. We address query processing in distributed databases in Section 19.7. In Section 19.8, we outline issues in handling heterogeneous databases. In Section 19.9, we describe directory systems, which can be viewed as a specialized form of distributed databases.

19.1 Homogeneous and Heterogeneous Databases

In a **homogeneous distributed database**, all sites have identical database management system software, are aware of one another, and agree to cooperate in processing users' requests. In such a system, local sites surrender a portion of their autonomy in terms of their right to change schemas or database management system software. That software must also cooperate with other sites in exchanging information about transactions, to make transaction processing possible across multiple sites.

In contrast, in a **heterogeneous distributed database**, different sites may use different schemas, and different database management system software. The sites may not be aware of one another, and they may provide only limited facilities for cooperation in transaction processing. The differences in schemas are often a major problem for query processing, while the divergence in software becomes a hindrance for processing transactions that access multiple sites.

In this chapter, we concentrate on homogeneous distributed databases. However, in Section 19.8 we briefly discuss query processing issues in heterogeneous distributed database systems. Transaction processing issues in such systems are covered later, in Section 24.6.

19.2   Distributed Data Storage

Consider a relation r that is to be stored in the database. There are two approaches to storing this relation in the distributed database:

- **Replication**. The system maintains several identical replicas (copies) of the relation, and stores each replica at a different site. The alternative to replication is to store only one copy of relation r.

- **Fragmentation**. The system partitions the relation into several fragments, and stores each fragment at a different site.

Fragmentation and replication can be combined: A relation can be partitioned into several fragments and there may be several replicas of each fragment. In the following subsections, we elaborate on each of these techniques.

19.2.1   Data Replication

If relation r is replicated, a copy of relation r is stored in two or more sites. In the most extreme case, we have **full replication**, in which a copy is stored in every site in the system.

There are a number of advantages and disadvantages to replication.

- **Availability**. If one of the sites containing relation r fails, then the relation r can be found in another site. Thus, the system can continue to process queries involving r, despite the failure of one site.

- **Increased parallelism**. In the case where the majority of accesses to the relation r result in only the reading of the relation, then several sites can process queries involving r in parallel. The more replicas of r there are, the greater the chance that the needed data will be found in the site where the transaction is executing. Hence, data replication minimizes movement of data between sites.

- **Increased overhead on update**. The system must ensure that all replicas of a relation r are consistent; otherwise, erroneous computations may result. Thus, whenever r is updated, the update must be propagated to all sites containing replicas. The result is increased overhead. For example, in a banking system, where account information is replicated in various sites, it is necessary to ensure that the balance in a particular account agrees in all sites.

In general, replication enhances the performance of read operations and increases the availability of data to read-only transactions. However, update transactions incur greater overhead. Controlling concurrent updates by several transactions to replicated data is more complex than in centralized systems, which we saw in Chapter 16. We can simplify the management of replicas of relation r by choosing one of them as the **primary copy** of r. For example, in a banking system, an account can be associated with the site in which the account has been opened. Similarly, in an airline-reservation system, a flight can be associated with the site at which the flight originates. We shall examine the primary copy scheme and other options for distributed concurrency control in Section 19.5.

19.2.2   Data Fragmentation

If relation r is fragmented, r is divided into a number of *fragments* $r_1, r_2, \ldots, r_n$. These fragments contain sufficient information to allow reconstruction of the original relation r. There are two different schemes for fragmenting a relation: *horizontal* fragmentation and *vertical* fragmentation. Horizontal fragmentation splits the relation by assigning each tuple of r to one or more fragments. Vertical fragmentation splits the relation by decomposing the scheme R of relation r.

We shall illustrate these approaches by fragmenting the relation *account*, with the schema

$$\textit{Account-schema} = (\textit{account-number, branch-name, balance})$$

In **horizontal fragmentation**, a relation r is partitioned into a number of subsets, $r_1, r_2, \ldots, r_n$. Each tuple of relation r must belong to at least one of the fragments, so that the original relation can be reconstructed, if needed.

As an illustration, the *account* relation can be divided into several different fragments, each of which consists of tuples of accounts belonging to a particular branch. If the banking system has only two branches—Hillside and Valleyview—then there are two different fragments:

$$account_1 = \sigma_{branch\text{-}name = \text{“Hillside”}}(account)$$
$$account_2 = \sigma_{branch\text{-}name = \text{“Valleyview”}}(account)$$

Horizontal fragmentation is usually used to keep tuples at the sites where they are used the most, to minimize data transfer.

In general, a horizontal fragment can be defined as a *selection* on the global relation r. That is, we use a predicate P_i to construct fragment r_i:

$$r_i = \sigma_{P_i}(r)$$

We reconstruct the relation r by taking the union of all fragments; that is,

$$r = r_1 \cup r_2 \cup \cdots \cup r_n$$

In our example, the fragments are disjoint. By changing the selection predicates used to construct the fragments, we can have a particular tuple of r appear in more than one of the r_i.

In its simplest form, vertical fragmentation is the same as decomposition (see Chapter 7). **Vertical fragmentation** of $r(R)$ involves the definition of several subsets of attributes $R_1, R_2, \ldots, R_n$ of the schema R so that

$$R = R_1 \cup R_2 \cup \cdots \cup R_n$$

Each fragment r_i of r is defined by

$$r_i = \Pi_{R_i}(r)$$

The fragmentation should be done in such a way that we can reconstruct relation r from the fragments by taking the natural join

$$r = r_1 \bowtie r_2 \bowtie r_3 \bowtie \cdots \bowtie r_n$$

One way of ensuring that the relation r can be reconstructed is to include the primary-key attributes of R in each of the R_i. More generally, any superkey can be used. It is often convenient to add a special attribute, called a *tuple-id*, to the schema R. The tuple-id value of a tuple is a unique value that distinguishes the tuple from all other tuples. The tuple-id attribute thus serves as a candidate key for the augmented schema, and is included in each of the R_is. The physical or logical address for a tuple can be used as a tuple-id, since each tuple has a unique address.

To illustrate vertical fragmentation, consider a university database with a relation *employee-info* that stores, for each employee, *employee-id*, *name*, *designation*, and *salary*. For privacy reasons, this relation may be fragmented into a relation *employee-private-info* containing *employee-id* and *salary*, and another relation *employee-public-info* containing attributes *employee-id*, *name*, and *designation*. These may be stored at different sites, again for security reasons.

The two types of fragmentation can be applied to a single schema; for instance, the fragments obtained by horizontally fragmenting a relation can be further partitioned vertically. Fragments can also be replicated. In general, a fragment can be replicated, replicas of fragments can be fragmented further, and so on.

19.2.3 Transparency

The user of a distributed database system should not be required to know either where the data are physically located or how the data can be accessed at the specific local site. This characteristic, called **data transparency**, can take several forms:

- **Fragmentation transparency.** Users are not required to know how a relation has been fragmented.

- **Replication transparency.** Users view each data object as logically unique. The distributed system may replicate an object to increase either system performance or data availability. Users do not have to be concerned with what data objects have been replicated, or where replicas have been placed.

- **Location transparency**. Users are not required to know the physical location of the data. The distributed database system should be able to find any data as long as the data identifier is supplied by the user transaction.

Data items—such as relations, fragments, and replicas — must have unique names. This property is easy to ensure in a centralized database. In a distributed database, however, we must take care to ensure that two sites do not use the same name for distinct data items.

One solution to this problem is to require all names to be registered in a central **name server**. The name server helps to ensure that the same name does not get used for different data items. We can also use the name server to locate a data item, given the name of the item. This approach, however, suffers from two major disadvantages. First, the name server may become a performance bottleneck when data items are located by their names, resulting in poor performance. Second, if the name server crashes, it may not be possible for any site in the distributed system to continue to run.

A more widely used alternative approach requires that each site prefix its own site identifier to any name that it generates. This approach ensures that no two sites generate the same name (since each site has a unique identifier). Furthermore, no central control is required. This solution, however, fails to achieve location transparency, since site identifiers are attached to names. Thus, the *account* relation might be referred to as *site17.account*, or *account@site17*, rather than as simply *account*. Many database systems use the internet address of a site to identify it.

To overcome this problem, the database system can create a set of alternative names or **aliases** for data items. A user may thus refer to data items by simple names that are translated by the system to complete names. The mapping of aliases to the real names can be stored at each site. With aliases, the user can be unaware of the physical location of a data item. Furthermore, the user will be unaffected if the database administrator decides to move a data item from one site to another.

Users should not have to refer to a specific replica of a data item. Instead, the system should determine which replica to reference on a read request, and should update all replicas on a write request. We can ensure that it does so by maintaining a catalog table, which the system uses to determine all replicas for the data item.

19.3 Distributed Transactions

Access to the various data items in a distributed system is usually accomplished through transactions, which must preserve the ACID properties (Section 15.1). There are two types of transaction that we need to consider. The **local transactions** are those that access and update data in only one local database; the **global transactions** are those that access and update data in several local databases. Ensuring the ACID properties of the local transactions can be done as described in Chapters 15, 16, and 17. However, for global transactions, this task is much more complicated, since several sites may be participating in execution. The failure of one of these sites, or the failure of a communication link connecting these sites, may result in erroneous computations.

In this section we study the system structure of a distributed database, and its possible failure modes. On the basis of the model presented in this section, in Section 19.4 we study protocols for ensuring atomic commit of global transactions, and in Section 19.5 we study protocols for concurrency control in distributed databases. In Section 19.6 we study how a distributed database can continue functioning even in the presence of various types of failure.

19.3.1 System Structure

Each site has its own *local* transaction manager, whose function is to ensure the ACID properties of those transactions that execute at that site. The various transaction managers cooperate to execute global transactions. To understand how such a manager can be implemented, consider an abstract model of a transaction system, in which each site contains two subsystems:

- The **transaction manager** manages the execution of those transactions (or subtransactions) that access data stored in a local site. Note that each such transaction may be either a local transaction (that is, a transaction that executes at only that site) or part of a global transaction (that is, a transaction that executes at several sites).

- The **transaction coordinator** coordinates the execution of the various transactions (both local and global) initiated at that site.

The overall system architecture appears in Figure 19.1.

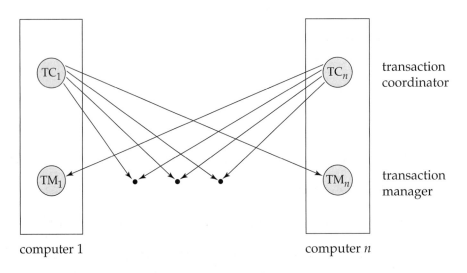

Figure 19.1 System architecture.

The structure of a transaction manager is similar in many respects to the structure of a centralized system. Each transaction manager is responsible for

- Maintaining a log for recovery purposes

- Participating in an appropriate concurrency-control scheme to coordinate the concurrent execution of the transactions executing at that site

As we shall see, we need to modify both the recovery and concurrency schemes to accommodate the distribution of transactions.

The transaction coordinator subsystem is not needed in the centralized environment, since a transaction accesses data at only a single site. A transaction coordinator, as its name implies, is responsible for coordinating the execution of all the transactions initiated at that site. For each such transaction, the coordinator is responsible for

- Starting the execution of the transaction

- Breaking the transaction into a number of subtransactions and distributing these subtransactions to the appropriate sites for execution

- Coordinating the termination of the transaction, which may result in the transaction being committed at all sites or aborted at all sites

19.3.2   System Failure Modes

A distributed system may suffer from the same types of failure that a centralized system does (for example, software errors, hardware errors, or disk crashes). There are, however, additional types of failure with which we need to deal in a distributed environment. The basic failure types are

- Failure of a site

- Loss of messages

- Failure of a communication link

- Network partition

The loss or corruption of messages is always a possibility in a distributed system. The system uses transmission-control protocols, such as TCP/IP, to handle such errors. Information about such protocols may be found in standard textbooks on networking (see the bibliographical notes).

However, if two sites A and B are not directly connected, messages from one to the other must be *routed* through a sequence of communication links. If a communication link fails, messages that would have been transmitted across the link must be rerouted. In some cases, it is possible to find another route through the network, so that the messages are able to reach their destination. In other cases, a failure may result in there being no connection between some pairs of sites. A system is **partitioned** if it has been split into two (or more) subsystems, called **partitions**, that lack any connection between them. Note that, under this definition, a subsystem may consist of a single node.

19.4 Commit Protocols

If we are to ensure atomicity, all the sites in which a transaction T executed must agree on the final outcome of the execution. T must either commit at all sites, or it must abort at all sites. To ensure this property, the transaction coordinator of T must execute a *commit protocol*.

Among the simplest and most widely used commit protocols is the **two-phase commit protocol** (**2PC**), which is described in Section 19.4.1. An alternative is the **three-phase commit protocol** (**3PC**), which avoids certain disadvantages of the 2PC protocol but adds to complexity and overhead. Section 19.4.2 briefly outlines the 3PC protocol.

19.4.1 Two-Phase Commit

We first describe how the two-phase commit protocol (2PC) operates during normal operation, then describe how it handles failures and finally how it carries out recovery and concurrency control.

Consider a transaction T initiated at site S_i, where the transaction coordinator is C_i.

19.4.1.1 The Commit Protocol

When T completes its execution—that is, when all the sites at which T has executed inform C_i that T has completed—C_i starts the 2PC protocol.

- **Phase 1**. C_i adds the record <prepare T> to the log, and forces the log onto stable storage. It then sends a prepare T message to all sites at which T executed. On receiving such a message, the transaction manager at that site determines whether it is willing to commit its portion of T. If the answer is no, it adds a record <no T> to the log, and then responds by sending an abort T message to C_i. If the answer is yes, it adds a record <ready T> to the log, and forces the log (with all the log records corresponding to T) onto stable storage. The transaction manager then replies with a ready T message to C_i.

- **Phase 2**. When C_i receives responses to the prepare T message from all the sites, or when a prespecified interval of time has elapsed since the prepare T message was sent out, C_i can determine whether the transaction T can be committed or aborted. Transaction T can be committed if C_i received a ready T message from all the participating sites. Otherwise, transaction T must be aborted. Depending on the verdict, either a record <commit T> or a record <abort T> is added to the log and the log is forced onto stable storage. At this point, the fate of the transaction has been sealed. Following this point, the coordinator sends either a commit T or an abort T message to all participating sites. When a site receives that message, it records the message in the log.

A site at which T executed can unconditionally abort T at any time before it sends the message ready T to the coordinator. Once the message is sent, the transaction is said to be in the **ready state** at the site. The ready T message is, in effect, a promise by a site to follow the coordinator's order to commit T or to abort T. To make such a promise, the needed information must first be stored in stable storage. Otherwise, if the site crashes after sending ready T, it may be unable to make good on its promise. Further, locks acquired by the transaction must continue to be held till the transaction completes.

Since unanimity is required to commit a transaction, the fate of T is sealed as soon as at least one site responds abort T. Since the coordinator site S_i is one of the sites at which T executed, the coordinator can decide unilaterally to abort T. The final verdict regarding T is determined at the time that the coordinator writes that verdict (commit or abort) to the log and forces that verdict to stable storage. In some implementations of the 2PC protocol, a site sends an acknowledge T message to the coordinator at the end of the second phase of the protocol. When the coordinator receives the acknowledge T message from all the sites, it adds the record <complete T> to the log.

19.4.1.2   Handling of Failures

The 2PC protocol responds in differenct ways to various types of failures:

- **Failure of a participating site**. If the coordinator C_i detects that a site has failed, it takes these actions: If the site fails before responding with a ready T message to C_i, the coordinator assumes that it responded with an abort T message. If the site fails after the coordinator has received the ready T message from the site, the coordinator executes the rest of the commit protocol in the normal fashion, ignoring the failure of the site.

  When a participating site S_k recovers from a failure, it must examine its log to determine the fate of those transactions that were in the midst of execution when the failure occurred. Let T be one such transaction. We consider each of the possible cases:

  □ The log contains a <commit T> record. In this case, the site executes redo(T).
  □ The log contains an <abort T> record. In this case, the site executes undo(T).
  □ The log contains a <ready T> record. In this case, the site must consult C_i to determine the fate of T. If C_i is up, it notifies S_k regarding whether T committed or aborted. In the former case, it executes redo(T); in the latter case, it executes undo(T). If C_i is down, S_k must try to find the fate of T from other sites. It does so by sending a querystatus T message to all the sites in the system. On receiving such a message, a site must consult its log to determine whether T has executed there, and if T has, whether T committed or aborted. It then notifies S_k about this outcome. If no site has the appropriate information (that is, whether T committed or aborted), then S_k can neither abort nor commit T. The decision concerning T is

postponed until S_k can obtain the needed information. Thus, S_k must periodically resend the querystatus message to the other sites. It continues to do so until a site that contains the needed information recovers. Note that the site at which C_i resides always has the needed information.

☐ The log contains no control records (abort, commit, ready) concerning T. Thus, we know that S_k failed before responding to the prepare T message from C_i. Since the failure of S_k precludes the sending of such a response, by our algorithm C_i must abort T. Hence, S_k must execute undo(T).

- **Failure of the coordinator**. If the coordinator fails in the midst of the execution of the commit protocol for transaction T, then the participating sites must decide the fate of T. We shall see that, in certain cases, the participating sites cannot decide whether to commit or abort T, and therefore these sites must wait for the recovery of the failed coordinator.

    ☐ If an active site contains a <commit T> record in its log, then T must be committed.

    ☐ If an active site contains an <abort T> record in its log, then T must be aborted.

    ☐ If some active site does *not* contain a <ready T> record in its log, then the failed coordinator C_i cannot have decided to commit T, because a site that does not have a <ready T> record in its log cannot have sent a ready T message to C_i. However, the coordinator may have decided to abort T, but not to commit T. Rather than wait for C_i to recover, it is preferable to abort T.

    ☐ If none of the preceding cases holds, then all active sites must have a <ready T> record in their logs, but no additional control records (such as <abort T> or <commit T>). Since the coordinator has failed, it is impossible to determine whether a decision has been made, and if one has, what that decision is, until the coordinator recovers. Thus, the active sites must wait for C_i to recover. Since the fate of T remains in doubt, T may continue to hold system resources. For example, if locking is used, T may hold locks on data at active sites. Such a situation is undesirable, because it may be hours or days before C_i is again active. During this time, other transactions may be forced to wait for T. As a result, data items may be unavailable not only on the failed site (C_i), but on active sites as well. This situation is called the **blocking** problem, because T is blocked pending the recovery of site C_i.

- **Network partition**. When a network partitions, two possibilities exist:

    1. The coordinator and all its participants remain in one partition. In this case, the failure has no effect on the commit protocol.

    2. The coordinator and its participants belong to several partitions. From the viewpoint of the sites in one of the partitions, it appears that the sites in other partitions have failed. Sites that are not in the partition containing the coordinator simply execute the protocol to deal with failure of the coordinator. The coordinator and the sites that are in the same partition as

the coordinator follow the usual commit protocol, assuming that the sites in the other partitions have failed.

Thus, the major disadvantage of the 2PC protocol is that coordinator failure may result in blocking, where a decision either to commit or to abort T may have to be postponed until C_i recovers.

19.4.1.3 Recovery and Concurrency Control

When a failed site restarts, we can perform recovery by using, for example, the recovery algorithm described in Section 17.9. To deal with distributed commit protocols (such as 2PC and 3PC), the recovery procedure must treat **in-doubt transactions** specially; in-doubt transactions are transactions for which a <ready T> log record is found, but neither a <commit T> log record nor an <abort T> log record is found. The recovering site must determine the commit–abort status of such transactions by contacting other sites, as described in Section 19.4.1.2.

If recovery is done as just described, however, normal transaction processing at the site cannot begin until all in-doubt transactions have been committed or rolled back. Finding the status of in-doubt transactions can be slow, since multiple sites may have to be contacted. Further, if the coordinator has failed, and no other site has information about the commit–abort status of an incomplete transaction, recovery potentially could become blocked if 2PC is used. As a result, the site performing restart recovery may remain unusable for a long period.

To circumvent this problem, recovery algorithms typically provide support for noting lock information in the log. (We are assuming here that locking is used for concurrency control.) Instead of writing a <ready T> log record, the algorithm writes a <ready T, L> log record, where L is a list of all write locks held by the transaction T when the log record is written. At recovery time, after performing local recovery actions, for every in-doubt transaction T, all the write locks noted in the <ready T, L> log record (read from the log) are reacquired.

After lock reacquisition is complete for all in-doubt transactions, transaction processing can start at the site, even before the commit–abort status of the in-doubt transactions is determined. The commit or rollback of in-doubt transactions proceeds concurrently with the execution of new transactions. Thus, site recovery is faster, and never gets blocked. Note that new transactions that have a lock conflict with any write locks held by in-doubt transactions will be unable to make progress until the conflicting in-doubt transactions have been committed or rolled back.

19.4.2 Three-Phase Commit

The three-phase commit (3PC) protocol is an extension of the two-phase commit protocol that avoids the blocking problem under certain assumptions. In particular, it is assumed that no network partition occurs, and not more than k sites fail, where k is some predetermined number. Under these assumptions, the protocol avoids blocking by introducing an extra third phase where multiple sites are involved in the decision to commit. Instead of directly noting the commit decision in its persistent storage, the coordinator first ensures that at least k other sites know that it intended to commit the transaction. If the coordinator fails, the remaining sites first select a new coordinator. This new coordinator checks the status of the protocol from the remaining sites; if the coordinator had decided to commit, at least one of the other k sites that it informed will be up and will ensure that the commit decision is respected. The new coordinator restarts the third phase of the protocol if some site knew that the old coordinator intended to commit the transaction. Otherwise the new coordinator aborts the transaction.

While the 3PC protocol has the desirable property of not blocking unless k sites fail, it has the drawback that a partitioning of the network will appear to be the same as more than k sites failing, which would lead to blocking. The protocol also has to be carefully implemented to ensure that network partitioning (or more than k sites failing) does not result in inconsistencies, where a transaction is committed in one partition, and aborted in another. Because of its overhead, the 3PC protocol is not widely used. See the bibliographical notes for references giving more details of the 3PC protocol.

19.4.3   Alternative Models of Transaction Processing

For many applications, the blocking problem of two-phase commit is not acceptable. The problem here is the notion of a single transaction that works across multiple sites. In this section we describe how to use *persistent messaging* to avoid the problem of distributed commit, and then briefly outline the larger issue of *workflows*; workflows are considered in more detail in Section 24.2.

To understand persistent messaging consider how one might transfer funds between two different banks, each with its own computer. One approach is to have a transaction span the two sites, and use two-phase commit to ensure atomicity. However, the transaction may have to update the total bank balance, and blocking could have a serious impact on all other transactions at each bank, since almost all transactions at the bank would update the total bank balance.

In contrast, consider how fund transfer by a bank check occurs. The bank first deducts the amount of the check from the available balance and prints out a check. The check is then physically transferred to the other bank where it is deposited. After verifying the check, the bank increases the local balance by the amount of the check. The check constitutes a message sent between the two banks. So that funds are not lost or incorrectly increased, the check must not be lost, and must not be duplicated and deposited more than once. When the bank computers are connected by a network, persistent messages provide the same service as the check (but much faster, of course).

Persistent messages are messages that are guaranteed to be delivered to the recipient exactly once (neither less nor more), regardless of failures, if the transaction sending the message commits, and are guaranteed to not be delivered if the transaction aborts. Database recovery techniques are used to implement persistent messaging on top of the normal network channels, as we will see shortly. In contrast, regular messages may be lost or may even be delivered multiple times in some situations.

Error handling is more complicated with persistent messaging than with two-phase commit. For instance, if the account where the check is to be deposited has been closed, the check must be sent back to the originating account and credited back there. Both sites must therefore be provided with error handling code, along with code to handle the persistent messages. In contrast, with two-phase commit, the error would be detected by the transaction, which would then never deduct the amount in the first place.

The types of exception conditions that may arise depend on the application, so it is not possible for the database system to handle exceptions automatically. The application programs that send and receive persistent messages must include code to handle exception conditions and bring the system back to a consistent state. For instance, it is not acceptable to just lose the money being transfered if the receiving account has been closed; the money must be credited back to the originating account, and if that is not possible for some reason, humans must be alerted to resolve the situation manually.

There are many applications where the benefit of eliminating blocking is well worth the extra effort to implement systems that use persistent messages. In fact, few organizations would agree to support two-phase commit for transactions originating outside the organization, since failures could result in blocking of access to local data. Persistent messaging therefore plays an important role in carrying out transactions that cross organizational boundaries.

Workflows provide a general model of transaction processing involving multiple sites and possibly human processing of certain steps. For instance, when a bank receives a loan application, there are many steps it must take, including contacting external credit-checking agencies, before approving or rejecting a loan application. The steps, together, form a workflow. We study workflows in more detail in Section 24.2. We also note that persistent messaging forms the underlying basis for workflows in a distributed environment.

We now consider the **implementation** of persistent messaging. Persistent messaging can be implemented on top of an unreliable messaging infrastructure, which may lose messages or deliver them multiple times, by these protocols:

- **Sending site protocol**: When a transaction wishes to send a persistent message, it writes a record containing the message in a special relation *messages-to-send*, instead of directly sending out the message. The message is also given a unique message identifier.

    A *message delivery process* monitors the relation, and when a new message is found, it sends the message to its destination. The usual database concurrency control mechanisms ensure that the system process reads the message only after the transaction that wrote the message commits; if the transaction aborts, the usual recovery mechanism would delete the message from the relation.

    The message delivery process deletes a message from the relation only after it receives an acknowledgment from the destination site. If it receives no acknowledgement from the destination site, after some time it sends the message again. It repeats this until an acknowledgment is received. In case of permanent failures, the system will decide, after some period of time, that the message is undeliverable. Exception handling code provided by the application is then invoked to deal with the failure.

Writing the message to a relation and processing it only after the transaction commits ensures that the message will be delivered if and only if the transaction commits. Repeatedly sending it guarantees it will be delivered even if there are (temporary) system or network failures.

- **Receiving site protocol**: When a site receives a persistent message, it runs a transaction that adds the message to a special *received-messages* relation, provided it is not already present in the relation (the unique message identifier detects duplicates). After the transaction commits, or if the message was already present in the relation, the receiving site sends an acknowledgment back to the sending site.

  Note that sending the acknowledgment before the transaction commits is not safe, since a system failure may then result in loss of the message. Checking whether the message has been received earlier is essential to avoid multiple deliveries of the message.

  In many messaging systems, it is possible for messages to get delayed arbitrarily, although such delays are very unlikely. Therefore, to be safe, the message must never be deleted from the *received-messages* relation. Deleting it could result in a duplicate delivery not being detected. But as a result, the *received-messages* relation may grow indefinitely. To deal with this problem, each message is given a timestamp, and if the timestamp of a received message is older than some cutoff, the message is discarded. All messages recorded in the *received-messages* relation that are older than the cutoff can be deleted.

19.5   Concurrency Control in Distributed Databases

We show here how some of the concurrency-control schemes discussed in Chapter 16 can be modified so that they can be used in a distributed environment. We assume that each site participates in the execution of a commit protocol to ensure global transaction atomicity.

The protocols we describe in this section require updates to be done on all replicas of a data item. If any site containing a replica of a data item has failed, updates to the data item cannot be processed. In Section 19.6 we describe protocols that can continue transaction processing even if some sites or links have failed, thereby providing high availability.

19.5.1   Locking Protocols

The various locking protocols described in Chapter 16 can be used in a distributed environment. The only change that needs to be incorporated is in the way the lock manager deals with replicated data. We present several possible schemes that are applicable to an environment where data can be replicated in several sites. As in Chapter 16, we shall assume the existence of the *shared* and *exclusive* lock modes.

19.5.1.1 Single Lock-Manager Approach

In the **single lock-manager** approach, the system maintains a *single* lock manager that resides in a *single* chosen site—say S_i. All lock and unlock requests are made at site S_i. When a transaction needs to lock a data item, it sends a lock request to S_i. The lock manager determines whether the lock can be granted immediately. If the lock can be granted, the lock manager sends a message to that effect to the site at which the lock request was initiated. Otherwise, the request is delayed until it can be granted, at which time a message is sent to the site at which the lock request was initiated. The transaction can read the data item from *any* one of the sites at which a replica of the data item resides. In the case of a write, all the sites where a replica of the data item resides must be involved in the writing.

The scheme has these advantages:

- **Simple implementation**. This scheme requires two messages for handling lock requests, and one message for handling unlock requests.

- **Simple deadlock handling**. Since all lock and unlock requests are made at one site, the deadlock-handling algorithms discussed in Chapter 16 can be applied directly to this environment.

The disadvantages of the scheme are:

- **Bottleneck**. The site S_i becomes a bottleneck, since all requests must be processed there.

- **Vulnerability**. If the site S_i fails, the concurrency controller is lost. Either processing must stop, or a recovery scheme must be used so that a backup site can take over lock management from S_i, as described in Section 19.6.5.

19.5.1.2 Distributed Lock Manager

A compromise between the advantages and disadvantages can be achieved through the **distributed lock-manager** approach, in which the lock-manager function is distributed over several sites.

Each site maintains a local lock manager whose function is to administer the lock and unlock requests for those data items that are stored in that site. When a transaction wishes to lock data item Q, which is not replicated and resides at site S_i, a message is sent to the lock manager at site S_i requesting a lock (in a particular lock mode). If data item Q is locked in an incompatible mode, then the request is delayed until it can be granted. Once it has determined that the lock request can be granted, the lock manager sends a message back to the initiator indicating that it has granted the lock request.

There are several alternative ways of dealing with replication of data items, which we study in Sections 19.5.1.3 to 19.5.1.6.

The distributed lock manager scheme has the advantage of simple implementation, and reduces the degree to which the coordinator is a bottleneck. It has a reasonably low overhead, requiring two message transfers for handling lock requests, and one message transfer for handling unlock requests. However, deadlock handling is more complex, since the lock and unlock requests are no longer made at a single site: There may be intersite deadlocks even when there is no deadlock within a single site. The deadlock-handling algorithms discussed in Chapter 16 must be modified, as we shall discuss in Section 19.5.4, to detect global deadlocks.

19.5.1.3 Primary Copy

When a system uses data replication, we can choose one of the replicas as the **primary copy**. Thus, for each data item Q, the primary copy of Q must reside in precisely one site, which we call the **primary site** of Q.

When a transaction needs to lock a data item Q, it requests a lock at the primary site of Q. As before, the response to the request is delayed until it can be granted.

Thus, the primary copy enables concurrency control for replicated data to be handled like that for unreplicated data. This similarity allows for a simple implementation. However, if the primary site of Q fails, Q is inaccessible, even though other sites containing a replica may be accessible.

19.5.1.4 Majority Protocol

The **majority protocol** works this way: If data item Q is replicated in n different sites, then a lock-request message must be sent to more than one-half of the n sites in which Q is stored. Each lock manager determines whether the lock can be granted immediately (as far as it is concerned). As before, the response is delayed until the request can be granted. The transaction does not operate on Q until it has successfully obtained a lock on a majority of the replicas of Q.

This scheme deals with replicated data in a decentralized manner, thus avoiding the drawbacks of central control. However, it suffers from these disadvantages:

- **Implementation**. The majority protocol is more complicated to implement than are the previous schemes. It requires $2(n/2 + 1)$ messages for handling lock requests, and $(n/2 + 1)$ messages for handling unlock requests.

- **Deadlock handling**. In addition to the problem of global deadlocks due to the use of a distributed lock-manager approach, it is possible for a deadlock to occur even if only one data item is being locked. As an illustration, consider a system with four sites and full replication. Suppose that transactions T_1 and T_2 wish to lock data item Q in exclusive mode. Transaction T_1 may succeed in locking Q at sites S_1 and S_3, while transaction T_2 may succeed in locking Q at sites S_2 and S_4. Each then must wait to acquire the third lock; hence, a deadlock has occurred. Luckily, we can avoid such deadlocks with relative ease, by requiring all sites to request locks on the replicas of a data item in the same predetermined order.

19.5.1.5   Biased Protocol

The **biased protocol** is another approach to handling replication. The difference from the majority protocol is that requests for shared locks are given more favorable treatment than requests for exclusive locks.

- **Shared locks**. When a transaction needs to lock data item Q, it simply requests a lock on Q from the lock manager at one site that contains a replica of Q.

- **Exclusive locks**. When a transaction needs to lock data item Q, it requests a lock on Q from the lock manager at all sites that contain a replica of Q.

As before, the response to the request is delayed until it can be granted.

The biased scheme has the advantage of imposing less overhead on read operations than does the majority protocol. This savings is especially significant in common cases in which the frequency of read is much greater than the frequency of write. However, the additional overhead on writes is a disadvantage. Furthermore, the biased protocol shares the majority protocol's disadvantage of complexity in handling deadlock.

19.5.1.6   Quorum Consensus Protocol

The **quorum consensus** protocol is a generalization of the majority protocol. The quorum consensus protocol assigns each site a nonnegative weight. It assigns read and write operations on an item x two integers, called **read quorum** Q_r and **write quorum** Q_w, that must satisfy the following condition, where S is the total weight of all sites at which x resides:

$$Q_r + Q_w > S \text{ and } 2 * Q_w > S$$

To execute a read operation, enough replicas must be read that their total weight is $\geq Q_r$. To execute a write operation, enough replicas must be written so that their total weight is $\geq Q_w$.

The benefit of the quorum consensus approach is that it can permit the cost of either reads or writes to be selectively reduced by appropriately defining the read and write quorums. For instance, with a small read quorum, reads need to read fewer replicas, but the write quorum will be higher, hence writes can succeed only if correspondingly more replicas are available. Also, if higher weights are given to some sites (for example, those less likely to fail), fewer sites need to be accessed for acquiring locks.

In fact, by setting weights and quorums appropriately, the quorum consensus protocol can simulate the majority protocol and the biased protocols.

19.5.2   Timestamping

The principal idea behind the timestamping scheme in Section 16.2 is that each transaction is given a *unique* timestamp that the system uses in deciding the serialization order. Our first task, then, in generalizing the centralized scheme to a distributed

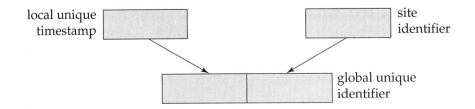

Figure 19.2   Generation of unique timestamps.

scheme is to develop a scheme for generating unique timestamps. Then, the various protocols can operate directly to the nonreplicated environment.

There are two primary methods for generating unique timestamps, one centralized and one distributed. In the centralized scheme, a single site distributes the timestamps. The site can use a logical counter or its own local clock for this purpose.

In the distributed scheme, each site generates a unique local timestamp by using either a logical counter or the local clock. We obtain the unique global timestamp by concatenating the unique local timestamp with the site identifier, which also must be unique (Figure 19.2). The order of concatenation is important! We use the site identifier in the least significant position to ensure that the global timestamps generated in one site are not always greater than those generated in another site. Compare this technique for generating unique timestamps with the one that we presented in Section 19.2.3 for generating unique names.

We may still have a problem if one site generates local timestamps at a rate faster than that of the other sites. In such a case, the fast site's logical counter will be larger than that of other sites. Therefore, all timestamps generated by the fast site will be larger than those generated by other sites. What we need is a mechanism to ensure that local timestamps are generated fairly across the system. We define within each site S_i a **logical clock** (LC_i), which generates the unique local timestamp. The logical clock can be implemented as a counter that is incremented after a new local timestamp is generated. To ensure that the various logical clocks are synchronized, we require that a site S_i advance its logical clock whenever a transaction T_i with timestamp $<x,y>$ visits that site and x is greater than the current value of LC_i. In this case, site S_i advances its logical clock to the value $x + 1$.

If the system clock is used to generate timestamps, then timestamps will be assigned fairly, provided that no site has a system clock that runs fast or slow. Since clocks may not be perfectly accurate, a technique similar to that for logical clocks must be used to ensure that no clock gets far ahead of or behind another clock.

19.5.3 Replication with Weak Degrees of Consistency

Many commercial databases today support replication, which can take one of several forms. With **master–slave replication**, the database allows updates at a primary site, and automatically propagates updates to replicas at other sites. Transactions may read the replicas at other sites, but are not permitted to update them.

An important feature of such replication is that transactions do not obtain locks at remote sites. To ensure that transactions running at the replica sites see a consistent (but perhaps outdated) view of the database, the replica should reflect a **transaction-consistent snapshot** of the data at the primary; that is, the replica should reflect all updates of transactions up to some transaction in the serialization order, and should not reflect any updates of later transactions in the serialization order.

The database may be configured to propagate updates immediately after they occur at the primary, or to propagate updates only periodically.

Master–slave replication is particularly useful for distributing information, for instance from a central office to branch offices of an organization. Another use for this form of replication is in creating a copy of the database to run large queries, so that queries do not interfere with transactions. Updates should be propagated periodically—every night, for example—so that update propagation does not interfere with query processing.

The Oracle database system supports a **create snapshot** statement, which can create a transaction-consistent snapshot copy of a relation, or set of relations, at a remote site. It also supports snapshot refresh, which can be done either by recomputing the snapshot or by incrementally updating it. Oracle supports automatic refresh, either continuously or at periodic intervals.

With **multimaster replication** (also called **update-anywhere replication**) updates are permitted at any replica of a data item, and are automatically propagated to all replicas. This model is the basic model used to manage replicas in distributed databases. Transactions update the local copy and the system updates other replicas transparently.

One way of updating replicas is to apply immediate update with two-phase commit, using one of the distributed concurrency-control techniques we have seen. Many database systems use the biased protocol, where writes have to lock and update all replicas and reads lock and read any one replica, as their currency-control technique.

Many database systems provide an alternative form of updating: They update at one site, with **lazy propagation** of updates to other sites, instead of immediately applying updates to all replicas as part of the transaction performing the update. Schemes based on lazy propagation allow transaction processing (including updates) to proceed even if a site is disconnected from the network, thus improving availability, but, unfortunately, do so at the cost of consistency. One of two approaches is usually followed when lazy propagation is used:

- Updates at replicas are translated into updates at a primary site, which are then propagated lazily to all replicas.

  This approach ensures that updates to an item are ordered serially, although serializability problems can occur, since transactions may read an old value of some other data item and use it to perform an update.

- Updates are performed at any replica and propagated to all other replicas.

  This approach can cause even more problems, since the same data item may be updated concurrently at multiple sites.

Some conflicts due to the lack of distributed concurrency control can be detected when updates are propagated to other sites (we shall see how in Section 23.5.4), but resolving the conflict involves rolling back committed transactions, and durability of committed transactions is therefore not guaranteed. Further, human intervention may be required to deal with conflicts. The above schemes should therefore be avoided or used with care.

19.5.4 Deadlock Handling

The deadlock-prevention and deadlock-detection algorithms in Chapter 16 can be used in a distributed system, provided that modifications are made. For example, we can use the tree protocol by defining a *global* tree among the system data items. Similarly, the timestamp-ordering approach could be directly applied to a distributed environment, as we saw in Section 19.5.2.

Deadlock prevention may result in unnecessary waiting and rollback. Furthermore, certain deadlock-prevention techniques may require more sites to be involved in the execution of a transaction than would otherwise be the case.

If we allow deadlocks to occur and rely on deadlock detection, the main problem in a distributed system is deciding how to maintain the wait-for graph. Common techniques for dealing with this issue require that each site keep a **local wait-for graph**. The nodes of the graph correspond to all the transactions (local as well as nonlocal) that are currently either holding or requesting any of the items local to that site. For example, Figure 19.3 depicts a system consisting of two sites, each maintaining its local wait-for graph. Note that transactions T_2 and T_3 appear in both graphs, indicating that the transactions have requested items at both sites.

These local wait-for graphs are constructed in the usual manner for local transactions and data items. When a transaction T_i on site S_1 needs a resource in site S_2, it sends a request message to site S_2. If the resource is held by transaction T_j, the system inserts an edge $T_i \rightarrow T_j$ in the local wait-for graph of site S_2.

Clearly, if any local wait-for graph has a cycle, deadlock has occurred. On the other hand, the fact that there are no cycles in any of the local wait-for graphs does not mean that there are no deadlocks. To illustrate this problem, we consider the local wait-for graphs of Figure 19.3. Each wait-for graph is acyclic; nevertheless, a deadlock exists in the system because the *union* of the local wait-for graphs contains a cycle. This graph appears in Figure 19.4.

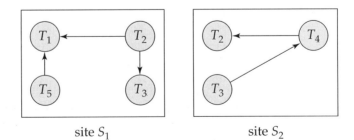

site S_1 site S_2

Figure 19.3 Local wait-for graphs.

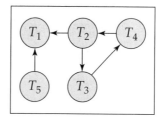

Figure 19.4   Global wait-for graph for Figure 19.3.

In the **centralized deadlock detection** approach, the system constructs and maintains a **global wait-for graph** (the union of all the local graphs) in a *single* site: the deadlock-detection coordinator. Since there is communication delay in the system, we must distinguish between two types of wait-for graphs. The *real* graph describes the real but unknown state of the system at any instance in time, as would be seen by an omniscient observer. The *constructed* graph is an approximation generated by the controller during the execution of the controller's algorithm. Obviously, the controller must generate the constructed graph in such a way that, whenever the detection algorithm is invoked, the reported results are correct. *Correct* means in this case that, if a deadlock exists, it is reported promptly, and if the system reports a deadlock, it is indeed in a deadlock state.

The global wait-for graph can be reconstructed or updated under these conditions:

- Whenever a new edge is inserted in or removed from one of the local wait-for graphs.

- Periodically, when a number of changes have occurred in a local wait-for graph.

- Whenever the coordinator needs to invoke the cycle-detection algorithm.

When the coordinator invokes the deadlock-detection algorithm, it searches its global graph. If it finds a cycle, it selects a victim to be rolled back. The coordinator must notify all the sites that a particular transaction has been selected as victim. The sites, in turn, roll back the victim transaction.

This scheme may produce unnecessary rollbacks if:

- **False cycles** exist in the global wait-for graph. As an illustration, consider a snapshot of the system represented by the local wait-for graphs of Figure 19.5. Suppose that T_2 releases the resource that it is holding in site S_1, resulting in the deletion of the edge $T_1 \rightarrow T_2$ in S_1. Transaction T_2 then requests a resource held by T_3 at site S_2, resulting in the addition of the edge $T_2 \rightarrow T_3$ in S_2. If the insert $T_2 \rightarrow T_3$ message from S_2 arrives before the remove $T_1 \rightarrow T_2$ message from S_1, the coordinator may discover the false cycle $T_1 \rightarrow T_2 \rightarrow T_3$ after the insert (but before the remove). Deadlock recovery may be initiated, although no deadlock has occurred.

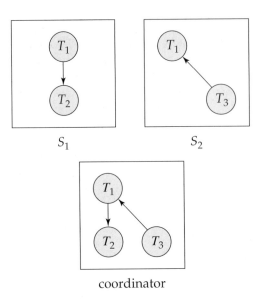

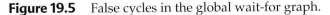

Figure 19.5 False cycles in the global wait-for graph.

Note that the false-cycle situation could not occur under two-phase locking. The likelihood of false cycles is usually sufficiently low that they do not cause a serious performance problem.

- A *deadlock* has indeed occurred and a victim has been picked, while one of the transactions was aborted for reasons unrelated to the deadlock. For example, suppose that site S_1 in Figure 19.3 decides to abort T_2. At the same time, the coordinator has discovered a cycle, and has picked T_3 as a victim. Both T_2 and T_3 are now rolled back, although only T_2 needed to be rolled back.

Deadlock detection can be done in a distributed manner, with several sites taking on parts of the task, instead of being done at a single site, However, such algorithms are more complicated and more expensive. See the bibliographic notes for references to such algorithms.

19.6 Availability

One of the goals in using distributed databases is **high availability**; that is, the database must function almost all the time. In particular, since failures are more likely in large distributed systems, a distributed database must continue functioning even when there are various types of failures. The ability to continue functioning even during failures is referred to as **robustness**.

For a distributed system to be robust, it must *detect* failures, *reconfigure* the system so that computation may continue, and *recover* when a processor or a link is repaired.

The different types of failures are handled in different ways. For example, message loss is handled by retransmission. Repeated retransmission of a message across a link, without receipt of an acknowledgment, is usually a symptom of a link failure. The network usually attempts to find an alternative route for the message. Failure to find such a route is usually a symptom of network partition.

It is generally not possible, however, to differentiate clearly between site failure and network partition. The system can usually detect that a failure has occurred, but it may not be able to identify the type of failure. For example, suppose that site S_1 is not able to communicate with S_2. It could be that S_2 has failed. However, another possibility is that the link between S_1 and S_2 has failed, resulting in network partition. The problem is partly addressed by using multiple links between sites, so that even if one link fails the sites will remain connected. However, multiple link failure can still occur, so there are situations where we cannot be sure whether a site failure or network partition has occurred.

Suppose that site S_1 has discovered that a failure has occurred. It must then initiate a procedure that will allow the system to reconfigure, and to continue with the normal mode of operation.

- If transactions were active at a failed/inaccessible site at the time of the failure, these transactions should be aborted. It is desirable to abort such transactions promptly, since they may hold locks on data at sites that are still active; waiting for the failed/inaccessible site to become accessible again may impede other transactions at sites that are operational.

  However, in some cases, when data objects are replicated it may be possible to proceed with reads and updates even though some replicas are inaccessible. In this case, when a failed site recovers, if it had replicas of any data object, it must obtain the current values of these data objects, and must ensure that it receives all future updates. We address this issue in Section 19.6.1.

- If replicated data are stored at a failed/inaccessible site, the catalog should be updated so that queries do not reference the copy at the failed site. When a site rejoins, care must be taken to ensure that data at the site is consistent, as we will see in Section 19.6.3.

- If a failed site is a central server for some subsystem, an *election* must be held to determine the new server (see Section 19.6.5). Examples of central servers include a name server, a concurrency coordinator, or a global deadlock detector.

Since it is, in general, not possible to distinguish between network link failures and site failures, any reconfiguration scheme must be designed to work correctly in case of a partitioning of the network. In particular, these situations must be avoided:

- Two or more central servers are elected in distinct partitions.

- More than one partition updates a replicated data item.

19.6.1 Majority-Based Approach

The majority-based approach to distributed concurrency control in Section 19.5.1.4 can be modified to work in spite of failures. In this approach, each data object stores with it a version number to detect when it was last written to. Whenever a transaction writes an object it also updates the version number in this way:

- If data object a is replicated in n different sites, then a lock-request message must be sent to more than one-half of the n sites in which a is stored. The transaction does not operate on a until it has successfully obtained a lock on a majority of the replicas of a.

- Read operations look at all replicas on which a lock has been obtained, and read the value from the replica that has the highest version number. (Optionally, they may also write this value back to replicas with lower version numbers.) Writes read all the replicas just like reads to find the highest version number (this step would normally have been performed earlier in the transaction by a read, and the result can be reused). The new version number is one more than the highest version number. The write operation writes all the replicas on which it has obtained locks, and sets the version number at all the replicas to the new version number.

Failures during a transaction (whether network partitions or site failures) can be tolerated as long as (1) the sites available at commit contain a majority of replicas of all the objects written to and (2) during reads, a majority of replicas are read to find the version numbers. If these requirements are violated, the transaction must be aborted. As long as the requirements are satisfied, the two-phase commit protocol can be used, as usual, on the sites that are available.

In this scheme, reintegration is trivial; nothing needs to be done. This is because writes would have updated a majority of the replicas, while reads will read a majority of the replicas and find at least one replica that has the latest version.

The version numbering technique used with the majority protocol can also be used to make the quorum consensus protocol work in the presence of failures. We leave the (straightforward) details to the reader. However, the danger of failures preventing the system from processing transactions increases if some sites are given higher weights.

19.6.2 Read One, Write All Available Approach

As a special case of quorum consensus, we can employ the biased protocol by giving unit weights to all sites, setting the read quorum to 1, and setting the write quorum to n (all sites). In this special case, there is no need to use version numbers; however, if even a single site containing a data item fails, no write to the item can proceed, since the write quorum will not be available. This protocol is called the **read one, write all** protocol since all replicas must be written.

To allow work to proceed in the event of failures, we would like to be able to use a **read one, write all available** protocol. In this approach, a read operation proceeds as in the **read one, write all** scheme; any available replica can be read, and a read lock is obtained at that replica. A write operation is shipped to all replicas; and write locks are acquired on all the replicas. If a site is down, the transaction manager proceeds without waiting for the site to recover.

While this approach appears very attractive, there are several complications. In particular, temporary communication failure may cause a site to appear to be unavailable, resulting in a write not being performed, but when the link is restored, the site is not aware that it has to perform some reintegration actions to catch up on writes it has lost. Further, if the network partitions, each partition may proceed to update the same data item, believing that sites in the other partitions are all dead.

The read one, write all available scheme can be used if there is never any network partitioning, but it can result in inconsistencies in the event of network partitions.

19.6.3 Site Reintegration

Reintegration of a repaired site or link into the system requires care. When a failed site recovers, it must initiate a procedure to update its system tables to reflect changes made while it was down. If the site had replicas of any data items, it must obtain the current values of these data items and ensure that it receives all future updates. Reintegration of a site is more complicated than it may seem to be at first glance, since there may be updates to the data items processed during the time that the site is recovering.

An easy solution is to halt the entire system temporarily while the failed site rejoins it. In most applications, however, such a temporary halt is unacceptably disruptive. Techniques have been developed to allow failed sites to reintegrate while concurrent updates to data items proceed concurrently. Before a read or write lock is granted on any data item, the site must ensure that it has caught up on all updates to the data item. If a failed link recovers, two or more partitions can be rejoined. Since a partitioning of the network limits the allowable operations by some or all sites, all sites should be informed promptly of the recovery of the link. See the bibliographical notes for more information on recovery in distributed systems.

19.6.4 Comparison with Remote Backup

Remote backup systems, which we studied in Section 17.10, and replication in distributed databases are two alternative approaches to providing high availability. The main difference between the two schemes is that with remote backup systems, actions such as concurrency control and recovery are performed at a single site, and only data and log records are replicated at the other site. In particular, remote backup systems help avoid two-phase commit, and its resultant overheads. Also, transactions need to contact only one site (the primary site), and thus avoid the overhead of running transaction code at multiple sites. Thus remote backup systems offer a lower-cost approach to high availability than replication.

On the other hand, replication can provide greater availability by having multiple replicas available, and using the majority protocol.

19.6.5 Coordinator Selection

Several of the algorithms that we have presented require the use of a coordinator. If the coordinator fails because of a failure of the site at which it resides, the system can continue execution only by restarting a new coordinator on another site. One way to continue execution is by maintaining a backup to the coordinator, which is ready to assume responsibility if the coordinator fails.

A **backup coordinator** is a site that, in addition to other tasks, maintains enough information locally to allow it to assume the role of coordinator with minimal disruption to the distributed system. All messages directed to the coordinator are received by both the coordinator and its backup. The backup coordinator executes the same algorithms and maintains the same internal state information (such as, for a concurrency coordinator, the lock table) as does the actual coordinator. The only difference in function between the coordinator and its backup is that the backup does not take any action that affects other sites. Such actions are left to the actual coordinator.

In the event that the backup coordinator detects the failure of the actual coordinator, it assumes the role of coordinator. Since the backup has all the information available to it that the failed coordinator had, processing can continue without interruption.

The prime advantage to the backup approach is the ability to continue processing immediately. If a backup were not ready to assume the coordinator's responsibility, a newly appointed coordinator would have to seek information from all sites in the system so that it could execute the coordination tasks. Frequently, the only source of some of the requisite information is the failed coordinator. In this case, it may be necessary to abort several (or all) active transactions, and to restart them under the control of the new coordinator.

Thus, the backup-coordinator approach avoids a substantial amount of delay while the distributed system recovers from a coordinator failure. The disadvantage is the overhead of duplicate execution of the coordinator's tasks. Furthermore, a coordinator and its backup need to communicate regularly to ensure that their activities are synchronized.

In short, the backup-coordinator approach incurs overhead during normal processing to allow fast recovery from a coordinator failure.

In the absence of a designated backup coordinator, or in order to handle multiple failures, a new coordinator may be chosen dynamically by sites that are live. **Election algorithms** enable the sites to choose the site for the new coordinator in a decentralized manner. Election algorithms require that a unique identification number be associated with each active site in the system.

The **bully algorithm** for election works as follows. To keep the notation and the discussion simple, assume that the identification number of site S_i is i and that the chosen coordinator will always be the active site with the largest identification number. Hence, when a coordinator fails, the algorithm must elect the active site that has the largest identification number. The algorithm must send this number to each active site in the system. In addition, the algorithm must provide a mechanism by which a site recovering from a crash can identify the current coordinator. Suppose that site S_i sends a request that is not answered by the coordinator within a prespecified time interval T. In this situation, it is assumed that the coordinator has failed, and S_i tries to elect itself as the site for the new coordinator.

Site S_i sends an election message to every site that has a higher identification number. Site S_i then waits, for a time interval T, for an answer from any one of these sites. If it receives no response within time T, it assumes that all sites with numbers greater than i have failed, and it elects itself as the site for the new coordinator and sends a message to inform all active sites with identification numbers lower than i that it is the site at which the new coordinator resides.

If S_i does receive an answer, it begins a time interval T', to receive a message informing it that a site with a higher identification number has been elected. (Some other site is electing itself coordinator, and should report the results within time T'.) If S_i receives no message within T', then it assumes the site with a higher number has failed, and site S_i restarts the algorithm.

After a failed site recovers, it immediately begins execution of the same algorithm. If there are no active sites with higher numbers, the recovered site forces all sites with lower numbers to let it become the coordinator site, even if there is a currently active coordinator with a lower number. It is for this reason that the algorithm is termed the *bully* algorithm.

19.7 Distributed Query Processing

In Chapter 14, we saw that there are a variety of methods for computing the answer to a query. We examined several techniques for choosing a strategy for processing a query that minimize the amount of time that it takes to compute the answer. For centralized systems, the primary criterion for measuring the cost of a particular strategy is the number of disk accesses. In a distributed system, we must take into account several other matters, including

- The cost of data transmission over the network

- The potential gain in performance from having several sites process parts of the query in parallel

The relative cost of data transfer over the network and data transfer to and from disk varies widely depending on the type of network and on the speed of the disks. Thus, in general, we cannot focus solely on disk costs or on network costs. Rather, we must find a good tradeoff between the two.

19.7.1 Query Transformation

Consider an extremely simple query: "Find all the tuples in the *account* relation." Although the query is simple — indeed, trivial—processing it is not trivial, since the *account* relation may be fragmented, replicated, or both, as we saw in Section 19.2. If the *account* relation is replicated, we have a choice of replica to make. If no replicas are fragmented, we choose the replica for which the transmission cost is lowest. However, if a replica is fragmented, the choice is not so easy to make, since we need to compute several joins or unions to reconstruct the *account* relation. In this case, the number of strategies for our simple example may be large. Query optimization by exhaustive enumeration of all alternative strategies may not be practical in such situations.

Fragmentation transparency implies that a user may write a query such as

$$\sigma_{branch\text{-}name\,=\,\text{"Hillside"}}\,(account)$$

Since *account* is defined as

$$account_1\,\cup\,account_2$$

the expression that results from the name translation scheme is

$$\sigma_{branch\text{-}name\,=\,\text{"Hillside"}}\,(account_1\,\cup\,account_2)$$

Using the query-optimization techniques of Chapter 13, we can simplify the preceding expression automatically. The result is the expression

$$\sigma_{branch\text{-}name\,=\,\text{"Hillside"}}\,(account_1)\,\cup\,\sigma_{branch\text{-}name\,=\,\text{"Hillside"}}\,(account_2)$$

which includes two subexpressions. The first involves only $account_1$, and thus can be evaluated at the Hillside site. The second involves only $account_2$, and thus can be evaluated at the Valleyview site.

There is a further optimization that can be made in evaluating

$$\sigma_{branch\text{-}name\,=\,\text{"Hillside"}}\,(account_1)$$

Since $account_1$ has only tuples pertaining to the Hillside branch, we can eliminate the selection operation. In evaluating

$$\sigma_{branch\text{-}name\,=\,\text{"Hillside"}}\,(account_2)$$

we can apply the definition of the $account_2$ fragment to obtain

$$\sigma_{branch\text{-}name\,=\,\text{"Hillside"}}\,(\sigma_{branch\text{-}name\,=\,\text{"Valleyview"}}\,(account))$$

This expression is the empty set, regardless of the contents of the *account* relation.

Thus, our final strategy is for the Hillside site to return $account_1$ as the result of the query.

19.7.2 Simple Join Processing

As we saw in Chapter 13, a major decision in the selection of a query-processing strategy is choosing a join strategy. Consider the following relational-algebra expression:

$$account \bowtie depositor \bowtie branch$$

Assume that the three relations are neither replicated nor fragmented, and that *account* is stored at site S_1, *depositor* at S_2, and *branch* at S_3. Let S_I denote the site at which the query was issued. The system needs to produce the result at site S_I. Among the possible strategies for processing this query are these:

- Ship copies of all three relations to site S_I. Using the techniques of Chapter 13, choose a strategy for processing the entire query locally at site S_I.

- Ship a copy of the *account* relation to site S_2, and compute $temp_1$ = *account* $\bowtie$ *depositor* at S_2. Ship $temp_1$ from S_2 to S_3, and compute $temp_2 = temp_1 \bowtie branch$ at S_3. Ship the result $temp_2$ to S_I.

- Devise strategies similar to the previous one, with the roles of S_1, S_2, S_3 exchanged.

No one strategy is always the best one. Among the factors that must be considered are the volume of data being shipped, the cost of transmitting a block of data between a pair of sites, and the relative speed of processing at each site. Consider the first two strategies listed. If we ship all three relations to S_I, and indices exist on these relations, we may need to re-create these indices at S_I. This re-creation of indices entails extra processing overhead and extra disk accesses. However, the second strategy has the disadvantage that a potentially large relation (*customer* $\bowtie$ *account*) must be shipped from S_2 to S_3. This relation repeats the address data for a customer once for each account that the customer has. Thus, the second strategy may result in extra network transmission compared to the first strategy.

19.7.3   Semijoin Strategy

Suppose that we wish to evaluate the expression $r_1 \bowtie r_2$, where r_1 and r_2 are stored at sites S_1 and S_2, respectively. Let the schemas of r_1 and r_2 be R_1 and R_2. Suppose that we wish to obtain the result at S_1. If there are many tuples of r_2 that do not join with any tuple of r_1, then shipping r_2 to S_1 entails shipping tuples that fail to contribute to the result. We want to remove such tuples before shipping data to S_1, particularly if network costs are high.

A possible strategy to accomplish all this is:

1. Compute $temp_1 \leftarrow \Pi_{R_1 \cap R_2}(r_1)$ at S_1.

2. Ship $temp_1$ from S_1 to S_2.

3. Compute $temp_2 \leftarrow r_2 \bowtie temp_1$ at S_2.

4. Ship $temp_2$ from S_2 to S_1.

5. Compute $r_1 \bowtie temp_2$ at S_1. The resulting relation is the same as $r_1 \bowtie r_2$.

Before considering the efficiency of this strategy, let us verify that the strategy computes the correct answer. In step 3, $temp_2$ has the result of $r_2 \bowtie \Pi_{R_1 \cap R_2}(r_1)$. In step 5, we compute

$$r_1 \bowtie r_2 \bowtie \Pi_{R_1 \cap R_2}(r_1)$$

Since join is associative and commutative, we can rewrite this expression as

$$\left(r_1 \bowtie \Pi_{R_1 \cap R_2}(r_1)\right) \bowtie r_2$$

Since $r_1 \bowtie \Pi_{(R_1 \cap R_2)}(r_1) = r_1$, the expression is, indeed, equal to $r_1 \bowtie r_2$, the expression we are trying to evaluate.

This strategy is particularly advantageous when relatively few tuples of r_2 contribute to the join. This situation is likely to occur if r_1 is the result of a relational-algebra expression involving selection. In such a case, $temp_2$ may have significantly fewer tuples than r_2. The cost savings of the strategy result from having to ship only $temp_2$, rather than all of r_2, to S_1. Additional cost is incurred in shipping $temp_1$ to S_2. If a sufficiently small fraction of tuples in r_2 contribute to the join, the overhead of shipping $temp_1$ will be dominated by the savings of shipping only a fraction of the tuples in r_2.

This strategy is called a **semijoin strategy**, after the semijoin operator of the relational algebra, denoted $\ltimes$. The semijoin of r_1 with r_2, denoted $r_1 \ltimes r_2$, is

$$\Pi_{R_1}(r_1 \bowtie r_2)$$

Thus, $r_1 \ltimes r_2$ selects those tuples of r_1 that contributed to $r_1 \bowtie r_2$. In step 3, $temp_2 = r_2 \ltimes r_1$.

For joins of several relations, this strategy can be extended to a series of semijoin steps. A substantial body of theory has been developed regarding the use of semijoins for query optimization. Some of this theory is referenced in the bibliographical notes.

19.7.4   Join Strategies that Exploit Parallelism

Consider a join of four relations:

$$r_1 \bowtie r_2 \bowtie r_3 \bowtie r_4$$

where relation r_i is stored at site S_i. Assume that the result must be presented at site S_1. There are many possible strategies for parallel evaluation. (We study the issue of parallel processing of queries in detail in Chapter 20.) In one such strategy, r_1 is shipped to S_2, and $r_1 \bowtie r_2$ computed at S_2. At the same time, r_3 is shipped to S_4, and $r_3 \bowtie r_4$ computed at S_4. Site S_2 can ship tuples of $(r_1 \bowtie r_2)$ to S_1 as they are produced, rather than wait for the entire join to be computed. Similarly, S_4 can ship tuples of $(r_3 \bowtie r_4)$ to S_1. Once tuples of $(r_1 \bowtie r_2)$ and $(r_3 \bowtie r_4)$ arrive at S_1, the computation of $(r_1 \bowtie r_2) \bowtie (r_3 \bowtie r_4)$ can begin, with the pipelined join technique of Section 13.7.2.2. Thus, computation of the final join result at S_1 can be done in parallel with the computation of $(r_1 \bowtie r_2)$ at S_2, and with the computation of $(r_3 \bowtie r_4)$ at S_4.

19.8   Heterogeneous Distributed Databases

Many new database applications require data from a variety of preexisting databases located in a heterogeneous collection of hardware and software environments. Manipulation of information located in a heterogeneous distributed database requires an additional software layer on top of existing database systems. This software layer is called a **multidatabase system**. The local database systems may employ different logical models and data-definition and data-manipulation languages, and may differ in their concurrency-control and transaction-management mechanisms. A multidatabase system creates the illusion of logical database integration without requiring physical database integration.

Full integration of heterogeneous systems into a homogeneous distributed database is often difficult or impossible:

- **Technical difficulties.** The investment in application programs based on existing database systems may be huge, and the cost of converting these applications may be prohibitive.

- **Organizational difficulties.** Even if integration is *technically* possible, it may not be *politically* possible, because the existing database systems belong to different corporations or organizations. In such cases, it is important for a multidatabase system to allow the local database systems to retain a high degree of **autonomy** over the local database and transactions running against that data.

For these reasons, multidatabase systems offer significant advantages that outweigh their overhead. In this section, we provide an overview of the challenges faced in constructing a multidatabase environment from the standpoint of data definition and query processing. Section 24.6 provides an overview of transaction management issues in multidatabases.

19.8.1 Unified View of Data

Each local database management system may use a different data model. For instance, some may employ the relational model, whereas others may employ older data models, such as the network model (see Appendix A) or the hierarchical model (see Appendix B).

Since the multidatabase system is supposed to provide the illusion of a single, integrated database system, a common data model must be used. A commonly used choice is the relational model, with SQL as the common query language. Indeed, there are several systems available today that allow SQL queries to a nonrelational database management system.

Another difficulty is the provision of a common conceptual schema. Each local system provides its own conceptual schema. The multidatabase system must integrate these separate schemas into one common schema. Schema integration is a complicated task, mainly because of the semantic heterogeneity.

Schema integration is not simply straightforward translation between data-definition languages. The same attribute names may appear in different local databases but with different meanings. The data types used in one system may not be supported by other systems, and translation between types may not be simple. Even for identical data types, problems may arise from the physical representation of data: One system may use ASCII, another EBCDIC; floating-point representations may differ; integers may be represented in *big-endian* or *little-endian* form. At the semantic level, an integer value for length may be inches in one system and millimeters in another, thus creating an awkward situation in which equality of integers is only an approximate notion (as is always the case for floating-point numbers). The same name may appear in different languages in different systems. For example, a system based in the United States may refer to the city "Cologne," whereas one in Germany refers to it as "Köln."

All these seemingly minor distinctions must be properly recorded in the common global conceptual schema. Translation functions must be provided. Indices must be annotated for system-dependent behavior (for example, the sort order of nonalphanumeric characters is not the same in ASCII as in EBCDIC). As we noted earlier, the alternative of converting each database to a common format may not be feasible without obsoleting existing application programs.

19.8.2 Query Processing

Query processing in a heterogeneous database can be complicated. Some of the issues are:

- Given a query on a global schema, the query may have to be translated into queries on local schemas at each of the sites where the query has to be executed. The query results have to be translated back into the global schema.

  The task is simplified by writing **wrappers** for each data source, which provide a view of the local data in the global schema. Wrappers also translate queries on the global schema into queries on the local schema, and translate results back into the global schema. Wrappers may be provided by individual sites, or may be written separately as part of the multidatabase system.

  Wrappers can even be used to provide a relational view of nonrelational data sources, such as Web pages (possibly with forms interfaces), flat files, hierarchical and network databases, and directory systems.

- Some data sources may provide only limited query capabilities; for instance, they may support selections, but not joins. They may even restrict the form of selections, allowing selections only on certain fields; Web data sources with form interfaces are an example of such data sources. Queries may therefore have to be broken up, to be partly performed at the data source and partly at the site issuing the query.

- In general, more than one site may need to be accessed to answer a given query. Answers retrieved from the sites may have to be processed to remove duplicates. Suppose one site contains *account* tuples satisfying the selection *balance* < 100, while another contains *account* tuples satisfying *balance* > 50. A query on the entire account relation would require access to both sites and removal of duplicate answers resulting from tuples with balance between 50 and 100, which are replicated at both sites.

- Global query optimization in a heterogeneous database is difficult, since the query execution system may not know what the costs are of alternative query plans at different sites. The usual solution is to rely on only local-level optimization, and just use heuristics at the global level.

Mediator systems are systems that integrate multiple heterogeneous data sources, providing an integrated global view of the data and providing query facilities on the global view. Unlike full-fledged multidatabase systems, mediator systems do not bother about transaction processing. (The terms mediator and multidatabase are often used in an interchangeable fashion, and systems that are called mediators may support limited forms of transactions.) The term **virtual database** is used to refer to multidatabase/mediator systems, since they provide the appearance of a single database with a global schema, although data exist on multiple sites in local schemas.

19.9   Directory Systems

Consider an organization that wishes to make data about its employees available to a variety of people in the organization; example of the kinds of data would include name, designation, employee-id, address, email address, phone number, fax number, and so on. In the precomputerization days, organizations would create physical directories of employees and distribute them across the organization. Even today, telephone companies create physical directories of customers.

In general, a directory is a listing of information about some class of objects such as persons. Directories can be used to find information about a specific object, or in the reverse direction to find objects that meet a certain requirement. In the world of physical telephone directories, directories that satisfy lookups in the forward direction are called **white pages**, while directories that satisfy lookups in the reverse direction are called **yellow pages**.

In today's networked world, the need for directories is still present and, if anything, even more important. However, directories today need to be available over a computer network, rather than in a physical (paper) form.

19.9.1   Directory Access Protocols

Directory information can be made available through Web interfaces, as many organizations, and phone companies in particular do. Such interfaces are good for humans. However, programs too, need to access directory information. Directories can be used for storing other types of information, much like file system directories. For instance, Web browsers can store personal bookmarks and other browser settings in a directory system. A user can thus access the same settings from multiple locations, such as at home and at work, without having to share a file system.

Several **directory access protocols** have been developed to provide a standardized way of accessing data in a directory. The most widely used among them today is the **Lightweight Directory Access Protocol (LDAP)**.

Obviously all the types of data in our examples can be stored without much trouble in a database system, and accessed through protocols such as JDBC or ODBC. The question then is, why come up with a specialized protocol for accessing directory information? There are at least two answers to the question.

- First, directory access protocols are simplified protocols that cater to a limited type of access to data. They evolved in parallel with the database access protocols.

- Second, and more important, directory systems provide a simple mechanism to name objects in a hierarchical fashion, similar to file system directory names, which can be used in a distributed directory system to specify what information is stored in each of the directory servers. For example, a particular directory server may store information for Bell Laboratories employees in Murray Hill, while another may store information for Bell Laboratories employees in Bangalore, giving both sites autonomy in controlling their local data. The directory access protocol can be used to obtain data from both directories, across a network. More importantly, the directory system can be set up to automatically forward queries made at one site to the other site, without user intervention.

For these reasons, several organizations have directory systems to make organizational information available online. As may be expected, several directory implementations find it beneficial to use relational databases to store data, instead of creating special-purpose storage systems.

19.9.2   LDAP: Lightweight Directory Access Protocol

In general a directory system is implemented as one or more servers, which service multiple clients. Clients use the application programmer interface defined by directory system to communicate with the directory servers. Directory access protocols also define a data model and access control.

The **X.500 directory access protocol**, defined by the International Organization for Standardization (ISO), is a standard for accessing directory information. However, the protocol is rather complex, and is not widely used. The **Lightweight Directory Access Protocol (LDAP)** provides many of the X.500 features, but with less complexity, and is widely used. In the rest of this section, we shall outline the data model and access protocol details of LDAP.

19.9.2.1   LDAP Data Model

In LDAP directories store **entries**, which are similar to objects. Each entry must have a **distinguished name (DN)**, which uniquely identifies the entry. A DN is in turn made up of a sequence of **relative distinguished names (RDNs)**. For example, an entry may have the following distinguished name.

cn=Silberschatz, ou=Bell Labs, o=Lucent, c=USA

As you can see, the distinguished name in this example is a combination of a name and (organizational) address, starting with a person's name, then giving the organizational unit (ou), the organization (o), and country (c). The order of the components of a distinguished name reflects the normal postal address order, rather than the reverse order used in specifying path names for files. The set of RDNs for a DN is defined by the schema of the directory system.

Entries can also have attributes. LDAP provides binary, string, and time types, and additionally the types tel for telephone numbers, and PostalAddress for addresses (lines separated by a "$" character). Unlike those in the relational model, attributes are multivalued by default, so it is possible to store multiple telephone numbers or addresses for an entry.

LDAP allows the definition of **object classes** with attribute names and types. Inheritance can be used in defining object classes. Moreover, entries can be specified to be of one or more object classes. It is not necessary that there be a single most-specific object class to which an entry belongs.

Entries are organized into a **directory information tree (DIT)**, according to their distinguished names. Entries at the leaf level of the tree usually represent specific objects. Entries that are internal nodes represent objects such as organizational units, organizations, or countries. The children of a node have a DN containing all the RDNs of the parent, and one or more additional RDNs. For instance, an internal node may have a DN c=USA, and all entries below it have the value USA for the RDN c.

The entire distinguished name need not be stored in an entry; The system can generate the distinguished name of an entry by traversing up the DIT from the entry, collecting the RDN=value components to create the full distinguished name.

Entries may have more than one distinguished name—for example, an entry for a person in more than one organization. To deal with such cases, the leaf level of a DIT can be an **alias**, which points to an entry in another branch of the tree.

19.9.2.2   Data Manipulation

Unlike SQL, LDAP does not define either a data-definition language or a data manipulation language. However, LDAP defines a network protocol for carrying out data definition and manipulation. Users of LDAP can either use an application programming interface, or use tools provided by various vendors to perform data definition and manipulation. LDAP also defines a file format called **LDAP Data Interchange Format (LDIF)** that can be used for storing and exchanging information.

The querying mechanism in LDAP is very simple, consisting of just selections and projections, without any join. A query must specify the following:

- A base—that is, a node within a DIT—by giving its distinguished name (the path from the root to the node).

- A search condition, which can be a Boolean combination of conditions on individual attributes. Equality, matching by wild-card characters, and approximate equality (the exact definition of approximate equality is system dependent) are supported.

- A scope, which can be just the base, the base and its children, or the entire subtree beneath the base.

- Attributes to return.

- Limits on number of results and resource consumption.

The query can also specify whether to automatically dereference aliases; if alias dereferences are turned off, alias entries can be returned as answers.

One way of querying an LDAP data source is by using LDAP URLs. Examples of LDAP URLs are:

> ldap:://aura.research.bell-labs.com/o=Lucent,c=USA
> ldap:://aura.research.bell-labs.com/o=Lucent,c=USA??sub?cn=Korth

The first URL returns all attributes of all entries at the server with organization being Lucent, and country being USA. The second URL executes a search query (selection) cn=Korth on the subtree of the node with distinguished name o=Lucent, c=USA. The question marks in the URL separate different fields. The first field is the distinguished name, here o=Lucent,c=USA. The second field, the list of attributes to return, is left empty, meaning return all attributes. The third attribute, sub, indicates that the entire subtree is to be searched. The last parameter is the search condition.

A second way of querying an LDAP directory is by using an application programming interface. Figure 19.6 shows a piece of C code used to connect to an LDAP server and run a query against the server. The code first opens a connection to an LDAP server by ldap_open and ldap_bind. It then executes a query by ldap_search_s. The arguments to ldap_search_s are the LDAP connection handle, the DN of the base from which the search should be done, the scope of the search, the search condition, the list of attributes to be returned, and an attribute called attrsonly, which, if set to 1, would result in only the schema of the result being returned, without any actual tuples. The last argument is an output argument that returns the result of the search as an LDAPMessage structure.

The first **for** loop iterates over and prints each entry in the result. Note that an entry may have multiple attributes, and the second **for** loop prints each attribute. Since attributes in LDAP may be multivalued, the third **for** loop prints each value of an attribute. The calls ldap_msgfree and ldap_value_free free memory that is allocated by the LDAP libraries. Figure 19.6 does not show code for handling error conditions.

The LDAP API also contains functions to create, update, and delete entries, as well as other operations on the DIT. Each function call behaves like a separate transaction; LDAP does not support atomicity of multiple updates.

19.9.2.3 Distributed Directory Trees

Information about an organization may be split into multiple DITs, each of which stores information about some entries. The **suffix** of a DIT is a sequence of RDN=value pairs that identify what information the DIT stores; the pairs are concatenated to the rest of the distinguished name generated by traversing from the entry to the root. For instance, the suffix of a DIT may be o=Lucent, c=USA, while another may have the suffix o=Lucent, c=India. The DITs may be organizationally and geographically separated.

A node in a DIT may contain a **referral** to another node in another DIT; for instance, the organizational unit Bell Labs under o=Lucent, c=USA may have its own DIT, in which case the DIT for o=Lucent, c=USA would have a node ou=Bell Labs representing a referral to the DIT for Bell Labs.

Referrals are the key component that help organize a distributed collection of directories into an integrated system. When a server gets a query on a DIT, it may

```
#include <stdio.h>
#include <ldap.h>
main() {
    LDAP *ld;
    LDAPMessage *res, *entry;
    char *dn, *attr, *attrList[] = {"telephoneNumber", NULL};
    BerElement *ptr;
    int vals, i;
    ld = ldap_open("aura.research.bell-labs.com", LDAP_PORT);
    ldap_simple_bind(ld, "avi", "avi-passwd") ;
    ldap_search_s(ld, "o=Lucent, c=USA", LDAP_SCOPE_SUBTREE, "cn=Korth",
                attrList, /*attrsonly*/ 0, &res);
    printf("found %d entries", ldap_count_entries(ld, res));
    for (entry=ldap_first_entry(ld, res); entry != NULL;
                        entry = ldap_next_entry(ld, entry)
    {
        dn = ldap_get_dn(ld, entry);
        printf("dn: %s", dn);
        ldap_memfree(dn);
        for (attr = ldap_first_attribute(ld, entry, &ptr);
                attr ! NULL;
                attr = ldap_next_attribute(ld, entry, ptr))
        {
            printf("%s: ", attr);
            vals = ldap_get_values(ld, entry, attr);
            for (i=0; vals[i] != NULL; i++)
                printf("%s, ", vals[i]);
            ldap_value_free(vals);
        }
    }
    ldap_msgfree(res);
    ldap_unbind(ld);
}
```

Figure 19.6   Example of LDAP code in C.

return a referral to the client, which then issues a query on the referenced DIT. Access to the referenced DIT is transparent, proceeding without the user's knowledge. Alternatively, the server itself may issue the query to the referred DIT and return the results along with locally computed results.

The hierarchical naming mechanism used by LDAP helps break up control of information across parts of an organization. The referral facility then helps integrate all the directories in an organization into a single virtual directory.

Although it is not an LDAP requirement, organizations often choose to break up information either by geography (for instance, an organization may maintain a directory for each site where the organization has a large presence) or by organizational structure (for instance, each organizational unit, such as department, maintains its own directory).

Many LDAP implementations support master–slave and multimaster replication of DITs, although replication is not part of the current LDAP version 3 standard. Work on standardizing replication in LDAP is in progress.

19.10 Summary

- A distributed database system consists of a collection of sites, each of which maintains a local database system. Each site is able to process local transactions: those transactions that access data in only that single site. In addition, a site may participate in the execution of global transactions; those transactions that access data in several sites. The execution of global transactions requires communication among the sites.

- Distributed databases may be homogeneous, where all sites have a common schema and database system code, or heterogeneous, where the schemas and system codes may differ.

- There are several issues involved in storing a relation in the distributed database, including replication and fragmentation. It is essential that the system minimize the degree to which a user needs to be aware of how a relation is stored.

- A distributed system may suffer from the same types of failure that can afflict a centralized system. There are, however, additional failures with which we need to deal in a distributed environment, including the failure of a site, the failure of a link, loss of a message, and network partition. Each of these problems needs to be considered in the design of a distributed recovery scheme.

- To ensure atomicity, all the sites in which a transaction T executed must agree on the final outcome of the execution. T either commits at all sites or aborts at all sites. To ensure this property, the transaction coordinator of T must execute a commit protocol. The most widely used commit protocol is the two-phase commit protocol.

- The two-phase commit protocol may lead to blocking, the situation in which the fate of a transaction cannot be determined until a failed site (the coordinator) recovers. We can use the three-phase commit protocol to reduce the probability of blocking.

- Persistent messaging provides an alternative model for handling distributed transactions. The model breaks a single transaction into parts that are executed at different databases. Persistent messages (which are guaranteed to be delivered exactly once, regardless of failures), are sent to remote sites to request actions to be taken there. While persistent messaging avoids the blocking problem, application developers have to write code to handle various types of failures.

- The various concurrency-control schemes used in a centralized system can be modified for use in a distributed environment.

  □ In the case of locking protocols, the only change that needs to be incorporated is in the way that the lock manager is implemented. There are a variety of different approaches here. One or more central coordinators may be used. If, instead, a distributed lock-manager approach is taken, replicated data must be treated specially.

  □ Protocols for handling replicated data include the primary-copy, majority, biased, and quorum-consensus protocols. These have different tradeoffs in terms of cost and ability to work in the presence of failures.

  □ In the case of timestamping and validation schemes, the only needed change is to develop a mechanism for generating unique global timestamps.

  □ Many database systems support lazy replication, where updates are propagated to replicas outside the scope of the transaction that performed the update. Such facilities must be used with great care, since they may result in nonserializable executions.

- Deadlock detection in a distributed lock-manager environment requires co-operation between multiple sites, since there may be global deadlocks even when there are no local deadlocks.

- To provide high availability, a distributed database must detect failures, reconfigure itself so that computation may continue, and recover when a processor or a link is repaired. The task is greatly complicated by the fact that it is hard to distinguish between network partitions or site failures.

  The majority protocol can be extended by using version numbers to permit transaction processing to proceed even in the presence of failures. While the protocol has a significant overhead, it works regardless of the type of failure. Less-expensive protocols are available to deal with site failures, but they assume network partitioning does not occur.

- Some of the distributed algorithms require the use of a coordinator. To provide high availability, the system must maintain a backup copy that is ready to assume responsibility if the coordinator fails. Another approach is to choose the new coordinator after the coordinator has failed. The algorithms that determine which site should act as a coordinator are called election algorithms.

- Queries on a distributed database may need to access multiple sites. Several optimization techniques are available to choose which sites need to be accessed. Based on fragmentation and replication, the techniques can use semi-join techniques to reduce data transfer.

- Heterogeneous distributed databases allow sites to have their own schemas and database system code. A multidatabase system provides an environment in which new database applications can access data from a variety of pre-existing databases located in various heterogeneous hardware and software environments. The local database systems may employ different logical models and data-definition and data-manipulation languages, and may differ in their concurrency-control and transaction-management mechanisms. A multidatabase system creates the illusion of logical database integration, without requiring physical database integration.

- Directory systems can be viewed as a specialized form of database, where information is organized in a hierarchical fashion similar to the way files are organized in a file system. Directories are accessed by standardized directory access protocols such as LDAP.

  Directories can be distributed across multiple sites to provide autonomy to individual sites. Directories can contain referrals to other directories, which help build an integrated view whereby a query is sent to a single directory, and it is transparently executed at all relevant directories.

Review Terms

- Homogeneous distributed database
- Heterogeneous distributed database
- Data replication
- Primary copy
- Data fragmentation
  - ☐ Horizontal fragmentation
  - ☐ Vertical fragmentation
- Data transparency
  - ☐ Fragmentation transparency
  - ☐ Replication transparency
  - ☐ Location transparency
- Name server
- Aliases
- Distributed transactions
  - ☐ Local transactions
  - ☐ Global transactions
- Transaction manager
- Transaction coordinator
- System failure modes
- Network partition
- Commit protocols
- Two-phase commit protocol (2PC)
  - ☐ Ready state

- ☐ In-doubt transactions
- ☐ Blocking problem
- Three-phase commit protocol (3PC)
- Persistent messaging
- Concurrency control
- Single lock-manager
- Distributed lock-manager
- Protocols for replicas
  - ☐ Primary copy
  - ☐ Majority protocol
  - ☐ Biased protocol
  - ☐ Quorum consensus protocol
- Timestamping
- Master−slave replication
- Multimaster (update-anywhere) replication
- Transaction-consistent snapshot
- Lazy propagation
- Deadlock handling
  - ☐ Local wait-for graph
  - ☐ Global wait-for graph
  - ☐ False cycles
- Availability
- Robustness

- ☐ Majority based approach
- ☐ Read one, write all
- ☐ Read one, write all available
- ☐ Site reintegration
- Coordinator selection
- Backup coordinator
- Election algorithms
- Bully algorithm
- Distributed query processing
- Semijoin strategy
- Multidatabase system
- Autonomy

- Mediators
- Virtual database
- Directory systems
- LDAP: Lightweight directory access protocol
    - ☐ Distinguished name (DN)
    - ☐ Relative distinguished names RDNs
    - ☐ Directory information tree (DIT)
- Distributed directory trees
- DIT suffix
- Referral

Exercises

19.1 Discuss the relative advantages of centralized and distributed databases.

19.2 Explain how the following differ: fragmentation transparency, replication transparency, and location transparency.

19.3 How might a distributed database designed for a local-area network differ from one designed for a wide-area network?

19.4 When is it useful to have replication or fragmentation of data? Explain your answer.

19.5 Explain the notions of transparency and autonomy. Why are these notions desirable from a human-factors standpoint?

19.6 To build a highly available distributed system, you must know what kinds of failures can occur.

    a. List possible types of failure in a distributed system.

    b. Which items in your list from part a are also applicable to a centralized system?

19.7 Consider a failure that occurs during 2PC for a transaction. For each possible failure that you listed in Exercise 19.6a, explain how 2PC ensures transaction atomicity despite the failure.

19.8 Consider a distributed system with two sites, *A* and *B*. Can site *A* distinguish among the following?

- *B* goes down.
- The link between *A* and *B* goes down.
- *B* is extremely overloaded and response time is 100 times longer than normal.

What implications does your answer have for recovery in distributed systems?

19.9 The persistent messaging scheme described in this chapter depends on timestamps combined with discarding of received messages if they are too old. Suggest an alternative scheme based on sequence numbers instead of timestamps.

19.10 Give an example where the read one, write all available approach leads to an erroneous state.

19.11 If we apply a distributed version of the multiple-granularity protocol of Chapter 16 to a distributed database, the site responsible for the root of the DAG may become a bottleneck. Suppose we modify that protocol as follows:

- Only intention-mode locks are allowed on the root.
- All transactions are given all possible intention-mode locks on the root automatically.

Show that these modifications alleviate this problem without allowing any nonserializable schedules.

19.12 Explain the difference between data replication in a distributed system and the maintenance of a remote backup site.

19.13 Give an example where lazy replication can lead to an inconsistent database state even when updates get an exclusive lock on the primary (master) copy.

19.14 Study and summarize the facilities that the database system you are using provides for dealing with inconsistent states that can be reached with lazy propagation of updates.

19.15 Discuss the advantages and disadvantages of the two methods that we presented in Section 19.5.2 for generating globally unique timestamps.

19.16 Consider the following deadlock-detection algorithm. When transaction T_i, at site S_1, requests a resource from T_j, at site S_3, a request message with timestamp n is sent. The edge (T_i, T_j, n) is inserted in the local wait-for of S_1. The edge (T_i, T_j, n) is inserted in the local wait-for graph of S_3 only if T_j has received the request message and cannot immediately grant the requested resource. A request from T_i to T_j in the same site is handled in the usual manner; no timestamps are associated with the edge (T_i, T_j). A central coordinator invokes the detection algorithm by sending an initiating message to each site in the system.

On receiving this message, a site sends its local wait-for graph to the coordinator. Note that such a graph contains all the local information that the site has about the state of the real graph. The wait-for graph reflects an instantaneous state of the site, but it is not synchronized with respect to any other site.

When the controller has received a reply from each site, it constructs a graph as follows:

- The graph contains a vertex for every transaction in the system.
- The graph has an edge (T_i, T_j) if and only if

☐ There is an edge (T_i, T_j) in one of the wait-for graphs.
☐ An edge (T_i, T_j, n) (for some n) appears in more than one wait-for graph.

Show that, if there is a cycle in the constructed graph, then the system is in a deadlock state, and that, if there is no cycle in the constructed graph, then the system was not in a deadlock state when the execution of the algorithm began.

19.17 Consider a relation that is fragmented horizontally by *plant-number*:

employee (name, address, salary, plant-number)

Assume that each fragment has two replicas: one stored at the New York site and one stored locally at the plant site. Describe a good processing strategy for the following queries entered at the San Jose site.

a. Find all employees at the Boca plant.
b. Find the average salary of all employees.
c. Find the highest-paid employee at each of the following sites: Toronto, Edmonton, Vancouver, Montreal.
d. Find the lowest-paid employee in the company.

19.18 Consider the relations

employee (name, address, salary, plant-number)
machine (machine-number, type, plant-number)

Assume that the *employee* relation is fragmented horizontally by *plant-number*, and that each fragment is stored locally at its corresponding plant site. Assume that the *machine* relation is stored in its entirety at the Armonk site. Describe a good strategy for processing each of the following queries.

a. Find all employees at the plant that contains machine number 1130.
b. Find all employees at plants that contain machines whose type is "milling machine."
c. Find all machines at the Almaden plant.
d. Find employee ⋈ machine.

19.19 For each of the strategies of Exercise 19.18, state how your choice of a strategy depends on:

a. The site at which the query was entered
b. The site at which the result is desired

19.20 Compute $r \bowtie s$ for the relations of Figure 19.7.

19.21 Is $r_i \bowtie r_j$ necessarily equal to $r_j \bowtie r_i$? Under what conditions does $r_i \bowtie r_j = r_j \bowtie r_i$ hold?

19.22 Given that the LDAP functionality can be implemented on top of a database system, what is the need for the LDAP standard?

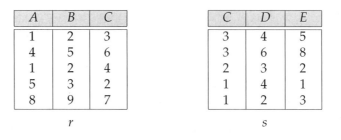

A	B	C
1	2	3
4	5	6
1	2	4
5	3	2
8	9	7

r

C	D	E
3	4	5
3	6	8
2	3	2
1	4	1
1	2	3

s

Figure 19.7   Relations for Exercise 19.20.

19.23 Describe how LDAP can be used to provide multiple hierarchical views of data, without replicating the base level data.

Bibliographical Notes

Textbook discussions of distributed databases are offered by Ozsu and Valduriez [1999] and Ceri and Pelagatti [1984]. Computer networks are discussed in Tanenbaum [1996] and Halsall [1992]. Rothnie et al. [1977] was an early survey on distributed database systems. Breitbart et al. [1999b] presents an overview of distributed databases.

The implementation of the transaction concept in a distributed database are presented by Gray [1981], Traiger et al. [1982], Spector and Schwarz [1983], and Eppinger et al. [1991]. The 2PC protocol was developed by Lampson and Sturgis [1976] and Gray [1978]. The three-phase commit protocol is from Skeen [1981]. Mohan and Lindsay [1983] discuss two modified versions of 2PC, called *presume commit* and *presume abort*, that reduce the overhead of 2PC by defining default assumptions regarding the fate of transactions.

The bully algorithm in Section 19.6.5 is from Garcia-Molina [1982]. Distributed clock synchronization is discussed in Lamport [1978]. Distributed concurrency control is covered by Rosenkrantz et al. [1978], Bernstein et al. [1978], Bernstein et al. [1980b], Menasce et al. [1980], Bernstein and Goodman [1980], Bernstein and Goodman [1981a], Bernstein and Goodman [1982], and Garcia-Molina and Wiederhold [1982].

The transaction manager of R* is described in Mohan et al. [1986]. Concurrency control for replicated data that is based on the concept of voting is presented by Gifford [1979] and Thomas [1979]. Validation techniques for distributed concurrency-control schemes are described by Schlageter [1981], Ceri and Owicki [1983], and Bassiouni [1988]. Discussions of semantic-based transaction-management techniques are offered by Garcia-Molina [1983], Kumar and Stonebraker [1988] and Badrinath and Ramamritham [1992].

Attar et al. [1984] discusses the use of transactions in distributed recovery in database systems with replicated data. A survey of techniques for recovery in distributed database systems is presented by Kohler [1981].

Recently, the problem of concurrent updates to replicated data has re-emerged as an important research issue in the context of data warehouses. Problems in this environment are discussed in Gray et al. [1996]. Anderson et al. [1998] discusses issues concerning lazy replication and consistency. Breitbart et al. [1999a] describe lazy update protocols for handling replication. The user manuals of various database systems provide details of how they handle replication and consistency.

Persistent messaging in Oracle is described in Gawlick [1998] while Huang and Garcia-Molina [2001] addresses exactly-once semantics in a replicated messaging system.

Distributed deadlock-detection algorithms are presented by Rosenkrantz et al. [1978], Menasce and Muntz [1979], Gligor and Shattuck [1980], Chandy and Misra [1982], Chandy et al. [1983], and Obermarck [1982]. Knapp [1987] surveys the distributed deadlock-detection literature, Exercise 19.16 is from Stuart et al. [1984].

Distributed query processing is discussed in Wong [1977], Epstein et al. [1978], Hevner and Yao [1979], Epstein and Stonebraker [1980], Apers et al. [1983], Ceri and Pelagatti [1983], and Wong [1983]. Selinger and Adiba [1980] and Daniels et al. [1982] discuss the approach to distributed query processing taken by R* (a distributed version of System R). Mackert and Lohman [1986] provides a performance evaluation of query-processing algorithms in R*. The performance results also serve to validate the cost model used in the R* query optimizer. Theoretical results concerning semijoins are presented by Bernstein and Chiu [1981], Chiu and Ho [1980], Bernstein and Goodman [1981b], and Kambayashi et al. [1982].

Dynamic query optimization in multidatabases is addressed by Ozcan et al. [1997]. Adali et al. [1996] and Papakonstantinou et al. [1996] describe query optimization issues in mediator systems.

Weltman and Dahbura [2000] and Howes et al. [1999] provide textbook coverage of LDAP. Kapitskaia et al. [2000] describes issues in caching LDAP directory data.

C H A P T E R   2 0

Parallel Databases

In this chapter, we discuss fundamental algorithms for parallel database systems that are based on the relational data model. In particular, we focus on the placement of data on multiple disks and the parallel evaluation of relational operations, both of which have been instrumental in the success of parallel databases.

20.1 Introduction

Fifteen years ago, parallel database systems had been nearly written off, even by some of their staunchest advocates. Today, they are successfully marketed by practically every database system vendor. Several trends fueled this transition:

- The transaction requirements of organizations have grown with increasing use of computers. Moreover, the growth of the World Wide Web has created many sites with millions of viewers, and the increasing amounts of data collected from these viewers has produced extremely large databases at many companies.

- Organizations are using these increasingly large volumes of data—such as data about what items people buy, what Web links users clicked on, or when people make telephone calls—to plan their activities and pricing. Queries used for such purposes are called **decision-support queries**, and the data requirements for such queries may run into terabytes. Single-processor systems are not capable of handling such large volumes of data at the required rates.

- The set-oriented nature of database queries naturally lends itself to parallelization. A number of commercial and research systems have demonstrated the power and scalability of parallel query processing.

- As microprocessors have become cheap, parallel machines have become common and relatively inexpensive.

As we discussed in Chapter 18, parallelism is used to provide speedup, where queries are executed faster because more resources, such as processors and disks, are provided. Parallelism is also used to provide scaleup, where increasing workloads are handled without increased response time, via an increase in the degree of parallelism.

We outlined in Chapter 18 the different architectures for parallel database systems: shared-memory, shared-disk, shared-nothing, and hierarchical architectures. Briefly, in shared-memory architectures, all processors share a common memory and disks; in shared-disk architectures, processors have independent memories, but share disks; in shared-nothing architectures, processors share neither memory nor disks; and hierarchical architectures have nodes that share neither memory nor disks with each other, but internally each node has a shared-memory or a shared-disk architecture.

20.2 I/O Parallelism

In it simplest form, **I/O parallelism** refers to reducing the time required to retrieve relations from disk by partitioning the relations on multiple disks. The most common form of data partitioning in a parallel database environment is *horizontal partitioning*. In **horizontal partitioning**, the tuples of a relation are divided (or declustered) among many disks, so that each tuple resides on one disk. Several partitioning strategies have been proposed.

20.2.1 Partitioning Techniques

We present three basic data-partitioning strategies. Assume that there are n disks, $D_0, D_1, \ldots, D_{n-1}$, across which the data are to be partitioned.

- **Round-robin**. This strategy scans the relation in any order and sends the ith tuple to disk number $D_{i \bmod n}$. The round-robin scheme ensures an even distribution of tuples across disks; that is, each disk has approximately the same number of tuples as the others.

- **Hash partitioning**. This declustering strategy designates one or more attributes from the given relation's schema as the partitioning attributes. A hash function is chosen whose range is $\{0, 1, \ldots, n - 1\}$. Each tuple of the original relation is hashed on the partitioning attributes. If the hash function returns i, then the tuple is placed on disk D_i.

- **Range partitioning**. This strategy distributes contiguous attribute-value ranges to each disk. It chooses a partitioning attribute, A, as a **partitioning vector**. The relation is partitioned as follows. Let $[v_0, v_1, \ldots, v_{n-2}]$ denote the partitioning vector, such that, if $i < j$, then $v_i < v_j$. Consider a tuple t such that $t[A] = x$. If $x < v_0$, then t goes on disk D_0. If $x \geq v_{n-2}$, then t goes on disk D_{n-1}. If $v_i \leq x < v_{i+1}$, then t goes on disk D_{i+1}.

  For example, range partitioning with three disks numbered 0, 1, and 2 may assign tuples with values less than 5 to disk 0, values between 5 and 40 to disk 1, and values greater than 40 to disk 2.

20.2.2   Comparison of Partitioning Techniques

Once a relation has been partitioned among several disks, we can retrieve it in parallel, using all the disks. Similarly, when a relation is being partitioned, it can be written
to multiple disks in parallel. Thus, the transfer rates for reading or writing an entire
relation are much faster with I/O parallelism than without it. However, reading an
entire relation, or *scanning a relation*, is only one kind of access to data. Access to data
can be classified as follows:

1. Scanning the entire relation

2. Locating a tuple associatively (for example, *employee-name* = "Campbell");
   these queries, called **point queries**, seek tuples that have a specified value
   for a specific attribute

3. Locating all tuples for which the value of a given attribute lies within a specified range (for example, $10000 < salary < 20000$); these queries are called
   range queries.

The different partitioning techniques support these types of access at different levels
of efficiency:

- **Round-robin.** The scheme is ideally suited for applications that wish to read
  the entire relation sequentially for each query. With this scheme, both point
  queries and range queries are complicated to process, since each of the n disks
  must be used for the search.

- **Hash partitioning.** This scheme is best suited for point queries based on the
  partitioning attribute. For example, if a relation is partitioned on the *telephone-
  number* attribute, then we can answer the query "Find the record of the employee with *telephone-number* = 555-3333" by applying the partitioning hash
  function to 555-3333 and then searching that disk. Directing a query to a single disk saves the startup cost of initiating a query on multiple disks, and
  leaves the other disks free to process other queries.

  Hash partitioning is also useful for sequential scans of the entire relation.
  If the hash function is a good randomizing function, and the partitioning attributes form a key of the relation, then the number of tuples in each of the
  disks is approximately the same, without much variance. Hence, the time
  taken to scan the relation is approximately $1/n$ of the time required to scan
  the relation in a single disk system.

  The scheme, however, is not well suited for point queries on nonparti-
  tioning attributes. Hash-based partitioning is also not well suited for answering range queries, since, typically, hash functions do not preserve proximity
  within a range. Therefore, all the disks need to be scanned for range queries
  to be answered.

- **Range partitioning.** This scheme is well suited for point and range queries on
  the partitioning attribute. For point queries, we can consult the partitioning
  vector to locate the disk where the tuple resides. For range queries, we consult

the partitioning vector to find the range of disks on which the tuples may reside. In both cases, the search narrows to exactly those disks that might have any tuples of interest.

An advantage of this feature is that, if there are only a few tuples in the queried range, then the query is typically sent to one disk, as opposed to all the disks. Since other disks can be used to answer other queries, range partitioning results in higher throughput while maintaining good response time. On the other hand, if there are many tuples in the queried range (as there are when the queried range is a larger fraction of the domain of the relation), many tuples have to be retrieved from a few disks, resulting in an I/O bottleneck (hot spot) at those disks. In this example of **execution skew**, all processing occurs in one—or only a few—partitions. In contrast, hash partitioning and round-robin partitioning would engage all the disks for such queries, giving a faster response time for approximately the same throughput.

The type of partitioning also affects other relational operations, such as joins, as we shall see in Section 20.5. Thus, the choice of partitioning technique also depends on the operations that need to be executed. In general, hash partitioning or range partitioning are preferred to round-robin partitioning.

In a system with many disks, the number of disks across which to partition a relation can be chosen in this way: If a relation contains only a few tuples that will fit into a single disk block, then it is better to assign the relation to a single disk. Large relations are preferably partitioned across all the available disks. If a relation consists of m disk blocks and there are n disks available in the system, then the relation should be allocated $\mathbf{min}(m, n)$ disks.

20.2.3 Handling of Skew

When a relation is partitioned (by a technique other than round-robin), there may be a **skew** in the distribution of tuples, with a high percentage of tuples placed in some partitions and fewer tuples in other partitions. The ways that skew may appear are classified as:

- Attribute-value skew
- Partition skew

Attribute-value skew refers to the fact that some values appear in the partitioning attributes of many tuples. All the tuples with the same value for the partitioning attribute end up in the same partition, resulting in skew. **Partition skew** refers to the fact that there may be load imbalance in the partitioning, even when there is no attribute skew.

Attribute-value skew can result in skewed partitioning regardless of whether range partitioning or hash partitioning is used. If the partition vector is not chosen carefully, range partitioning may result in partition skew. Partition skew is less likely with hash partitioning, if a good hash function is chosen.

As Section 18.3.1 noted, even a small skew can result in a significant decrease in performance. Skew becomes an increasing problem with a higher degree of parallelism. For example, if a relation of 1000 tuples is divided into 10 parts, and the division is skewed, then there may be some partitions of size less than 100 and some partitions of size more than 100; if even one partition happens to be of size 200, the speedup that we would obtain by accessing the partitions in parallel is only 5, instead of the 10 for which we would have hoped. If the same relation has to be partitioned into 100 parts, a partition will have 10 tuples on an average. If even one partition has 40 tuples (which is possible, given the large number of partitions) the speedup that we would obtain by accessing them in parallel would be 25, rather than 100. Thus, we see that the loss of speedup due to skew increases with parallelism.

A **balanced range-partitioning vector** can be constructed by sorting: The relation is first sorted on the partitioning attributes. The relation is then scanned in sorted order. After every $1/n$ of the relation has been read, the value of the partitioning attribute of the next tuple is added to the partition vector. Here, n denotes the number of partitions to be constructed. In case there are many tuples with the same value for the partitioning attribute, the technique can still result in some skew. The main disadvantage of this method is the extra I/O overhead incurred in doing the initial sort.

The I/O overhead for constructing balanced range-partition vectors can be reduced by constructing and storing a frequency table, or **histogram**, of the attribute values for each attribute of each relation. Figure 20.1 shows an example of a histogram for an integer-valued attribute that takes values in the range 1 to 25. A histogram takes up only a little space, so histograms on several different attributes can be stored in the system catalog. It is straightforward to construct a balanced range-partitioning function given a histogram on the partitioning attributes. If the histogram is not stored, it can be computed approximately by sampling the relation, using only tuples from a randomly chosen subset of the disk blocks of the relation.

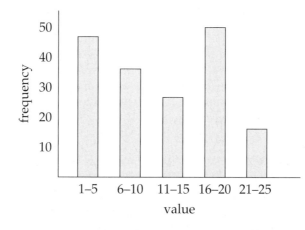

Figure 20.1   Example of histogram.

Another approach to minimizing the effect of skew, particularly with range partitioning, is to use *virtual processors*. In the **virtual processor** approach, we pretend there are several times as many *virtual processors* as the number of real processors. Any of the partitioning techniques and query evaluation techniques that we study later in this chapter can be used, but they map tuples and work to virtual processors instead of to real processors. Virtual processors, in turn, are mapped to real processors, usually by round-robin partitioning.

The idea is that even if one range had many more tuples than the others because of skew, these tuples would get split across multiple virtual processor ranges. Round robin allocation of virtual processors to real processors would distribute the extra work among multiple real processors, so that one processor does not have to bear all the burden.

20.3 Interquery Parallelism

In **interquery parallelism**, different queries or transactions execute in parallel with one another. Transaction throughput can be increased by this form of parallelism. However, the response times of individual transactions are no faster than they would be if the transactions were run in isolation. Thus, the primary use of interquery parallelism is to scaleup a transaction-processing system to support a larger number of transactions per second.

Interquery parallelism is the easiest form of parallelism to support in a database system—particularly in a shared-memory parallel system. Database systems designed for single-processor systems can be used with few or no changes on a shared-memory parallel architecture, since even sequential database systems support concurrent processing. Transactions that would have operated in a time-shared concurrent manner on a sequential machine operate in parallel in the shared-memory parallel architecture.

Supporting interquery parallelism is more complicated in a shared-disk or shared-nothing architecture. Processors have to perform some tasks, such as locking and logging, in a coordinated fashion, and that requires that they pass messages to each other. A parallel database system must also ensure that two processors do not update the same data independently at the same time. Further, when a processor accesses or updates data, the database system must ensure that the processor has the latest version of the data in its buffer pool. The problem of ensuring that the version is the latest is known as the **cache-coherency** problem.

Various protocols are available to guarantee cache coherency; often, cache-coherency protocols are integrated with concurrency-control protocols so that their overhead is reduced. One such protocol for a shared-disk system is this:

1. Before any read or write access to a page, a transaction locks the page in shared or exclusive mode, as appropriate. Immediately after the transaction obtains either a shared or exclusive lock on a page, it also reads the most recent copy of the page from the shared disk.

2. Before a transaction releases an exclusive lock on a page, it flushes the page to the shared disk; then, it releases the lock.

This protocol ensures that, when a transaction sets a shared or exclusive lock on a page, it gets the correct copy of the page.

More complex protocols avoid the repeated reading and writing to disk required by the preceding protocol. Such protocols do not write pages to disk when exclusive locks are released. When a shared or exclusive lock is obtained, if the most recent version of a page is in the buffer pool of some processor, the page is obtained from there. The protocols have to be designed to handle concurrent requests. The shared-disk protocols can be extended to shared-nothing architectures by this scheme: Each page has a **home processor** P_i, and is stored on disk D_i. When other processors want to read or write the page, they send requests to the home processor P_i of the page, since they cannot directly communicate with the disk. The other actions are the same as in the shared-disk protocols.

The Oracle 8 and Oracle Rdb systems are examples of shared-disk parallel database systems that support interquery parallelism.

20.4 Intraquery Parallelism

Intraquery parallelism refers to the execution of a single query in parallel on multiple processors and disks. Using intraquery parallelism is important for speeding up long-running queries. Interquery parallelism does not help in this task, since each query is run sequentially.

To illustrate the parallel evaluation of a query, consider a query that requires a relation to be sorted. Suppose that the relation has been partitioned across multiple disks by range partitioning on some attribute, and the sort is requested on the partitioning attribute. The sort operation can be implemented by sorting each partition in parallel, then concatenating the sorted partitions to get the final sorted relation.

Thus, we can parallelize a query by parallelizing individual operations. There is another source of parallelism in evaluating a query: The *operator tree* for a query can contain multiple operations. We can parallelize the evaluation of the operator tree by evaluating in parallel some of the operations that do not depend on one another. Further, as Chapter 13 mentions, we may be able to pipeline the output of one operation to another operation. The two operations can be executed in parallel on separate processors, one generating output that is consumed by the other, even as it is generated.

In summary, the execution of a single query can be parallelized in two ways:

- **Intraoperation parallelism**. We can speed up processing of a query by parallelizing the execution of each individual operation, such as sort, select, project, and join. We consider intraoperation parallelism in Section 20.5.

- **Interoperation parallelism**. We can speed up processing of a query by executing in parallel the different operations in a query expression. We consider this form of parallelism in Section 20.6.

The two forms of parallelism are complementary, and can be used simultaneously on a query. Since the number of operations in a typical query is small, compared to the number of tuples processed by each operation, the first form of parallelism can scale better with increasing parallelism. However, with the relatively small number of processors in typical parallel systems today, both forms of parallelism are important.

In the following discussion of parallelization of queries, we assume that the queries are **read only**. The choice of algorithms for parallelizing query evaluation depends on the machine architecture. Rather than presenting algorithms for each architecture separately, we use a shared-nothing architecture model in our description. Thus, we explicitly describe when data have to be transferred from one processor to another. We can simulate this model easily by using the other architectures, since transfer of data can be done via shared memory in a shared-memory architecture, and via shared disks in a shared-disk architecture. Hence, algorithms for shared-nothing architectures can be used on the other architectures too. We mention occasionally how the algorithms can be further optimized for shared-memory or shared-disk systems.

To simplify the presentation of the algorithms, assume that there are n processors, $P_0, P_1, \ldots, P_{n-1}$, and n disks $D_0, D_1, \ldots, D_{n-1}$, where disk D_i is associated with processor P_i. A real system may have multiple disks per processor. It is not hard to extend the algorithms to allow multiple disks per processor: We simply allow D_i to be a set of disks. However, for simplicity, we assume here that D_i is a single disk.

20.5   Intraoperation Parallelism

Since relational operations work on relations containing large sets of tuples, we can parallelize the operations by executing them in parallel on different subsets of the relations. Since the number of tuples in a relation can be large, the degree of parallelism is potentially enormous. Thus, intraoperation parallelism is natural in a database system. We shall study parallel versions of some common relational operations in Sections 20.5.1 through 20.5.3.

20.5.1   Parallel Sort

Suppose that we wish to sort a relation that resides on n disks $D_0, D_1, \ldots, D_{n-1}$. If the relation has been range partitioned on the attributes on which it is to be sorted, then, as noted in Section 20.2.2, we can sort each partition separately, and can concatenate the results to get the full sorted relation. Since the tuples are partitioned on n disks, the time required for reading the entire relation is reduced by the parallel access.

If the relation has been partitioned in any other way, we can sort it in one of two ways:

1. We can range partition it on the sort attributes, and then sort each partition separately.

2. We can use a parallel version of the external sort–merge algorithm.

20.5.1.1   Range-Partitioning Sort

Range-partitioning sort works in two steps: first range partitioning the relation, then sorting each partition separately. When we sort by range partitioning the relation, it is not necessary to range-partition the relation on the same set of processors or disks as those on which that relation is stored. Suppose that we choose processors $P_0, P_1, \ldots, P_m$, where $m < n$ to sort the relation. There are two steps involved in this operation:

1. Redistribute the tuples in the relation, using a range-partition strategy, so that all tuples that lie within the ith range are sent to processor P_i, which stores the relation temporarily on disk D_i.

   To implement range partitioning, in parallel every processor reads the tuples from its disk and sends the tuples to their destination processor. Each processor $P_0, P_1, \ldots, P_m$ also receives tuples belonging to its partition, and stores them locally. This step requires disk I/O and communication overhead.

2. Each of the processors sorts its partition of the relation locally, without interaction with the other processors. Each processor executes the same operation —namely, sorting—on a different data set. (Execution of the same operation in parallel on different sets of data is called **data parallelism**.)

   The final merge operation is trivial, because the range partitioning in the first phase ensures that, for $1 \le i < j \le m$, the key values in processor P_i are all less than the key values in P_j.

We must do range partitioning with a good range-partition vector, so that each partition will have approximately the same number of tuples. Virtual processor partitioning can also be used to reduce skew.

20.5.1.2   Parallel External Sort—Merge

Parallel external sort–merge is an alternative to range partitioning. Suppose that a relation has already been partitioned among disks $D_0, D_1, \ldots, D_{n-1}$ (it does not matter how the relation has been partitioned). Parallel external sort–merge then works this way:

1. Each processor P_i locally sorts the data on disk D_i.

2. The system then merges the sorted runs on each processor to get the final sorted output.

The merging of the sorted runs in step 2 can be parallelized by this sequence of actions:

1. The system range-partitions the sorted partitions at each processor P_i (all by the same partition vector) across the processors $P_0, P_1, \ldots, P_{m-1}$. It sends the tuples in sorted order, so that each processor receives the tuples in sorted streams.

2. Each processor P_i performs a merge on the streams as they are received, to get a single sorted run.

3. The system concatenates the sorted runs on processors $P_0, P_1, \ldots, P_{m-1}$ to get the final result.

As described, this sequence of actions results in an interesting form of **execution skew**, since at first every processor sends all blocks of partition 0 to P_0, then every processor sends all blocks of partition 1 to P_1, and so on. Thus, while sending happens in parallel, receiving tuples becomes sequential: first only P_0 receives tuples, then only P_1 receives tuples, and so on. To avoid this problem, each processor repeatedly sends a block of data to each partition. In other words, each processor sends the first block of every partition, then sends the second block of every partition, and so on. As a result, all processors receive data in parallel.

Some machines, such as the Teradata DBC series machines, use specialized hardware to perform merging. The Y-net interconnection network in the Teradata DBC machines can merge output from multiple processors to give a single sorted output.

20.5.2 Parallel Join

The join operation requires that the system test pairs of tuples to see whether they satisfy the join condition; if they do, the system adds the pair to the join output. Parallel join algorithms attempt to split the pairs to be tested over several processors. Each processor then computes part of the join locally. Then, the system collects the results from each processor to produce the final result.

20.5.2.1 Partitioned Join

For certain kinds of joins, such as equi-joins and natural joins, it is possible to *partition* the two input relations across the processors, and to compute the join locally at each processor. Suppose that we are using n processors, and that the relations to be joined are r and s. **Partitioned join** then works this way: The system partitions the relations r and s each into n partitions, denoted $r_0, r_1, \ldots, r_{n-1}$ and $s_0, s_1, \ldots, s_{n-1}$. The system sends partitions r_i and s_i to processor P_i, where their join is computed locally.

The partitioned join technique works correctly only if the join is an equi-join (for example, $r \bowtie_{r.A=s.B} s$) and if we partition r and s by the same partitioning function on their join attributes. The idea of partitioning is exactly the same as that behind the partitioning step of hash–join. In a partitioned join, however, there are two different ways of partitioning r and s:

- Range partitioning on the join attributes
- Hash partitioning on the join attributes

In either case, the same partitioning function must be used for both relations. For range partitioning, the same partition vector must be used for both relations. For hash partitioning, the same hash function must be used on both relations. Figure 20.2 depicts the partitioning in a partitioned parallel join.

Once the relations are partitioned, we can use any join technique locally at each processor P_i to compute the join of r_i and s_i. For example, hash–join, merge–join, or nested-loop join could be used. Thus, we can use partitioning to parallelize any join technique.

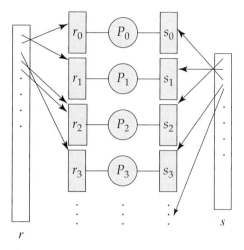

Figure 20.2   Partitioned parallel join.

If one or both of the relations r and s are already partitioned on the join attributes (by either hash partitioning or range partitioning), the work needed for partitioning is reduced greatly. If the relations are not partitioned, or are partitioned on attributes other than the join attributes, then the tuples need to be repartitioned. Each processor P_i reads in the tuples on disk D_i, computes for each tuple t the partition j to which t belongs, and sends tuple t to processor P_j. Processor P_j stores the tuples on disk D_j.

We can optimize the join algorithm used locally at each processor to reduce I/O by buffering some of the tuples to memory, instead of writing them to disk. We describe such optimizations in Section 20.5.2.3.

Skew presents a special problem when range partitioning is used, since a partition vector that splits one relation of the join into equal-sized partitions may split the other relations into partitions of widely varying size. The partition vector should be such that $|\ r_i\ | + |\ s_i\ |$ (that is, the sum of the sizes of r_i and s_i) is roughly equal over all the $i = 0, 1, \ldots, n - 1$. With a good hash function, hash partitioning is likely to have a smaller skew, except when there are many tuples with the same values for the join attributes.

20.5.2.2   Fragment-and-Replicate Join

Partitioning is not applicable to all types of joins. For instance, if the join condition is an inequality, such as $r \bowtie_{r.a < s.b} s$, it is possible that all tuples in r join with some tuple in s (and vice versa). Thus, there may be no easy way of partitioning r and s so that tuples in partition r_i join with only tuples in partition s_i.

We can parallelize such joins by using a technique called *fragment and replicate*. We first consider a special case of fragment and replicate—**asymmetric fragment-and-replicate join**—which works as follows.

1. The system partitions one of the relations—say, r. Any partitioning technique can be used on r, including round-robin partitioning.

2. The system replicates the other relation, s, across all the processors.

3. Processor P_i then locally computes the join of r_i with all of s, using any join technique.

The asymmetric fragment-and-replicate scheme appears in Figure 20.3a. If r is already stored by partitioning, there is no need to partition it further in step 1. All that is required is to replicate s across all processors.

The general case of **fragment and replicate join** appears in Figure 20.3b; it works this way: The system partitions relation r into n partitions, $r_0, r_1, \ldots, r_{n-1}$, and partitions s into m partitions, $s_0, s_1, \ldots, s_{m-1}$. As before, any partitioning technique may be used on r and on s. The values of m and n do not need to be equal, but they must be chosen so that there are at least $m * n$ processors. Asymmetric fragment and replicate is simply a special case of general fragment and replicate, where $m = 1$. Fragment and replicate reduces the sizes of the relations at each processor, compared to asymmetric fragment and replicate.

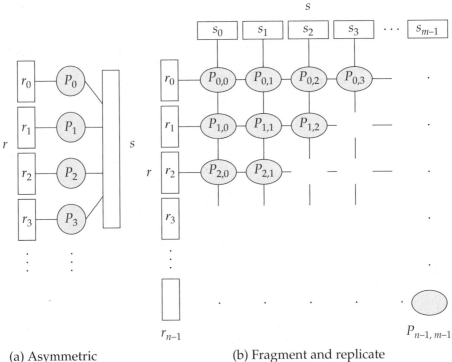

(a) Asymmetric fragment and replicate

(b) Fragment and replicate

Figure 20.3   Fragment-and-replicate schemes.

Let the processors be $P_{0,0}, P_{0,1}, \ldots, P_{0,m-1}, P_{1,0}, \ldots, P_{n-1,m-1}$. Processor $P_{i,j}$ computes the join of r_i with s_j. Each processor must get the tuples in the partitions it works on. To do so, the system replicates r_i to processors $P_{i,0}, P_{i,1}, \ldots, P_{i,m-1}$ (which form a row in Figure 20.3b), and replicates s_i to processors $P_{0,i}, P_{1,i}, \ldots, P_{n-1,i}$ (which form a column in Figure 20.3b). Any join technique can be used at each processor $P_{i,j}$.

Fragment and replicate works with any join condition, since every tuple in r can be tested with every tuple in s. Thus, it can be used where partitioning cannot be.

Fragment and replicate usually has a higher cost than partitioning when both relations are of roughly the same size, since at least one of the relations has to be replicated. However, if one of the relations—say, s—is small, it may be cheaper to replicate s across all processors, rather than to repartition r and s on the join attributes. In such a case, asymmetric fragment and replicate is preferable, even though partitioning could be used.

20.5.2.3   Partitioned Parallel Hash–Join

The partitioned hash–join of Section 13.5.5 can be parallelized. Suppose that we have n processors, $P_0, P_1, \ldots, P_{n-1}$, and two relations r and s, such that the relations r and s are partitioned across multiple disks. Recall from Section 13.5.5 that the smaller relation is chosen as the build relation. If the size of s is less than that of r, the parallel hash–join algorithm proceeds this way:

1. Choose a hash function—say, h_1—that takes the join attribute value of each tuple in r and s and maps the tuple to one of the n processors. Let r_i denote the tuples of relation r that are mapped to processor P_i; similarly, let s_i denote the tuples of relation s that are mapped to processor P_i. Each processor P_i reads the tuples of s that are on its disk D_i, and sends each tuple to the appropriate processor on the basis of hash function h_1.

2. As the destination processor P_i receives the tuples of s_i, it further partitions them by another hash function, h_2, which the processor uses to compute the hash–join locally. The partitioning at this stage is exactly the same as in the partitioning phase of the sequential hash–join algorithm. Each processor P_i executes this step independently from the other processors.

3. Once the tuples of s have been distributed, the system redistributes the larger relation r across the m processors by the hash function h_1, in the same way as before. As it receives each tuple, the destination processor repartitions it by the function h_2, just as the probe relation is partitioned in the sequential hash–join algorithm.

4. Each processor P_i executes the build and probe phases of the hash–join algorithm on the local partitions r_i and s_i of r and s to produce a partition of the final result of the hash–join.

The hash–join at each processor is independent of that at other processors, and receiving the tuples of r_i and s_i is similar to reading them from disk. Therefore, any of the optimizations of the hash–join described in Chapter 13 can be applied as well to the parallel case. In particular, we can use the hybrid hash–join algorithm to cache some of the incoming tuples in memory, and thus avoid the costs of writing them and of reading them back in.

20.5.2.4 Parallel Nested-Loop Join

To illustrate the use of fragment-and-replicate–based parallelization, consider the case where the relation s is much smaller than relation r. Suppose that relation r is stored by partitioning; the attribute on which it is partitioned does not matter. Suppose too that there is an index on a join attribute of relation r at each of the partitions of relation r.

We use asymmetric fragment and replicate, with relation s being replicated and with the existing partitioning of relation r. Each processor P_j where a partition of relation s is stored reads the tuples of relation s stored in D_j, and replicates the tuples to every other processor P_i. At the end of this phase, relation s is replicated at all sites that store tuples of relation r.

Now, each processor P_i performs an indexed nested-loop join of relation s with the ith partition of relation r. We can overlap the indexed nested-loop join with the distribution of tuples of relation s, to reduce the costs of writing the tuples of relation s to disk, and of reading them back. However, the replication of relation s must be synchronized with the join so that there is enough space in the in-memory buffers at each processor P_i to hold the tuples of relation s that have been received but that have not yet been used in the join.

20.5.3 Other Relational Operations

The evaluation of other relational operations also can be parallelized:

- **Selection**. Let the selection be $\sigma_\theta(r)$. Consider first the case where θ is of the form $a_i = v$, where a_i is an attribute and v is a value. If the relation r is partitioned on a_i, the selection proceeds at a single processor. If θ is of the form $l \leq a_i \leq u$—that is, θ is a range selection—and the relation has been range-partitioned on a_i, then the selection proceeds at each processor whose partition overlaps with the specified range of values. In all other cases, the selection proceeds in parallel at all the processors.

- **Duplicate elimination**. Duplicates can be eliminated by sorting; either of the parallel sort techniques can be used, optimized to eliminate duplicates as soon as they appear during sorting. We can also parallelize duplicate elimination by partitioning the tuples (by either range or hash partitioning) and eliminating duplicates locally at each processor.

- **Projection**. Projection without duplicate elimination can be performed as tuples are read in from disk in parallel. If duplicates are to be eliminated, either of the techniques just described can be used.

- **Aggregation**. Consider an aggregation operation. We can parallelize the operation by partitioning the relation on the grouping attributes, and then computing the aggregate values locally at each processor. Either hash partitioning or range partitioning can be used. If the relation is already partitioned on the grouping attributes, the first step can be skipped.

We can reduce the cost of transferring tuples during partitioning by partly computing aggregate values before partitioning, at least for the commonly used aggregate functions. Consider an aggregation operation on a relation r, using the **sum** aggregate function on attribute B, with grouping on attribute A. The system can perform the operation at each processor P_i on those r tuples stored on disk D_i. This computation results in tuples with partial sums at each processor; there is one tuple at P_i for each value for attribute A present in r tuples stored on D_i. The system partitions the result of the local aggregation on the grouping attribute A, and performs the aggregation again (on tuples with the partial sums) at each processor P_i to get the final result.

As a result of this optimization, fewer tuples need to be sent to other processors during partitioning. This idea can be extended easily to the **min** and **max** aggregate functions. Extensions to the **count** and **avg** aggregate functions are left for you to do in Exercise 20.8.

The parallelization of other operations is covered in several of the the exercises.

20.5.4   Cost of Parallel Evaluation of Operations

We achieve parallelism by partitioning the I/O among multiple disks, and partitioning the CPU work among multiple processors. If such a split is achieved without any overhead, and if there is no skew in the splitting of work, a parallel operation using n processors will take $1/n$ times as long as the same operation on a single processor. We already know how to estimate the cost of an operation such as a join or a selection. The time cost of parallel processing would then be $1/n$ of the time cost of sequential processing of the operation.

We must also account for the following costs:

- **Startup costs** for initiating the operation at multiple processors

- **Skew** in the distribution of work among the processors, with some processors getting a larger number of tuples than others

- **Contention for resources**—such as memory, disk, and the communication network—resulting in delays

- **Cost of assembling** the final result by transmitting partial results from each processor

The time taken by a parallel operation can be estimated as

$$T_{\text{part}} + T_{\text{asm}} + \max(T_0, T_1, \ldots, T_{n-1})$$

where T_{part} is the time for partitioning the relations, T_{asm} is the time for assembling the results and T_i the time taken for the operation at processor P_i. Assuming that the tuples are distributed without any skew, the number of tuples sent to each processor can be estimated as $1/n$ of the total number of tuples. Ignoring contention, the cost T_i of the operations at each processor P_i can then be estimated by the techniques in Chapter 13.

The preceding estimate will be an optimistic estimate, since skew is common. Even though breaking down a single query into a number of parallel steps reduces the size of the average step, it is the time for processing the single slowest step that determines the time taken for processing the query as a whole. A partitioned parallel evaluation, for instance, is only as fast as the slowest of the parallel executions. Thus, any skew in the distribution of the work across processors greatly affects performance.

The problem of skew in partitioning is closely related to the problem of partition overflow in sequential hash–joins (Chapter 13). We can use overflow resolution and avoidance techniques developed for hash–joins to handle skew when hash partitioning is used. We can use balanced range partitioning and virtual processor partitioning to minimize skew due to range partitioning, as in Section 20.2.3.

20.6 Interoperation Parallelism

There are two forms of interoperation parallelism: pipelined parallelism, and independent parallelism.

20.6.1 Pipelined Parallelism

As discussed in Chapter 13, pipelining forms an important source of economy of computation for database query processing. Recall that, in pipelining, the output tuples of one operation, A, are consumed by a second operation, B, even before the first operation has produced the entire set of tuples in its output. The major advantage of pipelined execution in a sequential evaluation is that we can carry out a sequence of such operations without writing any of the intermediate results to disk.

Parallel systems use pipelining primarily for the same reason that sequential systems do. However, pipelines are a source of parallelism as well, in the same way that instruction pipelines are a source of parallelism in hardware design. It is possible to run operations A and B simultaneously on different processors, so that B consumes tuples in parallel with A producing them. This form of parallelism is called **pipelined parallelism**.

Consider a join of four relations:

$$r_1 \bowtie r_2 \bowtie r_3 \bowtie r_4$$

We can set up a pipeline that allows the three joins to be computed in parallel. Suppose processor P_1 is assigned the computation of $temp_1 \leftarrow r_1 \bowtie r_2$, and P_2 is assigned the computation of $r_3 \bowtie temp_1$. As P_1 computes tuples in $r_1 \bowtie r_2$, it makes these tuples available to processor P_2. Thus, P_2 has available to it some of the tuples in $r_1 \bowtie r_2$ before P_1 has finished its computation. P_2 can use those tuples that are available to begin computation of $temp_1 \bowtie r_3$, even before $r_1 \bowtie r_2$ is fully computed by P_1. Likewise, as P_2 computes tuples in $(r_1 \bowtie r_2) \bowtie r_3$, it makes these tuples available to P_3, which computes the join of these tuples with r_4.

Pipelined parallelism is useful with a small number of processors, but does not scale up well. First, pipeline chains generally do not attain sufficient length to provide a high degree of parallelism. Second, it is not possible to pipeline relational operators that do not produce output until all inputs have been accessed, such as the set-difference operation. Third, only marginal speedup is obtained for the frequent cases in which one operator's execution cost is much higher than are those of the others.

All things considered, when the degree of parallelism is high, pipelining is a less important source of parallelism than partitioning. The real reason for using pipelining is that pipelined executions can avoid writing intermediate results to disk.

20.6.2   Independent Parallelism

Operations in a query expression that do not depend on one another can be executed in parallel. This form of parallelism is called **independent parallelism**.

Consider the join $r_1 \bowtie r_2 \bowtie r_3 \bowtie r_4$. Clearly, we can compute $temp_1 \leftarrow r_1 \bowtie r_2$ in parallel with $temp_2 \leftarrow r_3 \bowtie r_4$. When these two computations complete, we compute

$$temp_1 \bowtie temp_2$$

To obtain further parallelism, we can pipeline the tuples in $temp_1$ and $temp_2$ into the computation of $temp_1 \bowtie temp_2$, which is itself carried out by a pipelined join (Section 13.7.2.2).

Like pipelined parallelism, independent parallelism does not provide a high degree of parallelism, and is less useful in a highly parallel system, although it is useful with a lower degree of parallelism.

20.6.3   Query Optimization

Query optimizers account in large measure for the success of relational technology. Recall that a query optimizer takes a query and finds the cheapest execution plan among the many possible execution plans that give the same answer.

Query optimizers for parallel query evaluation are more complicated than query optimizers for sequential query evaluation. First, the cost models are more complicated, since partitioning costs have to be accounted for, and issues such as skew and resource contention must be taken into account. More important is the issue of how to parallelize a query. Suppose that we have somehow chosen an expression (from among those equivalent to the query) to be used for evaluating the query. The expression can be represented by an operator tree, as in Section 13.1.

To evaluate an operator tree in a parallel system, we must make the following decisions:

- How to parallelize each operation, and how many processors to use for it

- What operations to pipeline across different processors, what operations to execute independently in parallel, and what operations to execute sequentially, one after the other

These decisions constitute the task of **scheduling** the execution tree.

Determining the resources of each kind—such as processors, disks, and memory—that should be allocated to each operation in the tree is another aspect of the optimization problem. For instance, it may appear wise to use the maximum amount of parallelism available, but it is a good idea not to execute certain operations in parallel. Operations whose computational requirements are significantly smaller than the communication overhead should be clustered with one of their neighbors. Otherwise, the advantage of parallelism is negated by the overhead of communication.

One concern is that long pipelines do not lend themselves to good resource utilization. Unless the operations are coarse grained, the final operation of the pipeline may wait for a long time to get inputs, while holding precious resources, such as memory. Hence, long pipelines should be avoided.

The number of parallel evaluation plans from which to choose is much larger than the number of sequential evaluation plans. Optimizing parallel queries by considering all alternatives is therefore much more expensive than optimizing sequential queries. Hence, we usually adopt heuristic approaches to reduce the number of parallel execution plans that we have to consider. We describe two popular heuristics here.

The first heuristic is to consider only evaluation plans that parallelize every operation across all processors, and that do not use any pipelining. This approach is used in the Teradata DBC series machines. Finding the best such execution plan is like doing query optimization in a sequential system. The main differences lie in how the partitioning is performed and what cost-estimation formula is used.

The second heuristic is to choose the most efficient sequential evaluation plan, and then to parallelize the operations in that evaluation plan. The Volcano parallel database popularized a model of parallelization called the **exchange-operator** model. This model uses existing implementations of operations, operating on local copies of data, coupled with an exchange operation that moves data around between different processors. Exchange operators can be introduced into an evaluation plan to transform it into a parallel evaluation plan.

Yet another dimension of optimization is the design of physical-storage organization to speed up queries. The optimal physical organization differs for different queries. The database administrator must choose a physical organization that appears to be good for the expected mix of database queries. Thus, the area of parallel query optimization is complex, and it is still an area of active research.

20.7 Design of Parallel Systems

So far this chapter has concentrated on parallelization of data storage and of query processing. Since large-scale parallel database systems are used primarily for storing large volumes of data, and for processing decision-support queries on those data, these topics are the most important in a parallel database system. Parallel loading of data from external sources is an important requirement, if we are to handle large volumes of incoming data.

A large parallel database system must also address these availability issues:

- Resilience to failure of some processors or disks

- Online reorganization of data and schema changes

We consider these issues here.

With a large number of processors and disks, the probability that at least one processor or disk will malfunction is significantly greater than in a single-processor system with one disk. A poorly designed parallel system will stop functioning if any component (processor or disk) fails. Assuming that the probability of failure of a single processor or disk is small, the probability of failure of the system goes up linearly with the number of processors and disks. If a single processor or disk would fail once every 5 years, a system with 100 processors would have a failure every 18 days.

Therefore, large-scale parallel database systems, such as Compaq Himalaya, Teradata, and Informix XPS (now a division of IBM), are designed to operate even if a processor or disk fails. Data are replicated across at least two processors. If a processor fails, the data that it stored can still be accessed from the other processors. The system keeps track of failed processors and distributes the work among functioning processors. Requests for data stored at the failed site are automatically routed to the backup sites that store a replica of the data. If all the data of a processor A are replicated at a single processor B, B will have to handle all the requests to A as well as those to itself, and that will result in B becoming a bottleneck. Therefore, the replicas of the data of a processor are partitioned across multiple other processors.

When we are dealing with large volumes of data (ranging in the terabytes), simple operations, such as creating indices, and changes to schema, such as adding a column to a relation, can take a long time — perhaps hours or even days. Therefore, it is unacceptable for the database system to be unavailable while such operations are in progress. Many parallel database systems, such as the Compaq Himalaya systems, allow such operations to be performed **online**, that is, while the system is executing other transactions.

Consider, for instance, **online index construction**. A system that supports this feature allows insertions, deletions, and updates on a relation even as an index is being built on the relation. The index-building operation therefore cannot lock the entire relation in shared mode, as it would have done otherwise. Instead, the process keeps track of updates that occur while it is active, and incorporates the changes into the index being constructed.

20.8 Summary

- Parallel databases have gained significant commercial acceptance in the past 15 years.

- In I/O parallelism, relations are partitioned among available disks so that they can be retrieved faster. Three commonly used partitioning techniques are round-robin partitioning, hash partitioning, and range partitioning.

- Skew is a major problem, especially with increasing degrees of parallelism. Balanced partitioning vectors, using histograms, and virtual processor partitioning are among the techniques used to reduce skew.

- In interquery parallelism, we run different queries concurrently to increase throughput.

- Intraquery parallelism attempts to reduce the cost of running a query. There are two types of intraquery parallelism: intraoperation parallelism and interoperation parallelism.

- We use intraoperation parallelism to execute relational operations, such as sorts and joins, in parallel. Intraoperation parallelism is natural for relational operations, since they are set oriented.

- There are two basic approaches to parallelizing a binary operation such as a join.

  □ In partitioned parallelism, the relations are split into several parts, and tuples in r_i are joined with only tuples from s_i. Partitioned parallelism can only be used for natural and equi-joins.

  □ In fragment and replicate, both relations are partitioned and each partition is replicated. In asymmetric fragment-and-replicate, one of the relations is replicated while the other is partitioned. Unlike partitioned parallelism, fragment and replicate and asymmetric fragment-and-replicate can be used with any join condition.

  Both parallelization techniques can work in conjunction with any join technique.

- In independent parallelism, different operations that do not depend on one another are executed in parallel.

- In pipelined parallelism, processors send the results of one operation to another operation as those results are computed, without waiting for the entire operation to finish.

- Query optimization in parallel databases is significantly more complex than query optimization in sequential databases.

Review Terms

- Decision-support queries

- I/O parallelism

- Horizontal partitioning

- Partitioning techniques
  □ Round-robin

□ Hash partitioning
□ Range partitioning

- Partitioning attribute

- Partitioning vector

- Point query

- Range query
- Skew
  - □ Execution skew
  - □ Attribute-value skew
  - □ Partition skew
- Handling of skew
  - □ Balanced range-partitioning vector
  - □ Histogram
  - □ Virtual processors
- Interquery parallelism
- Cache coherency
- Intraquery parallelism
  - □ Intraoperation parallelism
  - □ Interoperation parallelism
- Parallel sort
  - □ Range-partitioning sort
  - □ Parallel external sort–merge
- Data parallelism
- Parallel join
- □ Partitioned join
- □ Fragment-and-replicate join
- □ Asymmetric fragment-and-replicate join
- □ Partitioned parallel hash–join
- □ Parallel nested-loop join
- Parallel selection
- Parallel duplicate elimination
- Parallel projection
- Parallel aggregation
- Cost of parallel evaluation
- Interoperation parallelism
  - □ Pipelined parallelism
  - □ Independent parallelism
- Query optimization
- Scheduling
- Exchange-operator model
- Design of parallel systems
- Online index construction

Exercises

20.1 For each of the three partitioning techniques, namely round-robin, hash partitioning, and range partitioning, give an example of a query for which that partitioning technique would provide the fastest response.

20.2 In a range selection on a range-partitioned attribute, it is possible that only one disk may need to be accessed. Describe the benefits and drawbacks of this property.

20.3 What factors could result in skew when a relation is partitioned on one of its attributes by:
  a. Hash partitioning
  b. Range partitioning
In each case, what can be done to reduce the skew?

20.4 What form of parallelism (interquery, interoperation, or intraoperation) is likely to be the most important for each of the following tasks.
  a. Increasing the throughput of a system with many small queries
  b. Increasing the throughput of a system with a few large queries, when the number of disks and processors is large

20.5 With pipelined parallelism, it is often a good idea to perform several operations in a pipeline on a single processor, even when many processors are available.

    a. Explain why.

    b. Would the arguments you advanced in part a hold if the machine has a shared-memory architecture? Explain why or why not.

    c. Would the arguments in part a hold with independent parallelism? (That is, are there cases where, even if the operations are not pipelined and there are many processors available, it is still a good idea to perform several operations on the same processor?)

20.6 Give an example of a join that is not a simple equi-join for which partitioned parallelism can be used. What attributes should be used for partitioning?

20.7 Consider join processing using symmetric fragment and replicate with range partitioning. How can you optimize the evaluation if the join condition is of the form $| r.A - s.B | \leq k$, where k is a small constant. Here, $| x |$ denotes the absolute value of x. A join with such a join condition is called a **band join**.

20.8 Describe a good way to parallelize each of the following.

    a. The difference operation

    b. Aggregation by the **count** operation

    c. Aggregation by the **count distinct** operation

    d. Aggregation by the **avg** operation

    e. Left outer join, if the join condition involves only equality

    f. Left outer join, if the join condition involves comparisons other than equality

    g. Full outer join, if the join condition involves comparisons other than equality

20.9 Recall that histograms are used for constructing load-balanced range partitions.

    a. Suppose you have a histogram where values are between 1 and 100, and are partitioned into 10 ranges, 1–10, 11–20, ..., 91–100, with frequencies 15, 5, 20, 10, 10, 5, 5, 20, 5, and 5, respectively. Give a load-balanced range partitioning function to divide the values into 5 partitions.

    b. Write an algorithm for computing a balanced range partition with p partitions, given a histogram of frequency distributions containing n ranges.

20.10 Describe the benefits and drawbacks of pipelined parallelism.

20.11 Some parallel database systems store an extra copy of each data item on disks attached to a different processor, to avoid loss of data if one of the processors fails.

    a. Why is it a good idea to partition the copies of the data items of a processor across multiple processors?

    b. What are the benefits and drawbacks of using RAID storage instead of storing an extra copy of each data item?

Bibliographical Notes

Relational database systems began appearing in the marketplace in 1983; now, they dominate it. By the late 1970s and early 1980s, as the relational model gained reasonably sound footing, people recognized that relational operators are highly parallelizable and have good dataflow properties. A commercial system, Teradata, and several research projects, such as GRACE (Kitsuregawa et al. [1983], Fushimi et al. [1986]), GAMMA (DeWitt et al. [1986], DeWitt [1990]), and Bubba (Boral et al. [1990]) were launched in quick succession. Researchers used these parallel database systems to investigate the practicality of parallel execution of relational operators. Subsequently, in the late 1980s and the 1990s, several more companies—such as Tandem, Oracle, Sybase, Informix, and Red-Brick (now a part of Informix, which is itself now a part of IBM)—entered the parallel database market. Research projects in the academic world include XPRS (Stonebraker et al. [1989]) and Volcano (Graefe [1990]).

Locking in parallel databases is discussed in Joshi [1991], Mohan and Narang [1991], and Mohan and Narang [1992]. Cache-coherency protocols for parallel database systems are discussed by Dias et al. [1989], Mohan and Narang [1991], Mohan and Narang [1992], and Rahm [1993]. Carey et al. [1991] discusses caching issues in a client–server system. Parallelism and recovery in database systems are discussed by Bayer et al. [1980].

Graefe [1993] presents an excellent survey of query processing, including parallel processing of queries. Parallel sorting is discussed in DeWitt et al. [1992]. Parallel join algorithms are described by Nakayama et al. [1984], Kitsuregawa et al. [1983], Richardson et al. [1987], Schneider and DeWitt [1989], Kitsuregawa and Ogawa [1990], Lin et al. [1994], and Wilschut et al. [1995], among other works. Parallel join algorithms for shared-memory architectures are described by Tsukuda et al. [1992], Deshpande and Larson [1992], and Shatdal and Naughton [1993].

Skew handling in parallel joins is described by Walton et al. [1991], Wolf [1991], and DeWitt et al. [1992]. Sampling techniques for parallel databases are described by Seshadri and Naughton [1992] and Ganguly et al. [1996]. The exchange-operator model was advocated by Graefe [1990] and Graefe [1993].

Parallel query-optimization techniques are described by H. Lu and Tan [1991], Hong and Stonebraker [1991], Ganguly et al. [1992], Lanzelotte et al. [1993], Hasan and Motwani [1995], and Jhingran et al. [1997].

PART 7

Other Topics

Chapter 21 covers a number of issues in building and maintaining applications and administering database systems. The chapter first outlines how to implement user interfaces, in particular Web-based interfaces. Other issues such as performance tuning (to improve application speed), standards issues in electronic commerce, and how to handle legacy systems are also covered in this chapter.

Chapter 22 describes a number of recent advances in querying and information retrieval. It first covers SQL extensions to support new types of queries, in particular queries typically posed by data analysts. It next covers data warehousing, whereby data generated by different parts of an organization are gathered centrally. The chapter then outlines data mining, which aims at finding patterns of various complex forms in large volumes of data. Finally, the chapter describes information retrieval, which deals with techniques for querying collections of text documents, such as Web pages, to find documents of interest.

Chapter 22 describes data types, such as temporal data, spatial data, and multimedia data, and the issues in storing such data in databases. Applications such as mobile computing and its connections with databases, are also described in this chapter.

Finally, Chapter 23 describes several advanced transaction-processing techniques, including transaction-processing monitors, transactional workflows, long-duration transactions, and multidatabase transactions.

Application Development and Administration

Practically all use of databases occurs from within application programs. Correspondingly, almost all user interaction with databases is indirect, via application programs. Not surprisingly, therefore, database systems have long supported tools such as form and GUI builders, which help in rapid development of applications that interface with users. In recent years, the Web has become the most widely used user interface to databases.

Once an application has been built, it is often found to run slower than the designers wanted, or to handle fewer transactions per second than they required. Applications can be made to run significantly faster by performance tuning, which consists of finding and eliminating bottlenecks and adding appropriate hardware such as memory or disks. Benchmarks help to characterize the performance of database systems.

Standards are very important for application development, especially in the age of the internet, since applications need to communicate with each other to perform useful tasks. A variety of standards have been proposed that affect database application development.

Electronic commerce is becoming an integral part of how we purchase goods and services and databases play an important role in that domain.

Legacy systems are systems based on older-generation technology. They are often at the core of organizations, and run mission-critical applications. We outline issues in interfacing with legacy systems, and how they can be replaced by other systems.

21.1 Web Interfaces to Databases

The **World Wide Web** (**Web**, for short), is a distributed information system based on hypertext. Web interfaces to databases have become very important. After outlining several reasons for interfacing databases with the Web (Section 21.1.1), we provide an overview of Web technology (Section 21.1.2) and then study Web servers (Section 21.1.3) and outline some state-of-the art techniques for building Web interfaces to databases, using servlets and server-side scripting languages (Sections 21.1.4 and 21.1.5). We describe techniques for improving performance in Section 21.1.6.

21.1.1 Motivation

The Web has become important as a front end to databases for several reasons: Web browsers provide a *universal front end* to information supplied by back ends located anywhere in the world. The front end can run on any computer system, and there is no need for a user to download any special-purpose software to access information. Further, today, almost everyone who can afford it has access to the Web.

With the growth of information services and electronic commerce on the Web, databases used for information services, decision support, and transaction processing must be linked with the Web. The HTML forms interface is convenient for transaction processing. The user can fill in details in an order form, then click a submit button to send a message to the server. The server executes an application program corresponding to the order form, and this action in turn executes transactions on a database at the server site. The server formats the results of the transaction and sends them back to the user.

Another reason for interfacing databases to the Web is that presenting only static (fixed) documents on a Web site has some limitations, even when the user is not doing any querying or transaction processing:

- Fixed Web documents do not allow the display to be tailored to the user. For instance, a newspaper may want to tailor its display on a per-user basis, to give prominence to news articles that are likely to be of interest to the user.

- When the company data are updated, the Web documents become obsolete if they are not updated simultaneously. The problem becomes more acute if multiple Web documents replicate important data, and all must be updated.

We can fix these problems by generating Web documents dynamically from a database. When a document is requested, a program gets executed at the server site, which in turn runs queries on a database, and generates the requested document on the basis of the query results. Whenever relevant data in the database are updated, the generated documents will automatically become up-to-date. The generated document can also be tailored to the user on the basis of user information stored in the database.

Web interfaces provide attractive benefits even for database applications that are used only with a single organization. The **HyperText Markup Language (HTML)** standard allows text to be neatly formatted, with important information highlighted. **Hyperlinks**, which are links to other documents, can be associated with regions of the displayed data. Clicking on a hyperlink fetches and displays the linked document. Hyperlinks are very useful for browsing data, permitting users to get more details of parts of the data as desired.

Finally, browsers today can fetch programs along with HTML documents, and run the programs on the browser, in safe mode—that is, without damaging data on the user's computer. Programs can be written in client-side scripting languages, such as Javascript, or can be "applets" written in the Java language. These programs permit the construction of sophisticated user interfaces, beyond what is possible with just HTML, interfaces that can be used without downloading and installing any software. Thus, Web interfaces are powerful and visually attractive, and are likely to eclipse special-purpose interfaces for all except a small class of users.

21.1.2 Web Fundamentals

Here we review some of the fundamental technology behind the World Wide Web, for readers who are not familiar with it.

21.1.2.1 Uniform Resource Locators

A **uniform resource locator** (URL) is a globally unique name for each document that can be accessed on the Web. An example of a URL is

http://www.bell-labs.com/topic/book/db-book

The first part of the URL indicates how the document is to be accessed: "http" indicates that the document is to be accessed by the HyperText Transfer Protocol, which is a protocol for transferring HTML documents. The second part gives the unique name of a machine that has a Web server. The rest of the URL is the path name of the file on the machine, or other unique identifier of the document within the machine.

Much data on the Web is dynamically generated. A URL can contain the identifier of a program located on the Web server machine, as well as arguments to be given to the program. An example of such a URL is

http://www.google.com/search?q=silberschatz

which says that the program search on the server www.google.com should be executed with the argument q=silberschatz. The program executes, using the given arguments, and returns an HTML document, which is then sent to the front end.

21.1.2.2 HyperText Markup Language

Figure 21.1 is an example of the source of an HTML document. Figure 21.2 shows the displayed image that this document creates.

The figures show how HTML can display a table and a simple form that allows users to select the type (account or loan) from a menu and to input a number in a text box. HTML also supports several other input types. Clicking on the submit button causes the program BankQuery (specified in the form action field) to be executed with the user-provided values for the arguments type and number (specified in the select and input fields). The program generates an HTML document, which is then sent back and displayed to the user; we will see how to construct such programs in Sections 21.1.3, 21.1.4, and 21.1.5.

HTML supports *stylesheets*, which can alter the default definitions of how an HTML formatting construct is displayed, as well as other display attributes such as background color of the page. The *cascading stylesheet (css)* standard allows the same

```
<html>
<body>
<table BORDER COLS=3>
<tr> <td>A-101</td> <td>Downtown</td> <td>500</td> </tr>
<tr> <td>A-102</td> <td>Perryridge</td> <td>400</td> </tr>
<tr> <td>A-201</td> <td>Brighton   </td> <td>900</td> </tr>
</table>
<center> The <i>account</i> relation </center>

<form action="BankQuery" method=get>
Select account/loan and enter number <br>
<select name="type">
     <option value="account" selected>Account
     <option value="loan"> Loan
</select>
<input type=text size=5 name="number">
<input type=submit value="submit">

</body>
</html>
```

Figure 21.1   An HTML source text.

stylesheet to be used for multiple HTML documents, giving a uniform look to all the pages on a Web site.

21.1.2.3   Client-Side Scripting and Applets

Embedding of program code in documents allows Web pages to be **active**, carrying out activities such as animation by executing programs at the local site, rather than just presenting passive text and graphics. The primary use of such programs is flexible interaction with the user, beyond the limited interaction power provided by HTML and HTML forms. Further, executing programs at the client site speeds up

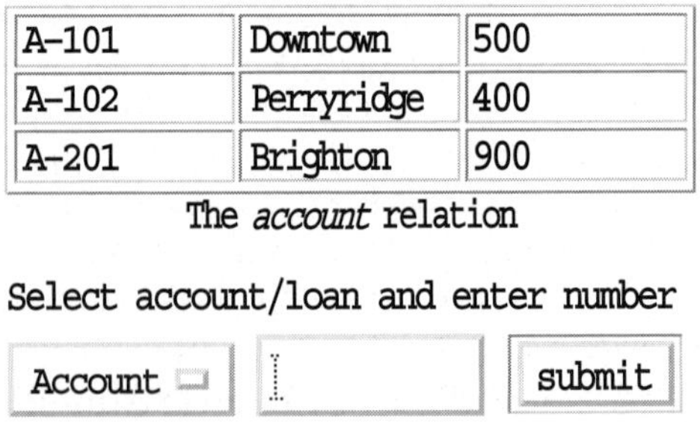

A–101	Downtown	500
A–102	Perryridge	400
A–201	Brighton	900

The *account* relation

Select account/loan and enter number

Account ⊟   [   ]   submit

Figure 21.2   Display of HTML source from Figure 21.1.

interaction greatly, compared to every interaction being sent to a server site for processing.

A danger in supporting such programs is that, if the design of the system is done carelessly, program code embedded in a Web page (or equivalently, in an e-mail message) can perform malicious actions on the user's computer. The malicious actions could range from reading private information, to deleting or modifying information on the computer, up to taking control of the computer and propagating the code to other computers (through e-mail, for example). A number of e-mail viruses have spread widely in recent years in this way.

The *Java* language became very popular because it provides a safe mode for executing programs on user's computers. Java code can be compiled into platform-independent "byte-code" that can be executed on any browser that supports Java. Unlike local programs, Java programs (applets) downloaded as part of a Web page have no authority to perform any actions that could be destructive. They are permitted to display data on the screen, or to make a network connection to the server from which the Web page was downloaded, in order to fetch more information. However, they are not permitted to access local files, to execute any system programs, or to make network connections to any other computers.

While Java is a full-fledged programming language, there are simpler languages, called **scripting languages**, that can enrich user interaction, while providing the same protection as Java. These languages provide constructs that can be embedded with an HTML document. **Client-side scripting languages** are languages designed to be executed on the client's Web browser. Of these, the *Javascript* language is by far the most widely used. There are also special-purpose scripting languages for specialized tasks such as animation (for example, Macromedia Flash and Shockwave), and three-dimensional modeling (Virtual Reality Markup Language (VRML)). Scripting languages can also be used on the server side, as we shall see.

21.1.3   Web Servers and Sessions

A **Web server** is a program running on the server machine, which accepts requests from a Web browser and sends back results in the form of HTML documents. The browser and Web server communicate by a protocol called the **HyperText Transfer Protocol (HTTP)**. HTTP provides powerful features, beyond the simple transfer of documents. The most important feature is the ability to execute programs, with arguments supplied by the user, and deliver the results back as an HTML document.

As a result, a Web server can easily act as an intermediary to provide access to a variety of information services. A new service can be created by creating and installing an application program that provides the service. The **common gateway interface (CGI)** standard defines how the Web server communicates with application programs. The application program typically communicates with a database server, through ODBC, JDBC, or other protocols, in order to get or store data.

Figure 21.3 shows a Web service using a three-tier architecture, with a Web server, an application server, and a database server. Using multiple levels of servers increases system overhead; the CGI interface starts a new process to service each request, which results in even greater overhead.

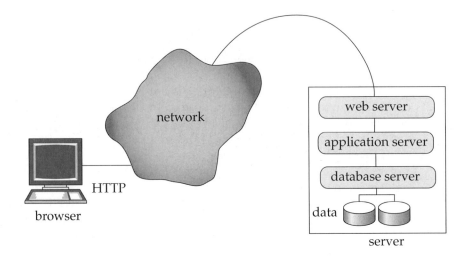

Figure 21.3   Three-tier Web architecture.

Most Web services today therefore use a two-tier Web architecture, where the application program runs within the Web server, as in Figure 21.4. We study systems based on the two-tier architecture in more detail in subsequent sections.

Be aware that there is no continuous connection between the client and the server. In contrast, when a user logs on to a computer, or connects to an ODBC or JDBC server, a session is created, and session information is retained at the server and the client until the session is terminated—information such as whether the user was authenticated using a password and what session options the user set. The reason that HTTP is **connectionless** is that most computers have limits on the number of simultaneous connections they can accommodate, and if a large number of sites on the Web open connections, this limit would be exceeded, denying service to further users. With a connectionless service, the connection is broken as soon as a request is satisfied, leaving connections available for other requests.

Most information services need session information. For instance, services typically restrict access to information, and therefore need to authenticate users. Authentication should be done once per session, and further interactions in the session should not require reauthentication.

To create the view of such sessions, extra information has to be stored at the client, and returned with each request in a session, for a server to identify that a request is part of a user session. Extra information about the session also has to be maintained at the server.

This extra information is maintained in the form of a **cookie** at the client; a cookie is simply a small piece of text containing identifying information. The server sends a cookie to the client after authentication, and also keeps a copy locally. Cookies sent to different clients contain different identifying text. The browser sends the cookie automatically on further document requests from the same server. By comparing the cookie with locally stored cookies at the server, the server can identify the request as

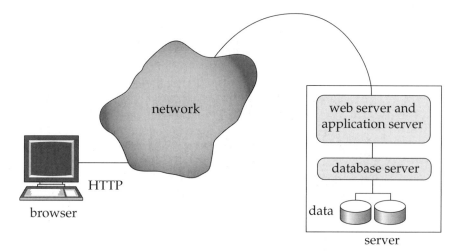

Figure 21.4   Two-tier Web architecture.

part of an ongoing session. Cookies can also be used for storing user preferences and using them when the server replies to a request. Cookies can be stored permanently at the browser; they identify the user on subsequent visits to the same site, without any identification information being typed in.

21.1.4   Servlets

In a two-tier Web architecture, the application runs as part of the Web server itself. One way of implementing such an architecture is to load Java programs with the Web server. The Java **servlet** specification defines an application programming interface for communication between the Web server and the application program. The word *servlet* also refers to a Java program that implements the servlet interface. The program is loaded into the Web server when the server starts up or when the server receives a Web request for executing the servlet application. Figure 21.5 is an example of servlet code to implement the form in Figure 21.1.

The servlet is called BankQueryServlet, while the form specifies that action="Bank-Query". The Web server must be told that this servlet is to be used to handle requests for BankQuery.

The example will give you an idea of how servlets are used. For details needed to build your own servlet application, you can consult a book on servlets or read the online documentation on servlets that is part of the Java documentation from Sun. See the bibliographical notes for references to these sources.

The form specifies that the HTTP get mechanism is used for transmitting parameters (post is the other widely used mechanism). So the doGet() method of the servlet, which is defined in the code, gets invoked. Each request results in a new thread within which the call is executed, so multiple requests can be handled in parallel.

Any values from the form menus and input fields on the Web page, as well as cookies, pass through an object of the HttpServletRequest class that is created for the

```
public class BankQueryServlet extends HttpServlet {
    public void doGet(HttpServletRequest request, HttpServletResponse result)
        throws ServletException, IOException
    {
        String type = request.getParameter("type");
        String number = request.getParameter("number");
        ... code to find the loan amount/account balance ...
        ... using JDBC to communicate with the database ..
        ... we assume the value is stored in the variable balance

        result.setContentType("text/html");
        PrintWriter out = result.getWriter();
        out.println("<HEAD><TITLE> Query Result</TITLE></HEAD>");
        out.println("<BODY>");
        out.println("Balance on " + type + number + " = " + balance);
        out.println("</BODY>");
        out.close();
    }
}
```

Figure 21.5 Example of servlet code.

request, and the reply to the request passes through an object of the class HttpServlet-Response.[1]

The doGet() method code in the example extracts values of the parameter's type and number by using request.getParameter(), and uses these to run a query against a database. The code used to access the database is not shown; refer to Section 4.13.2 for details of how to use JDBC to access a database. The system returns the results of the query to the requester by printing them out in HTML format to the HttpServlet-Response result.

The servlet API provides a convenient method of creating sessions. Invoking the method getSession(true) of the class HttpServletRequest creates a new object of type HttpSession if this is the first request from that client; the argument true says that a session must be created if the request is a new request. The method returns an existing object if it had been created already for that browser session. Internally, cookies are used to recognize that a request is from the same browser session as an earlier request. The servlet code can store and look up (attribute-name, value) pairs in the HttpSession object, to maintain state across multiple requests. For instance, the first request in a session may ask for a user-id and password, and store the user-id in the session object. On subsequent requests from the browser session, the user-id will be found in the session object.

Displaying a set of results from a query is a common task for many database applications. It is possible to build a generic function that will take any JDBC ResulSet as argument, and display the tuples in the ResulSet appropriately. JDBC metadata calls

---

1. The servlet interface can also support non-HTTP requests, although our examples only use HTTP.

can be used to find information such as the number of columns, and the name and types of the columns, in the query result; this information is then used to print the query result.

21.1.5   Server-Side Scripting

Writing even a simple Web application in a programming language such as Java or C is a rather time-consuming task that requires many lines of code and programmers familiar with the intricacies of the language. An alternative approach, that of **server-side scripting**, provides a much easier method for creating many applications. Scripting languages provide constructs that can be embedded within HTML documents. In server-side scripting, before delivering a Web page, the server executes the scripts embedded within the HTML contents of the page. Each piece of script, when executed, can generate text that is added to the page (or may even delete content from the page). The source code of the scripts is removed from the page, so the client may not even be aware that the page orignally had any code in it. The executed script may contain SQL code that is executed against a database.

Several scripting languages have appeared in recent years. These include Server-Side Javascript from Netscape, JScript from Microsoft, JavaServer Pages (JSP) from Sun, the PHP Hypertext Preprocessor (PHP), ColdFusion's ColdFusion Markup Language (CFML) and Zope's DTML. In fact, it is even possible to embed code written in older scripting languages such as VBScript, Perl, and Python into HTML pages. For instance, Microsoft's Active Server Pages (ASP) supports embedded VBScript and JScript. Other approaches have extended report-writer software, originally developed for generating printable reports, to generate HTML reports. These also support HTML forms for getting parameter values that are used in the queries embedded in the reports.

Clearly, there are many options from which to choose. They all support similar features, but differ in the style of programming and the ease with which simple applications can be created.

21.1.6   Improving Performance

Web sites may be accessed by millions or billions of people from across the globe, at rates of thousands of requests per second, or even more, for the most popular sites. Ensuring that requests are served with low response times is a major challenge for Web site developers.

Caching techniques of various types are used to exploit commonalities between transactions. For instance, suppose the application code for servicing each request needs to contact a database through JDBC. Creating a new JDBC connection may take several milliseconds, so opening a new connection for each request is not a good idea if very high transaction rates are to be supported. Many applications create a pool of open JDBC connections, and each request uses one of the connections from the pool.

Many requests may result in exactly the same query being executed on the database. The cost of communication with the database can be greatly reduced by caching the results of earlier queries, and reusing them, so long as the query result has not changed at the database. Some Web servers support such query result caching.

Costs can be further reduced by caching the final Web page that is sent in response to a request. If a new request comes with exactly the same parameters as a previous request, if the resultant Web page is in the cache it can be reused, avoiding the cost of recomputing the page.

Cached query results and cached Web pages are forms of materialized views. If the underlying database data changes, they can be discarded, or can be recomputed, or even incrementally updated, as in materialized view maintenance (Section 14.5). For example, the IBM Web server that was used in the 2000 Olympics can keep track of what data a cached Web page depends on and recompute the page if the data change.

21.2 Performance Tuning

Tuning the performance of a system involves adjusting various parameters and design choices to improve its performance for a specific application. Various aspects of a database-system design—ranging from high-level aspects such as the schema and transaction design, to database parameters such as buffer sizes, down to hardware issues such as number of disks—affect the performance of an application. Each of these aspects can be adjusted so that performance is improved.

21.2.1 Location of Bottlenecks

The performance of most systems (at least before they are tuned) is usually limited primarily by the performance of one or a few components, called **bottlenecks**. For instance, a program may spend 80 percent of its time in a small loop deep in the code, and the remaining 20 percent of the time on the rest of the code; the small loop then is a bottleneck. Improving the performance of a component that is not a bottleneck does little to improve the overall speed of the system; in the example, improving the speed of the rest of the code cannot lead to more than a 20 percent improvement overall, whereas improving the speed of the bottleneck loop could result in an improvement of nearly 80 percent overall, in the best case.

Hence, when tuning a system, we must first try to discover what are the bottlenecks, and then to eliminate the bottlenecks by improving the performance of the components causing them. When one bottleneck is removed, it may turn out that another component becomes the bottleneck. In a well-balanced system, no single component is the bottleneck. If the system contains bottlenecks, components that are not part of the bottleneck are underutilized, and could perhaps have been replaced by cheaper components with lower performance.

For simple programs, the time spent in each region of the code determines the overall execution time. However, database systems are much more complex, and can be modeled as **queueing systems**. A transaction requests various services from the database system, starting from entry into a server process, disk reads during execution, CPU cycles, and locks for concurrency control. Each of these services has a queue associated with it, and small transactions may spend most of their time waiting in queues—especially in disk I/O queues—instead of executing code. Figure 21.6 illustrates some of the queues in a database system.

As a result of the numerous queues in the database, bottlenecks in a database system typically show up in the form of long queues for a particular service, or, equivalently, in high utilizations for a particular service. If requests are spaced exactly uniformly, and the time to service a request is less than or equal to the time before the next request arrives, then each request will find the resource idle and can therefore start execution immediately without waiting. Unfortunately, the arrival of requests in a database system is never so uniform, and is instead random.

If a resource, such as a disk, has a low utilization, then, when a request is made, the resource is likely to be idle, in which case the waiting time for the request will be 0. Assuming uniformly randomly distributed arrivals, the length of the queue (and correspondingly the waiting time) go up exponentially with utilization; as utilization approaches 100 percent, the queue length increases sharply, resulting in excessively long waiting times. The utilization of a resource should be kept low enough that queue length is short. As a rule of the thumb, utilizations of around 70 percent are considered to be good, and utilizations above 90 percent are considered excessive, since they will result in significant delays. To learn more about the theory of queueing systems, generally referred to as **queueing theory**, you can consult the references cited in the bibliographical notes.

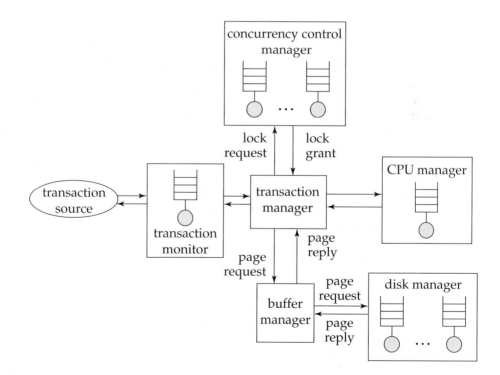

Figure 21.6   Queues in a database system.

21.2.2 Tunable Parameters

Database administrators can tune a database system at three levels. The lowest level is at the hardware level. Options for tuning systems at this level include adding disks or using a RAID system if disk I/O is a bottleneck, adding more memory if the disk buffer size is a bottleneck, or moving to a faster processor if CPU use is a bottleneck.

The second level consists of the database-system parameters, such as buffer size and checkpointing intervals. The exact set of database-system parameters that can be tuned depends on the specific database system. Most database-system manuals provide information on what database-system parameters can be adjusted, and how you should choose values for the parameters. Well-designed database systems perform as much tuning as possible automatically, freeing the user or database administrator from the burden. For instance, in many database systems the buffer size is fixed but tunable. If the system automatically adjusts the buffer size by observing indicators such as page-fault rates, then the user will not have to worry about tuning the buffer size.

The third level is the highest level. It includes the schema and transactions. The administrator can tune the design of the schema, the indices that are created, and the transactions that are executed, to improve performance. Tuning at this level is comparatively system independent.

The three levels of tuning interact with one another; we must consider them together when tuning a system. For example, tuning at a higher level may result in the hardware bottleneck changing from the disk system to the CPU, or vice versa.

21.2.3 Tuning of Hardware

Even in a well-designed transaction processing system, each transaction usually has to do at least a few I/O operations, if the data required by the transaction is on disk. An important factor in tuning a transaction processing system is to make sure that the disk subsystem can handle the rate at which I/O operations are required. For instance, disks today have an access time of about 10 milliseconds, and transfer times of 20 MB per second, which gives about 100 random access I/O operations of 1 KB each. If each transaction requires just 2 I/O operations, a single disk would support at most 50 transactions per second. The only way to support more transactions per second is to increase the number of disks. If the system needs to support n transactions per second, each performing 2 I/O operations, data must be striped (or otherwise partitioned) across $n/50$ disks (ignoring skew).

Notice here that the limiting factor is not the capacity of the disk, but the speed at which random data can be accessed (limited in turn by the speed at which the disk arm can move). The number of I/O operations per transaction can be reduced by storing more data in memory. If all data are in memory, there will be no disk I/O except for writes. Keeping frequently used data in memory reduces the number of disk I/Os, and is worth the extra cost of memory. Keeping very infrequently used data in memory would be a waste, since memory is much more expensive than disk.

The question is, for a given amount of money available for spending on disks or memory, what is the best way to spend the money to achieve maximum number of transactions per second. A reduction of 1 I/O per second saves (price per disk drive) / (access per second per disk). Thus, if a particular page is accessed n times per second, the saving due to keeping it in memory is n times the above value. Storing a page in memory costs (price per MB of memory) / (pages per MB of memory). Thus, the break-even point is

$$n * \frac{price\ per\ disk\ drive}{access\ per\ second\ per\ disk} = \frac{price\ per\ MB\ of\ memory}{pages\ per\ MB\ of\ memory}$$

We can rearrange the equation, and substitute current values for each of the above parameters to get a value for n; if a page is accessed more frequently than this, it is worth buying enough memory to store it. Current disk technology and memory and disk prices give a value of n around $1/300$ times per second (or equivalently, once in 5 minutes) for pages that are randomly accessed.

This reasoning is captured by the rule of thumb called the **5-minute rule**: If a page is used more frequently than once in 5 minutes, it should be cached in memory. In other words, it is worth buying enough memory to cache all pages that are accessed at least once in 5 minutes on an average. For data that are accessed less frequently, buy enough disks to support the rate of I/O required for the data.

The formula for finding the break-even point depends on factors, such as the costs of disks and memory, that have changed by factors of 100 or 1000 over the past decade. However, it is interesting to note that the ratios of the changes have been such that the break-even point has remained at roughly 5 minutes; the 5-minute rule has not changed to say, a 1-hour rule or a 1-second rule!

For data that are sequentially accessed, significantly more pages can be read per second. Assuming 1 MB of data is read at a time, we get the **1-minute rule**, which says that sequentially accessed data should be cached in memory if they are used at least once in 1 minute.

The rules of thumb take only number of I/O operations into account, and do not consider factors such as response time. Some applications need to keep even infrequently used data in memory, to support response times that are less than or comparable to disk access time.

Another aspect of tuning is in whether to use RAID 1 or RAID 5. The answer depends on how frequently the data are updated, since RAID 5 is much slower than RAID 1 on random writes: RAID 5 requires 2 reads and 2 writes to execute a single random write request. If an application performs r random reads and w random writes per second to support a particular throughput, a RAID 5 implementation would require $r + 4w$ I/O operations per second whereas a RAID 1 implementation would require $r + w$ I/O operations per second. We can then calculate the number of disks required to support the required I/O operations per second by dividing the result of the calculation by 100 I/O operations per second (for current generation disks). For many applications, r and w are large enough that the $(r + w)/100$ disks can easily hold two copies of all the data. For such applications, if RAID 1 is used, the required number of disks is actually less than the required number of disks if RAID 5 is used! Thus RAID 5 is useful only when the data storage requirements are very large, but the I/O rates and data transfer requirements are small, that is, for very large and very "cold" data.

21.2.4 Tuning of the Schema

Within the constraints of the chosen normal form, it is possible to partition relations vertically. For example, consider the *account* relation, with the schema

$$account\ (account\text{-}number,\ branch\text{-}name,\ balance)$$

for which *account-number* is a key. Within the constraints of the normal forms (BCNF and third normal forms), we can partition the *account* relation into two relations:

$$account\text{-}branch\ (account\text{-}number,\ branch\text{-}name)$$
$$account\text{-}balance\ (account\text{-}number,\ balance)$$

The two representations are logically equivalent, since *account-number* is a key, but they have different performance characteristics.

If most accesses to account information look at only the *account-number* and *balance*, then they can be run against the *account-balance* relation, and access is likely to be somewhat faster, since the *branch-name* attribute is not fetched. For the same reason, more tuples of *account-balance* will fit in the buffer than corresponding tuples of *account*, again leading to faster performance. This effect would be particularly marked if the *branch-name* attribute were large. Hence, a schema consisting of *account-branch* and *account-balance* would be preferable to a schema consisting of the *account* relation in this case.

On the other hand, if most accesses to account information require both *balance* and *branch-name*, using the *account* relation would be preferable, since the cost of the join of *account-balance* and *account-branch* would be avoided. Also, the storage overhead would be lower, since there would be only one relation, and the attribute *account-number* would not be replicated.

Another trick to improve performance is to store a **denormalized relation**, such as a join of *account* and *depositor*, where the information about branch-names and balances is repeated for every account holder. More effort has to be expended to make sure the relation is consistent whenever an update is carried out. However, a query that fetches the names of the customers and the associated balances will be speeded up, since the join of *account* and *depositor* will have been precomputed. If such a query is executed frequently, and has to be performed as efficiently as possible, the denormalized relation could be beneficial.

Materialized views can provide the benefits that denormalized relations provide, at the cost of some extra storage; we describe performance tuning of materialized views in Section 21.2.6. A major advantage to materialized views over denormalized relations is that maintaining consistency of redundant data becomes the job of the database system, not the programmer. Thus, materialized views are preferable, whenever they are supported by the database system.

Another approach to speed up the computation of the join without materializing it, is to cluster records that would match in the join on the same disk page. We saw such clustered file organizations in Section 11.7.2.

21.2.5   Tuning of Indices

We can tune the indices in a system to improve performance. If queries are the bottleneck, we can often speed them up by creating appropriate indices on relations. If updates are the bottleneck, there may be too many indices, which have to be updated when the relations are updated. Removing indices may speed up certain updates.

The choice of the type of index also is important. Some database systems support different kinds of indices, such as hash indices and B-tree indices. If range queries are common, B-tree indices are preferable to hash indices. Whether to make an index a clustered index is another tunable parameter. Only one index on a relation can be made clustered, by storing the relation sorted on the index attributes. Generally, the index that benefits the most number of queries and updates should be made clustered.

To help identify what indices to create, and which index (if any) on each relation should be clustered, some database systems provide *tuning wizards*. These tools use the past history of queries and updates (called the *workload*) to estimate the effects of various indices on the execution time of the queries and updates in the workload. Recommendations on what indices to create are based on these estimates.

21.2.6   Using Materialized Views

Maintaining materialized views can greatly speed up certain types of queries, in particular aggregate queries. Recall the example from Section 14.5 where the total loan amount at each branch (obtained by summing the loan amounts of all loans at the branch) is required frequently. As we saw in that section, creating a materialized view storing the total loan amount for each branch can greatly speed up such queries.

Materialized views should be used with care, however, since there is not only a space overhead for storing them but, more important, there is also a time overhead for maintaining materialized views. In the case of **immediate view maintenance**, if the updates of a transaction affect the materialized view, the materialized view must be updated as part of the same transaction. The transaction may therefore run slower. In the case of **deferred view maintenance**, the materialized view is updated later; until it is updated, the materialized view may be inconsistent with the database relations. For instance, the materialized view may be brought up-to-date when a query uses the view, or periodically. Using deferred maintenance reduces the burden on update transactions.

An important question is, how does one select which materialized views to maintain? The system administrator can make the selection manually by examining the types of queries in the workload, and finding out which queries need to run faster and which updates/queries may be executed slower. From the examination, the system administrator may choose an appropriate set of materialized views. For instance, the administrator may find that a certain aggregate is used frequently, and choose to materialize it, or may find that a particular join is computed frequently, and choose to materialize it.

However, manual choice is tedious for even moderately large sets of query types, and making a good choice may be difficult, since it requires understanding the costs of different alternatives; only the query optimizer can estimate the costs with reasonable accuracy, without actually executing the query. Thus a good set of views may only be found by trial and error—that is, by materializing one or more views, running the workload, and measuring the time taken to run the queries in the workload. The administrator repeats the process until a set of views is found that gives acceptable performance.

A better alternative is to provide support for selecting materialized views within the database system itself, integrated with the query optimizer. Some database systems, such as Microsoft SQL Server 7.5 and the RedBrick Data Warehouse from Informix, provide tools to help the database administrator with index and materialized view selection. These tools examine the workload (the history of queries and updates) and suggest indices and views to be materialized. The user may specify the importance of speeding up different queries, which the administrator takes into account when selecting views to materialize.

Microsoft's materialized view selection tool also permits the user to ask "what if" questions, whereby the user can pick a view, and the optimizer then estimates the effect of materializing the view on the total cost of the workload and on the individual costs of different query/update types in the workload.

In fact, even automated selection techniques are implemented in a similar manner internally: Different alternatives are tried, and for each the query optimizer estimates the costs and benefits of materializing it.

Greedy heuristics for materialized view selection operate roughly this way: They estimate the benefits of materializing different views, and choose the view that gives either the maximum benefit or the maximum benefit per unit space (that is, benefit divided by the space required to store the view). Once the heuristic has selected a view, the benefits of other views may have changed, so the heuristic recomputes these, and chooses the next best view for materialization. The process continues until either the available disk space for storing materialized views is exhausted, or the cost of view maintenance increases above acceptable limits.

21.2.7 Tuning of Transactions

In this section, we study two approaches for improving transaction performance:

- Improve set orientation
- Reduce lock contention

In the past, optimizers on many database systems were not particularly good, so how a query was written would have a big influence on how it was executed, and therefore on the performance. Today's advanced optimizers can transform even badly written queries and execute them efficiently, so the need for tuning individual queries is less important than it used to be. However, complex queries containing nested subqueries are not optimized very well by many optimizers. Most systems provide a mechanism to find out the exact execution plan for a query; this information can be used to rewrite the query in a form that the optimizer can deal with better.

In embedded SQL, if a query is executed frequently with different values for a parameter, it may help to combine the calls into a more set-oriented query that is executed only once. The costs of communication of SQL queries can be high in client−server systems, so combining the embedded SQL calls is particularly helpful in such systems.

For example, consider a program that steps through each department specified in a list, invoking an embedded SQL query to find the total expenses of the department by using the **group by** construct on a relation *expenses*(*date, employee, department, amount*). If the *expenses* relation does not have a clustered index on *department*, each such query will result in a scan of the relation. Instead, we can use a single SQL query to find total expenses of all departments; the query can be evaluated with a single scan. The relevant departments can then be looked up in this (much smaller) temporary relation containing the aggregate. Even if there is an index that permits efficient access to tuples of a given department, using multiple SQL queries can have a high communication overhead in a client−server system. Communication cost can be reduced by using a single SQL query, fetching its results to the client side, and then stepping through the results to find the required tuples.

Another technique used widely in client−server systems to reduce the cost of communication and SQL compilation is to use stored procedures, where queries are stored at the server in the form of procedures, which may be precompiled. Clients can invoke these stored procedures, rather than communicate entire queries.

Concurrent execution of different types of transactions can sometimes lead to poor performance because of contention on locks. Consider, for example, a banking database. During the day, numerous small update transactions are executed almost continuously. Suppose that a large query that computes statistics on branches is run at the same time. If the query performs a scan on a relation, it may block out all updates on the relation while it runs, and that can have a disastrous effect on the performance of the system.

Some database systems—Oracle, for example—permit multiversion concurrency control, whereby queries are executed on a snapshot of the data, and updates can go on concurrently. This feature should be used if available. If it is not available, an alternative option is to execute large queries at times when updates are few or nonexistent. For databases supporting Web sites, there may be no such quiet period for updates.

Another alternative is to use weaker levels of consistency, whereby evaluation of the query has a minimal impact on concurrent updates, but the query results are not guaranteed to be consistent. The application semantics determine whether approximate (inconsistent) answers are acceptable.

Long update transactions can cause performance problems with system logs, and can increase the time taken to recover from system crashes. If a transaction performs many updates, the system log may become full even before the transaction completes, in which case the transaction will have to be rolled back. If an update transaction runs for a long time (even with few updates), it may block deletion of old parts of the log, if the logging system is not well designed. Again, this blocking could lead to the log getting filled up.

To avoid such problems, many database systems impose strict limits on the number of updates that a single transaction can carry out. Even if the system does not impose such limits, it is often helpful to break up a large update transaction into a set of smaller update transactions where possible. For example, a transaction that gives a raise to every employee in a large corporation could be split up into a series of small transactions, each of which updates a small range of employee-ids. Such transactions are called **minibatch transactions**. However, minibatch transactions must be used with care. First, if there are concurrent updates on the set of employees, the result of the set of smaller transactions may not be equivalent to that of the single large transaction. Second, if there is a failure, the salaries of some of the employees would have been increased by committed transactions, but salaries of other employees would not. To avoid this problem, as soon as the system recovers from failure, we must execute the transactions remaining in the batch.

21.2.8 Performance Simulation

To test the performance of a database system even before it is installed, we can create a performance-simulation model of the database system. Each service shown in Figure 21.6, such as the CPU, each disk, the buffer, and the concurrency control, is modeled in the simulation. Instead of modeling details of a service, the simulation model may capture only some aspects of each service, such as the **service time**—that is, the time taken to finish processing a request once processing has begun. Thus, the simulation can model a disk access from just the average disk access time.

Since requests for a service generally have to wait their turn, each service has an associated queue in the simulation model. A transaction consists of a series of requests. The requests are queued up as they arrive, and are serviced according to the policy for that service, such as first come, first served. The models for services such as CPU and the disks conceptually operate in parallel, to account for the fact that these subsystems operate in parallel in a real system.

Once the simulation model for transaction processing is built, the system administrator can run a number of experiments on it. The administrator can use experiments with simulated transactions arriving at different rates to find how the system would behave under various load conditions. The administrator could run other experiments that vary the service times for each service to find out how sensitive the performance is to each of them. System parameters, too, can be varied, so that performance tuning can be done on the simulation model.

21.3 Performance Benchmarks

As database servers become more standardized, the differentiating factor among the products of different vendors is those products' performance. **Performance benchmarks** are suites of tasks that are used to quantify the performance of software systems.

21.3.1 Suites of Tasks

Since most software systems, such as databases, are complex, there is a good deal of variation in their implementation by different vendors. As a result, there is a significant amount of variation in their performance on different tasks. One system may be the most efficient on a particular task; another may be the most efficient on a different task. Hence, a single task is usually insufficient to quantify the performance of the system. Instead, the performance of a system is measured by suites of standardized tasks, called *performance benchmarks*.

Combining the performance numbers from multiple tasks must be done with care. Suppose that we have two tasks, T_1 and T_2, and that we measure the throughput of a system as the number of transactions of each type that run in a given amount of time —say, 1 second. Suppose that system A runs T_1 at 99 transactions per second, and that T_2 runs at 1 transaction per second. Similarly, let system B run both T_1 and T_2 at 50 transactions per second. Suppose also that a workload has an equal mixture of the two types of transactions.

If we took the average of the two pairs of numbers (that is, 99 and 1, versus 50 and 50), it might appear that the two systems have equal performance. However, it is *wrong* to take the averages in this fashion—if we ran 50 transactions of each type, system *A* would take about 50.5 seconds to finish, whereas system *B* would finish in just 2 seconds!

The example shows that a simple measure of performance is misleading if there is more than one type of transaction. The right way to average out the numbers is to take the **time to completion** for the workload, rather than the average **throughput** for each transaction type. We can then compute system performance accurately in transactions per second for a specified workload. Thus, system A takes 50.5/100, which is 0.505 seconds per transaction, whereas system B takes 0.02 seconds per transaction, on average. In terms of throughput, system A runs at an average of 1.98 transactions per second, whereas system B runs at 50 transactions per second. Assuming that transactions of all the types are equally likely, the correct way to average out the throughputs on different transaction types is to take the **harmonic mean** of the throughputs. The harmonic mean of n throughputs $t_1, \ldots, t_n$ is defined as

$$\frac{n}{\frac{1}{t_1} + \frac{1}{t_2} + \cdots + \frac{1}{t_n}}$$

For our example, the harmonic mean for the throughputs in system A is 1.98. For system B, it is 50. Thus, system B is approximately 25 times faster than system A on a workload consisting of an equal mixture of the two example types of transactions.

21.3.2   Database-Application Classes

Online transaction processing (OLTP) and **decision support** (including **online analytical processing (OLAP)**) are two broad classes of applications handled by database systems. These two classes of tasks have different requirements. High concurrency and clever techniques to speed up commit processing are required for supporting a high rate of update transactions. On the other hand, good query-evaluation algorithms and query optimization are required for decision support. The architecture of some database systems has been tuned to transaction processing; that of others, such as the Teradata DBC series of parallel database systems, has been tuned to decision support. Other vendors try to strike a balance between the two tasks.

Applications usually have a mixture of transaction-processing and decision- support requirements. Hence, which database system is best for an application depends on what mix of the two requirements the application has.

Suppose that we have throughput numbers for the two classes of applications separately, and the application at hand has a mix of transactions in the two classes. We must be careful even about taking the harmonic mean of the throughput numbers, because of **interference** between the transactions. For example, a long-running decision-support transaction may acquire a number of locks, which may prevent all progress of update transactions. The harmonic mean of throughputs should be used only if the transactions do not interfere with one another.

21.3.3 The TPC Benchmarks

The **Transaction Processing Performance Council** (TPC), has defined a series of benchmark standards for database systems.

The TPC benchmarks are defined in great detail. They define the set of relations and the sizes of the tuples. They define the number of tuples in the relations not as a fixed number, but rather as a multiple of the number of claimed transactions per second, to reflect that a larger rate of transaction execution is likely to be correlated with a larger number of accounts. The performance metric is throughput, expressed as **transactions per second** (TPS). When its performance is measured, the system must provide a response time within certain bounds, so that a high throughput cannot be obtained at the cost of very long response times. Further, for business applications, cost is of great importance. Hence, the TPC benchmark also measures performance in terms of **price per TPS**. A large system may have a high number of transactions per second, but may be expensive (that is, have a high price per TPS). Moreover, a company cannot claim TPC benchmark numbers for its systems *without* an external audit that ensures that the system faithfully follows the definition of the benchmark, including full support for the ACID properties of transactions.

The first in the series was the **TPC-A benchmark**, which was defined in 1989. This benchmark simulates a typical bank application by a single type of transaction that models cash withdrawal and deposit at a bank teller. The transaction updates several relations—such as the bank balance, the teller's balance, and the customer's balance—and adds a record to an audit trail relation. The benchmark also incorporates communication with terminals, to model the end-to-end performance of the system realistically. The **TPC-B benchmark** was designed to test the core performance of the database system, along with the operating system on which the system runs. It removes the parts of the TPC-A benchmark that deal with users, communication, and terminals, to focus on the back-end database server. Neither TPC-A nor TPC-B is widely used today.

The **TPC-C benchmark** was designed to model a more complex system than the TPC-A benchmark. The TPC-C benchmark concentrates on the main activities in an order-entry environment, such as entering and delivering orders, recording payments, checking status of orders, and monitoring levels of stock. The TPC-C benchmark is still widely used for transaction processing.

The **TPC-D benchmark** was designed to test the performance of database systems on decision-support queries. Decision-support systems are becoming increasingly important today. The TPC-A, TPC-B, and TPC-C benchmarks measure performance on transaction-processing workloads, and should not be used as a measure of performance on decision-support queries. The D in TPC-D stands for **decision support**. The TPC-D benchmark schema models a sales/distribution application, with parts, suppliers, customers, and orders, along with some auxiliary information. The sizes of the relations are defined as a ratio, and database size is the total size of all the relations, expressed in gigabytes. TPC-D at scale factor 1 represents the TPC-D benchmark on a 1-gigabyte database, while scale factor 10 represents a 10-gigabyte database. The benchmark workload consists of a set of 17 SQL queries modeling common tasks executed on decision-support systems. Some of the queries make use of complex SQL features, such as aggregation and nested queries.

The benchmark's users soon realized that the various TPC-D queries could be significantly speeded up by using materialized views and other redundant information. There are applications, such as periodic reporting tasks, where the queries are known in advance and materialized view can be carefully selected to speed up the queries. It is necessary, however, to account for the overhead of maintaining materialized views.

The **TPC-R benchmark** (where R stands for **reporting**) is a refinement of the TPC-D benchmark. The schema is the same, but there are 22 queries, of which 16 are from TPC-D. In addition, there are two updates, a set of inserts and a set of deletes. The database running the benchmark is permitted to use materialized views and other redundant information.

In contrast the **TPC-H benchmark** (where H represents **ad hoc**) uses the same schema and workload as TPC-R but prohibits materialized views and other redundant information, and permits indices only on primary and foreign keys. This benchmark models ad hoc querying where the queries are not known beforehand, so it is not possible to create appropriate materialized views ahead of time.

Both TPC-H and TPC-R measure performance in this way: The **power test** runs the queries and updates one at a time sequentially, and 3600 seconds divided by geometric mean of the execution times of the queries (in seconds) gives a measure of queries per hour. The **throughput test** runs multiple streams in parallel, with each stream executing all 22 queries. There is also a parallel update stream. Here the total time for the entire run is used to compute the number of queries per hour.

The **composite query per hour metric**, which is the overall metric, is then obtained as the square root of the the product of the power and throughput metrics. A **composite price/performance metric** is defined by dividing the system price by the composite metric.

The **TPC-W** Web commerce benchmark is an end-to-end benchmark that models Web sites having static content (primarily images) and dynamic content generated from a database. Caching of dynamic content is specifically permitted, since it is very useful for speeding up Web sites. The benchmark models an electronic bookstore, and like other TPC benchmarks, provides for different scale factors. The primary performance metrics are **Web interactions per second (WIPS)** and price per WIPS.

21.3.4   The OODB Benchmarks

The nature of applications in an object-oriented database, OODB, is different from that of typical transaction-processing applications. Therefore, a different set of benchmarks has been proposed for OODBs. The Object Operations benchmark, version 1, popularly known as the **OO1 benchmark**, was an early proposal. The **OO7 benchmark** follows a philosophy different from that of the TPC benchmarks. The TPC benchmarks provide one or two numbers (in terms of average transactions per second, and transactions per second per dollar); the OO7 benchmark provides a set of numbers, containing separate benchmark number for each of several different kinds of operations. The reason for this approach is that it is not yet clear what is the *typical* OODB transaction. It is clear that such a transaction will carry out certain operations, such as traversing a set of connected objects or retrieving all objects in a class, but it is not clear exactly what mix of these operations will be used. Hence, the benchmark provides separate numbers for each class of operations; the numbers can be combined in an appropriate way, depending on the specific application.

21.4   Standardization

Standards define the interface of a software system; for example, standards define the syntax and semantics of a programming language, or the functions in an application-program interface, or even a data model (such as the object-oriented-database standards). Today, database systems are complex, and are often made up of multiple independently created parts that need to interact. For example, client programs may be created independently of back-end systems, but the two must be able to interact with each other. A company that has multiple heterogeneous database systems may need to exchange data between the databases. Given such a scenario, standards play an important role.

Formal standards are those developed by a standards organization or by industry groups, through a public process. Dominant products sometimes become **de facto standards**, in that they become generally accepted as standards without any formal process of recognition. Some formal standards, like many aspects of the SQL-92 and SQL:1999 standards, are **anticipatory standards** that lead the marketplace; they define features that vendors then implement in products. In other cases, the standards, or parts of the standards, are **reactionary standards**, in that they attempt to standardize features that some vendors have already implemented, and that may even have become de facto standards. SQL-89 was in many ways reactionary, since it standardized features, such as integrity checking, that were already present in the IBM SAA SQL standard and in other databases.

Formal standards committees are typically composed of representatives of the vendors, and members from user groups and standards organizations such as the International Organization for Standardization (ISO) or the American National Standards Institute (ANSI), or professional bodies, such as the Institute of Electrical and Electronics Engineers (IEEE). Formal standards committees meet periodically, and members present proposals for features to be added to or modified in the standard. After a (usually extended) period of discussion, modifications to the proposal, and public review, members vote on whether to accept or reject a feature. Some time after a standard has been defined and implemented, its shortcomings become clear, and new requirements become apparent. The process of updating the standard then begins, and a new version of the standard is usually released after a few years. This cycle usually repeats every few years, until eventually (perhaps many years later) the standard becomes technologically irrelevant, or loses its user base.

The DBTG CODASYL standard for network databases, formulated by the Database Task Group, was one of the early formal standards for databases. IBM database products used to establish de facto standards, since IBM commanded much of the database market. With the growth of relational databases came a number of new entrants in the database business; hence, the need for formal standards arose. In recent years, Microsoft has created a number of specifications that also have become de facto standards. A notable example is ODBC, which is now used in non-Microsoft environments. JDBC, whose specification was created by Sun Microsystems, is another widely used de facto standard.

This section give a very high level overview of different standards, concentrating on the goals of the standard. The bibliographical notes at the end of the chapter provide references to detailed descriptions of the standards mentioned in this section.

21.4.1 SQL Standards

Since SQL is the most widely used query language, much work has been done on standardizing it. ANSI and ISO, with the various database vendors, have played a leading role in this work. The SQL-86 standard was the initial version. The IBM Systems Application Architecture (SAA) standard for SQL was released in 1987. As people identified the need for more features, updated versions of the formal SQL standard were developed, called SQL-89 and SQL-92.

The latest version of the SQL standard, called SQL:1999, adds a variety of features to SQL. We have seen many of these features in earlier chapters, and will see a few in later chapters. The standard is broken into several parts:

- SQL/Framework (Part 1) provides an overview of the standard.

- SQL/Foundation (Part 2) defines the basics of the standard: types, schemas, tables, views, query and update statements, expressions, security model, predicates, assignment rules, transaction management and so on.

- SQL/CLI (Call Level Interface) (Part 3) defines application program interfaces to SQL.

- SQL/PSM (Persistent Stored Modules) (Part 4) defines extensions to SQL to make it procedural.

- SQL/Bindings (Part 5) defines standards for embedded SQL for different embedding languages.

The SQL:1999 OLAP features (Section 22.2.3) have been specified as an amendment to the earlier version of the SQL:1999 standard. There are several other parts under development, including

- Part 7: SQL/Temporal deals with standards for temporal data.

- Part 9: SQL/MED (Management of External Data) defines standards for interfacing an SQL system to external sources. By writing wrappers, system designers can treat external data sources, such as files or data in nonrelational databases, as if they were "foreign" tables.

- Part 10: SQL/OLB (Object Language Bindings) defines standards for embedding SQL in Java.

The missing numbers (Parts 6 and 8) cover features such as distributed transaction processing and multimedia data, for which there is as yet no agreement on the standards. The multimedia standards propose to cover storage and retrieval of text data, spatial data, and still images.

21.4.2 Database Connectivity Standards

The **ODBC** standard is a widely used standard for communication between client applications and database systems. ODBC is based on the SQL **Call-Level Interface (CLI)** standards developed by the *X/Open* industry consortium and the SQL Access Group, but has several extensions. The ODBC API defines a CLI, an SQL syntax definition, and rules about permissible sequences of CLI calls. The standard also defines conformance levels for the CLI and the SQL syntax. For example, the core level of the CLI has commands to connect to a database, to prepare and execute SQL statements, to get back results or status values and to manage transactions. The next level of conformance (level 1) requires support for catalog information retrieval and some other features over and above the core-level CLI; level 2 requires further features, such as ability to send and retrieve arrays of parameter values and to retrieve more detailed catalog information.

ODBC allows a client to connect simultaneously to multiple data sources and to switch among them, but transactions on each are independent; ODBC does not support two-phase commit.

A distributed system provides a more general environment than a client–server system. The X/Open consortium has also developed the **X/Open XA standards** for interoperation of databases. These standards define transaction-management primitives (such as transaction begin, commit, abort, and prepare-to-commit) that compliant databases should provide; a transaction manager can invoke these primitives to implement distributed transactions by two-phase commit. The XA standards are independent of the data model and of the specific interfaces between clients and databases to exchange data. Thus, we can use the XA protocols to implement a distributed transaction system in which a single transaction can access relational as well as object-oriented databases, yet the transaction manager ensures global consistency via two-phase commit.

There are many data sources that are not relational databases, and in fact may not be databases at all. Examples are flat files and email stores. Microsoft's **OLE-DB** is a C++ API with goals similar to ODBC, but for nondatabase data sources that may provide only limited querying and update facilities. Just like ODBC, OLE-DB provides constructs for connecting to a data source, starting a session, executing commands, and getting back results in the form of a rowset, which is a set of result rows.

However, OLE-DB differes from ODBC in several ways. To support data sources with limited feature support, features in OLE-DB are divided into a number of interfaces, and a data source may implement only a subset of the interfaces. An OLE-DB program can negotiate with a data source to find what interfaces are supported. In ODBC commands are always in SQL. In OLE-DB, commands may be in any language supported by the data source; while some sources may support SQL, or a limited subset of SQL, other sources may provide only simple capabilities such as accessing data in a flat file, without any query capability. Another major difference of OLE-DB from ODBC is that a rowset is an object that can be shared by multiple applications through shared memory. A rowset object can be updated by one application, and other applications sharing that object would get notified about the change.

The **Active Data Objects (ADO)** API, also created by Microsoft, provides an easy-to-use interface to the OLE-DB functionality, which can be called from scripting languages, such as VBScript and JScript.

21.4.3 Object Database Standards

Standards in the area of object-oriented databases have so far been driven primarily by OODB vendors. The *Object Database Management Group* (ODMG) is a group formed by OODB vendors to standardize the data model and language interfaces to OODBs. The C++ language interface specified by ODMG was discussed in Chapter 8. The ODMG has also specified a Java interface and a Smalltalk interface.

The *Object Management Group* (OMG) is a consortium of companies, formed with the objective of developing a standard architecture for distributed software applications based on the object-oriented model. OMG brought out the *Object Management Architecture* (OMA) reference model. The *Object Request Broker* (ORB) is a component of the OMA architecture that provides message dispatch to distributed objects transparently, so the physical location of the object is not important. The **Common Object Request Broker Architecture (CORBA)** provides a detailed specification of the ORB, and includes an **Interface Description Language (IDL)**, which is used to define the data types used for data interchange. The IDL helps to support data conversion when data are shipped between systems with different data representations.

21.4.4 XML-Based Standards

A wide variety of standards based on XML (see Chapter 10) have been defined for a wide variety of applications. Many of these standards are related to e-commerce. They include standards promulgated by nonprofit consortia and corporate-backed efforts to create defacto standards. RosettaNet, which falls into the former category, uses XML-based standards to facilitate supply-chain management in the computer and information technology industries. Companies such as Commerce One provide Web-based procurement systems, supply-chain management, and electonic marketplaces (including online auctions). BizTalk is a framework of XML schemas and guidelines, backed by Microsoft. These and other frameworks define catalogs, service descriptions, invoices, purchase orders, order status requests, shipping bills, and related items.

Participants in electronic marketplaces may store data in a variety of database systems. These systems may use different data models, data formats, and data types. Furthermore, there may be semantic differences (metric versus English measure, distinct monetary currencies, and so forth) in the data. Standards for electronic marketplaces include methods for *wrapping* each of these heterogeneous systems with an XML schema. These XML *wrappers* form the basis of a unified view of data across all of the participants in the marketplace.

Simple Object Access Protocol (SOAP) is a remote procedure call standard that uses XML to encode data (both parameters and results), and uses HTTP as the transport protocol; that is, a procedure call becomes an HTTP request. SOAP is backed by the World Wide Web Consortium (W3C) and is gaining wide acceptance in industry (including IBM and Microsoft). SOAP can be used in a variety of applications. For instance, in business-to-business e-commerce, applications running at one site can access data from other sites through SOAP. Microsoft has defined standards for accessing OLAP and mining data with SOAP. (OLAP and data mining are covered in Chapter 22.)

The W3C standard query language for XML is called *XQuery*. As of early 2001 the standard was in working draft stage, and should be finalized by the end of the year. Earlier XML query languages include *Quilt* (on which XQuery is based), *XML-QL*, and *XQL*.

21.5 E-Commerce**

E-commerce refers to the process of carrying out various activities related to commerce, through electronic means, primarily through the internet. The types of activities include:

- Presale activities, needed to inform the potential buyer about the product or service being sold.

- The sale process, which includes negotiations on price and quality of service, and other contractual matters.

- The marketplace: When there are multiple sellers and buyers for a product, a marketplace, such as a stock exchange, helps in negotiating the price to be paid for the product. Auctions are used when there is a single seller and multiple buyers, and reverse auctions are used when there is a single buyer and multiple sellers.

- Payment for the sale.

- Activities related to delivery of the product or service. Some products and services can be delivered over the internet; for others the internet is used only for providing shipping information and for tracking shipments of products.

- Customer support and postsale service.

Databases are used extensively to support these activities. For some of the activities the use of databases is straightforward, but there are interesting application development issues for the other activities.

21.5.1 E-Catalogs

Any e-commerce site provides users with a catalog of the products and services that the site supplies. The services provided by an e-catalog may vary considerably.

At the minimum, an e-catalog must provide browsing and search facilities to help customers find the product they are looking for. To help with browsing, products should be organized into an intuitive hierarchy, so a few clicks on hyperlinks can lead a customer to the products they are interested in. Keywords provided by the customer (for example, "digital camera" or "computer") should speed up the process of finding required products. E-catalogs should also provide a means for customers to easily compare alternatives from which to choose among competing products.

E-catalogs can be customized for the customer. For instance, a retailer may have an agreement with a large company to supply some products at a discount. An employee of the company, viewing the catalog to purchase products for the company, should see prices as per the negotiated discount, instead of the regular prices. Because of legal restrictions on sales of some types of items, customers who are underage, or from certain states or countries, should not be shown items that cannot be legally sold to them. Catalogs can also be personalized to individual users, on the basis of past buying history. For instance, frequent customers may be offered special discounts on some items.

Supporting such customization requires customer information as well as special pricing/discount information and sales restriction information to be stored in a database. There are also challenges in supporting very high transaction rates, which are often tackled by caching of query results or generated Web pages.

21.5.2 Marketplaces

When there are multiple sellers or multiple buyers (or both) for a product, a marketplace helps in negotiating the price to be paid for the product. There are several different types of marketplaces:

- In a **reverse auction** system a buyer states requirements, and sellers bid for supplying the item. The supplier quoting the lowest price wins. In a closed bidding system, the bids are not made public, whereas in an open bidding system the bids are made public.

- In an **auction** there are multiple buyers and a single seller. For simplicity, assume that there is only one instance of each item being sold. Buyers bid for the items being sold, and the highest bidder for an item gets to buy the item at the bid price.

When there are multiple copies of an item, things become more complicated: Suppose there are four items, and one bidder may want three copies for $10 each, while another wants two copies for $13 each. It is not possible to satisfy both bids. If the items will be of no value if they are not sold (for instance, airline seats, which must be sold before the plane leaves), the seller simply picks a set of bids that maximizes the income. Otherwise the decision is more complicated.

- In an **exchange**, such as a stock exchange, there are multiple sellers and multiple buyers. Buyers can specify the maximum price they are willing to pay, while sellers specify the minimum price they want. There is usually a *market maker* who matches buy and sell bids, deciding on the price for each trade (for instance, at the price of the sell bid).

There are other more complex types of marketplaces.

Among the database issues in handling marketplaces are these:

- Bidders need to be authenticated before they are allowed to bid.

- Bids (buy or sell) need to be recorded securely in a database. Bids need to be communicated quickly to other people involved in the marketplace (such as all the buyers or all the sellers), who may be numerous.

- Delays in broadcasting bids can lead to financial losses to some participants.

- The volumes of trades may be extremely large at times of stock market volatility, or toward the end of auctions. Thus, very high performance databases with large degrees of parallelism are used for such systems.

21.5.3 Order Settlement

After items have been selected (perhaps through an electronic catalog), and the price determined (perhaps by an electronic marketplace), the order has to be settled. Settlement involves payment for goods and the delivery of the goods.

A simple but unsecure way of paying electronically is to send a credit card number. There are two major problems. First, credit card fraud is possible. When a buyer pays for physical goods, companies can ensure that the address for delivery matches the card holder's address, so no one else can receive the goods, but for goods delivered electronically no such check is possible. Second, the seller has to be trusted to bill only for the agreed-on item and to not pass on the card number to unauthorized people who may misuse it.

Several protocols are available for secure payments that avoid both the problems listed above. In addition, they provide for better privacy, whereby the seller may not be given any unnecessary details about the buyer, and the credit card company is not provided any unnecessary information about the items purchased. All information transmitted must be encrypted so that anyone intercepting the data on the network cannot find out the contents. Public/private key encryption is widely used for this task.

The protocols must also prevent **person-in-the-middle attacks**, where someone can impersonate the bank or credit-card company, or even the seller, or buyer, and steal secret information. Impersonation can be perpetrated by passing off a fake key as someone else's public key (the bank's or credit-card company's, or the merchant's or the buyer's). Impersonation is prevented by a system of **digital certificates**, whereby public keys are signed by a certification agency, whose public key is well known (or which in turn has its public key certified by another certification agency and so on up to a key that is well known). From the well-known public key, the system can authenticate the other keys by checking the certificates in reverse sequence.

The **Secure Electronic Transaction** (**SET**) protocol is one such secure payment protocol. The protocol requires several rounds of communication between the buyer, seller, and the bank, in order to guarantee safety of the transaction.

There are also systems that provide for greater anonymity, similar to that provided by physical cash. The **DigiCash** payment system is one such system. When a payment is made in such a system, it is not possible to identify the purchaser. In contrast, identifying purchasers is very easy with credit cards, and even in the case of SET, it is possible to identify the purchaser with the cooperation of the credit card company or bank.

21.6 Legacy Systems

Legacy systems are older-generation systems that are incompatible with current-generation standards and systems. Such systems may still contain valuable data, and may support critical applications. The legacy systems of today are typically those built with technologies such as databases that use the network or hierarchical data models, or use Cobol and file systems without a database.

Porting legacy applications to a more modern environment is often costly in terms of both time and money, since they are often very large, consisting of millions of lines of code developed by teams of programmers, over several decades.

Thus, it is important to support these older-generation, or legacy, systems, and to facilitate their interoperation with newer systems. One approach used to interoperate between relational databases and legacy databases is to build a layer, called a **wrapper**, on top of the legacy systems that can make the legacy system appear to be a relational database. The wrapper may provide support for ODBC or other interconnection standards such as OLE-DB, which can be used to query and update the legacy system. The wrapper is responsible for converting relational queries and updates into queries and updates on the legacy system.

When an organization decides to replace a legacy system by a new system, it must follow a process called **reverse engineering**, which consists of going over the code of the legacy system to come up with schema designs in the required data model (such as an E-R model or an object-oriented data model). Reverse engineering also examines the code to find out what procedures and processes were implemented, in order to get a high-level model of the system. Reverse engineering is needed because legacy systems usually do not have high-level documentation of their schema and overall system design. When coming up with the design of a new system, the design is reviewed, so that it can be improved rather than just reimplemented as is. Extensive coding is required to support all the functionality (such as user interface and reporting systems) that were provided by the legacy system. The overall process is called **re-engineering**.

When a new system has been built and tested, the system must be populated with data from the legacy system, and all further activities must be carried out on the new system. However, abruptly transitioning to a new system, which is called the **big-bang approach**, carries several risks. First, users may not be familiar with the interfaces of the new system. Second there may be bugs or performance problems in the new system that were not discovered when it was tested. Such problems may lead to great losses for companies, since their ability to carry out critical transactions such as sales and purchases may be severely affected. In some extreme cases the new system has even been abandoned, and the legacy system reused, after an attempted switchover failed.

An alternative approach, called the **chicken-little approach**, incrementally replaces the functionality of the legacy system. For example, the new user interfaces may be used with the old system in the back end, or vice versa. Another option is to use the new system only for some functionality that can be decoupled from the legacy system. In either case, the legacy and new systems coexist for some time. There is therefore a need for developing and using wrappers on the legacy system to provide required functionality to interoperate with the new system. This approach, therefore has a higher development cost associated with it.

21.7 Summary

- The Web browser has emerged as the most widely used user interface to databases. HTML provides the ability to define interfaces that combine hyperlinks with forms facilities. Web browsers communicate with Web servers by the HTTP protocol. Web servers can pass on requests to application programs, and return the results to the browser.

- There are several client-side scripting languages—Javascript is the most widely used—that provide richer user interaction at the browser end.

- Web servers execute application programs to implement desired functionality. Servlets are a widely used mechanism to write application programs that run as part of the Web server process, in order to reduce overheads. There are also many server-side scripting languages that are interpreted by the Web server and provide application program functionality as part of the Web server.

- Tuning of the database-system parameters, as well as the higher-level database design—such as the schema, indices, and transactions—is important for good performance. Tuning is best done by identifying bottlenecks and eliminating them.

- Performance benchmarks play an important role in comparisons of database systems, especially as systems become more standards compliant. The TPC benchmark suites are widely used, and the different TPC benchmarks are useful for comparing the performance of databases under different workloads.

- Standards are important because of the complexity of database systems and their need for interoperation. Formal standards exist for SQL. Defacto standards, such as ODBC and JDBC, and standards adopted by industry groups, such as CORBA, have played an important role in the growth of client–server database systems. Standards for object-oriented databases, such as ODMG, are being developed by industry groups.

- E-commerce systems are fast becoming a core part of how commerce is performed. There are several database issues in e-commerce systems. Catalog management, especially personalization of the catalog, is done with databases. Electronic marketplaces help in pricing of products through auctions, reverse auctions, or exchanges. High-performance database systems are needed to handle such trading. Orders are settled by electronic payment systems, which also need high-performance database systems to handle very high transaction rates.

- Legacy systems are systems based on older-generation technologies such as nonrelational databases or even directly on file systems. Interfacing legacy systems with new-generation systems is often important when they run mission-critical systems. Migrating from legacy systems to new-generation systems must be done carefully to avoid disruptions, which can be very expensive.

Review Terms

- Web interfaces to databases
- HyperText Markup Language (HTML)
- Hyperlinks
- Uniform resource locator (URL)
- Client-side scripting
- Applets
- Client-side scripting language
- Web servers
- Session
- HyperText Transfer Protocol (HTTP)
- Common Gateway Interface (CGI)
- Connectionless
- Cookie
- Servlets
- Server-side scripting
- Performance tuning
- Bottlenecks
- Queueing systems
- Tunable parameters
- Tuning of hardware
- Five-minute rule
- One-minute rule
- Tuning of the schema
- Tuning of indices

- Materialized views
- Immediate view maintenance
- Deferred view maintenance
- Tuning of transactions
- Improving set orientedness
- Minibatch transactions
- Performance simulation
- Performance benchmarks
- Service time
- Time to completion
- Database-application classes
- The TPC benchmarks
  - ☐ TPC-A
  - ☐ TPC-B
  - ☐ TPC-C
  - ☐ TPC-D
  - ☐ TPC-R
  - ☐ TPC-H
  - ☐ TPC-W
- Web interactions per second
- OODB benchmarks
  - ☐ OO1
  - ☐ OO7
- Standardization

- ☐ Formal standards
- ☐ De facto standards
- ☐ Anticipatory standards
- ☐ Reactionary standards
- Database connectivity standards
  - ☐ ODBC
  - ☐ OLE-DB
  - ☐ X/Open XA standards
- Object database standards
  - ☐ ODMG
  - ☐ CORBA
- XML-based standards
- E-commerce
- E-catalogs
- Marketplaces
  - ☐ Auctions
  - ☐ Reverse-auctions
  - ☐ Exchange
- Order settlement
- Digital certificates
- Legacy systems
- Reverse engineering
- Re-engineering

Exercises

21.1 What is the main reason why servlets give better performance than programs that use the common gateway interface (CGI), even though Java programs generally run slower than C or C++ programs.

21.2 List some benefits and drawbacks of connectionless protocols over protocols that maintain connections.

21.3 List three ways in which caching can be used to speed up Web server performance.

21.4   **a.** What are the three broad levels at which a database system can be tuned to improve performance?
  b. Give two examples of how tuning can be done, for each of the levels.

21.5 What is the motivation for splitting a long transaction into a series of small ones? What problems could arise as a result, and how can these problems be averted?

21.6 Suppose a system runs three types of transactions. Transactions of type A run at the rate of 50 per second, transactions of type B run at 100 per second, and transactions of type C run at 200 per second. Suppose the mix of transactions has 25 percent of type A, 25 percent of type B, and 50 percent of type C.

    a. What is the average transaction throughput of the system, assuming there is no interference between the transactions.

    b. What factors may result in interference between the transactions of different types, leading to the calculated throughput being incorrect?

21.7 Suppose the price of memory falls by half, and the speed of disk access (number of accesses per second) doubles, while all other factors remain the same. What would be the effect of this change on the 5 minute and 1 minute rule?

21.8 List some of the features of the TPC benchmarks that help make them realistic and dependable measures.

21.9 Why was the TPC-D benchmark replaced by the TPC-H and TPC-R benchmarks?

21.10 List some benefits and drawbacks of an anticipatory standard compared to a reactionary standard.

21.11 Suppose someone impersonates a company and gets a certificate from a certificate issuing authority. What is the effect on things (such as purchase orders or programs) certified by the impersonated company, and on things certified by other companies?

Project Suggestions

Each of the following is a large project, which can be a semester-long project done by a group of students. The difficulty of the project can be adjusted easily by adding or deleting features.

Project 21.1 Consider the E-R schema of Exercise 2.7 (Chapter 2), which represents information about teams in a league. Design and implement a Web-based system to enter, update, and view the data.

Project 21.2 Design and implement a shopping cart system that lets shoppers collect items into a shopping cart (you can decide what information is to be supplied for each item) and purchased together. You can extend and use the E-R schema of Exercise 2.12 of Chapter 2. You should check for availability of the item and deal with nonavailable items as you feel appropriate.

Project 21.3 Design and implement a Web-based system to record student registration and grade information for courses at a university.

Project 21.4 Design and implement a system that permits recording of course performance information—specifically, the marks given to each student in each assignment or exam of a course, and computation of a (weighted) sum of marks to get the total course marks. The number of assignments/exams should not be predefined; that is, more assignments/exams can be added at any time. The system should also support grading, permitting cutoffs to be specified for various grades.

You may also wish to integrate it with the student registration system of Project 21.3 (perhaps being implemented by another project team).

Project 21.5 Design and implement a Web-based system for booking classrooms at your university. Periodic booking (fixed days/times each week for a whole semester) must be supported. Cancellation of specific lectures in a periodic booking should also be supported.

You may also wish to integrate it with the student registration system of Project 21.3 (perhaps being implemented by another project team) so that classrooms can be booked for courses, and cancellations of a lecture or extra lectures can be noted at a single interface, and will be reflected in the classroom booking and communicated to students via e-mail.

Project 21.6 Design and implement a system for managing online multiple-choice tests. You should support distributed contribution of questions (by teaching assistants, for example), editing of questions by whoever is in charge of the course, and creation of tests from the available set of questions. You should also be able to administer tests online, either at a fixed time for all students, or at any time but with a time limit from start to finish (support one or both), and give students feedback on their scores at the end of the allotted time.

Project 21.7 Design and implement a system for managing e-mail customer service. Incoming mail goes to a common pool. There is a set of customer service agents who reply to e-mail. If the e-mail is part of an ongoing series of replies (tracked using the in-reply-to field of e-mail) the mail should preferably be replied to by the same agent who replied earlier. The system should track all incoming mail and replies, so an agent can see the history of questions from a customer before replying to an email.

Project 21.8 Design and implement a simple electronic marketplace where items can be listed for sale or for purchase under various categories (which should form a hierarchy). You may also wish to support alerting services, whereby a user can register interest in items in a particular category, perhaps with other constraints as well, without publicly advertising his/her interest, and is notified when such an item is listed for sale.

Project 21.9 Design and implement a Web-based newsgroup system. Users should be able to subscribe to newsgroups, and browse articles in newsgroups. The system tracks which articles were read by a user, so they are not displayed again. Also provide search against old articles.

You may also wish to provide a rating service for articles, so that articles with high rating are highlighted permitting the busy reader to skip low-rated articles.

Project 21.10 Design and implement a Web-based system for managing a sports "ladder." Many people register, and may be given some initial rankings (perhaps based on past performance). Anyone can challenge anyone else to a match, and the rankings are adjusted according to the result.

One simple system for adjusting rankings just moves the winner ahead of the loser in the rank order, in case the winner was behind earlier. You can try to invent more complicated rank adjustment systems.

Project 21.11 Design and implement a publications listing service. The service should permit entering of information about publications, such as title, authors, year, where the publication appeared, pages, and so forth. Authors should be a separate entity with attributes such as name, institution, department, e-mail, address, and home page.

Your application should support multiple views on the same data. For instance, you should provide all publications by a given author (sorted by year, for example), or all publications by authors from a given institution or department. You should also support search by keywords, on the overall database as well as within each of the views.

Bibliographical Notes

Information about servlets, including tutorials, standard specifications, and software, is available on java.sun.com/products/servlet. Information about JSP is available at java.sun.com/products/jsp.

An early proposal for a database-system benchmark (the Wisconsin benchmark) was made by Bitton et al. [1983]. The TPC-A,-B, and -C benchmarks are described in Gray [1991]. An online version of all the TPC benchmarks descriptions, as well as benchmark results, is available on the World Wide Web at the URL www.tpc.org; the site also contains up-to-date information about new benchmark proposals. Poess and Floyd [2000] gives an overview of the TPC-H, TPC-R, and TPC-W benchmarks. The OO1 benchmark for OODBs is described in Cattell and Skeen [1992]; the OO7 benchmark is described in Carey et al. [1993].

Kleinrock [1975] and Kleinrock [1976] is a popular two-volume textbook on queueing theory.

Shasha [1992] provides a good overview of database tuning. O'Neil and O'Neil [2000] provides a very good textbook coverage of performance measurement and tuning. The five minute and one minute rules are described in Gray and Putzolu [1987] and Gray and Graefe [1997]. Brown et al. [1994] describes an approach to automated tuning. Index selection and materialized view selection are addressed by Ross et al. [1996], Labio et al. [1997], Gupta [1997], Chaudhuri and Narasayya [1997], Agrawal et al. [2000] and Mistry et al. [2001].

The American National Standard SQL-86 is described in ANSI [1986]. The IBM Systems Application Architecture definition of SQL is specified by IBM [1987]. The standards for SQL-89 and SQL-92 are available as ANSI [1989] and ANSI [1992] respectively. For references on the SQL:1999 standard, see the bibliographical notes of Chapter 9.

The X/Open SQL call-level interface is defined in X/Open [1993]; the ODBC API is described in Microsoft [1997] and Sanders [1998]. The X/Open XA interface is defined in X/Open [1991]. More information about ODBC, OLE-DB, and ADO can be found on the Web site www.microsoft.com/data, and in a number of books on the subject that can be found through www.amazon.com. The ODMG 3.0 standard is defined in Cattell [2000]. *ACM Sigmod Record*, which is published quarterly, has a regular section on standards in databases, including benchmark standards.

A wealth of information on XML based standards is available online. You can use a Web search engine such as Google to search for more detailed and up-to-date information about the XML and other standards.

Loeb [1998] provides a detailed description of secure electronic transactions. Business process reengineering is covered by Cook [1996]. Kirchmer [1999] describes application implementation using standard software such as Enterprise Resource Planning (ERP) packages. Umar [1997] covers reengineering and issues in dealing with legacy systems.

Tools

There are many Web development tools that support database connectivity through servlets, JSP, Javascript, or other mechanisms. We list a few of the better-known ones here: Java SDK from Sun (java.sun.com), Apache's Tomcat (jakarta.apache.org) and Web server (apache.org), IBM WebSphere (www.software.ibm.com), Microsoft's ASP tools (www.microsoft.com), Allaire's Coldfusion and JRun products (www.allaire.com), Caucho's Resin (www.caucho.com), and Zope (www.zope.org). A few of these, such as Apache, are free for any use, some are free for noncommercial use or for personal use, while others need to be paid for. See the respective Web sites for more information.

Advanced Querying and Information Retrieval

Businesses have begun to exploit the burgeoning data online to make better decisions about their activities, such as what items to stock and how best to target customers to increase sales. Many of their queries are rather complicated, however, and certain types of information cannot be extracted even by using SQL.

Several techniques and tools are available to help with decision support. Several tools for data analysis allow analysts to view data in different ways. Other analysis tools precompute summaries of very large amounts of data, in order to give fast responses to queries. The SQL:1999 standard now contains additional constructs to support data analysis. Another approach to getting knowledge from data is to use *data mining*, which aims at detecting various types of patterns in large volumes of data. Data mining supplements various types of statistical techniques with similar goals.

Textual data, too, has grown explosively. Textual data is unstructured, unlike the rigidly structured data in relational databases. Querying of unstructured textual data is referred to as *information retrieval*. Information retrieval systems have much in common with database systems—in particular, the storage and retrieval of data on secondary storage. However, the emphasis in the field of information systems is different from that in database systems, concentrating on issues such as querying based on keywords; the relevance of documents to the query; and the analysis, classification, and indexing of documents.

This chapter covers decision support, including online analytical processing and data mining and information retrieval.

22.1 Decision-Support Systems

Database applications can be broadly classified into transaction processing and decision support, as we have seen earlier in Section 21.3.2. Transaction-processing systems are widely used today, and companies have accumulated a vast amount of information generated by these systems.

For example, company databases often contain enormous quantities of information about customers and transactions. The size of the information storage required may range up to hundreds of gigabytes, or even terabytes, for large retail chains. Transaction information for a retailer may include the name or identifier (such as credit-card number) of the customer, the items purchased, the price paid, and the dates on which the purchases were made. Information about the items purchased may include the name of the item, the manufacturer, the model number, the color, and the size. Customer information may include credit history, annual income, residence, age, and even educational background.

Such large databases can be treasure troves of information for making business decisions, such as what items to stock and what discounts to offer. For instance, a retail company may notice a sudden spurt in purchases of flannel shirts in the Pacific Northwest, may realize that there is a trend, and may start stocking a larger number of such shirts in shops in that area. As another example, a car company may find, on querying its database, that most of its small sports cars are bought by young women whose annual incomes are above $50,000. The company may then target its marketing to attract more such women to buy its small sports cars, and may avoid wasting money trying to attract other categories of people to buy those cars. In both cases, the company has identified patterns in customer behavior, and has used the patterns to make business decisions.

The storage and retrieval of data for decision support raises several issues:

- Although many decision support queries can be written in SQL, others either cannot be expressed in SQL or cannot be expressed easily in SQL. Several SQL extensions have therefore been proposed to make data analysis easier. The area of *online analytical processing* (OLAP) deals with tools and techniques for data analysis that can give nearly instantaneous answers to queries requesting summarized data, even though the database may be extremely large. In Section 22.2, we study SQL extensions for data analysis, and techniques for online analytical processing.

- Database query languages are not suited to the performance of detailed **statistical analyses** of data. There are several packages, such as SAS and S++, that help in statistical analysis. Such packages have been interfaced with databases, to allow large volumes of data to be stored in the database and retrieved efficiently for analysis. The field of statistical analysis is a large discipline on its own; see the references in the bibliographical notes for more information.

- Knowledge-discovery techniques attempt to discover automatically statistical rules and patterns from data. The field of *data mining* combines knowledge discovery techniques invented by artificial intelligence researchers and statistical analysts, with efficient implementation techniques that enable them to be used on extremely large databases. Section 22.3 discusses data mining.

- Large companies have diverse sources of data that they need to use for making business decisions. The sources may store the data under different schemas. For performance reasons (as well as for reasons of organization control), the data sources usually will not permit other parts of the company to retrieve data on demand.

To execute queries efficiently on such diverse data, companies have built *data warehouses*. Data warehouses gather data from multiple sources under a unified schema, at a single site. Thus, they provide the user a single uniform interface to data. We study issues in building and maintaining a data warehouse in Section 22.4.

The area of **decision support** can be broadly viewed as covering all the above areas, although some people use the term in a narrower sense that excludes statistical analysis and data mining.

22.2 Data Analysis and OLAP

Although complex statistical analysis is best left to statistics packages, databases should support simple, commonly used, forms of data analysis. Since the data stored in databases are usually large in volume, they need to be summarized in some fashion if we are to derive information that humans can use.

OLAP tools support interactive analysis of summary information. Several SQL extensions have been developed to support OLAP tools. There are many commonly used tasks that cannot be done using the basic SQL aggregation and grouping facilities. Examples include finding percentiles, or cumulative distributions, or aggregates over sliding windows on sequentially ordered data. A number of extensions of SQL have been recently proposed to support such tasks, and implemented in products such as Oracle and IBM DB2.

22.2.1 Online Analytical Processing

Statistical analysis often requires grouping on multiple attributes. Consider an application where a shop wants to find out what kinds of clothes are popular. Let us suppose that clothes are characterized by their item-name, color, and size, and that we have a relation *sales* with the schema *sales(item-name, color, size, number)*. Suppose that *item-name* can take on the values (skirt, dress, shirt, pant), *color* can take on the values (dark, pastel, white), and *size* can take on values (small, medium, large).

Given a relation used for data analysis, we can identify some of its attributes as **measure** attributes, since they measure some value, and can be aggregated upon. For instance, the attribute *number* of the *sales* relation is a measure attribute, since it measures the number of units sold. Some (or all) of the other attributes of the relation are identified as **dimension attributes**, since they define the dimensions on which measure attributes, and summaries of measure attributes, are viewed. In the *sales* relation, *item-name, color,* and *size* are dimension attributes. (A more realistic version of the *sales* relation would have additional dimensions, such as time and sales location, and additional measures such as monetary value of the sale.)

Data that can be modeled as dimension attributes and measure attributes are called **multidimensional data**.

size: | **all** |

color

	dark	pastel	white	Total
skirt	8	35	10	53
dress	20	10	5	35
shirt	14	7	28	49
pant	20	2	5	27
Total	62	54	48	164

item-name labels the rows.

Figure 22.1   Cross tabulation of *sales* by *item-name* and *color*.

To analyze the multidimensional data, a manager may want to see data laid out as shown in the table in Figure 22.1. The table shows total numbers for different combinations of *item-name* and *color*. The value of *size* is specified to be **all**, indicating that the displayed values are a summary across all values of *size*.

The table in Figure 22.1 is an example of a **cross-tabulation** (or **cross-tab**, for short), also referred to as a **pivot-table**. In general, a cross-tab is a table where values for one attribute (say A) form the row headers, values for another attribute (say B) form the column headers, and the values in an individual cell are derived as follows. Each cell can be identified by (a_i, b_j), where a_i is a value for A and b_j a value for B. If there is at most one tuple with any (a_i, b_j) value, the value in the cell is derived from that single tuple (if any); for instance, it could be the value of one or more other attributes of the tuple. If there can be multiple tuples with an (a_i, b_j) value, the value in the cell must be derived by aggregation on the tuples with that value. In our example, the aggregation used is the sum of the values for attribute *number*. In our example, the cross-tab also has an extra column and an extra row storing the totals of the cells in the row/column. Most cross-tabs have such summary rows and columns.

A cross-tab is different from relational tables usually stored in databases, since the number of columns in the cross-tab depends on the actual data. A change in the data values may result in adding more columns, which is not desirable for data storage. However, a cross-tab view is desirable for display to users. It is straightforward to represent a cross-tab without summary values in a relational form with a fixed number of columns. A cross-tab with summary rows/columns can be represented by introducing a special value **all** to represent subtotals, as in Figure 22.2. The SQL:1999 standard actually uses the **null** value in place of **all**, but to avoid confusion with regular null values, we shall continue to use **all**.

Consider the tuples (skirt, **all**, 53) and (dress, **all**, 35). We have obtained these tuples by eliminating individual tuples with different values for *color*, and by replacing the value of *number* by an aggregate—namely, sum. The value **all** can be thought of as representing the set of all values for an attribute. Tuples with the value **all** only for the *color* dimension can be obtained by an SQL query performing a group by on the column *item-name*. Similarly, a group by on *color* can be used to get the tuples with the value **all** for *item-name*, and a group by with no attributes (which can simply be omitted in SQL) can be used to get the tuple with value **all** for *item-name* and *color*.

item-name	color	number
skirt	dark	8
skirt	pastel	35
skirt	white	10
skirt	**all**	53
dress	dark	20
dress	pastel	10
dress	white	5
dress	**all**	35
shirt	dark	14
shirt	pastel	7
shirt	white	28
shirt	**all**	49
pant	dark	20
pant	pastel	2
pant	white	5
pant	**all**	27
all	dark	62
all	pastel	54
all	white	48
all	**all**	164

Figure 22.2   Relational representation of the data in Figure 22.1.

The generalization of a cross-tab, which is 2-dimensional, to n dimensions can be visualized as an n-dimensional cube, called the **data cube**. Figure 22.3 shows a data cube on the *sales* relation. The data cube has three dimensions, namely *item-name*, *color*, and *size*, and the measure attribute is *number*. Each cell is identified by values for these three dimensions. Each cell in the data cube contains a value, just as in a cross-tab. In Figure 22.3, the value contained in a cell is shown on one of the faces of the cell; other faces of the cell are shown blank if they are visible.

The value for a dimension may be **all**, in which case the cell contains a summary over all values of that dimension, as in the case of cross-tabs. The number of different ways in which the tuples can be grouped for aggregation can be large. In fact, for a table with n dimensions, aggregation can be performed with grouping on each of the 2^n subsets of the n dimensions.[1]

An online analytical processing or OLAP system is an interactive system that permits an analyst to view different summaries of multidimensional data. The word *online* indicates that the an analyst must be able to request new summaries and get responses online, within a few seconds, and should not be forced to wait for a long time to see the result of a query.

With an OLAP system, a data analyst can look at different cross-tabs on the same data by interactively selecting the attributes in the cross-tab. Each cross-tab is a

---

1.   Grouping on the set of all n dimensions is useful only if the table may have duplicates.

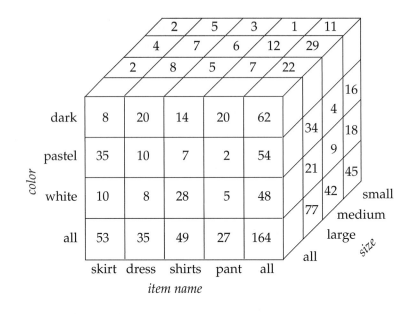

Figure 22.3 Three-dimensional data cube.

two-dimensional view on a multidimensional data cube. For instance the analyst may select a cross-tab on *item-name* and *size*, or a cross-tab on *color* and *size*. The operation of changing the dimensions used in a cross-tab is called **pivoting**.

An OLAP system provides other functionality as well. For instance, the analyst may wish to see a cross-tab on *item-name* and *color* for a fixed value of *size*, for example, large, instead of the sum across all sizes. Such an operation is referred to as **slicing**, since it can be thought of as viewing a slice of the data cube. The operation is sometimes called **dicing**, particularly when values for multiple dimensions are fixed.

When a cross-tab is used to view a multidimensional cube, the values of dimension attributes that are not part of the cross-tab are shown above the cross-tab. The value of such an attribute can be **all**, as shown in Figure 22.1, indicating that data in the cross-tab are a summary over all values for the attribute. Slicing/dicing simply consists of selecting specific values for these attributes, which are then displayed on top of the cross-tab.

OLAP systems permit users to view data at any desired level of granularity. The operation of moving from finer-granularity data to a coarser granularity (by means of aggregation) is called a **rollup**. In our example, starting from the data cube on the *sales* table, we got our example cross-tab by rolling up on the attribute *size*. The opposite operation—that of moving from coarser-granularity data to finer-granularity data—is called a **drill down**. Clearly, finer-granularity data cannot be generated from coarse-granularity data; they must be generated either from the original data, or from even finer-granularity summary data.

Analysts may wish to view a dimension at different levels of detail. For instance, an attribute of type **datetime** contains a date and a time of day. Using time precise to a second (or less) may not be meaningful: An analyst who is interested in rough time

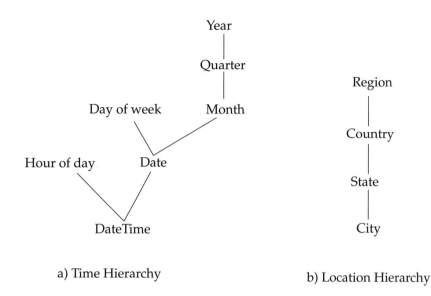

a) Time Hierarchy   b) Location Hierarchy

Figure 22.4 Hierarchies on dimensions.

of day may look at only the hour value. An analyst who is interested in sales by day of the week may map the date to a day-of-the-week and look only at that. Another analyst may be interested in aggregates over a month, or a quarter, or for an entire year.

The different levels of detail for an attribute can be organized into a **hierarchy**. Figure 22.4(a) shows a hierarchy on the **datetime** attribute. As another example, Figure 22.4(b) shows a hierarchy on location, with the city being at the bottom of the hierarchy, state above it, country at the next level, and region being the top level. In our earlier example, clothes can be grouped by category (for instance, menswear or womenswear); *category* would then lie above *item-name* in our hierarchy on clothes. At the level of actual values, skirts and dresses would fall under the womenswear category and pants and shirts under the menswear category.

An analyst may be interested in viewing sales of clothes divided as menswear and womenswear, and not interested in individual values. After viewing the aggregates at the level of womenswear and menswear, an analyst may *drill down the hierarchy* to look at individual values. An analyst looking at the detailed level may *drill up the hierarchy*, and look at coarser-level aggregates. Both levels can be displayed on the same cross-tab, as in Figure 22.5.

22.2.2 OLAP Implementation

The earliest OLAP systems used multidimensional arrays in memory to store data cubes, and are referred to as **multidimensional OLAP (MOLAP)** systems. Later, OLAP facilities were integrated into relational systems, with data stored in a relational database. Such systems are referred to as **relational OLAP (ROLAP)** systems. Hybrid

category	*item-name*	dark	pastel	white	total	
womenswear	skirt	8	8	10	53	
	dress	20	20	5	35	
	subtotal	28	28	15		88
menswear	skirt	14	14	28	49	
	dress	20	20	5	27	
	subtotal	34	34	33		76
total		62	62	48		164

Figure 22.5   Cross tabulation of *sales* with hierarchy on *item-name*.

systems, which store some summaries in memory and store the base data and other summaries in a relational database, are called **hybrid OLAP (HOLAP)** systems.

Many OLAP systems are implemented as client–server systems. The server contains the relational database as well as any MOLAP data cubes. Client systems obtain views of the data by communicating with the server.

A naïve way of computing the entire data cube (all groupings) on a relation is to use any standard algorithm for computing aggregate operations, one grouping at a time. The naïve algorithm would require a large number of scans of the relation. A simple optimization is to compute an aggregation on, say, (*item-name, color*) from an aggregation (*item-name, color, size*), instead of from the original relation. For the standard SQL aggregate functions, we can compute an aggregate with grouping on a set of attributes A from an aggregate with grouping on a set of attributes B if $A \subseteq B$; you can do so as an exercise (see Exercise 22.1), but note that to compute **avg**, we additionally need the **count** value. (For some non-standard aggregate functions, such as median, aggregates cannot be computed as above; the optimization described here do not apply to such "*non-decomposable*" aggregate functions.) The amount of data read drops significantly by computing an aggregate from another aggregate, instead of from the original relation. Further improvements are possible; for instance, multiple groupings can be computed on a single scan of the data. See the bibliographical notes for references to algorithms for efficiently computing data cubes.

Early OLAP implementations precomputed and stored entire data cubes, that is, groupings on all subsets of the dimension attributes. Precomputation allows OLAP queries to be answered within a few seconds, even on datasets that may contain millions of tuples adding up to gigabytes of data. However, there are 2^n groupings with n dimension attributes; hierarchies on attributes increase the number further. As a result, the entire data cube is often larger than the original relation that formed the data cube and in many cases it is not feasible to store the entire data cube.

Instead of precomputing and storing all possible groupings, it makes sense to precompute and store some of the groupings, and to compute others on demand. Instead of computing queries from the original relation, which may take a very long time, we can compute them from other precomputed queries. For instance, suppose a query requires summaries by (*item-name, color*), which has not been precomputed. The query result can be computed from summaries by (*item-name, color, size*), if that has been precomputed. See the bibliographical notes for references on how to select a good set of groupings for precomputation, given limits on the storage available for precomputed results.

The data in a data cube cannot be generated by a single SQL query using the basic **group by** constructs, since aggregates are computed for several different groupings of the dimension attributes. Section 22.2.3 discusses SQL extensions to support OLAP functionality.

22.2.3 Extended Aggregation

The SQL-92 aggregation functionality is limited, so several extensions were implemented by different databases. The SQL:1999 standard, however, defines a rich set of aggregate functions, which we outline in this section and in the next two sections. The Oracle and IBM DB2 databases support most of these features, and other databases will no doubt support these features in the near future.

The new aggregate functions on single attributes are standard deviation and variance (**stddev** and **variance**). Standard deviation is the square root of variance.[2] Some database systems support other aggregate functions such as median and mode. Some database systems even allow users to add new aggregate functions.

SQL:1999 also supports a new class of **binary aggregate functions**, which can compute statistical results on pairs of attributes; they include correlations, covariances, and regression curves, which give a line approximating the relation between the values of the pair of attributes. Definitions of these functions may be found in any standard textbook on statistics, such as those referenced in the bibliographical notes.

SQL:1999 also supports generalizations of the **group by** construct, using the **cube** and **rollup** constructs. A representative use of the **cube** construct is:

> **select** *item-name, color, size,* **sum**(*number*)
> **from** *sales*
> **group by cube**(*item-name, color, size*)

This query computes the union of eight different groupings of the *sales* relation:

> { (*item-name, color, size*), (*item-name, color*), (*item-name, size*),
> (*color, size*), (*item-name*), (*color*), (*size*), () }

where () denotes an empty **group by** list.

For each grouping, the result contains the null value for attributes not present in the grouping. For instance, the table in Figure 22.2, with occurrences of **all** replaced by *null*, can be computed by the query

> **select** *item-name, color,* **sum**(*number*)
> **from** *sales*
> **group by cube**(*item-name, color*)

---

2. The SQL:1999 standard actually supports two types of variance, called population variance and sample variance, and correspondingly two types of standard deviation. The definitions of the two types differ slightly; see a statistics textbook for details.

A representative **rollup** construct is

> **select** *item-name, color, size,* **sum**(*number*)
> **from** *sales*
> **group by rollup**(*item-name, color, size*)

Here, only four groupings are generated:

> { (*item-name, color, size*), (*item-name, color*), (*item-name*), () }

Rollup can be used to generate aggregates at multiple levels of a hierarchy on a column. For instance, suppose we have a table *itemcategory(item-name, category)* giving the category of each item. Then the query

> **select** *category, item-name,* **sum**(*number*)
> **from** *sales, category*
> **where** *sales.item-name = itemcategory.item-name*
> **group by rollup**(*category, item-name*)

would give a hierarchical summary by *item-name* and by *category*.

Multiple **rollup**s and **cube**s can be used in a single group by clause. For instance, the following query

> **select** *item-name, color, size,* **sum**(*number*)
> **from** *sales*
> **group by rollup**(*item-name*), **rollup**(*color, size*)

generates the groupings

> { (*item-name, color, size*), (*item-name, color*), (*item-name*),
> (*color, size*), (*color*), () }

To understand why, note that **rollup**(*item-name*) generates two groupings, {(*item-name*), ()}, and **rollup**(*color, size*) generates three groupings, {(*color, size*), (*color*), () }. The cross product of the two gives us the six groupings shown.

As we mentioned in Section 22.2.1, SQL:1999 uses the value **null** to indicate the usual sense of null as well as **all**. This dual use of **null** can cause ambiguity if the attributes used in a rollup or cube clause contain null values. The function **grouping** can be applied on an attribute; it returns 1 if the value is a null value representing **all**, and returns 0 in all other cases. Consider the following query:

> **select** *item-name, color, size,* **sum**(*number*),
>   **grouping**(*item-name*) **as** *item-name-flag,*
>   **grouping**(*color*) **as** *color-flag,*
>   **grouping**(*size*) **as** *size-flag*
> **from** *sales*
> **group by cube**(*item-name, color, size*)

The output is the same as in the version of the query without **grouping**, but with three extra columns called *item-name-flag, color-flag,* and *size-flag.* In each tuple, the value of a flag field is 1 if the corresponding field is a null representing **all**.

Instead of using tags to indicate nulls that represent **all**, we can replace the null value by a value of our choice:

$$\textbf{decode}(\textbf{grouping}(\textit{item-name}), 1, \text{'all'}, \textit{item-name})$$

This expression returns the value "all" if the value of *item-name* is a null corresponding to **all**, and returns the actual value of *item-name* otherwise. This expression can be used in place of *item-name* in the select clause to get "all" in the output of the query, in place of nulls representing **all**.

Neither the **rollup** nor the **cube** clause gives complete control on the groupings that are generated. For instance, we cannot use them to specify that we want only groupings {(*color, size*), (*size, item-name*)}. Such restricted groupings can be generated by using the **grouping** construct in the **having** clause; we leave the details as an exercise for you.

22.2.4 Ranking

Finding the position of a value in a larger set is a common operation. For instance, we may wish to assign students a rank in class based on their total marks, with the rank 1 going to the student with the highest marks, the rank 2 to the student with the next highest marks, and so on. While such queries can be expressed in SQL-92, they are difficult to express and inefficient to evaluate. Programmers often resort to writing the query partly in SQL and partly in a programming language. A related type of query is to find the percentile in which a value in a (multi)set belongs, for example, the bottom third, middle third, or top third. We study SQL:1999 support for these types of queries here.

Ranking is done in conjunction with an **order by** specification. Suppose we are given a relation *student-marks(student-id, marks)* which stores the marks obtained by each student. The following query gives the rank of each student.

> **select** *student-id*, **rank**() **over** (**order by** (*marks*) **desc**) **as** *s-rank*
> **from** *student-marks*

Note that the order of tuples in the output is not defined, so they may not be sorted by rank. An extra **order by** clause is needed to get them in sorted order, as shown below.

> **select** *student-id*, **rank** () **over** (**order by** (*marks*) **desc**) **as** *s-rank*
> **from** *student-marks* **order by** *s-rank*

A basic issue with ranking is how to deal with the case of multiple tuples that are the same on the ordering attribute(s). In our example, this means deciding what to do if there are two students with the same marks. The **rank** function gives the same rank to all tuples that are equal on the **order by** attributes. For instance, if the highest mark is shared by two students, both would get rank 1. The next rank given would be 3, not 2, so if three students get the next highest mark, they would all get rank 3, and the next student(s) would get rank 5, and so on. There is also a **dense_rank** function that does not create gaps in the ordering. In the above example, the tuples with the second highest value all get rank 2, and tuples with the third highest value get rank 3, and so on.

Ranking can be done within partitions of the data. For instance, suppose we have an additional relation *student-section(student-id, section)* that stores for each student the section in which the student studies. The following query then gives the rank of students within each section.

> **select** *student-id, section,*
> > **rank** () **over** (**partition by** *section* **order by** *marks* **desc**) **as** *sec-rank*
> **from** *student-marks, student-section*
> **where** *student-marks.student-id = student-section.student-id*
> **order by** *section, sec-rank*

The outer **order by** clause orders the result tuples by section, and within each section by the rank.

Multiple **rank** expressions can be used within a single select statement; thus we can obtain the overall rank and the rank within the section by using two **rank** expressions in the same **select** clause. An interesting question is what happens when ranking (possibly with partitioning) occurs along with a **group by** clause. In this case, the **group by** clause is applied first, and partitioning and ranking are done on the results of the group by. Thus aggregate values can then be used for ranking. For example, suppose we had marks for each student for each of several subjects. To rank students by the sum of their marks in different subjects, we can use a **group by** clause to compute the aggregate marks for each student, and then rank students by the aggregate sum. We leave details as an exercise for you.

The ranking functions can be used to find the top n tuples by embedding a ranking query within an outer-level query; we leave details as an exercise. Note that bottom n is simply the same as top n with a reverse sorting order. Several database systems provide nonstandard SQL extensions to specify directly that only the top n results are required; such extensions do not require the rank function, and simplify the job of the optimizer, but are (currently) not as general since they do not support partitioning.

SQL:1999 also specifies several other functions that can be used in place of **rank**. For instance, **percent_rank** of a tuple gives the rank of the tuple as a fraction. If there are n tuples in the partition[3] and the rank of the tuple is r, then its percent rank is defined as $(r - 1)/(n - 1)$ (and as null if there is only one tuple in the partition). The function **cume_dist**, short for cumulative distribution, for a tuple is defined as p/n where p is the number of tuples in the partition with ordering values preceding or equal to the ordering value of the tuple, and n is the number of tuples in the parti-

---

3. The entire set is treated as a single partition if no explicit partition is used.

tion. The function **row_number** sorts the rows and gives each row a unique number corresponding to its position in the sort order; different rows with the same ordering value would get different row numbers, in a nondeterministic fashion.

Finally, for a given constant n, the ranking function **ntile**(n) takes the tuples in each partition in the specified order, and divides them into n buckets with equal numbers of tuples.[4] For each tuple, **ntile**(n) then gives the number of the bucket in which it is placed, with bucket numbers starting with 1. This function is particularly useful for constructing histograms based on percentiles. For instance, we can sort employees by salary, and use **ntile**(3) to find which range (bottom third, middle third, or top third) each employee is in, and compute the total salary earned by employees in each range:

> **select** *threetile*, **sum**(*salary*)
> **from** (
>   **select** *salary*, **ntile**(3) **over** (**order by** (*salary*)) **as** *threetile*
>   **from** *employee*) **as** *s*
> **group by** *threetile*.

The presence of null values can complicate the definition of rank, since it is not clear where they should occur first in the sort order. SQL:1999 permits the user to specify where they should occur by using **nulls first** or **nulls last**, for instance

> **select** *student-id*, **rank** () **over** (**order by** *marks* **desc nulls last**) **as** *s-rank*
> **from** *student-marks*

22.2.5 Windowing

An example of a *window* query is query that, given sales values for each date, calculates for each date the average of the sales on that day, the previous day, and the next day; such moving average queries are used to smooth out random variations. Another example of a window query is one that finds the cumulative balance in an account, given a relation specifying the deposits and withdrawals on an account. Such queries are either hard or impossible (depending on the exact query) to express in basic SQL.

SQL:1999 provides a windowing feature to support such queries. In contrast to **group by**, the same tuple can exist in multiple windows. Suppose we are given a relation *transaction(account-number, date-time, value)*, where *value* is positive for a deposit and negative for a withdrawal. We assume there is at most one transaction per *date-time* value.

Consider the query

---

4.   If the total number of tuples in a partition is not divisible by n, then the number of tuples in each bucket can differ by at most 1. Tuples with the same value for the ordering attribute may be assigned to different buckets, nondeterministically, in order to make the number of tuples in each bucket equal.

> **select** *account-number, date-time,*
>   **sum**(*value*) **over**
>   (**partition by** *account-number*
>   **order by** *date-time*
>   **rows unbounded preceding**)
>   **as** *balance*
>   **from** *transaction*
>   **order by** *account-number, date-time*

The query gives the cumulative balances on each account just before each transaction on the account; the cumulative balance of the account is the sum of values of all earlier transactions on the account.

The **partition by** clause partitions tuples by account number, so for each row only the tuples in its partition are considered. A window is created for each tuple; the keywords **rows unbounded preceding** specify that the window for each tuple consists of all tuples in the partition that precede it in the specified order (here, increasing order of *date-time*). The aggregate function **sum**(*value*) is applied on all the tuples in the window. Observe that the query does not use a **group by** clause, since there is an output tuple for each tuple in the *transaction* relation.

While the query could be written without these extended constructs, it would be rather difficult to formulate. Note also that different windows can overlap, that is, a tuple may be present in more than one window.

Other types of windows can be specified. For instance, to get a window containing the previous 10 rows for each row, we can specify **rows** 10 **preceding**. To get a window containing the current, previous, and following row, we can use **between rows** 1 **preceding and** 1 **following**. To get the previous rows and the current row, we can say **between rows unbounded preceding and current**. Note that if the ordering is on a nonkey attribute, the result is not deterministic, since the order of tuples is not fully defined.

We can even specify windows by ranges of values, instead of numbers of rows. For instance, suppose the ordering value of a tuple is v; then **range between** 10 **preceding and current row** would give tuples whose ordering value is between $v - 10$ and v (both values inclusive). When dealing with dates, we can use **range interval** 10 **day preceding** to get a window containing tuples within the previous 10 days, but not including the date of the tuple.

Clearly, the windowing functionality of SQL:1999 is very rich and can be used to write rather complex queries with a small amount of effort.

22.3 Data Mining

The term **data mining** refers loosely to the process of semiautomatically analyzing large databases to find useful patterns. Like knowledge discovery in artificial intelligence (also called machine learning), or statistical analysis, data mining attempts to discover rules and patterns from data. However, data mining differs from machine learning and statistics in that it deals with large volumes of data, stored primarily on disk. That is, data mining deals with "knowledge discovery in databases."

Some types of knowledge discovered from a database can be represented by a set of **rules**. The following is an example of a rule, stated informally: "Young women with annual incomes greater than $50,000 are the most likely people to buy small sports cars." Of course such rules are not universally true, and have degrees of "support" and "confidence," as we shall see. Other types of knowledge are represented by equations relating different variables to each other, or by other mechanisms for predicting outcomes when the values of some variables are known.

There are a variety of possible types of patterns that may be useful, and different techniques are used to find different types of patterns. We shall study a few examples of patterns and see how they may be automatically derived from a database.

Usually there is a manual component to data mining, consisting of preprocessing data to a form acceptable to the algorithms, and postprocessing of discovered patterns to find novel ones that could be useful. There may also be more than one type of pattern that can be discovered from a given database, and manual interaction may be needed to pick useful types of patterns. For this reason, data mining is really a semiautomatic process in real life. However, in our description we concentrate on the automatic aspect of mining.

22.3.1 Applications of Data Mining

The discovered knowledge has numerous applications. The most widely used applications are those that require some sort of **prediction**. For instance, when a person applies for a credit card, the credit-card company wants to predict if the person is a good credit risk. The prediction is to be based on known attributes of the person, such as age, income, debts, and past debt repayment history. Rules for making the prediction are derived from the same attributes of past and current credit card holders, along with their observed behavior, such as whether they defaulted on their credit-card dues. Other types of prediction include predicting which customers may switch over to a competitor (these customers may be offered special discounts to tempt them not to switch), predicting which people are likely to respond to promotional mail ("junk mail"), or predicting what types of phone calling card usage are likely to be fraudulent.

Another class of applications looks for **associations**, for instance, books that tend to be bought together. If a customer buys a book, an online bookstore may suggest other associated books. If a person buys a camera, the system may suggest accessories that tend to be bought along with cameras. A good salesperson is aware of such patterns and exploits them to make additional sales. The challenge is to automate the process. Other types of associations may lead to discovery of causation. For instance, discovery of unexpected associations between a newly introduced medicine and cardiac problems led to the finding that the medicine may cause cardiac problems in some people. The medicine was then withdrawn from the market.

Associations are an example of **descriptive patterns**. **Clusters** are another example of such patterns. For example, over a century ago a cluster of typhoid cases was found around a well, which led to the discovery that the water in the well was contaminated and was spreading typhoid. Detection of clusters of disease remains important even today.

22.3.2 Classification

As mentioned in Section 22.3.1, prediction is one of the most important types of data mining. We outline what is classification, study techniques for building one type of classifiers, called decision tree classifiers, and then study other prediction techniques.

Abstractly, the **classification** problem is this: Given that items belong to one of several classes, and given past instances (called **training instances**) of items along with the classes to which they belong, the problem is to predict the class to which a new item belongs. The class of the new instance is not known, so other attributes of the instance must be used to predict the class.

Classification can be done by finding rules that partition the given data into disjoint groups. For instance, suppose that a credit-card company wants to decide whether or not to give a credit card to an applicant. The company has a variety of information about the person, such as her age, educational background, annual income, and current debts, that it can use for making a decision.

Some of this information could be relevant to the credit worthiness of the applicant, whereas some may not be. To make the decision, the company assigns a credit-worthiness level of excellent, good, average, or bad to each of a sample set of *current* customers according to each customer's payment history. Then, the company attempts to find rules that classify its current customers into excellent, good, average, or bad, on the basis of the information about the person, other than the actual payment history (which is unavailable for new customers). Let us consider just two attributes: education level (highest degree earned) and income. The rules may be of the following form:

$$\forall person \ P, \ P.degree = masters \textbf{ and } P.income > 75,000$$
$$\Rightarrow \ P.credit = excellent$$

$$\forall \ person \ P, \ P.degree = bachelors \textbf{ or}$$
$$(P.income \geq 25,000 \textbf{ and } P.income \leq 75,000) \ \Rightarrow \ P.credit = good$$

Similar rules would also be present for the other credit worthiness levels (average and bad).

The process of building a classifier starts from a sample of data, called a **training set**. For each tuple in the training set, the class to which the tuple belongs is already known. For instance, the training set for a credit-card application may be the existing customers, with their credit worthiness determined from their payment history. The actual data, or population, may consist of all people, including those who are not existing customers. There are several ways of building a classifier, as we shall see.

22.3.2.1 Decision Tree Classifiers

The decision tree classifier is a widely used technique for classification. As the name suggests, **decision tree classifiers** use a tree; each leaf node has an associated class, and each internal node has a predicate (or more generally, a function) associated with it. Figure 22.6 shows an example of a decision tree.

To classify a new instance, we start at the root, and traverse the tree to reach a leaf; at an internal node we evaluate the predicate (or function) on the data instance,

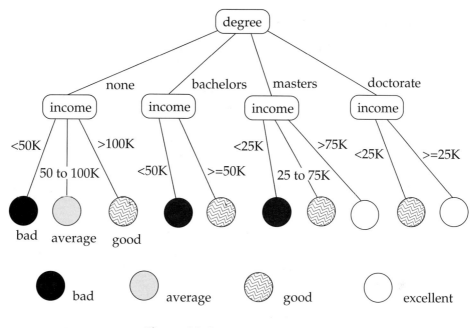

Figure 22.6 Classification tree.

to find which child to go to. The process continues till we reach a leaf node. For example, if the degree level of a person is masters, and the persons income is 40K, starting from the root we follow the edge labeled "masters," and from there the edge labeled "25K to 75K," to reach a leaf. The class at the leaf is "good," so we predict that the credit risk of that person is good.

Building Decision Tree Classifiers

The question then is how to build a decision tree classifier, given a set of training instances. The most common way of doing so is to use a **greedy** algorithm, which works recursively, starting at the root and building the tree downward. Initially there is only one node, the root, and all training instances are associated with that node.

At each node, if all, or "almost all" training instances associated with the node belong to the same class, then the node becomes a leaf node associated with that class. Otherwise, a **partitioning attribute** and **partitioning conditions** must be selected to create child nodes. The data associated with each child node is the set of training instances that satisfy the partitioning condition for that child node. In our example, the attribute *degree* is chosen, and four children, one for each value of degree, are created. The conditions for the four children nodes are *degree* = none, *degree* = bachelors, *degree* = masters, and *degree* = doctorate, respectively. The data associated with each child consist of training instances satisfying the condition associated with that child. At the node corresponding to masters, the attribute *income* is chosen, with the range of values partitioned into intervals 0 to 25,000, 25,000 to 50,000, 50,000 to 75,000, and over 75,000. The data associated with each node consist of training instances with the *degree* attribute being masters, and the *income* attribute being in each of these ranges, respectively. As an optimization, since the class for the range 25,000 to 50,000 and the range 50,000 to 75,000 is the same under the node *degree* = masters, the two ranges have been merged into a single range 25,000 to 75,000.

Best Splits

Intuitively, by choosing a sequence of partitioning attributes, we start with the set of all training instances, which is "impure" in the sense that it contains instances from many classes, and end up with leaves which are "pure" in the sense that at each leaf all training instances belong to only one class. We shall see shortly how to measure purity quantitatively. To judge the benefit of picking a particular attribute and condition for partitioning of the data at a node, we measure the purity of the data at the children resulting from partitioning by that attribute. The attribute and condition that result in the maximum purity are chosen.

The purity of a set S of training instances can be measured quantitatively in several ways. Suppose there are k classes, and of the instances in S the fraction of instances in class i is p_i. One measure of purity, the **Gini measure** is defined as

$$\text{Gini}(S) = 1 - \sum_{i-1}^{k} p_i^2$$

When all instances are in a single class, the Gini value is 0, while it reaches its maximum (of $1 - 1/k$) if each class has the same number of instances. Another measure of purity is the **entropy measure**, which is defined as

$$\text{Entropy}(S) = - \sum_{i-1}^{k} p_i \log_2 p_i$$

The entropy value is 0 if all instances are in a single class, and reaches its maximum when each class has the same number of instances. The entropy measure derives from information theory.

When a set S is split into multiple sets $S_i, i = 1, 2, \ldots, r$, we can measure the purity of the resultant set of sets as:

$$\text{Purity}(S_1, S_2, \ldots, S_r) = \sum_{i=1}^{r} \frac{|S_i|}{|S|} \text{purity}(S_i)$$

That is, the purity is the weighted average of the purity of the sets S_i. The above formula can be used with both the Gini measure and the entropy measure of purity.

The **information gain** due to a particular split of S into $S_i, i = 1, 2, \ldots, r$ is then

$$\text{Information-gain}(S, \{S_1, S_2, \ldots, S_r\}) = \text{purity}(S) - \text{purity}(S_1, S_2, \ldots, S_r)$$

Splits into fewer sets are preferable to splits into many sets, since they lead to simpler and more meaningful decision trees. The number of elements in each of the sets S_i may also be taken into account; otherwise, whether a set S_i has 0 elements or 1 element would make a big difference in the number of sets, although the split is the same for almost all the elements. The **information content** of a particular split can be defined in terms of entropy as

$$\text{Information-content}(S, \{S_1, S_2, \ldots, S_r\})) = -\sum_{i-1}^{r} \frac{|S_i|}{|S|} \log_2 \frac{|S_i|}{|S|}$$

All of this leads to a definition: The **best split** for an attribute is the one that gives the maximum **information gain ratio**, defined as

$$\frac{\text{Information-gain}(S, \{S_1, S_2, \ldots, S_r\})}{\text{Information-content}(S, \{S_1, S_2, \ldots, S_r\})}$$

Finding Best Splits

How do we find the best split for an attribute? How to split an attribute depends on the type of the attribute. Attributes can be either **continuous valued**, that is, the values can be ordered in a fashion meaningful to classification, such as age or income, or can be **categorical**, that is, they have no meaningful order, such as department names or country names. We do not expect the sort order of department names or country names to have any significance to classification.

Usually attributes that are numbers (integers/reals) are treated as continuous valued while character string attributes are treated as categorical, but this may be controlled by the user of the system. In our example, we have treated the attribute *degree* as categorical, and the attribute *income* as continuous valued.

We first consider how to find best splits for continuous-valued attributes. For simplicity, we shall only consider **binary splits** of continuous-valued attributes, that is, splits that result in two children. The case of **multiway splits** is more complicated; see the bibliographical notes for references on the subject.

To find the best binary split of a continuous-valued attribute, we first sort the attribute values in the training instances. We then compute the information gain obtained by splitting at each value. For example, if the training instances have values $1, 10, 15$, and 25 for an attribute, the split points considered are $1, 10$, and 15; in each case values less than or equal to the split point form one partition and the rest of the values form the other partition. The best binary split for the attribute is the split that gives the maximum information gain.

For a categorical attribute, we can have a multiway split, with a child for each value of the attribute. This works fine for categorical attributes with only a few distinct values, such as degree or gender. However, if the attribute has many distinct values, such as department names in a large company, creating a child for each value is not a good idea. In such cases, we would try to combine multiple values into each child, to create a smaller number of children. See the bibliographical notes for references on how to do so.

Decision-Tree Construction Algorithm

The main idea of decision tree construction is to evaluate different attributes and different partitioning conditions, and pick the attribute and partitioning condition that results in the maximum information gain ratio. The same procedure works recur-

procedure GrowTree(*S*)
    Partition(*S*);

procedure Partition (*S*)
    if (*purity*(*S*) > δ_p **or** $|S| < \delta_s$) **then**
        return;
    for each attribute *A*
        evaluate splits on attribute *A*;
    Use best split found (across all attributes) to partition
        S into $S_1, S_2, \ldots, S_r$;
    for $i = 1, 2, \ldots, r$
        Partition(S_i);

Figure 22.7   Recursive construction of a decision tree.

sively on each of the sets resulting from the split, thereby recursively constructing a decision tree. If the data can be perfectly classified, the recursion stops when the purity of a set is 0. However, often data are noisy, or a set may be so small that partitioning it further may not be justified statistically. In this case, the recursion stops when the purity of a set is "sufficiently high," and the class of resulting leaf is defined as the class of the majority of the elements of the set. In general, different branches of the tree could grow to different levels.

Figure 22.7 shows pseudocode for a recursive tree construction procedure, which takes a set of training instances *S* as parameter. The recursion stops when the set is sufficiently pure or the set *S* is too small for further partitioning to be statistically significant. The parameters δ_p and δ_s define cutoffs for purity and size; the system may give them default values, that may be overridden by users.

There are a wide variety of decision tree construction algorithms, and we outline the distinguishing features of a few of them. See the bibliographical notes for details. With very large data sets, partitioning may be expensive, since it involves repeated copying. Several algorithms have therefore been developed to minimize the I/O and computation cost when the training data are larger than available memory.

Several of the algorithms also prune subtrees of the generated decision tree to reduce **overfitting**: A subtree is overfitted if it has been so highly tuned to the specifics of the training data that it makes many classification errors on other data. A subtree is pruned by replacing it with a leaf node. There are different pruning heuristics; one heuristic uses part of the training data to build the tree and another part of the training data to test it. The heuristic prunes a subtree if it finds that misclassification on the test instances would be reduced if the subtree were replaced by a leaf node.

We can generate classification rules from a decision tree, if we so desire. For each leaf we generate a rule as follows: The left-hand side is the conjunction of all the split conditions on the path to the leaf, and the class is the class of the majority of the training instances at the leaf. An example of such a classification rule is

$$degree = masters \textbf{ and } income > 75,000 \Rightarrow excellent$$

22.3.2.2 Other Types of Classifiers

There are several types of classifiers other than decision tree classifiers. Two types that have been quite useful are *neural net classifiers* and *Bayesian classifiers*. Neural net classifiers use the training data to train artificial neural nets. There is a large body of literature on neural nets, and we do not consider them further here.

Bayesian classifiers find the distribution of attribute values for each class in the training data; when given a new instance d, they use the distribution information to estimate, for each class c_j, the probability that instance d belongs to class c_j, denoted by $p(c_j|d)$, in a manner outlined here. The class with maximum probability becomes the predicted class for instance d.

To find the probability $p(c_j|d)$ of instance d being in class c_j, Bayesian classifiers use **Bayes' theorem**, which says

$$p(c_j|d) = \frac{p(d|c_j)p(c_j)}{p(d)}$$

where $p(d|c_j)$ is the probability of generating instance d given class c_j, $p(c_j)$ is the probability of occurrence of class c_j, and $p(d)$ is the probability of instance d occurring. Of these, $p(d)$ can be ignored since it is the same for all classes. $p(c_j)$ is simply the fraction of training instances that belong to class c_j.

Finding $p(d|c_j)$ exactly is difficult, since it requires a complete distribution of instances of c_j. To simplify the task, **naive Bayesian classifiers** assume attributes have independent distributions, and thereby estimate

$$p(d|c_j) = p(d_1|c_j) * p(d_2|c_j) * \ldots * p(d_n|c_j)$$

That is, the probability of the instance d occurring is the product of the probability of occurrence of each of the attribute values d_i of d, given the class is c_j.

The probabilities $p(d_i|c_j)$ derive from the distribution of values for each attribute i, for each class class c_j. This distribution is computed from the training instances that belong to each class c_j; the distribution is usually approximated by a histogram. For instance, we may divide the range of values of attribute i into equal intervals, and store the fraction of instances of class c_j that fall in each interval. Given a value d_i for attribute i, the value of $p(d_i|c_j)$ is simply the fraction of instances belonging to class c_j that fall in the interval to which d_i belongs.

A significant benefit of Bayesian classifiers is that they can classify instances with unknown and null attribute values—unknown or null attributes are just omitted from the probability computation. In contrast, decision tree classifiers cannot meaningfully handle situations where an instance to be classified has a null value for a partitioning attribute used to traverse further down the decision tree.

22.3.2.3 Regression

Regression deals with the prediction of a value, rather than a class. Given values for a set of variables, $X_1, X_2, \ldots, X_n$, we wish to predict the value of a variable Y. For instance, we could treat the level of education as a number and income as another number, and, on the basis of these two variables, we wish to predict the likelihood of default, which could be a percentage chance of defaulting, or the amount involved in the default.

One way is to infer coefficients $a_0, a_1, a_1, \ldots, a_n$ such that

$$Y = a_0 + a_1 * X_1 + a_2 * X_2 + \cdots + a_n * X_n$$

Finding such a linear polynomial is called **linear regression**. In general, we wish to find a curve (defined by a polynomial or other formula) that fits the data; the process is also called **curve fitting**.

The fit may only be approximate, because of noise in the data or because the relationship is not exactly a polynomial, so regression aims to find coefficients that give the best possible fit. There are standard techniques in statistics for finding regression coefficients. We do not discuss these techniques here, but the bibliographical notes provide references.

22.3.3 Association Rules

Retail shops are often interested in **associations** between different items that people buy. Examples of such associations are:

- Someone who buys bread is quite likely also to buy milk

- A person who bought the book *Database System Concepts* is quite likely also to buy the book *Operating System Concepts*.

Association information can be used in several ways. When a customer buys a particular book, an online shop may suggest associated books. A grocery shop may decide to place bread close to milk, since they are often bought together, to help shoppers finish their task faster. Or the shop may place them at opposite ends of a row, and place other associated items in between to tempt people to buy those items as well, as the shoppers walk from one end of the row to the other. A shop that offers discounts on one associated item may not offer a discount on the other, since the customer will probably buy the other anyway.

Association Rules

An example of an association rule is

$$bread \Rightarrow milk$$

In the context of grocery-store purchases, the rule says that customers who buy bread also tend to buy milk with a high probability. An association rule must have an associated **population**: the population consists of a set of **instances**. In the grocery-store example, the population may consist of all grocery store purchases; each purchase is an instance. In the case of a bookstore, the population may consist of all people who made purchases, regardless of when they made a purchase. Each customer is an instance. Here, the analyst has decided that when a purchase is made is not significant, whereas for the grocery-store example, the analyst may have decided to concentrate on single purchases, ignoring multiple visits by the same customer.

Rules have an associated *support*, as well as an associated *confidence*. These are defined in the context of the population:

- **Support** is a measure of what fraction of the population satisfies both the antecedent and the consequent of the rule.

    For instance, suppose only 0.001 percent of all purchases include milk and screwdrivers. The support for the rule

$$milk \Rightarrow screwdrivers$$

    is low. The rule may not even be statistically significant—perhaps there was only a single purchase that included both milk and screwdrivers. Businesses are usually not interested in rules that have low support, since they involve few customers, and are not worth bothering about.

    On the other hand, if 50 percent of all purchases involve milk and bread, then support for rules involving bread and milk (and no other item) is relatively high, and such rules may be worth attention. Exactly what minimum degree of support is considered desirable depends on the application.

- **Confidence** is a measure of how often the consequent is true when the antecedent is true. For instance, the rule

$$bread \Rightarrow milk$$

    has a confidence of 80 percent if 80 percent of the purchases that include bread also include milk. A rule with a low confidence is not meaningful. In business applications, rules usually have confidences significantly less than 100 percent, whereas in other domains, such as in physics, rules may have high confidences.

    Note that the confidence of $bread \Rightarrow milk$ may be very different from the confidence of $milk \Rightarrow bread$, although both have the same support.

Finding Association Rules

To discover association rules of the form

$$i_1, i_2, \ldots, i_n \Rightarrow i_0$$

we first find sets of items with sufficient support, called **large itemsets**. In our example we find sets of items that are included in a sufficiently large number of instances. We will shortly see how to compute large itemsets.

For each large itemset, we then output all rules with sufficient confidence that involve all and only the elements of the set. For each large itemset S, we output a rule $S - s \Rightarrow s$ for every subset $s \subset S$, provided $S - s \Rightarrow s$ has sufficient confidence; the confidence of the rule is given by support of s divided by support of S.

We now consider how to generate all large itemsets. If the number of possible sets of items is small, a single pass over the data suffices to detect the level of support for all the sets. A count, initialized to 0, is maintained for each set of items. When a purchase record is fetched, the count is incremented for each set of items such that all items in the set are contained in the purchase. For instance, if a purchase included items a, b, and c, counts would be incremented for $\{a\}$, $\{b\}$, $\{c\}$, $\{a,b\}$, $\{b,c\}$, $\{a,c\}$, and $\{a,b,c\}$. Those sets with a sufficiently high count at the end of the pass correspond to items that have a high degree of association.

The number of sets grows exponentially, making the procedure just described infeasible if the number of items is large. Luckily, almost all the sets would normally have very low support; optimizations have been developed to eliminate most such sets from consideration. These techniques use multiple passes on the database, considering only some sets in each pass.

In the **a priori** technique for generating large itemsets, only sets with single items are considered in the first pass. In the second pass, sets with two items are considered, and so on.

At the end of a pass all sets with sufficient support are output as large itemsets. Sets found to have too little support at the end of a pass are eliminated. Once a set is eliminated, none of its supersets needs to be considered. In other words, in pass i we need to count only supports for sets of size i such that all subsets of the set have been found to have sufficiently high support; it suffices to test all subsets of size $i - 1$ to ensure this property. At the end of some pass i, we would find that no set of size i has sufficient support, so we do not need to consider any set of size $i + 1$. Computation then terminates.

22.3.4   Other Types of Associations

Using plain association rules has several shortcomings. One of the major shortcomings is that many associations are not very interesting, since they can be predicted. For instance, if many people buy cereal and many people buy bread, we can predict that a fairly large number of people would buy both, even if there is no connection between the two purchases. What would be interesting is a **deviation** from the expected co-occurrence of the two. In statistical terms, we look for **correlations** between items; correlations can be positive, in that the co-occurrence is higher than would have been expected, or negative, in that the items co-occur less frequently than predicted. See a standard textbook on statistics for more information about correlations.

Another important class of data-mining applications is sequence associations (or correlations). Time-series data, such as stock prices on a sequence of days, form an example of sequence data. Stock-market analysts want to find associations among stock-market price sequences. An example of such a association is the following rule: "Whenever bond rates go up, the stock prices go down within 2 days." Discovering such association between sequences can help us to make intelligent investment decisions. See the bibliographical notes for references to research on this topic.

Deviations from temporal patterns are often interesting. For instance, if a company has been growing at a steady rate each year, a deviation from the usual growth rate is surprising. If sales of winter clothes go down in summer, it is not surprising, since we can predict it from past years; a deviation that we could not have predicted from past experience would be considered interesting. Mining techniques can find deviations from what one would have expected on the basis of past temporal/sequential patterns. See the bibliographical notes for references to research on this topic.

22.3.5 Clustering

Intuitively, clustering refers to the problem of finding clusters of points in the given data. The problem of **clustering** can be formalized from distance metrics in several ways. One way is to phrase it as the problem of grouping points into k sets (for a given k) so that the average distance of points from the *centroid* of their assigned cluster is minimized.[5] Another way is to group points so that the average distance between every pair of points in each cluster is minimized. There are other definitions too; see the bibliographical notes for details. But the intuition behind all these definitions is to group similar points together in a single set.

Another type of clustering appears in classification systems in biology. (Such classification systems do not attempt to *predict* classes, rather they attempt to cluster related items together.) For instance, leopards and humans are clustered under the class mammalia, while crocodiles and snakes are clustered under reptilia. Both mammalia and reptilia come under the common class chordata. The clustering of mammalia has further subclusters, such as carnivora and primates. We thus have **hierarchical clustering**. Given characteristics of different species, biologists have created a complex hierarchical clustering scheme grouping related species together at different levels of the hierarchy.

Hierarchical clustering is also useful in other domains—for clustering documents, for example. Internet directory systems (such as Yahoo's) cluster related documents in a hierarchical fashion (see Section 22.5.5). Hierarchical clustering algorithms can be classified as **agglomerative clustering** algorithms, which start by building small clusters and then creater higher levels, or **divisive clustering** algorithms, which first create higher levels of the hierarchical clustering, then refine each resulting cluster into lower level clusters.

The statistics community has studied clustering extensively. Database research has provided scalable clustering algorithms that can cluster very large data sets (that may not fit in memory). The Birch clustering algorithm is one such algorithm. Intuitively, data points are inserted into a multidimensional tree structure (based on R-trees, described in Section 23.3.5.3), and guided to appropriate leaf nodes based on nearness to representative points in the internal nodes of the tree. Nearby points are thus clustered together in leaf nodes, and summarized if there are more points than fit in memory. Some postprocessing after insertion of all points gives the desired overall clustering. See the bibliographical notes for references to the Birch algorithm, and other techniques for clustering, including algorithms for hierarchical clustering.

An interesting application of clustering is to predict what new movies (or books, or music) a person is likely to be interested in, on the basis of:

1. The person's past preferences in movies

2. Other people with similar past preferences

3. The preferences of such people for new movies

---

5. The centroid of a set of points is defined as a point whose coordinate on each dimension is the average of the coordinates of all the points of that set on that dimension. For example in two dimensions, the centroid of a set of points $\{ (x_1, y_1), (x_2, y_2), \ldots, (x_n, y_n) \}$ is given by $\left(\frac{\sum_{i=1}^{n} x_i}{n}, \frac{\sum_{i=1}^{n} y_i}{n} \right)$

One approach to this problem is as follows. To find people with similar past preferences we create clusters of people based on their preferences for movies. The accuracy of clustering can be improved by previously clustering movies by their similarity, so even if people have not seen the same movies, if they have seen similar movies they would be clustered together. We can repeat the clustering, alternately clustering people, then movies, then people, and so on till we reach an equilibrium. Given a new user, we find a cluster of users most similar to that user, on the basis of the user's preferences for movies already seen. We then predict movies in movie clusters that are popular with that user's cluster as likely to be interesting to the new user. In fact, this problem is an instance of *collaborative filtering*, where users collaborate in the task of filtering information to find information of interest.

22.3.6 Other Types of Mining

Text mining applies data mining techniques to textual documents. For instance, there are tools that form clusters on pages that a user has visited; this helps users when they browse the history of their browsing to find pages they have visited earlier. The distance between pages can be based, for instance, on common words in the pages (see Section 22.5.1.3). Another application is to classify pages into a Web directory automatically, according to their similarity with other pages (see Section 22.5.5).

Data-visualization systems help users to examine large volumes of data, and to detect patterns visually. Visual displays of data—such as maps, charts, and other graphical representations—allow data to be presented compactly to users. A single graphical screen can encode as much information as a far larger number of text screens. For example, if the user wants to find out whether production problems at plants are correlated to the locations of the plants, the problem locations can be encoded in a special color—say, red—on a map. The user can then quickly discover locations where problems are occurring. The user may then form hypotheses about why problems are occurring in those locations, and may verify the hypotheses quantitatively against the database.

As another example, information about values can be encoded as a color, and can be displayed with as little as one pixel of screen area. To detect associations between pairs of items, we can use a two-dimensional pixel matrix, with each row and each column representing an item. The percentage of transactions that buy both items can be encoded by the color intensity of the pixel. Items with high association will show up as bright pixels in the screen—easy to detect against the darker background.

Data visualization systems do not automatically detect patterns, but provide system support for users to detect patterns. Since humans are very good at detecting visual patterns, data visualization is an important component of data mining.

22.4 Data Warehousing

Large companies have presences in many places, each of which may generate a large volume of data. For instance, large retail chains have hundreds or thousands of stores, whereas insurance companies may have data from thousands of local branches. Further, large organizations have a complex internal organization structure, and there-

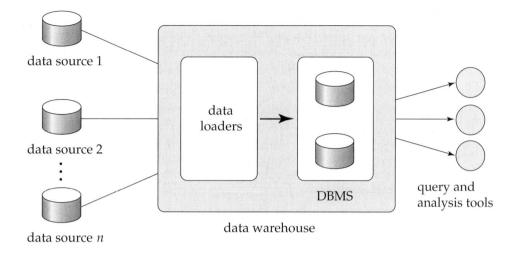

Figure 22.8   Data-warehouse architecture.

fore different data may be present in different locations, or on different operational systems, or under different schemas. For instance, manufacturing-problem data and customer-complaint data may be stored on different database systems. Corporate decision makers require access to information from all such sources. Setting up queries on individual sources is both cumbersome and inefficient. Moreover, the sources of data may store only current data, whereas decision makers may need access to past data as well; for instance, information about how purchase patterns have changed in the past year could be of great importance. Data warehouses provide a solution to these problems.

A **data warehouse** is a repository (or archive) of information gathered from multiple sources, stored under a unified schema, at a single site. Once gathered, the data are stored for a long time, permitting access to historical data. Thus, data warehouses provide the user a single consolidated interface to data, making decision-support queries easier to write. Moreover, by accessing information for decision support from a data warehouse, the decision maker ensures that online transaction-processing systems are not affected by the decision-support workload.

22.4.1   Components of a Data Warehouse

Figure 22.8 shows the architecture of a typical data warehouse, and illustrates the gathering of data, the storage of data, and the querying and data-analysis support. Among the issues to be addressed in building a warehouse are the following:

- **When and how to gather data.** In a **source-driven architecture** for gathering data, the data sources transmit new information, either continually (as transaction processing takes place), or periodically (nightly, for example). In a **destination-driven architecture**, the data warehouse periodically sends requests for new data to the sources.

Unless updates at the sources are replicated at the warehouse via two-phase commit, the warehouse will never be quite up to date with the sources. Two-phase commit is usually far too expensive to be an option, so data warehouses typically have slightly out-of-date data. That, however, is usually not a problem for decision-support systems.

- **What schema to use.** Data sources that have been constructed independently are likely to have different schemas. In fact, they may even use different data models. Part of the task of a warehouse is to perform schema integration, and to convert data to the integrated schema before they are stored. As a result, the data stored in the warehouse are not just a copy of the data at the sources. Instead, they can be thought of as a materialized view of the data at the sources.

- **Data cleansing.** The task of correcting and preprocessing data is called **data cleansing**. Data sources often deliver data with numerous minor inconsistencies, that can be corrected. For example, names are often misspelled, and addresses may have street/area/city names misspelled, or zip codes entered incorrectly. These can be corrected to a reasonable extent by consulting a database of street names and zip codes in each city. Address lists collected from multiple sources may have duplicates that need to be eliminated in a **merge–purge operation**. Records for multiple individuals in a house may be grouped together so only one mailing is sent to each house; this operation is called **householding**.

- **How to propagate updates.** Updates on relations at the data sources must be propagated to the data warehouse. If the relations at the data warehouse are exactly the same as those at the data source, the propagation is straightforward. If they are not, the problem of propagating updates is basically the *view-maintenance* problem, which was discussed in Section 14.5.

- **What data to summarize.** The raw data generated by a transaction-processing system may be too large to store online. However, we can answer many queries by maintaining just summary data obtained by aggregation on a relation, rather than maintaining the entire relation. For example, instead of storing data about every sale of clothing, we can store total sales of clothing by item-name and category.

  Suppose that a relation r has been replaced by a summary relation s. Users may still be permitted to pose queries as though the relation r were available online. If the query requires only summary data, it may be possible to transform it into an equivalent one using s instead; see Section 14.5.

22.4.2   Warehouse Schemas

Data warehouses typically have schemas that are designed for data analysis, using tools such as OLAP tools. Thus, the data are usually multidimensional data, with dimension attributes and measure attributes. Tables containing multidimensional data are called **fact tables** and are usually very large. A table recording sales information for a retail store, with one tuple for each item that is sold, is a typical example of a fact table. The dimensions of the *sales* table would include what the item is (usually an item identifier such as that used in bar codes), the date when the item is sold, which location (store) the item was sold from, which customer bought the item, and so on. The measure attributes may include the number of items sold and the price of the items.

To minimize storage requirements, dimension attributes are usually short identifiers that are foreign keys into other other tables called **dimension tables**. For instance, a fact table *sales* would have attributes *item-id*, *store-id*, *customer-id*, and *date*, and measure attributes *number* and *price*. The attribute *store-id* is a foreign key into a dimension table *store*, which has other attributes such as store location (city, state, country). The *item-id* attribute of the *sales* table would be a foreign key into a dimension table *item-info*, which would contain information such as the name of the item, the category to which the item belongs, and other item details such as color and size. The *customer-id* attribute would be a foreign key into a *customer* table containing attributes such as name and address of the customer. We can also view the *date* attribute as a foreign key into a *date-info* table giving the month, quarter, and year of each date.

The resultant schema appears in Figure 22.9. Such a schema, with a fact table, multiple dimension tables, and foreign keys from the fact table to the dimension tables, is called a **star schema**. More complex data warehouse designs may have multiple levels of dimension tables; for instance, the *item-info* table may have an attribute *manufacturer-id* that is a foreign key into another table giving details of the manufacturer. Such schemas are called *snowflake schema*s. Complex data warehouse designs may also have more than one fact table.

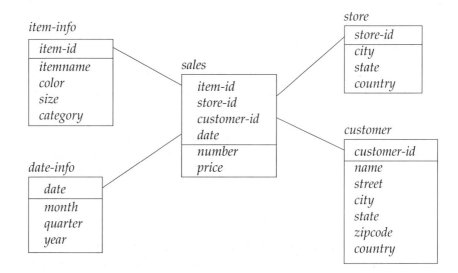

Figure 22.9   Star schema for a data warehouse.

22.5 Information-Retrieval Systems

The field of **information retrieval** has developed in parallel with the field of databases. In the traditional model used in the field of information retrieval, information is organized into documents, and it is assumed that there is a large number of documents. Data contained in documents is unstructured, without any associated schema. The process of information retrieval consists of locating relevant documents, on the basis of user input, such as keywords or example documents.

The Web provides a convenient way to get to, and to interact with, information sources across the Internet. However, a persistent problem facing the Web is the explosion of stored information, with little guidance to help the user to locate what is interesting. Information retrieval has played a critical role in making the Web a productive and useful tool, especially for researchers.

Traditional examples of information-retrieval systems are online library catalogs and online document-management systems such as those that store newspaper articles. The data in such systems are organized as a collection of *documents*; a newspaper article or a catalog entry (in a library catalog) are examples of documents. In the context of the Web, usually each HTML page is considered to be a document.

A user of such a system may want to retrieve a particular document or a particular class of documents. The intended documents are typically described by a set of **keywords**—for example, the keywords "database system" may be used to locate books on database systems, and the keywords "stock" and "scandal" may be used to locate articles about stock-market scandals. Documents have associated with them a set of keywords, and documents whose keywords contain those supplied by the user are retrieved.

Keyword-based information retrieval can be used not only for retrieving textual data, but also for retrieving other types of data, such as video or audio data, that have descriptive keywords associated with them. For instance, a video movie may have associated with it keywords such as its title, director, actors, type, and so on.

There are several differences between this model and the models used in traditional database systems.

- Database systems deal with several operations that are not addressed in information-retrieval systems. For instance, database systems deal with updates and with the associated transactional requirements of concurrency control and durability. These matters are viewed as less important in information systems. Similarly, database systems deal with structured information organized with relatively complex data models (such as the relational model or object-oriented data models), whereas information-retrieval systems traditionally have used a much simpler model, where the information in the database is organized simply as a collection of unstructured documents.

- Information-retrieval systems deal with several issues that have not been addressed adequately in database systems. For instance, the field of information retrieval has dealt with the problems of managing unstructured documents, such as approximate searching by keywords, and of ranking of documents on estimated degree of relevance of the documents to the query.

22.5.1 Keyword Search

Information-retrieval systems typically allow query expressions formed using keywords and the logical connectives *and, or,* and *not.* For example, a user could ask for all documents that contain the keywords "motorcycle *and* maintenance," or documents that contain the keywords "computer *or* microprocessor," or even documents that contain the keyword "computer *but not* database." A query containing keywords without any of the above connectives is assumed to have *and*s implicitly connecting the keywords.

In **full text** retrieval, all the words in each document are considered to be keywords. For unstructured documents, full text retrieval is essential since there may be no information about what words in the document are keywords. We shall use the word **term** to refer to the words in a document, since all words are keywords.

In its simplest form an information retrieval system locates and returns all documents that contain all the keywords in the query, if the query has no connectives; connectives are handled as you would expect. More sophisticated systems estimate relevance of documents to a query so that the documents can be shown in order of estimated relevance. They use information about term occurrences, as well as hyperlink information, to estimate relevance; Section 22.5.1.1 and 22.5.1.2 outline how to do so. Section 22.5.1.3 outlines how to define similarity of documents, and use similarity for searching. Some systems also attempt to provide a better set of answers by using the meanings of terms, rather than just the syntactic occurrence of terms, as outlined in Section 22.5.1.4.

22.5.1.1 Relevance Ranking Using Terms

The set of all documents that satisfy a query expression may be very large; in particular, there are billions of documents on the Web, and most keyword queries on a Web search engine find hundreds of thousands of documents containing the keywords. Full text retrieval makes this problem worse: Each document may contain many terms, and even terms that are only mentioned in passing are treated equivalently with documents where the term is indeed relevant. Irrelevant documents may get retrieved as a result.

Information retrieval systems therefore estimate relevance of documents to a query, and return only highly ranked documents as answers. Relevance ranking is not an exact science, but there are some well-accepted approaches.

The first question to address is, given a particular term t, how relevant is a particular document d to the term. One approach is to use the the number of occurrences of the term in the document as a measure of its relevance, on the assumption that relevant terms are likely to be mentioned many times in a document. Just counting the number of occurrences of a term is usually not a good indicator: First, the number of occurrences depends on the length of the document, and second, a document containing 10 occurrences of a term may not be 10 times as relevant as a document containing one occurrence.

One way of measuring $r(d, t)$, the relevance of a document d to a term t, is

$$r(d, t) = \log \left(1 + \frac{n(d, t)}{n(d)} \right)$$

where $n(d)$ denotes the number of terms in the document and $n(d, t)$ denotes the number of occurrences of term t in the document d. Observe that this metric takes the length of the document into account. The relevance grows with more occurrences of a term in the document, although it is not directly proportional to the number of occurrences.

Many systems refine the above metric by using other information. For instance, if the term occurs in the title, or the author list, or the abstract, the document would be considered more relevant to the term. Similarly, if the first occurrence of a term is late in the document, the document may be considered less relevant than if the first occurrence is early in the document. The above notions can be formalized by extensions of the formula we have shown for $r(d, t)$. In the information retrieval community, the relevance of a document to a term is referred to as **term frequency**, regardless of the exact formula used.

A query Q may contain multiple keywords. The relevance of a document to a query with two or more keywords is estimated by combining the relevance measures of the document to each keyword. A simple way of combining the measures is to add them up. However, not all terms used as keywords are equal. Suppose a query uses two terms, one of which occurs frequently, such as "web," and another that is less frequent, such as "Silberschatz." A document containing "Silberschatz" but not "web" should be ranked higher than a document containing the term "web" but not "Silberschatz."

To fix the above problem, weights are assigned to terms using the **inverse document frequency**, defined as $1/n(t)$, where $n(t)$ denotes the number of documents (among those indexed by the system) that contain the term t. The **relevance** of a document d to a set of terms Q is then defined as

$$r(d, Q) = \sum_{t \in Q} \frac{r(d, t)}{n(t)}$$

This measure can be further refined if the user is permitted to specify weights $w(t)$ for terms in the query, in which case the user-specified weights are also taken into account by using $w(t)/n(t)$ in place of $1/n(t)$.

Almost all text documents (in English) contain words such as "and," "or," "a," and so on, and hence these words are useless for querying purposes since their inverse document frequency is extremely low. Information-retrieval systems define a set of words, called **stop words**, containing 100 or so of the most common words, and remove this set from the document when indexing; such words are not used as keywords, and are discarded if present in the keywords supplied by the user.

Another factor taken into account when a query contains multiple terms is the **proximity** of the term in the document. If the terms occur close to each other in the document, the document would be ranked higher than if they occur far apart. The formula for $r(d, Q)$ can be modified to take proximity into account.

Given a query Q, the job of an information retrieval system is to return documents in descending order of their relevance to Q. Since there may be a very large number of documents that are relevant, information retrieval systems typically return only the first few documents with the highest degree of estimated relevance, and permit users to interactively request further documents.

22.5.1.2 Relevance Using Hyperlinks

Early Web search engines ranked documents by using only relevance measures similar to those described in Section 22.5.1.1. However, researchers soon realized that Web documents have information that plain text documents do not have, namely hyperlinks. And in fact, the relevance ranking of a document is affected more by hyperlinks that point *to* the document, than by hyperlinks going out of the document.

The basic idea of site ranking is to find sites that are popular, and to rank pages from such sites higher than pages from other sites. A site is identified by the internet address part of the URL, such as www.bell-labs.com in a URL http://www.bell-labs.com/topic/books/db-book. A site usually contains multiple Web pages. Since most searches are intended to find information from popular sites, ranking pages from popular sites higher is generally a good idea. For instance, the term "google" may occur in vast numbers of pages, but the site google.com is the most popular among the sites with pages that contain the term "google". Documents from google.com containing the term "google" would therefore be ranked as the most relevant to the term "google".

This raises the question of how to define the popularity of a site. One way would be to find how many times a site is accessed. However, getting such information is impossible without the cooperation of the site, and is infeasible for a Web search engine to implement. A very effective alternative uses hyperlinks; it defines $p(s)$, the **popularity of a site** s, as the number of sites that contain at least one page with a link to site s.

Traditional measures of relevance of the page (which we saw in Section 22.5.1.2) can be combined with the popularity of the site containing the page to get an overall measure of the relevance of the page. Pages with high overall relevance value are returned as answers to a query, as before.

Note also that we used the popularity of a *site* as a measure of relevance of individual pages at the site, not the popularity of individual *pages*. There are at least two reasons for this. First, most sites contain only links to root pages of other sites, so all other pages would appear to have almost zero popularity, when in fact they may be accessed quite frequently by following links from the root page. Second, there are far fewer sites than pages, so computing and using popularity of sites is cheaper than computing and using popularity of pages.

There are more refined notions of popularity of sites. For instance, a link from a popular site to another site s may be considered to be a better indication of the popularity of s than a link to s from a less popular site.[6] This notion of popularity

---

6. This is similar in some sense to giving extra weight to endorsements of products by celebrities (such as film stars), so its significance is open to question!

is in fact circular, since the popularity of a site is defined by the popularity of other sites, and there may be cycles of links between sites. However, the popularity of sites can be defined by a system of simultaneous linear equations, which can be solved by matrix manipulation techniques. The linear equations are defined in such a way that they have a unique and well-defined solution.

The popular Web search engine google.com uses the referring-site popularity idea in its definition **page rank**, which is a measure of popularity of a page. This approach of ranking of pages gave results so much better than previously used ranking techniques, that google.com became a widely used search engine, in a rather short period of time.

There is another, somewhat similar, approach, derived interestingly from a theory of social networking developed by sociologists in the 1950s. In the social networking context, the goal was to define the prestige of people. For example, the president of the United States has high prestige since a large number of people know him. If someone is known by multiple prestigious people, then she also has high prestige, even if she is not known by as large a number of people.

The above idea was developed into a notion of *hubs* and *authorities* that takes into account the presence of directories that link to pages containing useful information. A **hub** is a page that stores links to many pages; it does not in itself contain actual information on a topic, but points to pages that contain actual information. In contrast, an **authority** is a page that contains actual information on a topic, although it may not be directly pointed to by many pages. Each page then gets a prestige value as a hub (*hub-prestige*), and another prestige value as an authority (*authority-prestige*). The definitions of prestige, as before, are cyclic and are defined by a set of simultaneous linear equations. A page gets higher hub-prestige if it points to many pages with high authority-prestige, while a page gets higher authority-prestige if it is pointed to by many pages with high hub-prestige. Given a query, pages with highest authority-prestige are ranked higher than other pages. See the bibliographical notes for references giving further details.

22.5.1.3 Similarity-Based Retrieval

Certain information-retrieval systems permit **similarity-based retrieval**. Here, the user can give the system document A, and ask the system to retrieve documents that are "similar" to A. The similarity of a document to another may be defined, for example, on the basis of common terms. One approach is to find k terms in A with highest values of $r(d, t)$, and to use these k terms as a query to find relevance of other documents. The terms in the query are themselves weighted by $r(d, t)$.

If the set of documents similar to A is large, the system may present the user a few of the similar documents, allow him to choose the most relevant few, and start a new search based on similarity to A *and* to the chosen documents. The resultant set of documents is likely to be what the user intended to find.

The same idea is also used to help users who find many documents that appear to be relevant on the basis of the keywords, but are not. In such a situation, instead of adding further keywords to the query, users may be allowed to identify one or a few of the returned documents as relevant; the system then uses the identified documents to find other similar ones. The resultant set of documents is likely to be what the user intended to find.

22.5.1.4   Synonyms and Homonyms

Consider the problem of locating documents about motorcycle maintenance for the keywords "motorcycle" and "maintenance." Suppose that the keywords for each document are the words in the title and the names of the authors. The document titled *Motorcycle Repair* would not be retrieved, since the word "maintenance" does not occur in its title.

We can solve that problem by making use of **synonyms**. Each word can have a set of synonyms defined, and the occurrence of a word can be replaced by the *or* of all its synonyms (including the word itself). Thus, the query "motorcycle *and* repair" can be replaced by "motorcycle *and* (repair *or* maintenance)." This query would find the desired document.

Keyword-based queries also suffer from the opposite problem, of **homonyms**, that is single words with multiple meanings. For instance, the word object has different meanings as a noun and as a verb. The word table may refer to a dinner table, or to a relational table. Some keyword query systems attempt to disambiguate the meaning of words in documents, and when a user poses a query, they find out the intended meaning by asking the user. The returned documents are those that use the term in the intended meaning of the user. However, disambiguating meanings of words in documents is not an easy task, so not many systems implement this idea.

In fact, a danger even with using synonyms to extend queries is that the synonyms may themselves have different meanings. Documents that use the synonyms with an alternative intended meaning would be retrieved. The user is then left wondering why the system thought that a particular retrieved document is relevant, if it contains neither the keywords the user specified, nor words whose intended meaning in the document is synonymous with specified keywords! It is therefore advisable to verify synonyms with the user, before using them to extend a query submitted by the user.

22.5.2   Indexing of Documents

An effective index structure is important for efficient processing of queries in an information-retrieval system. Documents that contain a specified keyword can be efficiently located by using an **inverted index**, which maps each keyword K_i to the set S_i of (identifiers of) the documents that contain K_i. To support relevance ranking based on proximity of keywords, such an index may provide not just identifiers of documents, but also a list of locations in the document where the keyword appears. Since such indices must be stored on disk, the index organization also attempts to minimize the number of I/O operations to retrieve the set of (identifiers of) documents that contain a keyword. Thus, the system may attempt to keep the set of documents for a keyword in consecutive disk pages.

The *and* operation finds documents that contain all of a specified set of keywords $K_1, K_2, \ldots, K_n$. We implement the *and* operation by first retrieving the sets of document identifiers $S_1, S_2, \ldots, S_n$ of all documents that contain the respective keywords.

The intersection, $S_1 \cap S_2 \cap \cdots \cap S_n$, of the sets gives the document identifiers of the desired set of documents. The *or* operation gives the set of all documents that contain at least one of the keywords $K_1, K_2, \ldots, K_n$. We implement the *or* operation by computing the union, $S_1 \cup S_2 \cup \cdots \cup S_n$, of the sets. The *not* operation finds documents that do not contain a specified keyword K_i. Given a set of document identifiers S, we can eliminate documents that contain the specified keyword K_i by taking the difference $S - S_i$, where S_i is the set of identifiers of documents that contain the keyword K_i.

Given a set of keywords in a query, many information retrieval systems do not insist that the retrieved documents contain all the keywords (unless an *and* operation is explicitly used). In this case, all documents containing at least one of the words are retrieved (as in the *or* operation), but are ranked by their relevance measure.

To use term frequency for ranking, the index structure should additionally maintain the number of times terms occur in each document. To reduce this effort, they may use a compressed representation with only a few bits, which approximates the term frequency. The index should also store the document frequency of each term (that is, the number of documents in which the term appears).

22.5.3 Measuring Retrieval Effectiveness

Each keyword may be contained in a large number of documents; hence, a compact representation is critical to keep space usage of the index low. Thus, the sets of documents for a keyword are maintained in a compressed form. So that storage space is saved, the index is sometimes stored such that the retrieval is approximate; a few relevant documents may not be retrieved (called a **false drop** or **false negative**), or a few irrelevant documents may be retrieved (called a **false positive**). A good index structure will not have *any* false drops, but may permit a few false positives; the system can filter them away later by looking at the keywords that they actually contain. In Web indexing, false positives are not desirable either, since the actual document may not be quickly accessible for filtering.

Two metrics are used to measure how well an information-retrieval system is able to answer queries. The first, **precision**, measures what percentage of the retrieved documents are actually relevant to the query. The second, **recall**, measures what percentage of the documents relevant to the query were retrieved. Ideally both should be 100 percent.

Precision and recall are also important measures for understanding how well a particular document ranking strategy performs. Ranking strategies can result in false negatives and false positives, but in a more subtle sense.

- False negatives may occur when documents are ranked, because relevant documents get low rankings; if we fetched all documents down to documents with very low ranking there would be very few false negatives. However, humans would rarely look beyond the first few tens of returned documents, and may thus miss relevant documents because they are not ranked among the top few. Exactly what is a false negative depends on how many documents are examined.

    Therefore instead of having a single number as the measure of recall, we can measure the recall as a function of the number of documents fetched.

- False positives may occur because irrelevant documents get higher rankings than relevant documents. This too depends on how many documents are examined. One option is to measure precision as a function of number of documents fetched.

A better and more intuitive alternative for measuring precision is to measure it as a function of recall. With this combined measure, both precision and recall can be computed as a function of number of documents, if required.

For instance, we can say that with a recall of 50 percent the precision was 75 percent, whereas at a recall of 75 percent the precision dropped to 60 percent. In general, we can draw a graph relating precision to recall. These measures can be computed for individual queries, then averaged out across a suite of queries in a query benchmark.

Yet another problem with measuring precision and recall lies in how to define which documents are really relevant and which are not. In fact, it requires understanding of natural language, and understanding of the intent of the query, to decide if a document is relevant or not. Researchers therefore have created collections of documents and queries, and have manually tagged documents as relevant or irrelevant to the queries. Different ranking systems can be run on these collections to measure their average precision and recall across multiple queries.

22.5.4   Web Search Engines

Web crawlers are programs that locate and gather information on the Web. They recursively follow hyperlinks present in known documents to find other documents. A crawler retrieves the documents and adds information found in the documents to a combined index; the document is generally not stored, although some search engines do cache a copy of the document to give clients faster access to the documents.

Since the number of documents on the Web is very large, it is not possible to crawl the whole Web in a short period of time; and in fact, all search engines cover only some portions of the Web, not all of it, and their crawlers may take weeks or months to perform a single crawl of all the pages they cover. There are usually many processes, running on multiple machines, involved in crawling. A database stores a set of links (or sites) to be crawled; it assigns links from this set to each crawler process. New links found during a crawl are added to the database, and may be crawled later if they are not crawled immediately. Pages found during a crawl are also handed over to an indexing system, which may be running on a different machine. Pages have to be refetched (that is, links recrawled) periodically to obtain updated information, and to discard sites that no longer exist, so that the information in the search index is kept reasonably up to date.

The indexing system itself runs on multiple machines in parallel. It is not a good idea to add pages to the same index that is being used for queries, since doing so would require concurrency control on the index, and affect query and update performance. Instead, one copy of the index is used to answer queries while another copy is updated with newly crawled pages. At periodic intervals the copies switch over, with the old one being updated while the new copy is being used for queries.

To support very high query rates, the indices may be kept in main memory, and there are multiple machines; the system selectively routes queries to the machines to balance the load among them.

22.5.5   Directories

A typical library user may use a catalog to locate a book for which she is looking. When she retrieves the book from the shelf, however, she is likely to *browse* through other books that are located nearby. Libraries organize books in such a way that related books are kept close together. Hence, a book that is physically near the desired book may be of interest as well, making it worthwhile for users to browse through such books.

To keep related books close together, libraries use a **classification hierarchy**. Books on science are classified together. Within this set of books, there is a finer classification, with computer-science books organized together, mathematics books organized together, and so on. Since there is a relation between mathematics and computer science, relevant sets of books are stored close to each other physically. At yet another level in the classification hierarchy, computer-science books are broken down into subareas, such as operating systems, languages, and algorithms. Figure 22.10 illustrates a classification hierarchy that may be used by a library. Because books can be kept at only one place, each book in a library is classified into exactly one spot in the classification hierarchy.

In an information retrieval system, there is no need to store related documents close together. However, such systems need to *organize documents logically* so as to permit browsing. Thus, such a system could use a classification hierarchy similar to

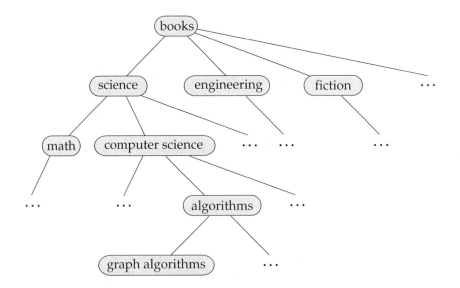

Figure 22.10   A classification hierarchy for a library system.

one that libraries use, and, when it displays a particular document, it can also display a brief description of documents that are close in the hierarchy.

In an information retrieval system, there is no need to keep a document in a single spot in the hierarchy. A document that talks of mathematics for computer scientists could be classified under mathematics as well as under computer science. All that is stored at each spot is an identifier of the document (that is, a pointer to the document), and it is easy to fetch the contents of the document by using the identifier.

As a result of this flexibility, not only can a document be classified under two locations, but also a subarea in the classification hierarchy can itself occur under two areas. The class of "graph algorithm" document can appear both under mathematics and under computer science. Thus, the classification hierarchy is now a directed acyclic graph (DAG), as shown in Figure 22.11. A graph-algorithm document may appear in a single location in the DAG, but can be reached via multiple paths.

A **directory** is simply a classification DAG structure. Each leaf of the directory stores links to documents on the topic represented by the leaf. Internal nodes may also contain links, for example to documents that cannot be classified under any of the child nodes.

To find information on a topic, a user would start at the root of the directory and follow paths down the DAG until reaching a node representing the desired topic. While browsing down the directory, the user can find not only documents on the topic he is interested in, but also find related documents and related classes in the classification hierarchy. The user may learn new information by browsing through documents (or subclasses) within the related classes.

Organizing the enormous amount of information available on the Web into a directory structure is a daunting task.

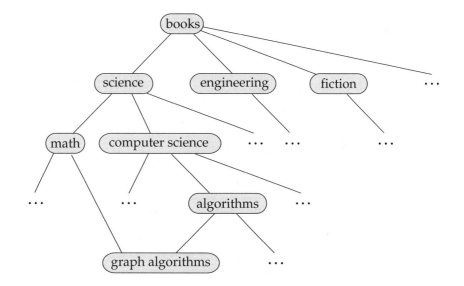

Figure 22.11   A classification DAG for a library information retrieval system.

- The first problem is determining what exactly the directory hierarchy should be.

- The second problem is, given a document, deciding which nodes of the directory are categories relevant to the document.

To tackle the first problem, portals such as Yahoo have teams of "internet librarians" who come up with the classification hierarchy and continually refine it. The *Open Directory Project* is a large collaborative effort, with different volunteers being responsible for organizing different branches of the directory.

The second problem can also be tackled manually by librarians, or Web site maintainers may be responsible for deciding where their sites should lie in the hierarchy. There are also techniques for automatically deciding the location of documents based on computing their similarity to documents that have already been classified.

22.6 Summary

- Decision-support systems analyze online data collected by transaction-processing systems, to help people make business decisions. Since most organizations are extensively computerized today, a very large body of information is available for decision support. Decision-support systems come in various forms, including OLAP systems and data mining systems.

- Online analytical processing (OLAP) tools help analysts view data summarized in different ways, so that they can gain insight into the functioning of an organization.

  - OLAP tools work on multidimensional data, characterized by dimension attributes and measure attributes.
  - The data cube consists of multidimensional data summarized in different ways. Precomputing the data cube helps speed up queries on summaries of data.
  - Cross-tab displays permit users to view two dimensions of multidimensional data at a time, along with summaries of the data.
  - Drill down, rollup, slicing, and dicing are among the operations that users perform with OLAP tools.

- The OLAP component of the SQL:1999 standard provides a variety of new functionality for data analysis, including new aggregate functions, cube and rollup operations, ranking functions, windowing functions, which support summarization on moving windows, and partitioning, with windowing and ranking applied inside each partition.

- Data mining is the process of semiautomatically analyzing large databases to find useful patterns. There are a number of applications of data mining, such as prediction of values based on past examples, finding of associations between purchases, and automatic clustering of people and movies.

- Classification deals with predicting the class of test instances, by using attributes of the test instances, based on attributes of training instances, and the actual class of training instances. Classification can be used, for instance, to predict credit-worthiness levels of new applicants, or to predict the performance of applicants to a university.

    There are several types of classifiers, such as

    □ Decision-tree classifiers. These perform classification by constructing a tree based on training instances with leaves having class labels. The tree is traversed for each test instance to find a leaf, and the class of the leaf is the predicted class.

    Several techniques are available to construct decision trees, most of them based on greedy heuristics.

    □ Bayesian classifiers are simpler to construct than decision-tree classifiers, and work better in the case of missing/null attribute values.

- Association rules identify items that co-occur frequently, for instance, items that tend to be bought by the same customer. Correlations look for deviations from expected levels of association.

- Other types of data mining include clustering, text mining, and data visualization.

- Data warehouses help gather and archive important operational data. Warehouses are used for decision support and analysis on historical data, for instance to predict trends. Data cleansing from input data sources is often a major task in data warehousing. Warehouse schemas tend to be multidimensional, involving one or a few very large fact tables and several much smaller dimension tables.

- Information retrieval systems are used to store and query textual data such as documents. They use a simpler data model than do database systems, but provide more powerful querying capabilities within the restricted model.

    Queries attempt to locate documents that are of interest by specifying, for example, sets of keywords. The query that a user has in mind usually cannot be stated precisely; hence, information-retrieval systems order answers on the basis of potential relevance.

- Relevance ranking makes use of several types of information, such as:

    □ Term frequency: how important each term is to each document.
    □ Inverse document frequency.
    □ Site popularity. Page rank and hub/authority rank are two ways to assign importance to sites on the basis of links to the site.

- Similarity of documents is used to retrieve documents similar to an example document. Synonyms and homonyms complicate the task of information retrieval.

- Precision and recall are two measures of the effectiveness of an information retrieval system.

- Directory structures are used to classify documents with other similar documents.

Review Terms

- Decision-support systems
- Statistical analysis
- Multidimensional data
  - ☐ Measure attributes
  - ☐ Dimension attributes
- Cross-tabulation
- Data cube
- Online analytical processing (OLAP)
  - ☐ Pivoting
  - ☐ Slicing and dicing
  - ☐ Rollup and drill down
- Multidimensional OLAP (MOLAP)
- Relational OLAP (ROLAP)
- Hybrid OLAP (HOLAP)
- Extended aggregation
  - ☐ Variance
  - ☐ Standard deviation
  - ☐ Correlation
  - ☐ Regression
- Ranking functions
  - ☐ Rank
  - ☐ Dense rank
  - ☐ Partition by
- Windowing
- Data mining
- Prediction
- Associations
- Classification
  - ☐ Training data
  - ☐ Test data
- Decision-tree classifiers

- ☐ Partitioning attribute
- ☐ Partitioning condition
- ☐ Purity
  - — Gini measure
  - — Entropy measure
- ☐ Information gain
- ☐ Information content
- ☐ Information gain ratio
- ☐ Continuous-valued attribute
- ☐ Categorical attribute
- ☐ Binary split
- ☐ Multiway split
- ☐ Overfitting
- Bayesian classifiers
  - ☐ Bayes theorem
  - ☐ Naive Bayesian classifiers
- Regression
  - ☐ Linear regression
  - ☐ Curve fitting
- Association rules
  - ☐ Population
  - ☐ Support
  - ☐ Confidence
  - ☐ Large itemsets
- Other types of associations
- Clustering
  - ☐ Hierarchical clustering
  - ☐ Agglomerative clustering
  - ☐ Divisive clustering
- Text mining
- Data visualization
- Data warehousing
  - ☐ Gathering data
  - ☐ Source-driven architecture

Exercises

22.1 For each of the SQL aggregate functions **sum, count, min** and **max**, show how to compute the aggregate value on a multiset $S_1 \cup S_2$, given the aggregate values on multisets S_1 and S_2.

Based on the above, give expressions to compute aggregate values with grouping on a subset S of the attributes of a relation $r(A, B, C, D, E)$, given aggregate values for grouping on attributes $T \supseteq S$, for the following aggregate functions:

  a. **sum, count, min** and **max**
  b. **avg**
  c. standard deviation

22.2 Show how to express **group by cube**(a, b, c, d) using **rollup**; your answer should have only one **group by** clause.

22.3 Give an example of a pair of groupings that cannot be expressed by using a single **group by** clause with **cube** and **rollup**.

22.4 Given a relation $S(student, subject, marks)$, write a query to find the top n students by total marks, by using ranking.

22.5 Given relation $r(a, b, d, d)$, Show how to use the extended SQL features to generate a histogram of d versus a, dividing a into 20 equal-sized partitions (that is, where each partition contains 5 percent of the tuples in r, sorted by a).

22.6 Write a query to find cumulative balances, equivalent to that shown in Section 22.2.5, but without using the extended SQL windowing constructs.

22.7 Consider the *balance* attribute of the *account* relation. Write an SQL query to compute a histogram of *balance* values, dividing the range 0 to the maximum account balance present, into three equal ranges.

22.8 Consider the *sales* relation from Section 22.2. Write an SQL query to compute the cube operation on the relation, giving the relation in Figure 22.2. Do not use the **with cube** construct.

22.9 Construct a decision tree classifier with binary splits at each node, using tuples in relation $r(A, B, C)$ shown below as training data; attribute C denotes the class. Show the final tree, and with each node show the best split for each attribute along with its information gain value.

$$(1, 2, a), (2, 1, a), (2, 5, b), (3, 3, b), (3, 6, b), (4, 5, b), (5, 5, c), (6, 3, b), (6, 7, c)$$

22.10 Suppose there are two classification rules, one that says that people with salaries between \$10,000 and \$20,000 have a credit rating of *good*, and another that says that people with salaries between \$20,000 and \$30,000 have a credit rating of *good*. Under what conditions can the rules be replaced, without any loss of information, by a single rule that says people with salaries between \$10,000 and \$30,000 have a credit rating of *good*.

22.11 Suppose half of all the transactions in a clothes shop purchase jeans, and one third of all transactions in the shop purchase T-shirts. Suppose also that half of the transactions that purchase jeans also purchase T-shirts. Write down all the (nontrivial) association rules you can deduce from the above information, giving support and confidence of each rule.

22.12 Consider the problem of finding large itemsets.

    a. Describe how to find the support for a given collection of itemsets by using a single scan of the data. Assume that the itemsets and associated information, such as counts, will fit in memory.

    b. Suppose an itemset has support less than j. Show that no superset of this itemset can have support greater than or equal to j.

22.13 Describe benefits and drawbacks of a source-driven architecture for gathering of data at a data-warehouse, as compared to a destination-driven architecture.

22.14 Consider the schema depicted in Figure 22.9. Give an SQL:1999 query to summarize sales numbers and price by store and date, along with the hierarchies on store and date.

22.15 Compute the relevance (using appropriate definitions of term frequency and inverse document frequency) of each of the questions in this chapter to the query "SQL relation."

22.16 What is the difference between a false positive and a false drop? If it is essential that no relevant information be missed by an information retrieval query, is it acceptable to have either false positives or false drops? Why?

22.17 Suppose you want to find documents that contain at least k of a given set of n keywords. Suppose also you have a keyword index that gives you a (sorted) list of identifiers of documents that contain a specified keyword. Give an efficient algorithm to find the desired set of documents.

Bibliographical Notes

Gray et al. [1995] and Gray et al. [1997] describe the data-cube operator. Efficient algorithms for computing data cubes are described by Agarwal et al. [1996], Harinarayan et al. [1996] and Ross and Srivastava [1997]. Descriptions of extended aggregation support in SQL:1999 can be found in the product manuals of database systems such as Oracle and IBM DB2. Definitions of statistical functions can be found in standard statistics textbooks such as Bulmer [1979] and Ross [1999].

Witten and Frank [1999] and Han and Kamber [2000] provide textbook coverage of data mining. Mitchell [1997] is a classic textbook on machine learning, and covers classification techniques in detail. Fayyad et al. [1995] presents an extensive collection of articles on knowledge discovery and data mining. Kohavi and Provost [2001] presents a collection of articles on applications of data mining to electronic commerce.

Agrawal et al. [1993] provides an early overview of data mining in databases. Algorithms for computing classifiers with large training sets are described by Agrawal et al. [1992] and Shafer et al. [1996]; the decision tree construction algorithm described in this chapter is based on the SPRINT algorithm of Shafer et al. [1996]. Agrawal and Srikant [1994] was an early paper on association rule mining. Algorithms for mining of different forms of association rules are described by Srikant and Agrawal [1996a] and Srikant and Agrawal [1996b]. Chakrabarti et al. [1998] describes techniques for mining surprising temporal patterns.

Clustering has long been studied in the area of statistics, and Jain and Dubes [1988] provides textbook coverage of clustering. Ng and Han [1994] describes spatial clustering techniques. Clustering techniques for large datasets are described by Zhang et al. [1996]. Breese et al. [1998] provides an empirical analysis of different algorithms for collaborative filtering. Techniques for collaborative filtering of news articles are described by Konstan et al. [1997].

Chakrabarti [2000] provides a survey of hypertext mining techniques such as hypertext classification and clustering. Chakrabarti [1999] provides a survey of Web resource discovery. Techniques for integrating data cubes with data mining are described by Sarawagi [2000].

Poe [1995] and Mattison [1996] provide textbook coverage of data warehousing. Zhuge et al. [1995] describes view maintenance in a data-warehousing environment.

Witten et al. [1999], Grossman and Frieder [1998], and Baeza-Yates and Ribeiro-Neto [1999] provide textbook descriptions of information retrieval. Indexing of documents is covered in detail by Witten et al. [1999]. Jones and Willet [1997] is a collection of articles on information retrieval. Salton [1989] is an early textbook on information-retrieval systems. The TREC benchmark (trec.nist.gov) is a benchmark for measuring retrieval effectiveness.

Brin and Page [1998] describes the anatomy of the Google search engine, including the PageRank technique, while a hubs and authorities based ranking technique called HITS is described by Kleinberg [1999]. Bharat and Henzinger [1998] presents a refinement of the HITS ranking technique. A point worth noting is that the PageRank of a page is computed independent of any query, and as a result a highly ranked page which just happens to contain some irrelevant keywords would figure among the top answers for a query on the irrelevant keywords. In contrast, the HITS algorithm takes the query keywords into account when computing prestige, but has a higher cost for answering queries.

Tools

A variety of tools are available for each of the applications we have studied in this chapter. Most database vendors provide OLAP tools as part of their database system, or as add-on applications. These include OLAP tools from Microsoft Corp., Oracle Express, Informix Metacube. The Arbor Essbase OLAP tool is from an independent software vendor. The site www.databeacon.com provides an online demo of the databeacon OLAP tools for use on Web and text file data sources. Many companies also provide analysis tools specialized for specific applications, such as customer relationship management.

There is also a wide variety of general purpose data mining tools, including mining tools from the SAS Institute, IBM Intelligent Miner, and SGI Mineset. A good deal of expertise is required to apply general purpose mining tools for specific applications. As a result a large number of mining tools have been developed to address specialized applications. The Web site www.kdnuggets.com provides an extensive directory of mining software, solutions, publications, and so on.

Major database vendors also offer data warehousing products coupled with their database systems. These provide support functionality for data modeling, cleansing, loading, and querying. The Web site www.dwinfocenter.org provides information datawarehousing products.

Google (www.google.com) is a popular search engine. Yahoo (www.yahoo.com) and the Open Directory Project (dmoz.org) provide classification hierarchies for Web sites.

Advanced Data Types and New Applications

For most of the history of databases, the types of data stored in databases were relatively simple, and this was reflected in the rather limited support for data types in earlier versions of SQL. In the past few years, however, there has been increasing need for handling new data types in databases, such as temporal data, spatial data. and multimedia data.

Another major trend in the last decade has created its own issues: the growth of mobile computers, starting with laptop computers and pocket organizers, and in more recent years growing to include mobile phones with built-in computers, and a variety of *wearable* computers that are increasingly used in commercial applications.

In this chapter we study several new data types, and also study database issues dealing with mobile computers.

23.1 Motivation

Before we address each of the topics in detail, we summarize the motivation for, and some important issues in dealing with, each of these types of data.

- **Temporal data**. Most database systems model the current state of the world, for instance, current customers, current students, and courses currently being offered. In many applications, it is very important to store and retrieve information about past states. Historical information can be incorporated manually into a schema design. However, the task is greatly simplified by database support for temporal data, which we study in Section 23.2.

- **Spatial data**. Spatial data include **geographic data**, such as maps and associated information, and **computer-aided-design data**, such as integrated-circuit designs or building designs. Applications of spatial data initially stored data as files in a file system, as did early-generation business applications. But as the complexity and volume of the data, and the number of users, have grown, ad hoc approaches to storing and retrieving data in a file system have proved insufficient for the needs of many applications that use spatial data.

Spatial-data applications require facilities offered by a database system—in particular, the ability to store and query large amounts of data efficiently. Some applications may also require other database features, such as atomic updates to parts of the stored data, durability, and concurrency control. In Section 23.3, we study the extensions needed to traditional database systems to support spatial data.

- **Multimedia data**. In Section 23.4, we study the features required in database systems that store multimedia data such as image, video, and audio data. The main distinguishing feature of video and audio data is that the display of the data requires retrieval at a steady, predetermined rate; hence, such data are called **continuous-media data**.

- **Mobile databases**. In Section 23.5, we study the database requirements of the new generation of mobile computing systems, such as notebook computers and palmtop computing devices, which are connected to base stations via wireless digital communication networks. Such computers need to be able to operate while disconnected from the network, unlike the distributed database systems discussed in Chapter 19. They also have limited storage capacity, and thus require special techniques for memory management.

23.2 Time in Databases

A database models the state of some aspect of the real world outside itself. Typically, databases model only one state—the current state—of the real world, and do not store information about past states, except perhaps as audit trails. When the state of the real world changes, the database gets updated, and information about the old state gets lost. However, in many applications, it is important to store and retrieve information about past states. For example, a patient database must store information about the medical history of a patient. A factory monitoring system may store information about current and past readings of sensors in the factory, for analysis. Databases that store information about states of the real world across time are called **temporal databases**.

When considering the issue of time in database systems, we must distinguish between time as measured by the system and time as observed in the real world. The **valid time** for a fact is the set of time intervals during which the fact is true in the real world. The **transaction time** for a fact is the time interval during which the fact is current within the database system. This latter time is based on the transaction serialization order and is generated automatically by the system. Note that valid-time intervals, being a real-world concept, cannot be generated automatically and must be provided to the system.

A **temporal relation** is one where each tuple has an associated time when it is true; the time may be either valid time or transaction time. Of course, both valid time and transaction time can be stored, in which case the relation is said to be a

account-number	branch-name	balance	from	to
A-101	Downtown	500	1999/1/1 9:00	1999/1/24 11:30
A-101	Downtown	100	1999/1/24 11:30	*
A-215	Mianus	700	2000/6/2 15:30	2000/8/8 10:00
A-215	Mianus	900	2000/8/8 10:00	2000/9/5 8:00
A-215	Mianus	700	2000/9/5 8:00	*
A-217	Brighton	750	1999/7/5 11:00	2000/5/1 16:00

Figure 23.1   A temporal *account* relation.

bitemporal relation. Figure 23.1 shows an example of a temporal relation. To simplify the representation, each tuple has only one time interval associated with it; thus, a tuple is represented once for every disjoint time interval in which it is true. Intervals are shown here as a pair of attributes *from* and *to*; an actual implementation would have a structured type, perhaps called *Interval*, that contains both fields. Note that some of the tuples have a "*" in the *to* time column; these asterisks indicate that the tuple is true until the value in the *to* time column is changed; thus, the tuple is true at the current time. Although times are shown in textual form, they are stored internally in a more compact form, such as the number of seconds since some fixed time on a fixed date (such as 12:00 AM, January 1, 1900) that can be translated back to the normal textual form.

23.2.1   Time Specification in SQL

The SQL standard defines the types **date**, **time**, and **timestamp**. The type **date** contains four digits for the year (1–9999), two digits for the month (1–12), and two digits for the date (1–31). The type **time** contains two digits for the hour, two digits for the minute, and two digits for the second, plus optional fractional digits. The seconds field can go beyond 60, to allow for leap seconds that are added during some years to correct for small variations in the speed of rotation of Earth. The type **timestamp** contains the fields of **date** and **time**, with six fractional digits for the seconds field.

Since different places in the world have different local times, there is often a need for specifying the time zone along with the time. The **Universal Coordinated Time (UTC)**, is a standard reference point for specifying time, with local times defined as offsets from UTC. (The standard abbreviation is UTC, rather than UCT, since it is an abbreviation of "Universal Coordinated Time" written in French as *universel temps coordonné*.) SQL also supports two types, **time with time zone**, and **timestamp with time zone**, which specify the time as a local time plus the offset of the local time from UTC. For instance, the time could be expressed in terms of U.S. Eastern Standard Time, with an offset of −6:00, since U.S. Eastern Standard time is 6 hours behind UTC.

SQL supports a type called **interval**, which allows us to refer to a period of time such as "1 day" or "2 days and 5 hours," without specifying a particular time when this period starts. This notion differs from the notion of interval we used previously, which refers to an interval of time with specific starting and ending times.[1]

23.2.2 Temporal Query Languages

A database relation without temporal information is sometimes called a **snapshot relation**, since it reflects the state in a snapshot of the real world. Thus, a snapshot of a temporal relation at a point in time t is the set of tuples in the relation that are true at time t, with the time-interval attributes projected out. The snapshot operation on a temporal relation gives the snapshot of the relation at a specified time (or the current time, if the time is not specified).

A **temporal selection** is a selection that involves the time attributes; a **temporal projection** is a projection where the tuples in the projection inherit their times from the tuples in the original relation. A **temporal join** is a join, with the time of a tuple in the result being the intersection of the times of the tuples from which it is derived. If the times do not intersect, the tuple is removed from the result.

The predicates *precedes*, *overlaps*, and *contains* can be applied on intervals; their meanings should be clear. The *intersect* operation can be applied on two intervals, to give a single (possibly empty) interval. However, the union of two intervals may or may not be a single interval.

Functional dependencies must be used with care in a temporal relation. Although the account number may functionally determine the balance at any given point in time, obviously the balance can change over time. A **temporal functional dependency** $X \xrightarrow{\tau} Y$ holds on a relation schema R if, for all legal instances r of R, all snapshots of r satisfy the functional dependency $X \to Y$.

Several proposals have been made for extending SQL to improve its support of temporal data. SQL:1999 Part 7 (SQL/Temporal), which is currently under development, is the proposed standard for temporal extensions to SQL.

23.3 Spatial and Geographic Data

Spatial data support in databases is important for efficiently storing, indexing, and querying of data based on spatial locations. For example, suppose that we want to store a set of polygons in a database, and to query the database to find all polygons that intersect a given polygon. We cannot use standard index structures, such as B-trees or hash indices, to answer such a query efficiently. Efficient processing of the above query would require special-purpose index structures, such as R-trees (which we study later) for the task.

Two types of spatial data are particularly important:

- **Computer-aided-design (CAD) data**, which includes spatial information about how objects—such as buildings, cars, or aircraft—are constructed. Other important examples of computer-aided-design databases are integrated-circuit and electronic-device layouts.

---

1.   Many temporal database researchers feel this type should have been called **span** since it does not specify an exact start or end time, only the time span between the two.

- **Geographic data** such as road maps, land-usage maps, topographic elevation maps, political maps showing boundaries, land ownership maps, and so on. **Geographic information systems** are special-purpose databases tailored for storing geographic data.

Support for geographic data has been added to many database systems, such as the IBM DB2 Spatial Extender, the Informix Spatial Datablade, and Oracle Spatial.

23.3.1   Representation of Geometric Information

Figure 23.2 illustrates how various geometric constructs can be represented in a database, in a normalized fashion. We stress here that geometric information can be represented in several different ways, only some of which we describe.

A *line segment* can be represented by the coordinates of its endpoints. For example, in a map database, the two coordinates of a point would be its latitude and longi-

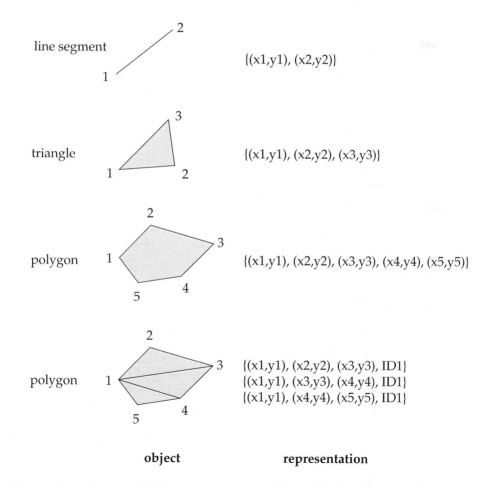

Figure 23.2   Representation of geometric constructs.

tude. A *polyline* (also called a *linestring*) consists of a connected sequence of line segments, and can be represented by a list containing the coordinates of the endpoints of the segments, in sequence. We can approximately represent an arbitrary curve by polylines, by partitioning the curve into a sequence of segments. This representation is useful for two-dimensional features such as roads; here, the width of the road is small enough relative to the size of the full map that it can be considered two dimensional. Some systems also support *circular arcs* as primitives, allowing curves to be represented as sequences of arcs.

We can represent a *polygon* by listing its vertices in order, as in Figure 23.2.[2] The list of vertices specifies the boundary of a polygonal region. In an alternative representation, a polygon can be divided into a set of triangles, as shown in Figure 23.2. This process is called **triangulation**, and any polygon can be triangulated. The complex polygon can be given an identifier, and each of the triangles into which it is divided carries the identifier of the polygon. Circles and ellipses can be represented by corresponding types, or can be approximated by polygons.

List-based representations of polylines or polygons are often convenient for query processing. Such non-first-normal-form representations are used when supported by the underlying database. So that we can use fixed-size tuples (in first-normal form) for representing polylines, we can give the polyline or curve an identifier, and can represent each segment as a separate tuple that also carries with it the identifier of the polyline or curve. Similarly, the triangulated representation of polygons allows a first-normal-form relational representation of polygons.

The representation of points and line segments in three-dimensional space is similar to their representation in two-dimensional space, the only difference being that points have an extra z component. Similarly, the representation of planar figures—such as triangles, rectangles, and other polygons—does not change much when we move to three dimensions. Tetrahedrons and cuboids can be represented in the same way as triangles and rectangles. We can represent arbitrary polyhedra by dividing them into tetrahedrons, just as we triangulate polygons. We can also represent them by listing their faces, each of which is itself a polygon, along with an indication of which side of the face is inside the polyhedron.

23.3.2 Design Databases

Computer-aided-design (CAD) systems traditionally stored data in memory during editing or other processing, and wrote the data back to a file at the end of a session of editing. The drawbacks of such a scheme include the cost (programming complexity, as well as time cost) of transforming data from one form to another, and the need to read in an entire file even if only parts of it are required. For large designs, such as the design of a large-scale integrated circuit, or the design of an entire airplane, it may be impossible to hold the complete design in memory. Designers of object-oriented databases were motivated in large part by the database requirements of CAD

2. Some references use the term *closed polygon* to refer to what we call polygons, and refer to polylines as open polygons.

systems. Object-oriented databases represent components of the design as objects, and the connections between the objects indicate how the design is structured.

The objects stored in a design database are generally geometric objects. Simple two-dimensional geometric objects include points, lines, triangles, rectangles, and, in general, polygons. Complex two-dimensional objects can be formed from simple objects by means of union, intersection, and difference operations. Similarly, complex three-dimensional objects may be formed from simpler objects such as spheres, cylinders, and cuboids, by union, intersection, and difference operations, as in Figure 23.3. Three-dimensional surfaces may also be represented by **wireframe models**, which essentially model the surface as a set of simpler objects, such as line segments, triangles, and rectangles.

Design databases also store nonspatial information about objects, such as the material from which the objects are constructed. We can usually model such information by standard data-modeling techniques. We concern ourselves here with only the spatial aspects.

Various spatial operations must be performed on a design. For instance, the designer may want to retrieve that part of the design that corresponds to a particular region of interest. Spatial-index structures, discussed in Section 23.3.5, are useful for such tasks. Spatial-index structures are multidimensional, dealing with two- and three-dimensional data, rather than dealing with just the simple one-dimensional ordering provided by the B^+-trees.

Spatial-integrity constraints, such as "two pipes should not be in the same location," are important in design databases to prevent interference errors. Such errors often occur if the design is performed manually, and are detected only when a prototype is being constructed. As a result, these errors can be expensive to fix. Database support for spatial-integrity constraints helps people to avoid design errors, thereby keeping the design consistent. Implementing such integrity checks again depends on the availability of efficient multidimensional index structures.

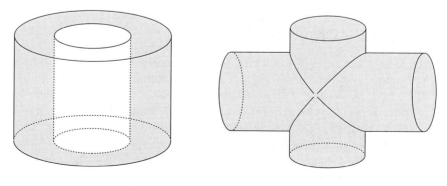

(a) Difference of cylinders   (b) Union of cylinders

Figure 23.3   Complex three-dimensional objects.

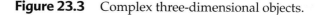

23.3.3 Geographic Data

Geographic data are spatial in nature, but differ from design data in certain ways. Maps and satellite images are typical examples of geographic data. Maps may provide not only location information—about boundaries, rivers, and roads, for example—but also much more detailed information associated with locations, such as elevation, soil type, land usage, and annual rainfall.

Geographic data can be categorized into two types:

- **Raster data.** Such data consist of bit maps or pixel maps, in two or more dimensions. A typical example of a two-dimensional raster image is a satellite image of cloud cover, where each pixel stores the cloud visibility in a particular area. Such data can be three-dimensional—for example, the temperature at different altitudes at different regions, again measured with the help of a satellite. Time could form another dimension—for example, the surface temperature measurements at different points in time. Design databases generally do not store raster data.

- **Vector data.** Vector data are constructed from basic geometric objects, such as points, line segments, triangles, and other polygons in two dimensions, and cylinders, spheres, cuboids, and other polyhedrons in three dimensions.

  Map data are often represented in vector format. Rivers and roads may be represented as unions of multiple line segments. States and countries may be represented as polygons. Topological information, such as height, may be represented by a surface divided into polygons covering regions of equal height, with a height value associated with each polygon.

23.3.3.1 Representation of Geographic Data

Geographical features, such as states and large lakes, are represented as complex polygons. Some features, such as rivers, may be represented either as complex curves or as complex polygons, depending on whether their width is relevant.

Geographic information related to regions, such as annual rainfall, can be represented as an array—that is, in raster form. For space efficiency, the array can be stored in a compressed form. In Section 23.3.5, we study an alternative representation of such arrays by a data structure called a *quadtree*.

As noted in Section 23.3.3, we can represent region information in vector form, using polygons, where each polygon is a region within which the array value is the same. The vector representation is more compact than the raster representation in some applications. It is also more accurate for some tasks, such as depicting roads, where dividing the region into pixels (which may be fairly large) leads to a loss of precision in location information. However, the vector representation is unsuitable for applications where the data are intrinsically raster based, such as satellite images.

23.3.3.2 Applications of Geographic Data

Geographic databases have a variety of uses, including online map services, vehicle-navigation systems; distribution-network information for public-service utilities such as telephone, electric-power, and water-supply systems; and land-usage information for ecologists and planners.

Web-based road map services form a very widely used application of map data. At the simplest level, these systems can be used to generate online road maps of a desired region. An important benefit of online maps is that it is easy to scale the maps to the desired size—that is, to zoom in and out to locate relevant features. Road map services also store information about roads and services, such as the layout of roads, speed limits on roads, road conditions, connections between roads, and one-way restrictions. With this additional information about roads, the maps can be used for getting directions to go from one place to another and for automatic trip planning. Users can query online information about services to locate, for example, hotels, gas stations, or restaurants with desired offerings and price ranges.

Vehicle-navigation systems are systems mounted in automobiles, which provide road maps and trip planning services. A useful addition to a mobile geographic information system such as a vehicle navigation system is a **Global Positioning System (GPS)** unit, which uses information broadcast from GPS satellites to find the current location with an accuracy of tens of meters. With such a system, a driver can never[3] get lost—the GPS unit finds the location in terms of latitude, longitude, and elevation and the navigation system can query the geographic database to find where and on which road the vehicle is currently located.

Geographic databases for public-utility information are becoming increasingly important as the network of buried cables and pipes grows. Without detailed maps, work carried out by one utility may damage the cables of another utility, resulting in large-scale disruption of service. Geographic databases, coupled with accurate location-finding systems, can help avoid such problems.

So far, we have explained why spatial databases are useful. In the rest of the section, we shall study technical details, such as representation and indexing of spatial information.

23.3.4 Spatial Queries

There are a number of types of queries that involve spatial locations.

- **Nearness queries** request objects that lie near a specified location. A query to find all restaurants that lie within a given distance of a given point is an example of a nearness query. The **nearest-neighbor query** requests the object that is nearest to a specified point. For example, we may want to find the nearest gasoline station. Note that this query does not have to specify a limit on the distance, and hence we can ask it even if we have no idea how far the nearest gasoline station lies.

- **Region queries** deal with spatial regions. Such a query can ask for objects that lie partially or fully inside a specified region. A query to find all retail shops within the geographic boundaries of a given town is an example.

---

3. Well, hardly ever!

- Queries may also request **intersections** and **unions** of regions. For example, given region information, such as annual rainfall and population density, a query may request all regions with a low annual rainfall as well as a high population density.

Queries that compute intersections of regions can be thought of as computing the **spatial join** of two spatial relations—for example, one representing rainfall and the other representing population density—with the location playing the role of join attribute. In general, given two relations, each containing spatial objects, the spatial join of the two relations generates either pairs of objects that intersect, or the intersection regions of such pairs.

Several join algorithms efficiently compute spatial joins on vector data. Although nested-loop join and indexed nested-loop join (with spatial indices) can be used, hash joins and sort–merge joins cannot be used on spatial data. Researchers have proposed join techniques based on coordinated traversal of spatial index structures on the two relations. See the bibliographical notes for more information.

In general, queries on spatial data may have a combination of spatial and nonspatial requirements. For instance, we may want to find the nearest restaurant that has vegetarian selections, and that charges less than $10 for a meal.

Since spatial data are inherently graphical, we usually query them by using a graphical query language. Results of such queries are also displayed graphically, rather than in tables. The user can invoke various operations on the interface, such as choosing an area to be viewed (for example, by pointing and clicking on suburbs west of Manhattan), zooming in and out, choosing what to display on the basis of selection conditions (for example, houses with more than three bedrooms), overlay of multiple maps (for example, houses with more than three bedrooms overlayed on a map showing areas with low crime rates), and so on. The graphical interface constitutes the front end. Extensions of SQL have been proposed to permit relational databases to store and retrieve spatial information efficiently, and also allowing queries to mix spatial and nonspatial conditions. Extensions include allowing abstract data types, such as lines, polygons, and bit maps, and allowing spatial conditions, such as *contains* or *overlaps*.

23.3.5 Indexing of Spatial Data

Indices are required for efficient access to spatial data. Traditional index structures, such as hash indices and B-trees, are not suitable, since they deal only with one-dimensional data, whereas spatial data are typically of two or more dimensions.

23.3.5.1 k-d Trees

To understand how to index spatial data consisting of two or more dimensions, we consider first the indexing of points in one-dimensional data. Tree structures, such as binary trees and B-trees, operate by successively dividing space into smaller parts. For instance, each internal node of a binary tree partitions a one-dimensional interval in two. Points that lie in the left partition go into the left subtree; points that lie in the right partition go into the right subtree. In a balanced binary tree, the partition is chosen so that approximately one-half of the points stored in the subtree fall in each partition. Similarly, each level of a B-tree splits a one-dimensional interval into multiple parts.

We can use that intuition to create tree structures for two-dimensional space, as well as in higher-dimensional spaces. A tree structure called a **k-d tree** was one of the early structures used for indexing in multiple dimensions. Each level of a k-d tree partitions the space into two. The partitioning is done along one dimension at the node at the top level of the tree, along another dimension in nodes at the next level, and so on, cycling through the dimensions. The partitioning proceeds in such a way that, at each node, approximately one-half of the points stored in the subtree fall on one side, and one-half fall on the other. Partitioning stops when a node has less than a given maximum number of points. Figure 23.4 shows a set of points in two-dimensional space, and a k-d tree representation of the set of points. Each line corresponds to a node in the tree, and the maximum number of points in a leaf node has been set at 1. Each line in the figure (other than the outside box) corresponds to a node in the k-d tree. The numbering of the lines in the figure indicates the level of the tree at which the corresponding node appears.

The **k-d-B tree** extends the k-d tree to allow multiple child nodes for each internal node, just as a B-tree extends a binary tree, to reduce the height of the tree. k-d-B trees are better suited for secondary storage than k-d trees.

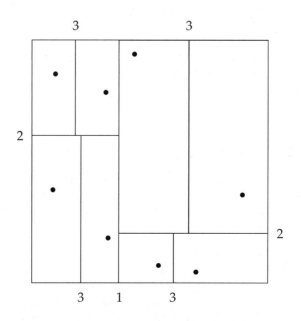

Figure 23.4   Division of space by a k-d tree.

23.3.5.2 Quadtrees

An alternative representation for two-dimensional data is a **quadtree**. An example of the division of space by a quadtree appears in Figure 23.5. The set of points is the same as that in Figure 23.4. Each node of a quadtree is associated with a rectangular region of space. The top node is associated with the entire target space. Each non-leaf node in a quadtree divides its region into four equal-sized quadrants, and correspondingly each such node has four child nodes corresponding to the four quadrants. Leaf nodes have between zero and some fixed maximum number of points. Correspondingly, if the region corresponding to a node has more than the maximum number of points, child nodes are created for that node. In the example in Figure 23.5, the maximum number of points in a leaf node is set to 1.

This type of quadtree is called a **PR quadtree**, to indicate it stores points, and that the division of space is divided based on regions, rather than on the actual set of points stored. We can use **region quadtrees** to store array (raster) information. A node in a region quadtree is a leaf node if all the array values in the region that it covers are the same. Otherwise, it is subdivided further into four children of equal area, and is therefore an internal node. Each node in the region quadtree corresponds to a subarray of values. The subarrays corresponding to leaves either contain just a single array element or have multiple array elements, all of which have the same value.

Indexing of line segments and polygons presents new problems. There are extensions of k-d trees and quadtrees for this task. However, a line segment or polygon may cross a partitioning line. If it does, it has to be split and represented in each of the subtrees in which its pieces occur. Multiple occurrences of a line segment or polygon can result in inefficiencies in storage, as well as inefficiencies in querying.

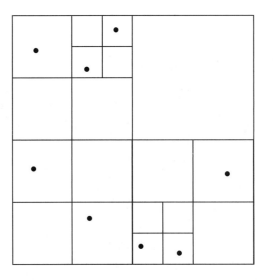

Figure 23.5   Division of space by a quadtree.

23.3.5.3   R-Trees

A storage structure called an **R-tree** is useful for indexing of rectangles and other polygons. An R-tree is a balanced tree structure with the indexed polygons stored in leaf nodes, much like a B$^+$-tree. However, instead of a range of values, a rectangular **bounding box** is associated with each tree node. The bounding box of a leaf node is the smallest rectangle parallel to the axes that contains all objects stored in the leaf node. The bounding box of internal nodes is, similarly, the smallest rectangle parallel to the axes that contains the bounding boxes of its child nodes. The bounding box of a polygon is defined, similarly, as the smallest rectangle parallel to the axes that contains the polygon.

Each internal node stores the bounding boxes of the child nodes along with the pointers to the child nodes. Each leaf node stores the indexed polygons, and may optionally store the bounding boxes of the polygons; the bounding boxes help speed up checks for overlaps of the rectangle with the indexed polygons—if a query rectangle does not overlap with the bounding box of a polygon, it cannot overlap with the polygon either. (If the indexed polygons are rectangles, there is of course no need to store bounding boxes since they are identical to the rectangles.)

Figure 23.6 shows an example of a set of rectangles (drawn with a solid line) and the bounding boxes (drawn with a dashed line) of the nodes of an R-tree for the set of rectangles. Note that the bounding boxes are shown with extra space inside them, to make them stand out pictorially. In reality, the boxes would be smaller and fit tightly on the objects that they contain; that is, each side of a bounding box B would touch at least one of the objects or bounding boxes that are contained in B.

The R-tree itself is at the right side of Figure 23.6. The figure refers to the coordinates of bounding box i as BB_i in the figure.

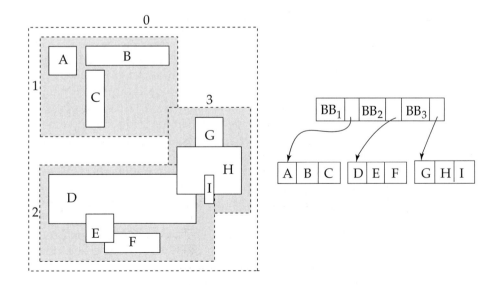

Figure 23.6   An R-tree.

We shall now see how to implement search, insert, and delete operations on an R-tree.

- **Search**: As the figure shows, the bounding boxes associated with sibling nodes may overlap; in B$^+$-trees, k-d trees, and quadtrees, in contrast, the ranges do not overlap. A search for polygons containing a point therefore has to follow *all* child nodes whose associated bounding boxes contain the point; as a result, multiple paths may have to be searched. Similarly, a query to find all polygons that intersect a given polygon has to go down every node where the associated rectangle intersects the polygon.

- **Insert**: When we insert a polygon into an R-tree, we select a leaf node to hold the polygon. Ideally we should pick a leaf node that has space to hold a new entry, and whose bounding box contains the bounding box of the polygon. However, such a node may not exist; even if it did, finding the node may be very expensive, since it is not possible to find it by a single traversal down from the root. At each internal node we may find multiple children whose bounding boxes contain the bounding box of the polygon, and each of these children needs to be explored. Therefore, as a heuristic, in a traversal from the root, if any of the child nodes has a bounding box containing the bounding box of the polygon, the R-tree algorithm chooses one of them arbitrarily. If none of the children satisfy this condition, the algorithm chooses a child node whose bounding box has the maximum overlap with the bounding box of the polygon for continuing the traversal.

  Once the leaf node has been reached, if the node is already full, the algorithm performs node splitting (and propagates splitting upward if required) in a manner very similar to B$^+$-tree insertion. Just as with B$^+$-tree insertion, the R-tree insertion algorithm ensures that the tree remains balanced. Additionally, it ensures that the bounding boxes of leaf nodes, as well as internal nodes, remain consistent; that is, bounding boxes of leaves contain all the bounding boxes of the polygons stored at the leaf, while the bounding boxes for internal nodes contain all the bounding boxes of the children nodes.

  The main difference of the insertion procedure from the B$^+$-tree insertion procedure lies in how the node is split. In a B$^+$-tree, it is possible to find a value such that half the entries are less than the midpoint and half are greater than the value. This property does not generalize beyond one dimension; that is, for more than one dimension, it is not always possible to split the entries into two sets so that their bounding boxes do not overlap. Instead, as a heuristic, the set of entries S can be split into two disjoint sets S_1 and S_2 so that the bounding boxes of S_1 and S_2 have the minimum total area; another heuristic would be to split the entries into two sets S_1 and S_2 in such a way that S_1 and S_2 have minimum overlap. The two nodes resulting from the split would contain the entries in S_1 and S_2 respectively. The cost of finding splits with minimum total area or overlap can itself be large, so cheaper heuristics, such as the *quadratic split* heuristic are used. (The heuristic gets is name from the fact that it takes time quadratic in the number of entries.)

The **quadratic split** heuristic works this way: First, it picks a pair of entries a and b from S such that putting them in the same node would result in a bounding box with the maximum wasted space; that is, the area of the minimum bounding box of a and b minus the sum of the areas of a and b is the largest. The heuristic places the entries a and b in sets S_1 and S_2 respectively.

It then iteratively adds the remaining entries, one entry per iteration, to one of the two sets S_1 or S_2. At each iteration, for each remaining entry e, let $i_{e,1}$ denote the increase in the size of the bounding box of S_1 if e is added to S_1 and let $i_{e,2}$ denote the corresponding increase for S_2. In each iteration, the heuristic chooses one of the entries with the maximum difference of $i_{e,1}$ and $i_{e,2}$ and adds it to S_1 if $i_{e,1}$ is less than $i_{e,2}$, and to S_2 otherwise. That is, an entry with "maximum preference" for one of S_1 or S_2 is chosen at each iteration. The iteration stops when all entries have been assigned, or when one of the sets S_1 or S_2 has enough entries that all remaining entries have to be added to the other set so the nodes constructed from S_1 and S_2 both have the required minimum occupancy. The heuristic then adds all unassigned entries to the set with fewer entries.

- **Deletion**: Deletion can be performed like a B$^+$-tree deletion, borrowing entries from sibling nodes, or merging sibling nodes if a node becomes underfull. An alternative approach redistributes all the entries of underfull nodes to sibling nodes, with the aim of improving the clustering of entries in the R-tree.

See the bibliographical references for more details on insertion and deletion operations on R-trees, as well as on variants of R-trees, called R*-trees or R^+-trees.

The storage efficiency of R-trees is better than that of k-d trees or quadtrees, since a polygon is stored only once, and we can ensure easily that each node is at least half full. However, querying may be slower, since multiple paths have to be searched. Spatial joins are simpler with quadtrees than with R-trees, since all quadtrees on a region are partitioned in the same manner. However, because of their better storage efficiency, and their similarity to B-trees, R-trees and their variants have proved popular in database systems that support spatial data.

23.4 Multimedia Databases

Multimedia data, such as images, audio, and video—an increasingly popular form of data—are today almost always stored outside the database, in file systems. This kind of storage is not a problem when the number of multimedia objects is relatively small, since features provided by databases are usually not important.

However, database features become important when the number of multimedia objects stored is large. Issues such as transactional updates, querying facilities, and indexing then become important. Multimedia objects often have descriptive attributes, such as those indicating when they were created, who created them, and to what category they belong. One approach to building a database for such multimedia objects is to use databases for storing the descriptive attributes and for keeping track of the files in which the multimedia objects are stored.

However, storing multimedia outside the database makes it harder to provide database functionality, such as indexing on the basis of actual multimedia data content. It can also lead to inconsistencies, such as a file that is noted in the database, but whose contents are missing, or vice versa. It is therefore desirable to store the data themselves in the database.

Several issues have to be addressed if multimedia data are to be stored in a database.

- The database must support large objects, since multimedia data such as videos can occupy up to a few gigabytes of storage. Many database systems do not support objects larger than a few gigabytes. Larger objects could be split into smaller pieces and stored in the database. Alternatively, the multimedia object may be stored in a file system, but the database may contain a pointer to the object; the pointer would typically be a file name. The SQL/MED standard (MED stands for Management of External Data), which is under development, allows external data, such as files, to be treated as if they are part of the database. With SQL/MED, the object would appear to be part of the database, but can be stored externally.

    We discuss multimedia data formats in Section 23.4.1.

- The retrieval of some types of data, such as audio and video, has the requirement that data delivery must proceed at a guaranteed steady rate. Such data are sometimes called **isochronous data**, or **continuous-media data**. For example, if audio data are not supplied in time, there will be gaps in the sound. If the data are supplied too fast, system buffers may overflow, resulting in loss of data. We discuss continuous-media data in Section 23.4.2.

- Similarity-based retrieval is needed in many multimedia database applications. For example, in a database that stores fingerprint images, a query fingerprint image is provided, and fingerprints in the database that are similar to the query fingerprint must be retrieved. Index structures such as B^+-trees and R-trees cannot be used for this purpose; special index structures need to be created. We discuss similarity-based retrieval in Section 23.4.3

23.4.1 Multimedia Data Formats

Because of the large number of bytes required to represent multimedia data, it is essential that multimedia data be stored and transmitted in compressed form. For image data, the most widely used format is *JPEG*, named after the standards body that created it, the *Joint Picture Experts Group*. We can store video data by encoding each frame of video in JPEG format, but such an encoding is wasteful, since successive frames of a video are often nearly the same. The *Moving Picture Experts Group* has developed the *MPEG* series of standards for encoding video and audio data; these encodings exploit commonalities among a sequence of frames to achieve a greater degree of compression. The *MPEG-1* standard stores a minute of 30-frame-per-second video and audio in approximately 12.5 megabytes (compared to approximately 75 megabytes for video in only JPEG). However, MPEG-1 encoding introduces some loss of video quality, to a level roughly comparable to that of VHS video tape.

The *MPEG-2* standard is designed for digital broadcast systems and digital video disks (DVD); it introduces only a negligible loss of video quality. MPEG-2 compresses 1 minute of video and audio to approximately 17 megabytes. Several competing standards are used for audio encoding, including *MP3*, which stands for MPEG-1 Layer 3, RealAudio, and other formats.

23.4.2 Continuous-Media Data

The most important types of continuous-media data are video and audio data (for example, a database of movies). Continuous-media systems are characterized by their real-time information-delivery requirements:

- Data must be delivered sufficiently fast that no gaps in the audio or video result.

- Data must be delivered at a rate that does not cause overflow of system buffers.

- Synchronization among distinct data streams must be maintained. This need arises, for example, when the video of a person speaking must show lips moving synchronously with the audio of the person speaking.

To supply data predictably at the right time to a large number of consumers of the data, the fetching of data from disk must be carefully coordinated. Usually, data are fetched in periodic cycles. In each cycle, say of n seconds, n seconds worth of data is fetched for each consumer and stored in memory buffers, while the data fetched in the previous cycle is being sent to the consumers from the memory buffers. The cycle period is a compromise: A short period uses less memory but requires more disk arm movement, which is a waste of resources, while a long period reduces disk arm movement but increases memory requirements and may delay initial delivery of data. When a new request arrives, **admission control** comes into play: That is, the system checks if the request can be satisfied with available resources (in each period); if so, it is admitted; otherwise it is rejected.

Extensive research on delivery of continuous media data has dealt with such issues as handling arrays of disks and dealing with disk failure. See the bibliographical references for details.

Several vendors offer video-on-demand servers. Current systems are based on file systems, because existing database systems do not provide the real-time response that these applications need. The basic architecture of a video-on-demand system comprises:

- **Video server**. Multimedia data are stored on several disks (usually in a RAID configuration). Systems containing a large volume of data may use tertiary storage for less frequently accessed data.

- **Terminals**. People view multimedia data through various devices, collectively referred to as *terminals*. Examples are personal computers and televisions attached to a small, inexpensive computer called a **set-top box**.

- **Network.** Transmission of multimedia data from a server to multiple terminals requires a high-capacity network.

Video-on-demand service eventually will become ubiquitous, just as cable and broadcast television are now. For the present, the main applications of video-server technology are in offices (for training, viewing recorded talks and presentations, and the like), in hotels, and in video-production facilities.

23.4.3 Similarity-Based Retrieval

In many multimedia applications, data are described only approximately in the database. An example is the fingerprint data in Section 23.4. Other examples are:

- **Pictorial data.** Two pictures or images that are slightly different as represented in the database may be considered the same by a user. For instance, a database may store trademark designs. When a new trademark is to be registered, the system may need first to identify all similar trademarks that were registered previously.

- **Audio data.** Speech-based user interfaces are being developed that allow the user to give a command or identify a data item by speaking. The input from the user must then be tested for similarity to those commands or data items stored in the system.

- **Handwritten data.** Handwritten input can be used to identify a handwritten data item or command stored in the database. Here again, similarity testing is required.

The notion of similarity is often subjective and user specific. However, similarity testing is often more successful than speech or handwriting recognition, because the input can be compared to data already in the system and, thus, the set of choices available to the system is limited.

Several algorithms exist for finding the best matches to a given input by similarity testing. Some systems, including a dial-by-name, voice-activated telephone system, have been deployed commercially. See the bibliographical notes for references.

23.5 Mobility and Personal Databases

Large-scale, commercial databases have traditionally been stored in central computing facilities. In distributed database applications, there has usually been strong central database and network administration. Two technology trends have combined to create applications in which this assumption of central control and administration is not entirely correct:

1. The increasingly widespread use of personal computers, and, more important, of laptop or notebook computers.

2. The development of a relatively low-cost wireless digital communication infrastructure, based on wireless local-area networks, cellular digital packet networks, and other technologies.

Mobile computing has proved useful in many applications. Many business travelers use laptop computers so that they can work and access data en route. Delivery services use mobile computers to assist in package tracking. Emergency-response services use mobile computers at the scene of disasters, medical emergencies, and the like to access information and to enter data pertaining to the situation. New applications of mobile computers continue to emerge.

Wireless computing creates a situation where machines no longer have fixed locations and network addresses. **Location-dependent queries** are an interesting class of queries that are motivated by mobile computers; in such queries, the location of the user (computer) is a parameter of the query. The value of the location parameter is provided either by the user or, increasingly, by a global positioning system (GPS). An example is a traveler's information system that provides data on hotels, roadside services, and the like to motorists. Processing of queries about services that are ahead on the current route must be based on knowledge of the user's location, direction of motion, and speed. Increasingly, navigational aids are being offered as a built-in feature in automobiles.

Energy (battery power) is a scarce resource for most mobile computers. This limitation influences many aspects of system design. Among the more interesting consequences of the need for energy efficiency is the use of scheduled data broadcasts to reduce the need for mobile systems to transmit queries.

Increasing amounts of data may reside on machines administered by users, rather than by database administrators. Furthermore, these machines may, at times, be disconnected from the network. In many cases, there is a conflict between the user's need to continue to work while disconnected and the need for global data consistency.

In Sections 23.5.1 through 23.5.4, we discuss techniques in use and under development to deal with the problems of mobility and personal computing.

23.5.1 A Model of Mobile Computing

The mobile-computing environment consists of mobile computers, referred to as **mobile hosts**, and a wired network of computers. Mobile hosts communicate with the wired network via computers referred to as **mobile support stations**. Each mobile support station manages those mobile hosts within its **cell**—that is, the geographical area that it covers. Mobile hosts may move between cells, thus necessitating a **handoff** of control from one mobile support station to another. Since mobile hosts may, at times, be powered down, a host may leave one cell and rematerialize later at some distant cell. Therefore, moves between cells are not necessarily between adjacent cells. Within a small area, such as a building, mobile hosts may be connected by a wireless local-area network (LAN) that provides lower-cost connectivity than would a wide-area cellular network, and that reduces the overhead of handoffs.

It is possible for mobile hosts to communicate directly without the intervention of a mobile support station. However, such communication can occur between only nearby hosts. Such direct forms of communication are becoming more prevalent with the advent of the **Bluetooth** standard. Bluetooth uses short-range digital radio to allow wireless connectivity within a 10-meter range at high speed (up to 721 kilobits per second). Initially conceived as a replacement for cables, Bluetooth's greatest promise is in easy ad hoc connection of mobile computers, PDAs, mobile phones, and so-called intelligent appliances.

The network infrastructure for mobile computing consists in large part of two technologies: wireless local-area networks (such as Avaya's Orinoco wireless LAN), and packet-based cellular telephony networks. Early cellular systems used analog technology and were designed for voice communication. Second-generation digital systems retained the focus on voice appliations. Third-generation (3G) and so-called 2.5G systems use packet-based networking and are more suited to data applications. In these networks, voice is just one of many applications (albeit an economically important one).

Bluetooth, wireless LANs, and 2.5G and 3G cellular networks make it possible for a wide variety of devices to communicate at low cost. While such communication itself does not fit the domain of a usual database application, the accounting, monitoring, and management data pertaining to this communication will generate huge databases. The immediacy of wireless communication generates a need for real-time access to many of these databases. This need for timeliness adds another dimension to the constraints on the system—a matter we shall discuss further in Section 24.3.

The size and power limitations of many mobile computers have led to alternative memory hierarchies. Instead of, or in addition to, disk storage, flash memory, which we discussed in Section 11.1, may be included. If the mobile host includes a hard disk, the disk may be allowed to spin down when it is not in use, to save energy. The same considerations of size and energy limit the type and size of the display used in a mobile device. Designers of mobile devices often create special-purpose user interfaces to work within these constraints. However, the need to present Web-based data has neccessitated the creation of presentation standards. **Wireless application protocol** (WAP) is a standard for wireless internet access. WAP-based browsers access special Web pages that use **wireless markup lanaguge** (WML), an XML-based language designed for the constraints of mobile and wireless Web browsing.

23.5.2 Routing and Query Processing

The route between a pair of hosts may change over time if one of the two hosts is mobile. This simple fact has a dramatic effect at the network level, since location-based network addresses are no longer constants within the system.

Mobility also directly affects database query processing. As we saw in Chapter 19, we must consider the communication costs when we choose a distributed query-processing strategy. Mobility results in dynamically changing communication costs, thus complicating the optimization process. Furthermore, there are competing notions of cost to consider:

- **User time** is a highly valuable commodity in many business applications

- **Connection time** is the unit by which monetary charges are assigned in some cellular systems

- **Number of bytes, or packets, transferred** is the unit by which charges are computed in some digital cellular systems

- **Time-of-day-based charges** vary, depending on whether communication occurs during peak or off-peak periods

- **Energy** is limited. Often, battery power is a scarce resource whose use must be optimized. A basic principle of radio communication is that it requires less energy to receive than to transmit radio signals. Thus, transmission and reception of data impose different power demands on the mobile host.

23.5.3 Broadcast Data

It is often desirable for frequently requested data to be broadcast in a continuous cycle by mobile support stations, rather than transmitted to mobile hosts on demand. A typical application of such **broadcast data** is stock-market price information. There are two reasons for using broadcast data. First, the mobile host avoids the energy cost for transmitting data requests. Second, the broadcast data can be received by a large number of mobile hosts at once, at no extra cost. Thus, the available transmission bandwidth is utilized more effectively.

A mobile host can then receive data as they are transmitted, rather than consuming energy by transmitting a request. The mobile host may have local nonvolatile storage available to cache the broadcast data for possible later use. Given a query, the mobile host may optimize energy costs by determining whether it can process that query with only cached data. If the cached data are insufficient, there are two options: Wait for the data to be broadcast, or transmit a request for data. To make this decision, the mobile host must know when the relevant data will be broadcast.

Broadcast data may be transmitted according to a fixed schedule or a changeable schedule. In the former case, the mobile host uses the known fixed schedule to determine when the relevant data will be transmitted. In the latter case, the broadcast schedule must itself be broadcast at a well-known radio frequency and at well-known time intervals.

In effect, the broadcast medium can be modeled as a disk with a high latency. Requests for data can be thought of as being serviced when the requested data are broadcast. The transmission schedules behave like indices on the disk. The bibliographical notes list recent research papers in the area of broadcast data management.

23.5.4 Disconnectivity and Consistency

Since wireless communication may be paid for on the basis of connection time, there is an incentive for certain mobile hosts to be disconnected for substantial periods. Mobile computers without wireless connectivity are disconnected most of the time when they are being used, except periodically when they are connected to their host computers, either physically or through a computer network.

During these periods of disconnection, the mobile host may remain in operation. The user of the mobile host may issue queries and updates on data that reside or are cached locally. This situation creates several problems, in particular:

- **Recoverability**: Updates entered on a disconnected machine may be lost if the mobile host experiences a catastrophic failure. Since the mobile host represents a single point of failure, stable storage cannot be simulated well.

- **Consistency**: Locally cached data may become out of date, but the mobile host cannot discover this situation until it is reconnected. Likewise, updates occurring in the mobile host cannot be propagated until reconnection occurs.

We explored the consistency problem in Chapter 19, where we discussed network partitioning, and we elaborate on it here. In wired distributed systems, partitioning is considered to be a failure mode; in mobile computing, partitioning via disconnection is part of the normal mode of operation. It is therefore necessary to allow data access to proceed despite partitioning, even at the risk of some loss of consistency.

For data updated by only the mobile host, it is a simple matter to propagate the updates when the mobile host reconnects. However, if the mobile host caches read-only copies of data that may be updated by other computers, the cached data may become inconsistent. When the mobile host is connected, it can be sent **invalidation reports** that inform it of out-of-date cache entries. However, when the mobile host is disconnected, it may miss an invalidation report. A simple solution to this problem is to invalidate the entire cache on reconnection, but such an extreme solution is highly costly. Several caching schemes are cited in the bibliographical notes.

If updates can occur at both the mobile host and elsewhere, detecting conflicting updates is more difficult. **Version-numbering**-based schemes allow updates of shared files from disconnected hosts. These schemes do not guarantee that the updates will be consistent. Rather, they guarantee that, if two hosts independently update the same version of a document, the clash will be detected eventually, when the hosts exchange information either directly or through a common host.

The **version-vector scheme** detects inconsistencies when copies of a document are independently updated. This scheme allows copies of a *document* to be stored at multiple hosts. Although we use the term *document*, the scheme can be applied to any other data items, such as tuples of a relation.

The basic idea is for each host i to store, with its copy of each document d, a **version vector**—that is, a set of version numbers $\{V_{d,i}[j]\}$, with one entry for each other host j on which the document could potentially be updated. When a host i updates a document d, it increments the version number $V_{d,i}[i]$ by one.

Whenever two hosts i and j connect with each other, they exchange updated documents, so that both obtain new versions of the documents. However, before exchanging documents, the hosts have to discover whether the copies are consistent:

1. If the version vectors are the same on both hosts—that is, for each k, $V_{d,i}[k] = V_{d,j}[k]$—then the copies of document d are identical.

2. If, for each k, $V_{d,i}[k] \leq V_{d,j}[k]$ and the version vectors are not identical, then the copy of document d at host i is older than the one at host j. That is, the copy of document d at host j was obtained by one or more modifications of the copy of the document at host i. Host i replaces its copy of d, as well as its copy of the version vector for d, with the copies from host j.

3. If there is a pair of hosts k and m such that $V_{d,i}[k] < V_{d,j}[k]$ and $V_{d,i}[m] > V_{d,j}[m]$, then the copies are *inconsistent*; that is, the copy of d at i contains updates performed by host k that have not been propagated to host j, and, similarly, the copy of d at j contains updates performed by host m that have not been propagated to host i. Then, the copies of d are inconsistent, since two or more updates have been performed on d independently. Manual intervention may be required to merge the updates.

The version-vector scheme was initially designed to deal with failures in distributed file systems. The scheme gained importance because mobile computers often store copies of files that are also present on server systems, in effect constituting a distributed file system that is often disconnected. Another application of the scheme is in groupware systems, where hosts are connected periodically, rather than continuously, and must exchange updated documents. The version-vector scheme also has applications in replicated databases.

The version-vector scheme, however, fails to address the most difficult and most important issue arising from updates to shared data—the reconciliation of inconsistent copies of data. Many applications can perform reconciliation automatically by executing in each computer those operations that had performed updates on remote computers during the period of disconnection. This solution works if update operations commute—that is, they generate the same result, regardless of the order in which they are executed. Alternative techniques may be available in certain applications; in the worst case, however, it must be left to the users to resolve the inconsistencies. Dealing with such inconsistency automatically, and assisting users in resolving inconsistencies that cannot be handled automatically, remains an area of research.

Another weakness is that the version-vector scheme requires substantial communication between a reconnecting mobile host and that host's mobile support station. Consistency checks can be delayed until the data are needed, although this delay may increase the overall inconsistency of the database.

The potential for disconnection and the cost of wireless communication limit the practicality of transaction-processing techniques discussed in Chapter 19 for distributed systems. Often, it is preferable to let users prepare transactions on mobile hosts, but to require that, instead of executing the transactions locally, they submit transactions to a server for execution. Transactions that span more than one computer and that include a mobile host face long-term blocking during transaction commit, unless disconnectivity is rare or predictable.

23.6 Summary

- Time plays an important role in database systems. Databases are models of the real world. Whereas most databases model the state of the real world at a point in time (at the current time), temporal databases model the states of the real world across time.

- Facts in temporal relations have associated times when they are valid, which can be represented as a union of intervals. Temporal query languages simplify modeling of time, as well as time-related queries.

- Spatial databases are finding increasing use today to store computer-aided-design data as well as geographic data.

- Design data are stored primarily as vector data; geographic data consist of a combination of vector and raster data. Spatial-integrity constraints are important for design data.

- Vector data can be encoded as first-normal-form data, or can be stored using non-first-normal-form structures, such as lists. Special-purpose index structures are particularly important for accessing spatial data, and for processing spatial queries.

- R-trees are a multidimensional extension of B-trees; with variants such as R+-trees and R*-trees, they have proved popular in spatial databases. Index structures that partition space in a regular fashion, such as quadtrees, help in processing spatial join queries.

- Multimedia databases are growing in importance. Issues such as similarity-based retrieval and delivery of data at guaranteed rates are topics of current research.

- Mobile computing systems have become common, leading to interest in database systems that can run on such systems. Query processing in such systems may involve lookups on server databases. The query cost model must include the cost of communication, including monetary cost and battery-power cost, which is relatively high for mobile systems.

- Broadcast is much cheaper per recipient than is point-to-point communication, and broadcast of data such as stock-market data helps mobile systems to pick up data inexpensively.

- Disconnected operation, use of broadcast data, and caching of data are three important issues being addressed in mobile computing.

Review Terms

- Temporal data
- Valid time
- Transaction time
- Temporal relation
- Bitemporal relation

- Universal coordinated time (UTC)
- Snapshot relation
- Temporal query languages
- Temporal selection
- Temporal projection

- Temporal join
- Spatial and geographic data
- Computer-aided-design (CAD) data
- Geographic data
- Geographic information systems
- Triangulation
- Design databases
- Geographic data
- Raster data
- Vector data
- Global positioning system (GPS)
- Spatial queries
- Nearness queries
- Nearest-neighbor queries
- Region queries
- Spatial join
- Indexing of spatial data
- k-d trees
- k-d-B trees
- Quadtrees
  - ☐ PR quadtree
  - ☐ Region quadtree
- R-trees
  - ☐ Bounding box
  - ☐ Quadratic split
- Multimedia databases
- Isochronous data
- Continuous-media data
- Similarity-based retrieval
- Multimedia data formats
- Video servers
- Mobile computing
  - ☐ Mobile hosts
  - ☐ Mobile support stations
  - ☐ Cell
  - ☐ Handoff
- Location-dependent queries
- Broadcast data
- Consistency
  - ☐ Invalidation reports
  - ☐ Version-vector scheme

Exercises

23.1 What are the two types of time, and how are they different? Why does it make sense to have both types of time associated with a tuple?

23.2 Will functional dependencies be preserved if a relation is converted to a temporal relation by adding a time attribute? How is the problem handled in a temporal database?

23.3 Suppose you have a relation containing the x, y coordinates and names of restaurants. Suppose also that the only queries that will be asked are of the following form: The query specifies a point, and asks if there is a restaurant exactly at that point. Which type of index would be preferable, R-tree or B-tree? Why?

23.4 Consider two-dimensional vector data where the data items do not overlap. Is it possible to convert such vector data to raster data? If so, what are the drawbacks of storing raster data obtained by such conversion, instead of the original vector data?

23.5 Suppose you have a spatial database that supports region queries (with circular regions) but not nearest-neighbor queries. Describe an algorithm to find the nearest neighbor by making use of multiple region queries.

23.6 Suppose you want to store line segments in an R-tree. If a line segment is not parallel to the axes, the bounding box for it can be large, containing a large empty area.
  - Describe the effect on performance of having large bounding boxes on queries that ask for line segments intersecting a given region.
  - Briefly describe a technique to improve performance for such queries and give an example of its benefit. Hint: you can divide segments into smaller pieces.

23.7 Give a recursive procedure to efficiently compute the spatial join of two relations with R-tree indices. (Hint: Use bounding boxes to check if leaf entries under a pair of internal nodes may intersect.)

23.8 Study the support for spatial data offered by the database system that you use, and implement the following:
  a. A schema to represent the geographic location of restaurants along with features such as the cuisine served at the restaurant and the level of expensiveness.
  b. A query to find moderately priced restaurants that serve Indian food and are within 5 miles of your house (assume any location for your house).
  c. A query to find for each restaurant the distance from the nearest restaurant serving the same cuisine and with the same level of expensiveness.

23.9 What problems can occur in a continuous-media system if data is delivered either too slowly or too fast?

23.10 Describe how the ideas behind the RAID organization (Section 11.3) can be used in a broadcast-data environment, where there may occasionally be noise that prevents reception of part of the data being transmitted.

23.11 List three main features of mobile computing over wireless networks that are distinct from traditional distributed systems.

23.12 List three factors that need to be considered in query optimization for mobile computing that are not considered in traditional query optimizers.

23.13 Define a model of repeatedly broadcast data in which the broadcast medium is modeled as a virtual disk. Describe how access time and data-transfer rate for this virtual disk differ from the corresponding values for a typical hard disk.

23.14 Consider a database of documents in which all documents are kept in a central database. Copies of some documents are kept on mobile computers. Suppose that mobile computer A updates a copy of document 1 while it is disconnected, and, at the same time, mobile computer B updates a copy of document 2 while it is disconnected. Show how the version-vector scheme can ensure proper updating of the central database and mobile computers when a mobile computer reconnects.

23.15 Give an example to show that the version-vector scheme does not ensure serializability. (Hint: Use the example from Exercise 23.14, with the assumption that documents 1 and 2 are available on both mobile computers A and B, and take into account the possibility that a document may be read without being updated.)

Bibliographical Notes

The incorporation of time into the relational data model is discussed in Snodgrass and Ahn [1985], Clifford and Tansel [1985], Gadia [1986], Gadia [1988], Snodgrass [1987], Tansel et al. [1993], Snodgrass et al. [1994], and Tuzhilin and Clifford [1990]. Stam and Snodgrass [1988] and Soo [1991] provide surveys on temporal data management. Jensen et al. [1994] presents a glossary of temporal-database concepts, aimed at unifying the terminology. a proposal that had significant impact on the SQL standard. Tansel et al. [1993] is a collection of articles on different aspects of temporal databases. Chomicki [1995] presents techniques for managing temporal integrity constraints. A concept of completeness for temporal query languages analogous to relational completeness (equivalence to the relational algebra) is given in Clifford et al. [1994].

Samet [1995b] provides an overview of the large amount of work on spatial index structures. Samet [1990] provides a textbook coverage of spatial data structures. An early description of the quad tree is provided by Finkel and Bentley [1974]. Samet [1990] and Samet [1995b] describe numerous variants of quad trees. Bentley [1975] describes the k-d tree, and Robinson [1981] describes the k-d-B tree. The R-tree was originally presented in Guttman [1984]. Extensions of the R-tree are presented by Sellis et al. [1987], which describes the R^+ tree; Beckmann et al. [1990], which describes the R^* tree; and Kamel and Faloutsos [1992], which describes a parallel version of the R-tree.

Brinkhoff et al. [1993] discusses an implementation of spatial joins using R-trees. Lo and Ravishankar [1996] and Patel and DeWitt [1996] present partitioning-based methods for computation of spatial joins. Samet and Aref [1995] provides an overview of spatial data models, spatial operations, and the integration of spatial and nonspatial data. Indexing of handwritten documents is discussed in Aref et al. [1995b], Aref et al. [1995a], and Lopresti and Tomkins [1993]. Joins of approximate data are discussed in Barbará et al. [1992]. Evangelidis et al. [1995] presents a technique for concurrent access to indices on spatial data.

Samet [1995a] describes research issues in multimedia databases. Indexing of multimedia data is discussed in Faloutsos and Lin [1995]. Video servers are discussed in Anderson et al. [1992], Rangan et al. [1992], Ozden et al. [1994], Freedman and DeWitt [1995], and Ozden et al. [1996b]. Fault tolerance is discussed in Berson et al. [1995] and Ozden et al. [1996a]. Reason et al. [1996] suggests alternative compression schemes for video transmission over wireless networks. Disk storage management techniques for video data are described in Chen et al. [1995], Chervenak et al. [1995], Ozden et al. [1995a], and Ozden et al. [1995b].

Information management in systems that include mobile computers is studied in Alonso and Korth [1993] and Imielinski and Badrinath [1994]. Imielinski and Korth [1996] presents an introduction to mobile computing and a collection of research papers on the subject. Indexing of data broadcast over wireless media is considered in Imielinski et al. [1995]. Caching of data in mobile environments is discussed in Barbará and Imielinski [1994] and Acharya et al. [1995]. Disk management in mobile computers is addressed in Douglis et al. [1994].

The version-vector scheme for detecting inconsistency in distributed file systems is described by Popek et al. [1981] and Parker et al. [1983].

Advanced Transaction Processing

In Chapters 15, 16, and 17, we introduced the concept of a transaction, which is a program unit that accesses—and possibly updates—various data items, and whose execution ensures the preservation of the ACID properties. We discussed in those chapters a variety of schemes for ensuring the ACID properties in an environment where failure can occur, and where the transactions may run concurrently.

In this chapter, we go beyond the basic schemes discussed previously, and cover advanced transaction-processing concepts, including transaction-processing monitors, transactional workflows, main-memory databases, real-time databases, long-duration transactions, nested transactions, and multidatabase transactions.

24.1 Transaction-Processing Monitors

Transaction-processing monitors (**TP monitors**) are systems that were developed in the 1970s and 1980s, initially in response to a need to support a large number of remote terminals (such as airline-reservation terminals) from a single computer. The term *TP monitor* initially stood for *teleprocessing monitor*.

TP monitors have since evolved to provide the core support for distributed transaction processing, and the term TP monitor has acquired its current meaning. The CICS TP monitor from IBM was one of the earliest TP monitors, and has been very widely used. Current-generation TP monitors include Tuxedo and Top End (both now from BEA Systems), Encina (from Transarc, which is now a part of IBM), and Transaction Server (from Microsoft).

24.1.1 TP-Monitor Architectures

Large-scale transaction processing systems are built around a client–server architecture. One way of building such systems is to have a server process for each client; the server performs authentication, and then executes actions requested by the client.

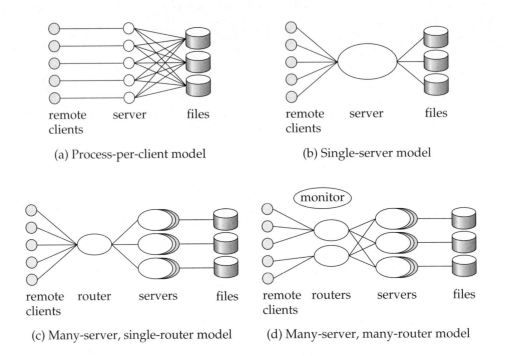

(a) Process-per-client model   (b) Single-server model

(c) Many-server, single-router model   (d) Many-server, many-router model

Figure 24.1   TP-monitor architectures.

This **process-per-client model** is illustrated in Figure 24.1a. This model presents several problems with respect to memory utilization and processing speed:

- Per-process memory requirements are high. Even if memory for program code is shared by all processes, each process consumes memory for local data and open file descriptors, as well as for operating-system overhead, such as page tables to support virtual memory.

- The operating system divides up available CPU time among processes by switching among them; this technique is called **multitasking**. Each **context switch** between one process and the next has considerable CPU overhead; even on today's fast systems, a context switch can take hundreds of microseconds.

The above problems can be avoided by having a single-server process to which all remote clients connect; this model is called the **single-server model**, illustrated in Figure 24.1b. Remote clients send requests to the server process, which then executes those requests. This model is also used in client–server environments, where clients send requests to a single-server process. The server process handles tasks, such as user authentication, that would normally be handled by the operating system. To avoid blocking other clients when processing a long request for one client, the server process is **multithreaded**: The server process has a thread of control for each client, and, in effect, implements its own low-overhead multitasking. It executes code on behalf of one client for a while, then saves the internal context and switches to the code for another client. Unlike the overhead of full multitasking, the cost of switching between threads is low (typically only a few microseconds).

Systems based on the single-server model, such as the original version of the IBM CICS TP monitor and file servers such as Novel's NetWare, successfully provided high transaction rates with limited resources. However, they had problems, especially when multiple applications accessed the same database:

- Since all the applications run as a single process, there is no protection among them. A bug in one application can affect all the other applications as well. It would be best to run each application as a separate process.

- Such systems are not suited for parallel or distributed databases, since a server process cannot execute on multiple computers at once. (However, concurrent threads within a process can be supported in a shared-memory multiprocessor system.) This is a serious drawback in large organizations, where parallel processing is critical for handling large workloads, and distributed data are becoming increasingly common.

One way to solve these problems is to run multiple application-server processes that access a common database, and to let the clients communicate with the application through a single communication process that routes requests. This model is called the **many-server, single-router model**, illustrated in Figure 24.1c. This model supports independent server processes for multiple applications; further, each application can have a pool of server processes, any one of which can handle a client session. The request can, for example, be routed to the most lightly loaded server in a pool. As before, each server process can itself be multithreaded, so that it can handle multiple clients concurrently. As a further generalization, the application servers can run on different sites of a parallel or distributed database, and the communication process can handle the coordination among the processes.

The above architecture is also widely used in Web servers. A Web server has a main process that receives HTTP requests, and then assigns the task of handling each request to a separate process (chosen from among a pool of processes). Each of the processes is itself multithreaded, so that it can handle multiple requests.

A more general architecture has multiple processes, rather than just one, to communicate with clients. The client communication processes interact with one or more router processes, which route their requests to the appropriate server. Later-generation TP monitors therefore have a different architecture, called the **many-server, many-router model**, illustrated in Figure 24.1d. A controller process starts up the other processes, and supervises their functioning. Tandem Pathway is an example of the later-generation TP monitors that use this architecture. Very high performance Web server systems also adopt such an architecture.

The detailed structure of a TP monitor appears in Figure 24.2. A TP monitor does more than simply pass messages to application servers. When messages arrive, they may have to be queued; thus, there is a **queue manager** for incoming messages. The queue may be a **durable queue**, whose entries survive system failures. Using a

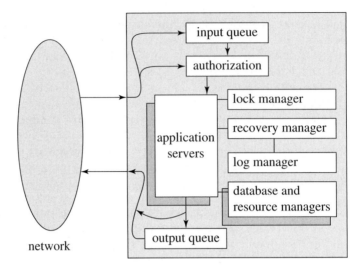

Figure 24.2 TP-monitor components.

durable queue helps ensure that once received and stored in the queue, the messages will be processed eventually, regardless of system failures. Authorization and application-server management (for example, server startup, and routing of messages to servers) are further functions of a TP monitor. TP monitors often provide logging, recovery, and concurrency-control facilities, allowing application servers to implement the ACID transaction properties directly if required.

Finally, TP monitors also provide support for persistent messaging. Recall that persistent messaging (Section 19.4.3) provides a guarantee that the message will be delivered if (and only if) the transaction commits.

In addition to these facilities, many TP monitors also provided *presentation facilities* to create menus/forms interfaces for dumb clients such as terminals; these facilities are no longer important since dumb clients are no longer widely used.

24.1.2 Application Coordination Using TP monitors

Applications today often have to interact with multiple databases. They may also have to interact with legacy systems, such as special-purpose data-storage systems built directly on file systems. Finally, they may have to communicate with users or other applications at remote sites. Hence, they also have to interact with communication subsystems. It is important to be able to coordinate data accesses, and to implement ACID properties for transactions across such systems.

Modern TP monitors provide support for the construction and administration of such large applications, built up from multiple subsystems such as databases, legacy systems, and communication systems. A TP monitor treats each subsystem as a **resource manager** that provides transactional access to some set of resources. The interface between the TP monitor and the resource manager is defined by a set of transaction primitives, such as *begin_transaction*, *commit_transaction*, *abort_transaction*, and *prepare_to_commit_transaction* (for two-phase commit). Of course, the resource manager must also provide other services, such as supplying data, to the application.

The resource-manager interface is defined by the X/Open Distributed Transaction Processing standard. Many database systems support the X/Open standards, and can act as resource managers. TP monitors—as well as other products, such as SQL systems, that support the X/Open standards—can connect to the resource managers.

In addition, services provided by a TP monitor, such as persistent messaging and durable queues, act as resource managers supporting transactions. The TP monitor can act as coordinator of two-phase commit for transactions that access these services as well as database systems. For example, when a queued update transaction is executed, an output message is delivered, and the request transaction is removed from the request queue. Two-phase commit between the database and the resource managers for the durable queue and persistent messaging helps ensure that, regardless of failures, either all these actions occur, or none occurs.

We can also use TP monitors to administer complex client–server systems consisting of multiple servers and a large number of clients. The TP monitor coordinates activities such as system checkpoints and shutdowns. It provides security and authentication of clients. It administers server pools by adding servers or removing servers without interruption of the system. Finally, it controls the scope of failures. If a server fails, the TP monitor can detect this failure, abort the transactions in progress, and restart the transactions. If a node fails, the TP monitor can migrate transactions to servers at other nodes, again backing out incomplete transactions. When failed nodes restart, the TP monitor can govern the recovery of the node's resource managers.

TP monitors can be used to hide database failures in replicated systems; remote backup systems (Section 17.10) are an example of replicated systems. Transaction requests are sent to the TP monitor, which relays the messages to one of the database replicas (the primary site, in case of remote backup systems). If one site fails, the TP monitor can transparently route messages to a backup site, masking the failure of the first site.

In client–server systems, clients often interact with servers via a **remote-procedure-call (RPC)** mechanism, where a client invokes a procedure call, which is actually executed at the server, with the results sent back to the client. As far as the client code that invokes the RPC is concerned, the call looks like a local procedure-call invocation. TP monitor systems, such as Encina, provide a **transactional RPC** interface to their services. In such an interface, the RPC mechanism provides calls that can be used to enclose a series of RPC calls within a transaction. Thus, updates performed by an RPC are carried out within the scope of the transaction, and can be rolled back if there is any failure.

24.2 Transactional Workflows

A **workflow** is an activity in which multiple tasks are executed in a coordinated way by different processing entities. A **task** defines some work to be done and can be specified in a number of ways, including a textual description in a file or electronic-mail message, a form, a message, or a computer program. The **processing entity** that

Workflow application	Typical task	Typical processing entity
electronic-mail routing	electronic-mail message	mailers
loan processing	form processing	humans, application software
purchase-order processing	form processing	humans, application software, DBMSs

Figure 24.3   Examples of workflows.

performs the tasks may be a person or a software system (for example, a mailer, an application program, or a database-management system).

Figure 24.3 shows examples of workflows. A simple example is that of an electronic-mail system. The delivery of a single mail message may involve several mailer systems that receive and forward the mail message, until the message reaches its destination, where it is stored. Each mailer performs a task—forwarding the mail to the next mailer—and the tasks of multiple mailers may be required to route mail from source to destination. Other terms used in the database and related literature to refer to workflows include **task flow** and **multisystem applications**. Workflow tasks are also sometimes called **steps**.

In general, workflows may involve one or more humans. For instance, consider the processing of a loan. The relevant workflow appears in Figure 24.4. The person who wants a loan fills out a form, which is then checked by a loan officer. An employee who processes loan applications verifies the data in the form, using sources such as credit-reference bureaus. When all the required information has been collected, the loan officer may decide to approve the loan; that decision may then have to be approved by one or more superior officers, after which the loan can be made. Each human here performs a task; in a bank that has not automated the task of loan processing, the coordination of the tasks is typically carried out by passing of the loan application, with attached notes and other information, from one employee to

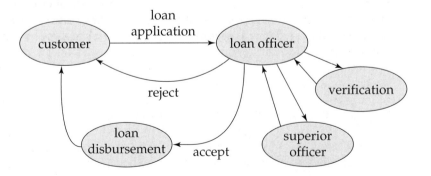

Figure 24.4   Workflow in loan processing.

the next. Other examples of workflows include processing of expense vouchers, of purchase orders, and of credit-card transactions.

Today, all the information related to a workflow is more than likely to be stored in a digital form on one or more computers, and, with the growth of networking, information can be easily transferred from one computer to another. Hence, it is feasible for organizations to automate their workflows. For example, to automate the tasks involved in loan processing, we can store the loan application and associated information in a database. The workflow itself then involves handing of responsibility from one human to the next, and possibly even to programs that can automatically fetch the required information. Humans can coordinate their activities by means such as electronic mail.

We have to address two activities, in general, to automate a workflow. The first is **workflow specification**: detailing the tasks that must be carried out and defining the execution requirements. The second problem is **workflow execution**, which we must do while providing the safeguards of traditional database systems related to computation correctness and data integrity and durability. For example, it is not acceptable for a loan application or a voucher to be lost, or to be processed more than once, because of a system crash. The idea behind transactional workflows is to use and extend the concepts of transactions to the context of workflows.

Both activities are complicated by the fact that many organizations use several independently managed information-processing systems that, in most cases, were developed separately to automate different functions. Workflow activities may require interactions among several such systems, each performing a task, as well as interactions with humans.

A number of workflow systems have been developed in recent years. Here, we study properties of workflow systems at a relatively abstract level, without going into the details of any particular system.

24.2.1 Workflow Specification

Internal aspects of a task do not need to be modeled for the purpose of specification and management of a workflow. In an abstract view of a task, a task may use parameters stored in its input variables, may retrieve and update data in the local system, may store its results in its output variables, and may be queried about its execution state. At any time during the execution, the **workflow state** consists of the collection of states of the workflow's constituent tasks, and the states (values) of all variables in the workflow specification.

The coordination of tasks can be specified either statically or dynamically. A static specification defines the tasks—and dependencies among them—before the execution of the workflow begins. For instance, the tasks in an expense-voucher workflow may consist of the approvals of the voucher by a secretary, a manager, and an accountant, in that order, and finally by the delivery of a check. The dependencies among the tasks may be simple—each task has to be completed before the next begins.

A generalization of this strategy is to have a precondition for execution of each task in the workflow, so that all possible tasks in a workflow and their dependencies are known in advance, but only those tasks whose preconditions are satisfied are executed. The preconditions can be defined through dependencies such as the following:

- **Execution states** of other tasks—for example, "task t_i cannot start until task t_j has ended," or "task t_i must abort if task t_j has committed"

- **Output values** of other tasks—for example, "task t_i can start if task t_j returns a value greater than 25," or "the manager-approval task can start if the secretary-approval task returns a value of OK"

- **External variables** modified by external events—for example, "task t_i cannot be started before 9 AM," or "task t_i must be started within 24 hours of the completion of task t_j"

We can combine the dependencies by the regular logical connectors (**or, and, not**) to form complex scheduling preconditions.

An example of dynamic scheduling of tasks is an electronic-mail routing system. The next task to be scheduled for a given mail message depends on what the destination address of the message is, and on which intermediate routers are functioning.

24.2.2   Failure-Atomicity Requirements of a Workflow

The workflow designer may specify the **failure-atomicity** requirements of a workflow according to the semantics of the workflow. The traditional notion of failure atomicity would require that a failure of any task results in the failure of the workflow. However, a workflow can, in many cases, survive the failure of one of its tasks—for example, by executing a functionally equivalent task at another site. Therefore, we should allow the designer to define failure-atomicity requirements of a workflow. The system must guarantee that every execution of a workflow will terminate in a state that satisfies the failure-atomicity requirements defined by the designer. We call those states **acceptable termination states** of a workflow. All other execution states of a workflow constitute a set of **nonacceptable termination states**, in which the failure-atomicity requirements may be violated.

An acceptable termination state can be designated as committed or aborted. A **committed acceptable termination state** is an execution state in which the objectives of a workflow have been achieved. In contrast, an **aborted acceptable termination state** is a valid termination state in which a workflow has failed to achieve its objectives. If an aborted acceptable termination state has been reached, all undesirable effects of the partial execution of the workflow must be undone in accordance with that workflow's failure-atomicity requirements.

A workflow must reach an acceptable termination state *even in the presence of system failures*. Thus, if a workflow was in a nonacceptable termination state at the time of failure, during system recovery it must be brought to an acceptable termination state (whether aborted or committed).

For example, in the loan-processing workflow, in the final state, either the loan applicant is told that a loan cannot be made or the loan is disbursed. In case of failures such as a long failure of the verification system, the loan application could be returned to the loan applicant with a suitable explanation; this outcome would constitute an aborted acceptable termination. A committed acceptable termination would be either the acceptance or the rejection of the loan.

In general, a task can commit and release its resources before the workflow reaches a termination state. However, if the multitask transaction later aborts, its failure atomicity may require that we undo the effects of already completed tasks (for example, committed subtransactions) by executing compensating tasks (as subtransactions). The semantics of compensation requires that a compensating transaction eventually complete its execution successfully, possibly after a number of resubmissions.

In an expense-voucher-processing workflow, for example, a department-budget balance may be reduced on the basis of an initial approval of a voucher by the manager. If the voucher is later rejected, whether because of failure or for other reasons, the budget may have to be restored by a compensating transaction.

24.2.3 Execution of Workflows

The execution of the tasks may be controlled by a human coordinator or by a software system called a **workflow-management system**. A workflow-management system consists of a scheduler, task agents, and a mechanism to query the state of the workflow system. A task agent controls the execution of a task by a processing entity. A scheduler is a program that processes workflows by submitting various tasks for execution, monitoring various events, and evaluating conditions related to intertask dependencies. A scheduler may submit a task for execution (to a task agent), or may request that a previously submitted task be aborted. In the case of multidatabase transactions, the tasks are subtransactions, and the processing entities are local database management systems. In accordance with the workflow specifications, the scheduler enforces the scheduling dependencies and is responsible for ensuring that tasks reach acceptable termination states.

There are three architectural approaches to the development of a workflow-management system. A **centralized architecture** has a single scheduler that schedules the tasks for all concurrently executing workflows. The **partially distributed architecture** has one scheduler instantiated for each workflow. When the issues of concurrent execution can be separated from the scheduling function, the latter option is a natural choice. A **fully distributed architecture** has no scheduler, but the task agents coordinate their execution by communicating with one another to satisfy task dependencies and other workflow execution requirements.

The simplest workflow-execution systems follow the fully distributed approach just described and are based on messaging. Messaging may be implemented by persistent messaging mechanisms, to provide guaranteed delivery. Some implementations use e-mail for messaging; such implementations provide many of the features of persistent messaging, but generally do not guarantee atomicity of message delivery and transaction commit. Each site has a task agent that executes tasks received through messages. Execution may also involve presenting messages to humans, who have then to carry out some action. When a task is completed at a site, and needs to be processed at another site, the task agent dispatches a message to the next site. The message contains all relevant information about the task to be performed. Such message-based workflow systems are particularly useful in networks that may be disconnected for part of the time, such as dial-up networks.

The centralized approach is used in workflow systems where the data are stored in a central database. The scheduler notifies various agents, such as humans or computer programs, that a task has to be carried out, and keeps track of task completion. It is easier to keep track of the state of a workflow with a centralized approach than it is with a fully distributed approach.

The scheduler must guarantee that a workflow will terminate in one of the specified acceptable termination states. Ideally, before attempting to execute a workflow, the scheduler should examine that workflow to check whether the workflow may terminate in a nonacceptable state. If the scheduler cannot guarantee that a workflow will terminate in an acceptable state, it should reject such specifications without attempting to execute the workflow. As an example, let us consider a workflow consisting of two tasks represented by subtransactions S_1 and S_2, with the failure-atomicity requirements indicating that either both or neither of the subtransactions should be committed. If S_1 and S_2 do not provide prepared-to-commit states (for a two-phase commit), and further do not have compensating transactions, then it is possible to reach a state where one subtransaction is committed and the other aborted, and there is no way to bring both to the same state. Therefore, such a workflow specification is **unsafe**, and should be rejected.

Safety checks such as the one just described may be impossible or impractical to implement in the scheduler; it then becomes the responsibility of the person designing the workflow specification to ensure that the workflows are safe.

24.2.4 Recovery of a Workflow

The objective of **workflow recovery** is to enforce the failure atomicity of the workflows. The recovery procedures must make sure that, if a failure occurs in any of the workflow-processing components (including the scheduler), the workflow will eventually reach an acceptable termination state (whether aborted or committed). For example, the scheduler could continue processing after failure and recovery, as though nothing happened, thus providing forward recoverability. Otherwise, the scheduler could abort the whole workflow (that is, reach one of the global abort states). In either case, some subtransactions may need to be committed or even submitted for execution (for example, compensating subtransactions).

We assume that the processing entities involved in the workflow have their own local recovery systems and handle their local failures. To recover the execution-environment context, the failure-recovery routines need to restore the state information of the scheduler at the time of failure, including the information about the execution states of each task. Therefore, the appropriate status information must be logged on stable storage.

We also need to consider the contents of the message queues. When one agent hands off a task to another, the handoff should be carried out exactly once: If the handoff happens twice a task may get executed twice; if the handoff does not occur, the task may get lost. Persistent messaging (Section 19.4.3) provides exactly the features to ensure positive, single handoff.

24.2.5 Workflow Management Systems

Workflows are often hand coded as part of application systems. For instance, enterprise resource planning (ERP) systems, which help coordinate activities across an entire enterprise, have numerous workflows built into them.

The goal of workflow management systems is to simplify the construction of workflows and make them more reliable, by permitting them to be specified in a high-level manner and executed in accordance with the specification. There are a large number of commercial workflow management systems; some, like FlowMark from IBM, are general-purpose workflow management systems, while others are specific to particular workflows, such as order processing or bug/failure reporting systems.

In today's world of interconnected organizations, it is not sufficient to manage workflows only within an organization. Workflows that cross organizational boundaries are becoming increasingly common. For instance, consider an order placed by an organization and communicated to another organization that fulfills the order. In each organization there may be a workflow associated with the order, and it is important that the workflows be able to interoperate, in order to minimize human intervention.

The Workflow Management Coalition has developed standards for interoperation between workflow systems. Current standardization efforts use XML as the underlying language for communicating information about the workflow. See the bibliographical notes for more information.

24.3 Main-Memory Databases

To allow a high rate of transaction processing (hundreds or thousands of transactions per second), we must use high-performance hardware, and must exploit parallelism. These techniques alone, however, are insufficient to obtain very low response times, since disk I/O remains a bottleneck—about 10 milliseconds are required for each I/O and this number has not decreased at a rate comparable to the increase in processor speeds. Disk I/O is often the bottleneck for reads, as well as for transaction commits. The long disk latency (about 10 milliseconds average) increases not only the time to access a data item, but also limits the number of accesses per second.

We can make a database system less disk bound by increasing the size of the database buffer. Advances in main-memory technology let us construct large main memories at relatively low cost. Today, commercial 64-bit systems can support main memories of tens of gigabytes.

For some applications, such as real-time control, it is necessary to store data in main memory to meet performance requirements. The memory size required for most such systems is not exceptionally large, although there are at least a few applications that require multiple gigabytes of data to be memory resident. Since memory sizes have been growing at a very fast rate, an increasing number of applications can be expected to have data that fit into main memory.

Large main memories allow faster processing of transactions, since data are memory resident. However, there are still disk-related limitations:

- Log records must be written to stable storage before a transaction is committed. The improved performance made possible by a large main memory may result in the logging process becoming a bottleneck. We can reduce commit time by creating a stable log buffer in main memory, using nonvolatile RAM (implemented, for example, by battery backed-up memory). The overhead imposed by logging can also be reduced by the *group-commit* technique discussed later in this section. Throughput (number of transactions per second) is still limited by the data-transfer rate of the log disk.

- Buffer blocks marked as modified by committed transactions still have to be written so that the amount of log that has to be replayed at recovery time is reduced. If the update rate is extremely high, the disk data-transfer rate may become a bottleneck.

- If the system crashes, all of main memory is lost. On recovery, the system has an empty database buffer, and data items must be input from disk when they are accessed. Therefore, even after recovery is complete, it takes some time before the database is fully loaded in main memory and high-speed processing of transactions can resume.

On the other hand, a main-memory database provides opportunities for optimizations:

- Since memory is costlier than disk space, internal data structures in main-memory databases have to be designed to reduce space requirements. However, data structures can have pointers crossing multiple pages unlike those in disk databases, where the cost of the I/Os to traverse multiple pages would be excessively high. For example, tree structures in main-memory databases can be relatively deep, unlike B^+-trees, but should minimize space requirements.

- There is no need to pin buffer pages in memory before data are accessed, since buffer pages will never be replaced.

- Query-processing techniques should be designed to minimize space overhead, so that main memory limits are not exceeded while a query is being evaluated; that situation would result in paging to swap area, and would slow down query processing.

- Once the disk I/O bottleneck is removed, operations such as locking and latching may become bottlenecks. Such bottlenecks must be eliminated by improvements in the implementation of these operations.

- Recovery algorithms can be optimized, since pages rarely need to be written out to make space for other pages.

TimesTen and DataBlitz are two main-memory database products that exploit several of these optimizations, while the Oracle database has added special features to support very large main memories. Additional information on main-memory databases is given in the references in the bibliographical notes.

The process of committing a transaction T requires these records to be written to stable storage:

- All log records associated with T that have not been output to stable storage

- The <T **commit**> log record

These output operations frequently require the output of blocks that are only partially filled. To ensure that nearly full blocks are output, we use the **group-commit** technique. Instead of attempting to commit T when T completes, the system waits until several transactions have completed, or a certain period of time has passed since a transaction completed execution. It then commits the group of transactions that are waiting, together. Blocks written to the log on stable storage would contain records of several transactions. By careful choice of group size and maximum waiting time, the system can ensure that blocks are full when they are written to stable storage without making transactions wait excessively. This technique results, on average, in fewer output operations per committed transaction.

Although group commit reduces the overhead imposed by logging, it results in a slight delay in commit of transactions that perform updates. The delay can be made quite small (say, 10 milliseconds), which is acceptable for many applications. These delays can be eliminated if disks or disk controllers support nonvolatile RAM buffers for write operations. Transactions can commit as soon as the write is performed on the nonvolatile RAM buffer. In this case, there is no need for group commit.

Note that group commit is useful even in databases with disk-resident data.

24.4 Real-Time Transaction Systems

The integrity constraints that we have considered thus far pertain to the values stored in the database. In certain applications, the constraints include **deadlines** by which a task must be completed. Examples of such applications include plant management, traffic control, and scheduling. When deadlines are included, correctness of an execution is no longer solely an issue of database consistency. Rather, we are concerned with how many deadlines are missed, and by how much time they are missed. Deadlines are characterized as follows:

- **Hard deadline**. Serious problems, such as system crash, may occur if a task is not completed by its deadline.

- **Firm deadline**. The task has zero value if it is completed after the deadline.

- **Soft deadlines**. The task has diminishing value if it is completed after the deadline, with the value approaching zero as the degree of lateness increases.

Systems with deadlines are called **real-time systems**.

Transaction management in real-time systems must take deadlines into account. If the concurrency-control protocol determines that a transaction T_i must wait, it may cause T_i to miss the deadline. In such cases, it may be preferable to pre-empt the transaction holding the lock, and to allow T_i to proceed. Pre-emption must be used with care, however, because the time lost by the pre-empted transaction (due to roll-back and restart) may cause the transaction to miss its deadline. Unfortunately, it is difficult to determine whether rollback or waiting is preferable in a given situation.

A major difficulty in supporting real-time constraints arises from the variance in transaction execution time. In the best case, all data accesses reference data in the database buffer. In the worst case, each access causes a buffer page to be written to disk (preceded by the requisite log records), followed by the reading from disk of the page containing the data to be accessed. Because the two or more disk accesses required in the worst case take several orders of magnitude more time than the main-memory references required in the best case, transaction execution time can be estimated only very poorly if data are resident on disk. Hence, main-memory databases are often used if real-time constraints have to be met.

However, even if data are resident in main memory, variances in execution time arise from lock waits, transaction aborts, and so on. Researchers have devoted considerable effort to concurrency control for real-time databases. They have extended locking protocols to provide higher priority for transactions with early deadlines. They have found that optimistic concurrency protocols perform well in real-time databases; that is, these protocols result in fewer missed deadlines than even the extended locking protocols. The bibliographical notes provide references to research in the area of real-time databases.

In real-time systems, deadlines, rather than absolute speed, are the most important issue. Designing a real-time system involves ensuring that there is enough processing power to meet deadlines without requiring excessive hardware resources. Achieving this objective, despite the variance in execution time resulting from transaction management, remains a challenging problem.

24.5 Long-Duration Transactions

The transaction concept developed initially in the context of data-processing applications, in which most transactions are noninteractive and of short duration. Although the techniques presented here and earlier in Chapters 15, 16, and 17 work well in those applications, serious problems arise when this concept is applied to database systems that involve human interaction. Such transactions have these key properties:

- **Long duration**. Once a human interacts with an active transaction, that transaction becomes a **long-duration transaction** from the perspective of the computer, since human response time is slow relative to computer speed. Furthermore, in design applications, the human activity may involve hours, days, or an even longer period. Thus, transactions may be of long duration in human terms, as well as in machine terms.

- **Exposure of uncommitted data**. Data generated and displayed to a user by a long-duration transaction are uncommitted, since the transaction may abort. Thus, users—and, as a result, other transactions—may be forced to read uncommitted data. If several users are cooperating on a project, user transactions may need to exchange data prior to transaction commit.

- **Subtasks**. An interactive transaction may consist of a set of subtasks initiated by the user. The user may wish to abort a subtask without necessarily causing the entire transaction to abort.

- **Recoverability**. It is unacceptable to abort a long-duration interactive transaction because of a system crash. The active transaction must be recovered to a state that existed shortly before the crash so that relatively little human work is lost.

- **Performance**. Good performance in an interactive transaction system is defined as fast response time. This definition is in contrast to that in a noninteractive system, in which high throughput (number of transactions per second) is the goal. Systems with high throughput make efficient use of system resources. However, in the case of interactive transactions, the most costly resource is the user. If the efficiency and satisfaction of the user is to be optimized, response time should be fast (from a human perspective). In those cases where a task takes a long time, response time should be predictable (that is, the variance in response times should be low), so that users can manage their time well.

In Sections 24.5.1 through 24.5.5, we shall see why these five properties are incompatible with the techniques presented thus far, and shall discuss how those techniques can be modified to accommodate long-duration interactive transactions.

24.5.1 Nonserializable Executions

The properties that we discussed make it impractical to enforce the requirement used in earlier chapters that only serializable schedules be permitted. Each of the concurrency-control protocols of Chapter 16 has adverse effects on long-duration transactions:

- **Two-phase locking**. When a lock cannot be granted, the transaction requesting the lock is forced to wait for the data item in question to be unlocked. The duration of this wait is proportional to the duration of the transaction holding the lock. If the data item is locked by a short-duration transaction, we expect that the waiting time will be short (except in case of deadlock or extraordinary system load). However, if the data item is locked by a long-duration transaction, the wait will be of long duration. Long waiting times lead to both longer response time and an increased chance of deadlock.

- **Graph-based protocols**. Graph-based protocols allow for locks to be released earlier than under the two-phase locking protocols, and they prevent deadlock. However, they impose an ordering on the data items. Transactions must lock data items in a manner consistent with this ordering. As a result, a transaction may have to lock more data than it needs. Furthermore, a transaction must hold a lock until there is no chance that the lock will be needed again. Thus, long-duration lock waits are likely to occur.

- **Timestamp-based protocols**. Timestamp protocols never require a transaction to wait. However, they do require transactions to abort under certain circumstances. If a long-duration transaction is aborted, a substantial amount of work is lost. For noninteractive transactions, this lost work is a performance issue. For interactive transactions, the issue is also one of user satisfaction. It is highly undesirable for a user to find that several hours' worth of work have been undone.

- **Validation protocols**. Like timestamp-based protocols, validation protocols enforce serializability by means of transaction abort.

Thus, it appears that the enforcement of serializability results in long-duration waits, in abort of long-duration transactions, or in both. There are theoretical results, cited in the bibliographical notes, that substantiate this conclusion.

Further difficulties with the enforcement of serializability arise when we consider recovery issues. We previously discussed the problem of cascading rollback, in which the abort of a transaction may lead to the abort of other transactions. This phenomenon is undesirable, particularly for long-duration transactions. If locking is used, exclusive locks must be held until the end of the transaction, if cascading rollback is to be avoided. This holding of exclusive locks, however, increases the length of transaction waiting time.

Thus, it appears that the enforcement of transaction atomicity must either lead to an increased probability of long-duration waits or create a possibility of cascading rollback.

These considerations are the basis for the alternative concepts of correctness of concurrent executions and transaction recovery that we consider in the remainder of this section.

24.5.2 Concurrency Control

The fundamental goal of database concurrency control is to ensure that concurrent execution of transactions does not result in a loss of database consistency. The concept of serializability can be used to achieve this goal, since all serializable schedules preserve consistency of the database. However, not all schedules that preserve consistency of the database are serializable. For an example, consider again a bank database consisting of two accounts A and B, with the consistency requirement that the sum $A + B$ be preserved. Although the schedule of Figure 24.5 is not conflict serializable, it nevertheless preserves the sum of $A + B$. It also illustrates two important points about the concept of correctness without serializability.

- Correctness depends on the specific consistency constraints for the database.

- Correctness depends on the properties of operations performed by each transaction.

In general it is not possible to perform an automatic analysis of low-level operations by transactions and check their effect on database consistency constraints. However, there are simpler techniques. One is to use the database consistency constraints as

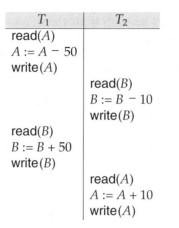

T_1	T_2
read(A)	
$A := A - 50$	
write(A)	
	read(B)
	$B := B - 10$
	write(B)
read(B)	
$B := B + 50$	
write(B)	
	read(A)
	$A := A + 10$
	write(A)

Figure 24.5   A non-conflict-serializable schedule.

the basis for a split of the database into subdatabases on which concurrency can be managed separately. Another is to treat some operations besides **read** and **write** as fundamental low-level operations, and to extend concurrency control to deal with them.

The bibliographical notes reference other techniques for ensuring consistency without requiring serializability. Many of these techniques exploit variants of multiversion concurrency control (see Section 17.6). For older data-processing applications that need only one version, multiversion protocols impose a high space overhead to store the extra versions. Since many of the new database applications require the maintenance of versions of data, concurrency-control techniques that exploit multiple versions are practical.

24.5.3   Nested and Multilevel Transactions

A long-duration transaction can be viewed as a collection of related subtasks or subtransactions. By structuring a transaction as a set of subtransactions, we are able to enhance parallelism, since it may be possible to run several subtransactions in parallel. Furthermore, it is possible to deal with failure of a subtransaction (due to abort, system crash, and so on) without having to roll back the entire long-duration transaction.

A nested or multilevel transaction T consists of a set $T = \{t_1, t_2, \ldots, t_n\}$ of subtransactions and a partial order P on T. A subtransaction t_i in T may abort without forcing T to abort. Instead, T may either restart t_i or simply choose not to run t_i. If t_i commits, this action does not make t_i permanent (unlike the situation in Chapter 17). Instead, t_i *commits to* T, and may still abort (or require compensation—see Section 24.5.4) if T aborts. An execution of T must not violate the partial order P. That is, if an edge $t_i \rightarrow t_j$ appears in the precedence graph, then $t_j \rightarrow t_i$ must not be in the transitive closure of P.

Nesting may be several levels deep, representing a subdivision of a transaction into subtasks, subsubtasks, and so on. At the lowest level of nesting, we have the standard database operations **read** and **write** that we have used previously.

If a subtransaction of T is permitted to release locks on completion, T is called a **multilevel transaction**. When a multilevel transaction represents a long-duration activity, the transaction is sometimes referred to as a **saga**. Alternatively, if locks held by a subtransaction t_i of T are automatically assigned to T on completion of t_i, T is called a **nested transaction**.

Although the main practical value of multilevel transactions arises in complex, long-duration transactions, we shall use the simple example of Figure 24.5 to show how nesting can create higher-level operations that may enhance concurrency. We rewrite transaction T_1, using subtransactions $T_{1,1}$ and $T_{1,2}$, which perform increment or decrement operations:

- T_1 consists of
    - □ $T_{1,1}$, which subtracts 50 from A
    - □ $T_{1,2}$, which adds 50 to B

Similarly, we rewrite transaction T_2, using subtransactions $T_{2,1}$ and $T_{2,2}$, which also perform increment or decrement operations:

- T_2 consists of
    - □ $T_{2,1}$, which subtracts 10 from B
    - □ $T_{2,2}$, which adds 10 to A

No ordering is specified on $T_{1,1}$, $T_{1,2}$, $T_{2,1}$, and $T_{2,2}$. Any execution of these subtransactions will generate a correct result. The schedule of Figure 24.5 corresponds to the schedule $< T_{1,1},\ T_{2,1},\ T_{1,2},\ T_{2,2} >$.

24.5.4 Compensating Transactions

To reduce the frequency of long-duration waiting, we arrange for uncommitted updates to be exposed to other concurrently executing transactions. Indeed, multilevel transactions may allow this exposure. However, the exposure of uncommitted data creates the potential for cascading rollbacks. The concept of **compensating transactions** helps us to deal with this problem.

Let transaction T be divided into several subtransactions $t_1, t_2, \ldots, t_n$. After a subtransaction t_i commits, it releases its locks. Now, if the outer-level transaction T has to be aborted, the effect of its subtransactions must be undone. Suppose that subtransactions $t_1, \ldots, t_k$ have committed, and that t_{k+1} was executing when the decision to abort is made. We can undo the effects of t_{k+1} by aborting that subtransaction. However, it is not possible to abort subtransactions $t_1, \ldots, t_k$, since they have committed already.

Instead, we execute a new subtransaction ct_i, called a *compensating transaction*, to undo the effect of a subtransaction t_i. Each subtransaction t_i is required to have a compensating transaction ct_i. The compensating transactions must be executed in the inverse order $ct_k, \ldots, ct_1$. Here are several examples of compensation:

- Consider the schedule of Figure 24.5, which we have shown to be correct, although not conflict serializable. Each subtransaction releases its locks once it completes. Suppose that T_2 fails just prior to termination, after $T_{2,2}$ has released its locks. We then run a compensating transaction for $T_{2,2}$ that subtracts 10 from A and a compensating transaction for $T_{2,1}$ that adds 10 to B.

- Consider a database insert by transaction T_i that, as a side effect, causes a B^+-tree index to be updated. The insert operation may have modified several nodes of the B^+-tree index. Other transactions may have read these nodes in accessing data other than the record inserted by T_i. As in Section 17.9, we can undo the insertion by deleting the record inserted by T_i. The result is a correct, consistent B^+-tree, but is not necessarily one with exactly the same structure as the one we had before T_i started. Thus, deletion is a compensating action for insertion.

- Consider a long-duration transaction T_i representing a travel reservation. Transaction T has three subtransactions: $T_{i,1}$, which makes airline reservations; $T_{i,2}$, which reserves rental cars; and $T_{i,3}$, which reserves a hotel room. Suppose that the hotel cancels the reservation. Instead of undoing all of T_i, we compensate for the failure of $T_{i,3}$ by deleting the old hotel reservation and making a new one.

If the system crashes in the middle of executing an outer-level transaction, its subtransactions must be rolled back when it recovers. The techniques described in Section 17.9 can be used for this purpose.

Compensation for the failure of a transaction requires that the semantics of the failed transaction be used. For certain operations, such as incrementation or insertion into a B^+-tree, the corresponding compensation is easily defined. For more complex transactions, the application programmers may have to define the correct form of compensation at the time that the transaction is coded. For complex interactive transactions, it may be necessary for the system to interact with the user to determine the proper form of compensation.

24.5.5   Implementation Issues

The transaction concepts discussed in this section create serious difficulties for implementation. We present a few of them here, and discuss how we can address these problems.

Long-duration transactions must survive system crashes. We can ensure that they will by performing a **redo** on committed subtransactions, and by performing either an **undo** or compensation for any short-duration subtransactions that were active at the time of the crash. However, these actions solve only part of the problem. In typical database systems, such internal system data as lock tables and transactions timestamps are kept in volatile storage. For a long-duration transaction to be resumed after a crash, these data must be restored. Therefore, it is necessary to log not only changes to the database, but also changes to internal system data pertaining to long-duration transactions.

Logging of updates is made more complex when certain types of data items exist in the database. A data item may be a CAD design, text of a document, or another form of composite design. Such data items are physically large. Thus, storing both the old and new values of the data item in a log record is undesirable.

There are two approaches to reducing the overhead of ensuring the recoverability of large data items:

- **Operation logging**. Only the operation performed on the data item and the data-item name are stored in the log. Operation logging is also called **logical logging**. For each operation, an inverse operation must exist. We perform **undo** using the inverse operation, and **redo** using the operation itself. Recovery through operation logging is more difficult, since **redo** and **undo** are not idempotent. Further, using logical logging for an operation that updates multiple pages is greatly complicated by the fact that some, but not all, of the updated pages may have been written to the disk, so it is hard to apply either the **redo** or the **undo** of the operation on the disk image during recovery.

    Using physical redo logging and logical undo logging, as described in Section 17.9, provides the concurrency benefits of logical logging while avoiding the above pitfalls.

- **Logging and shadow paging**. Logging is used for modifications to small data items, but large data items are made recoverable via a shadow-page technique (see Section 17.5). When we use shadowing, only those pages that are actually modified need to be stored in duplicate.

Regardless of the technique used, the complexities introduced by long-duration transactions and large data items complicate the recovery process. Thus, it is desirable to allow certain noncritical data to be exempt from logging, and to rely instead on offline backups and human intervention.

24.6 Transaction Management in Multidatabases

Recall from Section 19.8 that a multidatabase system creates the illusion of logical database integration, in a heterogeneous database system where the local database systems may employ different logical data models and data-definition and data-manipulation languages, and may differ in their concurrency-control and transaction-management mechanisms.

A multidatabase system supports two types of transactions:

1. **Local transactions**. These transactions are executed by each local database system outside of the multidatabase system's control.

2. **Global transactions**. These transactions are executed under the multidatabase system's control.

The multidatabase system is aware of the fact that local transactions may run at the local sites, but it is not aware of what specific transactions are being executed, or of what data they may access.

Ensuring the local autonomy of each database system requires that no changes be made to its software. A database system at one site thus is not able to communicate directly with a one at any other site to synchronize the execution of a global transaction active at several sites.

Since the multidatabase system has no control over the execution of local transactions, each local system must use a concurrency-control scheme (for example, two-phase locking or timestamping) to ensure that its schedule is serializable. In addition, in case of locking, the local system must be able to guard against the possibility of local deadlocks.

The guarantee of local serializability is not sufficient to ensure global serializability. As an illustration, consider two global transactions T_1 and T_2, each of which accesses and updates two data items, A and B, located at sites S_1 and S_2, respectively. Suppose that the local schedules are serializable. It is still possible to have a situation where, at site S_1, T_2 follows T_1, whereas, at S_2, T_1 follows T_2, resulting in a non-serializable global schedule. Indeed, even if there is no concurrency among global transactions (that is, a global transaction is submitted only after the previous one commits or aborts), local serializability is not sufficient to ensure global serializability (see Exercise 24.14).

Depending on the implementation of the local database systems, a global transaction may not be able to control the precise locking behavior of its local substransactions. Thus, even if all local database systems follow two-phase locking, it may be possible only to ensure that each local transaction follows the rules of the protocol. For example, one local database system may commit its subtransaction and release locks, while the subtransaction at another local system is still executing. If the local systems permit control of locking behavior and all systems follow two-phase locking, then the multidatabase system can ensure that global transactions lock in a two-phase manner and the lock points of conflicting transactions would then define their global serialization order. If different local systems follow different concurrency-control mechanisms, however, this straightforward sort of global control does not work.

There are many protocols for ensuring consistency despite concurrent execution of global and local transactions in multidatabase systems. Some are based on imposing sufficient conditions to ensure global serializability. Others ensure only a form of consistency weaker than serializability, but achieve this consistency by less restrictive means. We consider one of the latter schemes: *two-level serializability*. Section 24.5 describes further approaches to consistency without serializability; other approaches are cited in the bibliographical notes.

A related problem in multidatabase systems is that of global atomic commit. If all local systems follow the two-phase commit protocol, that protocol can be used to achieve global atomicity. However, local systems not designed to be part of a distributed system may not be able to participate in such a protocol. Even if a local system is capable of supporting two-phase commit, the organization owning the system may be unwilling to permit waiting in cases where blocking occurs. In such cases, compromises may be made that allow for lack of atomicity in certain failure modes. Further discussion of these matters appears in the literature (see the bibliographical notes).

24.6.1 Two-Level Serializability

Two-level serializability (2LSR) ensures serializability at two levels of the system:

- Each local database system ensures local serializability among its local transactions, including those that are part of a global transaction.

- The multidatabase system ensures serializability among the global transactions alone—*ignoring the orderings induced by local transactions.*

Each of these serializability levels is simple to enforce. Local systems already offer guarantees of serializability; thus, the first requirement is easy to achieve. The second requirement applies to only a projection of the global schedule in which local transactions do not appear. Thus, the multidatabase system can ensure the second requirement using standard concurrency-control techniques (the precise choice of technique does not matter).

The two requirements of 2LSR are not sufficient to ensure global serializability. However, under the 2LSR-based approach, we adopt a requirement weaker than serializability, called **strong correctness**:

1. Preservation of consistency as specified by a set of consistency constraints

2. Guarantee that the set of data items read by each transaction is consistent

It can be shown that certain restrictions on transaction behavior, combined with 2LSR, are sufficient to ensure strong correctness (although not necessarily to ensure serializability). We list several of these restrictions.

In each of the protocols, we distinguish between **local data** and **global data**. Local data items belong to a particular site and are under the sole control of that site. Note that there cannot be any consistency constraints between local data items at distinct sites. Global data items belong to the multidatabase system, and, though they may be stored at a local site, are under the control of the multidatabase system.

The **global-read protocol** allows global transactions to read, but not to update, local data items, while disallowing all access to global data by local transactions. The global-read protocol ensures strong correctness if all these conditions hold:

1. Local transactions access only local data items.

2. Global transactions may access global data items, and may read local data items (although they must not write local data items).

3. There are no consistency constraints between local and global data items.

The **local-read protocol** grants local transactions read access to global data, but disallows all access to local data by global transactions. In this protocol, we need to introduce the notion of a **value dependency**. A transaction has a value dependency if the value that it writes to a data item at one site depends on a value that it read for a data item on another site.

The local-read protocol ensures strong correctness if all these conditions hold:

1. Local transactions may access local data items, and may read global data items stored at the site (although they must not write global data items).

2. Global transactions access only global data items.

3. No transaction may have a value dependency.

The **global-read–write/local-read protocol** is the most generous in terms of data access of the protocols that we have considered. It allows global transactions to read and write local data, and allows local transactions to read global data. However, it imposes both the value-dependency condition of the local-read protocol and the condition from the global-read protocol that there be no consistency constraints between local and global data.

The global-read–write/local-read protocol ensures strong correctness if all these conditions hold:

1. Local transactions may access local data items, and may read global data items stored at the site (although they must not write global data items).

2. Global transactions may access global data items as well as local data items (that is, they may read and write all data).

3. There are no consistency constraints between local and global data items.

4. No transaction may have a value dependency.

24.6.2   Ensuring Global Serializability

Early multidatabase systems restricted global transactions to be read only. They thus avoided the possibility of global transactions introducing inconsistency to the data, but were not sufficiently restrictive to ensure global serializability. It is indeed possible to get such global schedules and to develop a scheme to ensure global serializability, and we ask you to do both in Exercise 24.15.

There are a number of general schemes to ensure global serializability in an environment where update as well read-only transactions can execute. Several of these schemes are based on the idea of a **ticket**. A special data item called a ticket is created in each local database system. Every global transaction that accesses data at a site must write the ticket at that site. This requirement ensures that global transactions conflict directly at every site they visit. Furthermore, the global transaction manager can control the order in which global transactions are serialized, by controlling the order in which the tickets are accessed. References to such schemes appear in the bibliographical notes.

If we want to ensure global serializability in an environment where no direct local conflicts are generated in each site, some assumptions must be made about the schedules allowed by the local database system. For example, if the local schedules are such that the commit order and serialization order are always identical, we can ensure serializability by controlling only the order in which transactions commit.

The problem with schemes that ensure global serializability is that they may restrict concurrency unduly. They are particularly likely to do so because most transactions submit SQL statements to the underlying database system, instead of submitting individual **read**, **write**, **commit**, and **abort** steps. Although it is still possible to ensure global serializability under this assumption, the level of concurrency may be such that other schemes, such as the two-level serializability technique discussed in Section 24.6.1, are attractive alternatives.

24.7 Summary

- Workflows are activities that involve the coordinated execution of multiple tasks performed by different processing entities. They exist not just in computer applications, but also in almost all organizational activities. With the growth of networks, and the existence of multiple autonomous database systems, workflows provide a convenient way of carrying out tasks that involve multiple systems.

- Although the usual ACID transactional requirements are too strong or are unimplementable for such workflow applications, workflows must satisfy a limited set of transactional properties that guarantee that a process is not left in an inconsistent state.

- Transaction-processing monitors were initially developed as multithreaded servers that could service large numbers of terminals from a single process. They have since evolved, and today they provide the infrastructure for building and administering complex transaction-processing systems that have a large number of clients and multiple servers. They provide services such as durable queueing of client requests and server responses, routing of client messages to servers, persistent messaging, load balancing, and coordination of two-phase commit when transactions access multiple servers.

- Large main memories are exploited in certain systems to achieve high system throughput. In such systems, logging is a bottleneck. Under the group-commit concept, the number of outputs to stable storage can be reduced, thus releasing this bottleneck.

- The efficient management of long-duration interactive transactions is more complex, because of the long-duration waits, and because of the possibility of aborts. Since the concurrency-control techniques used in Chapter 16 use waits, aborts, or both, alternative techniques must be considered. These techniques must ensure correctness without requiring serializability.

- A long-duration transaction is represented as a nested transaction with atomic database operations at the lowest level. If a transaction fails, only active short-duration transactions abort. Active long-duration transactions resume once any short-duration transactions have recovered. A compensating transaction is needed to undo updates of nested transactions that have committed, if the outer-level transaction fails.

- In systems with real-time constraints, correctness of execution involves not only database consistency but also deadline satisfaction. The wide variance of execution times for read and write operations complicates the transaction-management problem for time-constrained systems.

- A multidatabase system provides an environment in which new database applications can access data from a variety of pre-existing databases located in various heterogeneous hardware and software environments.

    The local database systems may employ different logical models and data-definition and data-manipulation languages, and may differ in their concurrency-control and transaction-management mechanisms. A multidatabase system creates the illusion of logical database integration, without requiring physical database integration.

Review Terms

- TP monitor
- TP-monitor architectures
    - ☐ Process per client
    - ☐ Single server
    - ☐ Many server, single router
    - ☐ Many server, many router
- Multitasking
- Context switch
- Multithreaded server
- Queue manager
- Application coordination
    - ☐ Resource manager
    - ☐ Remote procedure call (RPC)
- Transactional Workflows
    - ☐ Task
    - ☐ Processing entity
    - ☐ Workflow specification
    - ☐ Workflow execution
- Workflow state
    - ☐ Execution states
    - ☐ Output values
    - ☐ External variables
- Workflow failure atomicity

- Workflow termination states
    - ☐ Acceptable
    - ☐ Nonacceptable
    - ☐ Committed
    - ☐ Aborted
- Workflow recovery
- Workflow-management system
- Workflow-management system architectures
    - ☐ Centralized
    - ☐ Partially distributed
    - ☐ Fully distributed
- Main-memory databases
- Group commit
- Real-time systems
- Deadlines
    - ☐ Hard deadline
    - ☐ Firm deadline
    - ☐ Soft deadline
- Real-time databases
- Long-duration transactions
- Exposure of uncommitted data
- Subtasks

- Nonserializable executions
- Nested transactions
- Multilevel transactions
- Saga
- Compensating transactions
- Logical logging
- Multidatabase systems
- Autonomy
- Local transactions
- Global transactions

- Two-level serializability (2LSR)
- Strong correctness
- Local data
- Global data
- Protocols
  - ☐ Global-read
  - ☐ Local-read
  - ☐ Value dependency
  - ☐ Global-read–write/local-read
- Ensuring global serializability
- Ticket

Exercises

24.1 Explain how a TP monitor manages memory and processor resources more effectively than a typical operating system.

24.2 Compare TP monitor features with those provided by Web servers supporting servlets (such servers have been nicknamed *TP-lite*).

24.3 Consider the process of admitting new students at your university (or new employees at your organization).
  a. Give a high-level picture of the workflow starting from the student application procedure.
  b. Indicate acceptable termination states, and which steps involve human intervention.
  c. Indicate possible errors (including deadline expiry) and how they are dealt with.
  d. Study how much of the workflow has been automated at your university.

24.4 Like database systems, workflow systems also require concurrency and recovery management. List three reasons why we cannot simply apply a relational database system using 2PL, physical undo logging, and 2PC.

24.5 If the entire database fits in main memory, do we still need a database system to manage the data? Explain your answer.

24.6 Consider a main-memory database system recovering from a system crash. Explain the relative merits of
  - Loading the entire database back into main memory before resuming transaction processing
  - Loading data as it is requested by transactions

24.7 In the group-commit technique, how many transactions should be part of a group? Explain your answer.

24.8 Is a high-performance transaction system necessarily a real-time system? Why or why not?

24.9 In a database system using write-ahead logging, what is the worst-case number of disk accesses required to read a data item? Explain why this presents a problem to designers of real-time database systems.

24.10 Explain why it may be impractical to require serializability for long-duration transactions.

24.11 Consider a multithreaded process that delivers messages from a durable queue of persistent messages. Different threads may run concurrently, attempting to deliver different messages. In case of a delivery failure, the message must be restored in the queue. Model the actions that each thread carries out as a multilevel transaction, so that locks on the queue need not be held till a message is delivered.

24.12 Discuss the modifications that need to be made in each of the recovery schemes covered in Chapter 17 if we allow nested transactions. Also, explain any differences that result if we allow multilevel transactions.

24.13 What is the purpose of compensating transactions? Present two examples of their use.

24.14 Consider a multidatabase system in which it is guaranteed that at most one global transaction is active at any time, and every local site ensures local serializability.

  a. Suggest ways in which the multidatabase system can ensure that there is at most one active global transaction at any time.

  b. Show by example that it is possible for a nonserializable global schedule to result despite the assumptions.

24.15 Consider a multidatabase system in which every local site ensures local serializability, and all global transactions are read only.

  a. Show by example that nonserializable executions may result in such a system.

  b. Show how you could use a ticket scheme to ensure global serializability.

Bibliographical Notes

Gray and Edwards [1995] provides an overview of TP monitor architectures; Gray and Reuter [1993] provides a detailed (and excellent) textbook description of transaction-processing systems, including chapters on TP monitors. Our description of TP monitors is modeled on these two sources. X/Open [1991] defines the X/Open XA interface. Transaction processing in Tuxedo is described in Huffman [1993]. Wipfler [1987] is one of several texts on application development using CICS.

Fischer [2001] is a handbook on workflow systems. A reference model for workflows, proposed by the Workflow Management Coalition, is presented in Hollinsworth

[1994]. The Web site of the coalition is **www.wfmc.org**. Our description of workflows follows the model of Rusinkiewicz and Sheth [1995].

Reuter [1989] presents ConTracts, a method for grouping transactions into multi-transaction activities. Some issues related to workflows were addressed in the work on long-running activities described by Dayal et al. [1990] and Dayal et al. [1991]. The authors propose event–condition–action rules as a technique for specifying work-flows. Jin et al. [1993] describes workflow issues in telecommunication applications.

Garcia-Molina and Salem [1992] provides an overview of main-memory databases. Jagadish et al. [1993] describes a recovery algorithm designed for main-memory data-bases. A storage manager for main-memory databases is described in Jagadish et al. [1994].

Transaction processing in real-time databases is discussed by Abbott and Garcia-Molina [1999] and Dayal et al. [1990]. Barclay et al. [1982] describes a real-time data-base system used in a telecommunications switching system. Complexity and correctness issues in real-time databases are addressed by Korth et al. [1990b] and Soparkar et al. [1995]. Concurrency control and scheduling in real-time databases are discussed by Haritsa et al. [1990], Hong et al. [1993], and Pang et al. [1995]. Ozsoyoglu and Snodgrass [1995] is a survey of research in real-time and temporal databases.

Nested and multilevel transactions are presented by Lynch [1983], Moss [1982], Moss [1985], Lynch and Merritt [1986], Fekete et al. [1990b], Fekete et al. [1990a], Korth and Speegle [1994], and Pu et al. [1988]. Theoretical aspects of multilevel transactions are presented in Lynch et al. [1988] and Weihl and Liskov [1990].

Several extended-transaction models have been defined including Sagas (Garcia-Molina and Salem [1987]), ACTA (Chrysanthis and Ramamritham [1994]), the Con-Tract model (Wachter and Reuter [1992]), ARIES (Mohan et al. [1992] and Rothermel and Mohan [1989]), and the NT/PV model (Korth and Speegle [1994]).

Splitting transactions to achieve higher performance is addressed in Shasha et al. [1995]. A model for concurrency in nested transactions systems is presented in Beeri et al. [1989]. Relaxation of serializability is discussed in Garcia-Molina [1983] and Sha et al. [1988]. Recovery in nested transaction systems is discussed by Moss [1987], Haerder and Rothermel [1987], Rothermel and Mohan [1989]. Multilevel transaction management is discussed in Weikum [1991].

Gray [1981], Skarra and Zdonik [1989], Korth and Speegle [1988], and Korth and Speegle [1990] discuss long-duration transactions. Transaction processing for long-duration transactions is considered by Weikum and Schek [1984], Haerder and Rothermel [1987], Weikum et al. [1990], and Korth et al. [1990a]. Salem et al. [1994] presents an extension of 2PL for long-duration transactions by allowing the early release of locks under certain circumstances. Transaction processing in design and software-engineering applications is discussed in Korth et al. [1988], Kaiser [1990], and Weikum [1991].

Transaction processing in multidatabase systems is discussed in Breitbart et al. [1990], Breitbart et al. [1991], Breitbart et al. [1992], Soparkar et al. [1991], Mehrotra et al. [1992b] and Mehrotra et al. [1992a]. The ticket scheme is presented in Geor-gakopoulos et al. [1994]. 2LSR is introduced in Mehrotra et al. [1991]. An earlier ap-proach, called *quasi-serializability*, is presented in Du and Elmagarmid [1989].

PART 8

Case Studies

This part describes how different database systems integrate the various concepts described earlier in the book. Specifically, three widely used database systems—IBM DB2, Oracle, and Microsoft SQL Server—are covered in Chapters 25, 26, and 27. These three represent three of the most widely used database systems.

Each of these chapters highlights unique features of each database system: tools, SQL variations and extensions, and system architecture, including storage organization, query processing, concurrency control and recovery, and replication.

The chapters cover only key aspects of the database products they describe, and therefore should not be regarded as a comprehensive coverage of the product. Furthermore, since products are enhanced regularly, details of the product may change. When using a particular product version, be sure to consult the user manuals for specific details.

Keep in mind that the chapters in this part use industrial rather than academic terminology. For instance, they use table instead of relation, row instead of tuple, and column instead of attribute.

CHAPTER 25

Oracle

Hakan Jakobsson
Oracle Corporation

When Oracle was founded in 1977 as Software Development Laboratories by Larry Ellison, Bob Miner, and Ed Oates, there were no commercial relational database products. The company, which was later renamed Oracle, set out to build a relational database management system as a commercial product, and was the first to reach the market. Since then, Oracle has held a leading position in the relational database market, but over the years its product and service offerings have grown beyond the relational database server. In addition to tools directly related to database development and management, Oracle sells business intelligence tools, including a multidimensional database management system (Oracle Express), query and analysis tools, data-mining products, and an application server with close integration to the database server.

In addition to database-related servers and tools, the company also offers application software for enterprise resource planning and customer-relationship management, including areas such as financials, human resources, manufacturing, marketing, sales, and supply chain management. Oracle's Business OnLine unit offers services in these areas as an application service provider.

This chapter surveys a subset of the features, options, and functionality of Oracle products. New versions of the products are being developed continually, so all product descriptions are subject to change. The feature set described here is based on the first release of Oracle9i.

25.1 Database Design and Querying Tools

Oracle provides a variety of tools for database design, querying, report generation and data analysis, including OLAP.

25.1.1   Database Design Tools

Most of Oracle's design tools are included in the Oracle Internet Development Suite. This is a suite of tools for various aspects of application development, including tools for forms development, data modeling, reporting, and querying. The suite supports the UML standard (see Section 2.10) for development modeling. It provides class modeling to generate code for the business components for Java framework as well as activity modeling for general-purpose control flow modeling. The suite also supports XML for data exchange with other UML tools.

The major database design tool in the suite is Oracle Designer, which translates business logic and data flows into a schema definitions and procedural scripts for application logic. It supports such modeling techniques as E-R diagrams, information engineering, and object analysis and design. Oracle Designer stores the design in Oracle Repository, which serves as a single point of metadata for the application. The metadata can then be used to generate forms and reports. Oracle Repository provides configuration management for database objects, forms applications, Java classes, XML files, and other types of files.

The suite also contains application development tools for generating forms, reports, and tools for various aspects of Java and XML-based development. The business intelligence component provides JavaBeans for analytic functionality such as data visualization, querying, and analytic calculations.

Oracle also has an application development tool for data warehousing, Oracle Warehouse Builder. Warehouse Builder is a tool for design and deployment of all aspects of a data warehouse, including schema design, data mapping and transformations, data load processing, and metadata management. Oracle Warehouse Builder supports both 3NF and star schemas and can also import designs from Oracle Designer.

25.1.2   Querying Tools

Oracle provides tools for ad-hoc querying, report generation and data analysis, including OLAP.

Oracle Discoverer is a Web-based, ad hoc query, reporting, analysis and Web publishing tool for end users and data analysts. It allows users to drill up and down on result sets, pivot data, and store calculations as reports that can be published in a variety of formats such as spreadsheets or HTML. Discoverer has wizards to help end users visualize data as graphs. Oracle9i has supports a rich set of analytical functions, such as ranking and moving aggregation in SQL. Discoverer's ad hoc query interface can generate SQL that takes advantage of this functionality and can provide end users with rich analytical functionality. Since the processing takes place in the relational database management system, Discoverer does not require a complex client-side calculation engine and there is a version of Discoverer that is browser based.

Oracle Express Server is a multidimensional database server. It supports a wide variety of analytical queries as well as forecasting, modeling, and scenario management. It can use the relational database management system as a back end for storage or use its own multidimensional storage of the data.

With the introduction of OLAP services in Oracle9*i*, Oracle is moving away from supporting a separate storage engine and moving most of the calculations into SQL. The result is a model where all the data reside in the relational database management system and where any remaining calculations that cannot be performed in SQL are done in a calculation engine running on the database server. The model also provides a Java OLAP application programmer interface.

There are many reasons for moving away from a separate multidimensional storage engine:

- A relational engine can scale to much larger data sets.

- A common security model can be used for the analytical applications and the data warehouse.

- Multidimensional modeling can be integrated with data warehouse modeling.

- The relational database management system has a larger set of features and functionality in many areas such as high availability, backup and recovery, and third-party tool support.

- There is no need to train database administrators for two database engines.

The main challenge with moving away from a separate multidimensional database engine is to provide the same performance. A multidimensional database management system that materializes all or large parts of a data cube can offer very fast response times for many calculations. Oracle has approached this problem in two ways.

- Oracle has added SQL support for a wide range of analytical functions, including cube, rollup, grouping sets, ranks, moving aggregation, lead and lag functions, histogram buckets, linear regression, and standard deviation, along with the ability to optimize the execution of such functions in the database engine.

- Oracle has extended materialized views to permit analytical functions, in particular grouping sets. The ability to materialize parts or all of the cube is key to the performance of a multidimensional database management system and materialized views give a relational database management system the ability to do the same thing.

25.2 SQL Variations and Extensions

Oracle9*i* supports all core SQL:1999 features fully or partially, with some minor exceptions such as distinct data types. In addition, Oracle supports a large number of other language constructs, some of which conform with SQL:1999, while others are Oracle-specific in syntax or functionality. For example, Oracle supports the OLAP operations described in Section 22.2, including ranking, moving aggregation, cube, and rollup.

A few examples of Oracle SQL extensions are:

- **connect by**, which is a form of tree traversal that allows transitive closure-style calculations in a single SQL statement. It is an Oracle-specific syntax for a feature that Oracle has had since the 1980s.

- **Upsert** and **multitable inserts**. The upsert operation combines update and insert, and is useful for merging new data with old data in data warehousing applications. If a new row has the same key value as an old row, the old row is updated (for example by adding the measure values from the new row), otherwise the new row is inserted into the table. Multitable inserts allow multiple tables to be updated based on a single scan of new data.

- **with** clause, which is described in Section 4.8.2.

25.2.1 Object-Relational Features

Oracle has extensive support for object-relational constructs, including:

- **Object types**. A single-inheritance model is supported for type hierarchies.

- **Collection types**. Oracle supports **varrays** which are variable length arrays, and nested tables.

- **Object tables**. These are used to store objects while providing a relational view of the attributes of the objects.

- **Table functions**. These are functions that produce sets of rows as output, and can be used in the **from** clause of a query. Table functions in Oracle can be nested. If a table function is used to express some form of data transformation, nesting multiple functions allows multiple transformations to be expressed in a single statement.

- **Object views**. These provide a virtual object table view of data stored in a regular relational table. They allow data to be accessed or viewed in an object-oriented style even if the data are really stored in a traditional relational format.

- **Methods**. These can be written in PL/SQL, Java, or C.

- **User-defined aggregate functions**. These can be used in SQL statements in the same way as built-in functions such as **sum** and **count**.

- **XML data types.** These can be used to store and index XML documents.

Oracle has two main procedural languages, PL/SQL and Java. PL/SQL was Oracle's original language for stored procedures and it has syntax similar to that used in the Ada language. Java is supported through a Java virtual machine inside the database engine. Oracle provides a package to encapsulate related procedures, functions, and variables into single units. Oracle supports SQLJ (SQL embedded in Java) and JDBC, and provides a tool to generate Java class definitions corresponding to user-defined database types.

25.2.2   Triggers

Oracle provides several types of triggers and several options for when and how they are invoked. (See Section 6.4 for an introduction to triggers in SQL.) Triggers can be written in PL/SQL or Java or as C callouts.

For triggers that execute on DML statements such as insert, update, and delete, Oracle supports **row triggers** and **statement triggers**. Row triggers execute once for every row that is affected (updated or deleted, for example) by the DML operation. A statement trigger is executed just once per statement. In each case, the trigger can be defined as either a *before* or *after* trigger, depending on whether it is to be invoked before or after the DML operation is carried out.

Oracle allows the creation of **instead of** triggers for views that cannot be subject to DML operations. Depending on the view definition, it may not be possible for Oracle to translate a DML statement on a view to modifications of the underlying base tables unambiguously. Hence, DML operations on views are subject to numerous restrictions. A user can create an **instead of** trigger on a view to specify manually what operations on the base tables are to occur in response to the DML operation on the view. Oracle executes the trigger instead of the DML operation and therefore provides a mechanism to circumvent the restrictions on DML operations against views.

Oracle also has triggers that execute on a variety of other events, like database startup or shutdown, server error messages, user logon or logoff, and DDL statements such as **create**, **alter** and **drop** statements.

25.3   Storage and Indexing

In Oracle parlance, a *database* consists of information stored in files and is accessed through an *instance*, which is a shared memory area and a set of processes that interact with the data in the files.

25.3.1   Table Spaces

A database consists of one or more logical storage units called **table spaces**. Each table space, in turn, consists of one or more physical structures called **data files**. These may be either files managed by the operating system or raw devices.

Usually, an Oracle database will have the following table spaces:

- The **system** table space, which is always created. It contains the data dictionary tables and storage for triggers and stored procedures.

- Table spaces created to store user data. While user data can be stored in the **system** table space, it is often desirable to separate the user data from the system data. Usually, the decision about what other table spaces should be created is based on performance, availability, maintainability, and ease of administration. For example, having multiple table spaces can be useful for partial backup and recovery operations.

- Temporary table spaces. Many database operations require sorting the data, and the sort routine may have to store data temporarily on disk if the sort cannot be done in memory. Temporary table spaces are allocated for sorting, to make the space management operations involved in spilling to disk more efficient.

Table spaces can also be used as a means of moving data between databases. For example, it is common to move data from a transactional system to a data warehouse at regular intervals. Oracle allows moving all the data in a table space from one system to the other by simply copying the files and exporting and importing a small amount of data dictionary metadata. These operations can be much faster than unloading the data from one database and then using a loader to insert it into the other. A requirement for this feature is that both systems use the same operating system.

25.3.2 Segments

The space in a table space is divided into units, called **segments**, that each contain data for a specific data structure. There are four types of segments.

- **Data segments**. Each table in a table space has its own data segment where the table data are stored unless the table is partitioned; if so, there is one data segment per partition. (Partitioning in Oracle is described in Section 25.3.10.)

- **Index segments**. Each index in a table space has its own index segment, except for partitioned indices, which have one index segment per partition.

- **Temporary segments**. These are segments used when a sort operation needs to write data to disk or when data are inserted into a temporary table.

- **Rollback segments**. These segments contain undo information so that an uncommitted transaction can be rolled back. They also play an important roll in Oracle's concurrency control model and for database recovery, described in Sections 25.5.1 and 25.5.2.

Below the level of segment, space is allocated at a level of granularity called *extent*. Each extent consists of a set of contiguous database *blocks*. A database block is the lowest level of granularity at which Oracle performs disk I/O. A database block does not have to be the same as an operating system block in size, but should be a multiple thereof.

Oracle provides storage parameters that allow for detailed control of how space is allocated and managed, parameters such as:

- The size of a new extent that is to be allocated to provide room for rows that are inserted into a table.

- The percentage of space utilization at which a database block is considered full and at which no more rows will be inserted into that block. (Leaving some free space in a block can allow the existing rows to grow in size through updates, without running out of space in the block.)

25.3.3 Tables

A standard table in Oracle is heap organized; that is, the storage location of a row in a table is not based on the values contained in the row, and is fixed when the row is inserted. However, if the table is partitioned, the content of the row affects the partition in which it is stored. There are several features and variations.

Oracle supports nested tables; that is, a table can have a column whose data type is another table. The nested table is not stored in line in the parent table, but is stored in a separate table.

Oracle supports temporary tables where the duration of the data is either the transaction in which the data are inserted, or the user session. The data are private to the session and are automatically removed at the end of its duration.

A *cluster* is another form of organization for table data (see Section 11.7). The concept, in this context, should not be confused with other meanings of the word *cluster*, such as those relating to hardware architecture. In a cluster, rows from different tables are stored together in the same block on the basis of some common columns. For example, a department table and an employee table could be clustered so that each row in the department table is stored together with all the employee rows for those employees who work in that department. The primary key/foreign key values are used to determine the storage location. This organization gives performance benefits when the two tables are joined, but without the space penalty of a denormalized schema, since the values in the department table are not repeated for each employee. As a tradeoff, a query involving only the department table may have to involve a substantially larger number of blocks than if that table had been stored on its own.

The cluster organization implies that a row belongs in a specific place; for example, a new employee row must be inserted with the other rows for the same department. Therefore, an index on the clustering column is mandatory. An alternative organization is a *hash cluster*. Here, Oracle computes the location of a row by applying a hash function to the value for the cluster column. The hash function maps the row to a specific block in the hash cluster. Since no index traversal is needed to access a row according to its cluster column value, this organization can save significant amounts of disk I/O. However, the number of hash buckets and other storage parameters must be set carefully to avoid performance problems due to too many collisions or space wastage due to empty hash buckets.

Both the hash cluster and regular cluster organization can be applied to a single table. Storing a table as a hash cluster with the primary key column as the cluster key can allow an access based on a primary key value with a single disk I/O provided that there is no overflow for that data block.

25.3.4 Index-Organized Tables

In an *index organized* table, records are stored in an Oracle B-tree index instead of in a heap. An index-organized table requires that a unique key be identified for use as the index key. While an entry in a regular index contains the key value and row-id of the indexed row, an index-organized table replaces the row-id with the column values for the remaining columns of the row. Compared to storing the data in a regular heap table and creating an index on the key columns, index-organized table can improve both performance and space utilization. Consider looking up all the column values of a row, given its primary key value. For a heap table, that would require an index probe followed by a table access by row-id. For an index-organized table, only the index probe is necessary.

Secondary indices on nonkey columns of an index-organized table are different from indices on a regular heap table. In a heap table, each row has a fixed row-id that does not change. However, a B-tree is reorganized as it grows or shrinks when entries are inserted or deleted, and there is no guarantee that a row will stay in a fixed place inside an index-organized table. Hence, a secondary index on an index-organized table contains not normal row-ids, but **logical row-ids** instead. A logical row-id consists of two parts: a physical row-id corresponding to where the row was when the index was created or last rebuilt and a value for the unique key. The physical row-id is referred to as a "guess" since it could be incorrect if the row has been moved. If so, the other part of a logical row-id, the key value for the row, is used to access the row; however, this access is slower than if the guess had been correct, since it involves a traversal of the B-tree for the index-organized table from the root all the way to the leaf nodes, potentially incurring several disk I/Os. However, if a table is highly volatile and a large percentage of the guesses are likely to be wrong, it can be better to create the secondary index with only key values, since using an incorrect guess may result in a wasted disk I/O.

25.3.5 Indices

Oracle supports several different types of indices. The most commonly used type is a B-tree index, created on one or multiple columns. (Note: in the terminology of Oracle (as also in several other database systems) a B-tree index is what is referred to as a B^+-tree index in Chapter 12.) Index entries have the following format: For an index on columns col_1, col_2, and col_3, each row in the table where at least one of the columns has a nonnull value would result in the index entry

$$< col_1 >< col_2 >< col_3 >< row\text{-}id >$$

where $< col_i >$ denotes the value for column i and $< row\text{-}id >$ is the row-id for the row. Oracle can optionally compress the prefix of the entry to save space. For example, if there are many repeated combinations of $< col_1 >< col_2 >$ values, the representation of each distinct $< col_1 >< col_2 >$ prefix can be shared between the entries that have that combination of values, rather than stored explicitly for each such entry. Prefix compression can lead to substantial space savings.

25.3.6 Bitmap Indices

Bitmap indices (described in Section 12.9.4) use a bitmap representation for index entries, which can lead to substantial space saving (and therefore disk I/O savings), when the indexed column has a moderate number of distinct values. Bitmap indices in Oracle use the same kind of B-tree structure to store the entries as a regular index. However, where a regular index on a column would have entries of the form $< col_1 >< row\text{-}id >$, a bitmap index entry has the form

$$< col_1 >< startrow\text{-}id >< endrow\text{-}id >< compressedbitmap >$$

The bitmap conceptually represents the space of all possible rows in the table between the start and end row-id. The number of such possible rows in a block depends on how many rows can fit into a block, which is a function of the number of columns in the table and their data types. Each bit in the bitmap represents one such possible row in a block. If the column value of that row is that of the index entry, the bit is set to 1. If the row has some other value, or the row does not actually exist in the table, the bit is set to 0. (It is possible that the row does not actually exist because a table block may well have a smaller number of rows than the number that was calculated as the maximum possible.) If the difference is large, the result may be long strings of consecutive zeros in the bitmap, but the compression algorithm deals with such strings of zeros, so the negative effect is limited.

The compression algorithm is a variation of a compression technique called Byte-Aligned Bitmap Compression (BBC). Essentially, a section of the bitmap where the distance between two consecutive ones is small enough is stored as verbatim bitmaps. If the distance between two ones is sufficiently large—that is, there is a sufficient number of adjacent zeros between them—a runlength of zeros, that is the number of zeros, is stored.

Bitmap indices allow multiple indices on the same table to be combined in the same access path if there are multiple conditions on indexed columns in the **where** clause of a query. For example, for the condition

$$(col_1 = 1 \textbf{ or } col_1 = 2) \textbf{ and } col_2 > 5 \textbf{ and } col_3 <> 10$$

Oracle would be able to calculate which rows match the condition by performing Boolean operations on bitmaps from indices on the three columns. In this case, these operations would take place for each index:

- For the index on col_1, the bitmaps for key values 1 and 2 would be **or**ed.

- For the index on col_2, all the bitmaps for key values > 5 would be merged in an operation that corresponds to a logical **or**.

- For the index on col_3, the bitmaps for key values 10 and **null** would be retrieved. Then, a Boolean **and** would be performed on the results from the first two indices, followed by two Boolean minuses of the bitmaps for values 10 and **null** for col_3.

All operations are performed directly on the compressed representation of the bit-maps—no decompression is necessary—and the resulting (compressed) bitmap represents those rows that match all the logical conditions.

The ability to use the Boolean operations to combine multiple indices is not limited to bitmap indices. Oracle can convert row-ids to the compressed bitmap representation, so it can use a regular B-tree index anywhere in a Boolean tree of bitmap operation simply by putting a row-id-to-bitmap operator on top of the index access in the execution plan.

As a rule of thumb, bitmap indices tend to be more space efficient than regular B-tree indices if the number of distinct key values is less than half the number of rows in the table. For example, in a table with 1 million rows, an index on a column with less than 500,000 distinct values would probably be smaller if it were created as a bitmap index. For columns with a very small number of distinct values—for example, columns referring to properties such as country, state, gender, marital status, and various status flags—a bitmap index might require only a small fraction of the space of a regular B-tree index. Any such space advantage can also give rise to corresponding performance advantages in the form of fewer disk I/Os when the index is scanned.

25.3.7 Function-Based Indices

In addition to creating indices on one or multiple columns of a table, Oracle allows indices to be created on expressions that involve one or more columns, such as $col_1 + col_2 * 5$. For example, by creating an index on the expression *upper(name)*, where *upper* is a function that returns the uppercase version of a string, and *name* is a column, it is possible to do case-insensitive searches on the *name* column. In order to find all rows with name "van Gogh" efficiently, the condition

$$upper(name) = \text{'VAN GOGH'}$$

would be used in the **where** clause of the query. Oracle then matches the condition with the index definition and concludes that the index can be used to retrieve all the rows matching "van Gogh" regardless of how the name was capitalized when it was stored in the database. A function-based index can be created as either a bitmap or a B-tree index.

25.3.8 Join Indices

A join index is an index where the key columns are not in the table that is referenced by the row-ids in the index. Oracle supports bitmap join indices primarily for use with star schemas (see Section 22.4.2). For example, if there is a column for product names in a product dimension table, a bitmap join index on the fact table with this key column could be used to retrieve the fact table rows that correspond to a product with a specific name, although the name is not stored in the fact table. How the rows in the fact and dimension tables correspond is based on a join condition that is specified when the index is created, and becomes part of the index metadata. When a query is processed, the optimizer will look for the same join condition in the **where** clause of the query in order to determine if the join index is applicable.

Oracle allows bitmap join indices to have more than one key column and these columns can be in different tables. In all cases, the join conditions between the fact table on which the index is built and the dimension tables must refer to unique keys in the dimension tables; that is, an indexed row in the fact table must correspond to a unique row in each of the dimension tables.

Oracle can combine a bitmap join index on a fact table with other indices on the same table—whether join indices or not—by using the operators for Boolean bitmap operations. For example, consider a schema with a fact table for sales, and dimension tables for customers, products, and time. Suppose a query requests information about sales to customers in a certain zip code who bought products in a certain product category during a certain time period. If a multicolumn bitmap join index exists where the key columns are the constrained dimension table columns (zip code, product category and time), Oracle can use the join index to find rows in the fact table that match the constraining conditions. However, if individual, single-column indices exist for the key columns (or a subset of them), Oracle can retrieve bitmaps for fact table rows that match each individual condition, and use the Boolean and operation to generate a fact table bitmap for those rows that satisfy all the conditions. If the query contains conditions on some columns of the fact table, indices on those columns could be included in the same access path, even if they were regular B-tree indices or domain indices (domain indices are described below in Section 25.3.9).

25.3.9   Domain Indices

Oracle allows tables to be indexed by index structures that are not native to Oracle. This extensibility feature of the Oracle server allows software vendors to develop so-called **cartridges** with functionality for specific application domains, such as text, spatial data, and images, with indexing functionality beyond that provided by the standard Oracle index types. In implementing the logic for creating, maintaining, and searching the index, the index designer must ensure that it adheres to a specific protocol in its interaction with the Oracle server.

A domain index must be registered in the data dictionary, together with the operators it supports. Oracle's optimizer considers domain indices as one of the possible access paths for a table. Oracle allows cost functions to be registered with the operators so that the optimizer can compare the cost of using the domain index to those of other access paths.

For example, a domain index for advanced text searches may support an operator *contains*. Once this operator has been registered, the domain index will be considered as an access path for a query like

> **select** *
> **from** *employees*
> **where** *contains*(*resume*, 'LINUX')

where *resume* is a text column in the *employee* table. The domain index can be stored in either an external data file or inside an Oracle index-organized table.

A domain index can be combined with other (bitmap or B-tree) indices in the same access path by converting between the row-id and bitmap representation and using Boolean bitmap operations.

25.3.10 Partitioning

Oracle supports various kinds of horizontal partitioning of tables and indices, and this feature plays a major role in Oracle's ability to support very large databases. The ability to partition a table or index has advantages in many areas.

- Backup and recovery are easier and faster, since they can be done on individual partitions rather than on the table as a whole.

- Loading operations in a data warehousing environment are less intrusive: data can be added to a partition, and then the partition added to a table, which is an instantaneous operation. Likewise, dropping a partition with obsolete data from a table is very easy in a data warehouse that maintains a rolling window of historical data.

- Query performance benefits substantially, since the optimizer can recognize that only a subset of the partitions of a table need to be accessed in order to resolve a query (partition pruning). Also, the optimizer can recognize that in a join, it is not necessary to try to match all rows in one table with all rows in the other, but that the joins need to be done only between matching pairs of partitions (partitionwise join).

Each row in a partitioned table is associated with a specific partition. This association is based on the partitioning column or columns that are part of the definition of a partitioned table. There are several ways to map column values to partitions, giving rise to several types of partitioning, each with different characteristics: range, hash, composite, and list partitioning.

25.3.10.1 Range Partitioning

In range partitioning, the partitioning criteria are ranges of values. This type of partitioning is especially well suited to date columns, in which case all rows in the same date range, say a day or a month, belong in the same partition. In a data warehouse where data are loaded from the transactional systems at regular intervals, range partitioning can be used to implement a rolling window of historical data efficiently. Each data load gets its own new partition, making the loading process faster and more efficient. The system actually loads the data into a separate table with the same column definition as the partitioned table. It can then check the data for consistency, cleanse them, and index them. After that, the system can make the separate table a new partition of the partitioned table, by a simple change to the metadata in the data dictionary—a nearly instantaneous operation.

Up until the metadata change, the loading process does not affect the existing data in the partitioned table in any way. There is no need to do any maintenance of existing indices as part of the loading. Old data can be removed from a table by simply dropping its partition; this operation does not affect the other partitions.

In addition, queries in a data warehousing environment often contain conditions that restrict them to a certain time period, such as a quarter or month. If date range partitioning is used, the query optimizer can restrict the data access to those partitions that are relevant to the query, and avoid a scan of the entire table.

25.3.10.2   Hash Partitioning

In hash partitioning, a hash function maps rows to partitions according to the values in the partitioning columns. This type of partitioning is primarily useful when it is important to distribute the rows evenly among partitions or when partitionwise joins are important for query performance.

25.3.10.3   Composite Partitioning

In composite partitioning, the table is range partitioned, but each partition is subpartitioned by using hash partitioning. This type of partitioning combines the advantages of range partitioning and hash partitioning.

25.3.10.4   List Partitioning

In list partitioning, the values associated with a particular partition are stated in a list. This type of partitioning is useful if the data in the partitioning column have a relatively small set of discrete values. For instance, a table with a state column can be implicitly partitioned by geographical region if each partition list has the states that belong in the same region.

25.3.11   Materialized Views

The materialized view feature (see Section 3.5.1) allows the result of an SQL query to be stored in a table and used for later query processing. In addition, Oracle maintains the materialized result, updating it when the tables that were referenced in the query are updated. Materialized views are used in data warehousing to speed up query processing, but the technology is also used for replication in distributed and mobile environments.

In data warehousing, a common usage for materialized views is to summarize data. For example, a common type of query asks for "the sum of sales for each quarter during the last 2 years." Precomputing the result, or some partial result, of such a query can speed up query processing dramatically compared to computing it from scratch by aggregating all detail-level sales records.

Oracle supports automatic query rewrites that take advantage of any useful materialized view when resolving a query. The rewrite consists of changing the query to use the materialized view instead of the original tables in the query. In addition, the rewrite may add additional joins or aggregate processing as may be required to get the correct result. For example, if a query needs sales by quarter, the rewrite can take advantage of a view that materializes sales by month, by adding additional aggregation to roll up the months to quarters. Oracle has a type of metadata object called dimension that allows hierarchical relationships in tables to be defined. For example, for a time dimension table in a star schema, Oracle can define a dimension metadata object to specify how days roll up to months, months to quarters, quarters to years, and so forth. Likewise, hierarchical properties relating to geography can be specified —for example, how sales districts roll up to regions. The query rewrite logic looks at these relationships since they allow a materialized view to be used for wider classes of queries.

The container object for a materialized view is a table, which means that a materialized view can be indexed, partitioned, or subjected to other controls, to improve query performance.

When there are changes to the data in the tables referenced in the query that defines a materialized view, the materialized view must be refreshed to reflect those changes. Oracle supports both full refresh of a materialized view and fast, incremental refresh. In a full refresh, Oracle recomputes the materialized view from scratch, which may be the best option if the underlying tables have had significant changes, for example, changes due to a bulk load. In an incremental refresh, Oracle updates the view using the records that were changed in the underlying tables; the refresh to the view is immediate, that is, it is executed as part of the transaction that changed the underlying tables. Incremental refresh may be better if the number of rows that were changed is low. There are some restrictions on the classes of queries for which a materialized view can be incrementally refreshed (and others for when a materialized view can be created at all).

A materialized view is similar to an index in the sense that, while it can improve query performance, it uses up space, and creating and maintaining it consumes resources. To help resolve this tradeoff, Oracle provides a package that can advise a user of the most cost-effective materialized views, given a particular query workload as input.

25.4 Query Processing and Optimization

Oracle supports a large variety of processing techniques in its query processing engine. Some of the more important ones are described here briefly.

25.4.1 Execution Methods

Data can be accessed through a variety of access methods:

- **Full table scan.** The query processor scans the entire table by getting information about the blocks that make up the table from the extent map, and scanning those blocks.

- **Index scan.** The processor creates a start and/or stop key from conditions in the query and uses it to scan to a relevant part of the index. If there are columns that need to be retrieved, that are not part of the index, the index scan would be followed by a table access by index row-id. If no start or stop key is available, the scan would be a full index scan.

- **Index fast full scan.** The processor scans the extents the same way as the table extent in a full table scan. If the index contains all the columns that are needed in the index, and there are no good start/stop keys that would significantly reduce that portion of the index that would be scanned in a regular index scan, this method may be the fastest way to access the data. This is because the fast full scan can take full advantage of multiblock disk I/O. However, unlike a regular full scan, which traverses the index leaf blocks in order, a fast full scan does not guarantee that the output preserves the sort order of the index.

- **Index join.** If a query needs only a small subset of the columns of a wide table, but no single index contains all those columns, the processor can use an index join to generate the relevant information without accessing the table, by joining several indices that together contain the needed columns. It performs the joins as hash joins on the row-ids from the different indices.

- **Cluster and hash cluster access.** The processor accesses the data by using the cluster key.

Oracle has several ways to combine information from multiple indices in a single access path. This ability allows multiple **where**-clause conditions to be used together to compute the result set as efficiently as possible. The functionality includes the ability to perform Boolean operations **and**, **or**, and **minus** on bitmaps representing row-ids. There are also operators that map a list of row-ids into bitmaps and vice versa, which allows regular B-tree indices and bitmap indices to be used together in the same access path. In addition, for many queries involving **count**(*) on selections on a table, the result can be computed by just counting the bits that are set in the bitmap generated by applying the **where** clause conditions, without accessing the table.

Oracle supports several types of joins in the execution engine: inner joins, outer joins, semijoins, and antijoins. (An antijoin in Oracle returns rows from the left-hand side input that do not match any row in the right-hand side input; this operation is called anti-semijoin in other literature.) It evaluates each type of join by one of three methods: hash join, sort–merge join, or nested-loop join.

25.4.2 Optimization

In Chapter 14, we discussed the general topic of query optimization. Here, we discuss optimization in the context of Oracle.

25.4.2.1 Query Transformations

Oracle does query optimization in several stages. Most of the techniques relating to query transformations and rewrites take place before access path selection, but Oracle also supports several types of cost-based query transformations that generate a complete plan and return a cost estimate for both a standard version of the query and one that has been subjected to advanced transformations. Not all query transformation techniques are guaranteed to be beneficial for every query, but by generating a cost estimate for the best plan with and without the transformation applied, Oracle is able to make an intelligent decision.

Some of the major types of transformations and rewrites supported by Oracle are as follows:

- **View merging.** A view reference in a query is replaced by the view definition. This transformation is not applicable to all views.

- **Complex view merging.** Oracle offers this feature for certain classes of views that are not subject to regular view merging because they have a **group by** or **select distinct** in the view definition. If such a view is joined to other tables, Oracle can commute the joins and the sort operation used for the **group by** or **distinct**.

- **Subquery flattening.** Oracle has a variety of transformations that convert various classes of subqueries into joins, semijoins, or antijoins.

- **Materialized view rewrite.** Oracle has the ability to rewrite a query automatically to take advantage of materialized views. If some part of the query can be matched up with an existing materialized view, Oracle can replace that part of the query with a reference to the table in which the view is materialized. If need be, Oracle adds join conditions or **group by** operations to preserve the semantics of the query. If multiple materialized views are applicable, Oracle picks the one that gives the greatest advantage in reducing the amount of data that has to be processed. In addition, Oracle subjects both the rewritten query and the original version to the full optimization process producing an execution plan and an associated cost estimate for each. Oracle then decides whether to execute the rewritten or the original version of the query on the basis of the cost estimates.

- **Star transformation.** Oracle supports a technique for evaluating queries against star schemas, known as the star transformation. When a query contains a join of a fact table with dimension tables, and selections on attributes from the dimension tables, the query is transformed by deleting the join condition between the fact table and the dimension tables, and replacing the selection condition on each dimension table by a subquery of the form:

  $fact\_table.fk_i$ **in**
    (**select** pk **from** $dimension\_table_i$
    where $<$conditions on $dimension\_table_i >$)

  One such subquery is generated for each dimension that has some constraining predicate. If the dimension has a snow-flake schema (see Section 22.4), the subquery will contain a join of the applicable tables that make up the dimension.

Oracle uses the values that are returned from each subquery to probe an index on the corresponding fact table column, getting a bitmap as a result. The bitmaps generated from different subqueries are combined by a bitmap **and** operation. The resultant bitmap can be used to access matching fact table rows. Hence, only those rows in the fact table that simultaneously match the conditions on the constrained dimensions will be accessed.

Both the decision on whether the use of a subquery for a particular dimension is cost-effective, and the decision on whether the rewritten query is better than the original, are based on the optimizer's cost estimates.

25.4.2.2 Access Path Selection

Oracle has a cost-based optimizer that determines join order, join methods, and access paths. Each operation that the optimizer considers has an associated cost function, and the optimizer tries to generate the combination of operations that has the lowest overall cost.

In estimating the cost of an operation, the optimizer relies on statistics that have been computed for schema objects such as tables and indices. The statistics contain information about the size of the object, the cardinality, data distribution of table columns, and so forth. For column statistics, Oracle supports height-balanced and frequency histograms. To facilitate the collection of optimizer statistics, Oracle can monitor modification activity on tables and keep track of those tables that have been subject to enough changes that recalculating the statistics may be appropriate. Oracle also tracks what columns are used in **where** clauses of queries, which make them potential candidates for histogram creation. With a single command, a user can tell Oracle to refresh the statistics for those tables that were marked as sufficiently changed. Oracle uses sampling to speed up the process of gathering the new statistics and automatically chooses the smallest adequate sample percentage. It also determines whether the distribution of the marked columns merit the creation of histograms; if the distribution is close to uniform, Oracle uses a simpler representation of the column statistics.

Oracle uses both CPU cost and disk I/Os in the optimizer cost model. To balance the two components, it stores measures about CPU speed and disk I/O performance as part of the optimizer statistics. Oracle's package for gathering optimizer statistics computes these measures.

For queries involving a nontrivial number of joins, the search space is an issue for a query optimizer. Oracle addresses this issue in several ways. The optimizer generates an initial join order and then decides on the best join methods and access paths for that join order. It then changes the order of the tables and determines the best join methods and access paths for the new join order and so forth, while keeping the best plan that has been found so far. Oracle cuts the optimization short if the number of different join orders that have been considered becomes so large that the time spent in the optimizer may be noticeable compared to the time it would take to execute the best plan found so far. Since this cutoff depends on the cost estimate for the best plan found so far, finding a good plan early is important so that the optimization can be stopped after a smaller number of join orders, resulting in better response time.

Oracle uses several initial ordering heuristics to increase the likelihood that the first join order considered is a good one.

For each join order that is considered, the optimizer may make additional passes over the tables to decide join methods and access paths. Such additional passes would target specific global side effects of the access path selection. For instance, a specific combination of join methods and access paths may eliminate the need to perform an **order by** sort. Since such a global side effect may not be obvious when the costs of the different join methods and access paths are considered locally, a separate pass targeting a specific side effect is used to find a possible execution plan with a better overall cost.

25.4.2.3 Partition Pruning

For partitioned tables, the optimizer tries to match conditions in the **where** clause of a query with the partitioning criteria for the table, in order to avoid accessing partitions that are not needed for the result. For example, if a table is partitioned by date range and the query is constrained to data between two specific dates, the optimizer determines which partitions contain data between the specified dates and ensures that only those partitions are accessed. This scenario is very common, and the speedup can be dramatic if only a small subset of the partitions are needed.

25.4.3 Parallel Execution

Oracle allows the execution of a single SQL statement to be parallelized by dividing the work between multiple processes on a multiprocessor computer. This feature is especially useful for computationally intensive operations that would otherwise take an unacceptably long time to perform. Representative examples are decision support queries that need to process large amounts of data, data loads in a data warehouse, and index creation or rebuild.

In order to achieve good speedup through parallelism, it is important that the work involved in executing the statement be divided into granules that can be processed independently by the different parallel processors. Depending on the type of operation, Oracle has several ways to split up the work.

For operations that access base objects (tables and indices), Oracle can divide the work by horizontal slices of the data. For some operations, such as a full table scan, each such slice can be a range of blocks—each parallel query process scans the table from the block at the start of the range to the block at the end. For other operations on a partitioned table, like update and delete, the slice would be a partition. For inserts into a nonpartitioned table, the data to be inserted are randomly divided across the parallel processes.

Joins can be parallelized in several different ways. One way is to divide one of the inputs to the join between parallel processes and let each process join its slice with the other input to the join; this is the asymmetric fragment-and-replicate method of Section 20.5.2.2. For example, if a large table is joined to a small one by a hash join, Oracle divides the large table among the processes and broadcasts a copy of the small table to each process, which then joins its slice with the smaller table. If both tables are large, it would be prohibitively expensive to broadcast one of them to all processes. In that case, Oracle achieves parallelism by partitioning the data among processes by hashing on the values of the join columns (the partitioned hash-join method of Section 20.5.2.1). Each table is scanned in parallel by a set of processes and each row in the output is passed on to one of a set of processes that are to perform the join. Which one of these processes gets the row is determined by a hash function on the values of the join column. Hence, each join process gets only rows that could potentially match, and no rows that could match could end up in different processes.

Oracle parallelizes sort operations by value ranges of the column on which the sort is performed (that is, using the range-partitioning sort of Section 20.5.1). Each process participating in the sort is sent rows with values in its range, and it sorts the rows in its range. To maximize the benefits of parallelism, the rows need to be divided as evenly as possible among the parallel processes, and the problem of determining range boundaries that generates a good distribution then arises. Oracle solves the problem by dynamically sampling a subset of the rows in the input to the sort before deciding on the range boundaries.

25.4.3.1 Process Structure

The processes involved in the parallel execution of an SQL statement consist of a coordinator process and a number of parallel server processes. The coordinator is responsible for assigning work to the parallel servers and for collecting and returning data to the user process that issued the statement. The degree of parallelism is the number of parallel server processes that are assigned to execute a primitive operation as part of the statement. The degree of parallelism is determined by the optimizer, but can be throttled back dynamically if the load on the system increases.

The parallel servers operate on a producer/consumer model. When a sequence of operations is needed to process a statement, the producer set of servers performs the first operation and passes the resulting data to the consumer set. For example, if a full table scan is followed by a sort and the degree of parallelism is 12, there would be 12 producer servers performing the table scan and passing the result to 12 consumer servers that perform the sort. If a subsequent operation is needed, like another sort, the roles of the two sets of servers switch. The servers that originally performed the table scan take on the role of consumers of the output produced by the the first sort and use it to perform the second sort. Hence, a sequence of operations proceeds by passing data back and forth between two sets of servers that alternate in their roles as producers and consumers. The servers communicate with each other through memory buffers on shared-memory hardware and through high-speed network connections on MPP (shared nothing) configurations and clustered (shared disk) systems.

For shared nothing systems, the cost of accessing data on disk is not uniform among processes. A process running on a node that has direct access to a device is able to process data on that device faster than a process that has to retrieve the data over a network. Oracle uses knowledge about device-to-node and device-to-process affinity—that is, the ability to access devices directly—when distributing work among parallel execution servers.

25.5 Concurrency Control and Recovery

Oracle supports concurrency control and recovery techniques that provide a number of useful features.

25.5.1 Concurrency Control

Oracle's multiversion concurrency control differs from the concurrency mechanisms used by most other database vendors. Read-only queries are given a read-consistent snapshot, which is a view of the database as it existed at a specific point in time, containing all updates that were committed by that point in time, and not containing any updates that were not committed at that point in time. Thus, read locks are not used and read-only queries do not interfere with other database activity in terms of locking. (This is basically the multiversion two-phase locking protocol described in Section 16.5.2.)

Oracle supports both statement and transaction level read consistency: At the beginning of the execution of either a statement or a transaction (depending on what level of consistency is used), Oracle determines the current system change number (SCN). The SCN essentially acts as a timestamp, where the time is measured in terms of transaction commits instead of wall-clock time.

If in the course of a query a data block is found that has a higher SCN than the one being associated with the query, it is evident that the data block has been modified after the time of the original query's SCN by some other transaction that may or may not have committed. Hence, the data in the block cannot be included in a consistent view of the database as it existed at the time of the query's SCN. Instead, an older version of the data in the block must be used; specifically, the one that has the highest SCN that does not exceed the SCN of the query. Oracle retrieves that version of the data from the rollback segment (rollback segments are described in Section 25.5.2). Hence, provided that the rollback segment is sufficiently large, Oracle can return a consistent result of the query even if the data items have been modified several times since the query started execution. Should the block with the desired SCN no longer exist in the rollback segment, the query will return an error. It would be an indication that the rollback segment has not been properly sized, given the activity on the system.

In the Oracle concurrency model, read operations do not block write operations and write operations do not block read operations, a property that allows a high degree of concurrency. In particular, the scheme allows for long-running queries (for example, reporting queries) to run on a system with a large amount of transactional activity. This kind of scenario is often problematic for database systems where queries use read locks, since the query may either fail to acquire them or lock large amounts of data for a long time, thereby preventing transactional activity against that data and reducing concurrency. (An alternative that is used in some systems is to use a lower degree of consistency, such as degree-two consistency, but that could result in inconsistent query results.)

Oracle's concurrency model is used as a basis for the *Flashback Query* feature. This feature allows a user to set a certain SCN number or wall-clock time in his session and perform queries on the data that existed at that point in time (provided that the data still exist in the rollback segment). Normally in a database system, once a change has been committed, there is no way to get back to the previous state of the data other than performing point-in-time recovery from backups. However, recovery of a very large database can be very costly, especially if the goal is just to retrieve some data item that had been inadvertently deleted by a user. The Flashback Query feature provides a much simpler mechanism to deal with user errors.

Oracle supports two ANSI/ISO isolation levels, "read committed" and "serializable". There is no support for dirty reads since it is not needed. The two isolation levels correspond to whether statement-level or transaction-level read consistency is used. The level can be set for a session or an individual transaction. Statement-level read consistency is the default.

Oracle uses row-level locking. Updates to different rows do not conflict. If two writers attempt to modify the same row, one waits until the other either commits or is rolled back, and then it can either return a write-conflict error or go ahead and modify the row. Locks are held for the duration of a transaction.

In addition to row-level locks that prevent inconsistencies due to DML activity, Oracle uses table locks that prevent inconsistencies due to DDL activity. These locks prevent one user from, say, dropping a table while another user has an uncommitted transaction that is accessing that table. Oracle does not use lock escalation to convert row locks to table locks for the purpose of its regular concurrency control.

Oracle detects deadlocks automatically and resolves them by rolling back one of the transactions involved in the deadlock.

Oracle supports autonomous transactions, which are independent transactions generated within other transactions. When Oracle invokes an autonomous transaction, it generates a new transaction in a separate context. The new transaction can be either committed or rolled back before control returns to the calling transaction. Oracle supports multiple levels of nesting of autonomous transactions.

25.5.2 Basic Structures for Recovery

In order to understand how Oracle recovers from a failure, such as a disk crash, it is important to understand the basic structures that are involved. In addition to the data files that contain tables and indices, there are control files, redo logs, archived redo logs, and rollback segments.

The control file contains various metadata that are needed to operate the database, including information about backups.

Oracle records any transactional modification of a database buffer in the redo log, which consists of two or more files. It logs the modification as part of the operation that causes it and regardless of whether the transaction eventually commits. It logs changes to indices and rollback segments as well as changes to table data. As the redo logs fill up, they are archived by one or several background processes (if the database is running in **archivelog** mode).

The rollback segment contains information about older versions of the data (that is, undo information). In addition to its role in Oracle's consistency model, the information is used to restore the old version of data items when a transaction that has modified the data items is rolled back.

To be able to recover from a storage failure, the data files and control files should be backed up regularly. The frequency of the backup determines the worst-case recovery time, since it takes longer to recover if the backup is old. Oracle supports hot backups —backups performed on an online database that is subject to transactional activity.

During recovery from a backup, Oracle performs two steps to reach a consistent state of the database as it existed just prior to the failure. First, Oracle rolls forward by applying the (archived) redo logs to the backup. This action takes the database to a state that existed at the time of the failure, but not necessarily a consistent state since the redo logs include uncommitted data. Second, Oracle rolls back uncommitted transactions by using the rollback segment. The database is now in a consistent state.

Recovery on a database that has been subject to heavy transactional activity since the last backup can be time consuming. Oracle supports parallel recovery in which several processes are used to apply redo information simultaneously. Oracle provides a GUI tool, Recovery Manager, which automates most tasks associated with backup and recovery.

25.5.3 Managed Standby Databases

To ensure high availability, Oracle provides a managed standby database feature. (This feature is the same as remote backups, described in Section 17.10.) A standby database is a copy of the regular database that is installed on a separate system. If a catastrophic failure occurs on the primary system, the standby system is activated and takes over, thereby minimizing the effect of the failure on availability. Oracle keeps the standby database up to date by constantly applying archived redo logs that are shipped from the primary database. The backup database can be brought online in read-only mode and used for reporting and decision support queries.

25.6 System Architecture

Whenever an database application executes an SQL statement, there is an operating system process that executes code in the database server. Oracle can be configured so that the operating system process is *dedicated* exclusively to the statement it is processing or so that the process can be shared among multiple statements. The latter configuration, known as the *multithreaded server*, has somewhat different properties with regard to the process and memory architecture. We shall discuss the dedicated server architecture first and the multithreaded server architecture later.

25.6.1 Dedicated Server: Memory Structures

The memory used by Oracle falls mainly into three categories: software code areas, the system global area (SGA), and the program global area (PGA).

The system code areas are the parts of the memory where the Oracle server code resides. A PGA is allocated for each process to hold its local data and control information. This area contains stack space for various session data and the private memory for the SQL statement that it is executing. It also contains memory for sorting and hashing operations that may occur during the evaluation of the statement.

The SGA is a memory area for structures that are shared among users. It is made up by several major structures, including:

- **The buffer cache.** This cache keeps frequently accessed data blocks (from tables as well as indices) in memory to reduce the need to perform physical disk I/O. A least recently used replacement policy is used except for blocks accessed during a full table scan. However, Oracle allows multiple buffer pools to be created that have different criteria for aging out data. Some Oracle operations bypass the buffer cache and read data directly from disk.

- **The redo log buffer.** This buffer contains the part of the redo log that has not yet been written to disk.

- **The shared pool.** Oracle seeks to maximize the number of users that can use the database concurrently by minimizing the amount of memory that is needed for each user. One important concept in this context is the ability to share the internal representation of SQL statements and procedural code written in PL/SQL. When multiple users execute the same SQL statement, they can share most data structures that represent the execution plan for the statement. Only data that is local to each specific invocation of the statement needs to be kept in private memory.

  The sharable parts of the data structures representing the SQL statement are stored in the shared pool, including the text of the statement. The caching of SQL statements in the shared pool also saves compilation time, since a new invocation of a statement that is already cached does not have to go through the complete compilation process. The determination of whether an SQL statement is the same as one existing in the shared pool is based on exact text matching and the setting of certain session parameters. Oracle can automatically replace constants in an SQL statement with bind variables; future queries that are the same except for the values of constants will then match the earlier query in the shared pool. The shared pool also contains caches for dictionary information and various control structures.

25.6.2 Dedicated Server: Process Structures

There are two types of processes that execute Oracle server code: server processes that process SQL statements and background processes that perform various administrative and performance-related tasks. Some of these processes are optional, and in some cases, multiple processes of the same type can be used for performance reasons. Some of the most important types of background processes are:

- **Database writer.** When a buffer is removed from the buffer cache, it must be written back to disk if it has been modified since it entered the cache. This task is performed by the database writer processes, which help the performance of the system by freeing up space in the buffer cache.

- **Log writer.** The log writer process writes entries in the redo log buffer to the redo log file on disk. It also writes a commit record to disk whenever a transaction commits.

- **Checkpoint.** The checkpoint process updates the headers of the data file when a checkpoint occurs.

- **System monitor.** This process performs crash recovery if needed. It is also performs some space management to reclaim unused space in temporary segments.

- **Process monitor.** This process performs process recovery for server processes that fail, releasing resources and performing various cleanup operations.

- **Recoverer.** The recoverer process resolves failures and conducts cleanup for distributed transactions.

- **Archiver.** The archiver copies the online redo log file to an archived redo log every time the online log file fills up.

25.6.3 Multithreaded Server

The multithreaded server configuration increases the number of users that a given number of server processes can support by sharing server processes among statements. It differs from the dedicated server architecture in these major aspects:

- A background dispatch process routes user requests to the next available server process. In doing so, it uses a request queue and a response queue in the SGA. The dispatcher puts a new request in the request queue where it will be picked up by a server process. As a server process completes a request, it puts the result in the response queue to be picked up by the dispatcher and returned to the user.

- Since a server process is shared among multiple SQL statements, Oracle does not keep private data in the PGA. Instead, it stores the session-specific data in the SGA.

25.6.4 Oracle9*i* Real Application Clusters

Oracle9*i* Real Application Clusters is a feature that allows multiple instances of Oracle to run against the same database. (Recall that, in Oracle terminology, an instance is the combination of background processes and memory areas.) This feature enables Oracle to run on clustered and MPP (shared disk and shared nothing) hardware architectures. This feature was called Oracle Parallel Server in earlier versions of Oracle. The ability to cluster multiple nodes has important benefits for scalability and availability that are useful in both OLTP and data warehousing environments.

The scalability benefits of the feature are obvious, since more nodes mean more processing power. Oracle further optimizes the use of the hardware through features such as affinity and partitionwise joins.

Oracle9*i* Real Application Clusters can also be used to achieve high availability. If one node fails, the remaining ones are still available to the application accessing the database. The remaining instances will automatically roll back uncommitted transactions that were being processed on the failed node in order to prevent them from blocking activity on the remaining nodes.

Having multiple instances run against the same database gives rise to some technical issues that do not exist on a single instance. While it is sometimes possible to partition an application among nodes so that nodes rarely access the same data, there is always the possibility of overlaps, which affects locking and cache management. To address this, Oracle supports a distributed lock manager and the *cache fusion* feature, which allows data blocks to flow directly among caches on different instances using the interconnect, without being written to disk.

25.7   Replication, Distribution, and External Data

Oracle provides support for replication and distributed transactions with two-phase commit.

25.7.1   Replication

Oracle supports several types of replication. (See Section 19.2.1 for an introduction to replication.) In its simplest form, data in a master site are replicated to other sites in the form of *snapshots*. (The term "snapshot" in this context should not be confused with the concept of a read-consistent snapshot in the context of the concurrency model.) A snapshot does not have to contain all the master data—it can, for example, exclude certain columns from a table for security reasons. Oracle supports two types of snapshots: *read-only* and *updatable*. An updatable snapshot can be modified at a slave site and the modifications propagated to the master table. However, read-only snapshots allow for a wider range of snapshot definitions. For instance, a read-only snapshot can be defined in terms of set operations on tables at the master site.

Oracle also supports multiple master sites for the same data, where all master sites act as peers. A replicated table can be updated at any of the master sites and the update is propagated to the other sites. The updates can be propagated either asynchronously or synchronously.

For asynchronous replication, the update information is sent in batches to the other master sites and applied. Since the same data could be subject to conflicting modifications at different sites, conflict resolution based on some business rules might be needed. Oracle provides a number of of built-in conflict resolution methods and allows users to write their own if need be.

With synchronous replication, an update to one master site is propagated immediately to all other sites. If the update transaction fails at any master site, the update is rolled back at all sites.

25.7.2   Distributed Databases

Oracle supports queries and transactions spanning multiple databases on different systems. With the use of gateways, the remote systems can include non-Oracle databases. Oracle has built-in capability to optimize a query that includes tables at different sites, retrieve the relevant data, and return the result as if it had been a normal, local query. Oracle also transparently supports transactions spanning multiple sites by a built-in two-phase-commit protocol.

25.7.3   External Data Sources

Oracle has several mechanisms for supporting external data sources. The most common usage is in data warehousing when large amounts of data are regularly loaded from a transactional system.

25.7.3.1   SQL*Loader

Oracle has a direct load utility, SQL*Loader, that supports fast parallel loads of large amounts of data from external files. It supports a variety of data formats and it can perform various filtering operations on the data being loaded.

25.7.3.2   External Tables

Oracle allows external data sources, such as flat files, to be referenced in the **from** clause of a query as if they were regular tables. An external table is defined by metadata that describe the Oracle column types and the mapping of the external data into those columns. An access driver is also needed to access the external data. Oracle provides a default driver for flat files.

The external table feature is primarily intended for extraction, transformation, and loading (ETL) operations in a data warehousing environment. Data can be loaded into the data warehouse from a flat file using

> **create table** *table* **as**
>   **select** ... **from** < external table >
>   **where** ...

By adding operations on the data in either the **select** list or **where** clause, transformations and filtering can be done as part of the same SQL statement. Since these operations can be expressed either in native SQL or in functions written in PL/SQL or Java, the external table feature provides a very powerful mechanism for expressing all kinds of data transformation and filtering operations. For scalability, the access to the external table can be parallelized by Oracle's parallel execution feature.

25.8   Database Administration Tools

Oracle provides users a number of tools for system management and application development.

25.8.1 Oracle Enterprise Manager

Oracle Enterprise Manager is Oracle's main tool for database systems management. It provides an easy-to-use graphical user interface (GUI) and a variety of wizards for schema management, security management, instance management, storage management, and job scheduling. It also provides performance monitoring and tools to help an administrator tune application SQL, access paths, and instance and data storage parameters. For example, it includes a wizard that can suggest what indices are the most cost-effective to create under a given workload.

25.8.2 Database Resource Management

A database administrator needs to be able to control how the processing power of the hardware is divided among users or groups of users. Some groups may execute interactive queries where response time is critical; others may execute long-running reports that can be run as batch jobs in the background when the system load is low. It is also important to be able to prevent a user from inadvertently submitting an extremely expensive ad hoc query that will unduly delay other users.

Oracle's Database Resource Management feature allows the database administrator to divide users into resource consumer groups with different priorities and properties. For example, a group of high-priority, interactive users may be guaranteed at least 60 percent of the CPU. The remainder, plus any part of the 60 percent not used up by the high-priority group, would be allocated among resource consumer groups with lower priority. A really low-priority group could get assigned 0 percent, which would mean that queries issued by this group would run only when there are spare CPU cycles available. Limits for the degree of parallelism for parallel execution can be set for each group. The database administrator can also set time limits for how long an SQL statement is allowed to run for each group. When a users submits a statement, the Resource Manager estimates how long it would take to execute it and returns an error if the statement violates the limit. The resource manager can also limit the number of user sessions that can be active concurrently for each resource consumer group.

Bibliographical Notes

Up-to-date product information, including documentation, on Oracle products can be found at the Web sites http://www.oracle.com and http://technet.oracle.com.

Extensible indexing in Oracle8i is described by Srinivasan et al. [2000b], while Srinivasan et al. [2000a] describe index organized tables in Oracle8i. Banerjee et al. [2000] describe XML support in Oracle8i. Bello et al. [1998] describe materialized views in Oracle. Antoshenkov [1995] describes the byte-aligned bitmap compression technique used in Oracle; see also Johnson [1999b].

The Oracle Parallel Server is described by Bamford et al. [1998]. Recovery in Oracle is described by Joshi et al. [1998] and Lahiri et al. [2001]. Messaging and queuing in Oracle are described by Gawlick [1998].

IBM DB2 Universal Database

Sriram Padmanabhan
IBM T. J. Watson Research Center

IBM's DB2 Universal Database family of products consists of database servers and a suite of related products. The DB2 Universal Database Server is available on many hardware and operating system platforms, ranging from mainframes and large servers to workstations and even small hand-held devices. It runs on a variety of IBM and non-IBM operating systems. Everyplace Edition supports operating systems such as PalmOS, Windows CE, and others. Applications can migrate seamlessly from the low-end platforms to high-end servers. Besides the core database engine, the DB2 family consists of several other products that provide tools, administration, replication, distributed data access, pervasive data access, OLAP, and many other features. Figure 26.1 describes the different products in the family.

The origin of DB2 can be traced back to the System R project at IBM's Almaden Research Center (then called the IBM San Jose Research Laboratory). The first DB2 product was released in 1984 on the IBM mainframe platform. It was followed over time by versions for other platforms. IBM has continually enhanced the DB2 product in areas such as transaction processing (write-ahead logging and ARIES recovery algorithms), query processing and optimization (the Starburst research project), parallel processing (DB2 Parallel Edition), active database support (constraints and triggers), and object-relational support, by leveraging the innovations from its Research Division. See the bibliographical notes for references giving further details.

The DB2 database engine is available in four different code bases: (1) OS/390, (2) VM, (3) AS/400, and (4) all other platforms. Common elements in all these code bases are the external interfaces (specifically data definition language (DDL) and SQL) and basic tools such as administration. However, differences do exist as a result of the differing development histories of the code bases. The rest of this chapter will focus

Database Servers

DB2 UDB for Unix, Windows, OS/2, Linux
DB2 UDB for OS/390
DB2 UDB for AS/400
DB2 for VM/VSE

Application Development

VisualAge for Java, C++
VisualAge Generator
DB2 Forms for OS/390
Lotus Approach

Business Intelligence

DB2 OLAP Server
DB2 Intelligent Miner
DB2 Spatial Extender
DB2 Warehouse Manager
QMF for OS/390

EBusiness Tools

DB2 Net Search Extender
DB2 XML Extender
Net.Data
DB2 for Websphere

Data Integration

DB2 DataJoiner
DataLinks
Data Replication Services
DB2 Connect

Content Management

Content Manager
Content Manager VideoCharger

Database Management Tools

DB2 Control Center
DB2 Admin Tool for OS/390
DB2 Buffer Pool Tool
DB2 Estimator for OS/390
DB2 Performance Monitor
DB2 Visual Explain
DB2 Query Patroller
etc.

Mobile Data Access

DB2 EveryPlace
DB2 Satellite Edition

Multimedia Delivery

DB2 ObjectRelational Extenders
Digital Library

Figure 26.1 The DB2 family of products.

on the DB2 Universal Database System available on the Unix, Windows, and OS/2 platforms. Specific features of interest in other DB2 systems will be highlighted as appropriate.

26.1 Database Design and Querying Tools

Most of the database design and CASE tools can be used to design a DB2 database. In particular, the leading data modeling tools such as ERWin and Rational Rose allow the designer to generate DB2-specific DDL syntax. For instance, Rational Rose's UML Data Modeler tool can generate DB2-specific **create distinct type** DDL statements for user-defined types and use them subsequently in column definitions. Most design tools also support a reverse-engineering feature that reads the DB2 catalog tables and builds a logical design for additional manipulation. The tools can generate constraints and indices.

DB2 provides SQL constructs for supporting many logical database features, such as constraints, triggers, and recursion. Likewise, DB2 supports certain physical database features such as table spaces, buffer pools, and partitioning using SQL statements. The Control Center GUI tool for DB2 allows a designer or an administrator to issue the appropriate DDL for these features. Another tool allows the administrator to obtain a full set of DDL for a database including table spaces, tables, indices, constraints, triggers, and functions that create an exact replica of the database schema for testing or replication.

For data analysis, DB2 provides OLAP support through the DB2 OLAP server. The DB2 OLAP server can create a multidimensional data mart from an underlying DB2 database for analysis. The OLAP engine from the Essbase product is used in the DB2 OLAP server. DB2 also supports other OLAP engines from vendors such as Microstrategy and Cognos. In particular, DB2 provides native support for the **cube by** and **rollup** operations for generating aggregated cubes as well as aggregates along one or more hierarchies in the database engine. The Intelligent Miner or other data mining products can be used for deeper and complex analysis against DB2 data.

DB2 for OS/390 has a very rich set of tools. QMF is a widely used tool for generating ad hoc queries and integrating them into applications.

26.2 SQL Variations and Extensions

DB2 supports a rich set of SQL features for various aspects of database processing. Many of the DB2 features and syntax have provided the basis for standards in SQL-92 and SQL:1999. This section highlights the object-relational features in DB2 UDB Version 7. Readers can find references to complete description of IBM DB2 SQL support as well as extensions to support XML in the bibliographical notes.

26.2.1 Support for Data Types

DB2 supports user-defined data types. Users can define *distinct* or *structured* data types. Distinct data types are based on DB2 built-in data types. However, users can define additional or alternative semantics for these new types. For example, the user can define a distinct data type called US_DOLLAR as

create distinct type US_DOLLAR **as decimal**(9,2)

Subsequently, the user can create a field (for example, PRICE) in a table with type US_DOLLAR. Queries may use the typed field in predicates such as the following:

select Product
from US_Sales
where Price > US_DOLLAR(1000)

Structured data types are complex objects that usually consist of two or more attributes. The following code declares a structured type called department_t:

$$\textbf{create type}\ \text{department\_t}\ \textbf{as}$$
$$(\text{deptname}\ \textbf{varchar}(32),$$
$$\text{depthead}\ \textbf{varchar}(32),$$
$$\text{faculty\_count}\ \textbf{integer})$$
$$\textbf{mode db2sql}$$

Structured types can be used to define *typed tables*.

$$\textbf{create table}\ \text{dept}\ \textbf{of}\ \text{department\_t}$$

With the DDL, a system designer can create a type hierarchy and tables in the hierarchy that can inherit specific methods and privileges. Structured types can also be used to define nested attributes inside a column of a table.

26.2.2 User-Defined Functions and Methods

Another important feature is that users can define their own functions and methods. These functions can subsequently be included in SQL statements and queries. Functions can generate scalars (single attribute) or tables (multiattribute row) as their result. Users can register functions (scalar or table) by using the **create function** statement. They can write the functions in common programming languages such as C and Java, or scripting languages such as Rexx and Perl. User-defined functions (UDFs) can operate in *fenced* or *unfenced* modes. In fenced mode, the functions are executed by a separate thread in its own address space. In unfenced mode, the database processing agent is allowed to execute the function in the server's address space. UDFs can define a scratch pad (work) area where they can maintain local and static variables across different invocations.

Another feature is methods associated with objects, which define the behavior of the objects. Methods are associated with particular structured data types and are registered by using the **create method** statement.

26.2.3 Large Objects

New database applications require the manipulation of text, images, video, and other types of data that are typically quite large. DB2 supports these requirements by providing three different large object (LOB) types. Each LOB can be as large as 2 gigabytes in size. The large objects in DB2 are (1) Binary Large Objects (BLOBs), (2) Single Byte Character Large Objects (CLOBs), and (3) Double Byte Character Large Objects (DBCLOBs). DB2 organizes these LOBs as separate objects, with each row in the table maintaining pointers to its corresponding LOBs. Users can register UDFs that manipulate these LOBs according to application requirements.

26.2.4 XML support

DB2 integrates XML support into the server using the XML extender. The XML extender can extract XML elements and attributes into relational data columns and leverage SQL and indexing power of DB2. Alternatively, it can also store and retrieve XML documents as a single column in a table. It can index and provide text oriented search capability on this XML column. The extender provides a number of built-in functions and APIs for XML document composition, insert, update, and search. New features such as exposing DB2 data as a Web service via the SOAP protocol and XML query support are likely to be integrated soon.

26.2.5   Indexing Extensions and Constraints

A recent feature of DB2 provides a **create index extension** construct which helps create indices on attributes with structured datatypes, by generating keys from structured data types. For example, a user can create an index on an attribute whose type is department_t (defined in Section 26.2.1) by generating keys with the department name. DB2's spatial extender uses the index extension method to create indices on spatial data. DB2 also provides a rich set of constraint checking features for enforcing object semantics such as uniqueness, validity, and inheritance.

26.3   Storage and Indexing

IBM DB2 provides a variety of features for storing and indexing data.

26.3.1   Storage Architecture

DB2 provides storage abstractions for managing logical database tables in multinode (parallel) and multidisk environments. *Node groups* can be defined to support table partitioning across specified sets of nodes in a multinode system. This allows flexibility in allocating table partitions to different nodes in a system. For example, large tables may be partitioned across all nodes in a system while small tables may reside on a single node. Tables are hash-partitioned across the nodes in the node group using a subset of their attributes (the partitioning key).

Within a node, DB2 uses *table spaces* to organize tables. A table space consists of one or more *containers*, which are references to directories, devices, or files. A table space may contain zero or more database objects such as tables, indices, or LOBs (large objects). Figure 26.2 illustrates these concepts. In this figure, two table spaces are defined for a node group. The HUMANRES table space is assigned four containers, while the SCHED table space has only one container. The EMPLOYEE and DEPARTMENT tables are assigned to the HUMANRES table space, while the PROJECT table is in the SCHED table space. Data striping allocates fragments (extents) of the EMPLOYEE and DEPARTMENT table to the containers of the HUMANRES table space. DB2 permits the administrator to create either system managed or DBMS-managed table spaces. System-managed spaces (SMSs) are directories or file systems that the underlying operating system maintains. In a SMS, DB2 creates file objects in the directories and allocates data to each of the files. Data managed spaces (DMSs) are raw devices or preallocated files that are then controlled by DB2. The size of these containers can never grow or shrink. DB2 creates allocation maps and manages the DMS table space itself. In both cases, an extent of pages is the unit of space management. The administrator can choose the extent size for a table space.

DB2 supports striping across the different containers. For example, when data are inserted into a newly created table, DB2 assigns the first extent to a container. Once

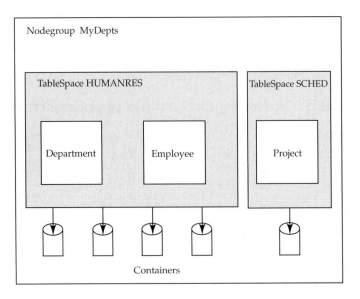

Figure 26.2 Table spaces and containers in DB2.

the extent is full, it allocates the next data items to the next container in round-robin fashion. Striping provides two significant benefits: parallel I/O and load balancing.

DB2 also supports prefetching and asynchronous writes using separate threads. The data manager component of DB2 triggers prefetching of data and index pages on the basis of query access patterns. For instance, a table scan always triggers prefetching of data pages. Index scans can trigger prefetching of index pages as well as data pages if they are being accessed in a clustered fashion. The number of concurrent prefetches as well as the prefetch size are configurable parameters that need to be initialized according to the number of disks or containers in the table space.

26.3.2 Tables, Records, and Indexes

DB2 organizes relational data as records in pages. Figure 26.3 shows the logical view of a table and an associated index. The table consists of a set of pages. Each page consists of a set of records—either user data records or special system records. Page zero of the table contains special system records about the table and its status. DB2 uses a space map record called the *Free Space Control Record* (FSCR) to find free space in the table. The FSCR record usually contains a space map for 500 pages. A FSCR entry consists of a few bits that provide an approximate indication of the percentage of free space in the page; for instance, with two bits, a bit pattern 11 would indicate most of the page may be free, while 01 would indicate about 25 percent of the space is free. To reduce update costs, the entries are not always kept up to date with the actual space usage, so the insert or update code must validate the FSCR entries by performing a physical check of the available space in a page.

Indices are organized as pages containing index records and pointers to child and sibling pages. DB2 provides support for the B^+-tree index mechanisms. The B^+-tree

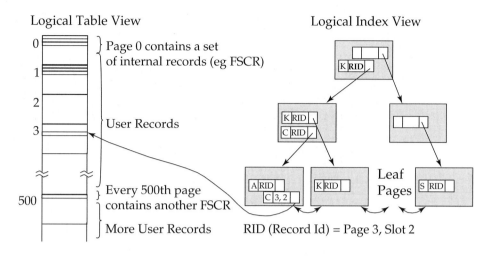

Logical Table View   Logical Index View

0 — } Page 0 contains a set of internal records (eg FSCR)

User Records

Every 500th page contains another FSCR

More User Records   RID (Record Id) = Page 3, Slot 2

Leaf Pages

Figure 26.3   Logical view of tables and indices in DB2.

index contains internal pages and leaf pages. The indices have bidirectional pointers at the leaf level to support forward and reverse scans. Leaf pages contain index entries that point to records in the table. Each record in a table has a unique *record identifier* (RID) constructed from its page identifier and slot identifier within the page (the slot structure of pages is described shortly). One index can be defined as the clustering index for the table. If so, the data records are maintained in a page-oriented clustering order based on the index keys.

DB2 indices can store extra columns along with the record identifiers at the leaf level of indices. For example,

create unique index I1 **on** T1 (C1) **include** (C2)

specifies that C2 is to be included as an extra column in an index on column C1. The included columns enable DB2 to use "index-only" query processing techniques (avoiding reading of the actual record) for queries that use the included columns, which would not be possible otherwise. (Index-only query processing is described in more detail shortly.) Additional directives such as MINPCTUSED and PCTFREE can be used to control the merging of index pages, and their initial space allocation during bulk load.

Figure 26.4 shows the typical data page format in DB2. Each data page contains a header and a slot directory. The slot directory is an array of 255 entries that points to record offsets in the page. The figure shows that page number 473 contains record zero at offset 3800 and record 2 at offset 3400. Page 1056 contains a record 1 at offset 3700, which really is a forward pointer to the record $< 473, 2 >$. Hence, record $< 473, 2 >$ is an overflow record that was created by an update operation of the original record $< 1056, 1 >$. DB2 supports different page sizes such as 4 KB, 8 KB, 16 KB, and 32 KB. However, each page may contain only 255 user records in it. Larger page sizes are useful in applications such as data warehousing where the table contains many columns. Smaller page sizes are useful for operational data with frequent updates.

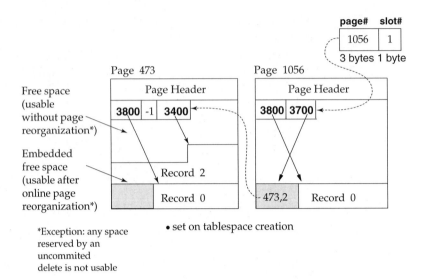

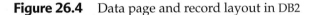

Figure 26.4   Data page and record layout in DB2

26.4 Query Processing and Optimization

DB2's query compiler transforms queries into a tree of operations; DB2 then uses the query operator tree at execution time for processing. DB2 supports a rich set of query operators which enable it to consider better processing strategies, and give it flexibility in executing complex queries.

Figures 26.5 and 26.6 show a query and its associated query plan. The query is a representative complex query (query 5) from the TPC-H benchmark and contains several joins and aggregations. The query plan in this example is rather simple, since only a few indices are defined, and auxiliary structures such as materialized views are not available for this query. DB2 provides various *explain* facilities including a powerful visual explain feature in the control center that can help users understand the details of a query execution plan. The query plan in the figure is based on the visual explain for the query. Visual explain allows the user to understand costs and other relevant properties of the different operations of a query plan.

DB2 transforms all SQL queries and statements, however complex they may be, into a query tree. The base or leaf operators of the query tree manipulate records in database tables. These operations are also called *access methods*. Intermediate operations of the tree include relational-algebra operations such as join, set operations, and aggregation. The root of the tree produces the results of the query or SQL statement.

26.4.1 Access Methods

DB2 supports a comprehensive set of access methods on relational tables, including:

- **Table scan.** This, the most basic method, accesses all records in the table page by page.

– 'TPCD Local Supplier Volume Query (Q5)';
select N_NAME,
        sum(L_EXTENDEDPRICE*(1-L_DISCOUNT)) **as** REVENUE
from TPCD.CUSTOMER, TPCD.ORDERS, TPCD.LINEITEM,
        TPCD.SUPPLIER, TPCD.NATION, TPCD.REGION
where C_CUSTKEY = O_CUSTKEY
        and O_ORDERKEY = L_ORDERKEY
        and L_SUPPKEY = S_SUPPKEY
        and C_NATIONKEY = S_NATIONKEY
        and S_NATIONKEY = N_NATIONKEY
        and N_REGIONKEY = R_REGIONKEY
        and R_NAME = 'MIDDLE EAST'
        and O_ORDERDATE >= **date**('1995-01-01')
        and O_ORDERDATE < **date**('1995-01-01') + 1 **year**
group by N_NAME
order by REVENUE DESC;

Figure 26.5   SQL query

- **Index scan**. DB2 uses an index to select the specific records that satisfy the query. It accesses the qualifying records using the RIDs in the index. DB2 detects opportunities to prefetch data pages when it observes a sequential access pattern.

- **Index-only**. This type of scan is used when the index contains all the attributes that the query requires. Hence, a scan of the index entries is sufficient, and there is no need to fetch the records. The index-only technique is usually a good choice from a performance viewpoint.

- **List prefetch**. This access method is a good choice for an unclustered index scan with a significant number of RIDs. DB2 collects the RIDs of relevant records using an index scan, then sorts the RIDs by page number, and finally performs a fetch of the records in sorted order from the data pages. Sorted access changes the I/O pattern from random to sequential and also offers prefetching opportunities.

- **Index anding**. DB2 uses this method when it determines that more than one index can be used to constrain the number of satisfying records in a base table. It processes the most selective index to generate a list of RIDs. It then processes the next selective index to return the RIDs that it finds. A RID qualifies for further processing only if it is present in the intersection (AND operation) of the index scan results. The result of an index AND operation is a small list of qualifying RIDs that is used to fetch the corresponding records from the base table.

- **Index or-ing**. This strategy is a good choice if two or more indices can be used to satisfy query predicates that are combined by using the OR operator. DB2 eliminates duplicate RIDs by performing a sort and then fetches the resulting set of records.

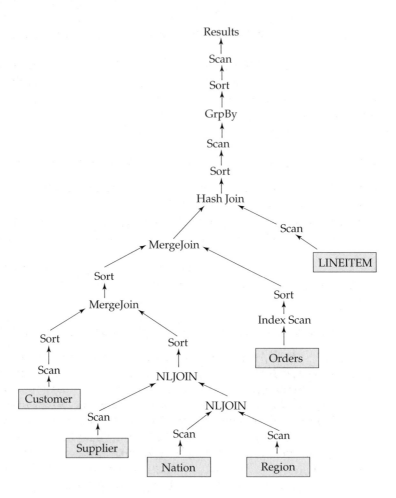

Figure 26.6   DB2 query plan (graphical explain).

DB2 usually pushes down all the selection and projection predicates of a query to the access methods. In addition, DB2 pushes down certain operations such as sorting and aggregation, where possible, in order to reduce the cost.

26.4.2   Join, Aggregation, and Set Operations

DB2 supports a number of techniques for join, aggregation and set operations. For join, DB2 can choose between nested loops, sort merge, and hashing techniques. In describing the join and set binary operations, we use the notation outer and inner tables to distinguish the two input streams. The nested loops technique is useful if the inner table is very small or can be accessed by using an index on a join predicate. Sort-merge join and hash join techniques are used for joins involving large outer and inner tables. DB2 implements set operations by using sorting and merging techniques. The merging technique eliminates duplicates in the case of union, while non-duplicates are eliminated in the case of intersection. DB2 also supports outer join operations of all kinds.

DB2 processes aggregation operations in early or push-down mode whenever possible. For instance, it can perform aggregation while sorting the aggregation input on the group by columns. The join and aggregation algorithms take advantage of superscalar processing in modern CPUs using block-oriented and memory-cache-conscious techniques.

26.4.3   Support for Complex SQL Processing

One of the most important aspects of DB2 is that it uses the query processing infrastructure in an extensible fashion to support complex SQL operations. The complex SQL operations include support for deeply nested and correlated subqueries, as well as constraints, referential integrity, and triggers. Constraints and integrity checks are built as query tree operations on insert, delete, or update SQL statements. By performing most of the constraint checking and triggering actions as part of the query plan, DB2 is able to provide better efficiency and scalability. DB2 also supports maintenance of materialized view by using built-in triggers.

26.4.4   Multiprocessor Query Processing Features

DB2 extends the base set of query operations with control and data exchange primitives to support SMP, MPP, and SMP-cluster modes of query processing. DB2 uses a *table-queue* abstraction for data exchange between threads on different nodes or on the same node. The table queue is a buffer that redirects data to appropriate receivers by using broadcast, one-to-one, or directed multicast methods. Control operations create threads and coordinate the operation of different processes and threads.

In all these modes, DB2 employs a coordinator process to control the query operations and final result gathering. Coordinator processes can also perform some global database processing actions if required. An example is the global aggregation operation to combine the local aggregation results. Subagents or slave threads perform the base operations in one or more nodes. In SMP mode, the subagents use shared memory to synchronize between themselves when sharing data. In an MPP, the table-queue mechanisms provide buffering and flow control to synchronize across different nodes during execution.

26.4.5   Query Optimization

DB2's query compiler uses an internal representation of the query, called *Query Graph Model* (QGM), in order to perform transformations and optimizations. After parsing the SQL statement, DB2 performs semantic transformations on the QGM to enforce constraints, referential integrity, and triggers. The result of these transformations is an enhanced QGM. Next, DB2 attempts to perform *query rewrite* transformations that are considered to be beneficial on most queries. Rewrite rules are fired, if applicable, to perform the required transformations. Examples of rewrite transformations include (1) decorrelation of correlated subqueries, (2) transformation of subqueries into joins where possible, (3) pushing group by operations below joins if applicable, and

(4) rewriting queries to make use of available materialized views or "summary tables" (materialized views using aggregation).

The query optimizer uses the enhanced and transformed QGM as its input for optimization. The optimizer is cost-based and uses an extensible, rule-driven framework. The optimizer can be configured to operate at different levels of complexity. At the highest level, it uses a dynamic programming algorithm to consider all query plan options and chooses the optimal cost plan. At an intermediate level, the optimizer does not consider certain plans or access methods (for example, index or-ing) as well as some rewrite rules. At the lowest level of complexity, the optimizer uses a simple greedy heuristic to choose a good but not necessarily optimal query plan. The optimizer uses detailed models of the query processing operations—taking into account details such as memory size and prefetching—to obtain accurate estimates of the I/O and CPU costs. It relies on the statistics of the data to estimate the cardinality and selectivities of the operations.

DB2 allows a user to generate histograms of column level distributions and combinations of columns by using the *runstats* utility. The histograms contain information about the most frequent value occurrences as well as quantile-based frequency distributions of the attributes. These statistics are used by the query optimizer.

The optimizer generates an internal query plan that it considers the best query plan, and then converts the query plan into threads of query operators and associated data structures, for execution by the query processing engine.

Consider an update of the form "Give a 10 percent raise to every employee earning less than 25000 dollars". In an early version of System R, the optimizer chose the salary index for access and processed the data from low to high (0 to 25000). The insertion of the new (higher) value for salary meant that the updated record was revisited again unless its salary value was greater than 25000. The cause of the revisitation is the use of the salary index for access in low-to-high order. The record would be revisited and the salary increased by 10 percent repeatedly until its salary value exceeded 25000. This bug occurred on Halloween day and so the members of the System R project called this bug the "*Halloween problem*".

DB2 addresses the Halloween problem by recognizing this situation in the query compiler. The optimizer generates a query plan that first materializes the RIDs of the qualifying rows before processing the updates. Each qualifying record is updated only once, as intended by the update statement.

26.5 Concurrency Control and Recovery

DB2 supports concurrency control techniques that provide a very high level of concurrency, coupled with an advanced recovery mechanism supporting a variety of features.

26.5.1 Concurrency and Isolation

DB2 supports a variety of modes of concurrency control and isolation. For isolation, DB2 supports the *repeatable read* (RR), *read stability* (RS), *cursor stability* (CS), and *uncommitted read* (UR) modes.

The definition of repeatable read in DB2 differs from that in Section 16.8, and corresponds closely to the *serializable* level described there. Specifically, RR in DB2 ensures that range scans will find the same set of tuples if repeated. If all transactions follow the RR protocol, then the resulting schedule would be serializable. CS and URmodes are as described in Section 16.8.

The RS isolation mode locks only the rows that an application retrieves in a unit of work. On a subsequent scan, the application is guaranteed to see all these rows (like RR) but might also see new rows that qualify. However, this might be an acceptable tradeoff for some applications with respect to strict RR isolation. Typically, the default isolation level is CS. Applications can choose the level of isolation they wish to run at. Also, most commercially available applications support the different isolation levels, and users can choose the right version of the application for their requirement.

The various isolation modes are implemented by using locks. DB2 supports record level and table level locks. It maintains a separate lock-table data structure with all the lock information. DB2 escalates from record-level to table-level locks if the space available for further locks in the lock table becomes low. DB2 implements strict two-phase locking for all update transactions. It holds write locks and update locks until commit or rollback time.

DB2 supports a variety of lock modes in order to maximize concurrency. Figure 26.7 shows the different lock modes and provides a short description of the purpose of each lock mode. We briefly outline some of the lock modes below; see the bibliographical references for more information on the lock modes. The lock modes include intent locks at table level to provide for multiple granularity locking. Also, DB2 implements next key locking for inserts and deletes affecting RR isolation level index

Lock Mode	Objects	Interpretation
IN (intent none)	Tablespaces, tables	Read with no row locks
IS (intent share)	Tablespaces, tables	Read with row locks
NS (next key share)	Rows	Read locks for RS or CS isolation levels
S (share)	Rows, tables	Read lock
IX (intent exclusive)	Tablespaces, tables	Intend to update rows
SIX (share with intent Exclusive)	Tables	No read locks on rows but X locks on updated rows
U (Update)	Rows, tables	Update lock but allows others to read
NX (next key exclusive)	Rows	Next key lock for inserts/deletes to prevent phantom reads during RR index scans.
X (exclusive)	Rows, tables	Only uncommitted readers allowed
Z (superexclusive)	Tablespaces, tables	Complete exclusive access

Figure 26.7 DB2 lock modes.

scans to eliminate the phantom read problem. See the bibliographical references for details. (A simple form of next key locking that eliminates the phantom problem is described in Section 16.9.)

The transaction can set the lock granularity to table level by using the **lock table** statement (an SQL extension). This is useful for applications that know their desired level of isolation is at the table level. Also, DB2 chooses the appropriate locking granularities when running utilities such as database reorganization and load. The offline versions of these utilities usually lock the table in exclusive mode. The online versions of the utilities allow other transactions to proceed concurrently by acquiring row locks.

A deadlock detection agent runs on each database, and periodically checks for deadlocks among transactions. The interval for deadlock detection is a configurable parameter. In case of a deadlock, the agent chooses a victim and aborts it. The victim gets an SQL error code indicating that the cause of failure was deadlock.

26.5.2 Commit and Rollback

Applications can commit or rollback by using explicit **commit** or **rollback** statements. Applications can also issue **begin transaction** and **end transaction** statements to control the scope of transactions. Nested transactions are not supported. Normally, DB2 releases all locks that it holds on behalf of a transaction at **commit** or **rollback**. However, if a cursor statement has been declared by the **withhold** clause, then some locks are maintained across commits.

26.5.3 Logging and Recovery

DB2 implements the ARIES logging and recovery schemes. (The ARIES scheme is briefly outlined in Section 17.9.6.) It employs write-ahead logging to flush log records to the persistent log file before data pages are written or at commit time. DB2 supports two types of log modes: circular logging and archive logging. In circular logging, DB2 uses a predefined set of primary and secondary log files. Circular logging is useful for crash recovery or application failure recovery. In archival logging, DB2 creates new log files and archives the old log files in order to free space in the file system. Archival logging is required for roll-forward recovery from an archival backup (described in more detail shortly). In both cases, DB2 allows the user to configure the number of log files and the sizes of the log files.

In update-heavy environments, DB2 can be configured to use group commits (Section 24.3) in order to combine log writes of multiple transactions and perform them using a single I/O operation.

DB2 supports transaction *rollback*, crash recovery, as well as *point-in-time*, or *roll-forward*, recovery. In the case of crash recovery, DB2 performs the standard phases of *undo* processing and *redo* processing up to and from the last checkpoint in order to recover the proper committed state of the database. For point-in-time recovery, DB2 can restore the database from a backup and roll it forward to a specific point in time by using the archived logs. The roll-forward recovery command supports both database and table-space levels. It can also be issued on specific nodes on a multinode system.

Recently, a parallel recovery scheme became available to improve performance in SMP multiprocessor systems by utilizing many CPUs. DB2 performs coordinated recovery across MPP nodes by a global checkpointing scheme.

26.6   System Architecture

Figure 26.8 shows some of the different processes, or threads, in a DB2 server. Remote client applications connect to the database server through communication agents such as *db2tcpcm*. Each application is assigned an agent (coordinator agent in MPP or SMP environments) called the *db2agent* thread. This agent and its subordinate agents perform the application-related tasks. Each database has a set of processes or threads that perform tasks such as prefetching, page cleaning from buffer pool, logging, and deadlock detection. Finally, there is a set of agents at the level of the server to perform tasks such as crash detection, process creation, control of system resources and license service. DB2 provides configuration parameters to control the number of threads and processes in a server. Almost all the different types of agents can be controlled by using the configuration parameters.

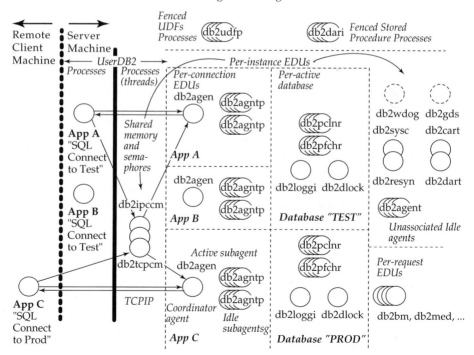

Figure 26.8   Process model in DB2.

Figure 26.9 shows the different types of memory segments in DB2. Private memory in agents or threads is mainly used for local variables and data structures that are relevant only for the current activity. For example, a private sort could allocate memory from the agent's private heap. Shared memory is partitioned into *server shared memory*, *database shared memory*, and *application shared memory*. The database level shared memory contains useful data structures such as the buffer pool, locklists, application package caches, and shared sort areas. The server and application shared memory areas are primarily used for common data structures such as server configuration parameters and communication buffers.

DB2 supports multiple buffer pools for a database. Buffer pools can be created by using the **create bufferpool** statement and can be associated with table spaces. Multiple buffer pools are useful for a variety of reasons, but they should be defined after a careful analysis of the workload requirements. DB2 also provides the extended store capability to exploit large memories (memories greater than 4 gigabytes) in systems that have 32-bit addressing capabilities only. The extended store is used as a shared backup buffer for active buffer pools. Pages that are flushed or replaced from an active buffer pool are written into the extended store area and can be copied back from there if required. Thus, the extended store can help avoid unnecessary I/Os in large memory systems.

DB2 supports a comprehensive list of memory configuration and tuning parameters. This includes parameters for all the large data structure heap areas such as the default buffer pool, the sort heap, package cache, application control heaps, lock list area, and so on.

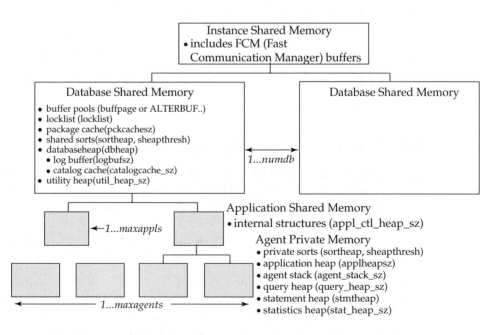

Figure 26.9   DB2 memory model.

26.7 Replication, Distribution, and External Data

DB2 Data Propagator is a product in the DB2 family that provides replication of data among DB2, other relational database systems such as Oracle, Microsoft SQL Server, Sybase SQL Server, and Informix, and nonrelational data sources such as IBM's IMS. Data Propagator consists of *capture* and *apply* components that are controlled by administration interfaces. The change-capture mechanisms are either *log-based* for DB2 tables or *trigger-based* in the case of other data sources. That is, for DB2 tables changes are detected by examining the database log, while triggers are used to detect changes for other data sources. The captured changes are stored in temporary staging-table areas under the control of DB2 data propagator, which then applies these staged intermediate tables, with changes, to destination tables by using SQL statements (inserts, updates, and deletes). SQL-based transformations can be performed on the intermediate staging tables using filtering conditions as well as aggregations. The resulting rows can be applied to one or more target tables. The administration facility controls all of these actions.

Another member of the DB2 family is the *Data Joiner* product, which provides federated and distributed database support. Data Joiner can integrate tables in remote DB2 or other relational databases into a single distributed database. Data Joiner provides a cost-based method for query optimization across the different data sites. Nonrelational data can also be integrated into Data Joiner by using wrappers to create tabular data.

DB2 supports user-defined table functions that can enable access to nonrelational and external data sources. DB2 creates user-defined table functions by using the **create function** statement with the clause **returns table**. With these features, DB2 is able to participate in the OLE-DB protocols.

Finally, DB2 provides full support for distributed transaction processing by using the two-phase commit protocol. DB2 can act as the coordinator or agent for distributed transaction support. As a coordinator, DB2 can perform all stages of the two-phase commit protocol. As a participant, DB2 can interact with any of the commercial distributed transaction managers.

26.8 Database Administration Tools

DB2 provides a number of tools for ease of use and administration. The core set of tools is augmented and enhanced by a large number of tools from vendors.

The DB2 control center is the primary tool for use and administration of DB2 databases. The control center runs on many workstation platforms. It has interfaces to administer objects of different types, such as servers, databases, tables, and indices. Additionally, it contains task-oriented interfaces to perform commands, and it allows users to generate SQL scripts.

Figure 26.10 is a a screen shot of the main panel of the control center. It shows a list of tables in the *Sample* database in the DB2 instance on node *Crankarm*. The administrator can use the menu to invoke a suite of component tools. The main components of the control center are command center, script center, journal, license management, alert center, performance monitor, visual explain, remote database management, stor-

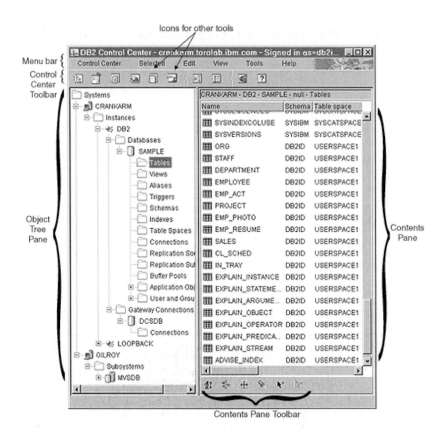

Figure 26.10   DB2 control center.

age management, and support for replication. The command center allows users and administrators to issue database commands and run SQL statements. The script center allows users to run SQL scripts constructed interactively or from a file. The performance monitor allows the user to monitor various events in the database system and obtain snapshots of performance. SmartGuides provide help on configuring parameters and setting up the DB2 system. A stored procedure builder helps the user to develop and install stored procedures. Visual explain gives the user graphical views of the query execution plan. An index wizard helps the administrator by suggesting indices for performance.

While the control center is an integrated interface for many of the tasks, DB2 also provides direct access to most tools. For users, tools such as the explain facility, explain tables, and graphical explain provide a detailed breakdown of the query plans. Users may use the control center to modify statistics (if modification is permitted) in order to generate the best query plans.

For administrators, DB2 provides comprehensive support for load, import, export, reorganization, redistribution, and other data-related utilities. Additionally, DB2 supports tools such as:

- Audit facility for maintaining the audit trace of database actions
- Governor facility for controlling the priority and execution times of different applications
- Query patroller facility for managing the query jobs in the system
- Trace and diagnostic facilities for debugging
- Event monitoring facilities for tracking the resources and events during system execution.

26.9 Summary

This chapter provides a very brief synopsis of the features that are available in the DB2 Universal Database System. In short, the DB2 Universal Database is a multi-platform, scalable, object-relational database server. More comprehensive books and guides on DB2 are cited in the bibliographical notes.

Bibliographical Notes

Chamberlin [1996] and Chamberlin [1998] provide a good review of DB2's SQL and programming features. Earlier books by Date [1989] and Martin et al. [1989] provide a good review of the features of DB2 Universal Database for OS/390. The DB2 manuals provide definitive views of various versions of DB2. Most of these manuals are available online at the site http://www.software.ibm.com/data/pubs. Recent books providing hands-on training for using and administering DB2 include Zikopoulos et al. [2000], Sanders [2000], and Cook et al. [1999]. Finally, Prentice Hall is publishing a complete series of books on enrichment and certification for various aspects of DB2.

IBM research on XML includes Shanmugasundaram et al. [2000] and Carey et al. [2000], and IBM has been an active participant in the standardization of XQuery. Details of the DB2 XML extender can be found online at the site

http://www.software.ibm.com/data/db2/extenders/xmlext.

For a detailed description of the lock modes and their usage see the DB2 *Administration Guide* (chapter on Application Considerations), which is available online at http://www.software.ibm.com/data/pubs. Mohan [1990a] and Mohan and Levine [1992] give detailed descriptions of index concurrency control in DB2.

IBM research contributions, some of which are listed below, have continually enhanced the DB2 product. Chamberlin et al. [1981] provide a history and evaluation of the System R project, which played a crucial role in the development of relational databases and lead to the development of the DB2 product. The Halloween problem and other aspects of System R history appear in

http://www.mcjones.org/System_R/SQL_Reunion_95/index.html.

Transaction processing techniques such as write-ahead logging and the ARIES recovery algorithms are described by Mohan et al. [1992]. Query processing and optimization in Starburst are described by Haas et al. [1990]. Parallel processing in the DB2 Parallel Edition is described by Baru et al. [1995]. Active database support, including constraints, and triggers, are described by Cochrane et al. [1996]. Carey et al. [1999] describe object-relational support in DB2.

CHAPTER 27

Microsoft SQL Server

Sameet Agarwal, José A. Blakeley, Thomas Casey,
Kalen Delaney, César Galindo-Legaria, Goetz Graefe,
Michael Rys, Michael Zwilling
Microsoft

Microsoft SQL Server is a relational database management system that scales from laptops and desktops to enterprise servers, with a compatible version, based on the PocketPC operating system, available for handheld devices such as PocketPCs and bar-code scanners. SQL Server was originally developed in the 1980s at Sybase for UNIX systems and later ported to Windows NT systems by Microsoft. Since 1994, Microsoft has shipped SQL Server releases developed independently of Sybase, which stopped using the SQL Server name in the late 1990s. The latest available release is SQL Server 2000, available in personal, developer, standard, and enterprise editions, and localized for many languages around the world. In this chapter, the term SQL Server refers to all of these editions of SQL Server 2000.

SQL Server provides replication services among multiple copies of SQL Server as well as with other database systems. Its Analysis Services, an integral part of the system, includes online analytical processing (OLAP) and data mining facilities. SQL Server provides a large collection of graphical tools and "wizards" that guide database administrators through tasks such as setting up regular backups, replicating data among servers, and tuning a database for performance. Many development environments support SQL Server, including Microsoft's Visual Studio and related products, in particular the .NET products and services.

27.1 Management, Design, and Querying Tools

SQL Server provides a suite of tools for managing all aspects of SQL Server development, querying, tuning, testing, and administration. Most of these tools center around the SQL Server Enterprise Manager. The Enterprise Manager is a snap-in accessory to Microsoft Management Console (MMC), a tool that provides a common interface for working with various server applications in a Windows network.

27.1.1   Database Development and Visual Database Tools

While designing a database, the database administrator creates database objects such as tables, columns, keys, indices, relationships, constraints, and views. To help create these objects, the SQL Server Enterprise Manager provides access to visual database tools. These tools provide three mechanisms to aid in database design: the Database Designer, the Table Designer, and the View Designer. The Visual Tools also provide a visual query tool that allows the database administrator to use the Windows drag-and-drop capability to build queries visually.

The Database Designer is a visual tool that allows the database administrator to create tables, columns, keys, indices, relationships, and constraints. Within the Database Designer, a user can interact with database objects through database diagrams, which graphically show the structure of the database. The user can create and modify objects that are visible on diagrams (tables, columns, relationships, and keys) and some objects that are not visible on diagrams (indices and constraints). Figure 27.1 shows a database diagram opened from the Enterprise Manager.

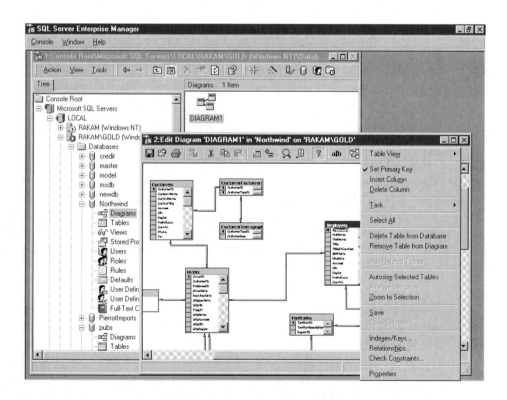

Figure 27.1   A diagram showing Table Designer options for the employees' table.

27.1.2 Database Query and Tuning Tools

SQL Server provides several tools to aid the application development process. Queries and stored procedures can be developed and tested initially using the SQL Server Query Analyzer, which also provides basic query analysis and tuning tools. Further analysis can be done using the SQL Server Profiler. Index tuning recommendations are provided by a third tool, the Index Tuning Wizard.

27.1.2.1 SQL Query Analyzer

SQL Query Analyzer provides a clean, simple, graphical user interface for running SQL queries and viewing the results. It allows for multiple windows so that simultaneous database connections (to one or more installations of SQL Server) can exist and be sized, tiled, or minimized separately. A query developer can choose to have query results displayed in a text window or in a grid. SQL Query Analyzer provides a graphical representation of **showplan**, the steps chosen by the optimizer for query execution. It also provides optional reports of the actual commands processed by SQL Server (a server-side trace) and of the work done by the client. SQL Query Analyzer comes with an object browser that lets a user drag and drop object or table names into a query window and helps build **select, insert, update,** or **delete** statements for any table. It also comes with a Transact-SQL Debugger tool. The debugger allows a user to single-step through any stored procedure, watching the behavior of parameters, local variables, and system functions as these steps execute.

A database administrator or developer can use SQL Query Analyzer to:

- Analyze queries: SQL Server Query Analyzer can show a graphical or textual execution plan for any query, as well as displaying statistics regarding the time and resources required to execute any query.

- Format SQL queries: the Query Analyzer allows indenting or unindenting lines of code, changing the case of words or sections of code, commenting a single line or multiple lines, and displaying queries with user-controlled color coding.

- Use templates for stored procedures, functions, and basic SQL statements: The Query Analyzer comes with dozens of predefined templates for building DDL commands, or users can define their own. When executing a template, users can supply specific values for object and column names, datatypes, and other specific information.

- Drag object names from the Object Browser to the Query window: Query Analyzer allows a developer to choose to see an object's definition, or for tables and views, to see templates for creating **insert, update, delete,** or **select** statements.

- Define personal keystroke and toolbar options: Query Analyzer allows defining hotkeys for quick execution of common queries, and gives complete control over what commands are available as toolbar buttons, and in what position those buttons appear.

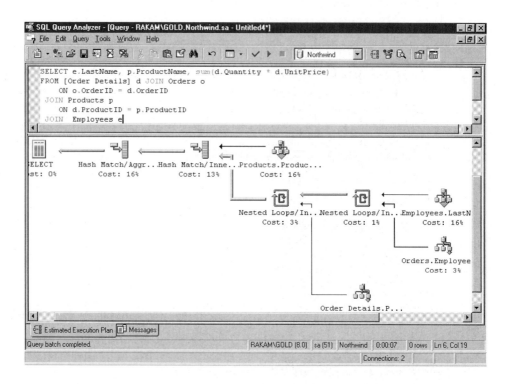

Figure 27.2   A showplan for a four-table join with **group by** aggregation.

Figure 27.2 shows the Query Analyzer displaying the graphical execution plan for a query involving a four-table join and an aggregation.

27.1.2.2 SQL Profiler

SQL Profiler is a graphical utility that allows database administrators to monitor and record database activity. SQL Profiler can display all server activity in real time, or it can create filters that focus on the actions of particular users, applications, or types of commands. SQL Profiler can display any SQL statement or stored procedure sent to any instance of SQL Server (if the security privileges allow it) as well as performance data indicating how long the query took to run, how much CPU and I/O was needed, and the execution plan that the query used.

SQL Profiler allows drilling down even deeper into SQL Server to monitor every statement executed as part of a stored procedure, every data modification operation, every lock acquired or released, or every occurrence of a database file growing automatically. Dozens of different events can be captured, and dozens of data items can be captured for each event. SQL Server actually divides the tracing functionality into two separate but connected components. The SQL Profiler is the client-side trace facility. Using SQL Profiler, a user can choose to save the captured data to a file or a table, in addition to displaying it in the Profiler user interface (UI). The Profiler tool displays every event that meets the filter criteria as it occurs. Once trace data are saved, SQL Profiler can read the saved data for display or analysis purposes.

On the server side is the SQL trace facility, which manages queues of events generated by event producers. A consumer thread reads events from the queues and filters them before sending them to the process that requested them. Events are the main unit of activity as far as tracing is concerned, and an event can be anything that happens inside SQL Server, or between SQL Server and a client. For example, creating or dropping an object is an event, executing a stored procedure is an event, acquiring or releasing a lock is an event, and sending a Transact-SQL batch from a client to the SQL Server is an event. There is a set of stored system procedures to define which events should be traced, what data for each event are interesting, and where to save the information collected from the events. Filters applied to the events can reduce the amount of information collected and stored. Figure 27.3 shows the events tab from the SQL Profiler's trace definition dialog.

SQL Server provides more than 100 predefined events, and a user can configure 10 additional events. Server-side traces run invisibly, and a trace can start automatically every time SQL Server starts. This guarantees that certain critical information will always be gathered, and can be used as a useful auditing mechanism. SQL Server is certified for C2-level security, and many of the traceable events are available solely to support C2-certification requirements.

27.1.2.3   The Index Tuning Wizard

With all of the possible query processing techniques available, the query optimizer can come up with a reasonably effective query plan even in the absence of well-planned indices. However, this does not mean that a well-tuned database doesn't benefit from good indices. Designing the best possible indices for the tables in a large database is a complex task; it not only requires a thorough knowledge of how SQL Server uses indices and how the query optimizer makes its decisions, but how the data will actually be used by applications and interactive queries. The SQL Server Index Tuning Wizard is a powerful tool for designing the best possible indices based on observed query and update loads.

The wizard tunes a single database at a time, and it bases its recommendations on a workload that can be a file of captured trace events or a file of SQL statements. SQL Profiler is designed to capture all SQL statements submitted by all users over a period of time. The wizard can then look at the data access patterns for all users, for all applications, for all tables, and make balanced recommendations.

27.1.3   SQL Server Enterprise Manager

In addition to providing access to the database design and visual database tools, the easy-to-use SQL Server Enterprise Manager supports centralized management of all aspects of multiple installations of SQL Server, including security, events, alerts, scheduling, backup, server configuration, tuning, full-text search, and replication. SQL Server Enterprise Manager allows a database administrator to create, modify, and copy SQL Server database schemas and objects such as tables, views, and trig-

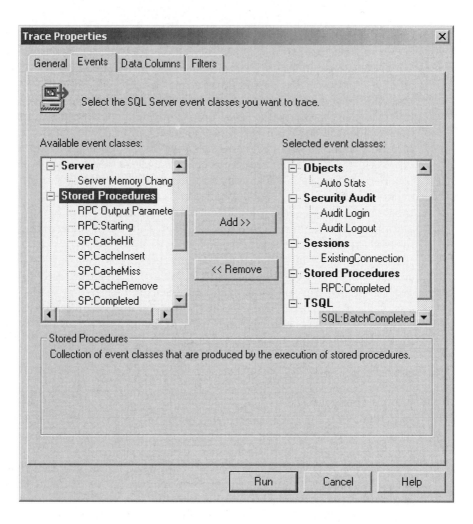

Figure 27.3   The Events tab of the Trace Properties dialog box.

gers. Because multiple installations of SQL Server can be organized into groups and treated as a unit, SQL Server Enterprise Manager can manage hundreds of servers simultaneously.

Although it can run on the same computer as the SQL Server engine, SQL Server Enterprise Manager offers the same management capabilities while running on any Windows NT/2000–based machine. SQL Server Enterprise Manager also runs on Windows 98, although a few capabilities aren't available in this environment (most notably the ability to use the Service Control Manager, a feature of Windows NT/2000, to start and stop SQL Server remotely). In addition, the efficient client/server architecture of SQL Server makes it practical to use the remote access (dial-up networking) capabilities of Windows NT/2000 as well as Windows 98 for administration and management.

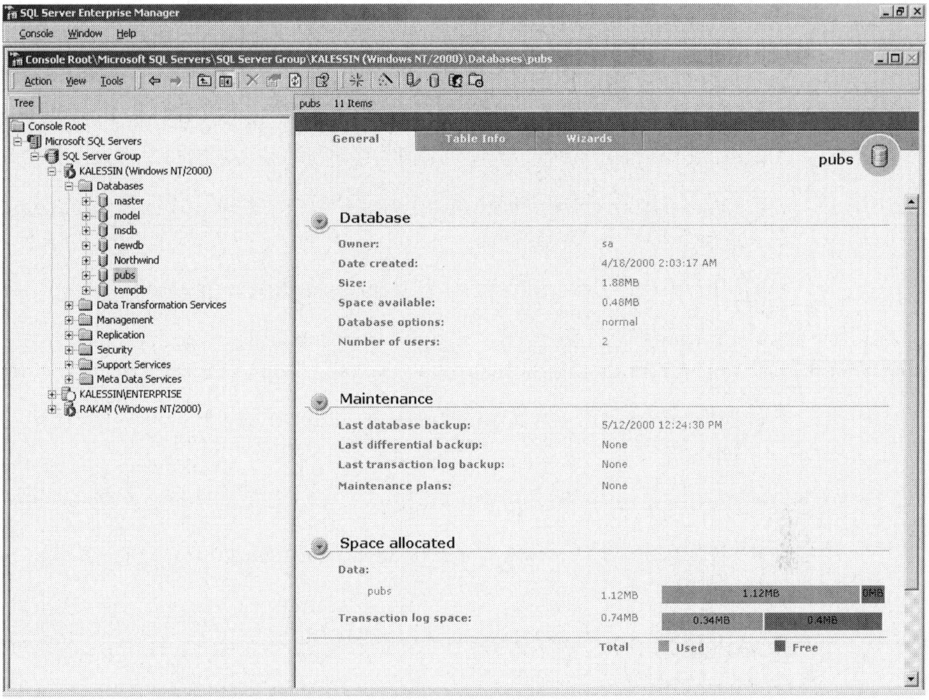

Figure 27.4   The SQL Server Enterprise Manager interface.

SQL Server Enterprise Manager relieves the database administrator from having to know the specific steps and syntax to complete a job. It provides more than 20 wizards to guide the database administrator through the process of setting up and maintaining an installation of SQL Server. Enterprise Manager's interface appears in Figure 27.4.

27.2   SQL Variations and Extensions

Transact-SQL is the database language supported by SQL Server. Transact-SQL is a complete database programming language that includes data definition and data manipulation statements, iterative and conditional statements, variables, procedures, and functions. Transact-SQL complies with the entry level of the SQL-92 standard, but also supports several features from the intermediate and full levels. Transact-SQL also supports extensions to the SQL-92 standard.

27.2.1   Data Types

SQL Server supplies a set of primitive data types that define all of the types of data that can be used with SQL Server. The set of primitive data types includes:

- A complete set of signed integer types with 1, 2, 4, and 8 bytes of precision (tinyint, smallint, int, and bigint)

- A bit data type with values 0 or 1 (bit)

- Decimal type with 38 digits of precision (decimal, numeric)

- Monetary types with accuracy to a ten-thousandth of a monetary unit (money, smallmoney)

- Date and time types with accuracy up to 3.33 milliseconds (datetime, small-datetime)

- Single- and double-precision floating-point types (real, float)

- Character string types of fixed and variable size up to $2^{30} - 1$ Unicode and non-Unicode characters (char/nchar, varchar/nvarchar, text/ntext)

- Byte strings of fixed and variable size up to $2^{31} - 1$ bytes (binary, varbinary, image)

- A cursor type that enables references to a cursor object (cursor)

- Database-wide and globally unique identifier data types (rowversion, unique-identifier)

In addition, SQL Server supports sql_variant and table types described in Sections 27.2.1.1 and 27.2.1.2.

27.2.1.1 Variant type

Sql_variant is a scalar data type that enables a column of a row, a variable, or a function argument to contain values of any SQL scalar type (except text, ntext, image, rowversion and sql_variant). It is used by applications that need to store data whose type cannot be anticipated at data definition time. Internally the system keeps track of the original type of the data. It is possible to filter, join, and sort on sql_variant columns. The system function sql_variant_property can return details on the actual data stored in a column of type sql_variant, including the base type and size information.

27.2.1.2 Table type

Table is a type that enables a variable to hold a set of rows. This type is used primarily to specify the return type of table-valued functions. A table variable behaves like a local variable. It has a well-defined scope, which is the function, stored procedure, or batch in which it is declared. Within its scope, a table variable may be used like a regular table. It may be applied anywhere a table or table expression is used in **select, insert, update,** and **delete** statements.

Table variables are cleaned up automatically at the end of the function, stored procedure, or batch in which they are defined. In addition, table variables used in stored procedures result in fewer recompilations of the stored procedures than when temporary tables are used. Transactions involving table variables last only for the duration of an update on the table variable, so table variables require less locking and logging resources.

27.2.2   User-Defined Functions

User-defined functions allow users to define their own Transact-SQL functions by using the **create function** statement. SQL Server supports functions whose return type can be a scalar or a table. Scalar functions can be used in any scalar expression inside a SQL DML, or DDL statement. Table-valued functions can be used anywhere a table is allowed in a **select** statement. Table-valued functions whose body contains a single SQL **select** statement are treated as a view (expanded inline) in the query that references the function. Since table-valued functions allow input arguments, inline table-valued functions can be considered parameterized views.

27.2.3   Views

A *view* is a virtual table whose contents are defined by a **select** statement. Views are a powerful data modeling and security mechanism. Indexed views (Section 27.2.3.1) can also provide a substantial performance benefit. The tables referenced by the view definition are known as the base tables. In the example that follows, *titleview* is a view that selects data from three base tables: *title*, *titleauthor*, and *titles*. These tables are part of the *pubs* sample database shipped with SQL Server.

```
create view titleview as
select title, au_ord, au_lname, price, ytd_sales, pub_id
from authors as a join titleauthor as ta on (a.au_id = ta.au_id)
         join titles as t on (t.title_id = ta.title_id)
```

The view *titleview* can be referenced in statements in the same way that a reference to a base table would be:

```
select *
from titleview
where price >= 30.00
```

A view can reference other views. For example, *titleview* presents information that is useful for managers, but a company typically discloses year-to-date figures only in quarterly or annual financial statements. A view can be built that selects all the titleview columns except au_ord and ytd_sales. This new view can be used by customers to get lists of available books without seeing the financial information:

```
create view Cust_titleview as
select title, au_lname, price, pub_id
from titleview
```

Queries that employ views are optimized by expanding the view definition into the query—in other words, the cost-based optimizer optimizes the entire query as if it had been stated without the use of views.

27.2.3.1 Indexed Views

In addition to traditional views as defined in ANSI SQL, SQL Server supports indexed (materialized) views. Indexed views can substantially enhance the performance of complex decision support queries that retrieve large numbers of base table rows and aggregate large amounts of information into concise sums, counts, and averages. SQL Server supports creating a clustered index on a view and subsequently any number of nonclustered indices. Once a view is indexed, the optimizer can use its indices in queries that reference the view or its base tables. Existing queries can benefit from the improved efficiency of retrieving data directly from the indexed view without having to be rewritten to reference the view. Update statements to the view's base tables are propagated automatically to the view's indices.

27.2.3.2 Partitioned Views

Partitioned views are used to partition data across multiple tables, databases, or SQL Server instances to distribute the workload. If the data are partitioned across multiple servers, they can provide the same performance benefits as a cluster of servers, and can be used to support the processing needs of the largest Web sites or corporate data centers. A base table can be partitioned into several member tables, each of which has a subset of rows from the original table. Each server must have the partitioned view definition. A partitioned view uses the **union** operator to combine all the partitions in the base tables into a single result set that behaves exactly like a copy of the complete original table. For example, a customer table can be partitioned across three servers. Each server must have a disjoint base table partition as follows:

- On Server1:

    ```
    create table Customer_33 (
        CustomerID integer primary key
            check (CustomerID between 1 and 32999),
    ... Additional column definitions )
    ```

- On Server2:

    ```
    create table Customer_66 (
        CustomerID integer primary key
            check (CustomerID between 33000 and 65999),
    ... Additional column definitions )
    ```

- On Server3:

    ```
    create table Customer_99 (
        CustomerID integer primary key
            check (CustomerID between 66000 and 99999),
    ... Additional column definitions )
    ```

After creating the member tables, the database administrator defines a distributed partitioned view on each server, with each view having the same name. The distributed partitioned view for Server1 would be defined as follows:

```
create view Customers as
select * from CompanyDatabase.TableOwner.Customers_33
union all
select * from Server2.CompanyDatabase.TableOwner.Customers_66
union all
select * from Server3.CompanyDatabase.TableOwner.Customers_99
```

Similar views would be defined on Server2 and Server3.

Having the view defined on each server allows queries referencing the distributed partitioned view name to run on any of the member servers. The system operates as if a complete copy of the original table is on each member server, although each server has only one local member table and a distributed partitioned view referencing that local table and two remote tables. The location of the data is transparent to the application. With these three views, any Transact-SQL statement on any of the three servers that reference Customers will see the same results as from the original table. Partitioned views can be accessed not only by **select** statements but also by **insert, update,** and **delete** statements, including statements that affect multiple partitions and even those that require moving rows from one partition to another.

27.2.3.3   Updatable Views

Generally, views can be the target of **update, delete**, or **insert** statements if the data modification applies to only one of the view's base tables. Updates to partitioned views can be propagated to multiple base tables. For example, the following **update** will increase the prices for publisher "0736" by 10 percent.

```
update titleview
set price = price * 1.10
where pub_id = '0736'
```

For data modifications that affect more than one base table, the view can be updated if there is an **instead** trigger (Section 27.2.4) defined for the operation: **instead** triggers for **insert**, **update**, or **delete** operations can be defined on a view, to specify the updates that must be performed on the base tables to implement the corresponding modifications on the view.

27.2.4   Triggers

Triggers are Transact-SQL procedures that are automatically executed when an **update, insert**, or **delete** statement is issued against a base table or view. Triggers are a mechanism that enables enforcement of business logic automatically when data are modified. Triggers can extend the integrity checking logic of declarative constraints, defaults, and rules, although declarative constraints should be used preferentially whenever they suffice.

There are two general kinds of triggers that differ in the time, relative to the triggering statement, at which the action is performed. **After** triggers execute after the triggering statement and subsequent declarative constraints are enforced. **Instead** triggers execute instead of the triggering action. **Instead** triggers can be thought of as similar to **before** triggers, but they actually replace the triggering action. In SQL Server, **after** triggers can be defined only on base tables, while **instead** triggers can be defined on base tables or views. **Instead** triggers allow practically any view to be made updatable.

27.3   Storage and Indexing

In SQL Server, a database refers to a collection of files, which contain data and are supported by a single transaction log. The database is the primary unit of administration in SQL Server and also provides a container for physical structures such as tables and indices and for logical structures such as constraints, views, etc.

27.3.1   FileGroups

In order to manage space effectively in a database, the set of data files in a database is divided into groups called filegroups. Each filegroup contains one or more operating system files.

Every database has at least one filegroup known as the primary filegroup. This filegroup contains all the metadata for the database in system tables. The primary filegroup may also store user data.

If additional, user-defined filegroups have been created, a user can explicitly control the placement of individual tables, indices, or the large-object columns of a table by placing them in a filegroup. For example, the user may choose to store a table in filegroupA, its nonclustered index in filegroupB, and the large-object columns of the table in filegroupC. The placing of these tables and indices in different filegroups allows the user to control the use of hardware resources (that is, disks and the I/O subsystem). One filegroup is always considered the default filegroup; initially, the default filegroup is the primary filegroup, but any user-defined filegroup can be given the default property. If a table or index is not placed specifically on a filegroup, it is created in the default filegroup.

27.3.2   Space Management within Filegroups

One of the main purposes for filegroups is to allow for effective space management. All data files are divided into fixed-size 8 Kbyte units called pages. The allocation system is responsible for allocating these pages to tables and indices. The goal of the allocation system is to minimize the amount of space wasted while, at the same time, keeping the amount of fragmentation in the database to a minimum to ensure good scan performance. In order to achieve this goal, the allocation manager usually allocates and deallocates all the pages in units of eight contiguous pages called extents.

The allocation system manages these extents through various bitmaps. These bitmaps allow the allocation system to find a page or an extent for allocation quickly. These bitmaps are also used when a full table or index scan is executed. The advantage of using allocation-based bitmaps for scanning is that it allows disk-order traversals of all the extents belonging to a table or index leaf level, which significantly improves the scan performance.

If there is more than one file in a filegroup, the allocation system allocates extents for any object on that filegroup using a "proportional fill" algorithm. Each file is filled up in the proportion of the amount of free space in that file compared to other files. This fills all the files in a filegroup at roughly the same rate and allows the system to utilize all the files in the filegroup evenly. During a scan using the allocation bitmaps, the scan algorithm takes advantage of the multiple files by issuing separate I/O against each of the files.

One of the biggest decisions in setting up a database is to determine how big to make it. SQL Server allows data files to change in size after the database is created. The user can even choose to have the data file automatically grow if the database is running out of space. Thus, the user can configure the database to a reasonable approximation of the expected size but set the database files to grow and adjust to the usage pattern, if the initial approximation is wrong. SQL Server allows files to shrink. In order to shrink a data file, SQL Server moves all the data from the physical end of the file to a point closer to the beginning of the file and then actually shrink the file, releasing space back to the operating system.

27.3.3 Tables

SQL Server supports two different organizations for tables: heaps and clustered indices. In a heap-organized table, the location of every row of the table is determined entirely by the system and is not specified in any way by the user. The rows of a heap have a fixed identifier known as the row (RID), and this value never changes unless the file is shrunk and the row is moved. If the row becomes large enough that it cannot fit in the page in which it was originally inserted, the record is moved to a different place but a forwarding stub is left in the original place so that the record can still be found by using its original RID.

In a clustered index organization for a table, the rows of the table are stored in a B^+-tree sorted by the clustering key of the index. The clustered index key also serves as the unique identifier for each row. The key for a clustered index can be defined to be nonunique, in which case SQL Server adds an additional hidden column to make the key unique. The clustered index also serves as a search structure to identify a row of the table with a particular key or scan a set of rows of the table with keys within a certain range.

27.3.4 Indices

The most common form of indexing is nonclustered indices, which are also known as secondary indices. These indices are B^+-trees on one or more columns of the base table. They allow efficient access of a base table row based on a search criterion on the indexed columns. In addition, queries that refer only to columns that are available through secondary indices are processed by retrieving pages from the leaf level of the indices without having to retrieve data from the clustered index or heap.

SQL Server supports the addition of computed columns to a table. A computed column is a column whose value is an expression, usually based on the value of other columns in that row. SQL Server allows the user to build secondary indices on computed columns.

27.3.5 Scans and Read-ahead

Execution of queries in SQL Server can involve a variety of different scan modes on the underlying tables and indices. These include ordered versus unordered scans, serial versus parallel scans, unidirectional versus bi-directional, forward versus backward, and entire table or index scan versus range or filtered scans.

Each of the scan modes has a read-ahead mechanism, which tries to keep the scan ahead of the needs of the query execution, in order to reduce seek and latency overheads and utilize disk idle time. The SQL Server read-ahead algorithm uses the knowledge from the query execution plan in order to drive the read-ahead and make sure that only data that is actually needed by the query is read. Also, the amount of read-ahead is automatically scaled according to the size of the buffer pool, the amount of I/O the disk subsystem can sustain, and the rate at which the data are being consumed by query execution.

27.4   Query Processing and Optimization

The query processor of SQL Server is based on an extensible framework that allows rapid incorporation of new execution and optimization techniques. Execution encapsulates data processing algorithms in *iterators*, which communicate with each other using a GetNextRow() interface. Optimization generates alternatives by using tree transformations, and it estimates execution cost by using detailed models of selectivities and iterator behavior.

27.4.1   Overview of Optimization Process

Complex queries present significant optimization opportunities that require reordering across query blocks, with plan selection based on estimated cost. SQL Server uses a purely algebraic framework. SQL Server's optimization framework is based on the Cascades optimizer prototype. An SQL statement is compiled as follows.

- **Parsing/binding**. The optimizer parses the statement, and resolves table and column names by using the catalogs. It resolves and incorporates views to generate an operator tree. It checks the procedure cache to see if there is already a plan for the query, in which case optimization is avoided. The operator tree uses an extended relational algebra where there is no notion of query block or derived table, but simply an arbitrary combination of relational operators.

- **Simplification/normalization**. The optimizer applies simplification rules on the operator tree, to obtain a normal, simplified form. These rules implement transformations such as pushing selections down and simplification of outer joins into joins. During simplification, the optimizer determines and loads statistics required for cardinality estimation. If required statistics are missing, the optimizer automatically creates them before continuing optimization.

- **Cost-based optimization**. The optimizer applies exploration and implementation rules to generate alternatives, estimates execution cost, and chooses the plan with cheapest anticipated cost. Exploration rules implement operator reordering, including join and aggregation reordering. Implementation rules introduce execution alternatives, such as merge join or hash join.

- **Plan preparation**. The optimizer creates query execution structures for the plan selected.

Cost-based optimization is not divided into phases that optimize different aspects of the query independently and it is not restricted to a single dimension such as join enumeration. Instead, a collection of transformation rules defines the space of interest, and cost estimation is used uniformly to select an efficient plan.

27.4.2 Query Simplification

During simplification, the optimizer pushes selects down the operator tree as far as possible. It checks predicates for contradictions, taking into account declared constraints. It uses contradictions to identify empty subexpressions, which it removes from the tree. A common scenario is the elimination of **union** branches that retrieve data from tables with different constraints.

A number of simplification rules are *context dependent*; that is, the substitution is valid only in the context of utilization of the subexpression. For example, an outer join can be simplified into an inner join if a later filter operation will discard nonmatching rules that were padded with **null**. Another example is elimination of joins on foreign-keys, which need not be performed if there are no later uses of columns from the referenced table. A third example is the context of duplicate-insensitivity, which specifies that delivering one or multiple copies of a row does not affect the query result. Subexpressions under semijoins and under **distinct** are duplicate insensitive, which allows turning **union** into **union all**.

For grouping and aggregation, the *GbAgg* operator is used, which creates groups and optionally applies an aggregate function on each group. Duplicate removal, expressed in SQL by the **distinct** keyword, is simply a *GbAgg* with no aggregate functions to compute. During simplification, information about keys and functional dependencies is used to reduce grouping columns.

Subqueries are normalized by removing correlated query specifications and using some join variant instead. Removing correlations is not a "subquery execution strategy," but simply a normalization step. A variety of execution strategies is then considered during cost-based optimization.

27.4.3 Reordering and Cost-Based Optimization

In SQL Server transformations are fully integrated into the cost-based generation and selection of execution plans. In addition to inner join reordering, the query optimizer employs reordering transformations for the operators outer join, semijoin, and antisemijoin, from the standard relational algebra (with duplicates, for SQL). *GbAgg* is reordered as well, by moving it below joins where possible. Partial aggregation, that is, introducing a new *GbAgg* with grouping on a superset of the columns of a *GbAgg* present higher up, is considered below joins and **union all**, and also in parallel plans. See the references given in the bibliographical notes for details.

Correlated execution is considered during plan exploration, the simplest case being index-lookup join. SQL Server models this using *Apply*, which operates on a table T and a parameterized relational expression $E(t)$. *Apply* executes E for each row of T, which provides parameter values. Correlated execution is considered as an execution alternative, regardless of the use of subqueries in the original SQL formulation. It is a very efficient strategy when the table T is small, and indices support efficient parameterized execution of $E(t)$. Furthermore, we consider reduction on the number of executions of $E(t)$ when there are duplicate parameter values, by means of two techniques: Sort T on parameter values so that a single result of $E(t)$ is reused while the parameter value remains the same; or else use a hash table that keeps track of the result of $E(t)$ for (some subset of) earlier parameter values.

Some applications select rows on the basis of some aggregate result for their group. For example, "Find customers whose balance is more than twice the average for their market segment". The SQL formulation requires a self-join. During exploration, this pattern is detected and per-segment execution is considered as an alternative to self-join.

Materialized view utilization is also considered during cost-based optimization. View matching interacts with operator reordering in that utilization may not be apparent until some other reordering has taken place. When a view is found to match some subexpression, the table that contains the view result is added as an alternative for the corresponding expression. Depending on data distribution and indices available, it may or may not be better than the original expression—selection will be based on cost estimation.

To estimate the execution cost of a plan, the model takes into account the number of expected rows to process, called the row goal, as well as the number of times a subexpression is executed. The row goal can be less than the cardinality estimate, in cases such as *Apply/semijoin*. *Apply/semijoin* outputs row t from T as soon as a single row is produced by $E(t)$ (that is, it tests **exists** $E(t)$). Thus, the row goal of the output of $E(t)$ is 1, and the row goals of subtrees of $E(t)$ are computed for this row goal for $E(t)$, and used for cost estimation.

27.4.4 Update Plans

Update plans optimize maintenance of indices, verify constraints, apply cascading actions, and maintain materialized views. For index maintenance, instead of taking each row and maintaining all indices for it, update plans apply modifications per index, sorting rows and applying the update operation in key order. This minimizes random I/O, especially when the number of rows to update is large. Constraints are handled by an **assert** operator, which executes a predicate and raises an error if the result is **false**. Referential constraints are defined by **exists** predicates, which in turn become semijoins and are optimized by considering all execution algorithms.

The Halloween problem is addressed by using cost-based choices. The Halloween problem refers to the following anomaly: Suppose a salary index is read in ascending order, and salaries are being raised by 10 percent. As a result of the update, rows will move forward in the index and will be found and updated again, leading to an infinite loop. One way to address this problem is to separate processing into two phases: First read all rows that will be updated and make a copy of them in some temporary place, then read from this place and apply all updates. Another alternative is to read from a different index where rows will not move as a result of the update. Some execution plans provide phase separation automatically, if they sort or build a hash table on the rows to be updated. In SQL Server's optimizer, Halloween protection is modeled as a property of plans. Multiple plans that provide the required property are generated, and one is selected on the basis of estimated execution cost.

27.4.5 Partial Search and Heuristics

Cost-based query optimizers face the issue of search space explosion, because applications do issue queries involving dozens of tables. To address this, SQL Server uses multiple optimization stages, each of which uses query transformations to explore successively larger regions of the search space.

There are simple and complete transformations geared toward exhaustive optimization, as well as smart transformations that implement various heuristics. Smart transformations generate plans that are very far apart in the search space, while simple transformations explore neighborhoods. Optimization stages apply a mix of both kinds of transformations, first emphasizing smart transformations, and later transitioning to simple transformations. Optimum results on subtrees are preserved, so that later stages can take advantage of results generated earlier.

Each stage needs to balance opposing plan generation techniques:

- **Exhaustive generation of alternatives**: To generate the complete space, the optimizer should use complete, local, nonredundant transformations—a transformation rule equivalent to a sequence of more primitive transformations only introduces additional overhead.

- **Heuristic generation of candidates**: A handful of interesting candidates (selected on the basis of estimated cost) are likely to be far apart in terms of primitive transformation rules. Here, desirable transformations are incomplete, global, and redundant.

Optimization can be terminated at any point after the first plan has been generated. Such termination is based on the estimated cost of the best plan found and the time spent already in optimization. For example, if a query requires only looking up a few rows in some indices, a very cheap plan will be produced quickly in the early stages, terminating optimization. This approach has allowed us to add new heuristics easily over time, without compromising either cost-based selection of plans, or exhaustive exploration of the search space, when appropriate.

27.4.6 Query Execution

Execution algorithms support both sort-based and hash-based processing, and their data structures are designed to optimize use of processor cache. Hash operations support basic aggregation and join, with a number of optimizations, extensions, and dynamic tuning for data skew. The *flow-distinct* operation is a variant of hash distinct, where rows are output early, as soon as a new distinct value is found, instead of waiting to process the complete input. This operator is effective for queries that use **distinct** and request only a few rows, say using the **top n** construct. Correlated plans specify executing $E(t)$, often including some index lookup based on the parameter, for each row t of a table T. *Asynchronous prefetching* allows issuing multiple index-lookup requests to the storage engine. It is implemented this way: A nonblocking index-lookup request is made for a row t of T, then t is placed in a prefetch queue. Rows are taken out of the queue and used by *Apply* to execute $E(t)$. Execution of $E(t)$ does not require that data be already in the buffer pool, but having outstanding prefetch operations maximizes hardware utilization and increases performance. The size of the queue is determined dynamically as a function of cache hits. If no ordering is required on the output rows of *Apply*, rows from the queue may be taken out of order, to minimize waiting on I/O.

Parallel execution is implemented by the *Exchange* operator, which manages multiple threads, partitions or broadcasts data, and feeds the data to multiple processes. The query optimizer decides *Exchange* placement on the basis of estimated cost. The degree of parallelism is determined dynamically at run time, according to the current system utilization.

Index plans are made up of the pieces described earlier. For example, we consider the use of index join to resolve predicate conjunctions (or index union, for disjunctions), in a cost-based way. Such a join can be done in parallel, using any of SQL Server's join algorithms. We also consider joining indices for the sole purpose of assembling a row with the set of columns needed on a query, which is sometimes faster than scanning a base table. Taking record ids from a secondary index and locating the corresponding row in a base table is effectively equivalent to peforming index-lookup join. For this, we use our generic correlated execution techniques such as asynchronous prefetch.

Communication with the storage engine is done through OLE-DB, which allows accessing other data providers that implement this interface. OLE-DB is the mechanism used for distributed and remote queries, which are driven directly by the query processor. Data providers are categorized according to the range of functionality they provide, ranging from simple row set providers with no indexing capabilities to providers with full SQL support.

27.5 Concurrency and Recovery

SQL Server's transaction, logging, locking, and recovery subsystems realize the ACID properties expected of a database system.

27.5.1 Transactions

In SQL Server, all statements are atomic and applications can specify various levels of isolation for each statement. Transactions are used to scope a sequence of statements, making the entire set atomic and controlling its isolation from other transactions. A single transaction can include statements that not only select, insert, delete, or update records, but also create or drop tables, build indices, and bulk-import data. Transactions can span databases on remote servers. When transactions are spread across servers, SQL Server uses a Windows operating system service called the Microsoft Distributed Transaction Coordinator (MS DTC) to perform two-phase commit processing. MS DTC supports the XA transaction protocol and, along with OLE-DB, provides the foundation for ACID transactions among heterogeneous systems.

27.5.1.1 Save-points

SQL Server supports two types of transaction save-points: statement and named. Statement save-points are implicit save-points taken at the beginning of a statement so that, if a statement fails, it can be rolled back without requiring the entire transaction to rollback. A named save-point is a **save transaction** statement issued by an application, which labels a point in the transaction. Later a **rollback** statement can be issued to rollback to the named save-point. Rolling back to a save-point does not release locks and cannot be used in distributed transactions.

27.5.1.2 Concurrency Options for Updates

SQL Server offers both optimistic and pessimistic concurrency control for update operations.

Optimistic concurrency control works on the assumption that resource conflicts between multiple users are unlikely (but not impossible), and allows transactions to execute without locking any resources. Only when attempting to change data are resources checked to determine if any conflicts have occurred. If a conflict occurs, the application must read the data and attempt the change again. Applications can choose whether changes are detected by comparing values or by checking a special rowversion column on a row. Optimistic concurrency control requires the use of cursors.

Pessimistic concurrency control locks resources as they are required, for the duration of a transaction. Unless deadlocks occur, a transaction is assured of successful completion. Pessimistic concurrency control is the default for SQL Server.

27.5.1.3 Isolation Levels

SQL-92 defines the following isolation levels, all of which are supported by SQL Server:

- Read uncommitted (the lowest level where transactions are isolated only enough to ensure that physically corrupt data are not read)
- Read committed (SQL Server default level)
- Repeatable read
- Serializable (the highest level, where transactions are completely isolated from one another)

Resource	Description
RID	Row identifier; used to lock a single row within a table
Key	Row lock within an index; protects key ranges in serializable transactions
Page	8 Kbyte table or index page
Extent	Contiguous group of eight data pages or index pages
Table	Entire table, including all data and indices
DB	Database

Figure 27.5   Lockable resources.

27.5.2 Locking

SQL Server provides multigranularity locking that allows different types of resources to be locked by a transaction (see Figure 27.5, where the resources are listed in order of increasing granularity). To minimize the cost of locking, SQL Server locks resources automatically at a granularity appropriate to the task. Locking at a smaller granularity, such as rows, increases concurrency, but has a higher overhead because more locks must be held if many rows are locked. Locking at a larger granularity, such as tables, is expensive in terms of concurrency because locking an entire table restricts access to any part of the table by other transactions, but has a lower CPU and memory overhead because fewer locks are being acquired.

The available lock modes are shared (S), update (U), and exclusive (X). Update locks are used to prevent a common form of deadlock that occurs when multiple sessions are reading, locking, and potentially updating resources later. Additional lock modes—called key-range locks—are taken only in serializable isolation level for locking the range between two rows in an index.

Multigranularity locking requires that locks be acquired in a strict hierarchy from largest to smallest granularity. The hierarchy is database, table, page, and row. When locking above the granularity at which shared, update, and exclusive locks are to be acquired, intent locks are used.

27.5.2.1 Dynamic Locking

Fine-granularity locking can improve concurrency at the cost of extra CPU cycles and memory to acquire and hold many locks. For many queries, a coarser locking granularity provides better performance with no (or minimal) loss of concurrency. Database systems have traditionally required query hints and table options for applications to specify locking granularity. In addition, there are configuration parameters (often static) for how much memory to dedicate to the lock manager.

In SQL Server, locking granularity is optimized automatically for optimal performance and concurrency for each index used in a query. In addition, the memory dedicated to the lock manager is adjusted dynamically on the basis of feedback from other parts of the system, including other applications on the machine.

Lock granularity is optimized before query execution for each table and index used in the query. The lock optimization process takes into account isolation level

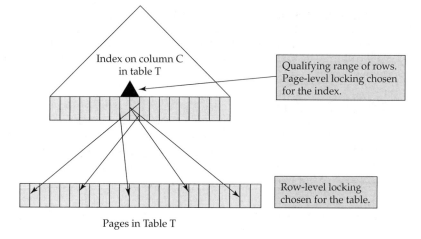

Index on column C
in table T

Qualifying range of rows.
Page-level locking chosen
for the index.

Row-level locking
chosen for the table.

Pages in Table T

Figure 27.6   Locking granularity.

(that is, how long locks are held), scan type (range, probe, or entire table), estimated number of rows to be scanned, selectivity (percentage of visited rows that qualify for the query), row density (number of rows per page), operation type (scan, update), user limits on the granularity, and available system memory.

Figure 27.6 shows an example query where qualifying rows are identified by a range scan of an index, and then the rows are retrieved from the base table. Here, page locks are used on the index because a dense range of index rows satisfies that portion of the query requiring only a few page locks. However, the base table rows are scattered throughout the table and thus row-level locking provides much higher concurrency. In general, lock optimization favors concurrency in its decisions.

Once a query is executing, the locking granularity is escalated automatically to table level if the system acquires significantly more locks than the optimizer expected or if the amount of available memory drops and cannot support the number of locks required.

27.5.2.2 Deadlock detection

SQL Server automatically detects deadlocks involving both locks and other resources. For example, if transaction A is holding a lock on Table1 and is waiting for memory to become available and transaction B has some memory it can't release until it acquires a lock on Table1, the transactions will deadlock. Threads and communication buffers can also be involved in deadlocks. When SQL Server detects a deadlock, it chooses as the deadlock victim the transaction that would be the least expensive to roll back, considering the amount of work the transaction has already done.

Frequent deadlock detection can hurt system performance. SQL Server automatically adjusts the frequency of deadlock detection to how often deadlocks are occurring. If deadlocks are infrequent, the detection algorithm runs every 5 seconds. If they are frequent it will begin checking every time a transaction waits for a lock.

27.5.3 Logging and Recovery

SQL Server is designed to recover from system and media failures, and the recovery system can scale to machines with very large buffer pools (100 Gbytes) and thousands of disk drives.

27.5.3.1 Logging

The transaction log records all changes made to the database and stores enough information to allow any changes to be undone (rolled back) or redone (rolled forward) in the event of a system failure or rollback request.

Logically, the log is a potentially infinite stream of log records identified by log sequence numbers (LSNs). Physically, a portion of the stream is stored in log files. Log records are saved in the log files until they have been backed up and are no longer needed by the system for rollback or replication. Log files grow and shrink in size to accommodate the records that need to be stored. Additional log files can be added to a database (on new disks, for example) while the system is running and without blocking any current operations, and all logs are treated as if they were one continuous file.

27.5.3.2 Crash Recovery

SQL Server's recovery system has many aspects in common with the ARIES recovery algorithm (see Section 17.9.6), and some of the key differences are highlighted in this section.

SQL Server has a configuration option called recovery interval, which allows an administrator to limit the length of time SQL Server should take to recover after a crash. The server dynamically adjusts the checkpoint frequency to reduce recovery time to within the recovery interval. Checkpoints flush all dirty pages from the buffer pool, and adjust to the capabilities of the I/O system and its current workload to effectively eliminate any impact on running transactions.

Upon startup after a crash, the system starts multiple threads (automatically scaled to the number of CPUs) to start recovering multiple databases in parallel. The first phase of recovery is an analysis pass on the log, which builds a dirty page table and active transaction list. The next phase is a redo pass starting from the last checkpoint and redoing all operations. During the redo phase, the dirty page table is used to drive read-ahead of data pages. The final phase is an undo phase where incomplete transactions are rolled back. The undo phase is actually divided into two parts as SQL Server uses a two-level recovery scheme. Transactions at the first level (those involving internal operations such as space allocation and page splits) are rolled back first, followed by user transactions.

27.5.3.3 Media Recovery

SQL Server's backup and restore capabilities allow recovery from many failures, including loss or corruption of disk media, user errors, and permanent loss of a server. Additionally, backing up and restoring databases is useful for other purposes, such as copying a database from one server to another and maintaining standby systems. Standby systems are created with a feature called log shipping, which continually backs up the transaction logs from a source database and then copies and restores the logs to one or more standby databases, keeping the standby databases synchronized with the source database. Standby systems can take over for a primary in a matter of minutes. In addition, a standby can be made available for read-only query processing.

SQL Server has three different recovery models that users can choose from for each database. By specifying a recovery model, an administrator declares the type of recovery capabilities required (such as point-in-time restore and log shipping) and the required backups to achieve them. Backups can be taken on databases, files, filegroups, and the transaction log. All backups are fuzzy and completely online; that is, they do not block any DML or DDL operations while they execute. Backup and restore operations are highly optimized and limited only by the speed of the media onto which the backup is targeted. SQL Server can back up to both disk and tape devices (up to 64 in parallel) and has high-performance backup APIs for use by third-party backup products.

27.6 System Architecture

A single SQL Server instance is a single operating system process that is also a named endpoint for requests for SQL execution. Applications interact with SQL Server via various client-side libraries (like ODBC and OLE-DB) in order to execute SQL.

27.6.1 Thread Pooling on the Server

In order to minimize the context switching on the server and to control the degree of multiprogramming, the SQL Server process maintains a pool of threads that execute client requests. As requests arrive from the client, they are assigned a thread on which to execute. The thread executes the SQL statements issued by the client and sends the results back to it. Once the user request completes, the thread is returned back to the thread pool.

In addition to user requests, the thread pool is also used to assign threads for internal background tasks:

- Lazywriter: This thread is dedicated to making sure a certain amount of the buffer pool is free and available at all times for allocation by the system. The thread also interacts with the operating system to determine the optimal amount of memory that should be consumed by the SQL Server process.

- Checkpoint: This thread periodically checkpoints all databases in order to maintain a fast recovery interval for the databases on server restart.

- Deadlock monitor: This thread monitors the other threads, looking for a deadlock in the system. It is responsible for the detection of deadlocks and also picking a victim in order to allow the system to make progress.

When the query processor chooses a parallel plan to execute a particular query, it can allocate multiple threads that work on behalf of the main thread to execute the query.

Since the Windows NT family of operating systems provides native thread support, SQL Server uses NT threads for its execution. However, SQL Server can be configured to run with user-mode threads in addition to kernel threads in very high end systems to avoid the cost of a kernel context switch on a thread switch.

27.6.2 Memory Management

There are many different uses of memory within the SQL Server process:

- **Buffer pool**: The biggest consumer of memory in the system is the buffer pool. The buffer pool maintains a cache of the most recently used database pages. It uses a clock replacement algorithm with a steal, no-force policy; that is, buffer pages with uncommitted updates may be replaced ("stolen"), and buffer pages are not forced to disk on transaction comming. The buffers also obey the write-ahead logging protocol to ensure correctness of crash and media recovery.

- **Dynamic memory allocation**: This is the memory that is allocated dynamically to execute requests submitted by the user.

- **Plan and execution cache**: This cache stores the compiled plans for various queries that have been previously executed by users in the system. This allows various users to share the same plan (saving memory) and also saves on query compilation time for similar queries

- **Large memory grants**: For query operators that consume large amounts of memory, such as hash join and sort.

SQL Server uses an elaborate scheme of memory management to divide its memory among the various uses described above. A single memory manager centrally manages all the memory used by SQL Server. The memory manager is responsible for dynamically partitioning and redistributing the memory between the various consumers of memory in the system. It distributes this memory in accordance with an analysis of the relative cost benefit of memory for any particular use.

The memory manager interacts with the operating system to decide dynamically how much memory it should consume out of the total amount of memory in the system. This allows SQL Server to be quite aggressive in using the memory on the system but still return memory back to the system when other programs need it without causing excessive page faults.

27.7 Data Access

This section describes the data access application programming interfaces (APIs) supported by SQL Server and how these APIs are used for communications among internal server components.

27.7.1 Data Access APIs

SQL Server supports a number of data access application programming interfaces (APIs) for building database applications, including:

- ActiveX Data Objects (ADO)

- OLE-DB

- Open Database Connectivity (ODBC) and the object APIs built over ODBC: Remote Data Objects (RDOs) and Data Access Objects (DAOs)

- Embedded SQL for C (ESQL)

- The legacy DB-Library for C API that was developed specifically to be used with earlier versions of SQL Server that predate the SQL-92 standard.

- HTTP and URLs

Internet applications can use URLs that specify internet information server (IIS) virtual roots that reference an instance of SQL Server. The URL can contain an XPath query, a Transact-SQL statement, or an XML template. In addition to using URLs, Internet applications can also use ADO or OLE-DB to work with data in the form of XML documents.

Application developers use APIs such as ADO and ODBC to access the capabilities of SQL Server from the middle tier. Some APIs such as OLE-DB are used internally to integrate core server components and enable replication and distributed access for SQL and other external sources.

27.7.2 Communication inside SQL Server

The database server of SQL Server has two main parts: the relational engine (RE) and the storage engine (SE) as shown in Figure 27.7. The architecture of SQL Server clearly separates the relational and storage engine components within the server, and these components use OLE-DB interfaces to communicate with each other.

The processing for a **select** statement that references only tables in local databases can be described as follows. The relational engine compiles the **select** statement into an optimized execution plan. The execution plan defines a series of operations against simple row sets from the individual tables or indices referenced in the **select** statement. The row sets requested by the relational engine return the amount of data needed from a table or index to perform the operations needed to build the **select** result set. For example, the following query computes the result from two indices:

select CompanyName, OrderID, ShippedDate
from Customers **as** Cst **join** Orders **as** Ord
on (Cst.CustomerID = Ord.CustomerID)

The relational engine requests two row sets, one for the clustered index on customers and the other on a nonclustered index on orders. The relational engine then uses the OLE-DB interfaces to request that the storage engine open row sets on these

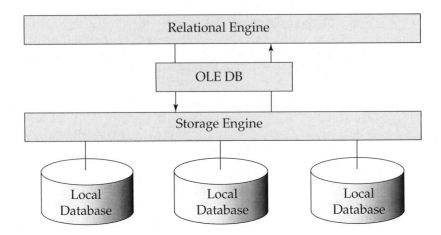

Figure 27.7   OLE-DB as an internal database management system interface.

indices. As the relational engine works through the steps of the execution plan and needs data, it uses OLE-DB to fetch the individual rows from the row sets. The storage engine transfers the data from its data buffers to the execution operators of the query, which is executing in the relational engine. The relational engine combines the data from the storage engine row sets into the final result set transmitted to the user.

This communication between the relational engine and the storage engine via OLE-DB interfaces enables the relational engine to process queries against any data source that exposes such interfaces. Such data sources can be other SQL Server systems (distributed queries) and other relational or nonrelational OLE-DB data providers (heterogeneous queries).

27.8   Distribution and Replication

This section describes SQL Server's capabilities for distributed and heterogeneous query processing as well as replication.

27.8.1   Distributed Heterogeneous Query Processing

SQL Server distributed heterogeneous query capability allows transactional queries and updates against a variety of relational and nonrelational sources via OLE-DB data providers running in one or more computers. SQL Server supports two methods for referencing heterogeneous OLE-DB data sources in Transact-SQL statements. The linked-server-names method uses system-stored procedures to associate a server name with an OLE-DB data source. Objects in these linked servers can be referenced in Transact-SQL statements using the four-part name convention described below. For example, if a linked server name of *DeptSQLSrvr* is defined against another copy of SQL Server, the following statement references a table on that server:

```
select *
from DeptSQLSrvr.Northwind.dbo.Employees
```

An OLE-DB data source is registered in SQL Server as a linked server. Once a linked server is defined, its data can be accessed using the four-part name <linked-server>.<catalog>.<schema>.<object>. The following example establishes a linked server to an Oracle server via an OLE-DB provider for Oracle:

exec sp_addlinkedserver OraSvr, 'Oracle 7.3', 'MSDAORA', 'OracleServer'

A query against this linked server is expressed as:

> **select** *
> **from** OraSvr.CORP.ADMIN.SALES

In addition, SQL Server supports built-in, parameterized table-valued functions called **openrowset** and **openquery**, which allow sending uninterpreted queries to a provider or linked server, respectively, in the dialect supported by the provider. The following query combines information stored in an Oracle server and a Microsoft Index Server. It lists all documents and their author containing the words Data and Access ordered by the author's department and name.

> **select** e.dept, f.DocAuthor, f.FileName
> **from** OraSvr.Corp.Admin.Employee e,
> **openquery**(EmpFiles,
>   '**select** DocAuthor, FileName
>   **from** scope("c:\EmpDocs")
>   **where** contains(' "Data" near() "Access" ')>0') **as** f
> **where** e.name = f.DocAutor
> **order by** e.dept, f.DocAuthor

The linked server name can also be specified in an **openquery** statement to open a row set from the OLE-DB data source. This row set can then be referenced like a table in Transact-SQL statements. The ad-hoc-connector-names method is used for infrequent references to a data source. This method uses a table-valued function called **openrowset**, where the information needed to connect to the data sources is provided as arguments to the function. The row set can then be referenced as a table is referenced in SQL statements. For example, the following query accesses scans the *employees* table stored in the *Northwind* database in a Microsoft Access data provider. Note that unlike the linked-server-name approach described earlier which encapsulates all information needed to connect to a data source, the ad-hoc-connector approach requires a user to specify the name of the data provider (Microsoft.Jet.OLE-DB.4.0), the complete path name of the data file, the user identifier, the password (empty in the example below), and the name of the table being accessed.

> **select** *
> **from openrowset**('Microsoft.Jet.OLE DB.4.0',
>   'c:\Samples\Northwind.mdb';'Admin';' '; Employees)

The relational engine uses the OLE-DB interfaces to open the row sets on linked servers, to fetch the rows, and to manage transactions. For each OLE-DB data source accessed as a linked server, an OLE-DB provider must be present on the server running SQL Server. The set of Transact-SQL operations that can be used against a specific OLE-DB data source depends on the capabilities of the OLE-DB provider. Whenever it is cost-effective, SQL Server pushes relational operations such as joins, restrictions, projections, sorts, and group by operations to the OLE-DB data source.

SQL Server uses Microsoft Distributed Transaction Coordinator and the OLE-DB transaction interfaces of the provider to ensure atomicity of transactions spanning multiple data sources.

Here is a typical scenario for using distributed queries: Consider a large insurance company that has subsidiaries in several countries. Each regional office selects the product that stores its sales data. The United Kingdom subsidiary stores its data in Oracle, the Australian subsidiary stores its data in Microsoft Access, the Spanish subsidiary stores data in Microsoft Excel, and the United States subsidiary stores its data in SQL Server. A worldwide sales executive wants a report that lists, on a quarterly basis for the last 3 years, the insurance policies, the subsidiaries, and the sales representatives with the highest quarterly sales figures. Each of these three queries can be accomplished by a single distributed query, running on SQL Server.

27.8.2   Replication

SQL Server replication provides a set of technologies for copying and distributing data and database objects from one database to another and then maintaining synchronization between databases.

Replication can roll up corporate data from geographically dispersed sites for reporting purposes and disseminate data to remote users on a local area network or mobile users on dial-up connections or the Internet. Microsoft SQL Server replication also enhances application performance by scaling out for improved total read performance among replicas, as is common in providing midtier data caching services for Web sites while maintaining transactional consistency within the replicated data set.

27.8.2.1   Replication Model

SQL Server introduced the *Publish–Subscribe* metaphor to database replication and extends this publishing industry metaphor throughout its replication administration and monitoring tools.

- The publisher is a server that makes data available for replication to other servers. The publisher can have one or more publications, each representing a logically related set of data and database objects. The discrete objects within a publication, including tables, stored procedures, user-defined functions, views, materialized views, and more, are called articles. The addition of an article to a publication allows for extensive customizing of the way the object is replicated, including the name and owner of destination objects, restrictions on which users can subscribe to receive its data, and how the data set should be filtered. For example, a table can have its entire data set or a horizontally partitioned subset of its data made available for distribution via its definition as an article. All forms of SQL Server replication support both horizontal and vertical partitioning from a published table.

- Subscribers are servers that receive replicated data from a publisher. Subscribers can conveniently subscribe to only the publications they require from one or more publishers regardless of the number or type of replication options each implements. Depending on the type of replication options selected, the subscriber either can be used as a read-only replica or can make data changes that are automatically propagated back to the publisher and subsequently to all other replicas. SQL Server replication supports true push and pull subscriptions; that is, the scheduling or initiation of the synchronization actions can be controlled either by the publisher or by its subscribers as business needs require. Subscribers can also republish the data they subscribe to, supporting as flexible a replication topology as the enterprise requires.

- The distributor is a server that hosts the distribution database and stores some replication metadata. The role of the distributor varies, depending on the replication options selected.

27.8.2.2   Replication Options

Microsoft SQL Server replication offers a wide spectrum of technology choices. To decide on the appropriate replication options to use, a database designer must determine the application's needs with respect to autonomous operation of the site involved and the degree of transactional consistency required.

- Snapshot replication copies and distributes data and database objects exactly as they appear at a moment in time. Snapshot replication does not require continuous change tracking because changes are not propagated incrementally to subscribers. Subscribers are updated with a complete refresh of the data set defined by the publication on a periodic basis. Options available with snapshot replication can filter published data and can enable subscribers to modify replicated data and propagate those changes back to the publisher.

- With transactional replication, the publisher propagates an initial snapshot of data to subscribers, then forwards incremental data modifications to subscribers as discrete transactions and commands. Incremental change tracking occurs inside the core engine of SQL Server, which marks transactions affecting replicated objects in the publishing database log. A replication agent reads these transactions from the database log, applies any partitioning logic, and stores them in the distribution database, which acts as the reliable queue supporting the store-and-forward mechanism of transactional replication. (Reliable queues are the same as durable queues, described in Section 24.1.1.) Another replication process, the distribution agent running at either the distributor (push) or subscriber (pull), then forwards the changes to each subscriber. Like snapshot replication, transactional replication offers subscribers the option to make immediate updates that use two-phase commit to reflect those changes consistently at the publisher and subscriber.

- Merge replication allows each replica in the enterprise to work with total autonomy whether online or offline. The system tracks metadata on the changes to published objects at publishers and subscribers in each replicated database, and the replication agent merges those data modifications together during synchronization between replicated pairs and ensures data convergence through automatic conflict detection and resolution. Numerous conflict resolution policy options are built into the replication agent used in the synchronization process, and custom conflict resolution can be written by using stored procedures or by using an extensible **component object model (COM)** interface.

27.9 Full-Text Queries on Relational Data

The full-text capability in Microsoft SQL Server supports the creation and maintenance of full-text indices on character string and image columns stored inside SQL Server tables, as well as full-text searches based on these indices. The full-text capability is implemented by the Microsoft Search service, developed independently of SQL Server, to enable full-text searches over file system data. The first step toward the integration of the search service with SQL Server was to transform the search service into an OLE-DB provider. This step allowed applications to be written in languages such as Visual Basic and C++ against data stored in the file system by using ADO, and also provided the ability to plug in the full-text provider into SQL Server as a heterogeneous data source. The second step involved a loosely coupled integration between SQL Server and the search service to enable full-text indexing of table content. This integration is loosely coupled in the sense that full-text indices are stored in the file system outside the database. Figure 27.8 illustrates the general architecture of this integration.

There are two aspects to full-text support: (1) index creation and maintenance and (2) query support. Indexing support involves creation, update, and administration of full-text catalogs and indices defined for a table or tables in a database. Query support involves processing of fulltext search queries. Given a full-text predicate, the search service determines which entries in the index meet the full-text selection criteria. For each entry that meets the selection criteria, the query component of the search service returns a row, in an OLE-DB row set, containing the identity of the row whose columns match the search criteria, and a ranking value. This row set is used as input to the query being processed by the SQL relational engine, just like any other row set originating from tables or indices inside the server. The relational engine joins this row set with the base table on the row identity and evaluates the execution plan that yields the final result set. The types of full-text queries this schema supports include searching for words or phrases, words in close proximity to each other, and inflectional forms of verbs and nouns.

The full-text catalogs and indices are not stored in an SQL Server database. They are stored in separate files managed by the Microsoft Search service. The full-text cat-

ject Model (COM) scripts. Each transformed source row is pushed into the OLE-DB destination data source.

27.10.2   Online Analytical Processing Services

SQL Server's OLAP services organize data from a data warehouse into multidimensional cubes with precomputed summary information to provide efficient answers to complex analytical queries. The primary OLAP object is the cube, a multidimensional representation of detail and summary data. A cube consists of a data source, dimensions, measures, and partitions. A data warehouse can support many different cubes. Multidimensional queries against cubes return dataset objects.

OLAP services provide server and client capabilities to create and manage multidimensional OLAP data (Figure 27.10). Server operations include creating multidimensional data cubes from relational data warehouse databases and storing cubes in multidimensional cube structures, in relational databases, and in combinations of both. Metadata for multidimensional cube structures is stored in a repository in a relational database. Client operations are provided by the PivotTable service, which is an OLE-DB provider that supports the OLE-DB for OLAP interface extensions. The PivotTable service is an in-process desktop OLAP server designed to provide online and offline data analysis and online access to OLAP data. PivotTable Service functions as a client of OLAP Services.

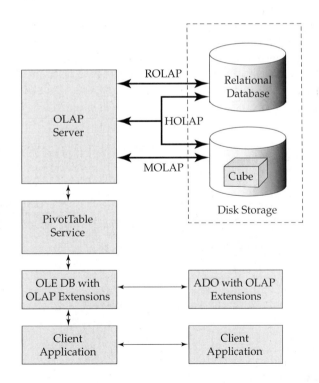

Figure 27.10   Integration of an OLAP server and a relational DBMS.

27.11 XML and Web Support

Many applications are built today as loosely-coupled, distributed systems where individual components (often called services) are combined together. Since many of these components will be reused for other applications, the architecture needs to be flexible enough to allow individual components to join or leave the heterogeneous conglomerate of services and components and to change their internal design and data models without jeopardizing the whole architecture.

SQL Server's XML and Web support simplifies the building of database-based components, and services that use XML for the integration layer. This layer hides the heterogeneity among the components and provides the glue that allows the individual components to take part in the loosely integrated system.

SQL Server provides mechanisms to produce XML from relational data and for consuming XML and mapping it to relational data. Together with the HTTP access component in the client access tools, this ability enables SQL Server to be used for both the data provider and consumer components of Web sites and services.

27.11.1 Architecture of the XML Access to SQL Server

Figure 27.11 shows a high-level architectural block diagram of SQL Server's XML support. Since different applications run their business logic in possibly different locations, the architecture provides for direct HTTP access when only visualization using XSLT needs to be performed on the midtier, and the rest of the business logic processing can be completely pushed either to the client or to the database server. For two-tier architectures or where the business logic needs to be performed on the middletier, a closer coupling of the business logic to the database access is often used for performance and programmability reasons. Thus, all access to the XML features

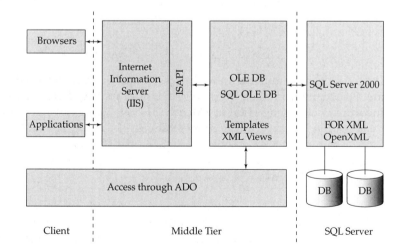

Figure 27.11   Architectural overview of the XML Access to SQL Server.

is through the SQL OLE-DB provider; this applies to both ADO access as well as HTTP access via the ISAPI extension to the Internet Information Server (IIS).

Several ways exist to access SQL Server via HTTP. The SQL Server ISAPI is registered with IIS to handle messages to a particular virtual root (vroot). The ISAPI receives the requests for that particular vroot, and, after performing authorization, passes the appropriate commands via the SQL OLE-DB provider to the database. The virtual root, as part of the URL, provides an abstraction mechanism that encapsulates the accessed database server and database instances, the access rights, and the enabled access methods. The major access methods provided by SQL Server are the template access and the XML view access.

Templates are XML documents that provide a parameterized query and update mechanism to the database. Since they hide the actual query (or update) from the user, they provide the level of decoupling that makes building loosely coupled systems possible. Elements containing queries are processed by the template processor and used to return database data as part of the resulting XML document. Elements not recognized by the template processor are returned unmodified. Templates can contain either Transact-SQL statements, updategrams (see Section 27.11.3), XPath queries, or a combination thereof.

XML views are defined by annotating an XML schema document with the mapping to the relational tables and columns. Hierarchies are mapped from and to the database using a relationship annotation that expresses the outer join between the parent and the children. This view can then be used to both query the database in the XPath 1.0 XML navigation language and to update it by using updategrams.

These XML features (as well as the server-side XML queries) are also accessible through SQL OLE-DB. Since XML data, unlike relational data, is not represented as a row set but as a marked-up stream of data, SQL Server's OLE-DB provider has been extended with a stream interface to expose XML results.

On the server side, SQL Server provides extensions to the **select** statement that simplify the transformation of relational data into XML and a mechanism to slice row sets out of XML documents and thus provides a relational view over XML data.

27.11.2 Serializing SQL Query Results into XML

People who are familiar with writing SQL select queries may need to be able to generate XML easily from their query result. Unfortunately, there are many different ways in which such a generation of XML can be done. SQL Server therefore provides three different modes for this with different levels of complexity and XML authoring capability. All three modes are provided via a new **select** clause called called FOR XML. The three modes are: *raw, auto,* and *explicit*. The following statement gives an example of an *auto* mode query:

> **select** Customers.CustomerID, OrderID
> **from** Customers **left outer join** Orders
>   **on** Customers.CustomerID = Orders.CustomerID
> **ordered by** Customers.CustomerID
> **for XML auto**

All three modes map rows to elements and column values to attributes. The optional directive *elements* in the *auto* mode changes the mapping of all column values to subelements. The *raw* and *auto* modes allow the simple generation of XML from existing relational queries. The *explicit* mode provides full column-specific control over the generated XML by taking a special form of a relational result set (called a universal table format) and transforming it into XML. All three modes stream data and thus avoid costly XML document build-ups on the server.

27.11.3   Providing XML Views over Relational Data

The previous section presented the SQL-centric approach to generating XML. SQL Server also provides a mechanism that allows defining virtual XML views over the relational database, which then can be queried and updated with XML-based tools.

The core mechanism of providing XML views over the relational data is the concept of an annotated schema. Annotated schemas consist of an XML-based schema description of the exposed XML view (in either the XML-Data Reduced or the W3C XML schema language) and annotations that describe the mapping of the XML schema constructs onto the relational schema constructs. To simplify the definition of the annotations, each schema provides a default mapping if no annotation is present. The default mapping maps an attribute or a noncomplex subelement (one whose content type is text only) to a relational column with the same name. All other elements map into rows of a table or view with the same name. Hierarchies are expressed with annotations. A downloadable visual tool called the SQL XML View Mapper provides a way to specify the mapping, and thus the annotations, graphically.

The annotated schema does not itself retrieve any data, but only defines a virtual view by projecting an XML view on the relational tables. The view can now be queried in an XML query language and updated in an XML-based update language. Updates are supported by so-called XML updategrams. Updategrams provide an intuitive way to perform an instance-based transformation from a before state to an after state by using optimistic concurrency control.

27.11.4   Providing Relational Views over XML

In many cases, data will be sent to the database server in the form of an XML message that needs to be integrated with the relational data after some optional business logic is performed on the data inside a stored procedure on the server. This requires programmatic access to the XML data from within a stored procedure. Unfortunately, neither DOM nor SAX (see Chapter 10) provides a well-suited API for dealing with XML data in a relational context. Instead, the new API needs to provide a relational view over the XML data; that is, it needs to allow the SQL programmer to shred an XML message into different relational views.

SQL Server provides a row set mechanism over XML by means of the OpenXML row set provider. The row set view utilizes an XPath expression (the row pattern) to identify the nodes in the XML document tree that will map to rows and uses a relative XPath expression (the column pattern) for identifying the nodes that provide the values for each column. The OpenXML row set provider can appear anywhere in an SQL expression where a row set can appear as a data source. In particular, it can appear in the **from** clause of any selection.

One of the advantages of this row set-oriented API for XML data is that it leverages the existing relational model for use with XML and provides a mechanism for updating database with data in XML format. Using XML in conjunction with OpenXML enables multirow updates with a single stored procedure call and multitable updates by exploiting the XML hierarchy. In addition, it allows the formulation of queries that join existing tables with the provided XML data.

27.12 Summary

Microsoft SQL Server is a complete data management package including relational database server, full text indexing and search, XML data import and export, distributed and heterogeneous data integration, analysis server and client for OLAP and data mining, replication among heterogeneous data stores, a programmable data transformation engine, and more. Thus, SQL Server serves as a foundation of Microsoft's suite of enterprise server products.

During the time that Microsoft has had full control over the code base (after acquiring it from Sybase), it has updated the code base and integrated the latest practical research in the product. SQL Server 2000 (shipped in August 2000) rounded out some of the feature groups started in earlier releases and added entirely new functionality, including XML support.

The release currently being implemented is designed to augument the product's ease of use, ease of applicaton development, robustness, performance, and scalability features.

Bibliographical Notes

The differences among the various editions of the SQL Server are desribed in Delaney [2000] and are also available on the Web at www.microsoft.com/sql.

Detailed information about using a C2 certified system with SQL Server is available at www.microsoft.com/Downloads/Release.asp?ReleaseID=25503.

SQL Server's optimization framework is based on the Cascades optimizer prototype, which Graefe [1995] proposed. Simmen et al. [1996] discusses the scheme for reducing grouping columns. Galindo-Legaria and Joshi [2001] presents the variety of execution strategies that SQL Server considers during cost-based optimization. Additional information on the self-tuning aspects of SQL server are discussed by Chaudhuri et al. [1999]. Chaudhuri and Shim [1994] and Yan and Larson [1995] discuss partial aggregation.

Chatziantoniou and Ross [1997] and Galindo-Legaria and Joshi [2001] proposed the alternative used by SQL Server for SQL queries requiring a self-join. Under this scheme, the optimizer detects the pattern and considers per-segment execution. Pellenkoft et al. [1997] discusses the optimization scheme for generating the complete space, where the optimizer uses complete, local, nonredundant transformations.

Graefe et al. [1998] offers discussion concerning hash operations that support basic aggregation and join, with a number of optimizations, extensions, and dynamic tuning for data skew. Graefe et al. [1998] present the idea of joining indices for the sole purpose of assembling a row with the set of columns needed on a query. It argues that this sometimes is faster than scanning a base table. Blakeley [1996] and Blakeley and Pizzo [2001] offer discussions concerning communication with the storage engine through OLE-DB.

Figure 27.11, which shows a high-level architectural block diagram of SQL Server's XML support is from Rys [2001].

Bibliography

[**Abbott and Garcia-Molina 1999**] R. Abbott and H. Garcia-Molina, "Scheduling Real-Time Transactions: A Performance Evaluation," *ACM Transactions on Database Systems*, Volume 17, Number 3 (1999), pages 513–560.

[**Abiteboul et al. 1995**] S. Abiteboul, R. Hull, and V. Vianu, *Foundations of Databases*, Addison Wesley (1995).

[**Acharya et al. 1995**] S. Acharya, R. Alonso, M. Franklin, and S. Zdonik, "Broadcast Disks: Data Management for Asymmetric Communication Environments," *Proc. of the ACM SIGMOD Conf. on Management of Data* (1995), pages 19 – 210. Also appears in Imielinski and Korth [1996], Chapter 12.

[**Adali et al. 1996**] S. Adali, K. S. Candan, Y. Papakonstantinou, and V. S. Subrahmanian, "Query Caching and Optimization in Distributed Mediator Systems," *Proc. of the ACM SIGMOD Conf. on Management of Data* (1996), pages 137–148.

[**Agarwal et al. 1996**] S. Agarwal, R. Agrawal, P. M. Deshpande, A. Gupta, J. F. Naughton, R. Ramakrishnan, and S. Sarawagi, "On the computation of multidimensional attributes," *Proc. of the International Conf. on Very Large Databases*, Bombay, India (1996), pages 506–521.

[**Agrawal and Gehani 1989**] R. Agrawal and N. Gehani, "ODE (Object Database and Environment): The Language and the Data Model," *Proc. of the ACM SIGMOD Conf. on Management of Data* (1989), pages 36–45.

[**Agrawal and Srikant 1994**] R. Agrawal and R. Srikant, "Fast Algorithms for Mining Association Rules in Large Databases," *Proc. of the International Conf. on Very Large Databases* (1994), pages 487–499.

[**Agrawal et al. 1992**] R. Agrawal, S. P. Ghosh, T. Imielinski, B. R. Iyer, and A. N. Swami, "An Interval Classifier for Database Mining Applications," *Proc. of the International Conf. on Very Large Databases* (1992), pages 560–573.

[**Agrawal et al. 1993**] R. Agrawal, T. Imielinski, and A. N. Swami, "Database Mining: A Performance Perspective," *IEEE Transactions on Knowledge and Data Engineering*, Volume 5, Number 6 (1993), pages 914–925.

[**Agrawal et al. 2000**] S. Agrawal, S. Chaudhuri, and V. R. Narasayya, "Automated Selection of Materialized Views and Indexes in SQL Databases," *Proc. of the International Conf. on Very Large Databases* (2000), pages 496–505.

[**Aho et al. 1979a**] A. V. Aho, C. Beeri, and J. D. Ullman, "The Theory of Joins in Relational Databases," *ACM Transactions on Database Systems,* Volume 4, Number 3 (1979), pages 297–314.

[**Aho et al. 1979b**] V. Aho, Y. Sagiv, and J. D. Ullman, "Equivalences among Relational Expressions," *SIAM Journal of Computing,* Volume 8, Number 2 (1979), pages 218–246.

[**Aho et al. 1986**] A. V. Aho, R. Sethi, and J. D. Ullman, *Compilers: Principles, Techniques, and Tools,* Addison Wesley (1986).

[**Aiken et al. 1995**] A. Aiken, J. Hellerstein, and J. Widom, "Static Analysis Techniques for Predicting the Behavior of Active Database Rules," *ACM Transactions on Database Systems,* Volume 20, Number 1 (1995), pages 3–41.

[**Akl 1983**] S. Akl, "Digital Signatures, A Tutorial Survey," *IEEE Computer,* Volume 16, Number 2 (1983), pages 15–24.

[**Alonso and Korth 1993**] R. Alonso and H. F. Korth, "Database System Issues in Nomadic Computing," *Proc. of the ACM SIGMOD Conf. on Management of Data* (1993), pages 388–392.

[**Anderson et al. 1992**] D. P. Anderson, Y. Osawa, and R. Govindan, "A File System for Continuous Media," *ACM Transactions on Database Systems,* Volume 10, Number 4 (1992), pages 311–337.

[**Anderson et al. 1998**] T. Anderson, Y. Breitbart, H. F. Korth, and A. Wool, "Replication, Consistency and Practicality: Are These Mutually Exclusive?," *Proc. of the ACM SIGMOD Conf. on Management of Data,* Seattle, WA (1998).

[**ANSI 1986**] *American National Standard for Information Systems: Database Language SQL.* American National Standards Institute. FDT, ANSI X3,135–1986 (1986).

[**ANSI 1989**] *Database Language SQL With Integrity Enhancement, ANSI X3, 135–1989.* American National Standards Institute, New York. Also available as ISO/IEC Document 9075:1989 (1989).

[**ANSI 1992**] *Database Language SQL, ANSI X3,135–1992.* American National Standards Institute, New York. Also available as ISO/IEC Document 9075:1992 (1992).

[**Antoshenkov 1995**] G. Antoshenkov, "Byte-aligned Bitmap Compression (poster abstract)," In *IEEE Data Compression Conf.* (1995).

[**Apers et al. 1983**] P. M. G. Apers, A. R. Hevner, and S. B. Yao, "Optimization Algorithms for Distributed Queries," *IEEE Transactions on Software Engineering,* Volume SE-9, Number 1 (1983), pages 57–68.

[**Apt and Pugin 1987**] K. R. Apt and J. M. Pugin, "Maintenance of Stratified Database Viewed as a Belief Revision System," *Proc. of the ACM Symposium on Principles of Database Systems* (1987), pages 136–145.

[**Aref et al. 1995a**] W. Aref, D. Barbará, D. Lopresti, and A. Tomkins, *Ink as a First-Class Multimedia Object,* Jajodia and Subramanian (1995).

[**Aref et al. 1995b**] W. Aref, D. Barbará, and P. Vallabhaneni, "The Handwritten Trie: Indexing Electronic Ink", *Proc. of the ACM SIGMOD Conf. on Management of Data* (1995), pages 151–162.

[**Armstrong 1974**] W. W. Armstrong, "Dependency Structures of Data Base Relationships," In *Proc. of the 1974 IFIP Congress* (1974), pages 580–583.

[**Astrahan et al. 1976**] M. M. Astrahan, M. W. Blasgen, D. D. Chamberlin, K. P. Eswaran, J. N. G. amd P. P. Griffiths, W. F. King, R. A. Lorie, P. R. McJones, J. W. Mehl, G. R. Putzolu, I. L. Traiger, B. W. Wade, and V. Watson, "System R, A Relational Approach to Data Base Management", *ACM Transactions on Database Systems,* Volume 1, Number 2 (1976), pages 97–137.

[**Astrahan et al. 1979**] M. M. Astrahan, M. W. Blasgen, D. D. Chamberlin, J. N. Gray, W. F. King, B. G. Lindsay, R. A. Lorie, J. W. Mehl, T. G. Price, G. R. Putzolu, M. Schkolnick, P. G. Selinger, D. R. Slutz, H. R. Strong, P. Tiberio, I. L. Traiger, B. W. Wade, and R. A. Yost, "System R: A Relational Database Management System," *IEEE Computer,* Volume 12, Number 5 (1979), pages 43–48.

[**Attar et al. 1984**] R. Attar, P. A. Bernstein, and N. Goodman, "Site Initialization, Recovery and Backup in a Distributed Database System," *IEEE Transactions on Software Engineering*, Volume SE-10, Number 6 (1984), pages 645–650.

[**Atzeni and Antonellis 1993**] P. Atzeni and V. D. Antonellis, *Relational Database Theory*, Benjamin Cummings, Menlo Park (1993).

[**Badal and Popek 1979**] D. S. Badal and G. Popek, "Cost and Performance Analysis of Semantic Integrity Validation Methods," *Proc. of the ACM SIGMOD Conf. on Management of Data* (1979), pages 109–115.

[**Badrinath and Ramamritham 1992**] B. R. Badrinath and K. Ramamritham, "Semantics-Based Concurrency Control: Beyond Commutativity," *ACM Transactions on Database Systems*, Volume 17, Number 1 (1992), pages 163–199.

[**Baeza-Yates and Ribeiro-Neto 1999**] R. Baeza-Yates and B. Ribeiro-Neto, *Modern Information Retrieval*, Addison Wesley (1999).

[**Bamford et al. 1998**] R. Bamford, D. Butler, B. Klots, and N. MacNaughton, "Architecture of Oracle Parallel Server," *Proc. of the International Conf. on Very Large Databases* (1998), pages 669–670.

[**Bancilhon and Buneman 1990**] F. Bancilhon and P. Buneman, *Advances in Database Programming Languages*, ACM Press, New York (1990).

[**Bancilhon and Ramakrishnan 1986**] F. Bancilhon and R. Ramakrishnan, "An Amateur's Introduction to Recursive Query-Processing Strategies," *Proc. of the ACM SIGMOD Conf. on Management of Data* (1986), pages 16–52.

[**Bancilhon and Spyratos 1981**] F. Bancilhon and N. Spyratos, "Update Semantics and Relational Views," *ACM Transactions on Database Systems*, Volume 6, Number 4 (1981), pages 557–575.

[**Bancilhon et al. 1989**] F. Bancilhon, S. Cluet, and C. Delobel, "A Query Language for the O_2 Object-Oriented Database," *Proc. of the Second Workshop on Database Programming Languages* (1989).

[**Banerjee et al. 1987**] J. Banerjee, W. Kim, H. J. Kim, and H. F. Korth, "Semantics and Implementation of Schema Evolution in Object-Oriented Databases," *Proc. of the ACM SIGMOD Conf. on Management of Data* (1987), pages 311–322.

[**Banerjee et al. 2000**] S. Banerjee, V. Krishnamurthy, M. Krishnaprasad, and R. Murthy, "Oracle8i—The XML Enabled Data Management System," *Proc. of the International Conf on Data Engineering* (2000), pages 561–568.

[**Barbará and Imielinski 1994**] D. Barbará and T. Imielinski, "Sleepers and Workaholics: Caching Strategies in Mobile Environments," *Proc. of the ACM SIGMOD Conf. on Management of Data* (1994), pages 1–12.

[**Barbará et al. 1992**] D. Barbará, H. Garcia-Molina, and D. Porter, "The Management of Probabilistic Data", *IEEE Transactions on Knowledge and Data Engineering*, Volume 4, Number 5 (1992), pages 487–502.

[**Barclay et al. 1982**] D. K. Barclay, E. R. Byrne, and F. K. Ng, "A Real-Time Database Management System for No.5 ESS," *Bell System Technical Journal*, Volume 61, Number 9 (1982), pages 2423–2437.

[**Baru et al. 1995**] C. Baru et al., "DB2 Parallel Edition," *IBM Systems Journal*, Volume 34, Number 2 (1995), pages 292–322.

[**Baru et al. 1999**] C. K. Baru, A. Gupta, B. Ludäscher, R. Marciano, Y. Papakonstantinou, P. Velikhov, and V. Chu, "XML-Based Information Mediation with MIX," *Proc. of the ACM SIGMOD Conf. on Management of Data* (1999), pages 597–599.

[**Bassiouni 1988**] M. Bassiouni, "Single-site and Distributed Optimistic Protocols for Concurrency Control," *IEEE Transactions on Software Engineering*, Volume SE-14, Number 8 (1988), pages 1071–1080.

[Batini et al. 1992] C. Batini, S. Ceri, and S. Navathe, *Database Design: An Entity-Relationship Approach*, Benjamin Cummings, Redwood City (1992).

[Bayer 1972] R. Bayer, "Symmetric Binary B-trees: Data Structure and Maintenance Algorithms," *Acta Informatica*, Volume 1, Number 4 (1972), pages 290–306.

[Bayer and McCreight 1972] R. Bayer and E. M. McCreight, "Organization and Maintenance of Large Ordered Indices," *Acta Informatica*, Volume 1, Number 3 (1972), pages 173–189.

[Bayer and Schkolnick 1977] R. Bayer and M. Schkolnick, "Concurrency of Operating on B-trees," *Acta Informatica*, Volume 9, Number 1 (1977), pages 1–21.

[Bayer and Unterauer 1977] R. Bayer and K. Unterauer, "Prefix B-trees," *ACM Transactions on Database Systems*, Volume 2, Number 1 (1977), pages 11–26.

[Bayer et al. 1978] R. Bayer, R. M. Graham, and G. Seegmuller, editors, *Operating Systems: An Advanced Course*, Springer Verlag (1978).

[Bayer et al. 1980] R. Bayer, H. Heller, and A. Reiser, "Parallelism and Recovery in Database Systems," *ACM Transactions on Database Systems*, Volume 5, Number 2 (1980), pages 139–156.

[Beckmann et al. 1990] N. Beckmann, H. P. Kriegel, R. Schneider, and B. Seeger, "The R*-tree: An Efficient and Robust Access Method for Points and Rectangles," *Proc. of the ACM SIGMOD Conf. on Management of Data* (1990), pages 322–331.

[Beech 1988] D. Beech, "OSQL: A Language for Migrating from SQL to Object Databases," *Proc. of the International Conf on Extending Database Technology* (1988).

[Beeri and Ramakrishnan 1991] C. Beeri and R. Ramakrishnan, "On the Power of Magic," *Journal of Logic Programming*, Volume 10, Number 3 and 4 (1991), pages 255–300.

[Beeri et al. 1977] C. Beeri, R. Fagin, and J. H. Howard, "A Complete Axiomatization for Functional and Multivalued Dependencies," *Proc. of the ACM SIGMOD Conf. on Management of Data* (1977), pages 47–61.

[Beeri et al. 1989] C. Beeri, P. A. Bernstein, and N. Goodman, "A Model for Concurrency in Nested Transactions Systems," *Journal of the ACM*, Volume 36, Number 2 (1989).

[Bell and Grimson 1992] D. Bell and J. Grimson, *Distributed Database Systems*, Addison Wesley (1992).

[Bell and LaPadula 1976] D. E. Bell and L. J. LaPadula, *Secure Computer Systems: Unified Exposition and Multics Interpretation*, Mitre Corporation, Bedford (1976).

[Bello et al. 1998] R. G. Bello, K. Dias, A. Downing, J. Feenan, J. Finnerty, W. D. Norcott, H. Sun, A. Witkowski, and M. Ziauddin, "Materialized Views in Oracle," *Proc. of the International Conf. on Very Large Databases* (1998), pages 659–664.

[Benneworth et al. 1981] R. L. Benneworth, C. D. Bishop, C. J. M. Turnbull, W. D. Holman, and F. M. Monette, "The Implementation of GERM, an Entity-Relationship Data Base Management System," *Proc. of the International Conf. on Very Large Databases* (1981), pages 478–484.

[Bentley 1975] J. L. Bentley, "Multidimensional Binary Search Trees Used for Associative Searching," *Communications of the ACM*, Volume 18, Number 9 (1975), pages 509–517.

[Berenson et al. 1995] H. Berenson, P. Bernstein, J. Gray, J. Melton, E. O'Neil, and P. O'Neil, "A Critique of ANSI SQL Isolation Levels," *Proc. of the ACM SIGMOD Conf. on Management of Data* (1995), pages 1–10.

[Bernstein and Chiu 1981] P. A. Bernstein and D. W. Chiu, "Using Semijoins to Solve Relational Queries," *Journal of the ACM*, Volume 28, Number 1 (1981), pages 25–40.

[Bernstein and Goodman 1980] P. A. Bernstein and N. Goodman, "Timestamp-based Algorithms for Concurrency Control in Distributed Database Systems," *Proc. of the International Conf. on Very Large Databases* (1980), pages 285–300.

[**Bernstein and Goodman 1981a**] P. A. Bernstein and N. Goodman, "Concurrency Control in Distributed Database Systems," *ACM Computing Survey*, Volume 13, Number 2 (1981), pages 185–221.

[**Bernstein and Goodman 1981b**] P. A. Bernstein and N. Goodman, "The Power of Natural Semijoins," *SIAM Journal of Computing*, Volume 10, Number 4 (1981), pages 751–771.

[**Bernstein and Goodman 1982**] P. A. Bernstein and N. Goodman, "A Sophisticate's Introduction to Distributed Database Concurrency Control," *Proc. of the International Conf. on Very Large Databases* (1982), pages 62–76.

[**Bernstein and Newcomer 1997**] P. A. Bernstein and E. Newcomer, *Principles of Transaction Processing*, Morgan Kaufmann (1997).

[**Bernstein et al. 1978**] P. A. Bernstein, N. Goodman, J. B. Rothnie, and C. H. Papadimitriou, "Analysis of Serializability of SDD-1: A System of Distributed Databases (the Fully Redundant Case)," *IEEE Transactions on Software Engineering*, Volume SE-4, Number 3 (1978), pages 154–168.

[**Bernstein et al. 1980a**] P. A. Bernstein, B. Blaustein, and E. Clarke, "Fast Maintenance of Semantic Integrity Assertions Using Redundant Aggregate Data," *Proc. of the International Conf. on Very Large Databases* (1980).

[**Bernstein et al. 1980b**] P. A. Bernstein, D. W. Shipman, and J. B. Rothnie, "Concurrency Control in a System for Distributed Databases (SDD-1)," *ACM Transactions on Database Systems*, Volume 5, Number 1 (1980), pages 18–51.

[**Bernstein et al. 1983**] P. A. Bernstein, N. Goodman, and M. Y. Lai, "Analyzing Concurrency Control when User and System Operations Differ," *IEEE Transactions on Software Engineering*, Volume SE-9, Number 3 (1983), pages 233–239.

[**Bernstein et al. 1987**] A. Bernstein, V. Hadzilacos, and N. Goodman, *Concurrency Control and Recovery in Database Systems*, Addison Wesley (1987).

[**Bernstein et al. 1998**] P. Bernstein, M. Brodie, S. Ceri, D. DeWitt, M. Franklin, H. Garcia-Molina, J. Gray, J. Held, J. Hellerstein, H. V. Jagadish, M. Lesk, D. Maier, J. Naughton, H. Pirahesh, M. Stonebraker, and J. Ullman, "The Asilomar Report on Database Research," *ACM SIGMOD Record*, Volume 27, Number 4 (1998).

[**Berson et al. 1995**] S. Berson, L. Golubchik, and R. R. Muntz, "Fault Tolerant Design of Multimedia Servers," *Proc. of the ACM SIGMOD Conf. on Management of Data* (1995), pages 364–375.

[**Bertino and Kim 1989**] E. Bertino and W. Kim, "Indexing Techniques for Queries on Nested Objects," *IEEE Transactions on Knowledge and Data Engineering* (1989).

[**Bharat and Henzinger 1998**] K. Bharat and M. R. Henzinger, "Improved Algorithms for Topic Distillation in a Hyperlinked Environment," *Proc. of the ACM SIGIR Conf. on Research And Development in Information Retrieval* (1998), pages 104–111.

[**Biliris and Orenstein 1994**] A. Biliris and J. Orenstein. "Object Storage Management Architectures," In *Dogac et al. [1994]*, pages 185–200 (1994).

[**Biskup et al. 1979**] J. Biskup, U. Dayal, and P. A. Bernstein, "Synthesizing Independent Database Schemas," *Proc. of the ACM SIGMOD Conf. on Management of Data* (1979), pages 143–152.

[**Bitton and Gray 1988**] D. Bitton and J. N. Gray, "Disk Shadowing," *Proc. of the International Conf. on Very Large Databases* (1988), pages 331–338.

[**Bitton et al. 1983**] D. Bitton, D. J. DeWitt, and C. Turbyfill, "Benchmarking Database Systems: A Systematic Approach," *Proc. of the International Conf. on Very Large Databases* (1983).

[**Bjork 1973**] L. A. Bjork, "Recovery Scenario for a DB/DC System," *Proc. of the ACM Annual Conf.* (1973), pages 142–146.

[Blakeley 1996] J. A. Blakeley, "Data Access for the Masses through OLE DB," *Proc. of the ACM SIGMOD Conf. on Management of Data* (1996), pages 161–172.

[Blakeley and Pizzo 2001] J. A. Blakeley and M. Pizzo, "Enabling Component Databases with OLE DB," In K. R.Dittrich and A. Geppert, editors, *Component Database Systems*, Morgan Kauffmann Publishers (2001), pages 139–173.

[Blakeley et al. 1986] J. A. Blakeley, P. Larson, and F. W. Tompa, "Efficiently Updating Materialized Views," *Proc. of the ACM SIGMOD Conf. on Management of Data* (1986), pages 61–71.

[Blakeley et al. 1989] J. Blakeley, N. Coburn, and P. Larson, "Updating Derived Relations: Detecting Irrelevant and Autonomously Computable Updates," *ACM Transactions on Database Systems*, Volume 14, Number 3 (1989), pages 369–400.

[Blakeley et al. 1993] J. A. Blakeley, W. J. McKenna, and G. Graefe, "Experiences Building the Open OODB Query Optimizer," *Proc. of the ACM SIGMOD Conf. on Management of Data*, Washington, DC. (1993), pages 287–295.

[Blasgen and Eswaran 1976] M. W. Blasgen and K. P. Eswaran, "On the Evaluation of Queries in a Relational Database System," *IBM Systems Journal,* Volume 16, (1976), pages 363–377.

[Boral et al. 1990] H. Boral, W. Alexander, L. Clay, G. Copeland, S. Danforth, M. Franklin, B. Hart, M. Smith, and P. Valduriez, "Prototyping Bubba, a Highly Parallel Database System," *IEEE Transactions on Knowledge and Data Engineering*, Volume 2, Number 1 (1990).

[Boyce et al. 1975] R. Boyce, D. D. Chamberlin, W. F. King, and M. Hammer, "Specifying Queries as Relational Expressions," *Communications of the ACM,* Volume 18, Number 11 (1975), pages 621–628.

[Breese et al. 1998] J. Breese, D. Heckerman, and C. Kadie, "Empirical Analysis of Predictive Algorithms for Collaborative Filtering," *Proc. of the Conf. on Uncertainty in Artificial Intelligence*, Morgan Kaufmann (1998).

[Breitbart et al. 1990] Y. Breitbart, A. Silberschatz, and G. Thompson, "Reliable Transaction Management in a Multidatabase System," *Proc. of the ACM SIGMOD Conf. on Management of Data* (1990).

[Breitbart et al. 1991] Y. Breitbart, D. Georgakopoulos, M. Rusinkiewicz, and A. Silberschatz, "On Rigorous Transaction Scheduling," *IEEE Transactions on Software Engineering*, Volume SE-17, Number 9 (1991), pages 954–961.

[Breitbart et al. 1992] Y. Breitbart, A. Silberschatz, and G. Thompson, "Transaction Management Issues in a Failure-prone Multidatabase System Environment," *VLDB Journal*, Volume 1, Number 1 (1992), pages 1–39.

[Breitbart et al. 1999a] Y. Breitbart, R. Komondoor, R. Rastogi, S. Seshadri, and A. Silberschatz, "Update Propagation Protocols For Replicated Databases," *Proc. of the ACM SIGMOD Conf. on Management of Data* (1999), pages 97–108.

[Breitbart et al. 1999b] Y. Breitbart, H. Korth, A. Silberschatz, and S. Sudarshan. "Distributed Databases," In *Encyclopedia of Electrical and Electronics Engineering*. John Wiley and Sons (1999).

[Bridge et al. 1997] W. Bridge, A. Joshi, M. Keihl, T. Lahiri, J. Loaiza, and N. MacNaughton, "The Oracle Universal Server Buffer," *Proc. of the International Conf. on Very Large Databases* (1997), pages 590–594.

[Brin and Page 1998] S. Brin and L. Page, "The Anatomy of a Large-Scale Hypertextual Web Search Engine," *Proc. of the International World Wide Web Conf.* (1998).

[Brinkhoff et al. 1993] T. Brinkhoff, H.-P. Kriegel, and B. Seeger, "Efficient Processing of Spatial Joins Using R-trees," *Proc. of the ACM SIGMOD Conf. on Management of Data* (1993), pages 237–246.

[Brown et al. 1994] K. P. Brown, M. Mehta, M. Carey, and M. Livny, "Towards Automated Performance Tuning for Complex Overloads,"

Proc. of the International Conf. on Very Large Databases (1994).

[**Buckley and Silberschatz 1983**] G. Buckley and A. Silberschatz, "Obtaining Progressive Protocols for a Simple Multiversion Database Model," *Proc. of the International Conf. on Very Large Databases* (1983), pages 74–81.

[**Buckley and Silberschatz 1984**] G. Buckley and A. Silberschatz, "Concurrency Control in Graph Protocols by Using Edge Locks," *Proc. of the ACM SIGMOD Conf. on Management of Data* (1984), pages 45–50.

[**Buckley and Silberschatz 1985**] G. Buckley and A. Silberschatz, "Beyond Two-Phase Locking," *Journal of the ACM*, Volume 32, Number 2 (1985), pages 314–326.

[**Bulmer 1979**] M. G. Bulmer, *Principles of Statistics*, Dover Publications (1979).

[**Burkhard 1976**] W. A. Burkhard, "Hashing and Trie Algorithms for Partial Match Retrieval," *ACM Transactions on Database Systems*, Volume 1, Number 2 (1976), pages 175–187.

[**Burkhard 1979**] W. A. Burkhard, "Partial-match Hash Coding: Benefits of Redundancy," *ACM Transactions on Database Systems*, Volume 4, Number 2 (1979), pages 228–239.

[**Cannan and Otten 1993**] S. Cannan and G. Otten, *SQL—The Standard Handbook*, McGraw Hill (1993).

[**Carey 1983**] M. J. Carey, "Granularity Hierarchies in Concurrency Control," *Proc. of the ACM SIGMOD Conf. on Management of Data* (1983), pages 156–165.

[**Carey et al. 1986**] M. J. Carey, D. DeWitt, J. Richardson, and E. Shekita, "Object and File Management in the EXODUS Extensible Database System," *Proc. of the International Conf. on Very Large Databases* (1986), pages 91–100.

[**Carey et al. 1990**] M. J. Carey, D. DeWitt, G. Graefe, D. Haight, D. S. J. Richardson, E. Shekita, and S. Vandenberg. "The EXODUS Extensible DBMS Project: An Overview," In *Zdonik and Maier [1990]*, pages 474–499 (1990).

[**Carey et al. 1991**] M. Carey, M. Franklin, M. Livny, and E. Shekita, "Data Caching Tradeoffs in Client-Server DBMS Architectures," *Proc. of the ACM SIGMOD Conf. on Management of Data* (1991).

[**Carey et al. 1993**] M. J. Carey, D. DeWitt, and J. Naughton, "The OO7 Benchmark," *Proc. of the ACM SIGMOD Conf. on Management of Data* (1993).

[**Carey et al. 1999**] M. J. Carey, D. D. Chamberlin, S. Narayanan, B. Vance, D. Doole, S. Rielau, R. Swagerman, and N. Mattos, "O-O, What have they done to DB2?," In *Proc. of the International Conf. on Very Large Databases* (1999), pages 542–553.

[**Carey et al. 2000**] M. J. Carey, J. Kiernan, J. Shanmugasundaram, E. J. Shekita, and S. N. Subramanian, "XPERANTO: Middleware for Publishing Object-Relational Data as XML Documents," *Proc. of the International Conf. on Very Large Databases* (2000), pages 646–648.

[**Cattell 2000**] R. Cattell, editor, *The Object Database Standard: ODMG 3.0*, Morgan Kaufmann (2000).

[**Cattell and Skeen 1992**] R. Cattell and J. Skeen, "Object Operations Benchmark," *ACM Transactions on Database Systems*, Volume 17, Number 1 (1992).

[**Ceri and Owicki 1983**] S. Ceri and S. Owicki, "On the Use of Optimistic Methods for Concurrency Control in Distributed Databases," *Proc. of the Sixth Berkeley Workshop on Distributed Data Management and Computer Networks* (1983).

[**Ceri and Pelagatti 1983**] S. Ceri and G. Pelagatti, "Correctness of Query Execution Strategies in Distributed Databases," *ACM Transactions on Database Systems*, Volume 8, Number 4 (1983), pages 577–607.

[**Ceri and Pelagatti 1984**] S. Ceri and G. Pelagatti, *Distributed Databases: Principles and Systems*, McGraw Hill (1984).

[Chakrabarti 1999] S. Chakrabarti, "Recent results in automatic Web resource discovery," *ACM Computing Surveys*, Volume 31, Number 4es (1999).

[Chakrabarti 2000] S. Chakrabarti, "Data mining for hypertext: A tutorial survey," *SIGKDD Explorations*, Volume 1, Number 2 (2000), pages 1–11.

[Chakrabarti et al. 1998] S. Chakrabarti, S. Sarawagi, and B. Dom, "Mining Surprising Patterns Using Temporal Description Length," *Proc. of the International Conf. on Very Large Databases* (1998), pages 606–617.

[Chakravarthy et al. 1990] U. S. Chakravarthy, J. Grant, and J. Minker, "Logic-Based Approach to Semantic Query Optimization," *ACM Transactions on Database Systems*, Volume 15, Number 2 (1990), pages 162–207.

[Chamberlin 1996] D. Chamberlin, *Using the new DB2: IBM's object-relational database system*, Morgan Kaufmann (1996).

[Chamberlin 1998] D. D. Chamberlin, *A complete guide to DB2 Universal Database*, Morgan Kaufmann (1998).

[Chamberlin and Boyce 1974] D. D. Chamberlin and R. F. Boyce, "SEQUEL: A Structured English Query Language," *ACM SIGMOD Workshop on Data Description, Access, and Control* (1974), pages 249–264.

[Chamberlin et al. 1976] D. D. Chamberlin, M. M. Astrahan, K. P. Eswaran, P. P. Griffiths, R. A. Lorie, J. W. Mehl, P. Reisner, and B. W. Wade, "SEQUEL 2: A Unified Approach to Data Definition, Manipulation, and Control," *IBM Journal of Research and Development*, Volume 20, Number 6 (1976), pages 560–575.

[Chamberlin et al. 1981] D. D. Chamberlin, M. M. Astrahan, M. W. Blasgen, J. N. Gray, W. F. King, B. G. Lindsay, R. A. Lorie, J. W. Mehl, T. G. Price, P. G. Selinger, M. Schkolnick, D. R. Slutz, I. L. Traiger, B. W. Wade, and R. A. Yost, "A History and Evaluation of System R," *Communications of the ACM*, Volume 24, Number 10 (1981), pages 632–646.

[Chamberlin et al. 2000] D. D. Chamberlin, J. Robie, and D. Florescu, "Quilt: An XML Query Language for Heterogeneous Data Sources," *Proc. of the International Workshop on the Web and Databases (WebDB)* (2000), pages 53–62.

[Chan and Ioannidis 1998] C.-Y. Chan and Y. E. Ioannidis, "Bitmap Index Design and Evaluation," In *Proc. of the ACM SIGMOD Conf. on Management of Data* (1998).

[Chan and Ioannidis 1999] C.-Y. Chan and Y. E. Ioannidis, "An Efficient Bitmap Encoding Scheme for Selection Queries," *Proc. of the ACM SIGMOD Conf. on Management of Data* (1999).

[Chandra and Harel 1982] A. K. Chandra and D. Harel, "Structure and Complexity of Relational Queries," *Journal of Computer and System Sciences*, Volume 15, Number 10 (1982), pages 99–128.

[Chandy and Misra 1982] K. M. Chandy and J. Misra, "A Distributed Algorithm for Detecting Resource Deadlocks in Distributed Systems," *Proc. of the ACM SIGMOD Conf. on Management of Data* (1982), pages 157–164.

[Chandy et al. 1975] K. M. Chandy, J. C. Browne, C. W. Dissley, and W. R. Uhrig, "Analytic Models for Rollback and Recovery Strategies in Database Systems," *IEEE Transactions on Software Engineering*, Volume SE-1, Number 1 (1975), pages 100–110.

[Chandy et al. 1983] K. M. Chandy, L. M. Haas, and J. Misra, "Distributed Deadlock Detection," *ACM Transactions on Database Systems*, Volume 1, Number 2 (1983), pages 144–156.

[Chatziantoniou and Ross 1997] D. Chatziantoniou and K. A. Ross, "Groupwise Processing of Relational Queries," *Proc. of the International Conf. on Very Large Databases* (1997), pages 476–485.

[Chaudhuri and Narasayya 1997] S. Chaudhuri and V. Narasayya, "An Efficient Cost-Driven Index Selection Tool for Microsoft SQL Server," *Proc. of the International Conf. on Very Large Databases* (1997).

[Chaudhuri and Shim 1994] S. Chaudhuri and K. Shim, "Including Group-By in Query Optimization," In *Proc. of the International Conf. on Very Large Databases* (1994).

[Chaudhuri et al. 1995] S. Chaudhuri, R. Krishnamurthy, S. Potamianos, and K. Shim, "Optimizing Queries with Materialized Views," *Proc. of the International Conf on Data Engineering*, Taipei, Taiwan (1995).

[Chaudhuri et al. 1999] S. Chaudhuri, E. Christensen, G. Graefe, V. Narasayya, and M. Zwilling, ""Self Tuning Technology in Microsoft SQL Server," *IEEE Data Engineering Bulletin*, Volume 22, Number 2 (1999).

[Chawathe 1999] S. S. Chawathe, "Describing and Manipulating XML Data," *IEEE Data Engineering Bulletin (Special Issue on XML)* (1999), pages 3–9.

[Chen 1976] P. P. Chen, "The Entity-Relationship Model: Toward a Unified View of Data," *ACM Transactions on Database Systems*, Volume 1, Number 1 (1976), pages 9–36.

[Chen and Patterson 1990] P. Chen and D. Patterson, "Maximizing Performance in a Striped Disk Array," *Proc. of the Seventeenth Annual International Symposium on Computer Architecture* (1990).

[Chen et al. 1994] P. M. Chen, E. K. Lee, G. A. Gibson, R. H. Katz, and D. A. Patterson, "RAID: High-Performance, Reliable Secondary Storage," *ACM Computing Survey*, Volume 26, Number 2 (1994).

[Chen et al. 1995] M.-S. Chen, H.-I. Hsiao, C.-S. Li, and P. S. Yu, "Using Rotational Mirrored Declustering for Replica Placement in a Disk Array Based Video Server," *Proc. of the ACM International Multimedia Conf.* (1995), pages 121–130.

[Cheng and Xu 2000] J. M. Cheng and J. Xu, "XML and DB2," *Proc. of the International Conf on Data Engineering* (2000), pages 569–573.

[Chervenak et al. 1995] A. L. Chervenak, D. A. Patterson, and R. H. Katz, "Choosing the Best Storage System for Video Service," *Proc. of the ACM International Multimedia Conf.* (1995), pages 109–120.

[Chiu and Ho 1980] D. M. Chiu and Y. C. Ho, "A Methodology for Interpreting Tree Queries into Optimal Semi-join Expressions," *Proc. of the ACM SIGMOD Conf. on Management of Data* (1980), pages 169–178.

[Chomicki 1992] J. Chomicki, "History-less checking of Dynamic Integrity Constraints," *Proc. of the International Conf on Data Engineering* (1992).

[Chomicki 1995] J. Chomicki, "Efficient Checking of Temporal Integrity Constraints Using Bounded History Encoding," *ACM Transactions on Database Systems*, Volume 20, Number 2 (1995), pages 149–186.

[Chou and Dewitt 1985] H. T. Chou and D. J. Dewitt, "An Evaluation of Buffer Management Strategies for Relational Database Systems," *Proc. of the International Conf. on Very Large Databases* (1985), pages 127–141.

[Chou et al. 1985] H. T. Chou, D. J. Dewitt, R. H. Katz, and A. C. Klug, "The Wisconsin Storage System Software," *Software—Practice and Experience*, Volume 15, Number 10 (1985), pages 943–962.

[Chrysanthis and Ramamritham 1994] P. Chrysanthis and K. Ramamritham, "Synthesis of Extended Transaction Models Using ACTA," *ACM Transactions on Database Systems*, Volume 19, Number 3 (1994), pages 450–491.

[Clifford and Tansel 1985] J. Clifford and A. Tansel, "On an Algebra for Historical Relational Databases: Two Views," *Proc. of the ACM SIGMOD Conf. on Management of Data* (1985), pages 247–267.

[Clifford et al. 1994] J. Clifford, A. Croker, and A. Tuzhilin, "On Completeness of Historical Relational Query Languages," *ACM Transactions on Database Systems*, Volume 19, Number 1 (1994), pages 64–116.

[Cochrane et al. 1996] R. Cochrane, H. Pirahesh, and N. M. Mattos, "Integrating Triggers and

Declarative Constraints in SQL Database Sytems," *Proc. of the International Conf. on Very Large Databases* (1996).

[**Codd 1970**] E. F. Codd, "A Relational Model for Large Shared Data Banks," *Communications of the ACM*, Volume 13, Number 6 (1970), pages 377–387.

[**Codd 1972**] E. F. Codd. "Further Normalization of the Data Base Relational Model," In *Rustin [1972]*, pages 33–64 (1972).

[**Codd 1979**] E. F. Codd, "Extending the Database Relational Model to Capture More Meaning," *ACM Transactions on Database Systems*, Volume 4, Number 4 (1979), pages 397–434.

[**Codd 1982**] E. F. Codd, "The 1981 ACM Turing Award Lecture: Relational Database: A Practical Foundation for Productivity," *Communications of the ACM*, Volume 25, Number 2 (1982), pages 109–117.

[**Codd 1990**] E. F. Codd, *The Relational Model for Database Management: Version 2*, Addison Wesley (1990).

[**Comer 1979**] D. Comer, "The Ubiquitous B-tree," *ACM Computing Survey*, Volume 11, Number 2 (1979), pages 121–137.

[**Comer and Droms 1999**] D. E. Comer and R. E. Droms, *Computer Networks and Internets*, 2nd edition, Prentice Hall (1999).

[**Cook 1996**] M. A. Cook, *Building Enterprise Information Architecture: Reengineering Information Systems*, Prentice Hall (1996).

[**Cook et al. 1999**] J. Cook, R. Harbus, and T. Shirai, *The DB2 Universal Database V6.1 certification guide: For UNIX, Windows, and OS/2*, Prentice Hall (1999).

[**Cormen et al. 1990**] T. Cormen, C. Leiserson, and R. Rivest, *Introduction to Algorithms*, MIT Press (1990).

[**Cosmadakis and Papadimitriou 1984**] S. S. Cosmadakis and C. H. Papadimitriou, "Updates of

Relational Views," *Journal of the ACM*, Volume 31, Number 4 (1984), pages 742–760.

[**Daemen and Rijmen 2000**] J. Daemen and V. Rijmen. "The Block Cipher Rijndael," In J.-J. Quisquater and B. Schneier, editors, *Smart Card Research and Applications (LNCS 1820)*, pages 288–296. Springer Verlag (2000).

[**Dalvi et al. 2001**] N. N. Dalvi, S. K. Sanghai, P. Roy, and S. Sudarshan, "Pipelining in Multi-Query Optimization," *Proc. of the ACM Symposium on Principles of Database Systems* (2001).

[**Daniels et al. 1982**] D. Daniels, P. G. Selinger, L. M. Haas, B. G. Lindsay, C. Mohan, A. Walker, and P. F. Wilms. "An Introduction to Distributed Query Compilation in R*," In *Schneider [1982]* (1982).

[**Dar et al. 1996**] S. Dar, H. V. Jagadish, A. Levy, and D. Srivastava, "Answering Queries with Aggregation Using Views," *Proc. of the International Conf. on Very Large Databases* (1996).

[**Date 1986**] C. J. Date, *Relational Databases: selected Writings*, Addison Wesley (1986).

[**Date 1989**] C. Date, *A guide to DB2*, Addison Wesley (1989).

[**Date 1990**] C. J. Date, *Relational Database Writings, 1985-1989*, Addison Wesley (1990).

[**Date 1993a**] C. J. Date, "How SQL Missed the Boat," *Database Programming and Design*, Volume 6, Number 9 (1993).

[**Date 1993b**] C. J. Date, "The Outer Join," In *IOCOD-2*, John Wiley and Sons (1993), pages 76–106.

[**Date 1995**] C. J. Date, *An Introduction to Database Systems*, 6th edition, Addison Wesley (1995).

[**Date and Darwen 1997**] C. J. Date and G. Darwen, *A Guide to the SQL Standard*, 4th edition, Addison Wesley (1997).

[**Davies 1973**] C. T. Davies, "Recovery Semantics for a DB/DC System," *Proc. of the ACM Annual Conference* (1973), pages 136–141.

[**Davis et al. 1983**] C. Davis, S. Jajodia, P. A. Ng, and R. Yeh, editors, *Entity-Relationship Approach to Software Engineering*, North Holland (1983).

[**Davison and Graefe 1994**] D. L. Davison and G. Graefe, "Memory-Contention Responsive Hash Joins," *Proc. of the International Conf. on Very Large Databases* (1994).

[**Dayal 1987**] U. Dayal, "Of Nests and Trees: A Unified Approach to Processing Queries that Contain Nested Subqueries, Aggregates and Quantifiers," *Proc. of the International Conf. on Very Large Databases* (1987), pages 197–208.

[**Dayal and Bernstein 1978**] U. Dayal and P. A. Bernstein, "The Updatability of Relational Views," In *Proc. of the International Conf. on Very Large Databases* (1978), pages 368–377.

[**Dayal et al. 1982**] U. Dayal, N. Goodman, and R. H. Katz, "An Extended Relational Algebra with Control over Duplicate Elimination," *Proc. of the ACM Symposium on Principles of Database Systems* (1982).

[**Dayal et al. 1990**] U. Dayal, M. Hsu, and R. Ladin, "Organizing Long-Running Activities with Triggers and Transactions," *Proc. of the ACM SIGMOD Conf. on Management of Data* (1990), pages 204–215.

[**Dayal et al. 1991**] U. Dayal, M. Hsu, and R. Ladin, "A Transactional Model for Long-Running Activities," *Proc. of the International Conf. on Very Large Databases* (1991), pages 113–122.

[**de Prycker 1993**] M. de Prycker, *Asynchronous Transfer Mode: Solution for Broadband ISDN*, 2nd edition, Ellis Horwood (1993).

[**Delaney 2000**] K. Delaney, *Inside Microsoft SQL Server 2000*, Microsoft Press (2000).

[**Denning and Denning 1979**] D. E. Denning and P. J. Denning, "Data Security," *ACM Computing Survey*, Volume 11, Number 3 (1979), pages 227–250.

[**Derr et al. 1993**] M. A. Derr, S. Morishita, and G. Phipps, "Design and Implementation of the Glue-Nail Database System," *Proc. of the ACM SIGMOD Conf. on Management of Data* (1993), pages 147–156.

[**Deshpande and Larson 1992**] V. Deshpande and P. A. Larson, "The Design and Implementation of a Parallel Join Algorithm for Nested Relations on Shared-Memory Multiprocessors," *Proc. of the International Conf on Data Engineering* (1992).

[**Deutsch et al. 1999a**] A. Deutsch, M. Fernandez, D. Florescu, D. M. Alon Levy, and D. Suciu, "Querying XML Data," *IEEE Data Engineering Bulletin (Special Issue on XML)* (1999), pages 10–18.

[**Deutsch et al. 1999b**] A. Deutsch, M. Fernandez, D. Florescu, A. Levy, and D. Suciu, "A Query Language for XML," *Proc. of the International World Wide Web Conf.* (1999). (XML-QL also submitted to the World Wide Web Consortium http://www.w3.org/TR/1998/NOTE-xml-ql-19980819).

[**Deux 1991**] O. Deux, "The O_2 System," *Communications of the ACM*, Volume 34, Number 10 (1991), pages 34–49.

[**DeWitt 1990**] D. DeWitt, "The Gamma Database Machine Project," *IEEE Transactions on Knowledge and Data Engineering*, Volume 2, Number 1 (1990).

[**DeWitt and Gray 1992**] D. DeWitt and J. Gray, "Parallel Database Systems: The Future of High Performance Database Systems," *Communications of the ACM*, Volume 35, Number 6 (1992), pages 85–98.

[**DeWitt et al. 1984**] D. DeWitt, R. Katz, F. Olken, L. Shapiro, M. Stonebraker, and D. Wood, "Implementation Techniques for Main Memory Databases," *Proc. of the ACM SIGMOD Conf. on Management of Data* (1984), pages 1–8.

[**DeWitt et al. 1986**] D. DeWitt, R. Gerber, G. Graefe, M. Heytens, K. Kumar, and M. Muralikrishna, "A High Performance Dataflow Database Machine," *Proc. of the International Conf. on Very Large Databases* (1986).

[**DeWitt et al. 1992**] D. DeWitt, J. Naughton, D. Schneider, and S. Seshadri, "Practical Skew Handling in Parallel Joins," *Proc. of the International Conf. on Very Large Databases* (1992).

[**Dias et al. 1989**] D. Dias, B. Iyer, J. Robinson, and P. Yu, "Integrated Concurrency-Coherency Controls for Multisystem Data Sharing," *Software Engineering*, Volume 15, Number 4 (1989), pages 437–448.

[**Diffie and Hellman 1979**] W. Diffie and M. E. Hellman, "Privacy and Authentication," *Proc. of the IEEE*, Volume 67, Number 3 (1979), pages 397–427.

[**Dijkstra 1965**] E. W. Dijkstra, "Cooperating Sequential Processes," Technical report, Technological University,Eindhoven, The Netherlands, EWD-123 (1965).

[**Dippert and Levy 1993**] B. Dippert and M. Levy, *Designing with FLASH Memory*, Annabooks (1993).

[**Dogac et al. 1994**] A. Dogac, M. T. Ozsu, A. Biliris, and T. Selis, *Advances in Object-Oriented Database Systems*, volume 130, Springer Verlag, Computer and Systems Sciences, NATO ASI Series F (1994).

[**Douglis et al. 1994**] F. Douglis, R. Caceres, B. Marsh, F. Kaashoek, K. Li, and J. Tauber, "Storage Alternatives for Mobile Computers," *Symposium on Operating Systems Design and Implementation* (1994), pages 25–37. An updated version appears as Douglis et al. [1996].

[**Douglis et al. 1996**] F. Douglis, R. Caceres, M. F. Kaashoek, P. Krishnan, K. Li, B. Marsh, and J. Tauber. "Storage Alternatives for Mobile Computers," In *Imielinski and Korth [1996], Chapter 18* (1996).

[**Draper et al. 2001**] D. Draper, A. Y. Halevy, and D. S. Weld, "The Nimble XML Data Integration system," *Proc. of the International Conf on Data Engineering* (2001), pages 155–160.

[**Du and Elmagarmid 1989**] W. Du and A. Elmagarmid, "Quasi Serializability: A Correctness Criterion for Global Database Consistency in In-

terBase," *Proc. of the International Conf. on Very Large Databases* (1989), pages 347–356.

[**Dubois and Thakkar 1992**] M. Dubois and S. Thakkar, editors, *Scalable Shared Memory Multiprocessors*, Kluwer Academic Publishers (1992).

[**Duncan 1990**] R. Duncan, "A Survey of Parallel Computer Architectures," *IEEE Computer*, Volume 23, Number 2 (1990), pages 5–16.

[**Eisenberg and Melton 1999**] A. Eisenberg and J. Melton, "SQL:1999, formerly known as SQL3," *ACM SIGMOD Record*, Volume 28, Number 1 (1999).

[**Ellis 1980a**] C. S. Ellis, "Concurrent Search and Insertion in 2–3 Trees," *Acta Informatica*, Volume 14, (1980), pages 63–86.

[**Ellis 1980b**] C. S. Ellis, "Concurrent Search and Insertion in AVL Trees," *IEEE Transactions on Computers*, Volume C-29, Number 3 (1980), pages 811–817.

[**Ellis 1987**] C. S. Ellis, "Concurrency in Linear Hashing," *ACM Transactions on Database Systems*, Volume 12, Number 2 (1987), pages 195–217.

[**Elmasri and Larson 1985**] R. Elmasri and J. Larson, "A Graphical Query Facility for E-R Databases," *Proc. of the International Conf. on Entity-Relationship Approach* (1985).

[**Elmasri and Navathe 2000**] R. Elmasri and S. B. Navathe, *Fundamentals of Database Systems*, 3rd edition, Benjamin Cummings (2000).

[**Elmasri and Wiederhold 1981**] R. Elmasri and G. Wiederhold, "GORDAS: A Formal High-Level Query Language for the Entity-Relationship Model," *Proc. of the International Conf. on Entity-Relationship Approach* (1981).

[**Eppinger et al. 1991**] J. L. Eppinger, L. B. Mummert, and A. Z. Spector, *Camelot and Avalon: A Distributed Transaction Facility*, Morgan Kaufmann (1991).

[**Epstein and Stonebraker 1980**] R. Epstein and M. R. Stonebraker, "Analysis of Distributed

Database Processing Strategies," *Proc. of the International Conf. on Very Large Databases* (1980), pages 92–110.

[Epstein et al. 1978] R. Epstein, M. R. Stonebraker, and E. Wong, "Distributed Query Processing in a Relational Database System," *Proc. of the ACM SIGMOD Conf. on Management of Data* (1978), pages 169–180.

[Escobar-Molano et al. 1993] M. Escobar-Molano, R. Hull, and D. Jacobs, "Safety and Translation of Calculus Queries with Scalar Functions," *Proc. of the ACM SIGMOD Conf. on Management of Data* (1993), pages 253–264.

[Eswaran and Chamberlin 1975] K. P. Eswaran and D. D. Chamberlin, "Functional Specifications of a Subsystem for Database Integrity," *Proc. of the International Conf. on Very Large Databases* (1975), pages 48–68.

[Eswaran et al. 1976] K. P. Eswaran, J. N. Gray, R. A. Lorie, and I. L. Traiger, "The Notions of Consistency and Predicate Locks in a Database System," *Communications of the ACM*, Volume 19, Number 11 (1976), pages 624–633.

[Evangelidis et al. 1995] G. Evangelidis, D. Lomet, and B. Salzberg, "The hB-Pi Tree: A Modified hB-tree Supporting Concurrency, Recovery and Node Consolidation," *Proc. of the International Conf. on Very Large Databases* (1995), pages 551–561.

[Fagin 1977] R. Fagin, "Multivalued Dependencies and a New Normal Form for Relational Databases," *ACM Transactions on Database Systems*, Volume 2, Number 3 (1977), pages 262–278.

[Fagin 1979] R. Fagin, "Normal Forms and Relational Database Operators," *Proc. of the ACM SIGMOD Conf. on Management of Data* (1979).

[Fagin 1981] R. Fagin, "A Normal Form for Relational Databases That Is Based on Domains and Keys," *ACM Transactions on Database Systems*, Volume 6, Number 3 (1981), pages 387–415.

[Fagin et al. 1979] R. Fagin, J. Nievergelt, N. Pippenger, and H. R. Strong, "Extendible Hashing

— A Fast Access Method for Dynamic Files," *ACM Transactions on Database Systems*, Volume 4, Number 3 (1979), pages 315–344.

[Faloutsos and Lin 1995] C. Faloutsos and K.-I. Lin, "Fast Map: A Fast Algorithm for Indexing, Data-Mining and Visualization of Traditional and Multimedia Datasets," In *Proc. of the ACM SIGMOD Conf. on Management of Data* (1995), pages 163–174.

[Fayyad et al. 1995] U. Fayyad, G. Piatetsky-Shapiro, P. Smyth, and R. Uthurusamy, *Advances in Knowledge Discovery and Data Mining*, MIT Press (1995).

[Fekete et al. 1990a] A. Fekete, N. Lynch, M. Merritt, and W. Weihl, "Commutativity-Based Locking for Nested Transactions," *Journal of Computer and System Science* (1990), pages 65–156.

[Fekete et al. 1990b] A. Fekete, N. Lynch, and W. Weihl, "A Serialization Graph Construction for Nested Transactions," *Proc. of the ACM SIGMOD Conf. on Management of Data* (1990), pages 94–108.

[Fernandez and Morishima 2001] M. F. Fernandez and A. Morishima, "Efficient Evaluation of XML Middle-ware Queries," *Proc. of the ACM SIGMOD Conf. on Management of Data* (2001).

[Fernandez et al. 1981] E. Fernandez, R. Summers, and C. Wood, *Database Security and Integrity*, Addison Wesley (1981).

[Fernandez et al. 2000] M. F. Fernandez, J. Siméon, and P. Wadler, "An Algebra for XML Query," *Proc. of the International Conf. on Foundations of Software Technology and Theoretical Computer Science* (2000), pages 11–45.

[Finkel and Bentley 1974] R. A. Finkel and J. L. Bentley, "Quad Trees: A Data Structure for Retrieval on Composite Keys," *Acta Informatica*, Volume 4, (1974), pages 1–9.

[Finkelstein 1982] S. Finkelstein, "Common Expression Analysis in Database Applications," *Proc. of the ACM SIGMOD Conf. on Management of Data* (1982), pages 235–245.

[Finkelstein et al. 1988] S. Finkelstein, M. Schkolnick, and P. Tiberio, "Physical Database Design for Relational Databases," *ACM Transactions on Database Systems*, Volume 13, Number 1 (1988), pages 53–90.

[Fischer 2001] L. Fischer, editor, *Workflow Handbook 2001*, Future Strategies (2001).

[Fischer and Thomas 1983] P. C. Fischer and S. Thomas, "Operators for Non-First-Normal-Form Relations," *Proc. of the International Computer Software Applications Conf.* (1983), pages 464–475.

[Fishman et al. 1990] D. Fishman, D. Beech, H. Cate, E. Chow, T. Connors, J. Davis, N. Derrett, C. Hoch, W. Kent, P. Lyngbaek, B. Mahbod, M. Neimat, T. Ryan, and M. Shan. "IRIS: An Object-Oriented Database Management System," In *Zdonik and Maier [1990]*, pages 216–226.

[Florescu and Kossmann 1999] D. Florescu and D. Kossmann, "Storing and Querying XML Data Using an RDBMS," *IEEE Data Engineering Bulletin (Special Issue on XML)* (1999), pages 27–35.

[Florescu et al. 2000] D. Florescu, D. Kossmann, and I. Monalescu, "Integrating keyword search into XML query processing," *Proc. of the International World Wide Web Conf.* (2000), pages 119–135. Also appears as a special issue of Computer Networks.

[Franklin et al. 1992] M. J. Franklin, M. J. Zwilling, C. K. Tan, M. J. Carey, and D. J. DeWitt, "Crash Recovery in Client-Server EXODUS," *Proc. of the ACM SIGMOD Conf. on Management of Data* (1992), pages 165–174.

[Franklin et al. 1993] M. J. Franklin, M. Carey, and M. Livny, "Local Disk Caching for Client-Server Database Systems," *Proc. of the International Conf. on Very Large Databases* (1993).

[Fredkin 1960] E. Fredkin, "Trie Memory," *Communications of the ACM*, Volume 4, Number 2 (1960), pages 490–499.

[Freedman and DeWitt 1995] C. S. Freedman and D. J. DeWitt, "The SPIFFI Scalable Video-on-Demand Server," *Proc. of the ACM SIGMOD Conf. on Management of Data* (1995), pages 352–363.

[Fry and Sibley 1976] J. Fry and E. Sibley, "Evolution of Data-Base Management Systems," *ACM Computing Survey*, Volume 8, Number 1 (1976), pages 7–42.

[Fushimi et al. 1986] S. Fushimi, M. Kitsuregawa, and H. Tanaka, "An Overview of the Systems Software of a Parallel Relational Database Machine: GRACE," *Proc. of the International Conf. on Very Large Databases* (1986).

[Fussell et al. 1981] D. S. Fussell, Z. Kedem, and A. Silberschatz, "Deadlock Removal Using Partial Rollback in Database Systems," *Proc. of the ACM SIGMOD Conf. on Management of Data* (1981), pages 65–73.

[Gadia 1986] S. K. Gadia, "Weak Temporal Relations," *Proc. of the ACM SIGMOD Conf. on Management of Data* (1986), pages 70–77.

[Gadia 1988] S. K. Gadia, "A Homogeneous Relational Model and Query Language for Temporal Databases," *ACM Transactions on Database Systems*, Volume 13, Number 4 (1988), pg. 418–448.

[Galindo-Legaria 1994] C. Galindo-Legaria, "Outerjoins as Disjunctions," *Proc. of the ACM SIGMOD Conf. on Management of Data* (1994).

[Galindo-Legaria and Joshi 2001] C. A. Galindo-Legaria and M. M. Joshi, "Orthogonal Optimization of Subqueries and Aggregation," *Proc. of the ACM SIGMOD Conf. on Management of Data* (2001).

[Galindo-Legaria and Rosenthal 1992] C. Galindo-Legaria and A. Rosenthal, "How to Extend a Conventional Optimizer to Handle One- and Two-Sided Outerjoin," *Proc. of the International Conf on Data Engineering* (1992), pages 402–409.

[Gallaire and Minker 1978] H. Gallaire and J. Minker, editors, *Logic and Databases*, Plenum Press, New York, NY (1978).

[Gallaire et al. 1984] H. Gallaire, J. Minker, and J. M. Nicolas, "Logic and Databases: A Deductive Approach," *ACM Computing Survey,* Volume 16, Number 2 (1984).

[Ganguly 1998] S. Ganguly, "Design and Analysis of Parametric Query Optimization Algorithms," *Proc. of the International Conf. on Very Large Databases,* New York City, New York (1998).

[Ganguly et al. 1992] S. Ganguly, W. Hasan, and R. Krishnamurthy, "Query Optimization for Parallel Execution," *Proc. of the ACM SIGMOD Conf. on Management of Data* (1992).

[Ganguly et al. 1996] S. Ganguly, P. Gibbons, Y. Matias, and A. Silberschatz, "A Sampling Algorithm for Estimating Join Size," *Proc. of the ACM SIGMOD Conf. on Management of Data* (1996).

[Ganski and Wong 1987] R. A. Ganski and H. K. T. Wong, "Optimization of Nested SQL Queries Revisited," *Proc. of the ACM SIGMOD Conf. on Management of Data* (1987).

[Garcia-Molina 1982] H. Garcia-Molina, "Elections in Distributed Computing Systems," *IEEE Transactions on Computers,* Volume C-31, Number 1 (1982), pages 48–59.

[Garcia-Molina 1983] H. Garcia-Molina, "Using Semantic Knowledge for Transaction Processing in a Distributed Database," *ACM Transactions on Database Systems,* Volume 8, Number 2 (1983), pages 186–213.

[Garcia-Molina and Salem 1987] H. Garcia-Molina and K. Salem, "Sagas," *Proc. of the ACM SIGMOD Conf. on Management of Data* (1987), pages 249–259.

[Garcia-Molina and Salem 1992] H. Garcia-Molina and K. Salem, "Main Memory Database Systems: An Overview," *IEEE Transactions on Knowledge and Data Engineering,* Volume 4, Number 6 (1992), pages 509–516.

[Garcia-Molina and Wiederhold 1982] H. Garcia-Molina and G. Wiederhold, "Read-only Transactions in a Distributed Database," *IEEE Transac-*

tions on Knowledge and Data Engineering, Volume 7, Number 2 (1982), pages 209–234.

[Gawlick 1998] D. Gawlick, "Messaging/Queuing in Oracle8," *Proc. of the International Conf on Data Engineering* (1998), pages 66–68.

[Geiger 1995] K. Geiger, *Inside ODBC,* Microsoft Press, Redmond, WA (1995).

[Georgakopoulos et al. 1994] D. Georgakopoulos, M. Rusinkiewicz, and A. Seth, "Using Tickets to Enforce the Serializability of Multidatabase Transactions," *IEEE Transactions on Knowledge and Data Engineering,* Volume 6, Number 1 (1994), pages 166–180.

[Gifford 1979] D. K. Gifford, "Weighted Voting for Replicated Data," *Proc. the ACM SIGOPS Symposium on Operating Systems Principles* (1979), pages 150–162.

[Gligor and Shattuck 1980] V. D. Gligor and S. H. Shattuck, "On Deadlock Detection in Distributed Systems," *IEEE Transactions on Software Engineering,* Volume SE-6, Number 5 (1980), pages 435–439.

[Goldberg and Robson 1983] A. Goldberg and D. Robson, *Smalltalk-80: The Language and Its Implementation,* Addison Wesley (1983).

[Goodman 1995] N. Goodman. "An Object-Oriented DBMS War Story: Developing a Genome Mapping Database in C++," In *Kim [1995],* pages 216–237 (1995).

[Graefe 1990] G. Graefe, "Encapsulation of Parallelism in the Volcano Query Processing System," *Proc. of the ACM SIGMOD Conf. on Management of Data* (1990), pages 102–111.

[Graefe 1993] G. Graefe, "Query Evaluation Techniques for Large Databases," *ACM Computing Survey,* Volume 25, Number 2 (1993), pages 73–170.

[Graefe 1995] G. Graefe, "The Cascades Framework for Query Optimization," *Data Engineering Bulletin,* Volume 18, Number 3 (1995), pages 19–29.

[Graefe and McKenna 1993] G. Graefe and W. McKenna, "The Volcano Optimizer Generator," *Proc. of the International Conf on Data Engineering* (1993), pages 209–218.

[Graefe et al. 1998] G. Graefe, R. Bunker, and S. Cooper, "Hash Joins and Hash Teams in Microsoft SQL Server," *Proc. of the International Conf. on Very Large Databases* (1998), pages 86–97.

[Graham et al. 1986] M. H. Graham, A. O. Mendelzon, and M. Y. Vardi, "Notions of Dependency Satisfaction," *Journal of the ACM*, Volume 33, Number 1 (1986), pages 105–129.

[Gray 1978] J. Gray. "Notes on Data Base Operating System," In *Bayer et al. [1978]*, pages 393–481 (1978).

[Gray 1981] J. Gray, "The Transaction Concept: Virtues and Limitations," *Proc. of the International Conf. on Very Large Databases* (1981), pages 144–154.

[Gray 1991] J. Gray, *The Benchmark Handbook for Database and Transaction Processing Systems*, 2nd edition, Morgan Kaufmann (1991).

[Gray and Edwards 1995] J. Gray and J. Edwards, "Scale Up with TP Monitors," *Byte,* Volume 20, Number 4 (1995), pages 123–130.

[Gray and Graefe 1997] J. Gray and G. Graefe, "The Five-Minute Rule Ten Years Later, and Other Computer Storage Rules of Thumb," *SIGMOD Record,* Volume 26, Number 4 (1997), pages 63–68.

[Gray and Putzolu 1987] J. Gray and G. R. Putzolu, "The 5 Minute Rule for Trading Memory for Disk Accesses and The 10 Byte Rule for Trading Memory for CPU Time," *Proc. of the ACM SIGMOD Conf. on Management of Data* (1987), pages 395–398.

[Gray and Reuter 1993] J. Gray and A. Reuter, *Transaction Processing: Concepts and Techniques*, Morgan Kaufmann (1993).

[Gray et al. 1975] J. Gray, R. A. Lorie, and G. R. Putzolu, "Granularity of Locks and Degrees of Consistency in a Shared Data Base," *Proc. of the International Conf. on Very Large Databases* (1975), pages 428–451.

[Gray et al. 1976] J. Gray, R. A. Lorie, G. R. Putzolu, and I. L. Traiger, *Granularity of Locks and Degrees of Consistency in a Shared Data Base*, Nijssen (1976).

[Gray et al. 1981a] J. Gray, P. Homan, H. F. Korth, and R. Obermarck, "A Straw Man Analysis of the Probability of Waiting and Deadlock," Technical report, IBM Research Laboratory, San Jose, Research Report RJ3066 (1981).

[Gray et al. 1981b] J. Gray, P. R. McJones, and M. Blasgen, "The Recovery Manager of the System R Database Manager," *ACM Computing Survey*, Volume 13, Number 2 (1981), pages 223–242.

[Gray et al. 1990] J. Gray, B. Horst, and M. Walker, "Parity Striping of Disc Arrays: Low-Cost Reliable Storage with Acceptable Throughput," *Proc. of the International Conf. on Very Large Databases* (1990), pages 148–161.

[Gray et al. 1995] J. Gray, A. Bosworth, A. Layman, and H. Pirahesh, "Data Cube: A Relational Aggregation Operator Generalizing Group-By, Cross-Tab and Sub-Totals," Technical report, Microsoft Research (1995).

[Gray et al. 1996] J. Gray, P. Helland, and P. O'Neil, "The Dangers of Replication and a Solution," *Proc. of the ACM SIGMOD Conf. on Management of Data* (1996), pages 173–182.

[Gray et al. 1997] J. Gray, S. Chaudhuri, A. Bosworth, A. Layman, D. Reichart, M. Venkatrao, F. Pellow, and H. Pirahesh, "Data Cube: A Relational Aggregation Operator Generalizing Group-by, Cross-Tab, and Sub Totals," *Data Mining and Knowledge Discovery*, Volume 1, Number 1 (1997), pages 29–53.

[Griffin and Libkin 1995] T. Griffin and L. Libkin, "Incremental Maintenance of Views with Duplicates," *Proc. of the ACM SIGMOD Conf. on Management of Data* (1995).

[Grossman and Frieder 1998] D. A. Grossman and O. Frieder, *Information Retrieval: Algorithms and Heuristics*, Kluwer Academic (1998).

[Gucht 1987] D. V. Gucht, "On the Expressive Power of the Extended Relational Algebra for the Unnormalized Relational Model," *Proc. of the ACM Symposium on Principles of Database Systems* (1987), pages 302–312.

[Gupta 1997] H. Gupta, "Selection of Views to Materialize in a Data Warehouse," In *Proc. of the International Conf. on Database Theory* (1997).

[Gupta and Mumick 1995] A. Gupta and I. S. Mumick, "Maintenance of Materialized Views: Problems, Techniques and Applications," *IEEE Data Engineering Bulletin,* Volume 18, Number 2 (1995).

[Guttman 1984] A. Guttman, "R-Trees: A Dynamic Index Structure for Spatial Searching," *Proc. of the ACM SIGMOD Conf. on Management of Data* (1984), pages 47–57.

[H. Lu and Tan 1991] M. S. H. Lu and K. Tan, "Optimization of Multi-Way Join Queries for Parallel Execution," *Proc. of the International Conf. on Very Large Databases* (1991).

[Haas et al. 1989] L. M. Haas, J. C. Freytag, G. M. Lohman, and H. Pirahesh, "Extensible Query Processing in Starburst," *Proc. of the ACM SIGMOD Conf. on Management of Data* (1989), pages 377–388.

[Haas et al. 1990] L. M. Haas, W. Chang, G. M. Lohman, J. McPherson, P. F. Wilms, G. Lapis, B. G. Lindsay, H. Pirahesh, M. J. Carey, and E. J. Shekita, "Starburst Mid-Flight: As the dust clears," *IEEE Transactions on Knowledge and Data Engineering*, Volume 2, Number 1 (1990), pages 143–160.

[Haerder and Reuter 1983] T. Haerder and A. Reuter, "Principles of Transaction-Oriented Database Recovery," *ACM Computing Survey*, Volume 15, Number 4 (1983), pages 287–318.

[Haerder and Rothermel 1987] T. Haerder and K. Rothermel, "Concepts for Transaction Recovery in Nested Transactions," *Proc. of the ACM SIGMOD Conf. on Management of Data* (1987), pages 239–248.

[Hall 1976] P. A. V. Hall, "Optimization of a Single Relational Expression in a Relational Database System," *IBM Journal of Research and Development*, Volume 20, Number 3 (1976), pages 244–257.

[Halsall 1992] F. Halsall, *Data Communications, Computer Networks, and Open Systems*, Addison Wesley (1992).

[Hammer and McLeod 1975] M. Hammer and D. McLeod, "Semantic Integrity in a Relational Data Base System," *Proc. of the International Conf. on Very Large Databases* (1975), pages 25–47.

[Hammer and McLeod 1980] M. Hammer and D. McLeod, "Database Description with SDM: A Semantic Data Model," *ACM Transactions on Database Systems*, Volume 6, Number 3 (1980), pages 51–386.

[Hammer and Sarin 1978] M. Hammer and S. Sarin, "Efficient Monitoring of Database Assertions," *Proc. of the ACM SIGMOD Conf. on Management of Data* (1978).

[Han and Kamber 2000] J. Han and M. Kamber, *Data Mining: Concepts and Techniques*, Morgan Kaufmann (2000).

[Harinarayan et al. 1996] V. Harinarayan, J. D. Ullman, and A. Rajaraman, "Implementing Data Cubes Efficiently," *Proc. of the ACM SIGMOD Conf. on Management of Data* (1996).

[Haritsa et al. 1990] J. Haritsa, M. Carey, and M. Livny, "On Being Optimistic about Real-Time Constraints," *Proc. of the ACM SIGMOD Conf. on Management of Data* (1990).

[Hasan and Motwani 1995] W. Hasan and R. Motwani, "Coloring Away Communication in Parallel Query Optimization," *Proc. of the International Conf. on Very Large Databases* (1995).

[Haskin and Lorie 1982] R. Haskin and R. A. Lorie. "On Extending the Functions of a Relational Database System," *Proc. of the ACM SIG-*

MOD Conf. on Management of Data, pages 207–212 (1982).

[Hevner and Yao 1979] A. R. Hevner and S. B. Yao, "Query Processing in Distributed Database Systems," *IEEE Transactions on Software Engineering*, Volume SE-5, Number 3 (1979), pages 177–187.

[Hinrichs 1985] K. H. Hinrichs, *The Grid File System:Implementation and Case Studies of Applications*. PhD thesis, Swiss Federal Institute of Technology, Zurich, Switzerland (1985).

[Hollinsworth 1994] D. Hollinsworth, *The Workflow Reference Model*, Workflow Management Coalition, TC00-1003 (1994).

[Holt 1971] R. C. Holt, "Comments on Prevention of System Deadlocks," *Communications of the ACM*, Volume 14, Number 1 (1971), pages 36–38.

[Holt 1972] R. C. Holt, "Some Deadlock Properties of Computer Systems," *ACM Computing Survey*, Volume 4, Number 3 (1972), pages 179–196.

[Hong and Stonebraker 1991] W. Hong and M. Stonebraker, "Optimization of Parallel Query Execution Plans in XPRS," *Proc. of the International Symposium on Parallel and Distributed Information Systems* (1991), pages 218–225.

[Hong et al. 1993] D. Hong, T. Johnson, and S. Chakravarthy, "Real-Time Transaction Scheduling: A Cost Conscious Approach," *Proc. of the ACM SIGMOD Conf. on Management of Data* (1993).

[Howes et al. 1999] T. A. Howes, M. C. Smith, and G. S. Good, *Understanding and Deploying LDAP Directory Services*, Macmillan Publishing, New York (1999).

[Hsu and Imielinski 1985] A. Hsu and T. Imielinski, "Integrity Checking for Multiple Updates," In *Proc. of the ACM SIGMOD Conf. on Management of Data* (1985), pages 152–168.

[Huang and Garcia-Molina 2001] Y. Huang and H. Garcia-Molina, "Exactly-once Semantics in a Replicated Messaging System," *Proc. of the International Conf on Data Engineering* (2001), pg. 3–12.

[Hudson and King 1989] S. E. Hudson and R. King, "Cactis:A Self-Adaptive, Concurrent Implementation of an Object-Oriented Database Management System," *ACM Transactions on Database Systems*, Volume 14, Number 3 (1989), pages 291–321.

[Huffman 1993] A. Huffman, "Transaction Processing with TUXEDO," *Proc. of the International Symposium on Parallel and Distributed Information Systems* (1993).

[IBM 1978] *Query-by Example Terminal Users Guide*. IBM Corporation. IBM Form Number SH20–20780 (1978).

[IBM 1987] IBM, "Systems Application Architecture: Common Programming Interface, Database Reference," Technical report, IBM Corporation, IBM Form Number SC26–4348–0 (1987).

[Imielinski and Badrinath 1994] T. Imielinski and B. R. Badrinath, "Mobile Computing — Solutions and Challenges," *Communications of the ACM*, Volume 37, Number 10 (1994).

[Imielinski and Korth 1996] T. Imielinski and H. F. Korth, editors, *Mobile Computing*, Kluwer Academic Publishers (1996).

[Imielinski et al. 1995] T. Imielinski, S. Viswanathan, and B. R. Badrinath, "Energy Efficient Indexing on the Air," *Proc. of the ACM SIGMOD Conf. on Management of Data* (1995), pages 25–36.

[Ioannidis and Christodoulakis 1993] Y. Ioannidis and S. Christodoulakis, "Optimal Histograms for Limiting Worst-Case Error Propagation in the Size of Join Results," *ACM Transactions on Database Systems*, Volume 18, Number 4 (1993), pages 709–748.

[Ioannidis and Kang 1990] Y. Ioannidis and Y. Kang. "Randomized Algorithms for Optimizing Large Join Queries," In *Proc. of the ACM SIGMOD Conf. on Management of Data*, pages 312–321 (1990).

[Ioannidis and Poosala 1995] Y. E. Ioannidis and V. Poosala. "Balancing Histogram Optimality and Practicality for Query Result Size Estimation," *Proc. of the ACM SIGMOD Conf. on Management of Data*, pages 233–244 (1995).

[Ioannidis and Wong 1987] Y. E. Ioannidis and E. Wong. "Query Optimization by Simulated Annealing," *Proc. of the ACM SIGMOD Conf. on Management of Data*, pages 9–22 (1987).

[Ioannidis et al. 1992] Y. E. Ioannidis, R. T. Ng, K. Shim, and T. K. Sellis, "Parametric Query Optimization," *Proc. of the International Conf. on Very Large Databases* (1992), pages 103–114.

[Ishikawa et al. 1993] H. Ishikawa, F. Suzuki, F. Kozakura, A. Makinouchi, M. Miyagishima, Y. Izumida, M. Aoshima, and Y. Yamana, "The Model, Language, and Implementation of an Object-Oriented Multimedia Knowledge Base Management System," *ACM Transactions on Database Systems*, Volume 18, Number 1 (1993), pages 1–50.

[Jaeschke and Schek 1982] G. Jaeschke and H. J. Schek. "Remarks on the Algebra of Non First Normal Form Relations," *Proc. of the ACM SIGMOD Conf. on Management of Data*, pages 124–138 (1982).

[Jagadish et al. 1993] H. V. Jagadish, A. Silberschatz, and S. Sudarshan, "Recovering from Main-Memory Lapses," *Proc. of the International Conf. on Very Large Databases* (1993).

[Jagadish et al. 1994] H. Jagadish, D. Lieuwen, R. Rastogi, A. Silberschat, and S. Sudarshan, *Dali: A High Performance Main Memory Storage Manager* (1994).

[Jain and Dubes 1988] A. K. Jain and R. C. Dubes, *Algorithms for Clustering Data*, Prentice Hall (1988).

[Jajodia and Sandhu 1990] S. Jajodia and R. Sandhu, "Polyinstantiation Integrity in Multilevel Relations," *Proc. of the IEEE Symposium on Research in Security and Privacy* (1990), pages 104–115.

[Jarke and Koch 1984] M. Jarke and J. Koch, "Query Optimization in Database Systems,"

ACM Computing Survey, Volume 16, Number 2 (1984), pages 111–152.

[Jensen et al. 1994] C. S. Jensen et al., "A Consensus Glossary of Temporal Database Concepts," *ACM Sigmod Record*, Volume 23, Number 1 (1994), pages 52–64.

[Jhingran et al. 1997] A. Jhingran, T. Malkemus, and S. Padmanabhan, "Query Optimization in DB2 Parallel Edition," *Data Engineering Bulletin*, Volume 20, Number 2 (1997), pages 27–34.

[Jin et al. 1993] W. Jin, L. Ness, M. Rusinkiewicz, and A. Sheth. "Concurrency Control and Recovery of Multidatabase Work Flows in Telecommunication Applications," *Proc. of the ACM SIGMOD Conf. on Management of Data* (1993).

[Johnson 1999a] T. Johnson, "Performance Measurements of Compressed Bitmap Indices," In *Proc. of the International Conf. on Very Large Databases* (1999).

[Johnson 1999b] T. Johnson, "Performance Measurements of Compressed Bitmap Indices," In *Proc. of the International Conf. on Very Large Databases* (1999).

[Johnson and Shasha 1993] T. Johnson and D. Shasha, "The Performance of Concurrent B-Tree Algorithms," *ACM Transactions on Database Systems*, Volume 18, Number 1 (1993).

[Jones and Willet 1997] K. S. Jones and P. Willet, editors, *Readings in Information Retrieval*, Morgan Kaufmann (1997).

[Joshi 1991] A. Joshi, "Adaptive Locking Strategies in a Multi-Node Shared Data Model Environment," *Proc. of the International Conf. on Very Large Databases* (1991).

[Joshi et al. 1998] A. Joshi, W. Bridge, J. Loaiza, and T. Lahiri, "Checkpointing in Oracle," *Proc. of the International Conf. on Very Large Databases* (1998), pages 665–668.

[Kaiser 1990] G. Kaiser, "A Flexible Transaction Model for Software Engineering," In *IEEE Transactions on Knowledge and Data Engineering* (1990).

[**Kambayashi et al. 1982**] Y. Kambayashi, M. Yoshikawa, and S. Yajima, "Query Processing for Distributed Databases Using Generalized Semijoins," *Proc. of the ACM SIGMOD Conf. on Management of Data* (1982), pages 151–160.

[**Kamel and Faloutsos 1992**] I. Kamel and C. Faloutsos. "Parallel -Trees," *Proc. of the ACM SIGMOD Conf. on Management of Data* (1992).

[**Kanne and Moerkotte 2000**] C.-C. Kanne and G. Moerkotte, "Efficient Storage of XML Data," *Proc. of the International Conf on Data Engineering* (2000), page 198.

[**Kapitskaia et al. 2000**] O. Kapitskaia, R. T. Ng, and D. Srivastava, "Evolution and Revolutions in LDAP Directory Caches," *Proc. of the International Conf on Extending Database Technology* (2000), pages 202–216.

[**Kedem and Silberschatz 1979**] Z. M. Kedem and A. Silberschatz, "Controlling Concurrency Using Locking Protocols," *Proc. of the Annual IEEE Symposium on Foundations of Computer Science* (1979), pages 275–285.

[**Kedem and Silberschatz 1983**] Z. M. Kedem and A. Silberschatz, "Locking Protocols: From Exclusive to Shared Locks," *ACM Press*, Volume 30, Number 4 (1983), pages 787–804.

[**Khoshafian and Copeland 1990**] S. Khoshafian and G. P. Copeland. "Object Identity," In *Zdonik and Maier [1990]*, pages 37–46 (1990).

[**Kifer et al. 1992**] M. Kifer, W. Kim, and Y. Sagiv, "Querying Object Oriented Databases," In *Proc. of the ACM SIGMOD Conf. on Management of Data* (1992), pages 393–402.

[**Kim 1982**] W. Kim, "On Optimizing an SQL-like Nested Query," *ACM Transactions on Database Systems*, Volume 3, Number 3 (1982), pages 443–469.

[**Kim 1984**] W. Kim. "Query Optimization for Relational Database Systems," In *Unger et al. [1984]* (1984).

[**Kim 1990**] W. Kim, *Introduction to Object-Oriented Databases*, MIT Press, Cambridge (1990).

[**Kim 1995**] W. Kim, editor, *Modern Database Systems*, ACM Press/ Addison Wesley (1995).

[**Kim and Lochovsky 1989**] W. Kim and F. Lochovsky, editors, *Object-Oriented Concepts, Databases, and Applications*, Addison Wesley (1989).

[**Kim et al. 1985**] W. Kim, D. S. Reiner, and D. S. Batory, editors, *Query Processing in Database Systems*, Springer Verlag (1985).

[**Kim et al. 1988**] W. Kim, N. Ballou, J. Banerjee, H. T. Chou, J. F. Garza, and D. Woelk, "Integrating an Object-Oriented Programming System with a Database System," *Proc. of the International Conf. on Object-Oriented Programming Systems, Languages, and Applications* (1988).

[**King 1981**] J. J. King, "QUIST: A System for Semantic Query Optimization in Relational Data Bases," *Proc. of the International Conf. on Very Large Databases* (1981), pages 510–517.

[**King et al. 1991**] R. P. King, N. Halim, H. Garcia-Molina, and C. Polyzois, "Management of a Remote Backup Copy for Disaster Recovery," *ACM Transactions on Database Systems*, Volume 16, Number 2 (1991), pages 338–368.

[**Kirchmer 1999**] M. Kirchmer, *Business Process Oriented Implementation of Standard Software : How to Achieve Competitive Advantage Efficiently and Effectively*, 2nd edition, Springer Verlag (1999).

[**Kitsuregawa and Ogawa 1990**] M. Kitsuregawa and Y. Ogawa, "Bucket Spreading Parallel Hash: A New, Robust, Parallel Hash Join Method for Skew in the Super Database Computer," *Proc. of the International Conf. on Very Large Databases* (1990), pages 210–221.

[**Kitsuregawa et al. 1983**] M. Kitsuregawa, H. Tanaka, and T. MotoOka, "Application of Hash to a Database Machine and its Architecture," *New Generation Computing,* Number 1 (1983), pages 62–74.

[Kleinberg 1999] J. M. Kleinberg, "Authoritative Sources in a Hyperlinked Environment," *Journal of the ACM*, Volume 46, Number 5 (1999), pages 604–632.

[Kleinrock 1975] L. Kleinrock, *Queuing Systems, Volume 1: Theory*, John Wiley and Sons (1975).

[Kleinrock 1976] L. Kleinrock, *Queuing Systems, Volume 2: Computer Applications*, John Wiley and Sons (1976).

[Klug 1982] A. Klug, "Equivalence of Relational Algebra and Relational Calculus Query Languages Having Aggregate Functions," *ACM Press*, Volume 29, Number 3 (1982), pages 699–717.

[Knapp 1987] E. Knapp, "Deadlock Detection in Distributed Databases," *ACM Computing Survey*, Volume 19, Number 4 (1987).

[Knuth 1973] D. E. Knuth, *The Art of Computer Programming*, volume 3, Addison Wesley, Sorting and Searching (1973).

[Kohavi and Provost 2001] R. Kohavi and F. Provost, editors, *Applications of Data Mining to Electronic Commerce*, Kluwer Academic Publishers (2001).

[Kohler 1981] W. H. Kohler, "A Survey of Techniques for Synchronization and Recovery in Decentralized Computer Systems," *ACM Computing Survey*, Volume 13, Number 2 (1981), pages 149–183.

[Konstan et al. 1997] J. A. Konstan, B. N. Miller, D. Maltz, J. L. Herlocker, L. R. Gordon, and J. Riedl, "GroupLens: Applying Collaborative Filtering to Usenet News," *Communications of the ACM*, Volume 40, Number 3 (1997), pages 77–87.

[Korth 1982] H. F. Korth, "Deadlock Freedom Using Edge Locks," *ACM Transactions on Database Systems*, Volume 7, Number 4 (1982), pages 632–652.

[Korth 1983] H. F. Korth, "Locking Primitives in a Database System," *Journal of the ACM*, Volume 30, Number 1 (1983), pages 55–79.

[Korth and Speegle 1988] H. F. Korth and G. Speegle. "Formal Model of Correctness Without Serializability," *Proc. of the ACM SIGMOD Conf. on Management of Data* (1988).

[Korth and Speegle 1990] H. F. Korth and G. Speegle, "Long Duration Transactions in Software Design Projects," *Proc. of the International Conf on Data Engineering* (1990), pages 568–575.

[Korth and Speegle 1994] H. F. Korth and G. Speegle, "Formal Aspects of Concurrency Control in Long Duration Transaction Systems Using the NT/PV Model," *ACM Transactions on Database Systems*, Volume 19, Number 3 (1994), pages 492–535.

[Korth et al. 1988] H. F. Korth, W. Kim, and F. Bancilhon, "On Long Duration CAD Transactions," *Information Science*, Volume 46, (1988), pages 73–107.

[Korth et al. 1990a] H. F. Korth, E. Levy, and A. Silberschatz, "A Formal Approach to Recovery by Compensating Transactions," *Proc. of the International Conf. on Very Large Databases* (1990).

[Korth et al. 1990b] H. F. Korth, N. Soparkar, and A. Silberschatz, "Triggered Real-Time Databases with Consistency Constraints," *Proc. of the International Conf. on Very Large Databases* (1990), pages 71–82.

[Kumar and Stonebraker 1988] A. Kumar and M. Stonebraker. "Semantics Based Transaction Management Techniques for Replicated Data," *Proc. of the ACM SIGMOD Conf. on Management of Data*, pages 117–125 (1988).

[Kung and Lehman 1980] H. T. Kung and P. L. Lehman, "Concurrent Manipulation of Binary Search Trees," *ACM Transactions on Database Systems*, Volume 5, Number 3 (1980), pages 339–353.

[Kung and Robinson 1981] H. T. Kung and J. T. Robinson, "Optimistic Concurrency Control," *ACM Transactions on Database Systems*, Volume 6, Number 2 (1981), pages 312–326.

[Labio et al. 1997] W. Labio, D. Quass, and B. Adelberg, "Physical Database Design for Data Warehouses," *Proc. of the International Conf on Data Engineering* (1997).

[Lahiri et al. 2001] T. Lahiri, A. Ganesh, R. Weiss, and A. Joshi, "Fast-Start: Quick Fault Recovery in Oracle," *Proc. of the ACM SIGMOD Conf. on Management of Data* (2001).

[Lai and Wilkinson 1984] M. Y. Lai and W. K. Wilkinson, "Distributed Transaction Management in JASMIN," *Proc. of the International Conf. on Very Large Databases* (1984), pages 466–472.

[Lamb et al. 1991] C. Lamb, G. Landis, J. Orenstein, and D. Weinreb, "The ObjectStore Database System," *Communications of the ACM,* Volume 34, Number 10 (1991), pages 51–63.

[Lamport 1978] L. Lamport, "Time, Clocks, and the Ordering of Events in a Distributed System," *Communications of the ACM,* Volume 21, Number 7 (1978), pages 558–565.

[Lampson and Sturgis 1976] B. Lampson and H. Sturgis, "Crash Recovery in a Distributed Data Storage System," Technical report, Computer Science Laboratory, Xerox Palo Alto Research Center,Palo Alto (1976).

[Langerak 1990] R. Langerak, "View Updates in Relational Databases with an Independent Scheme," *ACM Transactions on Database Systems,* Volume 15, Number 1 (1990), pages 40–66.

[Lanzelotte et al. 1993] R. Lanzelotte, P. Valduriez, and M. Zar, "On the Effectiveness of Optimization Search Strategies for Parallel Execution Spaces," *Proc. of the International Conf. on Very Large Databases* (1993).

[Larson 1978] P. Larson, "Dynamic Hashing," *BIT,* Volume 18, (1978).

[Larson 1982] P. Larson, "Performance Analysis of Linear Hashing with Partial Expansions," *ACM Transactions on Database Systems,* Volume 7, Number 4 (1982), pages 566–587.

[Larson 1988] P. Larson, "Linear Hashing with Separators — A Dynamic Hashing Scheme Achieving One-Access Retrieval," *ACM Transactions on*

Database Systems, Volume 19, Number 3 (1988), pages 366–388.

[Larson and Yang 1985] P. Larson and H. Z. Yang, "Computing Queries from Derived Relations," In *Proc. of the International Conf. on Very Large Databases* (1985), pages 59–269.

[Lecluse et al. 1988] C. Lecluse, P. Richard, and F. Velez, "O2: An Object-Oriented Data Model," *Proc. of the International Conf. on Very Large Databases* (1988), pages 424–433.

[Lee and Liou 1996] S. Y. Lee and R. L. Liou, "A Multi-Granularity Locking Model for Concurrency Control in Object-Oriented Database Systems," *IEEE Transactions on Knowledge and Data Engineering,* Volume 8, Number 1 (1996), pages 144–156.

[Lehman and Yao 1981] P. L. Lehman and S. B. Yao, "Efficient Locking for Concurrent Operations on B-trees," *ACM Transactions on Database Systems,* Volume 6, Number 4 (1981), pages 650–670.

[Lenzerini and Santucci 1983] M. Lenzerini and C. Santucci. "Cardinality Constraints in the Entity Relationship Model," In *Davis et al. [1983]* (1983).

[Lien and Weinberger 1978] Y. E. Lien and P. J. Weinberger. "Consistency, Concurrency and Crash Recovery," *Proc. of the ACM SIGMOD Conf. on Management of Data,* pages 9–14 (1978).

[Lin et al. 1994] E. T. Lin, E. R. Omiecinski, and S. Yalamanchili, "Large Join Optimization on a Hypercube Multiprocessor," *IEEE Transactions on Knowledge and Data Engineering,* Volume 6, Number 2 (1994), pages 304–315.

[Lindsay et al. 1980] B. G. Lindsay, P. G. Selinger, C. Galtieri, J. N. Gray, R. A. Lorie, T. G. Price, G. R. Putzolu, I. L. Traiger, and B. W. Wade. "Notes on Distributed Databases," In Draffen and P. 431, editors, *Distributed Data Bases,* pages 247–284. Cambridge University Press, Cambridge, England (1980).

[Litwin 1978] W. Litwin, "Virtual Hashing: A Dynamically Changing Hashing," *Proc. of the In-*

ternational Conf. on Very Large Databases (1978), pages 517–523.

[Litwin 1980] W. Litwin, "Linear Hashing: A New Tool for File and Table Addressing," *Proc. of the International Conf. on Very Large Databases* (1980), pages 212–223.

[Litwin 1981] W. Litwin. "Trie Hashing," *Proc. of the ACM SIGMOD Conf. on Management of Data*, pages 19–29 (1981).

[Liu et al. 2000] L. Liu, C. Pu, and W. Han, "XWRAP: An XML-Enabled Wrapper Construction System for Web Information Sources," *Proc. of the International Conf on Data Engineering* (2000), pages 611–621.

[Lo and Ravishankar 1996] M.-L. Lo and C. V. Ravishankar. "Spatial Hash-Joins," *Proc. of the ACM SIGMOD Conf. on Management of Data* (1996).

[Loeb 1998] L. Loeb, *Secure Electronic Transactions : Introduction and Technical Reference*, Artech House (1998).

[Lomet 1981] D. G. Lomet, "Digital B-trees," *Proc. of the International Conf. on Very Large Databases* (1981), pages 333–344.

[Lomet and Salzberg 1992] D. Lomet and B. Salzberg. "Access Method Concurrency with Recovery," *Proc. of the ACM SIGMOD Conf. on Management of Data*, pages 351–360. Also appears in The VLDB Journal (1997) (1992).

[Lopresti and Tomkins 1993] D. P. Lopresti and A. Tomkins, "Approximate Matching of Hand Drawn Pictograms," *Proc. of the INTERCHI 93 Conf.* (1993).

[Lorie 1977] R. A. Lorie, "Physical Integrity in a Large Segmented Database," *ACM Transactions on Database Systems*, Volume 2, Number 1 (1977), pages 91–104.

[Lorie et al. 1985] R. Lorie, W. Kim, D. McNabb, W. Plouffe, and A. Meier. "Supporting Complex Objects in a Relational System for Engineering Databases," In *Kim et al. [1985]*, pages 145–155 (1985).

[Lunt 1995] T. F. Lunt. "Authorization in Object-Oriented Databases," In *Kim [1995]*, pages 130–145 (1995).

[Lynch 1983] N. A. Lynch, "Multilevel Atomicity– A New Correctness Criterion for Database Concurrency Control," *ACM Transactions on Database Systems*, Volume 8, Number 4 (1983), pages 484–502.

[Lynch and Merritt 1986] N. A. Lynch and M. Merritt, "Introduction to the Theory of Nested Transactions," *Proc. of the International Conf. on Database Theory* (1986).

[Lynch et al. 1988] N. A. Lynch, M. Merritt, W. Weihl, and A. Fekete, "A Theory of Atomic Transactions," *Proc. of the International Conf. on Database Theory* (1988), pages 41–71.

[Lyngbaek and Vianu 1987] P. Lyngbaek and V. Vianu. "Mapping a Semantic Database Model to the Relational Model," *Proc. of the ACM SIGMOD Conf. on Management of Data*, pages 132–142 (1987).

[Mackert and Lohman 1986] L. F. Mackert and G. M. Lohman, "R* Optimizer Validation and Performance Evaluation for Distributed Queries," *Proc. of the International Conf. on Very Large Databases* (1986).

[Maier 1983] D. Maier, *The Theory of Relational Databases*, Computer Science Press, Rockville (1983).

[Maier and Stein 1986] D. Maier and J. Stein, "Indexing in an Object-Oriented DBMS," *Proc. of the International Workshop on Object-Oriented Database Systems* (1986).

[Maier et al. 1986] D. Maier, J. Stein, A. Otis, and A. Purdy, "Development of an Object-Oriented DBMS," *Proc. of the Object-Oriented Programming Languages, Systems and Applications Conf. (OOPSLA)* (1986), pages 472–482.

[Makinouchi 1977] A. Makinouchi, "A Consideration of Normal Form on Not-necessarily Normalized Relations in the Relational Data Model,"
*Proc. of the International Conf. on Very Large
Databases* (1977), pages 447–453.

[Markowitz and Raz 1983] V. Markowitz and
Y. Raz. "ERROL: An Entity-Relationship, Role
Oriented, Query Language," In *Davis et al. [1983]*
(1983).

[Markowitz and Shoshani 1992] V. M. Markowitz
and A. Shoshani, "Represented Extended
Entity-Relationship Structures in Relational
Databases," *ACM Transactions on Database
Systems*, Volume 17, (1992), pages 385–422.

[Martin et al. 1989] J. Martin, K. K. Chapman, and
J. Leben, *DB2: Concepts, Design, and Programming*,
Prentice Hall (1989).

[Mattison 1996] R. Mattison, *Data Warehousing:
Strategies, Technologies, and Techniques*, McGraw
Hill (1996).

[McCarthy and Dayal 1989] D. McCarthy and
U. Dayal, "The Architecture of an Active
Database Management System," *Proc. of the
ACM SIGMOD Conf. on Management of Data*
(1989), pages 215–224.

[McCune and Henschen 1989] W. W. McCune and
L. J. Henschen, "Maintaining State Constraints
in Relational Databases:A Proof Theoretic Basis,"
ACM Transactions on Database Systems, Volume
36, Number 1 (1989), pages 46–68.

[McHugh and Widom 1999] J. McHugh and
J. Widom, "Query Optimization for XML," *Proc.
of the International Conf. on Very Large Databases*
(1999), pages 315–326.

[Mehrotra et al. 1991] S. Mehrotra, R. Rastogi, H. F.
Korth, and A. Silberschatz, "Non-Serializable
Executions in Heterogeneous Distributed
Database Systems," *Proc. of the First International
Conf. on Parallel and Distributed Information
Systems* (1991).

[Mehrotra et al. 1992a] S. Mehrotra, R. Rastogi,
Y. Breitbart, H. F. Korth, and A. Silberschatz. "Ensuring Transaction Atomicity in Multidatabase Systems," In *Proc. of the ACM Symposium on Principles of Database Systems* (1992).

[Mehrotra et al. 1992b] S. Mehrotra, R. Rastogi,
H. F. Korth, A. Silberschatz, and Y. Breitbart.
"The Concurrency Control Problem in Multidatabases: Characteristics and Solutions," *Proc.
of the ACM SIGMOD Conf. on Management of Data*
(1992).

[Melton and Eisenberg 2000] J. Melton and
A. Eisenberg, *Understanding SQL and Java
Together: A Guide to SQLJ, JDBC, and Related
Technologies*, Morgan Kaufmann (2000).

[Melton and Simon 1993] J. Melton and A. R. Simon, *Understanding The New SQL: A Complete
Guide*, Morgan Kaufmann (1993).

[Menasce and Muntz 1979] D. A. Menasce and
R. R. Muntz, "Locking and Deadlock Detection
in Distributed Databases," *IEEE Transactions on
Software Engineering*, Volume SE-5, Number 3
(1979), pages 195–202.

[Menasce et al. 1980] D. A. Menasce, G. Popek,
and R. Muntz, "A Locking Protocol for Resource Coordination in Distributed Databases,"
ACM Transactions on Database Systems, Volume 5,
Number 2 (1980), pages 103–138.

[Microsoft 1997] Microsoft, *Microsoft ODBC 3.0
Software Development Kit and Programmer's Reference*, Microsoft Press (1997).

[Mistry et al. 2001] H. Mistry, P. Roy, S. Sudarshan,
and K. Ramamritham, "Materialized View Selection and Maintenance Using Multi-Query Optimization," *Proc. of the ACM SIGMOD Conf. on
Management of Data* (2001).

[Mitchell 1997] T. M. Mitchell, *Machine Learning*,
McGraw Hill (1997).

[Mohan 1990a] C. Mohan, "ARIES/KVL: A Key-
Value Locking Method for Concurrency Con-
trol of Multiaction Transactions Operations on
B-Tree indexes," *Proc. of the International Conf. on
Very Large Databases* (1990), pages 392–405.

[Mohan 1990b] C. Mohan, "Commit-LSN: A Novel and Simple Method for Reducing Locking and Latching in Transaction Processing Systems," *Proc. of the International Conf. on Very Large Databases* (1990), pages 406–418.

[Mohan 1993] C. Mohan. "IBM's Relational Database Products:Features and Technologies," *Proc. of the ACM SIGMOD Conf. on Management of Data* (1993).

[Mohan and Levine 1992] C. Mohan and F. Levine, "ARIES/IM:An Efficient and High-Concurrency Index Management Method Using Write-Ahead Logging," *Proc. of the ACM SIGMOD Conf. on Management of Data* (1992).

[Mohan and Lindsay 1983] C. Mohan and B. Lindsay, "Efficient Commit Protocols for the Tree of Processes Model of Distributed Transactions," *Proc. of the ACM Symposium on Principles of Distributed Computing* (1983).

[Mohan and Narang 1991] C. Mohan and I. Narang, "Recovery and Coherency-Control Protocols for Fast Intersystem Page Transfer and Fine-Granularity Locking in a Shared Disks Transaction Environment," *Proc. of the International Conf. on Very Large Databases* (1991).

[Mohan and Narang 1992] C. Mohan and I. Narang, "Efficient Locking and Caching of Data in the Multisystem Shared Disks Transaction Environment," *Proc. of the International Conf on Extending Database Technology* (1992).

[Mohan and Narang 1994] C. Mohan and I. Narang. "ARIES/CSA: A Method for Database Recovery in Client-Server Architectures," *Proc. of the ACM SIGMOD Conf. on Management of Data,* pages 55–66 (1994).

[Mohan et al. 1986] C. Mohan, B. Lindsay, and R. Obermarck, "Transaction Management in the R* Distributed Database Management System," *ACM Transactions on Database Systems,* Volume 11, Number 4 (1986), pages 378–396.

[Mohan et al. 1992] C. Mohan, D. Haderle, B. Lindsay, H. Pirahesh, and P. Schwarz, "ARIES: A Transaction Recovery Method Supporting Fine-Granularity Locking and Partial Rollbacks Using Write-Ahead Logging," *ACM Transactions on Database Systems,* Volume 17, Number 1 (1992).

[Mok et al. 1996] W. Y. Mok, Y.-K. Ng, and D. W. Embley, "A Normal Form for Precisely Characterizing Redundancy in Nested Relations," *ACM Transactions on Database Systems,* Volume 21, Number 1 (1996), pages 77–106.

[Moss 1982] J. E. B. Moss, "Nested Transactions and Reliable Distributed Computing," *Proc. of the Symposium on Reliability in Distributed Software and Database Systems* (1982).

[Moss 1985] J. E. B. Moss, *Nested Transactions: An Approach to Reliable Distributed Computing,* MIT Press,Cambridge (1985).

[Moss 1987] J. E. B. Moss, "Log-Based Recovery for Nested Transactions," *Proc. of the International Conf. on Very Large Databases* (1987), pages 427–432.

[Moss 1990] J. E. B. Moss, "Working with Objects: To Swizzle or Not to Swizzle," Technical report, Computer and Information Science, University of Massachusetts, Amherst, Technical Report COINS TR 90-38 (1990).

[Mumick et al. 1996] I. S. Mumick, S. Finkelstein, H. Pirahesh, and R. Ramakrishnan, "Magic Conditions," *ACM Transactions on Database Systems,* Volume 21, Number 1 (1996), pages 107–155.

[Nakayama et al. 1984] T. Nakayama, M. Hirakawa, and T. Ichikawa, "Architecture and Algorithm for Parallel Execution of a Join Operation," *Proc. of the International Conf on Data Engineering* (1984).

[Naqvi and Tsur 1988] S. Naqvi and S. Tsur, *A Logic Language for Data and Knowledge Bases,* Computer Science Press, Rockville (1988).

[Ng and Han 1994] R. T. Ng and J. Han, "Efficient and Effective Clustering Methods for Spatial Data Mining," *Proc. of the International Conf. on Very Large Databases* (1994).

[**Nievergelt et al. 1984**] J. Nievergelt, H. Hinterberger, and K. C. Sevcik, "The Grid File: An Adaptable Symmetric Multikey File Structure," *ACM Transactions on Database Systems*, Volume 9, Number 1 (1984), pages 38–71.

[**North 1995**] K. North, *Windows Multi-DBMS Programming: Using C++, Visual Basic, ODBC, OLE2, and Tools for DBMS Projects*, John Wiley and Sons (1995).

[**Obermarck 1982**] R. Obermarck, "Distributed Deadlock Detection Algorithm," *ACM Transactions on Database Systems*, Volume 7, Number 2 (1982), pages 187–208.

[**O'Neil and O'Neil 2000**] P. O'Neil and E. O'Neil, *Database: Principles, Programming, Performance*, 2nd edition, Morgan Kaufmann (2000).

[**O'Neil and Quass 1997**] P. O'Neil and D. Quass, "Improved Query Performance with Variant Indexes," *Proc. of the ACM SIGMOD Conf. on Management of Data* (1997).

[**Oracle 1997**] *Oracle 8 Concepts Manual*. Oracle Corporation, Redwood Shores (1997).

[**Orenstein 1982**] J. A. Orenstein, "Multidimensional Tries Used for Associative Searching," *Information Processing Letters*, Volume 14, Number 4 (1982), pages 150–157.

[**Ozcan et al. 1997**] F. Ozcan, S. Nural, P. Koksal, C. Evrendilek, and A. Dogac, "Dynamic Query Optimization in Multidatabases," *Data Engineering Bulletin*, Volume 20, Number 3 (1997), pages 38–45.

[**Ozden et al. 1994**] B. Ozden, A. Biliris, R. Rastogi, and A. Silberschatz, "A Low-cost Storage Server for a Movie on Demand Database," *Proc. of the International Conf. on Very Large Databases* (1994).

[**Ozden et al. 1995a**] B. Ozden, R. Rastogi, and A. Silberschatz, "A Framework for the Storage and Retrieval of Continuous Media Data," *Proc. of the IEEE International Conf. on Multimedia Computing and Systems* (1995).

[**Ozden et al. 1995b**] B. Ozden, R. Rastogi, and A. Silberschatz, "Research Issues in Multimedia Storage Servers," *ACM Computing Survey*, Volume 27, Number 4 (1995), pages 617–620.

[**Ozden et al. 1996a**] B. Ozden, R. Rastogi, P. Shenoy, and A. Silberschatz. "Fault-Tolerant Architectures for Continuous Media Servers," *Proc. of the ACM SIGMOD Conf. on Management of Data* (1996).

[**Ozden et al. 1996b**] B. Ozden, R. Rastogi, and A. Silberschatz, "On the Design of a Low-Cost Video-on-Demand Storage System," *Multimedia Systems Journal*, Volume 4, Number 1 (1996), pages 40–54.

[**Ozsoyoglu and Snodgrass 1995**] G. Ozsoyoglu and R. Snodgrass, "Temporal and Real-Time Databases: A Survey," *IEEE Transactions on Knowledge and Data Engineering*, Volume 7, Number 4 (1995), pages 513–532.

[**Ozsoyoglu and Yuan 1987**] G. Ozsoyoglu and L. Yuan, "Reduced MVDs and Minimal Covers," *ACM Transactions on Database Systems*, Volume 12, Number 3 (1987), pages 377–394.

[**Ozsoyoglu et al. 1987**] G. Ozsoyoglu, Z. M. Ozsoyoglu, and V. Matos, "Extending Relational Algebra and Relational Calculus with Set-Valued Attributes and Aggregate Functions," *ACM Transactions on Database Systems*, Volume 12, Number 4 (1987), pages 566–592.

[**Ozsu and Valduriez 1999**] T. Ozsu and P. Valduriez, *Principles of Distributed Database Systems*, 2nd edition, Prentice Hall (1999).

[**Pang et al. 1995**] H.-H. Pang, M. J. Carey, and M. Livny, "Multiclass Scheduling in Real-Time Database Systems," *IEEE Transactions on Knowledge and Data Engineering*, Volume 2, Number 4 (1995), pages 533–551.

[**Papadimitriou 1979**] C. H. Papadimitriou, "The Serializability of Concurrent Database Updates," *Journal of the ACM*, Volume 26, Number 4 (1979), pages 631–653.

[Papadimitriou 1982] C. H. Papadimitriou, "A Theorem in Database Concurrency Control," *Journal of the ACM*, Volume 29, Number 5 (1982), pages 998–1006.

[Papadimitriou 1986] C. H. Papadimitriou, *The Theory of Database Concurrency Control*, Computer Science Press, Rockville (1986).

[Papadimitriou et al. 1977] C. H. Papadimitriou, P. A. Bernstein, and J. B. Rothnie, "Some Computational Problems related to Database Concurrency Control," *Proc. of the Conf. on Theoretical Computer Science* (1977), pages 275–282.

[Papakonstantinou et al. 1996] Y. Papakonstantinou, A. Gupta, and L. Haas, "Capabilities-Based Query Rewriting in Mediator Systems," *Proc. of the International Conf. on Parallel and Distributed Information Systems* (1996).

[Parker et al. 1983] D. S. Parker, G. J. Popek, G. Rudisin, A. Stoughton, B. J. Walker, E. Walton, J. M. Chow, D. Edwards, S. Kiser, and C. Kline, "Detection of Mutual Inconsistency in Distributed Systems," *IEEE Transactions on Software Engineering*, Volume 9, Number 3 (1983), pages 240–246.

[Patel and DeWitt 1996] J. Patel and D. J. DeWitt, "Partition Based Spatial-Merge Join," *Proc. of the ACM SIGMOD Conf. on Management of Data* (1996).

[Patterson and Hennessy 1995] D. A. Patterson and J. L. Hennessy, *Computer Architecture: A Quantitative Approach*, 2nd edition, Morgan Kaufmann (1995).

[Patterson et al. 1988] D. A. Patterson, G. Gibson, and R. H. Katz, "A Case for Redundant Arrays of Inexpensive Disks (RAID)," *Proc. of the ACM SIGMOD Conf. on Management of Data* (1988), pages 109–116.

[Pellenkoft et al. 1997] A. Pellenkoft, C. A. Galindo-Legaria, and M. Kersten, "The Complexity of Transformation-Based Join Enumeration," *Proc. of the International Conf. on Very Large Databases*, Athens,Greece (1997), pages 306–315.

[Penney and Stein 1987] J. Penney and J. Stein, "Class Modification in the GemStone Object-Oriented DBMS," *Proc. of the Object-Oriented Programming Languages, Systems and Applications Conf. (OOPSLA)* (1987).

[Pless 1989] V. Pless, *Introduction to the Theory of Error-Correcting Codes*, 2nd edition, John Wiley and Sons (1989).

[Poe 1995] V. Poe, *Building a Data Warehouse for Decision Support*, Prentice Hall (1995).

[Poess and Floyd 2000] M. Poess and C. Floyd, "New TPC Benchmarks for Decision Support and Web Commerce," *ACM SIGMOD Record*, Volume 29, Number 4 (2000).

[Polyzois and Garcia-Molina 1994] C. Polyzois and H. Garcia-Molina, "Evaluation of Remote Backup Algorithms for Transaction-Processing Systems," *ACM Transactions on Database Systems*, Volume 19, Number 3 (1994), pages 423–449.

[Poosala et al. 1996] V. Poosala, Y. E. Ioannidis, P. J. Haas, and E. J. Shekita, "Improved Histograms for Selectivity Estimation of Range Predicates," *Proc. of the ACM SIGMOD Conf. on Management of Data* (1996), pages 294–305.

[Popek et al. 1981] G. J. Popek, B. J. Walker, J. M. Chow, D. Edwards, C. Kline, G. Rudisin, and G. Thiel, "LOCUS: A Network Transparent, High Reliability Distributed System," *Proc. of the Eighth Symposium on Operating System Principles* (1981), pages 169–177.

[Pu et al. 1988] C. Pu, G. Kaiser, and N. Hutchinson, "Split-transactions for Open-Ended Activities," *Proc. of the International Conf. on Very Large Databases* (1988), pages 26–37.

[Qian and Lunt 1996] X. Qian and T. F. Lunt, "A MAC Policy Framework for Multilevel Relational Databases," *IEEE Transactions on Knowledge and Data Engineering*, Volume 8, Number 1 (1996), pages 3–15.

[Rahm 1993] E. Rahm, "Empirical Performance Evaluation of Concurrency and Coherency Control Protocols for Database Sharing Systems,"

ACM Transactions on Database Systems, Volume 8, Number 2 (1993).

[Ramakrishna and Larson 1989] M. V. Ramakrishna and P. Larson, "File Organization Using Composite Perfect Hashing," *ACM Transactions on Database Systems*, Volume 14, Number 2 (1989), pages 231–263.

[Ramakrishnan and Gehrke 2000] R. Ramakrishnan and J. Gehrke, *Database Management Systems*, 2nd edition, McGraw Hill (2000).

[Ramakrishnan and Ullman 1995] R. Ramakrishnan and J. D. Ullman, "A Survey of Deductive Database Systems," *Journal of Logic Programming*, Volume 23, Number 2 (1995), pages 125–149.

[Ramakrishnan et al. 1992a] R. Ramakrishnan, D. Srivastava, and S. Sudarshan, *Controlling the Search in Bottom-up Evaluation* (1992).

[Ramakrishnan et al. 1992b] R. Ramakrishnan, D. Srivastava, and S. Sudarshan, "CORAL: Control, Relations, and Logic," *Proc. of the International Conf. on Very Large Databases* (1992), pages 238–250.

[Ramakrishnan et al. 1992c] R. Ramakrishnan, D. Srivastava, and S. Sudarshan. "Efficient Bottom-up Evaluation of Logic Programs," In *Vandewalle [1992]* (1992).

[Ramakrishnan et al. 1993] R. Ramakrishnan, D. Srivastava, S. Sudarshan, and P. Sheshadri, "Implementation of the CORAL Deductive Database System," *Proc. of the ACM SIGMOD Conf. on Management of Data* (1993), pages 167–176.

[Ramesh et al. 1989] R. Ramesh, A. J. G. Babu, and J. P. Kincaid, "Index Optimization: Theory and Experimental Results," *ACM Transactions on Database Systems*, Volume 14, Number 1 (1989), pages 41–74.

[Rangan et al. 1992] P. V. Rangan, H. M. Vin, and S. Ramanathan, "Designing an On-Demand Multimedia Service," *Communications Magazine*, Volume 1, Number 1 (1992), pages 56–64.

[Reason et al. 1996] J. M. Reason, L. C. Yun, A. Y. Lao, and D. G. Messerschmitt. "Asynchronous Video: Coordinated Video Coding and Transport for Heterogeneous Networks with Wireless Access," In *Imielinski and Korth [1996] Chapter 10* (1996).

[Reed 1978] D. Reed, *Naming and Synchronization in a Decentralized Computer System*. PhD thesis, Department of Electrical Engineering, MIT, Cambridge (1978).

[Reed 1983] D. Reed, "Implementing Atomic Actions on Decentralized Data," *Transactions on Computer Systems*, Volume 1, Number 1 (1983), pages 3–23.

[Reuter 1989] A. Reuter, "ConTracts: A Means for Extending Control Beyond Transaction Boundaries," *Proc. of the 3rd International Workshop on High Performance Transaction Systems* (1989).

[Richardson et al. 1987] J. Richardson, H. Lu, and K. Mikkilineni, "Design and Evaluation of Parallel Pipelined Join Algorithms," *Proc. of the ACM SIGMOD Conf. on Management of Data* (1987).

[Ries and Stonebraker 1977] D. R. Ries and M. Stonebraker, "Effects of Locking Granularity in a Database Management System," *ACM Transactions on Database Systems*, Volume 2, Number 3 (1977), pages 233–246.

[Rivest 1976] R. L. Rivest, "Partial Match Retrieval Via the Method of Superimposed Codes," *SIAM Journal of Computing*, Volume 5, Number 1 (1976), pages 19–50.

[Rivest et al. 1978] R. L. Rivest, A. Shamir, and L. Adelman, "On Digital Signatures and Public Key Cryptosystems," *Communications of the ACM*, Volume 21, Number 2 (1978), pages 120–126.

[Robinson 1981] J. Robinson, "The k-d-B Tree: A Search Structure for Large Multidimensional Indexes," *Proc. of the ACM SIGMOD Conf. on Management of Data* (1981), pages 10–18.

[Rosch and Wethington 1999] W. L. Rosch and A. Wethington, *The Winn L. Rosch Hardware Bible*,

5th edition, Que (1999).

[**Rosenblum and Ousterhout 1991**] M. Rosenblum and J. K. Ousterhout, "The Design and Implementation of a Log-Structured File System," *Proc. of the International Conf. on Architectural Support for Programming Languages and Operating Systems* (1991), pages 1–15.

[**Rosenkrantz et al. 1978**] D. J. Rosenkrantz, R. E. Stearns, and P. M. L. II, "System Level Concurrency Control For Distributed Data Base Systems," *ACM Transactions on Database Systems*, Volume 3, Number 2 (1978), pages 178–198.

[**Rosenthal and Reiner 1984**] A. Rosenthal and D. Reiner, "Extending the Algebraic Framework of Query Processing to Handle Outerjoins," *Proc. of the International Conf. on Very Large Databases* (1984), pages 334–343.

[**Ross 1990**] K. A. Ross. "Modular Stratification and Magic Sets for DATALOG Programs with Negation," *Proc. of the ACM SIGMOD Conf. on Management of Data* (1990).

[**Ross 1999**] S. M. Ross, *Introduction to Probability and Statistics for Engineers and Scientists*, Harcourt / Academic Press (1999).

[**Ross and Srivastava 1997**] K. A. Ross and D. Srivastava, "Fast Computation of Sparse Datacubes," In *Proc. of the International Conf. on Very Large Databases* (1997), pages 116–125.

[**Ross et al. 1996**] K. Ross, D. Srivastava, and S. Sudarshan, "Materialized View Maintenance and Integrity Constraint Checking: Trading Space for Time," *Proc. of the ACM SIGMOD Conf. on Management of Data* (1996).

[**Roth and Korth 1987**] M. A. Roth and H. F. Korth, "The Design of ¬1NF Relational Databases into Nested Normal Form," *Proc. of the ACM SIGMOD Conf. on Management of Data* (1987), pages 143–159.

[**Roth et al. 1988**] M. A. Roth, H. F. Korth, and A. Silberschatz, "Extended Algebra and Calculus for Nested Relational Databases," *ACM Transac-*

tions on Database Systems, Volume 13, Number 4 (1988), pages 389–417.

[**Roth et al. 1989**] M. A. Roth, H. F. Korth, and A. Silberschatz, "Null Values in Nested Relational Databases," *Acta Informatica*, Volume 26, (1989), pages 615–642.

[**Rothermel and Mohan 1989**] K. Rothermel and C. Mohan, "ARIES/NT: A Recovery Method Based on Write-Ahead Logging for Nested Transactions," *Proc. of the International Conf. on Very Large Databases* (1989), pages 337–346.

[**Rothnie et al. 1977**] J. B. Rothnie, Jr., and N. Goodman, "A Survey of Research and Development in Distributed Database Management," *Proc. of the International Conf. on Very Large Databases* (1977), pages 48–62.

[**Roy et al. 2000**] P. Roy, S. Seshadri, S. Sudarshan, and S. Bhobhe, "Efficient and Extensible Algorithms for Multi-Query Optimization," *Proc. of the ACM SIGMOD Conf. on Management of Data* (2000).

[**Ruemmler and Wilkes 1994**] C. Ruemmler and J. Wilkes, "An Introduction to Disk Drive Modeling," *IEEE Computer*, Volume 27, Number 3 (1994), pages 17–27.

[**Rusinkiewicz and Sheth 1995**] M. Rusinkiewicz and A. Sheth. "Specification and Execution of Transactional Workflows," In *Kim [1995]*, pages 592–620 (1995).

[**Rustin 1972**] R. Rustin, *Data Base Systems*, Prentice Hall (1972).

[**Rys 2001**] M. Rys, "Bringing the Internet to your Database: Using SQL Server 2000 and XML to build Web and B2B Applications," *Proc. of the International Conf on Data Engineering* (2001).

[**Sagiv and Yannakakis 1981**] Y. Sagiv and M. Yannakakis, "Equivalence among Relational Expressions with the Union and Difference Operators," *Proc. of the ACM SIGMOD Conf. on Management of Data*, Volume 27, Number 4 (1981).

[**Sahuguet 2001**] A. Sahuguet, "Kweelt: More than just "yet another framework to query XML"!," *Proc. of the ACM SIGMOD Conf. on Management of Data* (2001).

[**Salem and Garcia-Molina 1986**] K. Salem and H. Garcia-Molina, "Disk Striping," *Proc. of the International Conf on Data Engineering* (1986), pages 336–342.

[**Salem et al. 1994**] K. Salem, H. Garcia-Molina, and J. Sands, "Altruistic Locking," *ACM Transactions on Database Systems*, Volume 19, Number 1 (1994), pages 117–165.

[**Salton 1989**] G. Salton, *Automatic Text Processing*, Addison Wesley (1989).

[**Samet 1990**] H. Samet, *The Design and Analysis of Spatial Data Structures*, Addison Wesley (1990).

[**Samet 1995a**] H. Samet, "General Research Issues in Multimedia Database Systems," *ACM Computing Survey*, Volume 27, Number 4 (1995), pages 630–632.

[**Samet 1995b**] H. Samet. "Spatial Data Structures," In *Kim [1995]*, pages 361–385 (1995).

[**Samet and Aref 1995**] H. Samet and W. Aref. "Spatial Data Models and Query Processing," In *Kim [1995]*, pages 338–360 (1995).

[**Sanders 1998**] R. E. Sanders, *ODBC 3.5 Developer's Guide*, McGraw Hill (1998).

[**Sanders 2000**] R. E. Sanders, *DB2 Universal Database SQL Developer's Guide*, McGraw Hill (2000).

[**Sarawagi 2000**] S. Sarawagi, "User-Adaptive Exploration of Multidimensional Data," In *Proc. of the International Conf. on Very Large Databases* (2000), pages 307–316.

[**Schlageter 1981**] G. Schlageter, "Optimistic Methods for Concurrency Control in Distributed Database Systems," *Proc. of the International Conf. on Very Large Databases* (1981), pages 125–130.

[**Schmid and Swenson 1975**] H. A. Schmid and J. R. Swenson, "On the Semantics of the Rela-

tional Model," *Proc. of the ACM SIGMOD Conf. on Management of Data* (1975), pages 211–223.

[**Schneider 1982**] H. J. Schneider, *Distributed Data Bases* (1982).

[**Schneider and DeWitt 1989**] D. Schneider and D. DeWitt, "A Performance Evaluation of Four Parallel Join Algorithms in a Shared-Nothing Multiprocessor Environment," *Proc. of the ACM SIGMOD Conf. on Management of Data* (1989).

[**Schning 2001**] H. Schning, "Tamino - A DBMS designed for XML," *Proc. of the International Conf on Data Engineering* (2001), pages 149–154.

[**Selinger and Adiba 1980**] P. G. Selinger and M. E. Adiba, "Access Path Selection in Distributed Database Management Systems," Technical Report RJ2338, IBM Research Laboratory,San Jose (1980).

[**Selinger et al. 1979**] P. G. Selinger, M. M. Astrahan, D. D. Chamberlin, R. A. Lorie, and T. G. Price, "Access Path Selection in a Relational Database System," *Proc. of the ACM SIGMOD Conf. on Management of Data* (1979), pages 23–34.

[**Sellis 1988**] T. K. Sellis, "Multiple Query Optimization," *ACM Transactions on Database Systems*, Volume 13, Number 1 (1988), pages 23–52.

[**Sellis et al. 1987**] T. K. Sellis, N. Roussopoulos, and C. Faloutsos, "The R^+-Tree: A Dynamic Index for Multi-Dimensional Objects," *Proc. of the International Conf. on Very Large Databases* (1987), pages 507–518.

[**Seshadri and Naughton 1992**] S. Seshadri and J. Naughton, "Sampling Issues in Parallel Database Systems," *Proc. of the International Conf on Extending Database Technology* (1992).

[**Seshadri et al. 1996**] P. Seshadri, H. Pirahesh, and T. Y. C. Leung, "Complex Query Decorrelation," *Proc. of the International Conf on Data Engineering* (1996), pages 450–458.

[**Sha et al. 1988**] L. Sha, J. Lehoczky, and D. Jensen, "Modular Concurrency Control and Failure Recovery," *IEEE Transactions on Computing*, Volume 37, Number 2 (1988), pages 146–159.

[Shafer et al. 1996] J. C. Shafer, R. Agrawal, and M. Mehta, "SPRINT: A Scalable Parallel Classifier for Data Mining," *Proc. of the International Conf. on Very Large Databases* (1996), pages 544–555.

[Shanmugasundaram et al. 1999] J. Shanmugasundaram, G. He, K. Tufte, C. Zhang, D. DeWitt, and J. Naughton, "Relational Databases for Querying XML Documents: Limitations and Opportunities," *Proc. of the International Conf. on Very Large Databases* (1999).

[Shanmugasundaram et al. 2000] J. Shanmugasundaram, E. J. Shekita, R. Barr, M. J. Carey, B. G. Lindsay, H. Pirahesh, and B. Reinwald, "Relational Databases for Querying XML Documents: Limitations and Opportunities," *Proc. of the International Conf. on Very Large Databases* (2000), pages 65–76.

[Shapiro 1986] L. D. Shapiro, "Join Processing in Database Systems with Large Main Memories," *ACM Transactions on Database Systems*, Volume 11, Number 3 (1986), pages 239–264.

[Shasha 1992] D. Shasha, *Database Tuning: A Principled Approach*, Prentice Hall (1992).

[Shasha and Goodman 1988] D. Shasha and N. Goodman, "Concurrent Search Structure Algorithms," *ACM Transactions on Database Systems*, Volume 13, Number 1 (1988), pages 53–90.

[Shasha et al. 1995] D. Shasha, F. Llirabat, E. Simon, and P. Valduriez, "Transaction Chopping: Algorithms and Performance Studies," *ACM Transactions on Database Systems*, Volume 20, Number 3 (1995), pages 325–363.

[Shatdal and Naughton 1993] A. Shatdal and J. Naughton, "Using Shared Virtual Memory for Parallel Join Processing," *Proc. of the ACM SIGMOD Conf. on Management of Data* (1993).

[Sheard and Stemple 1989] T. Sheard and D. Stemple, "Automatic Verification of Database Trans-

action Safety," *ACM Transactions on Database Systems*, Volume 14, Number 3 (1989), pages 322–368.

[Sibley 1976] E. Sibley, "The Development of Database Technology," *ACM Computing Survey*, Volume 8, Number 1 (1976), pages 1–5.

[Signore et al. 1995] R. Signore, J. Creamer, and M. O. Stegman, *The ODBC Solution: Open Database Connectivity Distributed Environments*, McGraw Hill (1995).

[Silberschatz 1982] A. Silberschatz, "A Multiversion Concurrency Control Scheme With No Rollbacks," *Proc. of the ACM Symposium on Principles of Distributed Computing* (1982), pages 216–223.

[Silberschatz and Galvin 1998] A. Silberschatz and P. Galvin, *Operating System Concepts*, 5th edition, John Wiley and Sons (1998).

[Silberschatz and Kedem 1980] A. Silberschatz and Z. Kedem, "Consistency in Hierarchical Database Systems," *Journal of the ACM*, Volume 27, Number 1 (1980), pages 72–80.

[Silberschatz et al. 1990] A. Silberschatz, M. R. Stonebraker, and J. D. Ullman, "Database Systems: Achievements and Opportunities," *ACM SIGMOD Record*, Volume 19, Number 4 (1990).

[Silberschatz et al. 1996] A. Silberschatz, M. Stonebraker, and J. Ullman, "Database Research: Achievements and Opportunities into the 21st Century," Technical Report CS-TR-96-1563, Department of Computer Science, Stanford University, Stanford (1996).

[Simmen et al. 1996] D. Simmen, E. Shekita, and T. Malkemus, "Fundamental Techniques for Order Optimization," *Proc. of the ACM SIGMOD Conf. on Management of Data*, Montreal, Canada (1996), pages 57–67.

[Simmons 1979] G. J. Simmons, "Symmetric and Asymmetric Encryption," *ACM Computing Survey*, Volume 11, Number 4 (1979), pages 304–330.

[Skarra and Zdonik 1986] A. Skarra and S. Zdonik, "The Management of Changing Types in an

Object-Oriented Database," *Proc. of the Object-Oriented Programming Languages, Systems and Applications Conf. (OOPSLA)* (1986).

[Skarra and Zdonik 1989] A. Skarra and S. Zdonik. "Concurrency Control in Object-Oriented Databases," In *Kim and Lochovsky [1989]*, pages 395–421 (1989).

[Skeen 1981] D. Skeen, "Non-blocking Commit Protocols," *Proc. of the ACM SIGMOD Conf. on Management of Data* (1981), pages 133–142.

[Smith and Smith 1977] J. M. Smith and D. C. P. Smith, "Database Abstractions: Aggregation and Generalization," *ACM Transactions on Database Systems,* Volume 2, Number 2 (1977), pages 105–133.

[Snodgrass 1987] R. Snodgrass, "The Temporal Query Language TQuel," *ACM Transactions on Database Systems*, Volume 12, Number 2 (1987), pages 247–298.

[Snodgrass and Ahn 1985] R. Snodgrass and I. Ahn, "A Taxonomy of Time in Databases,," *Proc. of the ACM SIGMOD Conf. on Management of Data* (1985), pages 236–246.

[Snodgrass et al. 1994] R. Snodgrass et al., "TSQL2 Language Specification," *ACM SIGMOD Record*, Volume 23, Number 1 (1994), pages 65–86.

[Soo 1991] M. Soo, "Bibliography on Temporal Databases," *ACM SIGMOD Record*, Volume 20, Number 1 (1991), pages 14–23.

[Soparkar et al. 1991] N. Soparkar, H. F. Korth, and A. Silberschatz, "Failure-Resilient Transaction Management in Multidatabases," *IEEE Computer*, Volume 24, Number 12 (1991), pages 28–36.

[Soparkar et al. 1995] N. Soparkar, H. F. Korth, and A. Silberschatz, "Databases with Deadline and Contingency Constraints," *IEEE Transactions on Knowledge and Data Engineering*, Volume 7, Number 4 (1995), pages 552–565.

[Spector and Schwarz 1983] A. Z. Spector and P. M. Schwarz, "Transactions: A Construct for Reliable Distributed Computing," *Operating Sys-*

tems Review, Volume 17, Number 2 (1983), pages 18–35.

[Srikant and Agrawal 1996a] R. Srikant and R. Agrawal, "Mining Quantitative Association Rules in Large Relational Tables," *Proc. of the ACM SIGMOD Conf. on Management of Data* (1996).

[Srikant and Agrawal 1996b] R. Srikant and R. Agrawal, "Mining Sequential Patterns: Generalizations and Performance Improvements," *Proc. of the International Conf on Extending Database Technology* (1996), pages 3–17.

[Srinivasan et al. 2000a] J. Srinivasan, S. Das, C. Freiwald, E. I. Chong, M. Jagannath, A. Yalamanchi, R. Krishnan, A.-T. Tran, S. DeFazio, and J. Banerjee, "Oracle8i Index-Organized Table and Its Application to New Domains," *Proc. of the International Conf. on Very Large Databases* (2000), pages 285–296.

[Srinivasan et al. 2000b] J. Srinivasan, R. Murthy, S. Sundara, N. Agarwal, and S. DeFazio, "Extensible Indexing: A Framework for Integrating Domain-Specific Indexing Schemes into Oracle8i," *Proc. of the International Conf on Data Engineering* (2000), pages 91–100.

[Srivastava et al. 1995] D. Srivastava, S. Sudarshan, R. Ramakrishnan, and J. Naughton, "Space Optimization in Deductive Databases," *ACM Transactions on Database Systems*, Volume 20, Number 4 (1995), pages 472–516.

[Stachour and Thuraisingham 1990] P. D. Stachour and B. Thuraisingham, "Design of LDV: A Multilevel Secure Relational Database Management System," *IEEE Transactions on Knowledge and Data Engineering*, Volume 2, Number 2 (1990), pages 190–209.

[Stallings 1998] W. Stallings, *Cryptography and Network Security: Principles and Practice*, 2nd edition, Prentice Hall (1998).

[Stam and Snodgrass 1988] R. Stam and R. Snodgrass, "A Bibliography on Temporal Databases," *IEEE Transactions on Knowledge and Data Engi-*

neering, Volume 7, Number 4 (1988), pages 231–239.

[Stefik and Bobrow 1986] M. Stefik and D. G. Bobrow, "Object-Oriented Programming: Themes and Variations," *The AI Magazine* (1986), pages 40–62.

[Stone 1993] H. S. Stone, *High-Performance Computer Architecture*, 3rd edition, Addison Wesley (1993).

[Stonebraker 1975] M. Stonebraker, "Implementation of Integrity Constraints and Views by Query Modification," *Proc. of the ACM SIGMOD Conf. on Management of Data* (1975), pages 65–78.

[Stonebraker 1980] M. Stonebraker, "Retrospection on a Database System," *ACM Transactions on Database Systems*, Volume 5, Number 2 , Also appears in Stonebraker [1986b], Pages 46–62 (1980), pages 225–240.

[Stonebraker 1981] M. Stonebraker, "Operating System Support for Database Management," *Communications of the ACM*, Volume 24, Number 7 , Also appears in Stonebraker [1986b], pages 172-182 (1981), pages 412–418.

[Stonebraker 1986a] M. Stonebraker, "Inclusion of New Types in Relational Database Systems," *Proc. of the International Conf on Data Engineering* (1986), pages 262–269.

[Stonebraker 1986b] M. Stonebraker, editor, *The Ingres Papers*, Addison Wesley (1986).

[Stonebraker and Hellerstein 1998] M. Stonebraker and J. Hellerstein, *Readings in Database Systems*, 3rd edition, Morgan Kaufmann (1998).

[Stonebraker and Rowe 1986] M. Stonebraker and L. Rowe, "The Design of POSTGRES," *Proc. of the ACM SIGMOD Conf. on Management of Data* (1986).

[Stonebraker and Wong 1974] M. Stonebraker and E. Wong, "Access Control in a Relational Database Management System by Query Modification," *Proc. of the ACM National Conference* (1974), pages 180–187.

[Stonebraker et al. 1976] M. Stonebraker, E. Wong, P. Kreps, and G. D. Held, "The Design and Implementation of INGRES," *ACM Transactions on Database Systems*, Volume 1, Number 3 (1976), pages 189–222.

[Stonebraker et al. 1989] M. Stonebraker, P. Aoki, and M. Seltzer, "Parallelism in XPRS," *Proc. of the ACM SIGMOD Conf. on Management of Data* (1989).

[Stroustrup 1988] B. Stroustrup, *What Is Object-Oriented Programming?* (1988).

[Stroustrup 1997] B. Stroustrup, *The C++ Programming Language*, 3rd edition, Addison Wesley (1997).

[Stuart et al. 1984] D. G. Stuart, G. Buckley, and A. Silberschatz, "A Centralized Deadlock Detection Algorithm," Technical report, Department of Computer Sciences, University of Texas, Austin (1984).

[Sudarshan and Ramakrishnan 1991] S. Sudarshan and R. Ramakrishnan, "Aggregation and Relevance in Deductive Databases," *Proc. of the International Conf. on Very Large Databases* (1991).

[Swami and Gupta 1988] A. Swami and A. Gupta, "Optimization of Large Join Queries," *Proc. of the ACM SIGMOD Conf. on Management of Data* (1988), pages 8–17.

[Tanenbaum 1996] A. S. Tanenbaum, *Computer Networks*, 3rd edition, Prentice Hall (1996).

[Tansel et al. 1993] A. Tansel, J. Clifford, S. Gadia, S. Jajodia, A. Segev, and R. Snodgrass, *Temporal Databases: Theory, Design and Implementation*, Benjamin Cummings, Redwood City (1993).

[Tendick and Matloff 1994] P. Tendick and N. Matloff, "A Modified Random Perturbation Method for Database Security," *ACM Transactions on Database Systems*, Volume 19, Number 1 (1994), pages 47–63.

[Teorey et al. 1986] T. J. Teorey, D. Yang, and J. P. Fry, "A Logical Design Methodology for Relational Databases Using the Extended Entity-

Relationship Model," *ACM Computing Survey*, Volume 18, Number 2 (1986), pages 197–222.

[Thalheim 2000] B. Thalheim, *Entity-Relationship Modeling : Foundations of Database Technology*, Springer Verlag (2000).

[Thomas 1979] R. H. Thomas, "A Majority Consensus Approach to Concurrency Control," *ACM Transactions on Database Systems*, Volume 4, Number 2 (1979), pages 180–219.

[Thomas 1996] S. A. Thomas, *IPng and the TCP/IP Protocols: Implementing the Next Generation Internet*, John Wiley and Sons (1996).

[Todd 1976] S. J. P. Todd, "The Peterlee Relational Test Vehicle - A System Overview," *IBM Systems Journal*, Volume 15, Number 4 (1976), pages 285–308.

[Traiger et al. 1982] I. L. Traiger, J. N. Gray, C. A. Galtieri, and B. G. Lindsay, "Transactions and Consistency in Distributed Database Management Systems," *ACM Transactions on Database Systems*, Volume 7, Number 3 (1982), pages 323–342.

[Tsou and Fischer 1982] D. M. Tsou and P. Fischer, "Decomposition of a Relation Scheme into Boyce-Codd Normal Form," *ACM SIGACT News*, Volume 14, Number 3 (1982), pages 23–29.

[Tsukuda et al. 1992] S. Tsukuda, M. Nakano, M. Kitsuregawa, and M. Takagi, "Parallel Hash Join on Shared-Everything Multiprocessor," *Proc. of the International Conf on Data Engineering* (1992).

[Tsur and Zaniolo 1986] S. Tsur and C. Zaniolo, "LDL: A Logic-Based Data-Language," *Proc. of the International Conf. on Very Large Databases* (1986), pages 33–41.

[Tuzhilin and Clifford 1990] A. Tuzhilin and J. Clifford, "A Temporal Relational Algebra as a Basis for Temporal Relational Completeness," *Proc. of the International Conf. on Very Large Databases* (1990), pages 13–23.

[Ullman 1988] J. D. Ullman, *Principles of Database and Knowledge-base Systems*, volume 1, Computer Science Press, Rockville (1988).

[Ullman 1989] J. D. Ullman, *Principles of Database and Knowledge-base Systems*, volume 2, Computer Science Press, Rockville (1989).

[Umar 1997] A. Umar, *Application (Re)Engineering : Building Web-Based Applications and Dealing With Legacies*, Prentice Hall (1997).

[Unger et al. 1984] E. A. Unger, P. S. Fisher, and J. Slonim, *Advances in Data Base Management*, volume 2, John Wiley and Sons (1984).

[UniSQL 1991] *UniSQL/X Database Management System User's Manual: Release 1.2.* UniSQL Inc. (1991).

[US Dept. of Commerce 1977] *United States Department of Commerce, Data Encryption Standard.* National Bureau of Standards (1977).

[US Dept. of Defense 1985] *Department of Defense Trusted Computer System Evaluation Criteria.* National Computer Security Center (1985).

[Vandewalle 1992] J. Vandewalle, *The State of the Art in Computer Systems and Software Engineering*, Kluwer Academic (1992).

[Verhofstad 1978] J. S. M. Verhofstad, "Recovery Techniques for Database Systems," *ACM Computing Survey*, Volume 10, Number 2 (1978), pages 167–195.

[Vista 1998] D. Vista, "Integration of Incremental View Maintenance into Query Optimizers," *Proc. of the International Conf on Extending Database Technology* (1998).

[Wachter and Reuter 1992] H. Wachter and A. Reuter. "The ConTract Model," In A. K. Elmagarmid, editor, *Database Transaction Models for Advanced Applications*. Morgan Kaufmann (1992).

[Walton et al. 1991] C. Walton, A. Dale, and R. Jenevein, "A Taxonomy and Performance Model of Data Skew Effects in Parallel Joins," *Proc. of the International Conf. on Very Large Databases* (1991).

[Weihl and Liskov 1990] W. Weihl and B. Liskov. "Implementation of Resilient, Atomic Data Types," In *Zdonik and Maier [1990]*, pages 332–344 (1990).

[Weikum 1991] G. Weikum, "Principles and Realization Strategies of Multilevel Transaction Management," *ACM Transactions on Database Systems*, Volume 16, Number 1 (1991).

[Weikum and Schek 1984] G. Weikum and H. J. Schek, "Architectural Issues of Transaction Management in Multi-Level Systems," *Proc. of the International Conf. on Very Large Databases* (1984), pages 454–465.

[Weikum et al. 1990] G. Weikum, C. Hasse, P. Broessler, and P. Muth, "Multi-Level Recovery," *Proc. of the ACM SIGMOD Conf. on Management of Data* (1990), pages 109–123.

[Weltman and Dahbura 2000] R. Weltman and T. Dahbura, *LDAP Programming with Java*, Addison Wesley (2000).

[Whang and Krishnamurthy 1990] K. Whang and R. Krishnamurthy, "Query Optimization in a Memory-Resident Domain Relational Calculus Database System," *ACM Transactions on Database Systems*, Volume 15, Number 1 (1990), pages 67–95.

[White and DeWitt 1992] S. J. White and D. J. DeWitt, "A Performance Study of Alternative Object Faulting and Pointer Swizzling Strategies," *Proc. of the International Conf. on Very Large Databases* (1992).

[White and DeWitt 1994] S. J. White and D. J. DeWitt, "QuickStore: A High Performance Mapped Object Store," *Proc. of the ACM SIGMOD Conf. on Management of Data* (1994).

[Widom and Finkelstein 1990] J. Widom and S. Finkelstein, "Set-Oriented Production Rules in Relational Database Systems," *Proc. of the ACM SIGMOD Conf. on Management of Data* (1990).

[Widom et al. 1991] J. Widom, R. Cochrane, and B. Lindsay, "Implementing Set-Oriented Production Rules as an Extension to Starburst," *Proc.*

of the International Conf. on Very Large Databases (1991).

[Wilkinson et al. 1990] K. Wilkinson, P. Lyngbaek, and W. Hasan, "The Iris Architecture and Implementation," *IEEE Transactions on Knowledge and Data Engineering* (1990), pages 63–75.

[Wilschut et al. 1995] A. N. Wilschut, J. Flokstra, and P. M. Apers, "Parallel Evaluation of Multi-Join Queues," *Proc. of the ACM SIGMOD Conf. on Management of Data* (1995), pages 115–126.

[Wilson 1990] P. R. Wilson, "Pointer Swizzling at Page Fault Time: Efficiently Supporting Huge Address Spaces on Standard Hardware," Technical Report UIC-EECS-90-6, University of Illinois at Chicago (1990).

[Winslett et al. 1994] M. Winslett, K. Smith, and X. Qian, "Formal Query Languages for Secure Relational Databases," *ACM Transactions on Database Systems*, Volume 19, Number 4 (1994), pages 626–662.

[Wipfler 1987] A. J. Wipfler, *CICS: Application Development and Programming*, Macmillan Publishing, New York (1987).

[Witten and Frank 1999] I. H. Witten and E. Frank, *Data Mining: Practical Machine Learning Tools and Techniques with Java Implementations*, Morgan Kaufmann (1999).

[Witten et al. 1999] I. H. Witten, A. Moffat, and T. C. Bell, *Managing Gigabytes: compressing and indexing documents and images*, Morgan Kaufmann (1999).

[Wolf 1991] J. Wolf, "An Effective Algorithm for Parallelizing Hash Joins in the Presence of Data Skew," *Proc. of the International Conf on Data Engineering* (1991).

[Wong 1977] E. Wong, "Retrieving Dispersed Data from SDD-1: A System for Distributed Databases," *Proc. of the Berkeley Workshop on Distributed Data Management and Computer Networks* (1977), pages 217–235.

[Wong 1983] E. Wong, "Dynamic Rematerialization-Processing Distributed Queries Using Redundant Data," *IEEE Transactions on Software Engineering,* Volume SE-9, Number 3 (1983), pages 228–232.

[Wu and Buchmann 1998] M. Wu and A. Buchmann, "Encoded Bitmap Indexing for Data Warehouses," In *Proc. of the International Conf on Data Engineering* (1998).

[X/Open 1991] *X/Open Snapshot: X/Open DTP: XA Interface.* X/Open Company, Ltd. (1991).

[X/Open 1993] *X/Open Data Management: SQL Call Level Interface (CLI).* X/Open Company, Ltd. (1993).

[Yan and Larson 1995] W. P. Yan and P. A. Larson, "Eager Aggregation and Lazy Aggregation," In *Proc. of the International Conf. on Very Large Databases,* Zurich (1995).

[Yannakakis 1981] M. Yannakakis, "Issues of Correctness in Database Concurrency Control by Locking," *Proc. of the IEEE Symposium on the Foundations of Computer Science* (1981), pages 363–367.

[Yannakakis et al. 1979] M. Yannakakis, C. H. Papadimitriou, and H. T. Kung, "Locking Protocols: Safety and Freedom from Deadlock," *Proc. of the IEEE Symposium on the Foundations of Computer Science* (1979), pages 286–297.

[Zaniolo 1976] C. Zaniolo, *Analysis and Design of Relational Schemata for Database Systems.* PhD thesis, Department of Computer Science, University of California, Los Angeles (1976).

[Zaniolo 1983] C. Zaniolo, "The Database Language GEM," *Proc. of the ACM SIGMOD Conf. on Management of Data* (1983), pages 207–218.

[Zaniolo et al. 1997] C. Zaniolo, S. Ceri, C. Faloutsos, R. Snodgrass, R. Zicari, and V. S. Subrahmanian, *Advanced Database Systems,* Morgan Kaufmann (1997).

[Zdonik and Maier 1990] S. Zdonik and D. Maier, *Readings in Object-Oriented Database Systems,* Morgan Kaufmann (1990).

[Zeller and Gray 1990] H. Zeller and J. Gray, "An Adaptive Hash Join Algorithm for Multiuser Environments," *Proc. of the International Conf. on Very Large Databases* (1990), pages 186–197.

[Zhang and Mendelzon 1983] Z. Q. Zhang and A. O. Mendelzon. "A Graphical Query Language for Entity-Relationship Databases," In *Davis et al. [1983],* pages 441–448 (1983).

[Zhang et al. 1996] T. Zhang, R. Ramakrishnan, and M. Livny, "BIRCH: An Efficient Data Clustering Method for Very Large Databases," *Proc. of the ACM SIGMOD Conf. on Management of Data* (1996), pages 103–114.

[Zhuge et al. 1995] Y. Zhuge, H. Garcia-Molina, J. Hammer, and J. Widom, "View Maintenance in a Warehousing Environment," *Proc. of the ACM SIGMOD Conf. on Management of Data* (1995), pages 316–327.

[Zikopoulos et al. 2000] P. Zikopoulos, R. Melnyk, and L. Logomirski, *DB2 fof Dummies,* Hungry Minds Inc. (2000).

[Zloof 1977] M. M. Zloof, "Query-by-Example: A Data Base Language," *IBM Systems Journal,* Volume 16, Number 4 (1977), pages 324–343.

Index